CHILD PSYCHOLOGY

THE MODERN SCIENCE

CHILD PSYCHOLOGY

THE MODERN SCIENCE

THIRD EDITION

Ross Vasta
State University of New York at Brockport

Marshall M. Haith
University of Denver

Scott A. Miller
University of Florida

John Wiley & Sons, Inc.
New York Chichester Weinheim Brisbane Singapore Toronto

Acquisitions Editor	Ellen Schatz
Developmental Editor	Rachel Nelson
Senior Marketing Manager	Charity Robey
Senior Production Editor	Elizabeth Swain
Senior Designer	Kevin Murphy
Photo Editor	Kim Khatchatourian
Illustration Editor	Anna Melhorn

Cover photo by Charles Thatcher/Tony Stone Images, NYC.

Special thanks to Photo Researchers, a New York City photo agency, for their various contributions to this book, including consulting on the stock and location photography.

This book was set in 10/12 New Baskerville by LCI Design, and printed and bound by Von Hoffman Press. The cover was printed by Lehigh.

This book is printed on acid-free paper.

The paper in this book was manufactured by a mill whose forest management programs include sustained yield harvesting of its timberlands. Sustained yield harvesting principles ensure that the numbers of trees cut each year does not exceed the amount of new growth.

Library of Congress Cataloguing in Publication Data:
Vasta, Ross.
    Child Psychology: the modern science / Ross Vasta, Marshall M.
  Haith, Scott A. Miller. — 3rd ed.
      p. cm.
    Includes bibliographical references and index.
    ISBN 0-471-19221-X
    1. Child psychology.   I. Haith, Marshall M., 1937– .
  II. Miller, Scott A., 1944– .   III Title.

Printed in the United States of America

10 9 8 7 6 5 4 3 2 1

Preface

*T*he major goals of the first two editions of *Child Psychology: The Modern Science* were to serve instructors' needs, to maximize student learning, and to reflect accurately and comprehensively the discipline of developmental psychology as it exists today. In preparing the third edition, we expanded these goals to include a greater integration of contextual material, an increased emphasis on cross- and multicultural research, and even more real-world applications. In so doing, we have created a truly new edition of this textbook that captures the excitement and relevance of child psychology as the discipline enters the 21st century.

A Contextualist Approach

The most important and distinctive feature of *Child Psychology* remains its emphasis on the contextualist view of human development. Inspired by Urie Bronfenbrenner's seminal work, and fueled by the rediscovery of Lev Vygotsky's writings, modern developmental psychology has increasingly adopted a contextualist perspective. The child is not viewed as a passive recipient of environmental influences, but as an active producer of those influences. From the very beginning, the infant engages in a transactional "dance" with the caregiver, each regulating the behavior of the other. As the child grows, development interacts in critical ways with the social contexts in which it occurs, the three most important being the family system, the school, and the cultural environment.

Unfortunately, textbooks of child psychology have not kept pace with this trend. Too often, contextual material has been included simply in the form of separate chapters on family and school influences, appended to the end of the book. As such, the discussion of these influences comes too late to be of maximal pedagogical value. We feel strongly that determinants residing in these and other contextual settings should instead be interwoven in the study of child development and considered at the point where the relevant aspect of development is being discussed. If we wish to discuss, for example, the effects of junior high school practices and policies on the self-esteem of preadolescents, the place to present that material is in the chapter on the development of the self, not in a chapter on schools near the end of the course. One solution to this problem—undoubtedly employed by many instructors—is to extract pieces of material from the later chapters and insert them where they belong. This, however, is awkward and unsatisfying.

Here, as in the first two editions, *Child Psychology* offers a better solution. *Material on the family, school, and culture is integrated into the appropriate chapters of the text.* This allows the course to move from one area of development to another in a topical manner, while including the broad tapestry of variables that affect each area. In the third edition, we have increased our coverage of contextual influences and also presented detailed examples of them in separate sections titled "Development in Family Context," "Development in School Context," and "Development in Cultural Context" (see Pedagogical Features).

As in the previous editions, Chapter 2 introduces the contextualist theme in the presentation of Urie Bronfenbrenner's ecological systems model. Thereafter, each chapter includes one or more Development in Context sections relevant to the topic under consideration. For example, in Chapter 5 (Prenatal Development) we consider what life is like in families created by alternative methods of conception. In Chapter 7 (Sensory and Perceptual Development) we describe how cultural experiences can affect a baby's perception of music. And in Chapter 15 (Gender-Role Development) we examine whether the typical school environment and curriculum favors boys over girls. Even more importantly, we weave contextual material throughout the entire text, examining pertinent specific influences in every chapter.

Topical Organization

We have chosen to organize the book topically. By considering each topic area in a single chapter, we believe we can most effectively present and critique the full body of research and theorizing relevant to that area.

The 16 chapters can be grouped into four general parts:

• Chapters 1–3 provide the foundation of the discipline, covering history, theory, and research methods. In keeping with the research-oriented approach of the text, these topics are presented in some detail.

• Chapters 4–6 focus on biological and physical development, including genetics, prenatal development, birth, growth, and motor development.

• Chapters 7–11 cover sensory and perceptual development, three approaches to cognitive development, and language.

• Chapters 12–16 describe social and personality development, including emotional development, attachment, the self-system, moral reasoning, prosocial and antisocial behavior, gender-role development, and peer relations.

Although the overall organization is topical, the internal presentation of Chapters 7–16 is developmental. The topic area—be it language, gender roles, or whatever—begins with the newborn and describes development through adolescence. This approach helps the student to appreciate the continuity of growth within each area and also to understand the ongoing interactions between biological processes and contextual influences.

Cultural Diversity

The dramatic increase in cross-cultural and multicultural research within the discipline prompted us to expand even further our discussion of these influences. For example, we discuss cross-culture investigations of Piaget's theory (Chapter 8), we describe how different cultures foster different approaches to language learning (Chapter 11), we examine ethnic differences in infant temperment (Chapter 12), and we describe cross-cultural variations in early play (Chapter 16).

Scientific Orientation

In this text we treat child psychology as a natural science and present it in a way that reflects its scientific underpinnings. In addition to providing a full chapter on research methods (Chapter 3), we discuss specific methodological issues frequently throughout the book, such as comparing research designs for examining genetic influences on development in Chapter 4, describing computer simulations in Chapter 9, and considering contrasting approaches to assessing infant–caregiver attachment in Chapter 12.

State-of-the-Art Coverage

Information is being generated in developmental psychology at a staggering rate. To prepare a textbook of manageable proportions, authors must make some tough decisions. We have chosen to present a state-of-the-art treatment of child psychology that focuses on the very latest issues and findings. For example, Chapter 4 discusses Ceci and Bronfenbrenner's new model of gene–environment interactions; Chapter 6 describes Thelen's dynamic systems approach to motor development; Chapter 8 discusses the newest developments in theory of the mind; and Chapter 13 presents Dweck's latest model of motivational processes and academic achievement.

Some chapters include boxed sections titled "*On the Cutting Edge*" that describe new and exciting research developments (see Pedagogical Features). Also, to keep the third edition as up-to-date as possible, we have added hundreds of new references, many from 1995 through 1998.

Although our focus is on current work, we recognize that some truly classic studies should be known by every student of human development. In such cases, the material is presented in boxed sections titled "*Classics of Research*" (see Pedagogical Features).

Balanced Theoretical Presentation

Rather than emphasizing any single theoretical orientation, our book examines child psychology from the perspectives of the three principal traditions that characterize the discipline today—*the cognitive-developmental approach, the environmental/learning approach,* and *the ethological approach.* The fundamental tenets of these three orientations are first presented in Chapter 2. Then, most of the remaining chapters begin by examining what the three traditions have to say about that topic area and go on to consider relevant research findings and applications. As a consequence, the student can approach the substantive material in these chapters with a conceptual structure that facilitates interpretation, comparison, and critical analysis. For example, Chapter 14, on moral development, begins by outlining the theoretical models of Piaget, Kohlberg, and Turiel and then examines recent studies designed to test the validity and scope of these models.

Readability and Simplicity

We have worked hard to make our text, above all, interesting and accessible to the student reader. We believe that the text's comfortable writing style and the clarity with which concepts are introduced, discussed, and interrelated will enable students to read and understand a rigorous treatment of the issues.

In addition, rather than presenting long and tedious discussions of research findings that are likely to overwhelm students, we first decided what concepts and principles we wished students to come away with and then carefully selected research findings and real-world examples to illustrate and support this material. As a consequence, we believe that we have produced a text that communicates the essence and excitement of developmental psychology simply and efficiently.

Pedagogical Features

In our effort to be complete and up-to-date, we have not forgotten that this is a textbook whose audience includes college sophomores. We have designed into the book a number of features—some new to the third edition (designated by ** below)—to maximize the likelihood that students will learn the material.

Chapter-Opening Vignettes   Most of the chapters begin with a brief story or anecdote designed to capture the student's interest and to introduce the topic under consideration. In Chapter 4, for example, we open with the story of Dolly, the Scottish sheep that was cloned from a single cell, and we consider some of the intriguing ethical questions posed by the research. Or in Chapter 15, we describe a fascinating case study in which a male newborn is surgically altered and raised as a female.

"On the Cutting Edge" Boxes   We use boxes selectively in this text. The "On the Cutting Edge" boxes are designed to make students aware of recent research findings—such as the latest studies of newborn facial perception (Chapter 7), Goldin-Meadow's work on using gestures to assess cognitive status (Chapter 9), and Bem's new theory of sexual orientation (Chapter 15)—or important ongoing research programs—such as the Human Genome Project (Chapter 4).

"Classics of Research" Boxes   A highly praised feature of the first two editions was retained for this edition. The "Classics of Research" boxes present studies of enduring historical value, even though they are no longer of immediate relevance to contemporary thinking in the area. Examples include Arnold Gesell's research on motor development in twins (Chapter 6), Harlow's work with attachment in infant monkeys (Chapter 12), and Hartshorne and May's studies of moral character (Chapter 14).

"Applications" Sections   These sections present examples of research findings and programs that have been applied to work in schools, homes, hospitals, and other real-world settings. Whereas previous editions had this material separated out as boxes, here we integrated it into the main body of the text at the points where we felt it was most relevant and labeled them as Applications. Examples of these sections include caring for cocaine-exposed babies (Chapter 5), using picture-book reading to encourage language development (Chapter 11), and controlling gang violence (Chapter 16).

"Development in Context" Sections   In addition to describing the influences of contextual factors throughout the text, we also include more detailed discussions in separate sections labeled "Development in Family Context" (e.g., growing up in a single-parent household, in Chapter 15), "Development in School Context" (e.g., do schools depress adolescents' self-concept, in Chapter 13), and "Development in Cultural Context" (e.g., the effects of exposure to real-life violence, in Chapter 14). Like the Applications sections, these are integrated into the body of the text but are denoted by special headings and icons.

✓   ***"To Recap" Sections***   At the end of each major section in a chapter, a brief summary of the material is presented. This organization encourages students to pause and reflect on what they have just read and helps set the stage for the sections that follow. Feedback from the previous editions indicated that students found these sections very helpful.

Visual Summaries   Each chapter ends with a summary of the major points and issues. Using a visual layout, much like a flow chart, these summaries help students organize and review the chapter's material.

Running Glossary   Bold-faced glossary items in the text highlight terms of continuing importance to students. These items are defined in the margin on the same page, as well as at the end of the book, providing a convenient guide for reviewing the material.

Illustration Program   We reworked many of the figures and drawings from the previous edition to create new, effective illustrations in a full-color format. We also carefully selected many color photos that depict situations and events described in the text, along with some that illustrate laboratory techniques and other research methods.

Supplementary Materials

Accompanying the text is a full package of materials to support student learning and classroom teaching. The package includes the following:

The Student Study Guide contains chapter outlines, learning objectives, key terms, application exercises, critical thinking exercises, self-test questions, and practice exams. The study guide was again prepared by Alastair Younger of the University of Ottawa.

The Instructor's Resource Guide contains guidelines for the first-time instructor, chapter outlines, learning objectives, key terms, lecture topics, discussion questions, in-class and out-of-class activities, supplemental readings, videoguide, and media materials. It was prepared by Susan Siaw of the California State Polytechnic University, Pomona.

The Test Bank provides approximately 120 questions for each chapter, keyed to the text in a multiple-choice, true/false, and essay format. Each question notes the text page on which the answer can be found, and whether the question is factual or conceptual.

The Computerized Test Bank is available in IBM and Macintosh versions.

Overhead Transparencies present approximately 100 figures and tables from the text.

Video Library Instructor's can choose from a variety of videos and clips for class presentation from the Child Psychology Video Library. Please contact your local Wiley representative for more details about the different video options.

Web Site Using the Vasta Web site, located at http://www.wiley.com/college/vasta, students will be able to sample the study guide, and instructors can download the text supplements directly to their computers.

Ross Vasta
Marshall M. Haith
Scott A. Miller

Acknowledgments

A project of this size requires the participation of many people. We would like to thank the helpful staff at Wiley, especially Ellen Schatz, for all their advice and assistance. We are especially grateful to Alastair Younger, who prepared the Visual Summaries, and to Beverly Peavler, who helped create the vignettes. Thanks also to M. Jeffrey Farrar for his input on Chapter 11.

We would like to acknowledge the contributions of the following reviewers, whose many comments and suggestions were extremely helpful in preparing this revision of the text.

Linda Baker
University of Maryland, Baltimore County

Marie T. Balaban
John Hopkins University

Byron Barrington
University of Wisconsin-Marathon County

Sarah Bengston
Augustana College

Cynthia Berg
University of Utah

Rebecca Bigler
University of Wisconsin-Madison

Theodore Bosack
Providence College

Kristine Brady
Rider University

Stewart Cohen
University of Rhode Island

Jodi Compton
Framingham State University

K. Laurie Dickson
Northern Arizona University

Shelly Drazen
SUNY Binghamton

Shirlee Fenwick
Augustana College

Barry Ghoulson
University of Memphis

Yolanda Harper
University of Tulsa

Yvette R. Harris
Miami University

Melissa Heston
University of Northern Iowa

Kenneth I. Hoving
University of Oklahoma

Janice Kennedy
Georgia Southern University

Katherine Kipp
University of Georgia

Gerald Larson
Kent State University

Gary Levy
University of Wyoming

Pamela Ludeman
Framingham State University

Patricia McKane
Augustana College

Tammy A. Marche
University of Saskatchewan

Carolyn Mebert
University of New Hampshire

Morton J. Mendelson
McGill University

Derek Montgomery
Bradley University

Lynn Okagaki
Purdue University

Jeff Parker
Pennsylvania State University

Catherine Raeff
Indiana University of Pennsylvania

Jane Rysberg
California State University, Chico

Greg Simpson
University of Kansas

Beth Wildman
Kent State University

Kathy Stansbury
University of New Mexico

Martha Zlokovich
Southeast Missouri State University

Laura Thompson
New Mexico State University

We would also like to thank the following reviewers for their expert reviews of the cross-cultural coverage in the third edition and for their many suggestions.

Xinyin Chen
University of Western Ontario

Marite Rodriguez-Haynes
Clarion University

Catherine Raeff
Indiana University of Pennsylvania

We would like to thank the following consultants for their suggestions and feedback on the video selections to accompany the text.

Michelle Boyer
Middle Tennessee State University

Kristine Brady
Rider University

A group of students at Nassau Community College participated in a focus group to help us develop the design and pedagogy of the third edition, and we thank them for their time and feedback.

Amy Brooks
Olivia Figueras
Marianne Gobek-Craven

Linda Machado
Shaun Smith

We would also like to thank the following reviewers of the previous editions of this text.

Brian P. Ackerman
University of Delaware

Roger V. Burton
SUNY at Buffalo

Karen Bauer
University of Delaware

Bruce D. Carter
Syracuse University

Dan Bellack
College of Charleston

Stephen J. Ceci
Cornell University

Dana Birnbaum
University of Maine

Ed Cornell
University of Alberta

Fredda Blanchard-Fields
Louisiana State University

James Dannemiller
University of Wisconsin-Madison

Cathryn L. Booth
University of Washington

Beverly D. Eckhardt
Albuquerque Technical Institute

Theodore Bosack
Providence College

Melissa Faber
University of Toledo

Gordon F. Brown
Pasadena City College

Beverly I. Fagot
University of Oregon

Harriet Budd

Mary Ann Fischer
Indiana University-Northwest

Katherine W. Gibbs
University of California, Riverside

Gail S. Goodman
University of California, Davis

Terry R. Greene
Franklin & Marshall College

Vernon Hall
Syracuse University

William S. Hall
University of Maryland at College Park

Vernon Haynes
Youngstown University

Erika Hoff-Ginsburg
University of Wisconsin-Parkside

Marsha Ironsmith
East Carolina University

Jane Jakoubek
Luther College

Boaz Kahana
Cleveland State University

Kenneth Kallio
SUNY Geneseo

Christine Kenitzer
Texas Tech University

Wallace Kennedy
Florida State University

Marguerite D. Kermis
Canisius College

Elizabeth Lemerise
Western Kentucky University

Gary Levy
University of Wyoming

Angeline Lillard
University of San Francisco

Barbara Manning
University of Nebraska-Omaha

John C. Masters
Vanderbilt University

Kevin MacDonald
California State University, Long Beach

Robert G. McGinnis
Ancilla College

Margie McMahan
Cameron University

Richard Metzger
Mercer University

Barbar Moely
Tulane University

Ernst L. Moerk
California State University, Fresno

Derek Montgomery
Bradley University

Lisa Oakes
University of Iowa

Cynthia O'Dell
Indiana University

Vicky Phares
University of South Florida

Harvey A. Pines
Canisius College

Dina Raval
Towson State University

D. Dean Richards
University of California, Los Angeles

William L. Roberts
York University

Marite Rodriguez-Haynes
Clarion University

Karl Rosengren
University of Illinois

Nicholas R. Santilli
John Carroll University

Ellin Scholnick
University of Maryland

Frederick M. Schwantes
Northern Illinois University

Gayle Scroggs
Cayuga Community College

Kathleen Sexton-Radek
Elmhurst College

Harriet Shaklee
University of Iowa

Cecilia Shore
Miami University

Susan Siaw
California Polytechnic State University

Robert S. Sigeler
Carnegie Mellon University

Gregory Simpson
University of Kansas

Frank J. Sinkavich
York College of Pennsylvania

Rita Smith
Millersvile University of Pennsylvania

Thomoas R. Sommerkamp
Central Missouri State College

Debra Cowart Steckler
Mary Washington University

Nanci Stewart Woods
Austin Peay State University

Katherin Van Giffen
California State University, Long Beach

Diane N. Villwock
Moorehead State University

Leonard Volenski
Seton Hall University

Amye Warren-Leubecker
University of Tennessee at Chattanooga

Alastair Younger
University of Ottawa

About the Authors

Ross Vasta

is Distinguished Professor of Psychology at the State University of New York at Brockport. He received his undergraduate degree from Dartmouth College in 1969 and his Ph.D. in clinical and developmental psychology from the State University of New York at Stony Brook in 1974. He is a Fellow in the American Psychological Society and the American Psychological Association (Division 7). In 1987 he was awarded the SUNY Chancellor's Award for Excellence in Teaching. His previous books include *Studying Children: An Introduction to Research Methods, Strategies and Techniques of Child Study,* and *Six Theories of Child Development.* He is currently editor of the annual series *Annals of Child Development.*

Marshall M. Haith

is Professor of Psychology at the University of Denver. He earned his B.A. in 1959 from the University of Missouri and received his masters degree and Ph.D. from the University of California, Los Angeles, in 1964. After completing postdoctoral work at Yale University, he held positions at Harvard University, University of Geneva, and Rene Descartes University in Paris. He has been a Guggenheim Fellow and a Fellow at the Center for Advanced Study in the Behavioral Sciences. He has previously authored *Day Care and Intervention Programs for Infants Under Two Years of Age* and *Rules That Babies Look By: The Organization of Newborn Visual Activity.* Along with J.J. Campos, he edited Volume 2 of Mussen's *Handbook of Child Psychology.* His research interests include infant perception, the formation of expectations in early infancy, and the development of information-processing skills.

Scott A. Miller

is Professor of Psychology at the University of Florida. After completing his undergraduate work at Stanford University in 1966, he entered the Institute of Child Development at the University of Minnesota, where he earned his Ph.D. in 1971. His initial appointment was at the University of Michigan. He is a Fellow in the American Psychological Association (Division 7). He has previously authored *Developmental Research Methods,* 2nd edition, and coauthored (with John Flavell and Patricia Miller) *Cognitive Development,* 3rd edition. His research has been in the cognitive area, focusing on Piaget's work, children's understanding of logical necessity, theory of mind, and parents' beliefs about children.

Brief Contents

Contents

6 *Physical Development: Birth, Motor Skills, and Growth* 149

7 Sensory and Perceptual Development   195

8 Cognitive Development:
The Piagetian Approach   241

14 *Moral Development*   525

15 Gender-Role Development and Sex Differences — 571

16 Peer Relations — 613

Chapter *1*

Introduction and Perspective

This book presents the modern science of child psychology. In it, we trace the growing child's development from the embryo's earliest beginnings in the mother's womb to the child's eventual ascent into adolescence. We also describe the many factors that affect children's development, as well as how researchers go about the work of identifying them.

Attempts to explain children's development go as far back as history can trace. But child psychology as a science is only about 100 years old. What distinguishes our efforts during this past century is psychologists' use of the scientific method. *This approach involves rules that specify, for example, how research evidence should be gathered, how it may be analyzed, and what sorts of conclusions researchers may draw from their findings. Scientists have used this method to study an endless number of phenomena, from stars to starfish. In this book, we examine how they use it to study children.*

At first glance, understanding child development may not appear to be very difficult. Certainly the typical behaviors of infants and young children—including their physical abilities, their interactions with others, and even the ways they think—are simpler than those same behaviors in adults. But it is a mistake to conclude that the processes involved *are simple. Psychologists have learned that human development is a complex and intricate puzzle, and unraveling its mysteries has proved to be a major challenge. Since the methods of science were first applied to the study of children 100 years ago, we have learned a great deal. Yet the more we learn, the more apparent it becomes that we have only scratched the surface.*

Developmental Psychology

To begin, it is important to understand exactly what psychology is and what psychologists study. Psychology is the scientific study of behavior. The behavior that most psychologists study is human behavior. But any species—from mice to mynah birds to monkeys—can be examined legitimately from a psychological (and developmental) perspective.

Developmental psychology The branch of psychology devoted to the study of changes in behavior and abilities over the course of development.

Developmental psychology, one of the largest of psychology's many subfields, is concerned with *the changes in behavior and abilities that occur as development proceeds.* Developmental researchers examine both what the changes are and why they occur. To put it another way, developmental research has two basic goals. One is *description*—to identify children's behavior at each point in their development. This involves such questions as, When do babies begin to detect colors? What are the typical mathematical abilities of a 5-year-old? or How do sixth graders usually resolve conflicts with their peers? The second goal is *explanation*—determining the causes and processes that produce changes in behavior from one point to the next. This involves examining the effects of such factors as the genes children inherit from their parents, the biological characteristics of the human brain, the physical and social environment in which children live, and the types of experiences they encounter.

Developmental psychologists study behavior changes at all phases of the life cycle. Most, though, have focused on the childhood period, ending at adolescence. For this reason, *developmental psychology* and *child psychology* have traditionally referred to the same body of scientific knowledge. That situation has changed somewhat in recent years as increasing research is being directed toward issues of adulthood and old age. This book, however, focuses on the traditional early period (and so we have chosen the title *Child Psychology*).

Why Study Children?

If developmental psychologists can study any species of animal and any period in the life cycle, why has so much of their research traditionally concentrated on humans during the childhood years? We have at least five answers to this question.

Period of Rapid Development   Because developmental researchers are interested in studying change, it makes sense for them to focus on a period when much change occurs. During the first part of the life of most species, more developmental changes take place than during any other period. In humans, changes involving physical growth, social interactions, the acquisition of language, memory abilities, and virtually all other areas of development are greatest during childhood.

Long-Term Influences   Another important reason for studying children is that the events and experiences of the early years strongly affect an individual's later development. As the poet Wordsworth once noted (and many psychologists have since reiterated), "The child is father to the man." Almost all psychological theories suggest that who we are today depends very much on our development and experiences as children.

Insight into Complex Adult Processes   Not all psychologists are primarily concerned with early development. But even researchers who are attempting to understand complex adult behaviors often find it useful to examine those behaviors during periods when they are not so complex. For example, humans are capable of sophisticated communication because our languages follow systems of rules. But determining what these rules are has proved very difficult for researchers.

One approach to this problem is to study our language system as it is being acquired. Thus in language development, as well as in many other areas, the growing child is a "showcase" of developing skills and abilities, and researchers interested in different aspects of human development have taken advantage of this fact to help them understand adult behavior.

Real World Applications   Developmental psychologists often conduct their research in laboratory settings, where they investigate theoretical questions regarding basic psychological processes. Nevertheless, the products of this research can sometimes benefit children with real world problems, such as poverty, illiteracy, drugs, and crime. Legislators and other policy makers often turn to psychologists to provide them with usable knowledge regarding the effects of these problems on children and possible ways to treat them (Fisher & Lerner, 1994; Zigler & Finn-Stevenson, 1992). Developmental research is also being extended to such areas as the effects of day care, classroom teaching methods, and parental disciplinary techniques, among others. Simply put, one reason we study children is to make their lives better.

Children's fascinating behavior and inherent appeal undoubtedly contribute to their being of great interest to developmental researchers.

Interesting Subject Matter A final and important reason so many developmental psychologists have directed their efforts toward understanding children is that the human child is an intriguing and wondrous creature. When we consider that children have attracted attention from artists, writers, and scholars in many other fields of study, it is perhaps not surprising that psychologists, too, have found this subject matter appealing. Our own interest in pursuing this area of science reflects our personal love of children and our fascination with their behavior and development.

✓ *To Recap...*

Developmental psychologists use the scientific method to study changes in behavior and abilities. The two basic goals of their research are to describe children's behaviors at each point in development and to explain the changes that occur from one point to the next. Although any species at any age level is legitimate subject matter for developmental psychology, most research has involved children, for five reasons: childhood is a period of rapid development; early experiences have long-term effects; complex processes are easier to understand as they are forming; knowledge of basic processes can help solve some of the problems of childhood; and children are inherently interesting to study.

Historical Views of Childhood

Modern psychology considers childhood an extremely important period of human development. Western culture views children as vulnerable and requiring a great deal of attention, care, and shelter from harm. Many laws are designed to protect children from dangerous toys, dangerous substances, and even dangerous parents. Our belief that all children deserve a free public education and that they should remain in school until adolescence similarly reflects the view that childhood is a special and important time.

In contrast to earlier historical periods, children today are viewed as physically and psychologically vulnerable, and are accorded a special place in Western society.

But these attitudes toward children reflect a relatively recent conception of early development (Greenleaf, 1978; Hart, 1991). To understand our modern view of the child, it is helpful to examine briefly some views of childhood from earlier points in history. Because child psychology is a science whose roots are in Western culture, this survey will focus on that tradition. In the remainder of the text, however, we consider contemporary aspects of child development in cultures throughout the world.

Ancient Greece and Rome

The Greek and Roman civilizations, which extended from about 600 B.C. to about A.D. 400, are usually regarded as periods of great enlightenment. Yet the status of children during these times was hardly enviable.

Although such great Greek thinkers as Plato and Aristotle wrote of the importance of education, they also defended practices that today would seem unthinkable. *Infanticide*, the killing of newborns, was routine and viewed as an appropriate way to deal with babies who were illegitimate, unhealthy, or simply unwanted (Breiner, 1990; Langer, 1974).

Severe punishment and the sexual exploitation of children were neither uncommon nor considered wrong or cruel. The Romans, for example, bought and sold children for various purposes, including domestic work and service in brothels for the sexual pleasure of adults (Mounteer, 1987). And in neighboring Carthage, children were killed and buried in the foundations of public buildings as sacrifices to the gods (Weld, 1968). So although the ancient world recognized the importance of the childhood years, it clearly did not display the caring and protective attitudes toward children that exist today.

The Medieval and Renaissance Periods

Following the collapse of the Roman Empire, the Catholic Church attempted to improve the lives of children by promoting an image of them as pure and innocent. The Church took a strong stand against infanticide and offered parents of unwanted children the alternative of shipping them away to convents and monasteries—an arrangement that benefited both parties. (The Church, however, remained generally powerless in preventing the killing of twins, who were considered to be the obvious products of adultery.) Although educational training during this period reached one of its lowest levels in recorded history, the Church did provide simple reading and writing instruction to children involved in religious studies (Sommerville, 1982).

As the medieval period progressed, the view of childhood continued to improve. In the 12th century, for example, December 6 was set aside to honor the patron saint of all children, St. Nicholas. That holiday was later moved to coincide with the celebration of the birth of Christ and became the modern Christmas.

Unfortunately, the abuse and exploitation of children remained commonplace during this period of history. It has even been suggested that childhood as we know it did not exist during the Middle Ages. Once children were old enough to participate in household and community labor (at about the age of 7), they became a part of the larger society and were, according to some historians, treated simply as less experienced adults (Aries, 1962; McCoy, 1988). Although not all scholars agree entirely with this theory, there is little doubt that children of the medieval period had a very difficult life (Kroll, 1977; Pollock, 1983).

The Renaissance began early in the 14th century and extended into the 17th. It was marked by a revival of interest in Greco-Roman art, literature, and philosophy, which in turn prompted a general rebirth of Western civilization. This era also brought an increased concern for the welfare of children. In Florence, Italy—generally considered the birthplace of the Renaissance—charitable institutions known as *foundling homes* were set up by wealthy individuals to take in sick, lost, and unwanted children. Foundling homes, which eventually spread throughout western Europe, were significant in that they represented a new and growing belief that society had some responsibility for the care and protection of its youngsters (Trexler, 1973).

The Renaissance also saw the reemergence of scientific investigation in such fields as astronomy, medicine, and physics. The science of psychology did not yet exist, so the study of human development was primarily the concern of philosophers and religious scholars. Some early scientific thinkers, such as Galileo, believed that physical and biological mechanisms were the basis for understanding human behavior. The Church, however, disagreed with any nonspiritual explanations of behavior and, as it was a powerful social force at the time, was effective in discouraging their study.

The Reformation and the Puritans

Throughout the medieval period and much of the Renaissance, "the Church" referred to the Roman Catholic Church. But early in the 16th century, a variety of Protestant groups broke away. From the perspective of child development, the most important of these groups was the Puritans, led by John Calvin (1509–1564).

The Puritans were perhaps the first to offer a comprehensive model of child development. In many ways, their view was a rejection of the earlier belief in the child's purity. Instead of seeing them as innocents, Calvin argued that children are born with original sin and are naturally inclined toward evil unless given the proper guidance and instruction (Pollock, 1987). Yet he also believed that children have a great capacity for learning at an early age and that parents therefore have the opportunity (and the obligation) to train them properly.

The Puritans took child rearing very seriously. They were the first to write manuals to aid parents in this task. The Calvinist approach was to encourage the child to become independent and self-reliant and, most of all, to develop self-control. Because sin and evil were seen as ever-present problems, it was crucial that the child learn to resist temptations early and effectively.

The Puritans also put great emphasis on education, particularly on reading (Moran & Vinovskis, 1985), and were the first to write books specifically for children. Although most of the books had religious or moral themes, a few were somewhat entertaining in an attempt to make the task of learning a bit more pleasant.

Descartes's Dualistic Model

To understand the views of child development that emerged in the 17th century and beyond, we must take a short side trip to discuss the contribution of René Descartes (1596–1650). Descartes, a French mathematician and philosopher, was not specifically interested in child development, but his model of human behavior laid the groundwork for what would eventually become the science of psychology.

The essence of Descartes's philosophy is that the mind and the body are separate from each other. The human mind, he argued, is God given and therefore does not have a material form or follow the physical laws of nature. Its function is to reason and make decisions and then carry out these decisions by commanding the body—which is earthly and physical—to perform whatever is required.

Descartes's description of the human mind as nonphysical and dominant over people's material bodies was consistent with the Church's views, and so his ideas met with little religious opposition. This was important for science in general—and eventually for psychology—because it allowed Descartes to develop a theoretical model of the human body that was based solely on mechanical and physical principles.

In essence, then, Descartes divided the investigation of human behavior into two separate realms—one concerned with the psychological functioning of the mind and the other with the physical workings of the body. The concept that the mind exists independently of the body, referred to as **Cartesian dualism**, remains a matter of debate even today. But the historical importance of Descartes's mind–body division was that it removed the scientific investigation of the body from the scrutiny of the Church, thus permitting researchers to pursue whatever questions they saw fit to study. This new view of human behavior ushered in the modern study of psychology.

Cartesian dualism
René Descartes's idea that the mind and body are separate, which helped clear the way for the scientific study of human development.

✓ *To Recap...*

The concept of childhood has changed dramatically over time. The ancient Greeks and Romans viewed children largely as property that was both exchangeable and expendable. During the medieval period, the Church helped elevate the image of children by stressing their purity and innocence. At the same time, the Church hindered scientific study, which reemerged as an area of interest during the Renaissance, by permitting only religious explanations of human behavior. The Puritans, who arose out of the Reformation, constructed the first comprehensive model of child development. This model was based on the idea of the child's inherent evil and inclination toward sin. René Descartes cleared the way for the scientific study of human behavior by proposing a dualistic system in which the nonphysical mind governs the mechanical functioning of the physical body.

Early Theorists

Descartes's mind–body distinction fueled debate over the nature of human development, and several very different points of view emerged. Three early scholars—John Locke, Jean-Jacques Rousseau, and Charles Darwin—offered theories of human behavior that are the direct ancestors of the three major theoretical traditions found in child psychology today. These three modern traditions include one model that focuses on the influence of the child's environment, a second that emphasizes the role of the child's cognitive development, and a third that is most concerned with the evolutionary origins of behavior.

JohnLocke, a 17th-century British philosopher, foreshadowed later environmentalists by proposing that a newborn's mind was like a blank sheet of paper on which environment and experiences wrote the script of the child's life.

Tabula rasa
Latin phrase, meaning "blank slate," used to describe the newborn's mind as entirely empty of inborn abilities, interests, or ideas.

Jean Jacques Rousseau, an 18th-century French philosopher, described his nativistic views of human development in *Émile*, a novel about the growth and upbringing of a young French boy.

John Locke (1632–1704)

In 17th-century England, Descartes's theory was taken up by a group of philosophers. The most famous of these, John Locke, was a physician as well as a leading political figure of the time. Locke espoused the belief that "all men are created equal" in the eyes of the law. This principle eventually became the cornerstone of the new government developed by the colonists in America. It also found its way into Locke's views regarding human development.

According to Locke's theory, all children are created (born) equal, and the mind of a newborn infant is like a piece of white paper—a **tabula rasa** ("blank slate"). All knowledge comes to the child only through experience and learning. Children are therefore neither innately good nor innately evil; they are simply the products of their environment and upbringing. This environmentalist point of view also means that any child theoretically is capable of becoming anything—a surgeon, an actor, or a skilled artisan—if given the proper rearing and training. Similarly, the wrong environment can produce a scoundrel, beggar, or thief.

Locke's writings were not all scholarly. He also offered advice to parents on the best methods for raising their children. Although he stressed the use of rewards and punishments, Locke did not favor material rewards (e.g., candy and toys) or physical punishment. Discipline, he believed, should involve praise for appropriate behaviors and scolding for inappropriate behaviors. Locke also discussed the importance of stimulating children to begin learning at a very early age. Locke's ideas gained wide acceptance among British and European scholars as well as the general public. But in less than 100 years, this strong environmentalist model was to be replaced by a very different conception of the child.

Jean-Jacques Rousseau (1712–1778)

Jean-Jacques Rousseau was born in Switzerland but spent most of his life in France, where he became the leading philosopher of his day. He is considered the father of French romanticism, a movement in which artists and writers emphasized themes of sentimentality, naturalness, and innocence. These ideas were reflected in Rousseau's conception of the child.

Rousseau's views on development are presented in his well-known novel *Émile* (1762), in which he describes the care and tutoring of a male child from infancy to young adulthood. Using this literary vehicle, Rousseau outlined his views of human development and offered suggestions on the most appropriate methods of child rearing and education (Mitzenheim, 1985).

In contrast to Locke, Rousseau believed that children are born with knowledge and ideas, which unfold naturally with age. Development, in this view, follows a predictable series of stages that are guided by an inborn timetable. The child's innate knowledge includes such things as the principles of justice and fairness and, above all, a sense of conscience. In effect, Rousseau returned to the theme of the inborn goodness and purity of the child. Rousseau also believed that whatever knowledge the child does not possess innately is acquired gradually from interactions with the environment, guided by the child's own interests and level of development. Thus the wisest approach to child rearing is not to instruct children formally, but to have them learn through a process of exploration and discovery. By clearly emphasizing innate processes as the driving forces in human development, Rousseau's theory contrasted with the environmentalistic ideas of Locke and would today be referred to as **nativism**.

Rousseau further believed that the development of the child repeats the cultural history of the human race. Émile, he said, was a *noble savage*, much as the primitive cave dwellers were: they were noble because they possessed an innate goodness that characterizes all humans; they were savage because their ideas were simple and unsophisticated.

Rousseau's suggestions for educating Émile contain at least three ideas that are promoted by many educators today. First, children should be exposed to a new body of knowledge only after they display a cognitive "readiness" to learn it. Second, children learn best when they are allowed to acquire ideas or information through their own discovery process. Finally, both education and child rearing should encourage a permissive style that allows children to follow their own natural inclinations (Thomas, 1979).

Rousseau's ideas had a major impact in Europe, and his nativistic view of development was hailed by both scientific and political writers. His ideas, like Locke's, were both revolutionary and ahead of their time. And, as we will see, they would reappear 200 years later in the work of another Swiss theorist, Jean Piaget.

Charles Darwin (1809–1882)

The third major ancestor of modern developmental thought was the English biologist Charles Darwin. Although best known for his theory of evolution, presented in *The Origin of Species* (1859), Darwin was also a keen observer of child development. Indeed, his detailed record of the growth and behavior of his infant son, "Doddy," was one of the first developmental studies (Darwin, 1877).

Darwin's evolutionary theory begins with the assumption that individual members of a species vary in many characteristics, so that some are faster, some are stronger, some are lighter, and so on. A second assumption is that most species produce more offspring than their environment can support, which means that the individual members must compete for survival. Depending on the environment, some variations may increase the chances for survival, such as providing better ways of avoiding danger or acquiring food. If so, individuals possessing these traits are more likely to survive and so pass them along to future generations. Through this process, which Darwin called **natural selection**, the species continually evolves to evermore adaptive forms. At the same time, less useful variations gradually disappear. The evolutionary model thus suggests that some of the present-day behaviors of humans (or of any other animal) had their origins countless years ago, when they were important for the survival of an earlier form of our species.

Darwin's theory of evolution did not directly address the issue of child development, but his views led other biologists of the time, such as Ernst Haeckel, to propose the principle of **recapitulation** (Haeckel, 1906/1977). According to this theoretical notion, the development of the individual—that is, *ontogeny*—proceeds through stages that parallel the development of the entire species—that is, *phylogeny*. This principle is often stated as "ontogeny recapitulates phylogeny." As applied to our species, it means that human development—beginning with its earliest embryonic and prenatal forms and continuing with the physical, motor, and social development of the growing child—follows a progression similar to that which evolved through the various prehuman species (Wertheimer, 1985).

Although the recapitulation theory is no longer scientifically supported, the idea that the child's development repeats that of the species had great appeal for some early developmentalists. And by providing a theory that both explained the developing behaviors observed by Rousseau and others and served as a framework for future research on human development, Darwin's writings helped launch the scientific study of the child (Charlesworth, 1992).

Nativism
The theory that human development results principally from inborn processes that guide the emergence of behaviors in a predictable manner.

Charles Darwin's theory of evolution, developed in the mid-19th century, was quickly adopted by the early developmental psychologists and laid the foundation for the modern fields of ethology and sociobiology.

Natural selection
An evolutionary process proposed by Charles Darwin in which characteristics of an individual that increase its chances of survival are more likely to be passed along to future generations.

Recapitulation theory
An early biological notion, later adopted by psychologist G. Stanley Hall, that the development of the individual repeats the development of the species.

✓ *To Recap...*

Even before psychology emerged as a discipline, three early scholars presented important models of human development. John Locke based his approach on the strict environmentalist position that all knowledge is acquired through experience. Jean-Jacques Rousseau proposed a nativistic model in which development unfolds according to inborn processes. Charles Darwin's theory of evolution suggested that many human behaviors have their origins in the past, when they were valuable for our ancestors' survival.

Pioneers of Child Psychology

The belief that the development of the child is related to the evolution of the species gave birth to the science of developmental psychology. But the evolutionary perspective was soon joined by other theoretical models as child development quickly became the focus of increasing amounts of scientific debate and research. Only a few of the individuals who contributed to the rise of this movement are discussed here. Our purpose is not to provide a detailed history of child study, but to point out the origins of some important ideas and controversies that remain a part of modern developmental science.

G. Stanley Hall (1846–1924)

Referred to as the father of child psychology, G. Stanley Hall is credited with founding the field of developmental psychology (Appley, 1986). He conducted and published the first systematic studies of children in the United States.

Hall received his Ph.D. from Harvard in 1878 under the direction of the famous psychologist William James. He spent the next 2 years working in Germany, where he became interested in a child study project being conducted in Berlin. On his return to the United States, Hall administered questionnaires to all the first-grade children in the Boston school district to determine precisely what sorts of everyday knowledge American children usually possessed when they began school. The questions included such items as, What season is it? Where are your elbows? and Where does butter come from? Hall published the results of this research in 1883 under the title "The Contents of Children's Minds." Although interesting, the findings contained nothing particularly new or surprising.

In 1891, he began a larger project designed to gather data on children of all ages and from all regions of the country. Once again Hall used questionnaires, but this time he sent them to parents, teachers, and other adults who had frequent contact with children. Unfortunately, Hall's research was not well conceived. The information that poured in from these questionnaires took many forms, as the respondents approached the questions in a wide variety of ways. In the end, Hall was left with a vast accumulation of data that were difficult to interpret and impossible to summarize (White, 1992).

Hall's attempts to make a theoretical contribution to psychology were also not particularly successful. Excited by Darwin's writings, he adopted the view that children's development recapitulates the evolution of the species. Hall also felt that education and child rearing should encourage the "natural" tendencies of the child that reflect the behavior and development of earlier forms of the species. He was especially interested in the period of adolescence, which he believed marked the end of biological recapitulation and the first opportunity for the child to develop individual talents and abilities (Hall, 1904).

By the turn of the century, however, advances in biological research had made it clear that no simple recapitulation process exists in human development

Some of the pioneers of psychology invited by G. Stanley Hall to Clark University in 1909. Hall is seated front center, and Sigmund Freud is seated front left.

(Coleman, 1971). Furthermore, many American psychologists were beginning to favor the more environmentalist view that children acquire knowledge and skills through experience and that their behavior can be best explained by learning processes (Cairns, 1998).

Although neither his research nor his theoretical ideas ultimately had much impact, Hall did make some lasting contributions to the field (Hilgard, 1987; Ross, 1972). As an educator at Clark University in Worcester, Massachusetts, Hall trained the first generation of developmental researchers. He also established several scientific journals for reporting the findings of child development research, and he founded and became the first president of the American Psychological Association. Finally, a more indirect contribution was his invitation to Sigmund Freud to present a series of lectures in the United States—an event that, as we will see, led to the introduction of psychoanalytic theory into American psychology.

John B. Watson (1878–1958)

The theoretical idea that is generally shared by the scientists of a given period is referred to as its **Zeitgeist**—a German term meaning "the spirit of the times." When a science is very young, the Zeitgeist can change dramatically from one time to the next. Major shifts in thinking regarding one of the most basic issues of human development—what causes changes in behavior in growing children—had already occurred several times in the centuries before the science of developmental psychology emerged in the mid-1800s. We saw that the Zeitgeist of the 17th century was Locke's environmentalist view of human development. This model was replaced first by Rousseau's nativistic explanation and then by the evolutionary theories of Darwin and Hall. As the 20th century dawned, the pendulum began to swing away from biological interpretations of development and back toward the environmentalist position.

Zeitgeist
The spirit of the times, or the ideas shared by most scientists during a given period.

John B. Watson was the first major psychologist to adopt Locke's belief that human behavior can be understood principally in terms of experiences and learn-

Behaviorism
A theory of psychology, first advanced by John B. Watson, that human development results primarily from conditioning and learning processes.

ing. But his new approach, which he called **behaviorism**, also differed radically regarding what psychologists should study and which methods of investigation they should use (Horowitz, 1992).

Watson received his Ph.D. in 1903 from the University of Chicago. His early career was devoted to the study of animal psychology. Descartes's dualism was very evident among psychologists at this time. Some, like Watson, studied the physiological workings of the body. But many were exclusively concerned with the psychological functioning of the human mind and, in particular, with consciousness and such issues as how individual perceptions are combined to form ideas and thoughts. The most common research method was *introspection*, which involved engaging research participants in a task and then having them try to look inward and report on the processes occurring in their minds.

Watson found this approach unsatisfactory for a number of reasons. First, little agreement was ever found across participants' descriptions of their internal experiences. Further, Watson felt strongly that psychology should follow the example of the other natural sciences and deal only with objective, observable subject matter—in this case, observable behavior. Finally, his interest in animal psychology led him to reject any method that could not also be used to study other species.

These ideas were radical for the time, but Watson's persuasive writing style, combined with a bit of luck, soon propelled behaviorism into the forefront of psychological theory (Cohen, 1979). Watson joined the psychology faculty at Johns Hopkins University in 1908. Within several years he became chairman of the prestigious psychology department, president of the American Psychological Association, and editor of *Psychological Review*, the most important journal in the field. Watson used these positions as platforms from which to market behaviorism to the scientific community.

The basic tenet of behaviorism is that changes in behavior result primarily from conditioning processes. Watson argued that learning occurs through the process of association, as described in the work of the Russian physiologist Ivan Pavlov (1849–1936). Pavlov had shown that any simple reflex can be conditioned to many different stimuli—for example, he conditioned dogs to salivate to the sound of a bell.

Conditioned reflex method
John B. Watson's name for the Pavlovian conditioning process in which reflexive responses can be conditioned to stimuli in the environment.

Watson believed that this simple conditioning process, which he called the **conditioned reflex method**, explained how human behavior changes over time. All human behavior, he argued, begins as simple reflexes. Then, through an association process like the one Pavlov described, various combinations of simple behaviors become conditioned to many stimuli in the environment. Language ("verbal behavior," to Watson), for example, begins as simple infant sounds that grow in complexity as they continue to be conditioned to the objects and events in the surrounding environment. Furthermore, as speech grows more and more sophisticated, it gradually develops a subvocal (silent) form, which we know as thinking, reasoning, and problem solving. Watson therefore believed that it was crucial for psychologists to study infants and young children—not simply to observe early physical changes, but to study the first steps in the conditioning process that produces complex human behavior.

The Pavlovian conditioning process that formed the core of Watson's behavioristic theory was straightforward and easy to understand. And it was this simplicity, along with Watson's demand for strict experimental methods, that led American psychologists of the time to embrace behaviorism as a major advance in scientific thinking. A new Zeitgeist had emerged.

In 1920, however, Watson was forced to resign from Johns Hopkins when an affair with a graduate student and a divorce from his wife created a scandal. He left academic life and began writing magazine articles and books for the general public about his behavioristic approach. *Psychological Care of the Infant and Child*, published in 1928, presented his views on child rearing, and it proved to be a very successful and influential book. Watson's suggestions to parents were based on an almost pure environmentalism—that is, the belief that no abilities or personality characteristics are inborn, so children are entirely the products of their upbringing and environment. This view had great appeal for many parents, who delighted in believing that their children had the potential to become great athletes, scientists, or Supreme Court justices, if only given the proper training.

Watson's career was brief, but his contributions to psychology were significant. His call for objective methods of study, in particular, brought early experimental psychology in line with the other natural sciences. Today, virtually all experimental psychology is based on the methods that Watson espoused, including the precise specification of experimental procedures and the emphasis on observable and measurable behaviors. However, Watson's strict environmentalist views and the major role he assigned to conditioned reflexes are no longer taken very seriously.

Sigmund Freud (1856–1939)

In 1909, as Watson was introducing behaviorism to the scientific world, another important event took place. G. Stanley Hall invited some of the most eminent psychologists of the day, including Sigmund Freud and several other European scholars, to Clark University to celebrate the institution's 20th anniversary (Hall and Freud are seen seated together on page 11). It was on this occasion that Freud, in a series of five lectures, first outlined his grand theory of psychological development. American psychologists were not immediately receptive to Freud's model, and it proved to be no obstacle to Watson's emerging behavioral movement. But the seeds of psychoanalytic thought had been planted in U.S. soil, and in time Freud's views would attract a good deal of attention both inside and outside psychology.

Freud spent most of his early life in Vienna, Austria, where he trained as a medical student. In 1885, bored with medical practice, he traveled to Paris to learn the technique of hypnosis from the French physician Charcot. During this time Freud began to develop many of his ideas regarding the powerful role of the unconscious. On his return to Vienna, Freud established a private practice and began refining both his theory and the methods of psychoanalysis.

Freud made two major contributions to psychology. His greatest impact was in the area of clinical psychology, where his model of personality and his techniques of psychoanalysis continue to represent a major school of thought in psychotherapy. His contribution to developmental psychology was his stage theory of psychosexual development. Although he spent very little time observing children directly, he used his patients' and his own recollections of childhood experiences to construct a comprehensive model of child development.

The central theme of Freudian developmental theory is that each child is born with a certain amount of sexual energy, called **libido**, which is biologically guided to certain locations on the body, called the **erogenous zones**, as the child grows. Sexual energy, in this model, refers simply to the ability to experience physical pleasure. The arrival of the libido at each location marks a new stage in the child's psychosexual development, and during that stage the child receives the greatest physical pleasure in that erogenous zone.

Freud's model was not purely biological, however. He firmly believed that children's experiences during each stage strongly affect their later development. Successful movement from stage to stage requires that children receive the proper

Libido
Sigmund Freud's term for the sexual energy that he believed is possessed by all children from birth and then moves to different locations on the body over the course of development.

Erogenous zones
According to Freud's theory of psychosexual development, the areas of the body where the libido resides during successive stages of development. The child seeks physical pleasure in the erogenous zone at which the libido is located.

Freud proposed that, during the anal stage, successful toilet training is important to the child's psychosexual development.

Repression
Freud's term for the process through which desires or motivations are driven into the unconscious, as typically occurs during the phallic stage.

Identification
The Freudian process through which the child adopts the characteristics of the same-sex parent during the phallic stage.

Interactionist perspective
The theory that human development results from the combination of nature and nurture factors.

amount of physical pleasure from each erogenous zone. Freud therefore cautioned parents not to frustrate children by being overly strict, but he warned that being too indulgent or permissive could cause problems as well. In other words, children should experience enough pleasure, but not too much. Unfortunately, both Freud's advice and his theoretical predictions were always rather vague as to how much pleasure was enough.

According to the psychosexual model, human development unfolds in five stages. During the *oral stage*, from birth to about 18 months, the libido is located at the mouth. The infant's principal source of physical pleasure is sucking, and all objects tend to find their way into the child's mouth. When and how much infants are breast-fed and how they are eventually weaned are the events in this stage that, according to Freud, have the strongest long-term influence. The period from 18 months to 3 years marks the *anal stage*, in which the child attains physical pleasure first from having bowel movements and later from withholding them. Not surprisingly, positive toilet-training experiences are the major concern during this stage.

The most complex of Freud's stages is the *phallic stage*, which lasts roughly from age 3 to age 6 and the erogenous zone is the genital area. During this stage, according to Freud, children become sexually attracted to the parent of the opposite sex. But they soon experience feelings of conflict as they realize that the same-sex parent is a powerful rival. Children presumably resolve this conflict in two ways. First, they force their desires into the unconscious, a process called **repression**, which also wipes out their memory of these feelings. Then, they compensate for this loss by making a determined effort to adopt the characteristics of the same-sex parent, a process called **identification**.

The *latency stage* occurs in the middle and later childhood years, from age 6 to age 12. During this stage, the libido remains repressed and inactive. It reemerges at puberty in the *genital stage*, when once again the child develops an attraction toward the opposite sex. Now, however, it is more appropriately directed toward peers, rather than parents.

Freud's theory of child development is actually a theory of personality formation. It assumes that many aspects of the adult personality result from events during the childhood psychosexual stages. If the child's experiences during a stage are not what they should be, some portion of the libido will remain *fixated* in that erogenous zone, rather than moving on to the next one. For example, if a child is not given the appropriate amount of oral gratification during the first stage, the libido will remain partially fixated at the mouth. Later in life, this fixation will be manifested in the adult's continually seeking physical pleasure in this erogenous zone— perhaps by smoking, chewing on pencils, or having an unusual interest in kissing. Many everyday behaviors of this sort were explained by Freud as symptoms of early developmental difficulties.

Although Freud's theory had some influence on American developmentalists, they never fully accepted it, for several reasons. First, it is vague and its key elements cannot be scientifically verified or disproved. Furthermore, Freud's heavy reliance on unobservable mechanisms, such as unconscious motives, is not consistent with American psychology's belief that science should be based on measurable and verifiable observations.

In spite of its failings, though, Freud's theory of child development includes two fundamental concepts that are generally accepted today. The first is the rejection of both a purely nativistic and a strictly environmentalist explanation of human behavior. Freud was the first major developmentalist to argue for an **interactionist perspective**, which views both inborn processes and environmental factors as significant contributors to the child's development. Today almost all child psychologists subscribe to an interactionist position. The second fundamental concept is Freud's suggestion that early experiences can have important effects on behavior in later life. Again, most contemporary developmentalists agree with this idea, although few would explain these effects in terms of unresolved childhood conflicts hidden in the adult's unconscious (Beier, 1991; Emde, 1992).

Perhaps a third positive outcome of Freud's theory is that it inspired a number of related models of development that have achieved somewhat greater acceptance in developmental psychology. One of these, proposed by Erik Erikson, is described shortly.

Arnold Gesell (1880–1961)

In science, the pendulum of philosophical thought swings back and forth. Just as scientists begin to accept a particular way of looking at things, someone seems to come along with an important criticism of that view or with new evidence that supports some earlier position. So when the Zeitgeist swings back toward a prior point of view, it is usually because of new research findings or a more complete theoretical explanation of the facts. Accordingly, when developmentalists began returning to the biological model of child development in the 1930s, it was not because they once again accepted recapitulation theory. Rather, they were persuaded to reconsider the nativistic viewpoint by the research and ideas of one of G. Stanley Hall's most successful students, Arnold Gesell.

Gesell completed his doctoral work at Clark University in 1906 and obtained a medical degree at Yale University. In 1911, he established the Yale Clinic of Child Development, where he spent almost 50 years studying and describing the development of the typical child.

Although he did not agree with Hall's view that human development mirrors the evolution of the species, Gesell did believe that development is guided primar-

Among Arnold Gesell's most important contributions to developmental psychology were his innovative research techniques, including an observation dome that permitted photographing the child unobtrusively from any angle.

ily by biological processes. He therefore felt that growth and the emergence of motor skills (crawling and sitting, for example) should follow very predictable patterns. In his scheme, the environment plays only a minor role, perhaps affecting the age at which certain skills appear but never affecting the sequence or pattern of development. The complex of biological mechanisms that guide development Gesell described simply as **maturation**. The resulting patterns of growth and development were as yet unknown, and Gesell set about to identify them.

Maturation
The biological processes assumed by some theorists to be primarily responsible for human development.

Using observational methods and hundreds of children of many different ages as research participants, Gesell conducted the first large-scale study to examine children's behavior in great detail. This research revealed a high degree of uniformity in children's development. They did not all develop at the same rate—some walked earlier and others later—but the pattern of development was very consistent. For example, almost all children walked before they ran, ran before they skipped, and skipped before they hopped. From his work, Gesell established statistical **norms**—a sort of developmental timetable that describes the usual order in which children display various early behaviors and the age range within which each behavior normally appears (Gesell & Thompson, 1938). These norms proved very valuable to physicians and parents as general guidelines for evaluating developmental progress—so much so that they continue to be revised and used today.

Norms
A timetable of age ranges indicating when normal growth and developmental milestones are typically reached.

To acquire this sort of descriptive information, Gesell did not rely on the outdated research methods of the past. In fact, the sophisticated research techniques he developed for observing and recording children's behavior are among his most important contributions to psychology (Thelen & Adolph, 1992). Gesell pioneered in the use of film cameras to record children's behavior. He also developed one-way viewing screens, and he constructed a photographic dome that allowed observations from all angles without disturbing the child under study.

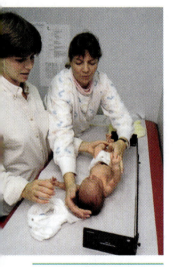

Gesell's method of comparing children's development to norms representing the average range of development continues to be used today.

Gesell wrote books containing advice for parents that could have been given by Rousseau 200 years earlier. He suggested, for instance, feeding babies only when they display signs of hunger and allowing them to sleep, play, and explore according to their own natural schedules. Parents should be patient, enjoying their children's current abilities and behaviors rather than trying to hurry them along toward more mature skills. Gesell did believe that parents need to include some limits and structure in the child's life, but he felt strongly that, if largely left alone, children will develop naturally and properly, according to their inborn biological plans (Gesell & Ilg, 1943).

Gesell's innovative methods of study and his establishment of developmental norms greatly expanded our knowledge of children's everyday skills and behavior. But his strongly biological philosophy, like most extreme viewpoints, was an oversimplification, because it largely neglected the crucial role of environmental factors. As a result, Gesell's theoretical model failed to have a long-term impact on developmental thought (Hilgard, 1987). His emphasis on patterns of unfolding behavior and his focus on similarities in children's development, however, may have helped prepare American psychologists to accept the more influential views of another of Rousseau's theoretical descendants, Jean Piaget.

Jean Piaget (1896–1980)

If we had to select the one psychologist whose work has had the greatest influence on the study of child development, we would have to consider Jean Piaget a very strong candidate. His ideas have inspired more research than those of any other theorist, and his conception of human development revolutionized thinking about children and their behavior. Piaget differs from the other pioneers discussed here in that his theoretical views are still widely accepted in some form by many of today's developmental psychologists. For this reason, we discuss Piaget in several places in this text. This chapter briefly describes his background and overall approach to psychology. Later chapters cover his theoretical views and the research that addresses them.

Piaget was born and raised in Switzerland. From boyhood, he was interested in science, particularly biology and animal behavior. Although he eventually left this area of study, his background in biology is reflected in his theory of child development. Piaget had always been drawn to the study of psychology, and after earning his doctorate in 1918, he moved from Switzerland to Paris, where he became involved in the development of intelligence tests for children.

Intelligence testing was a new field at this time, and two of its founders, Alfred Binet and Theodore Simon, were attempting to develop questionnaires that could predict children's success in school. Binet and Simon first devised questions that represented the knowledge typical of children at a given age. Then they developed norms so that any child's test performance—the number of correct answers—could be compared with the average performance of other children of the same age. These tests improved on Hall's early questionnaires by including precise testing and scoring procedures that did not allow for subjective interpretations.

Piaget was hired by Simon to administer the tests, which gave him his first real experience with developmental work. But unlike his employers, Piaget became less interested in the number of test items children answered correctly than in the reasons for their incorrect responses. Children of different ages, he observed, not only knew different amounts of information but also looked at the world in very different ways. Their answers revealed *qualitative* (style related) differences in thinking, beyond the *quantitative* (amount related) differences in factual information.

After two years in Paris, Piaget returned to Switzerland and began his own research on the development of children's knowledge. Piaget called his area of interest **genetic epistemology**, by which he meant the study of the nature of knowledge in young children and how it changes as they grow older. Unlike Hall, Piaget was interested not in the precise knowledge and facts that children possess—for example, *what* children know when they enter school—but rather in how they go about acquiring and using that knowledge—that is, *how children think*.

To find support for his theory, Piaget developed his own research technique. Whereas Gesell's methods involved observing children without interfering with them, Piaget challenged children (including three of his own) with simple tasks and verbal problems that required solutions and explanations. His technique, known as the **clinical method**, involved a loosely structured interview in which he asked a question or posed a problem and then, depending on the child's response, followed up with other questions that might reveal the child's reasoning or problem-solving approach.

Piaget's research initially attracted some attention in the United States during the 1920s and 1930s. But his writings were difficult for American psychologists to understand because they contained many terms and concepts that differed from the scientific language the Americans were using. And Piaget's somewhat informal methods of investigation were viewed as a problem by more rigorous experimental researchers. During the 1940s and 1950s, as American child psychology once again turned toward environmental and conditioning models, interest in Piaget's theory disappeared.

Beginning in the late 1950s, however, American psychologists began to rediscover Piaget's work. His theoretical writings were translated into more familiar concepts, and his studies were replicated under controlled experimental conditions (Flavell,

Jean Piaget is one pioneer of child psychology whose early ideas remain largely accepted today by many researchers.

Genetic epistemology
Jean Piaget's term for the study of children's knowledge and how it changes with development.

Clinical method
Piaget's principal research method, which involved a semistructured interview with questions designed to probe children's understanding of various concepts.

1963). Among the first to endorse Piaget's theories were educators, who began to develop school curricula based on his ideas. Research psychologists also became interested in Piaget's theoretical views. Their own experiments supported his predictions and confirmed the existence of qualitative differences in the thinking of children of different ages. In addition, his theory generated many new questions that psychologists felt could and should be investigated, questions about children's understanding of time, logic, causality, and other kinds of fundamental knowledge.

Piaget died in 1980 at the age of 84. As late as 1975, he was revising his model in response to new data and findings generated by his research team in Geneva (Beilin, 1989). Piaget's many books on child psychology remain the greatest contribution to the field by a single scholar (Beilin, 1992).

Erik Erikson (1902–1994)

Freud's psychoanalytic theory had problems that made it unacceptable to many American experimental psychologists. Some of Freud's ideas, nevertheless, were provocative enough to spur other child researchers to extend and refine them into new models of development. One of the most important of these *neo-analytic* models was that of Erik Erikson.

Erikson grew up in Germany just after the turn of the century. As a young man, he was a skilled artist, and he spent his early life wandering through Europe pursuing this work. His travels eventually took him to Vienna, where he began teaching art to children of Americans who had come to train with Freud and his colleagues. In time, Erikson also entered psychoanalytic training and studied under Freud's daughter, Anna, an accomplished analyst in her own right.

In 1933, Erikson traveled to the United States and accepted a position at Harvard Medical School. He was principally interested in children and became Boston's first child psychoanalyst. More important, he constructed a comprehensive model of human development that continues to be of interest to many psychologists.

Erikson's model, although based on Freud's theory, differed from it in some major ways. For one, he believed that development continues throughout life. He thus replaced Freud's five stages of development—which end in late adolescence—with an eight-stage model that continues into old age. Erikson also believed that personality development cannot be understood without considering the environment in which it develops. After studying a number of diverse cultures—including Native American tribes in California and South Dakota, inner-city youth, and the people of India—Erikson developed a psycho*social* model (in contrast to Freud's psycho*sexual* model) of personality that included a major role for social and cultural influences. Finally, Erikson's model was based on the study of normal individuals and emphasized the positive, healthy aspects of personality.

Epigenetic principle
According to Erikson, the genetic process that guides personality formation through its stages of development.

Identity
In Erikson's theory, the component of personality that develops across the eight stages of life and that motivates progress through the stages.

Like Freud, Erikson believed that all children progress through a predictable series of stages. This progression, he argued, is guided by an **epigenetic principle**, meaning that personality development is not random but follows a blueprint or timetable built into our genes. According to Erikson, each individual's ultimate goal is the quest for **identity**, which is accumulated gradually across the eight stages. But, at each stage, a positive personality characteristic associated with the search for identity conflicts with a negative one resulting from interaction with the social world. For example, in Erikson's second stage, the toddler's newfound physical abilities—such as walking and controlling bladder and bowel functions—lead to the positive feelings of *autonomy* as the child begins to exert more control over his or her life. But these new abilities also tend to cause conflict in the child's social world—with parents, for instance—leading to feelings of *shame* and *doubt*. According to Erikson, the best resolution of these conflicts would have the child leaving the stage with a strong

Table 1.1
Stages of Development: Erikson and Freud

Ages (yrs)	Erikson	Freud
Birth–1.5	Basic Trust vs. Mistrust	Oral
1.5–3	Autonomy vs. Shame	Anal
3–6	Initiative vs. Guilt	Phallic
6–12	Industry vs. Inferiority	Latency
12–18	Identity vs. Role Confusion	Genital
Young adult	Intimacy vs. Isolation	
Adult	Generativity vs. Stagnation	
Older adult	Ego Integrity vs. Despair	

sense of the positive personality characteristic, but also with a small degree of the negative characteristic. The eight stages are presented in Table 1.1, which includes a comparison with the stages proposed by Freud.

Erikson's theory is thus also interactionist, combining nature and nurture factors. Each person is guided through the psychosocial stages by genetic processes, but the individual's social and cultural surroundings help determine how the conflicts are resolved at each stage and so also contribute heavily to personality development.

Lev Vygotsky (1896–1934)

Another pioneer of child psychology whose ideas continue to find considerable acceptance is Lev Vygotsky. As with Piaget, we present Vygotsky's background and general theoretical approach here, and in later chapters we discuss his ideas in more detail.

Vygotsky was born in Russia in the same year as Piaget, and their early work occupied the same period. Yet their backgrounds were very different. These differences are reflected in the contrasting models of human development they constructed (Glassman, 1994; Kozulin, 1990).

Unlike Piaget, Vygotsky was not trained in science but instead received a law degree from Moscow University. He went on to study literature and linguistics and eventually received a Ph.D. for a book he wrote on the psychology of art.

A similarity between the two scholars, however, is that both received little attention from Western scientists until the 1960s, when their work was translated into English and their theories began to be tested experimentally. Piaget, of course, was still active at this time and continued to contribute to the scientific advances brought about by his theory. Vygotsky, however, had died at 37 and never saw his ideas pursued by other researchers. Initially, his writings were misunderstood, and they were banned in the former Soviet Union for over 20 years. Thus his work remained unknown even to many of his contemporary Soviet psychologists.

To understand Vygotsky's theory, it is important to appreciate the political environment of the time. Vygotsky began working in psychology shortly after the Russian Revolution, which replaced the rule of the czar with Marxism. The new philosophy stressed socialism and collectivism; individuals were expected to sacrifice their personal goals and achievements for the betterment of the larger society. Sharing and cooperation were encouraged, and the success of any individual was seen as reflecting the success of the culture. Marxists also placed a heavy emphasis on history, believing that any culture could be understood only through examination of the ideas and events that had shaped it.

Vygotsky's model of human development incorporated these elements and so has been termed a *sociocultural* approach. It holds that the individual's development

Lev Vygotsky's sociocultural theory of cognitive development, originally published more than fifty years ago, has generated great interest in modern developmentalists.

is a product of his or her culture. In this theory development refers largely to mental development, such as thought, language, and reasoning processes. Vygotsky assumed that these abilities develop through social interactions with others (especially parents) and thus represent the shared knowledge of the culture. Whereas Piaget believed that all children's cognitive development follows a very similar pattern of stages, Vygotsky saw intellectual abilities as much more specific to the culture in which the child was reared.

Today, the sociocultural approach has become one of the most influential movements in developmental psychology (Valsiner, 1998). We discuss the specific psychological mechanisms proposed by Vygotsky and others of this tradition in later chapters.

✓ *To Recap…*

The scientific study of children began with the questionnaire research of G. Stanley Hall, who also proposed a theory of development based on the principle of evolutionary recapitulation. John B. Watson helped make child psychology a natural science by introducing objective research methods based on observable and measurable behaviors. His behavioristic theory of development held that the conditioned reflex was the fundamental unit of development and that environmental and experiential factors were primarily responsible for changes in behavior. Sigmund Freud proposed a stage theory of child development that grew out of his clinical work in psychoanalysis. Modern developmentalists have little interest in Freud's theory, but his interactionist viewpoint and his emphasis on early experiences remain important concepts. Arnold Gesell's research with children renewed interest in the biological perspective by offering evidence that inborn maturational processes account for developmental changes. His observational studies produced age-related norms of behavior that have been valuable to both professionals and parents.

Jean Piaget is perhaps the most influential developmental theorist to date. His genetic epistemology was concerned with understanding the form of children's knowledge and the qualitative changes it undergoes as they develop. Erik Erikson offered a neo-analytic, stage model of development that similarly combined nature and nurture processes. Unlike Freud's theory, this model extended through adulthood, assigned a major role to social factors, and focused on the healthy aspects of personality. Lev Vygotsky proposed a sociocultural model of human, and especially mental, development that reflected Marxist beliefs in the social and cultural basis of individual development.

Issues in Developmental Psychology

As we described the views of some of the pioneers of developmental psychology, a number of questions arose repeatedly. Three issues in particular have run through scientific thinking about development almost from the very beginning, and they remain a source of debate today. These issues revolve around the questions of nature versus nurture, continuity versus discontinuity, and normative versus idiographic development.

Nature versus Nurture

Nature versus nurture debate
The scientific controversy regarding whether the primary source of developmental change rests in biological (nature) factors or in environmental and experiential (nurture) factors.

The most basic and long-standing issue in child psychology (and perhaps in all of psychology) involves the degree to which behavior and development result from inborn, biological, **nature** factors and the degree to which they reflect environmental, experiential, **nurture** factors. This debate has existed at least since Locke and Rousseau first proposed their rather pure environmental and nativistic models of child development. The nurture view was later taken up by Watson and other learning theorists, while the nature position formed the basis of the theories of Hall and Gesell. The modern debate, however, is far more complex than it was in these early days of psychology (Plomin & McClearn, 1993).

We noted earlier that virtually all child researchers today subscribe to some form of interactionist position, in which both nature and nurture are assumed to contribute to human development. Several theoretical models describing how our genes and environment may work together to guide our behavior are discussed in Chapter 4.

Nevertheless, the nature–nurture debate has not ended. There is still little agreement as to how and how much nature and nurture factors contribute to many areas of development. For example, when a kindergartner hits a classmate who has just taken away a toy, some psychologists are likely to believe that the child's aggressive response is principally a biological reaction to frustration and that it may have its roots in our evolutionary past. Others might argue that it probably represents a behavior the child learned by watching and interacting with others.

Another example can be found in the area of gender-role development. Once a sex difference in behavior has been identified—such as the finding that males are generally more adept than females at certain spatial tasks—explanations for the difference can take at least three different forms. The difference can be attributed to nature, as in the contention that the brains of males and females are structured differently. It can be attributed to environmental factors, as in the argument that boys receive more encouragement from parents and teachers to engage in activities that promote spatial skills. Or it can involve an interactionist explanation, such as the possibility that boys innately prefer activities involving spatial relations and, as a result, spend more time improving these skills.

Nature versus nurture questions arise in almost every topic we consider in this text. At times, however, they appear under different labels, such as heredity versus environment, maturation versus learning, or emergent abilities versus acquired skills. Whatever the name, these debates tend to involve the same fundamental issue.

The role of nature and nurture factors in human development has been at the heart of many theoretical debates in developmental psychology.

Continuity versus Discontinuity

A second long-standing issue in child psychology is whether development displays **continuity** or **discontinuity**. This debate actually has two components (Emde & Harmon, 1984). One involves the *pattern* of development. Is development smooth and stable, with new abilities, skills, and knowledge gradually added at a relatively uniform pace (continuous)? Or does development occur at different rates, alternating between periods of little change and periods of abrupt, rapid change (discontinuous)? The second component involves the *connectedness* of development. Continuity theorists contend that many of the behaviors and abilities we see in adolescents and adults can be traced directly back to development early in life. Discontinuity theorists, in contrast, suggest that some aspects of development emerge relatively independently of what has come before and cannot be predicted from the child's previous behavior (Clarke & Clarke, 1976).

The continuity model is often associated with the belief that human behavior consists of many individual skills that are added one at a time, usually through learning and experience. As children acquire more and more of these skills, they combine and recombine them to produce increasingly complex abilities. This approach emphasizes quantitative change—the simpler elements are essentially added together to produce the more advanced capabilities—and tends to characterize environmentalist models of development. In contrast, psychologists who favor the discontinuity model usually hold that development is guided primarily by internal biological factors. Stage theorists, for example, argue that the unevenness of children's development—relatively stable periods followed by abrupt changes—reflects the discontinuous nature of the changes taking place in the underlying structures of the body and brain. Thus, development is thought to involve qualitative changes in previous abilities or behaviors.

Like the nature versus nurture issue, the question of continuity versus discontinuity is not all-or-nothing. Psychologists on both sides of the debate agree that some developmental processes are more accurately described by one model and others by the competing model (Rutter, 1987).

Normative versus Idiographic Development

A third issue that commonly arises in child psychology is not a matter of debate so much as it is a description of a researcher's focus of study. Some psychologists are concerned with **normative** development, meaning what children have in common or how development is similar across them. Others focus on **idiographic** development, meaning the differences in development from one child to the next.

Normative research, such as the work of Gesell and, to a lesser degree, of Piaget, is often based on a biological view of development. This perspective thus focuses on the "average" child, with the primary goal of identifying and describing how normal development proceeds from step to step. A related issue involves the search for **universals of development**—behaviors or patterns of development that characterize all children, everywhere (which Piaget sought to identify).

Idiographic research centers on the individual child and the factors that produce human diversity. Genes are certainly responsible for some of the individual differences among people, but the idiographic perspective also considers the environmental and experiential processes that serve to mold and shape children into unique individuals. Researchers use this approach to study aspects of development that display **cultural relativism**—the way in which such aspects differ from one culture to another.

Research on language development illustrates these two approaches. Some theorists believe that language abilities develop in the same way for all children because they are controlled mainly by specific mechanisms in the brain. These

Normative research attempts to identify commonalities among children, whereas idiographic research is concerned with why one child is different from the next.

researchers therefore search for common patterns of linguistic development both in children who speak the same language and in children who speak different languages. Theorists concerned with individual differences in speech development are more apt to study environmental influences on language acquisition, such as the type of speech adults use when talking with children, in order to determine which factors cause language to develop differently from one child to the next.

✔ *To Recap…*

Three issues arise frequently in child psychology research. The nature versus nurture issue focuses on whether the primary source of developmental change is inborn and biological or environmental and experiential. The continuity versus discontinuity issue concerns whether the pattern of development is constant or uneven and whether development shows connectedness between early and later characteristics. The normative versus idiographic issue involves the researcher's preference for focusing either on the commonalities of children's development and the search for universals or on the factors that produce individual differences among children, such as cultural influences.

Conclusion

Our brief look backward in this chapter should have made one point clear—the more scholars have observed children and learned about early development, the more they have come to appreciate the importance of the childhood years for understanding all human behavior. As this fact became increasingly obvious, two things happened. First, we realized that because children are not fully developed organisms they are more vulnerable than adults, so we began to treat them better. Second, we began to study children much more closely, using all the available tools of science. Today, children are accorded a very special status in our society, and developmental psychology has taken its place among the other natural sciences.

Although child study is still young compared with other physical and biological sciences, our understanding of developmental processes is progressing so rapidly that it is difficult to keep up with the information that is being generated by researchers. The remainder of the text, therefore, focuses on the current state of the field rather than on historical issues and research. And yet, as we proceed from topic to topic, you may be struck by how familiar some of the recurring controversies sound, reminiscent of the fundamental differences that arose between Locke and Rousseau, Watson and Gesell, or Binet and Piaget.

Visual Summary for Chapter 1:
Introduction and Perspective

Developmental Psychology

| Two Basic Goals of Developmental Research | → | 1. To describe children's behavior at each point in development. |
| | → | 2. To explain developmental changes that occur from one point to the next. |

Why Study Children?

Five reasons why developmental psychology has traditionally involved children

Period of rapid development	→	More developmental changes take place in childhood than at any other time.
Long-term influences	→	Experiences of early years may affect the individual's later development.
Insight into complex adult processes	→	Complex processes are easier to understand as they are forming.
Real world applications	→	Knowledge of basic process can be used to help solve some of children's problems.
Interesting subject matter	→	Children are inherently interesting to study.

Historical Views of Childhood

Ancient Greece and Rome	→	Medieval Period	→	Renaissance	→	The Reformation	→	Descartes's Dualistic Model
Children were exchangeable, expendable property.	→	The Church stressed children's purity and innocence.	→	Foundling homes were set up to take in sick, lost, unwanted children.	→	The Puritans constructed the first comprehensive model of child development, based on the notion of original sin.	→	Descartes proposed a dualistic system, in which the nonphysical mind governed the mechanical functioning of the physical body.

Early Theorists

John Locke	→	Based his approach on the strict environmentalist position that all knowledge is acquired through experience.
Jean-Jacques Rousseau	→	Proposed a nativistic model in which development unfolds according to inborn processes.
Charles Darwin	→	His theory of evolution suggested that some human behaviors may have had their origins in the past, when they were valuable to our ancestors' survival.

Pioneers of Child Psychology

G. Stanley Hall	→	Credited with founding the field of developmental psychology. Proposed a theory of development based on the principle of evolutionary recapitulation.
John B. Watson	→	Proposed a behaviorist theory of development which held that the conditioned reflex was the fundamental unit of development and that experiential factors were primarily responsible for changes in behavior.
Sigmund Freud	→	Proposed a 5-stage psychosexual theory of development that emphasized the combined importance of early experiences and inborn processes.
Arnold Gesell	→	Proposed a biological perspective that stressed inborn maturational processes. Produced valuable age-related norms of development.
Jean Piaget	→	His genetic epistemology was concerned with understanding the form of children's knowledge and the qualitative changes it undergoes as they develop.
Erik Erikson	→	Developed an 8-stage theory that differed from Freud's in that it extended through adulthood, assigned a major role to social factors, and focused on the healthy aspects of personality.
Lev Vygotsky	→	Proposed a sociocultural model of human, and especially cognitive, development that reflected Marxist beliefs in the social and cultural bases of individual development.

Issues in Development Psychology

Nature versus nurture	→	This issue focuses on whether the primary source of developmental change is inborn and biological or environmental and experiential.
Continuity verus Discontinuity	→	This issue focuses on whether the pattern of development is constant or uneven, and whether there is a connectedness between early and later characteristics.
Normative versus Idiographic	→	This issue relates to the researcher's preference for focusing on the commonalities of child development or on factors that produce individual differences among children.

Chapter 2

Theories of Child Development

Developmental psychologists usually describe themselves in terms of their areas of research interest. One psychologist, for example, might concentrate on infants, studying how perceptual abilities develop during the first months of life. Another might be concerned with identifying the ways in which children's social skills affect their success in the classroom. But most psychologists also characterize themselves in terms of a particular theoretical orientation, that is, their view of how development occurs and which factors they believe are most responsible for changes in children's behavior.

Today, the large majority of child psychologists identify themselves with one of three general theoretical views: the cognitive-developmental approach, the environmental/learning approach, or the ethological approach. This chapter outlines the principal ideas and underlying assumptions of these three theories. Then, as we discuss various topics throughout the rest of the book, we will compare and contrast the approaches taken by each of the theories, including the types of questions they ask and the research methods they prefer.

Cognitive-Developmental Models

The cognitive-developmental approach actually includes several related theories. For years, it was most closely associated with the work of Piaget. Since the 1970s, however, information-processing and social models have also become very popular among cognitive developmentalists.

As we saw in Chapter 1, the roots of the cognitive-developmental tradition lie in the 18th-century writings of Jean-Jacques Rousseau. This early nativistic view suggested that human development unfolds predictably, with little or no environmental influence. Modern cognitive-developmental theorists assign a much greater role to environmental factors than did Rousseau, reflecting the interactionist perspective of all contemporary theories.

An important characteristic of this approach is its emphasis on cognition. According to these theories, the changes we witness in children's behaviors and abilities occur largely as a result of changes in their knowledge and intellectual skills. The major goals for psychologists of this tradition, therefore, are to specify what children know, how this knowledge is organized, and how it changes or develops.

Piaget's Theory

As a student of biology and zoology, Piaget learned that survival requires adaptation. Any individual organism, as well as any entire species, must adapt to constant changes in the environment. Piaget therefore viewed the development of human cognition (or intelligence) as the continual struggle of a very complex organism trying to adapt to a very complex environment (Piaget & Inhelder, 1968).

According to Piaget's theory, human development can be described in terms of *functions* and *cognitive structures*. The functions are inborn biological processes that are the same for everyone and remain unchanged throughout our lives. Their purpose is to construct internal cognitive structures. The structures, in contrast, change repeatedly as the child grows.

Cognitive Structures   The most fundamental aspect of Piaget's theory, and often the most difficult to understand, is the belief that intelligence is a process—not something that a child *has*, but something that a child *does*. Piaget's child does not possess knowledge passively, but understands the world by acting or operating on it.

For example, Piaget would describe an infant's knowledge of a ball in terms of the various actions the infant can perform with it—pushing the ball, throwing it, mouthing it, and so on. These actions represent the cognitive structures of infancy and are called **schemes**. Note that a scheme involves two elements: an object in the environment (such as a ball), and the child's reactions to the object. A scheme is therefore not a physical structure, but a psychological one. Early on, the infant has comparatively few of these schemes and they are related to one another in very simple ways. As development proceeds, however, schemes increase both in their number and in the complexity with which they are organized. These two characteristics of children's cognitive structures—number and complexity—define the child's intelligence at any point in development.

Schemes and other cognitive structures also display certain flexibilities. An infant does not perform exactly the same behavior with every ball she encounters—some may produce more squeezing, others more rolling—nor are the infant's reactions the same with every object. The way a ball is grasped may be somewhat different from the way a rattle is grasped, and the way either of these objects is sucked may be different from the way a nipple is sucked. Cognitive structures are flexible in another sense—they change over time. A particular scheme, such as grasping, reflects more and more skill as the infant applies it to more and more objects. In this way, schemes eventually become more individualized, or *differentiated*, so that a ball becomes primarily an object to be thrown, a rattle primarily an object to be shaken, and a nipple primarily an object to be sucked.

Beyond these simple schemes of infancy, new and higher-level cognitive structures gradually emerge. An 8-year-old confronted with a ball, for example, still has all the earlier schemes available (although sucking is not a very likely response), but the older child can also understand a ball by acting on it using mental operations, such as assigning it certain properties (color, size), actions (bouncing, hitting), or capabilities (being a member of the class "round things").

For Piaget, *development* referred to this continual reorganization of knowledge into new and more complex structures. Much of our discussion in Chapter 8 concerns what these structures are and how they change with development.

Functions   The functions that guide cognitive development are also central to Piaget's theory. Piaget stressed two general functions, both of which reflect his training in biology. One is **organization**. Because an individual's cognitive structures are interrelated, any new knowledge must be fitted into the existing system. According to Piaget, it is this need for integrating new information, rather than simply adding it on, that forces our cognitive structures to become ever more elaborately organized.

The second function is **adaptation**, which in general terms refers to an organism's attempt to fit with its environment in ways that promote survival. In Piaget's model, cognitive adaptation involves two processes. **Assimilation** entails trying to make sense of new experiences in terms of our existing cognitive structures. The infant who brings everything to his mouth to suck is demonstrating assimilation, as is the toddler who calls all men "Daddy." Note that assimilation may require some

Schemes
Piaget's term for the cognitive structures of infancy. A scheme consists of a set of skilled, flexible action patterns through which the child understands the world.

According to Piaget, babies' early schemes involve interactions with simple objects.

Organization
The tendency to integrate knowledge into interrelated cognitive structures. One of the two biologically based functions stressed in Piaget's theory.

Adaptation
The tendency to fit with the environment in ways that promote survival. One of the two biologically based functions stressed in Piaget's theory.

Assimilation
Interpreting new experiences in terms of existing cognitive structures. One of the two components of adaptation in Piaget's theory.

Accommodation
Changing existing cognitive structures to fit with new experiences. One of the two components of adaptation in Piaget's theory.

Constructivism
Piaget's belief that children actively create knowledge rather than passively receive it from the environment.

Periods
Piaget's term for the four general stages into which his theory divides development. Each period is a qualitatively distinct form of functioning that characterizes a wide range of cognitive activities.

Sensorimotor
Form of intelligence in which knowledge is based on physical interactions with people and objects. The first of Piaget's periods, extending from birth to about 2 years.

Preoperational
Form of intelligence in which symbols and mental actions begin to replace objects and overt behaviors. The second of Piaget's periods, extending from about 2 to about 6 years old.

Concrete operations
Form of intelligence in which mental operations make logical problem solving with concrete objects possible. The third of Piaget's periods, extending from about 6 to 11 years of age.

distortion of the new information in order to make it fit into the child's existing schemes. But trying to fit new things into what we already know is a necessary part of adapting to the world.

When new information is too different or too complex, **accommodation** occurs. Here, our cognitive structures change in order to integrate the new experiences. For example, the infant eventually learns that not all objects are to be sucked, just as the toddler learns that different labels or names need to be applied to different men. It is primarily through accommodation that the number and complexity of children's cognitive structures increase, that is, that intelligence grows.

Piaget assumed that assimilation and accommodation operate closely together. The growing child is continually making slight distortions of information to assimilate it into existing structures, while also making slight modifications in these structures to accommodate new objects or events. The interplay of these two functions illustrates another important aspect of Piaget's theory, the concept of **constructivism**. Children's knowledge of events in their environment is not an exact reproduction of those events—it is not like a perfect photograph of what they have seen or a precise recording of what they have heard. Children take information from the environment and bend, shape, or distort it until it fits comfortably into their existing cognitive organization. As we said earlier, they *operate* on it. Even when they accommodate structures to allow for new experiences, the accommodation is seldom complete, and some distortion of the information remains. Thus, when children 6, 8, and 10 years old watch a movie or hear a lecture, they come away with somewhat different messages, even though they may have seen or heard exactly the same stimulus input. Each child acts on the information somewhat differently, fitting it into his or her own existing set of structures. In this sense, the child *constructs* knowledge about the world, rather than simply receiving it.

The processes of assimilation, accommodation, and construction make the child's cognitive system increasingly more powerful and adaptive. However, these processes produce only small-scale changes. At certain points in development, Piaget argued, more major adjustments are required. At these points, the cognitive system, because of both biological maturation and past experiences, has completely mastered one level of functioning and is ready for new, qualitatively different challenges—challenges that go beyond what the current set of structures can handle. At such points, the child moves to a new stage of development.

Stages of Development   Piaget was a stage theorist. In his view, all children move through the same stages of cognitive development in the same order. At each stage, the child's cognitive functioning is qualitatively different and affects the child's performance in a wide range of situations.

There are four such general stages, or **periods**, in Piaget's model. Chapter 8 discusses the four periods in detail and also evaluates the general claim that development is divided into stages.

The **sensorimotor** period represents the first 2 years of life. The infant's initial schemes are simple reflexes and knowledge of the world is limited to physical interactions with people and objects. During the **preoperational** period, from roughly 2 to 6 years, the child begins to use symbols, such as words and numbers, to represent the world cognitively. The preoperational child is not yet skilled at symbolic problem solving, however. The period of **concrete operations** lasts approximately from age 6 to age 11. Children in this stage are able to perform mental operations on the pieces of knowledge they possess, permitting a kind of logical problem solving that was not possible during the preoperational period. The final stage, the period of

formal operations, extends from about age 12 through adulthood. This period includes all the higher-level abstract operations, enabling the child to deal with events or relations that are only possible, as opposed to those that actually exist.

The accuracy of Piaget's theory has been studied extensively over the years. In Chapter 8 we consider the evidence psychologists have gathered that both supports and questions various aspects of this theory.

Information-Processing Models

A second type of cognitive-developmental model is the information-processing approach, which we describe in detail in Chapter 9. Information-processing theorists view cognition as a system composed of three parts. First, information in the world provides the input to the system. Stimulation enters our senses in the form of sights, sounds, tastes, and so on. Second, processes in the brain act on and transform the information in a variety of ways, including encoding it into symbolic forms, comparing it with previously acquired information, storing it in memory, and retrieving it when necessary. Most psychologists working in the information-processing tradition have concentrated on this middle part of the system, designing their experiments to reveal the nature of these internal processes and how they interact with one another. The third part of the system is the output, which is our behavior—speech, social interactions, writing, and so on.

As you have probably noticed, there is an inescapable connection between the information-processing approach to cognition and the operation of a computer. Some psychologists make this connection very strongly. Their goal is to construct computer programs that simulate human behavior, so that ultimately we will be able to specify our cognitive processes in precise mathematical and logical terms. More often, however, researchers use the computer analogy simply as a way of thinking about information flowing through a system, where it is processed, and then reemerging in a different form. This approach has been useful in guiding psychological research on children's problem solving, memory, reading, and other cognitive processes (Kail & Bisanz, 1992; Klahr & MacWhinney, 1998).

In recent years, the information-processing view has probably become the leading approach to the study of human cognition. Its popularity reflects in part the growing interest in *cognitive science*, an interdisciplinary field in which researchers in biology, mathematics, philosophy, and neuroscience, among other disciplines, are attempting to understand the workings of the human mind (e.g., Keil, 1998; Osherson, 1990).

Not all information-processing research has been concerned with children, and much of it has not been directed toward developmental issues. Nevertheless, the approach has infused many areas of child psychology, and it will turn up throughout the text in topics as diverse as perception, language, gender roles, and aggression.

Social Models of Cognition

The cognitive-developmental tradition has always been most concerned with children's cognitive abilities, but in recent years it has also become involved with children's social development. This change has occurred for two reasons: On the one hand, cognitive processes have been shown to influence social experiences; on the other, social interactions are thought to influence cognitive development.

Social Cognition Many modern developmentalists believe that social development is affected by the nature and sophistication of the child's cognitive skills. How children interact with others depends, for example, on how they conceptualize

Formal operations
Form of intelligence in which higher-level mental operations make possible logical reasoning with respect to abstract and hypothetical events and not merely concrete objects. The fourth of Piaget's periods, beginning at about 11 years of age.

Information-processing models of development compare the functions of the human mind to those of a computer

interpersonal relationships, how accurately they interpret other children's behavior, how well they can apply information gained in previous situations to their current circumstances, and so forth. We will see in later chapters that such skills reflect fundamental aspects of children's emerging cognitive abilities.

This does not necessarily mean that the cognitive processes involved in social experiences are identical to those involved in nonsocial experiences. Although Piaget seemed to think they were (Piaget, 1964), most developmentalists today feel that the two are in some ways quite different. As a result, a new area of study, known as **social cognition,** has evolved (Flavell & Miller, 1998).

Social cognition
Knowledge of the social world and interpersonal relationships.

How might understanding the social world differ from understanding the physical world? One major difference is that people possess certain characteristics not found in nonliving things. For example, people have motives and intentions that may lead them to choose one behavior or another, sometimes in ways that are difficult to predict. Also, people have feelings and emotions that influence their behaviors and that may be important components of those behaviors. And, perhaps most important, people interact—that is, when acted on, people act back. An inanimate object, such as a leaf or a cup, may respond when we act on it. But when we act on a cup, we need not be concerned about what mood it is in, or what it hopes will happen, or what it will say in response. Nor, of course, do we need to be concerned about how *it* may act on *us*.

Although modern theorists recognize that there are important similarities between physical cognition and social cognition (Marini & Case, 1989, 1994), their primary interest is in the kinds of differences just described. Much research is presently under way to investigate children's understanding of their social world. You will encounter examples of such studies when we discuss children's beliefs regarding how the mind works (theory of mind) (Chapter 8), children's concept of self (Chapter 13), the ways in which children reason about moral issues (Chapter 14), and children's understanding of what it means to be a friend (Chapter 16).

Sociocultural Models   The kinds of research just described focus on how children's cognitive level enables them to understand their social world. But researchers have also been interested in the reverse process, that is, in how social experiences affect children's cognitive development.

The most influential contemporary theory of this type is that of the Soviet psychologist Lev Vygotsky, discussed briefly in Chapter 1. The theory itself is not new—as we saw, all of Vygotsky's work was conducted in the 1920s and 1930s—but only in recent years have developmental psychologists in the West begun to apply Vygotsky's ideas to children's cognitive and social development.

Tools of intellectual adaptation
Vygotsky's term for the techniques of thinking and problem solving that children internalize from their culture.

Vygotsky's theory emphasizes a number of related elements (Kozulin, 1990; Wertsch & Tulviste, 1992). Most important, it holds that culture is a major determinant of individual development. Humans are the only species that has created cultures, and every human child develops in the context of a culture. Culture makes two sorts of contributions to the child's intellectual development. First, children acquire much of the content of their thinking—that is, their knowledge—from the culture around them. Second, children acquire their thinking and reasoning processes—what Vygotskians call the **tools of intellectual adaptation**—from their culture. In short, culture teaches children both what to think and how to think.

Dialectical process
The process in Vygotsky's theory whereby children learn through problem-solving experiences shared with others.

How does culture exert its influences? Vygotsky believed that cognitive development results from a **dialectical process** in which the child learns through shared problem-solving experiences with someone else, usually a parent or teacher (Rogoff, 1998). Initially, the adult assumes most of the responsibility for guiding the

Vygotsky believed that children acquire cognition through shared experiences with others in their culture who are more knowledgeable.

problem they are working on. Gradually, however, the responsibility shifts partly and then completely to the child. Language plays a central role in this process in two ways. First, it describes and transmits to children the rich body of knowledge that exists in the culture. Second, it provides the means, or method, of problem solving, which is demonstrated by the adult and then adopted by the child, at first in vocal speech, and then in silent speech, to direct her own behavior.

This transfer of control from adult to child reflects the final Vygotskian theme, development as a process of **internalization** (Cox & Lightfoot, 1997). Bodies of knowledge and thinking tools at first exist outside the child, in the surrounding culture. Development, according to Vygotsky, consists of gradually internalizing them. This is what Vygotskians mean when they say that children's cognitive abilities grow directly out of their cultural experiences.

Undoubtedly much of the current popularity of this theory lies in its fit with contemporary ideas about the importance of contexts for understanding children's behavior. We have much to say about this issue throughout this book. And we return specifically to Vygotsky in Chapter 10, when we discuss theories of intelligence, and again in Chapter 13, when we examine the development of the self.

Internalization
Vygotsky's term for the child's incorporation, primarily through language, of bodies of knowledge and tools of thought from the culture.

✔ *To Recap…*

The cognitive-developmental approach is based on the belief that cognitive abilities are fundamental and that they guide children's behavior. The key to understanding changes in behavior across development, then, lies in understanding how children's knowledge is structured at any given time.

Piaget described human development in terms of inborn functions and changing cognitive structures. With development, the structures increase in number and complexity. Changes in structures are guided by two functions—organization and adaptation. Adaptation, in turn, consists of assimilation and accommodation. These processes reflect Piaget's constructivist view of development—the belief that children construct their understanding of the world rather than passively receive it from the environment. As children do this, they pass through four stages, or periods, of development: the sensorimotor period, the preoperational period, the period of concrete operations, and the period of formal operations.

Information-processing models conceptualize cognition as a computer-like system with three parts. Stimulation from the outside world makes up input, the first part; mental processes act on that information and represent the second part; and behavior of various sorts makes up the output of the system, the third part.

Social cognition refers to children's knowledge about people and social processes. Cognitive researchers have increasingly come to believe that understanding the social world differs in important ways from understanding the physical world. Psychologists favoring a sociocultural approach contend that social processes are crucial in the development of children's cognitive abilities. Vygotsky's theory stresses the role of culture in the child's gradual internalization of bodies of knowledge and tools of thought, primarily through shared experiences with parents and teachers.

Environmental/Learning Approaches

Just as Rousseau was the ancestor of the cognitive-developmental approach, so John Locke was the great-grandfather of the learning tradition. Locke's belief that environment and experiences are the keys to understanding human behavior—a view that John B. Watson translated into behaviorism early in this century—continues to be the guiding principle for many child psychologists today.

The essence of the environmental/learning view is that a great deal of human behavior, especially social behavior, is acquired rather than inborn. Of course, modern behavioral psychologists, like cognitive-developmental psychologists, are interactionists. They accept that biological and cognitive factors make important contributions to human development. But they do not share the belief that our biology and evolutionary history largely dictate our development (a view discussed in the next part of this chapter). Nor do they accept the idea that cognition is the fundamental process in psychological development and that changes in behavior always reflect or require advances in cognitive abilities.

Defining Learning

Learning
A relatively permanent change in behavior that results from practice or experience.

Behavioral psychologists believe that the changes in behavior that occur as children develop often are *learned*, meaning they result from conditioning and learning principles. When psychologists use the term **learning**, they are not referring simply to what goes on in a classroom (although, one hopes, a good deal of it takes place there, too). Instead, they view learning in a much more general sense, defining it as *a relatively permanent change in behavior that results from practice or experience.* This definition has three distinct elements.

The first part of the definition, "relatively permanent," distinguishes learned changes in behavior from changes that are only temporary and that often reflect physiological processes—such as when behavior changes as a result of sleep, illness, or fatigue. The second part, "change in behavior," means that learning must always be demonstrated through changes in observable behavior. If a psychologist were interested in determining whether a child had learned a list of words, for example, the child would need to demonstrate this learning through some aspect of behavior, such as writing, reciting, or recognizing the words. The final part of the definition, "results from practice or experience," is meant to separate learned changes in behavior from changes caused by more general biological processes, such as growth, pregnancy, or even death.

B. F. Skinner and Behavior Analysis

In Chapter 1 we saw that John B. Watson's attempt to build a comprehensive theory of child development based on learning principles failed, in part, because human behavior was too complex to be explained by Pavlovian conditioning. Watson's model was based on the conditioning of reflexes. Except in very young infants, though, reflexes account for only a small part of human behavior. How, then, can a learning theory attempt to explain the whole range of typical child behaviors? One answer emerged in the work of another pioneer of behaviorism, B. F. Skinner (Gewirtz & Pelaez-Nogueras, 1992).

B. F. Skinner's revision of Watson's early behavioristic views down-played the role of Pavlovian processes in human development and introduced principles of operant conditioning.

Skinner accepted the role of Pavlovian conditioning of reflexes, but he added to learning theory a second type of behavior and, correspondingly, a second type of learning. According to his model, all behavior falls into one of two categories. The first involves reflexes. A **reflex** is composed of a stimulus that reliably elicits a response. This relation is biological and inborn. The responses involved in the simple reflexes that all organisms display Skinner called **respondent behaviors**. The salivation response of Pavlov's dogs is an example. The most important characteristic of a respondent behavior is that it is completely controlled by the stimulus that elicits it; quite simply, the response occurs when the stimulus is present and does not occur when the stimulus is absent. In humans, respondent behaviors are particularly obvious during infancy and include such reflexive behaviors as sucking in response to a nipple's being placed in the mouth and grasping in response to an object's touching the palm of the hand. Older children and adults also display a few respondent behaviors, usually in the form of simple physiological responses (blinking and sneezing) and emotional responses (some aspects of fear, anger, and sexual arousal).

Operant behaviors are very different. We can think of them roughly as voluntary responses, and they include the vast majority of all human behaviors. Operant behaviors are controlled by their effects, that is, by the consequences they produce. In general, pleasant consequences make the behaviors more likely to occur again, whereas unpleasant consequences have the opposite result (Skinner, 1953).

Skinner's model of learning has been applied to children's development by Sidney Bijou and Donald Baer (Bijou, 1995; Rosales-Ruiz & Baer, 1996), who pioneered the environmental/learning approach to developmental psychology known as **behavior analysis**. The goal of behavior analytic theory is to explain how children's innate capabilities interact with their experiences and environment to produce changes in their behavior and development—which is, of course, remarkably similar to the goal of cognitive-developmental theory and most other interactional theories of child development. What distinguishes behavior analysis is that (1) it relies heavily on learning processes as explanations for developmental change and (2) it avoids explanations based on unobservable cognitive processes, such as Piaget's mental operations and the computer-like mental mechanisms of the information-processing approach.

Types of Learning

To understand environmental/learning accounts of child development, we must consider the various types of conditioning and learning that operate on the child. In this section, we examine three forms of learning: habituation, respondent conditioning, and operant learning.

Habituation   The simplest form of learning, called **habituation**, involves respondent behaviors. Habituation begins with a reflex. For example, if we clap our hands

---

Reflex
A biological relation in which a specific stimulus reliably elicits a specific response.

Respondent behaviors
Responses based on reflexes, which are controlled by specific eliciting stimuli. The smaller category of human behaviors.

Operant behaviors
Voluntary behavior controlled by its consequences. The larger category of human behaviors.

Behavior analysis
B. F. Skinner's environmental/learning theory, which emphasizes the role of operant learning in changing observable behaviors.

Habituation
The decline or disappearance of a reflex response as a result of repeated elicitation. The simplest type of learning.

Dishabituation
The recovery of a habituated response that results from a change in the eliciting stimulus.

Respondent (classical) conditioning
A form of learning, involving reflexes, in which a neutral stimulus acquires the power to elicit a reflexive response (UCR) as a result of being associated (paired) with the naturally eliciting stimulus (UCS). The neutral stimulus then becomes a conditioned stimulus (CS).

Unconditioned stimulus (UCS)
The stimulus portion of a reflex, which reliably elicits a respondent behavior (UCR).

Unconditioned response (UCR)
The response portion of a reflex, which is reliably elicited by a stimulus (UCS).

loudly near an infant, the infant will display a full-body *startle reflex*. If we continue to clap our hands at frequent intervals (say, every 15 seconds), the size of the startle response will decrease steadily until it may be difficult to detect at all. This simple change in behavior caused by repeatedly presenting a stimulus illustrates learning through habituation.

How do we know that habituation really represents some form of learning? Maybe the infant's muscles have simply become too fatigued to produce the response any longer—a change in behavior that, according to our earlier definition, we could not consider to be learned. To demonstrate that fatigue is not the reason for the decreased response, we need only change the stimulus. Assume, for instance, that the repeated hand clapping has reduced the startle to a very low level. Now, after waiting 15 seconds, we sound a loud buzzer instead of clapping our hands. With great reliability, the startle response will reappear at the same high level it showed when we first clapped our hands. The recovery of a habituated response that occurs as a result of a change in the eliciting stimulus is known as **dishabituation**.

Habituation plays only a small role in children's development. One common example is the way infants learn to sleep through routine household noises. If given enough exposure, babies habituate very quickly to slamming doors, ringing telephones, and similar sounds that might otherwise continually wake them. Unfortunately, many parents, unaware of the habituation process, try to keep everyone very quiet during nap times. The absence of typical household stimuli, however, may prevent the habituation process from occurring and, ironically, make the infant more likely to awaken at the first bark of the family dog.

Although habituation does not account for a great deal of children's development, psychologists have discovered that it can be a very useful technique for studying infants' sensory and memory abilities. We examine how this works in later chapters.

Respondent Conditioning   **Respondent conditioning**—sometimes called **classical conditioning**—was developed by Pavlov and also involves reflexes. In this type of learning, the stimulus is termed the **unconditioned stimulus (UCS)** and the elicited response is called the **unconditioned response (UCR)**. Respondent conditioning involves having another stimulus, which previously did not elicit the UCR, acquire

Habituation is a simple learning process that explains why babies can sleep in noisy surroundings.

the power to do so. The neutral (new) stimulus is paired or associated with the UCS. After a number of such pairings, it elicits the UCR (or a response very similar to it), at which point the previously neutral stimulus is termed a **conditioned stimulus (CS)**.

We can illustrate this process with an example involving children's emotional responses, the aspect of human development in which respondent conditioning plays its largest role. Fear responses, for instance, can be naturally elicited by a number of stimuli, a very common one being pain. Suppose a child visits the dentist for the first time. The stimuli in that environment—the dentist, the office, the instruments, and so forth—are neutral to the child and so have no particular emotional effect on his behavior. During the visit, however, suppose that the child experiences pain (UCS), which elicits fear (UCR). The various neutral stimuli become associated with the UCS, because they are paired with it, and thus may become conditioned stimuli (CS) for the fear response. After that, the sight of the dentist or sound of the drill, for example, will also elicit the fear response (UCR). In the same way, many common fears of childhood can be learned responses to places or objects that previously were not frightening. (See Box 2.1 for a classic demonstration of the conditioning of fear.)

Note that in habituation, learning results in a change in the response, which gradually gets weaker. By contrast, in respondent conditioning, the response remains the same and learning involves a change in the stimulus, which begins as neutral but becomes effective in producing the response.

Respondent conditioning often produces **stimulus generalization**, which means that stimuli similar to the CS also become conditioned. In our example, the child may come to fear not only his own dentist but all dentists, or perhaps even anyone wearing a white medical coat. Fortunately, the conditioned association also can be unlearned, a process called **respondent extinction**. Suppose the child in our example returns to the dentist often without experiencing any more pain. The dentist and other conditioned stimuli in the situation will then gradually cease to elicit fear and return to being neutral.

Respondent conditioning is somewhat more influential in children's development than is habituation. It most commonly plays a role in aspects of the child's emotional behavior.

Operant Learning

Operant Learning   A third type of learning is called **operant learning**. Unlike habituation and respondent conditioning, operant learning is assumed by learning theorists to be very important for understanding the typical behavior of children.

Operant behaviors are influenced by their effects, and many of the everyday behaviors of children occur simply because they resulted in desirable consequences in the past. Any consequence that makes a response more likely to occur again is called a *reinforcer*. Consider the following examples. The same child may (1) share her toys with a friend because doing so often produces similar sharing by the other child, (2) throw a temper tantrum in the supermarket because this usually results in getting candy from her parent, (3) twist and shake the knob of the playroom door because this behavior is effective in getting it open, (4) work hard at skating lessons because the coach praises her when she performs well, and (5) put a pillow over her head when her baby brother is crying because this behavior helps reduce the unpleasant sound.

It should be obvious from this list that reinforcers can take many forms. Nevertheless, they all fall into one of two categories: those that involve getting something good are called **positive reinforcers** and those that involve getting rid of something bad are called **negative reinforcers**.

Conditioned stimulus (CS)
A neutral stimulus that comes to elicit a response (UCR) through a conditioning process in which it is consistently paired with another stimulus (UCS) that naturally evokes the response.

Stimulus generalization
A process related to respondent conditioning in which stimuli that are similar to the conditioned stimulus (CS) also acquire the power to elicit the response.

Respondent extinction
A process related to respondent conditioning in which the conditioned stimulus (CS) gradually loses its power to elicit the response as a result of no longer being paired with the unconditioned stimulus (UCS).

Operant learning
A form of learning in which the likelihood of an operant behavior changes as a result of its reinforcing or punishing consequences.

Positive reinforcer
A consequence that makes the behavior it follows more likely through the presentation of something pleasant.

Negative reinforcer
A consequence that makes the behavior it follows more likely through the removal of something unpleasant.

BOX 2.1

LITTLE ALBERT AND LITTLE PETER: CONDITIONING AND COUNTERCONDITIONING FEAR

Perhaps the most famous research conducted by John B. Watson involved the conditioning of a fear response in an 11-month-old child named Albert B. (Watson & Rayner, 1920). The study was designed to show that fear is an unconditioned response that can be easily conditioned to a variety of common stimuli.

Watson believed that children fear dogs, dentists, and the like because they associate these objects or persons with an unconditioned stimulus for fear, such as pain or a sudden loud noise. To illustrate this process, Watson first exposed Albert to a tame white laboratory rat, which produced only mild interest in the child. On several later occasions, Watson presented the rat to Albert and then made a loud noise (UCS) behind Albert. The noise elicited a pronounced fear response (UCR) in the form of crying and trembling. Very soon, the sight of the rat alone was enough to make Albert cry in fear—it had become a conditioned stimulus (CS) for that response. Watson demonstrated stimulus generalization by showing that objects similar to the rat, such as cotton or a white fur coat, also elicited the fear response.

A few years later, Watson and an associate named Mary Cover Jones applied the fear-conditioning process in reverse (Jones, 1924). A 3-year-old named Peter was brought to them with an intense fear of rabbits and other furry creatures.

The researchers reasoned that if this fear had been learned (conditioned), it could be unlearned. They called their method for eliminating the fear response to the rabbit *counterconditioning*. It involved presenting the conditioned stimulus in such a way that it would not elicit the fear response but would instead elicit a competing emotional response—in this case, pleasure derived from eating.

On the first day of treatment, Peter was placed in a high chair and fed his lunch. At the same time, a caged rabbit was displayed on the other side of the room, far enough away so that the fear response did not occur. Each day, while Peter ate, the rabbit was moved slightly closer. In the end, Peter was not at all disturbed at having the rabbit sit next to him while he ate his lunch. The rabbit was no longer a conditioned stimulus for fear and had instead become associated with pleasure.

An experiment of the sort conducted with Little Albert, of course, would not be permitted today, because psychologists now have strict ethical guidelines for research that prohibit a child's being exposed to this type of fear experience (see Chapter 3). The experiment with Little Peter, however, is very similar to the type of fear-reduction therapy used today by clinical psychologists and would be considered a form of behavior modification.

It should also be apparent from our list of examples that the reinforcement process does not work only on desirable or beneficial responses. Reinforcement increases the likelihood of any behavior that leads to a pleasant consequence, whether we would typically view that behavior as appropriate (sharing toys), inappropriate (throwing a tantrum in a supermarket), or neutral (opening a door).

Not all consequences are reinforcing, however. Behavior sometimes produces effects that are unpleasant, and these *reduce* the likelihood that the behavior will occur again. Such consequences are called **punishers**. We usually think of punishment as something that is delivered by parents or teachers for misbehavior, but the principle of punishment, like the principle of reinforcement, is simply part of nature's learning process. Punishment teaches organisms which responses are wise to repeat and which are better to avoid. Punishment, too, can entail either getting something bad (such as a spanking, a failing grade, or a scraped knee) or losing

Punisher
A consequence that makes the behavior it follows less likely, either through the presentation of something unpleasant or the removal of something desirable.

something good (such as a baseball, a chance to sit by a friend at lunch, or television privileges for a week). Either way, behaviors that lead to punishing consequences become less likely to occur again.

Applications

Effects and Side Effects of Punishment by Parents or Teachers

Punishment is a consequence that makes behavior less likely to occur again. We typically think of punishment as the discipline dispensed by parents, such as spanking or confining the child to his or her room. Most parents use these techniques in the hope that the punished behavior will disappear. Indeed, moderate to strong punishment, if delivered clearly and consistently, is effective in reducing undesirable behaviors.

At the same time, punishment can produce a number of side effects that parents may not anticipate. First of all, strong punishers can elicit aggression and other emotional behaviors in children, including crying, tantrums, and head banging. Second, the individual who delivers the punishment sometimes becomes so closely associated with punishment in general that the child may begin to avoid interacting with that person. Third, punishment can reduce an entire class of responses, sometimes including behaviors that are not a problem. For example, the child who is punished by the teacher for speaking out of turn may react by decreasing all verbal participation in class. Fourth, parents who use punishment may be serving as models for behavior that they do not want to see their children imitate. The fact that many delinquent children were exposed to physical punishment in childhood and that abused children frequently grow up to be abusing parents may reflect, in part, the children's imitation of aggression by the parents. Fifth, punishment is not a good teaching device because it tells children only what they did wrong, not what they should be doing instead. Finally, punishment has an addictive quality. Because it often is successful in temporarily ending the child's unwanted behavior, parents who are unaware of other disciplinary techniques may come to rely on it heavily.

Punishment should always be used in combination with reinforcement for the appropriate behaviors we wish the child to display. Even then, it should be used sparingly, and preferably as a negative consequence, such as removing something desirable, rather than as a positive consequence, such as slapping or spanking.

Some activities, like putting together a puzzle, are reinforced simply by the consequence of achieving the solution.

Punishment should be used sparingly as a disciplinary tool because it can produce side effects.

Social-Learning Theory

Over the years, the environmental/learning tradition has grown more like the other two major traditions (in fact, all three approaches continue to move closer together). In this section, we consider a second approach within the behavioral tradition, **social-learning theory**, which has become increasingly concerned with how cognitive factors influence development (Grusec, 1992).

The leading spokesperson for the social-learning viewpoint has been Albert Bandura (1986, 1992). Like other behavioral psychologists, Bandura believes that cognitive development alone does not explain childhood changes in behavior and that learning processes are responsible for much of children's development. But some learning processes, he feels, are affected by the child's cognitive abilities. This is especially true for the more complex types of learning that Bandura believes are involved in children's development beyond the infant years. We turn to one of these types next.

Social-learning theory
A form of environmental/learning theory that adds observational learning to respondent and operant learning as a process through which children's behavior changes.

Observational Learning   Skinner's addition of operant learning to Watson's Pavlovian conditioning greatly expanded learning theory's ability to explain children's behavior. Nevertheless, some problems remained. One was that children sometimes acquire new behaviors simply by seeing someone else perform them. A second was that children sometimes become more or less likely to perform a behavior after seeing another person experience reinforcing or punishing consequences for that behavior. Neither of these facts is easily explained by a type of learning in which changes in behavior occur only when children experience direct consequences for their actions.

Observational learning
A form of learning in which an observer's behavior changes as a result of observing a model.

Bandura solved this problem by proposing that as children grow, their development is increasingly based on a fourth type of learning—**observational learning**. Learning by observation occurs when the behavior of an *observer* is affected by witnessing the behavior (and often its consequences) of a *model*. In developmental psychology, the observers are children, and the models include parents, teachers, siblings, classmates, sports celebrities, television personalities, and even cartoon characters—in short, just about anyone in the child's world.

Bandura and other researchers have studied three important questions regarding the modeling process: (1) Which models are most likely to influence a child's behavior? (2) Under what circumstances is this influence most likely to occur? (3) How does the child's behavior change as a result of observational learning?

The simple answer to the first question is that a model who possesses a characteristic that the child finds attractive or desirable—such as talent, intelligence, power, good looks, or popularity—is most likely to be imitated. Other issues can sometimes come into play, however, including the child's level of development and the types of behaviors being modeled.

Vicarious reinforcement
Reinforcing consequences experienced when viewing a model that affect an observer similarly.

The circumstances under which modeling is most effective also can vary, but one of the most important factors is whether the model receives reinforcing or punishing consequences for the behavior. One of Bandura's most significant contributions to social-learning theory was his demonstration that consequences of a model's behavior can affect the behavior of an observer. When a child sees a model receive reinforcement for a response, the child receives **vicarious reinforcement** and, like the model, becomes more likely to produce that same response. The opposite is true when the child receives **vicarious punishment** as a result of witnessing a model being punished. In some sense, then, observational learning is the same as operant learning, except that the child experiences the consequences vicariously rather than directly.

Vicarious punishment
Punishing consequences experienced when viewing a model that affect an observer similarly.

Imitation
Behavior of an observer that results from and is similar to the behavior of a model.

The most obvious and perhaps the most important result of modeling is **imitation**, which occurs when children copy what they have seen. Imitation can take such varied forms as eating the breakfast cereal a professional athlete claims to eat, climbing on a chair to steal a cookie from the shelf after seeing an older brother do it, or copying the problems a teacher is writing on the chalkboard.

Response inhibition
The absence of a particular response that has just been modeled; often the result of vicarious punishment.

A second result of modeling occurs when the observer becomes less likely to perform a behavior that has just been modeled. This effect, known as **response inhibition**, is a common result of vicarious punishment. The teacher who publicly disciplines an unruly child in order to set an example for the rest of the class is counting on observational learning to inhibit similar behaviors in the other children.

Children do not always immediately display behavior learned from models. A striking illustration of this point occurred in one of Bandura's early studies, in which one group of youngsters observed a model rewarded for displaying new aggressive behaviors toward an inflated toy clown, while a second group saw those same behaviors punished. When given an opportunity to play with the doll them-

Imitation is an important process by which children acquire new skills and behaviors.

selves, the children who witnessed the reinforcement imitated many of the model's aggressive acts toward the doll, whereas the group who observed punishment did not. But when later offered rewards for reproducing the aggressive behaviors, both groups were able to perform them quite accurately (Bandura, 1965). Obviously, all of the children had acquired (learned) the new behaviors, even though the vicariously experienced punishment had inhibited some children from performing them. This distinction between acquisition and performance has been of particular interest to researchers studying the potential effects of viewing television violence on children's aggressive behavior, which we discuss in Chapter 14.

Albert Bandura's early research showed that children exposed to filmed violence were capable of very accurately imitating of the model's aggressive acts when given the opportunity to reproduce them.

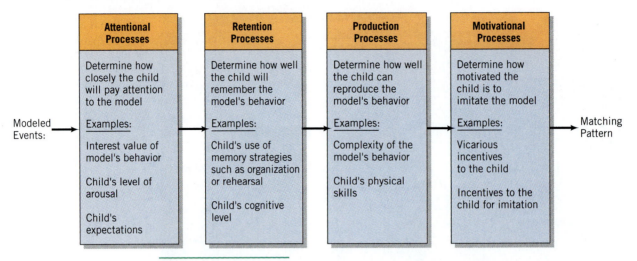

Figure 2.1
Bandura's model of observational learning. Adapted from Albert Bandura, *Social Learning Theory,* © 1977, p. 23. Reprinted by permission of Prentice-Hall, Inc., Upper Saddle River, New Jersey.

The acquisition–performance distinction is evident in Bandura's theoretical formulation of observational learning, depicted in Figure 2.1. Bandura believes that learning by observation involves four separate processes. The first two account for the acquisition, or learning, of a model's behavior, and the other two control the performance, or production, of these behaviors (Bandura, 1977b).

Attentional processes determine how closely the child pays attention to what the model is doing. *Retention processes* refer to how well the child can store the modeled information in memory for later use. *Production processes* control how well the child can reproduce the model's responses. *Motivational processes* determine who and what a child chooses to imitate.

One way to think of this formulation is to imagine a child viewing a model and then to consider why the child might *not* imitate the model's actions. The child might not have paid attention to what the model was doing, might not recall the model's responses, might not possess the physical skills to repeat the model's behaviors, or might feel little motivation to do what the model has done. In everyday life, children do not imitate everything they see. Bandura's theory suggests four important reasons why this is the case.

Reciprocal Determinism   Bandura's social-learning analysis is truly interactionist. It is based on his view that human development reflects the interaction of the person (P), the person's behavior (B), and the environment (E). Bandura describes this process of interaction as **reciprocal determinism** (Bandura, 1978).

As illustrated in Figure 2.2, the reciprocal determinism model forms a triangle of interactions. The person includes the child's cognitive abilities, physical characteristics, personality, beliefs, attitudes, and so on, which influence both the child's behavior and the child's environment. Children choose not only what they want to do (P→B), but also where and with whom to do it (P→E). These influences are reciprocal, however. Children's behavior (and the reactions it engenders) can affect their feelings about themselves and their attitudes and beliefs about other things (B→P). Likewise, much of children's knowledge about the world and other people

Reciprocal determinism Albert Bandura's proposed process describing the interaction of a person's characteristics and abilities (P), behavior (B), and environment (E).

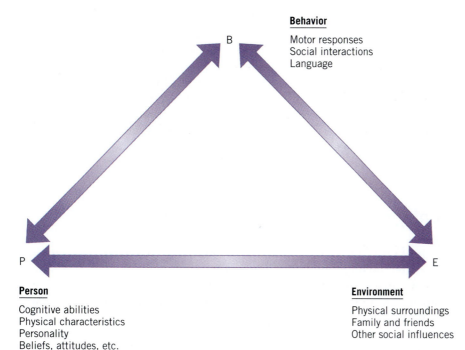

Behavior
Motor responses
Social interactions
Language

B

P

E

Person
Cognitive abilities
Physical characteristics
Personality
Beliefs, attitudes, etc.

Environment
Physical surroundings
Family and friends
Other social influences

Figure 2.2
Bandura's model of reciprocal determinism. Adapted from "Self System in Reciprocal Determinism" by Albert Bandura, 1978, *American Psychologist, 33*, p. 345. Copyright © 1978 by the American Psychological Association. Adapted by permission.

results from information they receive from television, parents, textbooks, and other environmental sources (E→P).

Environment also affects behavior. The consequences of children's behavior and the models they observe can powerfully influence what they do (E→B). But children's behavior also contributes to creating their environment. A child who shares and cooperates with classmates is likely to attract many friends, whereas the opposite may be the case for a child who behaves selfishly or aggressively (B→E).

Bandura's addition of observational learning to the environmental/learning tradition, along with his willingness to incorporate cognitive aspects of development, has greatly increased the explanatory power of social-learning theory and has made it the most important learning-based approach. We consider the role of this model in many aspects of children's development throughout the text.

✔ *To Recap...*

Environmental/learning theories begin with the assumption that much of children's typical behavior is acquired through conditioning and learning principles. Learned behaviors are distinguished from behaviors that are temporary, unobservable, or based solely on biological processes.

Behavior analysis is one form of learning theory. In this view, three types of conditioning and learning are assumed to operate on children: habituation (and dishabituation), respondent conditioning, and operant learning. Habituation and respondent conditioning involve reflexes. In contrast, operant learning is controlled by the consequences of behavior. Consequences that make behavior more probable are called reinforcers; those that make behavior less probable are called punishers.

Social-learning theory, based largely on the ideas of Albert Bandura, proposes a greater role for cognitive factors than does behavior analysis. According to this theory, observational learning occurs when an observer's behavior changes as a result of viewing the behavior of a model. Consequences experienced when viewing a model, called vicarious reinforcement and vicarious punishment, can affect the behavior of an observer. The most important result of modeling is imitation. Response inhibition occurs when imitation of an observed behavior becomes less likely—usually because the model has received punishment for it. Acquisition of a modeled behavior is determined by the observer's attentional and retentional processes, whereas performance of the behavior is controlled by the observer's production and motivational processes.

Bandura's theoretical model, reciprocal determinism, holds that human development results from the complex interaction of characteristics of the person, the person's behavior, and the environment.

Ethology

Ethology
The study of development from an evolutionary perspective.

Sociobiology
A branch of biology that attempts to discover the evolutionary origins of social behavior.

The third major theoretical approach in modern child psychology is **ethology**, the study of development from an evolutionary perspective. The historical roots of this tradition can be traced to the work of Charles Darwin (1809–1882). More recently, a similar approach has sprung up in the field of biology. Called **sociobiology**, this approach looks for evolutionary origins of social behavior (E. O. Wilson, 1975). Among the three theoretical models we are discussing in this chapter, the ethological tradition has the fewest followers, but their numbers are growing rapidly, and the ideas and findings of ethology are being applied to more and more areas of child development (MacDonald, 1988a; Miller, 1993).

Behavior and Evolution

When trying to understand the ethological approach, it is important to keep in mind that from an evolutionary perspective, our species is the product of millions of years of change. What we are today represents only a small part of an enormous process. Ethology views human beings as only one of the 5 million or so species that presently inhabit the earth, and it considers human development within the context of the entire animal kingdom. It should not be surprising, then, that much of the research conducted within this tradition involves nonhuman species.

Like the other theoretical models, ethology attempts to explain the changes in behavior that occur across development. According to ethological theorists, these changes have two kinds of determinants, or causes—immediate and evolutionary. The immediate determinants are the more obvious and include the environment in which the behavior occurs, the animal's recent experiences, and the state or condition of the animal—whether it is hungry, tired, or angry, for example. The evolutionary determinants of behavior are less clear. Presumably the behavior at some point contributed to the animal's chances of survival and so became more likely to be passed along to future generations through the natural selection process. To explain such behaviors as hunting for prey or constructing a dam, then, ethologists consider both the immediate circumstances, such as the availability of prey or of appropriate building materials, and factors in the animal's evolutionary past, such as the climate and terrain in which the behaviors evolved.

Classical Ethology

Ethology first gained scientific recognition in the 1930s with the work of two pioneers in animal study, Konrad Lorenz and Niko Tinbergen. Both men were zoologists by training, and their early investigations focused exclusively on nonhuman animals. Nevertheless, their research laid the groundwork for the growing trend toward the application of ethological principles to child development, and in 1973 they were jointly awarded a Nobel Prize for their pioneering research.

Innate Mechanisms   Ethologists have identified four qualities that characterize virtually all innate, or inborn, behaviors. First, they are *universal* to all members of the species. Second, since they are usually biologically programmed responses to very specific stimuli, they *require no learning or experience*. Third, they are normally *stereotyped*, meaning that they occur in precisely the same way every time they are displayed. Finally, they are only *minimally affected by environmental influences* (in the short run, that is; natural selection pressures affect them across generations) (Eibl-Eibesfeldt, 1989). Countless examples of these behaviors have been identified in virtually every known species, ranging from the nest-building behaviors of ants, to the pecking responses of chickens, to the herding behaviors of antelope.

In humans, such innate behaviors are most evident during infancy. An inborn response such as sucking, for example, is found in all babies, does not need to be learned, occurs in a stereotyped pattern, and is influenced very little by the environment (at least during the first weeks of life).

The idea of a stimulus that elicits a simple, reflexive, biological response, such as sucking, is neither new nor of interest only to ethologists (as the work of Pavlov and Watson clearly demonstrates). But ethologists have typically been interested in more complex *sequences* of innate behaviors, which they call **modal action patterns**. These are the chains of responses that we see, for example, when spiders spin webs, birds build nests, or bears care for newborn cubs. A modal action pattern is triggered by a specific stimulus in the animal's environment, what Lorenz called an **innate releasing mechanism**. A classic example of such a mechanism was demonstrated by Tinbergen (1973) in his work with the stickleback.

The stickleback is a freshwater fish with three sharp spines. In winter, the males stay in schools and are relatively inactive. In spring, the rising water temperature sets off a distinctive pattern of mating behaviors. Each stickleback leaves the school and builds a tunnel-like nest in the sand, which he defends as his own territory against other males. When a female approaches the area above the nest, the male begins his courtship by stabbing her with one of his spines. He then swims down to the nest in an unusual zigzag pattern. The stabbing and swimming motion apparently excite the female, who follows him to his nest. When she enters it, the male places his face against her tail and begins to quiver. This stimulates the female to release her eggs, which the male fertilizes by releasing his sperm. He then chases her away and waits for another female to approach. This ritual continues until five or so females have released eggs in the nest. The male subsequently cares for the developing eggs, driving away intruders and fanning the water with his tail to provide the eggs with sufficient oxygen.

In addition to observing this mating process in the wild, Tinbergen studied sticklebacks in the laboratory. There he exposed the fish to wooden models of other sticklebacks of various colors and shapes to determine experimentally which stimuli are necessary to trigger and maintain the chain of behaviors. The details of these experiments are not crucial for our purposes, but the work does raise several important issues.

One issue concerns the relevance of these sorts of modal action patterns for human development. Although the mating rituals of humans are (fortunately) very different from those of sticklebacks, ethologists believe that many response patterns in humans are triggered by very specific stimuli. These may include, for example,

Modal action pattern
A sequence of behaviors elicited by a specific stimulus.

Innate releasing mechanism
A stimulus that triggers an innate sequence or pattern of behaviors.

maternal responses to newborn babies or certain forms of aggression. A related issue concerns the nature versus nurture question. The stickleback does not need to learn the complex courtship responses; they are elicited biologically by stimuli in the environment. This does not mean, however, that other aspects of the stickleback's behavior do not change in response to experiences or consequences. From the opposite perspective, even though many aspects of human behavior clearly result from learning processes, ethologists contend that this does not rule out the possibility that other aspects of human behavior—perhaps even complex behavior patterns—are controlled by innate evolutionary processes. Thus modern ethologists, too, are interactionists, assuming important roles for both nature and nurture processes.

Tinbergen's research strategy also illustrates how ethologists combine naturalistic and laboratory methods. The great majority of their investigations involve the observation of behaviors in the natural settings where they evolved. In this way, the researcher can examine how an animal's responses typically occur. But the behaviors are also studied in more structured settings, where the researcher can control the conditions under which events take place and can subject an animal's rituals and routines to various experimental tests.

Sensitive Periods An important issue in psychology concerns how an animal's genetic or biological makeup can influence the learning process (Bolles & Beecher, 1988), that is, how nature and nurture work together to change behavior. Ethologists argue that animals are biologically programmed so that some things are learned most easily during certain periods of development. A dramatic example of this is illustrated by Lorenz's research on **imprinting**, the process by which newborns of some species form an emotional bond with their mothers.

Imprinting
A biological process of some species in which the young acquire an emotional attachment to the mother through following.

In many bird species, whose young can walk almost immediately after hatching, baby birds soon begin to follow the mother as she moves about. Lorenz guessed that this simple act of following was responsible for the strong social bond that developed between the newborn and the parent. To confirm his suspicion, Lorenz removed just-hatched goslings from their mother and had them follow another animal, or various nonliving objects that he pulled along, or even himself. As he predicted, the young birds quickly imprinted to whatever they followed and thereafter treated it as their mother (Lorenz, 1937).

Lorenz further discovered that one of the most important influences on imprinting was the age of the chicks. If the act of following occurred during a period that began several hours after birth and lasted until sometime the next day, the attachment bond reliably developed. When the following occurred only before or after this period, however, little or no imprinting resulted. Ethologists now use the term **sensitive periods** to describe points in development when learning is much easier than it is at earlier or later points. Sensitive periods are not restricted to imprinting or even to the area of mother–infant attachment. Child researchers have applied the concept to areas as diverse as language acquisition (Newport, 1991) and gender-role development (Money & Annecillo, 1987), as we will see in later chapters.

Sensitive period
A period of development during which certain behaviors are more easily learned.

Applications to Human Development

Our main interest in ethological theory is its application to child development, and modern researchers are finding many areas of development in which evolutionary processes may be important (DeKay & Buss, 1992; Scarr, 1992).

Sociobiology We said earlier that some biologists have attempted to apply evolutionary principles to human social behavior. This new area of research began

Konrad Lorenz found that newly hatched goslings, when permitted to follow him around for a short time, would imprint to him and thereafter treat him as their mother.

rather dramatically in 1975 with the publication of a book by a Harvard biologist, E. O. Wilson, entitled *Sociobiology: The New Synthesis*. According to Wilson's radical and somewhat controversial theory, genes are very selfish structures whose only interest is to ensure their own survival from generation to generation.

Many specific physical characteristics (color of fur, size of ears, and so on) are carried in an animal's genes. When a characteristic is valuable for survival or reproduction, the genes that produce it are more likely to be passed along to the next generation—Darwin's natural selection process. Sociobiologists believe that genes produce not only physical traits, but social behaviors (although these theorists admit that the process by which a gene can produce a behavior is not yet completely understood). Social behaviors that are more adaptive for survival thus are assumed to undergo the same natural selection process as physical traits.

The sociobiological view can be illustrated by a frequently cited example. Consider a mother who risks her life to save her child from danger. According to the traditional ethological model, this response by the mother should not have an evolutionary basis, because natural selection would not favor behaviors that reduce an individual's chances of survival. Sociobiologists, however, contend that the mother's genes have in some way programmed her to do whatever she can to ensure that her genes are passed on to future generations. Because her child carries many of those same genes, and because he would have many reproductive years ahead, evolutionary mechanisms drive the mother to sacrifice her life to save that of her child (Dawkins, 1976; Porter & Laney, 1980).

Ethologists believe that evolutionary processes play some role in the behavior of all species.

Wilson suggests that genetic effects on social behavior are better understood at the level of the culture or society, rather than of the individual. He claims, for example, that many of our cultural practices, such as taboos against incest and laws against murder or assault, reflect an evolutionary process that favors individuals whose social behaviors are in line with what is best for the survival of the species. The behaviors of these individuals are thus more likely to be passed along to future generations, whereas undesirable behaviors are not. This new theory has been both praised and criticized (Lerner & von Eye, 1992). But it has sparked a great deal of debate and has drawn additional attention to the evolutionary perspective.

Human Ethology   Ethological principles have increasingly been applied to our own species (Archer, 1992; Eibl-Eibesfeldt, 1989). As early as the 1940s, Lorenz suggested that physical characteristics of babies, such as the shape of their head and the sound of their cry, might serve as stimuli to trigger caregiving by mothers (Lorenz, 1950). Developmental psychologists likewise interpreted infants' early reflexive behaviors in terms of their evolutionary value to the species. Nevertheless, the scientific application of the ethological model to child development is usually considered to have begun in 1969, when John Bowlby published the first of his three volumes on the subject (Bowlby, 1969/1982, 1973, 1980).

Bowlby, an English physician and psychoanalyst, was the first to attract child psychologists to an evolutionary interpretation of human development. As a clinician, Bowlby had witnessed the emotional problems of children who had been raised in institutions. Such children often have difficulty forming and maintaining close relationships. Bowlby attributed this problem to the children's lack of a strong attachment to their mothers during infancy. His interest in this area eventually led him to an ethological explanation of how and why the mother–infant bond is established (Bretherton, 1995).

Bowlby's theory is an interesting mix of ethology and Freudian theory (Holmes, 1995; Sroufe, 1986). As did Freud, Bowlby believes that the quality of the early relationship (between baby and mother) is critical to later development and that these first experiences are carried forward by processes in the unconscious. Bowlby's theory also reflects the fundamental principle of classical ethology, that a close mother–infant bond is crucial in humans (and in most higher-level species) for the survival of the young. Infants who remain near the mother can be fed, protected, trained, and transported more effectively than can infants who stray from her side. The behaviors used by the mother and infant to keep the pair in close contact must therefore be innate and controlled by a variety of releasing stimuli (we discuss these behaviors in Chapter 12). Bowlby further maintains that the attachment bond develops easily during a sensitive period, but after this time it may become impossible for the child ever to achieve a truly intimate emotional relationship (Bowlby, 1988).

Bowlby's work has encouraged a great deal of additional research on attachment and bonding processes in humans. More important for this tradition, it began a general movement toward examining other aspects of child development within an evolutionary context (Blurton-Jones, 1972). Psychologists have since investigated children's aggression, peer interactions, cognitive development, and many other topics.

Ethologists have also influenced developmental research methods. Observational methods have always been used by child researchers, but there has been a renewed interest in studying children in their natural environments (Bronfenbrenner, 1979; McCall, 1977). Observational techniques that do not influence or intrude on children's normal social interactions are being added to more experimental approaches to studying these behaviors. The ethological tradition has clearly established itself as an important perspective in contemporary developmental psychology.

✔ *To Recap...*

Ethology is based on the principles of evolution as first proposed by Charles Darwin. Ethologists believe that behaviors have both immediate and evolutionary determinants. These scientists are primarily concerned with innate behaviors, and they attempt to explain complex response patterns in terms of their survival value for the species.

Lorenz and Tinbergen, two founders of the ethological movement, identified four characteristics of innate behavior: it is universal; it is stereotyped; it requires no learning; and it is minimally affected by the environment. Ethologists have described how complex sequences of inherited responses (modal action patterns) are triggered by stimuli in the environment and how innate mechanisms, such as imprinting, influence the learning process.

Sociobiology is a recent attempt to explain social behavior in terms of an evolutionary model in which the survival of the genes supersedes any other goal. This mechanism is believed to be principally expressed in cultural and social structures. Human ethology emerged largely as a result of Bowlby's research on the attachment process. Many aspects of child development now are being studied from an ethological perspective.

Development in Context
The Ecological Approach

*T*he three approaches we have just described guide most of the research conducted by child psychologists. But a fourth perspective that has recently emerged is proving very influential. This perspective is not a new theoretical model. Instead, it represents a different way of thinking about human development and a different approach to studying the factors that influence it (Moen, Elder, & Luscher, 1995).

Scientific research on children's development traditionally has taken place in laboratory settings. There are good reasons for this. The most important is that scientific investigation demands careful experimental control and, until recently, the laboratory has afforded the only setting in which such control could be achieved.

Some researchers, however, have questioned the wisdom of this practice, pointing to an obvious fact—children's development does not generally take place in laboratories. It takes place at home, with the family; at school, with classmates and teachers; in the park, with neighbors and peers; and, more generally, within a larger social and cultural environment. In short, *development always occurs in a context.* And, more important, the context often influences the course of that development. This realization has produced a growing interest in studying children in the settings in which their development typically occurs and in examining how the context influences, and is influenced by, the children's behavior.

The idea of studying development in context—called the **ecological approach**—is not new. Darwin argued that to understand the evolutionary value of any behavior, we must consider the ecological niche in which it evolved.

The recent resurgence of interest in the ecological perspective can be traced to two sources: the development of more sophisticated methods for studying behavior in the natural environment (Vasta, 1982a); and the publication of an influential book by Urie Bronfenbrenner, a psychologist at Cornell University. In *The Ecology of Human Development* (1979), Bronfenbrenner revitalized this field by providing researchers

Ecological approach
An approach to studying development that focuses on individuals within their environmental contexts.

Urie Bronfenbrenner's work has revitalized interest in the ecological approach to studying human development.

Transactional influence
A bidirectional, or reciprocal, relationship in which individuals influence one another's behaviors.

with a conceptual framework in which ecological issues could be studied. His approach, which he now describes as a *bioecological* model, has been revised several times (Bronfenbrenner, 1992; Bronfenbrenner & Ceci, 1994; Bronfenbrenner & Morris, 1998) and has generated a number of related efforts by other researchers (Leyendecker & Scholmerich, 1991; Moen et al., 1995).

The ecological approach is based on the notion that to understand development completely we must consider how the unique characteristics of a child interact with that child's surroundings. The child possesses a variety of personal characteristics; the most important of these are described by Bronfenbrenner as *developmentally generative*—capable of influencing other people in ways that are important to the child—and *developmentally disruptive*—capable of causing problems in the environment with corresponding negative effects on the child.

By instigating various responses and reactions from others, children in a sense become "producers" of their own environments—a concept we will come across again in later chapters. Examples of these characteristics include personality traits that are positive (sociability, cooperativeness, curiosity) or negative (impulsiveness, explosiveness, distractibility), physical appearance, and intellectual abilities. The environment, in this model, is viewed as a series of interrelated layers, with those closest to the child having the most direct impact and those farther away influencing the child more indirectly.

Bronfenbrenner contends that the child and the environment continually influence one another in a bidirectional, or **transactional**, manner. For example, suppose a child has the developmentally generative characteristics of being bright and articulate. These may affect the child's environment by resulting in the parents' sending her to a better school, which in turn may influence the child by resulting in improved academic skills, which again may affect her environment by attracting friends who have high career aspirations, and so forth, in an ongoing cycle of interaction and development. These sorts of interactions, Bronfenbrenner argues, are very difficult to study if the child is removed from the natural environment in which they occur.

Ecological theory holds that development varies depending on the context in which it occurs, including the people and the physical resources.

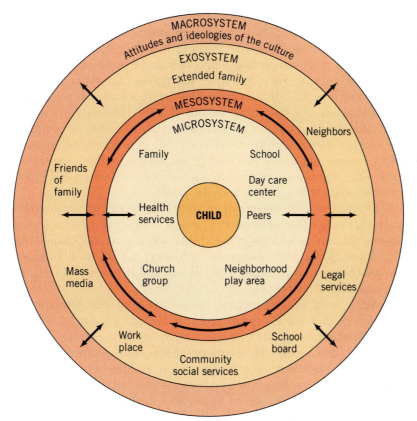

Figure 2.3
Bronfenbrenner's ecological model of the environment. U. Bronfenbrenner, from C. Kopp/Krakow, *Child Development in the Social Context* (figure 12.1), © 1982 by Addison-Wesley Publishing Co., Inc. Reprinted with permission of Addison Wesley Longman.

Figure 2.3 shows Bronfenbrenner's ecological model of development. At the center is the child and his or her physical and personal attributes. Nearest the child is the **microsystem**, which for most children includes the family, the school, the church, the playground, and so forth, along with the relationships that the child forms within these settings. The microsystem possesses physical characteristics, such as the size of the child's house, the amount of nearby playground equipment, and the number of books in the child's day-care center. It also consists of people, including the child's immediate family, the other children on the block, the child's teacher, and so on. These people, in turn, possess characteristics that may be relevant to the child's development, such as the socioeconomic status of the peer group, the educational background of the parents, and the political attitudes of the teacher. The microsystem is not constant, but changes as the child grows.

The **mesosystem** refers to the system of relationships among the child's microsystems. This might include the parents' relationship with the child's teacher and the relationship between the child's siblings and neighborhood friends. In general, the more interconnected these systems are, the more the child's development is likely to be supported in a clear and consistent way.

The **exosystem** refers to social settings that can affect the child but in which the child does not participate directly. Some examples are the local government, which decides how strictly air-pollution standards will be enforced or which families will be eligible for welfare payments; the school board, which sets teachers' salaries and recommends the budget for new textbooks and equipment; and the parents' places of employment, which establish policies regarding paid family leaves and on-site day-care facilities.

Microsystem
The environmental system closest to the child, such as the family or school. The first of Bronfenbrenner's layers of context.

Mesosystem
The interrelationships among the child's microsystems. The second of Bronfenbrenner's layers of context.

Exosystem
Social systems that can affect children but in which they do not participate directly. Bronfenbrenner's third layer of context.

Macrosystem
The culture or subculture in which the child lives. Bronfenbrenner's fourth layer of context.

Finally, there is the **macrosystem**, which involves the culture and subculture in which the child lives. The macrosystem affects the child through its beliefs, attitudes, and traditions. Children living in the United States may be influenced, for example, by beliefs regarding democracy and equality and perhaps the virtues of capitalism and free enterprise. In certain parts of the country, children may also be affected by regional attitudes regarding the importance of rugged individualism or the desirability of a slower pace of life. If a child lives in an ethnic or racially concentrated neighborhood, the values and cultural traditions of that group may add yet another source of influence. The macrosystem is generally more stable than the other systems, but it, too, can change as a society evolves—for example, from a liberal political era to a conservative one, or from economic prosperity to depression, or from peace to war (Elder & Caspi, 1988).

Not shown in the diagram is an additional factor that must be considered when studying human development: the passage of time. The interactions that take place among the various systems in the child's world gradually change over time and as the child grows. This source of influence, which Bronfenbrenner terms the **chronosystem**, adds even more complexity and richness to the challenge of analyzing children's development.

Chronosystem
Bronfenbrenner's term for the passage of time as a context for studying human development.

Along with his conceptual model for studying development in context, Bronfenbrenner has also proposed a theoretical account of how genes and environment operate together to guide human development. We will discuss that theory in Chapter 4, along with several other models of gene-environment interaction.

Context can affect any and all aspects of children's behavior and development. For that reason, we have spread our discussion of the many contextual influences over the various topics covered in this text. Each chapter that follows includes sections discussing specific examples of *development in context*, which focus on the three most important contexts for children: the family, the school, and the culture.

Conclusion

It may seem that ideas regarding child development have not changed very much in the past few hundred years. Locke, Rousseau, and Darwin offered explanations of human behavior that are, in essence, still with us today. Modern theories of development, however, are different from these early models in several important ways.

The first is that today's viewpoints are much less extreme. There are no longer pure nature or nurture theories, for example. Thus, although each of the theories described in this chapter has its own ideas, philosophy, and methods, each also accepts many of the ideas of the other models. As psychologists continue to add to our knowledge of child development, the overlap among the three approaches will undoubtedly grow.

A second difference is that today's psychologists no longer attempt to explain human development with only a few principles or processes. We have come to realize that behavior has many causes and that the mechanisms through which they operate are intricate and often interrelated. Modern theoretical explanations reflect this increasing complexity, and this trend, too, is likely to continue.

The final difference is that today's models are based on a great deal of scientific data. Early theories of human development were mostly the products of philosophical debates and logical deductions. Modern explanations, in contrast, have grown out of research findings, and they are continually being modified and revised in response to new observations and experimental data. A particular child psychologist may prefer one theoretical approach over another. In the final analysis, however, the evidence provided by research will determine which theories will survive and which will be abandoned.

Visual Summary for Chapter 2:
Theories of Child Development

Cognitive-Developmental Models

Cognitive abilities are fundamental and guide children's behavior. The key to understanding children's behavior lies in how their knowledge is structured at any given time, and how it changes as they grow.

Major Approaches

Key Assumptions

Piaget's Theory

Development can be described in terms of functions and cognitive structures. Changes in structures are guided by two functions: organization and adaptation. Adaptation consists of assimilation and accommodation. Development consists of movement through four stages: sensorimotor, preoperational, concrete operations, and formal operations.

Information-processing

Cognition is viewed in terms of a computer-like system with three parts: input from the senses, internal processes that act on and transform the information, output from the system in the form of behavior.

Social Models

Social cognition refers to children's knowledge about people and social processes. Vygotsky's sociocultural approach contends that social processes are crucial to the development of children's cognitive abilities and lead to the gradual internalization of culturally provided forms of knowledge and tools of adaptation.

Environmental/Learning Approaches

Much of children's typical behavior is acquired through conditioning and learning principles.

Major Approaches

Key Assumptions

Behavior Analysis

Three types of conditioning and learning are assumed to operate on children: habituation, respondent conditioning, and operant learning. Habituation and respondent conditioning involve reflexes, whereas operant learning is controlled by the consequences of behavior. Reinforcers are consequences that make behavior more probable; punishers are consequences that make behavior less probable.

Social-Learning Theory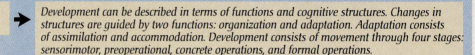

Bandura's theory stresses the role of observational learning. Vicarious reinforcement and vicarious punishment can affect the behavior of an observer. The distinction is made between the acquisition of a modeled response and its performance. Reciprocal determinism holds that human development results from the interaction of characteristics of the person, the person's behavior, and the environment.

Ethology

Ethology is based on the principles of evolution. Ethologists are primarily concerned with innate behaviors, and they attempt to explain complex response patterns in terms of their survival value for the species.

Major Approaches

Key Assumptions

Classical Ethology	➤	Lorenz and Tinbergen identified four characteristics of innate behavior: it is universal, it is stereotyped, it requires no learning, and it is minimally affected by the environment. Ethologists view complex sequences of inherited responses as modal action patterns that are triggered by innate releasing mechanisms in the organism's environment.
Sociobiology	➤	Sociobiology is a recent attempt to explain social behavior in terms of an evolutionary model in which the survival of the genes supersedes any other goal.
Human Ethology	➤	Human ethology emerged largely from the results of Bowlby's research on the attachment process. Many aspects of child development now are being studied from an ethological perspective.

Ecological Approach

Human development should be studied in the various contexts in which it occurs. Developmental interactions are transactional.

Bronfenbrenner's Model

Microsystem	➤	Layer of the environment that most directly affects the child. Examples include family, school, and neighborhood.
Mesosystem	➤	System of relationships among the child's microsystems.
Exosystem	➤	Social settings that affect the child indirectly. Examples include community services, mass media, and family friends.
Macrosystem	➤	Culture and subculture in which the child lives.
Chronosystem	➤	Interactions among the various systems over time.

Chapter *3*

Research Methods

The developing child may seem quite different from atoms fusing to produce nuclear energy or leaf cells using light and carbon dioxide to make food. Yet the research methods used by developmental psychologists to study children are essentially the same as those used by physicists, biologists, and other researchers in the natural sciences. In this chapter, we examine some of these methods and the ways child researchers can use them to unlock the mysteries of human development.

We saw in Chapter 1 that the study of the child became scientific in the 19th century, when G. Stanley Hall began using questionnaires to reveal children's everyday knowledge. Since then, the research methods used by child psychologists have advanced in many different ways. These advances have contributed importantly to the enormous growth in our knowledge and understanding of developmental processes (Miller, 1998).

We begin by outlining some of the ideas and concepts that are basic to all scientific research. We then consider the principal research methods used in developmental psychology. Last, we discuss the sometimes thorny issue of research ethics.

Scientific Research

Scientific method
The system of rules used by scientists to conduct and evaluate their research.

The approach scientists use to study any problem or issue is known as the **scientific method**. The method is really a system of rules that scientists use to design and conduct their research, to evaluate their results, and to communicate their findings to other scientists. These rules have evolved over hundreds of years, and they can be applied to the study of virtually anything.

The Role of Theory

Theory
A broad set of statements describing the relation between a phenomenon and the factors assumed to affect it.

In Chapter 2, we presented three major theories, but we did not actually define the term. In psychology, a **theory** is a set of statements describing the relation between behavior and the factors that influence it. A specific statement that is well supported by research evidence is called a **law** or **principle**—the principle of reinforcement is a good example. A statement that simply postulates, or proposes, a relation is called a **hypothesis**. Any individual study is usually designed to test a researcher's hypothesis regarding how some aspect of children's behavior is affected by some factor in their world.

Law (principle)
A predicted relation between a phenomenon and a factor assumed to affect it that is supported by a good deal of scientific evidence.

Theories have two important roles in scientific research. The first is to *organize research findings*. As investigators acquire knowledge, they use theories to fit the information together into a coherent explanation of the behaviors and processes being studied. Once the knowledge is organized, it is sometimes obvious that certain questions remain to be answered or that specific relations probably exist even though they do not yet have substantial supporting evidence. A second role of theories, then, is to *guide new research* by indicating to investigators which hypotheses should be tested next.

Hypothesis
A predicted relation between a phenomenon and a factor assumed to affect it that is not yet supported by a great deal of evidence. Hypotheses are tested in experimental investigations.

Psychologists do not investigate children's development by randomly studying any question that pops into their heads. Research is typically guided by an underlying theory and theoretical orientation. Thus, cognitive-developmentalists tend to investigate characteristics of children's knowledge; environmental/learning theorists study ways in which behavior is acquired through experience; and ethologists examine various innate patterns of responses.

Objectivity

Children are not of interest only to psychologists, of course. Scholars in literature, music, and art, for example, have devoted much attention to the developing child. But in these fields, the emphasis frequently is on individual tastes, personal opinions, and other subjective judgments. In psychology and the other natural sciences, the emphasis is on **objectivity**.

Objective methods of study have as their primary goal the opportunity for any other scientist, at least in principle, to conduct the same research in the same manner (and presumably arrive at the same results). In addition, objectivity helps to reduce potential sources of *bias* that may enter into the research, such as the experimenter's personal beliefs or preferences regarding what the results should be. These goals are achieved in a number of ways.

One is through a focus on *observable* behaviors. Recall that in child psychology our two primary goals—to describe children's behavior at each point in their development and to identify the causes and processes that produce changes in behavior from one point to the next—center on behavior. Even developmentalists who are concerned primarily with cognition observe the effects of internal cognitive processes on some aspect of behavior. For example, we study assimilation and accommodation by observing a child's reactions to new experiences; we study intelligence by calculating a child's performance on an IQ test; and we study self-esteem by examining how a child interacts in social situations.

A second requirement for ensuring objectivity is that the behaviors under study must be *measurable*. It is not enough that we can observe behavior; we must also feel confident as to when the behavior did or did not occur, when one behavior ended and the next one began, and so forth. Such confidence is achieved by defining and describing the behavior very precisely, so that independent observers would have no trouble agreeing on what happened in a given situation. For example, suppose we are interested in studying children's altruism—their willingness to help someone else. We might first define altruism in terms of sharing behaviors and then

Objectivity
A characteristic of scientific research; it requires that the procedures and subject matter of investigations should be formulated so that they could, in principle, be agreed on by everyone.

An important characteristic of psychological research is the focus on objective definitions and measurable behaviors.

develop a procedure that entails observing the number of pennies just won in a game that a child donates to a charity. Or, suppose we want to investigate an infant's attachment to her mother. We could define attachment in terms of specific behaviors, such as crying, smiling, and searching, and then measure the amount of time that elapses before the infant displays each of these behaviors after the mother has left the room. In this way, abstract concepts such as "altruism" and "attachment" become measurable in an objective, scientific way.

A third way to achieve objectivity is to make everything in the research study *quantifiable*, that is, able to be counted. The researcher must quantify not only the children's behaviors, but also the factors that the researcher hypothesizes may be affecting the behaviors. Usually such factors are physical. The number of children in a classroom, the length of time a child spends reading, or the amount of alcohol that a pregnant mother has consumed, for example, are relatively easy to define in this way. Factors that involve the behaviors of others—social approval, peer interactions, or modeling, for instance—are more difficult to deal with, but they, too, must be carefully defined so that they can be measured and counted.

Throughout this text, we describe many research studies. These studies vary greatly from one another in the issues under investigation, the methods used to collect data, and the types of research participants involved. All of them, however, share the characteristics we have just described. They focus on changes in observable responses, and they deal with behaviors and events that have been measured and quantified with as much precision as possible.

✔ To Recap...

The scientific method consists of the rules that researchers use to conduct and describe their investigations. Scientific theories play two important roles in the research process. First, they help to organize the information gathered from scientific studies. Second, they guide researchers to the important questions that need to be examined next.

Scientific research requires objectivity, which in psychology leads to a focus on observable behaviors and a need for behaviors and their determining factors to be described so that they are measurable and quantifiable.

Types of Research

Research in psychology generally falls into one of three categories: descriptive, correlational, or experimental. Here we briefly discuss each of these approaches as they apply to the study of children.

Descriptive Research

Descriptive research
Research based solely on observations, with no attempt to determine systematic relations among the variables.

The oldest form of psychological research is the purely descriptive approach. When applied to children, **descriptive research** consists of simply observing children and recording what is seen. The psychologist makes no formal attempt to identify relations among the children's behaviors and any other factors. Early *baby biographies*, such as those in which Darwin and others kept daily records of the behaviors of their infants, provided the first systematic descriptive data on human development. G. Stanley Hall's questionnaire findings and, later, Arnold Gesell's norms—both of which described the typical skills and abilities of children of various ages—also used the descriptive method.

Today, descriptive research of this sort is not very common. Normally it is conducted only when very little is known about a topic. Even then, it is often only a first step in a research plan that will go on to use more sophisticated methods of investigation.

Correlational Research

The step beyond observing and describing behaviors is identifying any systematic relations in the observations. Specifically, researchers attempt to identify correlations among variables. A **variable** is any factor that can take on different values along some dimension. Common examples include human physical characteristics—height, weight, age, and so on—and aspects of the environment—temperature, room size, distance to the nearest library, and number of people in a family, for instance. Human behaviors, if properly defined, can also be variables and can vary along several types of dimensions—for example, how many times a child asks the teacher for help (*frequency*), how loudly a baby cries (*intensity*), or how long a child practices the piano (*duration*).

A **correlation** is a statement that describes how two variables are related. Perhaps a psychologist would like to know whether children's ages are correlated with—systematically related to—their heights. The researcher might observe and record the heights of 100 children, aged 2 to 12, and examine whether changes in the one variable correspond to changes in the other. In this case, the psychologist could expect to find a clear relation between the variables of age and height—that is, as children increase in age, they generally increase in height as well. This type of relation, in which two variables change in the same direction, is described as a **positive correlation**.

What about the relation between a child's age and the number of hours each day that the child spends at home? Here we would also discover a systematic relation, but the variables involved would move in opposite directions—as a child's age increases, the amount of time the child spends at home generally decreases. This sort of relation is called a **negative correlation**.

Finally, we might investigate the relation between a child's height and the number of children in the child's classroom. In this case, we would likely find that the two variables are not related to one another at all and so have no correlation.

Correlations can be described not only in terms of their direction (positive or negative) but also in terms of their strength. A strong correlation means that two variables are closely related. In such cases, knowing the value of one gives us a good indication of the value of the second. As a correlation grows weaker, the amount of predictability between the two variables decreases. When the variables become completely unrelated, knowledge of the value of one gives us no clue as to the value of the other.

The direction of a correlation is indicated by a plus or minus sign, and its strength is indicated by a numerical value that can be calculated from a simple statistical formula. The result is called the **correlation coefficient (r)**, which can range between +1.00 and −1.00. A correlation coefficient of +.86 indicates a strong positive correlation, and +.17 indicates a weak positive correlation. Similarly, −.93, −.41, and −.08 denote, respectively, a strong, a moderate, and a weak negative correlation. A coefficient of 0.00 means that there is absolutely no correlation between two variables. Correlations can also be presented visually with a **scatter diagram**, some examples of which are shown in Figure 3.1.

To illustrate both the usefulness and the limitations of correlational research, let us consider a hypothetical example. Suppose a research team is interested in learning whether a relation exists between children's reading ability and the amount of

Variable
Any factor that can take on different values along a dimension.

Correlation
The relation between two variables, described in terms of direction and strength.

Positive correlation
A correlation in which two variables change in the same direction.

Negative correlation
A correlation in which two variables change in opposite directions.

Correlation coefficient (r)
A number between +1.00 and −1.00 that indicates the direction and strength of a correlation between two variables.

Scatter diagram
A graphic illustration of a correlation between two variables.

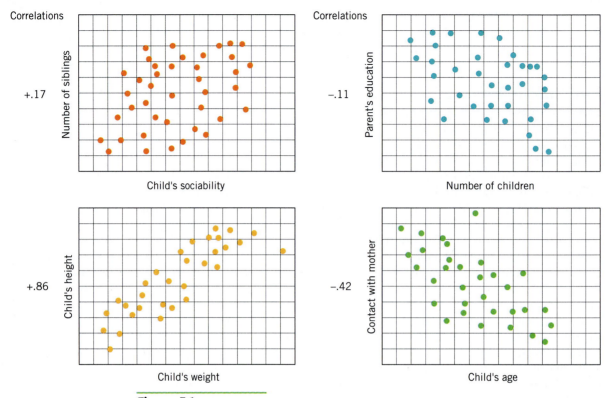

Figure 3.1
Scatter diagrams illustrating correlations between two variables. Each dot represents one child and shows the child's values for the two variables. One value is plotted from the vertical axis and the other from the horizontal axis. The left two graphs show positive correlations, and the right two graphs show negative correlations.

time they watch the educational television program *Sesame Street.* To begin, the researchers randomly select a number of children and measure each child's values on the reading-ability variable (perhaps by giving the children a reading test on which they can score between 0 and 100) and on the viewing variable (perhaps by having parents record the number of hours each week that the child watches *Sesame Street*). Then, the researchers calculate the correlation between the two sets of scores and discover that the variables have a correlation coefficient of +.78, as shown in Figure 3.2. What can the research team conclude from these findings?

Since the two variables display a strong positive correlation, we know that as one increases the other increases and also that knowing a child's value on one of the variables allows us to predict the child's value on the other variable fairly well. We therefore might be tempted to believe that the study shows that viewing *Sesame Street* leads to better reading skills, or in more general terms, that a change in one of the variables *causes* change in the other. Herein lies a major limitation of correlational research—*a correlation cannot be used to show causality between the variables.* The correlation in the example may accurately reveal the pattern and strength of the reading-viewing relation, but it cannot reveal cause and effect between the variables. Why not?

If we think carefully about the findings, we realize that some other conclusions cannot be ruled out. For example, rather than TV viewing's having an effect on the

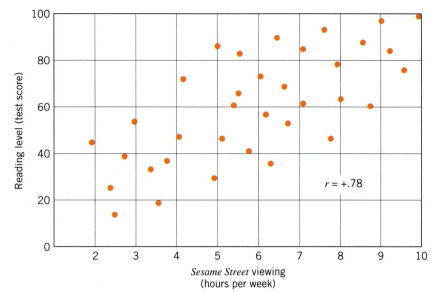

Figure 3.2
A scatter diagram of a hypothetical correlation between children's viewing of *Sesame Street* and their reading level. The correlation coefficient (*r*) shows a strong positive relation between the two variables.

reading, the reverse is equally plausible. That is, children who are better readers may watch *Sesame Street* more often than do children who are poorer readers (possibly because they enjoy it more). Another possibility is that the two variables are both influenced by some third variable that we have not measured. For instance, both might be affected by the educational background of the child's parents. Indeed, there is a good chance that the better educated a child's parents are, the more likely they are to encourage both reading and the viewing of educational television. Thus, although correlational research is a valuable tool for identifying and measuring systematic relations, it cannot be used to explain them. Explanation requires a more powerful research method—the experimental approach.

Nevertheless, correlational research can play an important role in the scientific research process. Like descriptive research, correlational studies sometimes raise interesting and provocative questions. These questions may be formed into specific research hypotheses that investigators can examine using more rigorous methods of research.

Experimental Research

The most popular and important type of research in developmental psychology is the experiment. A simple experiment often involves investigating the relation between just two variables, but, unlike correlational research, experimentation permits us to draw cause-and-effect conclusions about the variables.

The most important difference between a correlational study and an experimental study lies in how the information is gathered. Correlational research is usually based on simple observation. The two variables of interest are observed and recorded without any intrusion or interference by the researcher. In an experiment, however, the researcher systematically *manipulates*—changes—one variable and then looks for any effects (changes) in the second variable. The variable that is systematically manipulated is called the **independent variable**. The variable affected by the manipulation is called the **dependent variable**. In psychological research, the dependent variable is typically some aspect of behavior, whereas the independent variable is a factor the researcher suspects may influence that behavior.

Independent variable
The variable in an experiment that is systematically manipulated.

Dependent variable
The variable that is predicted to be affected by an experimental manipulation. In psychology, usually some aspect of behavior.

Group Studies Most experimental research conducted by developmental psychologists involves comparing the behavior of groups of research participants exposed to different manipulations of an independent variable.

Let us return to the previous example and consider how researchers might use the experimental method to address the question of whether watching *Sesame Street* affects reading level. First, the researchers need a hypothesis that clearly identifies the independent and dependent variables. If the hypothesis is that viewing the program *causes* improvements in reading ability, then the independent variable is the amount of viewing and the dependent variable is the child's reading level. The next step involves systematically manipulating the independent variable. As in the correlational approach, the researchers select a number of children, but in this case they randomly divide the children into, say, four groups. The first group is required to watch 2 hours of *Sesame Street* each week; the second group, 4 hours; the third group, 8 hours; and the fourth group, 10 hours. After perhaps 6 months, the researchers administer the reading test to all the children and examine how the different groups perform. Possible results are shown in Figure 3.3. If the differences in performance among groups are sufficiently large (as determined by the appropriate statistical tests), not only can the researchers conclude that the two variables are systematically related, but they can now also make the causal statement that viewing *Sesame Street* improves children's reading ability. That is, the psychologists' hypothesis now has been supported by experimental data.

Reversal-Replication Studies Although experimental research most often involves exposing groups of subjects to different values of an independent variable, there is an alternative called the **reversal-replication design** (or sometimes the **ABAB design**). In this method, the independent variable is systematically presented and removed and effects on the dependent variable are noted. The main advantage of this design is that fewer subjects are needed; for instance, it can be used in an experiment involving a single child. Consider how we might use this method to test the hypothesis that the presence of the mother causes infants to smile more often. In this experiment, the independent variable would be the presence or absence of the mother, and the dependent variable would be the amount the infant

Reversal-replication (ABAB) design
An experimental design in which the independent variable is systematically presented and removed several times. Can be used in studies involving very few research participants.

Figure 3.3
A bar graph illustrating an experimental test of the hypothesis that viewing *Sesame Street* improves reading test performance. Each bar shows the average test score for all the children in that experimental group.

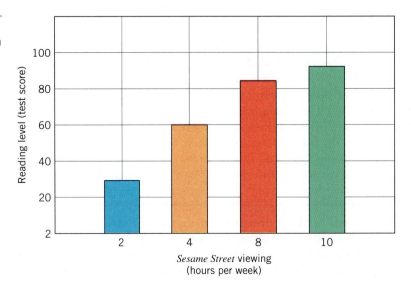

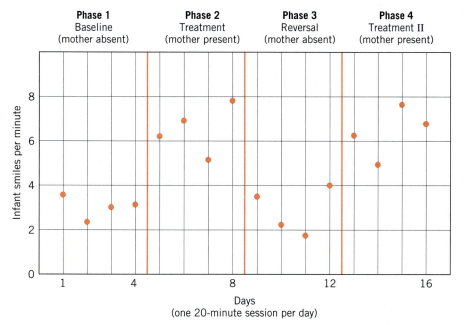

Phase 1
Baseline
(mother absent)

Phase 2
Treatment
(mother present)

Phase 3
Reversal
(mother absent)

Phase 4
Treatment II
(mother present)

Infant smiles per minute

Days
(one 20-minute session per day)

Figure 3.4
A reversal–replication design showing a causal relation between the presence of the mother (the independent variable) and the amount an infant smiles (the dependent variable). The third and fourth phases replicate the procedures and results of the first two phases.

smiles. As Figure 3.4 indicates, the basic procedure of the experiment involves counting the number of times the infant smiles per minute during a 20-minute daily session in which the mother is either present or absent.

To conduct the experiment, the researcher must first determine the *baseline*, or initial level of the behavior being observed. In this example, the baseline is the number of times the infant smiles when alone. In the second, or *treatment*, phase of the experiment, the independent variable is introduced. As shown in Figure 3.4, there is a clear increase in smiling when the mother is present. The change in the infant's behavior supports the researcher's hypothesis, but it is premature to conclude that a causal relation exists between the presence of the mother and the baby's smiling. Why? The change in the infant's behavior might have resulted from other factors—such as a better overall mood—that only coincidentally occurred when the mother was present.

To determine whether the change in behavior was only accidentally related to the change in the independent variable, the researcher attempts to *replicate* the procedure and results. In the next step, then, the independent variable is again removed. This is called the *reversal*, or withdrawal, phase. In our example, we can see that the infant's behavior returns to its baseline level. Finally, the independent variable is presented once more in a second treatment phase. If the subsequent change in behavior is the same as during the first treatment phase, then the researcher has enough evidence to infer a causal relation between the independent and dependent variables. Since the amount the infant smiles does indeed increase once again, the researcher can reasonably conclude that the baby's smiling is affected by the mother's presence.

Additional Considerations   Experimental research is a powerful scientific tool, not only because it can reveal cause-and-effect relations, but also because it can be applied to a wide variety of problems and settings. Much of the experimentation conducted by child psychologists takes place in laboratories, especially when conditions must be carefully controlled and monitored. But consistent with an ecological approach, experimental studies can also be conducted in field settings—playgrounds, classrooms, or children's homes, for example—where the child's behavior is studied under more natural conditions.

The experimental approach is of paramount importance in the study of child development, and examples of experiments are described frequently in the pages that follow. We have outlined here the most basic concepts involved in this method, but many detailed procedures not discussed must be followed before we can be confident that an experiment is scientifically sound. These involve such matters as how the research participants are selected and assigned to groups, under what conditions the data are gathered, which statistical tests are conducted, and so forth.

Furthermore, experimental studies—as well as correlational studies—are typically more complex than we have indicated. For one thing, a single study often involves a number of variables rather than just two, and sometimes several hypotheses are tested at once. Finally, no single experiment should ever be taken as definitive. Before science can feel confident about a finding, the results generally must be replicated several times and by different experimenters. Discussions of all these issues can be readily found in texts devoted to methodology in developmental psychology (e.g., Cozby et al., 1998; Miller, 1998; Vasta, 1982b).

✓ To Recap...

The three major research methods used by child psychologists are descriptive research, correlational research, and experimentation. The descriptive approach involves simple observation and is used today primarily as a first step in exploring areas about which little is known. Correlational studies are used to identify relations between variables and to describe them in terms of their direction and strength. This method does not permit conclusions regarding cause and effect. The experimental approach involves testing hypotheses by systematically manipulating the independent variable and examining its effects on the dependent variable. It allows researchers to draw conclusions regarding cause and effect. Experimental studies may involve groups of subjects exposed to different values of an independent variable. They may also involve only a few subjects, who are exposed to the repeated presentation and removal of an independent variable in a reversal-replication design.

Studying Development

Development, as we have seen, involves changes in behavior over time. Many of the issues of interest to developmental researchers therefore focus on how children's behavior at one age differs from their behavior at another age. Sometimes these issues are mainly descriptive, such as how a child's speech progresses from the one-word utterances of the toddler, to the ill-formed sentences of the preschooler, to the reasonably accurate sentences of the preadolescent. At other times the issues concern the causes of behavior, such as the possible effects of day-care programs on children's later social adjustment to school. For either type of question, however, the psychologist needs a research method that will allow the comparison of behaviors at different ages. Four methods are available for this purpose: the longitudinal study, the cross-sectional study, a method that combines the two, and the microgenetic technique.

Longitudinal Research

One approach to studying children's behavior at different ages is the **longitudinal design**. The logic of this approach is quite simple. The behaviors of interest are first measured when the child is very young and then measured again at various intervals as the child grows. The main advantage of this method is that it allows the researcher to study directly how each behavior changes as the child gets older (Menard, 1991).

The number of years required for a longitudinal study can vary considerably. Some questions can be explored within a relatively brief time frame. For example, determining whether different techniques of caring for premature infants have different effects on the age at which the babies begin to walk and talk should take only about 18 months to 2 years of observation. Other questions, such as whether a child's early disciplinary experiences influence his or her own use of punishment as a parent, may need to extend over decades.

Longitudinal studies can be either correlational or experimental. If we measure behaviors at one age and then again at a later age, we can determine the consistency of the behaviors by calculating the correlation between the two sets of measurements. Experimental longitudinal studies usually involve introducing a manipulation at one point in development and then examining its effects on the dependent variables of interest at some later point, or points, in development.

Two types of research questions are particularly well suited to the longitudinal approach (Magnusson et al., 1991). The first concerns the *stability*, or persistence, of behaviors. If, for instance, we wish to determine the extent to which a child's temperament (an aspect of personality) remains constant throughout life, the best approach is to measure this characteristic in the same children periodically and examine the correlations among the sets of scores.

The second type of question that works well with the longitudinal method involves the *effects of early experiences* on later behavior. If we wish to determine whether certain events or conditions that occur during a child's early years—divorce, an infant stimulation program, or the quality of diet, for instance—produce long-term effects, the clearest answers will be obtained with an experimental longitudinal approach. For example, we might identify children who have participated in an early stimulation program and children who have not and then follow both groups for a number of years to see whether differences emerge in their suc-

Longitudinal design
A research method in which the same individuals are studied repeatedly over time.

In longitudinal research, the same individuals are studied over a period of time, sometimes many years.

BOX 3.1

TERMAN'S STUDIES OF GENIUS

The first major longitudinal study in developmental psychology was Lewis Terman's investigation of intellectually gifted children. This classic research remains especially noteworthy because it followed a very large group of subjects for almost their entire lives and generated some fascinating findings (Cravens, 1992).

Terman was a psychologist at Stanford University and is best known for having developed one of the first IQ tests, the Stanford–Binet (which we will describe when we discuss intelligence testing in Chapter 10). In the course of administering his new test, Terman became interested in the children who scored at the very highest levels. In 1921 he selected approximately 1,400 extremely intelligent 11-year-olds in California to participate in a longitudinal project, which he titled *Genetic Studies of Genius* (Terman, 1925).

Terman was not interested only in the intelligence of these children. He also collected a great deal of information on their families, schools, physical characteristics, mental and medical health, personality traits, and more. At intervals of about 10 years, Terman readministered many of the same tests and measures to find out whether gifted children develop differently from their peers of normal intelligence.

The participants in this study, who became known as "Termites," proved to be quite different from what would have been predicted by the conventional wisdom of the time. They did not support the stereotype that genius children are sickly, meek, and social misfits. As they grew up, they were found to be healthier, wealthier, more successful professionally, and even happier than most of their peers in society.

Two of Terman's initial findings have been somewhat controversial. He reported that the gifted children came from wealthier, better educated families and that many more males than females had high IQ scores. Both of these findings today are regarded skeptically by psychologists and may have resulted from flaws or biases in the way in which Terman selected his research participants (Shurkin, 1992).

Terman died in 1957, but his research was continued by others, including Robert Sears, a Termite who became a developmental psychologist. In 1972, when the subjects had reached their 60s, they were asked to describe what aspects of their lives they had found most satisfying or rewarding. Interestingly, the majority of them pointed to their families—not their wealth, social status, or professional success—as having been their greatest source of happiness (Sears, 1977).

Although most of the Termites have now died, the vast amount of information collected by Terman's research team is still being studied, and scientists continue to generate new questions and better ways to look at the data (Friedman et al., 1995).

cess in school. Both questions also can be related to the more general issues of continuity and discontinuity, discussed in Chapter 1. (An early longitudinal study is presented in Box 3.1.)

Despite the obvious value of the longitudinal approach, the method does have certain disadvantages. One is the problem of *attrition*, the loss of individuals under study, which can occur for a variety of reasons. Families may move away, children may become ill or develop other problems that interfere with participation in the study, or parents may simply lose interest and withdraw from the project. Other problems may develop because of the repeated testing. For example, a study concerned with the stability of a child's intelligence requires that IQ tests be administered at regular intervals. But repeated experience with tests itself may make a child test wise to the types of responses that are expected and may thus artificially improve the child's performance.

A third disadvantage relates directly to the fact that longitudinal studies are often designed to last for many years. There is a very real possibility that the issues involved or the instruments used at the beginning of the study may become outdated. For example, the experimental questions posed at the outset of the project may become less important as the years pass and other research findings are published. Similarly, the tests and instruments used may become obsolete. Finally, there is a major practical disadvantage. Since it often requires a large research staff and many hours of observation or testing, longitudinal research can be very expensive.

Development in Cultural Context
Studying the Life Course

*O*ne interesting variation on longitudinal research is the study of the life course. Such investigations focus on how major personal and environmental events affect an individual. The dependent measures of interest here, however, are not the short-term impacts of these events, which psychologists usually study, but how these events can alter the course of the individual's entire life (Elder, 1998).

Generally such research is *archival* rather than experimental, that is, the investigators use existing longitudinal studies that have gone on for many years as their source of data. By examining the records of these studies—often tracing one individual's life at a time—the life-course researcher can study new questions of current interest that may not have been a specific focus of the original project. And, because the research uses data that have already been gathered, longitudinal issues can be studied in a fraction of the time normally required.

Studies of the life course have taken several forms. Some have examined the impact of major historical events or conditions on the lives of the people in a particular generation (Conger & Elder, 1994). Examples include the effects of the Great Depression of the 1930s and of World War II. Other studies have looked at the role of life transitions—for example, the age at which a woman decides to marry, to have her first child, or to enter the workforce (Elder, Caspi, & Downey, 1986); or the different effects of entering the military early or late, as reflected in the experiences of Terman's Termites (discussed in Box 3.1) (Elder, Shanahan, & Clipp, 1994).

A related interest of life-course researchers is the long-range effects of early personality characteristics (Caspi & Elder, 1988). A guiding assumption of research in this area is that an individual's relationship to his or her environment is transactional. Recall from Chapter 2 that this means that a person to some degree produces a certain type of environment to which he or she then continues to be exposed.

For example, studies have examined the lives of some shy children (Caspi, Elder, & Bem, 1988) and explosive children (Caspi, Elder, & Bem, 1987). Although few long-term effects of shyness in girls were identified, boys who were shy and unassertive later showed delays in marrying, fathering children, and establishing stable careers. Explosive, ill-tempered boys were more likely to drop out of school and ultimately to have poorer jobs, less job satisfaction, and more marital problems. Ill-tempered girls, too, tended to have less stable marriages as adults and to be married to men of lower socioeconomic status. The researchers believe these children, because of their shyness or explosiveness, engendered certain reactions in people and so gradually gravitated toward (or away from) certain social experiences and groups. These patterns, in turn, influenced the lives of these individuals for many years.

Research on the life course has investigated the effects of major historical events, such as the Great Depression of the 1930s, on the lives of individuals involved.

Cross-Sectional Research

Cross-sectional design
A research method in which people of different ages are studied simultaneously to examine the effects of age on some aspect of behavior.

An alternative to longitudinal research is the **cross-sectional design**, which allows researchers to examine developmental differences in behavior by studying children of different ages at the same point in time. In this type of experiment, the age of the children becomes an independent variable in the research design. The major advantage of this approach is that it is much less time-consuming than is the longitudinal method. Rather than waiting 5 years to determine, say, how memory processes in 3-year-olds differ from memory processes in 8-year-olds, we can simply study a group of 3-year-olds and a group of 8-year-olds at the same time. The relatively short time required also means that such experiments are rarely plagued by the problems of attrition, repeated testing, outdated issues and instruments, and high cost.

Still, the cross-sectional approach has two significant disadvantages. First, this method cannot be used to investigate questions of behavior stability and early experience, as it is impossible to determine persistence of an early trait or the impact of an early event by examining those behaviors in *different* older children.

Cohort effect
A problem sometimes found in cross-sectional research in which people of a given age are affected by factors unique to their generation.

Second is a problem known as the **cohort effect**, which occurs because certain aspects of people's behavior are influenced by the unique events and conditions experienced by their particular age group or generation. For example, suppose we were investigating the cognitive skills of individuals at ages 35, 45, and 65 and found that the 45-year-olds performed better on our various reasoning and problem-solving tests than did the younger or older groups. Would these results allow us to conclude that cognitive development improves into middle adulthood and then declines?

Such an interpretation is certainly consistent with our data, but another explanation arises when we consider the educational backgrounds of our three groups of subjects. The 65-year-olds were raised during the Depression, when many youngsters were forced to leave school early and find jobs. The 35-year-olds were raised during the late 1960s, when much greater emphasis was being placed on children's social and emotional development. But the 45-year-olds began attending school shortly after the launching of the Soviet satellite *Sputnik*, which stimulated a major U.S. effort to improve scientific and mathematical training. The point is that our research participants are members of three cohorts, or peer groups, which had different educational experiences. The performance differences we observe may not reflect the differences in their ages so much as their different life experiences.

Combining Longitudinal and Cross-Sectional Research

Cross-sequential design
A research method combining longitudinal and cross-sectional designs.

To obtain the best features of the longitudinal and cross-sectional designs, researchers sometimes combine the two methods into a **cross-sequential design**. The combined approach begins with a simple cross-sectional investigation, during which groups of children of different ages are studied simultaneously. The same groups are then studied again at one or more later times to provide a longitudinal perspective on the question.

For instance, an investigator might begin by measuring the amount of competitiveness displayed by 4-year-olds, 7-year-olds, and 10-year-olds playing a game. Three years later, the investigator retests the children, who are now 7, 10, and 13. This procedure makes a number of data comparisons possible. For example, cross-sectional comparisons among the children can be made at both the initial testing and the later testing to see whether children at the different ages show different levels of competitiveness. In addition, the stability of each child's competitiveness can be examined by a comparison of the child's scores at the two ages.

The combined design also permits the investigator to check directly for two of the common problems associated with the individual designs. If the data for the groups at ages 7 and 10 during the first testing differ from the data for these groups during the second testing, then these differences are very likely the result of either a cohort effect (a cross-sectional design problem) or a repeated-testing effect (a longitudinal design problem). In either case, the investigator will need to exercise caution in drawing conclusions regarding age-related differences in competitiveness or the stability of the behavior over time. But if the data from these corresponding groups are very similar, the researcher can have considerable confidence in the results of the study.

Microgenetic Studies

A somewhat newer approach to examining developmental change involves the intensive study of a small number of children over a brief period of time. The purpose of this **microgenetic method** is to investigate changes in important developmental processes *as they are occurring* (Kuhn, 1995; Siegler, 1995).

Recall from Chapter 1 that some aspects of human development are thought to be discontinuous—they are relatively stable for a period of time but then move abruptly to a higher level. Investigators attempting to understand the nature of such changes have used the microgenetic approach in the hope of examining the particular developmental process as it goes from one level to the next. Much of the research using this approach has been concerned with children's cognitive abilities, probably because the concept of discontinuous change is consistent with the view of development held by Piaget and most other cognitive-developmental psychologists.

A microgenetic study begins with several children who are about the age at which a developmental change is expected to occur. The behavior of interest is observed and measured repeatedly in these children. For example, if the experiment is concerned with the children's use of a particular cognitive strategy for solving a certain type of problem (a common focus of such research), the children may be asked to complete many such problems over a period of weeks. In such an experiment, the researcher not only notes the correctness of the children's solutions, but also examines precisely how they approach each problem, perhaps by asking them to describe what they are doing. In this way, the investigator attempts to identify when a child moves from the use of a simpler cognitive strategy to a more sophisticated one. By examining this process very carefully, the researcher may acquire a better understanding of exactly how it works.

Although the microgenetic method can yield a great deal of new information about a developmental process, it, too, has drawbacks. One practical problem is that making many observations over a compressed period of time can be expensive. Another consideration is that great care must be taken to ensure that the repeated assessment of the child's abilities does not itself cause changes in the behavior of interest (Pressley, 1992).

Microgenetic method
A research method in which a small number of individuals are observed repeatedly in order to study an expected change in a developmental process.

✔ To Recap...

Many developmental issues require comparisons of children's behavior at different ages. The longitudinal method assesses the behavior of the same children over a period of time. It is particularly useful for addressing the effects of early experience on later behavior and the stability of behavior. The longitudinal method commonly suffers from problems with attrition, the effects of repeated testing, and the fact that issues and instruments may become outdated. It is also expensive. Cross-sectional research is less time-consuming than longitudinal research because it involves simultaneously studying children of different ages. However, it is sometimes plagued by the cohort effect. The longitudinal and cross-sectional approaches can be combined into the cross-sequential design, which offers some of the advantages of both methods. The microgenetic method is used to study emerging developmental changes by intensive assessment of the behavior of a small number of children over a brief period of time.

Other Research Tactics

Many additional research methods are used by developmental psychologists. In this section we describe the case study, cross-cultural research, and comparative research, three popular approaches to investigating various developmental issues.

Case Studies

Case study

A research method that involves only a single individual, often with a focus on a clinical issue.

Sometimes research involves only a single individual who becomes the subject of a **case study**. Often these studies are concerned with clinical issues, such as when a child displays a rare disorder or when a new treatment approach is applied to a developmental problem. Occasionally, a child has encountered experiences so unusual as to attract the interest of psychologists for theoretical reasons.

Case study research can involve several different methods. At times it is purely descriptive, as with the early baby biographies we described in Chapter 1. But experimental research can also be conducted with only one child. We saw earlier, for example, that the reversal-replication design can be used in this way. At times case studies also represent natural experiments in the sense that a child has been exposed to a particular set of circumstances that could not have been otherwise arranged—usually for ethical reasons—but that offer researchers the opportunity to note the effects of these circumstances (independent variable) on one or more aspects of the child's behavior (dependent variable).

A dramatic example of such a situation is the case of "Genie," a child who was kept isolated by her parents and never spoken to until she was 14 years old (Curtiss, 1977). Genie presented language researchers with a unique opportunity to investigate whether being deprived from exposure to language early on can affect a child's ability to acquire verbal skills at an advanced age. Such a question, of course, could never have been studied in any conventional experimental way.

The major limitation of using only a single research participant is that the researcher must be very cautious about drawing conclusions from the case. Genie, for example, was not only deprived of language, but also experienced an extremely harsh and unusual childhood, because of her parents. Whether the data regarding her language abilities can be generalized to other children thus remains unclear.

Despite limitations, case studies can be valuable in the research process. They may raise new questions or issues that can be studied using more carefully controlled research methods.

Cross-Cultural Research

A major theme of modern child psychology is that development must be studied in context. We saw in Bronfenbrenner's model (Chapter 2) that an important context in which children develop is the culture of their people. How can we determine the influence of culture on a particular aspect of behavior or development?

Cross-cultural studies can sometimes help determine whether patterns of behavior among members of one culture are universal to humans or result from common environmental influences.

One approach is to study the same behavior in different cultures. **Cross-cultural studies** use the child's culture as an independent variable in the experiment and examine its effects on the dependent variable(s) of interest. Such studies have been conducted in areas as diverse as gender roles, moral reasoning, and perceptual abilities (Harkness & Super, 1987; Shweder et al., 1998).

An important use of this experimental method is to investigate nature–nurture questions. Language development again serves as a good example. English-speaking children generally follow a relatively predictable pattern of language acquisition. Certain grammatical structures are displayed before others (such as active sentences before passive sentences), and certain types of errors and omissions are common among all children of a given age. Do these similarities mean that language development is guided by inborn biological mechanisms and is therefore essentially the same for all humans? Or do they simply reflect the fact that most children in a given culture are exposed to similar language models in parents, teachers, and others?

One fruitful approach to answering this question is to examine patterns of language acquisition in several cultures. If children in different language environments display similar patterns in their development of grammar and speech distortions, we have good evidence that language development is genetically guided. If we find differences between cultural groups, however, we can conclude that environmental factors contribute to the language-acquisition process (an issue we pursue further in Chapter 11).

Comparative Research

Psychologists also study behaviors across species. Although **comparative research** of this sort has served many different purposes, developmentalists typically perform animal experiments for one of two reasons. First, researchers of the ethological tradition study animal behavior for clues to the evolutionary origins of similar human behaviors. For instance, determining how the imprinting process causes newborn birds to develop social attachments to their mothers may help child researchers

Cross-cultural studies Research designed to determine the influence of culture on some aspect of development and in which culture typically serves as an independent variable.

Comparative research Research conducted with nonhuman species to provide information relevant to human development.

Comparative research investigates similiar behaviors across different species.

understand the mechanisms involved in the development of attachment between human infants and their mothers. Similarly, studying the play fighting that commonly occurs among pups of many species may provide insights into the rough-and-tumble social interactions of young children.

More frequently, however, comparative research permits developmental psychologists to conduct studies that would be prohibited with humans for ethical reasons. What happens, for instance, to an infant who is reared for 6 months without a mother? Does the visual system develop normally in an infant raised in total darkness? Do injections of sex hormones during the mother's pregnancy affect the later social behavior of the offspring? These, as well as many other questions, would be impossible to address experimentally with humans. Using other species, however, researchers have studied each of these issues in the laboratory.

✓ To Recap...

Case studies involve a single individual and often are concerned with clinical issues. The generalizability of the findings is limited, but the results sometimes prompt more rigorous research on an issue. Cross-cultural research is useful for studying the influence of culture on development and for addressing some nature–nurture issues. Comparative research is conducted by ethologists to identify similarities in behavior processes of humans and non-human species. It also provides a way of experimentally addressing questions that would be unethical to investigate with humans.

Ethical Issues

No one would question the fact that psychological research often produces findings that benefit children, adults, and society as a whole. Nevertheless, almost any research involving humans can pose a variety of risks. Investigators have an obligation to determine exactly what potentially negative effects may result from their experiments and to consider whether these risks outweigh the potential value of the research findings (Fisher & Tryon, 1990; Rheingold, 1982a).

Concern over ethical issues has not always been as great as it is today. Early investigators had few restrictions on their research, as evidenced by such questionable experiments as John B. Watson's conditioning of 11-month-old Little Albert. Today, however, attention is increasingly focused on safeguarding children's rights and well-being (Sieber, 1992).

Potential Risks

An obvious concern in any experiment is the possibility of physical injury to the child, although this problem is relatively rare in developmental research. A more common, and often more subtle, issue involves potential psychological harm to the child. Some experimental hypotheses may require, for example, observing how children respond when they cannot solve a problem, are prohibited from playing with an attractive toy, or are exposed to violent behavior. These procedures may produce various negative emotions, such as feelings of failure, frustration, or stress. The concern is that the children may continue to experience these emotions for some time after leaving the experimental situation.

A less obvious category of problems involves violations of privacy. If a researcher secretly gains access to a child's school records, if observations are conducted without a child's knowledge, or if data regarding a child or a family become public knowledge, the legal and ethical rights of these individuals may be violated.

Safeguards

The concern for ethical research practices has led to the development of safeguards designed to avoid or eliminate potential risks. These safeguards have, by and large, become a routine part of modern research procedures. In addition, professional scientific organizations have developed codes of ethical standards to guide their members. *Ethical Principles in the Conduct of Research with Human Participants* (1982), published by the American Psychological Association, and "SRCD Ethical Standards for Research with Children" (1990), published by the Society for Research in Child Development and reproduced in part in Table 3.1, are two important examples.

Researchers who study children are required to ensure that neither physical nor psychological harm to the child is likely to result from their procedures.

Table 3.1
Ethical Standards for Research with Children, Society for Research in Child Development

Children as research participants present ethical problems for the investigator that are different from those presented by adult participants. Children are more vulnerable to stress than adults and, having less experience and knowledge than adults, are less able to evaluate the social value of the research and less able to comprehend the meaning of the research procedures themselves. In all cases, therefore, the child's consent or assent to participate in the research, as well as the consent of the child's parents or guardians, must be obtained.

In general, no matter how young children are, they have rights that supersede the rights of the investigator. The investigator is therefore obligated to evaluate each proposed research operation in terms of these rights, and before proceeding with the investigation, should obtain the approval of an appropriate Institutional Review Board.

The principles listed below are to be subscribed to by all members of the Society for Research in Child Development. These principles are not intended to infringe on the right and obligation of researchers to conduct scientific research.

Principle 1. Non-harmful Procedures:
The investigator should use no research operation that may harm the child either physically or psychologically. The investigator is also obligated at all times to use the least stressful research operation whenever possible. Psychological harm in particular instances may be difficult to define; nevertheless its definition and means for reducing or eliminating it remain the responsibility of the investigator. When the investigator is in doubt about the possible harmful effects of the research operations, consultation should be sought from others. When harm seems inevitable, the investigator is obligated to find other means of obtaining the information or to abandon the research.

Principle 2. Informed Consent:
Before seeking consent or assent from the child, the investigator should inform the child of all features of the research that may affect his or her willingness to participate and should answer the child's questions in terms appropriate to the child's comprehension. The investigator should respect the child's freedom to choose to participate in the research or not by giving the child the opportunity to give or not give assent to participation as well as to choose to discontinue participation at any time. Assent means that the child shows some form of agreement to participate without necessarily comprehending the full significance of the research necessary to give informed consent. Investigators working with infants should take special effort to explain the research procedures to the parents and be especially sensitive to any indicators of discomfort in the infant.

In spite of the paramount importance of obtaining consent, instances can arise in which consent or any kind of contact with the participant would make the research impossible to carry out. Nonintrusive field research is a common example. Conceivably, such research can be carried out ethically if it is conducted in public places, participants' anonymity is totally protected, and there are no foreseeable negative consequences to the participant.

Principle 3. Parental Consent:
The informed consent of parents, legal guardians or those who act in loco parentis (e.g., teachers, superintendents of institutions) similarly should be obtained, preferably in writing. Informed consent requires that parents or other responsible adults be informed of all the features of the research that may affect their willingness to allow the child to participate. Not only should the right of the responsible adults to refuse consent be respected, but they should be informed that they may refuse to participate without incurring any penalty to them or to the child.

Principle 4. Additional Consent:
The informed consent of any persons, such as school teachers for example, whose interaction with the child is the participant in the study, should also be obtained. As with the child and parents or guardians informed consent requires that the persons interacting with the child during study be informed of all features of the research which may affect their willingness to participate.

Perhaps the most important measure used to ensure that research is conducted ethically is *peer review*. Before beginning a research study, investigators are encouraged, and in many situations required, to submit the research plan to others for their comments and approval. This practice permits an objective examination of the procedures by knowledgeable individuals, including both scientists and community laypeople, who are not personally involved in the research. Peer review committees weigh the possible value of the research findings against potential risks. Sometimes they offer suggestions as to how negative effects might be prevented or minimized. Almost all research carried out at colleges and universities or funded by government organizations is subject to peer review.

Table 3.1
(Continued)

Principle 5. Incentives:
Incentives to participate in a research project must be fair and must not unduly exceed the range of incentives that the child normally experiences. Whatever incentives are used, the investigator should always keep in mind that the greater the possible effects of the investigation on the child, the greater is the obligation to protect the child's welfare and freedom.

Principle 6. Deception:
Although full disclosure of information during the procedure of obtaining consent is the ethical ideal, a particular study may necessitate withholding certain information or deception. Whenever withholding information or deception is judged to be essential to the conduct of the study, the investigator should satisfy research colleagues that such judgment is correct. If withholding information or deception is practiced, and there is reason to believe that the research participants will be negatively affected by it, adequate measures should be taken after the study to ensure the participant's understanding of the reasons for the deception.

Principle 7. Anonymity:
To gain access to institutional records, the investigator should obtain permission from responsible authorities in charge of records. Anonymity of the information should be preserved and no information used other than that for which permission was obtained.

Principle 8. Mutual Responsibilities:
From the beginning of each research investigation, there should be clear agreement between the investigator and the parents, guardians or those who act in loco parentis, and the child, when appropriate, that defines the responsibilities of each. The investigator has the obligation to honor all promises and commitments of the agreement.

Principle 9. Jeopardy:
When, in the course of research, information comes to the investigator's attention that may jeopardize the child's well-

being, the investigator has a responsibility to discuss the information with the parents or guardians and with those expert in the field in order that they may arrange the necessary assistance for the child.

Principle 10. Unforeseen Consequences:
When research procedures result in undesirable consequences for the participant that were previously unforeseen, the investigator should immediately employ appropriate measures to correct these consequences, and should redesign the procedures if they are to be included in subsequent studies.

Principle 11. Confidentiality:
The investigator should keep in confidence all information obtained about research participants. The participants' identities should be concealed in written and verbal reports of the results, as well as in informal discussion with students and colleagues.

Principle 12. Informing Participants:
Immediately after the data are collected, the investigator should clarify for the research participant any misconceptions that may have arisen. The investigator also recognizes a duty to report general findings to participants in terms appropriate to their understanding.

Principle 13. Reporting Results:
Because the investigator's words may carry unintended weight with parents and children, caution should be exercised in reporting results, making evaluative statements, or giving advice.

Principle 14. Implications of Findings:
Investigators should be mindful of the social, political and human implications of their research and should be especially careful in the presentation of findings from the research. This principle, however, in no way denies investigators the right to pursue any area of research or the right to observe proper standards of scientific reporting.

Source: Excerpted from "SRCD Ethical Standards for Research with Children," 1990, *SRCD Newsletter*, winter, pp. 5–6.

Another basic measure for protecting children's rights is the requirement that researchers obtain the *informed consent* of the participants in the study. Any research conducted with children requires the written permission of both the parents and the institution (school, day-care center, and so on) where the research will take place. In addition, each child must be made aware of the general procedures of the study. Most important, the child has the right to refuse to participate or to withdraw from the study at any time, even though the parents have given their permission.

If the research procedures may produce negative feelings in the child, the investigator must provide some means of reducing those feelings before the child leaves. For example, if a child is participating in an experiment in which he or she experiences failure, the investigator might end the research session by having the child perform a relatively easy task that will ensure success. Also, to whatever extent seems reasonable, the investigator should at some point explain to the child the purpose of the study and the child's role in it, a procedure called *debriefing*.

Maintaining *confidentiality* is also a crucial aspect of ethical research. Whenever possible, the identities of the participants and information about their individual performance should be concealed from anyone not directly connected with the research. Anonymity often is achieved through the practice of assigning numbers to the participants and then using these numbers instead of names during the analysis of the data.

Finally, all research psychologists have some ethical responsibilities that go beyond the protection of the individuals participating in the research. For example, scientists who report data that may be controversial or that may affect social-policy decisions have an obligation to describe the limitations and degree of confidence they have in their findings. In addition, investigators should normally provide their research participants with some general information about the final results of the research, as an acknowledgment of the importance of their contribution to the overall research process.

✓ *To Recap...*

Research with humans always involves a balance between the potential value of the findings and any risks that may be involved. The most common categories of risk include physical and psychological harm to the child and violations of privacy. Certain safeguards are now routinely used. They include prior review of research plans by other scientists; obtaining the informed consent of parents, teachers, and children involved in a research study; elimination of any experimentally produced negative feelings through extra procedures; debriefing as to the purpose of the research; and strict maintenance of confidentiality. Additional ethical requirements include taking some responsibility for the social ramifications of research findings and providing feedback to participants about the outcome of the research project.

Conclusion

Our purpose in devoting an entire chapter to research methods is to emphasize the fact that effective methods are crucial for advancing scientific knowledge. Unlocking the secrets of child development requires several elements. It begins, of course, with the perceptive insights of an astute researcher. But even the brightest researcher cannot answer important theoretical questions without the necessary research techniques. For example, researchers suspected the existence of atoms and genes many years ago. But it was not until the advent of the particle accelerator and the electron microscope that scientists could confirm these suspicions. In the same way, psychologists have long debated the capabilities of the newborn. Only since the 1960s, however, have research techniques been developed that permit many related questions to be studied scientifically.

Another reason for including this chapter is that the remainder of the text presents a good deal of research evidence regarding developmental progress and processes. This evidence, for the most part, has been gathered through the methods described here, so it is helpful to approach it with an understanding of the differences between the correlational and experimental designs, longitudinal and cross-sectional experiments, and so on. These basics will also pave the way for the many more specific techniques and procedures used in various areas, which we describe as they come into play.

Visual Summary for Chapter 3:
Research Methods

Scientific Research

Two roles of Theory

➜ 1. To organize research findings.

➜ 2. To guide new research.

Ways in which researchers ensure objectivity.

➜ Focus on observable behaviors.

➜ Ensure that the behaviors to be studied are measurable and quantifiable.

Types of Research

Method		Characteristics
Descriptive approach	➜	Involves simple observation. Used primarily as a first step in exploring areas about which little is known.
Correlational Studies	➜	Used to identify relations between variables and to describe them in terms of their direction and strength. Cannot produce conclusions regarding cause and effect.
Experimental Approach	➜	Involves systematically manipulating the independent variable and examining the effects produced on the dependent variable. Allows researchers to draw conclusions regarding cause and effect.

Studying Development

Method		Characteristics
Longitudinal Research	➜	Assesses the behavior of the same children over a period of time. Useful for looking at questions concerning the long-term effects of early experience and the stability of behavior. _Disadvantages:_ Subject attrition, effects of repeated testing, issues and instruments may become outdated, time- consuming and expensive.
Cross-Sectional Research	➜	Involves simultaneously studying children of different ages. Less time-consuming than longitudinal research. _Disadvantages:_ Cohort effects.
Cross-Sequential Design	➜	A combination of longitudinal and cross-sectional research offering some of the advantages of both methods.
Microgenetic Method	➜	Used to study emerging developmental changes by intensively assessing the behavior of small number of children over a brief period of time.

Other Research Tactics

Method		Characteristics
Case Study	➤	The study of a single individual, often focusing on clinical issues. Caution must be exercised in generalizing the findings to other individuals.
Cross-Cultural Research	➤	Designed to determine the influence of culture on some aspect of development. Can also address some nature-nurture issues.
Comparative Research	➤	Research conducted with nonhuman species in order to provide information relevant to human development.

Ethical Issues

Safeguards commonly used to reduce the risk of physical or psychological harm to the child and violations of privacy.

Peer review		Informed consent		Debriefing		Confidentiality
Have research plans reviewed by other individuals not personally involved in the research.	➤	Obtain the informed consent of children, parents, and teachers involved in a study.	➤	Explain to the child the purpose of the study and eliminate any experimentally produced negative feelings.	➤	Conceal identities of participants and details of their individual performance.

Chapter 4

Genetics:
The Biological Context
of Development

In February 1997, newspapers around the world reported the birth in Edinburgh, Scotland, of a lamb named Dolly. Such an event would not normally be considered newsworthy. Even the fact that Dolly had an identical (although somewhat older) twin would not typically have added much to the story. But the event was truly a landmark in science, because this lamb was not born in the usual way. Dolly was the first mammal ever to be cloned. Rather than being the product of a sperm and an egg from two parents, Dolly came into existence when the genetic material from an adult sheep was transplanted into a cell that developed into an exact copy, or clone, of that sheep.

The implications of this accomplishment are staggering, both scientifically and ethically. For the moment, most scientists are talking about relatively noncontroversial applications of the technology—such as cloning cows that are especially good milk producers—but the possibilities involving humans cannot be ignored. By January 1998, a scientist in Chicago had announced that he would begin experiments on human cloning, prompting President Clinton to urge Congress to pass a law prohibiting such experimentation. Within days, 19 European nations had signed an agreement banning human cloning in their countries. But it is undoubtedly just a matter of time before the technology is in place to create copies of other humans from the DNA in the nucleus of a single cell. What would this mean?

On the one hand, consider the potential benefits to society. We could make perfect (but younger) copies of brilliant scientists, surgeons, or even chefs. Infertile couples could be helped to bear children, and genetic diseases could perhaps be cured or prevented by manipulating the structure of the genes that cause them.

But there is another side to this potential. Picture a basketball team on which every player is Michael Jordan, or any combination of players that the owners choose to have. Or imagine people deciding to create clones of themselves so that, in a sense, they can go on living indefinitely. The possibilities of human cloning are limited only by one's imagination, and many of them raise serious ethical questions.

For the moment, there is little to fear. It took over 400 attempts to create Dolly, and no laboratory has yet to replicate the feat. But science fiction is quickly becoming reality. And the extraordinary birth of a lamb named Dolly serves as an appropriate entry into the relatively new and fascinating world of human genetics, the topic of this chapter.

Now that we have presented some history, theory, and methodology of child development, it is time to turn to the development of the individual child. Where do we begin? People often think of birth as the beginning of life. We will see in the next chapter, however, that by the time a baby comes into the world, a good deal of development has already taken place inside the mother's womb. Perhaps, then, we should consider that development begins when the father's sperm fertilizes the mother's egg at conception. But even this event is a continuation, rather than the start, of the developmental process. To understand the development of the child, we must begin with genetic processes inside the child's parents that determine how they pass their heredity on to the next generation.

But this starting point is just that. Our genes guide, regulate, and influence development throughout our lives. Precisely how they do so, and exactly how much of our behavior is affected by our genes are two exciting and controversial issues in modern child psychology.

Unlike most of the other topics in this book, genetics will take us briefly into the fields of biology and biochemistry. But our primary emphasis will remain on the psychological perspective and how our behavior is influenced by genetic processes. First, we discuss the basic concepts surrounding genes and their functions. Then we consider genetic disorders and why they occur. Third, we present several models that attempt to explain how genes and environment interact to produce behavior. Finally, we examine the methods psychologists use to study gene-environment interactions and some of what they have learned.

Mechanisms of Inheritance

How does a baby inherit the characteristics of his or her parents—black or white skin, red or brown hair? How does a fertilized human egg know to develop into a person rather than a chimpanzee? How does a single cell give rise to trillions of other cells that become different parts of the body—the fingers, the heart, the brain, and so on? Such questions lie at the heart of the puzzle of inheritance, a mystery that scientists are now slowly beginning to solve.

Cell Division

All living things are composed of cells. Adult humans, on average, possess about 10 trillion of them. Cells have three major subdivisions, shown in Figure 4.1: the nucleus; the cytoplasm, which surrounds the nucleus; and the cell membrane, which encases the cell.

Inside the nucleus lies the body's genetic material, DNA, which is organized into chemical strands called **chromosomes**. In humans, each cell nucleus contains 23 pairs of chromosomes, 46 in all. For each pair, one chromosome came from the father, the other from the mother. Twenty-two of the pairs are called **autosomes**. The members of these pairs are similar to one another and carry the same genes in the same locations. The twenty-third pair comprises the **sex chromosomes** which come in two varieties. The *X* chromosome is of about average size and carries a good deal of genetic material, whereas the *Y* chromosome is much smaller and has

Chromosomes
Chemical strands in the cell nucleus that contain the genes. The nucleus of each human cell has 46 chromosomes, with the exception of the gametes, which have 23.

Autosomes
The 22 pairs of human chromosomes, other than the sex chromosomes.

Sex chromosomes
The pair of human chromosomes that determines one's sex. Females have two X chromosomes, males and an X and a Y.

Figure 4.1
Major subdivisions of the cell.

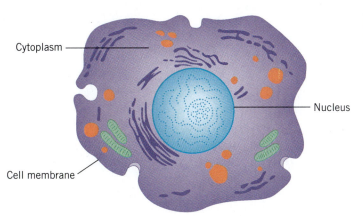

Cytoplasm

Nucleus

Cell membrane

many fewer genes. When the pair consists of two X chromosomes (XX), the person is female; when it comprises one of each type (XY), the person is male. We will discuss the role of the sex chromosomes in more detail in Chapter 15.

Although there are many specialized cells, they can be divided into two broad types—*body cells* and *germ cells*. These cells are distinguished principally by how they reproduce and the roles they play in hereditary transmission.

Cells constantly reproduce; their reproduction is probably the most fundamental genetic process that takes place in our bodies. In the time that it takes you to read this sentence, more than 100 million cells in your body will have reproduced. Body cells, by far the larger category, reproduce by a process called mitosis, whereas germ cells reproduce by a process called meiosis.

In **mitosis**, diagrammed on the left-hand side of Figure 4.2 (with only two pairs of chromosomes for simplicity), each parent cell produces two identical child cells

Mitosis
The process by which body cells reproduce, resulting in two identical cells.

Figure 4.2
Mitosis and meiosis. Mitosis results in two cells identical with the parent cell and with each other. Meiosis results in four cells different from the parent cell and from each other. Adapted from *Biology: Exploring Life* (p. 152) by G. D. Brum & L. K. McKane, 1989, New York: John Wiley & Sons. Copyright © 1989 by John Wiley & Sons, Inc. Adapted by permission of John Wiley & Sons, Inc.

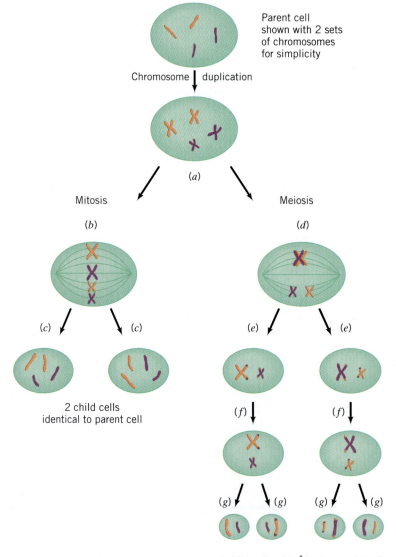

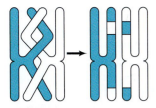

Figure 4.3
Crossing over results in the exchange of genetic material. After the crossover, all four strands are different. Adapted from *Biology: Exploring Life* (p. 44) by G. D. Brum and L .K. McKane, 1989, New York: John Wiley & Sons. Copyright © 1989 by John Wiley & Sons, Inc. Adapted by permission of John Wiley & Sons, Inc.

through a series of three phases. In the first phase (4.2*a*), each of the 46 chromosomes in the cell duplicates itself, producing two identical strands connected near their centers, like an X. Next, these joined strands line up at the cell's midline (4.2*b*). Each X splits and the two identical chromosomal strands move to opposite sides of the cell, a nucleus forms around each set of chromosomes, and the cell itself divides in two (4.2*c*). With mitosis complete, each new cell contains 46 chromosomes and is genetically identical to the parent cell.

In **meiosis**, the process by which germ cells reproduce, four child cells are produced that are all different from one another and that contain only 23 chromosomes each. These child cells, called *gametes*, are the sperm or the ova that will combine at conception to form a new individual with the full complement of 46 chromosomes. Meiosis, diagramed on the right side of Figure 4.2, requires several additional phases. The 46 chromosomes of the cell similarly duplicate themselves into two identical strands that remain attached like an X (4.2*a*). Then an important new process occurs. The X-shaped chromosomes pair up with their partners (remember, the 46 chromosomes are arranged in 23 pairs) and the strands of one X exchange pieces with the strands of the partner X (4.2*d*). This process, called **crossing over**, means that the two strands that form each X are no longer identical. (Figure 4.3 offers a greatly simplified representation of such an exchange). The Xs then line up at the midline of the cell. One X from each pair moves to one end of the cell, a nucleus forms around each half, and the cell divides (4.2*e*). This process is then repeated (4.2*f* and 4.2*g*). Thus, when meiosis is complete, the resulting four gametes possess 23 chromosomes each and are genetically unique. (In males, all four gametes become sperm; in females, three of the gametes disintegrate and only one ovum is produced.)

If we consider that every one of the 23 chromosomes in a gamete now represents a one-of-a-kind combination of genetic material and that these 23 chromosomes must combine with another set of original chromosomes from a gamete of the other parent, it should become clear why people come in so many sizes, colors, and shapes. Crossing over virtually assures that no two people (except identical twins produced from the same fertilized egg) will ever be exactly the same.

Inside the Chromosome

The idea that inheritance must involve genes on the chromosomes was generally accepted by the early 1940s, although no one had yet seen a **gene** or had any idea how it worked. The big breakthrough came in 1953, when James Watson and Francis Crick reported that they had uncovered the structure of a long and complicated molecule called **deoxyribonucleic acid (DNA)** that was the carrier of genet-

Meiosis
The process by which germ cells produce four gametes (sperm or ova), each with half the number of chromosomes of the parent cell.

Crossing over
The exchange of genetic material between pairs of chromosomes during meiosis.

Gene
A segment of DNA on the chromosome. The basic unit of inheritance.

Deoxyribonucleic acid (DNA)
A stairlike, double-helix molecule that carries genetic information on chromosomes.

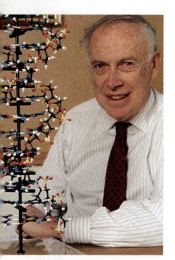

James Watson received the Nobel Prize with Francis Crick for discovering the structure of the DNA molecule.

ic information (Watson & Crick, 1953). The tale of their discovery is one of the most exciting detective stories in modern science (Watson, 1968), and the discovery itself earned them the Nobel Prize in 1962. Most important, their findings opened the door for an understanding of the basis of life itself.

Watson and Crick found that the DNA molecule has the structure of a double helix, much like the sides of a spiral staircase joined by rungs, as shown at the top of Figure 4.4. These rungs are composed of four bases: adenine (A), thymine (T), guanine (G), and cytosine (C). Each rung, called a *nucleotide*, consists of a pair of these bases linked together. Only two types of pairings occur, A–T and G–C. The *sequence* of these base pairs (rungs) determines the coded information carried by the gene.

Since each nucleotide base can link to only one other base, each half-rung of the DNA molecule can serve as a blueprint for the other half. Thus, during cell division, the chromosome "unzips" down the length of the staircase, breaking the links that connect the bases at the middle of each rung. The half-rungs then pair, base by base, with new material to form two new, identical copies of the original DNA sequence, as shown at the bottom of Figure 4.4.

What, then, is a gene? A gene is just a section of the DNA strand containing some set of these nucleotide rungs. On average, a gene contains about 1,000 nucleotides, although some contain as many as 2 million. Again, when we consider that the chromosomes in a human body cell together contain about 100,000 genes, and that each chromosome underwent the crossing-over process during meiosis, it is easy to understand why each individual person is truly unique.

The precise sequence of the nucleotides in a gene is extremely important. For example, 450 base pairs make up a gene that controls a characteristic of red blood cells. Only one base pair of the 450 differentiates a person who has normal blood from one who suffers from the devastating blood disease, sickle-cell anemia. In some genes, the sequence of nucleotides is so rigidly specified that it is essentially a family fingerprint. So-called DNA fingerprinting is increasingly used as forensic evidence (as in the O. J. Simpson trial) to convict murderers and rapists—or sometimes to free the innocent—and to help determine who may have fathered a child (Jeffreys, Brookfield, & Semeonoff, 1992).

The number and precise sequence of nucleotides in the genes also answers the question posed earlier about how the cell knows to develop into a human rather than a chimpanzee. The sequence is especially critical here because approximately 98% of human DNA is also found in the DNA of the chimpanzee ("Biological Systems," 1988).

Alleles
Genes for the same trait located in the same place on a pair of chromosomes.

The location of genes on the chromosome is likewise very important. For each pair of chromosomes, the genes for the same trait (eye color or nose shape) are in the same locations and are called **alleles**. We will see shortly that both genes are involved in how the trait is expressed, but that because the two alleles are not always the same, many different combinations of characteristics can result. Being located at the same place on the chromosome also makes possible the crossing-over process discussed earlier. In this way, variations of a trait are swapped between chromosomes but the trait itself remains a part of each and so gets passed on during reproduction. Finally, scientists have begun to map the precise locations of various genes on the human chromosomes, which will give them a clearer picture of the human genome (see Box 4.1) as well as make it possible to alter a person's hereditary code through genetic engineering (discussed in Chapter 5).

How do genes affect behavior? The answer to this question is complex and not yet entirely understood. It begins with the fact that there are two kinds of genes—structural genes and regulator genes. The job of the *structural genes* is to guide the

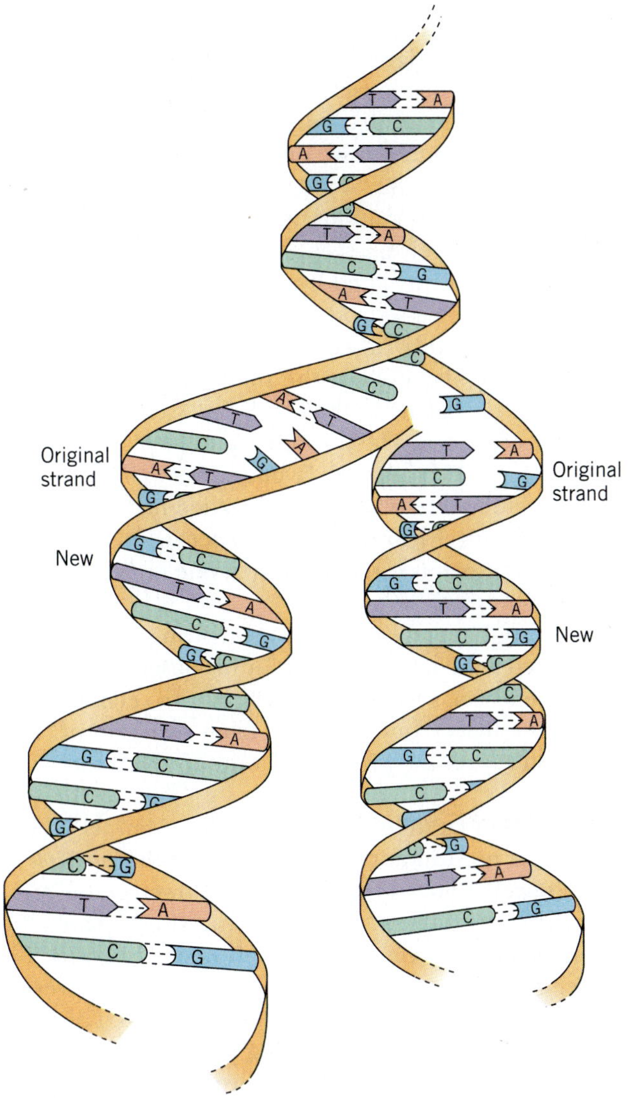

Figure 4.4
Structure and replication
of DNA.

Original
strand

Original
strand

New

New

production of proteins, which serve many different functions in various parts of the
body. The job of the *regulator genes* is to control the activities of the structural genes.
The regulator genes thus can selectively suppress the production of protein so that
the cells in a particular organ, such as the heart, liver, or brain, produce only proteins that are appropriate for that organ. The regulator genes also turn structural
genes on and off at different points in development—for example, initiating and
controlling the many changes that take place during puberty. They apparently do
this in response to what is going on in their environment—meaning the cells
around them—demonstrating that even at this molecular level, nature and nurture
always operate together.

Through these as yet poorly understood processes, our genes can affect our
sensory abilities, our nervous system, our muscles and bones, and so on, thus influencing our behavior and development in a reasonably direct manner. Later in the
chapter, we will see how genes also appear to affect human behavior through more
indirect processes.

Mendel's Studies

Scientists' knowledge of genetic processes has relied in recent years on the development of advanced research techniques and powerful laboratory instruments. Yet some of the fundamental principles of heredity have been understood since the mid-1800s, when they were discovered and described by an Austrian monk named Gregor Mendel (1822–1884). Working alone in his garden, Mendel used pea plants, careful observations, and brilliant logic to develop a theory of inheritance that remains largely correct today.

Mendel was intrigued by the process of hereditary transmission. He wondered how pea plants passed on such characteristics as flower color to the next generation. To study this process, Mendel mated purple-flowered and white-flowered plants. People believed at the time that when a mother and father had different traits, the traits blend in the child. But Mendell believed that the process must work in some other way. He knew that parent plants with purple and white flowers did not produce offspring with lavender flowers. In fact, all the offspring of the purple- and white-flowered plants that he mated had purple flowers. Had the white trait disappeared entirely? Apparently not, because when Mendel next mated the new purple-flowered plants with each other, one out of every four of the second-generation offspring were white.

Through many experiments involving color and other characteristics, Mendel developed a theory to account for his observations. He correctly deduced that each observable trait, such as color, requires two elements, which we now know are a pair of genes (alleles), one inherited from each parent. Today, we call the expressed, or observable, trait the **phenotype** and call the underlying genes the **genotype**.

Principles of Genetic Transmission

Mendel's theory involved several new principles, the most important of which was the *principle of dominance*. The alleles of a trait (purple-flower gene and white-flower gene) are not equal, and one usually dominates the other. As it turns out, in pea plants the gene for purple flowers is *dominant* and the gene for white flowers is *recessive*. Mendel discovered that when either gene is dominant, that characteristic is expressed; only when both genes are recessive is the other characteristic expressed. For example, if we think of the color trait in the pea plant as involving purple (P) or white (w) genes, then plants with the genotype PP, Pw, or wP will have purple flowers, and only those with the genotype ww will have white flowers. Plants thus can have the same phenotype (purple flowers) with different genotypes (PP, Pw, or wP).

Note how this principle explains what Mendel found when he mated the plants described earlier. As diagrammed in Figure 4.5, the genotypes of the original parent plants must have been PP and ww. When mated, each child plant then had one purple-flower gene and one white-flower gene (Pw), having received one from each parent. But because the purple-flower gene is dominant, the phenotype of all the first-generation plants was purple. From the next mating, however, four combinations could occur: purple from both parents; purple from parent 1 and white from parent 2; white from parent 1 and purple from parent 2; and white from both parents. Theoretically, since each of these four combinations has an equal chance of occurring, and since the purple gene dominates whenever it is present, three-fourths of the new plants should be purple, and one-fourth should be white. This is exactly what Mendel observed.

Mendel's theory included several other principles. The *principle of segregation* states that each inheritable trait is passed on to the offspring as a separate unit (the alleles that produce flower color are separate from one another and passed on that

The pioneering work of Gregor Mendel with pea plants paved the way for the modern science of genetics.

Phenotype
The characteristic of a trait that is expressed or observable.

Genotype
The arrangement of genes underlying a trait.

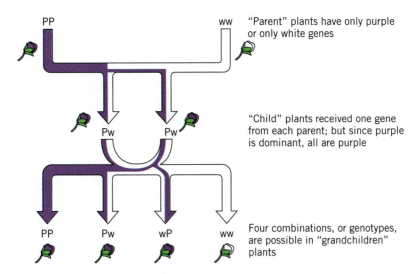

"Parent" plants have only purple or only white genes

"Child" plants received one gene from each parent; but since purple is dominant, all are purple

Four combinations, or genotypes, are possible in "grandchildren" plants

Figure 4.5
The four combinations of genes that can result after two generations when the original mating occurred between a plant with two dominant genes for color and a plant with two recessive genes for color.

way, which is why the blending idea was incorrect). The *principle of independent assortment* asserts that traits are passed on independently of one another (for example, which flower-color trait is passed on has no bearing on which stem-length trait is passed on).

Mendel's principles have proved to be surprisingly accurate, not just for pea plants, but throughout the huge variety of life-forms. Indeed, his discovery of dominant and recessive traits applies to many human characteristics, as shown in Table 4.1. One commonly cited example is eye color; the gene for brown eye color is dominant, while that for blue eye color is recessive. Thus, a mother and father who both possess brown–blue gene combinations for eye color have brown eyes themselves and are three times as likely to produce a brown-eyed child as a blue-eyed child.

Revisions of Mendel's Principles   Years of research have supported Mendel's basic ideas, but have also uncovered other processes involved in hereditary transmission. For instance, single traits are sometimes the product of more than one pair of genes—a process known as **polygenic inheritance**. In humans, intelligence and skin color are traits affected by a number of genes. Also, some traits result from genes that display **incomplete dominance**, that is, they are neither entirely dominant nor entirely recessive. For example, sickle-cell anemia is passed on through a recessive gene. However, the blood of people who have this recessive gene along

Polygenic inheritance
The case in which a trait is determined by a number of genes.

Incomplete dominance
The case in which a dominant gene does not completely suppress the effect of a recessive gene, which is then somewhat expressed in the phenotype.

Table 4.1
Some Common Dominant and Recessive Traits

Dominant	Recessive
Brown eyes	Blue, gray, or green eyes
Normal hair	Baldness (in men)
Dark hair	Blond hair
Normal color vision	Color blindness
Freckles	No freckles
Dimples	No dimples
Free earlobes	Attached earlobes
Double-jointed thumbs	Tight thumb ligaments

with a dominant normal gene will show some mild characteristics of the disease (this differs from the early idea of blending, however, because the two genes remain separate and are passed on that way to future generations).

Codominance
The case in which both alleles are dominant and each is completely expressed in the phenotype.

A third addition to Mendel's principles involves **codominance**, in which both genes of a trait are dominant and so both characteristics are expressed completely. For example, the genes for A and B blood types are codominant, so a person who inherits one from each parent will have blood type AB.

Mendel's principles must also be revised in another important way. Scientists now know that the environment can play a crucial role in the expression of genes. As just one example, the fur color of the Arctic fox changes with temperature from white in winter to brown in summer. In this way, the fox is camouflaged in both the winter snow and the brown underbrush of summer. Such gene-environment interactions affect the phenotypic characteristics of many species, the scope of which we are just beginning to appreciate.

✔ *To Recap…*

Genes carry hereditary information from one generation to the next and direct and regulate development throughout life.

Cell reproduction occurs by mitosis in body cells and by meiosis in germ cells. Mitosis results in two identical cells with 46 chromosomes apiece, whereas meiosis produces four different gametes, each with 23 chromosomes. Gametes are the sperm and ova that combine to form a new cell with the full 46 chromosomes.

The basis of life is DNA, a double-helix-shaped molecule in the cell nucleus that contains billions of nucleotides. The nucleotides on a chromosome are subdivided into genes. Alleles are pairs of genes on the chromosomes that determine a trait. The precise order of nucleotides is important in the gene's functioning and also can serve as a molecular fingerprint for forensic purposes. The fixed location of genes on the chromosomes permits the crossing-over process and also has prompted scientists' attempts to map the human genome and to alter its structure.

Structural genes direct the production of proteins. Regulator genes control the activity of the structural genes and also turn them on and off as required across development.

Mendel's research with pea plants led to the first scientific theory of inheritance, based on the concept of dominant and recessive genes. His principles of segregation and independent assortment are generally accepted today, although several other processes have been added: single traits may be affected by more than one gene; genes may be neither completely dominant nor completely recessive; the genes for some traits are both dominant; and the environment may influence phenotypic characteristics.

Genetic Disorders

Although in the great majority of cases a person's genetic makeup results in normal development, genes can occasionally be a source of problems. Some human disorders are entirely hereditary and are passed along according to the same principles of inheritance that determine eye color and nose shape. Other genetic disorders are not inherited but may result from errors during cell division in meiosis. Chromosomes and the genes they carry can also be made abnormal by radiation, drugs, viruses, chemicals, and perhaps even the aging process.

In this section, we examine the various kinds of genetic disorders and some common examples of each. We will limit our discussion here to genetic errors in the 22 pairs of autosomes. Problems related to the sex chromosomes will be described in Chapter 15.

Hereditary Disorders

Abnormal genes are typically passed along to offspring according to Mendel's principles as well. Whether defective genes are expressed in the phenotype depends on whether they are dominant or recessive. If a defective gene inherited from one parent is recessive, the dominant (and usually normal) allele from the other parent can prevent the problem. Of course, the problem gene still exists in the genotype and will be passed on to half the person's offspring.

Dominant Traits   Dominant genes that cause severe problems typically disappear from the species, because the affected people usually do not live to reproduce. In a few cases, however, severely disabling dominant genes are passed on because they do not become active until relatively late in life. People with these genes may reproduce before they know that they have inherited the disease.

An example is **Huntington's chorea**. The age of onset of this disease varies, but it typically strikes people between about 30 and 40 years of age. Quite suddenly, the nervous system begins to deteriorate, resulting in uncontrollable muscular movements and disordered brain function. In the 17th century, three brothers carrying the abnormal gene for this disorder came to North America from England. By 1965, more than 1,000 affected individuals could be traced directly to this family. The disease became well known to many Americans when it took the life of folksinger Woody Guthrie. Until recently, the children of a person stricken with Huntington's chorea had no way of knowing whether they also carried the gene and could pass it on to their offspring. Late in 1983, scientists discovered which chromosome carries the gene for Huntington's chorea, and 10 years later, they located the exact gene responsible for the disease and learned how to tell whether a person has inherited it (Morell, 1993).

Recessive Traits   Like Mendel's purple flowers, which did not reveal the white-flower gene they carried, parents can carry problem recessive genes that have no effect on them. If both parents carry such a gene, they can combine in the offspring to produce the disorder (just as two brown-eyed parents can produce a blue-eyed child). It has been estimated that on average, each of us carries four potentially lethal genes as recessive traits (Scarr & Kidd, 1983), but because most of these dangerous genes are rare, it is unlikely that we will mate with someone who has a matching recessive gene. Even then, the probability of a child's receiving both recessive genes is only 1 in 4.

Some diseases carried by recessive genes produce errors of metabolism, which cause the body to mismanage sugars, fats, proteins, or carbohydrates. With **Tay-Sachs disease**, the nervous system disintegrates because of the lack of an enzyme that breaks down fats in brain cells. The fatty deposits swell, and the brain cells die. Tay-Sachs disease is rare in the general population, occurring in only 1 in 300,000 births. However, among Ashkenazic Jews, who account for more than 90% of the Jewish population of the United States, it occurs in 1 in every 3,600 births. Infants afflicted with the disease appear normal at birth and through their first half-year. Then, at about 8 months of age, they usually become extremely listless, and often by the end of their first year, they are blind. Most stricken children die by the age of 6. At present, there is no treatment for the disorder.

Huntington's chorea
An inherited disease in which the nervous system suddenly deteriorates, resulting in uncontrollable muscular movements and disordered brain function. The disease typically strikes people between about 30 and 40 years of age and ultimately causes death.

Tay-Sachs disease
An inherited disease in which the lack of an enzyme that breaks down fats in brain cells causes progressive brain deterioration. Affected children usually die by the age of 6.

Phenylketonuria (PKU)
An inherited metabolic disease caused by a recessive gene. It can produce severe mental retardation if dietary intake of phenylalanine is not controlled for the first several years of life.

A more encouraging story is that of **phenylketonuria (PKU)**, a problem involving the body's management of protein. This disease occurs when the body fails to produce an enzyme that breaks down phenylalanine, an amino acid. As a result, abnormal amounts of the substance accumulate in the blood and harm the developing brain cells. Infants with PKU are typically healthy at birth but, if untreated, begin to deteriorate after a few months of life as the blood's phenylalanine level mounts. Periodic convulsions and seizures may occur, and the victims usually become severely retarded.

Our understanding of how PKU disrupts normal metabolism has resulted in one of the early victories of science over genetic abnormalities. Discovery of the mechanism of the disease led to the development of special diets, which are low in phenylalanine and thus prevent its accumulation in the bloodstream. Children placed on these special diets shortly after birth are able to develop normally. Because of the dramatic results of timely intervention in this disease, newborn babies are now routinely tested for PKU through a simple urine-screening procedure. The lesson in the PKU story is that genes are not necessarily destiny—how or whether a gene's influence is played out can depend on interactions with the environment.

Sickle-cell anemia (SCA)
An inherited blood disease caused by a recessive gene. The red blood cells assume a sickle shape and do not distribute oxygen efficiently to the cells of the body.

A recessive genetic abnormality that does not involve metabolism is **sickle-cell anemia (SCA)**. People who have inherited a gene for this recessive trait from both parents have red blood cells that do not contain normal hemoglobin, a protein that carries oxygen throughout the body. Instead, abnormal hemoglobin causes their red blood cells to become sickled, as shown in Figure 4.6. These sickled cells tend to clog small blood vessels instead of easily passing through them as normal cells do, thus preventing blood from reaching parts of the body. An unusual oxygen demand, such as brought on by physical exertion, may cause the sufferer to experience severe pain, tissue damage, and even death because of the inadequate supply of oxygen. As we indicated earlier, the gene for this disease is not entirely recessive (incomplete dominance), and people who have only one gene for SCA may show characteristics of the condition.

About 9% of African-Americans carry the recessive gene for SCA. Among the Bamba, a tribe in Africa, the incidence has been reported to be as high as 39%.

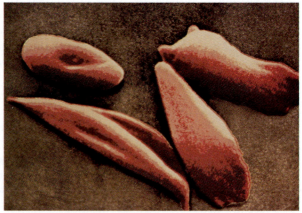

Figure 4.6
Scanning electron micrographs of red blood cells from normal individuals (*left*) and individuals with sickle-cell anemia (*right*).

Such a high rate of occurrence seems surprising from a Darwinian perspective, by which nonadaptive traits are weeded out through natural selection, because individuals who have two genes for SCA frequently die young and produce few children. How, then, could such a characteristic be preserved through evolution? The answer reveals a rare instance in which a gene is maladaptive for one purpose but adaptive for another. Scientists have noted that the Bamba live in areas where the incidence of malaria is high, but Bamba children who carry the SCA gene are about half as likely to have malarial parasites as those who do not. Although it is unclear how this gene offers resistance to malaria, its presence appears to permit more carriers to grow up and have children, even though 1 in 4 will have SCA. Apparently, the negative effects of malarial parasites on reproduction are greater than the effects of carrying the SCA gene.

It is likely that many new findings are on the horizon of genetic research. Within the last few years, investigators have discovered the gene for a type of Alzheimer's disease that runs in families. They also have located the genes for cystic fibrosis and for amytrophic lateral sclerosis (ALS), also known as Lou Gehrig's disease. The genetic locus of many other diseases may soon be discovered as part of the Human Genome Project, discussed in Box 4.1.

The discoveries of precise locations of genes that cause physical disorders has raised hope that we might also be able to find genes that account for behavioral problems. For example, there have been reports in recent years of discoveries of chromosomal locations for alcoholism, aggressiveness, manic-depressive disorder, schizophrenia, and hyperactivity. In addition, scientists have reported identifying a homosexuality gene on the X chromosome (Hamer et al., 1993). But we must be cautious in this area. Many scientists believe that no single gene will ever be found that alone accounts for a complex behavior, and not all early reports have been supported by subsequent research (Horan, 1993; Plomin, 1995b).

Structural Defects in the Chromosome

The genetic abnormalities we have discussed thus far are all passed along according to the regular principles of inheritance. But genetically based problems may also result from physical changes in chromosomes. These changes often occur during meiosis in one of the parents, and they can involve any of the 22 autosomes or the sex chromosome. As mentioned, environmental hazards can also damage chromosomes.

One of the most frequently observed effects of structural abnormality is **Down syndrome**, named after John Langdon H. Down, the physician who first described it. In Down syndrome, one of the pairs of chromosomes has a third member. Infants afflicted with this disorder are moderately to severely retarded and have a distinctive appearance that includes a flattened face and folded eyelids. They also tend to have poor muscle tone and problems with expressive language. The cause of Down syndrome was identified in 1957, marking the first time a human disease had been directly linked to a chromosomal disorder.

The likelihood that a couple will produce a child with Down syndrome increases dramatically with the age of the mother. Fewer than 1 in 1,000 babies of mothers under age 30 have Down syndrome, whereas the incidence is 74 times greater for women between the ages of 45 and 49. (Still, only a small proportion of births to these older mothers involve Down syndrome.) The age of the father is not as important, but the father contributes the extra chromosome in 20 to 30% of cases (Behrman & Vaughan, 1987).

Serious problems can also be caused when part of a chromosome is missing. For example, the deletion of a small amount of genetic material from one chro-

African children who carry a recessive gene for sickle-cell anemia have a reduced likelihood of contracting malaria.

Down syndrome
A chromosomal disorder caused by an extra chromosome. Its effects include mental retardation and a characteristic physical appearance.

Children with Down syndrome have physical features that include flattened faces and folds on the eyelids.

THE HUMAN GENOME PROJECT

If scientists knew where each of the genes were on the 24 human chromosomes (22 autosomes, plus X and Y), they would be in a better position to learn what each of these genes does. The potential benefits would be enormous. Health scientists, for example, would possess the tools to identify defective genes that produce many inherited diseases. In some cases, these defects could be detected even before people showed their effects, and preventive treatment might be possible. Locating the genes on the chromosomes is referred to as *mapping the genome.*

But such mapping is only one step toward understanding. If scientists knew the exact sequence of nucleotides in each gene, they would be able to specify how the gene is defective. This knowledge might, in turn, make it possible to correct the defective sequence. Identifying the sequence of the 3 billion nucleotides in the DNA molecule is called *sequencing the genome.*

In 1989 the United States launched the Human Genome Project, headed by James Watson, one of the discoverers of the DNA molecule (Cooper, 1994). The purpose of the research is to map and sequence human DNA. This project has been likened to the Manhattan Project, which produced the atomic bomb, or the Apollo program, which placed the first human being on the moon (Watson, 1990). One official exclaimed: "It's going to tell us everything. Evolution, disease, everything will be based on what's in that magnificent tape called DNA" (Jaroff, 1989, p. 63).

The task is not only exciting but overwhelming. At this point, about 2 million of the 3 billion nucleotides have been sequenced, and the capacity for sequencing has reached about 1 million per year. At this rate, it would take 3,000 years to sequence the whole genome (National Institutes of Health, 1993).

But the hope is that new technology will make it possible to complete the job of mapping and

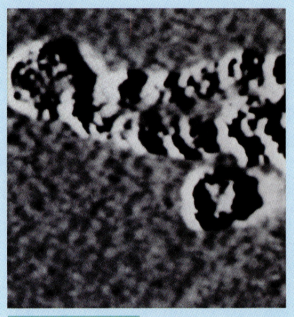

Figure 4.7
The first published high-resolution photograph of a strand of DNA, taken with a scanning tunneling microscope. From "Direct Observation of Native DNA Structures with the Scanning Tunneling Microscope" by T. P. Beebe et al., 1989, *Science, 243,* p. 371. Copyright © 1989 by the AAAS. Reprinted by permission.

sequencing the genome within 15 years at a cost to the U.S. government of $3 billion. Automatic sequencers are being developed that can sequence between 100,000 and 1 million nucleotides per day. Furthermore, scientists in the San Francisco area reported in 1989 that they had taken the first clear photograph of DNA—seen in Figure 4.7—through a revolutionary technique. It may be possible in the future for scientists to read the code of life from photographs of this type (Beebe et al., 1989).

mosome produces *cri du chat*, "cry of the cat," syndrome. Affected infants, who have a catlike cry, have mental retardation and neuromuscular problems. Another example is Wilms' tumor. Children who have this disorder have no iris, the colored part of the eye, and are more likely to have cancer of the kidney during infancy or early childhood.

Given the billions of sperm cells generated by the male and the 2 million or so ova generated by the female, we should not be surprised that genetic imperfections sometimes occur. These variations, or *mutations*, are the driving force behind evolution. When the "errors" turn out to be adaptive, they result in improvements in the species or the creation of a new species. The overwhelming majority of mutations, however, are maladaptive. Through a natural screening process in humans, about 90% of all genetic abnormalities result in miscarriage rather than live births. So although more than 5,000 single-gene disorders have been identified in humans (McKusick, 1994), only about 1% of all babies have detectable chromosomal abnormalities.

One important application of our rapidly accumulating knowledge about genetic disorders involves genetic counseling for couples and prospective parents. We discuss this topic in Chapter 5.

✓ *To Recap…*

Certain disorders are transmitted genetically on the autosomes according to Mendelian principles. Huntington's chorea is caused by a dominant gene that is expressed in all carriers, whereas Tay-Sachs disease, phenylketonuria, and sickle-cell anemia are caused by recessive genes expressed only when the individual inherits the defective gene from both parents. Other genetic diseases, such as Down syndrome, are caused by structural defects in chromosomes, which may occur during meiosis in one of the parents.

Models of Gene-Environment Interaction

We have seen what genes are and how they determine certain physical characteristics, such as eye and hair color. Genes also can cause physical abnormalities and intellectual deficits, as in Down syndrome. But psychologists have been most interested in the questions of how and how much genes typically affect human behavior and development.

When thinking about the role of genes in development, we must keep in mind an important distinction that we first discussed in Chapter 1. Recall that some psychologists focus on normative development—they are concerned with the ways in which humans are alike. Other psychologists are more interested in idiographic processes—they focus on what makes us different from one another. We can look at this issue in another way. Humans are different from other species, which are in turn different from one another. What gives a species its identity are the characteristics that all members *share*, that is, how they are alike. And there is no doubt that genes are responsible for making each species unique. Psychologists who study normative development thus are really trying to learn about humans as a species. But humans (and all other animals) also differ among themselves—not just in physical characteristics, but in behavior and development as well. These are the individual differences of interest to psychologists who take an idiographic approach. How much of a role do genes play in these sorts of differences? This is the main question being asked today by researchers in the field of **behavior genetics** and, in essence, it forms the basis of the modern nature–nurture debate (Scarr, 1992).

Behavior genetics
The field of study that explores the role of genes in producing individual differences in behavior and development.

All contemporary psychologists believe that genes (nature) and environment (nurture) interact to determine human behavior, but they differ as to which factor they feel has more influence. A related and perhaps even more useful question concerns *how* genes and environment exert their effects, that is, by what processes do these factors operate and how do they interact with one another?

In this section we examine four theoretical models that attempt to explain how genes and environment work together to determine any child's behavior and development. As the models are complex, we will present only their fundamental ideas. But they illustrate the increasing role that psychologists seem to be ascribing to genetic processes as this area is becoming better understood. In the final section, we examine the methods by which researchers have been testing these models and some of the evidence they have uncovered.

Gottesman's Limit-Setting Model

An early model proposed by Irving Gottesman (1974) suggested that genes interact with the environment by setting the upper and lower limits of our development. Our environment and experiences then presumably determine where in this **reaction range** we end up.

Reaction range
In Gottesman's model, the term for the range of ability or skill that is set by the genes.

Figure 4.8 illustrates this model by showing the ranges of possible basketball skill that might exist for groups of children born with different genotypes, representing different heights. Group A consists of children who carry a gene that makes them unusually short. Groups B and C represent typical girls and boys, respectively, who are of average height for their gender. Group D represents children who have inherited genes that make them unusually tall. Note that the reaction range (RR) of the groups varies, with the tallest individuals having the widest potential range of basketball abilities, and shortest having the narrowest. The graph also includes three

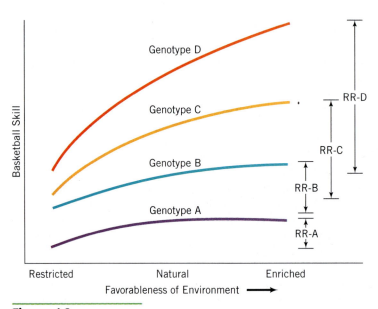

Figure 4.8
The reaction range concept, showing the simultaneous influences of genes and environment. Adapted from "Developmental Genetics and Ontogenetic Psychology: Overdue Détente and Propositions from a Matchmaker" by I. I. Gottesman, 1974. In A. D. Pick (Ed.), *Minnesota Symposia on Child Psychology*, Vol. 8, p. 60. Copyright © 1974 by the University of Minnesota Press. Adapted by permission.

levels of environment: restricted (where perhaps the child has no exposure to basketball at all), natural (the environment of a youngster growing up in a typical U.S. town), and enriched (such as when the child's father is a basketball coach).

Note how genes and environment interact in this model. The genes have set the limits on potential basketball skills such that very short children (Group A) will not become proficient at these skills regardless of their environment, whereas very tall children (Group D) have the greatest opportunity to benefit from a more supportive environment. But it is important to note also that the reaction ranges overlap. This means that either poor genes or a poor environment can be overcome somewhat by strength in the other. This model, of course, could be applied to many other behaviors and abilities, such as mathematics performance, musical ability, or any number of traits or skills.

In Gottesman's model, genes thus play a relatively passive role in human development, establishing our reaction range limits and then having no further influence. Newer models of gene-environment interaction view things very differently.

Scarr's Niche-Picking Model

In the model offered by Sandra Scarr, genes play a much more active role in development than simply setting limits (Scarr, 1992, 1993; Scarr & McCartney, 1983). They could almost be thought of as trying to take complete charge of the child's development—including the kind of environment that the child experiences.

The traditional view in psychology has been that different family environments cause children to develop in different ways. For example, we know that children whose parents provide books, educational activities, and encouragement to succeed tend to perform well in school, and children whose parents are harsh and punitive are more likely to be aggressive and to display various other behavior problems. The child's developmental outcome therefore was assumed to be rather directly determined by the child's family environment.

Scarr disagrees with this view. Her model invokes an important idea discussed in Chapter 2, namely, that children play a role in producing their own environments. This, she proposes, occurs through the genes. Consider the family example again. Although parents do provide children with their family environment, they also provide them with their genes. The child's genes, in turn, operate in three different ways—which Scarr believes change as the child grows from infancy to adolescence—to influence the family environment.

According to Scarr and McCartney's model, niche-picking occurs when children choose environments that reflect and support their genetic predispositions.

During infancy, genes exert their influence principally in a *passive* manner. The baby's environment is almost entirely dictated by the parents, but because the parents and child share so many of the same genes, the environment they create is usually very consistent with, and supportive of, the child's genotype. For example, musically inclined parents are likely both to give birth to musically inclined children and to provide a musical home environment for them.

As children get older, their genes operate through a more *evocative* process. Children now do things that evoke certain responses from the parents and others (recall Bronfenbrenner's notion of developmentally generative and developmentally disruptive behaviors, presented in Chapter 2). For example, a child who speaks and reads early—behaviors that likely have some genetic basis—may prompt parents to provide a rich language environment, including books, storytelling, and educational games. In this way, the child's genes help create an environment with which they are compatible and that serves to further their goals.

Finally, as children gain more independence, their genes can operate in a more *active* manner to produce environments that suit them. Children, on their own, can seek out the particular environments, or *niches*, that best fit their interests and talents—such as the library, the gym, or the rock concert.

Scarr's model of gene-environment interaction does not ignore the importance of the child's family environment, but it views the environment less as a direct cause of the child's development and more as a vehicle that enables the genes to guide the child along a particular developmental path. Scarr contends that genetic influences actually grow stronger with age, as children become better able actively to recruit the environments their genes demand. This prediction runs counter to the traditional view that our genes start us off in a particular direction and then our environment more or less takes over. We will examine the evidence on this and other aspects of the model in the next section.

Plomin's Environmental Genetics Model

A third model of gene-environment interaction has been presented by Robert Plomin (1994, 1995b; Plomin, DeFries, 1997). His approach shares many of the same ideas as Scarr's model. He believes that children's developmental outcomes are related to their family environments for two reasons: (1) children share many genes with their parents who, in turn, provide the environment for their children; and (2) children evoke from their parents the sorts of responses and surroundings that suit their genes.

Plomin has gone so far as to refer to his work as *environmental genetics*, which means the study of how our genes influence our environments in order to get what they want. Further, his model is not limited to parent–child interactions but also extends to other family members (Plomin et al., 1994).

Nonshared environment
A concept used in behavior genetics to refer to presumed aspects of the environment that children experience differently.

The most important addition in Plomin's model is the concept of **nonshared environment** (Hetherington, Reiss, & Plomin, 1994). This idea is most easily understood in terms of siblings. We know that children raised in the same family have many similarities. Psychologists have not been surprised to find that intelligence, physical abilities, personality, and other characteristics are generally more similar between brothers and sisters than they are between unrelated children. These similarities have always been assumed to result from siblings' sharing both many of the same genes (50%) and the same family environment. Given these two major sources of similarity, a more interesting question becomes why many siblings behave and develop so differently from one another.

Plomin's answer is that although these children live in the same family, they do not necessarily experience the same environments. Rather, parents often treat children differently from one another, and children frequently react to the same family events and experiences in different ways. Moreover, the source of both these differences, Plomin believes, is genetic. His argument is that although 50% of siblings' genes are the same, 50% are also different. These different genes, Plomin contends, lead siblings to evoke different treatment from their parents and to respond in different ways to the same events. In short, the aspects of the family environment that they experience differently—the nonshared aspects—are what make siblings different from one another.

What about siblings' similarities? Perhaps the most controversial aspect of this model is that, like Scarr and other behavior geneticists, Plomin believes that the similarities we see in siblings result mostly from their genetic similarity (the 50% of the genes they share). Their common family environment, by contrast, is thought to contribute very little to explaining why they are alike. Again, we will examine the research evidence on this idea later in the chapter.

Bronfenbrenner and Ceci's Bioecological Model

The most recent and perhaps most complex of the models we will consider is that of Urie Bronfenbrenner and Stephen Ceci (Bronfenbrenner & Ceci, 1994; Bronfenbrenner & Morris, 1998). This model derives from Bronfenbrenner's ecological approach, described in Chapter 2, and is strongly influenced by the development-in-context concept. We will see shortly why they call it a *bioecological model*.

Bronfenbrenner and Ceci assign much more importance to the environment than do the behavior geneticists. They agree with the idea that children's genes influence their development and that they do so, to some degree, by steering the environment in the right direction. But the bioecological model adds to this picture a more explicit description of how and when this occurs.

According to this analysis, genes can only exert their influence when certain experiences activate them. These experiences, called **proximal processes**, are interactions between the child and the child's direct-contact (microsystem) world—parents, siblings, toys, books, pets, and anything else of significance in the child's immediate environment—that have a positive effect on the child's psychological functioning. Such interactions may involve, for example, play with siblings, social activities with friends, reading and problem solving with parents, and other sorts of stimulating experiences. An additional requirement is that these interactions must take place fairly regularly and must continue for some time. When these requirements hold, the child's genes are able to use the experiences to achieve their ends, and, as a result, the child reaches his or her maximum genetic potential. But if proximal processes are weak or missing in the child's life, the genes cannot fully express themselves and so the child's development will remain below what it could have been.

Bronfenbrenner and Ceci also believe that proximal processes are valuable to the child in both high- and lower-quality environments, but in different ways. When the environment is stable and rich with resources—as is the case in many middle-class households—these interactions have the best opportunity to help children develop their fullest abilities (such as the example of musical talent described earlier). When the child's environment is disorganized and disadvantaged—as in many poor neighborhoods—proximal processes can help prevent undesirable genetic outcomes that might otherwise have occurred (such as aggression, violence, or other problem behaviors to which genes may have predisposed the child).

Note how the child's biology (genes) and ecology (immediate environment) contribute more equally and in greater interaction in this model than in either the

Proximal processes
Bronfenbrenner and Ceci's term for interactions between the child and aspects of the microsystem that have positive effects on psychological functioning and that help maximize expression of the child's genetic potential.

more strongly genetic or strongly environmental approaches. Perhaps for this reason, Bronfenbrenner and Ceci use the term *bioecological* to describe it.

✔ To Recap...

Four models attempt to explain how genes and environment interact to produce human development. In Gottesman's limit-setting model, genes play a passive role by setting the limits within which environmental effects can be observed. Genes play a more active role in Scarr's niche-picking model, controlling the child's environment through processes that move from passive (infancy) to evocative (early childhood) to active (later childhood). Plomin's model adds the concept of nonshared environment, whereby differences in the behavior of siblings are assumed to result from those aspects of the environment that they experience differently. Bronfenbrenner and Ceci's bioecological model proposes that genes exert their influence on the environment through proximal processes—stimulating interactions between the child and aspects of the microsystem—which must be frequent and continuing in the child's life.

Studying the Effects of Genes on Behavior

How do researchers study the influences of genes on behavior to determine which of these models is most accurate? Not easily. People are not pea plants, and scientists are not free to mate humans of their choice to see how the offspring will turn out. Researchers have to rely solely on observation, experiments of nature, and careful analyses of their data. Fortunately, scientists' statistical methods and their access to large populations of research participants have come a long way since Mendel's time.

The effects of genes on human behavior and development have been studied extensively over the years in three principal areas: intellectual abilities, psychiatric disorders (including children's behavior problems), and aspects of personality (including infant temperament). In this section we present some of what psychologists have learned about genetic contributions to these areas as we examine the four major methods that have been used in their investigation: family studies, adoption studies, twin studies, and combinations of these approaches.

Family Studies

Because children inherit 50% of their genes from each parent, similarities among family members are not surprising. The family-study approach looks for such similarities over generations in traits suspected to have a genetic basis.

One of the earliest reports claiming to demonstrate a genetic basis for intelligence was Henry Goddard's study of the Kallikak family, published in 1912. During the Revolutionary War, a soldier whom Goddard called Martin Kallikak (a pseudonym) had an illegitimate son by a retarded tavern maid. Later, Kallikak married a woman of normal intelligence from a respected family.

Goddard traced five generations of Kallikak's offspring from these two lines. Of the 480 or so descendants of the tavern maid, he identified many as criminal, alcoholic, or "immoral," and 25% as retarded. In contrast, the 496 descendants from Kallikak's marriage were all intellectually normal, according to Goddard, and most occupied respected positions in their communities. Since Kallikak was the father to both family lines, Goddard concluded that the differences between them must be due to the genetic differences between his two mates. Of course, this conclusion ignored the vastly different environments and upbringing of the two lines of descendants. Distinguishing between hereditary and environmental influences is a major limitation of the family-study method. As scientists have pointed out, lots of things run in families—names, religious beliefs, and cake recipes, for example. Not all of these are determined by our genes.

Family studies can be of value, however. Sometimes they point up characteristics that might have a genetic component and so encourage more definitive research using one of the more rigorous methods that we discuss next. For example, family studies have shown that children of mothers who have schizophrenia—a disorder that produces confused thought and language, hallucinations, and unpredictable actions—are about 10 times as likely as children of normal mothers to develop schizophrenia. Also, people who have schizophrenia are 8 times more likely to have a close relative with the disorder than are those who do not have schizophrenia (Gottesman & Shields, 1982). Do these statistics support a nature or nurture interpretation? Research using more sophisticated methods has been providing some answers.

Adoption Studies

Children are usually similar to their parents in a number of important and not-so-important ways. What is the source of these similarities? We have noted that parents share many of the same genes with their children and that they also share a similar environment. But our theoretical models suggest different contributions for nature and nurture. Which, in fact, is more influential? Or do they contribute equally?

The adoption-study method is designed to address this issue. Children who are living in adoptive homes are compared with their biological parents (who share their genes, but not their environments) and with their adoptive parents (who share their environments, but not their genes). If the correlation with one set of parents is stronger than that with the other, we have a good idea of which factor plays the larger role in the behavior or trait we are measuring.

Sometimes the method includes siblings, since many adoptive families go on to adopt a second child. These two children now share the same environment (although perhaps some of it is also nonshared), but none of the same genes. Their similarity on whatever behaviors we choose to study can thus be compared with the similarity of biological siblings in families used for comparison. Again, differences in the correlations between the two sets of siblings could shed light on whether environment or heredity has more influence on the behaviors of interest.

A major study that has employed this approach is the Colorado Adoption Project. This research, begun in 1975, is a longitudinal study of about 250 families with adopted children and, for comparison, 250 families with biological children. The children were first studied when they were infants and preschoolers, and they have been followed and studied since (DeFries, Plomin, & Fulker, 1994; Plomin & DeFries, 1985).

One focus of this project has been intelligence (we discuss methods of studying intelligence again in Chapter 10). The children have been tested using a variety of different instruments and on both general intellectual ability and specific cognitive skills (such as memory, vocabulary, spatial relations, and others). The findings clearly support a role for genetic processes. Stronger correlations have been found between the scores of biological siblings versus adoptive siblings, and between children and their biological parents versus their adoptive parents. These findings indicate that, at least to some degree, children inherit their intellectual abilities (Cardon, 1994; Cherny & Cardon, 1994).

But what about the role of the environment on intelligence? Does it operate completely independently of the child's genetic makeup? An additional question posed by the project has been whether Plomin is correct in his belief that children's genes help shape their environments. One study examined an instrument called the HOME (Home Observation for Measurement of the Environment), designed to assess the quality of children's family environments, including the amount and kinds of stimulation provided by the mother. Scores on this measure have repeatedly been found to correlate well with children's IQ scores, which seems to indicate that the quality of the early environment directly affects the child's intellectual development. Using the sibling-adoption method, however, project researchers found that biological siblings were more similar in their HOME scores than were adopted siblings (Braungart, Fulker, & Plomin, 1992; Saudino & Plomin, 1997). These findings can be interpreted as supporting the idea that children's genes sometimes play a passive role in producing their home and family environments—in this case because the mother's genes influenced both the biological children's intelligence and the environment she provided them. The previously found connections between the HOME and children's intelligence thus may involve more than just an environmental effect.

Adoption studies have also addressed the issue of schizophrenia, described earlier. Children of schizophrenic mothers who are placed in adoptive homes are around 10 times as likely to develop schizophrenia as are either the biological children of the adoptive parents or adopted children of normal mothers (Plomin et al., 1997). This finding suggests a major role for heredity in the development of the disease and is consistent with other research showing that psychological disorders can be inherited (Rutter et al., 1990).

Again we can ask the question, Can genetic processes be involved in what appear to be environmental influences on psychological problems? Evidence from adoption research suggests that they can. One recent study sought to explain the hostile and antisocial behaviors of a group of adolescents who had been adopted at birth. The researchers hypothesized that these behaviors could be connected to both their biological and their adoptive parents but that both connections involved the children's genes. The researchers first showed that these adolescents were more likely to have biological parents with psychiatric disorders than were a comparison group of adopted adolescents who showed no such problems. This finding simply demonstrates that some problem behaviors can be inherited (Rutter & Caesar, 1991). The researchers next showed that the troubled adolescents also were more likely to have adoptive parents who used harsh and inconsistent punishment. This apparent environmental influence also has been found many times before (Patterson, Reid, & Dishion, 1992).

What makes the study important is that, using sophisticated statistical methods, the researchers were able to relate the adoptive parents' disciplinary practices to the biological parents' history of psychiatric problems, but only in those children who displayed the behavior problems. Given that the only connection between the sets of parents was the child, the findings would seem to require a behavior-genetics explanation. Specifically, the researchers speculated that (1) the children initially inherited their behavior problems from their biological parents; (2) these problems then evoked responses (harsh discipline) from their adoptive parents; and (3) the parents' disciplinary practices then served to maintain the children's problem behaviors. In this way, genes connected the children's antisocial behaviors to the biological parents through a passive process and connected them to the adoptive parents through an evocative process (Ge et al., 1996).

Finally, adoption studies have produced two additional findings of importance to behavior geneticists: (1) adoptive (unrelated) siblings are more similar to one another in the early years than in adolescence, and (2) the psychological characteristics of an adopted child, with age, become increasingly similar to those of the biological mother and less similar to those of the adoptive mother. The first of these findings can be explained by the concept of nonshared environment, with family influences serving to separate the siblings rather than make them alike (Dunn & McGuire, 1994). The second finding seems to support the contention that genes play a stronger role in development as children get older. This may be because parents generally control children's environments at younger ages, but as children grow older, they are increasingly able to choose their own environments and experiences, thus permitting their genes to operate in a more active way to influence their behavior (McGue, 1993; Plomin, Fulker, et al., 1997).

Twin Studies

Approximately 1 of every 85 births yields twins, providing investigators with an interesting opportunity to study the role of genetic similarity. Twins come in two varieties. **Identical twins** develop from the same fertilized egg and are called **monozygotic twins (MZ)** (*mono*, "one"; *zygote*, "fertilized egg"). They have exactly the same genes. **Fraternal twins** develop from two different eggs and are called **dizygotic twins (DZ)** (*di*, "two"). Their genetic makeup is no more similar than that of any two children who have the same parents; on average, 50% of the genes of dizygotic twins are the same.

The logic of the twin-study approach begins with the assumption that fraternal twins share an environment that is as similar as the environment shared by identical twins. Researchers then look at a particular trait or behavior displayed by the sets of twins. If the trait is more similar in the identical twins than in the fraternal twins, we should be able to conclude that the greater similarity must result from the greater similarity of their genes.

Many twin studies have specifically targeted intelligence and its heritability. As shown in Table 4.2, hundreds of studies have been conducted, with virtually every one finding higher correlations between the IQ scores of MZ twins than between those of DZ twins (Bouchard & McGue, 1981; McGue et al., 1993). Clearly, intelli-

Identical (monozygotic [MZ]) twins
Twins who develop from a single fertilized ovum and thus inherit identical genetic material.

Fraternal (dizygotic [DZ]) twins
Twins who develop from separately fertilized ova and who thus are no more genetically similar than are other siblings.

Identical twins, whose genetic makeup is precisely the same, are commonly employed in research designs examining the effects of genes on human development.

Table 4.2
Average Correlations of Various Abilities from Several Twin Studies

Trait	Number of Studies	Average Correlation Identical Twins	Average Correlation Fraternal Twins
Ability			
General intelligence	30	.82	.59
Verbal comprehension	27	.78	.59
Number and mathematics	27	.78	.59
Spatial visualization	31	.65	.41
Memory	16	.52	.36
Reasoning	16	.74	.50
Clerical speed and accuracy	15	.70	.47
Verbal fluency	12	.67	.52
Divergent thinking	10	.61	.50
Language achievement	28	.81	.58
Social studies achievement	7	.85	.61
Natural science achievement	14	.79	.64
All abilities	211	.74	.54

Source: Adapted from "Heredity and Environment: Major Findings from Twin Studies of Ability, Personality and Interests" by R. C. Nichols, 1978, *Homo, 29*, Table 1, p. 163.

gence—at least when measured by IQ tests—has a genetic component. In recent work with infants, whose intelligence is assessed using instruments that rely less on language and verbal abilities and more on simple motor and perceptual responses (we discuss these differences more fully in Chapter 10), MZ twins also showed higher correlations than did DZ twins (Cherny, Fulker, Emde, et al., 1994).

Twin studies have also been used to address a variety of personality issues. Many such studies have been conducted with adults and have produced some unusual findings. For example, if one identical twin experiences divorce, the chance that the other twin will experience divorce is six times that of the general population; the likelihood falls to two times the population average for a fraternal twin. Of course, there is no such thing as a divorce gene; the increase in risk for divorce is probably related to personality characteristics affected by genetic inheritance (McGue & Lykken, 1992).

An important personality area in children involves their *temperament*. Babies come into the world with a particular style of responding. Some are irritable and cry frequently; some are easygoing and smile a lot; some are active; some are cuddly; and so forth. Aspects of temperament sometimes persist well into the early school years and may eventually form the basis for adult personality. (We take up this subject again in Chapter 12.) Do genes influence temperament? Apparently they do, at least to some extent. As early as 3 months of age, and throughout the first years of life, identical twins are more similar than fraternal twins on a variety of measures, including attention, activity, and involvement in testing (Braungart et al., 1992; Emde et al., 1992). One study looked at the trait of shyness, testing twin babies at 14 and 20 months in both the laboratory and at home. Genes were found to be strongly involved in this aspect of temperament at both ages and in both locations (Cherny, Fulker, Corley, et al., 1994).

Twin studies have also been used to look at developmental issues in older children and adolescents, including parent–child relationships. For example, a recent

Table 4.3
Average Correlations of Children's Ratings of Father–Son Relationships

Relationship factor	11-year-olds		17-year-olds	
	MZ	*DZ*	*MZ*	*DZ*
Conflict with father	.44	.36	.62	.01
Involvement with father	.46	.28	.64	.39
Son's regard for father	.32	.32	.58	.24
Father's regard for son	.34	.35	.53	.14
Structure provided by father	.27	.46	.43	.35
Support provided by father	.45	.31	.64	.15

Source: Adapted from "Genetic and Environmental Influences on Parent-Son Relationships: Evidence for Increasing Genetic Influence during Adolescence" by I. J. Elkins, M. McGue, and W. G. Iacono, 1997, *Developmental Psychology, 33,* 351–363. Adapted by permission.

study asked MZ and DZ boys, ages 11 and 17 years, to rate the quality of their relationships with their mothers and fathers. Two particularly clear findings were found on the ratings of the fathers, as shown in Table 4.3. The higher correlations between the identical twins demonstrate that genes must have contributed to these father–son relationships. And the higher correlations by the older MZ twins again offer evidence for the idea that gene effects get stronger over the course of development (Elkins et al., 1997).

Finally, behavior geneticists have used twins to examine whether genetic influences underlie certain changes we see in children's development and behavior. Physical development such as height and weight tends to occur in spurts and plateaus. The rhythm of these life events is called **developmental pacing**. Psychologists assume that developmental pacing is guided by the regulator genes, which turn the structural genes on and off at different points in development and thus control protein production. But what about similar sorts of changes in behavioral traits, such as intellectual abilities? Are they also controlled by our genes? One way to address this question is to see whether identical twins show more *concordance* (similarity) in these changes than do fraternal twins. The evidence suggests that they do. Figure 4.9 shows the results of a study comparing the intellectual development of almost 500 pairs of identical and fraternal twins, followed from the ages of 3 months to 15 years. The MZ twins clearly showed greater concordance in their shifts in performance than did the DZ twins, supporting the notion that genes direct the pacing of these abilities (Wilson, 1983, 1986).

Developmental pacing
The rate at which spurts and plateaus occur in an individual's physical and mental development.

Combined Twin-Study and Adoption-Study Approaches

There is one major problem with the twin-study approach: How do we know that a family treats a set of fraternal twins as similarly as a set of identical twins? Because identical twins look more alike, and perhaps because they know they are identical, parents and others may expect them to act the same. These expectations may influence how people behave toward the children and, as a result, may affect how the children themselves behave. A method that avoids these problems involves twins who are separated early in life and raised in different adoptive homes. If genes play a role in creating individual differences in behavior, then identical twins raised apart should still be more alike than are fraternal twins raised apart. Although this combined approach is the most desirable, it also is the most difficult to use, because so few twins are raised apart.

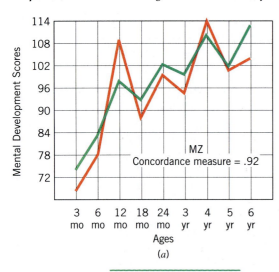

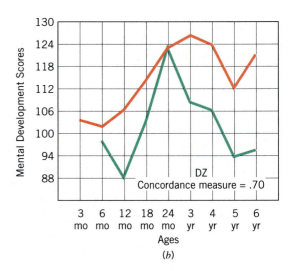

Figure 4.9

Concordance in IQ changes in (*a*) identical, or monozygotic (MZ), twins and (*b*) fraternal, or dizygotic (DZ), twins from 3 months to 6 years of age. The scales are different to accommodate different ranges of scores. The important point is that changes in performance are more similar for monozygotic twins. Adapted from "The Louisville Twin Study: Developmental Synchronies in Behavior" by R. S. Wilson, 1983, *Child Development, 54,* p. 301. Copyright © 1983 by The Society for Research in Child Development, Inc. Adapted by permission.

The best-known research project of this type is the Minnesota Study of Twins Reared Apart (Bouchard et al., 1990). The study involves 58 MZ and 46 DZ twins who are currently in their 40s. Supporting the role of genetics in personality characteristics, the identical twins have been found to be more similar in their religious interests, attitudes, and values than are the fraternal twins (Waller et al., 1990).

To study issues relating to early development the project used a retrospective approach in which twins were asked to recall and describe their family environments when they were children. Identical twins were more similar than fraternal twins in their reporting of family support, which included acceptance or rejection by their mothers and fathers as well as support provided by family members to one another. These results can be taken to mean that the identical twins were treated more similarly because their identical genotypes evoked the same sorts of responses from other family members. But not all the recollections showed this pattern. On questions relating to family organization and activities, the MZ and DZ twins did not differ (Hur & Bouchard, 1995). Once again, it appears that genes and environment probably exert their effects on different aspects of behavior.

✓ *To Recap...*

Psychologists have used four research strategies to study the influence of heredity on behavior: family studies, adoption studies, twin studies, and a combination of the twin study and the adoption study. In three areas in particular—psychiatric disorders, intellectual performance, and personality—genetic processes play a significant role.

Evidence gathered using the different methods supports behavior geneticists' belief that genes not only transmit traits from parents to children in a passive way, but also operate in more evocative and active ways to make children's environments compatible with their genotypes. This research also finds support for the hypothesis that genes exert stronger effects as children get older and for the idea that nonshared environments make adoptive siblings more dissimilar with age.

Conclusion

Much of what we have presented in this chapter is very new. Psychologists are just beginning to understand the various ways in which genes affect development, in part because we have only recently developed effective methods for studying genetic influences. But there can be little doubt that progress in this area will occur rapidly in the coming years. What will that likely mean for developmental psychology?

First, researchers may find that genetic processes reach into more areas of development than we now suspect. As we have seen, genes do more than transmit our ancestors' heritage to our children; they also continue to guide and regulate behavior throughout our lives. It is undoubtedly this second function that promises to bring the most surprises and exciting findings as behavior geneticists probe the limits of genetic forces.

On the other hand, genes will never be the whole story. The sheer volume of material in this chapter on genetic processes may give the false impression that environmental factors eventually will be reduced to minor players in the human drama. We certainly do not believe that. In the chapters that follow, we will see that environmental influences are crucial for understanding how our development unfolds. In fact, these influences likewise are being shown to exert effects in areas that we used to assume were governed exclusively by our biology.

Maybe the most important thing for developmental researchers to keep in mind is that any genetic process occurs within an environmental context. Rather than studying these two sources of influence in isolation, then, it is important to apply the development-in-context idea and focus on how nature and nurture combine to determine human development. This advice also makes sense for students of developmental psychology. If there is one message that you should take away from this course, it is this: At every point in development genes and environment work together to determine each and every aspect of our behavior. With that in mind, we move ahead to begin our look at the basics and the complexities of the growing child.

Visual Summary for Chapter 4:
Genetics: The Biological Context of Development

Mechanisms of Inheritance

Cell Division

Type of cell		Process		Outcome
Body cells	→	Mitosis	→	Two identical cells, each with 46 chromosomes.
Germ cells	→	Meiosis	→	Four different gametes, each with 23 chromosomes.

Inside the Chromosome

DNA	→	A double-helix shaped molecule that contains billions of nucleotides.
Gene	→	A segment of DNA on the chromosome. The basic unit of inheritance.
Alleles	→	Pairs of genes on the chromosomes that determine a trait.
Structural genes	→	Genes that direct the production of proteins.
Regulator genes	→	Genes that control the activity of structural genes, turning them on and off as required across development.

Principles of Genetic Transmission from Mendel's Studies

Principle of dominance	→	When one allele is dominant and the other recessive, only the characteristic associated with the dominant allele is expressed.
Principle of segregation	→	Each inheritable trait is passed on to the offspring as a separate unit.
Principle of independent assortment	→	Traits are passed on to the offspring independently of one another.

Revisions of Mendel's Principles

Polygenic inheritance	→	Single traits are sometimes the products of more than one pair of genes.
Incomplete dominance	→	Some genes are neither entirely dominant nor entirely recessive.
Codominance	→	For some traits, both members of a pair of genes are dominant.

Genetic Disorders

Cause of disorder		Explanation		Examples
Dominant traits	→	Caused by a dominant gene and therefore expressed in all carriers.	→	Huntington's chorea
Recessive traits	→	Caused by a recessive gene and therefore expressed only when the defective gene is inherited from both parents.	→	Tay-Sachs disease, phenylketonuria, sickle-cell anemia
Chromosome defects	→	Caused by a structural defect in the chromosome that may have occurred during meiosis in one of the parents.	→	Down syndrome

Models of Gene-Environment Interaction

Model		Explanation
Gottesman's Limit-Setting Model	→	Genes set the upper and lower limits for development; environmental influences determine development within this reaction range.
Scarr's Niche-Picking Model	→	Genes control the child's environment through processes that move from passive (infancy) to evocative (early childhood) to active (later childhood).
Plomin's Environmental Genetics Model	→	Differences in the behavior of siblings result from those aspects of the environment they experience differently (nonshared environment).
Brofenbrenner's and Ceci's Bioecological Model	→	Genes exert their influence on the environment through proximal processes stimulating interactions between the child and aspects of the microsystem which must be frequent and continuing in the child's life.

Studying Gene Effects on Behavior

Type of Study		Description		Assumption
Family studies	→	Look for similarities over generations of a family in traits suspected to have a genetic basis.	→	Similarities among family members are assumed to be the result of heredity. Limitation: It can be very difficult to distinguish between heredity and environmental influences in family studies.
Adoption studies	→	Adopted children are compared both with their biological parents and with their adoptive parents; they may also be compared with siblings in the adoptive home.	→	If the correlation with biological parents is greater, genetic factors are assumed to play the stronger role; if the correlation with adoptive parents is greater, environmental factors play the stronger role.
Twin studies	→	Monozygotic twins and dizygotic twins are compared in terms of their similarity on traits suspected to have a genetic basis.	→	If the correlation is greater between MZ twins than between DZ twins, genetic factors are assumed to play the stronger role. Limitation: MZ twins may have a more similar environment than DZ twins.
Combined twin and adoption studies	→	Compares twins separated early in life and raised in different adoptive homes.	→	Controls for the similar-environment limitation of twin studies. If MZ twins are more similar than DZ twins, even when raised apart, the greater similarity is assumed to be the result of genetic factors.

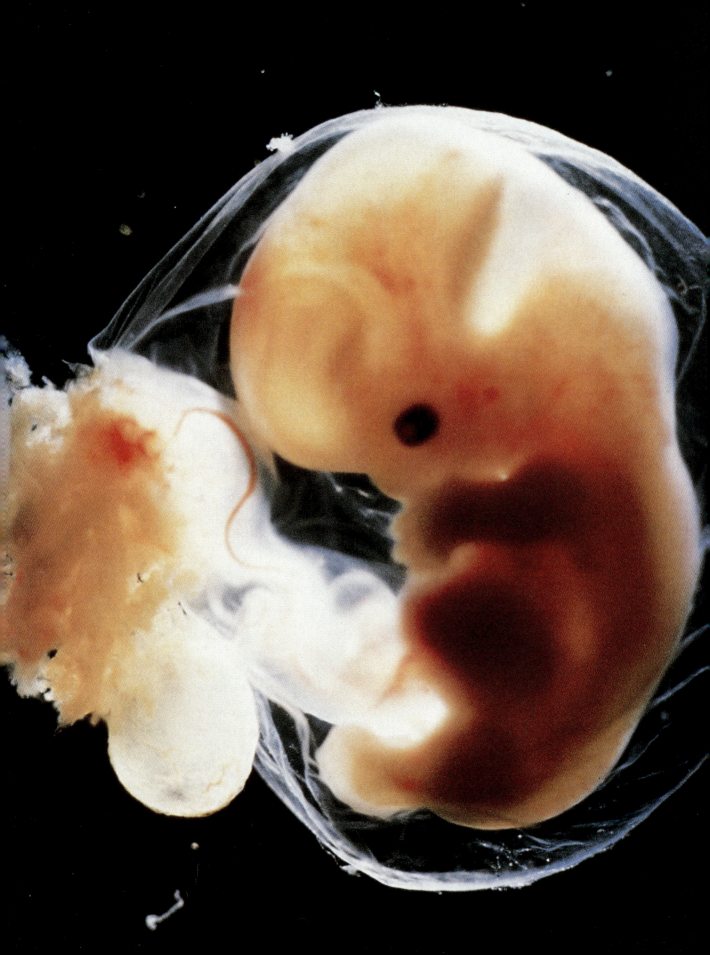

Chapter 5

Prenatal Development

In 1989, Jennifer Johnson of Sanford, Florida, became the first woman to be convicted of dealing cocaine to her newborn baby—through the umbilical cord! The case represented a relatively new trend in the war on drugs. Because no state laws made it illegal for women to pass drugs to fetuses, prosecutors had turned to laws aimed at dealers who sold drugs to minors. The case against Johnson, who had used cocaine during her pregnancy, essentially claimed that she had dealt drugs to her baby. A Florida appeals court upheld Johnson's conviction in 1991.

Law enforcement agencies in Florida and across the nation had good reason for concern about drug use among pregnant women. Experts had estimated that the number of babies born to women who used illegal drugs during their pregnancies had climbed to 375,000 a year. Some of these babies died, and others had various medical and behavioral problems. Many were abandoned, becoming boarder babies in public hospitals. Prosecuting mothers, some said, was one way to get the mothers into treatment and thus to protect their babies.

Many legal and medical professionals disagreed, however, arguing that pregnant women would be less—not more—likely to seek treatment if they feared prosecution. Legal experts also pointed out that drug-trafficking laws were never meant to be used to prosecute pregnant women. In 1992, the Florida Supreme Court struck down Johnson's conviction on precisely those grounds, holding that the Florida legislature had not intended state laws to be used in that way. Similar cases throughout the state were dropped as a result of the ruling.

A decade later, the problem of how fetuses can be legally protected from their mothers' drug use still has not been fully resolved. A central legal issue in this controversial area—and in the abortion controversy as well—is, What are a fetus's rights? However this question is eventually resolved in the U.S. legal system, one thing is certain: women who use drugs during pregnancy place their children at risk.

In this chapter we examine the development of the child during the nine-month prenatal period. Drugs, we will see, are only one of many risk factors a fetus may face while growing in the mother's womb.

When we consider the course of a child's life, the 9 months between conception and birth may be the most unappreciated period of development. This is probably because the events that occur during this time are largely hidden from view. Yet during these 9 months, what begins as a microscopic fertilized egg undergoes a series of dramatic changes and eventually emerges as a living, breathing baby.

You can probably imagine how people from ancient cultures must have struggled to explain how a fully formed creature could appear at birth. As late as the 18th century, some believed that people were completely formed even before conception. One theory, *homunculism*, proposed that each sperm cell contained a tiny individual, like the one shown in Figure 5.1, who would grow when deposited in a woman's womb. Another theory held that the fully formed baby resided instead in the ovum (Needham, 1959).

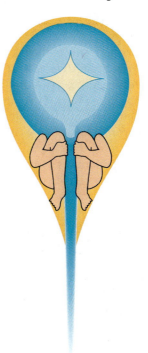

Figure 5.1
Copy of a seventeenth-century drawing of a sperm. The miniature human was thought to enlarge after entering the ovum.

Just a bit more than 100 years ago, a Swiss zoologist, peering through a microscope, became the first person to see a sperm enter an egg, fertilize it, and produce the cell for a new embryo. Such discoveries led to our current understanding of fertilization and prenatal development (Touchette, 1990; Wasserman, 1988). This understanding also includes knowledge about factors that impair development, such as genetic defects, infections, drugs, and environmental poisons.

Stages of Prenatal Development

Even though it is the largest cell in the body, the ovum is no larger than the period at the end of this sentence, and the sperm cell that fertilizes it weighs less than 1/30,000 as much. This tiny genetic package nevertheless grows into a baby billions of times larger in only 9 months.

Every stage of development along the journey from conception to birth represents a mix of the influences of nature and nurture. Even the genetic material that the mother and father contribute to the offspring can be affected by environmental factors, such as radiation. And other environmental factors, such as nutrition, infections, and drugs, can also influence development. In this section, we follow the baby's prenatal development through three stages, or periods—the period of the zygote, the period of the embryo, and the period of the fetus. First we consider the starting point of development—conception.

Conception

Prenatal development begins at **conception**, or fertilization, when a sperm unites with an ovum (egg) to form a single cell, called a **zygote**. The zygote receives 23 chromosomes from the mother and 23 from the father, to form a new and genetically unique person.

Conception
The combining of the genetic material from a male gamete (sperm) and a female gamete (ovum); fertilization.

Zygote
A fertilized ovum.

Millions of sperm from the father enter the vagina of the mother, but only several hundred reach the ovum and only one actually fertilizes it.

Once every 28 or so days, about halfway through a woman's menstrual cycle, an ovum is produced by either her left or right ovary (they alternate each month) and begins to travel through the fallopian tube toward the uterus, which at this point is only about the size of a plum. For the next 24 hours, the ovum is capable of being fertilized. Sperm from the male, which are deposited in the vagina, remain viable for 2 to 3 days. This time is crucial since their longer journey takes them through the cervix and the uterus before entering the fallopian tube where the ovum is located. Of the several million sperm that are typically deposited, only 100 to 200 of the strongest and healthiest make it all the way to the ovum, and only one actually penetrates its wall to fertilize it. Within about an hour of penetration, the genetic material from the sperm and the ovum have completely merged to form a zygote, and development of the baby begins.

The Period of the Zygote (Conception to Second Week)

The zygote multiplies rapidly as it continues its 4-day, 4-inch journey through the fallopian tube to the uterus. At first the zygote is a solid mass of cells, but it gradually changes into a hollow sphere as it prepares to implant into the wall of the uterus. Now the cells begin to specialize, some forming an inner cell mass, which will become the embryo, and some forming important structures that will support the embryo's development. Figure 5.2 diagrams the events of the first week of human development.

Implantation takes about a week. During this time, the zygote settles into the blood-enriched lining of the uterus, where it will remain attached for the duration of the pregnancy. The period of the zygote ends about 2 weeks after fertilization, which corresponds to the first missed menstrual period. By the time a woman suspects she may be pregnant, then, prenatal development is well under way.

The Period of the Embryo (Third to Eighth Week)

Embryo
The developing organism from the third week, when implantation is complete, through the eighth week after conception.

The period of the **embryo** begins when implantation is complete and lasts for around 6 weeks. Although the embryo at first is only the size of an apple seed, all major internal and external structures form during this period. For that reason, these weeks are the most delicate of the pregnancy and the time when the growing

Figure 5.2
Schematic representation of the events of the first week of human development.

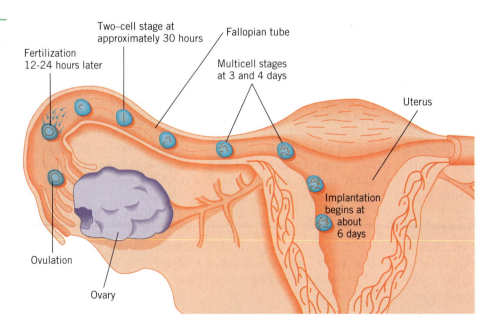

Fertilization
12-24 hours later

Two–cell stage at approximately 30 hours

Fallopian tube

Multicell stages at 3 and 4 days

Uterus

Implantation begins at about 6 days

Ovulation

Ovary

embryo is most vulnerable to threats from the internal and external environments (discussed shortly).

In the third week, the inner cell mass differentiates into three layers, from which all body structures will emerge. Two layers form first—the *endodermal* layer and the *ectodermal* layer. The endodermal cells will develop into some internal organs and glands. The ectodermal cells become the parts of the body that maintain contact with the outside world—the nervous system; the sensory parts of the eyes, nose, and ears; skin; and hair. The third cell layer then appears between the endodermal and ectodermal layers. This is the *mesodermal* layer, which will give rise to muscles, cartilage, bone, sex organs, and the heart. The heart is beating by the end of the third week.

Around the beginning of the fourth week, the embryo looks something like a tiny tube. The shape of the embryo gradually changes, however, because cell multiplication is more rapid in some locations than in others. By the end of the fourth week, the embryo assumes a curved form, as shown in Figure 5.3. We can distinguish a bump below the head, which is the primitive heart, and the upper and lower limbs, which have just begun to form as tiny buds.

The embryo's body changes less in the fifth week, but the head and brain develop rapidly. The upper limbs form, and the lower limbs appear and look like small paddles. In the sixth week, the head continues to grow rapidly, and differentiation of the limbs occurs as elbows, fingers, and wrists become recognizable. It is now possible to discern the ears and eyes. The limbs develop rapidly in the seventh week, and stumps appear that will form fingers and toes.

By the end of the eighth week, the embryo has distinctly human features. Almost half of the embryo consists of the head. The eyes, ears, toes, and fingers are easily distinguishable. All internal and external structures have formed. Thus, in 8 weeks, a single, tiny, undifferentiated cell has proliferated into a remarkably complex organism consisting of millions of cells differentiated into heart, kidneys, eyes, ears, nervous system, brain, and other structures. Its mass has increased a staggering 2 million percent. Figure 5.4 gives some indication of the magnitude of this change.

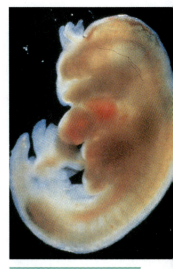

Figure 5.3
An embryo at 4 weeks.

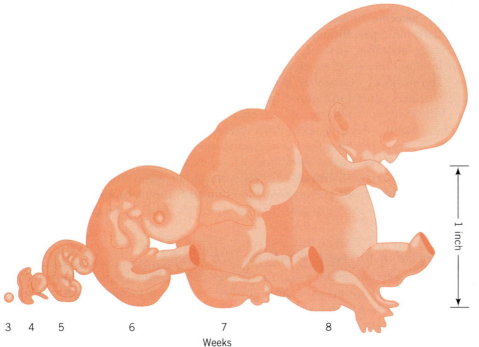

3 4 5 6 7 8
Weeks

1 inch

Figure 5.4
Human ova and embryos showing growth and body form from 3 to 8 weeks. Adapted from *Textbook of Embryology*, 5th ed. (p. 87), by H. E. Jordan and J. E. Kindred, 1948, New York: Appleton-Century-Crofts. Copyright © 1948 by Appleton-Century-Crofts. Adapted by permission.

Figure 5.5
Maternal structures that support the embryo and fetus include the placental villi, amniotic sac, placenta, and umbilical cord.

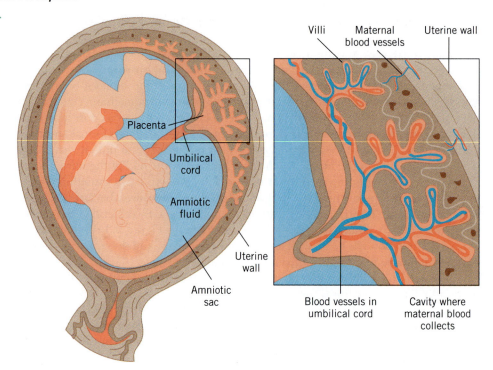

The Prenatal Environment   Just as the embryo's inner cell mass changes rapidly in the early weeks of development, so do its other cells. Three major structures arising from these cells develop by the end of the embryonic period: the amniotic sac, the placenta, and the umbilical cord, illustrated in Figure 5.5.

The **amniotic sac** is a watertight membrane filled with fluid. As the embryo grows, the amniotic sac surrounds it, cushioning and supporting it within the uterus and providing an environment with a constant temperature.

The **placenta**, formed from both the mother's tissue and the embryo's tissue, is a remarkable organ through which the mother and the embryo (later the fetus) exchange materials. Linking the embryo to the placenta is the **umbilical cord**, which houses the blood vessels that carry these materials.

The exchange of materials takes place in the placental villi. These ornate-looking structures (shown in Figure 5.5) are small blood vessels immersed in the mother's blood but separated from it by a very thin membrane. The membrane serves as a filter—nature's way of keeping many diseases, germs, and impurities in the mother's blood from reaching the baby. Unfortunately, as we will see shortly, it is not a perfect filter. Blood itself does not pass between the mother and the fetus (which is why the mother and baby can have different blood types); however, oxygen and nutrients do pass from the mother's blood through the placenta to the fetus, and waste products of the fetus pass into the mother's blood to be carried away and excreted.

The Period of the Fetus (Ninth to 38th Week)

At the end of the eighth week, the period of the **fetus** begins. The principal changes for the fetus are to develop further the already formed organ structures and to increase in size and weight. Beginning its third month weighing less than an ounce and measuring 2 inches in length, the average fetus will be born 266 days

Amniotic sac
A fluid-containing watertight membrane that surrounds and protects the embryo and fetus.

Placenta
An organ that forms where the embryo attaches to the uterus. This organ exchanges nutrients, oxygen, and wastes between the embryo or fetus and the mother through a very thin membrane that does not allow the passage of blood.

Umbilical cord
A soft cable of tissue and blood vessels that connects the fetus to the placenta.

Fetus
The developing organism from the ninth week to the 38th week after conception.

after conception weighing about 7 to 8 lb and measuring about 20 inches in length. Fetal growth begins to slow around the eighth month—which is good for both the mother and the fetus because if it did not, the fetus would weigh 200 lb at birth!

External Changes   During this period, the fetus's appearance changes drastically. The head grows less than do other parts of the body, so that its ratio decreases from 50% percent of the body mass at 12 weeks toward 25% at birth. The skin, which has been transparent, begins to thicken during the third month. Facial features, which appeared almost extraterrestrial at 6 weeks, become more human looking as the eyes move from the sides of the head to the front.

The eyelids seal shut near the beginning of the third month and remain that way for the next 3 months. Nails appear on fingers and toes by the fourth month, and pads appear at the ends of the fingers that will uniquely identify the individual for life. Head hair also begins to grow. A bone structure begins to support a more erect posture by 6 months.

Growth of Internal Organs   Changes in external appearance are accompanied by equally striking internal changes. By 3 months, the brain has organized into functional subdivisions—seeing, hearing, thinking, and so on. The 100 billion cells of the adult brain are already present in the fetus by the fifth month, but the 14 trillion connections they will make between themselves and incoming and outgoing nerve cells will not be completed until well after birth. Other nerve cells grow and establish connections throughout fetal development.

A major mystery facing scientists is how the single, undifferentiated zygote cell can give rise to billions of fibers that properly connect eyes, ears, touch sensors, muscles, and the parts of the brain. Although an inborn plan of some sort must guide how this wiring proceeds, it is clear that environmental factors and interactions between nerve cells also play a role, as no two brains are wired identically, not even those of identical twins, who have exactly the same genetic material (Edelman, 1993; Rakic, 1988).

Other internal organs continue to develop. Sexual development becomes apparent in males by the end of the third month with the appearance of external sexual organs. In females, the precursors of ova, or *oocytes*, form on the outer covering of the ovaries; all the oocytes the female will ever possess will be present at birth. The fallopian tubes, uterus, and vagina develop, and the external labia become discernible.

Early Signs of Behavior   Fetal activity begins in the third month, when the fetus is capable of forming a fist and wiggling the toes; the mother, however, feels none of this. The fetus also appears to become sensitive to environmental stimulation, moving its whole body in response to a touch stimulus.

By the fourth month the eyes are sensitive to light through the lids, and by the fifth month a loud noise may activate the fetus. During this same month, the fetus swims effortlessly, a luxury gradually lost later as quarters become increasingly cramped. The fetus is now capable of kicking and turning and may begin to display rhythms of sleep and activity. By the seventh month, brain connections are sufficient for the fetus to exhibit a sucking reflex when the lips are touched.

Toward Independence   The later stages of prenatal development ready the fetus to live outside the mother's body. Although separate from the mother in many ways during development, the fetus is nevertheless completely dependent on her for sur-

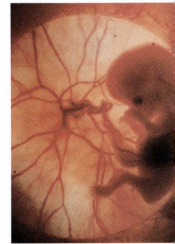

Until birth, the fetus remains immersed in fluid within the amniotic sac, receiving oxygen and nourishment through the umbilical cord. The fetus in the photo is 12 weeks into gestation.

vival during most of the prenatal period. Recall that the support system in the uterus provides oxygen, nutrients, waste disposal, and a constant temperature for the fetus. Although physicians have made marked progress in saving premature babies, they have been unable to lower the age of viability under around 23 to 24 weeks of fetal age.

The major obstacle to independent life for a fetus born prematurely is the immaturity of the air sacs of the lungs, which have to exchange carbon dioxide for oxygen. The fetus's inability to digest food or control body temperature is also a problem, and fat has not yet formed under the skin to assist in temperature regulation.

By 6 to 7 months of age, the fetus has a chance of survival outside the mother's body. The brain is sufficiently developed to provide at least partial regulation of breathing, swallowing, and body temperature. However, a baby born after only 7 months of development will need to be provided with extra oxygen, will have to take food in very small amounts, and will have to live for several weeks in an incubator for temperature control.

In the eighth month, fat appears under the skin, and although the digestive system is still too immature to extract nutrients from food adequately, the fetus begins to store maternal nutrients in its body. Even a baby born at 8 months, however, is susceptible to infection. Beginning in the eighth month, the mother's body contributes disease-fighting antibodies, which she has developed through her own exposure to foreign bodies, to the fetus. This process is not complete until 9 months of fetal age. It is an important process, because the antibodies help protect babies from infection until they are around 6 months of age when they can produce their own antibodies in substantial amounts.

Development in Family Context
Families Created by Alternative Methods of Conception

Infertility can be a frustrating problem for couples hoping to start a family. Sometimes the difficulty involves the woman's eggs (or lack of them); other times the problem lies in the quantity or quality of the male sperm. Fortunately, medical science today offers couples several alternative methods for conceiving a child.

When the problem involves the male, the most common solution is *donor insemination,* in which sperm donated from another male is injected into the female, where it initiates a pregnancy. Another popular method is *in vitro fertilization.* In this process, an egg and sperm (donated from either a third party or from one or both members of the couple) are combined in a laboratory procedure; then the fertilized egg is implanted in the female's uterus where, if all goes well, it begins to develop.

These new reproductive technologies have effectively solved a long-standing problem of biology. But what are the psychological implications of these procedures? What impact do they have on the children who are products of this technology and on their parents?

One study investigated this issue by comparing families with a child conceived by each of these two methods with both families whose children were conceived naturally and families whose children were adopted (Golombok et al., 1995). The focus of the study was social-emotional development and family functioning. Parents and children were interviewed, observed interacting with one another, and given a battery of tests.

The researchers wondered whether families formed with the help of new technologies might experience more difficulties than the natural-conception families, for several possible reasons. For one, the child in most cases was genetically unrelated to one or both of the parents, but in only one family was the child informed of this. Would the nongenetic parent have difficulty relating to the child? Would the child feel deceived when eventually made aware of the situation? Would the absence of a biological connection among all family members interfere with the establishment of the normal social and emotional bonds? Among the other concerns were whether the parents would feel unduly stressed by the unusual situation and whether the parents' relationship with one another would suffer if only one parent were genetically related to the child.

The results of the study are perhaps a little surprising. Parents of children conceived by the two alternative reproductive methods were found to be similar to the adoptive parents and superior to parents in the natural-conception families in a number of areas. Mothers in these families were rated as warmer and more emotionally involved with their children, and both mothers and fathers were found to interact more with their children. These parents also reported less stress than those in families with naturally conceived children. The children showed no ill effects of their unusual beginnings. Their feelings about themselves, their relations with their parents and with other children, and their overall psychological adjustment were no different from those of the children in the two comparison groups.

One conclusion drawn by the researchers was that genetic ties between parents and children may not be as important as the parents' strong commitment to parenthood. This seems reasonable, since parents who must seek special methods of conception would likely be heavily invested in the job of parenting. Their other major conclusion was that the new reproductive technologies appear to pose no serious threat to family functioning or harmony. Nevertheless, this area is still very new and will warrant continued evaluation as more children are conceived by these new techniques.

✔ *To Recap...*

Prenatal development begins with conception and proceeds through the period of the zygote, the period of the embryo, and the period of the fetus. At conception, a sperm cell penetrates an egg cell to form a zygote. The zygote multiplies rapidly as it migrates toward the uterus, where it becomes fully implanted by the end of the second week.

Now an embryo, the cell mass rapidly differentiates into organs (a heart, kidneys, eyes, ears, a nervous system, and a brain) and support structures (the amniotic sac, the placenta, and the umbilical cord). In the 6 weeks that make up the period of the embryo, a cluster of cells is transformed into a complex and differentiated organism.

At the end of the eighth week, the fetal period begins. The primary task for the fetus is growth and further development of organ systems. Behavior begins in the third month. The fetus grows toward increasing independence, but is unable to survive before about 23 to 24 weeks of fetal age. By 9 months following conception, the normal fetus is ready to face the external world.

Teratology: History, Principles, and Natural Events

It is natural to think that prenatal development depends only on genes and that the environment begins to affect the baby only after birth. Yet, although the uterus may not seem like an environment in the usual sense, it is the only home the embryo and fetus know. We will see that a number of factors affect the quality of this home and determine whether development is normal or abnormal—indeed, whether development can occur at all.

Approximately 3 to 5% of all live-born babies are identified as malformed at birth. Some malformations are difficult to detect at first, but become apparent with age. Thus, by the early school years, approximately 6 to 7% of children are identified as having *congenital malformations*—malformations that existed at birth. Many more babies would be born with malformations were it not for a natural prenatal process that results in miscarriage or spontaneous abortion. It is estimated that 90% of some kinds of malformations end in spontaneous abortions and that without this natural screening process, the observed incidence of congenital malformation would be 12% or more (Shepard, 1986).

We have already seen that some abnormalities are caused by genetic defects. Malformations may also be caused by infectious diseases, poor nutrition, age, and perhaps even the mother's emotional state, as well as by drugs and other environmental hazards. Nongenetic agents that can cause malformation in the embryo and fetus are referred to as **teratogens** (*tera* is a Latin base meaning "monster"). The term *teratology* refers to the study of the effect of teratogens on prenatal development.

Much of our discussion of teratogens will focus on their physical effects. Indeed, teratogens are defined in terms of their creation of physical malformations. However, psychologists have noted increasingly that teratogens can have psychological and behavioral effects as well. This realization has given rise to a new field, called **psychoteratology**. Researchers in this field use behavior rather than physical outcomes to study the potentially damaging effects of teratogens and have found that behavioral effects may show up even when physical effects do not. Thus in many cases, behavioral measures may be more sensitive than physical measures (Fein et al., 1983; Voorhees & Mollnow, 1987).

Teratogen
An agent that can cause abnormal development in the fetus.

Psychoteratology
The study of the harmful effects of teratogens through the use of behavioral measures, such as learning ability.

Historical Ideas

The field of teratology achieved scientific status only recently, but it has had an interesting history. The birth of malformed babies probably gave rise to at least some of the creatures of Greek mythology, such as the one-eyed cyclops and various creatures that are part human and part beast (Warkany, 1977). But although monsters were sometimes idolized in ancient times, people in the medieval period believed that the birth of malformed babies portended catastrophe, and malformed infants and children were often put to death. Some believed that these babies were produced through the mating of humans with animals, and it was not unusual for mothers and midwives who delivered malformed babies to be put on trial for witchcraft.

Such practices gradually gave way to the more benign belief that maternal fright, thoughts, and impressions could create a monster birth (Warkany, 1981). Running parallel to these theories were ancient beliefs that the food and drink a pregnant woman ingested could affect the fetus. In the Bible, an angel admonishes a man named Manoah that when his wife conceives a son, she should "drink no wine nor strong drink, and eat not any unclean thing" (Judges 13:4).

Despite the apparent fact that people of biblical times believed that maternal nourishment could affect the development of the fetus, a great deal of time elapsed before people fully realized the potential effects of the external world on the fetus. People generally believed that the embryo and fetus lived in a privileged environment, protected against harm by the placenta and its amniotic world.

By 1930, however, there was general recognition that X rays could produce intrauterine growth retardation, microcephaly (an abnormally small head and brain), and small eyes. By the mid-1940s, it had become obvious that a pregnant mother who contracted rubella (German measles) during the early months of pregnancy had a relatively high chance of producing a baby with congenital abnormalities of the eye, ear, heart, and brain.

Still, these events were seen as exceptional. A major disaster finally shook people's faith in the privileged-environment belief, but only as recently as the early 1960s. A mild and seemingly harmless sedative, thalidomide, was marketed in the late 1950s, and many pregnant women took it. Physicians soon noticed a sharp increase in the number of babies born with defective limbs. Careful questioning of mothers, analysis of doctors' prescriptions, and epidemiological research implicated thalidomide as the culprit. The field of teratology experienced a dramatic surge as a result of this event and has been expanding rapidly ever since.

General Principles

Many teratogens have been identified as causing defects in humans. Evaluating an agent for teratogenic effects, however, is fraught with problems. For obvious reasons, animals must be the "guinea pigs" for substance testing, but the potential teratogen may not have the same effect on animal and human fetuses. Furthermore, people often take more than one drug, and a particular drug may do damage only in combination with another drug, with a disease, or with stress. Some common teratogens and their effects are listed in Table 5.1.

Six principles capture important features of how teratogens act (Hogge, 1990).

1. A teratogen's effect depends on the genetic makeup of the organism exposed to it. A prime example is thalidomide. The human fetus is extremely sensitive to this substance, but rabbits and rats are not. One reason thalidomide was not initially suspected to be a teratogen was that testing on these animals revealed no ill effects. The principle of genetic differences in sensitivity also applies to individuals within a species. Some babies are malformed because their mothers drank alcohol during pregnancy, but others are apparently not affected by this practice.

2. The effect of a teratogen on development depends partly on timing. Even before conception, teratogens can affect the formation of the parents' germ cells. Formation of female germ cells begins during fetal life, and formation of sperm can occur up to 64 days before the sperm are expelled. Thus, a fetus can be affected by drugs that the pregnant grandmother took decades earlier or by X-ray exposure that the father experienced many weeks before conception.

For 2 to 3 weeks after conception, the zygote's fluids do not mix with those of the mother, so the zygote is relatively impervious to some teratogens. After the zygote has attached to the uterus, however, substances in the mother's bloodstream can pass through the placental barrier and mix with the blood of the embryo, and the embryo enters a particularly sensitive period. Teratogens can produce organ malformation from 2 to 8 weeks because this is a time when organs are forming. After the organs have formed, teratogens primarily produce growth retardation or tissue damage (Goldman, 1980).

Which organ is affected by a teratogen depends in part on which organ is forming. Rubella is an example of how crucial timing can be. Rubella affects only 2 to 3% of the offspring of mothers infected within 2 weeks after their last period, whereas it affects 50% of offspring when infection occurs during the first month following conception, 22% when it occurs during the second month, and 6 to 8% when it occurs during the third month. The incidence falls to very low levels thereafter. Whether ear, eye, heart, or brain damage occurs depends on the stage of the

Table 5.1
Some Teratogens and Conditions That May Harm the Fetus

Teratogen	*Potential Effect*
Therapeutic Drugs	
Aspirin	In large quantities, miscarriage, bleeding, newborn respiratory problems
Barbiturates	Newborn respiratory problems
Diethylstilbestrol (DES) (a drug to prevent miscarriage)	Genital abnormalities in both sexes, vaginal and cervical cancer in adolescent females
Isoretinoin (a vitamin A derivative for treating acne)	Malformations of the head and ears, heart and central nervous system defects, behavior problems
Phenytoin (an anticonvulsant drug)	Threefold increase in likelihood of heart defects and growth retardation
Streptomycin	Hearing loss
Tetracycline	Most commonly, staining of teeth; can also affect bone growth
Thalidomide	Deformed limbs, sensory deficits, defects in internal organs, death
Street Drugs	
Cocaine and crack	Growth retardation, premature birth, irritableness in the newborn, withdrawal symptoms
Heroin and methadone	Growth retardation, premature birth, irritableness in the newborn, withdrawal symptoms, sudden infant death syndrome
LSD and marijuana	Probable cause of premature birth and growth retardation when used heavily; originally implicated in chromosomal breakage, but this effect is uncertain
Maternal Condition	
Age	For teenage women and women over 35, lighter-weight babies than for women in the optimal childbearing years; likelihood of Down syndrome birth increases with advancing age
Alcohol use	Brain and heart damage, growth retardation, mental retardation, fetal alcohol syndrome
Diabetes	A threefold increase in all types of birth defects, including babies born without a brain, with spina bifida, and with heart defects
Malnutrition	Increased likelihood of growth retardation, prematurity, inattention; poor social interactive ability, especially when mother also has a history of malnutrition before pregnancy
Phenylketonuria (PKU)	Growth retardation of brain and head, mental retardation, heart defects
Smoking	Growth retardation, prematurity
Infections	
AIDS (acquired immunodeficiency syndrome)	Congenital malformations; leaves infant vulnerable to infections of all types
Cytomegalovirus	Deafness, blindness, abnormal head and brain growth, mental retardation
Herpes	Mental retardation, eye damage, death
Rubella	Mental retardation, eye damage, deafness, heart defects
Syphilis	Mental retardation, miscarriage, blindness, deafness, death
Toxoplasmosis	Abnormalities in brain and head growth, mental retardation
Environmental Hazards	
Lead	Miscarriage, anemia, mental retardation
Mercury	Abnormal head and brain growth, motor incoordination, mental retardation
PCBs	Growth retardation
Radiation	Leukemia, abnormal brain and body growth, cancer, genetic alterations, miscarriage, stillbirth

formation of each organ when the mother is infected (Murata et al., 1992; Whitley & Goldenberg, 1990).

3. *The effect of a teratogen may be unique.* For example, thalidomide produces gross limb defects, whereas rubella primarily affects sensory and internal organs.

4. *The abnormal development caused by teratogens may be severe.* Teratogenic effects may include malformation of limbs or other parts of the body, growth retardation, functional and behavioral disorders, or even death.

5. *Teratogens differ in how they gain access to the fetus.* Radiation passes to the fetus directly through the mother's body, for example, whereas chemicals usually travel to the fetus through the blood and across the placental membrane. Physical blows are partially cushioned by the mother's body and the amniotic fluid. The mother's blood may be able to filter some potentially harmful chemicals to protect the fetus. The placenta, too, serves as a filter, but not as a complete barrier; materials may be slowed by this filter, but will not necessarily be stopped. Some teratogens move past this filter faster than others.

6. *The likelihood and degree of abnormal development increase with the fetus's dosage of the harmful agent.* Depending on the amount of the teratogen to which the fetus is exposed, the outcome can range from no effect at all to death.

Natural Challenges

Much current media attention focuses on potential teratogens that mothers voluntarily consume or to which mothers are exposed in the modern industrial environment. Yet, the mothers and fetuses have always faced natural challenges from the environment. Infectious diseases can harm the fetus, and the quality of the mother's nutrition affects how the fetus develops. Parental age and even maternal experiences and stress may also have an effect.

Maternal Infectious Diseases Several viral and bacterial infections in the mother can damage the fetus. We discuss some of the more common ones here.

Rubella. Rubella virus can damage the central nervous system of the fetus, resulting in blindness, deafness, and mental retardation. The heart, liver, and bone structure may also be damaged, depending on the timing of infection.

Herpes. Two viruses in the herpes group can produce central nervous system damage. *Cytomegalovirus (CMV),* the most common intrauterine viral infection, may cause abnormal brain and head growth, encephalitis, blindness, and mental retardation. An estimated 33,000 infants are born with CMV each year, but only 10% of them are seriously affected.

Because pregnant mothers are often unaware that they have been infected by CMV, doctors have made little progress in discovering the specific effects of fetal exposure at particular ages. CMV can be transmitted by sexual contact, blood transfusions, or mixing of body fluids (Behrman & Vaughan, 1987).

Another herpes virus, *herpes virus type 2,* infects the genitals of adults. This virus had reached epidemic levels in the United States by the early 1980s. In the infant, herpes 2 can cause encephalitis, central nervous system damage, and blood-clotting problems. Most herpes 2 infections of infants occur following direct contamination by the mother's infected birth canal (Murata et al., 1992; Whitley & Goldenberg, 1990).

HIV. Another virus that reached epidemic levels in the 1980s is the human immunodeficiency virus (HIV), which causes acquired immunodeficiency syndrome, or AIDS. The virus is transmitted from one person to another exclusively through body fluids.

There are three major avenues for transmission. The first is through sexual intercourse by way of male semen or female vaginal fluids. The second is through blood exchange. Many people have been infected with the virus through transfusions of blood donated by infected individuals, but improved blood screening has reduced this threat dramatically. HIV-infected blood is exchanged most commonly through intravenous drug injection by addicts who share the same needle (Palca, 1990). The third means of transmission is from mother to infant through breast milk (European Collaborative Study, 1991).

In addition to causing AIDS, the human immunodeficiency virus can act as a teratogen. Some infected babies are born with facial deformities—larger-than-normal eye separation, boxlike foreheads, flattened nose bridges, and misshapen eye openings.

Syphilis and Gonorrhea. Syphilis and gonorrhea are sexually transmitted diseases. After declining for several years, the incidence of syphilis began to increase in the late 1980s. This disease is caused by a spirochete, a type of bacteria, which can infect the fetus and cause central nervous system damage, deformities of the teeth and skeleton, and even death. The fetus is relatively resistant to infection from the syphilis spirochete until the fourth or fifth month.

Gonorrhea is also caused by a bacterial agent. Its incidence has been reported to be as high as 30% in some populations. Premature birth, premature rupture of membranes, and spontaneous abortion are associated with gonorrhea. The fetus is affected in about 30% of cases. The most common problem is eye infection, which can lead to blindness if untreated. Fortunately, almost all newborns are treated with silver nitrate eyedrops at birth to prevent this problem (Murata et al., 1992; Whitley & Goldenberg, 1990).

Nutrition The original fertilized egg must multiply into trillions of cells to form the fully developed fetus. During prenatal development, cells increase not only in number but also in size. As Table 5.2 illustrates, the baby and its accompanying support system will weigh 25 to 30 lb by the ninth month of pregnancy, billions of times the weight of the fertilized egg.

Where does all of this mass come from? The answer is obvious—from the mother. Thinking about the issue this way brings home the importance of maternal nutrition. The quality of the fetus's cells can be no better than that of the nutrients the mother supplies through the placental circulation system. Oddly, this simple fact is often not fully appreciated. Earlier we said that, at least in the early stages of development, the functioning of cells depends on the environment they are in. The quality of the mother's nutrition is probably the most important environmental influence on the fetus and newborn baby (Morgane et al., 1993).

The prospective mother, then, must supply nutrients for the fetus and its support system. In part, her ability to do this depends on her nutrition during pregnancy. But it also depends to a great extent on her nutritional status *before* pregnancy. Both the mothers and their fetuses fare more poorly when the mother has had long-term malnutrition than when the mother has good prepregnancy nutrition (Rosso, 1990). Additionally, how well the placenta passes nutrients to the fetus, maternal disease, and genetic factors can affect fetal nutrition.

Maternal malnutrition can have devastating effects on the fetus. Autopsies of severely malnourished stillborn infants from third-world countries reveal that their

Table 5.2
Weight Gain during Pregnancy

Development	Weight Gain (lb)
Infant at birth	$7^1/_2$
Placenta	1
Increase in mother's blood volume to supply placenta	4
Increase in size of mother's uterus and muscles to support it	$2^1/_2$
Increase in size of mother's breasts	3
Fluid to surround infant in amniotic sac	2
Mother's fat stores	5–10
Total	25–30

Source: Reprinted by permission from page 495 of *Understanding Nutrition*, Fourth Edition, by E. N. Whitney and E. M. N. Hamilton; Copyright © 1987 by Wadsworth Publishing Co.

brains weighed up to one-third less than expected. Deficits in the size of major internal organs of between 6 and 25% have been found in the United States in infants born to urban poor families (Naeye, Diener, & Dellinger, 1969; Parekh et al., 1970). Malnutrition is associated with increased rates of spontaneous abortion, infant death, and congenital defects. Pregnant women who have inadequate diets are also more likely to have small and premature babies (Bauerfeld & Lachenmeyer, 1992). (Problems associated with low birth weight are discussed in Chapter 6.)

As is sometimes the case with teratogens, however, it can be difficult to isolate the effects of malnourishment from other factors. Malnutrition is often accompanied by inadequate housing and health care and inferior education and sanitation, as well as the daily stress of poverty. Catastrophes sometimes provide a means for separating out the influences of at least some of these factors. During World War II, for example, the entire populations of many countries had severely limited food supplies not associated with the other factors. Food supplies in the Netherlands were especially scarce, and, in addition to a decline in conceptions, there was a substantial increase in miscarriages, stillbirths, and congenital malformations.

Food quantity is not the only issue in maternal nutrition. The pregnant woman and her fetus have special dietary needs. Proteins, vitamins, and minerals are especially important. Animal studies reveal that protein deficits produce damage to the kidneys, intestines, and skeletal growth in the fetus. Low intake of certain vitamins can affect the eyes and internal organs and increase the number of malformations (Rosso, 1990).

Trace elements in the diet are also important. An absence of iron in the mother's blood can produce anemia in her baby. Diets lacking iodine are associated with an increased likelihood of cretinism, a severe thyroid deficiency that causes physical stunting and mental deficiency. Deficits of copper, manganese, and zinc produce central nervous system damage and other negative effects in rats, and zinc deficiency has been implicated in the occurrence of anencephaly (absence of the cortex of the brain) in people in Turkey and other Eastern countries. Vegetarians are vulnerable to deficiencies of vitamins, especially B12, iron, and zinc, as well as to inadequate caloric intake (Rosso, 1990).

Convincing evidence of the importance of one B vitamin, folic acid, has recently become available. Deficits of folic acid in pregnant mothers had been associated with neural tube defects—anencephaly and nonclosure of the spinal cord (spina bifida)—in babies.

What are the intellectual abilities of babies who are malnourished during fetal life? The outcome depends, to a large extent, on their childhood environments. Children who were malnourished as fetuses because of World War II but had adequate diet and stimulation as infants and children showed no long-term intellectual deficit. Many Korean children suffered malnutrition during the Korean War but were later adopted by families who provided them with good nutrition and education. These children later performed as well on intellectual and achievement tests as children who had not suffered early malnutrition. The general conclusion is that an enriched home environment may compensate for many of the effects of early malnutrition, but the outcome also depends on when during pregnancy the malnutrition occurred and how severe it was (Morgane et al., 1993; Vietze & Vaughan, 1988; Zeskind & Ramey, 1981).

On the other hand, babies who are malnourished both as fetuses and after birth are more likely to show delayed motor and social development. They become relatively inattentive, unresponsive, and apathetic (Bauerfeld & Lachenmeyer, 1992). Health organizations worldwide have recognized the lasting consequences of early nutritional deficits and have initiated attempts to supplement the diets of pregnant women and infants. Babies with supplemented diets are more advanced in motor development and more socially interactive and energetic, an encouraging sign that the consequences of bad nutrition may be avoided (Joos et al., 1983).

Excesses of nutrients can also be damaging. For example, recall from Chapter 4 that people with the disease phenylketonuria (PKU) are unable to break down the amino acid phenylalanine. Mothers who have phenylketonuria, even though they have protected themselves through early dietary restrictions, still have excesses of phenylalanine circulating in their blood. The fetus, though genetically normal, may suffer brain damage from intrauterine exposure to this excess product. Pregnant women can protect the fetus by maintaining a restricted diet during pregnancy (Koch & Dela Cruz, 1991).

Excesses of the sugar galactose in diabetic mothers may cause cataracts and other physical problems, even death, in fetuses; the babies at birth are more likely to have passive muscle tone and to be less attentive (Langer, 1990). Just as deficits in iodine can cause problems, excess iodine can have a detrimental affect on thyroid function in the fetus. Excess vitamin supplementation has been implicated in birth defects in both humans and animals (Rosso, 1990).

Maternal Experiences and Stress

Maternal Experiences and Stress Of all the factors that might influence the fetus, none has generated more speculation than that of the mother's own experiences. The belief that the mother's mental impressions could affect the fetus is quite old. We may chuckle when we hear that a pregnant woman's child will favor classical music if the mother listens to Beethoven. Yet surveys in modern times in the United States and Europe reveal that many people still believe that birthmarks are caused by maternal frights or unsatisfied food cravings; for example, an unsatisfied craving for strawberries may produce a strawberry-colored birthmark (Ferriera, 1969).

Modern investigators have dismissed beliefs in magical influences on the fetus and have focused on psychological factors that have fairly well documented influences on the body. For example, psychological stress increases the activity of the adrenal glands. The secretions from these glands enter the mother's blood and can be transmitted to the fetus through the placenta. Additionally, hormones released during stress can reduce the blood flow and oxygen available to the fetus. Thus, identifiable physical pathways exist by which maternal emotional states could affect the fetus.

Investigators have used various methods to assess the effects of stress in pregnant women and have examined the relation between the stress and abnormalities in the newborn. High levels of reported anxiety were related to such problems as increases in fetal activity, congenital malformations, irritability, and feeding and digestive difficulties in the baby (Ferriera, 1969; Sontag, 1944, 1966; Stott, 1969).

Again, there are problems in interpreting these relations because of limitations in researchers' ability to control all the factors that might be related to anxiety. Often mothers' reports of anxiety were obtained after their babies were born. These reports of anxiety might have been influenced by the babies' malformation or irritability rather than the other way around—the cause-and-effect problem mentioned in Chapter 3. Further, there is often no way to separate prenatal and postnatal influences on the infant. A mother who has reported a great deal of prenatal anxiety may handle her infant differently, for example, and it may be this handling that makes her baby irritable.

One study showed that women who reported marital difficulties and ambivalence about their pregnancies later reported more problems, including depression, when their babies were 5 months of age (Field et al., 1985). But depressed mothers' interactions with their babies are less optimal, and it appears that their negative judgments about their babies reflected their own states and their impact on the infants rather than their anxiety during pregnancy (Cohn et al., 1990; Vaughn et al., 1987).

Finally, the genetic relation between the mother and her baby, rather than the prenatal experience, may be the operative factor. A mother who is genetically predisposed to anxiety, which might reflect abnormal hormonal activity, could pass this genetic predisposition on to her fetus.

A recent study avoided some of the problems of prior studies by using low birth weight and early delivery as measures of the effects of stress on babies. These measures do not depend on the babies' postnatal interactions with their mothers or on the mothers' judgments of the babies. A group of women completed anxiety questionnaires during their pregnancies. Independent of other medical risk factors, there was a relation between a woman's reported anxiety and the likelihood that she would give birth early or have a baby with low birth weight. The physical pathways already described could have been responsible for these outcomes. It is also possible that women under stress do not look after their health—failing, for example, to get adequate rest or nutrition—which, in turn, might be responsible for the outcomes (Lobel, Dunkel-Schetter, & Scrimshaw, 1992).

The question of whether maternal experiences affect the fetus is a difficult one to answer. There seems little doubt that a relation exists between maternal stress and the likelihood of problems in the offspring, but we know neither why the relation exists nor how strong it is (Istvan, 1986).

Parental Age   The typical age at which a woman gives birth to her first child has risen dramatically in the United States since the 1970s. Between 1970 and 1986, the rate of first births to mothers between the ages of 30 and 39 rose 136%. Although the optimal childbearing years generally have been thought to be between ages 25 and 29, age has become less important in mothers who have chosen to delay their first birth past these years. These women today are better educated than were their counterparts decades ago, and they are more likely to seek early prenatal care and to be in good health. Babies born to mothers between 30 and 34 years of age are now almost as heavy as those born to mothers in the optimal range (Ventura, 1989). (Birth weight is a widely used indicator of newborn status.)

As we saw in Chapter 4, increased maternal age is associated with an increased likelihood of giving birth to a baby with Down syndrome. A mother's chances of giving birth to a Down syndrome infant are almost 74 times greater at age 49 than at age 30.

The father's age also carries a risk for the fetus, because the relative frequency of mutation in the father's sperm increases with age. Down syndrome is attributable to the father rather than the mother in 20 to 30% of cases (Behrman & Vaughan, 1987). Another genetic disorder related to the father's age is *achondroplasia*, a mutation that becomes dominant in the child who inherits it and causes bone deformities. The most obvious characteristics are dwarfism and a large head with a prominent forehead and a depressed bridge of the nose. As shown in Figure 5.6, the relative likelihood that a child will inherit achondroplasia increases with the father's age much as the relative likelihood of Down syndrome increases with the mother's age (Friedman, 1981).

In general, babies who are born to mothers in their teens are also at greater risk. Around 500,000 babies a year are born to teenage mothers in the United States, (Brooks-Gunn & Chase-Lansdale, 1995). There is some disagreement about whether the negative effect of early motherhood is due mostly to poorer prenatal care for teenage mothers or to their biological immaturity. One study showed that even when teenage mothers received the same prenatal care as older mothers, they were more likely to give birth to premature or underweight babies (Leppert, Namerow, & Barker, 1986). Other evidence, however, suggests that the less advan-

Figure 5.6
Relative frequency of Down syndrome and achondropiasia in the offspring of mothers (Down syndrome) and fathers (achondroplasia) of various ages. From "Paternal Age Effect" by J. M. Friedman. Reprinted with permission from The American College of Obstetricians and Gynecologists (*Obstetrics and Gynecology*, Vol. 57, 1981, p. 746).

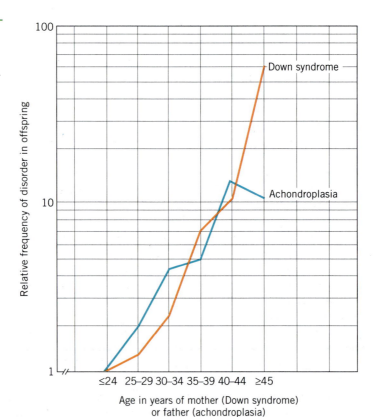

taged socioeconomic status of teenage mothers is responsible for the negative effect on their babies (Murata et al., 1992).

✓ *To Recap...*

Teratology is the study of agents that interfere with normal prenatal development. The emerging field of psychoteratology focuses on the behavioral effects of teratogens. These effects may not always be obvious at birth and do not always include physical problems.

Six principles describe how teratogens act: (1) the effect depends on the genetic makeup of the organism; (2) the effect depends on timing; (3) the effect may be unique to the teratogen; (4) the effect may include serious disorders or death; (5) teratogens gain access to the fetus in different ways; and (6) the effect increases with the level of exposure.

There are a number of natural challenges to the health of the embryo and the fetus. Infectious diseases, such as rubella and AIDS, can cause severe damage. Nutritional factors are important for normal fetal growth, so poor nutrition is also harmful. The ultimate effect of fetal malnutrition depends in part on postnatal nutrition and on the level of stimulation in the environment. Although there is strong suspicion that maternal stress and experiences during pregnancy can affect the fetus, more research is needed. Parental age is another risk factor for the fetus. As the age of the parents increases, there is increased risk of Down syndrome and achondroplasia. On average, teenage women are more likely to have premature or underweight babies than are women in the optimal childbearing age range, but the reasons might involve socioeconomic factors primarily.

Teenage pregnancy has skyrocketed in recent years. Babies of teenage mothers generally do less well than average. It is unclear what roles biological, social, and economic factors play in this outcome.

Teratology: Drugs and Environmental Chemicals

To this point we have considered natural challenges to the health of the fetus. There are also chemical hazards created by people. Such chemicals include those that people ingest—intentionally and accidentally—as well as substances released into the environment.

Drugs

"The desire to take medicine is, perhaps, the greatest feature which distinguishes us from animals." So said Sir William Osler, a medical historian (Finnegan & Fehr, 1980). People in our culture today consume chemicals not only as medicines to treat specific conditions but as means to induce various mental states. Many such substances—alcohol, caffeine, and nicotine—have become so much a part of daily life that we often do not think of them as drugs. A drug, however, can be defined as any substance other than food intended to affect the body. The average pregnant woman takes 4 to 10 drugs of some sort during pregnancy, and up to 80% of the drugs are not prescribed by a doctor.

We mentioned earlier that the effects of thalidomide dramatically increased awareness of the potential damage that chemicals can do to the fetus. The tragic consequences of the sedative became apparent in the early 1960s, soon after the drug appeared on the market. Depending on when a mother took the drug, her baby was born with malformations of the eyes and ears, deformation of the internal organs, or fused fingers and toes. Some babies were born with a rare defect called *phocomelia*, a condition in which the limbs are drastically shortened and the hands and feet are connected to the torso like flippers.

The teratogenic effects of thalidomide were especially surprising because doctors considered it a mild drug. The women who took it experienced no apparent side effects, and the drug produced no harmful effects in the offspring of pregnant animals on which it was tested. Clearly, we had a lot to learn about how chemicals affect the fetus, and we still do. This incomplete knowledge makes it all the more unwise for pregnant women to ingest drugs that they can avoid.

Street Drugs   The increasing availability of powerful mood- and mind-altering illegal drugs since the 1960s has been a major health concern in the United States and, unfortunately, has provided substantial evidence about the dangers of drug intake by pregnant women, both to themselves and to their fetuses. Addictive drugs have attracted the most attention.

Heroin addicts, for example, are more likely to have medical complications during pregnancy and labor, and their newborn babies are more likely to undergo drug-withdrawal symptoms. Frequently, addiction to heroin is compounded by poor nutrition and inadequate health care; almost 75% of addicts do not see a physician during pregnancy. Medical complications, including anemia, cardiac disease, hepatitis, tuberculosis, hypertension, and urinary infections, occur in 40 to 50% of heroin-dependent women who are observed during the prenatal period. These women are more likely to miscarry or to give birth prematurely. Their babies are usually lighter than normal and are more likely to have brain bleeding, low blood sugar, and jaundice.

Heroin-dependent expectant mothers may use methadone, a synthetic drug designed to help break the heroin habit, but methadone is also addictive and is associated with sudden infant death syndrome, or SIDS (in which the baby unexpectedly stops breathing and dies). Infants withdrawing from methadone may experience withdrawal symptoms even more severe than those associated with withdrawal from heroin (Chasnoff et al., 1984; Finnegan & Fehr, 1980). Offspring of heroin-addicted mothers are less well coordinated at 4 months of age and are less attentive at 1 year than are their agemates (Voorhees & Mollnow, 1987).

Applications
Beginning Life with Two Strikes: Cocaine-Exposed Babies

The story at the beginning of the chapter described the case of a pregnant woman passing cocaine to her fetus. Unfortunately, that case was not especially unusual. A conservative estimate is that at least 100,000 fetuses a year are exposed to cocaine (Hawley & Disney, 1992). The ready availability of cocaine, especially in the much cheaper form of hard crack, has increased use of the drug to epidemic proportions.

Cocaine affects the fetus indirectly through reduced maternal blood flow to the uterus, limiting the fetus's supply of nutrients and oxygen. Additionally, cocaine passes through the placenta and enters the fetus's bloodstream, where it gains direct access to the brain in as little as 3 minutes. In the brain, cocaine affects chemical nerve transmitters in addition to increasing heart rate and blood pressure.

Cocaine-exposed babies are more likely to be miscarried or born dead. If they are born alive, they are more likely to be premature or to suffer retarded growth. They also are more likely to be difficult to arouse and irritable, and they may frequently be jittery and shaky. They may have difficulty regulating their level of alertness and with their sleep patterns and they may be hard to handle (DiPietro et al., 1995; Phillips et al., 1996; Regalado et al., 1995).

Despite these problems, studies have turned up conflicting findings as to how babies exposed to cocaine turn out. Some studies have reported that exposed

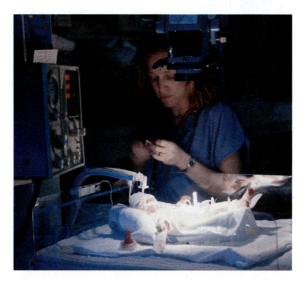

Newborn babies who have been exposed to cocaine as fetuses are more likely to be premature, jittery, and irritable and to have disrupted sleep patterns.

babies later are more impulsive than nonexposed babies and less able to function in unstructured settings. Other studies report few or no long-term effects that can be attributed to cocaine exposure alone. Cocaine research shares the same difficulties as research on many other teratogens. Mothers who use cocaine are more likely to use other drugs and to smoke and drink. They are also more likely to live in poverty and chaos, to be undernourished and in poor health, and to be depressed. Given this complex of factors, which often exist both before and after a child is born, it is difficult to pinpoint the role of prenatal cocaine exposure on the child's development (Barone, 1993; DiPietro et al., 1995; Hawley & Disney, 1992).

Investigators are becoming more sensitive to the effects of the postnatal environment on the cocaine-exposed child. Given an irritable baby who has difficulty falling into regular sleep patterns and a mother who is depressed, has few resources, and continues her drug habit, there is little likelihood that a healthy mother–infant interaction will develop. Many investigators believe that the quality of this relationship and the postnatal environment are the major determinants of the child's outcome (Mayes, 1992).

Some legal authorities believe that pregnant mothers who use drugs should be prosecuted, as was Jennifer Johnson. They believe that such mothers are unfit to care for their children. Others argue that it would be counterproductive, that a child's future prospects would worsen if the child were removed from his or her mother. They make the case that resources should be committed to helping these mothers kick the drug habit and providing them with education and support to enable them to provide a stable home for their children.

The use of marijuana and hallucinogens accelerated rapidly in the 1960s and 1970s, creating concern about their teratogenic potential. Early research suggested that chromosome breakage was more frequent in users of these drugs and that the users were more likely to experience miscarriages or to have babies with limb malformations. As with heroin and cocaine, however, the effects of the drugs are difficult to separate from other environmental and health-care practices.

Research suggests that the heavy use of marijuana may cause newborns to be jittery and to habituate poorly to visual stimuli (Jones & Lopez, 1990). However, other recent studies have found that moderate use of marijuana has much less extreme effects if the users otherwise engage in good health practices. A study in Ottawa, Canada, in which mothers had good prenatal care, found no effect on the offspring of maternal marijuana users at 2, 3, 5, or 6 years of age, although the exposed children did have lower verbal and memory scores when they were 4 years old (Fried, O'Connell, & Watkinson, 1992).

Development in Cultural Context
Ganja Use in Jamaica

A study in Jamaica underlines the importance of considering cultural context in health-care practices. As we have noted, one of the most difficult tasks that scientists face in evaluating effects on the fetus is separating these effects from other factors. In the U.S., marijuana consumption may be associated with alcohol consumption, smoking, poor nutrition and health care, antisocial behavior, and economic level. It is hard to separate these factors from the influence of marijuana alone.

In Jamaica, marijuana is referred to as ganja. Ganja use is very common among pregnant women in Jamaica and is not associated with the use of other drugs, smoking, or alcohol consumption. Furthermore, social disapproval is not a factor in ganja use in Jamaica. Smoking ganja is seen as a sign of independence from men, both economical and social. Often, women of lower economic status who smoke ganja sell it to earn money to provide food and housing—an option that is not available to nonsmokers.

An extensive study of offspring of ganja-using mothers found that they performed as well on assessments at 1 month and 5 years of age as did children of nonusers; in fact, on a few measures, they did better (although the differences were small and may have reflected the better access to resources of the ganja-using mothers). These data should *not* be taken to mean that marijuana use by pregnant women is safe—clearly, much more research needs to be done—but it does illustrate how studying the practices of different cultures can help us better evaluate the effects of drug use (Dreher & Hayes, 1993; Dreher, Nugent, & Hudgins, 1994; Hayes et al., 1991).

Therapeutic Drugs   Many pregnant women take prescribed drugs as part of a continuing regimen of health care—for example, to treat diabetes or blood-clotting tendencies—or as treatments for health problems brought on by the pregnancy. Some of these drugs may increase the risk of fetal problems, creating the need to weigh the risk to the fetus from taking the drug against the risk to the mother from not taking it.

Anticoagulants, anticonvulsants (for epileptics), antibiotics, and even heavy use of aspirin have been implicated in increased likelihood of fetal growth retardation, fetal malformations, and fetal and newborn death, especially when taken during the first 3 months of pregnancy. The action of these drugs is often not straightforward. For example, aspirin, which is harmless at a particular dosage in rats, can be teratogenic if administered with benzoic acid, a widely used food preservative. However, it is important to keep in mind that the danger from these drugs is fairly low and that by far the majority of mothers taking them have healthy infants. Indeed, there is still considerable controversy over whether some of these drugs are teratogenic at all (Hopkins, 1987; Jones et al., 1988).

The effects of sex hormones are more clear. These hormones are sometimes used to treat breast cancer in women and to reduce the likelihood of miscarriage. The use of sex hormones in early pregnancy has been associated with central nervous system malformations in offspring and, more frequently, with masculinization of the external genitalia of females.

Some pregnant women took a particularly damaging synthetic hormone, diethylstilbestrol (DES), in the 1950s and early 1960s to reduce the likelihood of miscarriage. Much later, physicians discovered that a high percentage of the female children of these women developed vaginal and cervical problems when they reached adolescence, and some of these offspring developed cancer of the cervix (Harper, 1981). Recently, evidence has accumulated that the male offspring of mothers who took DES are more likely to develop testicular cancer and to have a lowered sperm count (Sharpe & Skakkebaek, 1993). The studies of sex hormones illustrate yet another problem in detecting teratogenic agents—the possible delay by many years of any observable effect.

Some drugs offer unique benefits but are also powerful teratogens and thus considerably controversial. Accutane, a medication for the treatment of serious acne, came on the market in the early 1980s. Within a year, there were reports of birth defects associated with its use. By 1988, at least 62 deformed babies had been born to Accutane-using mothers, and the figure is now in the hundreds. Many people argue that the drug should be taken off the market, especially because young women who use it may become pregnant unknowingly or be unaware of its effects. Others argue that it is unfair to deprive people who are not at risk (e.g., males) of the unique therapeutic benefits of Accutane. The manufacturer of the drug has compromised by adding strong warning statements to the label and urging dermatologists to have women screened for pregnancy before they write a prescription for its use (Sun, 1988).

The effects of one prescription sedative, thalidomide, have already been described. Research on barbiturates and tranquilizers—both depressants—has turned up mixed results. Although some investigators have found associations between congenital defects and sedatives, others have not. Phenobarbital, however, has been associated with congenital defects and blood coagulation problems in newborns (Jones, Johnson, & Chambers, 1992). Tranquilizers such as diazepam (Valium) and chlordiazepoxide (Librium) are taken by millions of people each year. These tranquilizers they can produce a cleft palate in mice, and cleft palates in humans have been reported to be four times as frequent when these tranquilizers were taken in the first 3 months of pregnancy (Goldman, 1980; Voorhees & Mollnow, 1987).

Caffeine   Caffeine, a substance present in coffee, tea, chocolate, and some soft drinks, is the drug most commonly consumed during pregnancy. Strangely, the possible effect of caffeine on the fetus has received relatively little attention. As is often the case, one of the difficulties in determining the effect of caffeine is separating its effects from the effects of other drugs, such as nicotine and alcohol. Some studies have associated caffeine use with miscarriage, premature birth, lower birth weight, irritability, and poorer muscular development and reflexes in the newborn (Dlugosz & Bracken, 1992; Eskanazi, 1993; Heller, 1987). The potential problems seem to become more likely as the amount of caffeine increases (Infante-Rivard et al., 1993).

Nicotine   Between one-fourth and one-third of the women of childbearing age in North America smoke. The effects of nicotine and cigarette smoke on the fetus have been well investigated. Smoking is known to impair the functioning of the placenta, especially oxygen exchange. The following are some risks to women who smoke while they are pregnant:

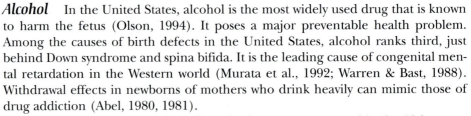

- On average, their babies are smaller.
- The likelihood of premature delivery and complications increases with the number of cigarettes they smoke per day (Cornelius et al., 1995).
- Their babies are 25 to 56% more likely to die at birth or soon thereafter (Murata et al., 1992).
- Their babies are as much as 50% more likely to develop cancer (Stjernfeldt et al., 1986).

According to longitudinal studies, detrimental effects on their children's height and reading ability may last into early adolescence (Fogelman, 1980). Other studies have found an association between a poorer performance on language and cognitive tasks and how much the mothers smoked while pregnant (Fried, O'Connell, & Watkinson, 1992). Impulsivity and attentional deficits have recently been found in 6-year-olds whose mothers smoked while pregnant (Fried, Watkinson, & Gray, 1992). Even passive exposure of pregnant, nonsmoking women to others' smoke apparently affects the growth of the fetus (Martin & Bracken, 1986).

Alcohol   In the United States, alcohol is the most widely used drug that is known to harm the fetus (Olson, 1994). It poses a major preventable health problem. Among the causes of birth defects in the United States, alcohol ranks third, just behind Down syndrome and spina bifida. It is the leading cause of congenital mental retardation in the Western world (Murata et al., 1992; Warren & Bast, 1988). Withdrawal effects in newborns of mothers who drink heavily can mimic those of drug addiction (Abel, 1980, 1981).

Although the effects of alcohol on the fetus were suspected in the 18th century, a clear picture of the consequences of chronic maternal alcoholism on the fetus did not emerge until 1973, when investigators described **fetal alcohol syndrome**, a unique set of features in the fetus caused by the mother's alcohol consumption (Jones et al., 1973). A photo of a child with this syndrome appears in Figure 5.7.

Limb and facial malformations, congenital heart disease, failure to thrive, anomalies of the external genitalia, growth retardation, mental retardation, and learning disabilities are associated with fetal alcohol syndrome. Behavior problems compound these difficulties, as infants with fetal alcohol syndrome are irritable, sleep less well, and are difficult to feed (Wekselman et al., 1995). By school age, these children are more likely to have difficulty sustaining effort and attention and to have language problems and motor-performance deficits (Larsson, Bohlin, & Tunell, 1985; Streissguth et al., 1985).

Research indicates that chronic alcohol use by the mother increases the risk to the fetus by almost 50%. Some of the effects just described, however, have been observed in infants whose mothers were not chronic alcohol users but who drank sporadically and heavily. Furthermore, the effects of alcohol can be increased by smoking and other drugs. What level of alcohol use during pregnancy is safe? One expert has cautioned against chronic use exceeding 45 drinks per month or 6 drinks at any one time; these levels double or triple the risk of congenital malformations, growth retardation, and functional abnormalities in the fetus.

The effects of relatively low levels of alcohol consumption are less clear. In one study, even alcohol consumption within the limits of what could be defined as social

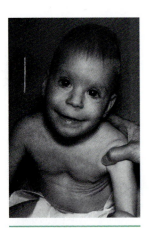

Figure 5.7
Infant born with fetal alcohol syndrome.

Fetal alcohol syndrome
A set of features in the infant caused by the mother's use of alcohol during pregnancy; typically includes facial malformations and other physical and mental disabilities.

drinking reduced alertness in newborns and their ability to habituate to a repeated stimulus, and some effects have been shown to be evident even in the teen years (Hunt et al., 1995; Streissguth et al., 1989). However, in two studies, children of low-risk women with good prenatal care who consumed less than one drink per day performed as well as the offspring of nondrinkers on tests of cognition and language and measures of attention and impulsivity (Fried, O'Connell, & Watkinson, 1992; Fried, Watkinson, & Gray, 1992).

Environmental Chemicals

The number and amount of chemicals in our environment have increased explosively since the beginning of the Industrial Revolution. Insecticides, herbicides, fungicides, solvents, detergents, food additives, and miscellaneous other chemicals have become common in our daily existence. Each year, thousands of new compounds are synthesized by industry or created as a result of reactions in the environment. It has been estimated that humans are exposed to significant amounts of approximately 5 million of these environmental chemicals. Only a small fraction of them are tested as potential teratogens in pregnant laboratory animals.

Researchers often find that chemicals are potentially teratogenic in animals, but the doses that they use are typically quite large. People generally experience comparable doses only in rare instances, such as industrial accidents or concentrated dumping (for example, in Love Canal, a former chemical dumping ground near Niagara Falls). The rates of defective births and spontaneous abortions are monitored routinely in many hospitals in the United States, providing a measure of protection against long-term chronic exposure of undiscovered teratogens. However, as we have seen, complex interactions among chemicals and delayed effects can often make detection difficult.

A clear example of the effects of environmental chemicals comes from Cubatão, a small town in an industrial valley in Brazil. Cubatão was slowly choking through pollution of its streams, air, and countryside. Thousands of tons of particulate matter were being discharged into the air from smokestacks, and huge amounts of organic matter and heavy metals were being dumped into the streams. Through an ambitious cleanup program the town reduced discharges of particulate matter by 72%, organic waste into rivers by 93%, and heavy metals by 97%. The infant mortality rate in Cubatão dropped to one-half the 1984 rate (Brooke, 1991).

Of the various chemicals present in the environment, metals have come under special scrutiny. Mercury and lead have been suspected teratogens for many years. A disaster comparable to that caused by thalidomide occurred in Japan between 1954 and 1960, when people ate fish from a bay that had been contaminated with mercury from industrial dumping. Many mothers who ate the fish gave birth to infants with severe neurological symptoms resembling cerebral palsy. Prenatal exposure to lead from automobile exhausts and lead-base paints has been implicated in miscarriages, neuromuscular problems, and mental retardation (Bellinger et al., 1986). Follow-ups of children who experienced high lead exposure as babies reveal negative effects even after 11 years on vocabulary, motor coordination, reading ability, and higher-level thinking (Needleman et al., 1990).

Another group of environmental chemicals that can harm fetuses consists of polychlorinated biphenyls (PCBs), widely used as lubricants, insulators, and ingredients in paints, varnishes, and waxes. Cooking oil used in Japan in 1968 and in Taiwan in 1979 was accidentally contaminated by PCBs, and pregnant women who used the oil were more likely to have stillborn infants and infants with darkly pigmented skin.

In the United States, PCB levels are relatively high in fish taken from Lake Michigan. Offspring of mothers who ate these fish were smaller at birth, had somewhat smaller heads, and were more likely to startle and be irritable. Babies who had detectable PCB levels in their blood at birth performed more poorly on various visual measures at both 7 months and 4 years of age (Jacobson & Jacobson, 1988; Jacobson et al., 1985; Jacobson et al., 1992). PCBs are widely distributed and appear to be well established in the food chain, though not at levels that are typically detrimental to fetuses (Rogan, 1982).

✓ *To Recap...*

Not only natural challenges, but also exposure to drugs and chemicals may pose risks to the developing embryo and fetus. Street drugs, although illegal, have become increasingly available over the past four decades and can have highly negative effects on the fetus. Babies of drug-addicted mothers may be born addicted, and they are likely to have many developmental problems. Therapeutic drugs may also be harmful, as was the case with thalidomide.

Some substances are so common in our daily lives that we may fail to think of them as drugs. Caffeine, nicotine, and alcohol are examples. No firm conclusions have been drawn regarding the effects of caffeine consumption during pregnancy, but smoking has consistently been shown to affect growth and to increase the risk of premature delivery and birth complications, and alcohol consumption can produce a range of physical malformations and intellectual consequences, including fetal alcohol syndrome.

Exposure to harmful chemicals can also occur when we take in the chemical by-products of industry through the food we eat and the air we breathe. Mercury and lead have been documented as particularly teratogenic, and PCBs also appear harmful.

Preventing, Detecting, and Treating Birth Defects

As research has furthered our knowledge of factors that can harm the fetus, agencies have become increasingly effective in alerting expectant mothers.

We noted earlier that spontaneous abortion ends fetal development in most cases in which the fetus has genetic abnormalities or a problem exists in the uterine environment. Although there are thousands of genetic abnormalities and challenges to the fetus, it is important to view these risks in perspective. More than 90% of infants are born healthy and normal, and the large majority of the remaining infants have minor problems that can be corrected or will be outgrown. Still, small percentages can translate to large numbers of people, and statistics provide little comfort to those affected. In a single year, as many as 200,000 babies may be born with birth defects in the United States, and 15 million Americans have some kind of handicap caused by a birth defect.

Can anything be done to prevent birth defects? How can a mother be sure the baby she is carrying is healthy? And how can birth defects be treated?

Prevention

At present, not all birth defects can be prevented. The causes of some are not controllable; the causes of others are not even known. Certain steps, however, can significantly lower the risk from teratogens. For example, a woman planning to become pregnant can avoid drinking alcohol, smoking, and taking unnecessary drugs, and she can eat prudently. Prenatal care is very important both for assessing risk and for monitoring the woman's progress and the fetus's development. Some experts advise women to see a physician even before they conceive (Murata et al., 1992).

Rapid progress in the area of genetics has made it possible for people to exert some control over the incidence of genetic problems. **Genetic counseling** involves a range of activities focused on determining the likelihood that a couple will conceive a child with a genetic disorder. Couples who are contemplating pregnancy often want to know the chances that their baby will be normal. DNA analysis of their blood may determine whether they are carriers of a defective dominant or recessive gene, as in the case of Tay-Sachs disease or cystic fibrosis. If one parent is a carrier of a defective dominant gene that is autosomal, the chances are 1 in 2 that their baby will be normal. If both parents are carriers of the same defective recessive gene, the chances are 3 in 4 that their baby will be healthy.

Defective genes on the sex chromosome affect the chances differently, depending on whether the fetus is a male or female and whether the mother or father is the carrier. When couples are at risk and the woman has become pregnant, parents often consider procedures for assessing whether the fetus is normal.

Screening for Abnormalities

Significant progress has been made in detecting problems in newborn infants, which opens up the possibility for early treatment. Phenylketonuria (PKU) again serves as an example. Although scientists understood at the beginning of the 1960s what caused PKU and how to treat it through diet, they had no method for determining which newborn infants had PKU. By the time they discovered the defect in a child, irreversible damage had occurred. Then, in 1961, a blood test was developed to detect excess phenylalanine in the blood. Infants with PKU were put on a special diet until they were around 7 years of age to prevent the severe retardation, seizures, and skin lesions characteristic of untreated PKU. By the late 1960s, approximately 90% of all babies in the United States were being screened at birth. Today, PKU is no longer a major health problem.

Even more dramatic advances permit parents to learn about the status of the fetus as early as 9 to 11 weeks into a pregnancy and, as we shall see, sometimes in the first days following conception.

Ultrasound Imaging **Ultrasound imaging** uses soundlike waves to provide a continuous picture of the fetus and its environment. The level of detail in this image permits identification of the sex of the fetus by 16 to 20 weeks and reveals abnormal head growth; defects of the heart, bladder, and kidneys; some chromosomal anomalies; and neural-tube defects (Anderson & Allison, 1990; Nakahara et al., 1993; Stoll et al., 1993). Ultrasound imaging is also helpful for diagnostic procedures that require collection of amniotic fluid or tissue, such as amniocentesis and chorionic villus sampling. Finally, ultrasound can determine whether there is more than one fetus.

As with many technological advances, concerns have arisen about how ultrasound imaging is used. Because China has developed a one-child policy and its citizens favor males, ultrasound imaging is being used there to determine the sex of the fetus in order to identify female fetuses for abortion. The practice is spreading in Asia, upsetting the ratio of male to female births. The ratio has reached 118.5 male per 100.0 female births in China (Kristof, 1993).

Amniocentesis An especially important tool for assessment is **amniocentesis**, because it provides samples of both the amniotic fluid and the fetal cells in it. A nee-

Genetic counseling
The practice of advising prospective parents about genetic diseases and the likelihood that they might pass on defective genetic traits to their offspring.

Ultrasound imaging
A noninvasive procedure for detecting physical defects in the fetus. A device that produces soundlike waves of energy is moved over the pregnant woman's abdomen, and reflections of these waves form an image of the fetus.

Amniocentesis
A procedure for collecting cells that lie in the amniotic fluid surrounding the fetus. A needle is passed through the mother's abdominal wall into the amniotic sac to gather discarded fetal cells. These cells can be examined for chromosomal and genetic defects.

Ultrasound imaging permits identification of abnormalities in the developing fetus, as well as of other characteristics, such as gender, size, and position.

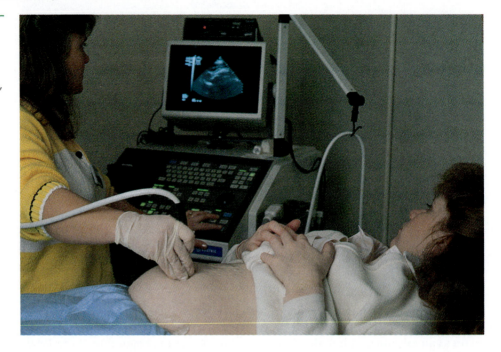

dle is passed through the mother's abdomen and into the amniotic cavity to collect the fluid. Analysis of the fluid can reveal abnormalities. For example, alpha-feto protein (FEP), a substance the fetus produces, circulates in the amniotic fluid. Abnormally high levels of FEP occur when the fetus has certain types of damage to the brain, the central nervous system, or the liver and kidneys. Chromosomal analysis of the fetal cells can also detect problems.

Women over the age of 35 frequently opt to have amniocentesis because of their heightened risk of having babies with Down syndrome, a defect that shows up in a chromosomal cell analysis. Interestingly, awareness of the risk associated with maternal age, coupled with the availability of amniocentesis and the option of terminating pregnancy, has completely changed the maternal age distribution of Down syndrome births. Now, 80% of babies with Down syndrome are delivered to mothers under age 35, because amniocentesis is not a routine procedure for these women (Behrman & Vaughan, 1987). Fetal cells can also be tested for genetic defects such as sickle-cell anemia, cystic fibrosis, and Duchenne muscular dystrophy (Winston & Handyside, 1993). The list of detectable diseases lengthens almost daily with increasing knowledge of which genes produce particular diseases.

The amniocentesis procedure does have its drawbacks. It increases the risk of miscarriage by around 0.5 percent (Cunningham, MacDonald, & Gant, 1989). Also, amniocentesis is most effective after the period during which abortion is safest for the mother. Chorionic villus sampling, a relatively new procedure, can make information about the fetus available much earlier.

Chorionic villus sampling (CVS)

A procedure for gathering fetal cells earlier in pregnancy than is possible through amniocentesis. A tube is passed through the vagina and cervix so that fetal cells can be gathered at the site of the developing placenta.

Chorionic Villus Sampling   In a procedure called **chorionic villus sampling (CVS)**, cells are collected from the chorion, a part of the placenta. A small tube is inserted through the cervix and into the fetal placenta to collect a sample of fetal cells. These cells reveal large-scale defects of the chromosomes or more minute defects in the DNA. CVS is possible as early as 9 to 11 weeks, but carries a slightly higher risk of miscarriage than amniocentesis, around 2% (Cunningham et al., 1989).

Test-Tube Screening   Scientists have succeeded in screening embryos in the test tube before they are implanted in the mother's uterus. Egg cells are collected from the mother and then fertilized in a petri dish through in vitro fertilization. One cell is removed from each embryo when it reaches the eight-cell stage. From this one cell, the sex of the embryo can be determined, and, within a few hours, the DNA of the cell can be checked for suspected anomalies.

Chloe O'Brien, born in the United Kingdom in April 1992, was the first baby to be born after in vitro fertilization following DNA analysis before implantation. The parents were carriers of the cystic fibrosis gene. If they had conceived in the normal fashion and had discovered that their fetus had cystic fibrosis by the other techniques described, they would have faced a decision on abortion. By this technique, they were assured that the embryo that was implanted was free of this disease. Chloe is doing fine (Fogle, 1992; Handyside et al., 1992).

It is possible to detect almost 200 disorders through various screening techniques. However, only around 10% of women who have at-risk pregnancies participate in prenatal screening. The risk of problem pregnancy is higher for a woman who (1) has had miscarriages or has had children with congenital disorders, (2) is outside the optimal childbearing age range, (3) has relatives (or is carrying a child whose biological father has relatives) with genetic abnormalities, (4) is poor and has inadequate medical supervision and nutrition, or (5) takes drugs during pregnancy.

Applications
A Population Approach to Genetic Screening

A highly successful program of genetic population screening has demonstrated the value of a well-publicized effort to inform parents of reproductive risks. The program, the first of its kind, was initiated in 1970 to identify carriers of Tay-Sachs disease. This disorder is carried as a recessive gene in about 1 of 29 American Jews. If two carriers mate, 1 of 4 of their children, on average, will have Tay-Sachs disease.

The effort to identify carriers, begun through a community education and neighborhood-based screening campaign in the Baltimore, Maryland–Washington, D.C., area, had tested more than 354,000 Jewish adults by 1981. Virtually all couples identified as carriers elected to have amniocentesis during their pregnancies, which numbered 912 by 1981, and 202 fetuses were diagnosed as having Tay-Sachs. All but 13 of these pregnancies were voluntarily terminated by the parents; the babies born to the remaining 13 were afflicted with Tay-Sachs, as predicted. The incidence of this fatal disease was thus reduced by 65 to 75% over the prior decade (Kaback, 1982).

In 1990, a similar program on a much larger scale was contemplated to screen parents for cystic fibrosis. The Tay-Sachs program had targeted 1 to 2 million people, but geneticists were considering screening the entire U.S. population of reproductive age—perhaps 100 to 200 million people. One in 25 Caucasians is a carrier of cystic fibrosis, which puts the level of risk in the general population near the level of risk for Tay-Sachs in American Jews. Current tests can identify about 70% of cystic fibrosis carriers, and efforts are under way to develop techniques for identifying the remaining 30% (Roberts, 1990).

Many ethical issues arise from our increasing skill in fetal screening. Should damaged fetuses be aborted? If so, how disabling must the genetic defect be? If a child is diagnosed as genetically damaged as a fetus, should insurance companies be able to deny the child insurance, given that the companies know that health expenses will be exorbitant compared with those of other children?

Treatment

The growing sophistication of diagnostic procedures has made early detection of developmental abnormalities more likely. But what happens when a fetus is found to be developing abnormally? The parents may decide to terminate the pregnancy, but there may be treatment alternatives. Developments in the medical treatment of fetuses parallel the rapid advances in early diagnosis. Current approaches to prenatal treatment fall into three categories: medical therapy, surgery, and genetic manipulation.

Medical Therapy   Medical therapy is currently the most widely available of the three methods. An example is providing extra vitamins to the mother when enzyme deficiencies are discovered in the blood of the fetus.

An exciting first in medical therapy was reported in mid-1989. Parents in Lyons, France, whose first child had died in infancy of a hereditary disorder, learned that the fetus the mother was carrying had the same disorder, involving an immune deficiency that leaves the infant open to almost any infection. Doctors decided to try to treat the fetus in the womb. They injected immune cells from the thymus and liver of two aborted fetuses into the umbilical cord, the first time this had been done. After the baby was born, the injected cells multiplied, as the doctors had hoped (Elmer-DeWitt, 1994).

Researchers recently discovered that women who have AIDS are less likely to pass the disease on to their fetuses if they have certain antibodies in their blood. It may be possible to immunize AIDS-carrying pregnant mothers to increase the number of these antibodies (Stephens, 1990).

Surgery   The use of fetal surgery is illustrated by the experience of a pregnant woman who had earlier given birth to an infant with hydrocephaly, an abnormal accumulation of fluid inside the skull that results in brain damage. An ultrasound diagnosis indicated that the fetus was accumulating fluid on the brain and would likely suffer brain damage if treatment was delayed until birth. Surgeons at the University of Colorado Medical School, working through a long, hollow tube inserted through the mother's abdomen and the amniotic sac, inserted a small valve in the back of the fetus's head to permit the excess fluid to drain, thereby relieving pressure on the brain. The fetus survived the surgery and, at 16 months of age, appeared to be normal (Clewell et al., 1982; Fadiman, 1983).

Physicians are now able to carry out surgery on fetuses to avoid the damage caused by blockage of the urinary tract and a small number of other problems (Ohlendorf-Moffat, 1991). In the near future, fetuses who have a neural-tube defect may also be treatable. Neural-tube defects often result in infants' being born with an opening in the back of the head through which part of the brain protrudes. The current treatment involves removing the external brain tissue and closing the skull after birth, which often leaves the infant blind and mentally retarded.

Working with monkeys, researchers at the National Institute of Child Health and Human Development have operated on fetuses by removing them from the uterus and conducting a similar operation, as shown in Figure 5.8. Apparently, the brain tissue at least partially regenerates, because the monkey fetuses, carried to term, are able to see. This treatment may someday be available for human fetuses.

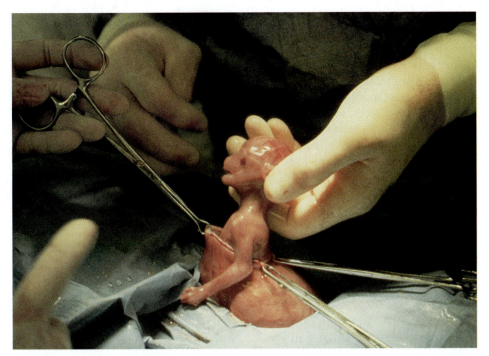

Figure 5.8
Brain surgery on a monkey fetus. The fetus was taken halfway out of the uterus for the procedure and then replaced to continue development inside the mother.

Genetic Engineering   Probably the greatest promise for prenatal treatment lies in the field of genetic engineering. Suppose we could detect, say, the lack of an enzyme in a fetus's blood and could identify the specific gene that caused the defect. Working in the laboratory with a blood sample from the fetus, we would clip out the defective gene and insert a synthetic gene. After producing many copies of the blood cells containing the repaired chromosome, we would inject them into the fetus, where they would survive and replicate and provide sufficient amounts of the enzyme for normal development.

In September 1990, scientists undertook the first federally approved attempt at human gene therapy of this kind. It involved a 4-year-old girl who suffered from ADA deficiency, a severe and incurable disease of the immune system. Cells were extracted from the girl, and harmless viruses were used to carry the needed ADA gene into the cells. The cells—a billion or so—were then reinjected into the child's bloodstream. The cells are producing the needed ADA, but the child will need repeated treatments. Scientists are working on techniques to make repeated treatments unnecessary by carrying out similar procedures during the fetal stage. They will try to replace the cells in the fetus that give rise to all the ADA-producing cells; thus these cells will not die during the lifetime of the patient (Capecchi, 1994; Karson, Polvino, & Anderson, 1992).

Ethical Considerations

The ability to diagnose abnormal development raises innumerable ethical questions—questions that people may find difficult to answer. Today's fetal-screening techniques can detect the presence of sickle-cell anemia, Huntington's chorea, Down syndrome, cystic fibrosis, and numerous other maladies. What are the consequences of this knowledge? If no treatment is possible, the options are to terminate the pregnancy or to bring a child with a serious disorder into the world.

Increasingly, special-interest groups and the federal government have become involved in this decision process. Movements to prevent the use of federal or state funds for abortions, and some that would make any abortion illegal, are underway. Proponents of these movements argue from a moral and ethical pro-life perspective. Opponents emphasize the individual mother's right to make a personal, moral, and ethical choice. Opponents also point out that prohibitions would discriminate against poorer citizens, who may not have personal funds to pay for abortion.

In a related area, two successive U.S. presidents have made different decisions regarding research on the use of aborted fetal tissue to treat various illnesses. President George Bush banned research with fetal tissue, and President Bill Clinton lifted this ban soon after he took office. Those who oppose such research argue that women might seek more abortions in order to sell their fetuses for research. Others claim that this is extremely unlikely and that the research could lead to humanitarian treatments for those who have debilitating diseases, such as Parkinson's, for whom fetal tissue provides the best hope.

The treatment of newborn infants with severe disorders is a controversial issue as well, as in the case of Baby Jane Doe. On October 11, 1983, on Long Island, Baby Jane Doe was born with hydrocephalus, spina bifida, and microcephaly. Her parents had two options. They could approve two operations, after which it was likely that she would live past age 20 but be paralyzed, severely retarded, and in pain; or they could refuse to permit surgery, in which case she would likely die before the age of 3. They chose not to allow surgery. But others felt it was not the parents' choice to make alone. Most significantly, the U.S. Justice Department, for the first time, sued on behalf of the medical rights of an infant with a disability. Ultimately, the U.S. Supreme Court ruled against the government and with the parents' right to choose (Holden, 1986).

Decisions regarding the health and life of a fetus or infant are intensely emotional and deeply embedded in social, ethical, and moral convictions. They are also very personal. As new technologies are developed, the fine line that separates these personal beliefs and feelings on the one side, and the government's role in protecting the rights of fetuses and infants on the other, may become increasingly blurred.

✓ *To Recap...*

We have progressed dramatically in our understanding of prenatal diseases and in our ability to diagnose and treat them. In some cases, the most useful approach is prevention, perhaps through genetic counseling.

During pregnancy, diagnostic procedures provide a window on prenatal development that was unknown only a few decades ago. Ultrasound imaging can detect growth anomalies, such as abnormal head growth. Amniocentesis and chorionic villus sampling provide fetal cells that can be analyzed for chromosomal defects and several genetic problems, as well as some other disorders. Screening has even been carried out on embryos in test tubes. When problems are detected, treatment can sometimes proceed even while the fetus is still in the uterus. Medical therapy is one possibility, as when there are chemical imbalances. Surgery is a second possibility. On the horizon is the possibility of gene therapy.

As we become more skilled at understanding genetics, screening for and diagnosing problems, and developing treatment alternatives, however, individuals and society at large face a new array of ethical dilemmas.

Conclusion

We live at a time when knowledge and technology in many fields are expanding at a dizzying pace. Nowhere are the effects of progress more dramatic than in biology and health-related fields. The field of prenatal development has benefited enormously from these advances.

Only relatively recently have we developed an understanding of the processes of conception and embryological development. It has been especially important for us to learn that differentiation of body parts and limbs occurs in the first 8 weeks or so after conception. With this knowledge, we have been better able to understand why infections and certain drugs have more devastating effects on the organism during the early prenatal period than later.

Our awareness that the placenta does not always filter out chemicals and toxins from the mother's blood and that these substances thus enter the bloodstream of the fetus has had profound effects. Scientists actively look for causes of abnormal development that were previously ignored. Environmental pollutants, drugs, and other chemicals are suspect, and it is now routine to test new chemicals for toxic effects on the fetus. The new field of psychoteratology may provide even more sensitive indicators of harmful substances. Although we may not always know how or why these substances affect the fetus, at least we are learning when they do. Partly because of this knowledge, the ratio of birth deaths to live births in the United States has reached an all-time low.

An important message from this information is that the baby is in an environment from the moment of conception. By the time of birth, interactions between genes and the environment have been at play during the full 9 months of development.

One might come away from this chapter fearful about all the things that threaten a baby's prenatal development. Keep in mind, though, that the very large majority of babies are born healthy and intact. Fortunately, as we have learned about the dangers that the fetus faces, we have been increasingly able to take precautions that will increase the likelihood that the newborn will get a healthy start.

Visual Summary for Chapter 5:
Prenatal Development

Stages of Prenatal Development

Period	Duration	Major Events of the Period
Zygote	Conception to 2nd week	At conception a zygote is formed, combining the 23 chromosomes from the father with the 23 chromosomes from the mother. The zygote becomes fully implanted in the uterus by the end of the second week.
Embryo	3rd to 8th week	All major internal and external structures, as well as support structures needed for protection and growth, form during this period.
Fetus	9th to 38th week	Development of the organ structures formed in the embryonic period continues, and the fetus increases in size and weight. The age of viability is considered to be 23 to 24 weeks of age.

Teratology: History, Principles, and Natural Events

Six Principles of How Teratogens Act

➡ 1. A teratogen's effect depends on the genetic makeup of the organism.

➡ 2. A teratogen's effect depends partly on timing.

➡ 3. The effect may be unique to the teratogen.

➡ 4. The effect may include death or serious disorders.

➡ 5. Teratogens gain access to the fetus in different ways.

➡ 6. The effect of a teratogen increases with the level of exposure to it.

Natural Challenges to the Health of the Embryo and Fetus

Challenge	Effect
Infectious Diseases	Diseases such as rubella, herpes, HIV, syphilis, and gonorrhea have the potential to harm a developing embryo or fetus.
Malnutrition	Maternal malnutrition may be associated with deficits in size of the brain and major internal organs in the fetus, small and premature babies, and increased rates of spontaneous abortion, infant death, and congenital defects.
Maternal Experiences and Stress	Maternal stress may be associated with abnormalities in the newborn, although more research is needed in this area.
Parental Age	Both the mother's and father's age are associated with increased risk for certain chromosomal or genetic abnormalities. Teenage mothers are also at higher risk for having premature or underweight babies, although the reasons may primarily involve socioeconomic factors.

Teratology: Drugs and Environmental Chemicals

Teratogen	Consequence
Street Drugs	Babies of drug-addicted mothers may be born addicted and are likely to have many developmental problems.
Therapeutic Drugs	Therapeutic drugs may also be harmful to the fetus, as was the case with thalidomide.
Caffeine	Some studies suggest risk associated with caffeine.
Nicotine	Can affect growth and can increase the risk of premature delivery and birth complications.
Alcohol	Can produce physical malformations and intellectual deficits, including fetal alcohol syndrome.
Environmental Chemicals	Mercury, lead, and PCBs appear to be harmful to the fetus.

Preventing, Detecting, and Treating Birth Defects

Methods of Screening for Abnormalities in the Fetus

Method	Description
Ultrasound Imaging	Uses soundlike waves to provide a continuous picture of the fetus and its environment. Can detect certain growth abnormalities.
Amniocentesis	Examines a sample of the amniotic fluid and the fetal cells contained in it. Can identify chromosomal defects and several genetic problems.
Chorionic Villus Sampling	Examines fetal cells collected from a sample of the chorion, a part of the placenta. Can identify chromosomal defects and several genetic problems.
Test-tube Screening	Embryos that are the result of in vitro fertilization can be screened for DNA abnormalities before being implanted into the mother's uterus.

Treatment of Abnormalities in the Fetus

Treatment of abnormalities in the fetus can involve in utero medical therapy or surgery. Genetic engineering holds promise as a treatment in the future.

Chapter 6

Physical Development: Birth, Motor Skills, and Growth

So-called miracles of medical science seem almost commonplace today. Even so, the birth of septuplets to an Iowa woman on November 19, 1997, took the world by surprise. The babies, four boys and three girls, were the first set of septuplets born alive in the United States.

The more fetuses a woman is carrying, the greater the risk to each one; so the risk with seven is extremely high. The only other known set of septuplets born alive in the world were born in Saudi Arabia earlier in 1997, and three of those babies died within a month of their birth. In the United States, no septuplets had been born since 1985. Of those septuplets, one was stillborn, three died within weeks, and the remaining three had medical and developmental problems. In contrast, the Iowa septuplets, born about 2 months prematurely, seemed surprisingly healthy. One doctor who helped deliver the babies said that they were "so well grown, so well developed, it just strikes me as a miracle."

But this miracle didn't happen without help. Advances not only in fertility treatments but also in prenatal and neonatal care made the pregnancy and the successful delivery possible. Bobbi McCaughey, the babies' mother, had been taking a fertility drug when the septuplets were conceived, and her pregnancy was carefully monitored by specialists. After the ninth week, she remained in bed. For a month before the babies' delivery, she was confined to a hospital.

At the 31st week—9 weeks short of the 40 weeks for a full-term pregnancy—doctors decided to deliver the babies when Mrs. McCaughey began having contractions. A team of more than 40 specialists were on hand for the delivery, which was performed by cesarean section. The babies ranged in size from 2.5 to 3.4 lb—normal for their gestational age, which is unusual in multiple pregnancies, but still small enough to require a long hospital stay and special treatment. In all, experts estimated that the cost of medical attention for mother and babies would reach $1 million.

Although septuplets are extremely rare, multiple births in general have become much more common as more and more women are using fertility drugs that increase the number of eggs produced in a single cycle. In the United States, the number of multiple births involving three or more babies has quadrupled since the 1970s. The high cost of medical care in many of these cases—and, more important, the high cost in terms of risk to the health of both the mother and the fetuses—has raised serious ethical questions. Is the promise of a medical miracle worth the cost and the risk? Should controls be placed on technology in this area? Debate on such questions is sure to continue as more multiple births occur.

We begin this chapter by examining the birth process, including the problems some newborns face, and how medical science has learned to deal with them.

*T*his chapter focuses on the child's physical development, beginning at birth and continuing through adolescence. Physical development involves more than just growth, although that is certainly an important part of it. We will also see how a baby acquires the motor skills to manipulate objects and to explore the environment, skills that have enormous psychological impact on development.

Psychological and physical growth depend crucially on the maturation of the brain, so we devote part of our discussion to how the brain develops and operates. Finally, we examine the physical changes during adolescence that prepare the body for reproduction but that also can affect the individual's self-image and identity.

Birth and the Perinatal Period

Our story starts with birth and its surrounding events—the **perinatal period**. Birth is truly a momentous event, as the child moves from a relatively sheltered and protected environment to the busy and much-less-predictable outside world, where the remainder of development will occur.

Perinatal period
The events and environment surrounding the birth process.

Typically, the birth process proceeds smoothly. In this technological age, we sometimes forget that humans have accomplished this feat over millions of years without hospitals, doctors, or elaborate equipment. Occasionally, however, modern technology is crucial for making the process work and even for saving the baby's life. After briefly describing the physical aspects of birth, we consider problems that can arise and the notion of infants at risk.

Labor and Delivery

Typically around 38 weeks after fertilization, a pregnant woman will go into labor, the first step in the birth process. Labor appears to be initiated by changes in the fetal brain (Nathanielsz, 1995). Chemicals are released that signal the muscles of the mother's uterus to start contracting rhythmically, initially every 15 to 20 minutes and then at shorter and shorter intervals. The complete birth process requires about 8 to 16 hours for the first baby and about half as much for later babies.

Labor consists of three stages, shown in Figure 6.1. The first and longest stage begins when the early contractions start to narrow the uterus and dilate (widen) the cervical opening through which the baby will pass. This stage ends when the cervix is fully dilated, usually about 10 cm. By the end of this stage, the contractions are very intense, occurring every 2–3 minutes. The second stage begins when the fetus starts to pass through the cervix and ends when the baby has been completely delivered into the world. During this stage, the contractions are long and closely spaced and the mother is encouraged to assist the process by pushing with each contrac-

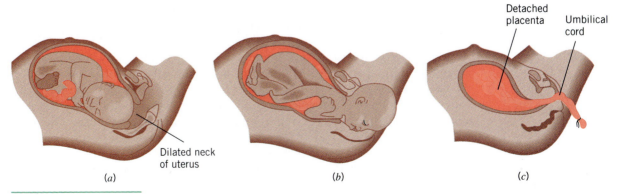

(a) (b) (c)

Figure 6.1
The three stages of labor: (a) the neck of the uterus dilates; (b) the baby is delivered; and (c) the placenta is expelled.

tion. The third stage, which often lasts only minutes, involves the delivery of the placenta and related other membranes, referred to as the *afterbirth.*

Technological advances permit the monitoring of the fetus's state during birth. Physicians can visualize the fetus, the umbilical cord, and the placenta by ultrasound to determine, for example, whether there is a danger that the umbilical cord will wrap around the fetus's neck (which can cause strangulation). They also can record electronically the heart rate and activity of the fetus through the mother's abdomen to determine whether there are signs of **fetal distress**, which would be indicated by an abnormally high or low heart rate (Anderson & Allison, 1990).

Fetal distress
A condition of abnormal stress in the fetus, reflected during the birth process in an abnormal fetal heart rate.

Cesarean section
Surgical delivery of the fetus directly from the uterus; performed when normal delivery is prohibited.

Sometimes birth cannot proceed according to nature's plan because, for example, the baby is lying in an unusual position in the uterus (such as sideways or buttocks down), delivery is proceeding too slowly, or the baby's head is too large to pass through the cervical opening. In such cases, the doctor often elects to perform a **cesarean section**, in which the baby is surgically removed directly from the uterus. The rate of cesarean deliveries skyrocketed from 5% in 1969 to 25% in 1990. Some critics charged that many of these procedures were performed for unjustifiable reasons, such as greater convenience for doctors or reduced risk of malpractice suits (Guillemin, 1993; Van Tuinen & Wolfe, 1993). Perhaps because of such criticism the rate fell back to 22% in 1993, and many public health officials are working toward having it decrease to about 15% by the year 2000 (Clarke & Taffel, 1995; Paul & Miller, 1995).

Although the stages of birth are the same in all cultures, there are many variations in how cultures think about and deal with birth. Practices have changed fairly rapidly in the United States. For instance, as recently as 1972, only 27% of U.S. hospitals permitted fathers or other family members in the delivery room. By 1980, 80% of U.S. hospitals had an open policy, and today very few do not.

Applications
Cultural Attitudes toward Birth

It has been said that in most Western countries, pregnancy, labor, and delivery are treated as if they were the symptoms of an illness. Pregnant women are encouraged to visit the doctor regularly. Most give birth in a hospital, lying down (some say for the convenience of the doctor), and having been given drugs to block pain. Often, after the baby is born doctors and nurses, not the baby's mother, take over the baby's care, at least for a while. Fortunately, this view of pregnancy and birth has begun to give way to a more realistic understanding that these processes are both normal and healthy.

Has Western civilization been unique in looking at pregnancy as a sort of disability and birth as a process requiring medical intervention? Not entirely. Among the Cuna Indians of Panama, for example, a pregnant woman must visit the medicine man daily for herbal medicines and women are given medication throughout labor. Various interventions during labor are practiced in many cultures: The pregnant woman's abdomen may be massaged, perhaps with masticated roots or melted butter, or even constricted to help push the baby out. For difficult cases, midwives of Myanmar (formerly Burma) tread on the woman's abdomen with their feet.

Nevertheless, the attitude of the West is often contrasted with that of cultures in which birth is seen as an everyday occurrence. Among the Jarara of South America, for example, labor and birth are so much a part of daily life that a woman may give birth in a passageway or shelter in view of everyone. In many cultures,

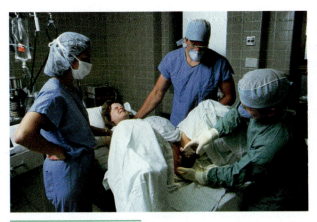 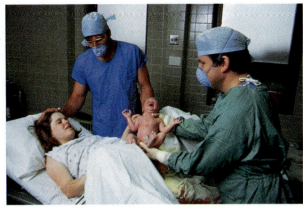

In Western society, birth typically takes place in a hospital with the mother lying on her back. Medication for pain, once administered routinely, has given way to more natural methods of dealing with the physical discomfort.

women give birth alone. And non-Western women commonly deliver in an upright position—kneeling, sitting, squatting, and even standing—rather than lying down (Mead & Newton, 1967).

There has been a trend in the West toward making birth more "natural." An English obstetrician, Grantly Dick-Read, wrote a book called *Natural Childbirth* in 1933 and a second, called *Childbirth without Fear*, in 1944 to put forth the view that Western societies had created an association between childbirth and pain. Fear of pain, he said, actually created tension and muscle cramping that produced pain unnecessarily. These ideas were reinforced by Dr. F. Lamaze in *Painless Childbirth* (1970). Lamaze's popular method of preparation for childbirth is based on conditioning through breathing and muscle exercises and on educating the mother about pregnancy and labor.

A parallel movement has emphasized the baby's experience of birth. In *Birth without Violence* (1975), Dr. F. Leboyer argued that the infant's transition into the outside world—already stressful because of the birth process itself—should not be made more difficult by bright lights, noise, and insensitive handling. Leboyer introduced a more gentle approach to limit the assault on the baby's senses—a darkened and quiet room, gentle massage, and a warm bath.

Other, related obstetric practices have emerged in recent years. One involves having the father present during the birth process, sometimes serving as the mother's breathing coach. Another is a return to giving birth at home, often with the assistance of a trained midwife rather than a doctor (O'Connor, 1993; Vedam & Kolodjii, 1995).

Is the naturalist trend right? Research in this field is inadequate at this point to allow us to draw any firm conclusions about what might be best for the mother or the baby. Maybe the truly remarkable fact is that mothers and newborns usually survive the birth process just fine, whatever the rituals with which their cultures surround them.

Culture also affects the likelihood that the mother will survive pregnancy and childbirth. In the United States, because of improved health care, maternal deaths per 100,000 pregnant women fell from approximately 660 in 1931 to 7.4 in 1986.

Table 6.1
U.S. Infant Mortality Rates 1915–1995 (deaths in the first year per 1,000 live births)

Year	*African-Americans*	*Whites*	*All Races*
1915	150.4	92.8	95.7
1925	105.3	65.0	69.0
1935	80.1	49.2	53.2
1945	56.2	35.6	38.3
1955	43.1	23.6	26.4
1965	41.7	21.5	24.7
1975	26.2	14.2	16.1
1985	18.2	9.3	10.6
1995	15.1	6.3	7.6

Source: Based on information from U.S. Department of Health and Human Services, National Center for Health Statistics, Vital Statistics of the United States, 1995, and Monthly Vital Statistics Reports from 1996.

But around the world even today, 500,000 women each year lose their lives from complications of pregnancy and labor. In Nigeria, for example, the death rate is still 800 per 100,000.

Often, health-care facilities simply are not available to pregnant women, or transportation to health facilities is a problem. But sometimes a cultural clash is the issue. A dramatic example comes from an area in Ghana that has a large population of Muslim refugees from Mali. It is the Muslim women's custom to wear long black dresses. For native Ghanans, however, the color black symbolizes evil and death. As a result, the local hospitals do not admit women dressed in black and try to get them to change their dress. The Muslim women resist these attempts and simply refuse to go to the hospitals, thus they often do not receive necessary care.

Babies face hazards during the birth process as well, and some do not survive. Scientists and physicians have devoted enormous efforts to addressing these problems and are making good progress. As shown in Table 6.1, infant mortality rates in the United States have dropped markedly in recent years, although less so for African-Americans than for whites. Still, in 1993, 21 countries had newborn mortality rates lower than that of the United States (Wegman, 1994).

The Concept of Risk

Parents worry about whether their baby will be normal. In more than 9 of 10 cases, the baby is born on time and healthy. But some parents and their babies are not so fortunate. Approximately 3% of all babies born in the United States each year—120,000 or so infants—are born with major physical malformations.

At risk
Describes babies who have a higher likelihood than other babies of experiencing developmental problems.

Whereas some babies have immediately obvious physical problems, other babies are considered **at risk** for developmental delays and cognitive and social problems. Psychologists believe that the earlier they can identify these babies, the earlier they can intervene to help. Thus, over the past few decades, hundreds of studies have attempted to discover what factors put infants in the highest category of risk. Three indicators seem to be most important: maternal and family characteristics, the physical compromise of the newborn, and the performance of the newborn on behavioral assessments.

Maternal and Family Characteristics   A baby's chances of developing problems can be predicted in part from the family context in which the child is born.

Around 85% of the risk of severe developmental problems can be attributed to what happens in the prenatal period. As mentioned in the preceding chapter, several maternal factors increase risk for the fetus, including the mother's use of drugs or alcohol, exposure to viral infections during pregnancy, smoking, and poor nutrition (Chomitz, Cheung, & Lieberman, 1995). A major factor in the United States is the failure of the mother to seek prenatal care from a physician. Of mothers who saw a doctor at any time during pregnancy, only 6% had babies with low birth weights, whereas the figure was 3.5 times greater for mothers who did not see a doctor (Bronfenbrenner, 1989).

Low birth weight is an important indicator of risk. We have already seen that the incidence of infant mortality is higher among African-Americans than among whites. So, too, is the incidence of low birth weight. This situation may reflect the fact that whereas only about 20% of pregnant white women fail to see a doctor in the first 3 months of pregnancy, the comparable figure for African-American women is 38% (Halpern, 1993; Kopp & Kaler, 1989).

Failure to see a doctor is in part attributable to lack of financial resources available to the mother. Financial problems increase the likelihood of low birth weight sixfold (Binsacca et al., 1987). Babies born to families who have strained financial resources, poor social support, and little education are more at risk than are those born to more advantaged families. One set of experts recently made the following projection of the percent of newborn babies that will face various risk factors by the year 2000 (Barnard, Morisset, & Spieker, 1993, p. 386):

Not wanted (12%)

Born at low birth weight and/or premature (7%)

Mothers are substance abusers (11%)

Parents are alcoholics (10%)

Mothers are teenagers (10%)

Mothers are not married (30%)

Mothers have not completed high school (20%)

Family income is below the federal poverty line (23%)

Physical Compromise of the Newborn   A second general indicator of risk is evidence of physical problems in the newborn, most frequently, low birth weight. Around 6 to 7% of the babies born in the United States each year (around 250,000) have a low birth weight, below 2,500 gr (about 5.5 lb). And low-birth-weight babies are about 40 times more likely to die in the first month of life than are babies with normal birth weight (Freda et al., 1990; Paneth, 1995). They also are at greater risk for many problems, large and small (Hack, Klein, & Taylor, 1995). Why is this so?

The newborn must make a number of adaptations to the outside world. Temperature control and nutrition are no longer provided by the mother's body, but these needs are rather easily met by the parents or other providers. Breathing, however, is a different story. After living in a water world for almost 9 months, the baby must draw the first breath of air within seconds after birth. Babies with low birth weight are more likely to have difficulty initiating or maintaining breathing. Failure to breathe prevents the delivery of oxygen to cells—a condition called **anoxia**—which can cause the cells to die. The brain cells are especially sensitive to oxygen deficits. Severe anoxia, for example, may damage the brain area that controls movement of the limbs, resulting in a spastic-type movement referred to as cerebral palsy (Vaughn, McKay, & Behrman, 1984).

Anoxia
A deficit of oxygen to the cells, which can produce brain or other tissue damage.

Preterm
Describes babies born
before the end of the
normal gestation period.

Low-birth-weight babies may be placed in two groups. One comprises babies whose birth weights are low because they were born **preterm**, meaning before the end of the normal 38 weeks of pregnancy. Preterm babies often have the breathing problems just described. In many, tiny blood vessels in the brain burst, causing bleeding and contributing to the infant's risk.

Even disregarding these physical challenges, development in the preterm baby may lag behind that in a full-term baby, at least for a time. Although we would expect the preterm infant, who is comparable to a fetus still in the womb, to be less advanced than the full-term baby, even when matched for the number of days following fertilization, the preterm infant usually has less mature brain patterns and is more disorganized and difficult to soothe (Als, Duffy, & McAnulty, 1988; Duffy, Als, & McAnulty, 1990). Longer term, these babies can be expected to have more frequent problems with growth and overall health issues. Studies indicate that by the elementary school years, preterm infants, especially boys, are at greater risk for both behavior and academic problems (Hack et al., 1995).

Small for gestational age (SGA)
Describes babies born at
a weight in the bottom
10% of babies of a particular gestational age.

The other group of babies born with a low birth weight are those whose fetal growth was retarded. These babies are considered **small for gestational age** (**SGA**). They may be born at the expected gestational age of 9 months, or they may be born earlier (and so be both SGA *and* preterm), but they are in this category because their weight places them among the bottom 10% of babies born at that particular gestational age. Although the cause is frequently unknown, several factors appear to increase the likelihood that a baby's prenatal growth will be delayed, including chromosomal abnormalities, infections, poor maternal nutrition, and maternal substance abuse.

SGA babies generally face fewer developmental risks than do preterm babies (Wilcox & Skjoerven, 1992), but some problems can be expected. For example, these infants do not arouse easily, and they tend to have poor muscle tone, appearing limp when held. They also are disadvantaged beyond the newborn period; for example, they show poorer recognition memory than do babies born at normal weight (Gotlieb, Baisini, & Bray, 1988). SGA babies who are preterm perform more poorly on verbal tests of IQ as preschoolers than do preterm babies whose weights were appropriate for their ages, although their eventual developmental course depends heavily on the quality of their postbirth environment (Dowling & Bendell, 1988; Gorman & Pollitt, 1992).

Steady improvement in technology has produced a dramatic decline in deaths resulting from low birth weight. Although a birth weight below 2,500 g (5.5 lb) is classified as low, babies weighing only 500 g (a little more than 1 lb) have at least a 25% chance of living, and the odds rise to more than 90% for babies who weigh at least 1,000 g (about 2.2 lb) (Minde, 1993).

Much of this progress can be attributed to the development of neonatal intensive care units (NICUs). In these facilities, low-birth-weight babies receive various forms of stimulation—rocking, sound recordings of the mother's heartbeat, high-contrast mobiles, gentle massage, and the like—which appear to assist their early development (Field, 1995; Mueller, 1996; Thoman, 1993). One consequence of these interventions is that very tiny babies who would once have died at birth are now kept alive. These babies, however, face strong challenges to life and well-being; the lighter the baby, the higher these risks.

Physical and Behavioral Assessment   A third indicator of risk is poor performance on standard assessments. Perhaps as a sign of things to come, almost all babies born in the United States begin life with a test. Tests are used to screen babies for disorders, to determine whether a baby's nervous system is intact, and to characterize how a newborn responds to social and physical stimuli. Even though newborns are new to the external world, they possess a surprising range of behaviors and functions. Newborn tests can assess more than 85% of such behaviors and functions (Francis, Self, & Horowitz, 1987). Here we consider the most often used tests: the Apgar exam, the Prechtl test, and the Brazelton Neonatal Behavioral Assessment Scale.

In 1953, Dr. Virginia Apgar introduced a test that permitted obstetricians to record objectively the status of the newborn. This test has become the standard for the baby's first assessment. The *Apgar exam* focuses on five of the newborn's vital functions, which are measured by heart rate, respiration, muscle tone, response to a mildly painful stimulus, and skin color. The newborn receives a score from 0 to 2 on each of these items. For example, the baby earns a 2 for the heart-rate category if the heart beats 100–140 times per minute; a 1 if the rate is less than 100; and a 0 if no beat is detectable. Babies are typically assessed on the five categories almost immediately after birth and then again 5 minutes later. The highest possible score is 10. On average, about 77% of newborns receive a score of 8–10, 17% a score of 3–7, and 6% a score of 0–2 (Apgar, 1953).

Investigators use the Apgar to identify babies who may need special monitoring and attention through early infancy. Several factors tend to lower the Apgar score, including maternal depression, anxiety, smoking, drinking, and labor medication. Psychologists have examined the relation between a newborn's Apgar score and intellectual functioning later in infancy and early childhood. The results have been mixed. Some investigators have reported a positive relation, but others report no relation when socioeconomic status, race, and gender are taken into consideration (Francis et al., 1987).

Low Apgar scores have also been related to sudden infant death syndrome (SIDS), defined as the sudden death of any infant under 1 year of age that cannot be explained by any physical or medical cause (Willinger, James, & Catz, 1991). SIDS is the leading cause of death among infants younger than 12 months, peaking between 2 and 4 months of age (Dwyer & Ponsonby, 1995; Guntheroth, 1995). Although the definitive cause of the disorder is unknown, effective preventive measures include placing babies on their backs to sleep; keeping them away from pillows, stuffed toys, or bedding; and maintaining a smoke-free environment (Fleming et al., 1996; Willinger, 1995).

The Apgar exam assesses vital life processes and can be quickly administered, but the results provide only limited information. An extensive assessment of neurological functioning, the *Prechtl test*, is much more informative (Prechtl, 1977; Prechtl & Beintema, 1964). This examination includes items similar to those in the Apgar but also assesses alertness, spontaneous movements and tremors, facial expressions, reactions to placement in various postures, and around 15 reflexes. Babies who show fetal distress during birth or who need assistance with instruments to pass through the birth canal earn lower scores on the Prechtl test (Leijon, 1980; Prechtl, 1968). Labor medication and premature birth also tend to depress Prechtl scores (Belsey et al., 1981; Forslund & Bjerre, 1983).

The questions addressed by the Apgar and Prechtl tests, such as how well the newborn is managing such functions as breathing, independent blood circulation, and certain reflexes, are obviously important. But such measurements may tempt us to think of the newborn as something of a machine whose vital functions operate at a certain level of efficiency and who responds in a fixed way to stimuli. The newborn is a much more complex creature, with a wealth of behavioral tools. Moreover, new-

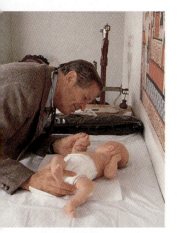

T. Berry Brazelton developed a widely used scale for assessing the newborn.

born babies differ substantially in how they behave, and these differences may affect how parents and others treat them. For these reasons, investigators have focused increasingly on tests of how well the newborn's behavior is *organized*.

The *Brazelton Neonatal Behavioral Assessment Scale* is the most comprehensive of the newborn tests. The main idea underlying this scale is that the seemingly helpless newborn actually possesses organized behaviors for dealing with both attractive stimuli—such as pleasant sights, sounds, and tastes—and offensive stimuli—such as loud noises and pinpricks (Brazelton, Nugent, & Lester, 1987). Assessors observe the baby in a number of states, or levels of alertness, to obtain a sense of the baby's style and temperament. An important feature of the exam is that it evaluates the newborn's ability to habituate. Recall from Chapter 2 that habituation is a simple form of learning in which a reflex response to a stimulus declines or disappears when the stimulus repeatedly occurs.

The exam includes items in four categories: attention and social responsiveness; muscle tone and physical movement; control of alertness (habituation, irritability, and excitability); and physiological response to stress. The baby's performance on these measures provides indicators of well-being and risk. For example, a baby who is unable to habituate to a repeated stimulus or to remain alert may fall into a higher risk category.

All the newborn assessments discussed here do a fairly good job of characterizing how a baby is doing in the early period. However, they are poor predictors of ultimate intelligence and personality, and none of the risk factors we have discussed is very dependable when considered in isolation. This fact may seem surprising to anyone who has seen a very low-weight baby in the newborn intensive-care nursery. A 2-lb baby, who is little more than tubes, able to breathe only with a respirator, and perhaps suffering internal brain bleeding, may seem to be on the verge of death. Amazingly, this baby is more than likely to turn out fine (Sostek et al., 1987). The best predictor of developmental difficulties is the *number* of risk factors to which an infant is subjected. The greater the number, the more likely that the infant will have problems (Sameroff et al., 1993).

Development in Family Context
Infants at Risk: Environment Holds the Key

Some babies who are born at risk have suffered brain or central nervous system damage that affects their functioning throughout life. However, in many cases, whether babies born at risk achieve normal development appears to depend largely on the context in which they are reared. Because most of the research supporting this finding has been carried out with preterm infants, we will focus on that work, but many of these factors play a role in determining the outcome of any baby at risk.

One factor in a baby's development progress is the quality of the relationship that forms between the parents and the baby (Mangelsdorf et al., 1996). At-risk babies often pose special challenges to this relationship. For example, the preterm baby may spend weeks in a plastic enclosure in a special-care hospital nursery that affords the parents little opportunity to hold and cuddle the baby. When finally at home, the baby is likely to have an irritating cry, be difficult to soothe, and have irregular patterns of sleep and wakefulness (Frodi et al., 1978; Parmelee & Garbanati, 1987).

These real problems are aggravated by people's reactions to preterm babies. In one study, several sets of parents were shown a film of a 5-month-old baby after they had been told that the baby was either normal, difficult, or premature (a term the researchers used for both SGA and preterm babies). Those who were told that the baby was premature judged crying segments of the film as more negative than did other parents, and physiological measures indicated that they experienced the baby's cries as more stressful (Frodi et al., 1978).

Other investigators have observed that parents treat their premature children differently even after apparent differences between them and full-term babies have disappeared (Barnard, Bee, & Hammond, 1984a; Beckwith & Parmelee, 1986). The tendency to expect negative behavior from premature infants has been referred to as "prematurity stereotyping" (Stern & Karraker, 1992). Such stereotypes increase the possibility that a negative cycle between parent and infant will be set in motion. Of course, the degree to which this occurs depends in part on the tolerance and flexibility of the caregivers, which is often related to their accurate understanding of the infant's needs (Benasich & Brooks-Gunn, 1996).

A contributor to disruption of the parent–infant relationship in the past was the policy of hospitals not to permit the parents to hold or touch their infant in the special-care nursery because of the fear of infection. We can easily imagine how a mother's confidence in caring for her newborn might be jeopardized after being limited for 6 to 8 weeks to watching the baby through a transparent incubator shield. As investigators began to recognize the importance of the very earliest social interactions between mother and infant, the situation changed. A group at Stanford University took the daring step of permitting parents to handle their infants in the special-care nursery and demonstrated that no increased danger of infection resulted (Barnett et al., 1970). Subsequent work demonstrated that handling enhanced mothers' self-confidence in responding to their babies (Leiderman & Seashore, 1975; Seashore et al., 1973).

A related factor is the lack of stimulation that infants often experience when they must spend time in the hospital. The temperature-controlled, patternless plastic chambers in which they are placed deprive them not only of human physical contact but of sensory input as well. As we have seen, intervention procedures introduced by NICUs have begun to address this problem.

There is concern, however, that, for some premature babies, added stimulation becomes overstimulation and has a negative rather than a positive effect. Investigators now tend to suggest that each baby must be considered individually. One creative idea is to provide stimulation that the babies themselves can decide to experience or avoid. For example, one investigator placed a "breathing" teddy bear in the baby's bed, which the baby could either contact or avoid. Premature babies who had the breathing bear tended to stay near it more than those who had a nonbreathing bear, and they spent a longer amount of time in quiet sleep (Thoman, 1993; Thoman, Ingersoll, & Acebo, 1991).

Another factor that may affect the development of the preterm infant is the family's socioeconomic status. By 2 to 3 years of age, children born preterm into families that have strong financial resources seem indistinguishable from children born at term. These more positive outcomes for infants of more advantaged parents might be related to the reduction of other stresses in the parents' lives—fewer financial problems and lower incidence of sickness, for example—and to their better access to and use of health and psychological professionals. Family stresses tend to reduce the emotional availability of parents for their infants, their tolerance for negative behavior, and their ability to organize family tasks (Hoy, Bill, & Sykes, 1988). Enrichment pro-

Premature babies benefit from opportunities to control their exposure to a mild stimulus that changes, such as the "breathing bear" discussed in the text.

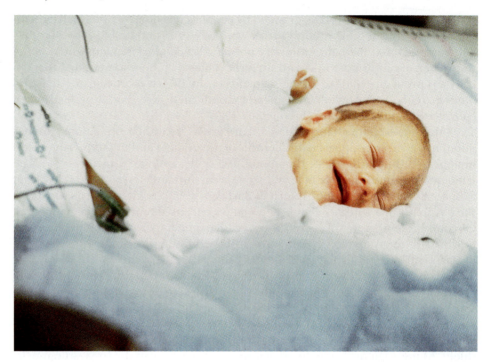

grams have been shown to be effective for families with low-birth-weight infants both for increasing the child's cognitive capabilities and for reducing behavior problems at 2 and 3 years of age (Brooks-Gunn et al., 1993; Dudley et al., 1993).

The contextual factors we have considered here affect the development of all babies. What recent research has told us is that these factors are especially important for babies born at risk (Hack et al., 1995).

✔ *To Recap...*

Labor begins with regular contractions of the uterus and passes through three stages. Most births proceed normally, and technological advances have helped improve the outcomes of those that do not. Cultures vary considerably in their attitudes and practices regarding birth.

Psychologists have been particularly interested in identifying babies born at risk for developmental problems. One indicator of risk is maternal and family characteristics. Whether the mother receives prenatal care from a physician seems especially important. A second indicator of risk is physical compromise of the newborn, most frequently identified by low birth weight. Low-birth-weight babies have more difficulties with breathing, which may lead to anoxia.

Babies have low birth weights for two reasons: preterm babies were born before the end of the normal gestation period; SGA babies are small for their gestational age because of growth retardation in the womb. Whatever the cause of low birth weight, these babies show differences from normal-weight infants, and these differences may persist for several years. However, at least for preterm babies, the differences may disappear by the early school years.

A third indicator of risk is provided by newborn assessments. These tests include the Apgar exam, the most common and easiest to use; the Prechtl test, which adds more neurological functions; and the Brazelton Neonatal Behavioral Assessment Scale, the most comprehensive test. No single risk indicator predicts intelligence or personality especially well, but the number of risk factors seems to be a good predictor of developmental problems.

The Organized Newborn

Look at a newborn baby and you will see that the baby's face, if he is awake, changes expression rapidly for no apparent reason and his legs and arms often flail around with no seeming purpose or pattern. A sleeping baby is less active, but her sleep is punctuated by twists, turns, startles, and grunts—a fairly unorganized picture. Seeing these behaviors, you can understand why, during most of the history of child psychology, people considered the newborn a passive and helpless creature whose activity was essentially random. Any organized behavior depended on external stimulation. Is it true that the newborn comes into the world with no organized patterns of behavior for sleeping, eating, getting the caregiver's attention, or even moving? Must caregivers teach the baby all these things?

Research on newborn behavior since the 1960s has drastically changed our views. Certainly the newborn is not as coordinated or predictable as the 2-year-old, but the behavior of the newborn is neither random nor disorganized. The newborn possesses natural rhythms of activity that generate patterns of sleeping and wakefulness, eating, and motion. Moreover, the newborn is equipped with many reflexive responses to external stimulation and a few organized behavioral patterns for investigating and controlling the environment through looking, sucking, and crying.

States of Alertness

Often the first question grandparents and friends ask the nurse about the new baby is, "Is the baby asleep or awake?" But there are other possibilities. Forty years ago, Peter Wolff, at the Harvard Medical School, carefully watched several newborn babies for many hours and was struck by how much their levels of alertness varied, yet how similar these levels were from one baby to another (Wolff, 1959, 1966). He captured these observations by defining six states of infant alertness: (1) quiet, or deep, sleep; (2) active, or light, sleep; (3) drowsiness; (4) alert inactivity; (5) alert activity; and (6) crying. These states are described in Table 6.2.

Table 6.2
States of the Infant

State	Characteristics
Deep Sleep	Regular breathing; eyes closed with no eye movements; no activity except for occasional jerky movements
Light sleep	Eyes closed but rapid eye movements can be observed; activity level low; movements are smoother than in deep sleep; breathing may be irregular
Drowsiness	Eyes may open and close but look dull when open; responses to stimulation are delayed, but stimulation may cause state to change; activity level varies
Alert inactivity	Eyes open and bright; attention focused on stimuli; activity level relatively low
Alert activity	Eyes open; activity level high; may show brief fussiness; reacts to stimulation with increases in startles and motor activity
Crying	Intense crying that is difficult to stop; high level of motor activity

Electroencephalograph (EEG)

An instrument that measures brain activity by sensing minute electrical changes at the top of the skull.

Rapid eye movement (REM) sleep

A stage of light sleep in which the eyes move rapidly while the eyelids are closed.

Several aspects of these states and how they change with age make them useful for understanding early development, for assessing the effects of various factors—such as teratogens—on development, and for comparing one infant with another. Recordings of brain activity by an **electroencephalograph (EEG)** reveal that states become increasingly distinct with age. Investigators believe this change reflects how the baby's brain matures (Sadeh & Anders, 1993). Similar information can also be obtained by examining the ease with which babies move from one state to the next (Halpern, MacLean, & Baumeister, 1995).

The time distribution of sleep states changes rapidly with age, as shown in Figure 6.2 (Groome et al., 1997). Whereas the fetus of 25 weeks gestational age engages almost exclusively in active sleep, the newborn spends only about half the time in active sleep and half in quiet sleep. By 3 months, quiet sleep occurs twice as much as active sleep (Berg & Berg, 1987; Gardner, Karmel, & Magnano, 1992). In active sleep, babies periodically move and breathe irregularly, but the most notable feature is that they frequently move their eyes back and forth with their eyelids closed (as do adults), so this sleep state is often called **rapid eye movement, or REM, sleep**.

The shift from dominantly active, or REM, sleep to dominantly quiet sleep has aroused considerable speculation about the function of REM sleep. In the adult, REM sleep constitutes only about 20% of total sleep time and is associated with

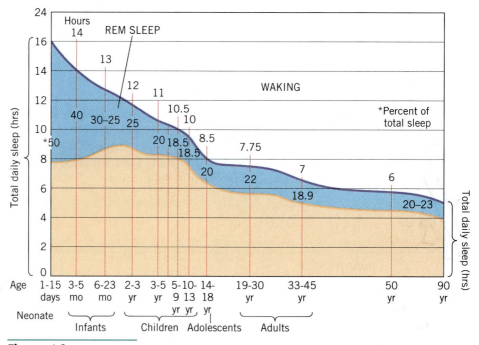

Figure 6.2

Although the total amount of sleep time declines with age, the drop is most noticeable for REM sleep during the first 2 to 3 years of life. The amount of quiet sleep is about the same for newborns and 3-year-olds, but the percentage of sleep time spent in the REM state declines from around 50% to around 25% over this time span. From "Ontogenic Development of the Human Sleep–Dream Cycle" by H. P. Roffwarg, J. N. Muzio, and W. C. Dement, 1966, *Science, 152* p. 608. Copyright © 1966 by the AAAS. Reprinted by permission. The figure reproduced here contains revisions made by Roffwarg et al. since the original publication in 1966.

dreaming. Research suggests that the high rate of REM activity in early development reflects a kind of internal motor that keeps nerve pathways active until the baby receives enough stimulation from the external world (Kandel & O'Dell, 1992). Consistent with this idea is the finding that babies who have longer awake periods, which presumably provide needed stimulation, have shorter REM periods during sleep (Boismer, 1977; Denenberg & Thoman, 1981).

Since the organization of sleep states—how well they are differentiated and their time distribution—reflects brain maturation, we might expect babies at risk to be less organized than other infants. Indeed, state organization is affected in babies of alcoholic and drug-addicted mothers, and babies who are unstable in their time distribution across various states between 2 and 5 weeks of life are more likely than are relatively stable babies to have later medical and behavioral problems (Halpern et al., 1995).

To this point, we have talked about infant states in terms of the internal processes they reflect. But states also play an important role in infants' interactions with the environment. When babies are in states of alertness—rather than crying, asleep, or drowsy—they are more receptive to stimuli and learn more readily (Berg & Berg, 1987; Thoman, 1990). Thus, states affect the impact of external events. External events, in turn, can affect an infant's state. For example, a crying baby will often shift to a quiet, alert state if picked up by an adult and gently rocked up and down on the adult's shoulder (Korner & Thoman, 1970; Pederson & Ter Vrugt, 1973).

Another external factor is where the baby sleeps. Although sleep and its various states have a strong biological basis, it is not clear where nature intended babies to sleep. In the United States, most middle-class families have babies sleep by themselves in their own beds. Among many lower-class families and some ethnic groups—such as African-Americans—babies are more likely to sleep with their parents. The most common reason given by middle-class mothers for the separate sleeping arrangements is the desire to build the infant's independence. The most common reasons given by mothers who prefer sharing a bed are the desire to develop a closeness with the infant as well as the ease of feeding and caregiving (Kawasaki et al., 1994; Lozoff, Wolff, & Davis, et al., 1984; Morelli et al., 1992). Not enough research has been directed toward this question to provide a good scientific answer as to what is best.

Rhythms

Most children and adults have regular patterns of daily activity. For the most part, they sleep at night, are awake during the day, and eat at fairly predictable times. We can say that their daily patterns obey a repeating rhythm. On the other hand, one need only look at the red, tired eyes of a new parent to know that the newborn baby's habits are not so regular. Can we conclude, then, that the baby enters the world with no rhythms at all and must be taught by the parents when to eat, when to sleep, and when to wake? Not at all. Newborn babies are rhythmic creatures. The newborn's biological clock just seems to tick at a different rate than ours, and it gradually shifts into synchrony with ours as the baby develops.

The newborn's states, like the adult's, occur as rhythms cycling within other rhythms. The baby engages in a cycle of active and quiet sleep that repeats each 50 to 60 minutes. This cycle is coordinated with a cycle of wakefulness that occurs once every 3 to 4 hours (Parmelee & Sigman, 1983). What produces this behavior? We might suspect that the sleep–wake cycle reflects a cycle of hunger or of external disruption by caregivers. However, the cycle seems to be internally controlled. Even before the first feeding and with external distractions held to a minimum, newborns still display roughly these same sleep–wake cycles (Emde, Swedberg, & Suzuki, 1975).

Much to the relief of their parents, infants gradually adapt to the 24-hour light–dark cycle. Sleep periods become longer at night, usually around 5 or 6 weeks of age, as awake periods lengthen during the day. By 12 to 16 weeks, the pattern of sleeping at night and being awake during the day is fairly well established, even though the baby still sleeps about the same amount as the newborn (Berg & Berg, 1987).

Although the rhythms of the newborn seem to be biologically programmed, they are not free from environmental influences. For example, newborn babies who stay in their mothers' rooms in the hospital begin to display day–night differences in their sleep cycles earlier than babies who stay in the hospital nursery. These rooming-in babies also spend more time in quiet sleep and less time crying than do babies in nursery groups (Keefe, 1987). Apparently, prenatal experience can also affect rhythmic activity. Newborns who have alcoholic or drug-dependent mothers have more difficulty synchronizing their various sleep–wake rhythms and adapting to the night–day cycle than do other babies (Parmelee & Sigman, 1983; Sander et al., 1977).

Reflexes

We have seen that the newborn baby has identifiable states of alertness and that these states fit into overall rhythms. Newborns are also equipped with a number of behaviors and behavior patterns. Some of these, called **reflexes**, are highly stereotyped and occur as brief responses to specific stimuli. As we discussed in Chapter 2, reflexes have evolved in humans over millions of years because they serve (or served at one time) an important survival function.

Reflexes are not of interest only to psychologists trying to understand early development; they can have applied value as well because their presence or absence provides information about the baby's brain and nervous system. For example, an infant should reflexively bend to the left side when the doctor runs a thumb along the left side of the baby's spinal column. If this reflex occurs on the left side but not on the right side, it may indicate damage to the nerves on the right side.

Some reflexes last throughout life, but the reflexes of most interest here are those that disappear in the first year of life, because their disappearance indicates the development of more advanced brain functions. Table 6.3 lists some of the more common reflexes as well as the stimuli that produce them and their developmental course. We discuss only a few of these reflexes here.

The **rooting reflex** is the first to appear. If we stroke a newborn's cheek next to the mouth, the baby will turn the head to that side and search with the mouth. This reflex is adaptive in an evolutionary sense because it helps the baby find the nipple of the mother's breast for feeding. This reflex appears as early as 2 to 3 months gestational age and represents the first indication that the fetus can respond to touch. Rooting generally disappears in infants around 3 to 4 months of age (Peiper, 1963).

The **palmar reflex** is elicited by pressure against the palm of a newborn's hand, such as with a finger, as shown in Figure 6.3*a*. The baby responds by grasping the finger tightly. Newborns are capable of supporting their own weight in this manner—a potentially important ability for babies of our evolutionary ancestors, who needed to cling tightly to the fur of their mothers as they moved along through the jungle. This reflex disappears at 3 to 4 months of age, and children will not again be able to support their own weight until around 4 or 5 years of age (McGraw, 1940).

The **Moro reflex** consists of a series of reactions to sudden sound or the loss of head support. The infant first thrusts her arms outward, opens her hands, arches

---

Reflex
An automatic and stereotyped response to a specific stimulus.

Rooting reflex
The turning of the infant's head toward the cheek at which touch stimulation is applied, followed by opening of the mouth.

Palmar reflex
The infant's finger grasp of an object that stimulates the palm of the hand.

Moro reflex
The infant's response to loss of head support or to a loud sound, consisting of thrusting the arms and fingers outward, followed by clenching the fists and making a grasping motion of the arms across the chest.

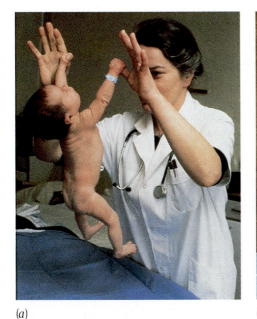

(a)

(b)

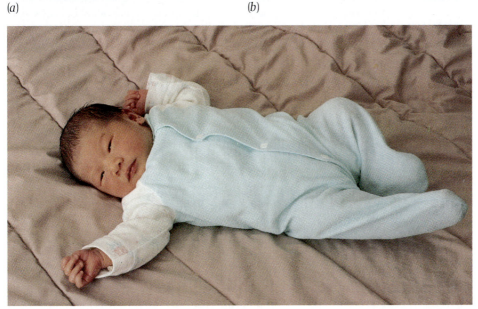

(c)

Figure 6.3
Some newborn reflexes:
(a) palmar, (b) stepping,
and (c) tonic neck.

her back, and stretches her legs outward, then she brings her arms inward in an embracing motion with fingers formed into fists. The absence of a Moro reflex is a sign of brain damage, and its failure to disappear after 6 or 7 months of age is also cause for concern. Moro, who first described the reflex (Moro, 1918), argued that it was a relic of an adaptive reaction by primates to grab for support while falling, but others have disputed this argument (e.g., Peiper, 1963). As with many newborn reflexes, the evolutionary roots of the Moro reflex are not certain.

When pressure is applied to the soles of the feet, the baby will flex her legs up and down in the **stepping reflex**, shown in Figure 6.3b. This reflex usually disappears by around 3 months of age. The disappearance of the reflex at this time

Stepping reflex
The infant's response to pressure on the soles of the feet, consisting of stepping (flexing) movements.

Table 6.3
Newborn Reflexes

Name	Testing Method	Response	Developmental Course	Significance
Blink	Flash a light in infant's eyes	Closes both eyes	Permanent	Protects eyes from strong stimuli
Biceps reflex	Tap on the tendon of the biceps muscle	Contracts the biceps muscle	Brisker in the first few days than later	Absent in depressed infants or those with congenital muscular disease
Knee jerk or patellar tendon reflex	Tap on the tendon below the patella or kneecap	Quickly extends or kicks the knee	More pronounced in the first 2 days than later	Absent or difficult to obtain in depressed infants or infants with muscular disease; exaggerated in hyperexcitable infants
Babinski	Gently stroke the side of the infant's foot from heel to toes	Flexes the big toe dorsally; fans out the other toes; twists foot inward	Usually disappears near the end of the 1st year; replaced by plantar flexion of big toe in the normal adult	Absent in infants with defects of the lower spine; retention important in diagnosing poor myelination of motor tracts of the brainstem in older children and adults
Withdrawal reflex	Prick the sole of the infant's foot with a pin	Flexes leg	Constantly present during the first 10 days; present but less intense later	Absent with sciatic nerve damage
Plantar or toe grasp	Press finger against the ball of the infant's foot	Curls all toes under	Disappears between 8 and 12 months	Absent in infants with defects of the lower spinal cord
Tonic neck reflex	Lay baby down on back	Turns head to one side; baby assumes fencing position, extending arm and leg on this side, bending opposite limbs, and arching body away from direction faced	Found as early as 28th prenatal week; frequently present in first weeks, disappears by 3 or 4 months	Paves way for eye-hand coordination

Tonic neck reflex
The infant's postural change when the head is turned to the side, consisting of extension of the arm on that side and clenching of the other arm in what looks like a fencer's position.

seems to result from the increasing weight of the baby's legs. Research has shown that if the legs are supported in water, the reflex can be demonstrated in older infants (Thelen & Fisher, 1982, 1983). Similarly, if the reflex is practiced, it can become stronger (Zelazo, Zelazo, & Kolb, 1972; Zelazo et al., 1993).

A few reflexes of the newborn occur in the absence of any obvious external stimulation. The **tonic neck reflex**, or fencer's position, is an example. When the head turns to one side, the newborn tends to extend the arm on that side while flexing the arm on the opposite side, as shown in Figure 6.3c.

Although there is an automatic quality to reflexes, environmental factors do affect them. For example, a baby who has just nursed may not show a rooting

Table 6.3
Newborn Reflexes

Name	Testing Method	Response	Developmental Course	Significance
Palmar or hand grasp	Press rod or finger against the infant's palm	Grasps the object with fingers; can suspend own weight for brief period of time	Increases during the 1st month and then gradually declines and is gone by 3 or 4 months	Weak or absent in depressed babies
Moro reflex (embracing reflex)	Make a sudden loud sound; let the baby's head drop back a few inches; or suspend baby horizontally, then lower hands rapidly about six inches and stop abruptly	Extends arms and legs and then brings arms toward each other in a convulsive manner; fans hands out at first, clenches them slightly	Begins to decline in third month, generally gone by fifth month	Absent or constantly weak Moro indicates serious disturbance of the central nervous system; may have originated with primate clinging
Stepping or automatic walking reflex	Support baby in upright position with bare feet on flat surface; move the infant forward and tilt him slightly from side to side	Makes rhythmic stepping movements	Disappears in 2 to 3 months	Absent in depressed infants
Swimming reflex	Hold baby horizontally on stomach in water	Alternates arm and leg movements, exhaling through the mouth	Disappears at 6 months	Demonstrates coordination of arms and legs
Rooting reflex	Stroke cheek of infant lightly with finger or nipple	Turns head toward finger, opens mouth, and tries to suck finger	Disappears at approximately 3 to 4 months	Absent in depressed infants; appears in adults with severe cerebral palsy
Babkin or palmarmental reflex	Apply pressure on both of baby's palms when lying on back	Opens mouth, closes eyes, and turns head to midline	Disappears in 3 to 4 months	Inhibited by general depression of central nervous system

Source: Excerpted from *Child Psychology: A Contemporary Viewpoint*, 2nd ed. (Table 4.1), by E. M. Hetherington and R. D. Parke, 1979, New York: McGraw-Hill. Copyright © 1979 by McGraw-Hill, Inc. Excerpted by permission of the McGraw-Hill Company.

response, and most other reflexes are also somewhat sensitive to the baby's biological state. Still, reflexes are generally tied to specific stimuli and are rarely seen in their absence. This is not the case for the behaviors we refer to as congenitally organized behaviors.

Congenitally Organized Behaviors

Not all early behaviors are responses to stimulation. The newborn also initiates activities and is capable of sustaining them over considerable periods of time. Such activities are called **congenitally organized behaviors**. Specifically, looking, sucking, and crying are three well-organized behaviors that, unlike reflexes, are often not elicited by a discrete, identifiable stimulus. These behaviors provide infants with means to get nourishment and to control and explore their environments.

Congenitally organized behavior
Early behaviors of newborns that do not require specific external stimulation and that show more adaptability than simple reflexes.

Looking   The newborn's looking behavior is often unexpected (Crouchman, 1985). New parents may be amazed when their baby, even in the first moments of life, will lie with eyes wide open, seemingly examining them and other objects in the room. In a room that is dimly lit, the light coming through the window may be an especially attractive target. And babies do not simply respond reflexively to light when they look. As early as 8 hours after birth, and in complete darkness, babies open their eyes wide and engage in frequent eye movements, as though they were searching for something to explore (Haith, 1991). We will have more to say about early perception in the next chapter. Our point now is that looking behavior shows that newborns possess tools for acting on their world, not just for reacting to it.

Sucking   In some respects, sucking seems to fit the definition of a reflex, since it is easily elicited by oral stimulation, at least when the newborn is hungry. In other respects, though, it is not reflexlike. Babies may suck spontaneously, even during sleep. The sucking act also is not stereotyped, but adapts to a variety of conditions, such as how much fluid can be obtained with each suck. In addition, sucking is sensitive to sensory events. Babies who are sucking tend to stop when they see something start to move or when they hear a voice (Haith, 1966). These characteristics set sucking apart from simpler reflexes.

Sucking is a marvelously coordinated act. Babies suck one to two times each second, and each suck requires an orchestration of actions. Milk is extracted from the nipple both by suction (as with a straw) and by a squeezing action, and these actions must be coordinated with both breathing and swallowing. Some babies show excellent sucking coordination from birth, whereas others may require a week or so of practice (Peiper, 1963).

No other newborn behavior seems to serve quite as many purposes as sucking. It is, of course, a way to get nourishment, but it is also a primary means by which babies begin to explore the world. Even at birth, many babies suck their fingers and thumbs, and it appears that some newborns have even practiced this as fetuses. Later, they will continue to explore with their mouths as they become better able to grasp and find new objects (Rochat, 1989).

Sucking also seems to buffer the infant against pain and overstimulation. Agitated babies quiet when they suck on a pacifier, especially when it contains a sweet substance (Smith & Blass, 1996). One study found that crying during circumcision was reduced by about 40% when babies were permitted to suck on a pacifier (Gunnar, Fisch, & Malone, 1984). This finding confirms experimentally what civilizations have known for some time; for thousands of years, Jewish babies have been encouraged to suck on wine-soaked cotton during circumcision. Finally, sucking plays a social role in the process of emotional attachment between infant and mother (Bowlby, 1969; Crook, 1979).

Crying   A third organized behavior of the newborn is crying. Like sucking, crying coordinates various components of behavior, such as breathing, vocalizing, and muscular tensing, in a rhythmic pattern. Psychologists have been interested in crying both as a diagnostic tool and for its social role.

Wolff (1969) distinguished three types of cries in the very young infant: a hungry, or basic, cry; a mad, or angry, cry; and a pain cry. The first two are similar in pitch but different in that the mad cry forces more air through the vocal cords, producing more variation. The pain cry has a more sudden onset with a much longer initial burst and a longer period of breath holding between cries. Other researchers have identified the types as expressing hunger, fear, or pain (Wasz-Hockert, Michelsson,

& Lind, 1985). Adults have little difficulty in distinguishing various cries based on their timing and patterning (Zeskind, Klein, & Marshall, 1992). We will discuss the role of crying as an early form of communication again in Chapter 11.

The crying of healthy, newborn infants is fairly characteristic in both pitch and rhythm. An unusual cry, therefore, can signal problems. Babies who are immature or brain damaged produce higher-frequency cries with abnormal timing patterns (Lester, 1976, 1984). Babies who show evidence of malnutrition at birth or who are preterm often also have higher-pitched cries with abnormal timing patterns (Zeskind, 1983). Infants who have genetic anomalies, such as the *cri du chat* syndrome (in which the infant's cry sounds like that of a cat) and Down syndrome, have atypical cries as well.

Some investigators have speculated that babies influence early social relationships with their caregivers by the nature of their cries (Lester, 1984). Cries of babies at risk are perceived as more grating, piercing, and aversive than the cries of other babies, and "difficult" babies seem to have more aversive cries than "easy" babies (Lounsbury & Bates, 1982). As noted earlier, cries experienced as aversive may set in motion a negative cycle between baby and caregiver.

More broadly, crying is a major factor in early social interaction because it is one of the infant's basic tools for getting the caregiver to come closer. Because adults dislike hearing babies cry, they typically do something to quiet the crying baby. Parents may try various techniques for soothing a baby who fusses for no apparent reason (Emde, Gaensbauer, & Harmon, 1976). Picking the baby up is an effective quieter, swaddling, or wrapping a baby snugly in a blanket, and pacifiers are also sometimes effective, as is continuous or rhythmic sound (Brackbill et al., 1966; Campos, 1989). Even in the first month of life, crying may be controlled by events other than food or pain relief; infants often stop crying if they have interesting things to watch or sounds to listen to (Wolff, 1969). Babies learn very early to use crying to control the social environment, sometimes producing what Wolff has called the fake cry, to get the caregiver's attention, as early as 3 weeks of age.

The three congenitally organized behaviors of looking, sucking, and crying are gradually fine-tuned by the infant to explore and control the physical and social world more effectively. Other skills, such as reaching, grasping, and walking, also play a role, and elaborate emotional behaviors, such as smiling and laughing, will enrich the social interactions of the developing infant. We will leave the more social components of early development to Chapter 12 and consider next some other physical accomplishments of the infant.

✔ *To Recap...*

The activity of newborns is not random, but is organized into states, rhythms, reflexes, and congenitally organized behaviors. The newborn's level of alertness is typically categorized according to six states, varying from quiet sleep to crying. Several aspects of these states change with age, providing information about early development. Although state organization is controlled primarily by internal factors, state can be affected by external stimulation. Conversely, the baby's response to stimulation is affected by the state the baby is in.

The newborn's states occur in rhythmic cycles. A basic rest–activity cycle is coordinated with a longer sleep–wake cycle. With age, the baby gradually adapts to the 24-hour, light–dark cycle.

Other evidence for behavioral organization is found in reflexes. Although some reflexes last through life, others, such as the rooting, palmar, Moro, and tonic neck reflexes, disappear during the first year. These reflexes and their developmental courses provide important information about the baby's central nervous system.

Congenitally organized behaviors such as looking, crying, and sucking are available at birth but, unlike reflexes, are not easily attributable to a particular stimulus. These are examples of inborn behaviors that the infant possesses for exploring and controlling the physical and social aspects of the world.

Motor Development

Looking, crying, and sucking are limited in their ability to control the environment. Imagine for a moment that you cannot move around or grasp and manipulate objects so that you must depend on others to provide interesting things for you to inspect. This is the state of the newborn baby. Before long, however, these limitations disappear and the infant is a go-for-everything, grab-anything 9-month-old.

The acquisition of motor skills is a key feature of development in human infancy, in effect giving the baby power tools for acquiring knowledge and gaining a sense of competence and self-control. These skills continue to development well into the childhood years, when they play important roles in other aspects of development.

Motor development can be divided into two general categories. The first comprises **postural development** and **locomotion**, which involve control of the trunk of the body and coordination of the arms and legs for moving around. The second category is **prehension**, the ability to use the hands as tools for such purposes as eating, building, and exploring.

Principles and Sequences

The progression of motor skills tends to follow two general principles. The first principle is that development proceeds in a **proximodistal** direction—that is, body parts closest to the center of the body come under control before parts farther out.

The acquisition of early prehensile skills provides a good example. In the first weeks, the newborn can position himself toward an object, but cannot reach it. Although his arm movements seem random, the infant does direct some movements toward the object. In the second month of life, the baby sweeps his hand more deliberately near the object and begins to contact it more consistently. By 4 months of age, the infant can often grab at objects in a way that looks convincingly deliberate, but he uses the whole hand, with as yet little individual finger control. Gradually, the baby coordinates his fingers, so that at 6 months of age, he may reach with one hand for a cube with all fingers extended. Once the object is in hand, the baby may transfer the cube from hand to hand and rotate his wrist so as to see it from various perspectives. By 9 months, the baby can grasp a small pellet neatly between forefinger and thumb, and the 1-year-old can hold a crayon to make marks on paper.

The second principle is that control over the body develops in a **cephalocaudal**, or head-to-foot, direction. The progression of early postural and locomotor skills illustrates this principle.

The newborn who is placed on her stomach can move her head from side to side, although her head must be supported when she is lifted to someone's shoulder. The 3-month-old infant first holds her head erect and steady in the vertical position, and then pushes off the mattress with her hands to lift her head and shoulders and look. At 6 months, the baby can pull herself to a sitting position and may even be able to drag herself around a bit by her arms (crawling). But only at around 8 months can the baby use her legs to move herself forward with her belly off the floor (creeping). By the time the infant is 1 year old, the parents are likely to find

Postural development
The increasing ability of the baby to control parts of their body, especially the head and the trunk.

Locomotion
The movement of a person through space, such as walking and crawling.

Prehension
The ability to grasp and manipulate objects with the hands.

Proximodistal
Literally, near to far. This principle of development refers to the tendency of body parts to develop in a trunk-to-extremities direction.

Cephalocaudal
Literally, head to tail. This principle of development refers to the tendency of body parts to mature in a head-to-foot progression.

her standing in the crib, rattling the side bars and perhaps distressed by being unable to figure out how to sit down again! Typically, soon after her first birthday, the baby is able to control the legs sufficiently to begin walking without support.

The top portion of Figure 6.4 shows a typical baby's stages of progression toward self-produced locomotion. The cephalocaudal progression just described is clearly evident, with the hands most active early on and responsibility for movement gradually transferring down to the legs. The lower portion of Figure 6.4 illustrates how babies can reach the same goal by following different routes (Largo et al., 1985). Some babies, for example, never crawl before walking. Psychologists now know that infants do not all develop a given motor skill (such as walking or standing) in the same way—a point to which we will return in a moment.

Table 6.4 presents some of the milestones of motor-skill acquisition, and, again, the proximodistal and cephalocaudal principles described earlier are apparent. The majority of babies follow these general sequences. It is important to note, however, that the ages given in the table are only approximate; some infants master these skills earlier, and others master them later. This variation in *when* motor skills are developed has taken on new significance since the recent discovery that infants also vary in *how* they develop specific skills. The result is that psychologists are now thinking about motor development very differently.

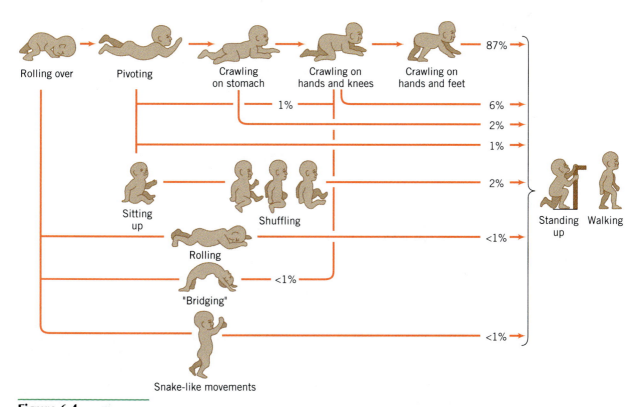

Figure 6.4

Most babies follow a fairly regular sequence in learning to walk, gradually transferring responsibility for movement from the arms to the feet. But some skip certain stages of crawling, and others never crawl at all. Adapted from "Early Development of Locomotion: Significance of Prematurity, Cerebral Palsy and Sex" by R. H. Largo, L. Molinari, M. Weber, L. C. Pinto, and G. Duc, 1985, *Developmental Medicine and Child Neurology, 27*, pp. 183–191, Figure 2. Copyright © 1985 by MacKeith Press. Adapted by permission.

Table 6.4
Motor Milestones

Age in Months	Locomotion and Postural Development	Prehension and Manipulative Skills
0	Turns head to side when lying on stomach; poor head control when lifted; alternating movements of legs when on stomach as if to crawl	Reflex grasp—retains hold on ring
3	Head erect and steady when held vertically; when on stomach, elevates head and shoulders by arms or hands or elbows; sits with support; anticipates adjustment of lifting	Grasps rattle; reaches for objects with two hands
6	Sits alone momentarily; pulls self to sitting position with adult's hand as puller; rolls from back to stomach	Grasps cube with simultaneous flexion of fingers; reaches with one hand and rotates the wrist; transfers cube between hands
9	Sits alone; pulls self to sitting position in crib; makes forward progress in prone position toward toy; walks holding on to furniture	Opposes thumb and finger in seizing cube; picks up pellet with forefinger and thumb
12	Stands alone; lowers self to sitting from a standing position; walks with help; creeping perfected; into everything	Holds crayon adaptively to make a mark
18	Walks well (since about 15 months) and falls rarely; climbs stairs or chair	Throws balls into box; scribbles vigorously; builds tower of three or more blocks
24	Walks up and down stairs; walks backward; runs	Places square in form board; imitates folding of paper; piles tower of six blocks; puts blocks in a row to form a train

Source: Based on information from *Manual for the Bayley Scales of Infant Development* by N. Bayley, 1969, New York: Psychological Corporation; and "The Denver Developmental Screening Test" by W. K. Frankenburg and J. Dodds, 1967, *Journal of Pediatrics, 71*, pp. 181–191.

The Nature and Nurture of Motor-Skills Development

Motor skills appear in a fairly predictable sequence and at similar times from one infant to another. Does this mean that sitting, crawling, reaching, and so forth are genetically programmed and simply emerge according to a biological set of instructions within the child? More and more, psychologists are answering this question no.

For one thing, different child-rearing experiences—often associated with different cultural practices—can clearly affect the timing of motor-skill development. For example, African infants generally sit, stand, and walk from one to several months earlier than do American infants (Konner, 1976; Super, 1981). But how the infants are dealt with, not heredity, seems to account for much of the difference.

One investigator reported that the Kipsigis in western Kenya believe their infants will not sit, stand, or walk without practice. Thus they energetically provide practice for their infants in these skills. For example, they dig a special hole in the ground using sand to reinforce their infants' sitting skills. In the development of skills that are not encouraged in this way, such as crawling and rolling over, Kenyan babies do not differ from American babies (Super, 1981). Mothers in Jamaica provide their babies with similar types of early physical stimulation, and these babies, too, develop motor skills earlier than do white infants in other cultures (Hopkins, 1991).

A glance back at Figure 6.4 shows a second reason that genetics cannot rigidly control motor development: Not all babies get to the same place by following the same path. Using the microgenetic method described in Chapter 3, researchers have carefully charted the development of motor skills in many individual infants. One study examined the development of reaching and grasping in four infants from ages 3 weeks to 1 year. Although all four eventually were able to reach out and grasp a toy, the manner in which they achieved this goal varied considerably from one child to the next (Thelen, Corbetta, & Spencer, 1996).

A Dynamic Systems Approach   These sorts of findings have prompted researchers to think about motor development in a new way. The **dynamic systems** approach was developed within the science of physics, but in developmental psychology it has been applied to children's motor development most extensively by Esther Thelen (Thelen, 1995; Thelen & Smith, 1994, 1998).

Thelen proposes that both nature and nurture contribute to the development of motor skills. Given that the emergence of these skills follows a predictable sequence for most babies, biological factors would seem to be strongly involved. Because practice and experience can affect motor-skills development and because children seem to acquire specific skills somewhat differently, environmental factors must be involved as well. Thelen argues that developmentalists need a model to help them understand the combined contributions of these two factors.

According to her dynamic systems analysis, the crucial element that unites the nature and nurture contributions and, more important, that stimulates the development of any particular skill, is the infant's "task." As babies mature biologically and cognitively, they become motivated to accomplish more and more things in the world around them. They seek to reach things, to grasp things, to move or shake things, to move themselves closer to things, and so on. These are the tasks of infancy. In order to accomplish such tasks, babies learn that various motor behaviors—such as those involving the arms, fingers, head, shoulders, and so on—can be useful.

Sometimes, though, the task requires a behavior that the child does not possess, so the infant must create such a behavior. To do this, the infant draws on the physical responses and abilities already available to her—what the baby can already do with arms, legs, hands, and fingers; muscle strength; balance and coordination; and so on. These abilities, of course, depend largely on age and biological maturation, but they also depend on the abilities the baby has created up to that point. A 9-month-old, therefore, should have many more physical responses and abilities on which to draw on than would, say, a 4-month-old. As a result, even when faced with the same task, the two children will likely create different new motor behaviors and so accomplish the task in different ways. Note that this is true not only for babies of different ages; *any* two children, even of the same age, will have different physical resources available to them as a result of both their genetic differences and their different experiences up to that point.

Thelen has found that as infants try to assemble a new motor behavior from the abilities currently available to them, they go through two stages. The first stage involves *exploration,* as the baby tries many different responses in a relatively random and uncoordinated fashion. In the second stage, *selection,* the baby learns exactly

Kipsigis (in Kenya, Africa), believe that their infants need practice to learn certain postural skills, such as sitting. Photo used by permission of Dr. Charles Super, Pennsylvania State University.

Dynamic systems
Thelen's model of the development of motor skills, in which infants who are motivated to accomplish a task create a new motor behavior from their available physical abilities.

BOX 6.1

DOES MOTOR DEVELOPMENT DEPEND ON PRACTICE OR ON MATURATION

The nature–nurture debate regarding motor development is very old. During the 1920s and 1930s, the Zeitgeist in developmental psychology leaned heavily toward biological explanations of children's development. We saw in Chapter 1 that G. Stanley Hall's early evolutionary views were revised and resurrected during this period by his student Arnold Gesell at Yale University.

One major theoretical issue of the time concerned children's motor-skills acquisition. Learning-oriented psychologists, such as John B. Watson, argued that the crawling, climbing, and walking displayed by all normal infants represented reflexes conditioned through experience and practice. But Gesell and other biologically oriented theorists believed that these behaviors emerged according to a genetic timetable. Simple biological maturation, not conditioning and learning principles, guide their appearance.

To compare these two theories, Gesell developed a research method called the *co-twin control*, which used identical twins so that biological factors would be the same for the two infants. Gesell then selected one infant, whom he termed twin T, to receive training and extra practice each day at climbing stairs and related motor skills. The control infant, twin C, received no extra practice.

After 6 weeks of training, twin T had become a very accomplished climber—but so had twin C. Gesell interpreted these findings to mean that the climbing skill must have been a result only of the children's biological development and not of their practice or experience (Gesell & Thompson, 1929). Studies of the same sort by other researchers appeared to confirm this conclusion (McGraw, 1935).

Later research, however, demonstrated that Gesell's conclusions had been a bit simplistic. Whereas extra training may not accelerate children's motor development, some amount of experience appears necessary for development to occur normally. Infants deprived of physical stimulation or the opportunity to move about were found to have delayed motor development (Dennis, 1960; Dennis & Najarian, 1957). When such infants were then given extra stimulation, their motor skills improved rapidly (Sayegh & Dennis, 1965).

The method of the co-twin control was a useful technique for comparing the effects of maturation and learning (which is, of course, a specific case of nature versus nurture). But as psychologists now agree, both of these processes are essential for normal motor development.

what works and what doesn't work and fine-tunes the many responses into an efficient package.

In short, the dynamic systems approach predicts that the motor skill a particular child develops at any given time will depend on (a) the task at hand, including how difficult it is and how motivated the child is to accomplish it, and (b) the physical abilities the child already possesses that form the starting point for creating the new behavior. The first of these (the task) is obviously very much influenced by the baby's environment and experiences; the second (the infant's physical abilities) is strongly influenced by the baby's biological maturation, but also by prior experiences.

Research Examples   Thelen demonstrated these principles in a clever laboratory study. Three-month-old infants were placed in cribs on their backs, where they could see a mobile suspended above them. The babies' feet were individually attached with cords to the mobile in such a way that either single kicks or alternating kicking movements were effective in making the mobile move. At first the babies explored different leg movements, but after a short while they learned to produce the necessary kicking behaviors, presumably because they were motivated to accomplish the task of moving the mobile. Thelen next tied each baby's feet loosely together, so that the motor behavior that would best move the mobile was a combined two-foot kick. Again the infants explored various leg movements before finally selecting a coordinated leg action that was effective in achieving their purpose (Thelen, 1994).

Another example involves locomotion. Researchers at the University of Denver videotaped the motions of babies' body parts as they learned to creep across the floor to reach an object. As shown in Figure 6.5, the babies wore black bodysuits that had small reflective markers (the kind bicyclists wear at night) at the shoulder, elbow, and other joints. Reflections from these markers were read by a computer and analyzed to determine the path, velocity, and timing of the children's movements.

The researchers found that once babies have the physical strength to move along with their bodies held above the floor, they begin to explore different patterns of arm-and-leg coordination and eventually settle on a diagonal pattern (right hand and left leg, then left hand and right leg) as the most efficient and stable way of locomotoring along, and thus reaching the object (Benson, 1990; Freedland & Bertenthal, 1994).

The essence of the dynamic systems approach, then, is that an infant does not simply wake up one morning with a new motor skill that has emerged spontaneously from her genetic code. Instead, a new skill is developed only when the infant is motivated to accomplish a task and has sufficient physical abilities to assemble into the necessary motor behavior.

Why, then, do most babies follow the same general sequence of motor development? The answer is probably simply that the physical resources of infants at the same points in development are reasonably similar and infants' tasks in any given culture tend also to be reasonably similar. On the other hand, Thelen's dynamic systems analysis shows why it also shouldn't be surprising that babies differ in the timing of their motor-skill development and in the manner in which they acquire these skills. Nature provides most of the raw material of motor development, but nurture determines the timing and direction development will take.

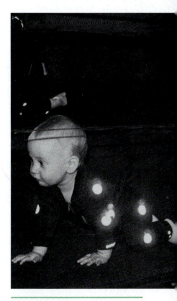

Figure 6.5
Scientists use computerized techniques to track light reflections on babies' joints to study how babies acquire skill in crawling. (Photo by permission of Dr. Janette Benson, University of Denver.)

The Psychological Implications of Motor Development

Learning to move around is not only a motor accomplishment for babies; it also helps them organize their world (Bertenthal, Campos, & Kermoian, 1994). For example, babies' self-produced locomotion seems to contribute to their spatial understanding (discussed in more detail in Chapter 7). In one study, a toy was hidden in one of two colored containers placed in front of an infant. Infants with crawling experience were better able to find the toy under a variety of conditions—such as when the babies were placed on the opposite side of the table (thereby reversing the left or right location of the toy from the baby's perspective)—than were babies of the same age who had not yet mastered crawling (Benson & Uzgiris, 1985).

A baby's control over body movement also helps her understand the meaning of distance and heights. Crawling seems to be related to infants' learning to fear heights (Campos, Bertenthal, & Kermoian, 1992). Later, when babies can control their distance from their mothers or other caregivers, they use their motor skills to venture off (when they feel safe) or to return for comfort (when they feel insecure), as we will see again in Chapter 12 (Ainsworth, 1983).

Motor Development in Childhood

Motor development has attracted the most attention from infant researchers, but motor skills continue to develop during the childhood years (Gallahue, 1989).

An infant's first steps are a major milestone of development.

By the second birthday, most children have overcome their battle with gravity and balance and are able to move about and handle objects fairly efficiently. Their early abilities form the basis for skills that appear between 2 and 7 years of age. Three sets of fundamental movement skills emerge: locomotor movements, manipulative movements, and stability movements.

Locomotor movements include walking, running, jumping, hopping, skipping, and climbing. Manipulative movements include throwing, catching, kicking, striking, and dribbling. Stability movements involve body control relative to gravity and include bending, turning, swinging, rolling, head standing, and beam walking. These fundamental skills typically appear in all children and can be further refined by adolescents, who may develop exceptional skills as skaters, dancers, and gymnasts.

The refinement of motor skills depends a great deal on the development of the muscles and the nerve pathways that control them, but other factors are important as well. Motor skills depend in part on sensory and perceptual skills, for example, and children acquire many of their motor skills in play, which involves social and physical interaction.

One important aspect of motor skills is reaction time—the time required for the external stimulus to trigger the ingoing nerve pathways, for the individual to make a decision, and for the brain to activate the muscles through the outgoing nerve pathways. Reaction time improves substantially through the preschool and elementary school years, even for simple motor movements (Bard, Hay, & Fleury, 1990; Dougherty & Haith, 1993).

✓ To Recap...

Motor development can be categorized as (1) locomotion and postural development or (2) prehension. In both, control over the body develops in a cephalocaudal and a proximodistal direction.

Infants' motor-skills development follows a reasonably predictable sequence, but differences in the timing and manner in which skills are acquired have led psychologists to doubt that motor development is rigidly genetically programmed.

Thelen's dynamic systems approach incorporates the contributions of both nature and nurture to motor development. The infant's task is viewed as the element that stimulates the development of new motor behaviors, as the baby attempts to accomplish the desired task by creating the necessary motor skill from the available physical resources. This process involves two stages: exploration and selection.

The infant's growing ability to act on the world has major psychological consequences. The infant gains knowledge of the environment, including spatial relations, height, and distance.

Motor development beyond infancy consists of increasing coordination of fundamental movement skills, including locomotor, manipulative, and stability movements.

The Human Brain

It is hardly necessary to say that the brain is central to every aspect of development and every sort of human function. Already we have mentioned connections between behavior and neurological maturity in newborns. In this section, we look more directly at the structure and development of the brain.

Structure of the Brain

The brain contains approximately 100 billion nerve cells, or **neurons**; each of these cells has around 3,000 connections with other cells, which adds up to several quadrillion message paths. No one completely understands how all these communication paths work, but we do know quite a bit.

Like every other cell, each neuron has a nucleus and a cell body. But neurons are unique among cells in that they develop extensions on opposite sides, as shown in Figure 6.6. On the incoming side, the extensions, called **dendrites**, often form a tangle of strands that look like the roots of plants. The outgoing extension, called

Neuron
A nerve cell, consisting of a cell body, axon, and dendrites. Neurons transmit activity from one part of the nervous system to another.

Dendrite
One of a net of short fibers extending out from the cell body in a neuron; receives activity from nearby cells and conducts that activity to the cell body.

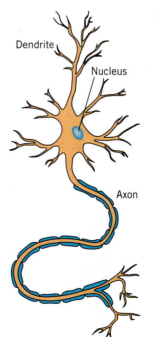

Figure 6.6
A nerve cell, or neuron.

Dendrite

Nucleus

Axon

Axon

A long fiber extending from the cell body in a neuron; conducts activity from the cell.

Myelin

A sheath of fatty material that surrounds and insulates the axon, resulting in speedier transmission of neural activity.

Synapse

The small space between neurons across which neural activity is communicated from one cell to another.

Neurotransmitter

A chemical that transmits electrical activity from one neuron across the synapse to another neuron.

Brain stem

The lower part of the brain, closest to the spinal cord; includes the cerebellum, which is important for maintaining balance and coordination.

Midbrain

A part of the brain that lies above the brain stem; serves as a relay station and as a control area for breathing and swallowing and houses part of the auditory and visual systems.

Cerebrum

The highest brain center; includes both hemispheres of the brain and the interconnections between them.

Cerebral cortex

The thin sheet of gray matter that covers the brain.

an **axon**, is more like a single strand. Axons usually extend farther from the cell than do dendrites and may be quite long. They are often covered by a sheath of a fatty substance, **myelin**, which insulates them and speeds message transmission. Cells do not quite touch one another, but are separated by fluid-filled gaps called **synapses**. Information is passed along a neuron as an electrical signal and crosses the synapse by the flow of chemicals called **neurotransmitters**.

The brain has three major parts. The **brain stem** includes the cerebellum, which controls balance and coordination. The **midbrain** serves as a relay station and controls breathing and swallowing. The **cerebrum**, the highest brain center, includes the left and right hemispheres and the bundle of nerves that connect them.

Of most interest to psychologists is the relatively thin shell of gray matter that covers the brain, called the **cerebral cortex**. This structure appears to be the most recently evolved part of the brain and is crucial for the functioning of the senses, language, memory, thought, and decision making, and the control of voluntary actions. Particular areas of the cerebral cortex have specific responsibilities, although some areas are more specialized than others. The cortex has more than 40 different functional areas. Some specialized tasks are identified in Figure 6.7.

Development of the Brain

Scientists only partially understand how the brain, in its amazing complexity, develops. It begins as a hollow tube. The neurons are generated along the outer walls of this tube and then travel to their proper locations (Kolb, 1989).

Scientists have identified three stages in this process. The first is *cell production*. Most neurons are produced between 10 and 26 weeks following conception, which means that the fetal brain generates these cells at a rate of 250,000 per minute. Cell production occurs from about 10 to 26 weeks, and then no more cells are produced for the rest of the person's life. The brain actually overproduces neurons and then trims them back by as much as 50% (Barinaga, 1993; Raff et al., 1993).

Once the cells have been produced near the center of the brain, they must migrate outward to their proper locations. This *cell migration* is the second stage of early brain development. How do the neurons know where to go? That question has not been answered. It seems likely that there is a chemical attraction between the target location and the migrating neuron. Migration is complete by 7 months gestational age (Huttenlocher, 1990).

When the neuron has found its home, the third stage, *cell elaboration*, begins. In this process, axons and dendrites form synapses with other cells. Cell elaboration continues for years after birth and produces as many as 100% more synapses than will eventually exist in the adult. Thus, as they are being formed, synapses are also being cut back. Experience plays an important role in the eventual sculpting of the connections of the brain through this process. Neurons and their connections compete for survival, and the ones that are used appear to survive, whereas those that are not used disappear (Diamond, 1991).

The fetus's brain grows faster than any other organ (except, perhaps, the eye), and this pace continues in infancy. At birth, the baby's body weight is only 5% of adult weight, whereas the brain weighs 25% of its adult value. By three years of age, the brain has attained 80% of its ultimate weight, compared with 20% for body weight (Morgan & Gibson, 1991; Tanner, 1990). However, the brain does not mature uniformly.

The first area to mature is the primary motor area. It may not be surprising to learn that within this area, the locations that control activity near the head mature first and maturation proceeds downward. This is the cephalocaudal direction in

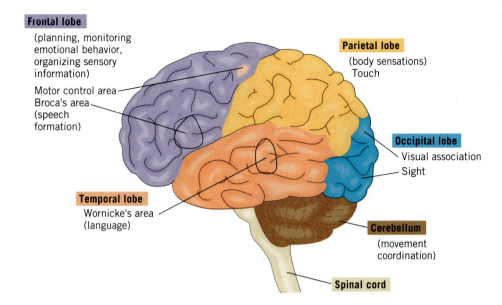

Frontal lobe
(planning, monitoring emotional behavior, organizing sensory information)

Motor control area
Broca's area
(speech formation)

Parietal lobe
(body sensations)
Touch

Occipital lobe
Visual association
Sight

Temporal lobe
Wornicke's area
(language)

Cerebellum
(movement coordination)

Spinal cord

Figure 6.7
Some areas of the cerebral cortex are specialized for particular functions; this diagram shows only a few.

which motor control proceeds. Similarly, the areas that correspond to the arms mature earlier than those that control the fingers, which corresponds to the proximodistal principle.

Not far behind the motor area in maturity are the major sensory areas—touch, vision, and hearing, in that order. Myelin formation, or *myelination*, indicates how mature an area is. For example, the tracts that control fine-motor movement continue to myelinate until about age 4, whereas the areas concerned with attention and consciousness continue to myelinate up to puberty (Tanner, 1990).

Hemispheric Specialization

The two hemispheres of the brain are not perfectly symmetrical, but are *lateralized*—meaning that the left brain and the right brain are somewhat specialized. The left side of the brain is usually more specialized for language performance and the right side for spatial and mathematical tasks. Another way to think about this distinction is that the left side is more oriented to words and concepts, and the right side is more oriented to images. Pictures of the brain produced by a technique called *positron emission tomography (PET)* have confirmed that the left side of the brain is typically more active during language tasks and the right side more active during mathematical tasks. At the same time, however, these pictures show that most tasks, such as reading and listening, involve many areas of the brain (Corina, Vaid, & Bellugi, 1992; Posner et al., 1988).

Also, in some people, the right rather than the left side of the brain appears to be dominant for language, or there is mixed dominance. Left-handers more frequently fall into these categories than do right-handers. Problems with reading performance are sometimes associated with mixed or right-side dominance for language. Children who have *dyslexia* (reading difficulties), but who have otherwise normal or superior intelligence, are more likely to lack strong left-brain dominance than are normal readers.

Hemispheric specialization appears quite early. For example, electrical brain recordings in newborn infants reveal more activity in response to speech sounds on the left than on the right side (Molfese & Molfese, 1979). In Chapter 15, we will see that hemispheric specialization may also play a role in certain gender differences in development.

✓ To Recap...

The brain operates through networks of communication that involve neurons and neuron pathways. Messages travel along neurons as electrical signals, which are picked up by the incoming dendrites and passed along by the outgoing axons. Neurotransmitters allow messages to travel across the synapses from cell to cell.

The brain has three major parts: the brain stem, the midbrain, and the cerebrum. Of most interest to psychologists is the cerebral cortex, which controls higher-level brain functions. Some areas of the cortex are specialized for various functions, including visual, auditory, and touch sensation.

Development of the fetal brain passes through three stages: cell production, cell migration, and cell elaboration. No neurons are produced after around 26 weeks of fetal age, but cell elaboration continues for years. Both neurons and synapses are overproduced and then cut back, and the cutting-back process continues into adolescence. Experience plays a role, affecting which neurons and synapses will die.

The left and right hemispheres of the brain are specialized to some extent. Evidence suggests that even at birth, the left side of the brain is usually prepared to control language functioning and the right side to control spatial and mathematical functioning.

Physical Growth

Physical growth does not proceed at a steady rate, but slows and speeds up throughout childhood.

Growth is perhaps the most fundamental aspect of child development. It is continuous throughout childhood, but it does not happen uniformly. Arnold Gesell once commented that growth does not proceed as a balloon inflates, with each part expanding equally fast (Gesell, 1954). Rather, the overall rate of growth fluctuates during the growth years, with different body parts growing at different rates. In this section, we discuss the unfolding of whole-body growth, adolescent sex differentiation, and factors that affect physical growth and development.

Growth in Size

We saw in Chapter 5 that the fetus's growth rate is dramatically high, although it necessarily slows as birth approaches. This general slowing trend characterizes growth up to adolescence.

Figure 6.8 shows an average growth curve for males and females. Boys and girls are approximately the same height until around 10 years of age. A growth spurt typically occurs between 10 and 12 years of age for girls and between 12 and 14 years of age for boys. This age difference accounts for the common observation that girls, on average, are taller than boys in grades 7 and 8, a relation that permanently reverses a few years later. In North America and northern and western Europe, where good records have been kept, we know that height increases are just about completed by 15.5 years of age in girls and 17.5 years in boys; less than 2% of growth is added afterwards (Malina, 1990; Tanner, 1990).

Charts like that in Figure 6.8 may give the impression that there is, or should be, a normal growth rate. But few children exactly fit the averages on these charts. Although it is obvious that individuals reach different ultimate heights and weights, it may be less apparent that their *rates* of growth may also differ. To illustrate, Figure 6.9 shows a growth curve for three girls. Girl B reached menarche, the onset of menstruation, before girls A and C. She was taller than both at age 12, but was ulti-

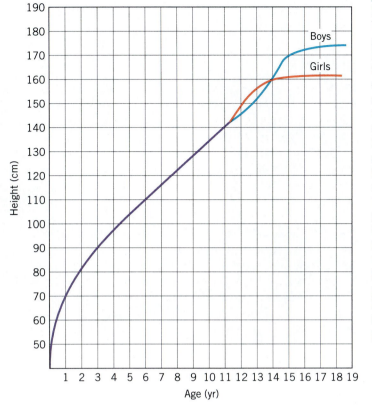

Figure 6.8
Typical male and female growth curves. Birth length doubles by around the 4th year, but growth slows, and length doubles again only around the 13th year. Adult height can be estimated by doubling the height of males at 24 months and of females at 18 months (Lowrey, 1978; Tanner, 1990). From "Standards for Growth and Growth Velocities" by J. M. Tanner, R. H. Whitehouse, and M. Takaishi, 1966, *Archives of Disease in Childhood, 41*, p. 467. Copyright © 1966 by *Archives of Disease in Childhood*. Reprinted by permission.

mately shorter than girl A. Such differences in age of onset of the growth spurt are likely to accompany differences in age of puberty. They may also have long-term implications for personality development, a topic to which we return later.

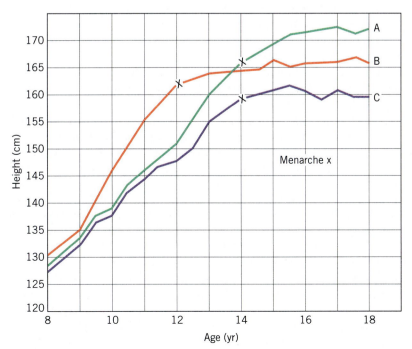

Figure 6.9
Curves showing the heights of three girls over time. Age of menarche is indicated by an *x*. Adapted from "Individual Patterns of Development" by N. Bayley, 1956, *Child Development, 27*, p. 52. Copyright © 1956 by The Society for Research in Child Development, Inc. Adapted by permission.

The pace of growth during childhood and adolescence is influenced by both nature and nurture factors.

Factors that may produce individual differences in growth rates include malnutrition and disease. For example, researchers recorded the growth rate of a child who suffered from two episodes of inadequate nutrition (Prader, Tanner, & von Harnack, 1963). The child's growth was severely affected. After the episodes were over, the child did not simply return to his normal rate of growth. Rather, he experienced a remarkable acceleration in growth, which returned him to his expected growth path. This *catch-up growth* is relatively common as an aftermath of disease or limited malnutrition (Tanner, 1963).

How might we distinguish a child whose rate of maturation is slow from a child who is genetically targeted for a small adult stature? A technique for making this distinction uses the child's skeletal maturity, or **bone age**, which may differ from the child's chronological age. Bones develop from the center and extend outward toward the bone ends, called the *epiphyses.* As a bone reaches its ultimate length, the epiphyses close and no further growth is possible. Scientists can use X-rays to determine how a child's bone development compares with that of his or her peers and approximately how much more growth remains to occur (Tanner, 1990).

Bone age
The degree of maturation of an individual as indicated by the extent of hardening of the bones.

Changes in Body Proportion and Composition

Another aspect of growth rate concerns the rates at which different parts of the body develop. Figure 6.10 shows a graph of proportional growth of the body. Most noticeably, the relative size of the head changes from 50% of total body length at 2 months fetal age, to 25% at birth, and to only about 10% by adulthood. This shift reflects the cephalocaudal, or top-down, sequence of development described earlier.

We have seen that a spurt in height accompanies adolescence. More of this height comes from trunk growth than from leg growth. However, in one of the few violations of the cephalocaudal and proximodistal principles, leg growth occurs

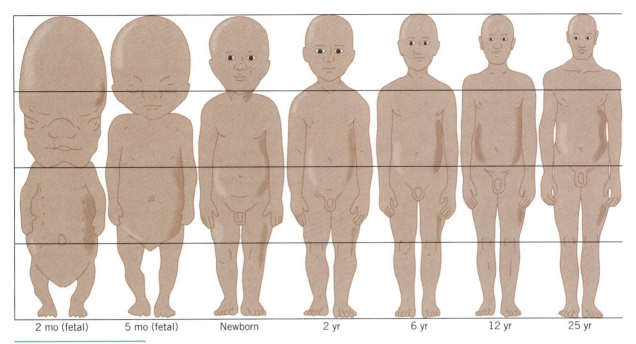

| 2 mo (fetal) | 5 mo (fetal) | Newborn | 2 yr | 6 yr | 12 yr | 25 yr |

Figure 6.10
Body proportions at several ages. From *Growth* by W. J. Robbins, S. Brady, A. G. Hogan, C. M. Jackson, and C. W. Greene, 1928, New Haven: Yale University Press, p. 118.

earlier than trunk growth by 6 to 9 months. Parents often wonder whether children at this stage will always be all hands and feet (Tanner, 1990).

Internal organs also follow individual paths of growth. Up to about 6 to 8 years of age, the brain grows much faster than the body in general and the reproductive organs grow much slower. Then the rate of brain growth slows to a gradual halt, whereas the reproductive system reaches a plateau between 5 and 12 years of age and surges at around 14 years of age.

The proportion of fat to muscle also changes with age and differs for boys and girls. The fetus begins to accumulate fat in the weeks before birth. This process continues until around 9 months after birth. After that, fat gradually declines until around 6 to 8 years of age. Girls have a bit more fat than boys at birth. This difference increases gradually through childhood until about 8 years of age and then increases more rapidly.

During the adolescent growth spurt, girls continue to gain fat faster than males. Muscle growth also occurs during adolescence, more strikingly for boys than for girls (Malina, 1990). However, because girls reach their growth spurt before males, there is a 2-year period in which girls, on average, have more muscle than boys. Changes in body proportions that occur in adolescence result in greater shoulder width and muscular development in males and broader hips and more fat in females.

Sex Differentiation and Puberty

We have seen that gender affects body size and composition. Now we look more closely at the physical aspects of gender in the growth years and especially in adolescence.

Early Sex Differentiation   We saw in Chapter 4 that the father's sperm determines the sex of the fetus by contributing either an X (female) or a Y (male) chromosome to the 23rd pair. In the fetus, the gonads (ovaries in females and testes in males) look the same for males and females when they first appear, but they develop somewhat faster in the male. It is interesting to note that every fetus is on a course to be female unless male hormones, secreted by the newly formed gonads, interrupt this process. Fetal hormones also affect brain wiring and appear responsible, for example, for the eventual sex differences in hemispheric specialization and for cyclic (menstruation) versus noncyclic hormone production in adulthood. We will have much more to say about early sex differentiation in Chapter 15.

Sex differentiation continues from birth until puberty. Although girls develop somewhat faster than boys, they share relatively similar heights, body proportions, and body composition in the years between birth and puberty, at least compared with the differences that occur during puberty.

Adolescence and Puberty   After the fetal period, puberty produces the greatest surge of differentiation between the two sexes. These changes occur when certain chemicals—hormones—provided by various endocrine glands, are released into the bloodstream. Especially important glands for growth and sexual differentiation in adolescence are the gonads, the adrenals, and the thyroid. In addition, growth hormone, secreted by the pituitary gland, helps stimulate bone growth (Kulin, 1991; Paikoff & Brooks-Gunn, 1990; Stanhope, 1989).

Puberty
The period in which chemical and physical changes in the body occur that enable sexual reproduction.

The most significant aspect of development during adolescence is **puberty**, the series of changes that culminate in sexual maturity and the ability to reproduce. Puberty usually begins between the ages of 10 and 14, typically earlier for girls than for boys.

In males, the first sign of puberty, which occurs at around age 11 on average, is an enlargement of the testes and a change in the texture and color of the scrotum. Later, the penis enlarges, pubic hair appears, and sperm production begins, followed by the appearance of hair under the arms and on the face. Near the end of puberty, the larynx lengthens, causing the male voice to become deeper. This lengthening is sometimes evident in a breaking of the voice.

For females, the first sign of puberty is breast budding, which may occur as early as 8 years of age and as late as 13 years, followed by the appearance of pubic hair. Menarche occurs relatively late in puberty. In northern and central Europe and North America, 95 percent of girls begin menarche between 11 and 15 years of age. Usually, ovulation follows the onset of menarche by 1 or 2 years.

How fast adolescents move through puberty varies as widely as when they start. For example, it may take a girl as few as 1.5 years or as many as 5 years to complete puberty. If we were to study a single class of boys and girls in elementary school, beginning when the first student began puberty and following the group until the last student finished puberty, chances are we would have to follow the group for a full 10 years (Petersen, 1987). We can imagine how much variation in maturation there would be in the middle years and how it might play out in social relations, self-image, and confidence.

Attitudes toward Puberty   Psychologists studying adolescence used to focus on physical changes. As investigators have learned more about the dynamics of adolescent change, however, they have increasingly emphasized social and cultural factors. More and more, investigators talk about biosocial or psychobiological factors in adolescence rather than only about biological factors (Lerner, Lerner, & Tubman, 1989; Smith, 1989).

Consider, for example, how girls react to the onset of menarche. This event usually heightens a girl's self-esteem and her prestige among peers. However, girls who are psychologically unprepared for menarche, perhaps because they lack information about it, have more negative feelings about its onset. Later in life, these girls are also more negative about menstruation, report more severe symptoms, and are more self-conscious about it than are other girls (Brooks-Gunn, 1987, 1991).

Social factors also influence how adolescents feel about the changes in their bodies and when they occur. At least in the United States, the ideal female is thin. But as we have seen, females add fat during puberty, and their hips broaden. In contrast, males add muscle and shoulder width, characteristics that better fit the preferred cultural image of males. Not surprisingly, then, early-maturing females tend to be more dissatisfied with their bodies during puberty than late-maturing females, whereas the opposite is true for males (Crockett & Petersen, 1987; Graber et al., 1994).

Only limited research exists on how early and late maturers succeed later in life. When studied as young adults, adolescent boys who had been early maturers had more stable careers than late maturers. They scored higher on tests of sociability, dominance, self-control, and responsibility. Late maturers had more negative self-concepts and more feelings of rejection by others and were more likely to have suffered maladjustment in late adolescence. On the positive side, late-maturing boys were more nurturant and seemed better able than earlier maturers to face their emotions and feelings (Brooks-Gunn & Reiter, 1990).

Factors That Affect Growth and Maturation

Our genes play a major part in our growth and physical maturation. Thus children tend to resemble their parents—tall parents, for example, usually have taller children than do short parents. But like every other aspect of human development, growth and maturation are also influenced by the context of development.

Heredity   Recall from Chapter 4 that investigators sometimes compare similarities in identical twins with similarities in fraternal twins to determine how much genetic factors influence particular behaviors. A similar strategy yields information about the role of heredity in the onset and pace of puberty and body structure.

One study of twins has been under way in Louisville, Kentucky, for over 30 years, and more than 500 twins have been studied. Identical twins have been found to become increasingly close in height up to around 4 years of age and to stabilize at a very high correlation of around .94. Fraternal twins of the same sex do the opposite. At birth, their correlation in height is about .77, but it drops to .59 at 2 years and to .49 at 9 years, at which point it stabilizes. A similar pattern exists for weight (Wilson, 1986b). Identical twins are also more similar than fraternal twins in their spurts and lags in growth (Mueller, 1986).

Several other measures support the role of heredity in the rate of maturation. Identical twins display much higher similarity in the age of eruption of their teeth than do fraternal twins, and they are more similar in the pace of bone development, as well as in breast development in girls and testicular development in boys. The age of onset of menarche differs by less than 4 months in identical twins. One study revealed that even when identical twins were raised apart, the onset of menarche differed by an average of only 2.8 months. In contrast, fraternal twins raised together typically differ by 6 to 12 months in the age of onset of menarche. These two studies imply that genes play a substantial role in maturation, a conclusion also supported by similarities in the age of onset of menarche between mothers and daughters (Bailey & Garn, 1986).

If genetic factors influence maturation and eventual stature, we might expect to find maturational differences among genetic groups. In fact, we do. Asians reach puberty faster than do Europeans and move through it more quickly (but achieve a smaller stature). Africans proceed through adolescence at about the same pace as Europeans and Americans, but when they have equivalent quality of life, they reach a taller stature (Evelyth, 1986).

Exercise   Physical activity generally has beneficial effects on development, but there is some evidence of negative effects if exercise is taken to extremes. Very strenuous exercise in highly intensive training programs (for example, training for wrestling) may reduce the rate of growth (Gallahue, 1989). Ballet dancers exercise strenuously and strive to keep their bodies slim, factors that seem to be related to their tendency to reach menarche at a later age than nondancers (Brooks-Gunn, 1987). Once menarche has begun, exercise affects the regularity of the menstrual cycle. Female athletes who train intensively often experience irregular menstrual periods during their training regime (Firsch, 1984).

Nutrition   It should come as no surprise that relations have been found between the adequacy of a child's nutrition and various measures of that child's growth and development. Considering that about 40% of the world's children below age 5 are underweight, this is not a minor issue (Pollitt et al., 1996).

Poor nutrition is thought to be especially damaging during gestation and the early years of life, because brain growth is so rapid during this period. For example, children in Chile who died from malnutrition in their first or second year showed lower brain weight, less brain protein, fewer brain cells, and less myelin than expected (Bálazs et al., 1986). Growth occurs in two ways: by increases in the number of cells and by increases in cell size. Increases in cell number usually characterize early growth, whereas increases in cell size are responsible for all growth after about 18 months. Thus the impact of malnutrition may be different at different ages.

Even mild-to-moderate malnutrition can cause problems in children (Ricciutti, 1993). A major research project investigated the diets of children in Kenya, Egypt, and Mexico. The report concluded that even when children were consuming ample quantities of food, the quality of their diets affected their scores on various tests of cognitive and intellectual development. Deficiencies in certain vitamins (principally, vitamins A, B12, and D) and minerals (especially calcium, iron, and zinc) seemed to be most clearly involved (Sigman, 1995).

Recent studies indicate, however, that the effects of early malnutrition are not as irreversible as was once thought. Dietary correction and stimulating environments can have remarkable recuperative effects, although prevention is clearly better than treatment. Research in Brazil and Colombia documents the effects of preventive measures. When food supplements were provided from midpregnancy to the time the child was 3 years of age, benefits for both growth and weight could be observed even 3 years after the intervention (Paine et al., 1992; Super, Herrera, & Mora, 1990).

Why does undernutrition affect intellectual development? Although direct biological effects on the brain seem to be involved, social and psychological factors may also play a role. For example, because poor nutrition reduces children's energy levels, it may limit their active exploration and learning. One theory also suggests

Zinc deficiency can produce abnormal metabolism and growth failure (child on left).

Eating disorders during adolescence often result from a preoccupation with weight and from distorted concepts of body image.

that babies who are smaller in size and delayed in motor abilities—two common effects of early undernutrition—tend to be treated and cared for more like younger infants, thereby receiving less verbal and cognitive stimulation (Pollitt et al., 1993).

Eating disorders represent an area of nutrition that has received increasing attention in recent years. With one such disorder, **anorexia nervosa**, the individual, most often a young female, voluntarily engages in severe dietary restriction in order to maintain a body physique that is extremely thin. The damaging effects of this self-starvation include muscle wasting, dry skin and hair, constipation, dehydration, and sleep disturbance. Sometimes growth and development are impaired, menstruation ceases, and breast development is permanently affected. Adolescent anorexics often have a distorted concept of nourishment and body image.

Another eating disorder is **bulimia**, which involves binging on large quantities of food and then self-induced vomiting to purge the excess calories and maintain a normal weight level. This disorder often results in damage to teeth and gums, cracked and damaged lips, and serious imbalances in body fluids. Bulimics, like anorexics, also frequently have distorted concepts of food and body image, and they often have guilt, anxiety, and depression (Hsu, 1990; Leon, 1991; Rees & Trahms, 1989).

Obesity, or excess fat storage, is one of the most common disorders in the United States today. Obesity is usually defined as weight 20% or more over a standard weight for height. Obesity appears to be a particular problem among Hispanic Americans (Olvera-Ezzell, Power, & Cousins, 1990). It may result from genetic predisposition, overeating, or a combination of both, and it frequently has an early onset, by 4 or 5 years of age (Eichorn, 1970, 1979).

Obesity has several effects on development. Obese females tend to begin puberty earlier than do nonobese females, for example, and obese males hit their growth spurt earlier than do their counterparts. Obesity has psychological consequences as well. Many obese children feel insecure and are overprotected by their parents. They frequently experience school difficulties, neuroses, and social problems. A vicious cycle may become established in which social and psychological problems induce eating, and weight gain further contributes to the problems.

Anorexia nervosa
A severe eating disorder, usually involving excessive weight loss through self-starvation, most often found in teenage girls.

Bulimia
A disorder of food binging and sometimes purging by self-induced vomiting, typically observed in teenage girls.

Obesity
A condition of excess fat storage; often defined as weight more than 20% over a standardized, ideal weight.

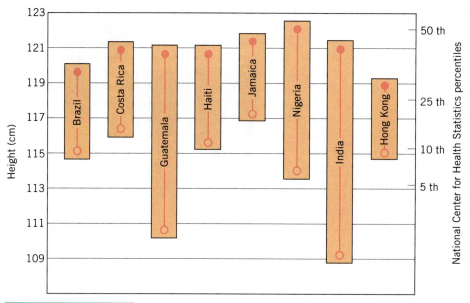

Figure 6.11
Average heights of 7-year-old boys in several countries. The solid circles at the top indicate the heights of boys from higher socioeconomic classes, and the open circles at the bottom indicate the heights of boys from lower socioeconomic classes. Adapted from "Genetics, Environment, and Growth: Issues in the Assessment of Nutritional Status" by R. Martorell, 1984. In A. Velasquez and H. Bourges (Eds.), *Genetic Factors in Nutrition* (p. 382), Orlando, FL: Academic Press. Copyright © 1984 by Academic Press. Adapted by permission.

Development in Cultural Context
Social Class and Poverty

The quality of life varies dramatically between rich and poor countries. The childhood death rate is 10 times higher in developing than in developed countries. One estimate is that 11 million fewer children would die each year if the poor countries of the world had the same death rates as the wealthy countries (Altman, 1993). However, even in the wealthiest countries, all citizens do not have equal access to resources.

In virtually every country in the world, there are differences in social classes, and these differences determine access to nutrition and health care. Differences in physical development between social classes are consistently found. As Figure 6.11 shows, for example, there is much less difference in height among young boys of the higher socioeconomic class across several countries than there is between higher and lower socioeconomic classes within a country. Social class itself is not the cause of such physical variations; rather, they result from the many differences in nutrition, health care, disease, environmental enrichment, and opportunity.

The United States is not immune to these problems. Some 14.3 million children under 18 years of age live in poverty, about one in every five U.S. children. And the likelihood of being poor is not evenly distributed among racial groups. Whereas approximately 40% of African-American families and 35% of Hispanic-American families with children are poor, only 13% of non-Hispanic white families live in poverty (Brooks-Gunn et al., 1995). Furthermore, poverty is a growing problem. In 1990, the poverty rate was one-third higher than what it was in the two preceding decades (Duncan, Brooks-Gunn, & Klebanov, 1994; Halpern, 1993).

Behind these grim statistics are children and parents who have inadequate access to health care, housing, and nutrition. The gravest consequence of these conditions is death. A recent study found that death rates among children were seven times higher in the poorest counties than in the richest counties (Halpern, 1993).

A child's well-being may be affected even before conception. Poor women are more likely to have inferior health before pregnancy and inadequate health care during pregnancy. They are also more likely to experience high levels of stress during pregnancy and to engage in behavior that is harmful to their health. Consequently, the fetus is more likely to experience intrauterine stress, a contributor to premature labor and delivery and to low birth weight (Chomitz et al., 1995).

The daily grind of poverty and typically overcrowded living conditions following birth can compound a baby's risk of problems. Poverty can drain parents' energy and undermine their self-confidence and feeling of control over their lives. Exhaustion, irritability, anger, and a feeling of futility are often the result, with consequences for the parent–child relationship. Parents may not have the psychological resources to share their infant's joy and pleasure, which would provide them positive feedback for meeting the infant's needs.

Not all poor families are the same, of course. Some children grow up poor in extended families where neighborhood and social support is ample and the social network pulls together to help them rise to the challenge of limited resources and excel. Still, these children and families face formidable odds.

The Clinton presidential administration has made several proposals to address some of the problems of the poor, including one that would make health care more accessible. But some people argue that caring for the poor is not the government's responsibility. Clearly, the problems of poverty and adequate health care for all will be with us for years to come.

Physical Abnormality Growth depends crucially on normal functioning of the pituitary and thyroid glands. In adolescence, sex-gland secretions play an important role in the growth spurt. Abnormalities in the functioning of any of these glands can produce dwarfism or giantism. If diagnosed in time, glandular abnormalities can be corrected. For example, some children fail to grow because of a deficit in growth hormone, perhaps as a result of a tumor of the hypothalamus in the brain. If this problem is discovered early enough, substances can be administered to stimulate the pituitary to produce growth hormone, often substantially speeding growth.

Growth problems can also be caused by diseases of organs such as the heart, liver, and kidneys and by various bone diseases (Kreipe & Strauss, 1989; Lowrey, 1978).

Abuse and Psychological Trauma We have focused up to now on physical aspects of the context of growth and development, but psychological trauma can also impair growth. A *failure-to-thrive* syndrome has been described in infants who fail to gain weight for no obvious reasons other than psychological disturbances or maltreatment and abuse by parents. Frequently, these babies gain weight readily when their care is transferred to hospital personnel (Benoit, 1993; Drotar et al., 1990).

A report on 13 children between the ages of 3 and 11 years provides an example of how psychological trauma can affect growth. These children lived in homes

Child abuse has reached alarming levels in the United States. Abuse can limit growth and can cause permanent brain and other physical damage.

that were unusually stressful as a result of marital problems or alcohol abuse, and there were several cases of child abuse. The children appeared to have abnormally low pituitary gland activity, and their growth rates were substantially impaired. Shortly after they were removed from their homes, the circulation of growth hormone from the pituitary increased, and the growth of most of the children accelerated (Powell, Brasel, & Blizzard, 1967). Thus, there is at least some environmental control over a characteristic that was once thought to be controlled almost exclusively by genetics.

This relationship between psychological environment and growth is of special concern in the United States, where child abuse is reaching alarming levels. The National Center on Child Abuse and Neglect reported 160,932 cases of confirmed abuse of children under age 3 in the United States in 1990, and a majority of the 1,200 children who died from abuse that year were under 3 (Mrazek, 1993). Because most cases are not reported, it is difficult to know how much abuse occurs, but it is estimated that 2.2 million children a year are abused, 25% of them under 2 years of age (Zigler, Hopper, & Hall, 1993).

Historical Trends   There is evidence that growth rates have changed over recent history in some parts of the world. In Europe and North America after about 1900 the average height of 5- to 7-year-olds increased 1 to 2 centimeters per decade and the average height of 10- to 14-year-olds increased 2 to 3 centimeters per decade. Adult height, however, increased only 0.6 cm per decade between 1880 and 1960. Thus the increase in children's heights apparently reflected a trend toward faster maturation more than a trend toward greater ultimate stature. Before this century it was fairly typical for people to grow until age 25 or so, whereas today growth usually continues only until about age 18 or 19.

The trend toward faster maturation has also been reflected in the age of menarche, which has decreased over the last century (Meredith, 1963; Tanner, 1987). Earlier maturation can be explained by better living conditions—better nourishment, better health care, and lowered incidence of disease. The trend began to level off in the 1970s.

✓ *To Recap...*

Growth is continuous through childhood but does not proceed uniformly. The rate of growth gradually slows, then experiences a spurt at adolescence, and stops soon afterward. Growth rates vary widely among children, as do the heights ultimately reached. Bone age is one way to distinguish a child who will be a short adult from one who is maturing slowly. Different parts of the body develop at different rates, following a cephalocaudal progression. Body organs also vary in rates of maturation; the brain, for example, develops very early.

Boys and girls grow fairly similarly until adolescence. Girls typically experience the adolescent growth spurt and puberty earlier than do boys. Boys add more height once their growth spurt has begun, as well as more muscle mass and shoulder width. Girls add relatively more fat and hip width. The adolescent's attitude toward these changes may reflect social and cultural factors, such as the amount of information he or she has about the changes and the body image that society holds up as ideal.

Many factors influence growth and maturation. Genetic processes are clearly important, but such environmental factors as exercise, nutrition, social class, disease, abuse, and psychological trauma also come into play. Some of these environmental variables, such as better nutrition, have accelerated growth rates in many developed countries during the 20th century.

Conclusion

This chapter concludes a set of three chapters that concern the more biological aspects of human development. In Chapters 4 and 5, we focused on genetics and prenatal development. In the present chapter, we discussed the behaviors and physical equipment the baby brings to the world and how this basic equipment develops through infancy, childhood, and adolescence.

Until recently, psychologists have not been very open to considering the physical and biological bases of behavior. Rather, a tension existed between the more physically based and the more psychologically based disciplines, with psychologists more focused on demonstrating that social and environmental factors influence behavior. However, the mood seems to be changing. As we have seen, biological influences that we might at first imagine would act on their own are found, on closer examination, to cooperate with environmental factors to produce their ultimate effect. We have seen many examples of this interdependence—for instance, in the effects of health care on birth mortality, of the family setting on the outcome of infants at risk, of prenatal exposure to cocaine on the newborn's state organization and rhythms, of practice on motor development, and of psychological trauma on growth. For this reason, many of the tensions that once existed between psychologists and biologists have largely disappeared, and the search is on to understand how biological factors and experience collaborate to influence human development.

No better evidence of this collaboration exists than in the successful efforts of psychologists, biologists, and neuroscientists to have the decade of the 1990s declared the decade of the brain. President George Bush signed a resolution to this effect in October 1989, committing the United States to the expenditure of significant research dollars and effort aimed at understanding both the psychological and the biological mysteries of this most important organ. Perhaps by the turn of the 21st century, exciting advances in our understanding of human development will reflect the wisdom of this national commitment to better understanding.

Visual Summary for Chapter 6:

Physical Development: Birth, Motor Development, and Growth

Birth and the Perinatal Period

Indicators of Risk for Developmental Problems

Maternal and Family Characteristics	→ A number of maternal and family factors, especially whether the mother receives prenatal care, are important in identifying babies at risk for developmental problems.
Physical Compromise of the Newborn	→ Low birthweight is an important indicator of risk. Low birthweight babies may be preterm, or they may be small for gestational age (SGA).
Physical and Behavioral Assessment	→ Newborn assessments, such as the Apgar exam, the Prechtl test, and the Brazelton Neonatal Behavioral Assessment Scale are also used to assess risk.

The Organized Newborn

Activity of Newborns

States	→ The newborn's level of alertness can be categorized according to six states varying from quiet sleep to crying.
Rhythms	→ The newborn's states occur in rhythmic cycles. A basic rest-activity cycle is coordinated with a longer sleep-wake cycle.
Reflexes	→ Newborns possess a number of reflexes, some that last through life, and others that disappear during the first year.
Congenitally Organized Behaviors	→ Congenitally organized behaviors are present in the newborn and differ from reflexes in that they are not easily attributable to a particular stimulus and are more adaptable.

Motor Development

Categories

Locomotion/Postural	→ Control of trunk of the body and arms and legs for moving around.
Prehension	→ Ability to use hands as tools.

Motor Development

Principles

Proximodistal	➤	Motor skills develop from center of the body to parts farther out.
Cephalocaudal	➤	Motor skills develop from head to feet.
Dynamic Systems Approach	➤	Individual motor skills develop when infants are motivated to accomplish a task and when they possess the sufficient physical resources.
Stages	➤	During exploration, many different responses are tried somewhat randomly; during selection, responses are fine-tuned and coordinated.

Motor Development in Childhood

Fundamental Movement Skills	➤	Locomotor, manipulative, and stability.
Reaction Time	➤	Improves through preschool and elementary years.

The Human Brain

Three Stages in the Development of the Fetal Brain

Cell Production	➤	Most neurons are produced between 10 and 26 weeks after conception.
Cell Migration	➤	Following production, cells migrate to their proper locations, a process that is completed by 7 months gestational age.
Cell Elaboration	➤	Axons and dendrites form synapses with other cells, a process that continues for years.

Hemispheric Specialization

Left Hemisphere	➤	Prepared at birth to control language function in most people.
Right Hemisphere	➤	Prepared at birth to control spatial and mathematical functioning in most people.

Human Growth

Growth in Size, Proportion, and Composition	➤	Growth is continuous, but not uniform, throughout childhood. The rate of growth gradually slows, then spurts at adolescence and stops soon afterwards. Different parts of the body, as well as body organs, develop at different rates.
Sex Differentiation and Puberty	➤	Boys and girls grow fairly similarly until puberty. Girls tend to experience the adolescence growth spurt and puberty earlier than boys. Once their growth spurt has begun, boys add more height, muscle mass, and shoulder width; girls add relatively more fat and hip width.
Factors Affecting Growth	➤	Human growth is influenced not only by heredity, but also by environmental factors such as nutrition, exercise, poverty, disease, and even abuse and psychological trauma.

Chapter 7

Sensory and Perceptual Development

In 1991, noted neurologist Oliver Sachs received a phone call offering him a rare opportunity for scientific study. A 50-year-old man, blind since early childhood, had just undergone an operation that restored his sight. Sachs was invited to visit the man, Virgil, and his family and to help assess Virgil's progress in the weeks following the recovery of his vision.

As Sachs noted, Virgil's case history presented a real-life instance of a hypothetical situation posed more than 300 years earlier by a philosopher named Molyneux. Molyneux directed this question to the famous empiricist philosopher John Locke: A man is born blind, but is suddenly able to see as an adult. The man had learned to distinguish a sphere and a cube by touch when he was blind. Will he be able to recognize which is which by sight alone? Locke (1694/1824) answered no, arguing that experience is necessary to understand the relation between vision and touch (the empiricist, or nurture, position). Others predicted that the previously blind man would be able to identify the two objects by vision alone, because knowledge of the relations among properties of objects is inborn (the nativist, or nature, position). At issue was a central question in philosophy, which was later carried over to psychology: Are people born with innate, organized categories for perceiving the world, or must everything be experienced to be known?

Sachs's summary of his observations was published as an article in the New Yorker *(Sachs, 1993). Virgil's experiences proved similar to those of other individuals who had gained or regained sight in adulthood (Gregory, 1978; von Senden, 1960). Virgil could certainly see from the moment the bandages were removed, and he was sensitive to and interested in colors, shapes, and movements. He could make little sense, however, of what he saw—not only initially but for some time—and he was quite unable to recognize through sight objects with which he was familiar through touch. Furthermore, the attempt to cope with the world through a new perceptual mode brought conflicts and disappointments as well as gains, and over time Virgil used his vision less and less. For example, he reverted to eating as he had when blind, and he began to turn away from the mirror and close his eyes while shaving.*

Cases such as Virgil's are fascinating, but they offer only indirect and imperfect evidence with respect to the nature–nurture issues that inspired Molyneux's query. There are, after all, enormous differences between a 50-year-old man and a newborn baby, even if both are experiencing the world of vision for the first time. More direct evidence would come from studies of what the newborn perceives of his or her world. This type of evidence was unavailable in Molyneux and Locke's time, and indeed for many years after, but it is no longer unavailable today. In this chapter we discuss some exciting discoveries about perceptual development, especially about perception in infancy, that have emerged from contemporary child psychology.

Sensation
The experience resulting from the stimulation of a sense organ.

In order to talk about perceptual development we must first distinguish among three processes: sensation, perception, and attention. **Sensation** refers to the detection and discrimination of sensory information—for example, hearing and distinguishing high and low tones. **Perception** refers to the interpretation of sensations and involves *recognition* ("I've heard that song before") and *identification* ("That was thunder"). **Attention** refers to the selectivity of perception, as when a child fails to hear a parent calling because he is watching television.

In this chapter, we examine the capacities that babies have for learning about the objects and people in their world and how these capacities develop. After we consider the perceptual modes (vision, touch, etc.) separately, we see how children coordinate information from these modes. We then discuss how the child integrates perception and attention with action in the smooth flow of behavior. We begin by taking a look at what the three major theories say about perceptual development.

Perception
The interpretation of sensory stimulation based on experience.

Attention
The selection of particular sensory input for perceptual and cognitive processing and the exclusion of competing input.

Theories of Sensory and Perceptual Development

The three theories of development that we have described—environmental/learning, ethological, and cognitive-developmental—have somewhat different ideas about perceptual development. As you might expect, however, they agree on several fundamental issues. All of these theories acknowledge that experience affects perceptual development, for example, and all of them acknowledge that our biological machinery plays an important role in how we experience the things that go on around us. Thus, all three theories adopt an interactionist perspective on the nature–nurture issue. As we will see, however, they differ in where they place their emphases.

Environmental/Learning Approaches

Learning theorists emphasize the role of experience in perceptual development. According to their view, a child builds perceptual impressions through associations. For example, a baby seeing a face for the first time sees no relation among the eyes, eyebrows, nose, mouth, ears, and hairline. After seeing many faces, the baby comes to see all of these elements as belonging together. Only then can the baby recognize a familiar face or distinguish one face from another (Hebb, 1949).

Babies are fascinated by faces of others and especially their eyes, while parents enjoy the social engagement that eye contact communicates.

[margin handwritten note: No to Molyneux ✓ Experience connects sight & hearing.]

Through experience babies also learn to connect sights with sounds, touch with vision, and so on. The sound of a human voice seems, at first, no more likely to accompany the sight of a face than does the sound of a horn. Only experience makes the combination of face and voice more natural than that of face and horn. So, along with John Locke, learning theorists would answer Molyneux's question regarding the integration of the senses with a resounding no: The blind man must see and feel the sphere and the cube at the same time to understand the relations between the visual and tactile sensations.

Learning theory helps make sense of such phenomena as our inability to distinguish easily among faces of people who belong to races that are unfamiliar. A person who is Asian, for example, may have difficulty distinguishing among Caucasian males of similar height and hair color, because she is relatively unfamiliar with the particular features of Caucasian faces.

Research on the central nervous system illustrates how experience affects even single sensory cells—both their survival and the connections that form among them. Experience produces a kind of Darwinian survival-of-the-fittest battle among brain cells (Edelman, 1993). As we noted in Chapter 6, many of the neurons we are born with die early in our life. Researchers believe that visual experience activates some cells, which survive, but that other cells are not activated, and these die or their synapses are trimmed back (Greenough & Black, 1992).

For example, each cell (neuron) in the visual area of the brain is stimulated by one type of visual element, such as vertical edges, but not by other elements, such as horizontal edges. Other brain cells respond to horizontal edges but are insensitive to vertical edges. Still other cells "like" angles, or diagonal lines, or other visual elements. Most theorists believe that when a stimulus repeatedly activates combinations of such cells—as when a baby looks at a square—the connections among these cells grow stronger. Eventually, the cells fire in synchrony, and a person sees a whole square rather than a combination of lines and intersections (Hebb, 1949). The important point here is that these cells are sensitive to experience at a very early age (Antonini & Stryker, 1993).

Ethological Theory

Ethological theorists emphasize the natural equipment that animals and humans have evolved for gathering information from their world. They pay special attention to how our sensory receptors are built to pick up physical energy and inform us about aspects of the physical world.

[margin handwritten note: Yes to Molyneux ✓ natural connection between vision & touch]

James and Eleanor Gibson have developed an ethological theory of perceptual development that contrasts strikingly with the learning approach (E. J. Gibson, 1969; J. J. Gibson, 1966). The Gibsons do not believe that perception involves combining pieces of input through experience. Instead, they argue that objects in the world give off physical energy that is already organized and can be perceived in its entirety. Perceptual development, they suggest, consists of a child's increasing sensitivity to the organization of this energy and to which properties of objects and people remain stable and which properties change. In general, ethological theorists would be more likely to answer Molyneux's question with a yes, because they would assume that natural relations exist between vision and touch.

The Gibsonian analysis suggests that even infants should be sensitive to the synchrony of visual and auditory events, and this appears to be the case. When young babies watch people speak, they can detect when speakers' lip movements are not synchronized with the sounds that they hear (Kuhl & Meltzoff, 1988). This ability is difficult to account for by traditional learning theories, which emphasize the need for certain sound–vision experiences. Such experiences are fairly limited for very young infants. Notice that theorists generally assume that the earlier in development a perceptual skill occurs, the less likely it is that it has been acquired by experience.

Cognitive-Developmental Theories

Cognitive theories of perception emphasize the role of knowledge in how we interpret the world. In a classic study illustrating the role of cognition in perception, Jerome Bruner had children from middle and low socioeconomic groups look at a quarter and then select a circle that they thought matched the size of the quarter. Children from the low socioeconomic group selected larger circles than did the children from the middle socioeconomic group, suggesting that the quarter looked larger to the former group, presumably because it was of greater relative value to them (Bruner & Goodman, 1947).

Bruner proposed, in fact, that cognitive processes precede perception rather than the other way around—that a person may not perceive an object until he or she has categorized it (Bruner, Goodnow, & Austin, 1956). Although this idea may seem unlikely, it is not difficult to demonstrate cognitive effects on perception. For example, look at the picture in Figure 7.1. What is it? Now, look at the upside-down word in the caption of the figure. Once you know what the picture is, you perceive it differently, and it is no longer possible to perceive it the way you did before. Clearly, cognitive categorization can affect perception.

Piaget also emphasized the role of cognition in perception. He believed that a child's stage of cognitive development controls how the child perceives the world. Through infancy, babies increasingly integrate perceptual modes, such as touch and vision, which helps them understand that, for example, a felt object and a seen object are the same. (Piaget, then, would answer Molyneux's question with a no: experience is necessary to properly identify previously felt objects by vision alone.)

Figure 7.1

A dalmatian.

The influence of cognition on perception continues well past infancy. For example, children in the early school years (the preoperational period) have difficulty attending to more than one perceptual dimension, which interferes with their ability to solve certain problems (Piaget & Inhelder, 1969). We pursue this research in more detail in the next chapter.

The information-processing model represents another cognitive approach to perception. Researchers who take this approach suggest that, like a computer, the brain processes information through a series of steps: perceptual input, internal modifications, memory, and output. The relevant questions about perceptual development, then, involve how these processes change with age and how these changes are related to the amount of information a child can process. For example, a child's improvement in reading may involve a number of cognitive and perceptual abilities, such as improved vision, recognition that clusters of lines and intersections form independent letters, skill in seeing several letters at the same time, and so on.

✓ *To Recap…*

The environmental/learning approach to perceptual development emphasizes the role of experience. In this view, development occurs as babies learn through experience to construct increasingly detailed and complex perceptions from the separate input of the senses. Experience appears to affect single sensory cells and connections among these cells.

Ethologists place less emphasis on experience and believe that even babies perceive sensory information comprehensively, not as separate pieces of input from different senses. Development consists of increasing sensitivity to the structure of incoming information and to which properties change and which remain constant.

Finally, the cognitive approach emphasizes how knowledge can affect perception. Piaget believed that the child's stage of development controls how she perceives the world. The information-processing approach focuses on how sensory information is transformed as it is processed by the brain.

Touch and Pain, Smell and Taste, Motion and Balance

Now we turn to an examination of what young babies actually perceive. We have much less information about the sensory modes of touch, smell, taste, and body balance and motion than about hearing or vision. Nevertheless, these sensory capacities are vitally important to the survival of young organisms. In most animals, these capacities develop earlier than hearing and vision, so we will consider them first.

Touch and Pain

Anyone who wonders whether the newborn baby senses touch or experiences pain should watch the baby's reaction to a heel prick for a blood sample or to circumcision (Hadjistavropoulos et al., 1994). The angry cry that follows the prick of the needle is a clear sign that the baby can feel pain, as are the physiological changes—for example, changes in blood cortisol level—that follow a medical procedure such as circumcision (Gunnar et al., 1985).

Newborn babies also show touch reflexes such as those described in Chapter 6. In fact, the fetus displays the first sign of sensitivity to external stimulation through reactions to touch. As early as the second month following conception, the fetus responds to stroking at the side of the mouth (tested in naturally aborted fetuses). Touch sensitivity increases over the first several days of life (Haith, 1986).

Touching is important for relations between children and adults. A hand placed on the newborn's chest can quiet a crying episode, and gentle stroking can soothe even premature babies (Oehler & Eckerman, 1988). For older infants, touching increases positive emotion and visual attention during interactions between infant and caregiver (Stack & Muir, 1992). It is interesting to note that parents can usually recognize their infant by touch alone within the first few days of life (Kaitz et al., 1993).

Psychologists refer to the active, exploratory use of touch as **haptic perception**. By the end of the first year of life, infants can recognize a familiar object by exploration with the hand alone (Rose, Gottfried, & Bridger, 1981). This perception improves with age. Young preschoolers tend to explore forms with their fingers haphazardly in comparison to the skilled exploration of older children. Nevertheless, even blind 3-year-olds can haptically explore a novel object in one orientation and then recognize that object in a new orientation, a skill that requires forming a mental image of the felt object and then transforming it mentally to the new orientation (Landau, 1991).

Haptic perception
The perceptual experience that results from active exploration of objects by touch.

Smell and Taste

When can babies smell odors? And how might we be able to tell? Researchers have examined this question by observing whether babies, when presented with a smell, will make a face, turn their heads, or do nothing at all. Even newborns turn their heads away from a cotton swab that smells bad (Rieser, Yonas, & Wikner, 1976). Babies produce positive facial expressions in response to banana, strawberry, and vanilla smells and negative expressions in response to smells of rotten eggs and fish (Crook, 1979; Steiner, 1979). Thus, the newborn's sense of smell is keen, and it improves over the first few days of life (Lipsitt, Engen, & Kaye, 1963).

The infant uses this ability as early as the first week of life to distinguish the mother's smell. One researcher placed a breast pad from the mother next to one cheek of her baby and a breast pad from another woman next to the other cheek. By the sixth day of life, the baby turned more frequently toward the mother's breast pad, a discrimination that could only have been made by smell (MacFarlane, 1975). Parents make use of olfactory cues as well. As with the sense of touch, parents can

Touching and stroking can calm babies and also increase their visual attention to the caregiver.

Figure 7.2

A newborn tasting (a) a sweet solution, (b) a bitter solution, and (c) a sour solution. From "Differential Facial Responses to Four Basic Tastes in Newborns" by D. Rosenstein and H. Oster, 1988, *Child Development, 59*, pp. 1561–1563. Copyright © 1988 by The Society for Research in Child Development, Inc. Reprinted by permission.

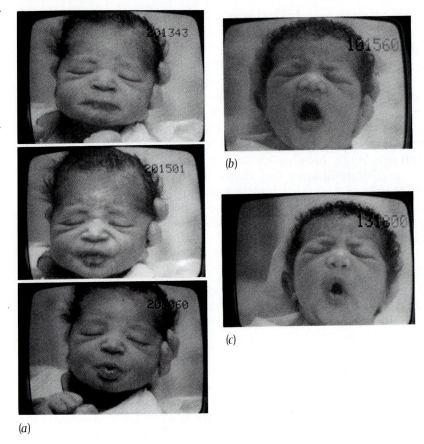

(b)

(c)

(a)

recognize their infant from smell alone within the first few days of life (Porter, Balogh, & Makin, 1988).

Babies are also sensitive to taste at birth. As the fluid that a baby sucks is sweetened, the baby sucks harder, consumes more, and tends to quiet faster from crying episodes (Blass & Smith, 1992; Smith et al., 1992). Interestingly, babies sometimes slow down their sucking rate with increasing sweetness, perhaps because they are taking time to savor the taste between sucks (Lipsitt, 1977).

As illustrated in Figure 7.2, newborn babies can distinguish among different tastes. Even at 2 hours of age, babies make different facial expressions when they taste sweet and nonsweet solutions, and they also differentiate sour, bitter, and salty tastes (Rosenstein & Oster, 1988). At around 4 months of age, they begin to prefer salty tastes, which they found aversive as newborns (Beauchamp et al., 1994).

The fact that newborns reject certain fluids and grimace in response to negative odors and tastes indicates that they come into the world with likes and dislikes. Within months, it can be a challenge to find the older infant's mouth with a spoon that contains something the infant has decided he dislikes just by looking at it.

Vestibular Sensitivity

Vestibular sensitivity
The perceptual experience that results from motion of the body and the pull of gravity.

Vestibular sensitivity refers to our ability to detect gravity and the motion of our bodies, which helps us maintain body posture. In adults, disturbance of the vestibular sense causes dizziness and an inability to remain standing in the dark.

Newborns are sensitive to vestibular stimulation along all three axes of motion—front to back, up and down, and side to side (Reisman, 1987). The sooth-

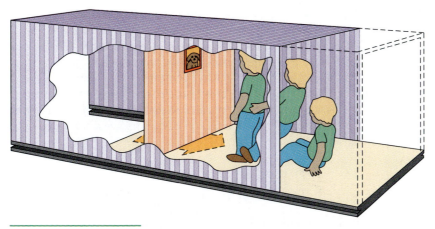

Figure 7.3
Apparatus for testing infants' response to a conflict between visual and vestibular cues. When the wall moves toward the child, the visual cues suggest that the child is swaying forward, and the child compensates by leaning back. From "Infants' Sensitivity to Optical Flow for Controlling Posture" by B. I. Bertenthal and D. L. Bai, 1989, *Developmental Psychology, 25*, p. 939. Copyright © 1989 by the American Psychological Association. Reprinted by permission.

ing properties of rocking and jiggling for crying babies clearly demonstrate this sensitivity. Postural adjustments can also affect a baby's alertness. For instance babies are often more alert when in a vertical than when in a horizontal position (Korner & Thoman, 1970).

Several investigators have examined the relation between vestibular and visual perception in providing the infant with a sense of self-motion. Usually, visual cues and vestibular cues are consistent in telling us whether we are moving or stationary. However, sometimes conflict between these cues produces confusing effects. For example, if you are seated in a stopped train next to another stopped train, and then the other train begins to move forward, your train may seem to you to move backward. Your vision tells you one thing, while your vestibular sense tells you another. Vision wins out for a moment, but your stomach may take a turn when you realize what has happened. Pilots are taught to trust their instruments rather than their impressions, as both their sight and their vestibular sense may mislead them.

Figure 7.3 shows an apparatus used to test the relation between visual and vestibular cues in infancy. Infants who have begun to walk (typically about a year to a year and a half old) are placed in a room with walls that can move as the floor remains stationary. When the front and side walls move, visual cues tell the infant that she is moving forward, while vestibular cues indicate she is not moving at all. Apparently, the visual cues win out, as babies often fall backward in this situation (Lee & Aronson, 1974). A similar phenomenon occurs in babies who are old enough only to sit up (Bertenthal & Bai, 1989). Indeed, even newborns show some adjustment of their heads in response to visual cues that signal movement (Bertenthal & Clifton, 1998). Thus, some ability to use visual information to judge bodily position seems to be present very early in life.

✔ *To Recap…*

Touch and pain, smell and taste, and body balance and motion (vestibular sensitivity) are well developed at birth. Even the fetus is sensitive to touch, and touch sensitivity increases over the first days of life. Touch is a vital component of several adaptive reflexes, and has important social effects as well. Babies use touch to explore the environment.

Newborns are sensitive to both smell and taste. They prefer pleasant odors to unpleasant ones and can distinguish their mother's body smells from those of other women. Similarly, babies suck harder to get sweeter fluid and consume more of it. As early as 2 hours after birth, babies can distinguish not only sweet but also sour, bitter, and salty tastes.

Newborns are also sensitive to vestibular stimulation, responding to both position and movement. Even older babies, however, tend to rely on vision when vestibular and vision cues contradict each other.

Hearing

Hearing is one of our most important senses, because a great deal of information about the world comes to us from sound alone. Cars approaching from behind, a ringing telephone, music from a stereo, and, most important, human speech—all are perceived through the sense of hearing.

How do we know that a newborn baby can hear? As with smell and taste, we can exploit babies' naturally occurring responses to changes in stimulation. The baby may tighten his eyelids, for example, in response to a sound, or turn his head and eyes toward the source of the sound, or perhaps become quiet. Changes in the baby's heart rate and breathing also occur in response to sounds (Aslin, Pisoni, & Jusczyk, 1983).

Imagine that we are interested not just in whether babies can detect sounds but in their ability to discriminate among different sounds. Here the *habituation–dishabituation* procedure described in Chapter 2 can be especially informative. We might first present a particular sound (sound A) repeatedly until the baby habituates to it—that is, no longer shows much, if any, response. Then we present sound B. If the baby dishabituates in response to this change in stimulus, then we have good evidence that she can hear a difference between A and B.

The habituation technique is a general methodology that can be applied to any of the sensory modes. It provided the basis for several of the conclusions about touch and smell summarized in the preceding section. It also, as we will see, has been important in the study of vision.

Prenatal Hearing

Even the fetus can hear. Electrical recordings of brain responses demonstrate sound reception in fetuses as early as the 25th week after conception, about 3.5 months before full-term birth (Parmelee & Sigman, 1983). These findings indicate that fetuses receive sound impulses. But how do they respond to sound?

Two investigators used ultrasound imaging to answer this question. (Ultrasound techniques, as mentioned in Chapter 5, create a picture of the fetus.) The images showed that although fetuses did not respond to auditory stimuli before 24 weeks after conception, after 28 weeks virtually all fetuses clamped their eyelids in response to sound. All the fetuses who did not respond (1 to 2%) were born with hearing deficits or serious impairments (Birnholz & Benacerraf, 1983).

But, we might ask, how good is the sound quality available to the fetus? One curious mother decided to answer this question by swallowing a microphone (she "drank the microphone," as she described it) and recording her own voice and other sounds. Although the stomach recording was muffled, various sounds could be discerned (Fukahara, Shimura, & Yamanouchi, 1988). As we might expect, the mother's speech was more audible than were sounds originating from outside, a finding that has emerged in other studies as well (Richards et al., 1992).

If some aspects of maternal speech are perceptible in the womb, might babies be affected by what they hear prenatally? A fascinating program of research by DeCasper, Fifer, and associates (DeCasper & Fifer, 1980; DeCasper & Spence, 1986; Fifer & Moon, 1995) suggests that the answer is yes. The initial study in the series (DeCasper & Fifer, 1980) reported a surprising finding: Babies less than 4 days old could discriminate their mothers' voices from strangers' voices (discrimination was shown by the fact that the babies altered their sucking rhythms more readily when their own mother's voice served as a reinforcer than they did when the reinforcer was the voice of a stranger).

One possible explanation for such early discrimination and preference for the mother is that the babies had become familiar with their mothers' voices in the womb. If this explanation is correct, we would expect no early preference for the father's voice, despite the fact that babies often hear the father in the days following birth. This, in fact, is the case: 4-day-old babies show no preference for their father's voice over that of a male stranger (DeCasper & Prescott, 1984).

The case for familiarity having come from fetal experience would be strengthened further if the infant could recognize a particular event that was *only* experienced before birth. DeCasper and Spence (1986) asked pregnant women to read aloud one of three stories each day in the last 6 weeks of pregnancy. When tested at 3 days of age, their babies showed a preference for the familiar story over a new story, whether it was the mother's voice reading the story or that of a stranger. This finding demonstrates a clear effect of prenatal experience, and it tells us as well that the fetus can become familiar not only with the mother's voice, but also with some of the specific sound patterns that the mother produces.

Other research suggests that fetuses may also pick up more general aspects of their own native languages. Newborn French babies can discriminate a woman speaking French from the same woman speaking Russian; babies of non-French-speaking mothers, however, do not make the discrimination (Mehler et al., 1988). Finally, a recent study from the DeCasper group (DeCasper et al., 1994) reports heart-rate change to a familiar passage in third trimester *fetuses*—and thus effects of auditory experience that are evident even prior to birth.

Research on prenatal hearing and learning is an ongoing enterprise, and most investigators are cautious in drawing conclusions. Nevertheless, it seems clear that fetuses can hear more than once believed.

Sensitivity to Sound

Newborn babies appear to be less sensitive to sound than are adults (Aslin et al., 1983). An adult, for example, can easily hear a whisper at a distance of about 4.5 feet; a newborn, however, requires a stimulus closer to normal conversational level to be able to hear at that distance. Fluid in the middle ear may be part of the problem.

How well a sound can be heard depends on its pitch. Adults can hear sounds of intermediate pitch better than sounds of high or low pitch. Newborn babies hear relatively better at low frequencies, but by 6 months of age their high-frequency sensitivity is as good as that of adults (Schneider & Trehub, 1985a, 1985b; Werner & Bargones, 1992). Sensitivity to sound increases until around 10 years of age. Sensitivity to higher frequencies, however, peaks earlier and does not improve beyond about 4 or 5 years of age (Trehub et al., 1988).

Sensitivity measurements determine how loud a sound must be for the infant to detect it. However, we are normally exposed to sounds that are much louder than this threshold level. For a full understanding of the infant's hearing capacity, we must also know how well the infant can discriminate sounds that differ in various characteristics, such as intensity, frequency, and duration.

Discriminating Sounds

Infants are able to distinguish differences in intensity, or loudness, at an early age. For example, after a 6-month-old becomes familiar with a sound approximately as loud as an ordinary conversation at a distance of about 3 feet, a small increase in intensity produces a noticeable change in heart rate (Moffitt, 1973). Twelve-month-olds can detect even very slight shifts in intensity (Trehub & Schneider, 1983).

How well do infants distinguish among sound frequencies? The fact that infants respond differently to sounds of different frequencies provides one kind of evidence of their ability to discriminate. Low-frequency tones are generally effective in quieting babies, whereas higher tones tend to distress them (Eisenberg, 1976). By 5 months of age, infants are almost as good as adults at distinguishing among high-frequency tones that vary only slightly (Werner & Bargones, 1992).

Babies are better at discriminating complex sounds than we might suspect. Infants as young as 6 months are sensitive to various properties of music, such as contour and rhythm, and they can pick out melodies, even when the key changes (Trehub & Schellenberg, 1995). This means that they can perceive the relations among the frequencies, even when the frequencies themselves change because of the key change. By 6 months babies can tell the difference between a lullaby and an adult-directed song, even when the song and lullaby are from a foreign culture (Trehub & Henderson, 1994).

Babies are especially sensitive to the characteristics of sound that will be important for language perception. Young infants prefer to listen to sounds that fall within the frequency range of the human voice, and they can distinguish different speech sounds as early as 1 month of age (Aslin, Jusczyk, & Pisoni, 1998). We consider the issue of perception of speech more fully in Chapter 11.

Development in Cultural Context
Music to Our Ears: Cultural Influences on Perception of Tunes

Perception seems so immediate and direct that it is natural to assume that what one person sees and hears is the same as what another person sees and hears. Yet this is not always the case. For example, native speakers of English easily perceive a stream of spoken English sounds as a string of distinctive words, but a similar stream spoken in German, Chinese, or Russian may sound to them like a bewildering flow of noise, with one word running into the next and little clue even for where one sentence ends and the next one begins. Clearly, language perception depends on the context in which it develops.

But might language be perceived in a special way because it is a social stimulus? Is it possible that our perceptions of other sound stimuli might be universal across cultures and not as sensitive to context? Some recent studies of music perception by Lynch and colleagues have examined these questions (Lynch & Eilers, 1992; Lynch, Short, & Chua, 1995; Lynch et al., 1990).

The initial study (Lynch et al., 1990) was carried out with 6-month-olds and adults. The investigators used seven-tone melodies based either on Western major and minor scales or on a Javanese scale of a different structure. To Western listeners, Javanese melodies sound odd.

Listeners heard a repeating melody from one of these scales, occasionally interrupted by a seven-note sequence that was mistuned in that the fifth note had a small frequency change. Babies had been trained to turn their heads to produce an animated toy sequence when they heard the mistuned sequence, and adults had been trained to raise their hands. The question was, could babies and adults pick up the same amount of mistuning for the Western and the Javanese scales?

The adults detected the mistuning much more easily in the Western melody than in the Javanese melody. The babies also detected the mistuned melodies, but they were no better at doing so for the Western than the Javanese melody. Subsequent studies (Lynch & Eilers, 1992; Lynch et al., 1995) have complicated the picture a bit, since in some instances 6-month-olds also do better with Western scales. In general, however, response to different musical scales is most similar early in infancy and gradually pulls apart as babies grow older. This conclusion holds not only for Western compared with Javanese scales but also for the familiar Western major scale in comparison with the less often heard Western augmented scale.

These results suggest that humans are born with the ability to perceive musicality across a wide range of sound structures, but that this ability gradually changes, becoming more sensitive for types of music often heard than for those seldom or never heard. Music perception, then, is apparently sensitive to cultural influences, as is language perception (Kuhl, 1993).

Sound Localization

An important property of sounds is the direction from which they come. Even newborns distinguish very general sound location (Morrongiello et al., 1994). They turn their eyes and heads toward a sound source to the left or right if the sound is relatively continuous. Rattles and human voices are most effective in eliciting this response (Braddick & Atkinson, 1988). Research indicates that the localization response disappears around the second month of life and reappears in the third or fourth month in a more vigorous form. When the response reemerges, it is faster and more skilled, suggesting that a different brain center has taken control of this ability (Muir & Clifton, 1985).

Over the first year and a half of life, babies make increasingly fine distinctions of auditory space (Ashmead et al., 1991; Morrongiello, 1988). To accomplish this feat, they must solve an interesting and very general problem of growing organisms, one of appropriate *recalibration*, or readjustment. The problem is that accurate sound localization depends in large part on the detection of the time difference between when sound arrives at the two ears. For example, a sound on the right produces energy that reaches the right ear before it reaches the left ear. With age, the head grows larger, so that the distance between the two ears increases. Therefore, a sound that comes from the same off-center location produces a greater time difference in an older child than in a younger child.

Since even the newborn displays some accuracy in locating sounds, the baby must perform a recalibration to accommodate growth at an older age, continually adjusting the relation between sound cues and what these cues mean for the location of the sound-producing object (Clifton et al., 1988; Morrongiello et al., 1994). The need for readjustment presents a general problem for the baby in many action systems—eye movements, head movements, reaching, and walking, to name a few. And researchers still do not know how it happens.

✔ *To Recap...*

The fetus can hear at least as early as several months prior to birth. Although newborns appear to be less sensitive to sound than are adults, within the first year the infant's hearing at high frequencies is as good as the adult's. The infant can discriminate sounds on the basis of intensity, frequency, and duration. Especially important are sound discriminations that are central to the perception of speech. The baby's ability to localize sounds is present at birth and then fades somewhat, to reappear at 4 months in a more efficient form. This ability becomes more precise over the first 18 months of life.

Vision

Take a moment to look around and appreciate the richness and complexity of your visual environment. You can see variations in brightness and color and texture, and you can tell which surfaces are hard and which are soft. You can see dozens of objects and many items of function—light switches that can be flicked, containers that hold objects, shelves that support books, chairs that support people. Vision provides an immense amount of information about the world, and you know how to interpret this information easily.

Now, consider what this world must look like to a newborn baby. First, can the newborn see? If so, how well? When the baby can see well enough to make out objects, how does he or she know that one object is in front of another, that an object can serve as a container, or even that the container—say, a cup—is separate from the table on which it rests? How does the baby know that a tree seen through a window is outside the room rather than part of the glass? From this small sample of questions, you can see how much the baby must come to understand. In the past 3 decades, we have discovered a great deal about how this understanding develops. Here, we first consider two basic questions: How good is the newborn baby's vision, and how quickly does it improve?

Sensory Capabilities

We have known for some time that newborn babies can see something. New parents notice their baby often turns her head toward a source of light, such as a window. In the first days of life, awake babies also distinguish light intensity. They open their eyes widely in darkness and close them in bright light; typically, they choose to look at moderate light levels (Haith, 1980). Babies find visual movement especially attractive even at birth, and they become increasingly sensitive to movement over the first several months of life (Aslin & Shea, 1990; Nelson & Horowitz, 1987).

Visual Acuity   The newborn baby will look more at patterned than at unpatterned displays. For example, if we show a baby a picture of a black-and-white bull's-eye and a gray card that are equally bright, the baby will look more at the pattern than at the plain card (Fantz, 1961). We can use this pattern-looking tendency to measure the baby's **visual acuity**, or how sharply he can see things. (Box 7.1 describes how the technique for doing such research was developed.)

To measure visual acuity, we show the baby a gray picture next to a second picture that contains vertical, black-and-white stripes. Ordinarily, the baby looks longer at the striped picture. Over repeated presentations, we make the stripes more narrow and compressed, which makes them more difficult to distinguish from the gray picture. Eventually, the baby no longer looks more at the striped pattern, presumably because he can no longer tell the difference between the two pictures.

Visual acuity
The clarity with which visual images can be perceived.

BOX 7.1

WHAT DO BABIES SEE? THE WORK OF ROBERT FANTZ

A key problem in understanding perceptual development is that we cannot easily communicate with infants. People have wondered since the beginning of time what the newborn baby can see and when the baby can tell one color or face or shape from another.

Through much of the modern era of psychology, researchers have approached these questions somewhat indirectly. For example, an investigator might measure the heart rate or respiration of a baby looking at a picture of a face and then see whether changes occur when the baby looks at a picture of the facial features (mouth, eyes, nose) scrambled up in a different pattern; if so, the investigator might conclude that there is something special about faces for the infant. Other indirect approaches use learning procedures. If a baby can learn to turn her head right when a red stimulus appears and left for a blue stimulus, presumably the baby can discriminate between red and blue.

Robert Fantz made a discovery that profoundly affected research on infant vision (Fantz, 1961). Fantz observed that babies look at different things for different periods of time. He suggested simply measuring the amount of time babies looked at one display rather than another to determine what babies could see and discriminate in the displays. This direct approach would eliminate the need to use cumbersome electrodes to measure physiological changes or the tedium of training and learning procedures.

The procedure for measuring where babies look is straightforward. The researcher shows the baby two displays, side by side. With properly adjusted lighting, the researcher can see the reflection of these displays on the surface of the baby's eye, much as you can see the reflection of a window in daylight in the eyes of a person to whom you are talking. When the baby looks at one of the displays, that display is reflected from the surface of the eye over the black pupil opening. The researcher, using two stopwatches, can record how long the baby looks at each display.

This approach is labeled the *preference method*, because what we are interested in is whether the infant will show a preference—that is, look longer at one stimulus than at the other. If the infant does show a preference, we conclude that she can discriminate between the stimuli.

Researchers have used this powerful technique to study a host of issues concerning infant vision, including visual acuity, color perception, form perception, face recognition, and picture perception. Because an infant's interest in a particular visual display declines over time and recovers for novel stimuli, investigators have also been able to use this technique to study how an infant's memory develops and how various types of developmental problems (such as Down syndrome and prematurity) affect perceptual processing and memory (Bornstein & Sigman, 1986).

A remarkable fact about the Fantz discovery is how obvious it seems after the fact. Many great contributors to science have been able to see the obvious among the complex and to find significance in what others have overlooked.

Using this approach, researchers have estimated that the newborn's acuity is about 20/400 to 20/800 (meaning that a normal-vision adult sees at 400 to 800 feet what the newborn sees at 20 feet), compared with normal adult acuity of 20/20 (Kellman & Banks, 1998). By 3 months of age, acuity improves to around 20/100; by 12 months, it approximates that of the adult (Banks & Salapatek, 1983). Figure 7.4 shows how a picture of a face might look to infants at 1, 2, and 3 months of age from a distance of about 6 inches.

Why do younger infants have poorer vision? Early studies of infants younger than 1 month of age suggested that the lens of the eye did not vary its focus with

Figure 7.4
Visual acuity improves dramatically during the first months of life, as illustrated in computer estimations of what a picture of a face looks like to 1-, 2-, and 3-month-olds at a distance of about 6 inches. All estimations were taken from the original, which illustrates adult acuity (seen on the far right). From "The Recognition of Facial Expressions in the First Two Years of Life: Mechanisms of Development" by Charles A. Nelson, *Child Development, 58*, Figure 1, p. 892. Copyright © 1987 by the Society for Research in Child Development, Inc. Reprinted by permission. These photos were made available by Martin Banks and Arthur Ginsburg.

Visual accommodation
The automatic adjustment of the lens of the eye to produce a focused image of an object on the light-sensitive tissue at the back of the eye.

distance, a process called **visual accommodation** (Haynes, White, & Held, 1965). Rather, the lens seemed to be fixed for optimal focus at a distance of about 7 to 8 inches. Because this is the typical distance of the mother's face from the baby's eyes during feeding, ethologists constructed a nice story about why evolution might use such a trick to assure that the baby would be attracted to the mother's face.

Evolutionary explanations are often very seductive, but they can also be wrong, as this one was. In fact, the baby's lens is not fixed, but it does not vary with distance as the adult's does. At birth, the brain circuits that are responsible for accommodation are simply not sufficiently mature to pick up minor differences in the precision of focus. Thus, variations for focal distance in the early weeks of life are relatively useless. It appears to be only happenstance that the lens has a relatively fixed focus at around 7 to 8 inches. Accommodation improves between 1 and 3 months of age and is almost adultlike by 6 months of age (Hainline & Abramov, 1992).

Peripheral Vision   The part of the eye that provides acute vision covers a very small portion of the visual field—a circular area about the size of a quarter at arm's length. Yet our visual world seems continuous and complete; we do not see it as if we were looking through a long, quarter-size tube. This is because our **peripheral vision**, which is less detailed, covers much more of the visual field. The peripheral vision of the 1-month-old is much smaller than that of the adult, but significant improvement occurs by 3 months of age (Braddick & Atkinson, 1988).

Peripheral vision
The perception of visual input outside the area on which the individual is fixating.

Color Vision   When can babies see color? Babies tend to look at colored objects, and that tendency has helped psychologists answer this question. Newborns can make some color discriminations—red from green, for example, and both red and green from white (Adams, 1989). In most respects, however, early color perception is limited. Aspects of the visual system that mediate color perception are not mature at birth, and newborns are unable to see many of the contrasts that are available to adults (Adams, 1995). Like many forms of perception, however, color perception improves rapidly in the early months, and by 4 months infants' ability to perceive color appears equivalent to that of an adult (Teller & Bornstein, 1987).

Visual Pattern and Contrast

For years, many people believed that newborn babies were blind or, at best, capable merely of reflexively looking at a source of light. As suggested in the discussion of visual acuity, Robert Fantz proved them wrong. Even newborn babies looked longer at a patterned display than at a nonpatterned display, as shown in Figure 7.5.

Investigators later developed the techniques shown in Figure 7.6 to measure what parts of displays newborns look at. They discovered that newborns look primarily at high-contrast edges—for example, where black and white meet—and move their eyes back and forth over those contrast edges (Haith, 1980, 1991).

As babies get older, they prefer patterns that are more densely packed. Whereas 3-week-olds look longer at a 6-by-6 checkerboard than at a 12-by-12 or a 24-by-24

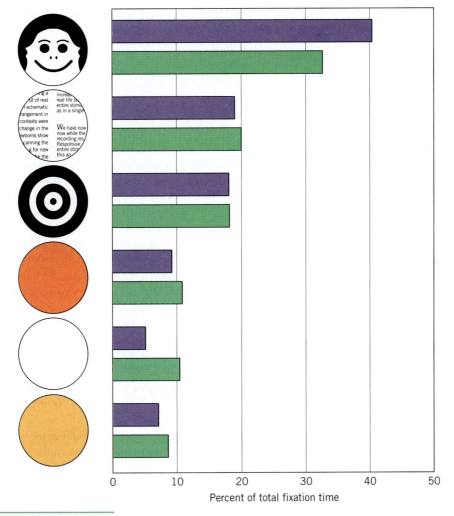

Figure 7.5

Stimuli that Robert Fantz showed to infants. The length of the purple bars indicates the average time that 2- to 3-month-olds looked at the stimulus, and the length of the green bars indicates looking time for 3- to 6-month-olds. From R. Fantz, 1961, "The origin of form perception," *Scientific American, 204*, p. 72. Copyright © 1961 by *Scientific American.* Reprinted by permission.

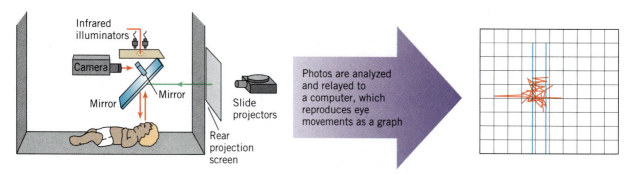

Figure 7.6

Studying how babies look at stimuli. A camera records the baby's eye movements as he looks at a reflected image. Pictures of the eye are then analyzed. Measurements of the positions of the center of the pupil and the reflected infrared light spots identify where the baby's eye fixated when the picture was taken. This information is relayed to a computer that reconstructs the baby's eye movements in graphic form. Shown is a reconstruction of a newborn's fixations on a vertical bar.

checkerboard, 6-week-olds are more likely to look longest at the intermediately complex display and 3-month-olds at the most complex display (Karmel & Maisel, 1975).

An early theory held that babies prefer increasing complexity (that is, more checks) as they get older and become more complex themselves. However, several investigators have pointed out that as the number of checks increases, so does the amount of black–white edge in the display. Most investigators now believe that babies are attracted to the displays that offer the most edge contrasts that they can see at a particular age (Banks & Ginsburg, 1985). Why? Perhaps these findings suggest what babies are trying to accomplish with their visual behavior.

When babies move their eyes over edges, they activate cells of the visual areas of the brain. The strongest brain activity occurs when the baby adjusts the eye so that images of the edges fall near the center of the eye—that is, when the baby looks straight at the edges. Also, the more detail the baby can see, the stronger the activation. Haith (1980) has suggested that the baby's visual activity in early infancy reflects a biological "agenda" for the baby to keep brain-cell firing at a high level. This agenda makes sense because, as we have seen, cells in the brain compete to establish connections to other cells. Activity tends to stabilize the required connections, while inactive pathways deteriorate (Greenough, Black, & Wallace, 1987). Fortunately, this agenda brings the baby to areas of the visual display that are also psychologically meaningful. Edges provide information about the boundaries of objects, their relation in depth, and where they can be grasped.

Thus, the baby appears to be "programmed" to engage in visual activity that is very adaptive. This activity produces the sensory input needed to maintain and tune the neural apparatus and also focuses the baby's attention on the most informative parts of the visual world. Once again, we can see that the young infant is anything but passive. Even the newborn possesses tools to get necessary experience for normal development. And we can see again the interplay of nature and nurture as the potential routes for development provided by biology are shaped by experience.

Visual Relations

The agenda that biology sets for the newborn makes sense initially, but growing babies must move beyond simply exciting their own brains and begin to appreciate

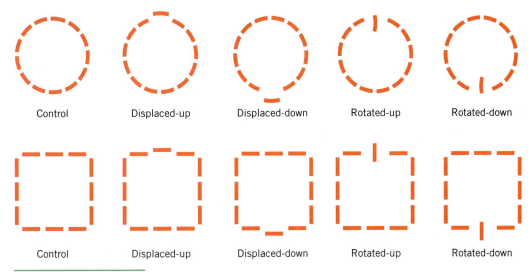

Figure 7.7
Stimuli used in the study by Van Giffen and Haith. Babies were shown the control stimulus three times, in alternation with one of the experimental figures. From "Infant Visual Response to Gestalt Geometric Forms" by K. Van Giffen and M. M. Haith, 1984, *Infant Behavior and Development, 7*, Figure 1, p. 338. Copyright © 1984 by Ablex Publishing Corp. Reprinted by permission.

the organization among parts of the visual world. Mother's face, for example, soon is seen as a whole, meaningful object rather than simply as eyebrows, eyes, ears, a nose, and so on.

Several lines of evidence suggest that although newborns are sensitive to very simple relations among stimuli, babies really begin to "put things together" between 1 and 3 months of age (Haith, 1986; Slater et al., 1991). One example of the kind of research from which this conclusion is drawn is pictured in Figure 7.7. Infants were shown an arrangement of bars that formed a circular or square pattern. In some patterns, one bar was misaligned. To an adult, the one misaligned bar seems strange, because the adult sees all the other bars as going together. The misalignment had no effect on the visual fixations of 1-month-olds, but 3-month-olds looked longer around the displaced bar than around the properly aligned ones (Van Giffen & Haith, 1984). Thus, between 1 and 3 months of age, babies begin to see the organization in visual displays rather than only the details.

Of course, babies do not appreciate all possible visual relations by 3 months of age. As you can demonstrate to yourself by walking into a modern art gallery, the perception of organization takes time and effort and, as we have seen, knowledge. Consider the display shown Figure 7.8*a*. Adults report perceiving a square that overlays full circles at each of the corners in this display. They also report faint edges that connect the corners of the square, even though no such edges exist. Adults, of course, have considerable knowledge about such things as squares and how a square might block the view of circles behind it.

Babies looked at the arrangement in 7.8*b* (the same elements, with some rotated to destroy the illusion) until their looking habituated. They then were tested for dishabituation with either the illusion stimulus in 7.8*a* or the second nonillusion stimulus shown in 7.8*c*. Both test stimuli involved a change in two corner elements, and hence we might expect them to be equally easy to discriminate. Five-month-old

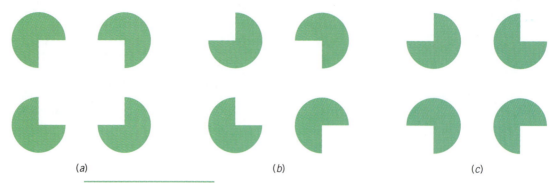

(a)   (b)   (c)

Figure 7.8
Stimuli used in studies by Bertenthal (all three stimuli) and Shapiro (*a* and *b* only). From "Development of Visual Organization: The Perception of Subjective Contours" by B. I. Bertenthal, J. J. Campos, and M. M. Haith, 1980, *Child Development, 51*, Figure 1, p. 1073. Copyright © 1980 by The Society for Research in Child Development, Inc. Reprinted by permission.

infants did not consistently detect either of these changes; however, 7-month-olds were able to detect the change when it involved the illusion in 7.8*a*, indicating that they were able to group its elements perceptually in a way that the younger infants were not yet able to do (Bertenthal, Campos, & Haith, 1980).

This study and others like it demonstrate an important point: The perception of visual organization, like most developmental phenomena, is not something that happens all at once for all displays. The ability to appreciate visual organization begins between 1 and 3 months of age, but this ability continues to improve and is affected by both knowledge and the cues the environment provides (Haith, 1993).

Psychologists exploit babies' natural inclination to look at patterned displays to learn what babies can see and discriminate.

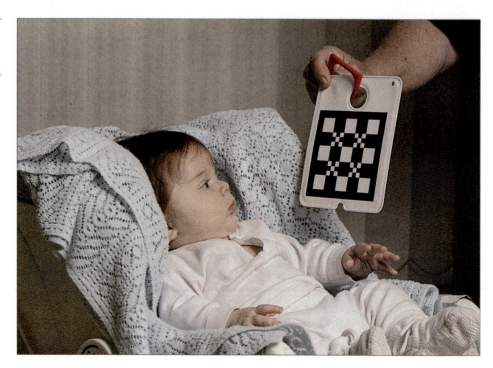

Face Perception

The face contains the arrangement of visual elements in which babies are most interested. Infants as young as 2 months of age appear to recognize the organization of facial features, as they look more at a schematic picture of a face than at the same features in a scrambled array. Facial features in these pictures change in importance with age; first the eyes, then the eyes and nose, and then the eyes, nose, and mouth assume importance in attracting attention and in eliciting smiling (Johnson & Morton, 1991).

A problem with this research is that most investigators have used pictures of faces or two-dimensional displays of black-and-white elements. Perhaps babies at earlier ages perceive real faces in a holistic fashion but cannot appreciate "faceness" in schematic, two-dimensional displays. That, in fact, seems to be the case.

Investigators used equipment similar to that described earlier to record exactly where infants looked on real, live faces (Figure 7.9). Babies at 5 weeks of age tended to look near the high-contrast borders of the face—the edges where skin and hair or chin and garment meet. However, babies only two weeks older spent most of their time looking at the internal features of the face, especially the eyes. Fixation on these internal features may reflect a new perceptual organization of the face into a whole rather than a collection of elements (Haith, Bergman, & Moore, 1977; Maurer & Salapatek, 1976).

Faces are not only interesting stimuli to view; they are also sources of social information. The sensitivity of babies to emotional expressions in faces grows slowly over the first 2 years of life (Walker-Andrews, 1997). Even 3-month-olds, however, may look longer at faces as the intensity of the smile increases. This tendency appears to depend on experience. Babies whose mothers call attention to themselves and smile when their babies look at them are the babies who show the strongest preferences for smiling faces (Kuchuk, Vibbert, & Bornstein, 1986). We

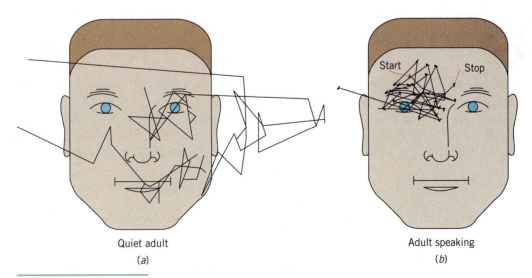

Quiet adult
(a)

Adult speaking
(b)

Figure 7.9
An apparatus similar to that shown in Figure 7.6 recorded a baby's fixations on a face. A computer reconstructed the baby's fixations on a face when (a) the adult was quiet and (b) the adult talked. A rotating arrow shows the sequence of fixations and where the baby began and ended looking.

BOX 7.2

NEWBORNS' RESPONSE TO FACES

No one has ever doubted that babies' perception of faces is influenced by experience—as the work that we have discussed clearly demonstrates. More controversial is the question of whether experience builds on some innate starting point—whether some interest in and response to faces is present from birth.

By most measures, the response of newborn babies to faces is limited. As we have seen, newborns seldom fixate on the internal features of faces, and data from the Fantz preference method reveal no preference for faces until at least 2 or 3 months of age. Given these findings, the results from a study by Johnson and colleagues (1991) are surprising. These investigators measured babies' tendency to track stimuli (by moving their eyes or heads) as the stimuli moved across their visual fields. Three stimuli were compared—all head-shaped, but differing in inner detail. In one, the elements were arranged in a facelike pattern; in another, the elements were scrambled; and in the third, the inner area was blank (see Figure 7.10). Johnson et al. reported that newborn infants tracked the face more than they did the other stimuli. Indeed, even babies who were only a few minutes old at the time of testing showed greater response to the face.

What does such an early interest in facelike stimuli mean? Johnson and colleagues are careful to emphasize that the primitive responses demonstrated in their research are far from the careful, selective processing of faces shown by 4- or 5-month-old infants. They suggest, in fact, that different brain centers may mediate early and later response to faces (a suggestion that, as we have seen, has also been proposed with regard to babies' localization of sounds). They also suggest, however, that the early responsiveness to facelike stimuli, limited and temporary though it may be, is adaptive, because it gets the baby started on the path toward more mature social perception.

Whatever the innate starting point for perception of faces may be, the preference for a familiar face must clearly depend on experience. We have seen that a preference for the mother's voice or the mother's odor emerges very early in life. Might a preference for the mother's face also be present very early?

Several recent studies suggest that the answer is yes. Babies as young as 2 days old have been shown to look more at their mother's face than at the face of a stranger (Bushnell, Sai, & Mullin, 1989). Newborn babies also alter their sucking patterns more readily to produce a view of their mother's face than to view the face of a stranger (Walton, Bower, & Bower, 1992).

Surprising as the Johnson et al. (1991) results may be, these results are perhaps even more surprising. Not only have 2-day-old infants had limited experience with their mothers' face, but we know that infants that young pay little attention to the inner details of faces and do not see such details at all clearly when they do fixate on them (recall Figure 7.4). How, then, can they recognize their own mother? A recent study by Pascalis et al. (1995) suggests an answer. These investigators

will see in Chapter 12 that by the end of the first year, babies can differentiate a number of other expressions of emotion.

There are, then, clear changes in how infants respond to faces across the first year or so of life. In Box 7.2 we consider some recent research that suggests that some aspects of face perception may be present from the earliest days of life.

Objects and Their Properties

The ability of babies to appreciate the relations among visual elements—for example, lines, angles, and edges—is important for their perception of the objects that

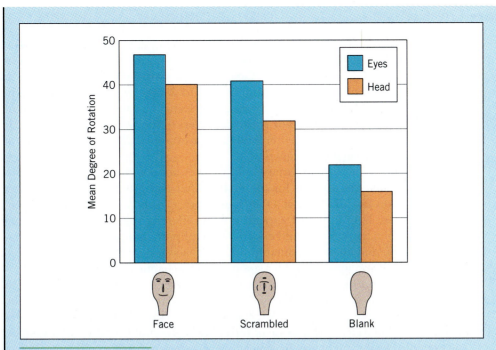

Figure 7.10
Stimuli and results from the Johnson et al. study of newborns' tendency to track moving objects. The babies moved their eyes and heads more in response to the face than in the response to the other two stimuli. Reprinted from "Newborns' Preferential Tracking of Facelike Stimuli and Its Subsequent Decline" by M. H. Johnson, S. Ddziurawiec, H. Ellis, and J. Morton, 1991, *Cognition, 40*, p. 6. Copyright © 1991 with kind permission of Elsevier Science Publishers–NL, Sara Burgerhartstraat 25, 1055 KV Amsterdam, The Netherlands.

found, as did earlier studies, that newborns look more at their mother's face than at the face of a stranger. The researchers then redid the experiment, but with one difference: Now the women wore scarves that covered their hair and part of their foreheads. With the scarves in place, newborns could no longer distinguish their mother from a stranger.

What the Pascalis et al. study suggests is that newborn recognition of the mother is not based on attention to the inner details of her face.

Newborns seem to rely instead on more peripheral information, such as hairline and shape of head. Early recognition of the mother, like the early interest in facelike stimuli, is therefore crude, and limited in comparison to the face perception of the older infant. Nevertheless, the recent research suggests that newborn infants are more responsive to faces than psychologists once believed. And this early responsiveness seems clearly conducive to the important task of forming emotional ties with others.

populate the world. But knowledge of objects involves more than the ability to perceive how the parts fit together to make a whole. In this section we discuss some further aspects of object perception that emerge during infancy.

The Constancies   As an object moves farther away from us, its image on the eye shrinks. Yet the object continues to appear the same size, at least up to a point. For example, a child standing in front of you seems shorter than an adult standing across the street, even though the child casts a larger image on your eyes than does the adult. This phenomenon is called **size constancy**.

Size constancy
The experience that the physical size of an object remains the same even though the size of its projected image on the eye varies.

217

Shape constancy
The experience that the physical shape of an object remains the same even though the shape of its projected image on the eye varies.

Brightness constancy
The experience that the brightness of an object remains the same even though the amount of light it reflects back to the eye changes (because of shadows or changes in the illuminating light).

Color constancy
The experience that the color of an object remains the same even though the wavelengths it reflects back to the eye change (because of changes in the color of the illuminating light).

Objects also change apparent shape as they rotate or as we move around them. **Shape constancy** refers to the stability of our perception in the face of changes in the shape of the image on the eye. Objects in the world continually change in brightness as well. Still, a dark dress continues to look dark whether it is dimly lit in a storeroom or brightly illuminated by direct sunlight. This is the phenomenon of **brightness constancy**. Finally, **color constancy** refers to the perception of a color as the same despite changes in the hue of light (for example, the fluorescent light of a department store versus sunlight).

Visual constancies are important because they address the fundamental question of how stable the world is for the infant. After all, without such constancies, each time a baby saw an object at a different distance, or in a different orientation, or in a different light, it would appear to be a different object. Instead of seeing only one mother, the infant would experience a different mother every time he saw her from a different angle. Fortunately for both baby and mother, the baby's visual world, as we will see, appears to be a good deal less chaotic than this.

Let us first consider size constancy. One approach to testing size constancy in very young infants is shown in Figure 7.11 (Slater, Mattock, & Brown, 1990). The stimuli are two cubes, one twice as large as the other. The baby first receives a series of familiarization trials in which one of the cubes is presented at different distances. For example, a baby might see the small cube at a distance of 23 cm, then at 53 cm, then at 38 cm, and so forth. Because both the distance and the size of the retinal image vary from trial to trial, the only constant element is the actual size of the cube. The test trials follow the familiarization phase. Now both cubes are presented simultaneously, but at different distances, with the larger cube twice as far away as the smaller one. The question of interest is whether the baby will show a preference by looking longer at one of the two cubes.

Before we describe the findings, it is worth taking a moment to think through the logic of the experiment. Why *might* the baby show a preference? The retinal image cannot be the basis for a preference, because the two cubes—as Figure 7.11*b* illustrates—project the same size image. The baby has not encountered the viewing distances before; thus there is no reason to think that distance will be important. On the other hand, one of the cubes is familiar and the other is novel, and hence we might see a preference based on relative familiarity. Note, however, that the small cube will be familiar only if the baby has been able to perceive its constant size during the familiarization trials. If, instead, size is perceived as changing every time distance changes, then both cubes will appear new on the test trials.

In fact, all of the newborn babies tested looked significantly longer at the larger cube. This finding tells us that they could see a difference between the two cubes, despite the equivalent retinal images. And the preference for the novel stimulus suggests that they did indeed find the small cube familiar and therefore less interesting. As noted, they could do so only if they perceived the constant size across presentations.

This study suggests, then, that some size constancy is present at birth. There is also evidence, based on a similar methodology, for some degree of shape constancy at birth (Slater & Morison, 1985). It is important to note, though, that "some constancy" is not *complete* constancy. Both size constancy and shape constancy are stronger and more easily demonstrated by 3 or 4 months of age than they are in the newborn. Indeed, the ability to judge the size of objects with changing distance improves up to at least 10 or 11 years of age (Day, 1987). Thus constancy, like other perceptual accomplishments, is not an all-or-nothing affair.

To date, there have been no demonstrations that the other forms of constancy we identified—brightness constancy and color constancy—are present from birth.

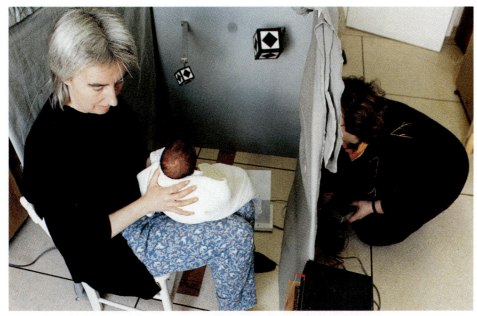

(a)

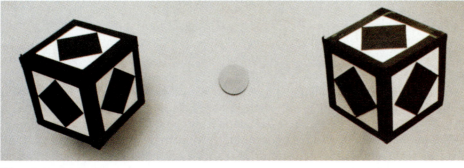

(b)

Figure 7.11

Procedure for testing size constancy in newborn babies. The top (a) shows the experimental arrangement, and the bottom (b) shows the stimuli for the critical test trial. From "Size Constancy at Birth: Newborn Infants' Responses to Retinal and Real Size" by A. Slater, A. Mattock, and E. Brown, 1990. *Journal of Experimental Child Psychology, 49*, pp. 317 and 318. Copyright © 1990 by Academic Press. Reprinted by permission.

Brightness constancy, however, is evident as early as 7 weeks for objects that are not too small (Dannemiller, 1985), and some degree of color constancy is available by 4 months of age (Dannemiller & Hanko, 1987).

Object Continuity   Our knowledge of objects extends beyond the various constancies. Because we understand principles of solidity and continuity, we see objects as continuous and whole even when our view is partially blocked. For example, when a person stands in front of a table, blocking the midsection of the table from our view, we naturally infer that the two ends of the table are connected. In a sense, we perceive a whole table. Do young infants also perceive objects as continuous and whole when they are partially blocked by other objects?

Figure 7.12

Some pictures used to study object perception in infants. From "Perception of Unity, Persistence, and Identity: Thoughts on Infants' Conceptions of Objects" by E. S. Spelke, 1985. In J. Mehler and R. Fox (Eds.), *Neonate Cognition: Beyond the Blooming Buzzing Confusion* (Figures 6.1, 6.2, and 6.3, pp. 91–93), Hillsdale, NJ: Erlbaum. Copyright © 1985 by Lawrence Erlbaum Associates. Reprinted by permission.

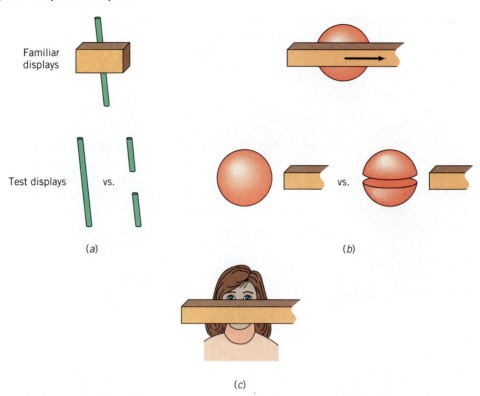

In one set of experiments, 4-month-old babies looked at a partially blocked object—for example, a long rod partly hidden by a block, as shown in the top of Figure 7.12*a*—until their interest declined. They then were shown the two stimuli at the bottom of Figure 7.12*a*: a continuous rod, paired with two rod pieces. Note that the latter stimulus is identical to what they were able to see with the block in place. Presumably, if the babies had perceived earlier that the rod was continuous, they should have looked longer at the two separated rods than at the more typical and familiar continuous rod. They did not, suggesting that they had not perceived a single whole rod behind the block (Spelke, 1985).

In a variation of this procedure, babies saw a bar move out from in front of a sphere that it had partially blocked, as illustrated in the top of Figure 7.12*b*. The movement of the bar revealed either a whole sphere or two separated sphere parts (bottom of 7.12*b*). Again, the babies paid no special attention to the separated parts. The researchers tried several displays—including a face, as shown in Figure 7.12*c*—but had no success in demonstrating that infants could infer more about the objects than what they could see (Kellman & Spelke, 1983).

These findings seem amazing. Is it possible that babies see people as cut into pieces when they stand behind a table? Probably not. In all these studies, the partially hidden object was stationary, and so was the baby. In the real world, when we see one object partially blocked by another, our own movement produces more displacement of the closer object than of the "pieces" of the farther object. This is a clue that the blocked object is continuous. Furthermore, the blocked object itself may move, providing another clue. For example, infants who saw a sphere move behind a blocking rod (that is, the two parts of the sphere moved simultaneously) later looked at the separated sphere parts as though they had not seen them before.

Under these conditions, infants apparently perceived the moving sphere as whole (Kellman, 1996; Spelke, 1988). Given movement and other optimal cues, infants as young as 2 months can perceive the continuity of partially visible objects (Johnson, 1997; Johnson & Aslin, 1995). Newborns, however, cannot, which suggests that some experience may be necessary for this accomplishment (Slater et al., 1994; Slater et al., 1996).

Based on several experiments of the kind just described, Spelke has argued that infants in the early months of life understand object continuity, along with several other basic properties of objects. Some other properties, however (such as the effects of gravity), are not understood until the second year of life (Spelke, 1991; Spelke & Hermer, 1996; Spelke et al., 1992). These ideas are controversial (in that others believe young babies have only a minimal understanding of continuity and other such properties) and await further investigation. We return to the question of what infants know about objects in Chapter 8.

The Spatial Layout

To this point, we have considered infants' fundamental perceptual capacities and their perception of patterns and objects. The visual world, however, consists of multiple objects—a landscape of objects and events that lie in particular spatial relations to one another (Gibson, 1988). To understand more about how babies perceive this richer world, we now consider the issues of depth and space perception.

Depth and Distance   As babies acquire the ability to move around, they also develop the capacity to get into trouble. One potential danger is falling over edges if they cannot perceive that a surface that supports them drops off. Eleanor Gibson and Richard Walk (1960) first tested infants' perception of depth by using a unique device called a *visual cliff*, shown in Figure 7.13.

The visual cliff consists of a sheet of plexiglass on which the infant can crawl. A patterned cloth lies just beneath the clear surface on one side. Under the other side is the same cloth pattern, but it lies several feet below the clear surface. Infants able to crawl were placed on a small platform just at the edge of the boundary between "safe" and "deep." Although their mothers called to them from across the deep side, most infants were unwilling to cross, apparently because they perceived the depth and danger. Subsequent research has confirmed the pattern identified by Gibson and Walk. Most babies old enough to be tested avoid the deep side of the cliff, and by 9 or 10 months this avoidance response is quite strong (Bertenthal, Campos, & Kermoian, 1994).

When does the ability to perceive the depth of the deep side develop? An ingenious approach to this question, one that can be used with infants too young to crawl, involves measuring infants' heart rates as the experimenter lowers them to the clear surface of the visual cliff on both the deep and the safe sides. The heart rates of infants as young as 2 months of age slow when they are lowered to the deep side. This finding tells us that the babies notice the difference and are interested in it; there is no evidence, however, that they fear the depth. By 9 months the response is quite different. Now heart rate increases over the drop-off, suggesting that babies are afraid, and now most infants are also unwilling to cross over to the deep side (Campos, Bertenthal, & Kermoian, 1992; Campos et al., 1978).

The shift from interest to fear in response to drop-offs occurs after about 7 months of age. This is also the time when babies begin to take responsibility for their own movements—for instance, by crawling or by pushing themselves around in walkers. Might the two developments be related? Various kinds of evidence sug-

Figure 7.13
Around the time that babies develop skill in crawling, they become fearful of heights in the absence of support, as they display in their reluctance to cross a visual cliff.

gest that they are (Campos et al., 1992). For example, there is a correlation between crawling experience and fear of depth: Babies who have been crawling the longest are most likely to show the fear response on the visual cliff. There is also experimental evidence for a relationship: Babies who have been provided with walkers in which they can move themselves around show the fear response earlier. Apparently, moving about on one's own furnishes information about drop-offs and falls that is less readily available to the nonmobile infant.

How are babies able to perceive depth? There are a number of perceptual cues for depth that babies might use. Some cues are referred to as **pictorial cues** because they are the kind of information that can be conveyed in a picture. For example, railroad tracks appear to converge at a distant point, and this apparent nonparallelism creates an impression of depth (see photo). Objects that are nearer may hide objects that are farther along the same line of sight (a dime, held in the right position, can block an object as large as the moon). Finally, the relative size of objects provides a cue about their distance. If we see a picture in which a dog is larger than a car, we assume the car is farther away, and we can even judge their relative distance from one another because we know how big cars and dogs are (remember size constancy).

Another class of cues is **kinetic cues**. These are cues which are produced by movement, either of the observer or of the objects. Probably the most important kinetic cue is **motion parallax**. When we move, nearer objects appear to change position faster than do farther objects; similarly, when two objects move within our visual field, the nearer object appears to move faster. (You can verify this phenomenon by moving your head from side to side and noting the appearance of near and far objects.) Such differences in apparent movement furnish information about relative depth.

Moving objects provide additional cues when their movement puts them on a collision course with the observer. In this situation, as the size of the object in the eye increases, it blocks more and more of the background, and all the parts of the object get larger. You blink when an object approaches in this way, and so, it turns out, do babies as young as 1 month of age (Yonas, 1981).

Sensitivity to different depth cues develops at different ages (Yonas & Owsley, 1987). Babies can make some use of kinetic depth cues between 1 and 3 months of age; response to static pictorial cues, however, is not evident until 6 or 7 months.

Pictorial cues
Visual cues that indicate the relative distances of objects through static, picturelike information—for example, interposition of one object in front of another.

Kinetic cues
Visual cues that indicate the relative distances of objects through movement either of the objects or of the observer.

Motion parallax
An observer's experience that a closer object moves across the field of view faster than a more distant object when both objects are moving at the same speed or when the objects are stationary and the observer moves.

At around 6–7 months of age, infants become sensitive to monocular cues for points with distance.

Similarly, by some behavioral measures (e.g., the blink response to an approaching object), perception of depth is present quite early; by others (e.g., fear on the visual cliff), it emerges considerably later. We can see again that there is no single answer to the "when" question for most developmental phenomena of interest. Perception of depth is a gradual, rather than instantaneous, achievement.

Keeping Track of Locations in Space We will see in Chapter 13 that the young infant only gradually learns the distinction between the self and the external world of objects. Early in development, the baby understands the world egocentrically—that is, the understanding of space and objects is tied to the baby's own actions and body. Thus, the baby who finds an object to her right expects to find that object on her right again, even if she rotates her body. Gradually, babies learn to use stable landmarks in the environment to find objects, because these provide reliable cues that do not change as the baby moves around (Piaget, 1954).

A clever study by Linda Acredolo (1978) examined this issue for infants at 6, 11, and 16 months of age. In the wall to each side of the infant was a window. Infants learned to turn and look at one window—say, the one on the left—to make an interesting visual display appear. For half the infants, a colored star around the window where the display would appear served as a landmark. The remaining infants had no landmark.

After infants learned the left-turn response, their chair was rotated 180 degrees so that the correct response was now a right turn. If the babies were responding with reference only to their own body, they would continue to look to the left. If they could use the landmark or if they could compensate for the rotation of their body, they would look to the right. Whether or not the landmark was present, 6-month-olds turned to the left side—that is, they used their bodies as the frame of reference rather than the landmark. The 11-month-olds also tended to turn left when no landmark was present, but were able to use the landmark to respond when it was present. Finally, the oldest group responded correctly whether the landmark was present or not. Thus, there was a clear progression with age in the ability to use external referents to judge spatial location.

We have seen that one factor that affects how infants respond to depth is the opportunity to move themselves around. It seems plausible that moving on their own might also help infants keep track of spatial locations. In contrast, like passengers in a car, passively moved babies might not understand how they got from one place to another or the spatial consequences of the move.

It turns out that self-produced movement does facilitate understanding of locations. Performance on tasks such as that used by Acredolo (1978) is better when infants move on their own than when they are carried around the display (Benson & Uzgiris, 1985). And infants who have begun to crawl do better on such measures than do infants who are not yet crawling (Bertenthal, Campos, & Barrett, 1984).

Finally, infants with motor disabilities are often delayed in mastering spatial-performance tasks, even though they are equivalent to babies without such disabilities on other cognitive measures (Telzrow et al., 1988). Babies' control over their own movement through space apparently plays an important role in how well they understand the spatial world.

✔ ***To Recap...***

Newborns can see, although visual acuity does not approach adult levels until about 12 months of age. Peripheral vision and color vision are present in the early months of life.

From birth, babies show interest in the visual contrasts presented by light–dark edges. One interpretation of this interest is that babies have an inborn agenda to engage in activity that stimulates their visual brain centers. At around 2 to 3 months of age, babies begin to prefer organized displays and faces to simple visual detail and contrast.

During the first 6 months of life, babies become quite sensitive to the properties of objects. They are able to appreciate that a single object offers many visual perspectives, as we can see in their ability to maintain size, shape, brightness, and color constancy. Babies in the first 6 months are also learning about further properties of objects, such as solidity and continuity. Initially, however, infants do not appear to infer that an object that is partially hidden from their view is continuous and whole unless they can see the object move.

Studies of how infants appreciate the spatial layout illustrate several important principles. Infants become sensitive to several kinds of cues for determining the distance of objects, with kinetic cues becoming effective prior to static pictorial cues. Although babies detect depth on a visual cliff at around 2 to 3 months of age, their fear of depth develops only around the time they learn to crawl. During the first half year, babies organize space and the objects in it with reference to their own bodies. Later, they can use landmarks in the visual field. This accomplishment permits them to appreciate that objects occupy a stable location independent of their own activity.

Intermodal Perception

Up to this point, we have discussed the various perceptual modes separately. But, of course, we actually perceive most objects, people, and events in our world through more than one mode. A dog, for example, provides a great deal of visual information. It also supplies auditory information by barking, panting, and moving around. Touch may provide another cue as the dog sidles up against your leg. Unfortunately, the dog may stimulate yet another perceptual mode, smell, from a distance of several feet. Although these perceptual cues may sometimes be available simultaneously, you probably can tell that the dog is nearby with only a few of them, maybe even with one alone.

How the child comes to realize that cues from different senses "go together" has puzzled psychologists and philosophers for some time (Bushnell, 1994). As we have seen, Piaget (1952) argued that the sensory modes are separate at birth and that the baby integrates them only through experience. For example, the baby can relate touch and vision only when he learns to look at objects as his hand grasps them. In contrast, other theorists, such as the Gibsons (e.g., Gibson, 1988), have argued that some coordination of the senses is present from the start. There is, as we will see, some truth to both positions.

Researchers generally have approached infants' understanding of intermodal relations in one of two ways (Rose & Ruff, 1987). Many studies focus on how exploring in one mode triggers exploration in a different mode. Other studies focus on how input from different senses comes to indicate a single mental representation— how we know, for example, that a particular sight, touch, and smell all come from the same dog.

Exploratory Intermodal Relations

We appreciate the spatial location of objects through many sensory modes—vision, audition, touch, and sometimes even smell. Investigators have asked whether infants are born with a knowledge of space that is used by all the different sensory modes. If so, this shared knowledge could provide a basis for the intercoordination of the senses. For example, you know where to look when a person calls your name from behind or to the side. Will a newborn baby, who has had no opportunity to associate sound location and visual location, do the same?

As we mentioned earlier, the answer is yes. The newborn turns her eyes and head toward the sound of a voice or a rattle if the sound continues for several seconds (Ennouri & Bloch, 1996; Morrongiello et al., 1994). And the interrelation among sensory modes is not limited to sound and vision. You will remember that one of the infant's earliest reflexes involves turning the head toward the cheek being stroked, an exploratory action that helps the newborn find the nipple. Similar relations exist between smell and vision—as noted, a 6-day-old baby will turn toward a breast pad that exudes the odor of the mother's milk (MacFarlane, 1975).

An important form of exploratory relations among perceptual modes is the relation between vision and reaching. Infants' reaching for a rattle that they see illustrates how vision can trigger tactile exploration. Babies do not reach and grasp objects accurately before 4 or 5 months of age, but much earlier they move their arms in the right direction, perhaps as early as birth (von Hofsten, 1982; White, Castle, & Held, 1964).

Such relations among the sensory modes are present at birth, presumably because they have evolutionary value. We call these *prepared relations*—relations for which the baby is predisposed by biology, but that are also modifiable by experi-

Babies explore novel objects with multiple modalities, including vision and touch (not necessarily a comforting tendency for household pets!).

ence. Some degree of modifiability is clearly necessary, so that the initially crude connections among perceptual modes can be sharpened by experience. Recall the notion of recalibration introduced earlier. If relations among the senses were fixed at birth, children would have no means by which they could adapt to such physical changes as the distance between their eyes and ears or the changing length of their arms and legs. In fact, all of the prepared relations that are evident in the newborn show substantial improvement across the course of infancy. Infants' localization of sounds, for example, is much more skilled and flexible by 5 or 6 months of age than at birth (Morrongiello, 1994). Visually directed reaching shows comparable advances, as infants gain more and more experience in acting on the world (Bertenthal & Clifton, 1998).

The examples of exploratory activity described here support the idea that relations among the sensory modes exist quite early. Next, though, we must ask whether babies realize they are exploring the same object in the two modes. This question raises the issue of mental representation (Rose & Ruff, 1987).

Intermodal Representation

How can we determine whether infants can use different perceptual modes to form a single mental representation of an object? Two kinds of evidence are informative. The first examines whether babies can transfer the benefit of experience from one mode to another. The second examines whether babies know that the same object is stimulating two modes. Psychologists have used these approaches to examine relations between haptic and visual perception and between vision and audition.

Haptic-Visual Relations
As noted earlier, haptic perception refers to active exploration by means of touch, as when a baby handles a rattle. Sucking can also be an important form of haptic exploration, especially for young infants.

Several researchers have investigated whether infants can transfer information gained from sucking to visual perception of the same object. Meltzoff and Borton (1979) provided 1-month-old infants an opportunity to suck on either a nubby (bumpy) nipple or a smooth nipple. They then presented the infants pictures of the nubby and smooth nipples, side by side. Infants looked longer at the nipple they had sucked. This finding suggests that cross-modal cues can specify the same object for infants at an amazingly early age, but we should be careful in reaching conclusions. Although some experimenters have reported similar findings (Gibson & Walker, 1984; Pecheux, Lepecq, & Salzarulo, 1988), others have been unable to replicate the results (Brown & Gottfried, 1986; Rose & Ruff, 1987), and thus at present it is not clear how early such oral-visual matching is possible.

Infants have also been tested for the ability to recognize objects visually that they have previously explored only by hand. Whether this ability is present in the first half year of life is in doubt, but babies between 6 and 12 months of age clearly demonstrate that they can make the match (Rose & Orlian, 1991; Ruff & Kohler, 1978). Babies are also able to learn about an object visually and then recognize that object by touch, but the vision-to-touch connection is more difficult to make than is the touch-to-vision connection. Infants typically succeed only if they are allowed more time to explore the object or if they are already somewhat familiar with it (Bushnell, 1994; Rose, 1994).

An ingenious study examined whether babies can detect differences between what they feel and what they see. Babies were given the impression that they were reaching for an object reflected in a mirror, but they were actually reaching for an object hidden behind the mirror. On trick trials, babies felt a furry object while viewing a smooth object or vice versa. On nontrick trials, the objects matched. Whereas 8-month-olds did not show different facial expressions for trick and non-trick trials, 9.5- and 11-month-olds showed more surprise during the trick trials, indicating that they perceived the mismatch (Bushnell, 1982).

Auditory-Visual Relations   Can babies detect a correspondence between a sound and a visual event? Interestingly, babies naturally look at visual events that correspond to the sounds they hear. For example, Spelke (1976) showed 4-month-old infants two films, side by side. One film showed a person playing peekaboo, and the other showed a hand hitting a wooden block and a tambourine. A sound track was played that was appropriate to one of the films. Babies looked more at the film that matched the sound track, suggesting that they recognized the sight-sound correspondence.

Babies can also match auditory and visual events when the matching involves tempo and rhythm and when it involves sounds that accompany a moving object's changes in direction (Bahrick & Pickens, 1994). And by 4 months of age, babies have some idea about the types of sounds new objects will make when they bang together, a feat that requires knowledge of several properties of objects—for example, their hardness and whether one item or several items are involved in the collision (Bahrick, 1983, 1992).

Babies also appreciate auditory-visual relations that involve people. Babies look longer at their mother's face when they hear her voice than when they hear a stranger's voice (Cohen, 1974). As early as 3.5 months of age, babies look more at their mother when they hear her voice and more at their father when they hear his voice (Spelke & Owsley, 1979). By 4 months of age, babies look more at a male face when they hear a male voice and more at a female face when they hear a female voice, even when both faces and voices are unfamiliar (Walker-Andrews et al., 1991).

Some sensitivities seem even more subtle. Infants between 2.5 and 4 months of age are sensitive to the lack of synchrony between the movement of lips and the sounds they hear, and they also respond to the match of mood in the voice and the face when sadness or happiness is expressed (Walker, 1982).

Infants, then, are surprisingly good at picking up the commonality in cues from different senses. The baby's awareness that different cues from the same objects are coordinated greatly simplifies the task of organizing the overwhelming number of stimuli in the world into more manageable chunks. It is important to remember, though, that intermodal capabilities emerge at different times. At first, for example, infants simply appreciate that synchrony exists between visual and auditory events. More subtle forms of intermodal perception appear in steps as the baby matures (Lewkowicz & Lickliter, 1994).

We have discussed two basic approaches to the study of intermodal perception. Research on intermodal exploration has shown that babies come into the world with a number of inborn relations among sensory modes. Yet it also seems that forming mental representations of objects from the inputs of many perceptual modes requires some experience. As always, nature and nurture work together to guide development.

✓ To Recap...

Most of our perceptual experience reflects the involvement of several sensory modes rather than a single one. Psychologists have wondered how children come to know that these perceptual cues "go together." In investigating this issue, they have focused on exploratory relations and mental representations.

Exploratory intermodal relations exist at birth, but they are tuned by experience. In the first half year of life, babies seem to have difficulty forming the same mental representation from different sensory modes. However, there is reasonable evidence that babies in the second half year do develop mental representations that bridge haptic and visual modes as well as auditory and visual modes. A general conclusion is that prepared relations between perceptual modes exist at birth, but that experience plays a significant role in tuning and elaborating these relations.

Attention and Action

Because sensory and perceptual processes are triggered by external stimuli, it may seem that these processes are passive and simply activated by events in the world. However, the perceptual modes are the mind's tools for gathering information about the environment, and the mind uses these tools actively. This is what we mean by *attention*: the active, selective taking in of some but not all of the potentially available information in a situation. Furthermore, perception is typically not an end in itself, but a means toward the goal of operating on the world effectively: "We perceive in order to act and we act to perceive" (Pick, 1992, p. 791). In this final section of the chapter we examine the dynamic aspect of perception, considering both how action affects perception and how perception guides action. We begin with infancy and then move on to older children.

Infancy

Orienting reflex
A natural reaction to novel stimuli that enhances stimulus processing and includes orientation of the eyes and ears to optimize stimulus reception, inhibition of ongoing activity, and a variety of physiological changes.

Defensive reflex
A natural reaction to novel stimuli that tends to protect the organism from further stimulation and that may include orientation of the stimulus receptors away from the stimulus source and a variety of physiological changes.

Selective attention
Concentration on a stimulus or event with attendant disregard for other stimuli or events.

Even newborn infants attend to mild sounds and sights. Their bodies become quieter, they stop what they are doing (such as sucking); they widen their eyes; and their heart rates slow (see Figure 7.14). These changes in behavior appear designed to optimize the baby's readiness to receive stimuli. First described by Sokolov (1960) as the **orienting reflex**, these changes can be observed, for example, when newborns attend to moving lights, to sounds that change gradually, or to sounds of low frequency (Haith, 1966; Kearsley, 1973). However, if the physical stimuli are too intense or the changes too abrupt, infants close their eyes and become agitated and their heart rates increase—a protective reaction called the **defensive reflex** (Finlay & Ivinskis, 1987; Graham & Clifton, 1966). The orienting and defensive reflexes appear to be the baby's earliest forms of positive and negative attention.

We have already discussed other indicators of newborns' attention, such as the tendency to look toward the location of a sound and to turn the head toward cheek stimulation or an attractive odor. Typically, however, investigators are more interested in the development of **selective attention**, the ability of the infant to focus on one stimulus rather than another. Even newborns have the capacity for at least a simple form of selective attention, choosing to look at displays of intermediate levels of brightness and pattern variability over extreme levels (Hershenson, 1964) and at patterned over nonpatterned displays (Fantz, 1963). Newborns also adjust their sucking activity to hear their mother's voice rather than the voice of a woman unknown to them (Cooper & Aslin, 1989; DeCasper & Fifer, 1980). This capacity for selective attention provides a powerful tool for investigating infant perception, as we have already seen.

What controls the infant's attention? This question has not yet been settled, but Jerome Kagan has provided one influential set of ideas. He suggests that from birth to around 3 months of age, infants attend to patterns that contain contour and

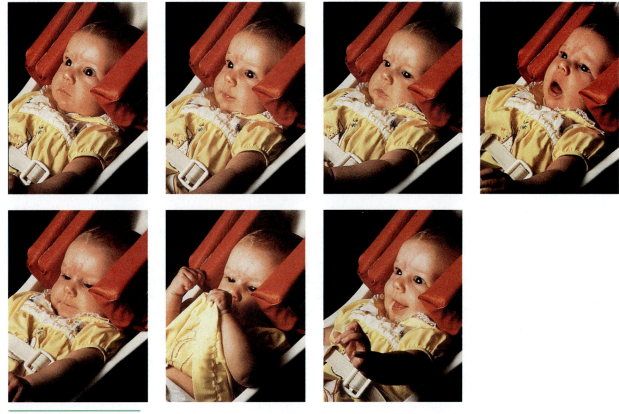

Figure 7.14
Examples of the orienting reflex in a young infant. Attention is high when a new stimulus first appears (pictures 1 and 2), then declines as the stimulus becomes familiar (pictures 4–6), then peaks again when the stimulus changes (picture 7). From *The World of the Newborn* (pp. 128–129) by D. Maurer and C. Maurer, 1988, New York: Basic Books. Copyright © 1988 by Daphe Maurer and Charles Maurer.

movement. From approximately 3 months to 12 months of age, they attend to things that seem surprising or discrepant from what they know. For example, when shown clay models of regular and distorted faces, babies looked more at the distorted faces. From 12 months on, babies attend to events that provoke them to form hypotheses, or guesses, about what is going on in their world. For example, a child might see his mother with a bandage on her face and try to figure out what happened (Kagan, 1970).

What babies attend to can also be affected by what other people attend to (Adamson, 1995; Butterworth, 1995). As infants develop, they become increasingly skilled at using cues from their mother or father to direct their own attentional activities. By 15 to 18 months the mother's glance at an object is likely to trigger similar exploration by the infant. This is the phenomenon of **joint attention**: the tendency to enter into the attentional focus of another. In addition to its role in directing exploration of the environment, joint attention marks an important advance in infants' understanding of other people, because it suggests that they are coming to realize that others are psychological beings who have perceptual experiences similar to their own.

Joint attention
Using cues (such as direction of gaze) to identify and share the attentional focus of another.

The looking activity of young infants is a good example of the role that action plays in perception. When alert and active, young infants make new visual fixations two or three times each second. Newborn infants even search actively with their eyes in darkness, indicating that their perceptual system is active even when there is no stimulus to produce a reaction. They continue to search when a light is turned on until they find light–dark edges. When they do, they cross back and forth over those edges, adjusting their visual scanning as necessary. They seem to come into the world with a set of rules for acting:

1. If awake and the light is not too bright, open eyes.
2. If in darkness, search around.
3. If find light, search for contrasting edges.
4. If find edges, stay near them and cross back and forth over them.
5. As the clustering of edges increases, scan the edges more and more narrowly.

This inborn set of rules serves the biological function of activating visual cells in the brain and assuring that cells form proper hookups with each other (Haith, 1980, 1991). Such rules also illustrate that from the earliest moments of a newborn's external life, action affects perception just as perception affects action.

Action can also anticipate perception. Recent research indicates that young infants can anticipate perceptual events before they occur, through the formation of expectations (Haith, 1994; Haith, Wentworth, & Canfield, 1993). Babies 3.5 months of age saw attractive pictures alternating in left-hand and right-hand positions on a computer screen. Each picture appeared for 0.7 second, followed by a delay of 1 second.

After about 15 seconds of experience with this series, most infants moved their eyes, during the 1-second delay, to the place where the next picture would appear.

Restaurants are favorite places for infants to practice their reaching and exploratory skills.

Even when they did not move their eyes during the delay, it was clear that they expected a picture to appear, because they responded to it within about 0.4 second on average—substantially faster than when the appearance of the pictures was unpredictable. One interpretation of this finding is that infants form expectations in order to free themselves from simply reacting to each event as it occurs. The ability to anticipate future events is an important component of many kinds of cognitive activity throughout the lifespan (Haith et al., 1994). Apparently, such "future-oriented processing" begins very early.

Most of our discussion so far has concerned vision. Babies also use other action tools to investigate objects—for example, their mouths and tongues (Rochat, 1993). And when they begin to move around by themselves, links between perception and action become even stronger. As we have seen, self-produced movement produces new experiences and sometimes new understandings—such as the onset of fear of heights (Campos et al., 1992).

Moving around independently also requires new perceptual learning. This is so because babies in the first year of life have difficulty separating their perception of space from the actions they perform. For example, babies who were able to reach around a barrier for a hidden object had to relearn the task when they were required to crawl around the barrier to get it (Lockman, 1984). Thus, what seem like very similar tasks to an adult—reaching around or moving around the same barrier—do not at first seem similar to the baby. As infants gain more experience with the effects of their own movements, they gradually develop a more unified understanding of space.

Older Children

Although infants are capable of selective attention, there is a general shift with age from control of attention by external stimuli to stronger self-regulation based on the individual's own goals and intentions. Flavell (1985) identified four important aspects of attention that develop with age.

1. *Control* of attention improves with age as attention span increases and distractibility decreases. For example, children under 2.5 years of age are easily distracted from watching television programs by toys in the room and other events in the house. Soon enough, however, it may become difficult to pull them away from the set (Anderson et al., 1986).

2. *Adaptability* of attention to the task also changes. When an experimenter tells children to pay attention to a particular task, older children do so and disregard things that are not central to it. Younger children, however, focus on many more of the irrelevant aspects and so do not perform as well on the main task (Hagen & Hale, 1973; Miller, 1990).

3. Another feature of attentional change is *planfulness*. When an experimenter asks children to judge whether two complex pictures are the same, younger children often use a haphazard comparison strategy, not examining all the details before making a judgment. Older children are more systematic, comparing each detail across pictures, one by one (Vurpillot, 1968).

4. Finally, children become better at *adjusting* their attentional strategies as they gather information from a task. For example, experienced readers change their reading speed as the difficulty of the text changes, while younger readers tend to maintain a fairly regular reading speed regardless of difficulty (Day, 1975).

Applications
ADHD: Helping Children with Attentional Problems

An important developmental achievement is the capacity to control and direct attention effectively. Not all children, however, master the challenges of attentional control as quickly or as fully as others. Anyone who has spent much time in elementary-school classrooms is familiar with children who constantly fidget and talk out inappropriately, who seem unable to stay in their seat or to concentrate for more than brief periods of time, and whose uncontrolled behavior detracts not only from their own but also from their classmates' learning.

Attention-deficit hyperactivity disorder (**ADHD**) is a relatively new label for what is almost certainly a very old problem. The term refers to a clinical syndrome characterized by the kinds of behavior patterns just described. Children with ADHD have great difficulty maintaining attention; they are often hyperactive; and their behavior has a generally uncontrolled and impulsive quality. These children perform poorly in school, and they often have difficulties in interpersonal relations as well. ADHD emerges early in childhood and can be a lifelong condition (American Psychiatric Association, 1994).

The diagnosis of ADHD has become increasingly common. Current estimates indicate that about 3 to 5% of school-age children in the United States have ADHD (American Psychiatric Association, 1994). Boys are diagnosed with the disorder more often than are girls; it is unclear, however, whether this disparity reflects a genuine difference between the sexes or simply the fact that boys are more likely to show the disruptive behaviors that lead to clinical evaluation (Silver, 1992).

The precise cause of ADHD has yet to be identified. The evidence suggests that in most cases both nature and nurture contribute. The fact that ADHD tends to run in families suggests a biological component. Approximately 20 to 30% of the parents of children with ADHD have ADHD themselves (Silver, 1992). In one study, 51% of identical twin pairs were concordant for ADHD—that is, if one twin had the disorder the other did as well (Goodman & Stevenson, 1989). Further evidence for the importance of biological factors comes from studies of brain structure and functioning. Individuals with ADHD often show abnormalities in the frontal lobe of the cortex—the part of the brain responsible for attention and inhibition of behavior (Riccio et al., 1993; Zametkin et al., 1990).

Experience can also be important. The home lives of children with ADHD tend to be characterized by high levels of stress and parental punitiveness (Bernier & Siegel, 1994; Jacobvitz & Sroufe, 1987). In some instances ADHD may have its origins even earlier—in the prenatal environment and the exposure of the fetus to teratogens such as alcohol and drugs (Silver, 1992).

Just as both nature and nurture may contribute to the emergence of ADHD, attempts to help children with ADHD may take both biological and environmental routes. One of the most common and effective treatments for these children is a biological one. Administration of stimulant drugs, such as Ritalin, has been used to treat ADHD since the 1930s. This treatment leads to improvement in 70 to 80% of cases (Silver, 1992). It may seem strange to prescribe a stimulant for children who already have an overabundance of energy. But in childhood stimulant medications tend to decrease activity level and heighten attention—which, of course, is precisely the sort of change that children with ADHD need (Rapoport et al., 1978).

Although drug treatment can be an important part of a therapy program for ADHD, medication does not cure the condition, and medication alone is unlikely

Attention-deficit hyperactivity disorder (ADHD) A developmental disorder characterized by difficulty in sustaining attention, hyperactivity, and impulsive and uncontrolled behavior.

to give children with ADHD all the help they need. The most effective treatment programs combine medication with changes in the child's environment. Environmental interventions can take many forms. Among the approaches that have proved beneficial are operant conditioning of appropriate behaviors, modeling, and family-oriented forms of therapy (Barkley, 1990; Pelham & Hinshaw, 1992). As we would expect, interventions that involve both the school and the home tend to be most effective.

At present, there is no known cure for ADHD, and not even the best treatment programs can guarantee long-term success. Still, recent years have seen important advances in our ability to help children and families cope with one of the most common and debilitating childhood disorders.

We saw that the study of children's eye movements demonstrates the interplay of action and perception very early in life. Eye movements are also informative in the study of older children. In one experiment, children were shown pairs of houses, such as those in Figure 7.15, and were asked to judge whether the houses in each pair were identical or different. The experimenter recorded the children's eye fixations and movements as they looked at the two houses. Each house had several windows of varying shapes with varying decorations. A thorough examination of the houses required comparing each window of the houses one by one.

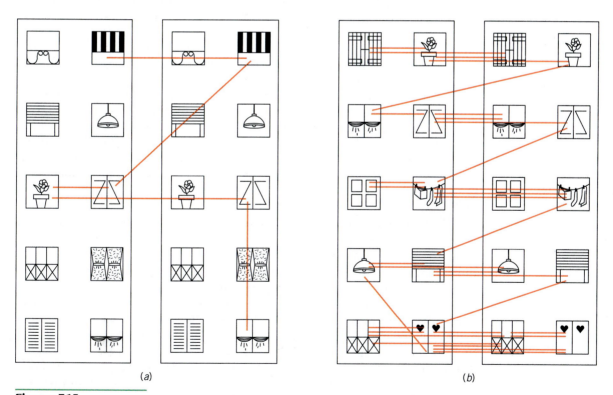

(a)   (b)

Figure 7.15

Reconstruction of a fixation sequence by (a) an inefficient child and (b) an efficient child. Their task was to judge whether the windows in two houses were identical or different. From E. Vurpillot, R. Castelo, and C. Renard, 1975, *Année Psychologique, 75,* Figure 2, pp. 362–363. Reprinted by permission of Presses Universitaires de France.

Striking differences were found between children 4 and 9 years of age. The younger children appeared to have little or no plan for the task. Rather than comparing the corresponding windows in a pair of houses, the younger children often looked at windows in different locations, in a haphazard order, and did not check all windows before deciding the houses were the same. Older children, in contrast, scanned comparable windows, systematically checking each pair of windows before making a "same" decision. They were also more efficient, ending their inspection as soon as a difference between windows permitted them to say "different" (Vurpillot & Ball, 1979).

In general, studies of scanning and other forms of perceptual activity reveal increased carefulness in gathering information, more flexibility in search, and lowered distractibility as children move from the preschool to the middle-elementary school years (Ruff & Rothbart, 1996). Such studies also reveal clear links between attention and learning and problem solving. Developmental improvements in attention are one contributor to differences between younger and older children in problem-solving prowess. And individual differences in attention at any age are one reason some children learn more effectively than others.

We turn finally to some research that examines the relation between perception and various forms of skilled motor behavior. Action skills—behaviors that require physical coordination, such as reaching, walking, and catching—involve a complex interplay between perception and various parts of the motor system (Bertenthal & Clifton, 1998). The development of these skills is made more complicated by the fact that the growing body and limbs change in size, weight, and proportion. Perception plays a key role in the continuing adjustment required for skill development, providing feedback about the relative accuracy of performance. Feedback indicates the difference between reaching a goal (such as catching a ball) and not reaching it (missed it by 6 inches!).

One study examined how children of different ages adjust action to perception in the development of skill (Hay, 1984). Glass wedges placed in front of the eyes of 5- to 11-year-old children created a shift in the apparent location of visual objects (much like the apparent shift of underwater objects as seen from above). If the child did not watch his arm as it moved toward the object, but simply reached directly for the object where it appeared to be, he would reach too far to one side and miss.

The 5-year-olds tended to make more direct reaches, correcting hand position only after the hand had reached the apparent position of the object. The 7-year-olds made slower or more-hesitant reaches, with starts and stops followed by small corrections near the end. Children 9 and 11 years of age were more likely to begin with a direct movement, gradually slowing their reach as they approached the object, and making corrective movements near the end. Apparently, the 5-year-olds paid little attention to feedback, whereas the 7-year-olds overemphasized it, much as an unpracticed driver oversteers a sliding car. By 9 years of age, children used feedback more effectively.

This study revealed an expected improvement with age in the coordination between perception and action. In some contexts, however, the perceptual-action skills of the young child seem to outshine those of the adult. A visit to the local video-game parlor will convince any doubter that children are capable of highly sophisticated forms of perceptual-motor coordination. In fact, it is commonly assumed that children are more competent in such skills than are adults. However, we should not forget that children have more practice and are more motivated to engage in such activities.

One research team developed a technology for exploring this issue, as illustrated in Figure 7.16 (Roberts et al., 1991). Adults and 4-, 7-, and 12-year-olds played the video game Asteroids over several sessions in the laboratory, so the researchers could observe them as the players evolved from novices to intermediates. None had ever played video games before. The tasks in the game are to maneuver a spaceship so that it is not hit by flying rocks and to try to shoot down the rocks. The fast movement of the game makes it perceptually demanding, and the player uses several buttons to control turning and flying the spaceship and shooting its gun. A computer recorded all the game displays and all the players' actions, including eye movements, for later analysis.

People in all age groups initially simplified the task by using as few controls as possible—for example, pressing only the spaceship's right-turn and fire buttons. The younger groups maintained this strategy throughout and therefore never got much better. The older groups, however, tried new strategies with time, learning to move or fly the spaceship around the screen. The shift to new strategies had a short-term cost, because new flyers tended to run into things and destroy the spaceship. Ultimately, however, the ability to fly produced better performance.

We can see similarities to the earlier discussion of attention and eye-movement strategies. Here, too, development consists of increasing flexibility in the use of skills and increasing use of strategies. There is hope beyond elementary school, after all!

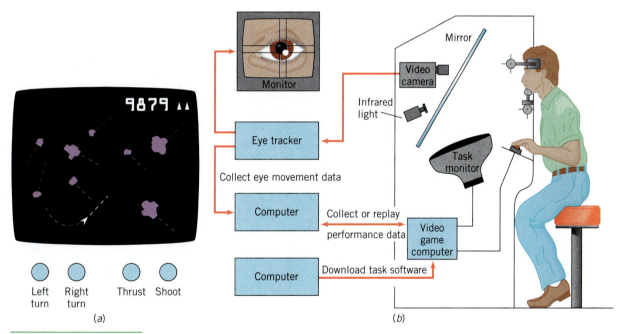

Figure 7.16

(*a*) In the Asteroids video game, a player controls a spaceship with buttons that can rotate the nose of the ship counterclockwise (left–turn button), rotate the nose clockwise (right–turn button), move the ship forward (thrust button), and fire missiles from the ship's nose. The object of the game is to destroy the moving asteroids with a missile and not to allow the asteroids to hit the ship. (*b*) As a person plays the game, a camera records the player's eye fixations. A computer records the screen presented to the player, the player's eye fixations, and the player's button presses 60 times each second. Researchers can analyze these data to find out precisely how looking and action are orchestrated.

✔ *To Recap...*

Perception, attention, and action are interwoven throughout life. From birth, some sensory stimuli arouse interest, or an orienting reflex, whereas others produce rejection, or a defensive reflex. Even newborns have some ability to be selective in what they attend to. One model proposes that infants first attend to patterns and contours, then to discrepant stimuli, and then to events that require cognitive effort to be understood.

Active use of perceptual skills is evident from birth. Newborns stimulate their developing brains through the inspection of high-contrast edges. Somewhat older babies develop expectations for regular events, which permit them to assume some control over their actions. Visually guided reach and self-produced locomotion dramatically change the opportunities that infants have to affect their own experience. Their control of their own movement through space contributes to their understanding of spatial stability.

Older children display better selective attention than do infants and young children. Four important aspects of attention that develop with age are control, adaptability, planfulness, and the ability to adjust with experience. Action tools also continue to develop through the school years. Increasingly, children make use of feedback to adapt to changing perception-action circumstances.

Conclusion

The issues that we have addressed in this chapter are long-standing—as the exchange between Molyneux and Locke with which we opened the chapter illustrates. What is new in the modern era are not the questions, but the method of answering them. The last three decades have seen the development of powerful scientific methods for addressing what were once matters for purely philosophical speculation.

This research has taught us that many earlier ideas about infants were wrong. Many experts thought babies were blind and deaf at birth, an idea that lent support to the empiricist view that perceptual capacities were based solely on experience and learning. We now know that all the perceptual systems function even before the fetus has reached the age of normal-term birth. We live in the age of the "competent infant," in which many new capabilities have been discovered and infancy seems much less a period of perceptual disability than was once believed.

At the same time, we must be careful not to attribute too much skill to the infant. A recent "superbaby" craze (reinforced by articles in such widely read publications as *Time* and *Newsweek* magazines) has led many people to think that babies can do almost anything. However, even in terms of very basic sensory processes—in detecting and discriminating the physical energies that stimulate the receptors—it is clear that the newborn baby has a great deal left to accomplish. And as we have seen, perceptual tools must be increasingly refined.

One of the most crucial problems in developmental psychology is that we have few concepts to enable discussion of partial accomplishments. We ask if the baby has color vision or melody perception or intermodal perception and so on. When we find evidence that the baby does, often that is the end of our questioning. But no one really believes, for example, that the melody perception of the infant is as good as the melody perception of the adult. The problem is that although we can understand how a baby can see more or less clearly, because we can experience out-of-focus images for ourselves, we do not have concrete examples of imperfect color vision, melody perception, or intermodal perception. Until we can find a way to talk about imperfect accomplishments clearly, we will not have a complete understanding of perceptual development.

It is useful to think of the baby as coming into the world with the essential *tools* for taking in and seeking out perceptual information. This is most obviously the case with eye movements. Other tools will soon mature, such as grasping, reaching, crawling, and walking. These tools are present at birth or mature during infancy in babies of every culture. However, the *content* of perception, the actual information gathered, is highly dependent on experience. Whether a baby becomes familiar with faces that are brown, yellow, or white or learns to understand French, Chinese, or English depends on the culture in which he or she is raised.

As in most cases, then, the diametrically opposed nature and nurture views are both correct. Evolution has provided a creature with all the tools necessary to collect information about the world. Experience determines exactly what that information will be.

Visual Summary for Chapter 7:
Sensory and Perceptual Development

Theories of Sensory and Perceptual Development

Theory	Emphasis	Explanation
Environmental/ Learning	Emphasizes the role of experience.	Development occurs as babies learn through experience to construct increasingly detailed and complex perceptions from the separate input of the senses.
Ethology	Emphasizes that even babies perceive sensory information comprehensively.	Development consists of increasing sensitivity to the structure of incoming information, as well as to which properties change and which remain constant.
Cognitive-Developmental	Emphasizes how knowledge can affect perception.	Piaget believed the child's stage of development controls how he/she perceives the world. Information-processing theories focus on how sensory information is transformed as it is processed by the brain.

Touch and Pain, Smell and Taste, Motion and Balance

Touch and Pain	The newborn is sensitive to touch, and this sensitivity increases over the first few days of life. Touch is important for several adaptive reflexes and for relations between children and adults. Infants and children use touch to explore the environment.
Smell and Taste	Newborns are sensitive to both smell and taste. They prefer pleasant smells and can distinguish their mother's smells from those of other women. They can distinguish among sweet, sour, bitter, and salty tastes.
Vestibular Sensitivity	Newborns respond to both position and movement, as evident in the soothing properties of rocking and jiggling. When vestibular and visual cues contradict one another, babies tend to rely on vision.

Hearing

Sensitivity to Sound	The fetus can hear several months prior to birth and may become familiar with sounds such as its mother's voice while in the womb. Newborns are not, however, as sensitive to sounds as adults. Sensitivity to sound, particularly high-pitched sounds, improves rapidly over the first year.
Discriminating Sounds	Infants can discriminate sounds on the basis of intensity, frequency, and duration. Babies are especially sensitive to the characteristics of sound that will be important for speech perception.
Sound Localization	The ability to localize sounds is present at birth, then fades somewhat, but reappears at 4 months in a more efficient form. This ability becomes more precise over the first 18 months of life.

Vision

Capabilities and Preferences Visual acuity in the newborn is poor, but improves with age, approaching adult levels at about 12 months of age. Peripheral vision and color vision are present in the newborn. Newborns are interested in high-contrast, light-dark edges; however, by 2 to 3 months organized displays and faces are of increasing interest.

Objects and Their Properties During the first half year of life, babies become quite sensitive to the properties of objects. They are able to appreciate that a single object offers many visual perspectives, as evident in their ability to maintain size, shape, brightness, and color constancy. They are also learning about the solidity and continuity of objects, although initially they do not appear to infer that an object that is partly hidden from view is continuous and whole unless they can see the object move.

Spatial Perception Babies use kinetic cues at an earlier age than static pictorial cues to judge depth and distance. Depth on the visual cliff can be detected by 2- to 3- month-old babies; however, fear of depth emerges onl later in infancy, at about the time when babies learn to crawl. Babies younger than 6 months organize space and objects in it with reference to their own bodies, but older babies use landmarks in the visual field. The accomplishment allows them to appreciate that objects occupy a stable location independent of their own activity.

Intermodal Perception

Exploratory Intermodal Relations Exploratory intermodal relations, such as turning toward a sound, are present in the newborn, but are tuned by experience.

Intermodal Representation In the first half year of life, babies have difficulty forming the same mental representation from different sensory modes. Older babies, however, develop mental representations that bridge haptic and visual modes, as well as the auditory and visual modes.

Attention and Action

Infancy Even newborns have some ability to be selective in what they attend to. One model proposes that infants first attend to patterns and contours, then to discrepant stimuli, and then to events that require cognitive effort in order to be understood. Active use of perceptual skills is evident from birth. Newborns stimulate their developing brains through the inspection of high-contrast edges. Older babies develop expectations for regular events, allowing them to assume some control over their actions. Visually guided reach and self-produced locomotion dramatically change the opportunities that infants have to affect their own experience.

Older Children Older children display better selective attention than do infants and young children. Four important aspects of attention that develop with age are control, adaptability, planfulness, and ability to adjust with experience. Action tools continue to develop through the school years. Increasingly, children make use of feedback to adapt to changing perception-action circumstances.

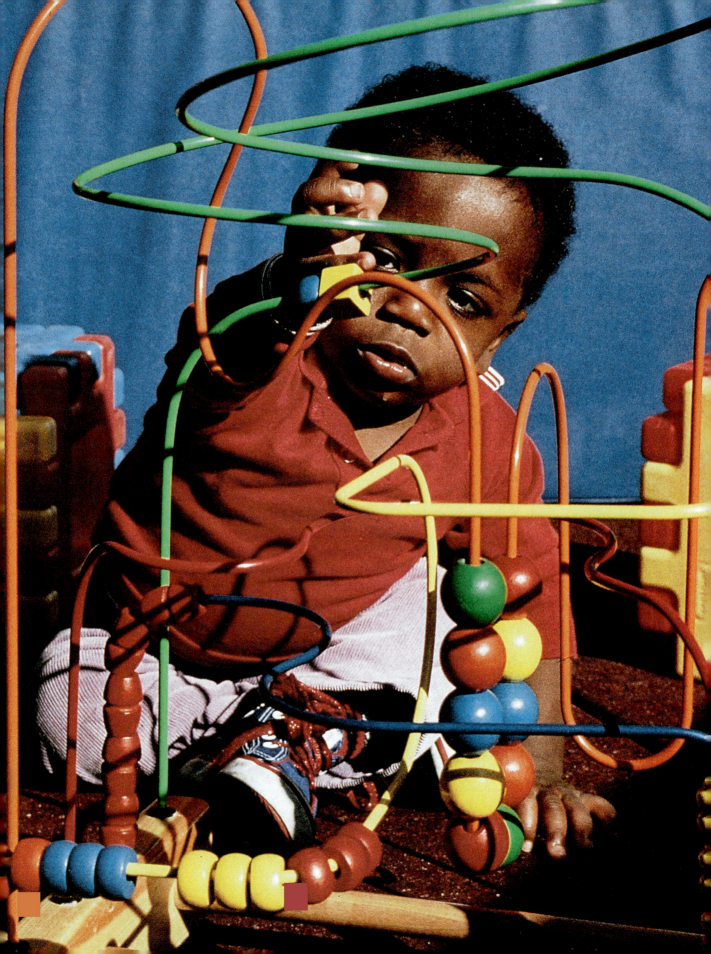

Chapter 8

Cognitive Development: The Piagetian Approach

Two-year-old Nathanial gazes at flashcards as his mother works at teaching him to read. Kira, almost 2, follows carpenter ants around the backyard, trying to touch each one she sees as she chants "little bug." Which toddler is learning more?

A generation ago, few parents would have considered teaching their baby to read a possibility, let alone a priority. But over the past decade or so, many parents have become convinced that they should be preparing their children for a lifetime of success by tutoring them from infancy in reading, math, computer skills, and the like. Books and articles offering advice on such matters as teaching babies to read, raising their IQs, and even getting them to pass entrance exams for exclusive preschools have proliferated.

Do parents who follow all this advice end up with a smarter child? Although some educators think so, many are dubious. For example, there is no evidence that a child who learns to read unusually early goes on to earn higher grades or experience more success later than children who learn to read on a more normal timetable, according to John Bruer, president of the James S. McDonnell Foundation, which conducts research into cognitive development.

The fact is, preschoolers are continually learning all kinds of important things as they conduct their own investigations of their environments. Toddlers, for example, enjoy repeating the same activity over and over. As they do so, they're learning that objects behave in certain predictable ways. Each small variation teaches them something new and interesting about how the world works. While banging a block on the table, a 1-year-old might learn how the sound changes when he bangs harder. By following carpenter ants, a 2-year-old learns something about the behavior of "little bugs."

In other words, in normal environments, children can't help learning lessons that will form the basis of later, more formal learning. In this chapter, we consider the theory and research that have provided the field with its richest source of ideas about such spontaneous, self-paced learning: the work of the Swiss psychologist Jean Piaget.

*W*e closed the last chapter with a message of both competence and limitations. We saw that the infant's perceptual abilities are considerably more impressive than psychologists once believed. But we saw as well that even the modern "superbaby" is not equivalent to an adult and that major improvements in perceptual ability occur within the short span of infancy. Determining the ways in which the perceptual world of the infant both resembles and differs from that of the adult is one of the most fascinating challenges in modern child psychology. So, too, is tracing the interplay of nature and nurture that transforms the "competent newborn" into the fully competent adult.

The same points apply, perhaps even more forcefully, to the subject of our next three chapters—children's cognitive development. By **cognition** we mean all the higher order mental processes by which humans attempt to understand and adapt to their world—processes that go by such labels as *thinking, reasoning, learning,* and

Cognition
Higher-order mental processes, such as reasoning and problem solving, through which humans attempt to understand the world.

problem solving. Here, too, the research of recent years has taught us that infants and young children are often far more competent than we used to believe. Yet the child's thinking may also differ from that of the adult in many ways, and these differences continue to intrigue and to baffle researchers and parents alike. Discovering the mixture of competence and limitations that characterizes thought at different points in childhood is one of the two great challenges that the researcher of cognitive development faces. The second is to discover how the limitations are overcome and how new forms of competence emerge. These challenges reflect the two general goals of developmental psychology identified in Chapter 1: to describe development, and to explain it.

Across the next three chapters, we consider three general approaches to these questions. First, we focus on the cognitive-developmental approach, as represented by the work of Jean Piaget. We examine both Piaget's original theory and research and more recent studies that in some way test, modify, or extend the Piagetian position. In Chapter 9, we shift our attention to another major representative of the cognitive-developmental approach—the information-processing perspective. Finally, in Chapter 10, we consider the intelligence-test approach. We will see that these perspectives are in many respects complementary rather than contradictory and that a full model of cognitive development requires insights gained from all three approaches.

Piaget's Theory

Piaget's training included heavy doses of both biology and philosophy. From philosophy came much of the content of his work. Piaget's goal throughout his career was to use the study of children to answer basic philosophical questions about the nature and origins of knowledge. His research thus shows a consistent focus on what have long been central topics in philosophy: the child's understanding of space, time, and causality, of number and quantity, of classes and relations, of invariance and change. Undoubtedly one reason Piaget's studies have attracted so much attention is that they identify such basic and important forms of knowledge. Another reason is Piaget's surprising, and controversial, claim that these basic forms of knowledge often take a long time to develop.

From biology Piaget took ideas about both the structure and the function of intelligence. A basic principle in biology is that of *organization*. An organism is never simply a random collection of cells, tissues, and organs; rather, organisms are always highly organized systems. One job of the biologist is to discover what the underlying organization is. Piaget maintains that the same principle applies to human intelligence. For Piaget, the essence of intelligence does not lie in individually learned responses or isolated memories; the essence lies in the underlying organization. This organization takes the form of the various *cognitive structures* that the developing child constructs. The job of the psychologist is to discover what these structures are.

Biology also contributed to the functional side of Piaget's theory. Another basic biological principle is that of *adaptation*. All organisms adapt to the environment in which they must survive, often by means of very complex mechanisms. The biologist tries to discover what these mechanisms of adaptation are. Human intelligence, according to Piaget, is an adaptive phenomenon—indeed, it may be the primary means by which humans adapt to the environmental challenges they face.

Adaptation occurs through the complementary processes of *assimilation* and *accommodation*. Whenever we interact with the environment, we assimilate the envi-

Table 8.1
Piaget's Four Periods of Development

Period	Ages (yrs)	Description
Sensorimotor	0–2	Infants understand the world through the overt actions performed on it. These actions reflect the sensorimotor schemes. Across infancy, the schemes become progressively more complex and interrelated. Decentering occurs, and the infant comes to understand object permanence.
Preoperational	2–6	The child can now use representations rather than overt actions to solve problems. Thinking is consequently faster, more efficient, more mobile, and more socially sharable. The child's initial attempts at representational functioning also show limitations, including egocentrism and centration.
Concrete operational	6–12	The advent of operations allows the child to overcome the limitations of preoperational thought. Operations are a system of internal mental actions that underlie logical problem solving. The child comes to understand various forms of conservation, as well as classification and relational reasoning.
Formal operational	12–adult	The further development of operations leads to a capacity for hypothetical-deductive reasoning. Thought begins with possibility and works systematically and logically back to reality. The prototype for such logical reasoning is scientific problem solving.

ronment to our current cognitive structures—that is, we fit it in or interpret it in terms of what we already understand. Yet at the same time we are continually accommodating our structures to fit with the environment—that is, altering our understanding to take account of new things. It is through innumerable instances of assimilation and accommodation that cognitive development occurs.

The term *development* reflects one final influence from biology. Organisms are not static. Rather, they change, both across the lifetime of the individual and across the history of the species. Still one more task for the biologist, therefore, is to describe and explain the changes that occur. Intelligence, too, changes as the child develops, and the child psychologist must describe and explain these changes. For Piaget, there is no single organization or set of cognitive structures that defines childhood intelligence. As children develop they construct qualitatively different structures, structures that allow a progressively better understanding of the world. These qualitatively different structures define the Piagetian *stages of development*. Thus Piaget, like many cognitive-developmentalists, was a stage theorist.

Piaget divided development into four general stages, or periods: sensorimotor, preoperational, concrete operational, and formal operational. These periods were introduced in Chapter 2 and are summarized in Table 8.1. Much of the rest of this chapter is devoted to a description of the Piagetian periods of development.

Although we focus on Piaget, we also consider related research by others as well. We will be able to see, therefore, how contemporary research is building on and extending the important work begun by Piaget.

✓ *To Recap...*

Piaget's approach to studying cognitive development was influenced by his training in both philosophy and biology. His training in philosophy led to an emphasis on basic forms of knowledge, such as concepts of space and causality. His training in biology led to the belief that intelligence reflects both organization—as knowledge is integrated into cognitive structures—and adaptation—as the child adjusts to challenges from the environment. Adaptation occurs through the complementary processes of assimilation and accommodation. As these processes lead to developmental change, children move through four qualitatively distinct stages, or periods, of cognitive functioning.

Cognition during Infancy: The Sensorimotor Period

The first of Piaget's periods is the sensorimotor period. It is the period of infancy, extending from birth until about age 2.

You can gain some idea of the magnitude of cognitive advance during this period by imagining (or remembering, if you are a parent) the following two scenes: bringing a newborn home from the hospital and planning a 2-year-old's birthday party. Only 2 years separate the two events, yet how different are the sorts of things that one can do with, say to, and expect of the two children! As Flavell, Miller, and Miller (1993) put it, "these two organisms scarcely seem to belong to the same species, so great are the cognitive as well as the physical differences between them" (p. 23). It is Piaget's work that provides us with our most complete picture of exactly what these differences are.

Studying Infant Intelligence

Piaget's conclusions about infant development are based on the study of his own three children from birth through the end of infancy (Piaget, 1951, 1952, 1954). We can add immediately that this restriction does *not* apply to his conclusions concerning later development, which are based on the study of thousands of children. For infancy, however, Piaget's research was limited to a sample of three.

Piaget's method of studying his infants combined naturalistic observation with experimental manipulation. Both Piaget and his wife, Valentine (herself a trained psychologist), spent many hours simply watching the everyday behavior of their babies. But these naturalistic observations were supplemented by frequent, small-scale experiments. If, for example, Piaget was interested in his daughter's ability to cope with obstacles, he would not necessarily wait until an obstacle happened along. Instead, he might interpose a barrier between daughter and favorite toy and then record her response to this challenge.

Piaget's methodology has both strengths and weaknesses. On the positive side, the method combines two attributes that are relatively rare in developmental research: the observation of behavior in the natural setting, and the longitudinal study of the same children as they develop. It seems clear that this approach (helped along, of course, by Piaget's genius) permitted insight into forms and sequences of development that could not have been gained solely from controlled laboratory study.

Piaget remains the field's most influential theorist of cognitive development. Many of his most important insights derived from his skill as an observer of children's behavior.

Perhaps the most obvious limitation of Piaget's method is his sample. A sample of three is a shaky basis for drawing conclusions about universals of human development—especially when all three are from the same family and are being observed by their own parents! It was clearly important for Piaget's observations to be replicated with larger and more representative samples and more objective techniques of data collection. A number of such replication studies now exist, and they are positive enough in general outline to tell us that Piaget's picture of infancy was reasonably accurate (Harris, 1983). The replications are by no means completely supportive, however. We will note corrections and extensions as we go.

The Six Substages

Piaget divided the sensorimotor period into six substages. In the descriptions that follow, the ages should be taken simply as rough averages. What is important in a stage theory is not the age but the *sequence*—the order in which the stages come—which is assumed to be the same for all children.

Substage 1: Exercising Reflexes (Birth to 1 Month)   Piaget's label for the first substage reflects his predominantly negative conception of the newborn's abilities. In his view, the newborn's adaptive repertoire is limited to simple, biologically provided reflexes. Thus the newborn sucks when a nipple rubs against the lips, grasps when an object grazes the palm, and orients when an appropriate visual stimulus appears. These behaviors are seen as automatic responses to particular environmental stimuli, and they show only slight change during the first month of life.

It should be clear from Chapter 6 that Piaget underestimated the newborn's behavioral competence. Indeed, most of what he labeled reflexes we would today refer to as congenitally organized behaviors, a term that reflects the complexity and the coordination that behaviors such as sucking and looking may show. Even in Piaget's view, however, these initial behaviors are important. They are important because they are the building blocks from which all future development proceeds. Development occurs as the behaviors are applied to more and more objects and events—in Piaget's terms, as babies assimilate more and more things—and as their behaviors begin to change in response to these new experiences—in Piaget's terms, as they begin to accommodate. As the initially inflexible behaviors begin to be modified by experience, the infant is entering the second of the sensorimotor substages.

Substage 2: Developing Schemes (1 to 4 Months)

As the infant changes, so does Piaget's terminology, from *reflexes* to *sensorimotor schemes*. We stressed earlier that Piaget sought to identify the cognitive structures that characterize a particular period of development. **Sensorimotor schemes** are the cognitive structures of infancy. The term refers to the skilled and generalizable action patterns with which the infant acts on and makes sense of the world. We can speak, for example, of a sucking scheme, in the sense that the infant has an organized pattern of sucking that can be applied to innumerable stimuli. Nipples, of course, are sucked, but so are rattles, stuffed toys, and fingers. Similarly, there is a grasping scheme, a skilled behavior of grasping that can be applied to virtually any object that the infant encounters.

Sensorimotor schemes
Skilled and generalizable action patterns by which infants act on and understand the world. In Piaget's theory, the cognitive structures of infancy.

The notion of scheme captures an emphasis central to Piaget's theory—the role of action in intelligence. For Piaget, intelligence at every period of development involves some form of action on the world. During infancy, the actions are literal and overt. The infant knows the world through behaviors such as sucking, grasping, looking, and manipulating.

Schemes undergo two sorts of development during the second substage. First, individual schemes become progressively refined. The grasping of the 1-month-old is a rather primitive affair; the hard, thin rattle and the soft, fat stuffed toy may both be grasped in essentially the same way. The grasping of the 4-month-old is considerably more skilled and attuned to environmental variation. Such development does not stop at 4 months, of course. Particular schemes may continue to evolve throughout infancy.

The second change involves the coordination of initially independent schemes. Rather than being performed in isolation, the schemes are now combined into larger units. Of particular importance is the fact that schemes involving the different sensory modes—sight, hearing, touch, taste, smell—begin to be brought together. Thus, the infant hears a sound and turns toward the source of the sound, a coordination of hearing and vision. Or the infant looks at an object and then reaches out to grasp and manipulate it, a coordination of vision and touch.

Recent studies indicate that Piaget underestimated the degree of early coordination between the senses. As we saw in Chapter 7, even newborns show a tendency to turn toward the source of a sound (Ennouri & Bloch, 1996). Other studies have suggested that the rudiments of visually directed reaching may be present quite early (von Hofsten, 1982), as may the ability to achieve a primitive matching of tactile and visual input (Kaye & Bower, 1994). The competencies identified in these studies are limited, and they certainly do not negate Piaget's claim that intermodal coordination improves across the early months. But they do suggest that the beginnings of such coordination are present earlier than he believed.

Substage 3: Discovering Procedures (4 to 8 Months)

Although infants act on the environment from birth, their behavior in the first few months has an inner-directed quality. When a young baby manipulates a stuffed toy, for example, the baby's interest seems to lie more in the various finger movements being performed than in the toy itself. In Piaget's terms, the substage 2 infant uses schemes for the pure pleasure of using them—grasping for the sake of grasping, sucking for the sake of sucking, and so on. One characteristic of substage 3 is that the infant begins to show a clearer interest in the outer world. The schemes begin to be directed away from the baby's own body and toward exploration of the environment. Thus, the substage 3 infant who manipulates a toy does so because of a real interest in exploring that object.

One manifestation of this greater awareness of the environment is that the infant discovers procedures for reproducing interesting events. For example, the infant might accidentally kick a doll suspended above the crib, making the doll jump, and then spend the next 10 minutes happily kicking and laughing. Or the infant might happen to create an interesting sound by rubbing a toy against the bassinet hood, thus initiating an activity that may continue indefinitely. The infant is beginning to develop a very important kind of knowledge—what he can do to produce desirable outcomes. That this knowledge is still far from perfectly developed is implied by the term *accidentally*. The substage 3 infant shows a kind of after-the-fact grasp of causality. Once the infant has accidentally hit upon some interesting outcome, he may be able to reproduce it. What the infant cannot yet do is figure out in advance how to produce interesting effects.

Substage 4: Intentional Behavior (8 to 12 Months)
During substage 4 this after-the-fact restriction disappears. Now the infant *first* perceives some desirable goal and *then* figures out how to achieve it. In so doing, the infant demonstrates the first genuinely **intentional behavior**.

Intentional behavior
In Piaget's theory, behavior in which the goal exists prior to the action selected to achieve it; made possible by the ability to separate means and end.

In Piaget's analysis, intentional behavior involves an ability to separate *means* and *end*. The infant must be able to use one scheme as a means to lead to some other scheme, which then becomes the goal, or end. The typical situation for studying intentional behavior involves response to obstacles. Suppose the baby is about to reach for a toy and we drop a pillow between hand and toy. How does the baby respond? Simple though this problem may seem, the infant before stage 4 cannot solve it. The younger infant may storm ineffectually at the pillow or may immediately activate the goal scheme—that is, do to the pillow what she would have done to the toy. What the substage 3 infant does *not* do—and the substage 4 infant does—is first push the pillow aside and then reach for the toy. This sort of adaptive problem solving requires a separation of means and end. The infant must use the push-aside scheme as a means to get to the reach-and-play scheme, the desired end.

Substage 5: Novelty and Exploration (12 to 18 Months)
Piaget's name for substage 5 is "the discovery of new means through active exploration." The word *new* conveys a major difference between substage 4 and substage 5. The behavior of the substage 4 infant, although certainly intelligent, is essentially conservative. The infant at this stage tends to use mostly familiar schemes to produce a small range of mostly familiar effects. The substage 5 infant, in contrast, begins deliberately and systematically to *vary* her behaviors, thus creating both new schemes and new effects.

The advances of substage 5 are evident when the infant has some problem to solve. The infant now is not limited to reproducing previously successful solutions or slight variants of them. Instead, the infant can discover completely new solutions through a very active process of trial and error. Piaget documented, for example, how infants at this stage come to discover that a faraway goal can be retrieved by means of a string and that a stick can be used to push, pull, or otherwise act on some distant object. Note that these behaviors can be considered the first instances of a very important human achievement—the ability to use tools (Flavell et al., 1993).

In Piaget's theory, babies act upon the world from birth. During stage 1 of the sensorimotor period these actions are limited to the exercise of inborn reflexes.

As infants progress through the sensorimotor substages, they become increasingly interested in the outer environment and increasingly skilled at acting upon it to produce interesting outcomes.

A hallmark of sensorimotor stage 5 is the ability to experiment in new ways to produce novel outcomes.

The substage 5 infant also experiments for the pure pleasure of experimentation. An example familiar to many parents is the "high-chair behavior" of the 1-year-old. The baby leans over the edge of her high chair and drops her spoon to the floor, carefully noting how it bounces. The parent retrieves and returns the spoon, whereupon the baby leans over the other side of the chair and drops the spoon again, perhaps with a bit more force this time. The parent again returns the spoon, and this time the baby flings it across the room—whereupon the exasperated parent gives up and removes either baby or spoon from the situation. For most of us, not being Piaget, it may be difficult to appreciate that cognitive development is occurring in this situation. Yet it is through such active experimentation that infants learn about the world.

Substage 6: Mental Representation (18 to 24 Months) The first five sensorimotor substages are a time of remarkable cognitive progress. Yet there is still one more great advance to be made.

During the first five substages all of the infant's adaptation to the world occurs through overt behavior. Even the substage 5 infant's problem solving is based on trying out one behavior after another until a solution is reached. The advance that occurs at substage 6 is that the infant becomes capable for the first time of **representation**—of thinking about and acting on the world *internally* and not merely externally. It is this advance that will bring the sensorimotor period to an end.

Let us consider two examples. One involves Piaget's daughter Jacqueline, who is carrying some blades of grass through the house. The numbers at the start indicate her age—1 year, 8 months, 9 days.

Representation
The use of symbols to picture and act on the world internally.

> *Jacqueline, at 1;8 (9) arrives at a closed door—with a blade of grass in each hand. She stretches out her right hand toward the knob but sees that she cannot turn it without letting go of the grass. She puts the grass on the floor, opens the door, picks up the grass again and enters. But when she wants to leave the room things become complicated. She puts the grass on the floor and grasps the doorknob. But then she perceives that in pulling the door toward her she will simultaneously chase away the grass which she placed between the door and the threshold. She therefore picks it up in order to put it outside the door's zone of movement. (Piaget, 1952, p. 339)*

When Jacqueline pauses with her hand on the doorknob the second time, she is apparently doing two things: She is imagining the problem—the door sweeping over the grass; and she is imagining the solution—moving the grass beyond the sweep of the door. She is thus engaged in a kind of mental problem solving, based on an internal use of representations or symbols, that is not possible earlier in infancy.

The second example involves Piaget's other daughter, Lucienne. Lucienne (who is 16 months old) and her father are playing a game in which he hides a watch chain in a matchbox and she attempts to retrieve it. After several easy versions of the game, Piaget makes it harder. He reduces the opening of the matchbox to only 3 millimeters, too narrow for Lucienne to perform her usual solution of inserting a finger to hook part of the chain. How does the child respond?

> *She looks at the slit with great attention; then, several times in succession, she opens and shuts her mouth, at first slightly, then wider and wider! Apparently Lucienne understands the existence of a cavity subjacent to the slit and wishes to enlarge that cavity.... Soon after this phase of plastic reflection, Lucienne unhesitatingly puts her finger in the slit and, instead of trying as before to reach the chain, she pulls so as to enlarge the opening. She succeeds and grasps the chain. (Piaget, 1952, pp. 337–338)*

In Piaget's analysis, the opening of the mouth is a symbol for the opening of the matchbox, and it is this symbol that allows Lucienne to solve the problem. Note that Piaget apparently caught Lucienne during a transitional period. Had he tried the game a month or so earlier, the mouth opening would have been unlikely. Instead, Lucienne would probably have approached the problem in typical substage 5 fashion, experimenting through overt trial and error. Had he tried the game a month or so later, the mouth opening would again have been unlikely. An older Lucienne could generate and use a purely internal symbol. It is because Lucienne is transitional, on the brink of using representations but not yet very good at it, that she still has to externalize her symbol.

For Piaget, the onset of representation defines the movement from the sensorimotor period to the next period of development, the preoperational. We will have more to say about representational ability when we discuss the preoperational period.

Table 8.2 summarizes the six sensorimotor substages.

Table 8.2
The Six Sensorimotor Substages

Stage	Ages (mos.)	Description
1. Exercising reflexes	0–1	The infant is limited to exercising inborn reflexes—for example, sucking and grasping.
2. Developing schemes	1–4	The reflexes evolve into adaptive schemes. The schemes begin to be refined and coordinated.
3. Discovering procedures	4–8	Behavior becomes more outwardly oriented. The infant develops procedures for reproducing interesting events.
4. Intentional behavior	8–12	The first truly intentional behavior emerges. The infant can separate means and end in pursuit of a goal.
5. Novelty and exploration	12–18	The infant begins to vary the schemes systematically to produce new effects. Problems are solved through an active process of trial and error.
6. Mental representation	18–24	The capacity for representational or symbolic functioning emerges. Mental problem solving begins to replace overt trial and error.

The Notion of Object Permanence

Any brief summary of Piaget's sensorimotor studies necessarily omits many interesting aspects of infant development. But one aspect must receive some attention, both because of its importance in Piaget's theory and because it has been the target of dozens of follow-up studies. This is the phenomenon of object permanence.

The term **object permanence** refers to our knowledge that objects have a permanent existence that is independent of our perception of them. It is the knowledge that a toy does not cease to exist just because one can no longer feel it, or a rattle just because one can no longer hear it, or Mommy just because one can no longer see her. It is hard to imagine a more basic piece of knowledge than this. Yet Piaget's research suggests that infants do not at first understand object permanence and that this understanding develops only gradually across the entire span of infancy.

Piaget described the development of object permanence in terms of the same six-stage progression that he used for the sensorimotor period as a whole. During the first two substages—that is, the first 3 or 4 months—babies show essentially no evidence that they realize objects exist apart from their own actions on them. Should a toy drop out of sight, for example, the 2-month-old acts for all the world as though it no longer exists. The young infant will not search for a vanished object and is likely instead to turn fairly quickly to some other activity. At most, the baby may follow an object with his eyes or stare for awhile at the place where an object has just disappeared.

It is only during the third substage, at about 4 to 8 months, that babies begin to search for vanished objects. At first, however, the search shows a number of curious limitations. The infant may search, for example, if the object is partially hidden but not if it is totally hidden. The search may even depend on how much of the object is hidden. If only a corner of a sought-after toy is visible, the baby may sit per-

Object permanence
The knowledge that objects have a permanent existence that is independent of our perceptual contact with them. In Piaget's theory, a major achievement of the sensorimotor period.

plexed. As soon as a bit more is revealed, however, the baby may happily reach out and retrieve the toy. Search may also depend on whether the infant's own action or something else makes the object disappear. The baby who pushes a toy over the edge of the high chair may look down at the floor to find it; should Papa Piaget do the pushing, however, search is less likely. For Piaget, this observation is evidence that the infant's knowledge of the object still depends on her action on it.

Substage 4 marks an important step forward with regard to object permanence. The infant now (at about 8 to 12 months) can search systematically and intelligently for hidden objects. The substage 4 infant searches even when the object is completely gone and even when it was not her own actions that made it disappear. Yet there are still limitations in the understanding of permanence, which are revealed when the infant must cope with more than one hiding place. Piaget might, for example, hide a toy under a pillow to his daughter's left two or three times, each time allowing her to retrieve it successfully. Then, with his daughter watching, he might hide the same toy under a blanket to her right. The baby would watch the toy disappear under the blanket and then turn and search under the pillow! What seemed to define the object was not its objective location, but the baby's previous success at finding it—it became "the thing that I found under the pillow." For Piaget, this behavior (which has come to be labeled the **A$\overline{\text{B}}$ error**—that is, A-not-B) is evidence that even at this substage, the baby's knowledge of objects is not freed from her own actions on them.

The infant does, of course, eventually overcome this limitation. The substage 5 infant (about 12 to 18 months) can handle the sort of multiple-hiding-place problems that baffle the younger baby. But there is still one more limitation. The infant can handle such problems only if the movements of the object are visible—that is, if he can see the object as it is moved from one hiding place to another. Suppose, however, that the movements are not visible—that the task involves what Piaget labeled *invisible displacements*. Piaget might hide a toy in his fist, for example, and then move the fist in succession through hiding places A, B, and C before bringing it out empty. To infer the movements of a hidden object, the infant must be able to represent the object when it is not visible. Solution of this problem is found only at substage 6, when the capacity for symbolic functioning emerges.

The work on object permanence illustrates two very general themes in Piaget's approach to development. One is the notion of development as a process of **progressive decentering**. According to Piaget, the infant begins life in a state of profound **egocentrism**; that is, he literally cannot distinguish between himself and the outer world. The newborn and the young infant simply do not know what is specific to the self (one's own perceptions, actions, wishes, and so on) and what exists apart from the self. This egocentrism is reflected most obviously in the absence of object permanence. For the young baby, objects exist only to the extent that he is acting on them. Only gradually, across infancy, does the baby decenter and grow more aware of both self and world.

The second theme is the importance of **invariants** in development. We live in a world of constant flux, a world in which all sorts of things (what we can or cannot see, how things look, etc.) change from one moment to the next. Piaget maintained that one important kind of knowledge that the child must acquire is a knowledge of what it is that stays the same—remains invariant—in the face of constant change. The first and most basic cognitive invariant is object permanence—the realization that the existence of objects is invariant despite changes in our perceptual experience of them. We will encounter other, more advanced invariants when we discuss the later Piagetian stages.

A$\overline{\text{B}}$ error
Infants' tendency to search in the original location in which an object was found rather than in its most recent hiding place. A characteristic of stage 4 of object permanence.

Progressive decentering
Piaget's term for the gradual decline in egocentrism that occurs across development.

Egocentrism
In infancy, an inability to distinguish the self (e.g., one's actions or perceptions) from the outer world. In later childhood, an inability to distinguish one's own perspective (e.g., visual experience, thoughts, feelings) from that of others.

Invariants
Aspects of the world that remain the same even though other aspects have changed. In Piaget's theory, different forms of invariants are understood at different stages of development.

Testing Piaget's Claims: More Recent Work on Infant Cognition

Piaget's studies continue to inspire a substantial proportion of the contemporary research on infant intelligence. Object permanence has been the most popular focus for such research, and we therefore begin with studies of infants' knowledge about objects, after which we broaden the discussion to other aspects of infant cognition.

Object Permanence   No researcher has questioned Piaget's assertion that the infant's understanding of objects is at first limited. Replication studies have amply confirmed Piaget's claims about the kinds of errors infants make when they must search for hidden objects (Harris, 1989b; Uzgiris & Hunt, 1975). Nevertheless, many researchers have wondered whether the infant's understanding is really *as* limited as Piaget believed. A particular concern has been Piaget's emphasis on motor search behaviors in assessing object permanence—that is, behaviors such as lifting a cloth or pushing aside a screen. It seems logically possible that an infant may know perfectly well that an object still exists but simply fail to show the kinds of active search behaviors that Piaget required.

How else might we assess what infants know about objects? The most informative approach has made use of the habituation phenomenon described in Chapter 2. *Habituation,* you may recall, refers to a decline in response to a repeated stimulus; conversely, *dishabituation* refers to the recovery of response when the stimulus changes. Researchers have probed infants' understanding of objects by seeing what sorts of changes in objects they are likely to notice and dishabituate to. Of particular interest are infants' responses to impossible changes—that is, events that seem to violate the laws of object permanence.

A study by Baillargeon (1987a) provides an example. In this study, babies were first shown a screen that rotated, like a drawbridge, though a 180-degree arc (see Figure 8.1*a*). Although this event was initially quite interesting, after a number of repetitions the babies' attention dropped off, showing that they had habituated to the rotation. At this point a wooden box was placed directly in the path of the screen (see Figure 8.1*b*). Note that the baby could see the box at the start of a trial but that the box disappeared from view once the screen had reached its full height. In one experimental condition, labeled the "Possible event" in the figure, the screen rotated to the point at which it reached the box and then stopped—as indeed it should, given the fact that a solid object was in its path. In the other condition, labeled the "Impossible event," the screen rotated to the point of contact with the box and then kept right on going through its full 180-degree arc! (This outcome was made possible by a hidden platform that dropped the box out of the way.)

Any adult confronted with such as event would probably be quite surprised, because he or she would know that the box still existed behind the screen, even though it could no longer be seen. Infants as young as 4.5 months apparently possess the same knowledge. Their attention did not increase when they viewed the possible event; looking times shot up, however, when the screen appeared to pass magically through a solid object. The most obvious explanation for such recovery of interest is that the infants knew that the box must still exist and therefore expected the screen to stop.

Young infants know something about not only the existence but also the properties of hidden objects. In a further experiment, Baillargeon (1987b) replaced the hard and rigid box with a soft and compressible ball of gauze. Infants were not surprised by the continued rotation of the screen in the soft-object case, indicating that they retained information about not only the presence, but also the compressibility of the hidden object.

Figure 8.1
The Baillargeon test of object permanence. Infants were first habituated to the event shown in part (a). Response was then measured to either the possible event in part (c), in which the screen rotates to point of contact with the box and stops, or the impossible event in part (b), in which the screen continues to move through the area occupied by the box. Adapted from "Object Permanence in 3½- and 4½-Month-Old Infants" by R. Baillargeon, 1987, *Developmental Psychology, 23*, p. 656. Copyright © 1987 by the American Psychological Association. Adapted by permission.

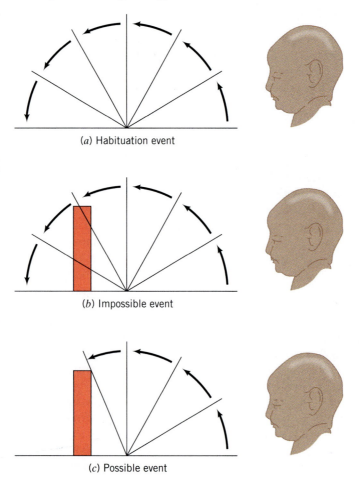

(a) Habituation event

(b) Impossible event

(c) Possible event

Infants can also retain and use information about the location of hidden objects. Baillargeon (1986) showed babies a toy car that moved along a track, disappeared behind a screen, and reemerged at the other end. Following habituation, the infants saw a box placed behind the screen, in one case next to the track (possible event) and in the other case directly on the track (impossible event). They then watched the car again make its journey from one side of the screen to the other. Infants looked longer at the impossible event, thus indicating that they remembered not only that the box still existed, but where it was, and that they drew different implications from the two locations.

The experiments just described are but a few examples of the ingenious ways in which modern researchers have attempted to discover what young babies know about objects (Baillargeon, 1993, 1995; Spelke & Hermer, 1996). Having emphasized the positive picture that emerges from these studies, we should add that the procedural innovations do not always lead to success. Baillargeon, for example, reports that young infants at first seem to possess a qualitative rather than quantitative appreciation of hidden objects—that is, they know that *some* object is still there, but have little ability to remember or reason about its quantitative properties once they can no longer see it. This means, for example, that they are not surprised if the drawbridge rotates somewhat farther than it should given the height of the concealed box, just so that it stops eventually; nor are they surprised if a large toy emerges from under a small cover, just so that *something* emerges (Baillargeon, 1994).

Findings such as these confirm a general tenet of Piaget's approach to infant intelligence—that new knowledge does not emerge full-blown, but only gradually and through a series of progressively more mature forms. Furthermore, no study to date has contradicted Piaget's claim that active search behaviors for hidden objects are absent prior to about 8 or 9 months. Why babies' ability to organize intelligent behaviors lags so far behind their initial knowledge is one of the most intriguing questions in modern infancy research (Bertenthal, 1996; Munakata et al., 1997).

Physical Knowledge Object permanence is one important kind of physical knowledge. In this section we review several other kinds that also emerge, at least in their initial forms, during infancy.

Understanding of causality is a classic philosophical issue, to which Piaget devoted much attention. His conclusions about infants' knowledge of cause and effect were based largely on their ability to act effectively to produce desired outcomes—for example, to push aside an obstacle to attain a goal. As with object permanence, later studies have reduced the response demands on the infant, and as with object permanence, later studies have furnished a more positive picture of infant knowledge. The habituation methodology has again been informative. The most common strategy has been to habituate the infant to an event with a particular causal structure (for example, a red ball that strikes and propels a green ball) and then test for dishabituation to events that either preserve or violate that structure (for example, a green ball that propels a red ball). If the events are simple enough, infants as young as 6 or 7 months are sensitive to the causal relations (Leslie & Keeble, 1987; Oakes & Cohen, 1995).

Infants also have some appreciation of the laws of inertia and gravity. One method for probing such knowledge is shown in Figure 8.2*a*. Infants are first habituated to the first event shown in the figure—that is, a ball that is dropped behind a screen (depicted by the broken lines) and then revealed, once the screen is removed, to be resting on the floor. Following habituation, a table is placed in the

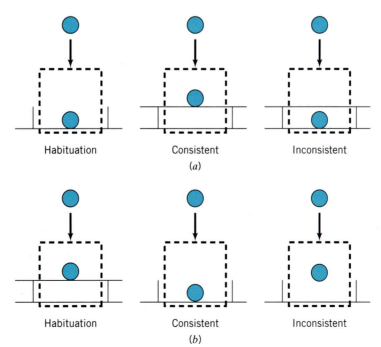

Habituation	Consistent	Inconsistent
	(*a*)	
Habituation	Consistent	Inconsistent
	(*b*)	

Figure 8.2
Consistent and inconsistent events in Spelke et al.'s study of infants' understanding of object movement and gravity. From "Origins of Knowledge" by E. Spelke, K. Breinlinger, J. Macomber, and K. Jacobson, 1992, *Psychological Review, 99,* pp. 611 and 621. Copyright © 1992 by the American Psychological Association. Reprinted by permission.

Possible Event

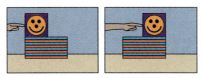

Impossible Event

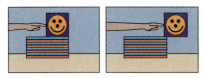

Figure 8.3
Possible and Impossible events in Baillargeon's study of infants' understanding of gravity and support. From *Current Directions in Psychological Science,* Vol. 3 (1994), p. 134, "How Do Infants Learn about the Physical World?" Fig. 1. Reprinted with permission of Cambridge University Press.

ball's path, and one of two new events is presented. In the Consistent event (i.e., consistent with the laws of physics), removal of the screen reveals the ball resting on the table; in the Inconsistent event, the ball is again on the floor. The latter outcome is in a sense more familiar, because the ball appears in the same position in which it appears during habituation; to get there, however, it has had to pass magically through another solid object. Spelke and colleagues (1992) report that 4-month-old infants look longer at the Inconsistent event, suggesting that they understand the principles of object movement and are surprised by the magical outcome.

Figure 8.3 depicts another method for studying infants' understanding of gravity and support. The contrast is again between a Possible event (amount of contact between box and platform sufficient to support box) and an Impossible event (amount of contact insufficient, yet box remains perched on platform). By 6.5 months of age infants look longer at the Impossible event, suggesting that they appreciate the relation between contact and support (Baillargeon, Kotovsky, & Needham, 1995).

We noted in discussing object permanence that the simplified procedures of modern research do not always lead to success, especially if the focus is on very young infants. The same point applies to the topics considered in the present section. Infants of 3 or 4 months, for example, are not fazed by the Impossible event of Figure 8.3; for them, *any* degree of contact, at any orientation, is sufficient to provide support (Baillargeon et al., 1995). Or consider the events shown in Figure 8.2*b*. Here, in contrast to the procedure described earlier, a table is removed rather than added, and the Inconsistent event consists of the ball's magically floating at the height at which it once rested on the table. Spelke et al. (1992) report that 4-month-olds are apparently insensitive to this violation of gravity; they look more attentively at the Consistent outcome than at the Inconsistent one. Such findings are a valuable reminder: Infants may be more competent than we once believed, but there are still many gaps in their knowledge and many important developments still to occur.

Imitation   Among the many topics that Piaget explored in his sensorimotor studies was the development of imitation. He reported that imitation, like other sensorimotor accomplishments, had an extended developmental history, beginning with rudimentary and limited forms early in life and only slowly progressing toward the skilled behavioral system of the toddler or preschool child. Imitations in the first 6 or 8 months he considered to be especially limited. Infants of this age, according to Piaget, imitate only those behaviors that they already produce spontaneously and that they can see and hear themselves perform. Thus, the infant might imitate a movement such as finger wiggling, for which there is perceptible feedback. But we would not expect a young baby to be able to imitate a facial expression, such as opening the mouth or sticking out the tongue.

Some recent evidence has provided a strong challenge to this view. Across a series of studies, Meltzoff and Moore (1977, 1983, 1985, 1989, 1994) have examined infants' ability to imitate facial expressions of a variety of sorts. Their procedure involves videotaping the infant's face as an adult model performs the target behaviors. The tapes are then scored by a rater who is unaware of the behavior being modeled (see Figure 8.4). Meltzoff and Moore report that even newborns can imitate both mouth opening and tongue protrusion, producing these behaviors reliably more often in response to the model than in the model's absence.

That modern research techniques often reveal greater competence than was evident to Piaget should be a familiar conclusion by now. The discrepancy in the Meltzoff and Moore studies, however, is especially striking—not just success far earlier than reported by Piaget, but the presence at birth of behavioral competencies that Piaget thought required many months of slow construction. In light of such a strong claim, it is not surprising that neonatal imitation has been the subject of dozens of recent studies. Some of this work provides support for Meltzoff and Moore's claims (e.g., Heimann, Nelson, & Schaller, 1989; Reissland, 1988); other investigators, however, have reported difficulties in replication or cautions about the genuineness of the phenomenon (e.g., Anisfeld, 1991, 1996; Jones, 1996). At present, therefore, the status of newborn imitation remains controversial. If valid, however, Meltzoff and Moore's findings would constitute perhaps the most dramatic example of competence that exists earlier than Piaget claimed.

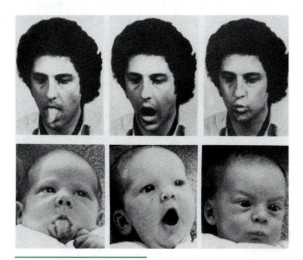

Figure 8.4
Adult model and infant response in Meltzoff and Moore's study of neonatal imitation. Even very young infants appear to imitate the adult's facial expressions. From "Imitation of Social and Manual Gestures by Human Neonates" by A. N. Meltzoff and M. K. Moore, 1977, *Science, 298*, p. 75. Copyright © 1977 by the American Association for the Advancement of Science. Reprinted by permission.

An Overall Evaluation

Piaget's work remains our most influential and informative account of infant cognitive development. Nevertheless, the more recent studies of infant cognition suggest several modifications to the initial Piagetian picture.

First, Piaget often underestimated the infant's ability. How great the underestimation is has been a matter of dispute. But when studies have suggested revisions in Piaget's age norms, the revisions have almost always been in a downward direction. This conclusion applies not just to the topics discussed here but to a wide range of infant developments (Bremner, 1996; Karmiloff-Smith, 1995).

Second, the primary reason for the discrepancy between Piaget's studies and modern work is methodological. Piaget's conclusions about infant knowledge were based largely on observations of overt motor behavior—that is, behaviors such as reaching, manipulating, bringing objects together, and in general acting on the world. With modern research techniques, such as the habituation procedure, the response demands on the infant are reduced considerably, and our picture of infant competence has correspondingly grown more positive.

A final conclusion is that this picture is not totally positive. Along with the demonstrations of unexpected competencies, modern studies have confirmed many of the limitations that were identified by Piaget. They also have at times revealed puzzling new gaps in infant competence—recall young infants' insensitivity to the quantitative features of objects, for example, or their apparent ignorance of the law of gravity. Our understanding of infant cognition has clearly progressed beyond the important beginning provided by Piaget; just as clearly, however, there is still much to learn.

✓ *To Recap...*

The first of Piaget's stages is the sensorimotor period, which extends from birth until about age 2. Infant intelligence is characterized in terms of sensorimotor schemes, and development occurs through the processes of assimilation and accommodation—incorporating new elements into the schemes and modifying the schemes in response to new experiences. This conception of infant intelligence reflects Piaget's emphasis on the child's own actions as a source of knowledge.

The sensorimotor period is divided into six substages. The starting point consists of various inborn reflexes. The reflexes evolve into adaptive schemes, and the schemes become more refined, externally oriented, and intercoordinated as the infant develops. The culmination of the sensorimotor period is the onset of mental representation at substage 6.

An especially important sensorimotor achievement is object permanence. Piaget's research suggests that infants only gradually come to understand object permanence through a series of stages in which the existence of the object is freed from the infant's actions on it.

Later studies have largely confirmed the descriptive picture provided by Piaget. Such studies also indicate, however, that Piaget's methods often failed to capture early forms of infant competence.

Thought in the Preschooler: The Preoperational Period

The preoperational period extends from about age 2 to about age 6. The "about" is again important. Piagetian age norms are always rough guidelines, and particular children may develop more quickly or more slowly than the average.

We noted at the beginning of the chapter that childhood cognition is a mixture of competence and limitations. At no other time during development is this mixture—surprisingly adultlike abilities on the one hand and glaring, hard-to-believe errors on the other—quite so striking or so challenging to explain as it is during the preoperational period. Some of the most fascinating contemporary research in child psychology is directed at exploring the mysteries of the preoperational mind.

More about Representation

As we saw, the defining characteristic of the movement from the sensorimotor to the preoperational period is the onset of representational ability, or what Piaget called the **symbolic function**. Piaget defined the symbolic function as the ability to use one thing to represent something else—that is, to use one thing as a symbol to stand for some other thing, which then becomes the symbolized. Symbols can take a variety of forms. They can be motor movements, as when the opening of Lucienne's mouth symbolized the opening of the matchbox. They can be mental images, as may have been the case when Jacqueline thought through the blades-of-grass problem. They can be physical objects, as when a 3-year-old grabs a broom and rides it as if it were a horse. And, of course, they can be words.

What is the evidence that a general capacity for representational functioning emerges near the end of infancy? Piaget (1951) cited five kinds of behavior that become evident at this time, all of which seem to require representational ability, and none of which he had observed earlier in infancy. We have discussed two of these behaviors: the internal problem solving of substage 6, and the ability to handle the invisible displacements version of the object permanence problem. Another, discussed in Chapter 11, is the first appearance of words. Here Piaget stressed the ability not simply to label present objects, but to talk about objects or events in their absence. The latter is clearly a symbolic achievement.

A fourth piece of evidence is the appearance of **deferred imitation**. Although babies imitate from early in life, they can at first imitate only models that are directly in front of them. It is only near the end of infancy, according to Piaget, that the baby begins to imitate models from the past—for example, some behavior that an older sibling performed the week before. The ability to imitate behavior from the past clearly implies the capacity to store that behavior in some representational form.

The final index of the symbolic function is familiar to any parent. It is the emergence of **symbolic play**. Now is the time that the child's play begins to be enriched by the ability to use one thing in deliberate pretense to stand for something else. Now is the time that sticks turn into boats, sandpiles into cakes, and brooms into horses.

Was Piaget correct about the emergence of representational ability? We have seen that a consistent theme from modern research is that babies are often more capable than Piaget indicated. Such is probably the case as well with respect to the onset of representation (Mandler, 1998). Although the importance of the transition described by Piaget is not in dispute, more recent research indicates that some forms of representational functioning almost certainly emerge earlier in infancy than he believed. The recent studies of object permanence, for example, seem to demonstrate some capacity to represent and reason about unseen objects considerably earlier than Piaget predicted. Deferred imitation has been shown in babies as young as 9 months of age (Meltzoff, 1988), and there is suggestive evidence that simple forms may be present as early as 3 months (Meltzoff & Moore, 1994). Finally, there is intriguing evidence from studies of infants learning American Sign

Symbolic function
The ability to use one thing (such as a mental image or word) as a symbol to represent something else.

Deferred imitation
Imitation of a model observed some time in the past.

Symbolic play
Form of play in which the child uses one thing in deliberate pretense to stand for something else.

One of the clearest signs of the preoperational child's representational skills is the emergence of symbolic play. With her newfound symbolic skills, the 2-year-old readily transforms a pot into a hat.

Language that the first genuinely symbolic signs may emerge as early as 6 or 7 months (Meier & Newport, 1990), and thus well before both the typical time for the first spoken words and the usual dating for Piaget's substage 6.

Strengths of Preoperational Thought

In Piaget's theory, the cognitive structures of later stages are always more powerful and more adaptive than those of earlier stages. Consequently, the onset of representational intelligence marks a major advance in the child's cognitive abilities.

Representational, in-the-head problem solving is superior to sensorimotor problem solving in a number of ways. Representational intelligence is considerably faster and more efficient. Rather than trying out all possible solutions overtly—a necessarily slow and error-prone process—the representational child can try them out internally, using representations rather than literal actions. When the representational child *does* act, the solution can be immediate and adaptive. Representational intelligence is also considerably more mobile. Sensorimotor intelligence is limited to the here and now—what is actually in front of the child to be acted on. With representational intelligence, however, the child can think about the past and imagine the future. The scope of cognitive activity is thus enormously expanded.

Representational intelligence is also socially sharable in a way that sensorimotor intelligence is not. With the acquisition of language, the child can communicate ideas to others and receive information from them in ways that are not possible without language. Piaget's theory does not place as much stress on either language or cultural transmission as do many other theories (for example, the Vygotskian position introduced in Chapters 1 and 2). Nevertheless, Piaget did consistently cite social experience as one of the factors that account for development (Piaget, 1964). And both the extent and the nature of social experience change greatly once the child has entered the preoperational period.

The preoperational period is also a time of specific cognitive acquisitions. It is the time during which the child develops a form of knowledge that Piaget labeled **qualitative identity** (Piaget, 1968). Qualitative identity refers to the realization that the qualitative, or generic, nature of something is not changed by a change in its appearance. It is the realization, for example, that a wire remains the same wire even after it has been bent into a different shape or that water remains the same water even though it may look different after being poured from a glass to a pie pan. (Note, though, that the child does not yet realize that the length of the wire or the quantity of water remains the same—this is a more advanced form of knowledge.) It should be clear that qualitative identity, like object permanence, reflects a central Piagetian theme: the importance of mastering invariants in the environment.

A striking illustration of the phenomenon of qualitative identity can be found in a study by DeVries (1969). DeVries first exposed her preschool participants to a docile black cat. The cat was then transformed, by means of a very realistic mask, into a fierce-looking dog (see Figure 8.5). Following the transformation, DeVries questioned the children about what kind of animal they now saw. What kind of sound would it make, for example, and what kind of food would it like to eat? Most of the 3-year-olds seemed quite convinced that the cat had become a dog. In contrast, most of the 5- and 6-year-olds were able to overcome the perceptual cues and affirm qualitative identity. They realized that the cat was still a cat and would always remain a cat.

A related, but more general, phenomenon that has received considerable research attention in recent years is labeled the **appearance–reality distinction**. As

---

Qualitative identity
The knowledge that the qualitative nature of something is not changed by a change in its appearance. In Piaget's theory, a preoperational achievement.

Appearance–reality distinction
Distinction between how objects appear and what they really are. Understanding the distinction implies an ability to judge both appearance and reality correctly when the two diverge.

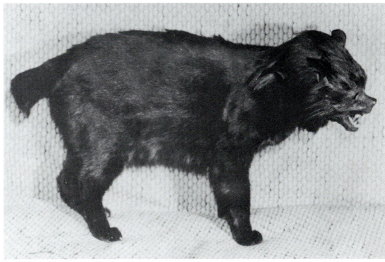

Figure 8.5
Cat transformed into dog, used by DeVries in the study of qualitative identity. Young preoperational children seem to believe that the cat has really become a dog; older preoperational children realize that the identity is unchanged. From "Constancy of Generic Identity in the Years Three to Six" by R. DeVries, 1969, *Monographs of the Society for Research in Child Development, 34,* (3, Serial No. 127), p. 8. Copyright © 1969 by the Society for Research in Child Development. Reprinted by permission.

the name suggests, the appearance–reality distinction concerns children's ability to distinguish between the way things appear and the way they really are. Suppose, for example, that we show a child a red car, cover the car with a filter that makes it look black, and then ask what color the car "really and truly is." A 3-year-old is likely to reply "black"; a 6-year-old will almost certainly (and perhaps scornfully) say "red." Suppose next that we present a stone disguised as an egg and ask what this strange object "looks like." The 3-year-old, knowing the "really and truly" in this case (the apparent egg really is a stone), answers "stone"; the 6-year-old, again showing a capacity to distinguish appearance from reality, replies "egg."

Problems in distinguishing appearance and reality are not limited to the visual realm. Children also come to realize that sounds or smells or touches may sometimes mislead, giving a false impression of their underlying source (Flavell, Flavell, & Green, 1983; Flavell, Green, & Flavell, 1989). And children must come to understand that people, as well as objects, can present misleading appearances—they may look nice, for example, when they are actually mean (Flavell et al., 1992).

It is important to note that the developmental progression from lack of understanding to eventual mastery in this area is not specific to American culture. Children from the People's Republic of China, for example, respond in the same way as American children to such tasks (Flavell, Zhang, et al., 1983), and Quechua Indian children in Peru show similar developmental changes (Vinden, 1996). In no culture do children completely master the distinction between appearance and reality by age 6; all of us remain susceptible to being fooled by misleading appearances. But the preoperational child makes major strides in mastering this important kind of knowledge (Flavell, 1986).

The examples discussed here hardly exhaust the list of preoperational accomplishments. Indeed, one of Piaget's efforts during the last part of his career was to identify preoperational achievements that had been missed in his earlier studies (Beilin, 1992a, 1992b; Piaget, 1979, 1980). And when we turn to language development in Chapter 11, we will see that the years from 2 to 6 constitute a time of truly remarkable progress with respect to this critical and uniquely human ability.

Limitations of Preoperational Thought

Despite the positive features just noted, most of what Piaget had to say about preoperational thought concerns weaknesses rather than strengths. The weaknesses all stem from the fact that the child is attempting to operate on a new plane of cognitive functioning, that of representational intelligence. The 3-year-old who is quite skilled at the sensorimotor level turns out to be not at all skilled at purely mental reasoning and problem solving. Hence the term *preoperational*—to refer to the fact that the child lacks the "operations" that allow effective problem solving at the representational level.

Egocentrism   We saw that infancy begins in a state of profound egocentrism and that a major achievement of infancy is the gradual decentering through which the infant learns what is specific to the self and what exists apart from the self. The preoperational period also begins in a state of egocentrism, but this time at a representational rather than a sensorimotor level. In Piaget's view, the young preoperational child has only a very limited ability to represent the psychological experiences of others—to break away from his own perspective to take the point of view of someone whose perspective is different from his own. Instead, the 3- or 4-year-old often acts as though everyone shares his particular point of view—sees what he sees, feels what he feels, knows what he knows, and so on. Note that egocentrism does not mean egotism or selfishness, but simply a difficulty in taking the point of view of another.

Table 8.3

Children Retell a Story: Some Piagetian Examples of Egocentric Speech

---

Story Presented to the Children

Once upon a time, there was a lady who was called Niobe, and who had 12 sons and daughters. She met a fairy who had only one son and no daughter. Then the lady laughed at the fairy because the fairy only had one boy. Then the fairy was very angry and fastened the lady to a rock. The lady cried for 10 years. In the end she turned to a rock, and her tears made a stream which still runs today.

Examples of Children's Reproductions

Met (6;4), talking of Niobe: "The lady laughed at this fairy because she [who?] only had one boy. The lady had 12 sons and 12 daughters. One day she [who?] laughed at her [at whom?]. She [who?] was angry and she [who?] fastened her beside a stream. She [?] cried for 50 months, and it made a great big stream." Impossible to tell who fastened, and who was fastened.

Gio (8 years old) "Once upon a time there was a lady who had 12 boys and 12 girls, and then a fairy a boy and a girl. And then Niobe wanted to have some more sons [than the fairy. Gio means by this that Niobe competed with the fairy, as was told in the text. But it will be seen how elliptical is his way in expressing it]. Then she [who?] was angry. She [who?] fastened her [whom?] to a stone. He [who?] turned into a rock, and then his tears [whose?] made a stream which is still running today."

Source: Adapted from *The Language and Thought of the Child* (pp. 99, 116, 121) by J. Piaget, 1926, New York: Harcourt Brace. Adapted by permission.

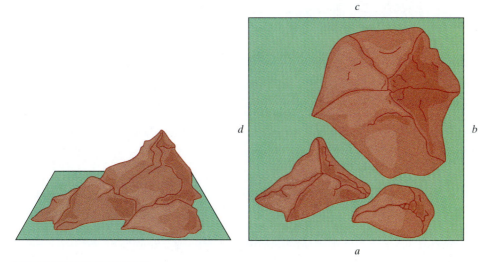

Figure 8.6

Piaget's three-mountains problem for assessing visual perspective taking. The child's task is to judge how the display looks to someone viewing it from a different perspective. From *The Child's Conception of Space* (p. 211) by J. Piaget and B. Inhelder, 1956, London: Routledge and Kegan Paul. Copyright © by Routledge and Kegan Paul. Reprinted by permission.

Preoperational egocentrism is evident in a variety of contexts. Perhaps the most apparent example is children's speech. Piaget's first book, *The Language and Thought of the Child* (1926), examined both naturally occurring conversations between children and experimentally elicited speech of various sorts. Piaget found that the children's speech was often hopelessly jumbled and hard to decipher, even when they clearly were trying their best to communicate.

Table 8.3 presents some examples from an experiment in which children attempted to retell a story (the phrases in brackets are Piaget's comments on their efforts). Piaget attributed such *egocentric speech* to the young child's basic cognitive egocentrism. Young children often fail to assume the perspective of their listener, acting instead as though the listener already knows everything that they know. Certainly anyone who has listened to a 3-year-old relate the events of her day has some appreciation for this claim.

Piaget also studied the child's ability to assume the visual perspective of another (Piaget & Inhelder, 1956). The best-known task for studying such visual perspective taking is the three-mountains problem pictured in Figure 8.6. After walking around the display, the child is seated on one side; the researchers then move a doll to various locations around the board. The child's task is to indicate what the doll would see from the different locations. For many young children, the answer is clear: The doll would see exactly what they see. Again, the young child acts as though his or her own perspective is the only one possible.

Centration   The concept of **centration** refers to the young child's tendency to focus on only one aspect of a problem at a time. As an example, let us consider what is perhaps the most famous Piagetian task—the **conservation** problem. Conservation is the realization that the quantitative properties of objects are not changed by a change in appearance.

Centration
Piaget's term for the young child's tendency to focus on only one aspect of a problem at a time, a perceptually biased form of responding that often results in incorrect judgments.

Conservation
The knowledge that the quantitative properties of an object or collection of objects are not changed by a change in appearance. In Piaget's theory, a concrete operational achievement.

CHILDREN'S COSMOLOGIES

However hazy their grasp of astronomy may be, most adults hold several beliefs with some certainty. They believe, for example, that the earth is round and that it revolves around another, larger round body (the sun), while a smaller round body (the moon) revolves around it. They believe as well that certain familiar phenomena (the day–night cycle, the seasons) depend on the movements and relative positions of Earth, sun, and moon. But how do adults come to form such beliefs? The facts of astronomy are hardly evident in everyday experience; if anything, the reverse could be argued to be true. Children experience an apparently flat earth from which they see the sun move across the sky, and they learn things (e.g., that unsupported objects fall) that seem incompatible with the notion that people could somehow live around the surface of a large ball. Is the development of adult-level understanding therefore simply a matter of suppressing childish beliefs and gradually incorporating what the adult society has to teach?

A recent program of research suggests that the answer to this question is "in part but not totally." Across a series of studies, Brewer, Vosniadou, and associates (Brewer, Herdrich, & Vosniadou, 1987; Samarapungavan, Vosniadou, & Brewer, 1996; Vosniadou & Brewer, 1992, 1994) have probed developmental changes in children's "cosmological beliefs." They have asked children, for example, about the shape of the earth, about why the sun disappears at night, and about whether the sun moves around the earth or the reverse. They have found, not surprisingly, that children's beliefs become more adultlike with increasing age. But their research also makes clear that the adult system is not simply imposed on a passive child mind. Throughout development, children strive to integrate adult teachings about the earth and sky with their own experiences and natural forms of thought. Many young children, for example, initially believe that the earth is a flattened sphere—that is, round along the sides but flat at the top and bottom. Such a

One of the most basic forms of conservation is the conservation of quantity. To conserve quantity, the child must avoid centering on the misleading perceptual appearance.

The example that we examine is a conservation of number problem (Piaget & Szeminska, 1952). To construct such a problem, we might begin by laying out two rows of five chips, as shown in the first column of Figure 8.7. As long as the chips are arranged in one-to-one correspondence, even a 3- or 4-year-old can tell us that the two rows have the same number. But suppose that, while the child watches, we spread one of the rows so that it is longer than the other and then ask the child again about the number. Virtually every 3- and 4-year-old will say that the longer row now has more. If we ask the child why, the child finds the answer obvious—because it is longer. In Piaget's terms, the child *centrates* on the length of the row and hence fails to conserve the number.

Centration, then, is a perceptually biased form of responding that is characteristic of young children. For the young child, what seems to be critical is how things look at the moment. The child's attention is captured by the most salient, or noticeable, element of the perceptual display, which in the number task is the length of the rows. Once her attention has been captured, the child finds it difficult to shift attention and take account of other information—for example, the fact that the rows differ not only in length but also in density. The result is that the child is easily fooled by appearance and often, as in the conservation task, arrives at the wrong answer.

Other Preoperational Limitations Piaget's studies identified several further confusions that preoperational thought may show (Piaget, 1929, 1951). Young children's conception fits with what they are told ("the earth is round") but also honors both their immediate perceptual experience (the earth looks flat) and their more general knowledge of physical principles (unsupported objects fall)—knowledge that, as the research discussed earlier in the chapter indicates, is present from early in life.

In general, children's thinking about cosmology is not simply a collection of isolated beliefs. Rather, such thinking coheres into what Brewer and associates refer to as *mental models*—organized systems of thought within which all the various contributors to a particular concept (personal experience, adult teaching, general developmental level) interact to yield the specific belief.

Children in every culture form cosmological beliefs of various sorts as they develop. Research to date suggests that these beliefs are in some respects the same and in some respects different across cultures. The grounding of such beliefs in basic and presumably universal forms of physical knowledge (e.g., objects move along continuous paths, unsupported objects fall) guarantees some similarity in children's thinking, whatever the cultural setting. But the way in which general principle is translated into specific belief may depend on the modes of thought prevalent in the surrounding culture.

Many young Indian children, for example, believe that the earth is a disk floating on a body of water—a belief not found among American children (Samarapungavan et al., 1996). This conception both honors the support principle (since not only objects on the earth but the earth itself are supported by a flat surface beneath) and accords with long-standing tenets of the Hindu belief system.

Some of Piaget's earliest studies concerned children's understanding of the physical world, including many of the astronomical phenomena that have been the focus of the recent cosmological studies (Piaget, 1929). Piaget would certainly agree with much in the contemporary research, including the notion that children are active, constructive participants in their own development and that their beliefs cohere in an organized system. But there are also some differences between the modern work and its Piagetian predecessors. Mental models, organized and inclusive though they may be, are a good deal more content-specific and limited in scope than are Piagetian stages. And the demonstration of specific cultural influences on children's thinking, while perhaps not incompatible with Piaget's theory, takes us well beyond Piaget's general statements about the role of culture.

thinking is often imbued with *animism*, or the tendency to endow inanimate objects with the qualities of life. The young child who indicates that the sun shines "because it wants to" is engaging in animistic thinking, as is the child who is concerned that a piece of paper will be hurt by being cut. A related phenomenon is *artificialism*, or the tendency to assume that natural objects and natural phenomena were created by human beings for human purposes. The child who believes that the night exists "so we can sleep" is showing artificialism, as is the child who believes that the moon was invented to light people's way after the sun goes down. The term *realism* refers to the tendency to believe that psychological phenomena have a real, material existence. A familiar example to parents of young children is the conviction that a dream is a real thing that is right there in the room (at the window? under the bed?). Finally, Piaget used the term *transductive reasoning* to describe a form of preoperational reasoning that qualifies neither as deduction (reasoning from general to particular) nor as induction (reasoning from particular to general). Transductive thought, in contrast, moves from particular to particular with no consideration of the general principles that link particular events. The result of transductive thinking is that the young child often shows confusion about how and why two events relate. Piaget's daughter Lucienne provides an example: "I haven't had my nap so it isn't afternoon."

Is the young child's thinking really as egocentric, centrated, and confused as Piaget claimed? A brief answer is "sometimes but by no means always." We provide a more complete answer after considering the next of the Piagetian periods.

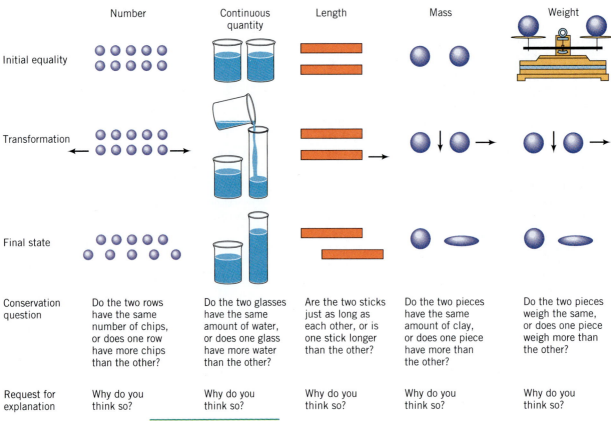

Figure 8.7
Examples of Piagetian conservation problems.

✓ *To Recap...*

The second developmental period in Piaget's progression is the preoperational period. The onset of representational intelligence marks a major advance over sensorimotor functioning. The child's intellectual adaptations are now faster, more efficient, more mobile, and more socially sharable. The preoperational period is also a time of specific cognitive acquisitions, including qualitative identity and the appearance–reality distinction.

The movement from sensorimotor to representational brings problems as well as advances, a fact that is signaled by the term *preoperational*. The young child's thinking is often egocentric, showing an inability to break away from his own perspective to adopt the perspective of others. The young child's thinking also shows centration, a tendency to be captured and misled by what is perceptually obvious. The child's failure to conserve is one manifestation of centration.

Middle-Childhood Intelligence: The Concrete Operational Period

The concrete operational period is the period of middle childhood. It extends from about age 6 to about age 11 or 12.

Discussions of the cognitive differences between preschoolers and grade-schoolers typically note a long list of contrasts (Flavell et al., 1993; Ginsburg &

Opper, 1988). If forced to sum up the differences in a single phrase, however, most child psychologists would probably say something like "The older child is just more *logical*." This is not to say that preschoolers are totally illogical; that would be far from the truth. But the preschooler's attempts at logical reasoning are often scattered and incomplete, working impressively in some contexts but going badly astray in others. The young child seems to lack an overall logical system that can be applied with confidence to a wide range of problems, particularly the kinds of scientific and logical problems that Piaget stressed. The older child, in contrast, does possess such a system.

To examine the differences between the preoperational and the concrete operational, we first present a sampling of the relevant Piagetian tasks. We then move on to Piaget's theory of the differences between the preoperational and concrete operational periods.

A Sampling of Tasks

For the most part, Piaget used the same tasks to study the preoperational and concrete operational periods. The difference between periods lies in the pattern of response. The preoperational child fails all the tasks, whereas the concrete operational child begins to succeed at them. The older child's success is not instantaneous, however. The concrete operational concepts differ in difficulty, and their mastery is spread across the entire period of middle childhood.

Conservation   The conservation of number problem described earlier is just one example of a conservation task. Conservation can be examined in any quantitative domain. And, indeed, Piaget and his coworkers studied just about every form of conservation that can be imagined. There are studies of conservation of mass, weight, and volume; of length, area, and distance; of time, speed, and movement (Piaget, 1969, 1970; Piaget & Inhelder, 1974; Piaget, Inhelder, & Szeminska, 1960). Some examples are shown in Figure 8.7. As can be seen, the typical starting point is a demonstration that two stimuli are equal on some quantitative dimension. While the child watches, one of the stimuli is transformed so that they no longer look equal. To conserve the quantity, the child must be able to overcome the misleading perceptual appearance. And this is precisely what the preoperational child cannot do.

Different forms of conservation are mastered at different times. Conservation of number is typically one of the first to be acquired, appearing by about age 5 or 6. Conservation of mass and conservation of continuous quantity are also relatively early achievements. Conservation of length and conservation of weight are more difficult, typically coming 2 or 3 years after the first conservations. Other forms of conservation emerge still later.

Conservation represents another form of invariant. During the sensorimotor period, the infant masters the invariant of object permanence—the knowledge that the existence of objects is invariant. During the preoperational period, the child comes to understand qualitative identity—the knowledge that the qualitative nature of objects is invariant. And during the concrete operational period, the child masters the various forms of conservation—the knowledge that quantitative properties of objects are invariant.

Classes   Piaget's major work on classes is described in a book entitled *The Early Growth of Logic in the Child* (Inhelder & Piaget, 1964). The word *logic* is important. A number of investigators, both before and since Piaget, have studied how children

Class inclusion
The knowledge that a subclass cannot be larger than the superordinate class that includes it. In Piaget's theory, a concrete operational achievement.

The ability to reason about classes is an important achievement of the concrete operational period.

Seriation
The ability to order stimuli along some quantitative dimension, such as length. In Piaget's theory, a concrete operational achievement.

Transitivity
The ability to combine relations logically to deduce necessary conclusions—for example, if A > B and B > C, then A > C. In Piaget's theory, a concrete operational achievement.

form groups or classes when asked to sort an array of objects. Do they sort on the basis of color or shape, for example, and can they consistently follow whatever criteria they select? Piaget's focus, however, was not simply on the child's ability to group objects sensibly. His interest was in the child's understanding of the structure or logic of any classification system formed.

The best-known task for probing the child's understanding of classes is the **class inclusion** problem. Suppose that we present the child with 20 wooden beads, 17 red and 3 white. The child agrees that some of the beads are red, some are white, and all are wooden. We then ask the child whether there are more red beads or more wooden beads. Or we might ask which would make a longer necklace, all the red beads or all the wooden beads.

However we word the question, the preoperational response is the same: "There are more red beads than wooden beads." The child is apparently unable to think about a bead as belonging simultaneously to both a subclass (all the red ones) and a superordinate class (all the wooden ones). Instead, once the child has focused on the perceptually salient subclass—the many red beads—the only comparison left is with the other subclass—the few white beads. Note again the role of centration in the preoperational child's thinking—the tendency to focus on what is perceptually obvious and to ignore other information. The result is that the child makes a fundamental logical error and judges that a subclass is larger than its superordinate class.

The concrete operational response is again quite different. The concrete operational child can solve this and other versions of the class inclusion problem. Furthermore, the concrete operational child, according to Piaget, appreciates the logical necessity of the class inclusion answer. The child knows not simply that there are not more roses than flowers or more dogs than animals. The child who truly understands the structure of classes knows that there can *never* be more roses or more dogs—that it is logically impossible for a subclass to be larger than the superordinate class (Miller, 1986).

Relations   In addition to understanding classes, the child must come to understand the relations between classes. Thus, another large set of Piagetian tasks has to do with various aspects of relational reasoning.

A deceptively simple-looking problem in relational reasoning is the **seriation** task (Piaget & Szeminska, 1952). To study seriation of length, we might present 10 sticks of different lengths haphazardly arranged on a table. The child's task is to order the sticks in terms of length. We might expect that any child who is persistent enough will eventually arrive at the correct solution through trial and error. Yet most young children fail the task. They may end up with just two or three groups of "big" and "little" sticks rather than a completely ordered array. Or they may line up the tops of the sticks but completely ignore the bottoms. Even if the child succeeds through trial and error, he is unlikely to be able to solve further variants of the problem—for example, to insert new sticks into a completed array. What seriation requires, according to Piaget, is a systematic and logical approach in which the child is able to think of each stick as being simultaneously longer than the one that precedes it and shorter than the one that comes after it. It is this sort of two-dimensional, noncentrated approach to problem solving that the preoperational child lacks.

The preoperational child also fails to appreciate the **transitivity** of quantitative relations (Piaget et al., 1960). Suppose we work with three sticks—A, B, and C—that differ only slightly in length. We show the child that A is longer than B and that B is longer than C. We then ask about the relative lengths of A and C but do not allow the child to compare them perceptually. Solving this task requires the ability to add together the two premises (A > B and B > C) to deduce the correct answer (A > C). The concrete operational child has this ability (though not immediately—transitivity emerges at about age 7 or 8). The preoperational child does not and so is likely to fall back on guessing or some other irrelevant strategy.

Note the similarity between transitivity and class inclusion. In both cases, the correct answer follows as a logically necessary implication from the information available. Thus, it is not simply a fact that A happens to be longer than C; if A is longer than B and B longer than C, then A *has* to be longer than C. We can see again Piaget's emphasis on very basic forms of logical reasoning.

The Concept of Operations

Interesting though the empirical studies may be, Piaget's primary purpose was never simply to document what children do or do not know. His goal was always to use children's overt performance as a guide to their underlying cognitive structures. During middle childhood, these structures are labeled *concrete operations.*

We will not attempt a complete presentation of Piaget's theory of concrete operations, both because the theory is very complicated and because the full model has not held up very well with time. Nevertheless, it is important to convey some idea of what Piaget meant by **operations**. Operations are in many respects similar to the sensorimotor schemes. One similarity is implied by the very name *operation.* An operation, like a sensorimotor scheme, always involves some form of action— *operating* on the world in order to understand it. Another similarity is that operations, like schemes, do not exist in isolation but are organized into a larger system of interrelated cognitive structures.

> **Operations**
> Piaget's term for the various forms of mental action through which older children solve problems and reason logically.

There are also differences between sensorimotor schemes and concrete operations. A major difference concerns how actions are expressed. Sensorimotor schemes are always expressed in overt action—reaching, grasping, manipulating, or the like. Operations, in contrast, are a system of *internal* actions. They are, in fact, the logical, in-the-head form of problem solving toward which the child has been slowly moving ever since the onset of representational intelligence.

Let us apply the notion of intelligence-as-internal-action to one of the concepts discussed earlier—working with classes, for example. Piaget argued that what a child knows about classes is a function of various mental actions that the child can perform. Simply to think about an object as belonging to a certain class is a form of action. Classes are not environmental givens; rather, they are cognitive constructions. To add together two subclasses (for example, red beads and white beads) to get the superordinate class (wooden beads) is a form of action. To compare the sizes of two subclasses, or of subclass and superordinate, is a form of action. In general, classification is a matter of mental activity—of creating and disbanding classes, comparing different classes, and logically adding, subtracting, or multiplying classes.

What about conservation? Piaget identified various mental actions through which the child might arrive at a correct conservation judgment. In the conservation of number task, the child might reason that the change in one dimension—say, the length of the row—is compensated by, or canceled out by, the change in the other dimension—the spacing between objects. Such reasoning by means of *compensation* involves a kind of logical multiplication of the two dimensions (increase in length times decrease in density implies no change in number). Or the child might reason that the spreading transformation can be undone and the starting point of equality reestablished, a form of reasoning that Piaget labeled *inversion* or *negation.*

Reversibility
Piaget's term for the power of operations to correct for potential disturbances and thus arrive at correct solutions to problems.

Both compensation and inversion are examples of a more general Piagetian notion, the concept of **reversibility**. Reversibility is a property of operational structures that allows the cognitive system to correct, or reverse, potential disturbances and thus to arrive at an adaptive, nondistorted understanding of the world. It is this power that concrete operational thought has and that preoperational thought lacks.

The Concept of Stage

Thus far in our review of the Piagetian stages we have not really discussed what it means to claim that there are stages of development. The concrete operational period provides a good context for discussion of this issue, because it is with regard to this period that the concept of stage has been most extensively debated.

Most theorists agree that a stage theory must meet at least three criteria to be valid. One is that development include *qualitative* as well as quantitative changes—that is, changes in how the child thinks and not merely in how much the child knows or how quickly the child can do things.

Piagetian theorists maintain that development does in fact show qualitative change from one period to the next. They would argue, for example, that there is a qualitative, in-kind difference between a sensorimotor child, who must act out all her adaptation to the world, and a preoperational child, who can solve problems mentally through the use of symbols. Similarly, there is a qualitative difference between the preoperational response to a conservation task and the concrete operational response. Younger children treat conservation as a problem in perceptual estimation, always judging in terms of how things look. Older children do not even need to look at the stimuli; for them, conservation is a matter of logical reasoning, not of perceptual judgment.

A second criterion is that the stages follow an *invariant sequence*—each stage builds on the one before, and no stage can be attained until the preceding one has been mastered. It is impossible, for example, for the child to become preoperational without the sensorimotor developments that make representational thought possible. Similarly, concrete operations build on the achievements of the preoperational period. This claim of sequence applies not only to the four general periods, but also to the substages within a period—for example, the six sensorimotor substages.

The final criterion has created the most problems. Piaget's theory maintains that each stage can be characterized by a set of interrelated cognitive structures—for example, the concrete operations of middle childhood. Once developed, these structures determine performance on a wide range of cognitive tasks. This position implies that there should be important *concurrences* in development. That is, if two or more abilities are determined by the same underlying structures, then they should emerge at the same time. Children's cognitive endeavors should show a good deal of consistency.

The problem for Piaget's theory is that children's performance is often far from consistent. They may, for example, succeed on some presumably concrete operational tasks yet fail totally on others. Piaget did not claim perfect consistency; he was the first, in fact, to demonstrate that various concrete operational concepts may be mastered at different times. Most commentators, however, believe that Piaget never satisfactorily explained the inconsistencies that his research uncovered. And research since his has revealed even more inconsistency in development, including instances in which abilities that Piaget explicitly claimed as concurrences are mastered at different times (de Ribaupierre, Rieben, & Lautrey, 1991; Jamison, 1977; Kreitler & Kreitler, 1989). The studies we describe in the next section raise even more questions about whether it makes sense to talk about a child being "in" the preoperational or concrete operational stage.

What, then, is the status of the concept of stage? The issue continues to be a source of debate (Fireman & Beilin, 1990; Lourenco & Machado, 1996; Miller, 1993). Some researchers believe that Piaget's stage model is basically accurate, even though specific details may need correcting. Others (including researchers whose work we discuss in the next chapter) believe that cognitive development does in fact occur in stages, but that the stages are different from those posited by Piaget. And still others believe that the concept of stage serves no useful purpose and should be abandoned.

More on the Preoperational–Concrete Operational Contrast

Is young children's thinking really as riddled with deficiencies as Piaget claimed? Are the differences between early childhood and later childhood really so great? A number of recent research programs have suggested that the answer to both questions is no. Here we discuss research directed to two of the topics reviewed earlier—perspective taking and number.

Perspective Taking We begin with the concept of visual perspective taking that Piaget's three-mountains task is meant to tap. As an examination of Figure 8.6 makes clear, the three-mountains task requires more than simply avoiding an egocentric response. To come up with the correct answer, the child must engage in a fairly complicated process of spatial calculation. Perhaps the young child's problems with this task tell us more about such spatial computation skills than about egocentrism.

When the task is simplified, young children often appear considerably less egocentric. Children as young as 3 can predict the other's viewpoint when familiar toys rather than Piagetian mountains serve as landmarks (Borke, 1975). Even 2-year-olds can demonstrate some awareness of the other's viewpoint in very simple situations (Klemchuk, Bond, & Howell, 1990). When asked to show another person a picture, for example, the 2-year-old holds the picture vertically so that its face is toward the viewer rather than toward the self (Lempers, Flavell, & Flavell, 1977). Similarly, 2-year-olds realize (popular myth notwithstanding) that the fact that *their* eyes are closed does not mean that other people also cannot see (Flavell, Shipstead, & Croft, 1980). Even 18-month-olds will point to objects that they want an adult to notice, a behavior that suggests some realization that the adult does not necessarily share their perspective (Rheingold, Hay, & West, 1976). All these behaviors represent only very simple forms of perspective taking; nevertheless, they imply some ability to separate another's point of view from one's own.

Children's ability to tailor their speech to the needs of others also turns out to be more advanced than one would expect from Piaget's accounts of egocentric speech. Four-year-olds use simpler speech when talking to 2-year-olds than when talking either to other 4-year-olds or to adults (Shatz & Gelman, 1973). Thus, they adjust the level of their communication to the cognitive resources of the listener. Indeed, even 2-year-olds talk somewhat differently to their infant siblings than to adults (Dunn & Kendrick, 1982). Children can also adjust to temporary variations in what the listener knows, as opposed to the general differences that exist between babies and adults. They describe an event differently, for example, depending on whether the adult to whom they are talking was present when the event occurred (Menig-Peterson, 1975), and they make different inferences about what listeners know and structure their communications differently in response to differences in listeners' past experiences (O'Neill, 1996).

Evidence for early perspective-taking skills is not limited to the studies reviewed here. The findings are quite general across a variety of different forms of perspective taking (Flavell, 1992b; Newcombe, 1989; Shantz, 1983). In no case is the 3- or 4-year-old's performance fully equivalent to that of the older child. But it is often more advanced than we once believed.

Number   As we saw, the aspect of numerical understanding that most interested Piaget was the child's ability to conserve number in the face of a perceptual change. Later studies have not disproved Piaget's contention that a full understanding of conservation of number—or, for that matter, any form of conservation—is a concrete operational achievement. Recent work does suggest, however, that there may be earlier, partial forms of understanding that were missed in Piaget's studies.

As with perspective taking, investigators have simplified the conservation task in various ways. They have reduced the usual verbal demands, for example, by allowing the child to pick candies to eat or juice to drink rather than answer questions about "same" or "more." Or they have made the context for the question more natural and familiar by embedding the task within an ongoing game. Although such changes do not eliminate the nonconservation error completely, they often result in improved performance by supposedly preoperational 4- and 5-year-olds (Donaldson, 1982; Galpert & Dockrell, 1995; Miller, 1976, 1982).

Researchers have studied other aspects of young children's understanding of number in addition to conservation. Gelman and associates, for example (Gelman, 1982, 1991; Gelman & Gallistel, 1978), have demonstrated that children's early counting is considerably less rote and confused than Piagetian theorists believed. Gelman and Gallistel identified five principles that a counting system must honor (see Table 8.4). Their research indicates that children as young as 3 or 4 have some understanding of these principles. Young children do not always follow the principles perfectly, and their specific ways of applying them may differ from those of adults (e.g., the 3-year-old who demonstrates the stable-order principle by always counting, "1, 2, 6"). Nevertheless, both Gelman's work and that of other researchers (e.g., Becker, 1993; Sophian, 1995) indicate that counting is a frequent, systematic, rule-governed behavior from early in life.

Gelman argues that children's early numerical abilities show a number of similarities to their early linguistic abilities. We will see in Chapter 11 that nativistic explanations have been common in the attempt to account for young children's remarkable language skills. Gelman suggests that there may be an important biological underpinning to human numerical competence as well.

The suggestion that biological factors contribute to numerical development finds dramatic support in recent research with infants. Investigators have used

---

Table 8.4
What Young Children Know About Number: The Gelman and Gallistel Counting Principles

Principle	*Description*
One–one	Assign one and only one distinctive number name to each item to be counted.
Stable-order	Always recite the number names in the same order.
Cardinal	The final number name at the end of a counting sequence represents the number of items in the set.
Abstraction	The preceding counting principles can be applied to any set of entities, no matter how heterogeneous.
Order-irrelevance	The items in a set can be counted in any order.

Source: Based on information from *The Child's Understanding of Number* by R. Gelman and C. R. Gallistel, 1978, Cambridge: Harvard University Press.

habituation to determine whether infants are sensitive to the numerical value of a set (Cooper, 1984; Starkey & Cooper, 1980; Trehub, Thorpe, & Cohen, 1991; van Loosbroek & Smitsman, 1990). In these studies, the infant is first repeatedly shown collections of a particular size until attention drops off. A new set size is then presented. Do infants notice the change? As long as the set sizes are small, infants as young as 3 months apparently do. One study (Antell & Keating, 1984), in fact, reports successful discrimination of 2 versus 3 by newborns!

That infants can discriminate differences in set size is certainly impressive. Even more impressive is the suggestion that babies may be capable of very simple forms of arithmetic. Evidence derives from an extension of the Baillargeon possible event–impossible event procedure. In this case, however, the impossible event involves a violation of the laws of arithmetic. Figure 8.8 shows an example.

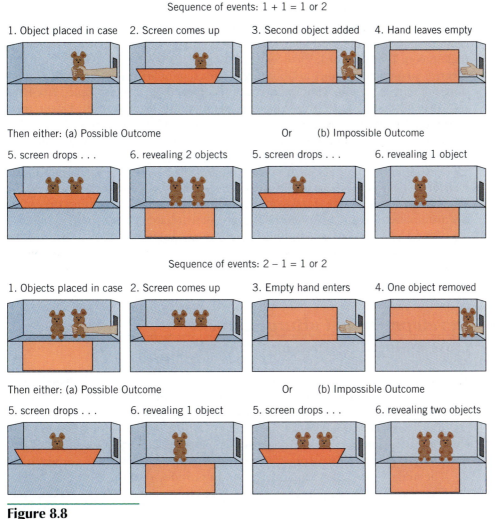

Figure 8.8
Possible and impossible outcomes in Wynn's study of infants' arithmetical competence. From "Addition and Subtraction by Human Infants" in *Nature* (1992) figure 1, p. 749. Reprinted by permission from *Nature*. Copyright 1992 Macmillan Magazines Ltd.

Wynn (1992, 1995*b*) reports that 5-month-old infants who witness such events react as we would expect them to react if they understood the arithmetical operations involved—that is, they show little dishabituation to the possible events, but a marked recovery of interest when the rules of addition or subtraction are apparently violated. This outcome is certainly compatible with the hypothesis of early arithmetical competence; unfortunately, it does not definitively establish it. As some thought about Figure 8.8 should reveal, the impossible events in these studies encompass not only arithmetical impossibilities, but also physical impossibilities—an object either magically disappears (in the Addition condition) or magically appears (in the Subtraction condition). It is possible, therefore, that the infants' apparent surprise reflects their knowledge about objects rather than anything specific about number (Haith & Benson, 1998). Pulling apart these possibilities is a challenging task, and efforts therefore continue to specify exactly what, if anything, babies know about arithmetic (Simon, 1997; Simon, Hespos, & Rochat, 1995).

An Overall Evaluation   The consistent message that emerges from the studies just described is that the preschool child is more competent than Piaget's research and theory would lead us to believe. The studies reviewed here represent just a small fraction of the evidence for this statement (Flavell, 1992a; Gelman & Baillargeon, 1983; Halford, 1989; Siegal, 1991; Wellman & Gelman, 1998), and perspective taking and number are but two of the content areas for which the conclusion holds true. Young children's relational reasoning, for example, has been shown to be more impressive than one might think from reading Piaget (e.g., Goswami, 1995), and the same is true for understanding of classes (e.g., Smith, 1979). In the concluding section of this chapter we will see still further examples of impressive cognitive achievements during the preschool period.

This is not to say that Piaget's description of preoperational thinking is totally inaccurate. It is not. Young children *are* often egocentric, centrated, and illogical. They fail in a wide range of tasks on which older children succeed, and they often need simplified situations or special help to show whatever competence they possess. Piaget was correct in asserting that there are important limitations in early childhood thinking and important developmental changes between early childhood and middle childhood. But he may have somewhat misjudged the nature of both the limitations and the change.

Development in Cultural Context
Cross-Cultural Research and Piaget

One of the general issues identified in Chapter 1 concerns normative versus idiographic approaches to the study of development. It should be clear that Piaget's work falls squarely under the normative heading. The emphasis in Piagetian research is always on similarities rather than on differences among children. All children are assumed to pass through the same stages of development, and all children are assumed to master concepts such as object permanence and conservation.

The study of development in other cultures provides a natural testing ground for the Piagetian claim of universality. We have long known that children growing up in the United States show the same basic patterns of development that Piaget first identified in children in Geneva, Switzerland, some 50 or 60 years ago. But suppose we consider a culture in which children's experiences are markedly different from those that are typical in Western societies. Will development still follow the Piagetian mold?

The answer turns out to be yes and no. A study by Dasen (1975) provides a good example. Dasen examined three groups of children: Canadian Inuits, Australian Aborigines, and Ivory Coast Africans. Both the Inuits and the Aborigines depend on hunting for their subsistence, and members of both groups lead a nomadic existence, moving from place to place as need dictates. Dasen hypothesized that such cultures might promote the development of spatial skills—abilities such as navigating through a strange environment, remembering and utilizing landmarks, and reversing one's route to get back to the starting point. In contrast, the Ivory Coast economy depends on agriculture rather than hunting, and the Ivory Coast way of life is correspondingly a good deal more sedentary, with an emphasis on accumulating and exchanging agricultural goods. Because of the emphasis on agricultural exchange, the hypothesis in this case was that the culture would promote concepts of quantity and volume.

Inuit children, and children of other nomadic cultures, have well-developed spatial abilities.

To test these predictions, Dasen administered a battery of Piagetian tasks to children from each of the three cultures. The children were between 6 and 14 years old, and the tasks were directed to forms of knowledge that Piaget had found to emerge during this period. The particular tasks were selected to reflect the aforementioned cultural emphases. Some of the tasks measured spatial skills—for example, the sorts of visual perspective taking tapped by Piaget's three-mountains problem. The Inuit and Aborigine children were expected to do well on these measures. Other tasks targeted quantitative skills—for example, conservation of weight and conservation of volume. The Ivory Coast children were expected to excel at these tasks. The results confirmed these expectations.

Dasen's study is by no means the only demonstration that specific experiences can affect the development of Piagetian concepts. Cross-cultural research indicates that development can be sped up or slowed down depending on the availability of certain experiences and that even the order in which certain abilities emerge may vary from one culture to another (Laboratory of Comparative Human Cognition, 1983; Mwamwenda, 1992).

At the same time, cross-cultural research also provides support for the Piagetian claim of universality. No one has found a culture in which children do not eventually acquire such basic forms of knowledge as object permanence and conservation, or in which children master conservation without going through an initial phase of nonconservation, or in which the order of the four general periods of development is reversed. Indeed, even some of the reported lags in rate of development disappear when the tests are made appropriate to the cultural setting—for example, when children are interviewed in their native language by a native speaker (Nyiti, 1982) or when the children themselves play an active role in the assessment situation (Greenfield, 1966).

Cross-cultural studies, then, reveal both variation and consistency, depending on which aspects of development we consider. And context undoubtedly contributes to both sorts of outcome. The particular context in which children grow up can nurture the development of particular skills, as studies such as Dasen's illustrate. But similarities in the contexts that children encounter also help create similarities in the ways in which children develop. There is no environment, after all, in which objects cease to exist when out of sight or in which quantities are not conserved in the face of a perceptual change. And there is no environment in which children cannot perform the kinds of actions on the world that Piaget considered critical to the development of intelligence. Thus, one explanation for similarities in human cognition lies in the similar contexts in which that cognition develops.

✓ *To Recap...*

The third developmental period in Piaget's theory is the period of concrete operations. During this period, the child gradually masters the different forms of conservation. The concrete operational child also comes to understand various aspects of classification (including class inclusion) and relational reasoning (including transitivity). Piaget attributed these and other achievements of middle childhood to the formation of concrete operations, an organized system of internal mental actions. One criticism of this theory is that development is not as consistent as the notion of underlying structure implies.

Recent research suggests that Piaget overstated the differences between early childhood and middle childhood. When tested in simplified situations, preschool children often show more competence than they show on standard Piagetian tasks. Young children are not as consistently egocentric as Piaget suggested, and they demonstrate the rudiments of skills that will develop more fully during middle childhood.

Adolescent and Adult: The Formal Operational Period

Formal operations is the final period in Piaget's stage hierarchy. It can be given a beginning but not an end point, because once acquired, formal operations are assumed to last throughout the lifetime. The onset of the period is usually dated at about age 12 or 13, around the beginning of adolescence. But formal operations may emerge later than this or not at all. As we will see, the evidence suggests that not everyone reaches the formal operational period.

Characteristics of Formal Operational Thought

We have already discussed the meaning of the term *operations*. But what about the term *concrete*? The concrete part of the label refers to the basic limitation of concrete operational thought. As we have seen, the concrete operational child, in contrast to the sensorimotor child, does operate cognitively by means of representations rather than overt actions. Nevertheless, concrete operational children are still limited to dealing largely with what is directly in front of them—with what is concrete, tangible, real. What the child at this stage cannot yet do at all well is deal with the hypothetical—with the whole world of possibility rather than immediate reality.

Formal operational thinkers show no such limitation. The distinguishing characteristic of the formal operational period is the capacity for **hypothetical-deductive reasoning**. The formal operational thinker moves easily and surely through the world of what-ifs, might-bes, and if-thens. The adolescent, in fact, often seems more at home with the hypothetical—with imagined worlds, counterfactual propositions, life dreams and schemes—than in the world of mundane reality.

The *deductive* part of *hypothetical-deductive* is also important. To qualify as formal operational, thought must do more than simply imagine possibilities. The formal operational thinker possesses a rigorous logical system for evaluating hypotheses and deducing necessary outcomes. As the term *operations* implies, this system again involves various forms of mental action.

Piaget's favorite way of characterizing the difference between concrete operations and formal operations was to talk about a reversal in the relation between reality and possibility. For the concrete operational child, the starting point is always immediate reality. From this point, the child can make very limited extensions into the hypothetical. In a conservation of number task, for example, the child who imagines pushing the chips back together *is* going beyond what is immediately

Hypothetical-deductive reasoning
A form of problem solving characterized by the ability to generate and test hypotheses and draw logical conclusions from the results of the tests. In Piaget's theory, a formal operational achievement.

given, but in a very limited way. For the formal operational thinker, in contrast, the starting point is the world of possibility—whatever it is that *might* be true. From this starting point in the possible, the thinker works back to what happens to be true in the situation under study.

A Research Example: Reasoning about Pendulums

Inhelder and Piaget's (1958) tasks for studying formal operations consist mostly of problems in scientific reasoning. In one task, for example, the participant must determine what factors (length, thickness, shape, and so on) influence the bending of a rod. In another, the task is to experiment with various chemical solutions to determine which combinations produce a specified outcome. Among the other content areas examined are projection of shadows, determinants of floating, conservation of motion, and laws of centrifugal force.

The example that we will describe is drawn from the domain of physics. In this task, the participant is shown a simple pendulum consisting of a weight hanging on a string. Various other weights and strings are also available for experimentation. The problem is to figure out what determines the frequency of oscillation of the pendulum—that is, how fast the pendulum swings back and forth. Is it the heaviness of the weight? The length of the string? The height from which the weight is dropped? The force with which it is pushed? Or perhaps some combination of two or more of these factors?

It turns out that the only factor that really has an effect is the length of the string. But the point is not that the formal operational thinker knows this in advance, because he probably does not. The point is that the formal operational subject possesses a set of cognitive structures that will allow systematic solution of the problem. The solution requires first identifying each of the potentially important variables—weight, length, and so on—and then systematically testing them out, varying one factor at a time while holding other factors constant. The subject must be able to generate all the possible variables (and sometimes combinations of variables), keep track of what has been done and what remains to be done, and draw logical conclusions from the overall pattern of results. In the case of the pendulum, the performance of all relevant tests will lead to the conclusion that if the string is short the pendulum swings fast, and only if the string is short does the pendulum swing fast. Thus, the length is both a necessary and a sufficient determinant of oscillation.

As with all Piagetian stages, the achievements of formal operations are clearest when contrasted with the preceding period. The concrete operational child is unlikely to solve the pendulum problem. The 9- or 10-year-old faced with such a task will do some intelligent things, including accurately testing some of the possible variables. But the younger child is not able to generate and examine the full range of possibilities on which a logical conclusion depends. Instead, the child may find that a heavy weight on a short string swings fast and conclude that both the weight and length are important, a conclusion that is not valid in the absence of further tests.

Note that the formal operational approach to the problem embodies the kind of reversal between reality and possibility that Piaget stressed. The formal operational thinker begins by considering all the various possibilities—maybe the weight is important, maybe the length is important, and so on. At first, these are merely hypotheses; none of them is anything that has yet been observed, and most of them will turn out to be false. Yet it is only by systematically considering all the possibilities that the subject can determine what happens to be true. Thus, the movement of thought is from the possible to the real.

More Recent Work on Formal Operations

Research on formal operations has addressed the same general issues that we discussed with respect to earlier Piagetian stages. A basic question is whether Piaget accurately diagnosed what his participants knew. Later studies using the Inhelder and Piaget tasks have typically found lower levels of performance than Inhelder and Piaget reported (Shayer, Kucheman, & Wylam, 1976; Shayer & Wylam, 1978). Indeed some studies have found substantial proportions of adults who fail the usual formal operational tasks (Commons, Miller, & Kuhn, 1982).

The suggestion that Piaget may have *overestimated* ability runs counter to what we identified earlier as a common conclusion about Piagetian procedures—namely, that they typically lead to some underestimation of children's competence. Some researchers have suggested that underestimation may also occur at the formal operational level. The Inhelder and Piaget tasks are unfamiliar to most people, and the usual method of administering them may not elicit the individual's optimal performance. Studies have shown that the addition of a simple hint or prompt concerning the appropriate procedure can lead to a marked improvement on later trials (Danner & Day, 1977; Stone & Day, 1978). More extended training procedures, as well as other sorts of procedural simplifications, have elicited at least some elements of formal operational performance in children as young as 9 or 10 (Fabricius & Steffe, 1989; Kuhn, Ho, & Adams, 1979).

Another possible approach is to vary the content of the tasks. Perhaps people tend to be formal operational when reasoning about content that is interesting and familiar to them. For some people, the natural science problems used by Inhelder and Piaget may provide such content; others, however, may require tasks in literary analysis, or auto mechanics, or cooking. Piaget himself, in fact, suggested this possibility in one of his later articles about formal operations (Piaget, 1972). Although research to date is limited, there is some support for the idea. For example, De Lisi and Staudt (1980) demonstrated that college students' ability to reason at a formal operational level depended on the fit between academic training and specific task: Physics majors did best on the Inhelder and Piaget pendulum task; English majors excelled on a task involving analysis of literary style; and political science majors earned their highest scores on a problem in political reasoning.

Findings from cross-cultural research also illustrate the importance of specific experience. Although people from non-Western cultures seldom do well on the Inhelder and Piaget problems, they may show impressive levels of performance when operating in more familiar and culturally significant domains. For example, prior to the availability of magnetic compasses, Micronesian navigators sailed their canoes for hundreds of miles from one island to another without the aid of instruments, an achievement no Western sailor would attempt to duplicate. The navigators' ability to maintain course depended on a complex—and culturally transmitted—computational system in which star positions, rate of movement, and fixed reference points were systematically combined in ways that seem fully equivalent to the highest levels of performance shown by Inhelder and Piaget's (1958) participants (Hutchins, 1983).

The importance of specific interests and training is also found in studies of logical reasoning (Moshman, 1998) and in work on scientific problem solving (Stanovich, 1993). Research in both areas shows the same variability in performance as does research on formal operations: surprisingly good performance by young children in some studies, surprisingly poor performance by older children and adults in others. Given appropriately supportive contexts, even preschoolers sometimes succeed in drawing logical conclusions from premises (e.g., Hawkins et

Formal-operational reasoning is not limited to the science laboratory. The navigational achievements of Micronesian sailors depend on a complex system of computations and logical deductions.

al., 1984), and in simple situations children as young as 6 may show the rudiments of scientific reasoning (e.g., Ruffman et al., 1993). On the other hand, adolescents and adults faced with reasoning tasks of the if-then sort often fail to draw logically valid conclusions from the available information. And even adults' scientific problem-solving efforts often go astray (Kuhn, 1991, 1992b). Such demonstrations of less-than-optimal performance fit with Piaget's suggestion that not everyone reaches the highest stage of cognitive functioning. At the least, they confirm De Lisi and Staudt's (1980) conclusion that we only sometimes operate at our best.

We can note, finally, that Piaget's theory of formal operations has been subject to some of the same criticisms made of his claims concerning concrete operations. The degree of within-stage consistency is again an issue. Although some studies report fairly strong correlations among formal operational tasks (Eckstein & Shemesh, 1992), low to moderate relations are probably a more common finding (Martorano, 1977). Furthermore, the specific logical structures that Piaget believed underlie formal operational performance have been severely criticized by logicians (Braine & Rumaine, 1983; Ennis, 1976; Parsons, 1960). As with earlier Piagetian stages, few dispute that Piaget identified interesting forms of thought or that his theory may partially explain what is happening. But the theory does not seem to be completely satisfactory, and debates about the best way to characterize this level of thinking therefore continue (Byrnes, 1988; Gray, 1990; Keating, 1988).

✓ *To Recap…*

The final period described by Piaget's theory is the period of formal operations, which typically begins around adolescence. The distinguishing characteristic of formal operations is the capacity for hypothetical-deductive reasoning. The formal operational thinker begins with possibility—all the hypotheses that might apply to the task under study—and ends with reality—the particular solution that a systematic and logical testing of hypotheses shows to be true. Such thinking is revealed most clearly in tasks that involve scientific reasoning, such as the pendulum problem.

Although later research has confirmed Piaget's general account of adolescent thought, questions have arisen concerning the adequacy of his assessment methods, with some researchers reporting poorer performance than that obtained by Piaget, and some reporting better performance. Questions have also arisen concerning the accuracy of Piaget's specific model of formal operations.

Cognitive Change

Our discussion thus far has been directed to one of the two basic questions in developmental psychology: What are the most important changes that occur in the course of development? We turn now to the second general question: How can we explain these changes?

Piaget's Theory

Piaget's position on the nature–nurture issue is definitely an interactionist one. In his theory, biology and experience act together to produce changes in the child's cognitive abilities.

More specifically, Piaget (1964, 1983) identified four general factors that contribute to cognitive change. Three of the factors are found to some extent in every theory of development. First, biological maturation plays a role. In any stage theory, biological factors contribute to both the nature and the timing of the stage changes. Learning and development occur within constraints set by the child's maturational level, and some kinds of development may be impossible until maturation has progressed sufficiently.

Experience is also important. Piaget divided experience into two categories: physical experience and social experience. The former includes the child's interactions with inanimate objects; the latter, the child's interactions with people. In both cases, Piaget stressed the importance of assimilation and action. Children must fit experiences, physical or social, into what they already understand. And they must actively construct new knowledge, as opposed to having knowledge imposed ready-made upon them.

Every theory talks in some way about maturation, physical experience, and social experience. The fourth factor is more uniquely Piagetian. **Equilibration** is another legacy of Piaget's biological training. Piaget used this term to refer to the general biological process of self-regulation. It was for him the most important of the four factors, the one that in a sense explained the other three.

What did Piaget mean by self-regulation? The notion is easiest to understand in conjunction with a closely related Piagetian construct, **equilibrium**. Equilibrium refers to balance within the cognitive system. It exists when the child's cognitive structures can respond to any environmental challenge without distortion or misunderstanding. In Piaget's theory, such an adaptive response implies a balance between assimilation and accommodation. The child neither distorts reality to make it fit existing structures (which would be an excess of assimilation) nor distorts current knowledge in an attempt to make sense of something new (which would be an excess of accommodation). It is the self-regulating process of equilibration that guards against such distortions and acts to maintain equilibrium.

Piaget cited equilibration as the ultimate explanation for several aspects of development. Equilibration accounts for the organization in development. As we

Equilibration
Piaget's term for the biological process of self-regulation that propels the cognitive system to higher and higher forms of equilibrium.

Equilibrium
A characteristic of a cognitive system in which assimilation and accommodation are in balance, thus permitting adaptive, nondistorted responses to the world.

saw, inputs from maturation and from various kinds of experience are not simply lumped together; rather, they are coordinated into cognitive structures. According to Piaget, there must be some more general factor that accounts for such coordination. This general factor is the self-regulating process of equilibration. Thus, it is equilibration that directs the integration of sensorimotor schemes during infancy and the coordination of knowledge about classes and knowledge about relations during middle childhood.

Equilibration also explains motivation. In Piaget's view, the cognitive system seeks always to reach and maintain states of equilibrium, because equilibrium characterizes adaptive behavior. Suppose, however, that the child encounters some new event that cannot immediately be understood. This new event will evoke disequilibrium, or cognitive conflict—some sort of disturbing imbalance within the cognitive system. The child will feel a need to get rid of the conflict and will continue to think and to act until the event is understood and equilibrium restored.

Equilibration accounts finally for the directionality in development—for the fact that development moves always in an upward, progressive direction. When disequilibrium exists, only certain kinds of resolution are satisfactory. Conceivably, the child could remove the disequilibrium by distorting the input or regressing to some lower level of understanding. But this does not happen. When equilibrium is restored, it exists at a higher, better level of understanding. It is in this way that misunderstanding evolves into understanding and lower stages into higher ones.

It should be clear that equilibration, at least as we have discussed it so far, is a *very* general notion. Even if the general construct makes sense, it does not tell us how specific cognitive changes come about. Piaget did attempt at various points to specify the equilibration process more exactly (Piaget, 1957, 1977). Most critics, however, have concluded that none of the versions is very satisfactory, and the theory remains vague and hard to test (Chapman, 1992; Rotman, 1977; Zimmerman & Blom, 1983). A reasonable conclusion is that Piaget provided a general framework within which a theory of change could be constructed, but that he himself never succeeded in filling in the framework.

Experimental Training Studies

We turn now from theory to evidence. How might we study the process of cognitive change? There are a number of possible approaches, some of which are discussed in the coming chapters. Here, we concentrate on the approach that has been most common in the Piagetian literature—the training study.

In a training study, we begin with a sample of children who have not yet mastered some Piagetian concept—say, some form of conservation. We begin also with some theory of what particular subskills or kinds of knowledge underlie conservation. We then provide the children, usually in a controlled laboratory setting, with experiences that we think might help them master these prerequisites and hence understand conservation. Following the training we administer a posttest to determine whether understanding has improved. If understanding *has* improved, it may be that our laboratory manipulation tells us something about the real-life routes to conservation.

Several hundred training studies have been carried out in the last 30 years or so. It seems fair to say that this massive effort has not led to the gains in knowledge for which researchers initially hoped (Flavell et al., 1993; Kuhn, 1992a). Nevertheless, three general conclusions can be drawn (Beilin, 1978; D. Field, 1987).

1. Training is difficult, but by no means impossible. Instilling a concept such as conservation is not a matter of simply pointing out the correct answer. A number of sensible-seeming procedures have had no success at all. Such negative outcomes are compatible with Piaget's theory, for they attest to the reality of preoperational thinking and to the slow, gradual nature of cognitive change. Nevertheless, the majority of training studies have reported positive outcomes. There is no longer any doubt that conservation and other Piagetian concepts *can* be experimentally taught.

2. *The success of training depends on the developmental level of the child.* Perhaps the clearest prediction that Piaget's theory makes about training is that the child's readiness should determine its success. Training is beneficial only if the child is already close to mastering the concept, because only then will the child be able to assimilate the new information and make the necessary accommodations to it. Training studies provide general support for this prediction. Training usually works best with older, more mature samples, and very young children are unlikely to be successfully trained. Piaget's theory, however, does not spell out the components of readiness very exactly. Hence, specific tests of readiness have been difficult to make, and the notion that learning must wait for development remains controversial. In some studies, children as young as 4 have been successfully trained in such concepts as conservation. This finding fits with an idea discussed earlier—namely, that preoperational children often possess more competence than Piaget believed.

3. *A wide variety of different training methods have had success.* Some successful training studies have used procedures derived from Piaget's theory—training in reversibility, for example (Wallach, Wall, & Anderson, 1967), or induction of cognitive conflict (Murray, 1982). But other successful studies have used procedures that seem quite distant from what Piaget stressed. Examples in this category include operant conditioning (Bucher & Schneider, 1973) and television modeling (Waghorn & Sullivan, 1970). It is difficult to see how Piaget's or any theory can encompass all the training methods that have proved, in laboratory settings, to be successful. How relevant these laboratory demonstrations are for real-life development remains debatable, because the laboratory situation is always somewhat different from the child's natural environment. To the extent that training studies *are* relevant, however, they suggest that there may be multiple routes to the mastery of concepts such as conservation. Some children may acquire conservation through one set of experiences and processes, other children through a different set, and other children through yet a different set.

Applications
Piaget and Education

The purpose of the sorts of training studies just discussed is not really to improve any individual child's cognitive functioning. The goal, rather, is a scientific one: to identify the processes through which cognitive change occurs. More generally, the Piagetian approach, with its grounding in basic issues in philosophy, has always been more theoretically than applicationally oriented. Yet Piaget wrote two books about education (Piaget, 1971, 1976), and others have written extensively about the educational implications of his work (Cowan, 1978; DeVries & Zan, 1994; Duckworth, 1987; Kamii & DeVries, 1993). In this section we consider what the Piagetian approach has to offer education.

Four principles are most often cited in discussions of Piagetian approaches to education. One is the importance of readiness. This principle follows from Piaget's

The Piagetian approach to education stresses the child's own exploration and self-discovery.

emphasis on assimilation. Experience—educational or otherwise—does not simply happen to the child; rather, it must always be assimilated to current cognitive structures. A new experience will be beneficial only if the child can make some sense of it. Teaching that is too far beyond the child's level is unlikely to have any positive impact.

A second, related principle concerns the motivation for cognitive activity. Educational content that is too advanced is unlikely to be interesting, but the same applies to content that is too simple. What is needed is content that is slightly beyond the child's current level, so that it provides experiences familiar enough to be assimilated, yet challenging enough to provoke disequilibrium.

We can hardly work at the child's level unless we know what that level is. A third contribution from Piaget is a wealth of information about what a child does or does not know at different points in development. The message, to be sure, is in part negative—constraints on what can be taught before certain points, cautions about how much development can be accelerated. More positively, Piaget's studies often identify steps and sequences through which particular content domains are mastered. We can thus determine not only where the child is, but also the natural next steps for development.

A final principle is more functional. It concerns Piaget's emphasis on intelligence as action. Piaget distrusted educational methods that are too passive, or too rote, or too verbal. In his view, education should build on the child's natural curiosity and natural tendency to act on the world in order to understand it. Knowledge is most meaningful when children construct it themselves rather than when it is imposed on them. This principle is expressed in the title of one of Piaget's books about education—*To Understand Is to Invent.*

✓ *To Recap…*

In addition to specifying important changes, a developmental theory must explain how the changes occur. Piaget identified four general factors that contribute to development: maturation, physical experience, social experience, and equilibration. Equilibration is the biological process of self-regulation—the tendency to move toward higher and higher levels of equilibrium. In Piaget's theory it accounts for the organization, motivation, and directionality of development.

The main methodology through which change has been examined is the training study. In a training study, we attempt to teach new knowledge (such as some form of conservation) to children who do not yet possess it. Such studies have demonstrated that training is possible, but they have not yet solved the problem of how real-life change comes about.

New Directions

As our discussions throughout this chapter should make clear, Piaget's tasks continue to be a fertile source for research in cognitive development. The influence of the Piagetian approach is not limited to the specific tasks and corresponding abilities examined in Piaget's own studies, however. The Piagetian legacy, rather, is a good deal more general, in that the basic cognitive-developmental approach initiated by Piaget has in recent years been extended to a number of interesting developments that received little if any attention in Piaget's own research. In this final section of the chapter we consider two such topics: children's understanding of concepts, and various developments that fall under the heading of "theory of mind."

Concepts

Take a moment to reflect on your experiences the next time you take a walk. Within a brief span of time you are likely to encounter dozens of distinct objects and events—grass, trees, dogs, and birds; running, flying, jumping; clouds, wind, and sun; perhaps happiness or excitement or fear. Some of these experiences will be identical to those you have encountered before (a familiar tree, for example), but most will be new—a bird you have never seen, a novel pattern of clouds. You will not be confused or overwhelmed by this newness, however; rather, you will automatically organize the ever-changing swirl around you into meaningful units that help you make sense of what is happening (a bird, a cloud, a smile, etc.).

Concept

A mental grouping of different items into a single category on the basis of some unifying similarity or set of similarities.

Your ability to cut the world up in this adaptive way is a reflection of the many concepts that you have developed and that you use every day. A **concept** is a mental grouping of different items into a single category on the basis of some underlying similarity—some common core that makes them all, in a sense, the same thing (all birds, all instances of happiness, etc.). Concepts are a fundamental way in which we organize the world, and thus their development in childhood is of clear interest. The question that we address now is how children organize their worlds. What bases do they use when judging things as similar, and how do these bases change with development?

Table 8.5 shows one approach to this question. The problems in the table are from an influential program of research by Gelman, Markman, and associates (Gelman, 1996; Gelman & Markman, 1986, 1987). The two possible bases for response should be clear. If perceptual similarity is taken to be critical, then the new item should be judged to be like the one that it most resembles. This means, for example, that the blackbird would be expected to have warm legs at night, just like the similar-looking bat. In contrast, if category membership is deemed more important, then the legs would be expected to be cold, just like those of the other bird. The contrast in these tasks is common in studies of children's concepts: between

Table 8.5

Sample Items from Gelman and Markman's Studies of Children's Concepts

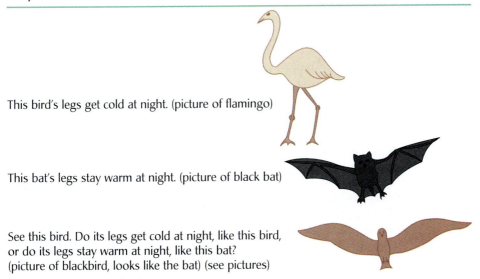

This bird's legs get cold at night. (picture of flamingo)

This bat's legs stay warm at night. (picture of black bat)

See this bird. Do its legs get cold at night, like this bird, or do its legs stay warm at night, like this bat? (picture of blackbird, looks like the bat) (see pictures)

This fish stays under water to breathe. (picture of tropical fish)
This dolphin pops above the water to breathe. (picture of dolphin)
See this fish. Does it breathe under water, like this fish, or does it pop above the water to breathe, like this dolphin? (picture of shark, looks like the dolphin)

This puppy hides bones in the ground. (picture of brown dachshund)
This fox hides food in the ground. (picture of red fox)
See this puppy. Does it hide bones in the ground, like this puppy, or does it hide food in the ground, like this fox? (picture of red dog, looks like the fox)

Source: From "Categories and Induction in Young Children" by S. A. Gelman and E. M. Markman, 1986, *Cognition, 23,* 183–209, with permission from Elsevier Science.

surface similarity and underlying essence as the basis for judging that things are the same.

Just as the contrast is common, so is the expectation that has guided much of the research on children's concepts. The expectation has been that young children will prove to be perceptually oriented, forming concepts on the basis of surface appearance rather than more basic commonalities. And there is, certainly, support for this expectation. Piaget's studies furnish many instances of preschool children's centrating on what is immediately obvious and ignoring what is beneath the surface. The young child's difficulties with the appearance–reality distinction, discussed earlier in this chapter, are another obvious example.

What has been striking and informative in recent research on children's concepts are demonstrations that in many cases young children are *not* perceptually bound. Often, in fact, preschool children seem to cut the world up in essentially the same way as do adults. This, for example, was the major conclusion from the Gelman and Markman research summarized in Table 8.5. Despite the compelling perceptual cues, most 4-year-olds opted for category membership as the relevant basis for inference, judging that the bird's legs would get cold, that the shark would breathe under water, and so forth. A subsequent study using simplified procedures showed that even 2.5-year-olds had some ability to overlook perceptual appearance in favor of category membership (Gelman & Coley, 1990).

Why the more positive picture of preschoolers' competence in recent research? Two factors are probably important. One is the methods used. We have seen repeatedly that simplified and sensitive procedures may reveal formerly unsuspected abilities, and such has proved to be the case in the study of concepts. Many of the older studies, for example, based their conclusions about early concepts on children's response to explicit instructions to sort items into categories (e.g., "Show me which ones go together"). The Gelman and Markman procedure, in contrast, is tied to a natural, everyday use of concepts—drawing inferences about new instances from what is already known. Our concept of "dog", for example, allows us to form expectations with respect to a number of attributes (likely behaviors, preferred diet, internal organs, etc.) even for dogs we have never met—indeed, even for breeds of dogs we have never seen. The grounding of the response measure in this natural function of concepts may be one explanation for the impressive performance in recent research.

The type of concept at issue is probably important as well. Some studies have used arbitrary concepts created on the spot for the purposes of research—for example, the category of blue circles in a study of sorting behavior. There is nothing arbitrary, however, about the concepts that children naturally form—such concepts reflect important commonalities among real-life experiences that children extract as they attempt to make sense of the world. The focus on familiar and interesting material may also contribute to the good performance in recent research.

As the vignette which opened this section should make clear, concepts are far too plentiful and diverse to permit a case-by-case discussion of their development. We will, however, single out one general category that has been the target of much interesting recent research: children's concepts of biology. Questions of life—of living versus nonliving, of origins, of growth—have fascinated children for as long as they have fascinated scientists. The Gelman and Markman research touches on such matters, and so, you may remember, did some of Piaget's (1929) earliest studies—recall our discussion of animism, or young children's tendency to attribute life to nonliving things. Such a tendency, it should be clear, signals an important gap in biological understanding.

Studies since Piaget's have confirmed that young children do sometimes manifest animism in their thinking, along with a number of other confusions and misunderstandings with regard to biological phenomena (Carey, 1985). Recent studies also indicate, however, that animism is less pervasive than Piaget believed and that the limitations in children's biological understanding are often accompanied by some unexpected strengths. Even 3-year-olds, for example, are fairly good at judging which things can move by themselves (i.e., animals) and which things cannot (e.g., statues, plants) (Massey & Gelman, 1988). Self-propelled movement is one distinguishing characteristic of animal life. Growth, in contrast, is a characteristic of both plants and animals, and preschool children also understand some of the basic facts about growth. They realize, for example, that only living things grow, that growth is inevitable (for example, you can't keep a baby pet small and cute just because you want to), and that growth is directional—that is, people, plants, and animals get bigger, not smaller, as they age (Inagaki & Hatano, 1987; Inagaki & Sugiyama, 1988; Rosengren et al., 1991). They also have some appreciation of origins and kinship, realizing that dogs produce baby dogs, not cats, and that offspring generally resemble their parents (Springer, 1996; Springer & Keil, 1991). This understanding is, to be sure, far from complete, and there are disagreements about exactly what knowledge to attribute to preschoolers (Solomon et al., 1996). Still, there is clearly a stronger starting point than we once believed.

Theory of Mind

We have seen that the preschool period is a time of impressive accomplishments in the domain of conceptual understanding. The preschool child also makes major strides with respect to a variety of forms of knowledge that fall under the heading of theory of mind. Psychologists use the term **theory of mind** to refer to children's understanding of the mental world—what they think about such phenomena as thoughts, beliefs, desires, and intentions. Do children realize, for example, that there is a distinction between the mental and the nonmental—that thoughts are in our minds and not part of the physical world? Do they realize, despite this distinction, that the mental and the nonmental are connected—that our experiences lead us to have certain thoughts and beliefs, and that these thoughts and beliefs in turn direct our behavior? Do they appreciate the distinctions among different mental states—the fact that to think something is not necessarily the same as to know something, or that the intention to achieve a goal is no guarantee that the goal will actually be reached?

Piaget (1929) was one of the first to explore questions of this sort in some of his earliest studies. Contemporary researchers, however, have gone well beyond these Piagetian beginnings. In just the last decade, theory of mind has emerged as one of the most active arenas for research in cognitive development (Astington, 1993; Flavell & Miller, 1998; Gopnik & Meltzoff, 1997; Mitchell, 1996; Taylor, 1996).

A topic of particular interest to theory-of-mind researchers has been the child's understanding of **false belief**: the realization that it is possible for people to hold beliefs that are not true. This topic is interesting because it provides evidence with respect to one of the issues identified in the preceding paragraph—the child's ability to separate the mental from the nonmental. Consider the scenario depicted in Figure 8.9. To any adult, the answer to the question of where Sally will search for her marble is obvious—in the basket, where she last saw it. She has no way, after all, of knowing that the marble has been moved during her absence. Note, however, that to arrive at this answer we must set aside our own knowledge of the true state of affairs to realize that Sally could believe something that differs from this true state—that she could hold a false belief. We can do this only if we realize that beliefs are mental representations that need not correspond to reality.

Three-year-old children typically have great difficulty understanding false beliefs. Most 3-year-olds will fail tasks such as the one in Figure 8.9. Most 3-year-olds also have difficulty recapturing their own false beliefs. In another common false-belief task, children are shown a container that turns out to have unexpected contents—for example, a crayon box that actually holds candles. When asked what they initially believed was in the box, most 3-year-olds reply "candles," answering in terms of their current knowledge rather than their original, false belief. Four-year-olds are much more likely to understand that they can hold a belief that is false and that a representation can change even when the reality does not. They are also more likely to realize that others could hold false beliefs in tasks of either the crayon-box or hidden-marble sort.

As noted, the false-belief task is of interest because it taps the very basic realization that mental representations are distinct from physical reality. But the task

Theory of mind
Thoughts and beliefs concerning the mental world.

False belief
The realization that people can hold beliefs that are not true. Such understanding, which is typically acquired during the preoperational period, provides evidence of the ability to distinguish the mental from the nonmental.

Figure 8.9

Example of a false–belief task. To answer correctly, the child must realize that beliefs are mental representations that may differ from reality. From *Autism: Explaining the Enigma* (p. 160) by U. Frith, 1989, Oxford: Basil Blackwell. Copyright © 1989 by Basil Blackwell. Reprinted with permission.

also speaks to a further important realization: the understanding that mental and physical, although separate, are also linked—that is, that what we believe follows from what we experience. This means, for example, that Sally, having seen the first but not the second placement of her marble, should expect to find it in the basket, whereas Anne (and also the child research participant), having seen the transfer, should realize that the box is the true location. As we saw, it is not until about age 4 that children are able to appreciate this connection between experience and belief.

Researchers have also probed more directly for children's understanding of where beliefs come from. Various questions have been of interest. Suppose, for example, that the child watches while one adult looks inside a box and a second adult merely stands by—can the child determine which adult now knows the contents of the box? Suppose that the child is one of the participants—can children make appropriate judgments of their own knowledge? Can children judge not only what they know but *how* they know? Can they recapture, for example, whether a particular belief was instilled through direct perception, or through inference, or through communication from someone else? Do they know what sorts of knowledge *can* come from different sources—for example, that vision is a good source for learning about color but not for learning about how objects feel—and that neither vision nor touch will work if the goal is to discover how something sounds?

Two general conclusions emerge from the studies of children's understanding of the origins of belief. First, the preschool period is again a time of important accomplishments. By age 5 most children have a basic understanding of how experience leads to belief and can handle at least most versions of the preceding problems. The second conclusion is perhaps more striking, given how obvious the experience-belief connection seems to any adult. The second conclusion is that this knowledge does in fact have to develop, for young preschoolers have only the shakiest grasp of how beliefs originate. Thus, 3-year-olds may be unable, seconds after learning the contents of a container, to indicate whether they learned through sight or touch or being told (O'Neill & Gopnik, 1991). Asked how to determine the color of an unseen object, 3-year-olds may be quite content to explore via touch rather than sight (O'Neill, Astington, & Flavell, 1992). And even 4-year-olds may report that they have always known a fact that the experimenter in fact taught them just moments before (Taylor, Esbensen, & Bennett, 1994).

The tasks and findings discussed here are but a small sampling of the kinds of research being conducted under the theory-of-mind heading. One of the most interesting of these ongoing efforts concerns possible relations between theory-of-mind understanding and social behavior. It is certainly plausible that there could be a relation, and in both directions—that children's understanding of the mental world can help them interact effectively with other people, but also that interactions with others can help teach children about belief and desire and other mental states. There is in fact evidence for both sorts of link. Several studies, for example, have reported a positive relation between number of siblings and false-belief understanding—that is, children from relatively large families are fastest, on the average, to master false belief (Jenkins & Astington, 1996; Perner, Ruffman, & Leekam, 1994; Ruffman et al., 1998). Presumably, growing up in a household with several siblings heightens the probability of experiences (quarrels, appeals, tricks, etc.) through which children can learn about mental states in both other people and themselves.

Further evidence for links between theory-of-mind understanding and social behavior is provided by the phenomenon of *childhood autism.* Autism is a severe disorder, almost certainly biological in origin, that is characterized by a number of abnormalities in development, prominent among which are difficulties in social interaction. From early in life, children with autism show little interest in other people and little ability to form interpersonal relationships. They also, as recent research (e.g., Baron-Cohen, 1995; Frith, 1989) demonstrates, show marked deficiencies with regard to theory-of-mind understanding. Even when other aspects of mental functioning are relatively unimpaired, children with autism typically perform very poorly on theory-of-mind tasks. As Baron-Cohen (1995) has observed, these children's insensitivity to the thoughts, wishes, and feelings of others is not surprising; they may literally not know that such psychological states exist. The consequences of such "mindblindness" (Baron-Cohen, 1995) are poignant testimony to the importance of theory of mind to normal social relations.

✔ *To Recap...*

The final section of the chapter considers ways in which modern researchers are building on and also extending the foundation laid down by Piaget. Studies of children's concepts examine the ways in which children organize their experiences into meaningful categories. Although such studies provide some support for Piaget's characterization of the perceptually oriented preschooler, they also have identified situations in which young children's concepts, like those of adults, reflect less obvious and more fundamental similarities among items.

Research under the theory-of-mind heading addresses children's knowledge about the mental world. Such research has revealed some striking limitations in young preschoolers' understanding of mental phenomena, including difficulties in appreciating false belief and in recognizing the sources of belief. Such research also reveals important advances in theory-of-mind understanding across the preschool years.

Conclusion

It is difficult in a single chapter to convey the impact of Piaget's work on the field of child psychology. American child psychologists began to discover Piaget in the late 1950s and the early 1960s, in part because translations of his books began to appear at this time and in part because of the publication of an excellent summary of Piaget's work by John Flavell (1963). Since that time, Piaget's writings have inspired literally thousands of studies of children's thinking. The tasks and findings described in this chapter are just a small sampling from this huge research yield (Chapman, 1988; Ginsburg & Opper, 1988; Miller, 1993; Modgil & Modgil, 1976).

Piaget's influence has also extended to the study of topics about which he himself had little to say. We considered two such topics—concepts and theory of mind—in the preceding section, and we will encounter many more in the chapters to come.

At the same time, the research effort of the last 25 years, perhaps inevitably, has revealed a number of problems in Piaget's research and theory. The major criticisms should be apparent by now. Piaget often underestimated children's ability, perhaps especially during the infant and preschool years. Development is not as orderly and consistent as Piaget's stage model seems to imply. Even if the concept of stages is valid, the logical models that Piaget used to characterize the stages are questionable. And Piaget never offered a completely satisfactory explanation of cognitive change.

The information-processing perspective, to which we turn in the next chapter, is a major contemporary alternative to Piaget. Psychologists in this tradition do not necessarily deny the insights of Piaget's work; indeed, one subset of information-processing theorists label themselves "neo-Piagetians" to indicate that they are building on a foundation laid by Piaget. The information-processing approach does, however, offer a number of contrasts to Piaget that modern researchers have found attractive.

Visual Summary for Chapter 8:
Cognitive Development: The Piagetian Approach

Piaget's Four Periods of Development

Period	Age	Description
Sensorimotor	0-2 years	Infants understand the world through overt actions. These sensorimotor schemes become progressively more complex across infancy.
Preoperational	2-6 years	The child can now use mental representations to solve problems. Thinking is more efficient and faster, but shows a number of limitations.
Concrete Operational	6-12 years	The use of operations – a system of internal mental actions – allows the child to overcome the limitations of preoperational thought.
Formal Operational	12-adult	The further development of operations leads to the capacity for hypothetical-deductive reasoning.

Cognition During Infancy: The Sensorimotor Period

The Six Substages of the Sensorimotor Period

Substage	Age	Description
1. Exercising Reflexes	Birth-1 month	The infant is limited to exercising inborn reflexes.
2. Developing Schemes	1-4 months	Reflexes evolve into adaptive schemes that begin to be refined and coordinated.
3. Discovering Procedures	4-8 months	Behavior becomes outwardly oriented and the infant develops procedures for reproducing interesting events.
4. Intentional Behavior	8-12 months	Intentional behavior emerges. The infant can separate means and end in pursuit of a goal.
5. Novelty and Exploration	12-18 months	The infant alters schemes to produce new effects. Trial and error is used to solve problems.
6. Mental Representation	18-24 months	The capacity for mental representation emerges. Mental problem solving begins to replace overt trial and error.

Development of Object Permanence

Object Permanence	An especially important achievement of the sensorimotor period is the understanding that objects have a permanent existence independent of our perceptual contact with them. Piaget suggested that infants only gradually come to understand object permanence through a series of stages in which the existence of an object is freed from the infant's actions on it.
Criticism of Piaget's Account	Although later studies have largely confirmed the descriptive picture provided by Piaget, they also indicate that Piaget's methods often failed to capture early forms of infant competence.

Thought in the Preschooler: The Preoperational Period

Strengths of Preoperational Thought	The child's intellectual adaptations are faster, more efficient, more mobile, and more socially sharable than in the sensorimotor period. The preoperational period is also a time of specific cognitive acquisitions, including qualitative identity and the appearance-reality distinction.
Limitations of Preoperational Thought	The child lacks the operations that allow effective problem solving at the representational level. She has difficulty taking the perspective of others (egocentrism), tends to be captured and misled by what is perceptually obvious (centration), and shows a failure to conserve.
Criticism of Piaget's Account	Recent research suggests that Piaget may have underestimated the abilities of the preoperational child. When tested in simplified situations, preschoolers often show more competence than on standard Piagetian tasks.

Middle Childhood Intelligence: The Concrete Operational Period

Strengths of Concrete Operational Thought	The child gradually masters the different forms of conservation, various aspects of classification, and relational reasoning. Piaget attributed these achievements to the formation of concrete operations, an organized system of internal mental actions.
Limitations of Concrete Operational Thought	Concrete operational children are limited to dealing with what is concrete, tangible, or real; they have difficulty thinking in terms of what is abstract or hypothetical.
Criticism of Piaget's Account	Many commentators feel that Piaget's account does not satisfactorily explain inconsistencies in the timing with which various concrete operational concepts emerge.

Adolescent and Adult: The Formal Operational Period

Strengths of Formal Operational Thought	The formal operational period is characterized by the capacity for hypothetical-deductive reasoning. Such thinking is revealed most clearly in tasks of scientific reasoning.
Criticism of Piaget's Account	Research has questioned the adequacy of some of Piaget's assessment methods. Some researchers report poorer performance than that obtained by Piaget, while others report better performance.

Cognitive Change

Factors that contribute to cognitive change	Piaget stressed the importance of four factors to cognitive change – biological maturation, physical experience, social experience, and equilibration.
Training Studies	Training studies have revealed that cognitive change is possible through training, but have not shed much light on how change comes about in real life.

New Directions

Children's Concepts	Studies of children's concepts provide some support for Piaget's characterization of the perceptually oriented preschooler. Such studies have also identified situations, however, in which young children's concepts, like those of adults, reflect less obvious and more fundamental similarities among items.
Theory of Mind	Research into children's knowledge about the mental world has revealed some striking limitations in young preschoolers' understanding of mental phenomena, including difficulties in appreciating false belief and in recognizing the sources of belief. Such research has also revealed important advances in theory-of mind-understanding across the preschool years.

Chapter *9*

Cognitive Development: The Information-Processing Approach

Out of the blue, Eileen Franklin-Lipsker of Los Angeles came forward with an amazing story in 1989. Twenty years earlier, as a child, she had seen her father rape her playmate, an 8-year-old girl, and then kill the child. Franklin-Lipsker had "recovered" this traumatic memory only recently, she said. For 20 years, it had been repressed—hidden somewhere out of her reach. Based on Franklin-Lipsker's story, the 20-year-old, unsolved murder case was reopened. Franklin-Lipsker's father, George Franklin, was arrested, tried, convicted, and sentenced to life in prison.

It was the first time that a recovered memory had been used as the basis for a criminal prosecution, but it would not be the last. Over the next several years, criminal charges based on recovered memories were brought in several states. In addition, hundreds of adults filed civil lawsuits, often against their parents, claiming to have recovered long-buried, painful memories of childhood molestation and abuse. Generally, these memories had been recovered with the aid of psychotherapy.

But as cases based on recovered memories multiplied, so did questions about the reliability of such memories. Although most mental-health experts accepted the idea that traumatic memories of childhood events might be repressed and later recalled, many cautioned against accepting every so-called recovered memory as fact. In particular, experts were concerned that some therapists, by using hypnosis and other suggestive techniques, were not recovering memories but creating them. Indeed, some people who had previously accused others of abuse began to retract their accusations. Some even sued their therapists for implanting false memories.

By the mid-1990s, courts were backing away from reliance on recovered memories. In 1995, a judge ruled that George Franklin must be given a new trial or be released. Recovered memories can be used in trials, the judge said, but admitting a recovered memory as evidence "does not establish that the memory is worthy of belief." George Franklin, who had always maintained his innocence, was set free in 1996, having spent 7 years in prison.

*E*xactly how does memory work? How are memories stored and how are they retrieved? These questions have important, real-life implications, as you can see in the discussion of recovered memory and as you will see again when we consider a related matter, children's eyewitness testimony, later in the chapter.

The workings of memory and other basic psychological processes are the focus of scientists seeking to understand children's cognitive development from the information-processing perspective. As we noted in the preceding chapter, information processing has emerged as a major contemporary approach to the study of children's thinking (Kail & Bisanz, 1992; Klahr & MacWhinney, 1998; Miller, 1993).

In this chapter, we first summarize some of the most important characteristics of information-processing theory and research. We then move on to aspects of child development that have especially intrigued information-processing researchers. We consider several important areas of development, including memory, problem solving, and academic skills. The chapter concludes, as did Chapter 8, with the challenging issue of cognitive change.

The Nature of the Approach

An example will help introduce some of the points to be made. Imagine a 6-year-old is about to set out for his second day of school. He pauses at the door to collect his backpack, carefully placed there the night before as a reminder to himself not to forget it. On the way to school, he notes the various landmarks that define his route—the sign at the corner that means turn left, the big tree that tells him that school is just around the bend. Once in the classroom, he struggles again with the task—a fairly new one for him and for most first graders—of sitting quietly and paying attention despite all the distracting events around him. There are, in fact, new and important things to which to pay attention—letters that must be distinguished from one another, numbers that add together to make other numbers. Not everything is work, however. At recess there is a chance—if only he can remember the rules—to play the interesting new game learned the day before.

Although much of the content of the first grader's experiences may be new, the psychological processes that underlie his behavior are long-standing ones. From early in life, the child has attended to some aspects of the surrounding environment and ignored others. From early in life, the child has stored information in memory and used this stored knowledge to guide future behavior. From the time that the child could first get around independently, he has needed to note and remember the spatial environment. And from early in life, the child has taken in information, learned rules, and solved problems—all with regard to both the physical and the social world.

Information processing is a general label for all the psychological activities touched on in our example. All involve information of some sort (a spatial landmark, a numerical symbol, an instruction from the teacher), and all involve some kind of processing of this information (attention to critical features, comparison with past memory input, selection of a response). The goal of the information-processing approach is to specify these underlying psychological processes—and the developmental changes they undergo—as exactly as possible.

Two images are instructive in characterizing the information-processing approach. One is the flowchart. The other is the computer.

Children's environments present information and cognitive challenges of many sorts. How children come to understand and to respond adaptively to these challenges are the concerns of the information-processing approach.

The Flowchart Metaphor

Figure 9.1 shows the symbolic representation of a typical information-processing theory. The particular theory, which deals with memory, contains a number of details that do not concern us here. But its general features are characteristic of the information-processing approach. The starting point is some environmental input, and the end point is some response output. Between stimulus and response a number of psychological processes intervene.

In the case of memory, the initial input is assumed to be acted on and transformed in various ways. Imagine, for example, that our first grader has just heard a word for the first time. This word enters the sensory register—in this case, the auditory register—where a literal image of a stimulus can be held for perhaps a second at most. The word then moves to short-term, or working, memory, which is the center for active and conscious processing. Although information typically stays for only a few seconds in short-term memory, various strategies (some of which we consider shortly) may prolong its lifetime considerably. Finally, the word may be transferred to long-term memory, where, as the name suggests, it can exist indefinitely. Getting the word to long-term memory is, of course, the teacher's goal when presenting a new term to be learned. And all of us in fact do have thousands of words stored in permanent memory.

As the figure indicates, more general psychological processes also play a role. Control processes of various sorts affect the maintenance of information and the movement from one store to another. Response-generating mechanisms are necessary to explain the eventual overt response—for example, the child's ability to say a recently learned word.

The origin of the term *flowchart* should be evident from this example. Information-processing theorists attempt to capture the orderly flow of information through the cognitive system. The origin of the term *information processing* should

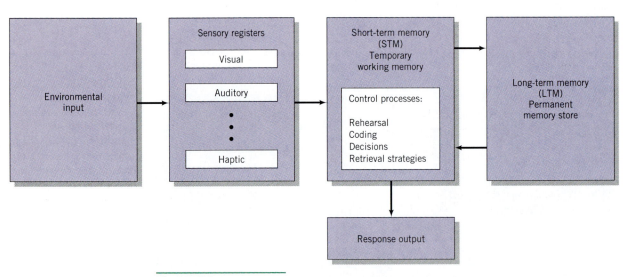

Figure 9.1

An example of an information-processing model of memory, which illustrates the kind of flowchart representation with which information-processing theorists attempt to describe the sequence of information processing. From "The Control of Short-Term Memory" by R. C. Atkinson and R. M. Shiffrin, 1971, *Scientific American, 225*, p. 82. Copyright credit Allen Beechel.

also be evident. Information is acted on, or processed, in various ways as it moves through the system. The external stimulus and external response—the concerns of traditional learning theory—are only the end points. The real goal of the psychologist—or so maintains the information-processing theorist—is to specify as completely and precisely as possible what comes between stimulus and response. And as our example suggests, even in a seemingly simple case, such as hearing a new word, quite a bit may be going on.

The Computer Metaphor

The preceding section described a cognitive system that can transform a variety of inputs into a variety of outputs in a systematic and intelligent way. In doing so, it uses stored information and stored rules of various sorts. What sort of intelligent system operates in this way? To anyone immersed in modern industrialized society, the answer should be obvious—a computer.

Information-processing theorists find the computer a useful tool on a variety of levels. At the most general level, the computer serves as a helpful metaphor for thinking about human cognition. Human and computer are alike in a number of ways. Both store representations or symbols and manipulate these symbols to solve problems. Both perform a variety of such manipulations in an incredibly rapid and powerful fashion. Despite this power, both are limited in the amount of information they can store and manipulate. Both, however, can learn from experience and modify their rule systems in a progressively adaptive direction. Understanding the operations of computer intelligence may thus lead to insights about human intelligence as well.

Information-processing theorists have drawn from computer technology in more specific ways as well. Any theorist of intelligence must decide on a language with which to formulate his or her theory. Information-processing theorists have often adopted preexisting computer languages for their theories. The kind of flow-chart language depicted in Figure 9.1, for example, was developed by workers in computer science. Such languages have the virtues of precision and (at least to the information-processing theorist) familiarity; they therefore are good vehicles for testing and communicating theories.

At the most specific level, the computer makes possible one of the prime methodologies of the information-processing approach—**computer simulation**. In a computer simulation, the researcher attempts to program a computer to produce some segment of intelligent behavior in the same way in which humans produce the behavior. The idea is to build into the computer program whatever knowledge and rules are thought to be important for the human problem solver. Suppose, for example, that we have a theory of how first graders solve simple addition problems. We might program our computer to apply the rules that we think children use and then see how *it* responds to the same tasks. How successfully the program generates the target behavior—in this case, the pattern of first-grade responses—then is a test of the investigator's theory of how children arrive at their answers.

Computer simulation Programming a computer to perform a cognitive task in the same way in which humans are thought to perform it. An information-processing method for testing theories of underlying process.

Comparisons with Piaget

Because our most complete discussion of intelligence to this point has involved the Piagetian approach, comparing the information-processing approach with this view is instructive.

Information-processing approaches to child development share several similarities with Piaget's approach. The first similarity is in the content studied. Information-processing researchers recognize the importance of the concepts identified by Piaget, and much of their research involves attempts to apply information-processing techniques to Piagetian tasks and abilities. Second, similarity exists at a general theoretical level. Information-processing theories, like Piagetian theory, fall within the cognitive-developmental approach to child development. Information-processing theorists agree with Piaget that a complex system of mental rules underlies cognitive performance and that one job of the theorist is to discover what these rules are. Finally, some information-processing theorists follow Piaget in dividing development into distinct stages. Although the stages are not identical to Piaget's, they typically show some important similarities. Because of their grounding in Piaget, this group of information-processing theorists is often referred to as *neo-Piagetian* (Case & Okamoto, 1996; Demetriou, Shayer, & Efklides, 1993; Fischer, 1980; Halford, 1993).

The issue of stages, however, also illustrates a difference between the information-processing and Piagetian approaches. Not all information-processing theorists subscribe to a stage model of development. And even those who may find stages useful differ in important ways from Piaget. The stages proposed by Piaget are the broadest, most general stages that the field of child psychology has seen. To say that a child is in the stage of concrete operations is to make a strong (and, as we saw, debatable) claim about how the child will perform on a wide range of cognitive tasks. Information-processing stage theories tend to be more limited in scope, focusing on specific skills and particular aspects of the child's development. A model might, for example, concentrate on the acquisition of spatial skills, without making any claims about the child's level of performance on other tasks. One way to summarize this difference is to say that the information-processing theorist's stages are more *domain-specific*—that is, more concerned with distinct aspects, or domains, of development.

Other differences between the information-processing and Piagetian approaches can be inferred from the flowchart and computer metaphors. Piaget's theoretical emphasis was always on the logical rules underlying problem solving, such as the concrete operations of middle childhood and the formal operations of adolescence. Piaget had little to say about many more process-oriented questions that are central to the information-processing researcher. How exactly does the child attend to new information? How is this information taken in and represented in memory? How is it retrieved in the service of problem solving? It would be difficult to construct a full flowchart model of problem solving, let alone a computer simulation, from Piaget's theoretical accounts. Information-processing theorists attempt to develop models that are both more specific and more complete than those offered by Piaget.

These goals have both methodological and theoretical implications. Methodologically, the emphasis on precision and testability has led to a number of distinctive methods for studying children's thinking. We have already mentioned one such method—the computer simulation technique—and we describe others later. Theoretically, the emphasis on completeness has meant a concern with a variety of aspects of children's development in addition to the kinds of logical reasoning stressed by Piaget. Much of the work on attention discussed in Chapter 7 was carried out within an information-processing perspective. The same is true for much of the work on memory that we consider next.

✓ To Recap...

The information-processing perspective is a major contemporary approach to the study of cognitive development. Information-processing researchers attempt to describe the underlying cognitive activities, or forms of information processing, that occur between stimulus input and response output. They draw from modern computer science, both for general ideas about human intelligence and for specific languages and methods with which to formulate and test their theories.

Like Piaget's theory, information-processing theories fall within the cognitive-developmental approach. In addition to sharing Piaget's emphasis on underlying rules or structures, information-processing researchers study many of the same concepts studied by Piaget, and some such researchers propose stage theories that have ties to Piaget's stages. Most information-processing theorists do not subscribe to the kinds of broad, general stages offered by Piaget, however. Their own models are more domain specific, and they attempt to construct models that are more precise, more complete, and more testable than those proposed by Piaget.

Memory in Infancy

Children can be affected by their experiences only if they can somehow retain information from these experiences over time. Questions of memory—of how information is taken in, stored, and retrieved—are therefore central to information-processing accounts of development. Because development starts in infancy, the examination of memory must also start with the infant.

We begin our discussion with a very basic question: Can babies remember? We have already encountered a number of findings that tell us the answer is yes. Many of the phenomena from Piaget's sensorimotor studies demonstrate the presence of memory—for example, the infant's ability to activate a familiar scheme when confronting a familiar object or to search for a plaything that has disappeared. Many of the findings from the study of infant perception discussed in Chapter 7 also imply the use of memory—for example, the infant's preference for the mother's voice. Much of the behavior that we as adults produce would be impossible if we did not remember and were not guided by past experience. The same is true of infants.

How well do babies remember? This question is harder to answer. Even a young infant's memory is in some respects surprisingly good. In other respects, however, infant memory is limited, and many important developmental advances have yet to come.

Psychologists distinguish between two basic forms of memory. **Recognition memory** refers to the realization that some perceptually present stimulus or event has been encountered before. You would be demonstrating recognition memory, for example, if you realized that you had already seen the flowchart memory model (Figure 9.1) when you encountered the same figure in some other book. **Recall memory** refers to the retrieval of some past stimulus or event when the stimulus or event is *not* perceptually present. You would be demonstrating recall memory if you were able to draw the flowchart model (or at least parts of it!) in the absence of any stimulus input. We begin with recognition, then move on to recall.

Recognition Memory

Methods of Study   How might we determine whether babies can recognize stimuli that they have encountered before? The most common method has been the habituation–dishabituation procedure. With this procedure, as you may recall, we examine the infant's response to a repeated stimulus; a decline in response as the stimulus becomes familiar is referred to as *habituation*. Such a decline in interest is possible only if the infant can recognize the repeated stimulus as something that

Recognition memory
The realization that some perceptually present stimulus or event has been encountered before.

Recall memory
The retrieval of some past stimulus or event that is not perceptually present.

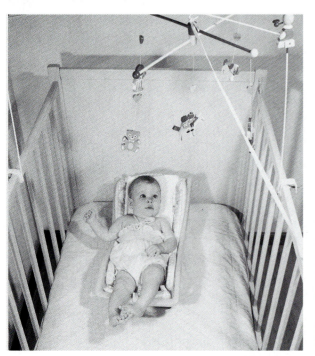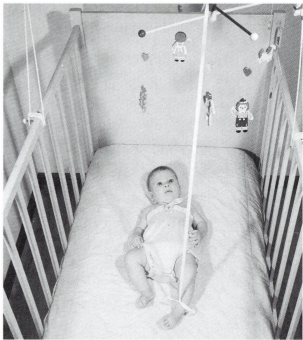

Figure 9.2

An experimental arrangement for studying infants' ability to learn and remember. When the ribbon is attached to the baby's ankle (as in the right-hand photo), kicking the leg makes the mobile above the crib move. Learning is shown by increased kicking whenever the ribbon is attached and the mobile is present. These photos were made available by Dr. C. K. Rovee-Collier.

has been experienced previously; if there were no such memory, every appearance of the stimulus would be experienced as a novel event. Similarly, dishabituation, or the recovery of response when the stimulus changes, can occur only if the infant is able to compare the new stimulus to some memory of the original.

Classical (or respondent) conditioning and operant conditioning have also been used to explore infant memory. As noted in Chapter 2, learning refers to the lasting effects of experience on behavior, and thus any demonstration of learning necessarily tells us something about memory as well.

One way in which operant conditioning has been employed to study infant memory is pictured in Figure 9.2. As the figure shows, the ribbon linking ankle and mobile confers a potential power on the infant—kicking the ankle will make the mobile jump. Infants as young as 2 months can learn this relation; the rate of kicking increases when the kicking pays off in the reinforcement of a dancing mobile (Rovee-Collier, 1987). Once this response has been established, various modifications can be introduced to probe the infant's memory. We can test for recognition of the training mobile, for example, by comparing response to a novel mobile with response to the familiar one. Or we can test the duration of the memory by seeing how the infant responds a day or a week or a month after the original conditioning.

Memory in Newborns   A number of questions about infant memory have been explored with these procedures. A natural first question is how early in life babies can remember. The answer seems clear—from birth (or possibly even earlier—

recall the suggestion in Chapter 7 that babies may remember some events that they experienced prenatally). Habituation studies are one basis for this conclusion. Habituation is not easy to demonstrate in newborns, and for years infant researchers disagreed about whether such early habituation was possible (Slater, 1995). It now seems clear, however, that a newborn infant—given optimal circumstances—can show habituation across a range of modalities: visual (Slater et al., 1991), auditory (Zelazo, Weiss, & Tarquino, 1991), and tactile (Kisilevsky & Muir, 1984). Thus newborns do possess some degree of recognition memory.

Conditioning studies are a further source of evidence for neonatal memory. As with habituation, conditioning can be difficult to produce in very young infants, and the question of whether newborns can be conditioned was a topic of debate for many years. Today, however, most researchers agree that both classical and operant conditioning are possible from birth (Lipsitt, 1990). We have already seen some examples of the latter. Recall the finding that newborns prefer a stimulus to which they have been exposed prenatally (DeCasper & Fifer, 1980). The newborns showed this preference by adjusting their sucking to produce the desired stimulus—for example, their own mothers' voices. Adjusting behavior to obtain reinforcement is a form of operant conditioning.

An example of classical conditioning in newborns is provided by a study in which 1- and 2-day-old infants received a sucrose solution delivered to the lips (Blass, Ganchrow, & Steiner, 1984). The solution functioned as an unconditioned stimulus that elicited the unconditioned response of sucking. The conditioned stimulus consisted of the experimenter's stroking the baby's forehead immediately before delivery of the sucrose. After a few pairings of the stroking with the solution, the babies began to suck in response to the stroking alone—a clear indication that conditioning had occurred.

Developmental Changes   Although memory may be present from birth, newborns' and young infants' memories are not as powerful as those of older infants.

One of the most rewarding signs of infant memory is the baby's pleasure at recognizing his parents.

Developmental improvements of various sorts occur during the first year or so of life. One important change is in how long material can be retained. Most demonstrations of memory in newborns involve only a few seconds between presentation of a stimulus and the test for recognition of that stimulus. What such studies show, then, is very short-term memory. As infants develop, the length of time across which they can remember their experiences steadily increases, soon reaching impressive levels. By 5 months of age, babies can recognize a photo of a face, initially viewed for only 2 minutes, after a delay of 2 weeks (Fagan, 1973). With a more dynamic, moving stimulus, recognition has been demonstrated across a 3-month delay for babies who were only 3 months old at the time of initial exposure (Bahrick & Pickens, 1995). We should add, however, that even the newborn is not limited to very brief memories. Newborns can remember speech stimuli across a period of at least 24 hours (Swain, Zelazo, & Clifton, 1993). And the studies of memory for speech sounds experienced prenatally (DeCasper & Spence, 1991; see Chapter 7) have typically involved even longer intervals between the last prenatal exposure and the first postnatal test.

The mobile procedure shown in Figure 9.2 provides another approach to assessing the durability of infant memory. The question is how long babies can remember the association between kicking and the movement of the mobile. This procedure, too, reveals both impressive early capacity and developmental improvements in long-term memory with age (Rovee-Collier & Bhatt, 1993). Two-month-olds, for example, can remember the association for 3 days; by 3 months of age the span has stretched to 8 days; and by 6 months some retention is still evident 21 days after conditioning (Rovee-Collier & Shyi, 1992).

Memory is even better if the infant is given a brief reminder during the delay period. In a study by Sullivan (1982), the experimenter jiggled the mobile on the 13th day of the delay period while the infant simply watched. Infants given this reminder showed much more kicking on day 14 than did a control group that received no such help. Such priming of memory through a brief reencounter with the original experience is referred to as **reactivation**. Naturally occurring instances of reactivation may be a major way in which forgetting is prevented and memories are kept alive (Rovee-Collier & Hayne, 1987).

In addition to the duration of memory, another basic question about memory concerns what information is retained. Babies' habituation to a stimulus tells us that they recognize *some* aspect of the stimulus, but it does not tell us exactly what they are remembering. This dimension of memory also shows developmental improvements across infancy. Older infants can remember both more information and more complex information than younger infants (Olson & Sherman, 1983). Older infants can also abstract and remember general categories of information and not just specific stimuli (Mandler, 1998). In one study, for example, 12- to 24-month-old infants were shown a series of pictures of various kinds of food (bread, hot dogs, salami, and so on). The infants were then given a choice of looking at either of two stimuli: a previously unseen item from the food category (an apple), or an item from a new category (a chair). Infants looked longer at the chair than at the apple, demonstrating that they recognized not just specific foods, but the general category of food, and that they found a new category more interesting than a familiar one (Ross, 1980).

Even earlier success has been demonstrated for other, perceptually simpler kinds of categorical distinctions. By 4 months, for example, infants shown a series of dog pictures look more at a picture of a bird than they do at one of another dog (Quinn & Eimas, 1996; we should add, however, that telling dogs and cats apart is

Reactivation
The preservation of the memory for an event through reencounter with at least some portion of the event in the interval between initial experience and memory test.

harder at this age). Infants as young as 3 months can form simple categories based on color or shape (Hayne, 1996).

The ability to move beyond specific experiences to abstract more general categories is an essential component in our attempts to make sense of the world. The studies just reviewed suggest that this ability emerges very early.

Recall Memory

The research that we have described indicates clearly that recognition memory is present from birth. But what about recall? Can infants not only recognize familiar stimuli or events, but also actively call such stimuli or events to mind?

Recall memory is considerably more difficult to study in infancy than is recognition memory, because infants cannot produce the responses that are used to study recall in older individuals (such as verbal reports or drawing). There is, in fact, no clear agreement on exactly what a young infant might do that would demonstrate recall and thus no agreement on exactly when recall emerges. It does seem clear that recall is present by the end of infancy, as many of the behaviors from Piaget's sensorimotor substage 6 imply. An infant could not show deferred imitation, for example, without the ability to recall a model from the past, nor could she produce words appropriately without some capacity for recall.

As we saw in our discussions of Piagetian research in Chapter 8, recent evidence suggests that simple forms of recall emerge earlier than Piaget proposed (Mandler, 1990). The infant's search for vanished objects is one kind of evidence. By the end of the first year most infants can find objects that are hidden in a single location (Piaget's substage 4 of object permanence). Most have also learned the permanent locations for familiar and valued objects, such as the cupboard in which a favorite cereal is kept (Ashmead & Perlmutter, 1980). The ability to find an object that one has not seen for days would certainly seem to imply some capacity for recall.

Studies of deferred imitation provide further evidence for recall memory in infancy. These studies indicate that the capacity to reproduce a model from the past emerges earlier than Piaget believed. By 9 months of age infants can imitate a novel action that they viewed a full 24 hours earlier (Meltzoff, 1988b). By 14 months the retention span has stretched to one week (Meltzoff, 1988a).

Infants can remember and imitate not only isolated behaviors, but also simple sequences of action. Thirteen-month-olds, for example, can reproduce three-action sequences for such events as giving a teddy bear a bath (first place in tub, then wash with sponge, then dry with towel) or constructing a simple rattle (place ball in large cup, invert small cup into large, shake) (Bauer & Mandler, 1992). By 24 months children can remember sequences of five actions (Bauer & Travis, 1993), and by 30 months children can retain as many as eight separate steps (Bauer & Fivush, 1992). Memory for the order in which events occur is an important form of knowledge to which we will return shortly. These studies indicate that such memory has its origins in infancy.

We saw that infants' ability to recognize familiar stimuli may eventually extend across a considerable period of time. The same appears to be true of early recall. Some memory for three-action sequences of the sort just described has been demonstrated after 8 months for infants who were only 16 months old at the time that they first learned the behaviors (Bauer, Hertsgaard, & Dow, 1994). Even more impressive long-term memory is suggested in a study by McDonough and Mandler (1994). These researchers first taught their 11-month-old participants to imitate simple sequences of actions, as in the teddy bear and rattle tasks described earlier. When the infants were retested as 23-month-olds, they showed some ability to reproduce

Memory for the order of events emerges early in life. Even 1-year-olds can remember simple sequences, such as the order to follow in giving a doll a bath.

individual actions that they had seen modeled a full year earlier! The question of the persistence of infant memories is another topic to which we will return shortly.

✓ To Recap...

Infants can remember from birth. Habituation, classical conditioning, and operant conditioning all imply memory, and all have been demonstrated in newborn babies. With development, the span of time across which the infant can retain material increases, as do the amount and the complexity of the material that can be retained.

Habituation and conditioning studies demonstrate recognition memory. Recall memory is more difficult to study in infancy, but recent research suggests that simple forms of recall may emerge by the end of the first year. Infants' ability to search for vanished objects provides one kind of evidence for this conclusion. Imitation of models from the past provides another.

Memory in Older Children

Beyond infancy, most studies of how children remember have concentrated on various forms of recall. The most general change in this type of memory is an obvious one: Older children remember better than younger children. This fact was undoubtedly apparent to parents and teachers long before there was research to verify it. It has also long been apparent to test makers. All the IQ tests described in Chapter 10 include memory as one of their components. On the average, the older the child, the better the performance on such memory measures.

Developmental improvements in memory are of considerable practical importance, because they influence what parents and teachers expect of children and how they treat children. The 10-year-old can be entrusted with a string of verbal instructions that would overtax the memory of a 4-year-old. Such improvements are also of theoretical interest. How can we explain the fact that older children remember better than younger ones? Several kinds of explanation have been offered, and each seems to capture part of the basis for developmental change. Here we consider three possible contributors to the developmental improvement in memory: greater use of mnemonic strategies, greater knowledge about memory, and more powerful cognitive structures.

The Role of Strategies

Imagine that you are confronted with the following task. A list of words, such as that in Table 9.1, is presented to you at the rate of one every 5 seconds. There is a 30-second delay following the last word, and you must then recall as many of the words as possible. How might you proceed?

Adults faced with such a task are likely to do any of a variety of things to help themselves remember. They may say the words over and over again as the list is presented and during the delay period. They may seek to make the list more memorable by grouping the words into categories—noting, for example, that several of the items name foods and several others name animals. Or they may attempt to create associations among the words by imagining a scenario in which several of the words are linked—for example, a mental image of a cow eating a banana while riding a bicycle.

The approaches just sketched are examples of **mnemonic strategies**. A mnemonic strategy is any technique that people use in an attempt to help them-

Mnemonic strategies
Techniques (such as rehearsal or organization) that people use in an attempt to remember something.

selves remember something. The examples just given correspond, in fact, to three of the most often studied strategies in research on memory: *rehearsal* of the items to be recalled (the saying-over-and-over technique), *organization* of the items into conceptual categories (grouping into foods, animals, and so on), and *elaboration* of the items by linkage in some more general image or story (the picture of the cow on the bicycle).

Developmental Changes in Strategy Use
An increase in the tendency to use strategies is one important source of the improvements in memory that come with age. Dozens of studies have demonstrated that older children are more likely than younger children to generate and employ mnemonic strategies (Bjorklund, 1990; Schneider & Bjorklund, 1998). This finding holds for the three strategies just mentioned—rehearsal (Flavell, Beach, & Chinsky, 1966), organization (Hasselhorn, 1992), and elaboration (Kee & Guttentag, 1994). It also holds for other mnemonic strategies that develop across childhood—for example, the ability to direct one's attention and effort in optimal ways, such as by attending to central rather than irrelevant information (Miller, 1990) or by concentrating on difficult rather than easy items (Dufresne & Kobasigawa, 1989).

Do strategies work? The answer in general is yes. Children who use strategies show better recall than children who do not. Children do not always benefit from their initial attempts to employ a strategy, perhaps because executing a new strategy places too great a demand on their limited information-processing resources. This failure of a recently developed strategy to facilitate recall is labeled a **utilization deficiency** (Bjorklund & Coyle, 1995; Miller & Seier, 1994). Usually, however, even young children derive some benefit from the use of strategies; their main problem is simply that they do not generate strategies in the first place. Before about age 5 or 6, it apparently simply does not occur to children that it makes sense to *do* something to help themselves remember. This failure to generate strategies spontaneously, even though the child is capable of executing and benefiting from a strategy, is referred to as a **production deficiency** (Flavell, 1970).

Strategies increase not only in frequency but also in complexity as children get older. Rehearsal is a relatively simple strategy and is, in fact, one of the first to emerge, typically appearing at about age 6 or 7. Organization appears somewhat later, and elaboration later still. There are also developmental changes in complexity within a particular strategy. Younger children's rehearsal efforts, for example, tend to be limited to naming each item as it appears. Older children are more likely to repeat larger chunks of the list each time ("cow," "cow-tree," "cow-tree-banana," and so on) (Ornstein, Naus, & Liberty, 1975). In general, older children can generate more complex strategies than can younger children, they are better able to match particular strategy to particular task, and they are more skilled at executing their strategies—all of which contributes to their superior memory performance.

We noted that on many memory tasks children younger than 5 or 6 do not display strategies. Does this mean that the young child is totally incapable of generating a mnemonic strategy? Not at all. If the task is sufficiently simplified, even quite young children may show rudimentary strategies. In one study, 3-year-olds played a game in which they had to keep track of a toy dog that had been hidden under one of several cups. During the delay between hiding and retrieval, many of the children sat with their eyes glued to the critical cup and a finger planted firmly on it (Wellman, Ritter, & Flavell, 1975). These are simple strategies, to be sure, but they *are* strategies, and they are available to even young children. Furthermore, they work. Children who produced such strategies showed better recall than children

Table 9.1
Items to Be Recalled on a Short-Term Memory Test

Cow	Truck
Tree	Hat
Banana	Bear
Bicycle	Apple
Dog	Flag
Orange	Horse

Utilization deficiency
The failure of a recently developed mnemonic strategy to facilitate recall.

Production deficiency
The failure to generate a mnemonic strategy spontaneously.

who did not. Other studies using a similar hide-and-seek procedure have demonstrated that children as young as 18 to 24 months can produce and benefit from simple strategies (Wellman, 1988). The general conclusion to be drawn from such research should sound familiar from the discussion of preschoolers' strengths in Chapter 8. Young children are by no means as competent as older children—in memory or in logical reasoning. When tested in simple and familiar contexts, however, they can sometimes show surprising abilities.

Cross-Cultural Studies of Strategy Use

Just as the specific context can affect what we conclude about differences between younger and older children, context can also be important when we compare children from different cultures. Children from non-Western cultures often do not perform well on list-learning tasks of the sort given in Table 9.1. Such children are less likely than their Western peers to generate effective mnemonic strategies on such tasks, and thus less likely to be successful in their recall efforts (Rogoff & Mistry, 1990).

Why might there be this cultural difference in strategy use? One factor, which we consider more fully in Chapter 10, is schooling. One of the most common activities in Western schools is committing information to memory—often information that (at least from the student's perspective) may seem disconnected and arbitrary. This experience instills skills that serve schooled children well when they respond to typical laboratory measures of memory, which, as we have seen, often involve somewhat arbitrary and context-free material. Children from non-Western cultures who have not been to school, or whose school experiences have not stressed such decontextualized learning, are at a relative disadvantage on such measures.

This analysis suggests that apparent cultural differences in mnemonic ability might disappear if we were to examine children's performance in more natural and familiar contexts. Such seems to be the case. In one study, for example, 9-year-old Guatemalan Mayan children were asked to reproduce the placement of 20 familiar objects that they had viewed within a scale model of a Guatemalan terrain (see Figure 9.3). Memory for spatial locations is a natural development in any culture, and the children showed impressive levels of recall; indeed, their performance was slightly better than that of a sample of American 9-year-olds who responded to a similar task using stimuli drawn from their culture (Rogoff & Waddell, 1982).

Many of the American children, it is interesting to note, were apparently hampered by an attempt to rehearse the information prior to the recall test. Although rehearsal is often a helpful strategy, it is not an optimal approach to problems of spatial memory. The Guatemalan children did not bring this bias to the task—and hence may have been quicker to hit on a more appropriate strategy.

Variability in Strategy Use

Although new and more complex strategies emerge with development, this does not mean that earlier strategies necessarily disappear. One interesting finding from recent memory research concerns the surprising variability in children's strategy use. Rather than employ a single preferred strategy, many children try out and combine several different approaches, sometimes generating as many as three or four strategies even within a single trial (Coyle & Bjorklund, 1997). A particular child, for example, might not only rehearse the items to be remembered, but also name the categories to which they belong and perhaps sort them into groups as well.

Why should children be so variable in their approach to memory tasks? It has been argued that such variability is adaptive, in that it provides experience from which children can eventually determine the optimal strategy for a particular task.

Figure 9.3
Mayan child and tester in the Rogoff and Waddell study of spatial memory. The child's task was to place the objects in their original positions in the panorama. From *Apprenticeship in Thinking* (p. 49) by B. Rogoff, 1990, New York: Oxford University Press. Copyright © 1990 by Oxford University Press. Reprinted by permission.

According to this view, there is a kind of survival of the fittest with respect to mnemonic strategies, with experience operating to select the most effective techniques from the many possibilities that children initially explore. We return to this argument later in the chapter.

Applications
Learning to Study

Just as strategies may begin to develop earlier than experts once thought, so they may continue to develop beyond the grade-school years that have been the focus of most memory research. Complex mnemonic strategies continue to be refined well into adolescence and even adulthood (Pressley, Levin, & Bryant, 1983). Of particular interest to both researchers and teachers have been the various **study strategies** that students develop to cope with school material. Study strategies include specific techniques, such as note taking and outlining. They also include more general methods, such as allocation of study time to important or not-yet-mastered material and self-testing to determine what has been learned and what needs to be studied further.

As with strategies in general, study strategies improve with age. As children develop, the frequency with which they use such techniques increases, as does the complexity of the strategies they generate. And, again as with strategies in general,

Study strategies
Mnemonic strategies (such as outlining and note taking) that students use in an attempt to remember school material.

Mnemonic strategies are not limited to laboratory settings. Study strategies can help to ensure that important material is remembered.

study strategies are beneficial. Research reveals a clear relation between the use of appropriate study techniques and the quality of the child's learning (Paris & Oka, 1986; Pressley, Forrest-Pressley, & Elliot-Faust, 1988).

Clearly, the work on study strategies is not only of scientific interest; it also speaks to important applied questions concerning the bases for children's academic performance. If we can identify and help children whose study strategies are poor, then perhaps we can improve their chances of success in school. More generally, if we can determine the kinds of experiences that nurture the development of good study skills, then perhaps we can alter children's environments in ways that will lead to general improvements in academic performance.

In recent years a number of research programs have addressed issues of this sort. Different researchers have taken different directions. Some have focused on the naturally occurring sources for study skills, looking in particular at what teachers or parents do to promote such behaviors. Observations of classrooms, for example (Moely et al., 1986; Moely, Santulli, & Obach, 1995), reveal that teachers vary considerably in the extent to which they attempt to teach study strategies, with variations as well across different grade levels and subject matters (math, for example, may be especially likely to elicit such instruction). Such studies also reveal cultural differences: German second and third graders are more likely to use organizational strategies for recall than are their counterparts in the United States, a difference that has roots both in the greater emphasis on such skills in German classrooms and in the greater concern with strategy instruction by German parents (Carr et al., 1989; Kurtz et al., 1990).

Other researchers have devised experimental interventions whose goal is to improve children's study skills (Brown & Campione, 1990; Pressley et al., 1988). One promising approach, for example, is labeled *reciprocal teaching*. As the name suggests, the emphasis in reciprocal teaching is on providing children experience with two roles: not only as students (which, of course, is their usual role) but also as teachers. By alternating roles with a supportive adult as they work together on a task, students have opportunities both to observe the modeling of adaptive study skills and to practice those skills themselves.

The particular strategies that are taught depend on the topic and the child's level of development. In an application of this approach to reading, for example, the emphasis was on strategies such as summarizing important points and self-testing to monitor understanding (Brown, Palincsar, & Armbruster, 1984). Seventh-graders who participated in a series of such reciprocal teaching sessions showed marked gains in both strategy use and reading comprehension. More generally, benefits from reciprocal teaching have been demonstrated across a range of study strategies and school content areas (Palincsar, 1992).

Reciprocal teaching is just one of a number of research-based programs that have proved helpful in classroom settings (Renninger, 1998). Such applications are, to be sure, far from complete: We still have much to learn about the determinants of study strategies, and translation of research findings to the complex world of the classroom is never an easy task. Nevertheless, the work on study strategies provides an encouraging illustration of how basic science can inform educational practice.

Research on strategies illustrates one important theme of the information-processing approach (Siegler, 1998). The child's—and, for that matter, the adult's—information-processing capacities are always limited. Only a limited amount of information can fit in short-term memory, for example, and this information typically can be held only briefly. If new information can be rehearsed, however, its lifetime can be extended considerably. If the child can think in terms of categories and not merely in terms of individual items, then much more can be retained. Much of development consists of the creation of techniques to overcome information-processing limitations and thereby increase the power of the cognitive system. Mnemonic strategies are a prime example of such techniques.

The Role of Metamemory

Although strategies are an important source of developmental improvements in memory, they are not the only contributor. What children know about memory also changes with age, and these changes in knowledge contribute to changes in memory.

Metamemory refers to knowledge about memory. It includes knowledge about memory in general—for example, the fact that recognition tasks are easier than recall tasks or that a short list of items is easier to memorize than a long list. It also includes knowledge about one's own memory—for example, the ability to judge whether one has studied an assignment long enough to do well on an exam.

Metamemory
Knowledge about memory.

Developmental Changes in Metamemory

Psychologists have been interested in metamemory for two general reasons. First, it is an important outcome of the child's cognitive development. Traditionally, research on cognitive development has concentrated on the child's understanding of external stimuli and events—in some cases physical stimuli (as in Piaget's conservation tasks) and in some cases social ones (as in studies of social cognition). Children's thinking is not limited to external stimuli, however; it also encompasses the internal, mental world. Flavell (1971) was among the first child psychologists to focus explicitly on "thinking about thinking," and he coined the term *metacognition* to refer to thoughts that have mental or psychological phenomena as their target. With metamemory, the focus is on thoughts about memory.

Children's thinking about memory changes in a variety of ways as they develop. Here we note just a few examples. A basic question is whether the child realizes that there is such a thing as memory. Even young children show some such knowledge. They may behave differently, for example, when told to remember something than when told simply to look, thus demonstrating some awareness that remembering may require special cognitive activities (Baker-Ward, Ornstein, & Holden, 1984). They also have some understanding of the relative difficulty of different memory tasks. By age 5 or 6, most children realize that familiar items are easier to remember than unfamiliar ones (Kreutzer, Leonard, & Flavell, 1975), that short lists are easier to learn than long ones (Wellman, 1977), that recognition is easier than recall (Speer & Flavell, 1979), and that forgetting becomes more likely over time (Lyon & Flavell, 1993).

In other respects, however, young children's metamemory is limited. They do not always behave differently when faced with an explicit request to remember (Appel et al., 1972). They do not yet understand many phenomena of memory, such as the fact that related items are easier to recall than unrelated ones (Kreutzer et al., 1975) or that remembering the gist of a story is easier than remembering the exact words (Kurtz & Borkowski, 1987). And their assessment of their own mnemonic abilities is far too optimistic. In one study, for example, over half of the preschool and kindergarten participants predicted that they would be able to recall all 10 items from a list of 10, a performance that no child in fact came close to achieving (Flavell, Friedrichs, & Hoyt, 1970). Furthermore, young children do not adjust their expectations readily in response to feedback; even after recalling only

2 or 3 items on one trial, they may blithely assert that they will get all 10 on the next attempt (Yussen & Levy, 1975). Older children are both more modest and more realistic in assessing their own memories (Schneider & Pressley, 1989).

Effects of Metamemory on Memory Performance The second general reason for interest in metamemory concerns its possible contribution to developmental changes in memory performance. We stated the argument at the beginning of this section. Older children know more about memory than do younger children; older children also remember better than do younger children. It is easy to see how these two facts might be related. Knowledge of the demands of different sorts of memory tasks should help the child select the best strategy for remembering. Knowledge of one's own memory should be important in deciding such things as how to allocate attention and what material to study further.

Obvious though the knowledge-behavior relationship seems, demonstrating it empirically has proved surprisingly difficult. Many early studies that assessed both metamemory and memory performance (usually focusing on the child's use of strategies) reported only modest correlations at best between the two (Cavanaugh & Perlmutter, 1982). Thus, the knowledge that children can demonstrate about memory does not always relate clearly to how they perform on memory tasks. The following quotation, taken from one of the first metamemory studies, suggests a possible reason for this discrepancy. Here, a little girl describes a wonderfully complex procedure for memorizing phone numbers (her metaknowledge), but then suggests at the end that her actual behavior might be quite different.

> *Say the number is 633–8854. Then what I'd do is—say that my number is 633, so I won't have to remember that, really. And then I would think now I've got to remember 88. Now I'm 8 years old, so I can remember, say my age two times. Then I say how old my brother is, and how old he was last year. And that's how I'd usually remember that phone number. [Is that how you would most often remember a phone number?] Well, usually I write it down. (Kreutzer et al., 1975, p. 11)*

Despite the difficulty in establishing knowledge-behavior links, most researchers remain convinced that the growth of metamemory is one source of developmental improvement in memory. It is simply hard to believe that what children know does not exert an important influence on how they behave. And indeed, more recent studies of the issue have been more successful than earlier work at identifying relations between knowledge and behavior (Fabricius & Cavalier, 1989; Melot & Corroyer, 1992). One promising approach has been to train children in various forms of metamemory and then look for possible effects on subsequent memory performance (Ghatala et al., 1985; Pressley, Borkowski, & O'Sullivan, 1985). Such training does in fact improve memory.

Like the work on mnemonic strategies, research such as this has applied as well as theoretical implications. For example, it may prove possible to help children with memory problems by teaching them about memory itself. Indeed, some of the most successful of the strategy training programs discussed earlier included instruction in metamemory. Apparently, children are most likely to benefit from memory training if they learn not only what to do, but also why to do it.

The studies of metamemory illustrate a second general theme of the information-processing approach. We have stressed the information-processing theorist's emphasis on the many different processes that go into intelligent behavior. These processes do not occur in isolation, however, nor do they occur without direction. The child must somehow select and coordinate specific cognitive activities, and a full model of intelligence must explain how this selection and coordination occur. The case of mnemonic strategies provides a good illustration. A strategy such as rehearsal does not simply happen. Rather, other cognitive processes must decide that rehearsal is an appropriate strategy, monitor its execution, and evaluate its success. In short, some sort of "executive" must control the more specific forms of information processing. Work on metamemory is directed toward one sort of executive control—the child's knowledge of memory as a determinant of the ways in which he goes about remembering.

The Role of Knowledge

Our final explanation for developmental improvements in memory is perhaps the most straightforward. It concerns the effects of knowledge on memory. Memory and knowledge are in fact closely related. What we know about a topic is an important determinant of how well we learn and remember information about that topic. Older children generally know more about all sorts of things than do younger children, and thus older children generally remember better than do younger children.

Studies that have attempted to specify the ways in which knowledge affects memory have taken a variety of directions. We discuss such research under three overlapping headings: constructive memory, expertise, and scripts.

Constructive Memory The notion of constructive memory is most easily introduced through example. Table 9.2 provides an example used in research with grade-school children. The children were first read the story and then asked the eight questions listed beneath it.

Any reader is likely to spot a difference between the first four questions and the last four. The first four tap verbatim memory for information that was given directly in the story. The last four, however, concern information that was never explicitly provided. We are never told, for example, that Linda likes to take care of animals. Yet any adult reader of the story knows that she does. And so, it turns out, do most young children.

The ability to answer questions 5 through 8 is a function of constructive memory. **Constructive memory** refers to the ways in which people's general knowledge system interprets the information they take in and thus affects what they remember.

> **Constructive memory**
> Effects of the general knowledge system on how information is interpreted and thus remembered.

Table 9.2
Story Used in Study of Constructive Memory with Children

Linda was playing with her new doll in front of her big red house. Suddenly she heard a strange sound coming from under the porch. It was the flapping of wings. Linda wanted to help so much, but she did not know what to do. She ran inside the house and grabbed a shoe box from the closet. Then Linda looked inside her desk until she found eight sheets of yellow paper. She cut the paper into little pieces and put them in the bottom of the box. Linda gently picked up the helpless creature and took it with her. Her teacher knew what to do.

1. Was Linda's doll new?
2. Did Linda grab a match box?
3. Was the strange sound coming from under the porch?
4. Was Linda playing behind her house?
5. Did Linda like to take care of animals?
6. Did Linda take what she found to the police station?
7. Did Linda find a frog?
8. Did Linda use a pair of scissors?

Source: From "Integration and Inference in Children's Comprehension and Memory" by S. G. Paris, 1975. In F. Restle, R. Shiffrin, J. Castellan, H. Lindman, and D. Pisoni (Eds.), *Cognitive Theory*, Vol. 1 (p. 233), Mahwah, NJ: Erlbaum. Copyright © 1975 by Lawrence Erlbaum Associates. Reprinted by permission.

The basic idea is that we do not simply record memories as a tape recorder would. Memory always involves acting on and integrating new experiences in light of what we already know—it always involves an attempt to *understand*, not merely record. In our attempt to understand, we continually draw inferences and go beyond the information given. The eventual memory is therefore truly a construction, and not merely a direct duplication of experience. And this is why we, and the 6-year-old, can come away from the story in Table 9.2 knowing that Linda likes to take care of animals.

Let us consider another example. Eleven-year-olds were read sentences such as "His mother baked a cake" and "Her friend swept the kitchen floor" (Paris & Lindauer, 1976). Later they were asked to recall the sentences. Half the children were given retrieval cues—hints that might help them remember. The retrieval cues were the names of the instruments implied by the sentences—"oven" for the sentence about baking, "broom" for the sentence about sweeping, and so on. Children given the cues recalled more than children who received no such help. But why should such cues be helpful? The sentences, after all, did not contain the words *oven* and *broom*. The cues were helpful because the children had gone beyond the information given in the sentences to fill in the missing elements. Having already inferred what the instrument must be, they were easily able to use "oven" or "broom" as a cue to what they had actually heard. Indeed, these implicit cues were just as effective as explicit cues drawn directly from the sentences ("cake," "floor," and so on).

It seems clear that memory is constructive from early in life. At every age, children filter new experiences through their existing knowledge systems, and what they ultimately remember depends on how they interpret experiences. Constructive memory does change across childhood, however, and the changes are of two general sorts.

First, with increased age memory becomes even more constructive, as children become increasingly active in processing information and increasingly likely to draw inferences that allow them to go beyond the literal input. In the retrieval-cues study described, for example, 7- and 9-year-olds showed little benefit from the implicit cues that were so helpful for 11-year-olds. Although certainly capable of inferring "oven" from "baked a cake," the younger children apparently did not spontaneously make such inferences. Second, with increased age the complexity of the inferences that children can draw increases as their cognitive abilities increase. In the injured-bird story, for example, even most 5-year-olds could answer questions 7 and 8. Questions 5 and 6, however, require a somewhat higher-order inference and hence were solved at a slightly later age.

Another example of constructive memory will help to make one final point. The example comes from Piaget's only research on memory. Piaget and Inhelder (1973) presented 3- to 8-year-old children with the stimulus shown in Figure 9.4. The sticks in the figure constitute a *seriated array*—that is, an array in which the stimuli are perfectly ordered along some quantitative dimension, in this case length. As we saw in Chapter 8, Piaget's previous research had established that an understanding of seriation is a concrete operational achievement, typically coming at age 6 or 7.

One week after they had seen the sticks, the children were asked to draw what they had seen. Figure 4.2*b* shows the kinds of drawings that the youngest children produced. It can be seen that the children's memories were not only wrong but systematically wrong. Their drawings, in fact, corresponded exactly to the various errors that preoperational children make in attempting to solve the seriation task. Piaget's interpretation was that the children assimilated the input to their preoperational understanding of seriation. In so doing, they reworked and distorted the

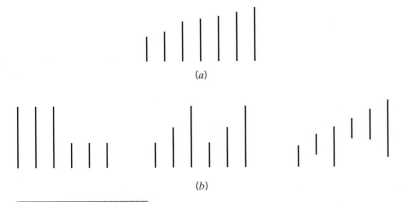

Figure 9.4

Stimulus and typical responses in Piaget and Inhelder's study of constructive memory: (*a*) the seriated array presented to the children and (*b*) what 4- and 5-year-olds remembered a week later. The memory distortions result from the young child's preoperational assimilation of the stimulus.

experience. The eventual memory thus reflected their understanding, and not simply the literal stimulus.

The point that the Piagetian research makes is that constructive memory can operate in a negative as well as a positive direction. When some new experience is too advanced for the child, the child's memory of the experience is likely to be simplified and perhaps even distorted. Other factors besides cognitive level can sometimes result in such "constructive" distortions. It has been shown, for example, that children's beliefs about gender differences may influence how they process information about males and females. Children who viewed pictures in which gender-stereotypic activities were reversed (e.g., a girl sawing and a boy playing with dolls) showed a tendency on a later memory test to "correct" these images, reporting, for example, that it was the boy who did the sawing (Martin & Halverson, 1983). Similarly, children's beliefs about different ethnic groups can influence what they remember about members of those groups (Bigler & Liben, 1993), just as their stereotypes about old age can color their memories for particular elderly individuals (Davidson, Cameron, & Jergovic, 1995).

The constructive nature of memory, then, is a mixed blessing. In general, constructive memory is a positive force, helping us understand experience more adaptively. But in particular instances, constructive memory can distort and mislead. In the next section, we discuss one situation in which it may be essential to know how accurate children's memories are.

Applications
Children's Eyewitness Testimony

It has been estimated that at least 100,000 children testify in court cases in the United States every year (Ceci & Bruck, 1995). This figure does not include the much larger number of instances in which children provide depositions or other kinds of evidence outside court. The cases in which children testify span a range of topics, but the most frequent category among criminal trials, accounting for about

13,000 cases each year, is child sexual abuse. In most instances of alleged abuse the child witness is also the target of the abuse. In many, the child is the only witness.

Often, the uncertain memories of young children are simply an interesting and perhaps even charming phenomenon. As the preceding paragraph illustrates, however, there are times when it is critically important to know how accurately children can recount their experiences. Can the testimony of a young child be trusted? Should such testimony be admissible in court?

In recent years, a number of researchers have attempted to provide evidence that speaks directly to this important question (Bottoms & Goodman, 1996; Ceci & Bruck, 1993, 1995, 1998). These researchers face an obvious challenge. Experiences of abuse are typically highly traumatic; they may continue for extended periods of time; and they involve the child as a participant and not merely as a bystander. Furthermore, what children say about abuse may involve more than simply what they remember. Complex social and emotional factors may be important, such as the child's guilt about being a participant or reluctance to implicate a parent or friend. Questioning by a parent or authority figure may lead the child to particular responses, especially if questioners believe that they already know the truth or if, as advocates within the court system, they have an interest in a particular outcome. All these characteristics make memory for abuse different from the kinds of memory that psychologists usually study—or that they *can* easily study in an ethically acceptable way.

Researchers have tried in various ways to discover or devise memory tests that bear some similarity to the abuse situation. Some have created experimental settings that reproduce some elements of the real-life situations of interest—for example, a Simon Says game in which child and experimenter touch parts of each other's bodies (Ceci, Leichtman, & White, in press). Others have focused on memory for naturally occurring traumatic experiences—for example, going to the dentist (Peters, 1991), receiving an injection (Goodman et al., 1991), or undergoing urinary catheterization (Goodman & Quas, 1997). Although such experiences can hardly equal the trauma of abuse, they do capture some of its characteristics.

In some studies, researchers have also attempted to simulate the types of questioning that suspected victims of abuse must undergo. A child may be questioned several times across a period of weeks, for example, or the interviewer may include some deliberately leading questions in an attempt to determine how suggestible the child is. Children may be told to "keep a secret" about what happened to them during the experimental session (Bottoms et al., 1990), or a police officer rather than research assistant may do the questioning (Tobey & Goodman, 1992).

Such studies suggest several conclusions about children as witnesses (Ceci & Bruck, 1995, 1998; Goodman & Tobey, 1994). First, research verifies that recall memory improves with age and that older children typically report more of their experiences than do younger children. The memories of 3-year-olds (the youngest age group tested in such research) are especially shaky. Second, in at least some cases, young children are more suggestible than are older children or adults—that is, they are more likely to be influenced by leading questions from an adult authority figure. These findings indicate the need for caution in accepting the reports of young children who have undergone repeated and leading questioning, as is often true in investigations of suspected abuse. On the other hand, in many studies, memory differences between children and adults are not very great. Furthermore, the memory problems that children do show are mainly errors of omission rather than of commission—that is, children are more likely to fail to report certain details than they are to introduce false information. This finding suggests that any clearly spontaneous mentions of abuse by children should be taken very seriously.

Having offered these conclusions, we should add that there remains much controversy about exactly what the research shows and what the implications are for children's legal testimony. The issue of suggestibility is especially controversial. It is clear—not only from laboratory studies but from court cases—that young children are sometimes suggestible, and, of course, even one false report may be devastating for the individual involved. On the other hand, there is also evidence that specific questioning may be necessary to elicit certain kinds of information from children—in particular, information about genital touch (Saywitz et al., 1991). Striking the right balance between helpful elicitation and misleading directiveness is clearly a very difficult task. Fortunately, one point on which all researchers agree is that more study is necessary, and the topic of eyewitness memory is currently the focus of an extraordinarily active research effort. Among the topics being explored in this research is the issue of how best to question children in court—for example, the possibility of obtaining testimony via videotape or closed-circuit television. Testifying in court can add to the trauma of an already traumatic situation (Goodman et al., 1992), and it is therefore important to devise procedures that can both maximize accuracy and minimize further stress.

Expertise   Like constructive memory, expertise is easiest to introduce through example. Imagine that you viewed each of the arrays pictured in Figure 9.5 for 10 seconds and then attempted to reproduce as much of each configuration as you could remember. If you do not play chess, the chances are that you would find the two arrays equally difficult to recall; both, after all, contain the same number and the same variety of stimuli. If you are a chess player, however, the top array would almost certainly be easier to remember. It would be easier because the pieces are in positions that might actually occur in a game, whereas those in the bottom array are randomly arranged. You could therefore draw on your knowledge of chess as you took in the information, stored it in memory, and retrieved it during reproduction.

Let us take our hypothetical study one step further. Imagine now that you are not only a chess player but an expert chess player. If so, several further predictions can be made. The odds are that your memory for the actual chess array will be even greater, that the discrepancy between actual and random will also be greater, and that you will easily surpass an average chess player, let alone a nonplayer, in your memory for the real positions.

As you may have guessed, the kinds of results just sketched are not purely hypothetical; such outcomes have emerged in a number of research projects. The examples pictured in Figure 9.5 are from a study by Schneider and associates (1993). As have several similar studies, this study provided support for each of the expectations just discussed: Expert chess players showed better memory for real chess positions than for random ones; chess experts remembered chess configurations better than did chess novices; and the expert–novice differences were especially marked when real positions were the target.

The Schneider et al. study demonstrates the effects of expertise on memory. The term **expertise** (also sometimes called *content knowledge* or the *knowledge base*) refers to organized factual knowledge about some content domain—that is, what we know about some subject. In contrast to the knowledge embodied in Piagetian stages, expertise is content specific. Someone's expertise may be high with regard to chess or dinosaurs or birds, but low when the topic turns to baseball or cooking or physics. When expertise is high, then memory also tends to be high. Variations in expertise contribute to variations in memory within individuals. Chess experts,

Expertise
Organized factual knowledge with respect to some content domain.

Figure 9.5
Meaningful and random configurations of chess pieces. Because they can make use of their knowledge of chess, chess players show better memory for the top array than for the bottom one. From "Chess Expertise and Memory for Chess Positions in Children and Adults" by W. Schneider, H. Gruber, A. Gold, and K. Opwis, 1993, *Journal of Experimental Child Psychology, 56*, p. 335. Copyright © 1993 by Academic Press. Reprinted by permission.

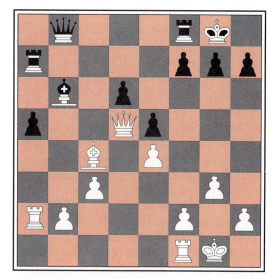

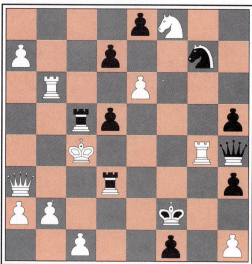

for example, show better memory for chess positions and other chess-related information than they do for most other topics. Variations in expertise also contribute to differences in memory across individuals. Thus, chess experts remember more about chess than do chess novices, just as experts in baseball or cooking or physics remember more about their specialty than do most people. Finally, variations in expertise contribute to the aspect of memory that is our main concern here: developmental changes in memory across the span of childhood. Older children possess more expertise for most topics than do younger children, and this greater expertise is one reason they remember more.

Expertise can affect memory in several ways. One way is through the form in which the knowledge is represented. In the case of chess, for example, experts store larger and more complex patterns of possible positions than do nonexperts, and this rich organizational structure helps them quickly make sense of positions that actually arise (Bedard & Chi, 1992). Another way is through effects on other contributors to memory, such as mnemonic strategies. Research has shown that children use strategies most effectively in content areas in which they are especially knowledgeable (Bjorklund, Muir-Broaddus, & Schneider 1990). Finally, perhaps the most general effect of expertise is on speed of processing. When knowledge about some domain is high, information relevant to that domain can be taken in and processed more rapidly, thus freeing cognitive resources for other activities, such as generating strategies (Bjorklund & Schneider, 1996).

An additional finding from the Schneider et al. study makes one more important point about expertise. In addition to the comparison of experts and novices, their study included an age dimension. Half the chess experts were adults and half were 10- to 13-year-old children; similarly, half the novices were adults and half were children. The design of the study (patterned after an earlier, classic study by Chi, 1978) therefore allowed the researchers to look separately at the effects of age and expertise, two factors that are usually closely linked and thus hard to pull apart. On memory tasks that did not involve chess, the adults, not surprisingly, demonstrated better memory than the children. On the memory-for-chess measure, however, expertise, not age, proved critical. Thus the 10-year-old experts outshone the adult novices in reproducing chess positions—despite the fact that the adults in general had greater memory spans.

The point that this study makes is that in at least some instances it is expertise, and not other factors associated with age, that is critical to memory. Other researchers have also found that young participants can equal or even outperform older ones when the content is something they know well. Among the content areas for which child superiority has been demonstrated are dinosaurs (Chi & Koeske, 1983), cartoon figures (Lindberg, 1980), baseball (Recht & Leslie, 1988), and soccer (Schneider, Korkel, & Weinert, 1987).

The work on expertise brings us to another general theme of the information-processing approach. The role of factual knowledge is heavily stressed in contemporary information-processing accounts of not only memory, but also reasoning and problem solving (Bjorklund, 1987; Chi, Glaser, & Farr, 1988). The argument is straightforward. The more children already know, the more they will understand of any new experience. The more they understand, the more they will remember. And the more they understand and remember, the more likely they are to reason and to solve problems in effective and adaptive ways.

Scripts   The main points of our discussion of knowledge and memory have been that knowledge affects memory and that as knowledge changes so does memory. Of course, as children develop, knowledge changes in many ways, including the buildup of expertise in numerous content areas. One such change, however, is worth singling out for special attention, both because of its general importance and because it has been the focus of much recent research on memory in early childhood. This is the development of scripts.

We can define a **script** formally as a representation of the typical sequence of actions and events in some familiar context. Less formally, a script refers to knowledge of the way things typically go. Each of us, for example, possesses a restaurant script, which represents the typical sequence of events in dining at a restaurant: entering the restaurant, sitting down, ordering the meal, eating, paying, and leaving. Our restaurant script, like scripts in general, is not tied to any specific example. Rather, it is a general representation that can apply to any number of specific restaurants.

Children also form scripts. Indeed, the emergence of scripts for a wide range of familiar experiences may be one of the most important achievements of early

Script
A representation of the typical sequence of actions and events in some familiar context.

Scripts are representations of the typical structure of familiar events. Even preschoolers may have learned a simple making-cookies script.

childhood cognitive development (Nelson, 1996). Among the scripts that have been studied are going to a restaurant, attending preschool, going to a birthday party, visiting a museum, eating dinner, making cookies, taking a bath, and going to bed at night (Farrar & Goodman, 1990; Nelson, 1986). Table 9.3 presents some examples of children's birthday-party scripts, elicited in response to the question, "What happens when you have a birthday party?" The numbers in parentheses indicate the age of the child. As you can see from the examples, scripts increase in both completeness and complexity as children develop.

Much of the interest in children's scripts concerns their effects on memory. Scripts are both product and process of the constructive nature of the memory system. They are product in the sense that they reflect the child's abstraction, from numerous specific experiences, of the essential general features of some familiar event. Scripts, as we have been stressing, are not reproductions of any specific episode; rather, they are constructions of what typically occurs. Once formed, however, scripts influence how future experiences are processed and remembered (Davidson, 1996). Children asked to remember stories based on familiar scripts show best recall for central events and poorer recall for details that are peripheral to the script (McCartney & Nelson, 1981). Stories that preserve the structure of familiar scripts are typically remembered better than stories that violate a script (Mandler, 1983), although sometimes a deviation from an expected script (e.g., a cat eating pickles) may be so striking that it proves especially memorable (Davidson & Hoe, 1993). Children may even rearrange details in their recall to make a story

Table 9.3
Examples of Children's Birthday Party Scripts

You cook a cake and eat it. (3 yr, 1 mo)

Well, you get a cake and some ice cream and then some birthday (?) and then you get some clowns and then you get some paper hats, the animal hats and then and then you sing, "Happy Birthday to you," and then then then they give you some presents and then you play with them and then that's the end and they they go home and they do what they wanta. (4 yr, 9 mo)

First, uhm…you're getting ready for the kids to come, like puttin' balloons up and and putting out party plates and making cake. And then all the people come you've asked. Give you presents and then you have lunch or whatever you have. Then…uhm…then you open your presents. Or you can open your presents anytime. Uhm…you could…after you open the presents, then it's probably time to go home. If you're like at Foote Park or something, then it's time to go home and you have to drive all the people home. Then you go home too. (6 yr, 7 mo)

Well, first you open your mail box, and you get some mail. And then you see that there's an invitation for you. Read the invitation. Then you ask your parents if you can go. Then you…uhm…go to the birthday party and you get a ride there, and after you get there you usually wait for everyone else to come. Then usually they always want to open one of the presents. Sometimes then they have three games, then they have the birthday cake, then sometimes they open up the other presents or they could open them up all at once. After that they like to play some more games and then maybe your parents come to pick you up. And then you go home. (8 yr, 10 mo)

Source: From "Generalized Event Representations: Basic Building Blocks of Cognitive Development" by K. Nelson and J. Gruendel, 1981. In M. E. Lamb and A. L. Brown (Eds.), *Advances in Developmental Psychology*, Vol. 1 (p. 135), Hillsdale, NJ: Erlbaum. Copyright © 1981 by Lawrence Erlbaum Associates. Reprinted by permission.

fit a script. In one study, for example, children heard a story in which the statement "Children brought presents" came at the end of a description of a birthday party. In later retelling the story, some children moved the present bringing earlier in the story, and others replaced it with "children took presents [party favors] home"—certainly a more natural conclusion to a birthday party (Hudson & Nelson, 1983).

In general, children seem to be especially sensitive to the order in which events occur, and they learn new scripts most readily when the events in the script follow a natural logical or causal sequence (Bauer, 1992; Fivush, Kuebli, & Clubb, 1992). Recall from our earlier discussion that even infants can learn the order of events for simple sequences of action.

As with constructive memory in general, the effects of scripts on memory are mixed. A script can sometimes lead to memory distortions, as when some unexpected event is reworked to fit an established script. In addition, young children who are just forming scripts may have difficulty separating the typical and the novel, and they may remember new events less well because they merge such events with the typical events of the script (Farrar & Goodman, 1990, 1992). For the most part, however, scripts—like knowledge in general—aid the memory process. Scripts free us from having to attend to the mundane and predictable, and they provide frameworks within which new experiences can be understood and thus remembered.

Development in Family Context
How Parents Teach Their Children to Remember

Memory is clearly a basic cognitive capacity. It is present from birth; it operates in much the same way in all infants and children; and it undergoes predictable changes as children develop. Furthermore, memory—as well as developmental changes in memory—is closely linked to the cognitive system as a whole, as revealed by the work we have just considered.

To say that memory is basic, however, is not to say that it is unaffected by experience. We have seen that there are seldom all-or-nothing answers to the nature–nurture question, and this holds true for the development of memory as well. Children's experiences affect their memories from early in life. In recent years there has been considerable interest in the effects of one particular type of experience: the way that parents talk about past events with their young children (Fivush, 1993; Fivush & Kuebli, 1997; Hudson, 1990; Welch-Ross, 1997).

Parents do in fact talk about the past with their children. Conversations about such matters as doctor visits, shopping excursions, and family trips are common occurrences in many households. Furthermore, different parents talk about the past in somewhat different ways. Table 9.4 presents examples of two styles of parental conversation that have been identified by researchers. These styles, we should note, are really points along a continuum. As the examples suggest, parents in the *elaborative* category provide a richer narrative structure than do parents in the *repetitive* category. Not only do they furnish more information in their own speech, but they make more extended and supportive efforts to elicit information from their children. They also talk more often about the past than do repetitive parents. The child of an elaborative parent is therefore given more chance to be an active participant in conversations about the past, as well as more chance to be successful in her recall efforts. Such a child is also provided with more general and more frequent models of how to remember and talk about past experience.

Parents often talk about past experiences with their children. Such conversations may be an important contributor to children's earliest memories.

Table 9.4

Examples of Elaborative and Repetitive Styles in Conversations between Parent (P) and Child (C)

Elaborative

P: Did we see any big fishes? What kind of fishes?

C: Big, big, big.

P: And what's their names?

C: I don't know.

P: You remember the names of the fishes. What we called them. Michael's favorite kind of fish. Big mean ugly fish.

C: Yeah.

P: What kind is it?

C: um, ba.,

P: A ssshark?

C: Yeah.

P: Remember the sharks?

C: Yeah.

P: Do you? What else did we see in the big tank at the aquarium?

C: I don't know.

P: Remember when we first came in, remember when we first came in the aquarium? And we looked down and there were a whole bunch of birdies in the water? Remember the names of the birdies?

C: Ducks!

P: Nooo! They weren't ducks. They had on little suits. Penguins. Remember, what did the penguins do?

C: I don't know.

P: You don't remember?

C: No.

P: Remember them jumping off the rocks and swimming in the water?

C: Yeah.

P: Real fast. You were watching them jump in the water, hm.

C: Yeah.

Repetitive

P: How did we get to Florida, do you remember?

C: Yes.

P: How did we get there? What did we do? You remember?

C: Yeah.

P: You want to sit up here in my lap?

C: No.

P: Oh, okay. Remember when we went to Florida, how did we get there? We went in the _____?

C: The ocean.

P: Well, be _____, when we got to Florida we went to the ocean, that's right, but how did we get down to Florida? Did we drive our car?

C: Yes.

P: No, think again, I don't thing we drove to Florida. How did we get down there, remember, we took a great big _____? Do you remember?

Source: From "Parental Styles of Talking about the Past" by E. Reese and R. Fivush, 1993, *Developmental Psychology, 29,* p. 606. Copyright © 1993 by the American Psychological Association. Reprinted by permission.

As we might expect, then, children of elaborative parents are generally more successful at recalling past events than are children of repetitive parents, not only in conversations with their own parents but also when tested by an independent adult (Fivush, 1991; Nelson, 1993a). Furthermore, differences are evident not only in the amount of recall, but also in the *style* of recall. Children of elaborative parents are more likely to approximate an adultlike narrative style, marked by clear temporal and causal relations and helpful orienting and contextual information (e.g., "Remember when we...?"). In general, children who engage in such conversations with their parents seem to be learning not only what to remember but *how* to remember—that is, how to organize and communicate their memories of the past. They are also learning something about the value of such memories and about the value of sharing one's memories with others.

To date, most of the research on early memory talk has focused on North American families. There is intriguing evidence, however, that this aspect of early socialization may vary across cultures. It has been argued that Asian cultures place less emphasis on an individual self, and more emphasis on the self's role within a broader social network, than do Western cultures (Markus & Kitayama, 1991). In support of this distinction, Mullen and Yi (1995) found that talk about past events involving the child was three times as frequent between American mothers and their 3-year-old children as between Korean mothers and their children. This finding helps explain another outcome from the same research program: Caucasian adults report earlier childhood memories than do Asian adults (Mullen, 1994).

The theoretical basis for much of the work on parents' contributions to memory has been Vygotsky's (1978) theory. The effects of parents on both what and how their children remember are clearly compatible with Vygotsky's emphasis on the social bases for individual development. Also compatible with Vygotskian theory are the developmental changes in parent–child interactions that this research reveals. When children are very young, the parent carries most of the burden, directing the conversation and drawing information from the child. As children develop, they gradually assume a more active and more equal role in discussions about the past.

Conversations with parents can encompass a variety of topics and can nurture memories of many different sorts. Such conversations contribute, for example, to the kinds of script memory discussed in the previous section. There has also been much recent interest in the effects of parental talk about emotions on emotional development in children, a topic that we consider in Chapter 13. Here we focus on an outcome for which memory talk has been argued to be especially important: the development of autobiographical memory.

The term **autobiographical memory** refers to memories that are specific, personal, and long-lasting—memories that are part of one's life history, that have to do with the self. A child who can recount the typical activities in a kindergarten day is demonstrating script memory. A child who can remember the time she spilled the paints or the day she won the big race is demonstrating autobiographical memory. What a number of theorists have suggested is that autobiographical memory may emerge in the context of conversations with parents (Bauer, 1993; Fivush, Haden, & Reese, 1996; Hudson, 1990; Nelson, 1993b; Welch-Ross, 1995). Such contexts provide a narrative framework within which personal memories can be elicited and rehearsed, as well as a motivation—sharing with others—for talking about and remembering one's past.

This proposal is relevant to the problem of **infantile amnesia**: the common inability to remember experiences from the first 2 or 3 years of life. The puzzle of why we cannot remember very early experiences has long intrigued theorists, dat-

Autobiographical memory
Specific, personal, and long-lasting memory regarding the self.

Infantile amnesia
The inability to remember experiences from the first 2 or 3 years of life.

ing back to Freud's proposal that such forgetting results from repression of forbidden sexual desires. A number of other explanations have been offered since Freud, and the topic remains the focus of a good deal of theoretical debate (Howe & Courage, 1993). The work on autobiographical memory provides another possible solution to the puzzle. One way to describe infantile amnesia is to say that there is no autobiographical memory for the events of infancy. If the emergence of autobiographical memory depends on the social sharing of memories, then its absence in the infant, who cannot use language, is understandable.

✓ *To Recap…*

Most examinations of memory beyond infancy have focused on recall memory, which improves with age across the childhood years. Three general explanations have been offered for this improvement. One source of improvement is the development of mnemonic strategies, such as rehearsal and organization. The tendency to use strategies, the complexity of the strategies, and the skill with which the strategies are executed all increase with age. The emphasis on strategies reflects one important theme of the information-processing approach—the existence of limits on information-processing resources and the need to develop techniques (such as mnemonic strategies) to overcome those limits.

A second approach to explaining developmental improvements stresses the child's metamemory, which includes knowledge about memory in general and about one's own memory in particular. Both sorts of knowledge increase with age. Although attempts to link metamemory to memory performance have sometimes been unsuccessful, recent evidence suggests that increases in knowledge do lead to improvements in performance. The work on metamemory reflects another theme of the information-processing approach—the need for executive control to select and coordinate cognitive activities.

A third approach stresses the effects of the general knowledge system on memory. Studies of constructive memory demonstrate that memory often involves inferences and constructions that go beyond the literal input. Older children are more likely to engage in such constructive processing than are younger children. Older children also possess greater content-specific expertise than do younger children, and this factor is another contributor to developmental improvements in memory. Finally, an aspect of cognitive development that appears to be especially closely related to memory is the emergence of scripts, or knowledge of the typical structure of familiar events.

Problem Solving

No one has to read a textbook to learn that children's problem-solving abilities improve dramatically across childhood. The tasks that the school system sets for its students, the ways in which parents attempt to reason with and control their children, the opportunities and the expectations that society in general holds—all are quite different for 15-year-olds than for 5-year-olds. As with the study of memory, the challenge for the researcher is to describe exactly how children's abilities change—and then to explain why these changes come about.

As you might expect, children's problem-solving abilities change in many ways as they develop (DeLoache, Miller, & Pierroutsaksos, 1998). Here we limit ourselves to discussing two such changes. We begin with the idea that some kinds of problem solving may be explained by the formation of rules for combining information and making judgments. We then consider a central theme in current information-processing theorizing—the contribution of memory to children's problem solving.

The Development of Rules

Robert Siegler (1978, 1981) has proposed that some important aspects of children's cognitive development can be characterized in terms of the construction of **rules**. Rules are procedures for acting on the environment and solving problems. They take the form of "if...then" statements. If A is the case, do X; if B is the case, do Y; and so forth. A simple and familiar example concerns the rules for behavior at traffic lights: If the light is green, proceed; if the light is red, stop (unfortunately, rules for yellow lights seem to be more variable!).

Many situations, of course, require more thought than does approaching a traffic light, and it is these more complex situations to which Siegler's research has been directed. Figure 9.6 presents one example—a balance-scale problem originally devised by Inhelder and Piaget (1958) to study formal operational reasoning. The child is shown a simple balance scale on which varying numbers of weights can be placed at varying distances from the fulcrum. The task is to predict whether the scale will balance or whether one side or the other will go down. Successfully performing the task requires that the child realize that both weight and distance are important and that she know how to combine the two factors in cases of conflict. The original Piagetian research revealed that children of different ages gave quite different responses to the task, which Piaget analyzed in terms of the logical structures of concrete and formal operations.

Siegler (1976, 1978) used the same task, but a different methodology and form of analysis. He began by carefully considering all the various ways in which children might go about attempting to solve the balance-scale problem. Such *task analysis* is a characteristic information-processing methodology (Kail & Bisanz, 1982). Based on this task analysis, Siegler identified four rules that children might use in solving balance problems.

At the simplest level, rule 1, the child judges that the side with more weights will go down or that, if the number of weights on each side is equal, the scale will balance. The child using rule 2 also judges solely in terms of number of weights when the weights on each side are different; if the weights are equal, however, the rule 2 child can also take distance into account. The rule 3 child always considers both weight and distance and is correct whenever one or both are equal. If the two factors are in conflict, however (i.e., more weight on one side, greater distance on the other), the child becomes confused, does not know how to resolve the conflict, and (in Siegler's words) "muddles through." Finally, the rule 4 child has mastered the weight-times-distance rule: Downward force equals amount of weight multiplied by distance from the fulcrum. The rule 4 child can therefore solve any version of the task.

A task analysis identifies possible ways of responding, but it does not tell us whether children actually use these approaches. Siegler's next step, therefore, was

Rules
Procedures for acting on the environment and solving problems.

Figure 9.6
Balance scale used in Siegler's research. Metal disks can be placed on any of the eight pegs.

Table 9.5

Types of Problems and Predicted Responses on the Siegler Balance–Scale Task

Problem Type	Rule			
	I	*II*	*III*	*IV*
Balance	100	100	100	100
Weight	100	100	100	100
Distance	0 (Should say "Balance")	100	100	100
Conflict-Weight	100	100	33 (Chance responding)	100
Conflict-Distance	0 (Should say "Right down")	0 (Should say "Right down")	33 (Chance responding)	100
Conflict-Balance	0 (Should say "Right down")	0 (Should say "Right down")	33 (Chance responding)	100

Source: From "The Origins of Scientific Reasoning" by R. S. Siegler, 1978. In R. S. Siegler (Ed.), *Children's Thinking: What Develops?* (p. 115), Mahwah, NJ: Erlbaum. Copyright © 1978 by Lawrence Erlbaum Associates. Reprinted by permission.

to test the psychological reality of the proposed rules. He devised six types of balance-scale problems, carefully constructed to yield different patterns of response across the different rules. Both the problem types and the predicted responses are shown in Table 9.5.

Siegler presented five versions of each problem type to children ranging in age from 5 to 17. Fully 90% of the children followed one of the four rules consistently. As expected, the complexity of the preferred rule increased with age; most 5-year-olds used rule 1, whereas by age 17, rules 3 and 4 were most common. Finally, a particularly interesting finding was that accurate performance on the problems involving conflict actually declined with age. Although declines with age are normally unexpected, this finding fit nicely with the predictions of the rule analysis. As you can see in Table 9.5, the developmentally primitive rules 1 and 2 yield perfect performance on these problems, whereas the more advanced rule 3 results only in chance performance.

Siegler and others have applied his rule-assessment methodology to a number of tasks in addition to the balance-scale task (Klahr & Robinson, 1981; Ravn & Gelman, 1984). Siegler's (1981) own research has demonstrated the value of rules in explaining performance on a variety of Piagetian problems—for example, conservation of number and conservation of continuous quantity. The explanation is, to be sure, in some respects similar to Piaget's. In the case of conservation, for example, Siegler and Piaget agree that children solve the problem through mental action that logically combines information from both relevant dimensions (e.g., height and width in the case of quantity). There are, however, two differences between Siegler's and Piaget's accounts, differences that in general divide the information-processing and Piagetian approaches. One concerns specificity and testability. Rules are more precisely defined than are Piagetian operations, and the rule-assessment methodology provides a more rigorous test of a proposed explanation than is typically the case in Piagetian research. The second difference is theoretical. Operations are general structures that are assumed to determine performance on a wide range of tasks, and the expectation therefore is that children will be consistent in their level of performance. Rules, however, may be more domain-specific, and there is no assumption that performance will necessarily be consistent from one task to another. And Siegler in fact finds that the same child may use rules of different levels on different tasks.

Although both this section and the next use Piagetian examples, we should stress that the approaches we consider have by no means been limited to Piagetian tasks. Siegler, for example, has recently extended his research to the study of academic skills, such as addition, subtraction, and reading. We consider some of this work later.

The Contribution of Memory to Problem Solving

We have noted that some information-processing theorists are labeled neo-Piagetian because their ideas are especially closely tied to those of Piaget. In this section we examine one such theory, that of Robbie Case (1985, 1992; Case & Okamoto, 1996).

Like Piaget, Case divides development into distinct stages—stages in many respects similar to Piaget's. A major difference between the two approaches is the emphasis that Case places on memory. In his theory, the total problem-solving resources available to the child are divided into two components—operating space and short-term storage space.

The term **operating space** refers to the resources necessary to carry out whatever cognitive operations are being employed for the problem at hand. In the case of the Siegler balance-scale task, for example, a child who used rule 2 would first count the number of weights on each side of the fulcrum. Assuming that the weights were equal, the child would then count the number of pegs from the fulcrum. Finally, the child would use the information about weight or distance to predict which side would go down. Each of these operations would require a certain amount of operating space. Note that the term *space* is used somewhat metaphorically, for there is no reference to some actual physical area in the brain. The reference, rather, is to how much of the available mental energy must be used for the activity in question.

Operating space
In Case's theory, the resources necessary to carry out cognitive operations.

Performing operations is one part of problem solving; remembering the results of those operations is another part. The phrase **short-term storage space** refers to the resources the child needs to store results from previous operations while carrying out new ones. The rule 2 child, for example, would need to remember both the overall goal of the task and the results of each preceding operation in order to execute the sequence just described. Without such memory, there could be little hope of a successful solution.

Short-term storage space
In Case's theory, the resources necessary to store results from previous cognitive operations while carrying out new ones.

Let us consider another example. Figure 9.7 shows a task in proportional reasoning. The dark beakers contain orange juice, and the clear beakers contain water. The child is asked to imagine that the beakers in each set are poured into a pitcher and to judge which mixture will taste more strongly of juice—that from set A or that from set B. One way to solve the most difficult versions of the task (such as problem *d*) is as follows: Count the number of juice beakers in each set and note

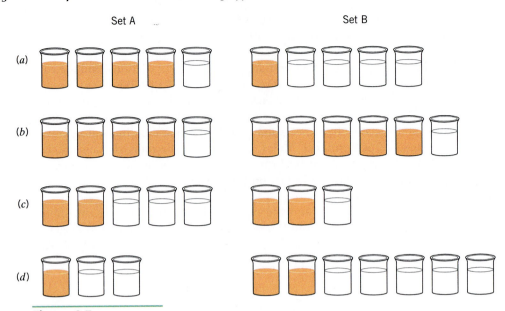

Figure 9.7
Example of a task in proportional reasoning. The dark beakers contain orange juice, and the clear beakers contain water. The child's task on each trial is to determine whether set A or set B will produce a juicier tasting drink. From *Intellectual Development* (p. 184) by R. Case, 1985, New York: Academic Press. Copyright © 1985 by Academic Press. Adapted by permission.

the size of the difference; count the number of water beakers in each set and note the size of the difference; compare the results of these two operations. If the juice difference is larger, decide that the set with more juice is juicier; if the water difference is larger (as is the case in the example), decide that the set with more water is less juicy. Thus, to solve the task, the child must both perform a number of distinct operations and remember the results of the operations.

The balance-scale and orange-juice tasks are just two of many problems whose solution depends on combining results from several cognitive operations. Such combining is possible only if short-term storage space is sufficient to hold all the relevant results. In Case's theory, limitations in short-term storage space are a major determinant of young children's difficulties in problem solving. Because they can keep track of only a few things at a time, young children can do only a few things at a time.

Correspondingly, advances in problem solving occur as short-term storage space expands, and the child can begin to combine operations that previously could only be performed separately. In the case of the juice problem, for example, it is not until age 9 or 10 that the child has sufficient storage space to combine all the operations described. More generally, the stage progressions in Case's theory are defined largely in terms of the new combinations made possible by increases in short-term storage capacity.

Why does short-term storage capacity increase? There are two possible explanations. One possibility, shown in Figure 9.8a, is that total problem-solving resources expand with age. As total resources grow, so does the space available for short-term storage. In this view, older children simply have more resources available to them. Thus, it is not surprising that they can remember more and do more.

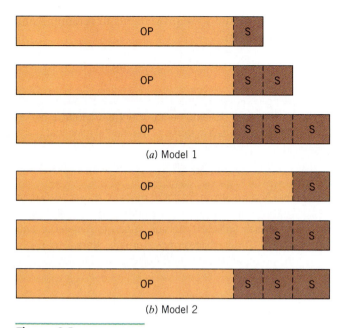

(a) Model 1

(b) Model 2

Figure 9.8
Two models for explaining developmental increases in short-term storage space. (a) In model 1, the total processing resources increase with age. (b) In model 2, processing resources remain constant, but operating space decreases.

Plausible though this model may seem, Case's research leads him to prefer a second possibility. This possibility, shown in Figure 9.8b, is that the growth in storage capacity results from a decrease in the space used to perform operations. Cognitive resources must always be divided between the two components of operations and storage; if fewer resources are needed for one component, then more are available for the other. In this second view, developmental changes in storage result from increases in the efficiency with which operations are performed. As children develop, they become more skilled at executing cognitive operations. Hence, they have more space left over for storage, and they can do more and more.

Accepting this second explanation leads naturally to another question: Why does operational efficiency increase? Case proposes two contributors. One is practice. With practice, cognitive activities of many sorts become more skilled and efficient. Thus, what once took effort and attention may eventually become automatic and routine. (We return to this notion, called *automatization*, in our discussion of cognitive change.) The second factor is biological maturation. Children develop at about the same pace, and this similarity suggests a biological contribution to development. Furthermore, Case notes that major changes in brain development occur at about the same time as the stage-to-stage transitions identified in his theory. Finally, research indicates that speed of information processing increases at a regular rate from early childhood to adulthood (Kail, 1991, 1995; Miller & Vernon, 1997). This increase in speed is so consistent across tasks and across samples that it appears to be maturational in origin.

Case's theory is one of the most ambitious information-processing efforts to date, and not all aspects of it have won acceptance (Keating, 1996; Siegler, 1996b). Its most general claim, however, is widely held: Memory improves as children develop, and improvements in memory contribute to improvements in reasoning and problem solving (Howe & Rabinowitz, 1990).

✓ To Recap...

Like memory, children's problem solving improves dramatically over the childhood years. The development of rules is one contributor to developmental change. Children's understanding of a variety of concepts can be formulated in terms of the mental rules that guide responding. Solution of balance-scale problems, for example, consistently follows one of four general rules, and the complexity and the appropriateness of the rules increase with age.

Short-term storage space is another important contributor to problem solving. Solutions to many problems require the ability to combine results from a number of cognitive operations. This is possible only if the child has sufficient storage space to remember past results while performing new operations. Older children have greater storage capacity than do younger children, and so they are capable of more complex forms of reasoning and problem solving.

Academic Abilities

Thus far our examples of information-processing research have been drawn largely from two content areas: the development of memory, and the understanding of Piagetian concepts. One of the strengths of the information-processing approach, however, is its applicability to a wide range of topics. In this section we discuss some information-processing research that has applied as well as theoretical interest—studies directed toward the development of skills stressed in school. We begin with arithmetic, then move to reading.

Arithmetic

Suppose you were asked how you come up with answers to simple addition problems, such as 4 + 2 and 3 + 5. Your response would probably be that you simply know—that you have memorized the answer to such often-encountered problems. And you would probably be right—all of us *have* memorized a number of basic arithmetical facts. But what about young children who are just beginning to learn about mathematics? How do they come up with *their* answers?

Many recent research programs have examined the strategies that children use to solve arithmetical problems (Ashcraft, 1990; Bisanz & LeFevre, 1990; Ginsburg, Klein, & Starkey, 1998; Widaman et al., 1992). Here we concentrate on some research by Robert Siegler and associates (Siegler & Jenkins, 1989; Siegler & Shipley, 1995; Siegler & Shrager, 1984). Table 9.6 shows strategies that young children might use to solve the 3 + 5 problem. The retrieval strategy corresponds to the expected strategy for adults—retrieving from memory a previously memorized answer. Other possible strategies vary in both sophistication and likelihood of success.

How can we determine which strategy a child is using? Siegler and colleagues use a variety of techniques. One approach is simply to watch children as they work on the problems. Some strategies (putting up fingers, counting out loud) are overt and thus directly observable. Another approach is to ask children how they arrive at their answers. Although verbal reports are not infallible guides to mental processes (in children or anyone), they can provide useful information. Table 9.7 presents some examples of children's self-reports on their use of the min strategy, or the

Table 9.6
Children's Strategies for Solving Simple Addition Problems

Strategy	Typical Use of Strategy to Solve 3 + 5
Sum	Put up 3 fingers, put up 5 fingers, count fingers by saying "1, 2, 3, 4, 5, 6, 7, 8."
Finger recognition	Put up 3 fingers, put up 5 fingers, say "8" without counting.
Short-cut sum	Say "1, 2, 3, 4, 5, 6, 7, 8," perhaps simultaneously putting up one finger on each count.
Count-from-first-addend	Say "3, 4, 5, 6, 7, 8" or "4, 5, 6, 7, 8," perhaps simultaneously putting up one finger on each count.
Min (count-from-larger-addend)	Say "5, 6, 7, 8," or "6, 7, 8," perhaps simultaneously putting up one finger on each count beyond 5.
Retrieval	Say an answer and explain it by saying "I just knew it."
Guessing	Say an answer and explain it by saying "I guessed."
Decomposition	Say "3 + 5 is like 4 + 4, so it's 8."

Source: Adapted from *How Children Discover New Strategies* (p. 59) by R. S. Siegler and E. Jenkins, 1989, Mahwah, NJ: Erlbaum. Copyright © 1989 by Lawrence Erlbaum Associates. Adapted by permission.

strategy of counting up from the larger of two addends (i.e., the two numbers to be added).

A third approach makes use of a central information-processing methodology: the measurement of response time as a guide to processes of solution. A child using the count-from-first-add end strategy, for example, should take longer to solve 3 + 7 than to solve 3 + 5; a child using the min strategy, however, should be equally quick on the two problems. Examination of response times across a range of problems can help to specify the strategies being used.

Finally, Siegler has tested his full model of children's knowledge of addition (only part of which is captured in Table 9.6) with another basic information-processing method, computer simulation. His success at programming a computer to generate the kinds of response patterns shown by children suggests that his theory really has identified the processes that guide behavior.

One of the most interesting findings from the Siegler program of research concerns the diversity of strategies that children use. We might have expected that a child at any point in development would have a single method of solving addition problems. In fact, children typically employ a number of different strategies, sometimes going with one approach, sometimes trying something different.

Children's selection among strategies is not random, but often adaptively geared to the problem at hand. They may, for example, use the retrieval strategy for simple and familiar problems but fall back on one of the more certain counting strategies when faced with a more complex task. In general, children seem to strive for a balance of speed and accuracy, selecting the fastest strategy that is likely to yield a correct response. With development, there is a predictable progression from less efficient to more efficient strategies, culminating in the ability to retrieve answers from memory rather than continually having to calculate them anew. With development, speed and accuracy increase as well. These increases come in part from the emergence of more efficient strategies and in part from increased skill in executing any particular strategy.

Counting on the fingers is one of the first arithmetical strategies that children develop.

Table 9.7
Protocols Illustrating Children's Use of the Min Strategy to Solve Addition Problems

Experimenter (E):	How much is 6 + 3?
Lauren (L):	(Long pause) Nine.
E:	OK, how did you know that?
L:	I think I said...I think I said...oops, um...I think he said...8 was 1 and...um...I mean 7 was 1, 8 was 2, 9 was 3.
E:	OK.
L:	Six and three are nine.
E:	How did you know to do that? Why didn't you count "1, 2, 3, 4, 5, 6, 7, 8, 9"? How come you did "6, 7, 8, 9"?
L:	Cause then you have to count all those numbers.
E:	OK, well how did you know you didn't have to count all of those numbers?
L:	Why didn't...well I don't have to if I don't want to.
Experimenter (E):	OK, Brittany, how much is 2 + 5?
Brittany (B):	2 + 5—(whispers)—6, 7—it's 7.
E:	How did you know that?
B:	(excitedly) Never counted.
E:	You didn't count?
B:	Just said it—I just said after six something—seven—six, seven.
E:	You did? Why did you say 6, 7?
B:	'Cause I wanted to see what it really was.
E:	OK, well—so, did you—what—you didn't have to count at one, you didn't count, 1, 2, 3, you just said 6, 7?
B:	Yeah—smart answer.
Experimenter (E):	OK, Christian, How much is 1 + 24?
Christian (C):	1 + 24!?
E:	Yep.
C:	Umm..............25.
E:	How did you know that?
C:	I...counted in my head.
E:	How did you count it in your head?
C:	What was it again?
E:	1 + 24.
C:	I went...1, 2, 3, 4, 5, si...I went, 24 + 1, I, well.... I'll try to get you to understand, ok?
E:	OK.
C:	I went 24 + 1...(whispers) 24...(whispers) 25...that's what I did.
E:	OK, that's good, well why didn't you count 1, 2, 3, 4, 5, 6, 7, 8, 9, 10, all the way to 24?
C:	Aww, that would take too long...silly.

Source: From *How Children Discover New Strategies* (pp. 66, 80, 91) by R. S. Siegler and E. Jenkins, 1989, Mahwah, NJ: Erlbaum. Copyright © 1989 by Lawrence Erlbaum Associates. Reprinted by permission.

Although variability in strategy use is common, it is not inevitable. In the previous section we discussed children's use of rules (which are a kind of strategy) to solve problems such as the balance scale or conservation. We saw that there is little variability on such tasks; rather, children tend to be quite consistent in the particular rule they use. Siegler (1996a) suggests that this consistency may result at least in part from the unfamiliarity of the problem. Because children have limited experience with balance scales or conservation tasks, they have not had a chance to try out a variety of different approaches. Thus, they construct a new strategy in response to the demands of the immediate task. In contrast, coping with addition problems is a common experience for any child who has started school, and attempts to commit material to memory are perhaps even more common. In these domains, therefore, children develop and use multiple strategies.

This argument suggests that we should expect to find variability in the strategies children develop to solve other familiar academic tasks as well. And this in fact is the case. Both subtraction and division, for example, are also characterized by the use of multiple strategies rather than a single, consistent approach (Siegler, 1996a). So, as we discuss shortly, is reading.

The conclusions noted thus far have been based on samples of American children. Research in China indicates that Chinese children develop very similar strategies when they are in the process of mastering arithmetic (Geary, Fan, & Bow-Thomas, 1992). Such research also shows, however, that Chinese children tend to be faster than American children at executing their strategies and that they move more quickly to the optimal strategy for a particular task—factors that contribute to their generally superior mathematical performance. In the next chapter we will return to the issue of cross-national differences in mathematics achievement when we consider some of the school and family experiences that may underlie these differences.

The research discussed in this section has implications for teaching arithmetic. Perhaps the most general implication is that teachers should be sensitive to the beliefs and strategies that children bring to the classroom setting. We saw in Chapter 8 that learning about numbers begins very early in life; thus it is not surprising that even first graders have their own strategies for solving arithmetic problems.

Teachers should realize, furthermore, that not all first graders will have the same strategies, and that instruction, as far as possible, should be adjusted to the individual child's level of development. As Siegler (1988) notes, lower-level strategies, such as counting on one's fingers, should not necessarily be discouraged; children may need experience with the simpler strategies to arrive at answers that they can eventually retrieve from memory. Recall that this same principle emerged in our discussion in Chapter 8 of the implications of Piaget's work for education: Be sensitive to the natural sequence of development and to the need for advanced knowledge to build on lower-level understanding.

Reading

Reading is a source of great joy for many people and a source of great sorrow for many others. Despite thousands of hours of school instruction, many children never develop satisfactory reading skills. Can research help identify problems and suggest solutions?

Reading as a cognitive activity is closely bound to many of the cognitive processes discussed throughout this chapter. Strategies are again important. Siegler's (1988) research has shown that children develop strategies for identifying words that are analogous to their strategies for adding numbers. They use retrieval from memory, for example, for high-certainty targets and fall back on slower, sounding-

Reading is one of the most important cognitive skills that children develop. Information-processing researchers attempt to identify the many specific components that make successful reading possible.

Phonological awareness
The realization that letters correspond to sounds and the ability to perform specific letter-to-sound translations.

Phonics
An approach to reading instruction that stresses letter–sound correspondences and the buildup of words from individual units.

Whole-word
An approach to reading instruction that stresses learning and visual retrieval of entire words.

out strategies when faced with less well known words. There are individual differences in strategy use, with good readers more likely to use retrieval than poor readers. Strategies are also important when children move beyond individual words and attempt to comprehend text. Comprehension monitoring is central to effective reading—that is, continual self-checking to be sure that what has been read is understood, coupled with rereading and other correction procedures when comprehension fails. Older children are generally better at comprehension monitoring than are younger children, and good readers are better than are poor readers (Garner, 1990). Monitoring their reading efforts may be the most important metacognitive skill that many people exercise.

The developments discussed in regard to memory and problem solving also play a role in reading. The knowledge base is again important. Knowledge of a variety of sorts can be brought to the task of comprehension, and there are both developmental and individual differences in the ability to use existing knowledge to make sense of new information (Siegler, 1991). The kind of short-term storage space stressed in Case's (1985) theory is important as well. To understand even a single sentence, readers must be able to hold in memory the first words read as they progress to later words in the sentence. Difficulties with short-term memory are one contributor to problems in reading (Siegel, 1993a).

Phonological Awareness   Thus far our focus has been on the ultimate goal in reading—namely, comprehension of text. But a number of more basic processing steps must be executed before comprehension becomes an issue: perception of letters, translation of letters into sounds, combination of individual sounds into words. Here, too, research has provided a wealth of information about how reading occurs and about differences between good and poor readers (Adams, 1990; Adams, Treiman, & Pressley, 1998; Rack, Hulme, & Snowling, 1993).

One finding in particular that emerges as important with respect to both developmental and individual differences concerns the role of phonological awareness. The term **phonological awareness** refers to both the general realization that letters correspond to sounds and the ability to perform specific letter-to-sound translations. It refers, in short, to children's ability to "crack the code"—to figure out how squiggles on paper can yield the sounds and words of the language. Table 9.8 presents examples of items used to assess such awareness in grade-school children. So defined, phonological awareness would appear to be central to reading, and research suggests that this is the case (Siegel, 1993b; Wagner & McBride-Chang, 1996). Deficits in phonological decoding skills are a major contributor to severe reading difficulties. And the early emergence of phonological awareness is a good predictor of eventual reading ability. Indeed, measures of phonological awareness in preschool are a better predictor of subsequent reading than are measures of IQ (Goswami & Bryant, 1990).

Approaches to Teaching Reading   The studies of phonological awareness are relevant to the long-standing debate between two approaches to teaching reading: the phonics and whole-word approaches. A **phonics** approach to reading instruction stresses letter–sound correspondences and the buildup of words from individual units; a **whole-word** approach stresses learning and visual retrieval of entire words without working through individual sounds. As Siegler (1998) notes, one reason that the debate has continued is that there is no simple right answer to the question of how best to teach reading. Both methods work well for some children and fail to work for others, and a full program of reading instruction must undoubt-

Table 9.8

Examples of Tasks Used to Assess Phonological Awareness in Children

What sound comes…	
skwupt	before /t/
glet	before /l/
nigz	after /g/
jeeld	after /l/
Say the following nonsense word without the ( ) sound…	
het(s)	
(s)plem	
me(v)z	
What sounds do you hear in…	
f-l-e-ss	
z-u-n	
l-e-k-t	

Source: From "What Is Phonological Awareness?" by C. McBride-Chang, 1995, *Journal of Educational Psychology, 87,* p. 191.

edly incorporate aspects of both approaches. Nevertheless, many researchers and practitioners believe that the findings from reading research indicate a need for a greater emphasis on phonics than exists in many school systems today (Chall, 1983; Perfetti, 1991).

Our emphasis on the contribution of basic information-processing skills to reading is not meant to deny the importance of the social context within which children learn to read. The social supports that children receive for reading are in fact quite important. In addition to the obvious contribution of the school, experiences within the home can nurture a love of reading—in some cases well before the child knows a single letter. One of the best predictors of pleasure in and skill at reading is growing up in a home in which books are valued and parents read to and with their children (Baker et al., 1994; McGee & Richgels, 1990).

✓ *To Recap…*

Studies of arithmetic indicate that children develop a variety of strategies to solve arithmetical problems and that they typically use several strategies rather than just one. With increased age, there is a gradual ascendance of more efficient strategies (such as retrieval) over less effective ones.

Studies of reading indicate that basic cognitive processes stressed in information-processing theory are important for reading. Strategies (such as comprehension monitoring), general knowledge, and short-term memory all contribute to reading comprehension. Also important is phonological awareness, the realization that letters correspond to sounds and the ability to perform specific letter-to-sound translations.

Cognitive Change

In Chapter 8 we concluded that Piaget never succeeded in providing a satisfactory theory of cognitive change. Much the same criticism has been leveled against information-processing theorists (Miller, 1993). Most information-processing accounts have been more successful at specifying the various levels or states of understand-

USING THE HANDS TO READ THE MIND

Cognitive change is a continual process that begins the moment the baby enters the world. Children—and indeed any of us—are continually adapting to new challenges and forging new forms of understanding. For any particular kind of cognitive advance, however, there often are especially sensitive periods for change—transitional phases during which children are ready to overcome past limits and benefit from new experiences. Identifying such transitional phases is important both theoretically, in terms of our understanding of how change comes about, and pragmatically, in terms of our ability to help children who are ready to learn.

A recent program of research by Goldin-Meadow, Perry, and associates (Goldin-Meadow, Alibali, DeChurch, 1993; Goldin-Meadow, Wein, & Chang, 1992; Perry, Woolley, & Ifcher, 1995) offers some intriguing evidence with respect to one possible index of readiness for change. Most assessments of children's knowledge focus on a single response measure—typically verbal judgments in response to some task. The Goldin-

Meadow group also elicits verbal judgments, but they add to such measures an observational recording of children's spontaneous gestures as they attempt to solve the problem. They are especially interested in what they label *gesture-speech mismatches*—that is, instances in which the information conveyed by the gesture does not match that expressed in the verbal judgment. These are cases in which the mouth is saying one thing and the hand something else.

One set of tasks used to explore such mismatches was drawn from Piaget's work (Church & Goldin-Meadow, 1986). The children in the study responded to a battery of conservation problems, and their gestures were recorded in addition to the standard judgments and explanations. Many of the children did in fact gesture when explaining their answers—for example, cupping their hands to indicate the width of the container on a continuous-quantity task. In many cases, the gesture was in accord with the verbal judgment; for some children, however, it was not. Some nonconservers, for example, referred only to the heights of the con-

ing through which the cognitive system moves than at explaining the transition from one state to another.

In this section we consider some of the explanations for cognitive change that *have* been offered in information-processing theories to date (Klahr & MacWhinney, 1998; Siegler, 1996a, 1998). As we did when examining the Piagetian approach to change, we begin by discussing the methods that researchers in this tradition use to study change. We then consider several specific mechanisms of change that have been proposed by information-processing theorists.

Methods of Study

Information-processing researchers have utilized a variety of techniques to study the process of change. Here we concentrate on two methods that have been emphasized in recent information-processing research: microgenetic techniques and the creation of self-modifying computer simulations.

Microgenetic Techniques   As we saw when we introduced the microgenetic method in Chapter 3, a microgenetic study begins with the selection of a sample of children who are thought to be in a transitional phase for the knowledge being studied—that is, close to moving to a higher level of understanding. The children are observed as they attempt to solve a variety of problems that assess the abilities tainers in their explanations, yet simultaneously signaled the difference in width with their accompanying gestures. Furthermore, a subsequent training study revealed that it was these "discordant" children who were most likely to benefit from conservation training. Thus, gesture-speech mismatch proved to be an index of readiness for change.

Why might gesture-speech mismatch be predictive of change? Goldin-Meadow et al.(1993) argue that such mismatches are a direct reflection of a knowledge state in transition. Children who are not yet close to mastering a concept are typically content with a simple and consistent basis for response—tall things have more, for example, in the case of conservation. The more advanced, transitional child, however, has reached the point of holding two conflicting beliefs about the phenomenon, and both beliefs come through in the response to the task. In the case of conservation, the discordant child, in contrast to his more solidly preoperational peer, has begun to sense that width as well as height is important and is struggling to reconcile these competing bases for response. Because both dimensions *are* in fact important, this child is closer to arriving at the correct answer than is the more confident and consistent nonconserver.

It is important to note that demonstrations of gesture-speech mismatch are not limited to conservation tasks. Indeed, one attractive feature of the measure as an index of readiness for change is that it is not tied to any particular task, or, for that matter to any particular age period. Among the other domains in which gesture-speech mismatches have been shown to be predictive of change are word learning in toddlers (Gershkoff-Stowe & Smith, 1991), arithmetical reasoning in grade-schoolers (Perry, Church, & Goldin-Meadow, 1988), and understanding of physics in adults (Perry & Elder, 1997).

We noted that researchers have been able to use mismatches to predict which children will benefit from experimentally provided training. But we must also ask whether the measure has any more general utility—that is, are these cues that teachers and parents can naturally detect and use in their interactions with children? Although evidence to date is limited, preliminary results are encouraging (Alibali, Flevares, & Goldin-Meadow, 1997; Goldin-Meadow et al., 1992; Perry et al., 1995). Adults have been shown to be sensitive to mismatches in their assessments of children's knowledge, and to be above chance, after watching both speech and gestures, in their predictions of which children are ready to master a new concept. The first step in helping children learn is knowing which children are ready to learn.

of interest. Typically, there are many such problems in each experimental session and several such sessions across a period of weeks or months. The goal is to observe processes of change as the change occurs—something that is usually not possible when we assess children only once or twice.

An analogy that Siegler (1996a) uses in contrasting microgenetic techniques with the standard longitudinal approach is the difference between a snapshot and a movie. With longitudinal research we get snapshots—pictures of the cognitive system at different points in time. With microgenetic research we get a movie—a continuous record of change over time.

An example of a microgenetic study is provided by some of the work on arithmetical strategies discussed in the previous section. Siegler and Jenkins (1989) selected 10 children who did not yet use the min strategy (that is, counting up from the larger addend) when solving simple arithmetic problems. These children then participated in three experimental sessions per week across a period of 11 weeks. During each session they attempted to solve seven addition problems; across sessions there was a gradual increase in the complexity of the problems presented. Both videotapes of the children's performance and direct questioning were used to infer the strategies underlying their answers. Through this approach, Siegler and Jenkins were able to document the gradual discovery of the min strategy by seven of the eight children who made it through all 11 weeks. Because of their extensive observational records, they knew when and how the strategy first appeared, as well as what preceded it and to what it subsequently led. The examples in Table 9.7 include the first appearance of the strategy for one of the children, Brittany.

In discussing the strengths of the microgenetic approach, Siegler (1996a) identifies five issues related to cognitive change for which microgenetic techniques can provide valuable data. Such techniques can inform us about the *path* of cognitive change: the sequences and levels through which children move in acquiring new knowledge. They can provide information about the *rate* of change: how quickly or slowly different forms of knowledge are mastered. Microgenetic findings speak to the issue of *breadth* of change: when a new competency (such as a particular arithmetical strategy) is acquired, how narrowly or broadly it is applied. They are relevant to the question of possible *variability* in the pattern of change: Do all children follow the same route in mastering a new concept? As we have seen, a major conclusion from microgenetic research is that often children do not; there can be substantial variability en route to the same end point. Finally, microgenetic methods can provide information about the *sources* of change: the experiences and processes through which new knowledge is constructed.

Self-Modifying Computer Simulations

Earlier in the chapter we described the computer simulation methodology—the creation of computer programs that attempt to reproduce certain aspects of human cognition. As we saw, such simulations offer a powerful method for testing theories of underlying process. Nevertheless, most simulations are limited in that they are static; at best they tell us what the cognitive system is like at one point in development. A relatively recent development is the creation of programs that can actually change from one level of understanding to another.

As you might expect, such simulations are difficult to produce, and their number to date is limited. Many of the most interesting efforts are collected in a book edited by Simon and Halford (1995). The research programs summarized vary in their underlying theoretical assumptions, in the computer languages in which they are written, and in the aspects of cognitive development to which they are directed. Among the forms of knowledge included are conservation, transitivity, physical reasoning, arithmetic, and language.

The programs also have several elements in common. Each includes a set of rules intended to model the starting-point level of understanding of a child who has not yet mastered the knowledge—for example, a rule system that uses only the length of the row when judging number and hence fails conservation-of-number tasks. Each also includes mechanisms for changing the initial rules in response to experience—for example, the capacity to benefit from experiences of counting and measurement in the case of conservation and thereby to construct more complex rules. Each includes tests in which the program is exposed to the relevant experiences and both its immediate and more long-term responses are recorded. Finally, each reports some success at modeling the acquisition of new knowledge—that is, in creating programs that modify their own rule systems with experience and hence change from lower to higher levels of understanding.

One other similarity among the research programs is important to note. All researchers who construct simulations acknowledge a basic point: that the success of a simulation does not guarantee that the theory underlying the simulation is correct. The fact, for example, that the computer program can learn conservation through particular experiences of counting and measurement does not mean that this is the way children learn to conserve. Children and computers may go about the task in quite different ways. Indeed, different children may take different paths to the same end point. A successful simulation identifies *one* way in which learning may occur, not necessarily *the* way. Still, to specify even one possible route is clearly an important accomplishment.

Mechanisms of Change

As noted, information-processing theorists have proposed a number of different change mechanisms. Here we discuss four: encoding, automatization, strategy construction, and strategy selection. We then consider a general characteristic that these and other specific mechanisms may have in common.

Siegler (1991) defines **encoding** as "identifying the most important features of objects and events and using the features to form internal representations" (p. 10). Encoding is thus related to what we normally mean by *attention*, but it carries some further implications as well. One is the idea that information processing is always active rather than passive, because the child attends to only some features of the environment and uses only some features to arrive at judgments. The other is the emphasis on how the child interprets or represents the encoded information. Encoding involves not simply attending, but also forming some sort of representation of what has been attended to, and it is this representation that guides subsequent problem solving.

Let us consider how the concept of encoding can be applied to Siegler's balance-scale task. Recall that children who use rule 1 base their judgments solely on the number of weights. Siegler (1976) tested such children's encoding of the relevant information. First, he allowed the children to observe an arrangement of the scale for 10 seconds. Then he covered the scale, brought another scale forward, and asked the children to reproduce the arrangement that they had just seen. Both 5-year-old and 8-year-old rule 1 users were tested.

Siegler found that the 5-year-olds could reproduce only the weights and not the distances, evidence that they had encoded only weight. The 5-year-olds also failed to benefit from training trials that showed them the results of various configurations of weight and distance. As Siegler notes, the children's failure to learn from training is not surprising given that they never encoded the critical information. The 8-year-olds, in contrast, were able to encode both weight and distance, even though they did not yet use distance information in making their judgments. Because of their sensitivity to both variables, the 8-year-olds were able to benefit from the same training that had been ineffective with the 5-year-olds.

A second mechanism is **automatization**. As noted in the context of Case's (1985) theory of the role of memory in problem solving, there is a characteristic progression in the development of any cognitive skill. At first, the skill—precisely because it is new—requires considerable attention and effort, and few resources may be left for any other sort of cognitive processing. With practice, however, execution of the skill becomes more and more automatic, cognitive resources are freed, and more advanced forms of problem solving become possible. Automatization is a primary mechanism by which the cognitive system overcomes inherent limitations on the amount of information that can be processed.

The same can be said for a third mechanism, **strategy construction**. Like automatization, strategies serve to overcome processing limitations by increasing the efficiency with which information is handled. The child who realizes the organization inherent in a set of items, for example, may need to remember only the general categories and not every individual item. Similarly, a child who has developed the min strategy for adding numbers will need to count just twice rather than eight times when adding 2 plus 8.

Encoding
Attending to and forming internal representations of certain features of the environment. A mechanism of change in information-processing theories.

Automatization
An increase in the efficiency with which cognitive operations are executed as a result of practice. A mechanism of change in information-processing theories.

Strategy construction
The creation of strategies for processing and remembering information. A mechanism of change in information-processing theories.

Strategy selection
Progressively greater use of relatively effective strategies in comparison to relatively ineffective ones. A mechanism of change in information-processing theories.

A final, closely related mechanism is **strategy selection**. As we have seen, children often try out a variety of strategies when they are in the process of developing a new form of competence. We discussed examples with respect to both memory and arithmetic, and the same finding has emerged for other kinds of problem-solving as well (Ellis, 1997). Given this multiplicity of approaches, a main task for development is selecting the strategy or combination of strategies that provides the optimal approach to problem solution. Over time, these relatively effective approaches come to be used more and more, whereas less effective strategies are gradually discarded. There is, in short, a survival of the fittest: Strategies that work are the ones that are maintained.

If the preceding passage reminded you of a theory from another discipline of science, the similarity was deliberate. Siegler (1996a) argues that cognitive development across the course of childhood is in many respects parallel to biological evolution in the history of a species. In both evolution and development, change builds on initial diversity and variation. In the case of evolution, the diversity is in the distribution of genes within a species; in development, it lies in the variation in problem-solving approaches (multiple strategies, different encodings, etc.) that characterize the initial response to a task. In both evolution and development, the initial variation is followed by selection based on differential success: reproductive success in the case of evolution, problem-solving success in the case of development. And in both evolution and development, successful variants are preserved and passed on—to the next generation in the evolution of species, to future problem-solving efforts in the development of the child. In Siegler's analysis, the parallels between biology and psychology are not surprising, because they follow from the similar tasks of evolution and development: to produce adaptive change over time.

✓ *To Recap...*

Information-processing researchers use a variety of methods to study cognitive change, two of which have been especially important in recent research. Microgenetic studies involve repeated observations, typically in multiple sessions across weeks or months, of children's problem-solving efforts. This approach offers the possibility of observing change as it occurs. Self-modifying computer simulations are computer programs whose purpose is to model the change from one level of understanding to another.

Mechanisms that seem to be important for cognitive change include encoding, automatization, strategy construction, and strategy selection. Developmental advances in encoding make developmental advances in reasoning possible. Automatization frees resources for other cognitive activities. Strategy construction helps overcome the limitations of the information-processing system, and strategy selection ensures that the most effective strategies are used. A set of general principles that may unite these and other change mechanisms can be drawn from the theory of biological evolution. Cognitive development, like evolution, involves the progressive selection and preservation of adaptive variations from an initial pool of possibilities.

Conclusion

As we saw in Chapter 8, the Piagetian approach to cognitive development is some 75 years old, dating back to Piaget's first studies in the 1920s. As we will see in Chapter 10, the intelligence-test approach, the third of the three general perspectives we examine, is even older.

Information processing is the relative newcomer among the major approaches to cognitive development. Despite its relative youth, it has already achieved some noteworthy successes, as our discussions throughout this chapter should make clear. Nevertheless, even its strongest advocates clearly regard their efforts as work in progress—already fruitful, to be sure, but with much still to be done. In that spirit, we focus here on some of the challenges that remain for workers in this tradition. We discuss three.

One challenge concerns scope. Information-processing research has addressed many different aspects of child development. Information-processing theories have been more limited. To date, information-processing theorists have been most successful at constructing precise models of specific, but also somewhat limited, aspects of child development—what Klahr and MacWhinney (1998) refer to as "toy versions" of the larger domains of interest. There is as yet no information-processing theory that rivals Piaget's theory in the scope of phenomena it encompasses.

A second challenge relates to the computer metaphor that has guided so much work in this tradition. One obvious difference between humans and computers concerns the social context for intelligent behavior. Humans, unlike computers, interact constantly with other humans, and these interactions are both an important context for exercising cognitive skills and one of the sources of those skills. Information-processing conceptions, it is true, have begun to influence the study of social cognition and social behavior; we will see a number of examples in the later chapters of the book. We saw in this chapter that researchers are beginning to explore the social contributors to information-processing skills—recall the work on memory talk, for example. Nevertheless, the social world has been a relatively neglected topic for most information-processing researchers.

A final challenge relates to the issue with which we concluded our discussion: cognitive change. Despite much recent attention to the question, information-processing theorists are still far from producing a completely satisfactory explanation of how cognitive change comes about. On the other hand, they *have* generated both specific models of the change process and the methods for testing the models. Thus they seem clearly to be moving in the right direction.

<u>Visual Summary for Chapter 9:</u>

Cognitive Development: The Information-Processing Approach

The Nature of the Approach

The Flowchart Metaphor → Information-processing theorists often employ a flowchart metaphor to describe the flow of information through the cognitive system, specifying the processes that occur between environmental input and response output.

The Computer Metaphor → The computer can serve as a useful metaphor for thinking about human cognition and can also provide a method for simulating the processes underlying cognition and cognitive change.

Comparisons with Piaget → Information-processing theories share Piaget's concern with cognitive development, his emphasis on underlying rules and structures, and, in some cases, his use of stages to describe development. Most information-processing theorists, however, do not subscribe to Piaget's broad, general stages, developing instead domain-specific models that are more precise, more complete, and more testable.

Memory in Infancy

Recognition Memory → Habituation and conditioning studies demonstrate recognition memory – the realization that a perceptually present stimulus or event has been encountered before – in newborns. With development, the span of time across which the infant can retain material increases, as does the amount and complexity of the material that can be retained.

Recall Memory → Recall memory – the retrieval of some past stimulus or event even when it is not perceptually present – is more difficult to study in infancy. Recent research suggests that simple forms of recall (e.g., the ability to search for vanished objects, or the imitation of models from the past) may emerge by the end of the first year.

Memory in Older Children

Three Sources of Improvement in Memory Across the Childhood Years

The Role of Strategies → One source of improvement is the development of mnemonic strategies, such as rehearsal and organization. The tendency to use strategies, the complexity of strategies, and the skill with which strategies are executed all increase with age. The emphasis on strategies reflects one important theme in information-processing research – the existence of limits in information-processing resources and the need to develop techniques to overcome the limits.

The Role of Metamemory → Metamemory includes knowledge about memory in general and one's own memory in particular. Such knowledge increases with age and can lead to improvements in memory performance. Research into metamemory reflects another theme of the information-processing approach – the need for executive control to select and coordinate cognitive activities.

The Role of Knowledge → Memory in older children is more likely to involve inferences and constructions that go beyond the literal input (constructive memory) than in younger children. Older children also possess greater content-specific expertise, which contributes to memory performance. The emergence of scripts, knowledge concerning the typical structure of events, also facilitates memory performance. Conversations with parents have been found to influence the development of various forms of memory, including scripts and autobiographical memory.

Children's Eyewitness Testimony

| Children's Eyewitness Testimony | | Children's memory is important in many real-life contexts, perhaps most critically when children offer testimony in cases of alleged abuse. Research directed to the issue suggests that children's memories are usually trustworthy; it also indicates, however, that suggestibility can be a danger, especially with young children. |

Problem Solving

Factors that Contribute to Age-Related Improvements in Problem Solving

| Development of Rules | | The development of mental rules that guide responding is one contributor to cognitive change. Solution of balance-scale problems, for example, consistently follows one of four general rules, and the complexity and appropriateness of the rules increase with age. |

| Contribution of Memory | | Older children have greater storage capacity needed to remember past results while performing new operations. They are thus capable of more complex forms of reasoning and problem solving than younger children. This growth in storage capacity results from an increase in operational efficiency, which in turn results from both biological maturation and practice at executing operations. |

Academic Abilities

| Arithmetic | | Children develop a variety of strategies to solve arithmetic problems and typically use several strategies rather than just one. With increased age, there is a gradual ascendance of more efficient strategies, such as retrieval, over less effective ones. |

| Reading | | Studies of reading indicate that the basic cognitive processes stressed in information-processing theory — strategies, general knowledge, and short-term memory — all contribute to reading comprehension. Also important is phonological awareness, the realization that letters correspond to sounds and the ability to perform specific letter-to-sound translations. |

Cognitive Change

| Methods of Study | | Microgenetic studies and self-modifying computer simulations are two methods of study that have been especially important in recent research studying cognitive change. Microgenetic studies offer the possibility of observing change as it occurs, through repeated observations across weeks or months of children's problem-solving efforts. Self-modifying computer simulations are computer programs whose purpose is to model the change from one level of understanding to another. |

| Mechanisms of Change | | Encoding, automatization, strategy construction, and strategy selection are mechanisms that seem important for cognitive change. Developmental advances in encoding make developmental advances in reasoning possible. Automatization frees resources for other cognitive activities. Strategy construction helps to overcome the limitations of the information-processing system, and strategy selection ensures that the most effective strategies are used. |

Chapter 10

Cognitive Development: The Intelligence-Test Approach

In the 1996 movie Phenomenon, *John Travolta plays a small-town mechanic who experiences a remarkable transformation. Knocked unconscious by a mysterious flash of light, George Malley awakens to find himself a genius. Formerly a man of simple interests and modest accomplishments, George is suddenly intellectually insatiable. He devours several books a day, creates invention after invention, embarrasses his former mentor at chess, and cracks security codes in his spare time. In addition to documenting these and other amazing feats, the movie dramatizes the many changes—not all of them positive— that George's newfound intellectual abilities bring to his life.*

To older moviegoers, parts of the Phenomenon *plot line may seem familiar. In the 1968 movie* Charly, *Cliff Robertson plays a mentally retarded man who undergoes a brain operation and emerges with the IQ of a genius.* Charly *depicts the profound transformations in its title character's life that result from this leap upward in IQ—as well as the further transformations when the effects of the operation fade and Charly's IQ returns to its initial level.*

Phenomenon *and* Charly *are both well-made movies that tell interesting stories. The appeal of these films, however, may have a deeper root as well. The plots of both tap into a pervasive fascination—at least in industrialized Western societies—with intelligence and the effects that intelligence has. For many people, individual differences in intelligence—what they are, where they come from, what they lead to—are issues of great personal and great scientific importance. For many people, IQ is the definition of intelligence, and high IQ is an unquestioned good. And for many, the possibility of raising IQ—and thereby of producing both individual and societal change—is one of the most promising scenarios that psychology has to offer.*

In this chapter we consider the issues sketched in the preceding paragraphs. Our focus is on the source of IQ scores: the **psychometric**, or intelligence-test, approach to cognition. As will become clear, we do not subscribe to the all-importance of IQ, nor do we have simple answers to offer for the large questions that the psychometric approach examines. The topics that we address in this chapter are among the most controversial in the field. What we *can* do is convey what research to date has and has not been able to establish—and thus help you form your own position on the various debates.

Why has the intelligence-test approach been so controversial? At least part of the answer lies in some important differences between this approach and the Piagetian and information-processing perspectives. Some of the differences relate to the distinction between normative and idiographic approaches to development, one of the general issues identified in Chapter 1. Piaget's approach falls clearly under the normative heading, in that his emphasis was always on similarities in children's development—that is, forms of knowledge that all children develop and stages all children move through. Although information-processing researchers have paid more attention to individual differences than did Piaget, they also have tended to concentrate on basic processes that are common to all children. In contrast, the main point of the intelligence-test approach is to identify differences in children's cognitive abilities. Furthermore, an IQ test identifies not merely differences, but *ordered* differences—it says that one child is more or less intelligent than another or that a particular child is above or below average in intelligence. IQ tests thus involve an evaluative component that is impossible to escape. The fact that such tests force us to make value judgments about children is one reason they have always been controversial.

Another difference between the intelligence-test approach and the Piagetian and information-processing approaches concerns purpose and uses. The research discussed in the two preceding chapters is very much theoretically oriented, its goal being to identify basic cognitive processes. We saw that such research has begun to have practical applications (e.g., effects on school curriculum); to date, however, such applications have been limited and secondary to the basic theoretical aims. In contrast, the psychometric approach has been pragmatically oriented from the start. As we will see, IQ tests were designed for practical purposes, and they have always had practical uses—most notably, to determine what kind of schooling a child is to receive. This factor, too, contributes to the controversy. Unlike many of psychologists' measures, IQ tests really can make a difference in a child's life.

In this chapter, we begin by reviewing what IQ tests for children look like, along with some of their strengths and weaknesses. We then move on to some of the theoretical issues that have been the focus of research in the psychometric tradition. Because of the importance of the question, we pay special attention to the role of experience in the development of intelligence, considering both the contribution of the family environment and the effects of schooling. Although our emphasis is on IQ, we occasionally broaden the scope to include other ways to assess differences in intellectual ability. And in the final part of the chapter, we break away from the traditional IQ approach to consider some recent and exciting alternative approaches to studying intelligence.

The Nature of IQ Tests

Before we consider the data that IQ tests yield, it is important to have some idea of how such tests are put together and what kinds of abilities they measure. We begin, therefore, with an overview of the history and construction of IQ tests. We take a brief look at several specific tests and then turn to the important question of how to evaluate such measures.

The Binet Approach to Measuring Intelligence

The first successful intelligence test was developed in Paris in 1905 by Alfred Binet and Theodore Simon. Binet and Simon had been hired by the Paris school authorities to develop a test that could be given to children who were having difficulty in school. The goal was to distinguish between children who were capable, perhaps with extra help, of succeeding in school and children who were simply not intelligent enough to cope with the regular curriculum. Once the latter group had been identified, they could be placed in special classes from which they might benefit. This sort of tracking based on test performance has become controversial in recent years (Dornbusch, Glasgow, & Lin, 1996), but originally it had a quite humanitarian purpose.

Binet and Simon took a pragmatic approach to their task. They tried out a large number of possible items for their test, looking at performance across both a range of ages and a range of ability levels (i.e., children who were known to do well in school

IQ tests were originally devised for purposes of school placement in Paris school systems in the early 1900s. Such educational applications remain important for contemporary IQ tests.

and children who were known to do poorly in school). All the items kept for the test were items on which older children, on the average, did better than younger children. Such improvement with age was one of Binet and Simon's criteria for a measure of childhood intelligence. These items also tended to differentiate between academically successful children and those who were less successful, which, of course, was the immediate purpose for which the test was designed. The test items, some of which appear in modified form on contemporary tests, included identification of parts of the body, naming of familiar objects, and distinguishing between abstract words—for example, indicating the difference between liking and respecting.

The Stanford–Binet Intelligence Scale (Thorndike, Hagen, & Sattler, 1986) is the direct descendant of the original Binet–Simon test. It was developed in 1916 by Lewis Terman at Stanford University and has been revised several times since. The Stanford–Binet shares several features with Binet's original instrument. It is a test of childhood intelligence, applicable to every age group within the span of childhood except infancy. It is a global measure of intelligence, designed to yield a single intelligence quotient, or IQ, score that summarizes the child's ability. And it stresses the kinds of verbal and academic skills that are important in school. Specifically, the current version of the Stanford–Binet assesses four general kinds of ability: verbal reasoning, quantitative reasoning, abstract/visual reasoning, and short-term memory.

The Stanford–Binet—and indeed every other standardized test of intelligence—shares one other important feature with Binet's original test. We saw that Binet's approach to measuring intelligence was based on comparing the performances of different groups of children. All contemporary tests of intelligence are comparative, or relative, measures. There is no absolute metric for measuring intelligence, as there is for measuring height or weight. Instead, a child's IQ is a function of how that child's performance compares with the performance of other children the same age. Children who perform at the average for their age group have average IQs, which by convention are set at 100. Children who outperform their

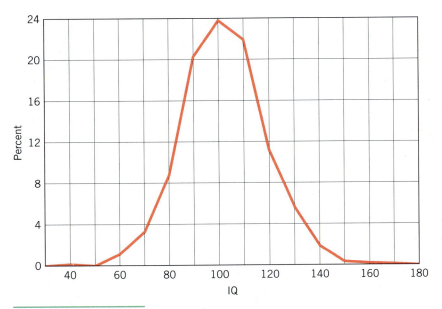

Figure 10.1
Typical distribution of IQ scores in a sample of children. Tests like the Stanford–Binet are designed to yield a normal distribution of IQs with a mean of 100. These data are from an early form of the Stanford–Binet Intelligence Scale (L–M). From *Stanford–Binet Intelligence Scale* (3rd ed., p. 18) by L.M. Terman and M.A. Merrill, 1973, Chicago: The Riverside Publishing Company. Copyright © 1973 by the Riverside Publishing Company. Reproduced with permission of the Riverside Publishing Company, 8420 W. Bryn Mawr Avenue, Chicago, IL 60631.

peers have above-average IQs; children who lag behind their age group have below-average IQs. The greater the discrepancy from average, the higher or lower the IQ will be. Figure 10.1 shows a typical distribution of IQ scores.

The Wechsler and Kaufman Tests

The leading alternative to the Stanford–Binet is a series of tests developed by David Wechsler. There are two Wechsler tests designed for childhood: the Wechsler Intelligence Scale for Children (WISC-III), which is intended for ages 6 to 16, and the Wechsler Preschool and Primary Scale of Intelligence (WPPSI), which is intended for ages 4 to 6.5 (Wechsler, 1989, 1991). The Wechsler test bears many similarities to the Stanford–Binet, including a focus on academically relevant skills. One difference between the two tests is that the Wechsler is divided into a verbal scale (which includes items such as vocabulary and general information) and a performance scale (which includes items such as assembling a puzzle and reproducing a design). The test therefore yields both an overall IQ and separate verbal and performance IQs. Some examples of the kinds of items included on the Wechsler test are shown in Table 10.1.

A relatively recent entry to the field of childhood assessment is a test developed by Kaufman and Kaufman (1983). The Kaufman Assessment Battery for Children, or K-ABC, marks an explicit effort to include cultural diversity and cultural fairness in the construction and administration of a test. The K-ABC thus attempts to answer one long-standing criticism of traditional IQ tests—namely, that such measures may discriminate against children from poor or minority families. The K-ABC also has a grounding in information-processing conceptions of intelligence, a grounding

Table 10.1
Types of Items Included on the Wechsler Intelligence Scale for Children–Third Edition

Subtest	Verbal Scale
Information	How many wings does a bird have? How many nickels make a dime? What is pepper?
Arithmetic	Sam had three pieces of candy and Joe gave him four more. How many pieces of candy did Sam have altogether? If two apples cost $.15, what will be the cost of a dozen apples?
Vocabulary	What is a _____? or What does ……….. mean? Hammer Protect Epidemic

Subtest	Performance Scale
Object assembly	Put the pieces together to make a familiar object.

Source: Adapted from *Wechsler Intelligence Scale for Children–Third Edition*. Copyright © 1991 by The Psychological Corporation. Reproduced by permission. All rights reserved.

motivated by another criticism leveled at traditional measures, that they are empirically derived instruments that lack a clear theoretical rationale. Items on the K-ABC are divided into two theoretically derived categories: the Sequential Processing Scale, which examines forms of problem solving for which the serial or temporal order of the information is important; and the Simultaneous Processing Scale, which examines forms of problem solving that require integration of simultaneously available information.

Other Tests of Childhood Intelligence

Other tests of childhood IQ differ in either the group at which they are targeted or the way in which they are administered. Some tests are directed toward infancy, the one age period not covered by the Stanford–Binet, Wechsler, or K-ABC tests. The best-known measure of infant development is the Bayley Scales of Infant Development (Bayley, 1993). Not surprisingly, measures of infant intelligence tend to stress sensorimotor skills, as opposed to the academic and verbal emphasis found in tests for older children. The Bayley test, for example, is divided into a motor scale (with items assessing control of the body, muscular coordination, manipulatory skill, and so on) and a mental scale (including items assessing sensory-perceptual acuity, vocalization, and memory). Table 10.2 presents some items from the mental scale.

In addition to individually administered tests, such as the Stanford–Binet and Wechsler, there are group tests of intelligence—that is, tests that can be administered

Table 10.2
Examples of Items from the Bayley Scales of Infant Development

Age Placement (in months)	*Ability Measured*	*Procedure*	*Credit*
1	Habituates to rattle	Shake rattle at regular intervals behind child's head	If child shows an initial alerting response that decreases over trials
6	Smiles at mirror image	Place mirror in front of child	If child smiles at image in mirror
12	Pushes car	Push toy car while child watches, then tell child, "Push the car, push the car like I did."	If child intentionally pushes car so that all four wheels stay on table
17–19	Uses two different words appropriately	Record the child's spontaneous word usage throughout the exam	If child uses two (nonimitative) words appropriately
23–25	Points to five pictures	Show pictures of 10 common objects (e.g., dog, book, car), say "Show me the _____."	If child either correctly points to or names at least five pictures

Source: From *Bayley Scales of Infant Development,* second edition. Copyright © 1993 by The Psychological Corporation. Reprinted by permission. All rights reserved.

to large numbers of children at the same time. Because of their ease of administration and efficiency, group tests are commonly used in school settings. Undoubtedly the majority of IQ scores that exist in school files derive from group tests.

Evaluating the Tests

How can we decide whether a test that claims to measure intelligence really does? A standardized test of intelligence—or indeed of any attribute—must meet two criteria: reliability and validity.

Reliability   The consistency or repeatability of measurement is referred to as **reliability**. Does the test give us a consistent picture of what the child can do? Or do scores on the test fluctuate from one testing occasion to the next, perhaps sometimes coming out very high and sometimes very low? Clearly, a test that lacks reliability can hardly give us an accurate measure of the child's ability.

The notion of reliability does not mean that children's IQ scores can never change. Scores often do go up or down as children develop. Reliability refers to short-term consistency—that is, to the constancy of the measuring instrument, not of the child. The major tests of childhood IQ, such as the Stanford–Binet and Wechsler, do possess good reliability.

Validity   The second criterion that a test must meet is **validity**. The issue of validity is easy to summarize: Does the test measure what it claims to measure? Do scores on the Stanford–Binet, for example, really reflect individual differences in children's

Reliability
The consistency or repeatability of a measuring instrument. A necessary property of a standardized test.

Validity
The accuracy with which a measuring instrument assesses the attribute that it is designed to measure. A necessary property of a standardized test.

intelligence? Or do the scores have some other basis—perhaps differences in motivation, or in general test-taking ability, or in familiarity with the specific test content?

The validity of a test can be determined in various ways. The approach most commonly used for IQ tests is labeled *criterion validity*. To determine criterion validity, we first specify some external measure, or criterion, of the attribute that we are attempting to assess. We then see whether scores on the test relate to performance on this external criterion. For tests of childhood IQ, the most common external criterion has been performance in school or on standardized tests of academic ability. Tests such as the Stanford–Binet do in fact relate to academic performance, with typical correlations of about .5 (Brody, 1997; Snow & Yalow, 1982). Thus, on the average, the higher the child's IQ, the better the child does in school.

Academic performance is not the only correlate of IQ. IQ also correlates with most standard laboratory measures of learning and cognitive performance—not perfectly, to be sure, but with typical values of around .5 (Jensen, 1981). IQ in adulthood correlates, again at a midrange level, with indices of occupational status and with measures of job performance (Hunter & Hunter, 1984). Indeed, as we saw in the discussion of the Terman study of genius (Chapter 3), high IQ is associated with a wide range of favorable life outcomes. It is this ability to predict important aspects of everyday intelligent behavior that constitutes the argument for IQ tests as valid measures of intelligence.

It is important to note some qualifications to the points just made. Consider the relation between IQ and performance in school. A correlation of .5 indicates a moderate relation between IQ and academic performance. But if the correlation is only .5, there must also be a number of exceptions to this on-the-average relation—children with high IQs who do poorly in school, children with average or below-average IQs who do well in school. Knowing a child's IQ does not allow us to predict that child's school performance (or, indeed, anything else) with certainty. Furthermore, as we saw in Chapter 3, a correlation in itself does not allow us to determine the cause and effect. Thus, simply knowing that IQ correlates with school performance does not allow us to conclude that children do well or poorly in school *because* of their IQs. This is one possible explanation for the correlation, but it is not the only one. All we know for certain is that there is some relation between the two variables.

IQ tests are most successful at measuring skills necessary for success in school. Such tests may not capture forms of intelligence that are important in other contexts.

We can note finally that there is a kind of inbred relation between IQ tests and school performance. IQ tests for children were devised to predict school performance, and this is what they do (although not perfectly). Performance in school is important in our culture; so, too, is performance in the occupational contexts to which school success often leads. It is reasonable to argue, therefore, that IQ tests do measure something of what we mean by intelligence in our culture. But the qualifications implied by this wording are important. IQ tests may not tap cognitive skills that are important in other cultures, for example (as discussed in Chapter 8), the ability to navigate in a society in which sailing is important or (as discussed later in this chapter) the ability to succeed as an urban candy vendor at an age when most Western children have barely started school. These tests may not even tap skills that are important for some subgroups within our culture, such as the ability to do chores on the family farm or to cope with the challenges of life in an inner-city ghetto. And for any individual, they at best measure *something* of intelligence, not everything that we would want this term to mean. The two preceding chapters considered numerous aspects of intelligence that are not well captured by IQ tests. Later in this chapter, we will see that even within the psychometric tradition there are a number of interesting alternatives to IQ.

✓ To Recap...

The psychometric, or intelligence-test, approach to intelligence is in several respects different from the Piagetian and information-processing approaches. The purpose of IQ tests is to measure individual differences in intellectual ability. Such tests were originally devised for practical purposes, and they have always had practical applications—school placement, for example. Such real-world applications contribute to the controversy that has always surrounded IQ tests.

Tests of intelligence must be both reliable and valid. The major IQ tests do possess satisfactory reliability. Whether the tests are valid measures of intelligence has been more difficult to determine. Tests of childhood IQ do relate to measures of academic performance, an important external criterion of childhood intelligence. The relation is not perfect, however. Furthermore, the academic focus of most IQ tests means that they may not be good measures of other kinds of intelligence.

Issues in the Study of Intelligence

We have emphasized the pragmatic origins and uses of IQ tests. But the early pioneers of intelligence testing, including Binet, were also interested in theoretical questions about the nature of intelligence. And IQ tests have long served as another context, in addition to Piagetian and information-processing measures, for trying to determine what intelligence is and how it changes with development. In this section, we consider some of the theoretical issues that have most intrigued researchers in the intelligence-test tradition.

The Organization of Intelligence

The question of the organization or structure of intelligence is a basic issue that any approach to intelligence must confront. We have seen how Piagetian and information-processing researchers have examined this question. Psychometric researchers also study the organization of intelligence, but the methods they use are different from those that we have encountered thus far.

In the psychometric approach, conclusions about the organization of intelligence are based on the individual differences that IQ tests elicit. The issue is whether these differences show consistent and interpretable patterns, patterns that can tell us something about how intelligence is organized.

Let us consider two opposed possibilities. Suppose that intelligence is a unitary trait—that is, that there is a single "general intelligence" that people possess in varying degrees. If so, then the particular task that we use to measure intelligence should not really matter. Some people—those who are high in general intelligence—will do well whatever the task, and some will do poorly whatever the task. This outcome would be reflected in uniformly high correlations among different measures of intelligence.

Consider now a very different hypothesis. Perhaps there is no such thing as general intelligence. Perhaps, instead, there are various specific intelligences—verbal intelligence, mathematical intelligence, spatial intelligence, and so on. People may be high in one form of intelligence but low in some other form. What happens, then, if we administer a test battery that assesses these different forms of intelligence? We no longer expect uniformly high correlations among our measures. Instead, a particular task should correlate most strongly with other tasks that are measuring the same kind of intelligence. Verbal tasks, for example, should correlate strongly with other verbal tasks, but weakly or not at all with measures of spatial ability.

The preceding example summarizes the psychometric approach to the organization of intelligence: determine how intelligence is organized by examining the pattern of correlations across different measures of intelligence. In practice, the approach is more complicated than this brief description suggests. Psychometric researchers use a complex statistical procedure, called *factor analysis*, to make sense of the large number of correlations that their research yields. There are disagreements about exactly how to carry out and interpret factor analyses, and results may vary depending on the method used. Results may also vary across different batteries of tasks or different samples of participants (Kail & Pellegrino, 1985). Thus, psychometric researchers provide no single, agreed-upon answer to the structure question. But they have offered some interesting theories and related findings.

General versus Specific   We have already previewed the question that has generated the most interest and debate among researchers of the organization of intelligence: Is intelligence a single general ability, or does intelligence consist instead of a number of specific abilities?

The earliest proponent of the general-intelligence view was the inventor of factor analysis, Charles Spearman. Spearman proposed what has come to be called a *two-factor theory of intelligence* (Spearman, 1927). One factor is general intelligence, or **g**. In Spearman's view, g permeates every form of intellectual functioning and is the most important determinant of individual differences on any test of intelligence. The second factor is *s*, Spearman's label for specific abilities that contribute to performance on particular tasks. Spearman used his newly invented technique of factor analysis to analyze correlations among different measures of intelligence. His conclusion was that the consistently positive correlations across measures were evidence for the existence and importance of g.

Other theorists have argued for a more differentiated model. Louis Thurstone, for example, developed an intelligence test designed to assess seven *primary mental abilities*: verbal comprehension, verbal fluency, number, spatial visualization, memory, reasoning, and perceptual speed (Thurstone, 1938; Thurstone & Thurstone,

g
General intelligence; g is assumed to determine performance on a wide range of intellectual measures.

1962). Thurstone regarded these seven abilities as largely independent and equally important.

Seven is by no means the maximum number of abilities that have been proposed. In J. P. Guilford's *structure of the intellect* model, there are at least 180 somewhat distinct mental abilities (Guilford, 1988)!

So what is the solution to the general versus specific dispute? As is often the case, the answer probably lies somewhere between extreme positions. The consistent finding of positive correlations among different measures of intelligence is evidence that something like general intelligence does exist. The fact that the correlations are far from perfect is evidence that more specific subskills also exist. This sort of solution is sometimes referred to as a **hierarchical model of intelligence**—intelligence is seen as organized in a hierarchical fashion, with broad, general abilities at the top of the hierarchy and more limited, specific skills nested underneath (Sternberg, 1985). This model probably corresponds to the intuitions that most of us hold about intelligence. We have some ability to order people, including ourselves, along some general dimension of intelligence. But we also realize that different people have different strengths and weaknesses and that we may outshine a particular peer in some respects yet lag behind in others.

Hierarchical model of intelligence
A model of the structure of intelligence in which intellectual abilities are seen as being organized hierarchically, with broad, general abilities at the top of the hierarchy and more specific skills nested underneath.

Developmental Changes in Structure Another question is particularly interesting to child psychologists: Does the structure of intelligence change as the child develops? If so, how?

Two kinds of developmental change have been suggested. One is a differentiation of abilities with increasing age. In this view, the young child's intellectual system is relatively undifferentiated, consisting mainly of general intelligence rather than distinct abilities. As the child develops, specific and at least somewhat separate abilities emerge, and the unified intelligence of early childhood gives way to a more differentiated system. This position predicts a change in the pattern of correlations across childhood. In early childhood, different measures of intelligence should correlate strongly, because all tap into the same general cognitive system. In later childhood, the correlations should drop as the child's abilities become more differentiated. Factor-analytic studies provide some support for this prediction (Kail & Pellegrino, 1985).

The first developmental change, then, is in the number of distinct factors of intelligence that can be identified. The second change concerns the nature of the factors. Various models have been proposed, but most seem to be variants of the same general theme (Sternberg & Powell, 1983). In infancy, intelligence consists mainly of perceptual and motor abilities. As the child develops, symbolic and verbal abilities emerge, and the sensorimotor functioning of infancy is supplanted by more abstract forms of thought. Thus, *intelligence* means somewhat different things at different ages. This claim, too, finds some support in factor-analytic research (Plomin, DeFries, & Fulker, 1988).

Stability of IQ

Do children's IQs remain stable as they develop, so that we can assume that a child who scores a 100 at age 4 will also score 100 at ages 8 or 12 or 20? Or can a child's IQ change? This is a question of both theoretical and practical importance.

Answering the question requires a longitudinal approach, in which the same children are tested repeatedly across some span of time. Researchers have conducted many longitudinal studies of IQ, including some essentially life-span efforts that began in the 1920s (Bayley, 1970). We therefore have quite a bit of data on this issue. Several conclusions emerge.

Prediction from Infancy   A first conclusion is that traditional tests of infant intelligence do not predict well to tests of later intelligence. The correlation between performance on the Bayley Scales, for example, and performance on later tests is typically close to 0 (Lipsitt, 1992; McCall, 1981). Thus, knowing how fast an infant is developing gives us no basis for predicting whether that infant will turn into an intelligent child or an intelligent adult.

There are some exceptions to this statement. Very low scores on infant tests sometimes indicate some problem in development (Siegel, 1989). Scores on particular subparts of an infant test (such as items dealing with fine motor skills) may relate to measures of similar skills on childhood tests (Siegel, 1992). For the most part, however, individual differences in infant scores do not tell us much about how children will differ later in development. Thus, there is little reason for the parents of a precocious 6-month-old to send away for college catalogs. And there is little reason for parents to become concerned just because their baby cannot stack blocks as early as the neighbors' babies.

Why should there be this gap between infant intelligence and later intelligence? The usual explanation stresses the differences in the content of infant tests and childhood tests (Brownell & Strauss, 1984). Tests such as the Stanford–Binet and WISC emphasize symbolic abilities (such as language) and abstract, higher-order reasoning and problem solving. Infant tests necessarily stress quite different things—manual dexterity, visual and auditory alertness, and so on. This explanation is related to the continuity–discontinuity issue introduced in Chapter 1. The argument is that there is a discontinuity in the nature of intelligence between infancy and later childhood. Intelligence in infancy requires different skills than those required by later intelligence, and thus it is not surprising that variations in infant development do not relate to variations in later development. The work on developmental changes in the structure of intelligence, discussed in the preceding section, is compatible with this hypothesis.

There is almost certainly some truth to the discontinuity argument. But to many psychologists, there is something unsatisfactory about any extreme version of the hypothesis. Surely there must be *some* continuity from infancy to childhood, *some* aspect of intelligence that is common across all age periods. But what might this common thread be?

Recent research suggests that the common thread may be *response to novelty*. This conclusion comes from longitudinal studies in which children who were first tested as infants are later assessed for childhood IQ. Investigators have reported positive relations between various measures of interest in and response to novelty in infancy and later measures of intelligence (Colombo, 1993; McCall & Carriger, 1993; Slater, 1995). For example, babies who show an especially strong preference for new compared with familiar stimuli tend to do well on later IQ tests (Fagan, 1992; Rose & Feldman, 1995). Similarly, babies who are especially quick to habituate to familiar stimuli tend to perform well on later tests (Slater et al., 1989). The relations that have been demonstrated are modest in size (typical correlations are about .35 to .40) and do not extend beyond age 11 or 12 in the follow-ups available to date. Nevertheless, these findings provide a first piece of evidence for some continuity in intelligence from infancy to later childhood.

Why might response to novelty in infancy relate to later IQ? A number of hypotheses have been proposed, and there is still no consensus among researchers as to the best explanation (McCall, 1994; McCall & Mash, 1994). Perhaps the leading candidate is speed of processing. Infants who are quick to habituate to the familiar and to turn to something new are apparently taking in information more rapid-

Figure 10.2
The Fagan Test of Infant Intelligence. Infants are first exposed to one of the two members of each stimulus pair, then given a chance to look at either the familiar stimulus or the novel alternative. A relatively strong preference for novelty correlates positively with later IQ. From "Predictive Validity of the Fagan Test of Infant Intelligence" by J. F. Fagan III, P. Shepherd, and C. Knevel, 1991, Meeting of the Society for Research in Child Development, Seattle. Copyright © 1993 by J. F. Fagan III. Reprinted by permission.

ly than are their slower-to-habituate peers. It is certainly plausible that speed of processing new information would be a component of intelligence at any point in the life span. And there is in fact evidence for such a relation in older individuals: In both children and adults, various measures of speed of processing have been found to correlate with IQ (Deary, 1995; Vernon, 1993). In addition, one recent study reports a relation between reaction time in infancy and both reaction time and IQ at age 4 (Dougherty & Haith, 1997). It may be that the response-to-novelty measures are predictive because they tap into this basic component of the intellectual system.

As might be expected, the studies of response to novelty have led to the creation of a new approach to assessing infant intelligence. In the Fagan Test of Infant Intelligence (Fagan & Detterman, 1992; Fagan & Shepherd, 1986), babies are shown a picture to look at for a brief period, after which the original picture is paired with a slightly different, novel picture (see Figure 10.2). The measure of interest is how long the baby looks at the novel compared with the familiar. The greater the interest in novelty, the higher the score on the test. And the higher the Fagan score, the higher, on the average, the later IQ.

Prediction across Childhood   After infancy, scores from traditional IQ tests begin to correlate significantly from one age period to another. The correlation is not perfect, however. A typical set of findings is shown in Table 10.3.

Two rules for predicting stability in IQ can be abstracted from the data in the table. A first rule is that the degree of stability decreases as the time period between tests increases. Thus, we typically find more similarity in IQ between ages 3 and 6

Table 10.3
Correlations in IQ across Different Ages

Age	3	6	9	12	18
3		.57	.53	.36	.35
6			.80	.74	.61
9				.90	.76
12					.78

Source: Based on information from "The Stability of Mental Test Performance between Two and Eighteen Years" by M. P. Honzik, J. W. MacFarlan, and L. Allen, *Journal of Experimental Education, 17,* p. 323, 1948. Reprinted with permission of the Helen Reid Educational Foundation. Published by Heldref Publications, 1319 Eighteenth St., N.W., Washington, D.C. 20036–1802. Copyright © 1948.

than between ages 3 and 12. This pattern fits what we would expect from common sense: The longer we wait between tests, the more chance there is for some change to occur. Indeed, this pattern is not limited to IQ, but applies generally whenever we measure stability or change across varying time periods (Nunnally, 1982).

As an illustration of the second rule, consider a comparison between the 3-to-6 correlation and the 9-to-12 correlation. Both reflect a 3-year interval, and hence by our first rule we would expect them to be equivalent. But the correlation is greater between 9 and 12 than it is between 3 and 6. In general, the older the child, the higher the correlation in IQ for any given span of time. This pattern, too, fits common sense. As children get older, major changes in their abilities relative to those of other children become less and less likely.

Another way to examine the stability question is to ask about the magnitude of changes in IQ. If children's IQs do change (and the less-than-perfect correlations tell us that they do), how large can the changes be? One study found that 79% of a sample of children shifted at least 21 points in IQ between the ages of 2.5 and 17. For 14% of the children, the change was 40 points or more (McCall, Applebaum, & Hogarty, 1973).

In summary, probably the most reasonable position on the stability issue is one that avoids extreme statements. It is not correct to suggest that IQ varies wildly as children develop and that childhood IQ therefore has no predictive value. IQ shows moderately good stability, and the stability increases as the child gets older. Furthermore, at least some apparent change found in longitudinal research may reflect random fluctuations or measurement error (since the tests are not perfectly reliable) rather than genuine change (Moffitt et al., 1993). On the other hand, it is also not correct to suggest that a child's IQ is fixed and unchangeable. IQs do change, and in some cases they change dramatically. We consider some of the reasons for change shortly.

Origins of Individual Differences

Our discussion of IQ has already touched on two of the issues introduced in Chapter 1—normative versus idiographic emphasis and continuity versus discontinuity. We turn next to the third and most general issue—nature versus nurture. The question of the origin of differences in intelligence has been perhaps the most common—and certainly the most heated—context for debates about the relative contributions of biology and experience to human development.

We first considered this question in Chapter 4 in the discussion of hereditary transmission. As we noted, researchers use three main approaches to study this question: family studies, adoption studies, and twin studies.

Table 10.4

Correlations in IQ as a Function of Degree of Genetic Relation

Relation	*Median Correlation*
Siblings	.55
Parent–child	.50
Grandparents–grandchild	.27
First cousins	.26
Second cousins	.16

Source: Adapted from "Genetics and the Development of Intelligence" by S. Scarr-Salapatek, 1975. In F. D. Horowitz (Ed.), *Review of Child Development Research* (Vol. 4, p. 33), Chicago: University of Chicago Press. Copyright © 1975 by the University of Chicago Press. Adapted by permission.

Family Studies   Family studies (also labeled kinship studies) capitalize on our knowledge of the degree of genetic relation among different sorts of relatives. Parent and child, for example, have 50% of their genes in common. Two siblings also share an average of 50% of their genes. For grandparent and grandchild, the average genetic overlap is 25%. For first cousins, the overlap is 12.5%. In general, if we know the type of relation between two people, we know their degree of genetic similarity. We can then see whether similarity in IQ relates to similarity in genes.

Similarity in IQ *does* relate to similarity in genes. Typical correlations in IQ across different degrees of relation are shown in Table 10.4. These findings fit nicely with what would be expected from a genetic model of intelligence (Scarr & Kidd, 1983).

Adoption Studies   The problem in interpreting the family studies, of course, is that genetic similarity is not the only possible explanation for similarity in IQ. The pattern shown in Table 10.4 might also be accounted for by environmental factors. Siblings, after all, usually share similar experiences. Parents are typically an important part of their children's environments. We would expect some relation between the parent's IQ and the child's IQ solely for environmental reasons.

You may recall that studies of adopted children offer a way to disentangle the genetic and environmental explanations for parent–child similarity. Two sets of correlations are relevant. One is the correlation between the adopted child's IQ and the biological parents' IQs. In this case, the usual genetic basis for a correlation remains, but the environmental basis is ruled out. The other correlation of interest is that between the adopted child's IQ and the adoptive parents' IQs. In this case, the environmental basis remains, but the genetic contribution is ruled out.

Before discussing findings, we should note that adoption studies are not really as easy to interpret as this description suggests. In some cases, for example, when the separation of mother and infant does not occur at birth, the biological mother provides part of the postbirth environment. In all cases, the biological mother provides the prenatal environment, which—as we saw in Chapter 5—can be important. There is also the possibility of selective placement, through which adoption agencies attempt to match characteristics of the adoptive parents with characteristics of the biological parents. To the extent that selective placement occurs, parent–child correlations cannot be clearly interpreted as either genetic or environmental (Horn, 1983).

Two main findings emerge from adoption studies (Plomin et al., 1997; Turkheimer, 1991). One concerns the pattern of correlations. Typically, the adopted child's IQ correlates more strongly with the IQs of the biological parents than

Adoptive homes often offer intellectually stimulating environments, and children who grow up in such homes tend to have above-average IQs.

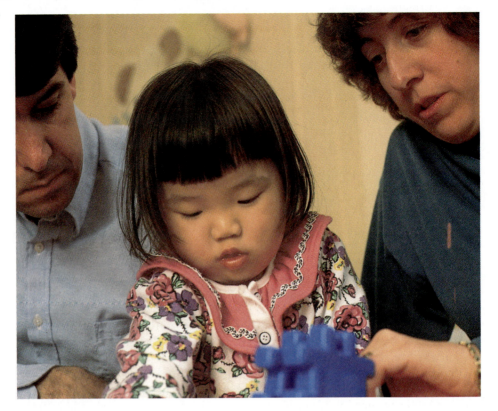

with the IQs of the adoptive parents. This finding provides evidence for the importance of genetic factors. The biological parents make relatively little contribution to an adopted child's environment, but they do provide the child's genes. Recall from our discussion in Chapter 4 that studies of siblings paint a similar picture: stronger correlations for biological siblings than for children adopted into the same home.

The second finding concerns average level of IQ. In most studies the mean IQ for samples of adopted children falls in the range of 105 to 110 (Capron & Duyme, 1989; Scarr & Weinberg, 1983). Adopted children thus tend to have above-average IQs. Why should this be? The most plausible explanation is an environmental one. Parents who adopt children are not a random subset of the population of parents, nor are adoptive homes a random subset of the population of homes. Adoptive parents tend to be highly motivated parents, and adoptive homes tend to be privileged in various ways (such as having a large number of books available and access to good-quality of schools for the children). These factors apparently boost the IQs of children who grow up in such settings. Thus, the adoption studies provide evidence for both genetic and environmental effects.

Twin Studies   The logic of the twin-study approach was explained in Chapter 4. There are two types of twins: monozygotic, or identical, twins, who are genetically identical, and dizygotic, or fraternal, twins, who have only a 50% genetic overlap and thus are no more related than are ordinary siblings. Researchers have compared correlations in IQ for members of identical twin pairs with correlations in IQ for members of fraternal twin pairs. If genes are important, the first set of correlations should be higher than the second.

The results from many such studies were summarized in Table 4.2 (see page 106). The consistent finding is that identical twins *are* more similar (McGue et al., 1993; Nichols, 1978). The same pattern emerges for tests of more specific abilities—for example, verbal and mathematical skills or spatial reasoning ability (Plomin, 1990).

Like family studies, twin studies are compatible with a genetic model, but they do not prove it correct. Environmental factors again provide an alternative explanation. Perhaps identical twins are treated more similarly than are fraternal twins. If so, the greater similarity in IQ may have an environmental rather than a genetic basis.

Researchers have tried in various ways to control for this environmental alternative. Some have attempted to measure aspects of the twins' environments to see whether identical twins are in fact treated more similarly than are fraternal twins. Investigators have concluded that such differential treatment is less marked than is often claimed; furthermore, to the extent that it does occur, it appears to be elicited by preexisting characteristics of the twins, such as the greater physical similarity or more similar temperaments of identical twins. In this view, then, the similarity between identical twins leads to their being treated similarly, not the reverse (Lytton, 1977, 1980).

The most widely cited attempt to control for environmental factors comes in the study of twins reared apart. If identical twins are separated early in life and reared in unrelated environments, then there is no environmental basis (other than prenatal experiences) for their developing similarly. The twins still share 100% of their genes, however. Should they still correlate in IQ, powerful evidence for the importance of genes would be gained.

Table 10.5 summarizes results from studies of twins reared apart. The values in the table indicate that separated twins correlate quite substantially in IQ. Indeed, the reported correlations are higher for identical twins reared apart than they are for fraternal twins reared in the same home!

We noted that some caution is necessary in interpreting the results of adoption studies. The same point applies to studies of twins reared apart. Many of the results summarized in Table 10.5 come from older studies that are subject to a number of methodological criticisms (Farber, 1981; Taylor, 1980). Separated twins are not easy to find, and they often have not been studied well once found. On the other hand, two ongoing studies of twins reared apart appear methodologically sound, and these studies confirm the conclusions from the older research: strong similarity in IQ for identical twins, even when the twins have been separated since early in life (Bouchard, 1997; Bouchard et al., 1996; Pederson et al., 1984).

Table 10.5

Correlations in IQ of Related and Unrelated Children Reared Together or Apart

Relationship and Rearing Condition	Average Correlation	Number of Pairs
Identical twins reared together	.86	4,672
Fraternal twins reared together	.60	5,533
Siblings reared together	.47	26,473
Unrelated children reared together	.32	714
Identical twins reared apart	.72	65

Source: Adapted from "Familial Studies of Intelligence: A Review" by T. J. Bouchard, Jr. and M. McGue, 1981, *Science*, p. 1056. Copyright © 1981 by the American Association for the Advancement of Science. Adapted by permission.

The Concept of Heritability

The three kinds of evidence that we have considered all point to the same conclusion: Both differences in genes and differences in environments can lead to differences in IQ. This conclusion is important, but very general. Can we go beyond a general statement that both factors are important to say something about their relative importance?

It is important to emphasize that the question of relative importance makes sense only when we are talking about differences among people. Any individual's intelligence clearly depends on both genes and environment, and there is no way, when talking about individual development, to disentangle the two factors or to label one factor as more important than the other. We simply would not exist without both genes and environment, let alone have a height or weight or an IQ to explain.

Suppose, however, that we are studying a sample of people who differ in IQ and we wish to determine the origin of these differences. In this case, the question of relative importance *does* make sense. The differences among the members of our sample may be totally or predominantly genetic in origin, totally or predominantly environmental in origin, or a reflection of some more even mixture of genetic and environmental factors.

Researchers who attempt to determine relative importance make use of exactly the sorts of data that we have been discussing—kinship correlations, adoption studies, and twin studies. What they add to these data is a set of statistical procedures for calculating the heritability of IQ. The term **heritability** refers to the proportion of variance in a trait that can be attributed to genetic variance in the sample being studied. It is, in other words, an estimate of the extent to which differences among people come from differences in their genes as opposed to differences in their environments. The heritability statistic ranges from 0 (all of the differences are environmental in origin) to 1 (all of the differences are genetic in origin).

The most widely accepted contemporary estimates of the heritability of IQ place the value at about .4 to .7, with figures toward the lower end of the range more typical in childhood and somewhat higher values for adult samples (McGue et al., 1993; Plomin, 1990). By these estimates, then, approximately half the variation in people's IQs results from differences in their genes. The conclusion that genes are important should come as no surprise in light of the evidence that we have reviewed. The heritability estimates follow directly from the findings just discussed—the similarity in IQ between identical twins, the correlations in IQ between adopted children and their biological parents, and so on.

It is important to note some limitations of the heritability statistic. First, heritability can be calculated in different ways, and the value obtained may vary depending on the method used and on the particular data that the researcher decides to emphasize. Published heritability estimates for IQ in fact range from as high as .8 (Herrnstein, 1973) to as low as 0 (Kamin, 1974). Second, whatever the heritability may be, the value is specific to the sample studied and cannot be generalized to other samples. The value is specific to the sample studied because it depends on two factors: the range of environmental differences in the sample, and the range of genetic differences in the sample. If we increase either range we give that factor more chance to have an effect; conversely, if we decrease either range we give that factor less chance to have an effect. In either case, we change the heritability.

Let us consider an example of this point, using not intelligence, but height as the outcome we wish to explain. Imagine an island on which every person receives exactly 100% of his or her nutritional needs (Bjorklund, 1995). In this case, the heritability for height has to be close to 1, since there is no variability in the main

Heritability
The proportion of variance in a trait (such as IQ) that can be attributed to genetic variance in the sample being studied.

environmental contributor to differences in height. If a factor does not vary in some sample of people, it cannot produce differences among those people. Suppose, however, that famine strikes the island. Some people still receive 100% of their nutritional needs; others, however, fall well short of this ideal. Over time, people in the first group grow taller than people in the second group. In this case, the heritability for height becomes less than 1, because environmental as well as genetic differences are now contributing to variations in height. Because the range of environmental differences has grown, the relative importance of genes and environment has changed.

The sample-specific nature of heritability has two further important implications. First, a particular heritability value—based as it is on the current range of genes and environments—tells us nothing for certain about what might happen in the future. In particular, heritability does not tell us about the possible effects of improvements in the environment. Height, for example, typically shows high heritability, yet average height has increased over the last 100 years, presumably because of improvements in nutrition (Angoff, 1988). Indeed, performance on IQ tests has improved steadily ever since the tests were first introduced, with an average gain of about 3 points per decade, which is one reason that the tests must be periodically revised and renormed (Flynn, 1987). Thus, however high heritability may be, improvements in the environment could still lead to gains in children's intelligence.

Second, heritability tells us nothing for certain about comparisons between samples that were not included in the heritability estimate. Knowing what the heritability for height is on Island A, for example, does not tell us why its residents are taller or shorter than residents of Island B. Whatever the heritability may be within one group, differences between groups could result solely from differences in their genes, solely from differences in their environments, or from some combination of genes and environment. We will return to this point about comparisons between groups in our discussion of racial differences in IQ.

✔ *To Recap...*

Organization is one major issue in the study of intelligence. Psychometric researchers draw inferences about how intelligence is organized from patterns of correlations across different measures of intelligence. Factor analyses of such correlations provide evidence both for general intelligence, which affects performance on many tasks, and for more specific abilities, which contribute to performance on specific tasks. Such studies have also identified developmental changes in the structure of intelligence across childhood. As children develop, their cognitive abilities become more differentiated, and sensorimotor kinds of functioning give way to more abstract, symbolic skills.

The question of the stability of IQ is another central issue in the psychometric approach to intelligence. Longitudinal studies indicate that infant IQ has little relation to later IQ. This apparent discontinuity in development is usually attributed to the differences in content between infant and childhood intelligence. Recent evidence suggests, however, that response to novelty may provide a link between infancy and later childhood. After infancy, IQ begins to correlate from one age to another, and the stability increases as the child gets older. The correlations are not perfect, however, and substantial changes in IQ do sometimes occur.

The third classic issue in the psychometric approach concerns the origins of individual differences. Three methods of study have been prominent: family studies, adoption studies, and twin studies. All three methods suggest a substantial genetic contribution to individual differences in intelligence, yet all three also indicate the importance of the environment. Estimates of the heritability of IQ suggest that 40 to 70% of the variation among people is genetic in origin.

Experience and Intelligence

Although we have just discussed some of the limitations of the heritability statistic, we have yet to note what is perhaps the most important limitation. At best, heritability estimates answer the question of how much: How much of the variation among people can be attributed to genetic or environmental factors? Such estimates tell us nothing about the processes by which genes or environments exert their effects. *How* is a genotype translated into a particular level of intelligence? And *how* do different environments shape different kinds of cognitive development?

We saw in Chapter 4 that researchers are just beginning to unravel the mysteries of genetic transmission. Some of the basic principles and mechanisms have been discovered, and more seem likely to yield their secrets in the near future. In this section, we focus on the ways in which the environment affects intelligence.

Our starting point is the fact that no two children encounter exactly the same environment as they grow up. The world is, in fact, a natural laboratory for the study of experience and intelligence, offering natural variations in children's experiences on the one hand, and variations in children's intellectual development on the other. The psychologist's task is to discover the relations between the two. Several kinds of evidence have been important in this attempt.

Natural Deprivations

In chapter 5 we pointed out that the belief that the placental "barrier" protects the fetus from all harm has only gradually been replaced by an appreciation of the importance of prenatal experience. Much the same historical progression can be traced in the study of early experience and intelligence. Through at least the first third of this century, psychologists showed little concern with the possibility that the early environment might affect later intelligence. Instead, the development of intelligence was believed to be largely under genetic and maturational control, and any effects of early experience were assumed to be minor and transitory.

Institutionalization studies
Examinations of the effects of naturally occurring deprivation (such as in certain kinds of orphanage rearing) on children's development.

The first important challenge to this view came from so-called **institutionalization studies** (Hunt, 1961; Thompson & Grusec, 1970). During the 1930s and 1940s, researchers discovered a number of orphanages in which early rearing experiences departed sharply from those typical in a home setting. Such orphanages (which, unfortunately, are still found in parts of the world, as recent reports from Romania make clear [Carlson & Earls, 1997]) were characterized by very high child-to-caretaker ratios and by frequent changes in caretakers. The children thus had minimal social stimulation and little opportunity to form relationships with others. They also received little perceptual-cognitive input. In some institutions, sheets were hung over the sides of the cribs, preventing the children from seeing out. In one orphanage, the children lay so long in one place that they hollowed out a depression in the mattress. When the children reached the age at which they should have been able to turn over and look around, they could not, because they were trapped in the depression (Spitz, 1945).

In retrospect, it is not surprising that these barren environments had detrimental effects on children's development. The effects were wide-ranging and severe. Children subjected to deprived orphanage rearing showed problems on a number of aspects of later development, including performance on IQ tests and

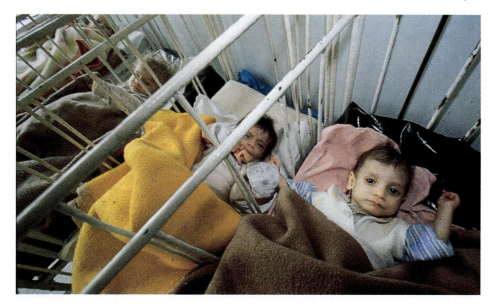

Studies of natural deprivations—such as rearing in the Romanian orphanage shown here—provide dramatic evidence for the negative effects of a bad environment on intellectual development.

other cognitive measures. In one study, for example, the mean IQ of a group of children reared in a Lebanese orphanage was 50, and no child in the sample reached an IQ of 100 (Dennis, 1973).

One positive finding emerged from the orphanage studies, however. Strong and persistent though the results of early deprivation might have been, the effects were not necessarily permanent. If the children's environments were significantly improved, then at least some of the damage could be undone. This same heartening message is evident in studies of Romanian infants who have been removed from their orphanages and adopted into supportive homes (Marcovitch et al., 1997). The institutionalization studies thus provide evidence about the effects of experience in both directions. Bad early environments can depress children's intelligence, but later improvements in the environment can lead to gains in intellectual performance.

The conclusions that emerged from the orphanage studies are paralleled in occasional case study reports of "attic" or "closet" children (e.g., Davis, 1947). We discussed one such case, that of the little girl called Genie, in Chapter 3 (Curtiss, 1977). Such reports confirm that an extremely deprived environment (such as being chained in an attic) can result in greatly lowered intelligence. Yet these studies also have a more hopeful side in that therapeutic efforts with such children have succeeded, at least sometimes, in producing remarkable gains (Clarke & Clarke, 1976). So, again, we see that early experience is important, but not all-important. The later environment also plays a role.

Most children, of course, do not encounter such extreme deprivation. What do we know about the less extreme variations in experience that characterize the lives of most children? We consider findings with respect to two central contexts for development: family and school.

Contributions of the Family

For most children, the home environment is one important context within which intellectual skills develop. Several kinds of research provide evidence about the contribution of family experience to intellectual development.

Longitudinal Studies The longitudinal studies mentioned earlier are one source of evidence. Such studies have shown that IQ is not perfectly stable as children develop and that a particular child's IQ may go up or down by 30 or 40 points across childhood. Researchers have sought to discover whether these changes in IQ can be linked to characteristics of the children's environments.

Sameroff and associates, for example (Sameroff et al., 1993), followed a sample of children and their parents from the time the children were 4 until they reached the age of 14. Included at both time periods was an assessment of the extent to which the child's family life was characterized by each of the 10 risk factors listed in Table 10.6. At both age periods, the children's IQs were negatively related to the number of risk factors; that is, the more risk factors present, the lower, on average, the IQs. No single category of risk emerged as critical; rather, what seemed important was the accumulation of different forms of risk. Furthermore, risk at age 4 proved predictive of IQ at age 13. Children with difficult early environments were most likely to experience continued problems in intellectual adaptation. The negative impact of early risk, it is important to note, is not limited to IQ scores, but extends to performance in school as well (Caughy, 1996).

McCall and colleagues (1973) focused more directly on parents' contribution to stability or change in IQ. They analyzed patterns of IQ change for 80 children participating in a long-term longitudinal study. They found that two aspects of parental behavior showed the strongest relation to IQ change. Children who declined in IQ tended to have parents who made relatively little effort to stimulate them or to accelerate their development and who also fell at the extremes in their use of punishment, either very high or very low. In contrast, children who increased in IQ tended to have parents who emphasized intellectual acceleration and who were intermediate in the severity of their discipline. Thus, the most adaptive parental pattern appeared to be one that stressed stimulation and intellectual encouragement within a general context of structure and control. Similar conclu-

Table 10.6
Risk Factors in the Sameroff et al. Study of Family Environment and IQ

Risk Factor	Description
Minority status	Family is African American or Puerto Rican.
Occupation	Head of household is unemployed or holds low-skilled occupation.
Mother's education	Mother did not complete high school.
Family size	Family has four or more children.
Father absence	Father is not present in the home.
Stressful life events	Family experienced at least 20 stressful events during the child's first 4 years.
Parenting perspectives	Parents hold relatively rigid and absolutist conceptions of children and child rearing.
Maternal anxiety	Mother is unusually high in anxiety.
Maternal mental health	Mother has relatively poor mental health.
Mother–child interaction	Mother shows little positive affect toward child.

Source: Adapted from "Stability of Intelligence from Preschool to Adolescence: The Influence of Social and Family Risk Factors" by A. J. Sameroff, R. Seifer, A. Baldwin, and C. Baldwin, 1993, *Child Development, 64,* p. 85. Copyright © 1993 by the Society for Research in Child Development. Adapted by permission.

sions have emerged from other studies of the child-rearing antecedents of intellectual competence (Wachs, 1992; White et al., 1978).

Research with the HOME   To identify the environmental contributors to intellectual development, we must have a way to assess the quality of the child's environment. Undoubtedly the most popular contemporary approach to measuring the home environment is an instrument called the **HOME** (Home Observation for Measurement of the Environment. In this section we review findings from research with the HOME.

The infant version of the HOME, developed by Caldwell and Bradley (1979), consists of 45 items intended to tap the quality of the child's environment during the first 3 years. Each item is scored either yes (this feature is characteristic of the child's environment) or no (this feature is not characteristic). The 45 items are in turn grouped into six general subscales. The items and corresponding subscales are shown in Table 10.7. Scoring on the HOME is accomplished during a 1-hour home visit and is based on a combination of interviews with the mother and observation of mother–child interaction. Part of the appeal of the instrument is that such a wide range of information can be elicited in such a short time.

Of course, the infant environment, important though it may be, is not our only concern. There has long been a preschool version of the HOME as well. The preschool HOME is similar in structure to the infant scale, but includes 55 items and eight subscales. More recent developments are HOME scales for the periods of middle childhood and adolescence (Bradley, 1994).

Do scores on the HOME relate to children's IQs? Many studies indicate that they do (Bradley, 1994; Elardo & Bradley, 1981; Gottfried, 1984a). In general, the higher the score on the HOME (that is, the greater the number of "yes" answers), the better the child's development. There is some evidence that each of the subscales correlates with IQ, although which scales predict most strongly varies some across studies and across age periods. Perhaps the most consistently important dimensions are parental involvement, play materials, and variety of stimulation (Gottfried, 1984b).

Measures on the HOME relate to contemporaneous measures of the child's intelligence. That is, scores on the infant version of the HOME correlate with infant intelligence (Barnard, Bee, & Hammond, 1984), scores on the preschool version correlate with preschool intelligence (Siegel, 1984), and scores on the middle childhood version correlate with childhood intelligence (Luster & Denbow, 1992). Measures on the HOME also relate to future intelligence. In one study, for example, the correlation between HOME score at 6 months and IQ at 4.5 years was .50; the correlation between HOME at 24 months and IQ at 4.5 years was .63 (Bradley & Caldwell, 1984a). Other studies have demonstrated relations between HOME scores in infancy and both IQ and school performance during the grade-school years (Bradley & Caldwell, 1984b; Olson, Bates, & Kaskie, 1992). Thus, the quality of the child's early environment is predictive of various aspects of the child's later intelligence.

Although the HOME is a valuable source of evidence with respect to experience and intelligence, one caution should be noted. As we discussed in Chapter 4, research suggests that genetic factors may also contribute to findings with the HOME (Braungart, Fulker, & Plomin, 1992; Cherny, 1994; Plomin & Neiderhiser, 1992). Genetically based characteristics of children may influence the HOME score itself, since such characteristics will affect the treatment that children receive from their parents (recall Bronfenbrenner's notion of developmentally generative characteristics, discussed in Chapter 2). And genetic characteristics of the parents may affect both the home environment and the child's intelligence, thus contributing

HOME (Home Observation for Measurement of the Environment) An instrument for assessing the quality of the early home environment. Included are dimensions such as maternal involvement and variety of play materials.

Table 10.7

Items and Subscales on the HOME (Infant Version)

I. Emotional and Verbal Responsivity of Mother
1. Mother spontaneously vocalizes to child at least twice during visit (excluding scolding).
2. Mother responds to child's vocalizations with a verbal response.
3. Mother tells child the name of some object during visit or says name of person or object in a "teaching" style.
4. Mother's speech is distinct, clear, and audible.
5. Mother initiates verbal interchanges with observer—asks questions, makes spontaneous comments.
6. Mother expresses ideas freely and easily and uses statements of appropriate length for conversation (e.g., gives more than brief answers).
7. Mother permits child occasionally to engage in "messy" types of play.
8. Mother spontaneously praises child's qualities or behavior twice during visit.
9. When speaking of or to child, mother's voice conveys positive feelings.
10. Mother caresses or kisses child at least once during visit.
11. Mother shows some positive emotional responses to praise of child offered by visitor.

II. Avoidance of Restriction and Punishment
12. Mother does not shout at child during visit.
13. Mother does not express overt annoyance with or hostility toward child.
14. Mother neither slaps nor spanks child during visit.
15. Mother reports that no more than one instance of physical punishment occurred during the past week.
16. Mother does not scold or derogate child during visit.
17. Mother does not interfere with child's actions or restrict child's movements more than three times during visit.
18. At least 10 books are present and visible.
19. Family has a pet.

III. Organization of Physical and Temporal Environment
20. When mother is away, care is provided by one of three regular substitutes.

21. Someone takes child into grocery store at least once a week.
22. Child gets out of house at least four times a week.
23. Child is taken regularly to doctor's office or clinic.
24. Child has a special place in which to keep his toys and "treasures."
25. Child's play environment appears safe and free of hazards.

IV. Provision of Appropriate Play Materials
26. Child has some muscle-activity toys or equipment.
27. Child has push or pull toy.
28. Child has stroller or walker, kiddie car, scooter, or tricycle.
29. Mother provides toys or interesting activities for child during interview.
30. Provides learning equipment appropriate to age—cuddly toy or role-playing toys.
31. Provides learning equipment appropriate to age—mobile, table and chairs, high chair, play pen.
32. Provides eye–hand coordination toys—items to go in and out of receptacle, fit together toys, beads.
33. Provides eye–hand coordination toys that permit combinations—stacking or nesting toys, blocks or building toys.
34. Provides toys for literature or music.

V. Maternal Involvement with Child
35. Mother tends to keep child within visual range and to look at him often.
36. Mother "talks" to child while doing her work.
37. Mother consciously encourages developmental advances.
38. Mother invests "maturing" toys with value via her attention.
39. Mother structures child's play periods.
40. Mother provides toys that challenge child to develop new skills.

VI. Opportunities for Variety in Daily Stimulation
41. Father provides some caretaking every day.
42. Mother reads stories at least three times weekly.
43. Child eats at least one meal per day with mother and father.
44. Family visits or receives visits from relatives.
45. Child has three or more books of his or her own.

Source: From "174 Children: A Study of the Relationship between Home Environment and Cognitive Development during the First 5 Years" by R. H. Bradley and B. M. Caldwell, 1984. In A. W. Gottfried (Ed.), *Home Environment and Early Cognitive Development* (pp. 7–8), New York: Academic Press. Copyright © 1984 by Academic Press. Reprinted by permission.

to the correlation between HOME measures and children's IQs. The conclusion that both genes and environment are important for intelligence—and that the two factors are often very difficult to separate—should be familiar by now.

Development in Cultural Context
Families and Achievement:
The Message from Cross-Cultural Research

American children, on average, do not perform well in mathematics. This conclusion has emerged from several surveys of cross-national differences in mathematics ability in recent years. The contrast with children from Asian countries is especially marked. For example, in one study of mathematics achievement in 20 countries, American 8th and 12th graders scored below the international average on virtually every measure taken (Garden, 1987; McKnight et al., 1987). Children from China and Japan, in contrast, were consistently near the top of the range. Other studies across the last two decades have provided a similar picture—disappointingly poor performance by American children, coupled with exceptional achievement for children from Asian countries (Geary, 1996).

Why do American children do so poorly in mathematics? It is tempting to indict the school system; and schools, as we discuss more fully in the next section, can be quite important. Some differences between Asians and Americans, however, are evident by age 5, before most children have even started school (Stevenson, Lee, & Stigler, 1986). Furthermore, Asian-American students in the United States often outperform Caucasian students, even though both groups are moving through the same school systems (Sue & Ozaki, 1990). These findings suggest that schools are not the sole explanation; the family environment also contributes.

The most ambitious attempt to identify family bases for academic achievement is a program of research by Stevenson and associates (Chen & Stevenson, 1995; Stevenson, Chen, & Lee, 1993; Stevenson et al., 1990). The child participants for the initial phase of the project were first and fifth graders from the United States, China, and Japan. The children took a variety of achievement tests, and the results fit those of previous research—poorer performance in mathematics by American children than by children from China or Japan. Many of the first graders were retested in 5th and 11th grade, and the original results were confirmed; if anything, the cross-national gap in achievement had widened.

The children's mothers also participated in the study, and it was their beliefs and practices that constituted the main focus of the research. The maternal interviews included a variety of questions designed to reveal differences among families and among cultures that might lead to differences in academic performance. Mothers were asked, for example, to judge how well their children were doing in school and to indicate how satisfied they were with this progress. They were asked to give their beliefs about the bases for school success—in particular, to judge the relative contributions of ability and effort to doing well in school. And they were asked about various experiences at home that might contribute to school success, such as parental help with homework or the provision of a quiet place to study.

The Stevenson group's assessments made clear that mothers in all three cultures are interested in and supportive of their children's academic development. At the same time, the maternal interviews revealed cross-cultural differences in beliefs and practices that might well contribute to the superior performance of Asian children. Asian mothers, for example, were more likely than American mothers to regard effort as more important than ability for success in school. The emphasis on effort in the Chinese and Japanese families appears to fit with general and long-standing cultural beliefs about the malleability of human nature and the possibility of improving oneself through hard work (Munro, 1977). In line with these beliefs, Asian mothers were more likely than American mothers to provide help for their children's academic endeavors. In China, for example, 96% of the children received help with homework (the figure in the United States was 67%), and fully 95% of Chinese fifth graders and 98% of Japanese fifth graders had their own desk at home at which to work (the figure for American children was 63%). Similar results emerged from a measure of time spent on academically related activities (e.g., reading, doing workbooks) outside school; Asian children spent more time in such endeavors than did American children.

Given the relatively poor performance of their children, American mothers might have been expected to be least satisfied with their children's academic achievement. In fact, just the reverse was true. American mothers were more satisfied with both their children's performance and their children's schools than were Chinese or Japanese mothers. American mothers also gave higher, and therefore less realistic, evaluations of their children's cognitive and academic abilities than did mothers in the other two cultures. This pattern suggests a basis for the failure of many American mothers to nurture optimal academic performance in their children. These mothers may believe that their children are doing better than they are doing and thus may be satisfied with levels of performance that are not that high. Furthermore, these mothers may believe that academic success is primarily a function of immutable ability rather than changeable effort and thus may see little point in encouraging their children to try harder.

Having presented the main conclusions of Stevenson et al.'s study, we should also note some qualifications (see also Hatano, 1990). The research does not claim that the child-rearing practices of the Asian cultures are producing generally superior children. American children do just as well as Chinese and Japanese children on measures of general intelligence, and differences in other domains of academic achievement are less marked and less consistent than those found for mathematics. Nor does the research claim that the differences in mathematics result solely from differences among families. Schools are also important, and schools contribute to the superior performance of Asian children in mathematics. Finally, Asian superiority in mathematics may be bought at some cost. Although they were more likely to engage in outside-of-school academic activities, the Asian children in the study were considerably less likely than their American counterparts to be involved in art, music, or sports. As is always the case in child rearing, decisions about practices are intertwined with decisions about values and goals. Children's development is multifaceted, and parents must decide how much emphasis to place on each of the many facets.

Contributions of the School

The average American child spends approximately 15,000 hours in school between the ages of 5 and 18. Clearly, school is a major setting within which children in our society exercise—and develop—their intellectual abilities. What do we know about the impact of schooling on cognitive development? In addressing this question, we draw from the same two general kinds of evidence that were the focus of our discussions of the family. In this case we begin with comparisons of different cultures, after which we turn to variations within our own culture.

Cross-Cultural Studies   A difficulty in determining the effects of schooling in Western culture is its pervasiveness: Virtually every child goes to school. When we broaden our scope to encompass other cultures, this uniformity no longer holds. Of course, if we simply compare cultures with and without schooling, it will be difficult to interpret our results, because the cultures may differ in a number of ways apart from the presence or absence of school. Most informative, therefore, are cases in which only some children within a culture go to school or in which schooling has been recently introduced, allowing us to make a before-and-after comparison. Psychologists have been able to find and to study a number of such cases (Ceci, 1990; Cole, 1998). Several conclusions emerge.

A first conclusion is that some aspects of children's cognitive development seem to be more strongly and consistently affected by schooling than others. Many of the kinds of knowledge studied by Piaget fall in the relatively unaffected category. Schooling does sometimes influence the development of Piagetian concepts—most obviously, effects on the rate at which knowledge is acquired. Most studies, however, report no clear qualitative differences between schooled children and unschooled children in their mastery of such concepts as conservation, nor any lasting advantage for children who have been to school.

Other aspects of cognitive development appear to be affected more by schooling. Skill at various kinds of perceptual analysis can be facilitated by schooling—for example, the ability to match stimuli or to construct models of familiar patterns. Schooling can affect memory. Schooled children not only perform better on a variety of memory tasks, but they are also more likely to use mnemonic strategies to help themselves remember. Schooling affects how children classify objects. Children who have been to school are more likely to group objects in terms of general categories (e.g., all of the foods together) rather than functional or thematic relations (e.g., ice cream and spoon together). Similarly, schooling affects how children think about words and use language, with schooled children more likely to think in terms of general categories and abstract relations. And perhaps most generally, schooling improves children's ability to reflect on their own cognitive processes—to think about thinking. As we saw in Chapter 9, such *metacognition* has emerged as an active area of current research interest.

Why does schooling produce these effects? Rogoff (1981) discusses four factors that may play roles. Perhaps the most obvious explanation is that schooling directly teaches many of the specific skills on which schooled children excel. Classification, for example, is a common activity in school, and committing material to memory is even more common. A more general proposal is that schooling exerts its effects through its emphasis on the search for general rules—for universal systems of knowledge (such as mathematics) within which specific instances can be understood. A third possibility stresses the differences between teaching in school and teaching outside school. Teaching in school often involves the verbal transmission of information that is far removed from its everyday context, a style of instruction that may promote verbally based, abstract modes of thought. Finally, perhaps the most general explanation concerns a primary goal of most forms of schooling, the development of literacy. It has been argued that literacy, like verbally based teaching, promotes abstract, reflective styles of thinking. And reading, of course, can also be the door to a vast world of experiences and knowledge that could never be acquired firsthand (Stanovich, 1993).

Cross-cultural examinations of schooling are not limited to comparisons of present versus absent. Even when all children go to school, the type of schooling that children receive may vary across cultures, and these variations can be a source of cognitive differences. This point is relevant to the discrepancy in mathematics achievement between Chinese and Japanese children and American children.

Studies of education in the three cultures make clear that the differences in family life discussed earlier are built on and magnified by the kinds of schooling that children in the three countries receive (Geary, 1995a; Stevenson & Stigler, 1992; Stigler & Fernandez, 1995). Classrooms in China and Japan, for example, typically devote more instructional time to mathematics than do classrooms in the United States; teachers and children in China and Japan spend a higher proportion of the allotted time actually teaching and doing mathematics as opposed to peripheral activities (e.g. handing out papers); children from China and Japan do more math homework than do American children; and mathematics textbooks and curricula are more challenging in Asia than they are in the United States. In light of these and other differences, it is perhaps not surprising that the achievement gap persists.

Schooling in the United States   We touched on some evidence about schooling in the United States in the points just made about cross-national differences. Here we take up the topic more fully. We begin with research on the amount of schooling, after which we turn to the more difficult question of the quality of schooling.

It has long been known that there is a positive relation between number of years of education completed and IQ—that is, the more years of schooling people complete, the higher (on the average) are their IQs (Jencks, 1972). The usual explanation has been that more intelligent people stay in school longer. This factor is almost certainly part of the basis for the correlation. Recently, however, Stephen Ceci (1991, 1992; Ceci & Williams, 1997) has argued that the cause and effect may also flow in the opposite direction—that is, that schooling may actually increase IQ.

Ceci cites a variety of evidence in support of his conclusion. Here are three examples. First, children who drop out of school decline in IQ relative to children who stay in school, even when the two groups are initially equal in IQ. Second, children's IQs have been shown to decline slightly across the months of summer vacation and then to rise again during the school year. Third, children whose birthdays make them just barely old enough to qualify for school entry obtain higher IQ scores by age 8 than children whose birthdays make them fall just short. The point is that the two groups are virtually the same age, but one group has had a year more of schooling. Indeed, Morrison and colleagues (Morrison, Griffith, & Alberts, 1997; Morrison, Smith, Dow-Ehrensberger, 1995) have demonstrated, using this "school cut-off" approach, that starting school relatively early can nurture a number of specific cognitive abilities.

Not only do IQ tests predict success in school, recent evidence suggests that schooling can increase IQ.

In speculating about why schooling boosts IQ, Ceci draws on the cross-cultural evidence just discussed. We saw that schooling affects perceptual analysis, memory, language use, and classification. These skills, Ceci notes, are precisely the kinds of abilities that are stressed on IQ tests. This overlap is, of course, no accident: IQ tests were designed, in part, to predict school performance. It is not surprising, therefore, that being good at IQ-type skills is helpful in school. But it is also not surprising that experiences in school can nurture IQ.

As might be expected, quality of schooling is more difficult than quantity to define and study (Fuller, 1987; Good & Brophy, 1997). Despite the difficulties, however, few doubt that there can be important differences in the quality of the education that different children receive. Some schools consistently produce more successful outcomes than others—doing so even when the children being served are initially equivalent. And some teachers within a school consistently have happier and more productive classrooms than others.

Michael Rutter (1983) has provided one of the most helpful surveys of the research directed to quality of schooling. One of the interesting messages from his review concerns factors that do *not* make much of a difference. Rutter has found little evidence, for example, that variations in school success (such as performance on standardized tests, attendance rates, and graduation rates) are associated with the financial or physical resources available to the school, with the overall size of the school, or with the size of the class within the school. This conclusion does not mean that such factors are never important—no one would advocate a class size of 50 for kindergartners. But the variations that are normally found along these dimensions do not seem to have much effect on school success.

What factors *do* influence school success? The dimensions that emerge as important in Rutter's review have to do mainly with emphasis and organization. Successful schools have a clear emphasis on academic goals, accompanied by clearly defined procedures for achieving those goals. Teachers plan the curriculum together, actively teach important content, assign and grade homework regularly, and in general hold high but realistic expectations for their students. Discipline within successful schools tends to be firm but fair—sufficient to maintain a focus on the task at hand, but not so punitive as to arouse anxiety or resentment. Students in successful schools are helped to feel part of the school through opportunities to participate in school-related activities, as well as by the chance to have a voice in decisions concerning the school. Finally, teachers in successful schools manage their classrooms in an organized and efficient manner, maximizing the time spent on the lesson of the moment rather than on peripheral concerns (e.g., distributing papers, setting up equipment). As we saw, this same variable of classroom management proved important in the comparison of Asian and U.S. schools.

One final point about quality is important. How well school works for a particular child depends not only on general factors, such as classroom management, but also on the fit between the school experience and the child's background and expectations. This principle is expressed in the **cultural compatibility hypothesis**: Classroom instruction is most effective when it matches patterns of learning that are familiar in the child's culture (Slaughter-DeFoe et al., 1990; Tharp, 1989).

A nice example of the principle is found in a study of *wait-time*—the length of time one participant in a dialogue waits before responding to the other (White & Tharp, 1988). Navajo children tend to pause when giving answers, creating the impression (at least for Anglo teachers) that they have finished responding. The result is that Navajo children are often interrupted before they have completed their answers. In this case, the teacher's wait-time is too short. In contrast, native

Cultural compatibility hypothesis
The hypothesis that schooling will be most effective when methods of instruction are compatible with the child's cultural background.

BOX 10.1

PYGMALION IN THE CLASSROOM

Teachers naturally welcome information about their students that might help them to teach more effectively. For many, results from standardized assessment tests—such as IQ and academic achievement measures—are one useful source of information. Normally, of course, such tests are designed to be as accurate as possible. One of the most famous experiments in child psychology, however, was built around the provision of deliberately *inaccurate* test information to teachers.

Robert Rosenthal and Lenore Jacobson (1968) informed a group of elementary-school teachers that a new test of intellectual potential had been developed to measure children's readiness to "bloom." The test, the teachers were told, could identify those children who were most likely to show spurts or leaps forward in their academic performance during the coming year. Each teacher was also given a list of the children from his or her classroom whom the test had identified as likely bloomers. In fact, however, a random-numbers table had been used to select the supposed bloomers. These children were no different from any other children in the class.

What is the point of deliberately misleading teachers in this way? Rosenthal and Jacobson's study grew out of previous research by Rosenthal on a phenomenon known as the *researcher expectancy effect*. Across a series of experiments, Rosenthal

(1976) had demonstrated that researchers' expectations can affect the results they obtain. For example, testers who believe that their subjects will perform well on some cognitive measure typically elicit better performance than do testers who believe that their subjects will perform poorly. The effect extends even to animal research. Testers who are told that they are working with "maze-bright" rats obtain better performance than testers who believe that their rats are "maze-dull."

The work on researcher expectancy effects is of considerable methodological significance, for it identifies a source of bias that may seriously affect the outcomes of research. The point of the Rosenthal and Jacobson study was to see whether expectancy effects extend beyond the laboratory to the real-life settings within which children develop. Do the expectancies teachers hold about their students affect the way the students perform? In particular, can the creation of positive expectancies—as was done with respect to the bloomers—lead to positive outcomes for the children?

The answer to this question turned out to be a qualified yes. Rosenthal and Jacobson did not find any effects of expectancies for the older children in the study. In first and second grade, however, the effects were dramatic. Children who had been identified as bloomers easily outperformed their classmates on an IQ test given at the end of

---

Hawaiian children prefer a short wait-time, because in their culture prompt response and overlapping speech patterns are signs of interest and involvement. Teachers, however, often interpret the Hawaiian child's quick responses as rude interruptions, and their attempts to curtail such behavior may lead to general uncertainty and inhibition. Thus in both cases, although in different ways, the teacher's unfamiliarity with the child's cultural background can create problems for the child in school. (Box 10.1 discusses a famous study of the effects of teachers' expectations about their pupils.)

Experimental Interventions

Studies of naturally occurring variations in experience, whether at home or at school, are important but also incomplete. Such studies lack experimental control, and therefore it is difficult to be certain of cause-and-effect relations. We may know, for example, that verbal stimulation from the mother relates to the child's IQ, but

Teachers are an important part of any child's life. The Pygmalion study suggests that the expectations teachers form can affect their behavior toward their students.

The Rosenthal and Jacobson study is not only one of the most famous, but also one of the most controversial experiments in child psychology. The original study has been subjected to a number of criticisms, and its results have not always been replicated in follow-up research (Good, 1993; Wineberg, 1987). Clearly, children's intellectual performance has many determinants, and teachers' expectancies are at best one of many contributors. Nevertheless, the weight of the evidence has convinced most critics that expectancies can make a difference—not always, certainly, but in some classrooms and for some children. What teachers expect of their students has been shown to affect how they behave toward those students, and the teachers' behavior has in turn been shown to affect, for better or for worse, how the children perform.

Expectancies themselves can have many bases. Among the sources that have been identified are standardized test scores (the basis explored in the Rosenthal and Jacobson study), gender, social class, race, physical attractiveness, and presence of an older sibling in the school system (Dusek & Joseph, 1983). Anyone who has ever followed an older sibling through school should be able to appreciate this last factor.

Rosenthal and Jacobson entitled their book *Pygmalion in the Classroom.* In the Pygmalion legend, a sculptor's skill and devotion transform a mass of stone into a perfect, living woman. Teachers' effects on students are neither this powerful nor (unfortunately) this positive. But teachers can have effects, and the expectancies that they form are one determinant of what these effects may be.

the year. By the end of the year, the bloomers were also earning better grades in reading and arithmetic. Apparently, the teachers' expectancies acted as self-fulfilling prophecies. Children who were expected to perform well did perform well.

why is this? Is it because the mother's verbal input enhances the child's intelligence? Or is it because children who are intelligent elicit a high degree of speech from their mothers? Or does the relation result from some third factor—for example, that mothers who engage in verbal stimulation have genes conducive to intelligence, which they pass on to their children, who therefore have high IQs? If we could experimentally manipulate the child's experiences, we could be much more certain about what the causal relations are.

For obvious ethical reasons, experimental manipulations of children's environments take one direction only. No researcher deliberately makes a child's environment worse. A number of investigators, however, have sought to improve children's environments and thereby enhance their intellectual development. We saw early attempts of this sort when we considered the orphanage and case-study reports of severe deprivation. Next, we examine more recent and more large-scale intervention projects.

An Illustrative Intervention Project   The decade of the 1960s saw the birth of dozens of intervention programs directed toward children who were perceived to be at risk for school failure. The Early Training Project (Gray & Ramsey, 1982; Gray, Ramsey, & Klaus, 1982) was one of the first, and it is in many ways a typical example. The participants in the project were ninety 3- and 4-year-old children of mothers of low socioeconomic status. Half of the children were randomly assigned to the intervention condition; the other half constituted an untreated control group.

The intervention consisted of two 10-week summer programs in which the children met in small groups with trained teachers. Emphasized in the summer programs were basic skills that the children would need when they started school—perceptual analysis, numerical concepts, linguistic abilities. Also emphasized was the development of general attitudes necessary for school success, such as achievement motivation. Throughout, the researchers attempted to give the children many one-on-one experiences with a helpful adult in a generally supportive environment. Although the focus was on the summer programs, home visits were made throughout the remainder of the year in an attempt to keep any gains from dissipating.

Effects of the Early Training Project were assessed in various ways. On IQ tests given when the children entered first grade, the intervention group outperformed the control group by approximately 10 points. By fourth grade, the difference had shrunk to 7 points, but was still statistically significant. By age 17, when the last follow-up measures were taken, there were no longer any significant IQ differences; both groups had mean IQs of about 80. On various measures of academic performance, however, effects of the intervention were still evident even a dozen years after its completion. Children in the intervention group were less likely than children in the control group to be placed in special education classes. They were also more likely than those in the control group to graduate from high school .

Overview   Intervention projects of the sort just described have been in existence for over 30 years. What have they told us about the possibility of modifying intelligence by changing the environment? In answering this question, we draw especially from two sources—a report from the Consortium for Longitudinal Studies (1983; Lazar & Darlington, 1982) and a more recent review by Barnett (1995). Both the Consortium report and the Barnett review collate information from a large number of independent intervention projects, looking for both immediate and long-term effects of the interventions. Both sources support several general conclusions.

First, participation in intervention projects has an immediate positive effect on children's IQs. Children who have received intervention typically have higher IQs than do children who have not, and the differences typically persist for at least a year or two after the program has ended. The effects, however, do show a definite tendency to diminish with time; in most projects, no differences between experimental and control groups are evident in long-term follow-ups. Furthermore, no project has produced a generally superior level of intellectual functioning in its participants. The main effect of intervention seems to be to minimize the declines in IQ that the children would otherwise experience.

Second, positive effects of intervention are often more marked on other measures than IQ. The major finding of the Consortium report concerned impact on school performance. Participation in early intervention was associated with higher scores on standardized achievement tests, lower probability of being assigned to special education classes, and lower probability of being retained in a grade. There was also evidence for positive effects on self-concept, achievement motivation, and maternal attitudes toward school. Other studies have also documented beneficial effects of intervention even in the absence of IQ gain. Such findings have reinforced long-standing criticisms of the practice of using IQ scores as the main index of the success of intervention (Schweinhart & Weikart, 1991; Travers & Light, 1982). Not only is IQ an incomplete measure of intellectual ability, but other kinds of effects (such as the effect on school performance) may be more important for the child's development. Furthermore, IQ tests cannot measure the nonintellectual benefits that some programs may have (improved nutritional status, better social competence, and so on).

Third, identifying the specific features of intervention that produce positive effects is difficult. It appears, in fact, that a variety of approaches can be beneficial. The common feature may be the opportunity for close and extended interaction with a supportive adult. Benefits also relate to the intensity of the intervention. Programs that begin in infancy or extend into grade school have greater impact than do more short-term efforts, and programs that produce large-scale changes in the child's environment have greater impact than do programs whose intervention is more limited. Involvement of family members, particularly the mother, is beneficial, especially in ensuring that effects do not disappear once the program ends. In addition to promoting positive forms of mother–child interaction, programs that emphasize parents may produce other changes in the parent's life (such as completion of school or successful employment) that in turn have a positive effect on the child's development (Benasich, Brooks-Gunn, & Clewell, 1992; Larner, Halpern, & Harkavy, 1992). Finally, with regard to the specific content of the program, an emphasis on language appears to characterize many of the most successful programs. More generally, an explicit focus on academically relevant skills (language, reading, number, and so on) seems, not surprisingly, to increase the chances of later school success.

Applications

Project Head Start

The sample size for the Early Training Project was 90 mothers and children. Similarly modest sample sizes are true of most of the programs whose results were reviewed in the previous section. Investigators seldom have the resources to include more than a fraction of the families that might benefit from their efforts. The hope has been that such programs can at least help some of the children in need, while perhaps also identifying general principles of intervention that can eventually be applied more broadly.

Project Head Start is enormously larger in scope. Head Start is a nationwide, federally funded intervention program directed primarily toward low-income preschool children and their families. It was launched in 1965 as part of President Lyndon Johnson's War on Poverty and, unlike many components of the War on Poverty, it continues today. There are more than 2000 Head Start centers spread across all 50 states.

Because Head Start is many centers rather than one, it can be difficult to say what Head Start "is." Nevertheless, several elements have characterized Head Start classrooms since the beginning of the program (Zigler & Muenchow, 1992). Head Start emphasizes family and community involvement. Parents are encouraged to volunteer in their children's classrooms and parents are also given a voice in decisions about the direction of the program. As part of this emphasis on family and

Although preschool intervention projects typically have limited effects on IQ, they can increase children's chances for later success in school.

community, Head Start attempts to avoid the "deficit" orientation that has characterized some interventions: Rather than seeking only to correct deficiencies in the child's background, Head Start is designed to build on existing interests and strengths. Although academic readiness is always part of a Head Start curriculum, other aspects of the child's development are stressed as well. Social skills are important, as is the development of self-confidence and motivation. So, too, is the child's physical development—an emphasis on nutrition and dental and medical care has been part of Head Start since its inception.

Does Head Start work? We saw that this question can be difficult to answer for any intervention. It is especially difficult in the case of Head Start, given the many different aspects of development that are stressed in the program, as well as the variations in how the general philosophy is implemented across centers. Initial evaluations of Head Start focused on IQ gain, and many commentators were dismayed when Head Start failed to produce lasting improvements in children's IQs (Westinghouse Learning Center, 1969). In the years since the initial assessment, however, it has become clear that Head Start, like intervention programs in general, can have a number of beneficial effects that are not captured by IQ scores (Lee et al., 1990; Zigler & Finn-Stevenson, 1992; Zigler & Styfco, 1993). These effects include greater success in school, better health status, gains in social competence, and increased involvement of the family in the child's education.

One other benefit of Head Start is worth noting. In addition to directly serving some 11 million children across the last 30 years, Head Start has functioned as a kind of national laboratory for designing and testing intervention programs for children and families (Zigler & Finn-Stevenson, 1992). A number of current social-policy initiatives had their origins in programs introduced as part of Head Start, including support programs for needy families and techniques for mainstreaming children with disabilities in regular classrooms. Head Start thus qualifies as not only the nation's largest social-policy effort, but also its largest scientific experiment.

Race and Intelligence

The intervention programs we have just discussed have been directed overwhelmingly toward poor African-American children. This emphasis reflects the fact that African-American children are more likely than are Caucasian children to have problems in school. African-American children also tend to perform more poorly than Caucasian children on IQ tests; the average difference is about 10 to 15 points (Loehlin, Lindzey, & Spuhler, 1975). There is some evidence that the gap may have narrowed slightly in recent years (Vincent, 1991).

Before we discuss possible bases for this finding, we should note an important point about what such average differences do and do not tell us. The ranges of performance for different ethnic groups on IQ tests are completely overlapping, and there is much more variation within groups (that is, among Caucasian children or among African-American children) than there is between groups (Suzuki & Valencia, 1997). There is no way, therefore, simply from knowing a child's race to predict anything about that child's abilities.

The issue of why average racial differences in IQ exist is perhaps the most controversial topic in developmental psychology. For years the commonly accepted explanation was an environmentalist one: The environments that African-American children encounter are less likely than those of Caucasian children to promote the skills needed to do well on IQ tests. In 1969, however, Arthur Jensen published an article in which he suggested that genetic differences between races might also play a role (Jensen, 1969)—a position that he has since elaborated in a number of publications (Jensen, 1972, 1973, 1980, 1981). The recent appearance of the book *The Bell Curve* (Herrnstein & Murray, 1994) has further fueled the debate. While the authors of *The Bell Curve* are careful to state that the issue of racial differences remains unresolved, they do offer a variety of seemingly progenetic kinds of evidence—in the context of a generally strong statement about the importance both of IQ for success in society and of the genes as determinants of individual differences in IQ.

Why might anyone believe that genes contribute to racial differences in IQ? We can only briefly summarize this complex argument here. The starting point is the consistency of the racial differences in IQ. Such differences have appeared in dozens of studies and on a wide variety of tests. The differences do not seem to relate to the cultural loading of the test; they are found, for example, on nonverbal as well as verbal tests, and on test items that do not seem to require any culture-specific knowledge. Nor are the differences explained by differences in social class, since controlling for social class results in only a small decrease in the discrepancy.

A further component of the argument comes from the data concerning heritability. Heritability for Caucasian samples, as we saw earlier, is high. Comparable studies with African-American samples have also yielded substantial heritabilities (Scarr, 1981). It appears, therefore, that genes are an important source of individual differences within a race. Both Jensen and the authors of *The Bell Curve* acknowledge the points we made earlier—that heritability is always sample-specific and that heritability within one group cannot be applied directly to a comparison between two groups. What they offer, however, is a kind of plausibility argument. If genes are so important to differences within races, is it plausible that they make absolutely no contribution to differences between races? In support of this position, they argue that the environmental factors known to be important for intelligence have not been shown to vary appreciably between Caucasians and African-Americans. And they maintain that intervention programs designed to increase the intelligence of African-American children have failed to do so. Thus, the environmentalist position, they maintain, has been tested and has failed.

Most developmental psychologists have not been persuaded by these arguments. Various replies are possible (Ceci, 1996; Fraser, 1995; Mackenzie, 1984; Scarr, 1981). Many would contend that the plausibility argument drawn from the heritability data is simply not plausible. A high heritability value means simply that environmental differences are relatively unimportant *in the sample studied.* Even if differences among

Caucasian children's environments have little impact, it is still possible that environmental differences between African-Americans and Caucasians could produce a 10 to 15 point difference in IQ. Recall our example of Island A and Island B. Marked nutritional differences between the two islands might well lead to marked differences in height, no matter how high the heritabilities for each island alone. The same point applies to environmental effects on IQ. To many, this position is more plausible than is the claim that African-American children's experiences do not differ in important ways from those of Caucasian children.

More direct evidence can also be cited.

1. Race is more a social classification than a biologically determined category. Many African-Americans in the United States in fact have Caucasian ancestry in varying degrees. If genes contribute to group differences in IQ, then IQ scores among African-Americans should be positively correlated with degree of Caucasian ancestry. So-called admixture studies, however, provide no support for this prediction (Scarr et al., 1977).

2. We noted that adopted children tend to have superior IQs. Similar effects have been reported in studies of transracial adoption—that is, African-American children adopted into Caucasian homes. Although the interpretation of this research is somewhat controversial (Levin, 1994; Scarr & Weinberg, 1983; Waldman, Weinberg, & Scarr, 1994), it appears that rearing in what Scarr and Weinberg call the "culture of the test" (that is, homes and schools that promote the kinds of knowledge emphasized on IQ tests) diminishes the racial differences in IQ. Clearly, this finding is compatible with an environmentalist position.

3. Although intervention programs have not been as successful as hoped, at least some programs have produced genuine and long-term gains in African-American children's intellectual competence. Furthermore, intervention programs to date do not exhaust what might be done. It is quite possible that future programs, building on the knowledge that has been gained, may yield more impressive effects.

✓ *To Recap...*

The issue of experience and intelligence can be studied in two general ways: through examination of the effects of naturally occurring variations in children's experiences and by experimental interventions that change children's environments.

The study of naturally occurring deprivations (such as orphanage rearing) first alerted psychologists to the possible importance of early experience. These studies demonstrated both the negative effects of a deprived environment and the positive effects of an improvement in environment. Subsequent research has revealed significant, although less dramatic, effects of more normal variations in experience within the home setting. Such studies (often using the HOME instrument) suggest that the quality of the home environment influences both current and future intellectual competence.

Schools as well as homes can affect children's intellectual development. Cross-cultural studies indicate that schooling promotes a number of cognitive skills, including memory, classification, and metacognition. Studies within our culture verify that both the quantity and the quality of schooling can be important.

Experimental interventions have been directed mainly toward children who are perceived as being at risk for school failure. A variety of intervention programs have had positive effects on children's development. Immediate effects are generally greater than are long-term ones, and effects on school performance are generally greater than are effects on IQ. Programs that introduce the greatest changes in the child's environment have generally had the greatest impact.

On average, African-American children score lower than Caucasian children on IQ tests. Drawing on the generally high heritability of IQ, some authors have suggested that genetic factors may contribute to this difference. Most developmental psychologists disagree. Counterarguments include the inappropriateness of applying within-race heritabilities to between-race differences and the positive effect of transracial adoption on African-American children's IQs.

Alternatives to IQ

In the discussion of intervention programs, we touched on some ways other than IQ to assess children's competence. In this section, we broaden the scope to consider some recent theories and programs of research that represent significant departures from the traditional IQ perspective.

Vygotsky and the Zone of Proximal Development

As we saw in Chapter 2, Lev Vygotsky was a Russian psychologist who was a contemporary of Piaget (both were born in 1896) but who died when he was only 37. Vygotsky therefore never had a chance to complete his theorizing or program of research. Nevertheless, he is an important figure, for his ideas have helped shape the development of modern Soviet child psychology. And in recent years, as translations of his writings have appeared (Vygotsky, 1934, 1962, 1978, 1987), Vygotsky has begun to influence Western thinking as well.

A central construct in Vygotsky's theory is the **zone of proximal development**. The zone is defined as the difference between what children can do on their own and what children can do with help. Vygotsky refers to what children can do on their own as the *level of actual development*. In his view, this is what standard IQ tests measure. Such a measure is undoubtedly important, but it is also incomplete. Two children might have the same level of actual development, in the sense of being able to solve the same number of problems on some standardized test. Given appropriate help from an adult, however, one child might be able to solve an additional dozen problems, whereas the other child might be able to solve only two or three more. What the child can do with help is referred to as the *level of potential development*. The difference between actual and potential development defines a particular child's zone of proximal development.

The emphasis on what the child can do with help is a reflection of a central theme in the theorizing of Vygotsky and later Soviet psychologists, a theme that we first encountered in Chapter 2 in our discussion of sociocultural approaches to development. Soviet psychologists believe strongly in the cultural determination of individual development. In their view, much of what children learn is acquired from the culture around them, and much of the child's problem solving is mediated through adult help. Focusing on the child in isolation (as in IQ testing) is therefore misleading. Such a focus at best captures the products of learning; it does not reveal the processes by which children acquire new skills. Furthermore, such a focus may miss important differences among children. In the example just given, the two children appeared equally intelligent when working alone, yet their ability to benefit from help was quite different—they had different zones of proximal development.

In recent years, a number of researchers have attempted to develop **dynamic assessments**—methods of assessing intelligence that build on the concept of the zone

Zone of proximal development
Vygotsky's term for the difference between what children can do by themselves and what they can do with help from an adult.

Dynamic assessment
Method of assessing children's abilities derived from Vygotsky's concept of the zone of proximal development. Measures the child's ability to benefit from adult-provided assistance, typically in a test-train-retest design.

In Vygotsky's theory, guidance from a more competent adult is an important source of children's problem-solving skills.

Scaffolding
A method of teaching in which the adult adjusts the level of help provided in relation to the child's level of performance, the goal being to encourage independent performance.

of proximal development and the child's ability to profit from instruction (Brown & Ferrara, 1985; Feuerstein, 1979; Lidz, 1992; Swanson, 1996). A common research strategy has been a test-train-test procedure. With this approach, the child first attempts to solve a set of problems on her own, much as on a standard IQ test. Following this determination of actual level, the experimenter provides a standardized set of prompts designed to help the child arrive at an answer. The prompts are arranged in a graduated series, starting out fairly subtle and indirect and becoming progressively more explicit until the solution is reached. The child's zone for that kind of problem solving can be determined from the number of hints needed—the fewer the hints, the wider the zone. In the final phase, the child is presented with problems that vary in their similarity to those on which help was given. This final phase provides a measure of the child's ability to transfer the skills learned with adult help.

Assessments of this sort are difficult to carry out, and the approach has yet to result in a generally accepted method of testing intelligence (for critiques, see Paris & Cross, 1988; Sternberg, 1991). Nevertheless, studies using the approach have confirmed Vygotsky's claim that IQ tests provide an incomplete picture of children's intelligence. IQ scores do relate to both speed of initial learning and breadth of transfer. The relation is not perfect, however, and many children's ability to profit from help is not predicted by their IQs. Children, in short, are a good deal more variable than IQ tests indicate. In a sense, of course, this fact has always been known; we saw that IQ scores are a far from perfect predictor of school performance or any other important outcome. What dynamic assessments do is to specify one of the important dimensions not captured by IQ—the ability to profit from help provided by other people.

Our emphasis so far has been on the zone of proximal development as a method for assessing intelligence. In Vygotsky's theory, however, social interaction is not only a context within which children demonstrate their intelligence; it is also the primary mechanism through which that intelligence develops. Children acquire knowledge and tools of intellectual adaptation from their interactions with other people, most notably (especially for young children) with their own parents. This aspect of the theory has also been the focus of much recent research, as investigators have sought to determine when and how parents teach things to their children and what children take away from such interactions (Diaz, Neal, & Vachio, 1991; Freund, 1990; Rogoff, 1998). This work has confirmed that children can often perform tasks with appropriate adult help that they are unable to carry out on their own. Of particular interest has been a form of teaching known as **scaffolding**, in which the parent continually adjusts the level of help in response to the child's level of performance, moving to more direct, explicit forms of teaching if the child falters and to less direct, more demanding forms of teaching as the child moves closer to independent mastery. Scaffolding appears to be effective not only in producing immediate success but in instilling the skills necessary for independent problem solving in the future. We consider some specific aspects of this process in the next chapter, when we discuss children's language development.

Although parents have been the focus for much of the research inspired by Vygotsky's theory, other social agents have also received attention. Teachers are important as well, and in recent years Vygotsky's writings, like those of Piaget, have begun to have an impact on educational practice (Bodrova & Leong, 1996). Vygotsky also suggested that interactions with more competent peers contribute to children's intellectual development, and recent research supports this idea—benefits from peer teaching have been shown in both experimental studies of problem solving and naturalistic research in classroom settings (Forman, 1992; Phelps & Damon, 1991; Tudge

& Rogoff, 1989). More generally, Vygotsky's writings emphasize the importance not only of specific social agents, such as parents or peers, but also of the broader culture within which the child develops. Much of the cross-cultural research that we discuss throughout this book has a grounding in Vygotsky's theory, including the work that we describe shortly in the Development in Cultural Context section.

The scope of the Vygotskian approach is broad, and we have considered only some of the ideas and applications in our present discussion. We will return to Vygotsky's theory in Chapter 13, when we discuss the development of children's ability to regulate their own behavior. We will see some further aspects of the theory then. We will also see some interesting contrasts between Vygotsky's theory and that of his famous contemporary, Piaget.

Development in Cultural Context
Mathematics in School and on the Streets: Brazilian Candy Vendors

The importance of mathematics in school curricula is reflected in the enshrinement of "'rithmetic" as one of the traditional three Rs. But school is not the only place in which children learn about math. A striking example of out-of-school learning is provided by studies of child candy vendors on the urban streets of Brazil (Nunes, Carraher, & Schliemann, 1993; Saxe, 1988, 1991).

In Brazil, candy selling is one of the occupations available to poor children (usually boys) who need to earn money to help their families survive. Children may enter the selling practice as early as age 5, and they may eventually work as many as 14 hours per day and 60 or 70 hours per week. Many vendors either never go to school or leave school after a few years. In addition to the sheer physical demands of the job, candy selling poses cognitive challenges. Figure 10.3 summarizes the steps that the youthful candy vendor must execute.

During the *purchase phase* the seller must buy the candies that he will eventually sell from one of the many available stores. During the *prepare-to-sell phase* the seller must price the candy, translating the wholesale price he has paid for a multi-unit box to a retail price for individual units, including a sufficient mark-up to ensure a profit. During the *sell phase* the seller must negotiate with customers, handling currency and making change as needed and perhaps bargaining on the price as well. Such transactions may take place wherever potential customers are to be found: on the streets, in line at theaters, on buses waiting to depart. Finally, during the *prepare-to-purchase phase* the seller must decide what kind of candies he will buy for his next outing and which store is likely to give him the best price. All of this is complicated by two further factors indicated in the figure: the competition from the many peers who are also engaged in the candy-selling business, and the need to cope with Brazil's spiraling inflation rate (250% or higher in recent years).

As this description should make clear, the mathematics involved in candy selling is not of the abstract sort that children often encounter in school. Rather, the mathematical goals that must be met emerge in the context of the candy-selling practice, and children can succeed as candy sellers only if they achieve these goals. That they do succeed is demonstrated both by naturalistic observations of candy vendors at work and by more formal experimental tests of their mathematical ability.

On the streets, child candy vendors perform a number of mathematical operations both quickly and accurately: representing the numerical values of different

Child candy vendors in Brazil must develop a number of mathematical skills in order to perform their task successfully.

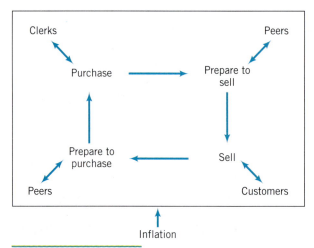

Figure 10.3

Model of the candy-selling practice engaged in by child vendors in Brazil. The children must perform mathematical operations at each phase of the process (purchase, sell, etc.), while interacting with various social agents and adjusting over time to the effects of inflation. From "Candy Selling and Math Learning" by G. B. Saxe, 1988, *Educational Researcher*, August–September, p. 15. Copyright © 1988 by the American Educational Research Association. Reprinted by permission of the publisher.

forms of currency, adding and subtracting units of various sizes, comparing ratios to determine optimal buying or selling prices (e.g., 3 for 500 versus 7 for 1,000), and adjusting over time for the ever-present inflation. In experimental tests, child candy vendors perform well on problems similar to those they encounter during selling but perform poorly on traditional school-type problems—just the reverse of the pattern shown by nonvendors who go to school. Neither candy selling nor schooling produces a generally superior level of mathematical functioning; rather, children in both groups do best when operating in the contexts with which they are most familiar (Carraher, Carraher, & Schliemann, 1985; Saxe, 1991).

In addition to demonstrating the importance of cultural context, the candy-selling studies illustrate a further Vygotskian theme. This theme concerns the nurturing of children's intellectual development through the teaching and guidance provided by more competent members of the society. Candy vendors, especially the youngest ones, are not expected to master all the mathematical tasks on their own. Help of various sorts is often provided. Parents may set the day's selling price before the child leaves the house. Storekeepers may help with various calculations. Peers and older siblings may provide both on-the-spot assistance and general models of how to proceed. As the child grows older, these forms of assistance are gradually cut back. Older children are expected to do on their own what they once could do only with help.

One more change that comes with age is worth noting. In general, younger children are less competent vendors than are older ones. For example, they often offer just one price ratio rather than several, which might be expected to make their wares less attractive to prospective customers. Despite this seeming disadvantage, 6- to 7-year-old vendors make twice as many sales as do 12- to 15-year-olds. Clearly, being young and cute is one way to elicit help from adults.

Ceci's Bioecological Theory

The work just discussed represents the rediscovery and elaboration of a theory that made its first appearance some 70 years ago. In contrast, the approach to which we turn next, Stephen Ceci's **bioecological theory** (Bronfenbrenner & Ceci, 1994; Ceci, 1993, 1996), is one of the newest entrants to the field of intelligence theories.

Ceci's theory is characterized by several distinct emphases, each of which provides a contrast with traditional psychometric approaches. We considered some of these emphases in Chapter 4 in the discussion of gene-environment models. Here we pick up two further themes, each of which is implied by the label *bioecological.* One is an emphasis on the biological underpinnings of intelligent behavior. In Ceci's view, the basic cognitive processes that make intellectual adaptation possible are a reflection of the biological heritage of the species, and the intellectual adaptations that children show are constrained always by their level of biological maturation. This biological substrate, however, is explicitly not the all-purpose mental power implied by the psychometrician's g. The conception, rather, is closer to the information-processing perspective—an emphasis on a variety of fundamental processes (encoding, storage, retrieval, etc.) that work together to produce intelligent behavior. Furthermore—and this is the meaning of the "ecological" part of the label—these processes may work more or less well across the various contexts, or ecologies, with which children must cope. A particular child might appear quite intelligent in one context, but not at all intelligent when faced with a different task. As Bjorklund (1995, p. 396) has summarized the argument, "There are no intelligent people, only people who behave intelligently on various tasks."

Why should cognitive performance be variable across different contexts? Ceci's answer evokes another information-processing emphasis discussed in Chapter 9: the importance of domain-specific knowledge. Children's (or, for that matter, adults') ability to utilize basic cognitive processes effectively depends on the knowledge that they already possess about the task or domain in question. There is no intelligence in isolation, only intelligence in context, and all of us know more about some contexts than others.

Note that this position does not deny the importance, at least within our culture, of IQ and its various correlates. For Ceci, however, IQ tests, as well as the academic and occupational settings to which they relate, are just one of many contexts within which intelligence operates. Because IQ tests and school tasks are such similar contexts, it is not surprising that they correlate. But this correlation does not mean that IQ provides an exhaustive or even especially interesting sampling of intelligent behavior. Furthermore, as we saw earlier in the chapter, Ceci has collected evidence to show that the IQ-school relation goes in both directions: Schooling nurtures the kinds of performance that lead to high IQ scores. Thus IQ is not some immutable quantity that children carry inside them; like other forms of intelligent behavior, it reflects experience and context.

We have already seen a number of examples of the importance of domain-specific knowledge, both in Chapter 9 and earlier in this chapter (recall Brazilian street vendors' arithmetical proficiency in the context of the candy-selling operation). Here we add two examples from Ceci's own research.

One comes from a study of handicapping experts—that is, horse racing devotees with a special expertise in evaluating horses and setting the odds for a race. Ceci and Liker (1986) compared the approach taken by such experts with that of a group of equally experienced, but much less successful, race track patrons. They found that the experts' success resulted from use of a remarkably complex system

Bioecological theory
Theory of intelligence that emphasizes the interplay of domain-specific knowledge and basic cognitive processes in the generation of intelligent behavior.

Figure 10.4
Children's ability to predict the position of a moving object in two contexts: a laboratory task with geometric shapes and a video game with flying animals. Reprinted by permission of the publisher from *On Intelligence: A Bioecological Treatise on Intellectual Development* by Stephen J. Ceci, Cambridge, Mass.: Harvard University Press, Copyright © 1990, 1996 by the President and Fellows of Harvard College.

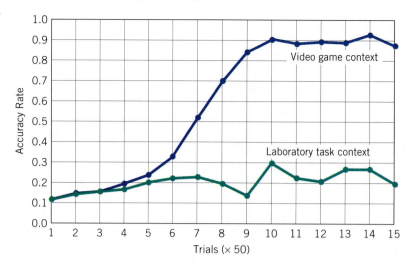

of reasoning in which numerous potential determinants of racing success were weighted and combined in mathematically sophisticated ways. This impressive cognitive achievement was not a reflection of general intelligence: There were no differences in IQ between experts and nonexperts, and there was no relation within the group of experts between IQ and level of success. Rather, the experts' achievement was a reflection of the importance of domain-specific knowledge: When operating in a highly familiar and highly motivating context, these men showed levels of reasoning that far surpassed their norm in other settings.

The other example will probably seem more directly relevant to parents and teachers. Ceci (1990) reported a study in which 10-year-olds attempted to predict the movement of a geometric shape across a computer screen. The movements were based on a system of underlying rules (squares go up, circles go down, dark-colored objects move right, etc.), and hence with experience the children could potentially discover the system and predict perfectly. As the lower line in Figure 10.4 shows, however, most did not. Even after 750 trials with feedback, accuracy was at only 22%.

But consider what happened when the context changed. Ceci and associates replaced the computer screen with a video game, changed the geometric shapes to butterflies and other small creatures, and altered the task: Now the child used a joystick to move a butterfly net across the screen, the goal being to anticipate the butterfly's movement and thereby position the net correctly to catch it. Note that the patterns of movements and the rules governing them were identical to those in the geometric-shapes form of the task; thus the two forms of the problem might be expected to be equally difficult. As Figure 10.4 shows, however, they were not: Children did much better when catching butterflies than when tracking abstract shapes. Again, we can see the importance of context: Children's abilities are most likely to be revealed when the contexts for exercising those abilities are familiar and engaging ones.

Gardner's Multiple Intelligences

Howard Gardner (1983, 1993) has proposed a theory of intelligence that is in some respects similar to those of factor-analytic theorists such as Thurstone and Guilford. Like these theorists, Gardner believes that intelligence is considerably more diversified and multifaceted than the notion of general intelligence admits. Unlike most psychometric researchers, however, Gardner does not rely solely on factor analyses of standardized tests to draw conclusions about different forms of intelligence. And the kinds of intelligence that he proposes go well beyond the ones that psychometric theorists usually consider.

Gardner's general thesis is that humans possess at least seven relatively distinct *intelligences*, defined as the "ability to solve problems or fashion products that are of consequence in a particular cultural setting or community" (Gardner, 1993, p. 15). We consider what some of these intelligences are shortly. First, however, we must ask about evidence. How can the existence of a distinct intelligence be demonstrated? Gardner suggests a number of kinds of evidence, or *signs*, that can help point the way. First, there must be experimental evidence in support of the intelligence. The factor-analytic studies discussed earlier in the chapter are one possible experimental approach to distinguishing different sorts of intelligence; information-processing demonstrations of the distinctiveness of different cognitive domains (see Chapter 9) are another. Next, the intelligence should be specifiable in terms of a set of distinct core operations—that is, it should be possible to say what it "is." Third, the intelligence should show a distinct developmental history, progressing predictably from rudimentary to advanced. In addition, it should show a distinct evolutionary history, growing in complexity as the species grows more complex in the course of its evolution.

Two final signs discussed by Gardner concern deviations from the normal developmental path. Gardner argues that isolation by brain damage can be informative. The fact, for example, that linguistic abilities can be either selectively impaired or selectively spared in cases of brain injury is evidence for a separate linguistic intelligence. Similarly, the existence of individuals with exceptional talents in one particular domain is a possible sign. In so-called savants, for example, remarkable mathematical ability may be coupled with subnormal general intelligence, suggesting that a distinct mathematical intelligence exists. And children who compose symphonies at age 10, as did Mozart and Mendelssohn, are evidence for a musical intelligence.

As noted, Gardner uses such evidence to propose the existence of at least seven distinct human intelligences. He marshals evidence in support of a linguistic intelligence, a spatial intelligence, and a logical-mathematical intelligence. Although the evidence that he uses is sometimes unusual (for example, an analysis of the drawings of a child with autism in the discussion of spatial intelligence; see Figure 10.5), these are forms of intelligence that are talked about in some way by every theorist.

Other intelligences are less familiar. We have already mentioned, for instance, the idea of a musical intelligence. In Gardner's view, musical ability meets all the signs for consideration as a distinct form of intelligence. Musical ability has both an evolutionary and a developmental history, it can appear in isolated form in cases of brain injury or musical prodigy, and it can be analyzed in terms of a set of core elements (pitch, rhythm, timbre, and so on). Similar arguments are offered in support of a bodily-kinesthetic intelligence and two forms of personal intelligence—one (intrapersonal intelligence) concerned with understanding of the self, and one (interpersonal intelligence) concerned with understanding others. In his recent writings, Gardner (1995) speculates that an eighth form of intelligence may eventually prove identifiable: the "naturalist's intelligence," or skill at recognizing flora and fauna.

We noted that the Vygotskian approach is beginning to have an impact on both psychological assessment and educational practice. The same is true of the theory of multiple intelligences. Recent years have seen the formation of a number of schools inspired by Gardner's framework, as well as the creation of methods of

Figure 10.5
Drawing made by a 5-year-old girl with autism—one kind of evidence offered by Gardner in support of his theory of a distinct form of spatial intelligence. From *Frames of Mind: The Theory of Multiple Intelligence* (p. 189) by H. Gardner, 1983, New York: Basic Books. Copyright © 1983 by Basic Books. Reprinted by permission.

assessing children's abilities that encompass a wider range of skills and contexts than do IQ tests (Kornhaber, 1994; Kornhaber, Krechevsky, & Gardner, 1990). As with the dynamic assessments inspired by Vygotsky, such efforts face formidable practical obstacles, and applications to date have been limited. Both approaches, however, have the potential to enrich our understanding of how children differ in intelligence.

The Ethological Approach to Intelligence

As we stress throughout this book, the ethological perspective has emerged in recent years as one of the dominant approaches in child psychology. Thus far, ethologists have devoted more attention to aspects of social development (such as attachment and prosocial behavior) than to the development of cognitive abilities. Recently, however, several ethologically oriented writers have begun to address issues of intelligence.

Theorists who discuss intelligence from an ethological perspective emphasize the same themes that characterize ethology in general (Bjorklund, 1997; Charlesworth, 1995; Geary, 1995b; Jerison, 1982). A basic theme involves the evolutionary basis for behavior. Intelligent behavior is seen as having evolved, and as having done so because it was adaptive in the history of the human species. This emphasis on evolutionary shaping does not mean that ethologists see intelligent behavior as automatic and rigid—humans are above all flexible, learning organisms. But the very capacity for such powerful learning, ethologists maintain, has evolved in response to the varied environmental challenges with which humans have had to cope.

A second theme follows from the first. It is an emphasis on the innate bases for intelligent behavior. This biological emphasis is compatible with the evidence that we have discussed indicating an important genetic contribution to individual differences in intelligence. The ethological approach, however, differs from all the other approaches considered in this chapter in that ethologists' main concern is not with differences, but with commonalities. In their view, human intelligence is in basic respects the same the world around, involving the same problem-solving capacities and the same environmental challenges. For ethologists, these similarities stem from the common biological mechanisms and biological heritage of the species.

A third theme is methodological. Ethologists emphasize the naturalistic study of behavior in its natural setting. It is only through naturalistic study that the full range of the organism's behavioral repertoire, as well as the adaptive significance of that repertoire, can be revealed. This emphasis is directly opposed to the psychometric concern with response to standardized tests. Ethologists are doubtful that performance on a single laboratory test can capture much of the range of human intelligence. It should be clear that this concern is shared by all the approaches considered in this section.

Let us briefly consider two examples of how ethological thinking has been applied to the study of cognitive development. One concerns the naturalistic methodology. William Charlesworth (1978, 1983) has collected hundreds of hours of observational data of children's problem-solving behavior in the natural environment. In his research, a problem is defined as any block to ongoing behavior (for example, a stuck door that refuses to open) that elicits an attempt at solution (for example, asking a parent for help). Analyses have focused on the frequency and types of problems that children encounter, on the ways in which they respond, and on the success or failure of the response. One finding is that real-life problems often do not look much like those on intelligence tests. Charlesworth reports, for example, that a high proportion of the problems that young children encounter involve social blocks and social interaction, a dimension of intelligence that is sel-

Ethologists believe that sensorimotor forms of intelligence are similar across babies and across species.

dom tapped on IQ tests. Other observational studies confirm the frequency of social problems in children's natural environments (Scott, 1997). Such studies also demonstrate that the social world can be a source of solutions as well as problems: Seeking parental help is an adaptive problem-solving strategy from early in life (De Cooke & Brownell, 1995). Note that the emphasis on the social context for intelligence is compatible with the Vygotskian position discussed earlier.

The second application is more theoretical. We have seen that variations in sensorimotor forms of intelligence in infancy have little relation to variations in later intelligence. Sandra Scarr (1983) has offered an ethological explanation for this discontinuity. She suggests that the sensorimotor intelligence of infancy evolved earlier in our primate history than did later representational intelligence. Sensorimotor forms of intelligence are, in fact, quite similar across different primates, in contrast to the marked interspecies differences in adult intelligence. They also are quite similar across human infants, appearing in essentially the same form in every human culture. Scarr suggests that infant intelligence has been shaped through evolution to develop in the same form in any normal environment. Because infant intelligence is so invariable, and because its evolutionary history is so distinct from that of later intelligence, there is little reason to expect infant IQ to predict later IQ. Thus, ethologists offer a theoretical explanation for what to many has been a puzzling empirical finding. More generally, ethology brings a strong theoretical perspective to a field of study that has often been more pragmatic than theoretical.

✓ To Recap…

Dissatisfaction with the traditional IQ approach is reflected in four recent alternative approaches to intelligence. Vygotsky and later Soviet psychologists emphasize what children can do with appropriate help from adults. The distinction between what children can do on their own and what they can do with help constitutes the zone of proximal development. Children may differ in their zones of proximal development, even though by standard IQ measures they look equivalent. And appropriate help from an adult or a more competent peer may lead to new forms of intellectual competence.

Ceci's bioecological theory departs in two major ways from the notion of general intelligence, or g, stressed by psychometric theorists. In Ceci's view, intelligent behavior results from the conjunction of numerous basic cognitive processes, not a single g factor, and the ability to utilize such processes adaptively varies across contexts or domains. Domain-specific knowledge is an important source of these variations.

Gardner's theory of multiple intelligences suggests that certain forms of intelligence fall outside the scope of standard psychometric assessments. Based on a variety of evidence, Gardner posits the existence of seven relatively distinct human intelligences: linguistic, spatial, logical-mathematical, musical, bodily-kinesthetic, intrapersonal, and interpersonal.

The ethological approach to intelligence stresses themes important to ethological theorizing in general. Among the points emphasized are the evolutionary history of intelligence, the biological bases for intelligent behavior, and the methodological importance of studying intelligence in its natural context.

Conclusion

In 1994 the Board of Scientific Affairs of the American Psychological Association, impelled in part by the controversy surrounding *The Bell Curve*, formed a task force whose goal was to clarify the issues raised by the book. The committee set out, therefore, to summarize and to evaluate the evidence with respect to the questions that have concerned us throughout this chapter: What is intelligence, where does it come from, why are there differences among individuals and among groups, and what effects does intelligence have? The task force was chaired by Ulric Neisser, and its members included many of the theorists and researchers whose work we have discussed.

The committee's report was published in the January 1996 issue of the *American Psychologist* (Neisser et al., 1996), and we recommend it highly for those with a continuing interest in the issues addressed in this chapter. We will not attempt to summarize all of the points made in the report, but we will note three of the general conclusions that the task force emphasizes, because they mirror conclusions that we have attempted to convey in our own discussion of the issues.

A first conclusion is that we have learned much about intelligence in the 80 or so years since intelligence tests first appeared. Much of the Neisser et al. article, like much of the current chapter, is devoted to documenting these gains in knowledge. As we noted at the outset of the chapter, the impact of the approach has been applied as well as theoretical—effects on school curricula, for example, or on the design and evaluation of intervention programs. Whether intelligence tests really rank, as one of their proponents has claimed, as "psychology's most telling accomplishment to date" (Herrnstein, 1971, p. 45) is debatable. But they certainly are among the most influential.

A second conclusion is that these undeniable achievements are accompanied by large areas of uncertainty and debate. The greatest uncertainty, not surprisingly, is associated with the hardest-to-study topics. Thus we know, for example, that both genes and environment contribute to differences in IQ, as well as something about their typical relative contribution. But we still have much to learn about how genes or environments produce their effects. Nor do we know why there are on-average group differences on some measures of intellectual performance.

A final conclusion concerns limitations of another sort. IQ tests provide a sampling of intellectual abilities, but they do not exhaust the domain of human intelligence. As Neisser et al. (1996, p. 95) note, "We know much less about the forms of intelligence that tests do not easily assess: wisdom, creativity, practical knowledge, social skill, and the like." Furthermore, the psychometric focus on individual differences may cause us to lose track of the important ways in which all children are similar in their intellectual development. Similarly, the frequent focus on problems in development may cause us to miss the strengths that particular children possess. It is in this respect that the Piagetian and information-processing approaches provide a valuable complement to the intelligence-test perspective. These approaches concentrate on basic developments common to all children, and they remind us that all children show impressive intellectual achievements.

These points emerge even more clearly in the next chapter, when we turn to the topic of language development. We will see that the focus of most research on language has been on similarities rather than on differences among children. And we will see that mastery of language is a remarkable cognitive achievement—perhaps the most impressive achievement that the human species shows.

Visual Summary for Chapter 10:

Cognitive Development: The Intelligence-Test Approach

The Nature of IQ Tests

| The Binet Approach to Measuring Intelligence | → | The first successful intelligence test was developed in 1905 by Alfred Binet and Theodore Simon. Its purpose was to measure individual differences in intellectual ability, to assist in school placement. The Stanford-Binet test is a direct descendant of Binet's test. Like other standardized tests of intelligence, it compares a child's performance with that of other children of the same age. |

| The Wechsler and Kaufman Tests | → | The leading alternative to the Stanford-Binet is a series of tests developed by David Wechsler, which include the Wechsler Intelligence Scale for Children (WISC) and the Wechsler Preschool and Primary Scales of Intelligence (WPPSI). The Kaufman Assessment Battery for Children (K-ABC) includes an explicit attempt at cultural diversity and cultural fairness and has grounding in information-processing conceptions of intelligence. |

| Other Tests of Childhood Intelligence | → | Other tests include the Bayley Scales of Infant Development, which stresses sensorimotor skills in infancy. In addition to individually administered tests, there are a number of group tests of intelligence that can be administered to large numbers of children at the same time. |

| Evaluating the Tests | → | The major IQ tests possess satisfactory reliability. Whether they are valid measures of intelligence has been more difficult to determine. Tests of childhood IQ do relate to measures of academic performance; however, the relation is not perfect. Moreover, the academic focus of most IQ tests means that they may not be good measures of other kinds of intelligence. |

Issues in the Study of Intelligence

| The Organization of Intelligence | → | Factor analysis provides evidence for both general intelligence, which affects performance on many tasks, and more specific abilities which contribute to performance on specific tasks. As children develop, their cognitive abilities become more differentiated, and sensorimotor kinds of functioning give way to more abstract, symbolic skills. |

| Stability of IQ | → | Infant IQ appears to have little relation to later IQ, a discontinuity in development usually attributed to differences in content between infant and childhood intelligence. Recent evidence suggests, however, that response to novelty may provide a link between infancy and later childhood. Beyond infancy, IQ does correlate from one age to another, although the correlations are not perfect. The stability of IQ increases with age. |

| Origins of Individual Differences | → | Family studies, adoption studies, and twin studies all suggest a substantial genetic contribution to individual differences in intelligence. All three methods also indicate the importance of the environment. It is estimated that 40 to 70% of the variation in IQ among people is genetic in origin. |

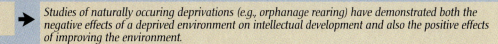

Experience and Intelligence

Natural Deprivations → Studies of naturally occuring deprivations (e.g., orphanage rearing) have demonstrated both the negative effects of a deprived environment on intellectual development and also the positive effects of improving the environment.

Contributions of the Family → Variations in experience within the home setting have also been found to be important. Longitudinal studies, as well as studies using the HOME instrument, suggest that the quality of the home environment can influence both current and future intellectual competence.

Contributions of the School → Schools can affect intellectual development. Cross-cultural studies indicate that schooling promotes a number of cognitive skills, including memory, classification, and metacognition. North American studies indicate that both quantity and quality of schooling can be important.

Experimental Interventions → Experimental interventions have been directed mainly toward children perceived to be at risk for school failure. A variety of programs have had positive effects. In general, immediate effects are greater than long-term effects, and effects on school performance are greater than effects on IQ.

Race and Intelligence → On the average, African-American children score lower than White children on IQ tests. Some authors have suggested that genetic factors may contribute to this difference. Most developmental psychologists disagree. Counterarguments include the inappropriateness of applying within-race heritabilities to between-race differences, and the positive effect of transracial adoption on African-American children's IQs.

Alternatives to IQ

Vygotsky and the Zone of Proximal Development → Vygotsky emphasized what children can do with appropriate help from adults. The zone of proximal development is defined as the difference between what children can do on their own (level of actual development) and what they can do with help (level of potential development). Children who look equivalent in terms of standard IQ measures may actually differ in their zones of proximal development. Appropriate help from an adult or more competent peer may lead to new forms of intellectual competence.

Ceci's Bioecological Theory → Ceci's bioecological theory departs in two major ways from the notion of general intelligence, or g, stressed by psychometric theorists. According to the bioecological view, intelligent behavior results from the conjunction of numerous basic cognitive processes, not a single g factor, and the ability to utilize such processes adaptively varies across contexts or domains. Domain-specific knowledge is an important source of these variations.

Gardner's Multiple Intelligences → Gardner's theory of multiple intelligences suggests that certain forms of intelligence fall outside the scope of standard IQ assessments. Gardner proposes the existence of seven relatively distinct human intelligences: linguistic, spatial, logical-mathematical, musical, bodily-kinesthetic, intrapersonal, and interpersonal.

The Ethological Approach to Intelligence → The ethological view of intelligence stresses the same themes that characterize ethological theorizing in general. Among the points emphasized are the evolutionary history of intelligence, the biological bases for intelligent behavior, and the methodological importance of studying intelligence in its natural context.

Language Development

In the fifth century B.C. the Greek historian Herodotus reported what may have been the first scientific experiment. According to Herodotus, the Egyptian pharaoh Psammentichus had sought to determine which was the earliest, and therefore the most natural, human language. To answer this question, the pharaoh ordered that two infants be reared in an isolated mountain hut without any exposure to language. If the infants nevertheless learned to speak, as the pharaoh believed they would, then the language that emerged must be the original human tongue. The infants did in fact eventually speak, and the first word uttered was "bekos," which, it turned out, was the word for "bread" in the ancient language of Phrygia (now part of Turkey). The honor of the original language was therefore ceded to the Phrygians (Fromkin & Rodman, 1988).

The report by Herodotus is just one of many accounts of attempts, spread across many centuries, to identify the first human language. The reported results have varied. One experiment, carried out by King James IV of Scotland, led to the conclusion that the original language was Hebrew (Fromkin & Rodman, 1988). Another study was inconclusive because the isolated babies, deprived of social contact, died before they could produce any words (Ross & McLaughlin, 1949).

We will not attempt to solve the mystery of the first human language in this chapter. Our focus will be on how children today master the particular language to which they are exposed. We will see, however, that this problem is perhaps no less difficult than the one that confronted Psammentichus. The question of how children learn language is one of the most challenging and fascinating topics in the modern science of child psychology.

Any student who has spent 4 years in high school or college attempting to learn a second language can appreciate the struggle of trying to memorize how each verb is conjugated or what endings signify past, future, and subjunctive forms. Yet that very same student, during the first 4 years of life, very likely acquired the rudiments of her native language rather easily, with no textbooks, classroom instruction, or studying. How is such an impressive feat accomplished?

We can immediately rule out simple explanations of either the nature or nurture sort. The remarkable feat of language development would be easy to understand if language were simply an inherited ability that is passed along in the genes, emerging according to a biological timetable. As we saw in Chapter 2, even animals with very limited cognitive capabilities can display extremely complex behavior if it is the product of millions of years of evolution. Various properties of language rule out such an explanation, however. One is its **productivity**. Whereas communication in other species involves a small set of inborn messages that the animal can send and also recognize, humans can produce—and comprehend—an infinite number of sentences. Many of the statements we speak and hear every day are ones we have never used or encountered in exactly the same form, yet they give us little trouble. Such statements are obviously not the sorts of messages that are passed along genetically from generation to generation.

A second property of language that argues against a purely genetic explanation is its variety. Language consists not of one tongue used by all members of the

Productivity
The property of language that permits humans to produce and comprehend an infinite number of statements.

species, but of thousands of languages. Furthermore, different languages do not simply substitute one word for another; they use different grammatical structures. The word order used to ask a question in Japanese, for example, is different from the corresponding order in French. Yet children readily learn the particular language to which they are exposed. And a child of Japanese parents growing up in a French-speaking home will learn French, not Japanese. We are reminded of the story of the little American girl whose parents had just adopted a baby from Korea. "I can't wait until he gets older," she remarked, "so that he can teach me to speak Korean."[1] Whatever language abilities children inherit from their parents, the ability to speak and comprehend their native tongue is not one of them.

We can begin, then, by ruling out a simple nature solution to the fascinating puzzle of human language. Clearly, language must be at least in part learned. But some of the same properties of language that argue against a direct genetic explanation also pose problems for any simple learning account. Language, as we said, is infinitely productive, and children continually produce and understand sentences that they have not encountered before. The rules that underlie such sentences are quite complex, yet children master them very quickly. And they do so even though their parents do not explicitly teach them most of the rules, nor (as we will see) do they necessarily provide clear models or reinforcements from which children might learn the rules. These arguments suggest that there may indeed be a strong biological basis on which experience operates.

Our coverage of the active field of language development focuses on the two traditional developmental issues. One is a description of the typical course of language development, beginning with the infant's earliest recognition abilities and continuing through children's first words, sentences, and more complex utterances. The second involves proposed explanations of language acquisition and the research findings that support them.

The chapter is divided into five parts. We begin by considering modern theories of language development. Next, we examine what is known about the period before the child begins to speak—a period that many researchers feel is important in laying the groundwork for language development. In the remaining sections, we discuss the development of the three principal areas of language: its meaning (semantics), its structure (grammar), and its functions (pragmatics).

Theories of Language Development

As we saw in our discussion of pharaoh Psammentichus and other early researchers, the theoretical debate over language development is not a new one. Today, the theoretical approaches to language follow roughly the three traditions we described in Chapter 2, including a biologically oriented model, cognitive approaches, and environmental analyses. Here we outline the fundamental ideas of these theories, and in later sections we examine what the data from research with children have to say about them.

Nativistic Theory

The modern debate over language development began around 1960. Before then, most American psychologists viewed language learning in terms of conditioning and learning principles. In his book *Verbal Behavior* (1957), B. F. Skinner had argued

---

[1] We thank Harriet Rheingold for this story.

that the same operant principles used to explain other forms of human behavior could be used to explain the acquisition of language.

The first important challenge to Skinner's views came from Noam Chomsky, a linguist at the Massachusetts Institute of Technology (MIT). The **nativistic theory** of language development proposed by Chomsky puts heavy emphasis on inborn processes and biological mechanisms, in contrast to the environmentalist emphasis of Skinner's theory. Chomsky and other nativistic theorists contend that language acquisition must have a strong biological basis, because young children acquire language so rapidly and so easily, and during a period of development when their cognitive abilities are still rather unsophisticated (Chomsky, 1959, 1965; Lenneberg, 1967; Pinker, 1984). These theorists rule out the possibility that language is acquired by means of rewards, punishments, and imitation for several reasons.

First, adults do not appear to reinforce or punish children for the accuracy of their speech (a point we will discuss again shortly), as an environmental analysis would seem to suggest. In addition, learning by imitation would require that children be exposed to consistently good models of speech and language. However, much of the everyday adult speech that children hear is not well formed and accurate, but includes short pieces of sentences, hesitating stops and starts, slang words, and errors of many types. The productivity property of language also argues against learning by imitation because children produce many statements they have never heard spoken precisely in that way. Similarly, they cannot be imitating adult speech when they produce forms such as "Mommy goed here" or "me up."

A final argument comes from linguistic analyses of human language. Such analyses reveal that the rules we use in speaking or comprehending language are extremely complex. But adults do not specifically teach children these rules. None of us, in fact, could accurately describe the intricate system of language regulations we use so effortlessly to produce and understand good speech and to recognize when speech is not good. These problems and others have led theorists in this tradition to conclude that environmental/learning accounts of language development are inadequate. The only alternative, they suggest, is that children are born with special brain mechanisms—separate from other cognitive processes—that allow them to acquire language quickly and easily.

According to Chomsky's original model, language can be described in terms of two types of structures. A language's **surface structure** consists of the rules governing the way that words and phrases can be arranged, which may vary considerably from one language to another. The **deep structure** of language, in contrast, refers to the inborn rules humans possess that underlie *any* language system. Language acquisition, therefore, requires a speech-analyzing mechanism, which Chomsky called the **language acquisition device (LAD)**. Whenever a child hears speech—good, bad, or whatever—this hypothetical brain mechanism begins to develop a **transformational grammar** that translates the surface structure of the language into the deep structure that the child can comprehend. The development of these transformational rules is assumed to take place over several years, explaining why the child's initial language skills are rather limited, but also why they progress so rapidly.

It should be noted that more recent models in this tradition have diverged in various ways from Chomsky's original formulation. Chomsky's own theory has undergone many specific changes over the years, but the general claims about language and language acquisition have remained the same (Chomsky, 1995). Thus, the current version of the theory still maintains that language consists of a very complex system of rules, that many of these rules are universal across the languages of the world, and that children start the task of language learning with innate

Nativistic theory
A theory of language development, originated by Chomsky, that stresses innate mechanisms separate from cognitive processes.

Surface structure
Chomsky's term for the way words and phrases are arranged in spoken languages.

Deep structure
Chomsky's term for the inborn knowledge humans possess about the properties of language.

Language acquisition device (LAD)
Chomsky's proposed brain mechanism for analyzing speech input; the mechanism that allows young children to acquire quickly the language to which they are exposed.

Transformational grammar
A set of rules developed by the LAD to translate a language's surface structure to a deep structure that the child can innately understand.

knowledge of these universal features. Experience, then, does not teach children language; rather, it simply tells them how the universal features are expressed in the language that they are learning. This emphasis on the natural, biologically prepared nature of language development is well captured in the title of a recent book devoted to this position: *The Language Instinct* (Pinker, 1994).

A relatively recent development within the nativistic perspective is an approach called **learnability theory** (Morgan, 1986; Pinker, 1989). Learnability theory is based on mathematical analyses of the kinds of evidence that children would need to learn various aspects of language. According to such analyses, some linguistic rules could be learned only if children received *negative evidence*—that is, explicit correction when they make errors. But such evidence, these theorists claim, is not available to children, yet all children quickly master the rules in question. The conclusion is that the rules must be innately given rather than derived from experience. We will return to this argument later.

The nativistic model solves several of the problems of an environmental approach. For one, children need only a few critical bits of speech input to develop a grammar and thus to trigger a great deal of language development. Once children grasp the structural rules, or grammar, of the language, they can understand and produce an infinite number of sentences. In addition, according to this model, the analyzing and processing mechanisms needed have evolved specifically for language acquisition and are concerned only with the abstract structure of speech (e.g., subject-verb-object), not with its meaning or content. These two points mean that language acquisition should put few demands on children's cognitive abilities, making highly sophisticated language learning possible in a cognitively immature organism. The nativistic approach also emphasizes the comprehension side of language—children are assumed to acquire language primarily through hearing it, rather than through speaking it. The rewards and punishments that would be necessary to operantly condition children's speech are thus not important to this model.

Noam Chomsky's nativistic theory dominated research on language acquisition throughout the 1960s.

Learnability theory
A nativistic theory of language acquisition that uses mathematical models to determine the kinds of evidence necessary to learn grammatical rules.

Cognitive-Developmental Models

Chomsky's approach dominated language research and theory throughout the 1960s. Beginning around 1970, however, alternative views of language development began to emerge. Some of these grew out of the cognitive-developmental tradition (Rice, 1989).

Whereas nativistic theorists believe that language does not depend on children's cognitive abilities and is more or less separate from them, cognitive theorists assume that even very young children have a good deal of knowledge about the world and that they use this knowledge to help them learn language. These researchers contend that children do not simply acquire a set of abstract linguistic rules. Rather, they acquire language forms that they can "map onto" cognitive concepts they already possess (Bruner, 1979; Johnston, 1986).

Some cognitive language research has been based on Piaget's theory (Tomasello, 1996). Most interest has centered on the transition from the later sensorimotor abilities of the toddler to the early preoperational abilities of the preschooler—a time when children are just beginning to combine words into two- and three-word phrases. This research has examined the relations between certain mental operations and corresponding language forms (Gopnik & Meltzoff, 1996; Tamis-Lemonda & Bornstein, 1994). For example, it appears that infants need a concept of object permanence before they begin using disappearance words such as *all-gone* (Gopnik & Meltzoff, 1987). Similarly, the kinds of meanings that children convey in their earliest sentences (e.g., agents acting on objects) correspond closely to the kinds of understanding that they have developed during the sensorimotor period.

A second cognitive approach is based on a belief that children actually use their early cognitive concepts as a means of extracting the rules of language from the speech they hear. Recall that the nativistic view is that children analyze speech into its abstract, grammatical structure. This cognitive model, in contrast, holds that children first analyze speech into meaning-based, or *semantic*, concepts that involve relations among objects, actions, and events. According to this view, children have a very early understanding of concepts such as *agent* (the person who performs an action), *action* (something that is done to a person or object), and *patient* (the person who is acted on). When young children hear speech, they presumably analyze it into these cognitive concepts, focusing, for example, on who did what to whom. They then develop simple rules regarding these concepts—such as "agents are usually named at the beginning of a statement"—that they use to guide their own speech (Bowerman, 1976).

Even cognitive theorists believe that children eventually become more attuned to the structural aspects of language, as nativistic theorists suggest. But the essence of the cognitive approach is that children's early knowledge of how the world operates is what they use to "crack the code" of the speech they hear (Bowerman, 1988; Schlesinger, 1988).

Environmental/Learning Approaches

Whereas some psychologists emphasize the biological or cognitive bases of language, others seek the major sources of influence in the child's environment and social interactions. These models fall into two categories: the learning approach, and the functionalist approach.

Learning-Based Analyses We saw that Skinner's analysis of language behavior fell out of favor when Chomsky convincingly argued that the environment alone cannot explain the facts of normal language development. Nevertheless, learning-based approaches to this topic did not stop. Contemporary work in this tradition differs in two main ways from its predecessors. First, although some learning-based research has remained close to Skinner's original operant model (Michael, 1984; Vargas, 1986), most is now directed by more cognitively oriented theories of learning. In particular, much recent work has been grounded in Bandura's social-cognitive model (see Chapter 2), with its emphasis on observational learning and related cognitive processes (Zimmerman, 1983).

The second difference concerns evidence for the role of environmental factors. As we saw, one of Chomsky's most important criticisms of Skinner's approach was that the environment does not present the child with a good model of language from which to learn. But research has shown that people do not talk to infants in the same way that they talk to proficient speakers. Instead, mothers (and fathers, and even older children) use a distinct style of speech termed **motherese**. Motherese (also referred to as *infant-directed speech*) is characterized by slow, careful pronunciation and exaggerated intonation. It consists primarily of familiar words, there is much repetition, and sentences tend to be short, simple, and grammatically accurate (Hampson & Nelson, 1993; Snow & Ferguson, 1977). These findings indicate that the input children receive may well be clearer and more helpful than Chomsky claimed.

Chomsky also argued that children cannot learn language simply by imitating what they hear because they can produce and understand an unlimited number of new sentences. But as we saw in Chapter 2, social-learning theorists have shown that learning by imitation need not involve exact copying. They argue, therefore, that

Motherese
Simplified speech directed at very young children by adults and older children.

modeling may account for the kind of rule-based system that children come to use (Bandura, 1986; Whitehurst & DeBaryshe, 1989).

Finally, nativistic theorists have argued that parents do not specifically train children in the rules of language. Yet recent analyses of parent–child interactions indicate that parents do sometimes respond to the grammatical accuracy of their children's speech, providing them a variety of forms of feedback and instruction (Bohannon & Stanowicz, 1988; Furrow et al., 1993; Moerk, 1996). Taken together, these findings suggest that social and environmental factors may play a significant role in children's language acquisition.

Functionalist Theories   A final theoretical view of language development is the **functionalist model**. This approach is not based on learning principles and, in fact, has a distinctly cognitive flavor (Budwig, 1995; Ninio & Snow, 1988). Nevertheless, we have chosen to consider it within the environmental tradition because it emphasizes the social context in which language develops (Hickmann, 1986; Lempert, 1984).

Functionalists hold that the child's primary motivation for acquiring language is to communicate ideas and to be understood. The emphasis here is on *pragmatics*, or the functional uses of language. Like the cognitive approach, this model argues that children extract meaning, rather than structure, from speech. But functionalists assign a much larger role to children's social interactions in the language learning process (Bates & MacWhinney, 1982; Bretherton, 1988; MacWhinney & Bates, 1993).

Jerome Bruner has proposed that the typical social environment of infants (in most cases their parents) in fact provides many structured opportunities for language learning to take place. These opportunities make up the **language acquisition support system (LASS)**, whose function is to assist children in their efforts to acquire meaning, and eventually grammatical rules, from speech input (Bruner, 1983).

The central component of the LASS is the *format*. Formats are similar to the scripts we discussed in Chapter 9 and consist of structured social interactions, or routines, that commonly take place between infants and their mothers. Familiar

Functionalist model
A theory of language development that stresses the uses of language and the context in which it develops.

Language acquisition support system (LASS)
Bruner's proposed process by which parents provide children assistance in learning language.

Jerome Bruner believes that young children learn language through structured play experiences called formats.

formats include looking at books together, playing naming games ("Where's your nose?" "Where's your mouth?") and action games (peekaboo and hide-and-seek), and singing songs with gestures ("The Itsy Bitsy Spider"). Such activities appear to be common across a range of cultures. Variations of the peekaboo game, for example, were found in all 17 cultural settings examined by Fernald and O'Neill (1993).

The format allows a child to learn specific language elements within a very restricted context—usually simply by memorizing words and their corresponding actions. Gradually, the parent may change the formats so that they include more elements or require a greater contribution from the child. In this way, additional language can be learned and previously acquired responses can be applied in new ways. Within these formatted interactions, the parent also provides other sorts of scaffolding for language acquisition, such as simplifying speech, using repetition, and correcting the child's inaccurate or incomplete statements (Snow, Perlmann, & Nathan, 1987).

✓ To Recap...

Until about 1960, the leading theory of language development was Skinner's conditioning and learning account. Since then, the three major traditions have offered additional models.

The evolutionary tradition is represented by Chomsky's nativistic theory. This model holds that learning explanations are inadequate to account for language development. Instead, nativistic theorists propose that language is acquired by way of an inborn language acquisition device (LAD), which transforms the surface structure of the language into an internal deep structure that the child innately understands. This hypothetical brain mechanism presumably responds only to the structure, not the meaning, of speech, so language learning is essentially independent of the child's cognitive development.

Cognitive-developmental theorists believe that children's early knowledge and concepts play an important role in language development. Piagetians have attempted to link advances in sensorimotor and early preoperational abilities to corresponding language skills. Others contend that when children hear speech, they analyze it according to its content before extracting its grammatical structure.

Environmental/learning accounts emphasize the social context in which language learning occurs. Learning-based theories contend that the environment can provide children with the experiences necessary to acquire language and that social-learning principles play a part in this process. Functionalists argue that children's primary motivation to acquire language is to gain a tool for communication. Parents facilitate this process by providing a language acquisition support system (LASS), through which children acquire specific language elements as parts of games or songs.

The Preverbal Period

From the abstract world of theories, we turn to the real world of children learning language. Development in most other areas begins at birth or even before. But children typically do not produce their first identifiable word until about 1 year of age, and they do not begin to combine words until about 18 months. Just how important is the preverbal period in language development?

Some theorists have argued that the process of language development is discontinuous, with the events of the preverbal period having little connection to later language learning (Bickerton, 1984; Shatz, 1983). Most, however, believe that language acquisition represents a continuous process and that abilities developed during infancy form the building blocks of the language skills that appear later on (Bloom, 1998; Hirsh-Pasek & Golinkoff, 1996). Although scientists have not yet resolved this issue, we will see that infants display some remarkable linguistic skills even before many of the typical signs of language appear.

Speech Perception

Before babies can learn language, they must be able to perceive the sounds through which language works. How early is perception of speech sounds apparent? The answer to this question takes us into the area of **phonology**, the study of speech sounds.

Human speech actually consists of a continuous stream of sound. In order to comprehend language, the listener therefore must divide this stream into segments of various sorts, including syllables, words, and statements. The listener must also attend to other characteristics of speech, such as rising and falling intonations, pauses between words and phrases, and stress placed at different points.

Phonologists characterize speech in several ways. Speech therapists, for example, are most concerned with **phonetic** properties, which refer to the different kinds of sounds that can be articulated by our vocal apparatus—the lips, tongue, larynx, and so on. Articulation skills develop in a predictable order, with some sounds, such as *r*, appearing later than others (which explains why a young child might be heard to say, "The wabbit is wunning").

A more important characteristic of speech for infants learning language, however, is its **phonemic** properties. These are the contrasts in speech sounds that change the *meaning* of what is heard. Not all sound differences produce different meanings. The *a* in the word *car*, for example, sounds very different when spoken by someone from Mississippi and someone from Brooklyn. But they represent a single **phoneme** because they fall within a class of sounds that all convey the same meaning. As a result, an English-speaking listener would recognize both words as meaning "automobile."

If a sound variation crosses the boundary from one phoneme category to another, however, a different meaning is produced, as when *car* becomes *core*. The sound difference between these two words may actually be smaller than that between the two regional pronunciations of *car* we just described. But *car* and *core* are perceived as different words—that is, words with different meanings—because in English they represent different phoneme categories. The English language, in fact, uses about 45 phonemes. Other languages use more or fewer. According to Pinker (1994), the range extends from as few as 11 (in Polynesian) to as many as 141 (in the Khoisan or "Bushman" language).

This topic is important for our understanding of language development because research has shown that babies are surprisingly skilled in this area. From an early age, they show evidence of **categorical perception**—the ability to discriminate when two sounds represent two different phonemes and when, instead, they lie within the same phonemic category. This ability has been investigated extensively in infants and has been demonstrated across a wide range of speech sounds in babies as young as 1 month (Aslin, Jusczyk, & Pisoni, 1998; Jusczyk, 1997). Indeed, infants have been shown to display categorical perception of some speech contrasts found only in languages they have never heard (Trehub, 1976). These findings suggest that categorical perception is an innate ability and thus universal among children. But biology is only part of the story.

Experience also plays a role in early speech perception. Two-day-old infants already show a preference for hearing their own language (Moon, Cooper, & Fifer,

Phonology
The study of speech sounds.

Phonetics
The branch of phonology that deals with articulation skills.

Phonemics
The branch of phonology that deals with the relation between speech sounds and meaning.

Phoneme
A sound contrast that changes meaning.

Categorical perception
The ability to detect differences in speech sounds that correspond to differences in meaning; the ability to discriminate phonemic boundaries.

1993). Indeed, studies indicate that the more babies are exposed to a language, the sharper their phonemic discriminations become (Eilers & Oller, 1988). Conversely, lack of exposure may dull these abilities. For example, the distinction between the sounds *r* and *l*, which is not a phonemic contrast in the Japanese language, is a well-known problem for Japanese speakers. Studies show that adult Japanese not only have difficulty pronouncing these sounds, but also struggle to discriminate them (Miyawaki et al., 1975). Young infants, however, have no difficulty discriminating this contrast, suggesting that children learning Japanese gradually *lose* the ability as a result of having little need to use it (Eimas, 1975). In fact, more recent research specifies exactly when the loss occurs: 6-month-old Japanese infants can make the *r* versus *l* discrimination; 12-month-olds, however, cannot (Tsushima et al., 1994). This pattern turns out to be a general one, now demonstrated across a variety of speech contrasts and a variety of languages. By the end of the first year, babies lose a good deal of their ability to discriminate sound contrasts that are not present in the language to which they have been exposed (Best, 1995; Werker & Desjardins, 1995).

Experience with language also helps babies conquer the formidable task, mentioned earlier, of segmenting the continuous stream of speech they hear into individual words. One cue that babies use to accomplish this is the location of a word's stress. In English, for example, most words are stressed on the first syllable. One study found that when American babies were exposed to words stressed on either the first or last syllable, 6-month-olds showed no preference, but 9-month-olds preferred listening to the words stressed at the beginning, presumably because that was the pattern they were used to hearing (Jusczyk, Cutler, & Redanz, 1993). These results support the conclusion that infants' speech-perception abilities improve as they are exposed to language.

Research on infant speech perception, then, suggests the influence of both nature and nurture. Perhaps from birth, babies possess an ability to discriminate a wide range of speech contrasts. They are, in the words of one leading researcher, "universal linguists" (Kuhl, 1991). But the environment very quickly begins to fine-tune these discriminations, eliminating those that are not needed and improving the child's ability to use those that remain.

Listening Preferences

Babies not only discriminate various types and properties of speech, but they prefer some to others. It may not be surprising to learn that infants prefer listening to their mothers' voices over virtually any other type of sound (DeCasper & Fifer, 1980; Mehler et al., 1978). Also as might be expected, they prefer normal speech to either jumbled words or music (Colombo & Bundy, 1981; Glenn, Cunningham, & Joyce, 1981).

Perhaps even more theoretically important is the *type* of speech that infants prefer. We noted earlier that adults talk to babies differently than they talk to other adults, utilizing the style of speech that has been labeled motherese. Several research teams have presented babies with recordings of mothers speaking to their infants and mothers speaking to other adults. These investigators report that infants consistently prefer the mother-to-baby talk (Cooper & Aslin, 1990; Fernald, 1993; Pegg, Werker, & McLeod, 1992). This preference is evident in the first days of life, although young infants are not yet sensitive to all the tone-of-voice cues to which older babies respond (Cooper & Aslin, 1994). Interestingly, the phenomenon is not limited to the auditory medium. Deaf mothers of deaf infants use a form of motherese in the sign language they direct to their babies, slowing down and exaggerating their gestures, and their babies are more attentive to such input than they are to adult-directed signs (Masataka, 1996).

Babies have identifiable listening preferences, such as preferring the mother's voice to that of other adults.

The findings from studies of motherese are important because they suggest that the adjustments speakers make when talking to an infant may actually increase the likelihood that the baby will be listening. But the benefits of motherese extend beyond simply heightening interest in the speech signal. Infants make a variety of discriminations more readily when the input takes the form of motherese than when the speech is of the adult-to-adult sort. For example, the early preferences we noted for the mother's voice or for one's own native language are most evident when the speech is in motherese (Mehler et al., 1978). Similarly, infants discriminate phonemic categories more easily when listening to motherese than when listening to adult-directed speech (Karzon, 1985), and they are better at detecting boundaries between clauses (Kemler Nelson et al., 1989). Thus, adults' natural way of talking to babies may help babies take the initial steps toward making sense of speech.

Early Sounds

Before babies speak words, they produce other sounds. On this topic, the discontinuity view argues that babies' early vocalizations are random and unrelated to their eventual production of words (Studdert-Kennedy, 1986). Continuity theorists, in contrast, feel that early sounds provide the basis for later speech and that the emergence of words represents the continuation of a developmental process that began shortly after birth (Vihman, Ferguson, & Elbert, 1986).

Children's preverbal sounds, in fact, are not random; they follow a reasonably predictable course (Oller & Eilers, 1982; Stark, 1986). The very earliest sounds consist of nonspeech utterances that include whimpers and cries, burps, grunts, and other physiological noises. At about 2 months of age, babies begin to produce one-syllable vowel sounds known as **cooing**—*ah, oo,* and occasionally a consonant-vowel combination such as *goo.* Whereas the earlier sounds usually signaled some form of

Cooing
A stage in the preverbal period, beginning at about 2 months, when babies primarily produce one-syllable vowel sounds.

discomfort, these new sounds frequently are accompanied by smiling or laughing and seem to convey more positive emotions (Blount, 1982).

At about 6 months of age, **reduplicated babbling** appears (Ferguson, 1983). Here, the infant strings together several identical sounds, as in *bababababa*. In the months that follow, the baby adds more and more sounds, including some that occur only in other languages. Research indicates, in fact, that the babbling of children from different language backgrounds is very similar (Locke, 1989).

As infants approach the end of the first year, their babbling loses its duplicated quality, and they begin to combine different sounds, as in *da-doo* or *boo-nee*. This later phase of babbling is characterized by "speechiness"—that is, it begins to include certain fundamental qualities of speech. For example, babies add changing intonation to their sounds, so that their babbling includes the same patterns of rising and falling pitch that we might hear in adult speech (Clumeck, 1980). In addition, many of the sounds that infants produce late in the babbling period are sounds that they will display when they first begin to produce words (Vihman & Miller, 1988).

Babbling is so similar among infants of different language groups that biological mechanisms undoubtedly play a major role. But when infants finally begin to speak, they say only words from the language they have been hearing. Does this mean that speech emerges separately from babbling? Or, instead, does the form of babbling steadily gravitate toward the language the child hears—a theoretical notion called **babbling drift** (Brown, 1958b)? Evidence has been reported on both sides of this issue, but it seems to be accumulating in favor of the drift hypothesis (Blake & Boysson-Bardies, 1992; Levit & Utman, 1992; Locke, 1993). In either case, this issue nicely illustrates the difference between the continuity and discontinuity views of children's preverbal abilities.

The possible role of environmental factors in babbling has also led researchers to examine the vocalizations of deaf infants. If babies do not hear speech, will they still display babbling? The answer is yes, but the nature and course of babbling are not identical to the typical pattern for hearing children. Differences are most marked near the end of the babbling stage and include a delay in the onset of reduplicated babbling and a reduced number of well-formed syllables (Oller & Eilers, 1988). Such findings suggest that although early babbling is probably guided by innate mechanisms, hearing speech may be a necessary environmental experience for the emergence of the more complex aspects of later babbling.

What about infants who are prevented from babbling? This unusual situation can occur, for example, in children who have severe respiratory problems and must breathe through a surgically implanted tube in the trachea. Clinical studies of such cases show that when the tube is eventually removed and normal breathing is

Reduplicated babbling
A stage in the preverbal period, beginning at about 6 months, when infants produce strings of identical sounds, such as *dadada*.

Babbling drift
A hypothesis that infants' babbling gradually gravitates toward the language they are hearing and soon will speak.

Research indicates that the babbling of infants from different language environments is very similar.

MARVIN

BY TOM ARMSTRONG

Reprinted with permission of North American Syndicate

resumed, the child's ability to articulate words lags behind that of age-mates for some time. This finding suggests that the opportunity to babble may provide important practice in the development of articulation. Also, the sounds produced by these children resemble those of deaf children, suggesting further that hearing one's own speech (that is, babbling), along with the speech of others, may be necessary for articulatory skills to develop properly (Locke & Pearson, 1990).

At least one type of babbling, however, does not require vocal skills. Deaf children learning sign language have been shown to display a sort of gestural babbling, producing partial forms of appropriate hand and finger gestures (Petitto & Marentette, 1991). This finding, too, supports the belief that early babbling has a strong biological basis.

Gestures and Nonverbal Responses

Gestures are an important component of human communication (McNeill, 1992). As early as the preverbal period, hearing infants use gestures, combined with other nonverbal responses, to perform many of the functions of vocal language (Acredolo & Goodwyn, 1990; Adamson, 1995). These behaviors have been of particular interest to continuity theorists, who believe that later language is built on early nonverbal skills of this sort (Harding, 1983; Zinober & Martlew, 1985).

Infants first use gestural responses for communicating requests at about 8 to 10 months, usually with their mothers (Bruner, Roy, & Ratner, 1982). Babies who want their mother to bring a toy, join in a game, or open a box learn to signal these desires with various nonverbal behaviors. For example, a baby who wants a toy may reach toward it while looking back and forth between the toy and his mother. Sometimes the reaching includes fussing or crying, which stops when the mother complies with the request (Bates, Camaioni, & Volterra, 1975).

A second function of early gestures is *referential communication*—that is, talking about something in the environment (Bates, O'Connell, & Shore, 1987). This form of behavior usually appears at about 11 or 12 months and may initially involve only *showing*, in which the baby holds up objects for adults' acknowledgment. From showing, it may evolve into *giving*, in which the baby offers objects to the adult, again apparently for approval or comment. Eventually, infants develop *pointing* and *labeling*—the baby uses a gesture to draw attention to an object, such as a cat that has just walked into the room, while producing a vocalization and alternating glances between the adult and the object (Leung & Rheingold, 1981).

For these sorts of nonverbal responses to continue, someone must respond to them. A child is not likely to keep requesting toys, for example, unless her mother provides them at least some of the time. In fact, studies have demonstrated that mothers typically react appropriately to their infants' nonverbal behaviors, such as by getting and labeling the object to which the child has just pointed (Ninio & Bruner, 1978). And, importantly, this sort of appropriate responding appears to have a positive effect on the child's use of these and related language forms (Masur, 1982).

Not all infant gestures are used for communicating; some are used for *symbolizing* objects or events. For example, a child may put her fist to her ear and speak into it as if it were a telephone or hold her arms out to signify an airplane. Children also use gestures to label events (clapping hands to mean "game show") or to label attributes of objects (raising arms to mean "big"). These gestures frequently are not directed at anyone else—in fact, they often occur when the child is alone—and serve primarily to name things, not to communicate the names to others.

Several other aspects of gestural naming are worth noting (Acredolo & Goodwyn, 1988). Gesture labeling and word labeling tend to be positively correlated, so that

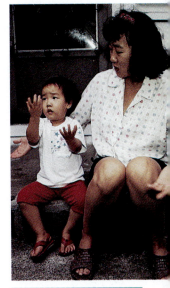

During language acquisition, children used gestures both to communicate their wants and also to label things.

children who do more of one also do more of the other. And once a child acquires a word for an object or event, its gesture label usually disappears. These findings also support the contention of cognitive language theorists that an emerging cognitive skill—the ability to use symbols to represent things in the world—is related to an emerging language ability—the labeling of objects, people, and their characteristics. And they suggest continuity in language development, with gestures serving as a crude form of communication that with time is largely supplanted by the more efficient and powerful system of spoken language (Harding, 1983; Pettito, 1992).

Studies of deaf children provide an interesting addendum to work on the development of gestures. Deaf children who learn sign language do, of course, eventually master a gestural system that far surpasses that of hearing children. The striking finding concerns deaf children who, at least for a while, are *not* exposed to a conventional sign system. Despite the absence of the usual supports for language, many such children spontaneously develop a complex gestural system with many of the properties of spoken language (Goldin-Meadow & Mylander, 1984). We can see again a conclusion that emerged from studies of babbling in deaf children: Humans seem to be born with a strong tendency to develop language if at all possible.

Transition to Words

At about 12 months of age, most children utter what their parents consider to be their first word. Students unfamiliar with infants might assume that one morning a baby looks up from his cereal and says "granola." But in fact, the production of words appears to involve a more gradual and continuous process (Bates et al., 1987; Vihman & Miller, 1988).

Late in their first year, infants begin to utter specific sounds (or sound combinations) with increasing frequency—for example, *dee-dee*. Parents often notice that these sounds have become favorites for the child. Soon the baby begins to attach these utterances to particular objects, situations, or people, such as calling the television *dee-dee* (Kent & Bauer, 1985). At this point, such sounds would seem to be functioning as words for the child. But parents may not attribute much significance to this phase, because none of the infant's words correspond to any of their own. Finally, though, the child begins to produce an utterance, even if it is a bit distorted, that the parents recognize, calling the television *dee-vee*. The parents jubilantly record this event as a milestone in the baby's development (Dore, 1985).

The continuity view of language development finds support during this period as well. For example, children more quickly learn words that involve sounds and syllables they are already using, suggesting that early speech builds on babbling skills (Schwartz et al., 1987). Additional evidence is that other preverbal communication forms do not immediately stop when words appear. For some time after the baby's first words, babbling continues, along with communicative and symbolic gesturing (Vihman & Miller, 1988). Together, these findings suggest that the transition between the preverbal period and the emergence of speech is relatively smooth and continuous rather than abrupt and discontinuous. And they add to the growing belief that the preverbal period serves as an important jumping-off point for later language development.

✔ To Recap...

The importance of the preverbal period in language development has been a subject of interest to both discontinuity theorists, who see preverbal abilities as unrelated to later language, and continuity theorists, who view language development as growing out of earlier nonverbal communication.

Research in early speech perception has shown that babies are born with categorical perception of many speech contrasts, including some that do not occur in their own language. Exposure to specific contrasts of their own language sharpens their ability to discriminate these contrasts, while the ability to discriminate other contrasts declines. Babies prefer speech to other sounds and particularly like the rising and falling intonations many adults use when speaking to young children. This motherese also enhances their ability to make various speech discriminations.

The first sounds of newborns are cries and physiological noises. Cooing sounds appear at about 2 months. Reduplicated babbling begins at 6 months and includes a wide variety of sounds. Near the end of the first year, babbling becomes more speechlike in its sounds and intonations.

Gestures serve many pragmatic functions for infants; preverbal gestures initially take the form of requests and referential communication and later function as symbols to label objects, events, and attributes. Characteristics of early gestures support the cognitive view that gestural and vocal communication are both based on advances in cognitive development.

Early words only gradually replace babbling, gestures, and other nonverbal forms of communication. The combined evidence appears to support a growing consensus that the preverbal period is important for the development of later language.

Semantics

Once children have begun speaking, their use of language expands at a breathtaking rate. We begin our look at this period of language development with the concept of **semantics**, the study of how children acquire words and their meanings.

A well-known investigator of children's language recounts how her 18-month-old daughter began to use the word *hi* to mean that some sort of cloth was covering her hands or feet (for example, her hands were inside a shirt or a blanket was laid across her feet). The child apparently had come to make this unlikely association as a result of her mother's showing her a finger puppet that nodded its head and said "hi." Rather than interpreting the word as a greeting, the child had instead assumed that it meant the mother's fingers were covered by a cloth (Bowerman, 1976).

This anecdote illustrates two points about semantic development. The first is that learning the meaning of words is not as simple a task as it might appear, especially around the age of 2. Not only do children hear adults speaking thousands of different words, but they also must learn that words are of different types, such as those that stand for objects ("hat" and "Mommy"), actions ("eat" and "talk"), and states ("happy" and "red") (Clark, 1983).

Second, the more psychologists study word learning, the more they come to realize how closely this process is tied to children's concept development. Names of things (such as "cat") usually label an entire class of things (the family's pet kitten, a stuffed toy, Garfield), as do names of actions, states, and so on. Furthermore, the same thing can be called by many different names (for example, animal, horse, stallion, and Champ). How the young child knows what class of things to attach a new word to and how this learning develops are issues of considerable importance to understanding language acquisition (Bloom, 1993).

Early Lexical Development

The acquisition of words and their meanings typically begins in the baby's second year. Infants' first words usually name things that are familiar or important to them, such as food, toys, and family members. These words, we will see, also serve a vari-

Semantics
The study of how children acquire words and their meanings.

Children's first words usually label common objects.

Lexicon
A vocabulary, or repertoire of words.

Naming explosion
A period of language development, beginning at about 18 months, when children suddenly begin to acquire words (especially labels) at a high rate.

ety of pragmatic functions, including requesting things, asking questions, and complaining (Griffiths, 1985). In this section, we examine the emergence of children's first words and the importance of the errors children make when attempting to relate words to objects and events in their world.

First Words and the Naming Explosion

By the age of 18 months, children possess an average **lexicon**, or vocabulary, of about 50 spoken words and about 100 words that they understand (Benedict, 1979). There are, however, substantial individual differences; some children have lexicons that number in the hundreds, whereas others still know only a handful of words (Fenson et al., 1994).

At around this time, many children display what has been termed the **naming explosion**, in which they begin to label everything in sight. Some psychologists believe that this burst of vocabulary is related to the child's emerging ability to categorize objects (Goldfield & Reznick, 1990; Gopnik & Meltzoff, 1992; Poulin-Dubois, Graham, & Sippola, 1995). Word learning continues rapidly for the next few years, and by the age of 6, children have a lexicon of about 10,000 words (Anglin, 1993)—which means that they have learned, on average, six new words a day between the ages of 18 months and 6 years.

Semantic development proceeds faster for comprehension than for production. Children typically comprehend words before they begin to produce them, and they comprehend more words than they normally speak (Benedict, 1979; Rescorla, 1981). This pattern is evident from the very beginning and continues into adulthood.

What sorts of words are present in children's early lexicons? Table 11.1 provides some typical examples. For most children, nouns (especially object words) predominate, and nouns remain more common than verbs and action words throughout language development. In most languages, in fact, nouns are understood earlier, spoken earlier and more frequently, and even pronounced better (Camarata & Leonard, 1986; Gentner, 1982; Nelson, Hampson, & Shaw, 1993).

Individual Differences

Despite the commonalities just noted, children do not all follow the same pattern of lexical development. Indeed, one of the major changes in the study of language development in recent years has been the realization that there are important individual differences in how children go about the task of learning language (Pine, Lieven, & Rowland, 1997; Shore, 1995).

With regard to early word learning, the nouns-first pattern is not universal. Two types of early development have been identified (McCabe, 1989; Nelson, 1973).

Table 11.1
Typical Early Words: The First Words in Five Children's Lexicons

Child	Words
Jane	Daddy, Mommy, Daniel, girl, ball, cracker, cookie, that, school, bye
Leslie	Daddy, ball, duck, doggie, kitty, donkey, bottle, apple, thank you, bowwow
Lisa	Daddy, Mommy, Daisy, puppy, ball, see, hi, yes, where
Paul	Daddy, Mommy, Papa, boat, truck, map, this, sit, umm
Mark	Ma, dog, milk, water, car, here, bye-bye, no

Source: Adapted from "Structure and Strategy in Learning to Talk" by K. Nelson, 1973, *Monographs of the Society for Research in Child Development, 38* (Serial No. 149). Copyright © 1973 by the Society for Research in Child Development Inc. University of Michigan, Center for Human Growth & Development.

Some children, who display what is called a **referential style**, do follow the nouns-first mode. These children produce a large proportion of nouns, especially object names, and use language primarily to label things. Other children display an **expressive style**. This style includes a larger mix of word types, more "frozen phrases" (e.g., "What's that?" "Lemmee see"), and a greater emphasis on language as a pragmatic tool for expressing needs and for social interaction. The two groups seem to have somewhat different ideas about the purpose of language, with referential children focusing on its informational function and expressive children more concerned with interpersonal uses. On average (and, of course, with many exceptions), referential children are more likely to be girls, to be firstborns, to have good articulation skills, and to be from middle- or upper-class homes.

What could produce these two different patterns of early language acquisition? Although researchers have yet to reach agreement, one influential model stresses the contexts within which language learning takes place and the interplay of biological and environmental factors (Nelson, 1985; Shore, 1995). This contextual explanation stresses the *transactional* nature of development discussed in Chapter 2. Certain characteristics that differentiate children with the two styles—such as gender, birth order, and articulation abilities—are thought to affect the type of language environment to which the children are exposed. These different environments, in turn, lead the children to develop either a referential or an expressive pattern of vocabulary acquisition.

Evidence of several types supports this analysis. Parents tend to speak to their infant daughters more than to their infant sons, using more complex speech and better articulation (Cherry & Lewis, 1976; Gurman Bard & Anderson, 1983). Furthermore, the types of activities in which children engage affect the kinds of speech parents direct toward them. Doll play, for example, evokes a greater use of nouns, whereas toy-vehicle play results in less parent speech altogether (O'Brien & Nagle, 1987). Children's gender, then, can affect the sorts of language interactions they have with their parents.

Similar arguments can be offered with regard to birth-order differences. Parents tend to spend more time with firstborns than with later-born children, and speech to firstborns includes more learning devices and greater attention to the development of language abilities (Jones & Adamson, 1987). In addition, firstborns get most of their language input from their parents, whereas later-born children get a good deal of it from older brothers and sisters. Once again, characteristics of the child affect the context within which language learning takes place, which, in turn, in a transactional fashion, affects the child's further development.

The Nature of Children's Early Words

Psychologists have learned a great deal about children's semantic development by examining the kinds of errors they make. Word learning typically begins with a child's attaching a specific label to a specific object, such as learning that the pet poodle is a "doggie." Next, the child begins to extend that label to other examples of the same object, using "doggie" to label the dogs he sees in books or on television. These extensions demonstrate that the child is forming an object category called *doggie* that is defined by certain features.

Most children, however, make errors when attempting to extend these early labels and may also use "doggie" to describe a cat, a fox, a rabbit, and so on. Such **overextensions** are very common in the early stages of semantic development in many languages (Rescorla, 1980). Why they occur is not certain. One obvious possibility is that children's initial categories are simply too broad; they do not yet understand the specific features that define the concept. However, this explanation

---

Referential style
Vocabulary acquired during the naming explosion that involves a large proportion of nouns and object labels.

Expressive style
Vocabulary acquired during the naming explosion that emphasizes the pragmatic functions of language.

Overextension
An early language error in which children use labels they already know for things whose names they do not yet know.

When young children encounter an object whose name they do not know, they often overextend a label they already have.

Underextension

A language error in which children fail to apply labels they know to things for which the labels are appropriate.

Coining

Children's creation of new words to label objects or events for which the correct label is not known.

Holophrase

A single word used to express a larger idea; common during the second year of life.

does not fit very well with the fact that overextensions are more common in production than in comprehension. For example, a child who calls an apple a ball might, if shown an apple, a ball, and a pear, be able to *point* to the apple (Naigles & Gelman, 1995; Thomson & Chapman, 1977).

If overextensions do not always reflect a lack of understanding, then maybe they reflect a lack of vocabulary. If she does not know the word *apple*, a child may use the name of a similar object, such as "ball," simply to achieve the communication function of talking about the object. Most likely, both of these reasons are involved in overextension errors (Behrend, 1988; Hoek, Ingram, & Gibson, 1986).

Another type of semantic error involves applying labels too narrowly, rather than too broadly. A child who has learned to apply the label "bird" to robins and wrens, for example, may not apply it to ostriches. Such **underextensions** are less common in production than are overextensions. Underextensions are frequent, however, in comprehension. For example, when shown a group of different animals, young children often do not point to the ostrich in response to the instruction "Show me a bird," but instead select a nonmember of the category, such as a butterfly (Kay & Anglin, 1982).

Both overextensions and underextensions are indications that children, for a while, use words differently than do adults. **Coining** occurs when children create new words that are not part of the adult language (Becker, 1994; Clark, 1982). We saw earlier that children sometimes name an unfamiliar object by overextending the label of a similar object. Thus, a child who sees a lawn rake for the first time may call it a fork, even though the child understands that the label is not correct. But another device that children use to deal with gaps in their vocabulary is simply to coin a new name for the object. Our first-time viewer of a rake might instead call it a grass-comb. Word coining is common in young children, gradually decreasing as their lexicon grows (Windsor, 1993). Such inventiveness provides a nice example of a point that we will reencounter frequently: the creativity that children bring to the task of language learning.

A final characteristic of children's utterances during the one-word phase concerns their communicative function. We might expect that when children produce one-word utterances they are simply labeling objects in their environment—thus "ball" means "That's a ball," "Daddy" means "That's Daddy," and so forth. Although this is sometimes true, it is not always the case, especially near the end of the one-word phase. Instead, sometimes young children use one word to express an entire sentence or idea—thus "ball" might mean "I want the ball," or "The ball hit me," or perhaps any of several other meanings. We call such words **holophrases**, meaning single-word sentences (Dore, 1985). Making sense of them—for either parent or psychologist—must clearly depend on context and the use of whatever extralinguistic cues there may be to the child's intended meaning.

First Word Combinations   Children begin to combine words as they approach age 2. As with holophrases, they may sometimes use the same phrase to express different meanings, depending on its function. For example, "Daddy hat" may represent a name for an article of clothing, a demand for the father to take off his hat, or perhaps a simple description of the father's putting on his hat (Bloom, 1973). Again, contextual cues are important in interpreting what the child is trying to communicate.

Some functions of early word combinations are given in Table 11.2. Studies in various cultures reveal that the same dozen or so functions appear first in a variety of languages (Bowerman, 1975; Brown, 1973). This cross-language commonality

Table 11.2
Some Functions of First Word Combinations

Function	Purpose	Examples
Nomination	Naming, labeling, or identifying	Bunny Ernie
Negation	Rejecting or denying	No nap No wet
Nonexistence	Describing something that is gone or finished	No milk All-gone story
Recurrence	Describing or demanding the repetition of something	More pat-a-cake More drink
Entity–attribute	Describing a characteristic of an object	Ball big
Possessor–possession	Naming two nouns, the first possessing the second	Mommy sock
Agent–action	Describing a person performing an action	Daddy jump
Action–object	Describing an action being performed on an object	Hit ball
Agent–patient	Describing a person doing something to another person	Oscar Bert
Action–patient	Describing an action being performed on a person	Feed baby
Entity–location	Naming a noun and its place	Ball up Baby chair

suggests that the kinds of things children attempt to communicate during this period probably are influenced by their level of cognitive development (Bowerman, 1981). Because cognitive development is similar across different cultures, so too are aspects of early language.

Mechanisms of Semantic Development

Since the early 1970s, a variety of explanations have been proposed to account for how children learn words. Here we discuss three general approaches to explaining semantic development. We begin with the proposal that children use grammatical cues to help determine the meanings of certain words. We then consider the claim that children are predisposed, perhaps by biology, to interpret words in certain ways. Finally, we consider the environmental contributors to word learning, focusing especially on what parents do to help their children learn words.

Grammatical Cues   In our discussion of theories, we saw that cognitive-developmental theorists have argued that children use their knowledge of the meaning or semantics of utterances to help figure out the grammatical structure. In such cases, learning of grammar builds on a prior knowledge of semantics. But the reverse direction is also possible. Perhaps once children have mastered some aspects of grammar, they can use this knowledge to make sense of new words.

How might this process work? Imagine that a child who does not yet know the word *spatula* hears the sentence, "Give me the spatula." From its placement following "the," the child can use her knowledge of grammar to infer that *spatula* is a noun, and probably the name of an object. If the spatula is the only nearby object whose name she does not know, then the child is in position to make a correct name-object pairing and thus learn a new word. Suppose instead that the child already knows the word *spatula* and hears the sentence "Give me the gray spatula." From the fact that it follows an article and precedes a noun, the child can determine that *gray* must be an adjective. If further cues indicate what type of adjective is at issue (e.g., "Give me the gray spatula, not the white one."), then the child may learn a new color term.

There are, in fact, numerous grammatical cues to word meaning, in English and in other languages (Bloom, 1996). The *ing* ending, for example, signals that a word is a verb, and probably labels some sort of action. The contrast between "a" and "some" signals the difference between count nouns (a dog, a book) and mass nouns (some water, some sand). The presence or absence of an article (a collie, Collie) can mark the difference between a count noun and the name of a particular individual.

Can children use such information? The usual approach to this question has been to do experimental studies in which children have a chance to learn a new word based on the grammatical cues available in a sentence. Studies of this sort demonstrate that children can exploit a variety of grammatical cues—including all those discussed in the preceding paragraph—to narrow down the possible meanings of new words (Bloom, 1996; Gleitman, 1990). This process is called **syntactic bootstrapping** because the child's prior knowledge of grammar underlies, or "bootstraps," learning of semantics. Young children, with their more limited grasp of grammar, utilize such cues less successfully than do older children, and grammar alone is seldom a sufficient basis for determining meaning. But it can be helpful.

Constraints We saw that most children have learned thousands of words by the time they start school. Most of these are words that no one has explicitly taught them. And in some cases the learning is quite rapid. Children as young as 3 can sometimes acquire at least a partial meaning of a word after only one exposure to it, a process called **fast-mapping** (Carey, 1977; Heibeck & Markman, 1987). Preschoolers can even use this process when watching television programs, demonstrating in some studies a very rapid acquisition of new words used by the story characters (Rice & Woodsmall, 1988).

But note how difficult this task really is. When a child sees a cat and hears Mommy say, "There's kitty," how does the child know that "kitty" refers to the cat rather than, say, its fur, its color, or its behavior? How does the child know that the reference is to the cat alone, and not to the cat on the sofa, or the cat with its toy? In any situation in which a child hears a new word, there are many logically possible meanings for that word. How does the child avoid the many false directions and zero in on the one correct meaning?

Some psychologists who have studied this question contend that children can accomplish this task only if they are predisposed to relate labels to objects in particular ways. That is, when children hear a new word, they automatically make certain assumptions (usually accurate) regarding what it probably means. The assumptions, or **constraints**, rule out the many false possibilities and thus permit children to acquire the meanings of new words quickly (Markman, 1991; Waxman, 1990). Several such constraints have been proposed to govern early word learning (Woodward & Markman, 1998). Here we consider two.

According to **lexical contrast theory** (Clark, 1987, 1993), when children hear an unfamiliar word, they automatically assume the new word has a meaning different from that of any word they already know. This assumption motivates them to learn exactly what the new word means. A second part of this theory holds that

---

Syntactic bootstrapping
A proposed mechanism of semantic development in which children use syntactic cues to infer the meanings of words.

Fast-mapping
A process in which children acquire the meaning of a word after a brief exposure.

Constraints
Implicit assumptions about word meanings that are hypothesized to narrow down the possibilities that children must consider and hence to facilitate the task of word learning.

Lexical contrast theory
A theory of semantic development holding that (1) children automatically assume that a new word has a meaning different from that of any other word they know and (2) children always choose word meanings that are generally accepted over more individualized meanings.

when a choice must be made, children always replace their current meanings or categories with those they decide are more conventional or accepted. For example, a child who has been assuming that foxes are called "dogs" should, on learning that "fox" has its own separate meaning, replace the incorrect label, "dog," with the correct label, "fox". This mechanism helps bring the child's categories in line with those of adults. There is evidence from both naturalistic and experimental studies that children often do honor the principle of contrast.

The **principle of mutual exclusivity** (Markman, 1989, 1991) states simply that children believe that objects can have only one name. So, when a youngster hears a new word, she is more likely to attach it to an unknown object than to an object for which she already has a label. This strategy has the advantage of limiting the possible choices when a child is trying to attach meaning to a new word. Suppose, for example, that a toddler knows "kitty," but not "doggie." If her mother points at a cat and dog and says, "See the doggie," the child should assume, based on mutual exclusivity, that "doggie" cannot refer to the cat, since she already knows a name for cats. She is therefore more likely to attach the label to the correct referent.

As with lexical contrast, research indicates that young children often do adhere to the principle of mutual exclusivity, and that doing so can be helpful in learning new words (Merriman, 1997; Woodward & Markman, 1998). Interestingly, some of the support for the principle comes not from the successes, but from the difficulties that young children sometimes have in learning words. For example, the strategy causes temporary problems as children encounter the hierarchical nature of word categories. A dog, for instance, can also be called an animal, a mammal, a beagle, and so forth. Two-year-olds sometimes balk at referring to their pet pooches by more than one name, which is what we would expect if they believe that objects can have only a single label (Gelman, Wilcox, & Clark, 1989; Mervis, 1987).

Although mutual exclusivity and other proposed constraints seem to account well for some aspects of early word learning, we should note that not all psychologists are convinced that the notion of constraints is really helpful (Bloom, 1998; Nelson, 1988). Disagreements revolve around several points: whether children's word learning biases really are as consistent and strong as the label "constraint" implies; whether, assuming that constraints exist, they are present from the start of word learning or emerge only later; and whether, again assuming their existence, constraints are innate or derived from experience. There are also concerns about the scope of such explanations—that is, how much of early word learning they can account for. Constraints positions have focused on how children learn nouns, yet children clearly must learn other types of words as well (Tomasello & Merriman, 1995). Finally, even if constraints provide a helpful start toward word learning, we still need to know how children use the speech around them to figure out exactly what words mean. We turn to this question next.

Environmental Bases Whatever innate predispositions children may bring to the task of semantic development, experience is clearly necessary to complete the process. Children are not born knowing the meanings of any specific words; rather, they can learn words only if their social environment provides them with sufficient information about what different words mean. What do parents do that might help their children in this task?

Undoubtedly one important process is *modeling*. Although children sometimes make up their own words, much of what they say reflects what they have heard. In fact, children's early words tend to be those used most frequently by their mothers (Harris et al., 1988; Ninio, 1992); and the more speech parents address to infants,

Children can sometimes acquire the meaning of a new word from only a brief exposure, a process called fast-mapping.

Principle of mutual exclusivity
A proposed principle of semantic development stating that children assume that an object can have only one name.

the faster their early vocabularies grow (Dunham & Dunham, 1992; Huttenlocher et al., 1991). There is also evidence that infants' first lexicons contain so many object words because objects are what parents usually talk to babies about (Bridges, 1986; Goldfield, 1993).

The specific labels that children attach to objects can also be affected by parental modeling. Not surprisingly, children tend to learn such words as *dog* before they learn either *animal* (the superordinate category under which dogs fall) or *poodle* (a subordinate category within the category of dogs). At least part of the basis for this ordering lies in parents' labeling practices—parents are more likely to say, "Look at the dog," than either, "Look at the animal," or, "Look at the poodle" (Callanan, 1985). Furthermore, when parents do use subordinate labels for objects, they usually do so for nontypical examples—such as identifying a robin as a bird but an ostrich as an ostrich (White, 1982). This suggests one explanation for children's underextensions: They may fail to extend a label to nontypical examples of a category because they seldom hear anyone use the label for such examples. If a child has never heard ostriches called birds, it is not surprising if his own use of "bird" does not include ostriches.

Parents' modeling of words can occur either incidentally, in the normal course of conversation, or explicitly, in an attempt to teach the child a new word. In what has been called the Original Word Game (Brown, 1958a), parents sometimes do, in fact, specifically show a child an object, tell the child its name, encourage the child to say the name, and then provide feedback as to the accuracy of the child's responses. This kind of modeling is given most often to infants and occurs less as children grow older (Goddard, Durkin, & Rutter, 1985). With older children, most labels occur in a less structured fashion, simply in everyday conversations between parent and child (Howe, 1981). Whether intended as teaching or not, however, such conversations can be a rich source of information about word meaning. Indeed, as we saw earlier, even labels encountered on television can help children learn new words.

Whatever the source or intent of a label, children can learn its meaning only if they can figure out what the speaker is referring to. This is the problem we considered earlier in our discussion of constraints: How does the child know that "kitty" refers to the cat rather than to any number of other logically possible alternatives? At least part of the answer to this puzzle may lie in parents' sensitivity to their child's interest and attention. Studies of parent–child interaction indicate that parents talk most about objects or events to which their children are already attending (Harris, Jones, & Grant, 1983), and that children are most successful at learning new words when parents have accurately judged their focus of attention (Tomasello & Farrar, 1986). Furthermore, children themselves play an active role in this process. Even infants are surprisingly good at discerning a parent's attentional focus and thereby linking what the parent says with the correct object or event (Baldwin, 1991, 1995). And from early in life it is children, not parents, who initiate and direct many of the conversations from which words and other aspects of language are learned (Bloom et al., 1996).

✓ *To Recap...*

Semantic development is the study of how children learn words and their meanings. At first, children acquire words slowly. But when their lexicons reach about 50 spoken words, their vocabularies typically increase rapidly, a phenomenon known as the naming explosion. Comprehension of words generally precedes production, and both children and adults understand more words than they speak. Nouns make up the majority of children's early lexicons, but even very early there are differences among children in the proportion of nouns used, which relate to factors such as social class, gender, and birth order.

Children's language errors help explain their learning processes. Overextension, a common error, appears to occur for two reasons: Sometimes children do not understand a concept, and sometimes they lack the vocabulary necessary to express the concept. Underextensions are less common in word production than are overextensions, although they occur frequently in comprehension. Children sometimes fill gaps in their vocabularies by coining new words. They also may use their one-word utterances as holophrases that convey a meaning similar to a full sentence.

Several models of word learning have been proposed. Some researchers have examined children's ability to use grammatical information to infer the meanings of new words. Experimental studies indicate that grammatical cues of a variety of sorts can be helpful. Other researchers have argued that various predispositions or constraints are necessary to explain how children rule out the many logically possible meanings for any word. Lexical contrast theory is based on two ideas: Children assume that new words have different meanings from familiar words, and they adopt generally accepted meanings over more individualized meanings. The mutual exclusivity hypothesis holds that children believe that objects can have only one name.

Children's learning of category labels is aided by parents' modeling, whether direct or in the course of day-to-day interaction. Children play an active part in this process, initiating conversations and following the parent's attentional focus.

Grammar

All human languages are structured and follow certain rules called **grammar**. Many of these rules seem arbitrary, such as the English rule that adding *ed* to a verb puts it in the past tense. But, as nativistic theorists suggest, some rules may have a biological basis—that is, languages appear to be structured in such a way that humans learn them very easily.

Children must, of course, learn something about the structure of language to comprehend and speak it. Understanding the acquisition of grammar, however, has posed one of the major challenges to language researchers. As noted at the beginning of the chapter, children are not explicitly taught the structure of their language (at least, not before school age), yet they learn it very quickly. And making this feat all the more impressive is the fact that most adults, even those who are well educated, cannot describe our complex linguistic rules in any detail.

The grammar of most languages involves three principal devices: word order, inflections, and intonation. Word order, called **syntax**, is most important for the English language and thus the aspect of grammar on which we focus here. The sentences "John hit the car" versus "The car hit John" or "I did pay" versus "Did I pay?" illustrate how necessary it is to take into account the order of words. **Inflections** are certain endings added to words to modify their meanings. Common examples

Grammar
The study of the structural properties of language, including syntax, inflection, and intonation.

Syntax
The aspect of grammar that involves word order.

Inflections
The aspect of grammar that involves adding endings to words to modify their meaning.

include plural endings (cat*s*), possessive endings (Mary*'s*), and past-tense endings (work*ed*). Some languages rely much more heavily than does English on inflections to communicate meaning. (In Turkish, a verb can have up to 3,000 different inflections!) Finally, intonation can alter grammar. A rising tone at the end of a sentence, for example, can transform a statement into a question. Again, some languages make greater use of this device than does English. In Chinese, for example, rising or falling tones serve to distinguish certain vowels from others.

Development of Grammar

Children's acquisition of knowledge about the structure of their language involves several distinct phases. And as with semantic development, children's errors often reveal a great deal about the rule-learning processes they are using.

Most children do not begin to combine words into the first simple sentences until about 18 months. Various precursors to sentence formation may be evident prior to this point, however. As we saw, the meanings and pragmatic functions that children convey with their one-word utterances expand across the one-word phase, moving from simple labels to more sentencelike communications. Also, near the end of this period many children begin to produce many single-word utterances in a row. Now the child may use one word to call the mother's attention to an object, and then a second word to comment on the object (e.g., "milk hot"). These multiple one-word utterances can be distinguished from the two-word sentences that will soon appear by the longer pause that occurs between the words (Branigan, 1979). The child seems to be on the brink of producing sentences—just not quite ready to put the parts together.

Early Word Combinations   By age 2, most children have overcome this limitation and are producing two- and three-word sentences, such as "Mommy chair" and "all-gone cookie." Investigators have discovered that children's first word combinations are not random, but follow certain patterns or orders. As a result, much research has been devoted to trying to understand these earliest indications of grammatical knowledge.

The principal method of investigation used has been to collect samples of a child's speech—usually in the natural environment—and to analyze its structure. Many such studies are longitudinal, with samples gathered over a period of months or years in order to examine how grammar evolves (Bates & Carnevale, 1993; MacWhinney, 1991). Researchers have also devised a number of ingenious experimental techniques to probe for knowledge that may not be evident in spontaneous speech—for example, children's comprehension of different linguistic forms (McDaniel, McKee, & Cairns, 1997).

The first syntactic rules that many children develop seem to be built around individual words. For example, a child may say "all-gone doggie," "all-gone milk," and "all-gone Mommy," using "all-gone + _____" as a basic rule (Maratsos, 1983). Children display a degree of individuality in these rules, however. Another child might develop rules around other words, for example "_____ + on" or "I + _____" (Bloom, Lightbrown, & Hood, 1975; Braine, 1976). Furthermore, not all children begin with the "familiar word + _____" formula; some show a greater variety of items and combinations in their initial sentences. We can see again that there are individual differences in how children go about learning language.

The next phase of grammatical development is the emergence of **telegraphic speech**. As the child's sentences grow from two to three or four words and beyond, they begin to resemble telegram messages. That is, they leave out unnecessary func-

Telegraphic speech Speech from which unnecessary function words (e.g., *in, the, with*) are omitted; common during early language learning.

tion words, such as *a*, *the*, and *of*, and also certain parts of words, such as endings and unstressed syllables. Thus, a child who hears "Billy, we're going to the parade" may repeat "Billy go 'rade." Over time, however, the telegraphic nature of children's speech greatly diminishes, as children expand their utterances and add more and more elements of the adult language (Bowerman, 1982).

We noted that children take somewhat different approaches to early sentence construction. One consistent characteristic, however, is an emphasis on word order. No child ever generates sentences by randomly combining all the words in her lexicon in all possible ways; rather, only certain orders and certain combinations appear in children's early utterances. Indeed, even children who are not yet producing sentences are responsive to word order in the sentences they hear (Golinkoff et al., 1987; Mandel, Kemler Nelson, & Jusczyk, 1996). From the start, therefore, children seem to be sensitive to one of the basic properties of grammar.

Overregularization   As mentioned, the rule learning at the core of children's acquisition of grammar also is evident in certain types of mistakes they make. A good example involves inflections (Kuczaj, 1977). The English language uses inflectional rules to change a verb to the past tense (*ed* is added, as in talk*ed* and play*ed*) and a noun from singular to plural (*s* or *es* is added, as in cup*s* and dish*es*). But unfortunately for English-speaking children, our language also contains a large number of irregular forms that are exceptions to these rules—the verb forms *go-went*, *eat-ate*, and *see-saw*, for example, and the noun forms *mouse-mice*, *foot-feet*, and *sheep-sheep*.

At first, children may produce a correct irregular form if it is part of a chunk of adult speech that they are copying. Thus, even 2-year-olds may be heard to say "ate" or "feet." But as they begin to learn the inflectional rules of the language, children **overregularize**, sometimes applying the rules to nouns and verbs that have irregular forms. Now the child will be heard to say "I knowed her" or "Look at the mans." Interestingly, the correct forms do not altogether disappear, so that a child may at one time say "I ate" and at another time say "I eated." Eventually, the correct and incorrect forms may merge, and the child may begin to produce words such as "wented" and "mices." The final disappearance of the overregularized forms seems to take place word by word, with some errors persisting longer than others (Marcus, 1996).

Although such forms as "mans" or "eated" may be quite noticeable to the adults around the child, overregularizations in fact occur in only a minority of the cases in which children cope with irregular words. One extensive survey, based on more than 11,000 past tense utterances, reported overregularizations in only about 4% of the possible instances (Marcus et al., 1992). Nevertheless, overregularizations are informative because they tell us something about the creativity of child language. A word such as "eated" could not be an imitation of anything the child has heard. Instead, the errors children make suggest that they are not merely imitating, but developing a system of rules.

Overregularizations are not limited to grammar. Similar phenomena are evident in phonological and semantic development. An example from the latter domain is the child who creates "yesternight" in analogy with "yesterday" (Maratsos, 1976). Nor are overregularizations limited to children who are learning English; indeed, such errors may be more striking in more highly inflected languages that offer more opportunity for children to go astray (Slobin, 1985). (An early study of children's understanding of inflections is described in Box 11.1.)

Characterizing Children's Language   All researchers of child language agree that some sort of structured rule system underlies even the earliest sentences that

Overregularization
An early structural language error in which children apply inflectional rules to irregular forms (e.g., adding *-ed* to *say*).

BOX 11.1

ADDING ENDINGS TO "WUGS" AND THINGS

Even before the appearance of Chomsky's critique of learning theories of language acquisition, other researchers had questioned the early view that language is learned piecemeal through reinforcement of early babbling or imitation of adult speech. One alternative possibility was that children develop general rules that regulate their early speech productions.

To explore this possibility, Jean Berko, a doctoral student at MIT, conducted a simple but ingenious experiment (Berko, 1958). Children ages 4 through 7 were shown a series of pictures of nonsense objects and activities that had been given nonsense names—the most famous perhaps was a small, birdlike creature that Berko called a "wug," shown in Figure 11.1.

The aspect of grammar that Berko examined was inflectional endings—such as adding the *s* or *z* sound to create the plural (cat*s*, dog*s*) and the *d* or *t* sound to create the past tense (play*ed*, walk*ed*). To investigate a child's use of inflectional endings, Berko might have presented the child with a sequence similar to the following: "This is a cup. Now there is another one. There are two of them. There are two _____."

But what if the child added the correct ending sound to the word? Would that demonstrate that the child knew the rule for plurals? Perhaps. But it could simply mean that the child had previously been reinforced for saying "cups" when more than one was present or that the child was imitating her parents' use of this plural form.

To eliminate these alternative explanations, Berko used nonsense terms. For example, on one trial examining possessive endings, the children were told: "This is a bik who owns a hat. Whose hat is it? It is the _____." As predicted, on this and many of the other trials, children supplied the correct inflectional ending. Since these terms were new, the children could not have learned

This is a wug.

Now there is another one.

There are two of them.

There are two _____.

Figure 11.1

An example of a stimulus used to demonstrate that children's early use of inflectional endings involves rules. From "The Child's Learning of English Morphology" by J. Berko, 1958, *Word, 14*, p. 155. Copyright © 1958 by the International Linguistic Association. Reprinted by permission.

them either through reinforcement or through imitation of what they had heard. Rather, this classic study showed that the children had acquired a set of inflectional rules that they could systematically apply even to unfamiliar words.

children produce. What they do not agree on is how best to characterize the structure. Two opposing positions exist.

One possibility, favored by cognitively oriented researchers, is that children's early sentences are organized in terms of meaning-based, or semantic, categories

Table 11.3
Sample Sentences

Jamie hits ball.	Jamie is hit.
Baby drinks juice.	Jamie has freckles.
Mommy play.	Baby liked juice.
Throw ball.	Thunder scary.

(Schlesinger, 1988). These categories, in turn, reflect the kinds of cognitive concepts that the 2- or 3-year-old child has come to understand. The small set of basic meanings that appear consistently in children's first sentences are compatible with this cognitive model (see Table 11.2).

The other possibility, favored by nativistic researchers, is that even the earliest sentences reflect knowledge of abstract grammatical categories, such as subject, verb, and object (Valian, 1986). In this view, syntax, not semantics, underlies sentence formation.

As an example of how these models differ, consider the sentences in Table 11.3. The sentences in the left-hand column all lend themselves to a similar semantic description. Each includes at least two components of a basic three-part structure: an *agent* (e.g., Jamie) who *acts* (e.g., hits) on a *patient*, or recipient of the action (e.g., ball). Each sentence can also be analyzed as consisting of certain syntactic categories (nouns and verbs) and syntactic relations (subject-verb, verb-object). But—or at least so most researchers argue—there is no reason to credit the child with such abstract grammatical knowledge as long as a simpler, semantically based system can account for all the sentences that we hear.

But consider now the sentences in the right-hand column. Now there is no longer a one-to-one relation between a semantic description and a syntactic one. In the first sentence, for example, "Jamie" is the semantic patient (since she is the one receiving the action), but the grammatical subject. In the second sentence, "Jamie" is again the subject, but now is the possessor of an attribute rather than an agent who performs an action. In both the second and third sentences, the verb is no longer an action word, and in the fourth, the subject is no longer an object name.

The debate about how to characterize early language centers on whether children's initial knowledge about language is limited to consistent meanings or extends to the abstract categories represented in the second group of sentences. As you might expect, semantic analyses find their strongest support with regard to children's *initial* sentences, which are much more likely to consist of combinations of the "Mommy play" sort than they are to include constructions such as "is hit" or "baby liked" (deVilliers, 1980; Maratsos, 1988). Even in this case, however, there are disputes about whether a semantic analysis is sufficient to capture the child's knowledge (Radford, 1990). And exactly when, and how, knowledge of syntax eventually emerges remains a topic of much current debate (Maratsos, 1998).

Mechanisms of Grammar Acquisition

No area of language development is more complex than that of grammar. As with semantics, many explanations for this complexity have been proposed. Rather than attempting to examine them all, we focus on those that are currently of greatest interest to language researchers.

Semantic Bootstrapping One proposed model of the acquisition of grammar grows out of the semantics versus syntax debate discussed in the preceding section.

Even cognitively oriented researchers agree that children eventually master a system of grammatical rules. What they maintain, however, is that this acquisition builds upon prior semantic understanding. According to this view, children first learn semantic categories, such as agent and action, which follow naturally from early achievements in cognitive development. Once these categories are established, young language learners can begin to note that other words can perform the same roles in sentences as the words that make up their own utterances. For example, nouns in general, and not just object labels, can serve as the subject of a sentence or can follow the word *the*. Similarly, verbs in general, and not just action words, can be the predicate of a sentence or can precede the object or patient. In this way, abstract grammatical categories slowly grow out of what was at first a purely semantic system.

Earlier we discussed the notion of syntactic bootstrapping: the idea that children use their knowledge of grammar to help learn about semantics. The form of learning just discussed is known as **semantic bootstrapping**: use of knowledge of semantics to help learn about grammar (Bowerman, 1988; Grimshaw, 1981). The two kinds of learning are not, of course, incompatible; as language develops, the various components might well build on each other in a back-and-forth, reciprocal fashion. Given the complexity of language acquisition, it certainly makes sense that children would make use of any source of information available to them.

Semantic bootstrapping has a role even in many nativistic accounts of language acquisition (Pinker, 1987). Theorists in this tradition, however, do not believe that children's initial categories are purely semantic, or that meaning alone is sufficient to teach children about syntax. Their view, rather, is that much of the basic structure of language—in particular, those aspects that are universal across languages—is innate. The reasons for this claim are the arguments given earlier: the apparent unlearnability of many language rules, given the complex, nonobvious nature of the rules and the very limited evidence available to children. Experience remains necessary in this view—not to teach the child the rules, however, but simply to indicate how the rules are expressed in his language.

Strategies The position just discussed assumes that children possess innate knowledge about the rules of language. An alternative possibility is that children's innate endowment consists not of rules, but of cognitive *strategies* that allow them to acquire the rules rapidly.

One proposal of this type is based on the notion of **operating principles** (Slobin, 1982, 1985). After studying more than 40 languages, Slobin extracted a number of strategies, which he called operating principles, that describe how to learn the rules of almost any language. Among the most important strategies are (1) "Pay attention to the order of words," (2) "Avoid exceptions," and (3) "Pay attention to the ends of words."

We have already seen that children increasingly focus on word order, or syntax, in speech. And children's overregularizations may result, in part, from their avoiding exceptions and applying inflectional rules across the board. Evidence supporting children's use of the third operating principle has been reported in an interesting study.

The method used to address this issue involved teaching English-speaking children several artificial language rules and examining which were acquired most easily. First, the children were taught the names of two new animals—"wugs" and "fips" (Figure 11.2). Next, they learned two new verbs—"pum" (meaning to toss an animal vertically into the air) and "bem" (meaning to toss an animal horizontally across the table surface). Finally, the children were taught two variations of these verbs. If the animal's actions were observed by one other animal, the verbs describ-

Semantic bootstrapping
A proposed mechanism of grammatical development in which children use semantic cues to infer aspects of grammar.

Operating principle
A hypothetical innate strategy for analyzing language input and discovering grammatical structure.

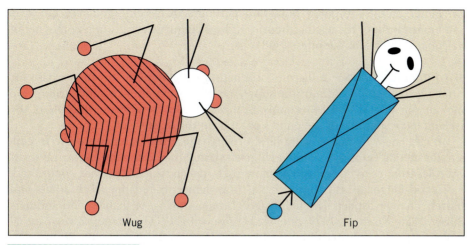

Figure 11.2
Artificial language concepts, along with these two imaginary animals, were used to compare children's acquisition of suffixed and prefixed verbs. From "Syntactic Form, Semantic Complexity, and Short-Term Memory: Influences on Children's Acquisition of New Linguistic Structures" by M. Daneman and R. Case, 1981, *Developmental Psychology, 17*, p. 369. Copyright © 1981 by the American Psychological Association. Reprinted by permission.

ing them were "pumabo" or "bemabo"; if the animal's actions were observed by several other animals, the verbs became "akipum" or "akibem." The researchers hypothesized that if children use a strategy of paying attention to the ends of words, the verbs with a suffix (*-abo*) should be acquired more quickly than the verbs with a prefix (*aki-*). In support of Slobin's model, children learned the suffixed verbs more easily (Daneman & Case, 1981).

A more recent proposal that involves strategies for acquiring grammar is the **competition model** (Bates & MacWhinney, 1987; MacWhinney, 1987; MacWhinney & Chang, 1995). The competition model is a blend of functionalist approaches and information-processing theory. According to this account, young children hearing speech examine the various grammatical cues of their language, such as word order, endings, and intonation, and then focus on the one they believe is most useful for learning the structure of the language. The cue they select can vary from one language to another and significantly, is thought to change as the child matures.

Initially, children focus on the cue that is most *available*. In English and French, for example, children's first attempts to learn grammar involve word order. Because word order is important in these languages, it is a cue that is frequently available to provide information useful for learning language rules. In Turkish, in contrast, word order is less important, and language-learning children typically focus first on the inflections in the speech they hear. In the second stage, children select the cues that are most *reliable*, meaning those that most consistently provide clues to grammatical structure. And in the final stage, children note cues that are in *conflict* with one another and then focus on the one that most often "wins out" and best reveals the language's structure.

Tests of specific claims from this model often take the form of computer simulations—for example, demonstrations that a computer programmed with the strategies described and given appropriate linguistic input shows the same patterns in mastery of the English past tense as do children (MacWhinney & Leinbach, 1991).

Competition model
A proposed strategy children use for learning grammar in which they weight possible cues in terms of availability and reliability.

Motherese and other forms of speech adjustment to babies are not exclusive to English-speaking mothers.

More generally, the computer-simulation methodology has emerged in recent years as an important tool for testing theories of how language acquisition comes about (McDonald, 1997; MacWhinney, 1998).

Environmental Bases As is true for semantic development, any innate basis for grammatical development must be supplemented by experience and learning. We conclude our discussion of mechanisms, therefore, by considering the role of the environment, especially of the child's parents, in the mastery of grammar.

We can begin by asking what kind of language input parents provide to children. Recall that Chomsky claimed children should have difficulty extracting structural rules from everyday speech because such speech typically provides poor models of good language. But research has now demonstrated that both adults and children change aspects of their speech when talking to babies and toddlers (Messer, 1980; Newport, 1977; Snow & Ferguson, 1977). This is the *motherese* speaking style, already discussed at various points. Motherese, you may recall, includes helpful-looking adjustments of a variety of sorts. Mothers tend to speak slowly and use short utterances, often three words or fewer. Usually the words are pronounced very clearly, and the speech rarely contains grammatical errors. When talking about an object or situation, mothers label it frequently and use a good deal of repetition in their descriptions and comments. And the focus of their speech usually is on the here and now, rather than on more distant or abstract events.

Fathers display many of the same speech adjustments, although they generally are less sensitive to the infant's level of linguistic development (McLaughlin et al., 1983; Ratner, 1988). In fact, some researchers have suggested that the father's speech serves as a bridge between the fine-tuned adjustments of the mother and the complex and erratic speech of the outside world (Gleason & Weintraub, 1978; Mannle & Tomasello, 1987; Tomasello, Conti-Ramsden, & Ewert, 1990).

But do all these speech adjustments have any effect on the child's language development? We noted earlier that some aspects of phonological development, such as the ability to discriminate phonemes, can be facilitated by motherese. The evidence with respect to grammatical development is less clear. Attempts to find a convincing connection between the overall degree of maternal speech adjustment and the child's level of language development have failed to discover a strong relation (Gleitman, Newport, & Gleitman, 1984; Murray, Johnson, & Peters, 1990). And attempts to uncover positive effects of more specific speech changes (length of utterance, amount of repetition, and so on) have offered only scattered support (Furrow, Nelson, & Benedict, 1979; Hoff-Ginsberg, 1990; Hoff-Ginsberg & Shatz, 1982).

Do these results mean that simplifications in the speech directed toward language-learning children are of little value? Not necessarily. One possibility is that some *minimum* amount of simplification is important, but that the additional degree of motherese provided to some children is of no extra benefit (Scarborough & Wyckoff, 1986). Another possibility is that the methods and measures used by researchers have simply not been appropriate or sensitive enough to detect all the relations that exist between the adults' input and the children's output (Schwartz & Camarata, 1985; Snow et al., 1987). At present, therefore, the role of motherese in grammatical development remains to be established.

We turn next to one of the contributors discussed with respect to semantic development: *parental modeling*. The fact that parents present children with a simplified model of language suggests a possible role for imitation. To what extent do young children acquire grammatical rules by imitating the speech of their parents and other adults?

We know, of course, that imitation cannot be the whole story. As Chomsky pointed out, our ability to produce entirely novel statements means that language must be based on more than merely copying what we hear. In addition, young children produce word combinations that they have probably not heard ("all-gone Daddy"), along with overregularizations not found in adult speech ("I hurted my foots"). These forms clearly do not arise from imitation in any simple sense.

But perhaps those imitations that occur are *progressive*. That is, perhaps when youngsters do repeat their parents' comments, they tend to imitate language structures more complex than those they use themselves. These structures may then begin to find their way into the children's own spontaneous speech. Whether this is the case seems to depend on how *imitation* is defined (Clark, 1977; Whitehurst & DeBaryshe, 1989).

When imitation is defined as immediate and exact copying of an utterance, several findings emerge. The first is that most children display very little imitation, although a few imitate a great deal (Bloom, Hood, & Lightbrown, 1974). Furthermore, such imitations are rarely progressive. In fact, they often are even shorter and less complex than the syntax the child usually uses (Ervin, 1964; Tager-Flusberg & Calkins, 1990). Finally, the proportion of immediate and exact imitations declines over the first few years of language learning (Kuczaj, 1982).

A different picture emerges when imitation is defined more broadly. For example, we might look for *expanded imitations*, in which the child adds something to the utterance that was just heard; or *deferred imitations*, in which the copying occurs at some later time; or *selective imitations* (which can also be deferred), in which the child imitates the general form of a language structure, such as a prepositional phrase, but uses different words (Snow, 1983; Whitehurst & Novak, 1973). The research evidence suggests that these forms of imitation sometimes *are* progressive. Thus, at least in some cases, a more advanced language structure does first appear in a child's imitation of adult speech and then gradually finds its way into the child's spontaneous, nonimitative speech (Bloom et al., 1974; Snow & Goldfield, 1983). Moreover, in the speech of young children who imitate frequently, the proportion of expanded imitations generally increases with age, suggesting that these children may have adopted imitation as a mechanism for learning syntax (Kuczaj, 1982; Snow, 1981).

The final mechanism we consider that might help children master grammar is feedback, or correction in response to statements that are grammatically incorrect. Such feedback is called *negative evidence* because it provides information about what is *not* correct in language (in contrast, parental modeling of correct language provides what is called *positive evidence*). As we noted in the Theories section, nativistic theorists maintain that some grammatical rules could be learned only if children received negative evidence. As we also saw, they claim that such evidence is not available—and thus that knowledge of the rules must be innate.

Do children receive negative evidence? We know that systematic reinforcement for correct utterances and disapproval or correction for incorrect utterances can be an effective method of teaching language in applied contexts—in work with language-impaired children, for example (Whitehurst et al., 1989), or in programs for children learning vocabulary in a second language (Whitehurst & Valdez-Menchaca, 1988). But does this sort of process operate in the natural environment? Do parents respond to the accuracy of their children's grammar? Once again, the answer to these questions is neither a simple yes or no (Snow et al., 1987). Indeed, the issue of negative evidence is one of the most controversial topics in the study of language development (Bohannon et al., 1996; Morgan, Bonamo, & Travis, 1995; Valian, 1996).

Parents rarely respond to their children's ungrammatical statements with simple disapproval, such as "No, you didn't say that right." Instead, feedback regarding the accuracy of a child's remark usually involves its content, or truth value, such as "No, the block isn't red, it's blue" (Brown & Hanlon, 1970; Demetras, Post, & Snow, 1986). Thus, most children apparently do not receive the kind of negative evidence that nativistic theorists have stressed. But parents do provide helpful feedback in more subtle ways (Bohannon & Stanowicz, 1988; Moerk, 1996).

Research has shown, for example, that mothers frequently respond to their children's ill-formed statements (such as "Mouses runned in hole, Mommy!") in one of three ways. **Expansions** involve repeating the child's incorrect statement in a corrected or more complete form ("Yes, the mice ran into the hole!"). **Recasts** involve restating the child's remark using a different structure ("Didn't those mice run into that hole!"). And **clarification questions** signal that the listener did not understand the comment and that the child should attempt the communication again ("What happened? What did those mice do?") (Demetras et al., 1986; Hirsh-Pasek, Treiman, & Schneiderman, 1984; Penner, 1987).

Are these forms of feedback helpful? Research suggests that they are. Children appear to be sensitive to such parental responses; it has been shown, for example, that they are much more likely to imitate a correct grammatical form following a parental recast than following ordinary speech (Farrar, 1992). And there is evidence, from both experimental and correlational studies, that providing children with such feedback can accelerate the development of correct grammar (Farrar, 1990, 1992; Moerk, 1996).

Expansion
A repetition of speech in which errors are corrected and statements are elaborated.

Recast
A response to speech that restates it using a different structure.

Clarification question
A response that indicates that a listener did not understand a statement.

Development in Cultural Context
Cultural Variations in Language-Learning Experiences

Children in every human culture master the language they hear around them, and in some respects the process is the same the world over. But language learning can also vary in interesting ways across different societies and cultural settings. Some variations, of course, follow from differences in the language being learned—a child acquiring Russian or Turkish, for example, must pay closer attention to inflections than a child learning English. Some differences, however, are a reflection less of language per se than of cultural practices and ways in which parents socialize babies and young children in different cultures.

Consider first the words that appear in children's early lexicons. We saw that children learning English tend (with some exceptions) to learn nouns, especially object names, first. This is not surprising, since American parents include a high proportion of object labels in speech to their children. In contrast, Japanese mothers place more emphasis on using objects to engage their baby in social routines—for example, turn taking and sharing. They are consequently less likely to provide labels, and Japanese toddlers are slower to acquire names for objects (Fernald & Morikawa, 1993). Similarly, Korean mothers provide fewer object names than do English-speaking mothers; at the same time, they are more likely to use verbs that refer to ongoing actions. Compared with children learning English, Korean children are slower to acquire nouns but faster to learn verbs of action (Choi, 1997; Choi & Gopnik, 1995).

The way in which parents talk to children can also convey information about how to use language to influence others—a topic that falls under the heading of *pragmat-*

ic development. An interesting example can be seen in a comparison of middle-class American and German mothers (Shatz, 1991). Both groups represent Western, industrialized societies, and their languages are structurally similar to one another. One cultural difference between them, however, lies in their philosophies of discipline and socialization. American mothers tend to stress teaching children to express their emotional needs, whereas German mothers display more interest in teaching obedience and self-reliance. Of interest to the investigators was whether these differences in cultural values would be reflected in the style of speech the mothers used with their 2-year-old children. The study focused on verb forms that serve different functions—for example, expressing permission ("you *may* choose"), obligation ("you *must* put"), and possibility ("this *can* fit"). As predicted, the German mothers tended to focus on obligation verbs and used more negatives than did the American mothers; the latter group, in turn, asked more questions and focused more on permission and possibility. These differences, moreover, were reflected in the children's language. For example, many German toddlers were already producing obligation statements, whereas not a single American child was as yet using this form.

Perhaps the most striking cultural difference in the language input children receive comes from the study of children learning Kaluli, a language spoken in Papua New Guinea (Schieffelin, 1985). Kaluli mothers regard infants as helpless and incapable of any sort of understanding; as a result, they never direct speech toward their babies. All the speech the infant hears, therefore, is of the sort that is intended for older children or adults, which means that it lacks the simplifying motherese features that are common in parental speech in Western cultures. Yet Kaluli children learn language quite readily—an outcome that has also been reported in other settings in which motherese is apparently absent or rare (Heath, 1983; Ochs, 1982). (We should note, however, that not all investigators are convinced that speech simplifications are really totally lacking in these cultures [Fernald, 1991].)

These findings make two important points about language development. First, the fact that children can acquire language in at least somewhat similar ways across so many different environmental settings suggests that there is indeed, as nativistic theorists argue, a strong biological basis for language learning. Second, the process of acquiring language, as we noted before, cannot be completely biological, and every human culture provides experiences from which children can learn the culture's language and more generally become productive members of their society. It is good to be reminded that there can be different routes to the same end point, and that practices common in Western cultures, sensible and helpful though they may be in particular settings, are not necessarily universal.

Applications
Picture-Book Reading as a Context for Language Learning

As we have just seen, one of the striking features of language acquisition is that it occurs in at least somewhat similar ways across so many different human environments. This is not to say, however, that the process is impervious to experience, or that it always proceeds smoothly and satisfactorily. A program of research by Grover Whitehurst and associates (Whitehurst, 1997) illustrates both the problems that can arise when language is acquired under difficult circumstances and some possible ways to overcome the problems.

Picture-book reading offers a good opportunity for parents to provide scaffolding to language-learning youngsters.

Dialogic reading
Form of joint picture-book reading in which the adult uses open-ended questions and other prompts to encourage the child to tell the story, with the goal of promoting linguistic skills.

The sample for the Whitehurst research consists of preschool children who are growing up in conditions of extreme poverty. In one study, for example, all the families have incomes below the $14,000 cutting point that determines eligibility for the local Head Start program. Many of the mothers are single, and virtually all are required to work outside the home. Given the challenges with which they must cope, such parents often have limited time and resources to devote to their children, and the children's verbal environments tend to be a good deal less rich than those of the middle-class children who have been the subjects of most language-development research.

The children's own language also turns out to be less rich. On various measures of semantic and pragmatic development, these children score well below the norms for more privileged samples. Their scores consistently place them in the lowest 15% of the population in general, and on some measures they fall in the bottom 2%. It is interesting to note that the children's grammatical development is less affected than other aspects of their language. Even in this area, however, they often lag behind their middle-class peers.

In attempting to devise a way to help such children, Whitehurst and colleagues draw on both theory and research. We saw earlier that functionalist theorists emphasize the various *formats*, or structured interactions, through which parents convey information about language to their children. One such format is reading picture books together. By one estimate, a typical middle-class child in the United States has experienced 1,000 to 1,700 hours of one-on-one picture-book reading by the time he enters first grade (Adams, 1990). The comparable figure for children from low-income families is about 25 hours. If reading together really does contribute to language learning, it is not hard to see how such a staggering difference in experience (along, of course, with many other differences) could eventually lead to differences in the quality of language development.

Research with middle-class samples provides evidence that frequency of book reading does in fact relate positively to measures of language competence (Crain-Thoreson & Dale, 1992; Whitehurst & Lonigan, in press). One step in the Whitehurst research program was to verify that a similar relation held in their sample. Payne, Whitehurst, and Angell (1994) collected measures not only of book reading but of various other indices of the children's "literacy environments" (e.g., number of picture books in the home, frequency of trips to the library). These measures showed substantial relations to individual differences in the children's language development: The more positive the literacy environment, the better, on average, the children's language.

Because the Payne et al. study was correlational, it could not establish cause-and-effect relations with certainty. The next step, therefore, was to manipulate book reading experimentally. The Whitehurst group has now done so across several different studies and samples, in some cases using research assistants as the readers and in others training the child's teachers or parents to perform the role (Lonigan & Whitehurst, in press; Valdez-Menchaca & Whitehurst, 1992; Whitehurst, Arnold, et al., 1994; Whitehurst, Epstein, et al., 1994). They have emphasized what the researchers label **dialogic reading**. In typical book reading, the adult takes the lead role—the adult reads and the child listens. Dialogic reading involves a shift in roles, so that the child becomes the storyteller. In dialogic reading, the adult assumes the part of an active listener, posing questions, adding information, and prompting the child to increase the sophistication of his descriptions. Open-ended rather than yes/no questions are emphasized, as are questions that move the child beyond specific details to more general issues of motivation and meaning. And as the child's competence as a storyteller increases, so does the level of the adult's prompts and expectations.

The results of this sort of experience have been consistent across the program of research. In each study, the children who received the picture-book intervention outperformed a matched control group on subsequent measures of language development. Benefits have been demonstrated on a range of different language measures, with effects on semantic development perhaps most impressive. Furthermore, the gains, as Whitehurst (1997) stresses, are not merely statistically significant; they are large enough to constitute meaningful improvements in the children's everyday linguistic functioning.

Clearly, the Whitehurst studies address only one of the environmental bases for individual differences in language development—and only one possible approach to helping children whose language skills lag behind those of their peers. Still, the studies do suggest that a common and enjoyable parent–child activity can be a source not only of pleasure, but of significant learning as well.

✓ *To Recap...*

Grammar is the study of the rules of language structure. These rules include such devices as word order (syntax), inflections, and intonation. The growth of grammar can be seen as children's speech steadily increases in length and complexity. Children's two-word utterances, which appear around the end of the second year, often display rules built around individual words—for example, combining "all-gone" with various nouns. As sentences grow longer, telegraphic speech emerges. When children first learn inflectional rules, they overregularize them, applying the regular forms even to irregular words. Children's early sentences are systematic and rule governed, but researchers disagree as to whether semantic or grammatical knowledge accounts for their systematic nature.

Many explanations of how grammar develops have been proposed. The semantic bootstrapping hypothesis maintains that children use their knowledge of semantics (e.g., that agents act on objects) to figure out rules of syntax (e.g., the categories of nouns and verbs). In contrast, nativistic theorists maintain that children's language reflects syntactic and not merely semantic knowledge from the start and that innate knowledge about the principles of grammar makes language acquisition possible.

An alternative to inborn knowledge is inborn linguistic strategies. Operating principles for acquiring language have been derived from the study of many languages and are supported by observations and experimental investigations of children's language learning. The competition model, which focuses on how cues to grammatical structure are selected, finds support in computer simulations of grammatical change.

Environmental influences on grammatical development have also been investigated. Both mothers and fathers use motherese in talking to babies and young children. Attempts to link the use of this simplified speech style to progress in language development have met with mixed success.

Imitation can take several forms. Most important for language learning are the expanded, deferred, and selective forms, which introduce new grammatical constructions to some children. Another environmental factor is feedback. Although parents rarely respond to children's ungrammatical statements with disapproval, they commonly expand, recast, or ask for clarification of ill-formed statements. Such responses have been shown to be of some value for children's language development.

Pragmatics

Pragmatics
The study of the social uses of language.

We have seen that language has both structure (grammar) and meaning (semantics). But it also performs functions, in that it gets people to do things we would like them to do. When a toddler points to the refrigerator and says "cup," for example, she is not as likely to be labeling the refrigerator as she is to be asking her mother to fetch her cup of juice. The study of the social uses of language is called **pragmatics** (Ninio & Snow, 1996).

Pragmatics is a relatively new area of study and, as a result, we know less about it than we know about semantics or grammar. But it is one of the most rapidly growing approaches to language study, perhaps because psychologists are focusing more and more on the context in which children learn. As mentioned, functionalist theories have been especially important in this area.

Pragmatics grows out of the functionalists' belief that children continually strive to find better ways of communicating their ideas, requests, and objections to others. From this perspective, children do not learn language simply because of an innate quest to understand linguistic structure. Instead, they are motivated to acquire language because it provides them with a very powerful tool—the ability to communicate with others easily and to achieve their goals effectively (Hickmann, 1986; Ninio & Snow, 1988).

To be effective communicators, children first must learn to express their needs or desires in ways that can be understood by others. In the beginning, babies cannot always accomplish this, and sometimes their attempts to convey their wants are frustrated by their parents' failure to understand exactly what is being requested. This frustration is an important motivator for the child to acquire skills that will make communication easier. But the process operates in the other direction as well. Effective communication also involves understanding what parents and others are saying in order to follow their directions, answer their questions, or comply with their requests. Communication, of course, is a two-way street.

We begin our discussion of pragmatics with a look at how children use speech to control others and to get their own way. Then we examine the development of conversation skills and the ability to communicate effectively with others.

Speech Acts

Speech act
An instance of speech used to perform pragmatic functions, such as requesting or complaining.

Before acquiring speech, infants use other tools for communication, such as crying, facial expressions, and gestures. In one study, mothers engaged in a turn-taking game (for example, taking turns squeezing a squeak toy) with their 1-year-old babies. Once the game was going smoothly, they were instructed not to take a turn and simply to sit silently and motionlessly. The babies reacted by performing a variety of behaviors clearly designed to communicate to the mother that it was her turn. These included vocalizing at her, pointing to the toy, and picking up the toy and giving it to her (Ross & Lollis, 1987).

With the acquisition of language, children add verbal responses to this repertoire of communication devices. Now children achieve various goals by directing words and phrases at other people. Functionalists refer to these pragmatic uses of language as **speech acts** (Astington, 1988; Dore, 1976). Researchers have found that even the earliest words that infants utter usually serve several pragmatic functions (Bretherton, 1988). "Mama," for example, is generally first used both to call the mother and to request things from her (as when the baby says "mama" while pointing to a toy on a shelf). In time, this word also begins to serve the more common purpose of naming the parent (Ninio & Snow, 1988). Later in the one-word peri-od, babies begin to use *relational words*—those connecting several objects or events—in a number of pragmatic ways. For example, "more" may be used to request that an activity be continued as well as to describe a block being added to a pile (McCune-Nicolich, 1981).

As children's cognitive and linguistic abilities grow, so, too, do the range and effectiveness of their speech acts. In one longitudinal study, the number of com-municative attempts per minute more than doubled between 14 and 32 months, and the number of different types of speech acts more than tripled. In addition, the proportion of attempts that were judged as interpretable—and therefore more like-ly to be successful—rose from 47% to 94% (Snow et al., 1996).

Mothers also produce speech acts, which must be comprehended by the lan-guage-learning infant if mother and child are to communicate effectively (Ninio & Wheeler, 1984). The comprehension side of communication also improves greatly with development. The child's task is complicated, however, by the fact that the function of some speech she hears may not be obvious. When a mother says, "May I open it for you?" she is not really asking the child a question as much as she is offering help. And when she says, "I didn't mean to break it," she is doing more than describing her intentions; she is actually apologizing to the baby. Researchers are just beginning to study this aspect of pragmatics, as we will see shortly.

Discourse

Regardless of what theory of language acquisition they favor, all researchers agree that language is most often used in social contexts. Speech during social interaction is called **discourse** or, more commonly, conversation (Hicks, 1996).

When people have conversations, they must, of course, adhere to the gram-matical rules of the language if they are to understand one another. But they also must follow certain social rules of discourse. The most obvious of these is turn tak-ing, with each participant alternating between the roles of speaker and of listener. This basic rule of conversation is one of the first acquired by children. As we have seen, it may actually be learned during the preverbal period (Collis, 1985).

Some other rules of discourse are more difficult, however, and are learned later. One of these is the "answer obviousness" rule. Some statements that are phrased as questions may actually be intended as directives, such as, "Could you hand me that pencil?" How do listeners know in these situations which function the speaker intends? Most often, we solve the problem by considering the context in which the remark is made (Shatz & McCloskey, 1984). For example, we would very likely treat the remark as a directive if the speaker were about to write a note, if a pencil were visible but out of the speaker's reach, and if the pencil were within our reach. Another kind of cue we often use in such situations, however, is the obvi-ousness of the answer. Since we realize that the speaker in our example knows that we *could* pass the pencil, we do not treat the remark as a request for information. Instead, we view it as a directive. Discourse rules of this sort are clearly more diffi-cult to learn than is turn taking, and the answer-obviousness rule is not apparent in children until about age 5 (Abbeduto, Davies, & Furman, 1988).

Other discourse rules appear even later. For example, understanding that in a conversation one should (1) say something that relates to what the speaker has just said, (2) say something that is relevant to the topic under discussion, and (3) say something that has not already been said involves discourse rules that most chil-dren do not use consistently until 6 or 7 years of age (Conti & Camras, 1984).

Discourse
Language used in social interactions; conversation.

Social Referential Communication

An even more advanced conversational skill involves the ability to effectively communicate information about something that is not known to the other participant in the conversation, as when one child describes his new computer game to a classmate in such a way that the other child understands how it is played. This form of communication is called **social referential communication**. In formal terms, such communication occurs when a *speaker* sends a *message* that is comprehended by a *listener*. The communication is social because it occurs between two people (rather than between a person and a machine, for example); it is referential because the message is in a symbolic form (the child is using language to convey the information and not simply showing the classmate what to do); and it is communication because it is understood by the listener (Whitehurst & Sonnenschein, 1985).

Research on social referential communication has been conducted primarily in laboratory settings. To study this process, researchers have generally used a task of the following sort (see Figure 11.3). Two children sit across from one another at a table, separated by a screen or partition. One child is designated as the speaker, the other as the listener. Both children are given identical sets of stimuli, such as blocks of different sizes, patterns, or colors. The speaker's task is to send messages that describe a block. The listener's task is to use the messages to select the correct block from the available array. In some experiments, the listener can ask questions or comment on the usefulness of the speaker's descriptions. The success of the communication is measured by how often the listener selects the correct item. Using this procedure, psychologists have been able to identify many of the factors that influence children's communication abilities.

In order for children to engage in social referential communication effectively—as speakers or as listeners—they must learn a number of important skills. In the

Social referential communication
A form of communication in which a speaker sends a message that is comprehended by a listener.

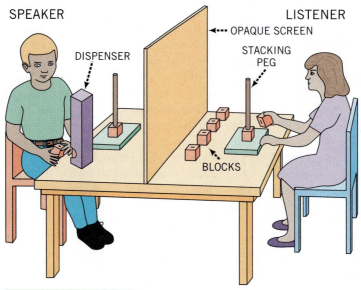

Figure 11.3
Example of an arrangement used to study social referential communication in children. The speaker's task is to describe the target object in his set clearly enough so that the listener can pick the same object in her set. From "The Development of Communication: Competence as a Function of Age" by R. M. Krauss and S. Glucksberg, 1969, *Child Development, 40*, p. 259. Copyright © 1969 by the Society for Research in Child Development. Reprinted by permission.

To become effective communicators, young children must acquire both speaker skills and listener skills.

role of speaker, children must become aware of *listener cues*, meaning simply that they must adjust messages to meet the needs of the listener. For example, if the listener is far away, the message should be loud; if the listener is running out the door, the message should be brief; and if the listener is someone of high status (for example, a teacher or a preacher), the message should be polite.

A good example of a young child's failure to take listener cues into account is the little boy who talks with his grandmother on the telephone and answers her questions by nodding his head. The same phenomenon is evident in experimental tasks of the sort pictured in Figure 11.3 when young children in the speaker role say, "It's this one," or perhaps simply point to the intended target.

Although children are often insensitive to the characteristics of the listener, they do sometimes adjust their speech in response to one important listener characteristic—namely, age. We have seen that adults tend to use the simplified motherese style of speech when talking to young children. So, it turns out, do children; children as young as 4 simplify their speech when addressing toddlers or infants (Sachs & Devin, 1976; Shatz & Gelman, 1973). As we would expect, this ability improves as children grow older. Fifth graders, for example, make more effective speech modifications when talking to younger children than do first graders (Sonnenschein, 1988). Even grade-schoolers, however, still show a tendency to overestimate the comprehension abilities of young listeners (Montgomery, 1993).

Another useful listener cue involves *common ground*, the information shared by the speaker and listener. If the listener, for example, knows the speaker's birthday, then the message "Come over on my birthday" will be sufficient; if the listener does not possess the information, the message will be inadequate. Kindergartners have some understanding of the common-ground principle, but this ability, too, improves with age (Ackerman & Silver, 1990; Ackerman, Szymanski, & Silver, 1990).

Perhaps the most important listener cues involve feedback. If the listener does not appear to be comprehending, the speaker should change the message and try again. In simple situations with very clear cues, even 2-year-olds show some ability to adjust their messages when a listener has misunderstood (Shwe & Markman, 1997). In general, however, sensitivity to listener feedback is limited in young children, who often persist with the same types of messages even when the listener is clearly not understanding (Robinson, 1981).

As listeners, children need to learn certain rules as well. Like speakers, listeners must be aware of context cues, including the information that has previously been sent and the nature of the array from which the referent is to be chosen. In addition, when a message is not informative, the child must learn to recognize this fact and to communicate the problem. Children as young as 5 can sometimes detect when a message is poorly constructed or when critical information is missing. At this age, however, they will often proceed with the inadequate information, whereas by age 7 they are more likely to seek clarification or additional information from the speaker (Ackerman, 1993).

Most of the conclusions just discussed were derived from the sorts of experimental measures pictured in Figure 11.3. We should add, therefore, that children's communicative performance, as either speaker or listener, is often more impressive in the natural environment (e.g., talking with a parent, playing with friends) than it is on unfamiliar laboratory tasks (Warren-Leubecker & Bohannon, 1989). As is often the case, what we conclude about children's abilities depends on the context in which we assess those abilities. On the other hand, difficulties in communicating clearly do not disappear in the natural setting—as anyone who has tried to carry on a conversation with a 4-year-old can attest.

How referential communication skills develop is clearly an important question. Such skills must depend in part on the emergence of certain cognitive abilities. For example, as children's egocentric view of the world decreases, they develop a better appreciation for how another person might view a situation. And as their theory-of-mind understanding improves (see Chapter 8), they come to realize that listeners with different cognitive capabilities (such as children versus adults) may interpret the same information differently (Chandler & Lalonde, 1996; Taylor, Cartwright, & Bowden, 1991). But environmental factors also appear to play a role. One study, for example, found that children whose mothers provided them specific feedback regarding how their messages were inadequate developed their communication skills most rapidly (Robinson, 1981).

Development in School Context
Language Differences in School: Teaching (and Learning) One Language or Two?

Almost 5 million children in the United States live in households in which more than one language is spoken. A similar situation exists in many other countries, such as Canada, where a significant minority of the population speaks both English and French. Most of these children eventually acquire elements of both languages, and many become fluent bilingual speakers (Hyltenstam & Obler, 1989). How should the educational system deal with such children?

Approaches to this problem range from "immersion" programs, in which children are taught in both languages with the goal of making them bilingually fluent, and "transitional" programs, in which minority children are first taught in their own language with the goal of having them later become fluent in the majority language, to "majority-only" policies in which the use of minority languages is explicitly discouraged (Bialystok & Cummins, 1991). Although the types of programs employed often reflect political rather than educational factors, policy makers typically attempt to support their decisions with scientific data regarding bilingual learning. One of the most important questions has been whether children learning two languages

Research indicates that teaching nonnative children in their own language does not interfere with their learning of the majority language

have more difficulty learning the majority language. For many scientists, answering this question requires a basic understanding of how the bilingual process works.

One theory has been that bilingual children initially approach the task of learning two languages as if they were learning only one. That is, they do not separate the two forms of speech input, but develop a single language system that includes elements of each. Only with increasing age do these children presumably learn to differentiate the two tongues, gradually treating them as independent languages (Swain, 1977; Volterra & Taeschner, 1978).

This theory has principally grown out of the observation that younger bilingual children display a good deal of *mixing* (also referred to as *code-switching*), or combining forms from the two languages within the same utterance (Lanza, 1992; Redlinger & Park, 1980). Mixing occurs at all levels of speech, including articulation, vocabulary, inflections, and syntax. The assumption has been that mixing reflects confusion on the part of the bilingual child, who cannot separate the two languages. A related finding is that children in bilingual homes acquire both languages more slowly than do peers who are learning only one language, although this lag gradually disappears and the children's proficiency in both languages eventually reaches that of monolingual children.

Recent research has begun to challenge the single-system hypothesis and to offer alternative interpretations (Genesee, 1989; Pye, 1986). Studies of infant speech perception, for example, indicate clearly that babies can differentiate sounds and phonemes found in different languages (Eilers & Oller, 1988; Moon et al., 1993). Hence, perceptual confusion does not appear to be a problem. It has also been suggested that children's substitution of a word in one language for the same word in the second language may simply reflect the overextension principle. Thus, the child may substitute in this way if she does not know the appropriate word in the second language or if it is simply easier to do so (Vihman, 1985). Furthermore, modeling by parents has been implicated in children's language mixing. Detailed studies of bilingual children's home environments indicate that their parents often speak to them using parts of both languages simultaneously (Goodz, 1989). Finally, bilingualism does not result in cognitive deficits, as might be implied by the slower growth of language skills in bilingual children and the suggestion that hearing two languages confuses children. Bilingual children, in fact, have been shown to be more advanced in some areas of cognition than monolingual children (Diaz, 1983, 1985; Johnson, 1991).

It appears, then, that exposure to two languages does not present an unusually difficult challenge to young children, who can apparently separate and acquire both systems (Cummins, 1991; Umbel et al., 1992). This would suggest that majority-only educational policies, in which nonnative children are required from the start of school to use and learn only the majority language, may be misguided. Indeed, research that compares different approaches to educating bilingual children generally favors the transitional approach, in which both languages are utilized at the early grades and children can gradually develop competence in their nonpreferred language (Genesee, 1994). Note that in addition to its purely academic benefits, this approach has the virtue of acknowledging the value of the child's family and cultural background.

The long-standing debate about bilingual education is relevant to a more recent controversy—the question of how best to structure the early school environment for young African-American children. Many African-American children, especially those from poor inner-city areas, grow up in homes and neighborhoods in which they learn a form of English popularly known as *Ebonics* (the linguists' term for this speech style is *African-American Vernacular English*). Ebonics is not, of course, a separate language from English in the sense that French or Spanish is; it is merely one of a number of dialectical variations of English spoken in the United States (which, indeed, is true of so-called Standard English as well).

Most linguists agree that Ebonics is as fully formed, complex, and effective a language as is Standard English. Nevertheless, the differences between Ebonics and Standard English are marked, and they occur along every dimension of language— phonology, semantics, grammar, and interpersonal, pragmatic uses (Dandy, 1991). The result is that African-American children often face the same challenges in school faced by bilingual children—the need to master material that is presented in a relatively unfamiliar language, within an environment in which their own language is discouraged, if not actively disparaged.

In 1996 the Oakland, California, school board adopted a policy of treating Ebonics as a second language, with instruction in Standard English intended to build gradually on initial instruction in Ebonics. This policy elicited a firestorm of controversy, some of which reflected genuine differences in educational philosophy, but much of which was politically motivated. Bills were introduced in the state senate to prohibit the use of Ebonics in school, the Oakland school board was eventually forced to revise its policy, and the implementation of the approach—in Oakland and elsewhere—remains limited.

The research on bilingual education that we have reviewed certainly does not answer the question of how best to educate African-American children whose home language is Ebonics. But such research does make two points that seem relevant: First, children are quite capable of mastering two language systems simultaneously; and second, at least sometimes, instruction in the majority language can profitably build on the skills in the language of their home that children from nonmajority backgrounds bring to school.

In January 1997, William Labov, a leading researcher of African-American dialects, testified before a United States Senate committee convened to consider the Ebonics controversy. His testimony included the following passage:

At the heart of the controversy, there are two major points of view taken by educators. One is that any recognition of a nonstandard language as a legitimate means of expression will only confuse children, and reinforce their tendency to use it instead of standard English. The other is that children learn most rapidly in their home language, and that they can benefit in both motivation and achievement by getting a head start in learning to read and write in this way. Both of these views are honestly held and deserve a fair hearing. But until now, only the first has been tried in the American public school system. (Labov, 1997)

✓ *To Recap...*

Pragmatics is the study of the social uses of language. It is based on the functionalist view that children are motivated to acquire language in order to communicate their wants and needs more effectively. Effective communication abilities involve both speaker skills and listener skills.

Infants at first communicate with crying, gestures, and so on. As they acquire language, they add speech acts to their nonverbal communication skills. They also learn to comprehend speech acts of others.

The ability to communicate effectively involves learning rules of discourse. Turn taking is one of the earliest discourse rules acquired by infants. Others, such as the answer-obviousness rule, are more difficult to learn and are not apparent in children until several years later.

Social referential communication occurs when a speaker sends a message that is understood by a listener. Effective communication of this sort involves speaker skills, such as adjusting the messages to the demands of the listener and the context, and listener skills, such as recognizing and communicating when messages are ambiguous.

Conclusion

Developmental psychologists, like researchers in the other natural sciences, attempt to identify processes that are general and fundamental. Rather than considering each event or behavior unique, scientists search for principles and laws that can explain and interrelate them across the many domains of human development.

During the 1960s, the study of language became an exception to this approach. Language was believed to be different, requiring special mechanisms and processes independent of other behaviors. The basic cognitive and learning processes that psychologists used to explain other aspects of development were thought to be inadequate, and even irrelevant, in explaining language acquisition. Perhaps this separation occurred because the nativistic model was developed outside traditional psychology, by theorists who were trained primarily in linguistic structure rather than human behavior. As we have seen throughout this chapter, however, the situation has changed considerably.

With the development of new theoretical models and better research techniques, language study has come back into the mainstream of child psychology. The view that language is either independent of cognitive abilities or insensitive to social and environmental factors no longer finds much support among developmental researchers. This is not to say that language does not possess its own unique characteristics, which need to be more clearly understood. But there can be little doubt that language development is very much interrelated with other developmental processes, which both affect and are affected by it.

Visual Summary for Chapter 11:
Language Development

Theories of Language Development

Theory   *Explanation*

Nativistic 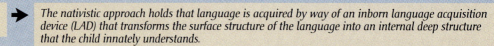 The nativistic approach holds that language is acquired by way of an inborn language acquisition device (LAD) that transforms the surface structure of the language into an internal deep structure that the child innately understands.

Cognitive-Developmental 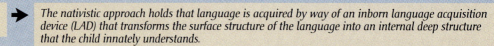 Piagetians link advances in cognitive abilities to language development. Other hold that when children hear speech, they analyze it according to its content before extracting its grammatical structure.

Environmental/ Learning 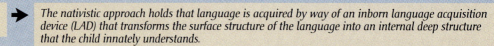 Learning theories contend that the environment provides children with the experiences necessary to acquire language and that social-learning principles play a part in this process. Functionalists argue that the primary motivation to acquire language is to gain a tool for communication and that parents facilitate this process by providing a language acquisition support system (LASS).

The Preverbal Period

Speech Perception and Listening Preferences 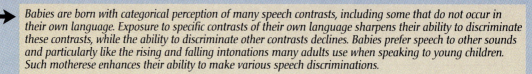 Babies are born with categorical perception of many speech contrasts, including some that do not occur in their own language. Exposure to specific contrasts of their own language sharpens their ability to discriminate these contrasts, while the ability to discriminate other contrasts declines. Babies prefer speech to other sounds and particularly like the rising and falling intonations many adults use when speaking to young children. Such motherese enhances their ability to make various speech discriminations.

Early Sounds and Gestures 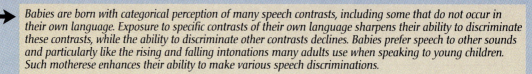 The first sounds of newborns are cries and physiological noises. Cooing appears at about 2 months, while reduplicated babbling begins at 6 months. Near the end of the first year, babbling becomes more speechlike in sound and intonation. Gestures serve many pragmatic functions for infants, initially taking the form of requests and referential communication, and later functioning as symbols to label objects, events, and attributes.

Semantics

Early Lexical Development 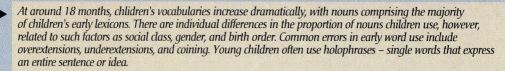 At around 18 months, chlidren's vocabularies increase dramatically, with nouns comprising the majority of children's early lexicons. There are individual differences in the proportion of nouns children use, however, related to such factors as social class, gender, and birth order. Common errors in early word use include overextensions, underextensions, and coining. Young children often use holophrases – single words that express an entire sentence or idea.

Mechanisms of Semantic Development 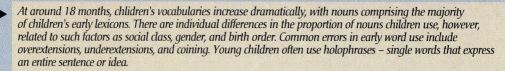 Some researchers have proposed that children use grammatical information to infer the possible meanings of new words, a process labeled syntactic bootstrapping. Other have argued that various constraints are necessary to explain how children rule out the many possible meanings for any word. Lexical contrast theory holds that children assume that new words have different meanings from familiar words and that they adopt generally accepted meanings over more individualized meanings. The mutual exclusivity hypothesis holds that children believe that objects have only one name. Children's learning of category labels is aided by parents' modeling, whether direct or in the course of day-to-day interactions.

Grammar

Development of Grammar Two-word utterances appear around the end of the second year. As sentences grow longer, telegraphic speech emerges. When children first learn inflectional rules, they overregularize them, applying regular forms even to irregular words.

Mechanisms of Grammar Acquisition → The semantic bootstrapping hypothesis holds that children use their knowledge of semantics to figure out rules of syntax. Nativistic theorists maintain that innate knowledge about the principles of grammar makes language acquisition possible. Some researchers have argued for the importance of innate strategies such as operating principles for acquiring language and the competition model. Grammar acquisition may also be facilitated by environmental factors such as motherese, imitation, and feedback.

Pragmatics

Speech Acts Infants at first communicate with crying, gestures, etc.. As they acquire language, they add speech acts - pragmatic uses of language - to their nonverbal communication skills, and they learn to comprehend speech acts of others.

Discourse → To communicate effectively, children must learn rules of discourse. Some rules are simple and are acquired early, while others are complex and are learned later.

Social Referential Communication → Social referential communication involves sending a message that is understood by a listener. Effective social referential communication requires speaker skills, such as adjusting the message to the demands of the listener , as well as listener skills, such as recognizing and communicating when messages are ambiguous.

Chapter 12

Early Social and Emotional Development

Every day in the United States, millions of infants and preschool children spend time in day care centers—it's a reality of life in the 1990s. But how does day care affect a young child's social and emotional development, and how does it compare with being raised at home? Jennifer Ireland was a 19-year-old college student in 1994 when her baby daughter, Maranda, became the focus of a custody battle centering on precisely these issues.

Shortly after Maranda was born to Jennifer and her boyfriend, the couple split up. Jennifer went on to start her freshman year at the University of Michigan, taking Maranda with her. The two lived in campus housing, and Maranda was cared for in the university's child care center. Maranda's father—who was still living at home with his parents—responded by suing for custody of the toddler. He claimed that Maranda would be better off living with him and being cared for by his mother, a full-time homemaker. The judge agreed and placed Maranda in her father's custody, ruling that a child is better off being raised in a home with a single caregiver than in a group setting.

Does the research evidence support the judge's claim? And what effect would such a decision have on life in the United States today? In the view of a lawyer for the American Civil Liberties Union, which helped Jennifer appeal the court's decision, "[the judge's] ruling had to be overturned, or else it would have sent shock waves to every single parent who works and uses day care." In 1995, the state court of appeals reversed the judge's order, holding that there is no convincing evidence that day care is harmful to young children or is necessarily less beneficial than being raised at home.

In this chapter, we explore the issues at the center of this case, along with related issues, as we examine children's early social and emotional development. Family life in recent years has certainly been changing in some fundamental ways, and understanding the role played by the mother and other caregivers during the child's first months and years of life is thus more important than ever to psychologists, policymakers, and parents. As we will see, this area is very complex, and many questions—including those surrounding day care—have not been entirely resolved. Nevertheless, research is yielding some interesting and important answers.

*H*umans are a very social species. We organize into groups ranging in size from families to communities to nations, and we spend a good deal of time interacting with one another. From early on, children form many social relationships. Some of these relationships, such as those with occasional baby-sitters, are very brief and of little consequence. But others, such as those with family members and certain friends, will last for many years and may affect children's later development and personality in important ways (Caspi, 1998; Thompson, 1998).

Understanding social development has not been easy, however, because the complexity of social interaction poses certain obstacles to its scientific study. Consider the following mother–infant interaction, which represents the relatively simple *dyadic*, or two-person, situation. A mother talks to her baby and he begins to smile; when she moves a toy in front of him, the baby follows it with his eyes; and when she makes a strange face at him, he becomes still and stares attentively.

What causes these changes in the baby's behavior? Clearly the changes are being determined, or caused, by what the mother is doing. But there is more to the interaction than that because the influence here is undoubtedly bidirectional. That is, the baby's responses also influence the mother's behavior. For example, if the baby gazes at her with apparent interest, the mother is likely to continue what she is doing. If the baby begins to act bored, she may step up her actions, perhaps tickling him or adding attention-getting vocalizations. And if the baby begins to fret, the mother may tone down her responses or even end the interaction altogether.

Children's social interactions are transactional. They not only respond to their environment, they also influence it.

This relatively simple example illustrates the challenge that faces psychologists in their attempts to identify the determinants of social interactions. In the case of the baby's behavior, certainly one determinant is the mother's behavior. But the baby's behavior and personal characteristics affect the kinds of things the mother does. In that sense, then, the baby is a *producer* of his own environment (Lerner, 1982).

We have already encountered this general idea in earlier chapters—first, in Chapter 2, when we discussed Bandura's model of reciprocal determinism and Bronfenbrenner's notion of developmentally generative and disruptive behaviors, and then in Chapter 4, in the behavior-genetic models of Scarr and Plomin. The essential point here is that psychologists have come to understand that human social behavior is *transactional*—each person's actions both affect and are affected by the actions of others. We will see many examples of this in the remainder of the book.

This chapter is the first of five that deal with children's social and personality development. We focus here on social interactions during the child's first 2 years of life. To begin, we survey the approaches of the three major theoretical traditions to infant social development. Next, we consider how the infant and caregiver develop an early communication system as they learn to regulate one another's behavior. Then we look at the baby's temperament, or individual style of responding. Finally, we examine the topic that traditionally has been of greatest interest to researchers—the nature of the attachment process that produces the unique emotional bond between caregiver and child.

Theories of Early Social Development

Social development during the first 2 years of life is distinctive in several important ways. First, although children eventually come to have many social contacts—family, friends, teachers, and so on—the social world of infants in most Western cultures typically consists of only a few significant individuals, such as the mother, father, and siblings. Second, despite their small number, these initial relationships appear to be more influential and to have longer term effects on the child's social, personality, and even cognitive development than do many of the relationships that develop later on. Finally, children appear to develop strong emotional relationships—especially with the mother but also with the father and others—more easily and intensely during the infant years, suggesting that early social development may involve psychological processes that are different from those that operate later in life.

Researchers from each of the three major theoretical approaches have taken an interest in early social development. And, as you might expect, their different views have led them to pursue different questions and aspects of this area. Much of the focus has been on the attachment process, which we discuss in detail later in the chapter.

Ethology

The ethological explanation of early social interactions is the most extensively developed of the three major theories. Ethological researchers are, of course, most concerned with the evolutionary origins of development, arguing that the social behaviors we observe in today's infants and caregivers represent millions of years of gradual adaptation to the environment (Eibl-Eibesfeldt, 1989; Hess & Petrovich, 1991). Much of this work has involved other species, with theorizing regarding human development based largely on the views of John Bowlby, discussed in Chapter 2 (Bretherton, 1995).

In contrast to the young of many other species, human infants are relatively helpless at birth and for years remain unable to survive on their own. If babies are not fed, sheltered, and protected, they will certainly die. And because humans produce comparatively few offspring (whereas fish, for example, lay thousands of eggs), our species would quickly become extinct if a high percentage of babies did not survive long enough to reproduce.

Ethologists believe that the process of natural selection has provided infants and mothers with an innate system of behaviors designed to ensure the infant's survival (Ainsworth & Bowlby, 1991). Sociobiologists, you may recall, describe this process a little differently, arguing that evolutionary mechanisms see to it that the species' genes are passed on; the child just happens to be carrying them. By either account, evolution is assumed to have provided a number of built-in responses for the task at hand.

Perhaps the most important of these built-in responses is for the infant to develop a relationship with the **primary caregiver**—usually the mother—that accomplishes two goals: keeps her nearby, and motivates her to provide adequate caregiving. For the first 6 or 7 months, the baby can remain close to the mother only by drawing her near. Crying is by far the most effective behavior for doing this. Later, as locomotor abilities develop, the child can stay near the mother by crawling or running after her.

The infant promotes caregiving behaviors in several ways. One is by making interactions very pleasant for the mother, such as by smiling, vocalizing, and making eye contact with her. Some ethologists believe that the physical appearance of babies—large heads, round faces, and chubby legs—may also serve to maintain the mother's interactions, because she innately finds these features "cute" (Alley, 1983; Fullard & Reiling, 1976). Proper caregiving is also encouraged when babies reduce signs of distress in response to the mother's attention, such as when they stop fussing when picked up.

The caregiver, too, presumably has built-in mechanisms for doing what is necessary for the infant's survival. Her job is to "read" the infant's signals and decide what is wrong, what she should do in response, and when it has been effective. Innate caregiving patterns are obvious with other mammals, where mothers of even first litters appear to know exactly how to care for their young. As we saw in Chapter 2, ethologists characterize these more complex sequences of innate behaviors as modal action patterns and assume that they are triggered by certain stimuli (such as the sound or smell of the newborn pups). It is not easy to determine what portion of the caregiving provided by human mothers is innate, however, because new mothers in most cultures typically acquire much of this information through social sources (e.g., by observing or conversing with other mothers).

These behaviors that serve to keep mother and baby together during the early weeks and months of life emerge as part of an *attachment process* that also includes a strong emotional bond (Grossmann, 1995; Isabella, 1994). The baby, at first, emits

Primary caregiver
The person, usually the mother, with whom the infant develops the major attachment relationship.

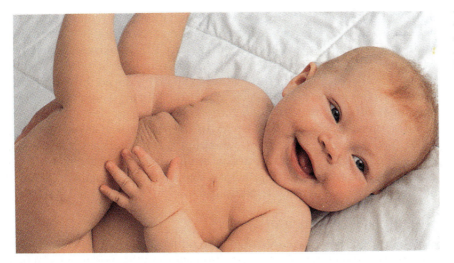

According to ethologists, aspects of babies' physical appearance may be innately "cute" and so elicit caregiving.

care-seeking behaviors to virtually anyone. But if the mother responds to these bids in a sensitive and consistent way (and sometimes even when she is not so sensitive), the baby gradually focuses them on her, and she becomes the primary caregiver. Bowlby and others of this tradition believe further that the attachment process in humans occurs during a sensitive period in the baby's development, as is the case for the imprinting process that produces attachment in some other species (Scott, 1987). We discuss the attachment process in detail later in the chapter.

Environmental/Learning Approaches

Environmentally oriented theorists do not deny that infants and mothers possess many built-in responses that may contribute to early caregiving and the attachment process. But the main concern of these theorists is with the infant's **socialization—the process by which a child's behavior is molded to fit with the society's roles, beliefs, and expectations** (Bugenthal & Goodnow, 1998; Maccoby, 1992). Socialization is assumed to continue throughout childhood and later on affects many of the child's more complex social behaviors, such as moral development and interactions with peers. The process, however, begins in infancy and can be observed in the way the baby's first social interactions are influenced by others.

According to the environmental/learning view, caregiver–infant social behaviors result from interaction between the two individuals, with each influencing the behavior of the other. Rather than appealing to special evolutionary mechanisms unique to this area, however, psychologists of this tradition assume that these interactions can be explained by social-learning processes, including reinforcement, punishment, and observational learning (Gewirtz & Pelaez-Nogueras, 1992a; Hay et al., 1985).

For example, this approach contends that infants produce behaviors that encourage the mother to approach and remain close (crying, smiling, vocalizing, and so on) because these behaviors result in either positive reinforcement (milk, a rattle, or being rocked) or negative reinforcement (the removal of a wet diaper). Similarly, the mother learns to respond to these behaviors because they also result in either negative reinforcement (the baby stops crying) or positive reinforcement (the baby smiles, coos, and clings).

Much of the evidence supporting the social-learning model derives from studies showing that infant social behaviors can be influenced by reinforcement

Socialization
The process through which society molds the child's beliefs, expectations, and behavior.

processes. Infant vocalizations, for example, will increase if reinforced and decrease if subjected to an extinction procedure (Poulson & Nunes, 1988). The same is true for infant smiling (Etzel & Gewirtz, 1967; Zelazo, 1971). Likewise, certain behaviors common in infants, such as separation protest and social referencing (both of which we will discuss later in the chapter), can be produced through conditioning processes (Gewirtz & Pelaez-Nogueras, 1991a, 1992b). And similar experiments have demonstrated that infant behaviors can serve to increase (reinforce) or decrease (punish) the social behavior of the caregiver (Gewirtz & Boyd, 1976, 1977). Taken together, these studies show that it is theoretically possible to explain changes in caregiver–infant interaction by applying social-learning principles. But exactly how important such principles are in the development of the typical infant–caregiver relationship remains unresolved (Hay, 1986; Schaffer, 1986).

Cognitive-Developmental Models

The third major tradition contends that to understand children's early social development we should search for the cognitive processes that underlie social behaviors. This approach is based on the concept of social cognition (Flavell & Miller, 1998), which, as noted in Chapter 2, refers to children's and adults' understanding of human behavior and social interactions.

As applied to attachment, the cognitive tradition overlaps somewhat with the ethological approach in that both are concerned with how infants and mothers cognitively *represent* their relationships with each other (Main, Kaplan, & Cassidy, 1985). Some theorists believe that infants and caregivers develop **internal working models** of each other and use these models to interpret events and predict what will happen (Bowlby, 1973; Bretherton, 1987, 1993). For example, an infant may develop expectations regarding the mother's behavior as a result of the type of treatment she provides. If she responds quickly and reliably to the infant's signals of distress or care seeking, the baby may develop the expectation that the mother will be available if needed and so will be less likely to cry when left alone (Lamb, Ketterlinus, & Fracasso, 1992; Pipp, 1990). Likewise, the caregiver may develop an internal working model of the infant that leads her to expect the baby will be eager to interact with her. As a result, she may become more likely to play with the infant (Crowell & Feldman, 1991; George & Solomon, 1989). Internal working models are also important for the infant's development of a sense of self, a topic we consider in the next chapter.

Internal working model
An infant's and a caregiver's cognitive conception of each other, which they use to form expectations and predictions.

Another perspective that fits within the cognitive-developmental model is that of Vygotsky. Psychologists working within this tradition have been concerned less with the attachment process and more with how infants acquire new social (and cognitive) skills through shared activities with adults and older peers (Rogoff, 1991, 1997). Using an "apprenticeship" model and a process called *guided participation,* the baby and caregiver jointly engage in an activity, with the adult at first directing the learning experience and then gradually transferring control and responsibility to the child (Rogoff, 1990). As we noted in Chapter 2, Vygotsky believed that infants acquire various tools to help them develop. Among these tools are the other people in their social world. Beginning at about age 1, infants increasingly attempt to manipulate adults to help them achieve their goals, using techniques such as facial expressions, vocalizations, and various gestures (Rogoff et al., 1992).

An important aspect of the Vygotskian model of early social development is that it puts less emphasis on the mother–infant relationship and recognizes that in many cultures the baby learns a great deal through interactions with others. Across cultures there is considerable variation in how parents and other adults interact with babies, in who is responsible for child care, and in the kinds of opportunities babies have for interacting with other members of the community (Whiting & Edwards, 1988). In some cultures, for example, children spend a great deal of time with members of their extended family, whereas in others much of the child care is the responsibility of the entire community, including older children. These relationships, too, are assumed to play an important role in the child's early socialization (Rogoff et al., 1991, 1993).

Cognitive models of early social development appear to be gaining in popularity (Bretherton, 1993; Thompson, 1998). This shift is due largely to the increasing interest in children's social cognition as psychologists continue to tear down the artificial wall that has traditionally separated research in social development and research in cognitive development.

✓ *To Recap…*

Early social development differs from later social interactions in that infants have fewer social relationships; these relationships often have long-term significance; and infants form them very easily. The transactional nature of social interactions has made social development a challenge to researchers.

Ethologists contend that evolution has provided many of the responses necessary for the infant's survival. Babies are programmed by nature to produce behaviors that keep the mother close at hand and encourage her to provide appropriate caregiving. The mother, in turn, is biologically predisposed to read and respond to the infant's signals. Infant–mother attachment results from these innate behaviors.

Social-learning theorists favor a less biological explanation. They assume that mother–infant attachment responses result from social-learning processes, with the infant and caregiver each providing consequences for the other's behavior.

Cognitive explanations of early social development consider cognitive development the foundation on which social development is built. Some psychologists contend that children's social behavior reflects their social cognition and that babies and mothers develop expectations, or internal working models, regarding each other's behavior. Vygotskian theorists contend that parents and others assist infants in acquiring social skills and knowledge through a process of guided participation.

Mutual Regulation between Infants and Caregivers

The attachment process that becomes so evident by the end of the baby's first year has roots in early infancy (Malatesta et al., 1989). Right from birth, mothers and newborns begin to interact in ways that will draw them into a close emotional relationship. A most important feature of these early interactions is that each individual both influences the other's behavior and adjusts to it, producing a smooth-running system of *mutual regulation* (Bornstein & Tamis-LeMonda, 1990; Tronick, 1989).

The key to the development of this two-way system is effective communication between the infant and the caregiver. Chapter 11 described how babies use gestures and babbling to send messages even before they can speak. But the baby's ability to convey wants and needs and to mobilize the caregiver into action begins even earlier.

Crying

By far the most important form of communication for the newborn is crying. Not only is crying one of the baby's strongest and clearest responses, but it is one to which caregivers appear to be especially responsive (Demos, 1986). Crying is part of the infant's larger affective communication system, which we discuss next. But because it has generated so much research on its own, we consider crying here separately.

Darwin believed that crying in newborns evolved as a means of providing the mother with information about the baby's state or condition (Darwin, 1872). Ethologists today continue to assume that crying serves as a stimulus to trigger innate caregiving behaviors by the mother (Eibl-Eibesfeldt, 1989). Learning theorists point out that crying (like sucking and some other early, reflexlike behaviors) also soon comes under the baby's voluntary control. When this occurs, crying becomes modifiable by its consequences—that is, it can be conditioned. If a baby's crying results in his caregiver's presence (as it often does), he may learn to use this response purposefully, as a way of summoning care (Gewirtz, 1991).

For crying to serve as a form of communication, two conditions are necessary. First, different types of cries should communicate different messages. And they do; babies have separate cries for pain, hunger, and fear (Wasz-Hockert, Michelsson, & Lind, 1985). In addition, variations in cries can convey other information. For example, as the pitch of crying increases, adult listeners tend to perceive the baby's problem as becoming more serious and urgent (Leger et al., 1996; Zeskind & Marshall, 1988).

The other condition necessary for crying to be communicative is that listeners must be able to discriminate one type from another. Caregivers must understand whether the baby is saying, for example, "I'm hungry," "I'm wet," or "I'm frightened." Here, too, a number of studies have reported that adult listeners can be quite good at interpreting babies' cries. This ability is based in part on experience. In general, parents and other adults who have spent time around newborns are better at decoding infant crying than are adults with little experience (Green, Jones, & Gustafson, 1987; Gustafson & Harris, 1990). Similarly, mothers of 4-month-olds are better skilled in this area than are mothers of 1-month-olds (Freeburg & Lippman, 1986).

The communication role of crying thus has elements of both nature and nurture. At first, crying is innately elicited by various internal stimuli (such as hunger) and external stimuli (such as a diaper pin). Such crying serves primarily to draw the mother near. With experience, however, the caregiver becomes more accurate at reading the information in these signals, and babies learn to use the crying response as a means of controlling the mother's attention and care.

Emotions and the Affective System

Research on crying indicates that many of the early messages sent by babies involve "dislikes." Newborns also can communicate "likes," using behaviors such as smiling, vocalizing, and gazing at an object they find interesting (Brazelton, 1982). These aversions and preferences are the internal reactions, or feelings, we call **emotions**. On seeing his mother, for example, an infant might experience joy, which might be followed by anger as she prepares to leave, sadness when she is gone, and fear when he hears an unfamiliar sound. Some researchers believe that emotions also carry with them a readiness for action—the child experiences a particular feeling in preparation for doing something (Campos et al., 1994; Saarni, Mumme, & Campos, 1998).

The outward expression of emotions is called **affect**. Many theorists believe that initially a close correspondence exists between what babies feel and what they express. That is, early on, affect accurately reveals emotion (Malatesta et al., 1989). It is now widely believed that the infant's ability to display different affective states is an important component in the mutual regulation between babies and their mothers (Adamson & Bakeman, 1991; Fogel & Thelen, 1987).

> **Emotion**
> An internal reaction or feeling, which may be either positive (such as joy) or negative (such as anger), and may reflect a readiness for action.

> **Affect**
> The outward expression of emotions through facial expressions, gestures, intonation, and the like.

Development and Expression of Emotions   Although affective responses can take a number of forms, such as gestures and vocalizations, much of our understanding of babies' early emotional development has come about through the study of facial expressions (Malatesta, Izard, & Camras, 1991). Even newborns possess all the facial muscle movements necessary to produce virtually any adult emotional expression. Researchers have developed detailed coding procedures for assessing babies' facial expressions, involving separate ratings for the brow, eye, and mouth regions (Izard, 1989).

Babies' facial expressions of the basic emotions first appear at different points in development (Camras, Malatesta, & Izard, 1991; Ekman, 1993). Researchers do not agree exactly on what these basic emotions are (Izard, 1993; Sroufe, 1996), but we will consider several that have been mentioned frequently.

From birth, babies can indicate *distress* by crying and *interest* by staring attentively. As we saw in Chapter 7, one stimulus that reliably elicits this expression is the human face, illustrating how evolution encourages infant–mother interaction right from the beginning. Another inborn facial expression is *disgust,* which is elicited by unpleasant tastes or odors, usually signaling to the caregiver that feeding is not going the way it should (Rosenstein & Oster, 1988; Steiner, 1979).

By 10 to 12 weeks of age, smiling (reflecting *pleasure*) appears in response to the human voice or a moving face (Haviland & Lelwica, 1987). Some smiles may be seen before this age, but those occur spontaneously during sleep and are apparently not related to external stimulation (Emde, Gaensbauer, & Harmon, 1976). *Sadness* and *anger*—demonstrated experimentally by removing a teething toy or by restraining the baby's arm—are first evident in facial expressions at 3 or 4 months (Lewis, Alessandri, & Sullivan, 1990; Stenberg, Campos, & Emde, 1983). Facial expressions indicating *fear* do not appear until about 7 months, and more complex affective responses, such as those for *guilt, shame,* and *embarrassment,* are not apparent until near the end of the baby's first year (Tangney & Fischer, 1995).

The emergence of these emotions is probably guided primarily by biological processes and thus is universal across cultures (Izard, 1995). For example, one study reported the same progression of facial expressions in Japanese and American infants (Camras et al., 1992).

Since they are assumed to reflect the infant's emotions, an infant's expression can be used to infer how the baby is feeling about a situation. For example, researchers taught babies to pull a string tied to one arm to produce a pleasant visual and auditory stimulus. The babies displayed expressions of joy during the learning process, but displays expressions of anger when the pulling no longer produced a reward (Lewis, et al., 1990; Sullivan, Lewis, & Alessandri, 1992). Thus the infants appeared to experience the two situations in much the same way as adults would. Nevertheless, researchers cannot be certain that babies' affective responses are identical to those of adults, and we clearly have more to learn in this area (Izard et al., 1995; Oster, Hegley, & Nagel, 1992).

Socialization of Emotions   Emotional responses do not emerge simply as a result of a biological timetable. Their development is influenced by the social and cultural environment (Parke, 1994; Saarni et al., 1998).

Some of this influence may occur through modeling. Most mothers, for example, display only a few facial expressions to their babies, most of which are positive (Malatesta, 1985). The babies, in turn, tend to match these expressions (Haviland & Lelwica, 1987). In contrast, infants of depressed mothers display more sad expressions, probably in part because they imitate the expressions they are seeing (Pickens & Field, 1993).

Whether or not the result of modeling, smiling in 10-month-olds clearly is influenced by social factors and not simply controlled by the emotion the baby is experiencing. One study found that babies this age who were playing with (and smiling at) attractive toys smiled much more when they looked up and found their mother looking at them than when they found she was looking away. These findings suggest that babies' smiles indeed reflect their positive emotions, but also serve as a form of communication with the mother (Jones, Collins, & Hong, 1991).

Socialization of emotions also occurs through reinforcement processes. Mothers more often respond positively to infants' expressions of pleasure than to their displays of distress (Keller & Scholmerich, 1987; Malatesta, 1985). This process, perhaps in combination with the modeling just described, may be one reason that over the course of the first year infants' positive emotional signals typically increase, while their negative responses decrease (Malatesta et al., 1989).

Older infants and preschoolers generally learn to identify and label their emotions through everyday experiences. For example, parents frequently point out how a child is feeling ("You seem to be angry with Mommy" or "That baby must be feeling upset about dropping her ice cream cone") (Denham, Zoller, & Couchoud, 1994; Smiley & Huttenlocher, 1989).

At first, babies' affective expressions closely mirror their emotions, but with time children learn to control their affective displays, so that what they express may not necessarily reflect what they are feeling (Saarni, 1989, 1990). Such attempts to conceal emotions often result from children's increased understanding of their culture's emotional **display rules—the expectations or attitudes regarding the expression of affect** (Davis, 1995; Malatesta & Haviland, 1982; Underwood, Coie, & Herbsman, 1992). For example, boys may learn that displaying fear or pain is not seen as appropriate for them, and so they often try to inhibit such expressions of emotion.

Display rules
The expectations and attitudes a society holds toward the expression of affect.

Recognizing Emotions

Just as the baby influences the mother through the display of affective responses, the mother can influence the baby. But before this form of regulation can occur, the baby must be able to recognize and interpret the mother's responses.

An infant's ability to recognize facial expressions of emotion seems to develop in stages (Baldwin & Moses, 1996; Nelson, C. A., 1987; Walker-Andrews, 1997). Babies younger than 6 weeks are not very good at scanning faces for detail. As a result, they do not recognize different emotional expressions (Field & Walden, 1982). Soon after, however, infants begin to show evidence of discriminating facial expressions of emotions. For example, babies who have been habituated to a photo of a smiling face show renewed attention when the photo is changed to one depicting a frowning face (Barrera & Maurer, 1981). Babies of this age discriminate even better when they view talking faces displaying various emotions—although under these circumstances the voice may also provide important cues (Caron, Caron, & MacLean, 1988).

But do babies in this second stage have any real *understanding* of the emotions that are being expressed? Probably not. It is more likely that they simply can tell that the faces look different, without appreciating that a sad look represents unhappiness or a smiling face, joy. Once infants reach 5 to 6 months of age, however, they appear to develop a clearer understanding of the meanings of emotional expressions. This is shown, for example, by the fact that at this age babies begin to display the same emotion as displayed on the face they are viewing (smiling at a happy face) and prefer some emotional expressions to others (Balaban, 1995; Haviland & Lelwica, 1987; Izard et al., 1995; Ludemann, 1991).

Near the end of the first year, infants begin to use information about other people's emotional expressions to regulate their own behavior, a process called **social referencing** (Feinman et al., 1992; Klinnert et al., 1983). Babies are especially likely to look to their mothers or fathers for this type of guidance when they are uncertain what to do next, such as when they encounter an unfamiliar object or person. They then use the parent's expression as a guide to how to react in the situation.

In a study that illustrates this process very clearly, 1-year-old infants and their mothers were studied as they interacted on the visual-cliff apparatus described in Chapter 7. The baby was placed on the shallow side, and the mother and an attractive toy were positioned at the deep end. This situation appeared to produce uncertainty in the infants, who generally responded cautiously and frequently looked up at their mothers as if attempting to gain information as to how to respond. The mothers were trained to produce a number of affective facial expressions, including fear, happiness, anger, interest, and sadness.

The question of interest to the researchers was whether the mother's expression would regulate the infant's behavior on the visual cliff. The results indicate that it did. When the mother expressed joy or interest, most babies crossed over to the deeper side to reach her. If she expressed fear or anger, however, very few of them ventured onto the deep portion of the apparatus (Sorce et al., 1985). Similar results have been found when mothers were instructed to express different emotions toward an unfamiliar person or a new toy—babies' willingness to approach and interact with the person or toy depended on the nature of the mother's reaction (Baldwin & Moses, 1994; Boccia & Campos, 1989; Mumme, Fernald, & Herrera, 1996). Thus, babies as young as 1 year old appear to be able to use facial expressions as a cue for understanding the environment and adjusting to it.

Finally, mothers have been shown to use the infant's tendency for social referencing to their advantage. In a study examining the emergence of emotions, mothers were asked how they usually responded when an event—such as abruptly encountering an unfamiliar animal or hearing a loud sound—caused their baby to display surprise. Many mothers reported that immediately after exhibiting surprise, the baby appeared for a moment uncertain as to how to respond and then entered a state of either joy or distress. If during that brief moment the mother communicated a positive reaction to the infant, perhaps by smiling or speaking in a pleasant voice, the baby's response was more likely to be a pleasant one, and distress avoided (Klinnert et al., 1984). This study and others suggest that mothers intuitively understand (or perhaps have learned through experience) that their baby looks to them when feeling uncertain and that they have some ability to influence the infant's response to the situation (Hornik & Gunnar, 1988).

Face-to-Face Interactions

During the first 3 or 4 months of life, much of the infant's contact with the caregiver involves face-to-face interactions, such as those that occur during feeding, diapering, and many kinds of play. Psychologists have come to attach considerable significance to these early interactions, believing that they are fundamental to the development of an effective communication system between mother and baby and ultimately to the development of a strong attachment relationship (Brazelton & Yogman, 1986; Isabella, 1993, 1994).

To understand how these early dyadic interactions develop, researchers have employed a clever laboratory method. The baby and mother sit facing each other, with the mother typically instructed to play with the infant in her normal fashion. As they interact, one camera videotapes the mother's face, and another videotapes the

Social referencing
Using information gained from other people to regulate one's own behavior.

Face-to-face interactions during the early months appear to play an important role in the development of infant-caregiver attachment.

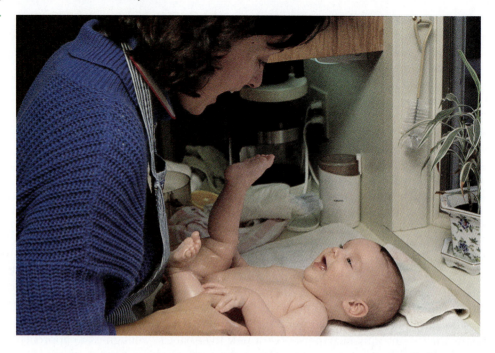

baby's. By replaying the two tapes side by side—often comparing only one frame at a time—investigators can examine the interactions in great detail. This technique, known as **microanalysis**, has helped reveal the subtle ways in which infant and mother influence one another (Kaye, 1982; Lamb, Thompson, & Frodi, 1982).

Microanalysis
A research technique for studying dyadic interactions, in which two individuals are simultaneously videotaped with different cameras, and then the tapes are examined side by side.

Two aspects of these early interactions are important. We saw in Chapter 6 that the behavior of newborns is characterized by cycles and rhythms. Sleep and feeding are common examples, in that both usually follow regular patterns. But newborns also display other behavior cycles that may be important for understanding their social interactions. For example, they appear to cycle from states of attention and interest to states of inattention and avoidance. During the attention phase, they make eye contact with the caregiver and often display positive affect, such as by smiling and vocalizing, whereas during the inattention phase they avoid eye contact and are more likely to show distress.

Some psychologists believe that periods of attention can become too arousing and stressful for infants and that infants keep this stimulation under control by turning away and perhaps by self-comforting, for instance, by putting the thumb in the mouth (T. M. Field, 1987; Gianino & Tronick, 1988). Early face-to-face interactions are important therefore because they reveal the baby's capability for *emotion regulation,* whereby the infant increases positive feelings and decreases negative feelings, by adjusting her behavior (Fox, 1994; Thompson, Flood, & Lundquist, 1995).

Interactional synchrony
The smooth intermeshing of behaviors between mother and baby.

The other important aspect of early interactions is that they produce *patterns* of behavior between the caregiver and the infant. As the mother comes to recognize the baby's cycles of attention and inattention, she adjusts her behavior to them. Microanalytic studies of mother–infant interaction during the first 4 months have shown that mothers gradually learn to concentrate their affective displays (talking, tickling, and smiling) during those times when the baby is attending to them. When the baby looks away, the mother's responses decline. Soon the infant and mother develop an **interactional synchrony** in behavior, so that they are both "on" or both "off" at about the same time (Kaye, 1982). In this way, the mother maximizes her opportunities to "teach" the baby and the baby can regulate the amount of interaction that takes place.

An interesting sidelight involves the issue of child abuse. Although it is not clear why, preterm infants have been shown to be at greater risk for abuse than are full-term babies. It is possible that this problem results in part from a failure of the infant and caregiver to develop a good communication system. In support of this view, studies have shown that preterm babies spend more time asleep, are less alert when awake, are more quickly overaroused by social stimulation, and spend more time averting their gaze from the caregiver. In turn, their mothers spend less time in face-to-face interaction with them, smile at and touch them less, and are less skilled at reading their emotional signals (Kropp & Haynes, 1987; Lester, Hoffman, & Brazelton, 1985; Malatesta et al., 1986). It is important to point out that prematurity does not necessarily prevent the development of a secure attachment relationship (van IJzendoorn et al., 1992). Nevertheless, the apparent disruption of normal face-to-face affective interaction that results from prematurity may interfere with the establishment of a strong mutual regulation system between mother and baby, possibly increasing the likelihood of abuse. We consider this issue again later in the chapter.

Once a synchronous pattern has developed between mother and baby, a second pattern begins to emerge. The mother waits for the baby to respond, and then she responds back. Sometimes these responses are imitative (the mother produces the same sound that the baby has just made), sometimes they are repetitive (she wiggles the baby's toes after each response), and sometimes they take other forms. But all of them serve to "answer" the infant's responses. This *turn-taking* pattern between caregivers and babies may represent the first conversational "dialogues," which later become more obvious as speech and language develop (Beebe et al., 1988; Mayer & Tronick, 1985). This pattern is not exclusive to English-speaking pairs; it has also been reported in Japanese mothers and their infants (Masataka, 1993). Babies appear to enjoy turn-taking episodes, often displaying a good deal of smiling and positive vocalizations.

A revealing experimental technique involves having the mother present the baby with no expression at all. The results of this *still-face* procedure have been fairly consistent across a number of studies (Cohn & Tronick, 1983; Ellsworth, Muir, & Hains, 1993; Segal et al., 1995; Toda & Fogel, 1993). Generally, babies at first attempt to engage the mother's attention, sometimes by pointing, vocalizing, or looking at her inquisitively. When the mother fails to respond, the infants usually begin to show signs of distress and protest, and they reduce their overall level of positive affect and often gaze in a different direction. These findings are consistent with the belief that the infant and mother develop an interaction pattern within the first few months that becomes comfortable for both of them. When one member of the pair (in this case, the mother) violates that pattern, however, the system is disrupted, and the other member (here, the baby) has difficulty coping with the new interactional style.

The importance of a smooth-running pattern of infant–caregiver interactions can also be seen in studies with mothers who are clinically depressed. These mothers have been found to be much less positive or responsive to their babies, and they do not synchronize well with the infants' behaviors. The babies, in turn, are less active and attentive and spend much of their time crying or displaying other forms of distress (Cohn et al., 1990; Field et al., 1990; Murray et al., 1996). Importantly, however, such infants do not display this sort of behavior with their nursery teachers (Pelaez-Nogueras et al., 1994), suggesting that it is indeed the absence of a synchronous relationship with the *caregiver* that causes the infants to respond in this way.

Simple face-to-face interaction between the mother and baby peaks at about 3 to 4 months. After that, the baby becomes more interested in objects, and the focus of infant–mother interaction is directed toward other things (Adamson & Bakeman, 1991; Lamb, Morrison, & Malkin, 1987). But the establishment of the reciprocal infant–caregiver relationship appears to lay the groundwork for the attachment bond that will soon emerge.

✓ *To Recap…*

The attachment between mother and infant begins at birth and depends on communication. At first, babies use crying to communicate. But soon, other elements of the affective system come into play. The mother and infant regulate each other's behavior through their affective expressions and their recognition of the affective expressions of the other.

Babies begin to express relatively simple emotions facially within the first 3 months; expression of emotions that require more cognitive sophistication occur later. Infants also begin to discriminate facial expressions within the first half year of life. Their understanding of these expressions is not obvious until the second half year, however, and they do not use this understanding to guide their own behavior until the end of the first year.

Microanalysis has been used to study face-to-face interactions, the most common interactions of the first 3 or 4 months. These studies reveal that as babies cycle between states of attention and inattention, mothers synchronize their own behavior to match these cycles. Such interactions eventually develop into a turn-taking pattern, which may represent the earliest form of conversation. They also reflect infants' ability to regulate their emotions. Experimentally altering the mother's natural behavior toward the child has produced negative reactions in the infant, suggesting that the mother–infant system evolves into a relationship that is comfortable for both of them.

Temperament

The child's role in infant–caregiver interactions is greatly influenced by her personality. For example, mothers often respond differently to happy, friendly babies who like to cuddle than to fussy, irritable, babies who squirm when held. For infants, personality does not yet include many components that are evident later on, such as beliefs, attitudes, and values. For this reason, the study of infant personality is generally restricted to emotional expressiveness and responsiveness to environmental stimulation. These components of personality are called **temperament** (Rothbart & Bates, 1998).

Temperament
The aspect of personality studied in infants, which includes their emotional expressiveness and responsiveness to stimulation.

Temperament is meant to describe the baby's behavioral style, reflecting not so much *what* babies do as *how* they do it. For example, two babies may both enjoy riding in a mechanical swing, but one may react exuberantly, shrieking with delight, while the other may remain calm and even fall asleep. Most researchers view temperament as simply one of the many individual differences, or traits, that make each child unique (Bates & Wachs, 1994).

Defining Temperament

Psychologists' definitions of temperament vary considerably (Goldsmith et al., 1987). We begin, therefore, simply by considering three questions that have guided their attempts to define this concept.

Is Temperament Inherited?   A fundamental question is whether babies inherit their response styles, just as they inherit the shapes of their noses or the color of their hair. There is considerable support for this idea.

We saw in Chapter 4 that studies comparing identical, or monozygotic, twins with fraternal, or dizygotic, twins provide strong evidence that at least some portion of temperament is transferred through the genes. Identical twins have been found to be more similar to each other than fraternal twins on a variety of behavioral measures, ranging from descriptions by parents of the baby's irritability, to ratings by trained observers of the child's reactions to strangers, to laboratory tests of the infant's fear responses on the visual-cliff apparatus. Twin studies likewise have found genetic effects in temperament traits among toddlers and preschoolers (Emde et al., 1992; Goldsmith, Buss, & Lemery, 1997; Plomin et al., 1993; Robinson et al., 1992).

We will see, though, that there is some disagreement over which behaviors best represent an infant's temperament, and not all these behaviors have been shown to have a genetic basis (Goldsmith et al., 1997). In addition, even if aspects of temperament are inherited, they may also be influenced by the child's environment.

Is Temperament Stable?   Regardless of the origins of temperament, another theoretical question is whether it remains constant over the years. Does the fearful baby who cries at an unfamiliar face at 6 months also shy away from new people at 20 months and avoid playmates at 42 months? This kind of stability over time and across situations has traditionally been viewed as an important defining component of responses that reflect temperament.

Research suggests that certain aspects of infants' behavioral style do indeed remain reasonably stable over time. The most common of these are negative emotionality (such as fear or fussiness), reactions to new situations or people, attention span, and activity level (Guerin & Gottfied, 1994; Pedlow et al., 1993; Ruddy, 1993). Not all measures of temperament, however, display this sort of stability.

The question of stability—or the lack of it—has been of interest to both nature and nurture theorists (Hooker et al., 1987). Those who favor a genetic model of temperament argue that when some aspect of a child's response style is found to be stable across years, this stability is most easily explained by assuming that the trait is simply part of the child's genetic structure. Environmentalists, however, contend that such stability could just as easily result from the child's remaining in a fairly constant environment (Bates, 1987; Wachs, 1988).

Lack of stability in temperament likewise can be handled by both nature and nurture models. Changes in behavioral style obviously could result from changes in the child's environment. But studies have also shown that genetically related children tend to show similar *patterns of change* in some temperamental behaviors, which could mean that temperament develops according to some genetic plan (Eaton, 1994; Matheny, 1989). More research on this issue is needed.

Is Temperament Evident Early in Life?   A third question that has been important in defining temperament is whether the child's response style is apparent from very early on. Again, the evidence is mixed. Recent research has found that certain characteristics of the fetus—such as heart rate and activity level—are reasonably stable during the last months of pregnancy and also fairly good predictors of how the mother later rates her infant's temperament (DiPietro et al., 1996; Eaton & Saudino, 1992). These data would seem to suggest that temperament begins in the womb. However, only some of the temperamental differences among newborns—usually those involving irritability and other forms of negative responding—are still observable after several years (Plomin et al., 1993; Riese, 1987; Stifter & Fox, 1990; Worobey & Blajda, 1989); most early differences disappear. In addition, not all behaviors that are assumed to reflect temperament are evident this early (Bates, 1987).

In sum, although many psychologists believe that temperamental behaviors are genetic, stable, and apparent early, not all agree. And the research evidence at this point does not settle the issue. We will see in the sections that follow, however, that the absence of a formal, agreed-upon definition has not prevented researchers from pursuing many investigations of children's temperament.

Types of Temperament

Inasmuch as definitions of temperament have not been consistent from one research team to another, not all investigators have treated temperament in the same way. In this section, we examine three current approaches to this area, including both the behaviors studied and the methods employed.

NYLS   The oldest and perhaps most widely used classification of temperament was developed in the 1950s by two pediatricians, Alexander Thomas and Stella Chess. Their research project, named the **New York Longitudinal Study** (NYLS), has continued for more than 30 years and represents one of the most important longitudinal efforts in modern child psychology (Thomas & Chess, 1986; Thomas, Chess, & Birch, 1968).

The research began as an effort to predict children's psychological adjustment by identifying potential problems early. The strategy was to develop categories of infant temperament and then to examine whether these categories related to the child's social and emotional development at later ages. After extensive interviews with parents of infants, Thomas and Chess identified three clusters of characteristics that occurred frequently, leading them to conclude that they had identified three early behavioral styles. They labeled these styles "easy," "difficult," and "slow to warm up."

The *easy baby* is rhythmic and usually has regular patterns of eating, sleeping, and toileting. She adapts well to changing situations and generally has a positive, happy mood. Easy babies are willing to approach new objects or people, and their reactions (of all types) are typically of low to moderate intensity. About 40% of the babies studied were classified by Thomas and Chess as this type.

The *difficult baby* is just the opposite. His schedules are less predictable, he is uncomfortable when situations change, and he often cries or displays a negative mood. He also withdraws from new experiences and reacts intensely to most environmental stimulation. This pattern was evident in about 10% of the infants.

The *slow-to-warm-up baby*, too, adapts poorly to changing situations and tends to withdraw from unfamiliar people or objects. She is typically less active, however, and responds at a relatively low intensity. About 15% of the babies were classified as this type. (The remaining 35% of the infants in the project did not fit into any of these three categories.)

As we will see in the sections that follow, Thomas and Chess (1977) proposed that the infant's temperament influences his later development according to the **goodness of fit** between the baby's response style and his physical and social surroundings. This notion meshes well with the transactional view of early social development and has become an important concept in temperament research (Wachs, 1994; Windle & Lerner, 1986).

Although the NYLS approach remains a widely used method of categorizing infant temperament, it does have its critics. One problem is its heavy reliance on parental report as a means of obtaining information. Parents' descriptions of their babies' behavior have the advantage of reflecting a wide range of situations, but this method also is open to biases of several sorts. Some parents are undoubtedly more

New York Longitudinal Study (NYLS)
A well-known longitudinal project conducted by Thomas and Chess to study infant temperament and its implications for later psychological adjustment.

Goodness of fit
A concept describing the relation between a baby's temperament and her social and environmental surroundings.

objective than others, and some are better than others at observing and describing what their children do. Parents also may tend to report what they assume the researchers would like to hear, presenting, for example, a consistent description of the infant from one interview to the next or portraying the child in a more positive than realistic light. And parents' descriptions sometimes reflect their own reactions to the infant's behavior. Some parents, for example, might describe a response style as "stubborn" that other parents would describe as "self-assured" (Bates & Bayles, 1984; Kagan, 1994).

An alternative to the interview is the questionnaire, which asks parents to respond to a series of objective questions about the child's typical behavior and reactions to situations. The best-known questionnaires have been designed according to the NYLS classification scheme (Carey & McDevitt, 1978; Fullard, McDevitt, & Carey, 1984; Medoff-Cooper, Carey, & McDevitt, 1993). Questionnaires offer the advantage of producing quantitative information that can be easily summarized and compared. But they suffer from some of the same potential biases as parent interviews, and they involve additional issues, including how well the parents understand the questions, how well they can compare their child with others (as some of the items require), and how they are feeling about the child when they fill out the instrument (Mebert, 1991; Rothbart & Goldsmith, 1985).

EAS Model   Another popular method of classifying infant temperament, which also uses a parent questionnaire, has been developed by a research team headed by Robert Plomin (Buss & Plomin, 1984, 1986). This model is strongly biological in its approach, viewing temperament as inherited personality traits that show an early onset. According to these researchers, a baby's temperament can be measured along three dimensions—emotionality, activity, and sociability. Consequently, this classification is commonly referred to as the **EAS model**.

Emotionality in this model refers to how quickly a baby becomes aroused and responds negatively to stimulation from the environment. A baby rating high on this dimension, for example, would be awakened easily by a sudden noise and would cry intensely in reaction. Plomin believes that differences on this dimension represent inherited differences in infants' nervous systems, with some infants having a quicker "trigger" and automatically experiencing greater arousal than others. During the first few months of life, emotionality is revealed through general distress reactions (such as crying) in unpleasant situations. Later in the first year, emotionality begins to evolve toward either fear or anger responses. Which behavioral style develops, Plomin contends, depends on the infant's experiences.

Activity describes the baby's tempo and energy use. Babies rating high on this dimension are moving all the time, exploring new places, and frequently seeking out vigorous activities. Like most definitions of temperamental traits, this one describes only how the baby behaves and not precisely what the baby likes to do. The researchers use the analogy of the controls of an automobile: The activity level presumably determines how fast the infant can go, but the environment determines the direction that the infant will take.

Sociability refers to an infant's preference for being with other people. Babies rating high on this dimension do not like to spend time alone and often initiate contact and interaction with others. This trait is not meant to describe the closeness of a baby's relationship with the caregiver or other significant people, which is assumed to be greatly influenced by the child's experiences. It is simply a measure of how much a given child innately prefers the stimulation derived from people rather than from things, and it is perhaps most clearly assessed in the baby's reac-

EAS model
Plomin and Buss's theory of temperament, which holds that temperament can be measured along the dimensions of emotionality, activity, and sociability.

tions to unfamiliar people, when the strength of a prior relationship does not come into play.

Although the EAS model views temperament as a biological concept, the researchers are interactionist in their conception of social development. In their view, although the baby's levels of emotionality, activity, and sociability may be determined by his genes, the baby's overall social development will depend on how these characteristics interact with characteristics of the social and physical environment.

Rothbart's Model   A third model of temperament has been proposed by Mary Rothbart. This model also has a strong biological flavor, viewing temperament as reflecting inborn differences in infants' physiological functioning. It, too, employs a parent questionnaire to assess an infant's temperament, although this information is supplemented by laboratory measures and by data collected in the home by professional observers (Goldsmith & Rothbart, 1991). Rothbart views temperament as consisting of individual differences in two areas—reactivity and self-regulation (Rothbart & Bates, 1998).

Reactivity is similar to Plomin's dimension of emotionality in that it refers to how easily and intensely a baby responds to stimulation. The major difference is that Rothbart also includes positive arousal, as illustrated by a baby's smiling and laughing at a new toy.

The other component of temperament according to this model is the baby's ability to increase or reduce this reactivity. This ability, termed *self-regulation,* is assumed to be inborn and to vary from child to child. Control of arousal by infants can take a number of forms, such as how long a baby looks at a stimulating object before turning away or how she approaches and explores it. The specific behaviors used for self-regulation change as the baby gets older, but the underlying temperamental trait presumably determines the infant's success in achieving it (Rothbart & Posner, 1985).

In a study that illustrates reactivity and self-regulation (LaGasse, Gruber, & Lipsitt, 1989), 2-day-old babies were tested to determine how intensely they sucked on an artificial nipple to obtain sweetened water. Individual babies' reactions to this positive stimulation differed considerably. At 18 months, the intensity of the same babies' reactions to unfamiliar people and situations was examined and found to be positively correlated with their earlier behavior—that is, those who had reacted intensely to the positive stimulation also responded intensely to the aversive stimulation. The researchers interpreted these results as reflecting a stable temperamental trait involving both reactivity and self-regulation. Babies who rated high on this trait were better able both to maximize their exposure to the positive stimulation (by sucking harder) and to minimize their exposure to the aversive stimulation (by withdrawing and hiding).

Like the other schemes, Rothbart's model is interactionist. Even though the reactivity and self-regulation abilities of babies differ from birth, the child's caregivers and physical surroundings are assumed to play major roles in determining the path that development will take.

Temperament and Social Interactions

It should be clear by now that virtually all researchers who study temperament have an interactional view of its relation to early social development. An infant's social interactions are influenced not only by her personality, but also by the degree to which these characteristics match the demands or expectations of the environment (Sanson & Rothbart, 1995). For example, if a mother's personality is very methodical, she may have considerable difficulty with a baby whose behavioral style is irregular and unpatterned. As a result, she may frequently attempt to do certain things, such as feed or put the baby down for a nap, when the child is not interested, perhaps producing repeated conflict and tension for both of them. That same baby, however, may develop a smoother relationship with a mother whose own behavior is not very structured. A mismatch can similarly occur with the physical environment. A baby who has a high activity level, for example, may have trouble living in a small apartment, and a baby who has a low threshold for distraction may not do well in a noisy neighborhood.

The quality of children's social interactions, as we have seen, can also affect their cognitive development. Thus, temperamental characteristics of the child come into play in this area of development as well. One research team found that when mothers viewed their infants as having a more difficult temperament, they tended to provide them with fewer learning and discovery opportunities during their daily interactions (Gauvain & Fagot, 1995). Importantly, follow-up observations at age 5 revealed that these children did not perform as well on tasks involving cognitive problem solving (Fagot & Gauvain, 1997).

The interactional model of temperament and social relationships has implications for the role that infant personality may play in the attachment process too. We consider this issue later in the chapter.

The match between the baby's temperament and the mother's personality can influence how successfully attachment develops.

Temperament and Behavior Problems

The NYLS project has not been the only research motivated by the search for early predictors of children's psychological adjustment. Other investigators have taken a similar clinical approach to investigations of temperament. Most work has focused on two categories of infant personality: the level of difficulty and the level of inhibition (Bates, Wachs, & Emde, 1994; Newman et al., 1997).

Difficult Infants   Thomas and Chess reported early in their longitudinal study that babies classified as "difficult" displayed more behavior problems during early childhood than did infants in the other categories (Thomas et al., 1968). This finding has spurred a number of investigations aimed at determining whether this classification scheme might serve as an early screening device for identifying children at risk for later problems (Rothbart, Posner, & Hershey, 1995).

Interestingly, in a follow-up of their longitudinal subjects, Thomas and Chess (1984) indicated that the majority of those who displayed temperamental difficulties during early childhood showed no evidence of these difficulties by early adulthood. Others have reported similar findings (Korn, 1984; Lee & Bates, 1985). Nevertheless, it remains useful to ask whether assessments of a difficult temperament during infancy and early childhood correlate positively with reports of behavior and adjustment problems in later childhood, adolescence, or even adulthood. Some studies have indeed reported such correlations (e.g., Bates et al., 1991; Caspi et al., 1995, 1996; Rothbart, Ahadi, & Hershey, 1994; Tubman et al., 1992). But exactly why difficult infants tend to develop these sorts of problems later on remains unresolved.

One possibility is that those aspects of the baby's temperament that produce the classification of difficult, such as frequent crying and irritability, increase the chances that parents will respond to the infant in a less than optimal manner, leading to problems in the child–caregiver relationship and ultimately to behavior problems in the child. This explanation is related to the goodness-of-fit concept described earlier (Bates, 1990; Chess & Thomas, 1987).

A very different explanation is that the positive correlation lies primarily in the eyes of the beholders (that is, the parents). According to this analysis, the fact that some parents rate their babies as difficult and later report them as having behavior problems results from the parents' attitudes, expectations, or approaches to child rearing, not from the child's characteristics (Garrison & Earls, 1987; Sanson, Prior, & Kyrios, 1990). Several studies, for example, have found that a baby's temperament during the first year—as measured by parent questionnaires—could be accurately predicted by assessment of the mother's personality characteristics and expectations when the child was still in the uterus (e.g., Diener, Goldstein, & Mangelsdorf, 1995; Mebert, 1989, 1991; Vaughn et al., 1987)!

Finally, having a "difficult" temperament—although perhaps posing certain long-term risks—nevertheless may afford children some ethological advantages. For example, a cross-cultural study of babies during a drought in East Africa found that those classified as difficult were most likely to survive, presumably because they were most demanding of attention and care from their mothers (DeVries & Sameroff, 1984).

Inhibited Infants   Another problem personality characteristic that researchers believe may be linked to temperament involves **inhibition** (Asendorpf, 1990, 1994; Kagan, Snidman, & Arcus, 1993). With babies, this trait is evidenced as being quick to respond negatively to anything new, such as crying when presented with a new toy. As they approach one year of age, these children become more timid, shy, and fearful, especially when encountering new situations or people (Schmidt & Fox, 1997). Like difficult babies, inhibited infants also are at risk for a variety of behavior problems in later childhood and beyond (Kagan, 1997; Rubin & Asendorpf, 1993).

The best-known research on inhibited children has been conducted by Jerome Kagan and his colleagues (Kagan, 1994, 1998). Kagan's research has involved an impressive longitudinal study designed to determine whether certain behaviors and physiological responses of inhibited children display an early onset and are stable over childhood (Kagan, Snidman, & Arcus, 1992).

Kagan's approach was to first identify groups of 2-year-olds who were either very inhibited or very uninhibited. He did this by observing how a large group of children reacted in a laboratory setting with unfamiliar people or objects. About 15% of the children responded to the new situations in a very timid manner and were

Inhibition
Kagan's proposed temperamental response style characterizing infants who react to unfamiliar events and people with timidity and avoidance.

Inhibition is a personality style that appears to have a biological basis, but it is likely also affected by socialization influences.

thus selected for study. The 15% who responded in the most outgoing and fearless manner were used for comparison. The children were studied again at 5.5 years and at 7.5 years to see whether their early response styles were still apparent, as we would expect if inhibition is a stable trait (Reznick et al., 1986).

Two sorts of measurement were used. The first was a set of behavioral measures, including children's performance on a series of problem-solving tasks with an unfamiliar adult, their interactions with unfamiliar peers, and their social behavior in school. On these measures, about 75% of the children who had been identified as inhibited or uninhibited displayed behaviors consistent with their classification even 6 years later. In addition, most of the inhibited children were found to have developed other fears or anxieties, such as fear of the dark or fear of going away to camp (Kagan, Reznick, Snidman, Gibbons, & Johnson, 1988).

Suspecting that inhibition might have a biological basis, the researchers also looked at a number of physiological responses (such as heart rate and pupil dilation) that are commonly associated with human stress reactions (Kagan, Reznick, & Snidman, 1987; Schmidt & Fox, 1997). The physiological data were reasonably consistent with the behavioral findings. Children identified at age 2 as being inhibited continued to show evidence of greater physiological arousal in new situations as second graders (Kagan, Reznick, & Snidman, 1988). These studies suggest that some timid children may be displaying a temperamental trait that has been apparent from infancy, that has remained reasonably stable over the years, and that has a biological basis. Recent findings in Sweden by other researchers support these conclusions (Broberg, Lamb, & Hwang, 1990; Kerr, Lambert, & Bem, 1996; Kerr, et al., 1994).

Even if true, however, these results tell only part of the story. For example, only those children at the extremes of inhibition displayed the sort of stability that is presumed characteristic of a temperamental trait; the rest of the children's levels of inhibition varied considerably over time (Kagan, Reznick, & Gibbons, 1989; Reznick et al., 1989). And even within the extreme groups, some children's inhibition did not remain constant.

Shyness and timidity, like a difficult temperament, also can be influenced by factors related to experience and socialization. Several studies have found, for example, that babies who display the negative emotionality that is characteristic of this trait during the early months are more likely to reduce their crying and fussing if their mothers are sensitive, responsive, and highly involved with them (Belsky, Fish, & Isabella, 1991; Matheny, 1986; Washington, Minde, & Goldberg, 1986).

An inhibited behavioral style likewise may be of some benefit to the child. Recent research has found that inhibited children more quickly and more strongly develop a sense of conscience, especially when exposed to particular forms of discipline (Kochanska, 1997; Kochanska, Murray, & Coy, 1997). We discuss this issue in more detail in Chapter 14 when we consider children's moral development.

Development in Cultural Context
Ethnic Differences in Temperament: Biology or Culture?

If temperament is indeed inherited to a degree, is it possible that different races and ethnicities could display different behavior styles? Some research evidence comparing Asian and Caucasian (usually American) children seems to point to that conclusion. But, as always, separating the contributions of nature and nurture is not a simple task.

Table 12.1
Mean Behavioral Scores for Motor Activity, Crying, Fretting, Vocalizing, and Smiling for Caucasian-American and Chinese 4-Month-Old Infants

Behavior	*Caucasian-American*	*Chinese*
Motor activity	48.6	11.2
Crying (in seconds)	7.0	1.1
Fretting (% trials)	10.0	1.9
Vocalizing (% trials)	31.4	8.1
Smiling (% trials)	4.1	3.6

Source: From "The Idea of Temperament: Where Do We Go from Here" by J. Kagan, D. Arcus, and N. Snidman, 1993. In R. Plomin & G. E. McClearn (Eds.), *Nature, Nurture, and Psychology*, Washington, DC: Copyright © 1993 by the American Psychological Association. Reprinted with permission.

Several investigators over the years have reported that Asian babies tend to be calmer, less active, less vocal, and more difficult to upset (such as by inoculations) than Caucasian babies (Camras et al., 1992; Kagan, Kearsley, & Zelazo, 1978; Kagan et al., 1994; Lewis, Ramsey, & Kawakami, 1993). Some illustrative data are presented in Table 12.1. These findings could be interpreted as temperamental differences, such as described by Rothbart's reactivity and self-regulation.

The idea that the genes of Asian and Caucasian babies may support different temperamental traits is not altogether unreasonable; their genes obviously distinguish the two groups on some physical characteristics. But before accepting a biological conclusion of this sort, it is wise to consider whether cultural influences may underlie some or all of these differences.

An important factor may be the value that society places on traits in different cultures (Chen, Rubin, & Sun, 1992). Many parents in the United States, for example, view shyness and inhibition in their children as weaknesses, perhaps reflecting a social deficit of some sort. Behaviors consistent with this style therefore are not likely to be encouraged or approved of by these parents. An inhibited response style is viewed more positively in Asian cultures, however, where it is seen as a virtue and sign of competence. Parents of these children, then, should be more likely to socialize them to behave in this manner (Chen, Rubin, & Li, 1995).

Similarly, in Thailand much emphasis is placed on raising children to be obedient, nonaggressive, and respectful of authority figures. Studies have found that Thai children have fewer behavior problems in school than do American children (Weisz et al., 1995) and that the problems they display typically involve social withdrawal and anxiety-related issues, rather than acting out or disruptive behaviors (Weisz et al., 1993). Similar findings have been reported in comparisons with Japanese and American children (Stevenson & Stigler, 1992).

These differences in Western versus Asian cultural values do not rule out the possibility of genetic involvement, but they do suggest that the context of development should always be taken into account when evaluating temperamental, or any other, characteristics of the developing child.

✓ To Recap...

Temperament refers to an infant's overall style of responding. No single definition of temperament exists, but many researchers assume it is genetically based, stable, and evident early in life.

Investigators have taken different approaches to temperament research. The NYLS project involved a longitudinal study designed to identify the early correlates of later social and emotional problems. Based on parent interviews, this approach has identified three temperament types: the easy baby, the difficult baby, and the slow-to-warm-up baby. It has been criticized, however, for its overreliance on parental reports. Plomin's EAS model has a strong biological orientation. It defines temperament as the baby's emotionality, activity, and sociability. Rothbart contends that temperament reflects the infant's reactivity (emotionality) and self-regulation (ability to control the emotionality).

Temperament is assumed to affect mother–child interactions through goodness-of-fit—the degree to which there is a match between the infant's temperamental characteristics and the physical and social environment. The quality of these interactions, in turn, can influence the child's cognitive development. Temperament is also assumed to be involved in children's later behavioral problems. Infants classified as difficult have been shown to be at risk for behavior disorders. Timid children may be displaying an early temperamental trait, inhibition, which is apparent in both their behavioral interactions and their physiological responses to stressful situations.

Attachment

We come at last to the topic that is most central to this chapter. How do mothers and babies develop the intense emotional relationship that characterizes infancy and early childhood? We have seen that this process appears to be a continuous one, beginning with the earliest mother–infant interactions. In particular, the development of the affective system—which is at the heart of infant–caregiver mutual regulation—is important in setting the stage for the social relationship that is about to form. The baby's temperament undoubtedly plays a role in this process as well.

Developmental Course of Attachment

The infant's attachment to the caregiver can first be clearly observed at 6 to 8 months of age. However, the actual process begins shortly after birth and continues well beyond this time. Here we describe three general phases of attachment development that roughly correspond to those proposed in several theoretical models of this process (Bowlby, 1982; Schaffer & Emerson, 1964).

Phase 1 (birth–2 months): Indiscriminate Social Responsiveness   At first, babies do not focus their attention exclusively on their mothers and will at times respond positively to anyone. Nevertheless, they do behave in ways that are important for the development of an attachment relationship with the caregiver. Infants come into the world with a number of built-in responses designed to draw the mother near (such as crying) and to keep her close at hand (quieting and smiling, for example). And although babies in this stage may not reserve their sociability solely for the caregiver, they clearly can recognize her. As we saw in Chapter 7, the newborn prefers to look at the mother (or at a photograph of her) rather than at a stranger within only a few days after birth (Bushnell, Sai, & Mullin, 1989; Pascalis et al., 1995).

Caregivers, too, very quickly learn to recognize their babies. Within hours after giving birth, for example, mothers can identify their own children solely on the basis of smell (Kaitz et al., 1987) or by touching a hand or cheek (Kaitz et al., 1992; Kaitz, et al., 1993).

An important difference, however, is that although the baby displays attachment only after some months have passed, the mother's emotional bond to the

Maternal bonding
The mother's emotional attachment to the child, which appears shortly after birth and which some theorists believe develops through early contact during a sensitive period.

baby develops very quickly. Some believe that **maternal bonding** occurs during a sensitive period immediately following birth and requires skin-to-skin contact with the baby (Klaus & Kennell, 1976; Klaus, Kennell, & Klaus, 1995). Based on this view, many hospitals and neonatal intensive care units (NICUs) have made it easier for mothers to spend more time with their newborns during the presumably crucial first hours and days of life.

Research indicates, however, that although such early contact may be important for some mothers under some circumstances, it certainly does not appear *necessary* for a strong maternal bond (Eyer, 1992; Goldberg, 1983; Lamb & Hwang, 1982; Myers, 1987; Svejda, Pannabecker, & Emde, 1982). Mothers and babies separated during the first days after birth by illness are just as likely as pairs not separated to develop strong attachment relationships (Rode et al., 1981). This also holds true for mothers and their adopted babies (Brodzinsky, Lang, & Smith, 1995).

Phase 2 (2–7 months): Discriminate Social Responsiveness

During the second stage, infants become more interested in the caregiver and other familiar people and direct their social responses to them. Although strangers continue to be accepted, they now assume a second-class status.

Across this period the infant and caregiver develop interactional patterns that permit them to communicate and that establish a unique relationship between them. The child develops a cognitive representation, or internal working model, of the caregiver based on how reliable and trustworthy she is seen to be (Bretherton, 1993). The baby also looks to the mother when anxious or uncertain for information regarding how he should feel—the social-referencing process described earlier—and the mother uses this communication system to exert some control over the child (Ainsworth, 1992).

Also important to the attachment process, babies now begin to develop a sense of self and to understand that they are separate from the rest of the world and that they can do things to affect it. We discuss these processes in detail in the chapter that follows.

Phase 3 (8–24 months): Focused Attachment

The attachment bond becomes clearest in the third quarter of the first year and remains very strong until about age 2. The appearance of attachment behaviors is very much tied to development in two other areas—one of these is emotional. At about this time, fear begins to emerge as a dominant emotion. With improvements in memory and other cognitive functions, babies begin to recognize what is strange or unfamiliar, and they generally react to such experiences negatively (Thompson & Limber, 1990). **Wariness of strangers** becomes common, often causing the baby to cry and retreat to the mother. Being apart from the caregiver produces **separation protest**, which also involves crying and sometimes searching after the mother. Both forms of distress are typically reduced once the baby is back in contact with the caregiver.

Wariness of strangers
A general fear of unfamiliar people that appears in many infants at around 8 months of age and indicates the formation of the attachment bond.

The other related development is physical. At about 6 to 8 months, most babies begin to crawl. This ability gives infants their first opportunity to have considerable control over where they are, and it is crucial in the attachment process—the baby no longer needs to rely on crying or related behaviors to gain proximity to his mother, but can crawl to her and follow her around.

Separation protest
Crying and searching by infants separated from their mothers; an indication of the formation of the attachment bond.

The full-blown attachment process becomes evident when the infant puts these two developments together and begins to treat the mother as a *secure base.* Now the infant's increased mobility allows her to regulate feelings of fear and insecurity by controlling the distance between her and the caregiver. When she is feeling secure, she ventures boldly from the mother to explore her environment, but when an unfamiliar person or situation appears, she returns to the mother for comfort and security (Bowlby, 1988).

The development of this sort of attachment bond between infant and caregiver is now well established. But psychologists are still learning exactly how it develops and what effects it has on the child's later development (Thompson, 1998; Waters et al., 1995).

Assessing Attachment

In order to study the attachment process, researchers must have reliable and valid methods for assessing the nature and quality of the infant–caregiver relationship. Two major methods have been developed for this purpose.

Strange Situation Procedure   The older and more popular way of assessing the strength and quality of the attachment relationship is the **Strange Situation procedure**. This method was developed in the 1960s by Mary Ainsworth as part of a longitudinal study of the attachment process (Ainsworth & Wittig, 1969).

The Strange Situation is a laboratory procedure that involves studying the child interacting with the mother and with an adult stranger in an unfamiliar setting. This approach ensures that the situation will be at least mildly stressful for the child and so will elicit secure-base attachment behaviors toward the caregiver. The procedure is typically conducted when the infant is about 12 months of age, a point at which the attachment relationship should be clearly established. Of particular interest are the baby's reactions when separated from the mother and when reunited with her.

The method consists of eight episodes, summarized in Table 12.2. Episode 1 simply involves introducing the caregiver and baby to the laboratory room, which contains several chairs and an array of toys and is designed to encourage exploration by the infant. Observers are positioned behind one-way windows, where they can observe and videotape the behaviors of the infant for later scoring. The next two episodes provide preseparation experiences for the baby. In episode 2, the caregiver and infant are alone, and the observers note the baby's willingness to explore the new toys and situation. In episode 3, a stranger joins them; after one minute of silence the stranger begins a conversation with the caregiver and also attempts to engage the baby in play.

Episode 4 represents the first separation, in which the caregiver leaves the child alone with the stranger. This episode may last for 3 minutes, but is cut short if the baby shows too much distress. Episode 5 involves the return of the caregiver and the departure of the stranger. How the infant reacts to the reunion with the caregiver is carefully noted. The caregiver remains with the infant for at least 3 minutes, offering comfort and reassurance, and attempts to get the baby reinvolved with the toys.

In episode 6, the second separation takes place. Now the caregiver leaves the baby alone in the room, again for a maximum of 3 minutes, depending on the child's level of distress. The stranger returns in episode 7 and attempts to interact with the baby. Episode 8 is the second reunion, during which the caregiver greets and picks up the baby, while the stranger leaves.

Three patterns of responses have generally been found to describe most infants who have undergone this procedure (Ainsworth, 1983; Thompson, 1998). Infants exhibiting pattern B are considered to be *securely attached* to the caregiver. They feel secure enough to explore freely during the preseparation episodes, but they display distress when the caregiver leaves and respond enthusiastically when she returns. About 65% of babies tested react in this manner. Pattern A babies are described as *insecure–avoidant.* They generally show little distress at separation, and when the

One clear sign that attachment has developed is the infant's reluctance to separate from her caregiver.

Strange Situation procedure Ainsworth's laboratory procedure for assessing the strength of the attachment relationship by observing the infant's reactions to a series of structured episodes involving the mother and a stranger.

Table 12.2
Strange Situation Procedure

Episode Number	Persons Present	Duration	Brief Description of Action
1	Mother, baby, and observer	30 sec.	Observer introduces mother and baby to experimental room, then leaves.
2	Mother and baby	3 min.	Mother is nonparticipant while baby explores. If necessary, play is stimulated after 2 min.
3	Stranger, mother, and baby	3 min.	Stranger enters. Min. 1: stranger silent. Min. 2: stranger converses with mother. Min. 3: stranger approaches baby. After 3 min., mother leaves unobtrusively.
4	Stranger and baby	3 min. or less [a]	First separation episode. Stranger's behavior is geared to that of baby.
5	Mother and baby	3 min. or more [b]	First reunion episode. Mother greets and comforts baby, then tries to settle baby again in play. Mother then leaves, saying bye-bye.
6	Baby alone	3 min. or less [a]	Second separation episode.
7	Stranger and baby	3 min. or less [a]	Continuation of second separation. Stranger enters and gears behavior to that of baby.
8	Mother and baby	3 min.	Second reunion episode. Mother enters, greets baby, then picks baby up. Meanwhile, stranger leaves unobtrusively.

[a] Episode is curtailed if the baby is unduly distressed.

[b] Episode is prolonged if more time is required for the baby to become reinvolved in play.

caregiver returns, they tend to avoid her. This pattern represents about 20% of infants. Pattern C babies are termed *insecure–resistant.* They give evidence of distress throughout the procedure, but particularly during separation. Reunions with the caregiver produce a mixture of relief at seeing her and anger directed toward her. Only about 15% of infants respond in this way.

It is important to understand that although the Strange Situation focuses on the infant's behavior, it is designed to assess the quality of the *relationship* between caregiver and baby. Pattern B infants are assumed to have developed a secure, healthy attachment to the caregiver, whereas the relationships developed by pattern A and C infants are assumed to be less than optimal.

An important advantage of this procedure is that it is very structured and so can be applied in the same way at different times and by different researchers. Because it is videotaped, it also can be reobserved by other researchers or for other reasons. The major disadvantages are that it involves only a very brief sampling of the child's interactions (usually less than 30 minutes), it occurs in an unfamiliar setting and environment, and the mother's behavior is strictly directed.

Attachment Q-Set
A method of assessing attachment in which cards bearing descriptions of the child's interactions with the caregiver are sorted into categories to create a profile of the child.

Attachment Q-Set   An alternative approach to assessing attachment that avoids the problems just mentioned is the **Attachment Q-Set (AQS)** (Waters, 1995; Waters & Deane, 1985). Rather than studying attachment in the laboratory, this evaluation is conducted in the home and over a much longer period of time.

The procedure usually involves trained observers who visit the infant and mother in their own home, sometimes more than once, and observe their interactions in a variety of typical activities. After completing several hours of observation, each observer evaluates the nature and quality of the mother–baby relationship using the *Q-sort method*—a rating technique used in social science research in which prepared statements are sorted into categories. Sometimes the mothers themselves serve as the observers and evaluators.

The *AQS* consists of 90 items, each describing the behavior of an infant or young child (ages 1–5) interacting with the mother (e.g., "Child enjoys climbing all over the mother when they play" or "When child returns to mother after playing, he is sometimes fussy for no clear reason"). Each item is printed on a card, and the observer is instructed to sort the 90 cards into 9 piles ranging from "least like the child" (piles 1–3) to "most like the child" (piles 7–9).

When the cards have all been sorted, the researcher compares the observer's profile of the child with a profile of a "securely attached child" prepared by experts in the field. The higher the correlation with the expert description, the more securely attached the child is assumed to be.

The *AQS* would seem to offer an important advantage over the Strange Situation procedure in that it involves a much wider array of behaviors on the part of both the mother and the baby (Pederson & Moran, 1995). Nevertheless, studies that have included both methods have generally found that they classify children in about the same way (Pederson & Moran, 1996; Seifer et al., 1996; Vaughn & Waters, 1990). More important than the differences between the methods are the issues that they raise. What factors produce different patterns of attachment between infant and caregiver and what significance do they have for the child's development?

Determinants of Attachment

The first issue involves the origin of patterns of attachment. Several factors have been suggested as determining what kind of attachment relationship develops (Belsky, Rosenberger, & Crnic, 1995).

Maternal Responsiveness Many theorists believe that the major influence on the quality of attachment is the mother's responsiveness to the baby. (We will consider the role of fathers in attachment in a later section.) Mothers who are more sensitive to their infants' needs and who adjust their behavior to that of their babies are believed more likely to develop a secure attachment relationship (Ainsworth, 1983; Isabella, 1994; Pederson & Moran, 1995).

Examples of such interactions can be seen in certain everyday situations, such as feeding. Pattern B infants have mothers who are more responsive to their signals—feeding them at a comfortable pace, recognizing when they are done or ready for more, and recognizing their taste or texture preferences (Ainsworth et al., 1978; Egeland & Farber, 1984). Another revealing situation involves responsiveness to crying. Mothers of pattern B babies are less likely to ignore their crying, are quicker to respond, and are more effective in comforting the child (Belsky, Rovine, & Taylor, 1984; Del Carmen et al., 1993). A third situation involves the mother's bodily contact with the infant. When mothers of pattern B babies are holding them, they tend to be more affectionate, playful, and tender toward the children (Anisfeld et al., 1990; Tracy & Ainsworth, 1981).

In face-to-face interactions, pattern B infants have caregivers who more easily synchronize their actions to mesh with those of the baby (interactional synchrony and turn taking), which also serves to lengthen their time together (Isabella &

BOX 12.1

MOTHER LOVE: HARLOW'S STUDIES OF ATTACHMENT

Much of the early work on attachment involved other species, in part, because this research often was conducted by ethologists—scientists who traditionally study behavior in a wide range of animal species. But the focus on other species also reflects the fact that some questions cannot easily be addressed by research with humans. A classic study conducted in the 1950s by Harry Harlow at the University of Wisconsin illustrates this point.

Harlow was interested in determining the role of feeding in the attachment process. Many psychologists at that time accepted the learning-theory view that a baby's emotional attachment to the mother is based on her role as a powerful reinforcer. Not only does she provide the infant with social stimulation, remove his wet diapers, and comfort him when he is upset, she is, perhaps

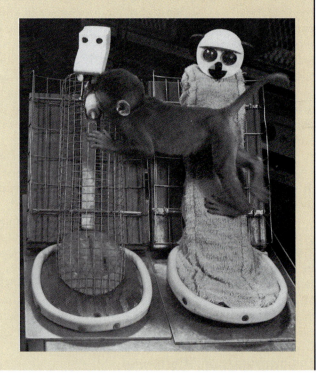

Harry Harlow found that contact comfort, rather than feeding, was the most important determinant of a rhesus monkey's attachment to its caregiver.

Secure attachments are most likely to develop when the caregiver is sensitive and responsive to the infant's needs.

most important, the source of the baby's nourishment. Because food is so fundamental to sustaining life, many researchers assumed that the baby becomes emotionally drawn to the mother as a result of her being associated with food.

To test this hypothesis, a psychologist would need to manipulate when, how, and by whom a baby is fed. For ethical reasons, we cannot conduct such research with human babies. Harlow approached the issue using what he felt was the best available alternative—baby rhesus monkeys. In addition to feeding, Harlow suspected that the opportunity to cuddle with the mother would also influence the attachment process. So he conducted the following study.

A group of rhesus monkeys were removed from their mothers immediately after birth and raised in a laboratory with two surrogate "mothers" constructed of wood and wire. One of the surrogates was covered with terry cloth to which the baby monkey could cling; the other surrogate was made only of a wire mesh. For half the infants, food was made available in a bottle on the cloth mother; for the other monkeys, food was attached to the wire mother. To assess the infant's "love" for the mothers, Harlow used two measures: the amount of time spent with each surrogate, and the degree to which the mother provided the baby monkey with security in fear-producing situations.

The results were dramatic and surprising. The baby monkeys spent an average of 17 to 18 hours a day on the cloth mother and less than 1 hour a day on the wire mother, regardless of which mother provided the food. Likewise, when frightened, the monkeys consistently sought out the cloth mother for security; and when only the wire mother was available to them, the infants seemed to find little comfort in its presence (Harlow & Harlow, 1966). Harlow's research thus demonstrated that the most important factor in the development of attachment in rhesus monkeys is not feeding, but the opportunity to cling and snuggle, which he called *contact comfort*.

The relevance of these findings to our species remains unclear, partly because we cannot replicate Harlow's procedures by depriving human babies of contact with their caregivers. But this classic research did prompt investigators to begin examining factors other than conditioning and learning principles in their search for the determinants of human attachment. And it also served as a reminder that even widely held ideas regarding the causes of behavior should not be accepted without scientific verification.

Belsky, 1991; Isabella, Belsky, & von Eye, 1989; Kiser et al., 1986). Finally, overall levels of acceptance, rejection, and sensitivity by mothers across a variety of everyday activities have been shown to predict which of the three attachment classifications their babies will exhibit in the Strange Situation (De Wolff & van IJzendoorn, 1997; Pederson & Moran, 1996; Rosen & Rothbaum, 1993; Seifer et al., 1996).

Still other kinds of evidence link the caregiver's behavior to the quality of the attachment relationship. For example, babies can develop different attachment relationships with different caregivers (e.g., the mother, the father, professional caregivers), which should not be surprising if caregivers respond differently to the child (Howes & Hamilton, 1992; Sagi et al., 1995; van IJzendoorn & De Wolff, 1997).

Also, the proportion of infants in different attachment classifications varies from culture to culture, again presumably as a result of different caregiving practices (we consider this research again shortly) (Sagi et al., 1995; van Ijzendoorn & Kroonenberg, 1988). Finally, interventions designed to increase mothers' sensitivity to their infants have also produced more secure attachment relationships between them (van den Boom, 1994, 1995; van IJzendoorn, Juffer, & Duyvesteyn, 1995).

It seems clear, then, that the security of the relationship between the infant and the caregiver depends heavily on the kinds of care the child receives. Yet it should also be clear by this point that the infant has more than a little to do with how her mother treats her.

469

Adult Attachment Interview (AAI)
An instrument used to assess an adult's childhood recollections of the attachment relationship with the primary caregiver.

Attachment across Generations   It is reasonable to ask why some mothers respond more sensitively to their babies than do others. One answer seems to involve the mother's recollections of her own childhood experiences. Using an instrument called the **Adult Attachment Interview**, researchers have had mothers describe their childhood attachment relationships and have then classified them into four groups (George, Kaplan, & Main, 1985; Main & Goldwyn, 1998).

Autonomous mothers present an objective and balanced picture of their childhood, noting both the positive and negative experiences; *dismissing* mothers claim to have difficulty recalling their childhoods and appear to assign little significance to them; *preoccupied* mothers tend to dwell on their early experiences, often describing them in a confused and highly emotional manner; and *unresolved* mothers have experienced attachment-related trauma that they have not yet resolved, such as the loss of, or abuse from, a mother or father.

The assumption underlying this research is that mothers' memories and feelings regarding their own attachment security will be expressed in their caregiving toward their child and so affect the infant–caregiver relationship. Several studies have shown that these classifications are indeed reasonably good predictors of the patterns of attachment these mothers form with their own babies (Posada et al., 1995; van IJzendoorn, 1992, 1995). Even more impressive, they can predict both forward and backward—that is, mothers' interviews during pregnancy predict their later attachment to their infants (Steele, Steele, & Fonagy, 1996; Ward & Carlson, 1995) and mothers' interviews when their children are age 6 correlate positively with their attachments when the children were only 12 months old (Main et al., 1985).

Temperament and Attachment   We have seen that an infant's temperament can affect how the child interacts with the caregiver, as well as in other social situations. Some researchers believe that temperament may therefore play a role in the attachment process. This could happen in two different ways (Seifer & Schiller, 1995).

The infant's temperament may interfere with a valid assessment of his attachment classification. For example, some researchers suspect that infants who are fearful and inhibited tend frequently to be classified as pattern C in the Strange Situation procedure—not because they actually have this sort of relationship with the caregiver, but because their overreaction to the unfamiliar situation gives the *appearance* of their being insecurely attached to her (Calkins & Fox, 1992; Kagan, 1994; Thompson, Connell, & Bridges, 1988). Temperamental characteristics involving activity level, distractibility, or soothability likewise are suspected to affect ratings in the Strange Situation (Goldsmith & Harman, 1994). This problem does not appear to be serious, however, and use of the Q-Set methodology has helped address it (Rothbart & Bates, 1998).

The more important role for temperament is that it may directly affect the type of attachment relationship the child develops with the caregiver. This idea relates to the goodness-of-fit concept discussed earlier in the chapter. For example, babies who are irritable or have other characteristics of a difficult temperamental style might be a challenge to respond to in a prompt and sensitive manner. Another possibility is that a baby's temperament may influence how sensitive the child is to the mother's caregiving—such that the same type of caregiving could be received differently by different infants. Either of these situations could result in a child's being less likely to develop a secure attachment with the mother.

There seems to be increasing evidence that temperament may affect the attachment relationship in the second, more direct, way (Seifer et al., 1996; van den

Boom, 1994), but the precise processes responsible for its influence remain to be identified (Thompson, 1998).

Development in Cultural Context
Attachment across Cultures

The attachment theory originally proposed by Bowlby and Ainsworth would seem to predict that the process should work the same way for all children and caregivers everywhere. After all, the biological mechanisms that underlie this process presumably evolved over millions of years and well before the rise of the cultures that exist today. But many modern researchers believe that the theory has room for some variation and that the discovery of cultural differences in how infants and caregivers relate need not undermine its basic elements.

Most of the early work on attachment was done in the United States. But as this research spread to other countries and cultures, it became obvious that attachment to some degree varies with the cultural context in which it develops (Harwood, Miller, & Irizarry, 1995; Main, 1990). This conclusion was initially based on studies using the Strange Situation procedure, but has since been confirmed by research involving the Q-Set approach (Sagi et al., 1995).

Germany, for example, represents a Western industrialized culture whose attachment patterns we might expect to be similar to those in the United States. However, researchers have found that fewer infant–caregiver pairs display the secure (pattern B) attachment relationship than in U.S. samples and that more are classified as pattern A, or insecure–avoidant. This difference does not appear to result from less maternal sensitivity among German mothers. Rather, the investigators speculated that German mothers' emphasis on building independence in their children resulted in the infants' appearing less interested in their mothers during reunions (Grossmann & Grossmann, 1990; Grossmann et al., 1985).

Very different results have been reported in studies of Japanese children, which have found a higher percentage of pattern C, or insecure–resistant, attachments. In the Japanese culture, mothers rarely leave their babies with others, so the Strange Situation procedure may prove more stressful for the infants (Miyake, Chen, & Campos, 1985; Takahashi, 1986, 1990).

Yet a third child-rearing situation exists in Israel, where a baby is often cared for with many other infants in a communal *kibbutz*. Because these infants spend most of their time with a single caregiver, they generally have limited exposure to strangers or unfamiliar settings. Perhaps for this reason, infants in this culture also respond poorly to the Strange Situation procedure, with the majority displaying pattern C attachment (Sagi, 1990; Sagi & Lewkowicz, 1987).

Cultural differences need not always mean differences in nationality. Even within the United States, differences in attachment can be found among certain groups. Among African-Americans, for example, child care is commonly shared by multiple family members, rather than left primarily to the mother. As a result, African-American infants often do not seem to find the Strange Situation procedure especially stressful (Jackson, 1993).

Similarly, Puerto Rican mothers and Anglo-American mothers tend to differ in how they expect their infants to behave in the Strange Situation. Anglo mothers, who stress activity and individualism in their children, rated active exploration as the most desirable infant response in the Strange Situation; Puerto Rican mothers, who emphasize self-control and respect in their children, preferred infant behaviors that maintained appropriate public demeanor (such as the absence of crying) and that kept the baby in close contact with them (Harwood, 1992; Harwood & Miller, 1991).

The message from all these studies is one of caution. Most researchers agree that the Strange Situation and Attachment Q-Set remain valid measures of the quality of the infant–caregiver relationship (Bretherton, 1995), and evidence gathered across many cultures suggests that the attachment process is reasonably similar from country to country (Sagi et al., 1995; Wartner et al., 1994). Nevertheless, differences do exist. Investigators therefore must be careful not to assume that the values and practices of their own culture are universal and that any deviations from them represent problems or nonoptimal development. What appears to be insecure–avoidance or insecure–resistance may have a very different meaning when viewed from within another culture.

Effects of Attachment on Other Behaviors

The other major issue in attachment research concerns the effects of a secure or insecure attachment on other aspects of the infant's functioning. Many studies have reported that securely attached infants display a variety of other positive characteristics not found in infants whose caregiver relationships are of lower quality.

One of these characteristics involves the child's cognitive competence. Several experiments have shown that securely attached infants later become better problem solvers (Frankel & Bates, 1990; Jacobsen, Edelstein, & Hofmann, 1994; Matas, Arend, & Sroufe, 1978). Pattern B infants also have been reported to be more curious and to do more exploring than other infants (Hazen & Durrett, 1982; Slade, 1987). Finally, one study reported that the cognitive competence of children at 4 years of age can be predicted by their mothers' responsiveness toward them (and presumably the eventual quality of their attachment relationship) at 3 months of age (Lewis, 1993).

Securely attached infants also seem to be more socially competent. For example, they tend to be more cooperative and obedient, and they have better relations with their peers (Cassidy et al., 1996; Fagot, 1997; Kerns, 1994). In addition, pattern B babies are less likely to develop emotional or behavior problems than are pattern A or C infants (Erickson, Sroufe, & Egeland, 1985; Lewis et al., 1984). This does not mean, however, that insecurely attached babies are doomed to problems. It has been shown, for example, that these babies seem to benefit more from day-care experiences, suggesting that environmental influences play an important role in the development of their later social competence (Egeland & Heister, 1995).

Precisely why a secure attachment with the caregiver has these effects is not entirely understood. But it is likely that as a result of being secure in the caregiver's presence, the infant feels comfortable in exploring the surrounding social and physical environment and thus develops important cognitive and social skills.

✓ To Recap...

Infant–caregiver attachment develops in three stages. Between birth and 2 months of age, babies respond socially to almost anyone. From ages 2 to 7 months, infants direct social responses principally to familiar people, and they develop a unique affective communication system with the caregiver. Clear-cut attachment becomes evident at 6 to 8 months. At this point, the infant is wary of strangers, protests separation, and uses the mother as a source of comfort and a secure base. The appearance of attachment is related to the emergence of two other developmental milestones: the emergence of fear as a major emotion, and the ability to crawl.

Two principal methods are used to assess the quality of the infant–caregiver attachment relationship. Ainsworth's Strange Situation procedure is conducted in the laboratory and produces three common patterns of infant response: pattern A, or insecure–avoidant; pattern B, or securely attached; and pattern C, or insecure–resistant. Most babies display pattern B, but the proportion of infants in each classification varies across cultures, apparently reflecting different attitudes toward child rearing. The Attachment Q-Set method assesses the infant-caregiver relationship over a wider range of behaviors and situations.

The quality of the infant–caregiver attachment relationship appears to result primarily from the caregiver's responsiveness. Mothers who are more sensitive to their babies' signals and who adjust their behavior to mesh with that of their children are more likely to develop secure attachment relationships. The mother's recollections of her childhood and the infant's temperament also play a role.

Secure attachment to the mother has several positive effects on the child's development. Pattern B babies generally display greater cognitive and social competence than do babies who are less securely attached.

Family Influences

Social development, like every other aspect of the child's development, is influenced by the context in which it occurs. During the early years, the most important context is the family. This is where young children spend most of their time, acquire many important social and cognitive skills, and develop—for better or for worse—various attitudes, beliefs, and values. Recall from Chapter 2 that the family, along with the school, the neighborhood, the church, and so on, is part of Bronfenbrenner's microsystem—the layer of environment that affects the child most directly. But the family itself is a dynamic system, with every member exerting influence on every other member and with the entire system evolving over time (Garbarino & Abramowitz, 1992; Lerner et al., 1995).

The transactional nature of the *family system* means that events or changes in any part of it tend to affect everyone—for example, when a new baby comes home, when

The transactional nature of the family system means that events like the addition of a new baby can alter the interplay among family members.

a child leaves for college, when a disabled grandparent comes to live with the family, when a father loses his job, or when parents get divorced (Cowan & McHale, 1997; Minuchin, 1985). Understanding the family's effects on the developing child, therefore, requires that we consider the reciprocal influences, not only between child and parent, but also between siblings, between parents, and so forth (Cowan et al., 1991).

Because the family undoubtedly is the most influential element of the microsystem, it has been studied extensively by developmental researchers (Cowan et al., 1991; Grotevant, 1989). This research has focused on topics ranging from simple parent–child interactions (Parke & Buriel, 1998), to children's conceptions of the family (Bretherton & Watson, 1990), to the relation of the family to the community and larger society (Goodnow, 1988). In this section, we consider some of the ways in which children's development is influenced in both positive and negative ways by the family context.

The Changing American Family

Adding to the complexity of studying the family system is the fact that the family as an institution has undergone some radical changes in the past several decades. The "traditional" two parent–two child family, idealized in the 1950s, has become increasingly less common as changing values and lifestyles have resulted in a wide range of family types. Today, approximately 50% of children spend some portion of their childhood living with only one parent, usually the mother. And some children's two parents may be two mothers or two fathers, as gay and lesbian couples are increasingly choosing to have or adopt children (Patterson, 1994, 1995). Also, whereas traditionally fathers were the family breadwinners, today about 60% of women with children are employed. In some families, fathers are opting to stay home with the children.

The soaring rate of divorce means that many remarriages are occurring, often producing blended families that include children from different parents. Today's children can also expect to have older parents, as many mothers are waiting longer to have their first child, and they can expect to have fewer siblings, as many parents are choosing to have fewer children (U.S. Bureau of the Census, 1990).

The impact of these changes on children's development has been of great interest to developmental psychologists, for both theoretical and applied reasons. Much of what psychologists know about child development they have learned by studying children in traditional family contexts. But do these conclusions continue to hold when children are reared in nontraditional contexts? More and more, the answer appears to be no, as researchers repeatedly discover the importance of understanding development in context (Moen et al., 1995).

Applied interest in the changing family grows out of the sobering reality that many of today's children are being reared in what are undoubtedly less-than-optimal conditions. Children of single parents, as well as children in two-parent homes whose parents are both employed, frequently are latchkey children, who come home to an empty house and must largely care for themselves (Cowan, Powell, & Cowan, 1998). Hard economic times have resulted in poverty for 14 million children in the United States (McLoyd, 1998). Child abuse is at epidemic levels and appears to be rising (Emery & Laumann-Billings, 1998). And drugs, crime, and AIDS have become a part of many children's everyday lives. Child psychologists must inform policy makers on how such conditions affect children and what interventions are needed to deal with them (Garbarino & Kostelny, 1995).

Styles of Parenting

Early social development is very much influenced by parents' child-rearing attitudes and practices (Cowan & McHale, 1997). Parents' beliefs regarding the degree to which their behavior determines the child's success in life affect how they approach the task of socializing the child (Goodnow & Collins, 1990; Murphey, 1992). And the child-rearing practices parents employ—such as making and enforcing rules, offering support and encouragement, or providing guidance, structure, and predictability in the child's life—can greatly influence the child's development (Chamberlain & Patterson, 1995; Parke & Buriel, 1998).

Approaches to parenting are individual and vary across cultures (Bornstein, 1991; Maccoby, 1992). Two dimensions of parenting appear to be especially important for the child's development (Maccoby & Martin, 1983). One is *parental warmth*—the amount of support, affection, and encouragement the parent provides, as opposed to hostility, shame, or rejection. The other is *parental control*—the degree to which the child is monitored, disciplined, and regulated rather than being largely unsupervised. The combination of these two dimensions produces four general styles of parenting, which have been found to produce different outcomes in children (Baumrind, 1971, 1989; Dornbusch et al., 1985; MacDonald, 1992).

Parents who are high in both warmth and control are referred to as *authoritative* parents. These parents tend to be caring and sensitive toward their children but set clear limits and maintain a predictable environment. This parenting style clearly has the most positive effects on early social development. Children of authoritative parents generally are the most curious, self-confident, academically successful, and independent.

Parents who are low in warmth but high in control are termed *authoritarian* parents. Authoritarian parents are very demanding, exercising strong control over their children's behavior and enforcing their demands with threats and punishment. Most children do not respond well to this approach. Children of authoritarian parents often are easily upset, displaying moodiness, aggression, and conduct problems.

Parents who are high in warmth but low in control are called *permissive* parents. These parents are loving and emotionally sensitive but set few limits on behavior. Though they provide acceptance and encouragement to their children, they provide little in the way of structure or predictability. Interestingly, children of permissive parents in some ways resemble those of authoritarian parents; they are often impulsive, immature, and out of control.

Finally, parents who are low on both dimensions are termed *indifferent* parents. These parents set few limits on their children, but they also provide little in the way of attention, interest, or emotional support. This detached style of parenting does not foster healthy social development. Children of indifferent parents tend to be demanding and disobedient and tend not to participate effectively in play and social interactions.

It appears, then, that optimal parenting involves both warmth and control. It is crucial that children feel loved and accepted, but they must also understand the rules of conduct and believe that their parents will require that the rules be followed. Moreover, the different outcomes produced by these four styles of parenting persist well beyond the early years of social development. Clear differences in social and even cognitive development during adolescence can be traced to the parenting style children experienced early on (Fletcher et al., 1995; Steinberg et al., 1994; Steinberg et al., 1995).

warmth + control

Why do parents differ so much in their parenting styles? We saw earlier that mothers' sensitivity to their infants results, in part, from their recollections of their own attachment relationships. These recollections similarly appear to influence the interaction styles of both parents with their children. One longitudinal study compared responses by mothers and fathers on the AAI prior to becoming parents with their later parenting styles with their first child (Cohn et al., 1992; Cowan & Cowan, 1992). The greatest warmth was displayed when both parents were classified as autonomous, and the least when neither was classified as autonomous. Interestingly, even when only the father was autonomous, the mother displayed the same high level of warmth, suggesting that support from the spouse may serve to decrease a mother's feelings of insecurity and thus enhance her relationship with her child.

Applications
Maternal Employment, Day Care, and Attachment

One of the most obvious recent societal changes involves the increased number of women working outside the home and leaving some of the job of child rearing to others, such as those who provide care in day-care centers (Scarr, 1998). One topic that has generated a great deal of interest and debate concerns what happens to the mother–infant attachment process under these circumstances (Clarke-Stewart, Gruber, & Fitzgerald, 1994; Lamb, 1998; McCartney, 1990). This question is not a minor one, in that in the United States by 19953 more than 50% of married women with children under 5 were regularly receiving care from someone other than the mother (Bachu, 1995; Scarr, 1998).

Over the years, a number of studies have reported that infants whose mothers are employed are less likely than those whose mothers stay at home to be classified as securely attached in the Ainsworth Strange Situation procedure (e.g., Barglow, Vaughn, & Molitor, 1987; Belsky, 1988; Belsky & Rovine, 1988; Lamb, Sternberg, & Prodromidis, 1992). And infants whose mothers work full-time are less likely to be securely attached than those whose mothers work part-time (Clarke-Stewart, 1989). Such evidence appears to suggest that leaving infants with day-care providers may be unadvisable, but not all psychologists agree that a problem exists (Jaeger & Weinraub, 1990; Weinraub & Jaeger, 1990).

One of the main points of contention involves what these findings really mean. As indicated earlier, the Strange Situation has been used frequently to assess the attachment relationship, and there is some disagreement about exactly what it measures. We have also seen that an important requirement of Ainsworth's method is that the infant experience it as somewhat stressful. This experience of stress is what causes the baby to show anxiety when the mother leaves and to greet her enthusiastically when she returns—reactions that lead to the baby's being classified as securely attached.

The problem with using this method to assess the impact of maternal employment is that infants left frequently in day care may not find the Strange Situation particularly stress inducing. After all, their mothers routinely leave them with others and then later return to pick them up. Perhaps after babies have gained enough experience with this routine, the Strange Situation does not evoke the level of anxiety necessary for them to display the secure-base behaviors normally indicating secure attachment.

But suppose that day-care infants are not in fact as strongly attached to their mothers. Not all psychologists believe that even this indicates a serious problem.

There is evidence, for example, that infants can develop secure attachments to their day-care providers, thus perhaps partially compensating for the typical mother–infant relationship (Goossens & van IJzendoorn, 1990). Alternatively, or perhaps as a result, day-care infants may be more independent and more confident in dealing with their social environments. For example, among older children, those who have been in day care have been reported in some research to be more sociable, to have better language skills, and to be more skillful in social interactions (Clarke-Stewart et al., 1994; Lamb & Sternberg, 1997). Two longitudinal projects in Sweden have found that early day-care experiences produce positive social and cognitive effects during later childhood and adolescence (Andersson, 1992; Broberg et al., 1997).

Another problem with interpreting the effects of day care on attachment involves the mothers themselves. Some mothers are forced to work for economic reasons, whereas others choose to work because their careers are important to them. Conversely, some mothers who stay home prefer not to work, whereas others would like to work but feel they should remain home to care for the infant. The point is that whether a mother is employed may not be as important as how she feels about her situation (Hock & DeMeis, 1990).

This issue sometimes becomes evident when employment produces **maternal separation anxiety** (Hock & Schirtzinger, 1992; McBride, 1990). For some mothers, separation from their babies causes a great deal of emotional distress. High levels of anxiety, in turn, often interfere with optimal caregiving. One study found that among employed women, those experiencing the most separation anxiety exhibited an insensitive style of caregiving and had infants who were more likely to be classified as pattern A (Stifter, Coulehan, & Fish, 1993). In these cases, the problem was not the employment itself, but the effect it had on the mother, and ultimately on the infant–mother relationship.

Related to all these findings are issues regarding the day-care setting and staff. The number of children in a classroom, the number of adults supervising them, and the methods of discipline and teaching (if any) all affect the quality of children's day-care experiences (Howes, 1997; Lamb & Sternberg, 1998; Rosenthal & Vandell, 1996). And these factors may ultimately have as much impact on the child's development as whether the child is with or without the mother.

The controversy surrounding the appropriateness of the Strange Situation procedure for measuring attachment in children in day care has now been somewhat resolved. A recent large-scale study suggests that placing a child in day care does not in itself affect the security of the child's attachment to the caregiver one way or the other (NICHD Early Child Care Research Network, 1997). The report does indicate, however, that a child whose mother is low in sensitivity is more likely to be classified as insecurely attached when (1) the day-care center also does not provide a high level of care, (2) the child spends a great deal of time in day care, or (3) the child has had many different child-care arrangements. A related finding is that boys are more likely to be classified as insecurely attached when they spend a great deal of time in day care, whereas girls are more likely to receive such a classification when they spend little time in day care.

This issue is obviously complex, and despite a great deal of study, it remains unresolved. Yet unless major governmental or business policy changes permit mothers (or perhaps fathers) to be supported while they stay at home with their newborns, maternal employment will continue to occur in most families (Carnegie Task Force, 1994; Clark et al., 1997). The day-care question will thus likely remain a topic of concern for some time to come.

Maternal separation anxiety
Strong negative emotional reactions experienced by some mothers when separated from their children.

Infants also develop attachment relationships with their fathers, although not necessarily of the same type as with their mothers.

The Role of Fathers

Most of the research we have discussed has involved mothers. But fathers, too, play a major part in most families and certainly are important figures for young children. This is especially the case today, as many fathers are assuming a greater role in child rearing (Hewlett, 1992; Parke, 1996; Russell & Radojevic, 1992).

Fathers generally spend less time with their children than do mothers, even when both parents are at home (Belsky, Gilstrap, & Rovine, 1984; Biernat & Wortman, 1991). Evidence suggests that fathers do have the ability to be good caregivers (Belsky, Gilstrap, & Rovine, 1984; Parke, 1995, 1996). But the caregiving role is not the one fathers typically assume to interact with infants. More often, father–infant interactions involve physical stimulation and play, especially with boys (Lamb, 1986; MacDonald & Parke, 1986).

Attachment between infants and their fathers has been the subject of much interest (Belsky, 1996). One question has been whether the infant will develop a strong emotional attachment to someone other than the primary caregiver (who is usually the mother). The answer is clearly yes. Infants can become very securely attached to their fathers; fathers, in turn, report similar feelings (Fox, Kimmerly, & Schafer, 1991; Palkovitz, 1984). In fact, fathers report levels of *paternal separation anxiety* that are as high as those of mothers (Deater-Deckard et al., 1994).

A second major question has been whether the infant's relationship with the father is necessarily the same as that with the mother. In fact, it appears that an infant's attachment to the father can be quite different (Bridges, Connell, & Belsky, 1988; Fox et al., 1991) and that it, too, reflects the father's sensitivity and responsiveness toward the baby (Cox et al., 1992; Easterbrooks & Goldberg, 1984). These findings are important because they offer support for the hypothesis that the security of an infant's attachment to the caregiver depends on the caregiver's responsiveness to the infant. Nevertheless, even when father and baby have a very secure relationship, it is probably not as strong as the baby's relationship with the mother (Parke, 1995, 1996).

Unfortunately, fathers can also be a source of negative influence on children. Although most of the research examining the effects of parental depression, psychopathology, and maltreatment has involved mothers, the presence of such problems in fathers also can have harmful effects on children's development (Phares, 1992; Phares & Compas, 1992). Finally, fathers appear to play a role in children's development of gender roles. We discuss that issue in Chapter 15.

Development in Cultural Context
The Changing Roles of Fathers in China

Technology is modernizing the world in dramatic ways. Societies that once were rural are quickly becoming urban. Societies whose economies once were based on farming and fishing are now becoming industrialized. And with these developments have come important changes in the social fabric of these cultures, especially concerning the family (MacFarlane, 1987). Nowhere has this trend been more apparent than in China, where the changing roles of fathers serve to illustrate what is happening in many other cultures around the world (Whyte & Parish, 1984).

The Chinese culture is one of the oldest in the world; for the past 2,000 years or so its family structure has been rooted in the philosophy of Confucius, which dictated family roles that were, by Western standards, rigid and traditional. Until recently, the Chinese family was characterized by a strict division of labor between parents. The father was viewed as the major economic provider and absolute head of the household. Children were expected to respect his authority and to obey him without question. His major role was as disciplinarian, and his most important responsibility was to ensure the character development of the child, which included fostering independence, self-sufficiency, and motivation to succeed. In this role, he tended to remain emotionally aloof and to avoid displays of affection.

Chinese fathers were also responsible for the child's education. Not only were they expected to instruct the child in many areas themselves, but they were also expected to oversee the child's formal schooling and eventual entry into the career world. In contrast, the mother's job was to be the nurturant caregiver, who provided children with affection and emotional support and who attended to their daily needs (Ho, 1987).

The rapid industrialization and urbanization of China in the past few decades has produced several trends that are changing this traditional family structure (Jankowiak, 1992). First, many mothers are now entering the workforce, leaving some of the child care to fathers. Thus, fathers' roles have had to extend beyond disciplinarian and educator to include many of the caretaking duties of the mother. In addition, Chinese fathers are becoming involved with their children's education at an earlier age. And with many Chinese families now living in small, urban apartments, fathers are almost forced into more frequent everyday interactions with their children. Also, there is a growing attitude in the modern Chinese culture that the father–child relationship should be one of greater warmth and emotionality. Finally, the Chinese government's policy of encouraging only one child per family (Falbo & Poston, 1993) has meant that in most families, the father's entire parenting focus has been directed toward a single son or daughter.

These changes do not mean that Chinese fathers have suddenly become interchangeable with Chinese mothers, who continue to display more patience and affection toward their children. Much of the traditional thinking remains, as illustrated by one anthropologist's recent observations of Chinese parents:

> *Whenever a child was with both parents, it was assumed and expected that the mother would perform all the necessary caretaking acts, the same acts she performed within the home. This is especially so if the child becomes cranky and starts to cry, a behavior that immediately activates the mother's involvement as it rapidly disengages the father's interest. During the summer [observations] I never saw a father, in a home or in public, holding a crying child in the presence of his wife.* (Jankowiak, 1992, p. 353)

Nevertheless, a new breed of fathers in China does appear to be emerging. Unfortunately, with change sometimes come problems. One ironic development is that Chinese schoolteachers are complaining that children are too spoiled and indulged by their parents. Although this trend was assumed to be the result of many parents' having only a single child, the research has not supported this idea (Falbo & Poston, 1993; Yang et al., 1995). Rather, it more likely can be attributed to modern fathers, who have largely abandoned their traditional role as strict disciplinarians and become more affectionate and permissive with their children.

The Role of Grandparents

In some families, grandparents play many important roles. They can be a source of emotional or financial support for the parents, and they can be mentors, playmates,

As boys reach adolescence, they often become closer to their grandfathers.

baby-sitters, or substitute parents for the grandchildren (Smith, 1995; Tinsley & Parke, 1988). The roles they play and the nature of their relationships with their children and grandchildren appear to depend in part on several factors (Clingempeel et al., 1992).

One such factor is the family structure. In families with two parents, grandparents tend to stay more in the background and have less direct involvement with the grandchildren. When one parent is absent, however, the role of grandparents generally increases and children similarly report an increased closeness to them. This trend is especially evident for grandfathers. If the lone parent remarries, however, grandparents tend to retreat once again to more distant roles.

Grandparents' involvement with their grandchildren also has been found to be related to the children's age and gender. At younger ages, boys and girls generally have equally close relations with their grandparents. But as the children reach puberty, boys tend to become closer to their grandparents, whereas girls become more distant, especially with their grandfathers. One proposed explanation for this difference is that puberty is a time of emotional stress that leads children to distance themselves somewhat from their parents and to seek support elsewhere (Anderson et al., 1989; Steinberg, 1988). Young males apparently seek out available grandparents to serve this function, whereas young females are more likely to seek support from their girlfriends.

The role of grandparents is not always positive, however. Several studies have examined the influence that a grandmother may have when the daughter is an adolescent with a new baby. Because teenage mothers are often poor and single, it is not uncommon for them to live with their own mothers. In these cases, the grandmother sometimes has the effect of interfering with the mother's becoming comfortable and effective in the parenting role. As a result, children in these situations are more likely to display behavioral problems and less likely to be securely attached (Spieker & Bensley, 1994; Unger & Cooley, 1992).

Abusive Parents

Although the family is typically a source of security and protection for the young child, sometimes it can be just the opposite. Child abuse is a tragic reality of some households, and it is a problem that may be growing (Emery & Laumann-Billings, 1998).

Abuse and neglect have major developmental consequences for growing children. By 1 year of age, maltreated infants tend to lag in both social and cognitive development, and these problems typically continue into childhood and adolescence (Trickett & McBride-Chang, 1995). Many developmental researchers believe that these deficits result from the lack of a secure attachment relationship with the mother. A great deal of recent research has focused on the attachment process in infants who have been abused or are at risk for abuse (Cicchetti & Carlson, 1989; Rogosch et al., 1995).

Sensitive and responsive caregiving growing out of mutual infant–caregiver regulation is thought to provide the basis for secure attachment. But, as noted, many abusive mothers fail to develop a smooth and effective communication system with their infants. Although babies will become attached even to mothers whose quality of caregiving is poor, the quality of the attachment relationship suffers. Perhaps for this reason, the insecure attachment patterns occur more frequently among maltreated infants (Carlson et al., 1989; Rogosch et al., 1995).

Some mothers maltreat their infants in ways that involve physical punishment, active hostility, and intrusiveness into the baby's world. Rather than synchronizing their behavior with that of the child, they often insensitively forge ahead with whatever they are doing (such as feeding a baby before she is hungry), focusing more on their own needs than on those of the infant. This caregiving style has been referred to as *overstimulating* and has been linked to physical abuse, such as beating and battering, and to the insecure–avoidant pattern of attachment (pattern A). In contrast, the insensitive care of some mothers takes the form of withdrawal and underinvolvement. This style, termed *understimulating*, has been associated with physical and emotional neglect and appears to be a cause of the insecure–resistant pattern of attachment (pattern C) (Belsky, Rovine, & Taylor, 1984; Lyons-Ruth, Connell, & Zoll, 1989).

Maltreated infants cannot always be classified according to Ainsworth's three original patterns because they often fail to display any coherent pattern of reactions to the Strange Situation. These infants frequently exhibit elements of each category, sometimes accompanied by bizarre responses, such as freezing, assuming unusual postures or expressions, and making interrupted or mistimed movements. Such behaviors, which are sometimes also seen in nonabused children, have led to a fourth classification, *disorganized and disoriented*, or pattern D (Main & Solomon, 1986, 1990). These children are especially at risk for developing aggression and antisocial behavior problems (Lyons-Ruth, Alpern, & Repacholi, 1993).

The conclusions that can be drawn from research on abused children support a transactional model of attachment (Crittenden & Ainsworth, 1989). Evolution has provided that babies will become attached even to caregivers who provide minimal or deviant care, but the interactions between these mothers and babies clearly affect the quality of the relationship that develops. This in turn, affects the child's later social, emotional, and cognitive development (van IJzendoorn et al., 1992).

✓ *To Recap...*

The family is the most important context in which early social development occurs. The traditional family has changed dramatically in recent years. Psychologists are interested in these changes as a way of validating previous conclusions regarding human development and also because they involve important societal issues.

One set of findings indicates that children's social behavior is influenced by the parents' style of child rearing. The dimensions of parental warmth and control produce four general styles of parenting. Authoritative parents produce the most independent and socially competent children and adolescents. Children of authoritarian, indifferent, or permissive parents often display social and behavioral problems. Parenting styles are influenced by parents' attitudes and beliefs, as well as by their recollections of their early attachment relationships.

A fairly new factor in early social development is the current trend for mothers to work outside the home. Some studies have found weaker attachment relationships between mothers and their infants who spend time in day care, but the meaning and import of these findings are not yet clear.

Infants can develop strong attachment relationships to their fathers, apparently based on the father's level of responsiveness. Even secure infant–father attachments, however, are not likely to be as strong as the infant–mother relationship.

Grandparents generally are most involved in children's lives when only a single parent is in the home. At puberty, boys tend to become closer to their grandparents, whereas girls tend to distance themselves. The presence of a grandmother can sometimes interfere with the parenting effectiveness of a single, adolescent daughter.

Child abuse can harm children's cognitive and social development. Infants form attachments to abusive mothers, but the attachment relationships are not secure. Children of mothers who use the overstimulating style of care tend to show the A pattern of attachment, and children of understimulating mothers show the C pattern. The D, or disoriented and disorganized, pattern often characterizes abused children.

Conclusion

We said at the beginning of the chapter that social development is a complex topic. By now, that should be very clear. But it is important to understand that this complexity is of two different types.

The first concerns social interactions themselves. Because these behaviors are transactional—with people continually affecting one another—it becomes difficult to separate the causes of social behaviors from their effects. Even in the infant–mother relationship, as we have seen, social influences can be subtle and highly interrelated. Identifying the determinants of the baby's and the mother's behavior thus can be a very challenging task.

The second reason this topic is so complex is that social development is affected by more than social influences. How the child interacts with other people is the result of biological processes, cognitive abilities, and nonsocial environmental factors—in addition to the influences of others in the child's world. Only recently have psychologists begun to appreciate the extent to which these nonsocial factors are involved in the development of social relationships, as we shall continue to see in later chapters.

In this chapter, we have focused on the attachment process and the developmental events that lead up to it. Other social relationships and processes also occur during infancy, and we consider those in the chapters that follow. In addition, we examine social development beyond the early years as the child grows away from the caregiver and the home to become a member of the larger society.

Visual Summary for Chapter 12:
Early Social and Emotional Development

Theories of Early Social Development

Theory	Explanation
Ethology	Babies are biologically programmed to produce behaviors that keep the mother close by and that encourage her to provide appropriate caregiving. The mother, in turn, is biologically predisposed to read and respond to the infant's signals.
Environmental/ Learning Approaches	Mother–infant attachment responses result from social-learning processes, with the infant and caregiver each providing consequences for the other's behavior.
Cognitive-Developmental Models	Some theorists contend that babies and mothers develop internal working models regarding each other's behavior. Vygotskian theorists hold that, through guided participation, parents and others assist infants in acquiring social skills and knowledge.

Mutual Regulation between Infants and Caregivers

Crying	Babies use different cries to communicate different messages. Caregivers, with experience, become more accurate at reading these messages.
Emotions and the Affective System	Babies begin to express relatively simple emotions within the first 2 months. Infants also begin to discriminate facial expressions within the first half-year of life, although their understanding of these expressions is not obvious until the second half-year.
Face-to-Face Interactions	Face-to-face interactions are the most common interactions of the first 3 or 4 months. As babies cycle between states of attention and inattention, mothers synchronize their own behavior to match these cycles.

Temperament

Types of Temperament	The NYLS identified three temperament types: the easy baby, the difficult baby, and the slow-to-warm-up baby. Plomin's EAS model defines temperament in terms of emotionality, activity, and sociability. Rothbart contends that temperament reflects the infant's reactivity and self-regulation.
Consequences of Temperament	Temperament may influence mother–child interactions through goodness-of-fit, the match between the infant's temperament and the physical and social environment. The quality of these interactions, in turn, can influence the child's cognitive development. Temperament may also be involved in children's later behavior problems and in how they react to stressful situations.

Attachment

Developmental Course of Attachment	*Infant–caregiver attachment develops in three stages. In the first stage, indiscriminate social responsiveness (birth–2 months), infants respond socially to almost anyone. In the second stage, discriminate social responsiveness (2–7 months), infants direct social responses principally to familiar people and develop a unique affective communication system with their caregiver. In the third stage, focused attachment (8–24 months), infants are wary of strangers, protest separation, and use the mother as a source of comfort and a secure base.*
Assessing Attachment	*Ainsworth's Strange Situation procedure is conducted in the laboratory and produces three patterns of responses: pattern A, or insecure–avoidant; pattern B, or securely attached; and pattern C, or insecure–resistant. The AQS procedure involves observing infants and their mothers in their home, and evaluating the nature and quality of the mother–baby relationship using the Q-sort method.*
Determinants and Consequences of Attachment	*The quality of the infant–caregiver attachment relationship appears to result primarily from the caregiver's responsiveness. The infant's temperament also plays a role, as does the mother's recollections of her own childhood. Secure attachment has positive cognitive and social effects on the child's development.*

Family Influences

Styles of Parenting	*Authoritative parents produce the most independent and socially competent children and adolescents. Children of authoritarian, indifferent, or permissive parents often display social and behavioral problems.*
The Role of Fathers	*Infants can develop strong attachment relationships to their fathers; however, even secure infant–father attachments are not likely to be as strong as the infant–mother relationship.*
The Role of Grandparents	*Grandparents generally are most involved in children's lives when only a single parent is in the home. At puberty, boys tend to become closer to their grandparents, whereas girls tend to distance themselves.*
Abusive Parents	*Infants form insecure attachments to abusive mothers. Children of mothers who are overstimulating tend to show the A pattern of attachment; those of understimulating mothers show the C pattern. The D, or disoriented and disorganized, pattern often characterizes abused children.*

Chapter 13

Development of the Self

Megan looks in the mirror, opens her mouth wide, and picks food from her teeth. After inspecting a spot on her eye, she begins to make faces at herself. These simple behaviors, crude as they may seem, are significant to the researchers who are studying Megan because they indicate that she recognizes herself in the mirror. They are even more significant because Megan is a chimpanzee.

Self-recognition may not seem very impressive until you realize how very rare it is in the animal kingdom. None of the mammals we usually consider intelligent—dogs, cats, and horses, for example—can recognize themselves in mirrors. Only our close phylogenetic relatives, chimpanzees and orangutans, show evidence of this ability, along with children beyond about 18 months of age.

What is the importance of these findings? Many scientists believe it means that only these few species possess a degree of self-awareness. That is, only these species appear to understand that they exist as individuals separate from the world around them.

That does not mean, however, that chimps and children are at the same level in this area. Humans, for example, not only display self-awareness but also have feelings about themselves, compare themselves with others, and control and manage themselves—abilities not observed in any other species.

In this chapter, we will see that, in fact, the self is a complex and wide-ranging topic. Only recently have developmental researchers even begun to understand when and how the self emerges in infancy. Today, many more questions and issues are under study in this fascinating area.

Existential self
The "I" component of the self, which is concerned with the subjective experience of existing.

Categorical self
The "Me" component of the self, which involves one's objective personal characteristics.

Self-system
The set of interrelated processes—self-knowledge, self-evaluation, and self-regulation—that make up the self.

Self-knowledge (self-awareness)
The part of the self-system concerned with children's knowledge about themselves.

*B*etween infancy and adolescence, as children learn about the physical and social world around them, they also seek answers to questions about themselves. Three such questions might be: What am I really like? How do I feel about myself? and Can I exert control over my life? We will see shortly that these questions in fact, represent the three aspects of the self on which developmental psychologists have focused a great deal of attention—self-knowledge, self-evaluation, and self-control (Bracken, 1996; Damon & Hart, 1992; Rochat, 1995).

Over the years, psychologists have conceptualized the self using several schemes. The more traditional view divides the self into two domains: the "I," or **existential self**, and the "Me," or **categorical self** (James, 1890; Lewis & Brooks-Gunn, 1979). The *I* refers to the *subjective* experience of existing, which includes a sense of personal identity, a sense of being able to do things (personal agency), and an awareness of one's continuing existence across time (Blasi & Glodis, 1995). The *Me* refers to a more *objective* understanding of one's personal characteristics, such as physical appearance, personality traits, and cognitive abilities (Lewis, 1994). As we will see, most modern theorists do not assume that the child's awareness of the self is innate. Rather, the I-self is thought to develop during the first months of life, and the Me-self to emerge sometime during the infant's second year (Harter, 1998; Lewis, 1995a).

A more recent classification scheme for studying the self is the **self-system** (Harter, 1983). This scheme holds that the self is embedded in a system of interrelated processes—some that affect it, others that are affected by it. The self-system has three components. The first is **self-knowledge** (also referred to as **self-aware-**

ness). What do children know about themselves and when do they acquire this knowledge? How is this knowledge related to their understanding of other aspects of their social and physical environment? A second component is **self-evaluation**. What factors influence children's opinions of themselves? How do these opinions affect their behavior? The third component is **self-regulation**. How and when do children acquire self-control? What variables influence this process?

Our coverage of the self in this chapter follows the self-system. Throughout the chapter, we also maintain our interest in the themes that have guided our discussions in other areas: what the three principal theoretical traditions have to say about this topic, how it looks from the nature and the nurture perspectives, and how researchers have investigated it.

Self-evaluation
The part of the self-system concerned with children's opinions of themselves and their abilities.

Self-regulation
The part of the self-system concerned with self-control.

Theories of the Self

The three components of the self-system cover a very broad range of topics and issues. Perhaps for this reason, none of the three major theories has attempted to explain all aspects of this complex area. In this section, we only briefly consider what each of the major theories has to say about the self. More theoretical ideas and models will be presented in later sections of the chapter.

Cognitive-Developmental Approaches

The concept of the self and its relation to other aspects of development have been of considerable interest to cognitive-developmental psychologists. Some researchers have studied the development of the self within the context of Piaget's stages of cognitive growth (discussed in Chapter 8). We consider their ideas later in the chapter. Other cognitive researchers have constructed separate models of the self. Here, we describe Selman's model, the information-processing model, and the Vygotskian approach.

Selman's Work on Self-Awareness   The most detailed account of children's self-awareness has been presented by Robert Selman (1980). In the tradition of other cognitive-developmental theorists (such as Piaget), the model was developed from extensive clinical interviews with children.

Selman presented children of various ages with brief stories in which the main character faces a conflict or dilemma. The children were then asked a series of questions regarding what the character was thinking and feeling and how the dilemma would be resolved. The focus was not so much on the children's solutions as on the type of reasoning they used to arrive at the solutions.

From his interview data, Selman developed a five-stage model of children's awareness of the self. The model includes some assumptions that are common to most stage theories. That is, the stages (1) follow a fixed sequence through which all children pass with no regression to earlier stages, (2) are consistent across different problems and situations, (3) are universal across cultures, and (4) develop as a result of changes in the child's cognitive abilities (Gurucharri & Selman, 1982).

The five stages can be summarized briefly as follows:

Level 0 (infancy): Children understand their physical existence but do not display an awareness of a separate psychological existence. The child does not, for example, distinguish between physical behavior (such as crying) and simultaneous emotional feelings (such as being sad).

Level 1 (early childhood): The child now separates psychological states from behavior and believes that thoughts can control actions. But the child also believes that inner thoughts and feelings are directly represented in outward appearance and behavior, so that someone's self can be known simply by observing the person's actions and statements (for example, that a person who is whistling and smiling *must* be happy).

Level 2 (middle childhood): The child appreciates that feelings and motives can be different from behavior and thus that the self can to some degree be hidden from others; it cannot, however, be hidden from oneself.

Level 3 (preadolescence): Children in later childhood show a growing belief that the self represents a stable component of personality. They believe that people can observe and evaluate their inner selves, suggesting that the mind (which does the observing) is somehow separate from the self (which is observed).

Level 4 (adolescence): Ultimately, the adolescent comes to believe that the self cannot ever be completely known because some aspects of personality remain at an unconscious level.

Here is one of the stories Selman used in developing his model:

The Puppy Story

Tom has just saved some money to buy Mike Hunter a birthday present. He and his friend Greg go downtown to try to decide what Mike will like. Tom tells Greg that Mike is sad these days because Mike's dog Pepper ran away. They see Mike and decide to try to find out what Mike wants without asking him right off. After talking to Mike for a while the kids realize that Mike is really sad because of his lost dog. When Greg suggests that he get a new dog, Mike says he can't just get a new dog and have things be the same. Then Mike leaves to run some errands. As Mike's friends shop some more they see a puppy for sale in the pet store. It is the last one left. The owner says that the puppy will probably be sold by tomorrow. Tom and Greg discuss whether to get Mike the puppy. Tom has to decide right away. What do you think Tom will do?

The questions Selman asked of the child listeners were designed to help classify each of them into one of the five stages, as you can see from the following examples:

If Mike is smiling, could he still be sad?

Could someone be happy on the outside, but sad on the inside?

Is it possible that Mike doesn't know how he feels?

Can you tell what kind of person someone is from a situation like this?

How does one get to know someone else's personality?

(Selman, 1980, pp. 318–319)

Selman's model is most concerned with children's knowledge and reasoning about the self. Like other cognitive-developmental theories, it has had little to say about children's actual behavior, such as self-regulation.

Information-Processing Model   In the view of psychologists who favor an information-processing model of cognitive development, the self-system is part of the larger memory system (Greenwald & Pratkanis, 1984; Lapsley & Quintana, 1985).

According to this model, each individual develops a **self-schema** of who she is. A self-schema is an internal self-portrait that includes the various features and characteristics we ascribe to our personalities. Self-schemas are constructed over time and serve primarily to organize self-related information. Whenever we encounter new events or information, then, we attempt to understand them in terms of these cognitive structures (Larsen, 1992; Markus, Cross, & Wurf, 1990).

Support for the existence of such structures is found in studies showing that people are better able to recall words and events that they can apply to themselves than to recall descriptors that do not seem to relate to them (Pullybank et al., 1985; Skowronski et al., 1995). For example, researchers wondered whether children's levels of self-esteem and depression would influence their memory for certain types of words. The words were presented one at a time. Half of them were followed by the question, "Is this word like you?" and the other half were followed by the question, "Is this a long word?" As the self-schema model would predict, all children later were better able to recall the words that they had been asked to relate to themselves.

A second variable involved the type of words that were presented. Half the words described positive personal traits (*brave, helpful,* and so on); the other half described negative personal traits (such as *lonely* and *ugly*). Again as predicted, children who were high in self-esteem and were not depressed showed better recall of the positive traits, whereas depressed children with low self-esteem showed better recall of the negative traits (Hammen & Zupan, 1984; Zupan, Hammen, & Jaenicke, 1987). Other studies have similarly shown that depression in children is linked to negative self-schemas (Gotlib & Hammen, 1992).

This research illustrates how powerfully children's self-schemas can influence the manner in which they relate to the world around them. Children whose self-esteem is high are apparently more attuned to information that is consistent with their positive view of themselves. They are likely, for example, to notice compliments, which, in turn, should further enhance their self-image. Children low in self-esteem, in contrast, are more aware of information that confirms their negative feelings and very likely serves to decrease them even more.

The Vygotskian Approach   Researchers working in the tradition of Vygotsky have also been interested in the self, with memory processes once again being viewed as very important for children's self-understanding. Recall that according to Vygotsky, children's cognitive abilities are acquired through social interaction and guided participation by parents, teachers, and other experienced adults. One of these abilities, discussed in Chapter 9, is *autobiographical memory*—children's memories of events and personal experiences in their past (Fivush, Haden, & Reese, 1996; Thompson et al., 1996). The development of this type of memory, perhaps not surprisingly, appears closely related to the development of children's knowledge about the self.

Children's ability to recall and recount the past is typically thought to result from conversational interactions with a parent, and it appears to develop across three stages (Fivush, 1994). Between the ages of 1 1/2 and 2 1/2 years, toddlers cannot yet tell stories about themselves without a parent or other adult directly guiding the narration and providing most of the content. A parent–child conversation at this age might go as follows:

> *Mother:* Do you remember when we went to Grandma's farm last summer?
> *Child:* Yup.
> *Mother:* And who else was there?
> *Child:* I don't know.

Self-schema
An internal cognitive portrait of the self used to organize information about the self.

> Mother: *Grandpa. Remember grandpa was there, too?*
> Child: *Yeah, Grandpa.*
> Mother: *And what was Grandma baking?*
> Child: *What?*
> Mother: *Pies. She was baking pies with apples and cherries from the farm.*
> Child: *Pies.*

Beginning at about age 2 1/2, children begin to *coconstruct* autobiographical narratives with the parent. Now the adult continues to guide the conversation, but the child contributes a fair amount of the content and, to some degree, the direction that the narrative takes. Two aspects of this process are important from the Vygotskian perspective. One is that, by being a major participant in the autobiographical memory process, the parent strongly influences how the past events are remembered and interpreted. The memories the child hears and recites are therefore more than just an objective account of what happened in the past; they undoubtedly also reflect the parent's own views and feelings about the child.

The second important aspect of this process is that different cultures structure their autobiographical narratives in different ways. Some are fairly objective, whereas others permit some amount of exaggeration and embellishment; some put the emphasis on the story's entertainment value, whereas others are concerned with teaching a lesson; some focus on a single topic, while others tend to recount a series of events or episodes (Gergen, 1994; Rogoff & Mistry, 1990).

By about age 4, the final stage, most children have internalized the structure of the narrative as it typically is presented in their culture. They also can now recount many personal experiences completely on their own and with a reasonable amount of detail.

Autobiographical memory is important to psychologists working in the Vygotskian tradition because they believe that children develop an understanding of who they are through the memories and stories they recount from their past. That is, children's view of the self is to a large degree defined by these coconstructed narratives about their personal experiences (Miller, 1994; Sperry & Sperry, 1995). Note, then, that because this process involves considerable input by the parent and the culture, the conception of the self that the child internalizes strongly reflects the context in which it develops—a characteristic common in the Vygotskian view of development.

Environmental/Learning Theories

Social-learning theorists have proposed a number of psychological processes that are relevant to the self. Two theoretical models have been developed by Albert Bandura, one involving self-evaluation, the other, self-regulation.

Self-efficacy
Bandura's term for people's ability to succeed at various tasks, as judged by the people themselves.

Bandura's self-evaluation model is built around the concept of **self-efficacy**, a person's ability, as judged by that person, to carry out various behaviors and acts (Bandura, 1997). Bandura observes that just as infants and young children do not understand the operations of the physical and social world very well, they do not know much about their own skills and abilities. Studies have shown, for example, that parents (and teachers) can predict how well children will perform on academic tasks much better than can children themselves (Miller & Davis, 1992; Stipek & MacIver, 1989). Similarly, in everyday situations parents must frequently warn children, for example, that they are swimming out too far, or that a particular library book will be too difficult for them to understand, or that they can never finish the largest ice cream sundae on the menu. Such verbal instructions from parents, along with many trial-and-error experiences, help young children gradually learn the limits of their talents and capabilities—that is, accurately judge their self-efficacy (Plumert, 1995).

As children grow, two other mechanisms promote the development of self-efficacy judgments. One is modeling, which children come to use as a way of estimating the likelihood of success at a task. For example, a child might reason, "If that little girl (who is my size and age) can jump over that fence, I can probably do it, too." Using vicarious experiences in this way obviously involves somewhat sophisticated cognitive abilities, in that the child must determine the appropriate models and situations for making comparisons.

Another way in which children learn to estimate their potential for success is through awareness of internal bodily reactions. For example, feelings of emotional arousal (e.g., tension, a nervous stomach, or a fast heart rate) frequently become associated with failures. Bandura believes that as a result, children begin to interpret these feelings as indications of fear, anxiety, or lack of confidence, and they learn to use them to decide that failure is close at hand. Again, using this type of information requires a fairly high level of cognitive processing and so is more common in older children (Bandura & Schunk, 1981; Schunk, 1983).

Self-efficacy judgments are important because they are believed to affect children's behavior significantly. Bandura contends, for example, that greater feelings of self-efficacy produce increased effort and persistence on a task and thus, ultimately, a higher level of performance. This concept is especially relevant in the area of children's academic achievement and how it relates to their self-evaluations—a topic we discuss later in the chapter.

Bandura also has proposed a theoretical mechanism to explain the development of self-regulation (Bandura, 1991a). Early on, children's behavior is only externally controlled, through such processes as modeling, consequences (reinforcement and punishment), and direct instruction. With experience, however, children learn to anticipate the reactions of others, and they use this knowledge to self-regulate their behavior. For example, as a child learns (through external processes) how the teacher expects her to behave in the classroom, she begins to monitor her behavior to conform to these expectations. Gradually, the child internalizes the rules, and they become her own personal standards. Now the child's behavior comes under the control of her **evaluative self-reactions**—that is, the child notes whether her behavior has met her personal standards and then applies *self-sanctions* in the form of self-approval ("I did well today") or self-disapproval ("I shouldn't have done that"). According to Bandura, self-regulation occurs as children become motivated to behave in ways that match their internal standards and that lead to feelings of self-satisfaction.

Ethological Theory

Classical ethologists have displayed the least interest in the self-system. Their focus on the entire range of species has tended to discourage their studying the self, which many scientists of this tradition believe is a concept unique to humans (Krebs, Denton, & Higgins, 1987).

Bowlby's writings on attachment, however, discussed his belief that the sense of self begins to develop within the context of infant–caregiver interactions and is promoted by responsive caregiving. These ideas have been elaborated by more recent developmental theorists (Bretherton, 1993; Cicchetti, 1991; Lewis, 1987b). For example, responsive caregiving leads to a more secure attachment between baby and mother, which in turn should affect the infant's development of an internal

According to Albert Bandura, children learn to self-regulate their behavior by internalizing the rules and standards of adults.

Evaluative self-reactions Bandura's term for consequences people apply to themselves as a result of meeting or failing to meet their personal standards.

working model of the self (as well as of the mother) (Bretherton, 1993; Pipp, 1990, 1993). Babies whose caregivers are sensitive and responsive should construct an internal model of the self as lovable and worthy of attention; babies whose caregivers are neglectful and insensitive should form models of the self as unworthy (Sroufe, 1990). We will see shortly that evidence from both normal and clinical populations of children provides support for these ideas.

✓ *To Recap...*

The self-system can be divided into three components: self-knowledge, self-evaluation, and self-regulation. Cognitive-developmental theorists have offered several models concerning self-development. Based on interviews with children, Selman proposed a five-stage model that begins with the infant's being unable to differentiate the physical and psychological selves and ends with the adolescent's believing that aspects of the self remain unconscious and unknowable. Information-processing theorists view the self as part of the larger memory system. Children are believed to construct self-schemas, which they use to organize information related to the self and which influence how they perceive and interact with the world. Researchers in the Vygotskian tradition believe that children's understanding of the self results from autobiographical memories that have been coconstructed with parents.

Social-learning theory has contributed two models of the self, both proposed by Bandura. Self-efficacy judgments are assumed to be inaccurate in early childhood but to improve gradually with the help of four processes: verbal instruction from parents and other adults, success and failure experiences, observation of relevant models, and monitoring of internal bodily reactions. Self-efficacy judgments appear to have important influences on children's behavior. Self-regulation is assumed to occur when children internalize standards they have acquired through external processes and then use evaluative self-reactions to keep their behavior consistent with these standards.

Ethologists have had the least to say regarding the self-system, but some have suggested that responsive caregiving and a secure attachment relationship may facilitate aspects of the child's self-development.

Self-Knowledge

Our look at the research evidence on the self-system begins with perhaps the most basic questions: What do children know about the self, and when do they know it? It is not uncommon to hear a toddler proudly announce that he is a big boy or that his name is Jeremy. But he may, as yet, have very little understanding of his physical characteristics (heavy or slight), his personality (shy or bold), or his living conditions (middle-class or poor). As we will see, children's self-knowledge develops steadily across the childhood years and is interwoven with the development of other cognitive and socialization processes.

Discovery of the Self in Infancy

When does a baby first understand that he exists separately from the surrounding world? This question has long been of interest in developmental psychology. Some researchers believe that babies have an inborn awareness of their existence or at least that awareness develops within the first weeks of life (Butterworth, 1995; Gibson, 1993; Samuels, 1986). Others argue that none of what babies do requires us to assume they have self-awareness prior to their first birthday (Kagan, 1991). Unfortunately, like many issues involving nonverbal infants, this one is not easily settled.

The Role of Perception Perceptual processes are thought to play an important role in infants' first coming to recognize their separateness (Butterworth, 1990, 1995; Neisser, 1993, 1995). For example, we have seen that within only weeks after birth, infants can imitate certain adult facial expressions. This finding has been interpreted to mean that newborns can connect sensory (visual) input with the corresponding motor responses—a capability that lays the groundwork for their realizing that they can interact with and affect the world around them (Meltzoff & Moore, 1995).

By 3 months of age, infants seem to perceive that they control their own body movements. One study had babies seated in an apparatus in which they could see live images of their legs transmitted on two television monitors in front of them. Different images—sometimes reversed or upside down—were presented on each TV, and it was clear from the babies' looking responses that they could easily detect when the timing or direction of the leg movements they viewed did not correspond to what they were doing (Rochat & Morgan, 1995). Similar research has reported the same findings with infants' arm movements (Schmuckler, 1995).

Studies of perception also have shown that in the months that follow the self becomes much more clearly defined. As we saw in Chapter 7, when 6-month-olds are taught to look for an object located in one position relative to themselves—say, to the left—and then are rotated to the opposite orientation—so that the object is to their right—they continue to search for the object by looking left. The addition of visual cues or landmarks to encourage more appropriate searching has little effect on babies of this age (Acredolo, 1985). This approach, of course, results in unsuccessful searching and gradually gives way to more effective, environmentally guided perceptual strategies as the baby approaches 1 year. But in using themselves as anchor points when searching, young infants demonstrate at least a crude awareness of their own separate existence.

Personal Agency Along with infants' knowledge that they exist apart from the things around them comes an understanding of **personal agency**—that is, an understanding that they can be the agents or causes of events that occur in their worlds. Now babies move toys and put things in their mouths and bang blocks, all suggesting an awareness both that they are separate from these things and that they can do something with them (Case, 1991; Connell & Wellborn, 1991).

Personal agency
The understanding that one can be the cause of events.

Personal agency also appears to develop through babies' early interactions with caregivers (Emde et al., 1991; Sroufe, 1990). Theorists from all three major traditions concur that when parents are more sensitive and responsive to their infants' signals, babies more quickly develop an understanding of the impact they can have on their environments (e.g., "I can make Mommy come by crying").

A related question has been whether babies first acquire an understanding of the self or of the mother. In one study, babies aged 6 months and older watched an adult model eat a Cheerio. They were then given one and instructed either to feed it to themselves or to feed it to their mothers. Significantly more babies at each age level were able to follow the first instruction than were able to follow the second (Pipp, Fischer, & Jennings, 1987).

These findings are consistent with others in showing that infants learn to direct actions or speech toward themselves before they direct those same responses toward their mothers or others (Bretherton & Beeghly, 1982; Huttenlocher, Smiley,

& Charney, 1983), suggesting that, with respect to agency, self-knowledge ("I can do it to me") precedes mother-knowledge ("I can do it to her"). This difference reverses by age 2 when toddlers are better able to direct actions toward their mothers and other objects than toward themselves. This change may result from older infants' becoming more self-conscious (Lewis, 1993, 1995b) and therefore less comfortable with directing actions toward themselves. Or it may reflect the child's increasing focus on interpersonal relations and newly emerging capacity for play (Pipp-Siegel & Foltz, 1997).

Mastery motivation
An inborn desire to affect or control one's environment.

A sense of personal agency gradually evolves into **mastery motivation** in the child (Jennings, 1991). The child begins to do things simply for the pleasure of observing the reactions they produce and for the satisfaction of accomplishing a goal. Recall from Chapter 8 that Piaget discussed the emergence of such behavior during the sensorimotor period. The level of a child's mastery motivation may also influence the child's cognitive development. For example, one study found that infants who were more persistent in trying to solve a challenging task also scored higher on measures of cognitive competence several years later (Messer et al., 1986). This relation corresponds with the belief that an early sense of mastery motivation is responsible for infants' first attempts to seek help from caregivers and others when trying to solve a problem (De Cooke & Brownell, 1995)—a process that Vygotskians believe leads to the important guided participation process discussed in Chapter 12.

Self-Recognition

As babies approach age 2, many display an increasing awareness of the self through their use of pronouns, such as *me* and *mine*, as well as the use of their own names—although at first these terms are not always used appropriately (Bates, 1990; Stipek, Gralinski, & Kopp, 1990). But the form of self-knowledge during this period that has attracted the most research is infants' ability to recognize what they look like.

Visual self-recognition
The ability to recognize oneself; often studied in babies by having them look into mirrors.

Visual Self-Recognition
A number of researchers have investigated the development of **visual self-recognition** by examining babies' reactions to mirror reflections. The major issue in this research concerns whether babies actually recognize the reflected images as themselves (Brooks-Gunn & Lewis, 1984; Loveland, 1986).

During their first year, babies will smile and vocalize at their mirror reflections (Fischer, 1980; Schulman & Kaplowitz, 1977). Whether babies this young realize that what they are seeing is themselves, however, is not known. They may be intrigued by the reflections simply because they can control them.

Infants' interest in controlling outcomes becomes more clearly evident as they move into the second year of life. This phenomenon was illustrated by a clever experiment in which a 14-month-old baby with a toy was seated across a table from two adults with identical toys. Whenever the baby moved or manipulated the toy, the two adults immediately responded—one imitating the baby's actions, the other performing a different action with the toy. The babies in the study smiled and looked longer at the adult who imitated them, indicating not only that they discriminated between the two behaviors, but also that they preferred the imitative to the nonimitative behavior (Meltzoff, 1990). These results suggest that infants' early interest in mirrors may be based on their understanding that what they do in front of the mirror and what they see in it are the same. But does this mean that they also understand that the infants in the mirrors are themselves?

To investigate this issue more specifically, psychologists have used an ingenious procedure. A colored mark is surreptitiously placed on the infant's face in a location where she could not normally see it, such as on her forehead. The baby is then placed before a mirror, and the investigators note whether she attempts to touch the mark. If she does, they conclude that she understands that the marked face in the mirror is her own. Using this measure, researchers have not found self-recognition in infants under 15 months of age; self-recognition does not occur reliably until about 24 months (Brooks-Gunn & Lewis, 1984; Bullock & Lutkenhaus, 1990).

Visual self-recognition has also been investigated with a variety of other techniques, including comparing infants' reactions to videotapes or photographs of themselves with their reactions to tapes or photos of similar peers (Bigelow, 1981; Johnson, 1983) and having infants point to pictures of themselves in a group after hearing their names (Bertenthal & Fischer, 1978; Damon & Hart, 1982). Evidence from these measures places self-recognition several months later than did the mirror-technique findings (Fischer, 1980).

When the marked-face type of procedure includes a delay, the age of self-recognition rises even further. One study had 2-, 3-, and 4-year-old children play a simple game, during which the experimenter frequently patted the child on the head and at some point surreptitiously placed a large sticker on the child's head. Shortly thereafter, the child was invited to watch a videotape of the game, which clearly showed the experimenter placing the sticker on the child's head. None of the 2-year-olds searched for the sticker on their own bodies; only the 4-year-olds did so consistently (Povinelli, 1995).

Regardless of the method used, self-recognition appears at different ages for different infants. What could be the source of these differences? One "nature" hypothesis is that self-recognition relates to temperament. Specifically, babies who react strongly in stress situations (and so are usually classified as difficult) are thought to develop a sense of self earlier than do other babies in order to deal better with the intensity of the stimulation they experience. Consistent with this idea, infants who react most strongly to vaccinations at 6 months of age also are most likely to show mirror self-recognition at 18 months of age (Lewis & Ramsey, 1997).

The age differences in the emergence of visual self-recognition have also been the subject of a "nurture" hypothesis—perhaps the appearance of self-recognition is affected by how much experience a baby has had with mirrors. This question was investigated in an interesting naturalistic study. Researchers compared infants from a nomadic desert culture in Israel, who had had no previous experience with mirrors or other reflective surfaces, with a matched group of Israeli children from a nearby city, again using the marked-face measure. The researchers found no self-recognition differences between the two groups (Priel & de Schonen, 1986), suggesting that experience with mirrors does not accelerate the appearance of visual self-recognition.

Other research, however, raises the possibility that babies do benefit from seeing themselves in mirrors. When infants as young as 3 months of age are shown still images of themselves and another baby, they exhibit a clear preference for looking at the other child, indicating not only that they can discriminate between the two images but that their own is familiar to them. The researchers suggest that early experience with mirrors perhaps plays some role in this process. By about 5 months of age, this procedure reveals another interesting finding. When the image a baby normally sees in a mirror is distorted (such as by placing colored marks on the cheeks of both babies), the looking preference changes, and infants spend more time looking at their own images. The results from these and related studies raise the possibility that visual self-recognition may actually occur earlier than psychologists have previously assumed (Bahrick, 1995; Legerstee, Anderson, & Schaffer, 1998).

Visual self-recognition has been the most commonly used method of assessing toddlers' self-awareness.

Self-Recognition in Maltreated Infants

Infants may differ also in their self-recognition as a result of the infant–caregiver relationship. As we indicated earlier, some psychologists believe that the infant first develops a concept of a separate self through mother–child interaction. And as mentioned in Chapter 12, a secure attachment to the caregiver promotes exploration and cognitive development in the baby. Thus we might predict that more securely attached infants would show greater self-recognition than would less securely attached infants of the same age.

Using the Strange Situation procedure (described in Chapter 12) as the measure of attachment and the marked-face technique as the measure of self-recognition, one research team compared the responses of infants who had been abused and neglected with those who had experienced more normal interactions with their caregivers. The maltreated infants were found to be less securely attached and displayed less evidence of self-recognition (Schneider-Rosen & Cicchetti, 1984, 1991). Moreover, the maltreated infants responded more negatively to their mirror reflections, which the researchers speculate may indicate the beginnings of a low sense of self-worth (Cicchetti et al., 1990).

Other research with abused children has found that their language is less likely to involve descriptions of themselves or of their internal states and feelings (Cicchetti, 1991; Coster et al., 1989). Recent studies with nonabused children have confirmed that those who are securely attached have a better understanding of both personal agency and physical characteristics than do children in other classifications (Pipp, Easterbrooks, & Harmon, 1992; Verschueren, Marcoen, & Schoefs, 1996). Thus, a secure attachment relationship appears to promote the development of the self.

Self-Recognition and the Awareness of Others

One result of infants' increasing awareness of their own identities may be a greater awareness of the separateness and distinctiveness of others. That is, as we become more self-aware, we should simultaneously become more other-aware. Evidence for children's developing appreciation of the existence and individuality of others is found in several sources.

One source involves *synchronic imitation,* in which two preverbal children play with similar toys in a similar fashion that involves coordinated action (Eckerman & Stein, 1990; Nadel & Fontaine, 1989). To synchronize his play with that of a peer, a child must have some understanding of the other child's intentions and behavior. This type of play would thus seem to require some degree of self- and other-awareness. Consistent with this view, 18-month-olds who give evidence of mirror self-recognition display more synchronic imitation with same-age peers (and also with adults) than do infants who do not recognize themselves in the mirror (Asendorpf & Baudonniere, 1993; Asendorpf, Warkentin, & Baudonniere, 1996).

Other-awareness has also been demonstrated by young children's reactions to another person's distress. If the emergence of the self leads to an increased understanding of the separate feelings of others, we might expect this to be reflected in greater concern for someone in pain or discomfort. This prediction, too, has been supported. Research has shown that 2-year-olds who display mirror self-recognition are more likely than others to help someone in distress (Zahn-Waxler et al., 1992).

Developmental Changes in Self-Descriptions

Psychologists have typically assessed older children's self-knowledge by examining their descriptions of themselves. This method has taken various forms, ranging from very unstructured interviews, which might include such general questions as "Who are you?" to very structured questionnaires, which might require answers to such written items as "How old are you?" and "What is your favorite outdoor game?" Regardless of the method used, researchers have found a relatively predictable pattern of development (Damon & Hart, 1992; Harter, 1998).

By the age of 2, many children display knowledge of some of their most basic characteristics. For example, they know whether they are girls or boys and that they are children rather than adults (Harter, 1988; M. Lewis, 1981). These category labels are undoubtedly learned through modeling and other learning processes, as children repeatedly hear themselves referred to with phrases such as "my little boy" or as they receive approval when they correctly state their age or other personal characteristic. But as we will see, cognitive development also plays a role in the self-discovery process.

In the preschool years, as shown in Table 13.1, self-descriptions usually involve physical features, possessions, and preferences (Case, 1992; Hart & Damon, 1985). Thus a 4-year-old might say that she lives in a big house, has a dog, and likes ice cream. This information, however, is not always completely accurate, and children's descriptions are often unrealistically positive. During this period there is a focus on objective, here-and-now attributes—a finding that corresponds well with Piaget's description of preoperational children's view of the world.

But it is incorrect to assume, as some psychologists have, that children of this age can comprehend only specific characteristics of themselves and do not understand more general traits, such as being messy or having a big appetite. The self-description a young child offers seems to depend heavily on how the information is sought. Children give more general responses when questions are structured to encourage generality ("Tell me how you are at school with your friends") than when questions seek more specific information ("Tell me what you did at school with friends today") (Eder, 1989, 1990).

In middle childhood, self-descriptions change in several ways, reflecting the shift to concrete operational abilities (Harter, 1994; Markus & Nurius, 1984). Rather than limiting their statements to the here and now and the physical, 6- to 10-year-olds begin to talk about less tangible characteristics such as emotions ("Sometimes I feel sad"), and to combine separate attributes (good at climbing, jumping, and running) into an overall category ("I'm a good athlete"). The accuracy of children's information also improves during this period, although they gen-

Table 13.1

Children's Self-Descriptions during Three Age Periods

Age Period	Piagetian Stage	Focus of Self-Descriptions	Examples
Early childhood	Preoperational	Physical characteristics, possessions, preferences	"I have freckles" "My cat is white" "I like pizza"
Middle and later childhood	Concrete Operations	Behavioral traits and abilities, emotions, category membership	"I'm a good singer" "I'm a happy kid" "I'm a cheerleader"
Adolescence	Formal Operations	Attitudes, personality attributes (sometimes opposing or associated with different roles), beliefs	"I'm patriotic" "I can be persuasive" "I support gun control"

erally continue to stress their positive, rather than negative, characteristics (Phillips & Zimmerman, 1990; Ruble & Dweck, 1995). During this time children begin to internalize the opinions of others and to relate them to their own conceptions of the self, resulting in the earliest instances of self-regulation (discussed shortly) (Harter, 1998; Higgins, 1991).

In later childhood, descriptions may be based on social comparisons with others, as children evaluate their skills or talents relative to those of friends or classmates ("I'm the best skater on the street") (Moretti & Higgins, 1990; Ruble & Frey, 1991). Children also can include opposing attributes, such as "I'm good at spelling, but bad at math," in their descriptions. But the earlier tendency to stress positive attributes now sometimes gives way to more intense negative self-evaluations and more general feelings of low self-worth (Harter, 1998).

As children enter adolescence, their self-descriptions continue to change (Harter & Monsour, 1992). The formal operational child thinks and self-describes in more abstract and hypothetical terms. Rather than focusing on physical characteristics and possessions (as in early childhood) or on behavioral traits and abilities (as in middle and later childhood), the adolescent is concerned with attitudes ("I hate chemistry"), personality attributes ("I'm a curious person"), and beliefs involving hypothetical situations ("If I meet someone who has a different idea about something, I try to be tolerant of it") (Hart & Fegley, 1995; Rosenberg, 1986b).

By middle adolescence, the self typically differentiates into more roles. For example, adolescents give different responses when asked to describe themselves in the classroom, at home, and with friends. Sometimes these differences involve opposing or conflicting attributes, such as being shy in the classroom but outgoing with friends which, for the first time, produce feelings of confusion and distress (Harter & Monsour, 1992).

Later in adolescence, these opposing characteristics are often combined into single personality styles ("cheerful" and "sad" are combined into "moody"), and this more complex view of the self comes to be viewed as legitimate and normal (Harter, 1997). Adolescents now can display **false self behavior**, meaning that, when necessary, they can purposely behave ("act") in ways that do not reflect their true selves (Harter et al., 1996). The limits of self-development are not yet known, but the self apparently continues to differentiate throughout adolescence and adulthood (Block & Robins, 1993; Hart & Yates, 1996).

False self behavior
Behaving in a way that is knowingly different from how one's true self would behave.

Development in Cultural Context
Self-Understanding among Exceptional Inner-City Adolescents

Children growing up in the poverty and chaos of some inner-city neighborhoods typically spend much of their energy dealing with such issues as crime, drugs, and AIDS. In light of the high drop-out rates often found in these urban neighborhoods, it might be considered a success for a child simply to complete high school. But for teenagers reared in these stressful conditions to become outstanding citizens, devoted to the care and service of those less fortunate than themselves, would truly be extraordinary.

A recent study investigated a group of adolescents who did just that (Hart & Fegley, 1995; Hart et al., 1995). The research took place in Camden, New Jersey, a city that by some accounts is the poorest in the United States (Kozol, 1991). The first goal of the investigators was to identify a group of adolescents who had in some way demonstrated an exceptional level of caring, compassion, and willingness to help those in need. Community leaders in schools, churches, and civic organizations were asked to nominate such individuals and ultimately 15 African-American and Latino adolescents were selected for study. These adolescents were labeled *care exemplars.* For the purpose of comparison, a control group of 15 other youths were matched to the first group in terms of age, sex, ethnicity, and local neighborhood.

The principal question of the research was, "What is different about the way the care exemplars think about themselves that leads to, or supports, their unusual behavior?" (Hart & Fegley, 1997, p. 139). To address this question, each adolescent was interviewed extensively across four to six sessions. The sessions included open-ended interview questions, such as, "What kind of person are you?" and "What kind of goals do you have for yourself?" as well as more specific questions contained in an instrument called the Self-Understanding Interview (Damon & Hart, 1988).

The investigators found that as expected, the conceptions of the self held by the care exemplars were quite different from those of the adolescents in the control group. For example, the care exemplars described themselves using more positive, caring personality traits, and their goals were more likely to be of a moral nature. This group perceived the self as having greater stability and continuity across time than did the controls. They also were more likely to believe that their actual self was closely related to their ideal, or wished-for, self. Finally, the care exemplars usually described their *theory of the self* as involving their personal beliefs and philosophies, whereas the control adolescents' theories more often stressed acceptance by their social network of friends.

What is fascinating about this remarkable group of teenagers is that, despite the hardships and struggles they faced in their everyday lives, they nevertheless directed their time and energies toward others in need of their help. If the researchers are correct, it was the way in which the exemplars viewed themselves that prompted these altruistic activities. But, of course, the other intriguing possibility is that it was, instead, the charitable activities that fostered these very different conceptions of the self.

✓ To Recap...

Children's knowledge about the self increases steadily through childhood. It is not yet known whether babies are born with any understanding of the self. Perceptual processes, such as those involved in neonatal imitation and early space perception, likely play an important role in early self-development. During the second half of the first year, babies begin to display a sense of personal agency by acting on toys and other objects in their environments. A sense of agency evolves into mastery motivation, as infants begin to engage in activities simply for the sake of mastering them.

As infants approach the end of their second year, they begin to show recognition of themselves. Research with mirrors, videotapes, and photographs indicates reliable self-recognition by about 2 years of age. The development of self-recognition may occur earlier in babies with difficult temperaments but does not appear to be related to experience with mirrors. Research with maltreated infants suggests that self-recognition is influenced by the security of the infant–caregiver attachment.

Increases in self-awareness are accompanied by increases in other-awareness. Infants who display self-recognition are also more likely to engage in synchronic imitation and to help someone in distress.

Self-knowledge in children beyond the infant years has been assessed principally through examination of their self-descriptions. Self-descriptions by preschoolers reflect preoperational thinking and typically include references only to objective, here-and-now characteristics. In middle childhood, the concrete operational child focuses to a greater degree on nontangible characteristics, such as emotions, and on membership in various categories. Adolescents' formal operational abilities lead to more abstract and hypothetical self-descriptions, concerned often with attitudes, personality characteristics, and personal beliefs, sometimes involving conflicting attributes.

Self-Evaluation

As children grow, they not only come to understand more about themselves, but they also begin to evaluate this information. Social involvements, as in school or on athletic teams, encourage children to compare themselves with other children and also with their images of who they would like to be. Such self-evaluations usually bring both good news and bad, as children come to recognize their strengths and weaknesses and their positive and negative attributes. Self-evaluation, like self-knowledge, develops as children grow, and is influenced by both cognitive and socialization variables (Ruble et al., 1990).

Measuring Self-Esteem

Self-esteem (self-worth)
A person's evaluation of the self, and the affective reactions to that evaluation.

Looking-glass self
The conception of the self based on how one thinks others see him or her.

Competence
Self-evaluation that includes both what one would like to achieve and one's confidence in being able to achieve it.

The opinions children develop about themselves have been referred to as their **self-esteem**, or **self-worth** (Harter, 1985a, 1987). Self-esteem is assumed to include not only children's cognitive judgments of their abilities, but also their affective reactions (pride, shame, etc.) to these self-evaluations.

This concept is not new. Two traditional views of self-esteem have long been part of the developmental literature. According to the **looking-glass self** (Cooley, 1902), the psychological portraits we paint of ourselves are based on how we think others see us. That is, we view other people's reactions to us as "reflections" of who we are. The **competence** view of the self (James, 1892) holds that our level of self-esteem results from a combination of what we would like to achieve and how confident we feel about achieving it—an idea very similar to the more recent concept of self-efficacy (Harter, 1988; Novick, Cauce, & Grove, 1996).

Methods   The most common method of assessing children's self-esteem has been through questionnaires. Typically, such instruments present children with a list of questions designed to tap their opinions of themselves in a variety of situations or contexts (such as, "Are you usually willing to help when a friend needs a favor?" and "Do you think you are artistic?"). The responses to these questions can be combined and analyzed to produce an overall score that represents the child's level of self-esteem (Keith & Bracken, 1996).

Attempts to capture self-esteem in a single score, however, have met with the same problems as attempts to describe children's intelligence with a single IQ score. Intuitively, it seems unlikely that children would evaluate themselves similarly in all areas—academics, appearance, athletics, and so on. And research has demonstrated that evaluations across different areas are usually not consistent (Harter, 1985a; Rosenberg, 1986a).

An alternative to the single-score method is to divide children's lives conceptually into a number of domains (social skills, physical skills, and so on) and then to assess children's self-evaluations separately in each. The results are then reported as a profile across the various domains. We consider an example of this approach next.

Harter's Self-Perception Profile for Children   Susan Harter has developed a popular instrument for measuring children's self-esteem. The *Self-Perception Profile for Children* (Harter, 1985b) is a questionnaire designed for children ages 8 and older that assesses their opinions of their overall worth as well as their self-evaluations in five separate domains: scholastic competence, athletic competence, social acceptance, behavioral conduct, and physical appearance.

Each item on the questionnaire presents two related statements, one describing a competent child and the other a less competent child. A child completing the instrument selects the statement that best describes him and then marks the box indicating whether the statement is "really true for me" or "sort of true for me." Figure 13.1 shows sample items from the scholastic competence area and the domain of behavioral conduct.

Children respond to six items in each of the six areas, and their scores are used to construct a profile of their self-esteem. The sample profiles depict one child (A) who has a relatively consistent view of her competence across the five domains and

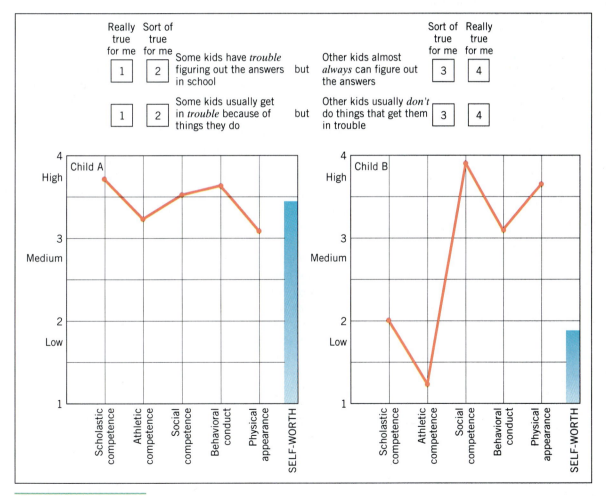

Figure 13.1

Two sample items from the Self-Perception Profile and examples of the scoring profiles from two children.

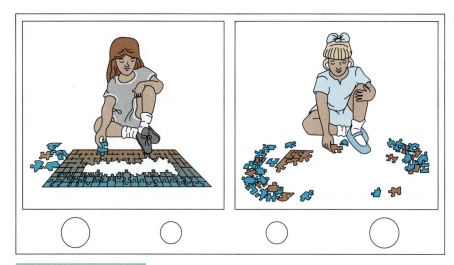

Figure 13.2
A sample item from the version of the Self-Perception Profile used with younger children.

whose self-worth is very high. The other child (B) has self-evaluations that vary considerably among the five areas and a low level of global self-worth.

The scores for self-worth do not simply reflect a composite of the child's other five scores. Harter has explained this by examining the degree to which children's global self-worth is influenced by the two traditional models just described.

To assess the looking-glass self, she constructed additional items that asked children to rate how they believed other people felt about them. Consistent with that model, youngsters who felt others had high regard for them also rated themselves high on the self-worth items. To examine the competence view of the self, she asked children to rate how important each of the five areas was to them. In support of this model, children who rated themselves as very competent in areas they felt were important also had high self-worth scores (Harter, 1986). Harter concluded from her research that older children's feelings of self-esteem are based on *both* how they believe others evaluate them and how they evaluate themselves (Harter, 1988, 1990).

For children between the ages of 4 and 7, Harter modified the instrument into the *Pictorial Scale of Perceived Competence and Social Acceptance*, as shown in Figure 13.2 (Harter & Pike, 1984). Its items consist of pictures—for example, a girl who is good at puzzles (*left*) and a girl who is not good at puzzles (*right*). The child points to the circle indicating whether a picture is a little like her (small circle) or a lot like her (large circle). Because children below age 8 cannot form an overall judgment of their self-worth, only the five individual areas are assessed.

This scale has been used widely to assess children's self-evaluations in early-childhood education and intervention programs. Some evidence suggests, however, that it may not be well suited for some minority populations, such as children in urban Head Start programs (Fantuzzo et al., 1996).

The Stability of Self-Esteem

The results of many studies give a relatively clear picture of the development of self-esteem across the childhood years. Children under about 8 years of age do not have a well-developed sense of overall self-worth (Harter, 1988). We do know, however, that kindergartners' self-esteem scores tend to be reasonably high and related to a secure attachment to the caregiver (Cassidy, 1988) and a general optimism about the future (Fischer & Leitenberg, 1986). During middle and later childhood, self-esteem scores are generally stable, with perhaps a small trend toward improvement (Cairns & Cairns, 1988; Dunn, 1994). But the transition to adolescence often poses problems. Many investigators have found that at about age 11 or 12, self-esteem scores dip, only to increase again during the high-school years (Harter, 1990; Nottleman, 1987; Wigfield et al., 1991).

One factor that may play a role in this temporary deterioration of self-esteem is the child's level of **self-consciousness**, or concern about the opinions of others (Tangney & Fischer, 1995). Cognitive-developmentalists suggest that this tendency increases with the emergence of formal operational abilities. At this stage, children become so much better at taking the perspective of others that they develop a pre-occupation with how other people regard their appearance, behavior, and so forth (Elkind, 1980; Hart, 1988a). The increased self-consciousness leads to more critical self-evaluations, which in turn lower self-esteem (Adams, Abraham, & Markstrom, 1987; Rosenberg, 1985). This process appears to be especially true of girls, who display both greater self-consciousness (Gray & Hudson, 1984) and lower self-esteem (Block & Robins, 1993) during this period than do boys.

Self-consciousness
A concern about the opinions others hold about one.

The dip in self-worth among early adolescents may also be caused, in part, by the biological changes associated with puberty. Some researchers have suggested that pubertal changes produce physical and psychological stress in children that leads to depression and other negative emotional states (Simmons & Blyth, 1987).

An environmental variable that has been found to contribute to the drop in self-esteem involves whether children remain in their own school during this period or move to a new one following sixth grade. Several studies report that moving to a new school usually produces a noticeable decline in self-esteem scores, especially if the new school is large and ethnically diverse (Blyth, Simmons, & Carlton-Ford, 1983; Simmons, Carlton-Ford, & Blyth, 1987). Children who remain in the same school show no such change (Rosenberg, 1986b). We consider the role that changing schools plays in academic problems in a later section.

Conformity to peer pressure during adolescence may result from an increase in self-consciousness and a dip in self-esteem

Academic Self-Concept

Academic self-concept
The part of self-esteem involving children's perceptions of their academic abilities.

The factors affecting self-esteem have also been investigated in the classroom, especially with regard to children's perceptions of their academic competence, or **academic self-concept** (Byrne, 1996; Marsh, 1993; Stipek, 1992).

Age and Gender Differences   Prior to entering school, children have no basis for an academic self-concept. Some research has examined the reactions of infants and preschoolers to other sorts of achievement tasks, however, and has found that a developmental progression does exist (Stipek, Recchia, & McClintic, 1992). Infants, for example, have little understanding of success and failure and so do not behave in ways that give any evidence of self-evaluation. However, even before the age of 2, children begin to show that they anticipate how adults will react to their (often small) achievements, such as when they look up for approval after making a stack of blocks. They also express delight at their successes and display negative reactions to their failures. By age 3, most children prefer to engage in activities at which they win rather than lose.

Children's academic self-concept generally is highest in kindergarten and steadily declines through at least fourth grade. This trend has been noted in children's spontaneous classroom comments to other students (Ruble & Frey, 1987), in their statements during interviews (Benenson & Dweck, 1986), and in their responses to questionnaires (Butler, 1990; Eccles et al., 1993a). One cause of this decline may be as simple as the fact that older children realize that bragging is not socially appropriate and so increasingly avoid giving glowing descriptions of their abilities (Ruble & Frey, 1987).

During this period, boys express more self-competence in sports and mathematics, whereas girls are more positive regarding their abilities in reading and music (Eccles, Wigfield, et al., 1993; Frey & Ruble, 1987). Girls, however, tend to base their academic self-image largely on classroom conduct and much less on academic achievement. The reverse is true for boys (Entwistle et al., 1987). This gender difference is not completely understood, but it may be related to the different ways in which teachers respond to boys and girls, as we will see shortly.

Development in Family Context
Children's Self-Evaluations in Single-Parent Families

Millions of children, many of them living in poverty, grow up in families in which the mother is the only parent. This social context would appear to put children at risk for problems in development and adjustment (L. W. Hoffman, 1984, 1989). For this reason, psychologists have been interested in determining whether being raised in a mother-headed household affects children's evaluations of their personal and academic competence. As it turns out, a crucial factor is whether the mother is employed.

In one study, inner-city children in Philadelphia were given Harter's Self-Perception Profile (Alessandri, 1992). All the children lived in single-parent households and had been raised from birth by their mothers alone. For one-third of the subjects, the mother was employed full-time; for another third, she worked part-time; and for the final third, she stayed at home and received public assistance. The three groups of mothers did not differ in age, ethnic background, or education.

Children whose mothers worked either full- or part-time had more favorable self-perceptions of global self-worth than did children whose mothers stayed at home. Mothers who worked appeared to be especially good role models for their daughters; the researchers also found that these girls evaluated themselves significantly higher in scholastic competence than did the girls whose mothers were unemployed. Moreover, school records showed the academic achievement of daughters of working mothers to be higher than that of any other children in the study.

Finally, the researchers examined how mothers described their children's characteristics, as well as how children described their own characteristics. Families with working mothers were found to show a better correspondence between the mothers' descriptions and the children's self-descriptions; this was especially true for mothers and daughters. This finding suggests that these families were more in tune with one another and shared more similar beliefs and expectations.

It seems, then, that when single mothers play the dual roles of wage earner and parent, their children's development does not necessarily suffer. Inconveniences that result from mothers' work schedules (such as difficulty scheduling meals and transportation problems) appear to be compensated for by children's greater self-esteem and, in the case of girls, by higher academic self-concept and achievement.

When mothers play the roles of both wage-earner and parent, their children's development does not necessarily suffer.

Dweck's Motivational Model of Achievement

Children's academic self-concept, of course, derives mainly from their academic performance. Those who do well in school are likely to develop high opinions of their competence, whereas poor performers are likely to develop low opinions. How well a child performs in school depends partly on his academic abilities and partly on the amount of effort and motivation the child puts forth.

Based on over 20 years of research, Carol Dweck and her colleagues have developed a theoretical model that attempts to explain the complex role that motivation plays in children's academic success (Burhans & Dweck, 1995). The model focuses on two patterns of motivation that have been observed in both younger and older children and that are reflected in their affect, cognitions, and behavior.

Children in achievement situations generally react to failure experiences in one of two ways (Diener & Dweck, 1978, 1980). Some children display a *mastery-oriented* pattern. Despite having just failed at a task or problem, these children retain a positive mood and express high expectations for success on future attempts. As a result, they tend to persist at the task and they seek out similar challenging problems. This motivational pattern usually leads to improved academic performance over time.

Other children, however, display a *helpless* pattern. When they encounter failure, their affect conveys sadness or disappointment, and they express doubt that they can ever succeed at the task. These children show little persistence on the activity and tend to avoid similar challenges in the future. Academic performance in these children often remains considerably below what it could be. What could produce these very different responses to failure?

Dweck's model proposes that at the heart of the problem are children's feelings of self-worth. Children who develop the helpless pattern typically believe that their self-worth depends on the approval and positive judgments of others. As a way of validating their self-worth, they seek out situations in which success involves receiving such approval. If the situation instead produces failure, these children view the absence of approval as a blow to their "goodness" as a person (self-worth), which then leads to the helpless pattern of negative affect, low expectations for future success, low persistence, and avoidance of similar situations.

In contrast, children who develop the mastery-oriented pattern do not believe that their self-worth depends on the opinions of others. They tend to seek out situations in which, whether successful or not, they will learn from their experiences. When these children fail, therefore, they view it simply as an opportunity to improve their ability on the task, and so display the opposite pattern of affect, expectations, and persistence.

This portion of the model can account for the development of the motivational patterns observed in younger children. Support for it comes from several studies in which 4- and 5-year-olds were asked to solve a number of puzzles, only one of which could actually be solved. When later given the opportunity to play with any one of the puzzles again, children who chose the solved puzzle (nonpersisters) also displayed negative affect toward the task and expressed lower expectations for success on another task. Children who chose to persist on one of the unsolved puzzles showed the more positive pattern of reactions (Dweck, 1991; Smiley & Dweck, 1994).

In older children, the model becomes more complex. Beyond 10 years of age or so, children's cognitive abilities permit them to develop certain self-conceptions (Dweck & Leggett, 1988). One of these is a "theory of intelligence." Some children come to believe in an *entity* model, in which the amount of a person's intelligence is fixed and unchangeable. Others subscribe to an *incremental* model, in which a person's intelligence can grow with experience and learning. A second self-conception involves children's "attributions for success or failure." Some children believe that success or failure results primarily from the amount of *ability* a person has; other children believe it depends on the amount of *effort* a person applies to a task.

Children who develop the helpless pattern, as we might expect, generally believe that the amount of their intelligence is fixed (entity model) and that their lack of success derives from a lack of ability. These two beliefs combine to give the child little reason for optimism in the face of failure—after all, ability is unchangeable and the child simply has too little of it. Predictably, then, these children feel helpless and hopeless. A very different outlook, however, results from the two opposite beliefs, which are generally held by mastery-oriented children. If intelligence can grow (incremental model) and success depends largely on one's effort, then failure experiences need not lead to feelings of despair or pessimism. These children believe they can do better next time simply by trying harder.

Research has likewise supported this portion of the model. For example, one study found that fifth-grade children who displayed elements of the helpless pattern (nonpersistence and low expectations for future success) following failure on a task were more likely to hold the entity view of intelligence, whereas children displaying the mastery-oriented pattern tended to believe in the incremental view (Cain & Dweck, 1995). Evidence supporting the effects of different attributions for success and failure derives from an early finding that the helpless pattern is more common in girls (Dweck & Gilliard, 1975; Dweck & Reppucci, 1973). This gender difference was subsequently shown to involve the way in which teachers typically provided feedback to boys and girls. When boys failed, they were more often told that they did not try hard enough (indicating a lack of effort); when girls failed, they usually were told simply that they had the wrong answers (implying a lack of ability) (Dweck & Goetz, 1980; Dweck et al., 1978).

Because all children sometimes fail, all receive such feedback, and all can thus be influenced by it. In general, then, girls may eventually come to believe that their

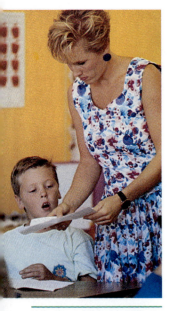

Whether children attribute failure to effort or ability can strongly affect their academic self-concept.

abilities are inadequate ("I failed because I'm lousy at math") and therefore approach new tasks in a pessimistic manner, whereas boys may continue to assume that their failures result from too little effort ("I could have done better if I had studied harder") and so remain motivated in the face of new challenges. Fortunately, feelings of helplessness based on these sorts of attributions have been shown to be treatable, such as by training teachers to provide feedback in more appropriate ways (Dweck et al., 1978), or by retraining helpless children to attribute their failures to effort rather than to ability (Dweck, 1975).

The Role of Social Comparisons   We have seen that academic self-image is affected by children's academic performance and by the types of attributions they make regarding failure. But the general decline over the elementary grades in children's self-evaluations of competence may involve yet another factor.

Children, like adults, evaluate their abilities at least partly by comparing them with those of others—a process called **social comparison** (Suls & Wills, 1991). This process begins as early as kindergarten, but its function changes with age (Pomerantz et al., 1995; Stipek, 1992).

Social comparison
Comparing one's abilities to those of others.

Kindergartners use what their classmates are doing or saying primarily as a way of making friends or learning how things are done. For example, a child may comment to a classmate that they are coloring on the same page of their books. Social comparisons, at this point, do not appear to have much impact on the child's self-image (Aboud, 1985; Stipek & Tannatt, 1984). As children proceed through the early grades, however, their social comparisons increasingly involve academic performance, and they begin to use the comparisons to evaluate their own competence relative to others (Butler, 1992; Pomerantz et al., 1995).

By second grade, children's spontaneous self-evaluative remarks become positively correlated with the number of social comparisons they make; that is, children with lower opinions of their competence make fewer social comparisons (Ruble & Frey, 1991). Why? One interpretation of this finding is that in continually comparing their performance with that of peers, many children unhappily discover that their work is not as good as they had believed. A child who once found great pleasure in drawing may discover that his artwork is not as attractive as that of his classmates. As a result, he may lower his opinion of his drawings but also begin to avoid comparing his work with that of other children. If this interpretation is correct, we would expect academically successful children to seek out more information about their performance than children who are lower achievers. And research has found just that: high-achieving students show more interest in comparing their perfor-

Children's willingness to make social comparisons is related to their academic competence.

mance with that of classmates and also in discovering the correct answers to problems (Ruble & Flett, 1988).

This developmental change in the use of social comparisons is not inevitable, however, and can be influenced by the atmosphere of the educational environment. For example, in Israel the communal kibbutz environment places more emphasis on cooperative than on competitive learning and fosters concern with mastering skills rather than with surpassing others. As a result, even older children in the kibbutz environment have been found to use social comparison primarily as a means of acquiring new abilities and much less for self-evaluation (Butler & Ruzany, 1993).

The relation between social comparison and academic self-concept, then, is bidirectional. Social comparisons can affect children's self-image by giving them information about how they are performing relative to other children. But children's self-image may affect their willingness to engage in social comparisons, depending on how pleasant or unpleasant they expect the resulting information to be (Pomerantz et al., 1995).

Parenting Styles   Children's academic self-concept is also affected by the attitudes, expectations, and behaviors of their parents. Studies have shown that parents' perceptions of their children's academic abilities are one of the best predictors of the children's self-perceptions of ability (Lamborn et al., 1991; Oosterwegel & Oppenheimer, 1993; Phillips & Zimmerman, 1990). And, as we will see in Chapter 15, parents generally hold higher opinions and expect greater achievements of their sons than of their daughters (Phillips, 1987; Phillips & Zimmerman, 1990).

How do such expectations produce their effects on children's self-perceptions? One likely possibility lies in the way in which parents interact with children on academic tasks. For example, we know that parents who display an authoritative style of discipline and child rearing tend to use more scaffolding techniques when working with their children (Pratt et al., 1988), and that these children, in turn, tend to be more cognitively competent (Baumrind, 1989, 1991).

To determine whether differences in parents' interaction styles also influence academic self-concept, researchers in one study observed academically successful students working on several tasks with either their mothers or their fathers (Wagner & Phillips, 1992). The children were divided into those whose academic self-concepts were high and those whose academic self-concepts were low. No differences in interaction style were found among the mothers of these two groups; however, marked differences were found among the fathers. The fathers of children with high academic self-concept were warmer and more supportive in their interactions than were the fathers of the other children. This finding is consistent with other research in which college students recalled that continuing support from their fathers was instrumental in their success in school (Schaffer & Blatt, 1990).

Effects of Academic Self-Concept   Children's perception of their academic competence has perhaps been of such interest to psychologists because of its applied value—academic self-concept strongly influences academic achievement (Byrne, 1996; Nolen-Hoeksema, Girgus, & Seligman, 1986). Studies examining feelings of competence and perceived self-efficacy report that children who view themselves as academically skilled are more motivated to succeed, more persistent in their work, and more willing to seek out challenging tasks or problems (Boggiano, Main, & Katz, 1988; Harter, 1988; Harter & Connell, 1984; Schunk, 1984). A high academic self-concept, even when it is an overestimate of the child's abilities, also correlates positively with (and probably contributes to) a high level of self-esteem (Connell & Ilardi, 1987; Harter, 1985a).

As significant, children with low opinions of their academic abilities are less motivated to work. One study found that even among children whose academic skills were high, those who held an incorrectly low opinion of their competence approached new tasks with less effort and optimism than did their classmates (Phillips, 1984, 1987). Thus, for some children, academic success may hinge as much on academic self-concept as it does on academic ability.

The value of academic success to the child may seem obvious, but its effects can reach beyond the classroom. For example, research indicates that when children have academic (and social) failure experiences at school, their relations with their parents often suffer—the children tend to become more demanding and unreasonable, while the parents become more disapproving and punitive (Repetti, 1996). These home experiences, in turn, may further erode the child's attitude toward school, in effect, producing a vicious cycle.

Development in School Context

Do U.S. Schools Depress Adolescents' Academic Self-Concept?

The dip in self-esteem that is common during early adolescence usually includes a decline in feelings of academic competence and motivation (Eccles, Midgley, & Adler, 1984; Harter, 1981). Some have attributed this decline to the physical and emotional changes associated with puberty or to other developmental processes (Simmons & Blyth, 1987).

An alternative explanation, however, views the problem more as a mismatch between the predictable developmental changes of adolescence and the educational context to which students are exposed (Seidman et al., 1994). Specifically, Jacquelynne Eccles contends that most junior high schools are not well suited to the developmental needs of adolescents, resulting in what she describes as a poor *stage/environment fit* (Eccles, Midgley, et al., 1993).

Eccles argues that the typical junior high school environment produces mismatches in several areas. First, junior high teachers tend to put more emphasis on teacher control and discipline at a time when the adolescent is attempting to become more independent and self-reliant. A related problem is that teachers at this level frequently report feeling discouraged and ineffective, especially in their attempts to teach lower ability students, whereas students during this period particularly need support and encouragement. Third, having students move from class to class and grouping them according to their abilities tend to encourage social comparisons among adolescents at a time when their feelings of self-consciousness are just beginning to emerge. Finally, junior high teachers tend to use higher standards of grading than do their elementary-school counterparts, which results in some students' suddenly encountering more failures than they had previously (Eccles & Midgley, 1990).

Eccles supports these contentions with data from a longitudinal study across a number of sixth- and seventh-grade classrooms. The study investigated the beliefs and behaviors of teachers and students regarding mathematics. One finding was that seventh-grade math teachers reported having less trust and confidence in their students and feeling less effective in working with them than did the sixth-grade teachers (Midgley, Feldlaufer, & Eccles, 1988b). The students, in turn, viewed teach-

The increased emphasis on classroom control and discipline in many junior high schools may serve to depress self-esteem in adolescent students, who are in the process of developing independence and self-reliance.

ers in seventh grade as being less supportive, less friendly, and less fair (Feldlaufer, Midgley, & Eccles, 1988).

The researchers also compared the self-efficacy levels of the teachers with those of their students. Students who had moved from a sixth-grade teacher whose self-efficacy level was high to a seventh-grade teacher whose level was low ended the year with lower expectations regarding their abilities in math than did students whose seventh-grade teacher reported high self-efficacy. This pattern was most pronounced among students at lower ability levels (Midgley et al., 1988b).

Finally, the students' perceptions of how much support they received from their teachers were compared with the value the students attached to mathematics. When students moved to a seventh-grade teacher they viewed as higher in support, their view of math was enhanced; when they moved to a teacher they viewed as nonsupportive, the value they attached to math declined (Midgley, Feldlaufer, & Eccles, 1988a).

These results suggest that at least some declines in academic self-concept and motivation that occur during adolescence may not be inevitable. What seems to be necessary is for educational policy makers to adjust school environments to fit the developmental needs of young adolescents better. Such changes might include keeping students together in the same classrooms, fostering better student–teacher relationships, and adjusting grading standards to more closely match those to which students have been accustomed (Eccles, Midgley, et al., 1993). These changes may not eliminate all the problems associated with adolescence, but they can help provide a more appropriate educational context in which learning can take place.

✓ *To Recap...*

The opinions children form about themselves constitute their self-esteem. Researchers have typically measured self-esteem through questionnaires. The most popular of these is Susan Harter's *Self-Perception Profile for Children*, which creates a profile of children's self-esteem across a number of different domains.

Kindergartners tend to have a relatively high level of self-esteem, which remains stable until early adolescence. At about age 12, children report a dip in self-esteem, which has been attributed to several changes that typify adolescence, including an increase in self-consciousness.

An important component of self-esteem is a feeling of competence. Academic self-concept, representing the child's perceived competence in the classroom, has been of particular interest to researchers. The academic self-image of the kindergartner is high, but it steadily decreases over the elementary school years. Girls display lower academic self-images during these years than do boys.

Dweck has developed a theoretical model describing the complex role that motivation plays in academic achievement. According to the model, mastery-oriented children remain positive and persistent because they view failure experiences as opportunities to learn, whereas helpless children become pessimistic and avoid future challenges because they view failures as signs of low self-worth. In older children, conceptions of intelligence and attributions for failure (effort or ability) affect their academic motivation.

As children move through the early grades, they increasingly use social comparisons in developing academic self-concepts. This process may explain the general decline in academic self-image, because many children must lower their assessments of their abilities as they compare them with those of other children. Parents' (especially fathers') interaction styles also influence children's academic self-concept.

Academic self-concept influences children's academic achievement. High self-image improves motivation and success, and low self-image reduces them, even among children whose low self-image inaccurately reflects their high academic ability.

Self-Regulation

We have examined how growing children gain knowledge of the self and how their continual evaluation of this knowledge produces a positive or negative view of the self. In this section, we consider a third process—how the self comes to regulate, or control, children's behavior.

Self-regulation is a crucial aspect of human development. If children did not learn to control their own behavior—to avoid the things they must avoid, to wait for the things they cannot have right away, to alter strategies that are not working—they would be constantly at the mercy of the moment-to-moment pushes and pulls of their environments. They would simply be "weathervanes," as Bandura puts it (1986, p. 335). The development of self-control is one of the child's most impressive accomplishments. Self-control indicates at the very least that the child knows what demands are made by the surrounding world, realizes what behaviors relate to those demands, and understands how to adjust behaviors to meet the demands (Vaughn, Kopp, & Krakow, 1984). How does such self-control develop, and what are its effects?

The Emergence of Self-Control

Many theoretical models have been proposed to explain the emergence of self-regulation (e.g., Bandura, 1991a; Harter, 1982; Kopp, 1991; Mischel, Shoda, & Rodriguez, 1989; Vygotsky, 1934/1962), and all of them share a common belief. Children's behavior is assumed to be completely controlled at first by external sources. Then, gradually, some of this control is internalized. Although the theories disagree on the contributions of biological, cognitive, and social influences to this process, they all propose this fundamental shift from external to internal regulation.

Self-regulation is primitive during early infancy and mostly involves involuntary biological processes (Rothbart & Posner, 1985; Stifter & Braungart, 1995). As we have seen, babies reflexively squint in response to a bright light and turn away when the caregiver is providing too much verbal stimulation. Such responses serve important regulatory functions, but they offer no evidence that the infants who engage in them are cognitively aware of what is happening.

By the beginning of the second year, babies have developed many voluntary behaviors and can act on their environments in purposeful ways. Children act in order to accomplish things or to reach goals, as when a baby grabs for a toy he would like to play with or pushes over a tower of blocks to watch it crash to the floor. But at this point, the child's ability to monitor his behaviors and to adjust them as necessary is still not very impressive (Bullock & Lutkenhaus, 1988).

Self-control becomes more effective and obvious during the third year, as children begin to resist having everything done for them and to assert their desire to do things themselves (Bullock & Lutkenhaus, 1990; Grolnick, Bridges, & Connell, 1996). Much of the external control these children have experienced has involved verbal instruction from the parent. In asserting their independence, children sometimes attempt to take on this role themselves, and they adopt some of the same regulating commands. A 2-year-old might, for example, say "no, no," as she reaches for a forbidden object. Or she may direct her own behavior much as her mother has directed it previously ("Put the spoon in the bowl").

At this point, then, some verbal control over the child's behavior has begun to move from external sources to the child herself. But the progression is not yet complete. The final step comes when the child internalizes the control, directing her behavior silently with thought rather than with speech. This form of self-regulation generally is not apparent before 3 years of age.

Beyond age 3, self-control quickly becomes much more elaborate and sophisticated. Children develop strategies to resist the many temptations they encounter every day. They also learn to delay gratification by passing up smaller, immediate rewards in exchange for larger, delayed ones. And they acquire a host of additional techniques for guiding other aspects of their behavior. We consider some of these more complex forms of self-regulation a little later in the chapter.

The Role of Private Speech

Many psychologists believe that the transition from external control to self-control is guided primarily by the child's language. This proposition has been most clearly articulated in the writings of two Russian psychologists, Lev Vygotsky and Alexander Luria.

Vygotsky's Model   Earlier, we noted that Vygotsky was a contemporary of Piaget. Like Piaget, he believed that a good way to learn about young children's development is by observing them in problem-solving situations (Vygotsky, 1934/1962). Vygotsky was intrigued by the common observation that preschoolers sometimes talk to themselves while working on a task—a behavior now generally referred to as **private speech** (Diaz & Berk, 1992; Zivin, 1979). Piaget had labeled this self-directed behavior *egocentric speech* and believed that it was only minimally relevant to children's cognitive development and self-regulation (Hodapp & Goldfield, 1985).

Vygotsky did not agree. He argued that young children's private speech grows out of their interactions with parents and other adults as they work together on various tasks (Behrend, Rosengren, & Perlmutter, 1992; Rizzo & Corsaro, 1988). Much of a parent's speech in such situations involves guiding and regulating the child. Over the course of many such interactions, children begin to use their parents' instructional

Private speech
Speech children produce and direct toward themselves during a problem-solving activity.

comments (although not always in versions as complete or well formed) to direct their own behavior. Gradually, the controlling speech becomes internalized as thought, and children eventually produce silent statements similar to the verbal ones (Berk, 1994). Vygotsky thus viewed self-regulation as developing out of the child's social interactions—a process he called **sociogenesis** (Van der Veer & Valsiner, 1988).

Research is finding increasing support for Vygotsky's model (Cox & Lightfoot, 1997). If the model is correct, we would expect children's production of private speech to expand over the early years, as they more and more adopt the language of adults, and then to diminish gradually as the speech "goes underground." Developmental studies have shown that this pattern is indeed apparent across ages 4 to 10 (Bivens & Berk, 1990; Frauenglass & Diaz, 1985; Kohlberg, Yaeger, & Hjertholm, 1968). Researchers have also found that in middle and later childhood a greater proportion of private speech takes the form of whispering, presumably also reflecting its gradual internalization (Frauenglass & Diaz, 1985). Furthermore, private speech is most evident at the beginning of a new task and at other times when children have the greatest difficulty, but it decreases (becomes internalized) as they master the task (Behrend et al., 1992; Meichenbaum & Goodman, 1979).

Finally, a number of studies have closely examined parent–child interaction during problem-solving activities, with a special focus on the changes that occur over time. Parents have been found to adjust their behaviors to the demands of the situation—for example, being more directive with children who are younger or who are just learning a task—and children have shown evidence of taking on the regulating role and guiding their own behavior to solve the problems (Berk & Spuhl, 1995; Freund, 1990; Pratt et al., 1988).

Luria's Model   Vygotsky's interest in verbal regulation was carried on by his colleague Alexander Luria (1961, 1982). Whereas Vygotsky focused on the transfer of parental speech to children, Luria was more interested in the role speech plays in controlling young children's behavior. And whereas Vygotsky's work was based largely on naturalistic observations of children at play, Luria used a simple but ingenious laboratory method of study (Vocate, 1987).

The behavior of interest was the way in which children pressed a rubber bulb with their hands. The bulb allowed Luria to investigate, among other things, what factors were effective in getting the child either to start pressing the bulb or to inhibit (either stop or not start) pressing it. Here we consider only two of the factors Luria studied. The first involved whether the child responded to the *semantic content* (the meaning) of a spoken command or instead responded only to its sound or rhythm, which Luria called *its pulse*. The second factor was whether the command was given by someone else or was spoken by the child. The results of Luria's many studies indicate that verbal regulation of this sort changes as the child grows (Waters & Tinsley, 1982; Zivin, 1979).

Between 18 months and 3 years of age, only adult, external speech can influence the child's responding; self-verbalizations are ineffective. Furthermore, speech can only start the behavior; it cannot inhibit it. If a 2-year-old is pressing the bulb, for example, the instruction "Stop!" usually leads to even harder pressing, because the aspect of speech that controls behavior during this period is its pulse, rather than its meaning. For the same reason, these youngsters are just as likely to begin pressing when they hear the command "Don't press!" as when they hear the command "Press!"

From ages 3 to 4 1/2, external speech can control both starting and inhibiting, indicating that the semantic content of commands presented by others has become relevant. Children's own self-directed speech (under the experimenter's instruc-

Sociogenesis
The process of acquiring knowledge or skills through social interactions.

tions) can cause them to start pressing the bulb. But because children during this period respond only to the pulse of their own speech, they cannot yet produce self-controlled inhibiting.

By 5 years of age, children's self-directed speech can control their behavior almost as well as speech from the experimenter can. Luria contended that at this point children's vocal speech becomes internalized as they begin to guide their responses with silent instructions. His own research, however, did not examine this final part of the process.

Luria's model has inspired a great deal of investigation, although not all of it has supported his views (Miller, Shelton, & Flavell, 1970). We consider one study here and discuss some others in the following section. This experiment nicely illustrates Luria's distinction between the semantic content and the pulse of speech.

Children in the study participated in a game similar to Simon Says. On each turn, the experimenter modeled a response—for example, touched her toes—and simultaneously gave either a command to start ("Touch your toes!") or to inhibit ("Don't touch your toes!"). For one-third of the children, the experimenter used a soft voice; for one-third, a medium voice; and for one-third, a loud voice. The dependent measures of interest were the number of starting errors (not responding when they should) and the number of inhibiting errors (responding when they should not).

Luria's model would predict more inhibiting errors, because verbal control over inhibition develops later. And indeed, the children made about seven times as many inhibiting errors. The researchers also predicted that for younger children, louder commands, which are more effective in grabbing the children's attention, should produce more inhibiting errors, because these children should be responding only to the pulse aspect of the speech and not to its content. For older children, to whom the content is relevant, louder commands should be better for controlling behavior. The results of this study, depicted in Figure 13.3, confirmed these predictions (Saltz, Campbell, & Skotko, 1983).

Luria's research adds further support to Vygotsky's belief that self-regulation begins as external control and is gradually internalized. But perhaps more important, it illustrates the limited information-processing capabilities of younger children, who tend to respond more to the presence or absence of a command than to its content. As the data from the study described suggest, shouting at a toddler to inhibit a response ("Don't touch the stove!") may actually make the child more likely to carry out a dangerous act.

Resistance to Temptation

Luria's laboratory studies of self-regulation were somewhat abstract and were not designed to deal directly with everyday events or problems. In contrast, researchers in the United States have used experimental procedures that bear a closer resemblance to situations that children commonly encounter in their daily lives. One such situation arises when children must resist the temptation to do something that they are prohibited from doing. Babies have no self-control in this regard and immediately go after whatever appeals to them. The only deterrent is control by the parent, who either prevents or punishes the response. Children, however, eventually learn to inhibit forbidden behaviors, even when no one is watching them. How does this kind of self-control come about?

A common method for studying resistance to temptation uses the **forbidden-toy technique**. Typically, an experimenter puts a child in a room where there is an attractive toy and tells the child not to touch or play with the toy. Outside the room, observers monitor the child's behavior through a two-way mirror. The investigators

Forbidden-toy technique
An experimental procedure for studying children's resistance to temptation in which the child is left alone with an attractive toy and instructed not to play with it.

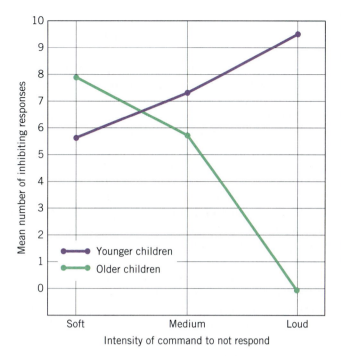

Figure 13.3
Mean number of inhibiting errors for younger and older children as a function of the intensity of the verbal command not to respond. From "Verbal Control of Behavior: The Effects of Shouting" by E. Saltz, S. Cambell, and D. Skotko, 1983, *Developmental Psychology, 19*, pp. 461–464. Copyright © 1983 by the American Psychological Association. Reprinted by permission.

usually are interested in how long the child waits before breaking the rule or how much time the child spends playing with the forbidden toy.

One example of this type of research has some relevance for Luria's analysis. The researchers wanted to find out whether having children produce self-instructional statements during their waiting time would affect their ability to resist temptation. The children were placed in a room with several attractive toys on a table behind them and were instructed not to turn around and look at the toys while the experimenter was out of the room. Some of the children were also told that, to help them keep from looking, they should repeat out loud a relevant statement, such as "I must not turn around." Children in a second group were told to use an irrelevant self-instruction, such as "hickory, dickory, dock." Those in a third group were given no self-instructional advice and waited silently. For younger children, producing a verbal self-instruction led to greater resistance than remaining silent. But the semantic content of the instruction did not matter—the relevant and irrelevant instructions worked equally well. For older children, the content of the self-instruction did make a difference, with the relevant statement proving most effective (Hartig & Kanfer, 1973).

Several other factors have also been shown to influence children's behavior in forbidden toy settings. For example, seeing an adult model break the rule and play with the toy makes children more likely to do so (Grusec et al., 1979). On the other hand, providing children with a good rationale for following the prohibition ("Don't touch the toy; it's fragile and might break") increases the likelihood that they will resist (Parke, 1977), as does teaching children to develop their own plans or strategies for dealing with the temptation (C. J. Patterson, 1982).

Delay of Gratification

Another popular approach to studying children's self-control has been the **delay-of-gratification technique**. Typically, the child is presented with two choices: a small reward that is available immediately or a larger reward that can only be obtained

Delay-of-gratification technique
An experimental procedure for studying children's ability to postpone a smaller, immediate reward in order to obtain a larger, delayed one.

later. This situation is analogous to many choices children (and adults) encounter every day. Should I use this week's allowance to buy a small toy or combine it with next week's and buy a larger toy? Should I eat this snack now or save my appetite for a better meal later? Perhaps because this experimental task is a bit more complex than that involving resistance to temptation, more factors have been shown to influence children's ability to delay gratification (Mischel et al., 1989).

Here, too, Luria's model has found support. In one study, while waiting for the better reward, children were directed to produce either a relevant statement ("I am waiting for the marshmallow"), an irrelevant statement ("one, two, three"), or nothing. Once again, either of the self-statements increased waiting time for younger children, but only the relevant verbalizations were of assistance to the older children (Karniol & Miller, 1981).

Another method for helping children delay gratification is to reduce or alter the attention they pay to the tempting object (the smaller but immediately available reward) (Mischel et al., 1989). When the object is out of sight, for example, children will wait much longer. The same is true when they spend the waiting time playing with a toy or engaging in some other distracting activity. Even when they are thinking about the tempting object, children will wait longer if they are instructed to think only about certain of its objective properties (say, the shape or color of a candy bar) rather than about its appealing properties (the candy bar's smell or taste).

As children grow older, their understanding of these delay strategies increases. For example, when presented with various waiting techniques and asked to select the ones that would work best, preschoolers display little knowledge of what strategies would be more effective. Third graders, however, show an impressive understanding. And by sixth grade, the large majority of children clearly seem to know that redirecting one's attention from the reward and various other forms of distraction are the methods most useful in delaying gratification (Mischel et al., 1989; Yates, Yates, & Beasley, 1987).

The ability to delay gratification has been linked to children's social competence as well. Children who respond impulsively often experience problems in their social interactions with other children, in part because they fail to acquire all the necessary information about a situation before making a decision (Moore, Hughes, & Robinson, 1992). One study investigated the relation between a child's ability to

The ability to delay gratification appears to be a personality trait that remains quite stable over the years.

delay gratification (in the standard tasks described here) and how many witness statements the child chose to hear before deciding whether another child was guilty of having caused a problem. As predicted, those children who were good at delaying gratification also waited to hear more testimony before making their decisions (Gronau & Waas, 1997).

Finally, children's ability to cope with temptation in this type of experimental situation appears to reflect a surprisingly stable personality characteristic. In a recent study, adolescents who had participated as preschoolers in delay-of-gratification research of the type described earlier were studied again 10 years later. Parents were asked to complete several questionnaires concerned with aspects of their children's present cognitive skills, social competence, and ability to cope with stress.

The results indicated that children who had been better at delaying gratification in their early years were much more likely to be rated by parents as stronger in each of these three areas. For example, the children who had waited the longest during the experimental procedures (especially those who had spontaneously developed good coping strategies) were now reported to be the most academically successful, the best at getting along with peers, the best at coping with problems, and the most confident and self-reliant (Mischel, Shoda, & Peake, 1988; Mischel et al., 1991). These rather remarkable findings indicate that a child's early ability to delay gratification may be one long-term predictor of that child's eventual success and happiness.

Applications

Teaching Children to Talk to Themselves

An exciting outgrowth of research on children's self-control has been the application of self-regulation procedures to problems in the classroom. Much of this work has been concerned with behavior problems and has trained children to monitor the appropriateness of their own behavior and to dispense self-rewards accordingly (Kendall & Braswell, 1985; Rosenbaum & Drabman, 1979). An interesting study illustrates how these methods can also be applied to children's academic performance (Roberts, Nelson, & Olson, 1987).

The subjects were first and second graders who were having difficulty with math skills. The researchers believed that the children's performance could be improved if they were taught to approach each problem in a systematic, step-by-step manner, which would be guided by self-instructional statements.

Following a baseline period in which the researchers simply observed the children's unaided performance, the training began with the modeling of self-instructions. For a simple addition problem, the approach modeled to the child might be as follows:

$$8 + \underline{\hspace{2cm}} = 15$$

"First, I have to read the problem. Eight plus some number equals 15. This is an addition problem, so I have to circle the sign. I circle the plus. Now I put eight sticks over the 8 and put sticks over the box until I get 15: 1, 2, 3, 4, 5, 6, 7, 8 and 9, 10, 11, 12, 13, 14, 15. Now I count the sticks over the box. 1, 2, 3, 4, 5, 6, 7. There are seven sticks over the box. Seven is my answer, so I write it in the box: 8 plus 7 equals 15."

Children then practiced and were given feedback on more problems until they could reliably produce the correct self-instructions on their own. At this point, a rein-

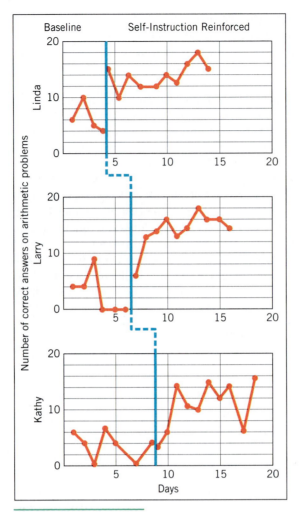

Figure 13.4
Number of math problems solved by three first and second graders participating in the self–instructional training project. During the baseline period, when no training was involved, per–formance was low. When children were taught to self-instruct and were reinforced for doing so correctly, the number of problems they solved increased markedly. From "Self-instruction: An analysis of the differential effects of instruction and reinforcement" by R. N. Roberts, R. O. Nelson, and T. W. Olson, 1987, *Journal of Applied Behavior Analysis, 20*, pp. 235–242. Copyright © 1987 by the Society for the Experimental Analysis of Behavior.

forcement system was introduced. The experiment involved several conditions, but of particular interest is the condition in which children earned rewards simply for con-tinuing to use the self-instructions as they performed their daily math problems.

The data from three of these students over several weeks are presented in Figure 13.4. The dependent variable (on the vertical axis) indicates the number of math problems solved correctly during the baseline condition and then during the reward procedures. Recall that these children did not receive reinforcement for the accu-racy of their math answers; they were rewarded only for producing the self-instruc-tional statements. Their improvement in math performance thus can be attributed directly to the production of self-guiding verbalizations. These results illustrate clearly how training in self-regulation can be used as a tool in the classroom.

✓ *To Recap…*

The development of self-regulation is a major achievement that represents a shift from external environmental control to internal regulation. Little meaningful self-regulation is evident during the first year of life. During the second year, children's voluntary behaviors are principally under environmental control, but some of this control gradually moves to the child during the third year in the form of self-directing speech and, eventually, self-directing thought. Self-control strategies after age 3 become more numerous and increasingly complex.

Verbal self-regulation has been investigated extensively by Russian psychologists. Lev Vygotsky studied children's private speech, concluding that through social interactions and shared problem-solving activities, children gradually adopt the regulating speech of parents and internalize it as thought. Alexander Luria studied the effects of speech on children's starting and inhibiting behaviors. His contention is that children at about 5 years of age can control their behavior using internalized, self-directed speech.

Resistance-to-temptation studies examine the common situation in which children must withhold a prohibited behavior. Using the forbidden-toy technique, investigators have found that the ability to resist temptation is influenced by a number of factors, including appropriate self-statements, modeling, and a good rationale or plan for resisting the prohibited act.

Delay-of-gratification studies examine children's ability to forgo smaller, immediate rewards in order to receive larger, delayed ones. Factors that affect waiting time include self-statements and various methods of reducing attention to the tempting, immediately available reward. Children's understanding of effective delay strategies increases as they get older. The ability to delay gratification during the preschool years has been linked with parents' ratings of their adolescents' cognitive, social, and coping abilities.

Conclusion

This chapter has covered a variety of topics that may seem only loosely connected to one another. Why a baby watches herself in a mirror may seem unrelated to why the child does or does not give up a smaller reward to wait for a larger one in kindergarten or why she lowers her opinion of herself in junior high school. The lack of an immediately obvious connection between these aspects of child development reflects the fact that the self has only recently become a topic of major research interest (Hattie & Marsh, 1996).

Our examination of the self has, however, nicely illustrated an important theme of this book and of modern child psychology: social and cognitive development are so interdependent that it is difficult to study either one alone. Although for clarity we have often discussed these two domains separately, it should be apparent that one cannot be completely understood without the other. We have seen, for example, that children's growing knowledge about themselves and their increasingly accurate evaluations of their abilities have major influences on their interactions with other people. On the other hand, Vygotsky and others have demonstrated that social interactions play an important role in the development of children's thinking and problem-solving skills. This theme emerged in earlier chapters and will continue to find its way into our discussions as we look further at children's social development.

Visual Summary for Chapter 13:
Development of the Self

Theories of the Self

Cognitive-Developmental Approaches ➤ Cognitive-developmental theorists have offered several models concerning self-development. Selman proposed a 5-stage model of self-awareness. Information-processing theorists view the self as part of the larger memory system. Vygotskians believe that children's understanding of the self results from autobiographical memories that have been constructed with parents.

Environmental/Learning Theories ➤ Bandura proposed a model of self-evaluation built around children's developing sense of self-efficacy. Bandura also proposed an explanation for the development of self-regulation that involves a shift from external control of behavior to internal control.

Ethological Theory ➤ Some ethologists have suggested that responsive caregiving and a secure attachment relationship may facilitate aspects of the child's self-development.

Self-Knowledge

Discovery of the Self in Infancy ➤ It is not yet known whether newborns have any understanding of the self. During the second half of the first year, babies begin to display a sense of personal agency by acting on toys and other objects in their environments. This evolves into mastery motivation, as infants engage in activities simply for the sake of mastering them. Toward the end of the second year, infants begin to recognize themselves in mirrors, pictures, and videotapes.

Developmental Changes in Self-Descriptions ➤ Self-descriptions by preschoolers reflect preoperational thinking and typically include references only to objective, here-and-now characteristics. In middle childhood, the concrete operational child focuses to a greater degree on nontangible characteristics, such as emotions, and on membership in various categories. Adolescents' formal operational abilities lead to more abstract and hypothetical self-descriptions, concerned with attitudes, personality characteristics, and personal beliefs, sometimes involving conflicting attributes.

Self-Evaluation

Measuring Self-Worth ➤ The opinions children form about themselves comprise their self-esteem. The most popular measure of self-esteem is Susan Harter's Self-Perception Profile for Children, which creates a profile of children's self-esteem across a number of different domains.

The Stability of Self-Worth ➤ Kindergartners tend to have a relatively high level of self-esteem, which remains stable until early adolescence. At about age 12, children report a dip in self-esteem, which has been attributed to several changes that typify adolescence, including an increase in self-consciousness.

Academic Self-Concept

Dweck's Motivational Model of Achievement ➤ Dweck's model distinguishes between mastery-oriented and helpless patterns. Mastery-oriented children remain positive and persistent because they view failure experiences as opportunities to learn, whereas helpless children become pessimistic and avoid future challenges because they view failures as signs of low self-worth.

Self-Evaluation

Influences on Academic Self-Concept → As children move through the early grades, they increasingly use social comparisons in developing academic self-concepts. Many children must lower their assessments of their abilities as they compare them with those of other children. Parents' interaction styles also influence children's academic self-concept. The predictable decline in self-esteem during early adolescence may result from a mismatch between the developmental characteristics of children of this age and the requirements of the typical school environment.

Effects of Academic Self-Concept → Academic self-concept influences children's academic achievement. High self-image improves motivation and success, and low self-image reduces them, even among children whose low self-image inaccurately reflects their high academic ability.

Self-Regulation

The Emergence of Self-Control → Little self-regulation is evident in the 1st year of life. During the 2nd year, children's voluntary behaviors are principally under environmental control. Some of this control gradually moves to the child during the 3rd year in the form of self-directing speech and, eventually, self-directing thought. Self-control strategies after age 3 become more numerous and increasingly complex.

The Role of Private Speech → Vygotsky studied children's private speech, concluding that, through social interactions and shared problem-solving activities, children gradually adopt the regulating speech of parents and internalize it as thought. Luria studied the effects of speech on children's starting and inhibiting behaviors. He contends that children at about 5 years of age can control their behavior using internalized, self-directed speech.

Resistance to Temptation → Resistance to temptation studies examine situations in which children must withold a prohibited behavior. The ability to resist temptation is influenced by a number of factors, including appropriate self-statements, modeling, and a good rationale for resisting the prohibited act.

Delay of Gratification → Delay of gratification studies examine children's ability to forgo smaller immediate rewards in order to receive larger delayed ones. Factors that affect waiting time include self-statements and various methods of reducing attention to the tempting, immediately available reward. Children's understanding of effective delay strategies increases as they get older. The ability to delay gratification during the preschool years has been linked with cognitive, social, and coping abilities in adolescence.

Chapter 14

Moral Development

Why did they do it?

They were high-school sweethearts in their first year of college—bright, popular, well-to-do, and apparently well adjusted. Yet one night in November 1996, Amy Grossberg and Brian Peterson disposed of a 6-lb, 2-oz newborn boy—their child—in a dumpster outside a Comfort Inn in Delaware. Grossberg, with Peterson's help, had just delivered the baby in one of the rooms at the motel. Afterward, they drove back to their dormitories, as if hoping they could simply forget what had happened. When police found the infant the next day, he was dead, and an autopsy later revealed that death had been caused by shaking and skull fractures. Grossberg and Peterson were charged with murder.

The case attracted the attention of virtually every major news provider, and all asked the same question: Why did two well-educated, upper-middle-class teenagers, who had so many alternatives, choose this one? Some infanticides have always occurred, but, as a Newsweek article pointed out, "There is a pattern to these deaths. The parents are usually young and poor; the mother frequently acts alone." Grossberg and Peterson certainly didn't fit that pattern.

But perhaps a new pattern was emerging. In June 1997, a middle-class high-school girl from a small town in New Jersey gave birth in a restroom while attending the senior prom, placed the baby in the trash, and returned to the dance floor. The baby was dead when janitors discovered it, either strangled or suffocated in a plastic bag. At about the same time, similar cases were reported in New Jersey, in the Boston area, and in Seattle.

How can all these "nice, normal kids" be killers? If they had grown up disadvantaged, we might assume that somehow they had simply failed to develop an understanding of the difference between right and wrong. But that wasn't the case. These young persons clearly knew right from wrong, yet they acted in ways that seem entirely inconsistent with this knowledge. Understanding what factors affect these two aspects of moral development—moral reasoning and moral behavior—is one of the major tasks for developmental researchers, as we will see in this chapter.

Morality involves issues of right and wrong, good and evil. If any society is going to survive, it must have rules that make clear to its citizens what is permitted and what is prohibited. Children's moral development involves the ways in which they come to understand and follow (or not follow) the rules of their social world. Until early in this century, the study of moral development was left primarily to philosophers and religious scholars. Today, developmental psychologists also have a great deal of interest in this topic.

Researchers who study moral development generally divide social rules into two main types (Tisak, 1995; Turiel, Killen, & Helwig, 1987). **Moral rules** involve broad issues of fairness and justness. They protect the welfare of individuals and guarantee their rights. In most societies, for example, people are not permitted to kill or harm one another or to steal one another's property. **Social conventions** focus on keeping the system running smoothly and maintaining order in society. Such conventions might include giving up a seat to an older person, saying "please" and "thank you," and waiting in line for one's turn.

Moral rules
Rules used by a society to protect individuals and to guarantee their rights.

Social conventions
Rules used by a society to govern everyday behavior and to maintain order.

526

Both moral rules and social conventions can vary from one setting to another. Thus, in addition to learning the rules, children must learn that important differences may exist, for example, between the rules of their family and those of their classroom, or between the behavior expected by parents and the behavior encouraged by peers. Acquiring all this knowledge about social rules constitutes a very important part of children's development (Gralinski & Kopp, 1993; Turiel, 1998).

Contemporary research in moral development falls into two major categories. Researchers who focus on **moral conduct** are interested in explaining children's behavior—for example, why children steal, which children are more likely to start fights, and what factors promote sharing and cooperation among youngsters. Researchers concerned with **moral reasoning** investigate how children think about what they and others do. Studies of this type focus on children's ability to examine a situation and to decide such questions as whether a person's behavior was appropriate and whether the person should be punished.

Moral conduct
The aspect of children's moral development concerned with behavior.

Moral reasoning
The aspect of children's moral development concerned with knowledge and understanding of moral issues and principles.

We begin this chapter by considering the approaches to moral development taken by the three major theoretical traditions. Then we examine what psychologists have learned about the development of moral reasoning abilities. Next, we focus on issues of moral conduct; we look at the factors affecting children's *prosocial*, or desirable, behaviors, and then at the causes of aggression and other *antisocial* behaviors—the behaviors that cause so much concern in the United States today.

Theories of Moral Development

Two theoretical issues have dominated the study of moral development (Gibbs & Schnell, 1985; Krebs & Van Hesteren, 1994; Wainryb, 1993). One issue is whether children's moral beliefs and behaviors reside in the child and simply emerge over time or whether they reside in the culture and are transmitted to the child. You will recognize this issue as a form of the nature–nurture debate. The second issue involves the generality of moral rules. If they emerge from the child, they must have a large biological component, making them universal for all members of our species. On the other hand, if they develop within the social group, they are more arbitrary and thus can vary from one culture to the next. These two questions lie at the heart of much of the research on this topic.

Cognitive-Developmental Models

The cognitive tradition has been most concerned with the development of children's moral reasoning as they struggle with issues involving moral rules and social conventions. Some of these issues, such as abortion rights, gun control, and the death penalty, can be complex, with compelling arguments on both sides. Older children and adults will often examine the various arguments and weigh the evidence on all sides. Young children, in contrast, have difficulty appreciating that an issue may look very different from another person's perspective, and so they tend to base their opinions on only certain aspects of the information and to arrive at simplistic conclusions (Turiel, Hildebrandt, & Wainryb, 1991). Based on these observations, cognitive-developmentalists have concluded that advances in moral reasoning abilities depend heavily on children's improving cognitive abilities. Their advancing moral understanding, in turn, is thought to produce more mature moral behaviors (DeVries, 1991; Krebs & Van Hesteren, 1994).

Three models have guided most of the cognitive research on moral development. Here we simply describe the models; in the next section, we will examine some of the research findings that relate to them.

Piaget's Theory   Piaget's model of moral development grew out of his early work with children in Geneva, Switzerland, during the 1920s and 1930s. To investigate how children's conceptions of morality develop, Piaget used two very different methods.

One was a naturalistic approach in which he observed children playing common street games, such as marbles. Piaget closely examined how youngsters created and enforced the rules of their games, and he questioned them about circumstances under which the rules could be modified or even ignored. The second approach was more experimental and involved presenting individual children with **moral dilemmas** to solve. These took the form of short stories in which the child had to determine which of two characters was "naughtier." For example, in one story a little boy named Augustine accidentally makes a large ink stain on the tablecloth while trying to be helpful and fill his father's ink pot, whereas a little boy named Julian makes a small ink spot on the tablecloth while engaging in the forbidden act of playing with his father's pen.

From this research, Piaget developed a four-stage model of moral development that focused on the way children follow rules (Damon, 1983; Piaget, 1932). In the first stage (2 to 4 years), children have no real conception of morality. Much of their behavior involves play and imaginative games that have no formal rules, although at times they may invent certain restrictions as part of the play (e.g., all green blocks must be put in the same pail). The idea of following someone else's rules does not appear consistently until the second stage (5 to 7 years). When rule following emerges, children approach the concept in an absolute manner. Social rules are viewed as *heteronomous*, or externally dictated, commands presented by people in authority (usually parents), and they cannot be changed. Children in this second stage, called the stage of **moral realism**, do not think to question the purpose or correctness of a rule, even though they may not like to follow it. Thus, Piaget observed that younger children playing marble games were usually very inflexible about changing any rules, even if it would have made the game more convenient or more fun.

Moral dilemmas
Stories used by Piaget and others to assess children's levels of moral reasoning.

Moral realism
Piaget's second stage of moral development, in which children's reasoning is based on objective and physical aspects of a situation and is often inflexible.

Piaget studied common street games as a way of examining children's conceptions of rules.

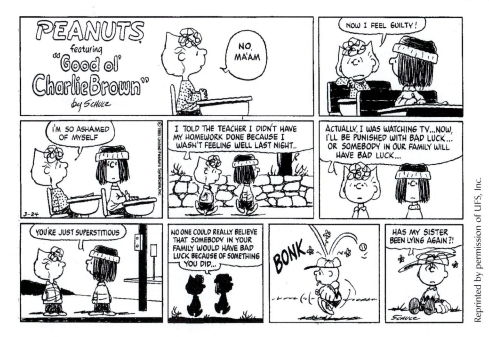

A belief in immanent justice characterizes children's reasoning in Piaget's stage of moral realism.

Piaget noted two interesting characteristics that grow out of this absolutist orientation. Most children in the second stage display **objective responsibility**, meaning that they evaluate moral situations only in terms of their physical and objective consequences. In the moral dilemmas, for example, these children saw acts causing more damage as more morally wrong than acts causing less damage, regardless of the character's motives or intentions. Hence, the helpful Augustine was usually seen as naughtier than the disobedient Julian because he made the larger ink stain.

Another characteristic of this stage is **immanent justice**. Because these children believe so firmly in the authority of a rule, they feel that punishment must always occur when the rule is broken. Thus, if a child steals a cookie when no one is looking and then loses his baseball the following day, he may assume that he has been punished for the theft.

In Piaget's third stage (8 to 11 years), the child gradually realizes that rules are agreements created by people to help or protect one another. Obeying these rules is no longer viewed as simply following someone else's orders, but as an *autonomous*, or personal, decision to cooperate with others. Piaget observed, for example, that third-stage children could adapt marble-game rules if necessary to fit the circumstances of the moment (too many players, too few marbles, and so on).

Furthermore, at this stage children's more advanced cognitive abilities allow new factors to enter into their moral evaluations. What a person was trying or meaning to do—that is, the person's motives or intentions—may become as important as the outcome of the behavior. Accordingly, with increasing age, children were more likely to judge Julian's forbidden behavior naughtier, even though it caused less damage. Because the morality of following a rule is now evaluated in relation to other factors in the situation, Piaget referred to this third level as the stage of **moral relativism**.

In the final stage, which Piaget discussed only briefly, children become capable of developing new rules when the circumstances require it. They also begin to extend their moral reasoning beyond the personal level to larger societal and political concerns.

Objective responsibility
Responsibility assigned solely in terms of an action's objective and physical consequences. Children in Piaget's stage of moral realism evaluate situations using this concept.

Immanent justice
Literally, inherent justice; refers to the expectation of children in Piaget's stage of moral realism that punishment must follow any rule violation, including those that appear to go undetected.

Moral relativism
Piaget's third stage of moral development, in which children view rules as agreements that can be altered and consider people's motives or intentions when evaluating their moral conduct.

Piaget believed that moral reasoning, like cognitive development, is guided by both innate and environmental factors. On the nature side, children's advancing cognitive abilities, including their movement away from egocentric thinking, enable them to consider more information and several different perspectives when evaluating the morality of a situation. Thus, the narrow focusing on unchangeable rules and objective consequences gives way to a broader and more flexible view of the world as the child gets older.

From the nurture perspective, Piaget believed that social experiences play an important role in the child's movement from stage to stage. During their early years, children learn that parents usually dictate and enforce the rules of behavior. In their desire to please their parents, children adopt the belief that they live in a world where rules must be followed. But the one-way nature of this rule system keeps children from expressing their own points of view or appreciating that there can be different opinions on moral questions. Gradually, interactions with peers become an important socializing factor. As Piaget discovered by observing street games, through peer interactions children learn that there can be several perspectives on an issue and that rules are the result of negotiating, compromising, and respecting the points of view of other people.

Kohlberg's Model

A second influential cognitive theory of moral development was proposed by Lawrence Kohlberg. Kohlberg's model grew out of his 1958 doctoral dissertation, in which he attempted to examine Piaget's theory using newer research methods. The theory has since been revised several times (Kohlberg, 1969, 1984, 1986; Kohlberg, Levine, & Hewer, 1983).

Kohlberg's method, like Piaget's, involved presenting research participants with moral dilemmas to assess their level of moral reasoning. But Kohlberg's stories did not require a simple choice as to who was naughtier. Instead, they presented the child with a dilemma in which a story character must choose, for example, between obeying a law (or rule) and breaking the law for the benefit of an individual person. For example, in one story a poor man named Heinz must choose between stealing medicine from a drugstore to save the life of his sick wife and letting her die. For each dilemma, the child is asked to indicate what the character should do and why. In Kohlberg's model, the second question is more important because it presumably reveals the subject's level of reasoning.

From his research, Kohlberg concluded that moral reasoning develops in three predictable levels, termed **preconventional**, **conventional**, and **postconventional**. Within each level are two stages, each of which can be divided into a social perspective component and a moral content component. The model is described in Table 14.1. In his later writings, Kohlberg suggested that the sixth stage is actually more theoretical than real. Few individuals attain this level, and none of the individuals that Kohlberg studied ever displayed it. Nevertheless, Kohlberg speculated that a seventh stage of moral development might also exist that goes beyond conventional moral reasoning and enters the realm of religious faith (Kohlberg et al., 1983).

An important aspect of Kohlberg's model is how the two components of each stage interact. The social perspective component indicates the point of view from which the moral decision is made. For example, the child in the first stage is egocentric and sees all situations from a personal point of view. With development, the child becomes better able to appreciate the dilemma from the perspective of others or in terms of what is best for society as a whole. Advances in this area are thought to be related to the individual's cognitive development and to have a strong biological basis. But advances in perspective taking are not sufficient for

Preconventional level
Kohlberg's first two stages of moral development. Moral reasoning is based on the assumption that individuals must serve their own needs.

Conventional level
Kohlberg's third and fourth stages of moral development. Moral reasoning is based on the view that a social system must be based on laws and regulations.

Postconventional level
Kohlberg's final stages of moral development. Moral reasoning is based on the assumption that the value, dignity, and rights of each individual person must be maintained.

Table 14.1
Kohlberg's Stage Model of Moral Reasoning

	Social Perspective	*Moral Content*
Level I Preconventional		
Stage 1: Heteronomous morality ("Morality derives from power and authority.")	Children cannot consider more than one person's perspective. They tend to be egocentric, assuming that their feelings are shared by everyone.	This stage is equivalent to Piaget's moral realism. Evaluations of morality are absolute and focus on physical and objective characteristics of a situation. Morality is defined only by authority figures, whose rules must be obeyed.
Stage 2: Individualism and instrumental purpose ("Morality means looking out for yourself.")	Children understand that people have different needs and points of view, although they cannot yet put themselves in the other's place. Other people are assumed to serve their own self-interests.	Moral behavior is seen as valuable if it serves one's own interests. Children obey rules or cooperate with peers with an eye toward what they will get in return. Social interactions are viewed as deals and arrangements that involve concrete gains.
Level II Conventional		
Stage 3: Interpersonal conformity ("Morality means doing what makes you liked.")	People can view situations from another's perspective. They understand that an agreement between two people can be more important than each individual's self-interest.	The focus is on conformity to what most people believe is right behavior. Rules should be obeyed so that people you care about will approve of you. Interpersonal relations are based on the Golden Rule ("Do unto others…").
Stage 4: Law and order ("What's right is what's legal.")	People view morality from the perspective of the social system and what is necessary to keep it working. Individual needs are not considered more important than maintaining the social order.	Morality is based on strict adherence to laws and on performing one's duty. Rules are seen as applying to everyone equally and as being the correct means of resolving interpersonal conflicts.
Level III Postconventional		
Stage 5: Social contract ("Human rights take precedence over laws.")	People take the perspective of all individuals living in a social system. They understand that not everyone shares their own values and ideas but that all have an equal right to exist.	Morality is based on protecting each individual's human rights. The emphasis is on maintaining a social system that will do so. Laws are created to protect, rather than restrict, individual freedoms, and they should be changed as necessary. Behavior that harms society is wrong, even if it is not illegal.
Stage 6: Universal ethical principles ("Morality is a matter of personal conscience.")	People view moral decisions from the perspective of personal principles of fairness and justice. They believe each person has personal worth and should be respected, regardless of ideas or characteristics. The progression from stage 5 to stage 6 can be thought of as a move from a socially directed to an inner-directed perspective.	It is assumed that there are universal principles of morality that are above the law, such as justice and respect for human dignity. Human life is valued above all else.

Source: Based on information from L. Kohlberg, "Moral Stages and Moralization: The Cognitive-Development Approach," 1976. In T. Likona (Ed.), *Moral Development and Behavior: Theory, Research, and Social Issues*, New York: Holt, Rinehart and Winston.

moral reasoning to advance. They must be accompanied by development of the moral content component, which is assumed to be more strongly influenced by the child's experiences with moral situations. Kohlberg's theory thus resembles Piaget's in assuming that moral development results from a combination of improving cognitive skills and repeated encounters with moral issues.

Movement from stage to stage in Kohlberg's model closely follows the Piagetian process of accommodation. Movement occurs when the child can no longer handle new information within her current view of the world—or in Piagetian terms, when she can no longer assimilate new information within her existing structure of schemes. Kohlberg's model places particular importance on *role-taking* opportunities, which occur when children participate in decision-making situations with others and exchange differing points of view on moral questions. The contrasting viewpoints produce cognitive conflict, which the child eventually resolves by reorganizing her thinking into a more advanced stage of reasoning. This process occurs gradually, so although any individual's reasoning can be generally classified into one of the stages, she may approach certain moral issues at a higher or lower stage.

Several other characteristics of Kohlberg's stage model are similar to Piaget's theory. For instance, each stage forms a *structured whole*, with children in that stage generally responding consistently to different dilemmas and situations. Also, the stages follow an *invariant sequence*, so all children experience them in the same order and with no regression to earlier stages. Finally, the progression of stages is *universal* for all people and all cultures.

Kohlberg did not attempt to construct a model that deals with all aspects of moral reasoning. He developed his dilemmas specifically to assess children's *justice reasoning*—how children decide which of the story characters has the most valid rights and claims (for example, Heinz's sick wife or the druggist who owns the store). Kohlberg assumed that this aspect of moral development would be most likely to display the Piagetian stage characteristics just described, because justice reasoning emphasizes children's abstract cognitive approach to the moral issue rather than their emotional feelings about it. Moral decisions in which the child has a more personal stake were not of interest to Kohlberg, although we will see shortly that they have been to other researchers.

Turiel's Model   The most recent of the cognitive-developmental models of moral reasoning has been offered by Elliot Turiel (1998; Turiel et al., 1987; Turiel, et al., 1991). Turiel's model has much in common with those of Piaget and Kohlberg but makes several additional claims. The first of these is that children's moral reasoning involves a number of different *domains* of social cognition, the two most important being the moral domain and the societal domain.

The moral domain is concerned with people's rights and welfare. Issues concerning fairness and justice, such as lying, stealing, and killing, fall into this category. The societal domain involves rules that guide social relations among people. Being polite, wearing appropriate clothing, and addressing people using the proper titles (*Mrs.* Jones, *Dr.* Brown, etc.) are behaviors that characterize this domain. In Turiel's model, these two domains correspond to the moral rules and social conventions described earlier. In the models of Piaget and Kohlberg, in contrast, these rules and conventions fall within a single domain for children and do not divide into separate cognitive categories until later on.

A related claim of Turiel's model is that children can distinguish between the moral and societal domains from a very early age. Until the mid-1970s, the same methods were used to study children's and adults' moral reasoning—especially involving Kohlberg's model. Probably for this reason children were believed unable to distinguish between moral rules and social conventions until at least adolescence. Using different interview, observation, and scoring methods with children, however, Turiel has demonstrated that their moral reasoning is more sophisticated than formerly believed, as we shall see shortly (Tisak, 1995).

A third claim of the domain model is that children's understanding of moral and societal issues is very much influenced by the contexts in which they arise and by personal experiences (Smetana, 1994). Children's understanding of issues within the moral domain is thought to result from their social interactions—especially with peers—both through being victims of immoral acts and through witnessing the consequences of such acts for others. Interactions with parents can also play a role in that parents often point out why an immoral act was wrong (Smetana, 1989, 1994). Children's understanding of social conventions is assumed to result from their having experiences in a variety of social settings, where the conventions often differ from one context to another. One very important context involves culture. The domain model predicts that children in all cultures will distinguish between the moral and conventional domains at an early age but that particular social conventions may vary from one culture to the next (Turiel & Wainryb, 1994; Wainryb, 1993).

The cognitive models of Piaget, Kohlberg, and Turiel have inspired most of the research on children's moral reasoning. We examine how well the three theories have held up to experimental scrutiny when we review the research findings later in the chapter.

Environmental/Learning Theories

The social-learning tradition also has had a great deal to say about moral development, and most of it contrasts sharply with the cognitive-developmental perspective. The essence of the social-learning view is that the social behaviors we traditionally label in terms of moral development are acquired and maintained through the same principles that govern most other behaviors. Although social-learning theorists agree that these processes are affected by developmental advances in cognitive abilities (Perry & Perry, 1983), they emphasize environmental mechanisms such as reinforcement, punishment, and observational learning (modeling and imitation). This emphasis argues against a stage model of development in which moral behaviors emerge according to an internal timetable that is universal for all children. Instead, it predicts that behaviors should develop more individually, depending primarily on each child's social environment and personal experiences.

Most of the research within the social-learning tradition has involved moral conduct—both prosocial and antisocial behaviors—rather than moral reasoning. This difference has resulted principally because social-learning theorists, unlike cognitive developmentalists, believe that moral reasoning and moral conduct are somewhat independent processes that can be influenced by different factors. As a result, social-learning theorists are less inclined to expect a child's moral behavior to show consistency across situations or between knowledge and conduct (Gewirtz & Pelaez-Nogueras, 1991b).

The principal spokesperson for the social-learning account of moral development has been Albert Bandura, and most of the research conducted within this tradition is based on his views (Bandura, 1986, 1989, 1991b). Bandura's theory, described in Chapter 2, holds that reinforcement and punishment are major processes by which children acquire moral behaviors. In simplest terms, children are more likely to produce behaviors (prosocial or antisocial) that are approved or rewarded and tend to inhibit behaviors that are ignored or punished. In addition, children come to discriminate the reinforcement possibilities that exist in different settings, such as the praise parents provide for good grades versus the pressure peers may exert for skipping school.

Another process that Bandura considers crucial for understanding moral development is observational learning. Children learn many of the rules and practices of their social world by watching others, such as parents and peers (Brody & Shaffer, 1982; Mills & Grusec, 1988). Also of interest is the role of the media and how children's behavior is affected by what they observe on television or read in books and magazines (Eron & Huesmann, 1986; Williams, 1986).

With development, reinforcement and observational processes become internalized, and children learn to use them to regulate their own behavior. As we saw in Chapter 13, Bandura proposes that, through the use of evaluative self-reactions and self-sanctions, children come to regulate their behavior to match the moral standards they set for themselves.

We will have much to say about the contributions of social-learning researchers when we discuss children's prosocial development and aggression later in the chapter.

The Ethological Perspective

Both human ethologists and sociobiologists have investigated aspects of moral conduct. Much of their work has involved relating the behavior observed in other species to the moral conduct of humans. Two areas of particular interest have been altruism and aggression (De Waal, 1996; Hinde, 1986; MacDonald, 1988b, 1988c).

Paradox of altruism
The logical dilemma faced by ethological theorists who try to reconcile self-sacrificial behavior with the concepts of natural selection and survival of the fittest.

Kin selection
A proposed mechanism by which an individual's altruistic behavior toward kin increases the likelihood of the survival of genes similar to those of the individual.

Reciprocal altruism
A proposed mechanism by which an individual's altruistic behavior toward members of the social group may promote the survival of the individual's genes through reciprocation by others or may ensure the survival of similar genes.

Altruism   Altruistic behaviors are those that benefit someone else but offer no obvious benefit—and perhaps even some cost—to the individual performing them. Giving money to a charity, sharing a candy bar, and risking one's life to save someone else's are examples. As mentioned in Chapter 2, this prosocial behavior has been a particular challenge to classical evolutionary models, because self-sacrifice would not seem to fit with Darwin's proposed mechanisms. How can a behavior that does not increase a person's own chances of survival and reproduction be passed on in the species? It would seem, instead, that people who act selfishly and think first about themselves would be more likely to survive to pass along their genes. This dilemma, called the **paradox of altruism**, was discussed by Darwin and has been studied and debated ever since (Campbell & Christopher, 1996; Krebs, 1987; MacDonald, 1988a).

Sociobiologists have attempted to resolve this problem by adding two concepts to Darwin's notion of survival of the fittest (Dawkins, 1976; Maynard Smith, 1976). **Kin selection** proposes that humans, and some other animals, behave in ways that increase the chances for the survival and reproduction of their genes rather than of themselves. A person can pass on his genes either by reproducing himself *or* by increasing the reproductive chances of someone who has the same or similar genes. The more genes the second individual shares with the first, the more reasonable it becomes to try to save that individual's life (and reproductive capability). Therefore, we would predict that a mother should be more likely to risk her life for her child than for her husband, because her child shares many of her genes. Similarly, any family member, or *kin*, should be favored over any unrelated individual.

But people perform acts of altruism directed toward nonfamily members every day. How does evolutionary theory explain such behavior? Here a process called **reciprocal altruism** comes into play. According to this idea, people are genetically programmed to be helpful because (1) it increases the likelihood that they will someday in turn receive aid from the person they helped or from some other altruistic member of their group, or (2) by helping someone else in their social group, they help ensure that genes similar to their own will be passed on in the species (Trivers, 1971, 1983). We have more to say about altruistic behavior later in the chapter.

Aggression Aggression and dominance relationships have been another favorite area of research for human ethologists (Cairns, 1986; Omark, Strayer, & Freedman, 1980). One function of aggression is, again, to increase the likelihood of survival of an individual's genes—believed by some to be the most important evolutionary function of any behavior. Aggression serves this purpose in many ways, such as by helping the individual obtain food, protect the young, or preserve valuable hunting territory. In such cases, evolutionary processes clearly favor the stronger, smarter, or more skillful members of the species.

Aggression in many species can lead to physical combat. Some conflicts, however, do not progress to this point, but are resolved when one animal displays threatening gestures (such as certain facial expressions and body postures) and the other animal backs down, perhaps making submissive gestures. Such behaviors also have adaptive value for both individuals—the attacker gains possession of the desired property, while the retreating animal avoids injury or death. In some species that form social groups, such as monkeys, a **dominance hierarchy** develops, in which each member of the group fits somewhere on a dominance ladder. Each monkey controls those lower in the hierarchy (often simply by threats) but submits to those higher on the ladder. Even though initially created through aggression, such a structure ultimately reduces the overall physical conflict that might otherwise occur in the group. The structure and function of dominance hierarchies in children's social interactions has been a favorite focus of ethologists (Lore & Schultz, 1993), as we will see in Chapter 16.

Dominance hierarchy
A structured social group in which members higher on the dominance ladder control those who are lower, initially through aggression and conflict, but eventually simply through threats.

Development in Family Context
An Evolutionary Account of the Development of Antisocial Behavior

A newer evolutionary model, proposed by Jay Belsky and his colleagues (Belsky, Steinberg, & Draper, 1991), is concerned with the development of "reproductive strategies," the behaviors and attitudes children display regarding interpersonal relationships, mating, and parenting. According to this model, evolution has primed humans to be sensitive to their early rearing experiences and to develop, in response, behavior patterns or strategies that maximize their chances of successful reproduction. Such strategies thus result from a combination of the child's evolutionary heritage and early experiences, and they are assumed to emerge during the first 5 to 7 years of life.

Two behavior patterns in particular are most common. Children who are raised in secure and supportive environments, with ample food, clothing, and other resources, are likely to develop more positive attitudes toward family life and toward personal relationships in general. As a result, they focus on finding a single mate for a long-term relationship and invest heavily in raising their children. In contrast, children who have stressful, unstable early home experiences and who fail to develop close emotional bonds with caregivers and others develop reproductive patterns that are more individualistic and oriented toward personal survival. These children have less interest in forming long-term interpersonal relationships. They tend to seek many sexual partners but have minimal interest in their offspring.

The relevance of this evolutionary theory to moral development lies in its prediction that children (especially males) displaying the second pattern of development will be more likely to engage in antisocial behaviors, such as aggression, delinquency, and generally self-oriented conduct. Children reared in more nurturant environments, on the other hand, should display more interpersonal cooperation, altruism, and other-oriented behaviors.

Belsky's model is contextualist in that he argues that the two behavior patterns should not be viewed as better or worse, but simply as two strategies for coping with very different environmental contexts. For children who experience nurturant caregiving and secure attachments, developing trust and concern for others may be a sensible approach to life. But for children raised in unpredictable environments, where resources are scarce and others cannot necessarily be trusted, developing an opportunistic lifestyle may have evolutionary survival value by offering a realistic and effective response to the situation. This model, then, suggests that understanding children's moral behavior requires an appreciation of how evolutionary mechanisms promote development in context.

✓ *To Recap...*

Research in moral development falls into two major categories: studies of moral conduct and studies of moral reasoning. Cognitive developmentalists are most concerned with moral reasoning, and they argue that moral development depends on cognitive development. It is marked by consistency across situations and between moral thought and moral conduct, and it proceeds through stages.

Piaget proposed a four-stage model. Children in the first stage show very little understanding of rule following. In the stage of moral realism, children view rules as absolute and base their moral evaluations largely on physical and objective aspects of a situation. Increased interaction with peers combines with a movement away from egocentric thinking in the stage of moral relativism, during which children approach rules more flexibly and are able to take subjective factors into account. In the final stage, moral reasoning can extend to hypothetical situations and to issues in the larger society.

Kohlberg's model consists of three levels of moral reasoning—preconventional, conventional, and postconventional—each composed of two stages. The two components of each stage, social perspective and moral content, represent inborn and environmental influences, respectively. According to Kohlberg, movement from stage to stage occurs when the child experiences cognitive conflict; each stage represents a structured whole; the stages follow an invariant sequence; and the model is universal across cultures and sexes.

Turiel believes that children's moral reasoning involves several domains of social cognition, that even very young children can distinguish issues in the moral and societal domains, and that understanding such issues is influenced by their context and situational factors.

Social-learning theory emphasizes environmental influences on moral development and is most concerned with moral conduct. Bandura has been the most influential proponent of this view. Reinforcement and punishment principles, along with observational learning processes and self-regulation, are assumed to be the major determinants of children's moral behavior according to the social-learning model.

The ethological tradition has attempted to explain patterns of moral development in terms of evolutionary principles. For the so-called paradox of altruism, sociobiologists have argued that self-sacrificial behavior can be explained by a focus on the survival of the genes, rather than of the individual, through the processes of kin selection and reciprocal altruism. In the area of aggression, ethologists have been especially interested in how aggression reduces the overall level of conflict in a social group through the formation of dominance hierarchies.

Moral Reasoning

How well has research evidence supported the theoretical positions of the theories we have just examined? We investigate this question, along with other issues, with reference to three important topic areas: moral reasoning, prosocial behavior, and aggression. We begin with a discussion of research on children's moral reasoning.

Evaluating Piaget's Model

Some studies of moral reasoning have specifically addressed Piaget's model. One focus has been whether Piaget's research methods distorted his conclusions to some extent. Consider an example.

In Piaget's stories, the character's intentions were always stated before the amount of damage was described. Thus, children were first told that Julian was disobeying his father and then that he caused little damage. Because very young children may have difficulty processing much information at one time, the part of the story they hear last might be the one they remember best. So if the damage done is always mentioned at the end, younger children may focus on this factor. Studies have shown that if the character's motives or intentions are presented at the end of Piaget's stories, children as young as 5 years old may decide that the naughtier character was not the one who did less damage but the one who had bad motives (Karniol, 1978; Moran & McCullers, 1984).

These results, combined with results from related experiments, suggest that Piaget somewhat underestimated younger children's moral reasoning abilities (Grueneich, 1982; Karniol, 1978). Even very young children seem capable of taking into account a number of factors when making a moral judgment. But for a younger child to use a piece of information (such as a character's motives), that information must be made *salient*—clear and noticeable. Some techniques that have been used successfully to increase the salience of a character's intentions include (1) placing the information at the end of the story, (2) adding pictures, slides, or videotapes to the stories, as shown in Figure 14.1 (Chandler, Greenspan, & Barenboim, 1973; Nelson, 1980), (3) training the child to examine the story carefully before making a moral judgment (Rotenberg, 1980), and (4) asking the child to describe the character's intentions (Brandt & Strattner-Gregory, 1980).

Research designed to improve on Piaget's methods has now provided a more complete picture of how moral reasoning typically develops. Although they are capable of using motives and intentions earlier, children up to 5 or 6 years of age nevertheless base their moral evaluations primarily on the amount of damage produced by the story character. From that point until they are 8 to 10 years of age, children consider damage and motives about equally. And beginning at about age 10, the character's motives become the most important factor (Surber, 1982; Zelazo, Helwig, & Lau, 1996).

Children use other factors in addition to motives and damage to assess a story character's morality. For example, they judge the breaking of moral rules more harshly than the violation of social conventions (Smetana & Braeges, 1990; Smetana, Schlagman, & Adams, 1993); they evaluate a harmful act less severely if it involves retaliation (getting back at someone for an earlier wrongdoing) (Ferguson & Rule, 1988); and they view acts intended to cause harm more critically if they involved a

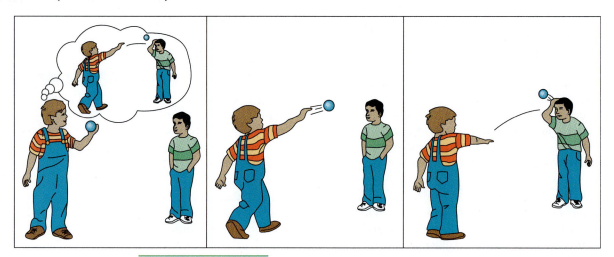

Figure 14.1

An example of drawings used to convey motive, action, and outcome in stories. When pictures such as these accompany stories involving moral dilemmas, even 4- to 6-year-olds sometimes use story characters' motives as a basis for evaluating their behavior. From "Factors Influencing Young Children's Use of Motives and Outcomes as Moral Criteria" by S. A. Nelson, 1980, *Child Development, 51*, pp. 823–829. Copyright © 1980 by The Society for Research in Child Development. Reprinted by permission.

great deal of effort (Jones & Nelson-Le Gall, 1995). But children are more tolerant of acts that were unforeseeable (such as accidentally hitting someone who has just come around the corner) (Sanvitale, Saltzstein, & Fish, 1989; Yuill & Perner, 1988) or that were followed by an apology or an admission of guilt (Leon, 1982; Nunner-Winkler & Sodian, 1988). Younger children also believe that taking a toy from a friend is more wrong than taking a toy from a nonfriend (Slomkowski & Killen, 1992).

Evaluating Kohlberg's Model

A great deal more research has been directed toward studying Kohlberg's model, and it, too, has been the target of some criticism.

Some problems Kohlberg addressed himself in his revisions of the model. For example, the original scoring method by which he determined the stage of each subject's reasoning was faulted for requiring a great deal of subjective interpretation (Kurtines & Grief, 1974; Liebert, 1984). In response, Kohlberg and his associates developed a new scoring procedure, the *Moral Judgment Interview (MJI)*, which is considerably more objective and precise (Colby & Kohlberg, 1987). Another criticism was that the existence of Kohlberg's highest stage of reasoning, the sixth stage, has not been demonstrated. As we saw earlier, Kohlberg conceded that this stage is more theoretical than actual.

Other questions regarding specific elements of Kohlberg's model can only be answered with data from well-conducted experiments. The most important of these questions involve five characteristics of the model, several of which we discussed earlier: prerequisite abilities, structured wholeness, invariant sequence, universal stages, and movement through stages as the result of cognitive conflict.

Prerequisite Abilities   A fundamental tenet of any cognitive-developmental model, including Kohlberg's, is that advances in cognitive and perspective-taking abilities form the basis for advances in moral reasoning. Researchers have tested this belief in two ways. One has been to determine whether children at more advanced levels of moral reasoning also display greater cognitive and perspective-taking abilities. Several studies have found that they do (Krebs & Gillmore, 1982; Rowe & Marcia, 1980). But, as discussed in Chapter 3, such correlational findings cannot confirm that improved cognitive and perspective-taking abilities *cause* improvements in moral reasoning abilities. All these abilities could simply advance at about the same time (or, for that matter, cognitive advances might be brought on by advances in moral reasoning).

A better way to approach this question would be to induce advances in cognitive and perspective-taking abilities experimentally—for example, through educational programs—and then examine whether increases in moral reasoning follow. Several studies of this sort have been conducted and appear to support Kohlberg's claims (Arbuthnot et al., 1983; Walker, 1980; Walker & Richards, 1979).

Structured Wholeness   A second issue is whether Kohlberg was correct in his belief that each stage of moral reasoning forms a structured whole, with the child using the same level of reasoning to approach most problems and situations. Research using Kohlberg's original scoring system failed to find this sort of consistency (Rest, 1983). However, recent studies employing the newer scoring method suggest that children's reasoning does generally follow this pattern (Walker, 1988; Walker & Taylor, 1991b). A typical study, for example, found that 60% of the time, the reasoning of research participants across a series of moral dilemmas involved only one stage, and 90% of the time it involved two adjacent stages (Walker, deVries, & Trevarthen, 1987). Nevertheless, an individual's level of reasoning is not always consistent and can even be influenced by characteristics of the dilemma itself, such as whether it involves general moral issues or personally experienced problems (Carpendale & Krebs, 1995; Teo, Becker, & Edelstein, 1995).

Invariant Sequence   Another source of controversy has involved the assertion that stages follow an invariant sequence through which all children proceed in the same order without regressing. Again, longitudinal investigations using Kohlberg's earlier scoring system reported that stage skipping and regression to lower stages were frequent (Holstein, 1976; Kuhn et al., 1977). But more recent research seems to indicate that such violations of sequence are actually uncommon (Page, 1981; Walker, 1986, 1989).

Universal Stages   The two issues just discussed can also be examined with regard to a larger question raised by Kohlberg's theory: Is the model universal, applying equally well to people of all cultures? Cross-cultural studies have examined the issues of consistency across situations (Bersoff & Miller, 1993; Lei & Cheng, 1989; Snarey, Reimer, & Kohlberg, 1985) and invariant sequence (Edwards, 1986; Lei & Cheng, 1989; Snarey et al., 1985; Tietjen & Walker, 1985) and have found these characteristics in cultures as diverse as those in Israel, Indonesia, and the Bahamas.

But some cultural differences have been found. In many nonindustrial societies, for example, individuals rarely progress to the fifth stage, although many people in more technologically advanced cultures do make this progression (Snarey, 1985). This finding is not a major problem for Kohlberg's theory, which incorporates the idea that culture and experiences help determine what stage a person ultimately reaches (Kohlberg, 1984). A more serious concern is that Kohlberg's moral dilemmas do not adequately address certain moral issues and concepts found in other cultures (Snarey & Keljo, 1991).

In some Chinese cultures, for example, the conflict between what is right for the individual and what is right for society is not ideally resolved by choosing one over the other (as is required in Kohlberg's hypothetical dilemmas). Instead, the most appropriate solution is thought to be a reconciliation of the two interests by arriving at a compromise solution (Dien, 1982). And according to Hindu beliefs in India, the very fact that Heinz finds himself in a dilemma is an indication of his prior sins or negligence, which he will not escape by committing further sinful actions, such as stealing (Shweder & Much, 1987). Kohlberg's model, then, is not applicable to everyone in these cultures.

What about generalizing principles of morality from one culture to another? Kohlberg's theory would predict that moral reasoning is universal in that an individual should view a particular behavior in the same way regardless of the customs or standards of the culture in which the behavior takes place. Research with children and adolescents in the United States, however, indicates that most children do not feel that they must impose their own moral beliefs on the behavior of individuals in cultures very different from their own (Wainryb, 1993).

Applicability should be universal not only across cultures but between sexes as well. Recall that Kohlberg's theory focuses on justice reasoning as the best indicator of moral development. In some early research, Kohlberg reported that the moral reasoning of females generally was not as advanced as that of males (Kohlberg, 1969; Kohlberg & Kramer, 1969) because the responses they gave to the dilemmas appeared to reflect lower stages. One of Kohlberg's students, however, subsequently conducted a study that challenged this suggestion.

In a book entitled *In a Different Voice*, Carol Gilligan (1982) argues that women's moral reasoning is not lower than that of males, just different from it. Specifically, she contends that Kohlberg's model underestimates the moral reasoning of females because their moral orientation is less concerned with justice—whether someone has the *right* to do something based on laws or rules—and more concerned with issues of responsibility and care—whether someone has an *obligation* to do something based on the value of a personal relationship. For example, arguing that Heinz should steal the drug because saving a life is more important than obeying laws reflects a justice orientation, whereas arguing that Heinz should steal the drug because he has an obligation to help someone he loves represents a care orientation. This book sparked a heated debate that continues today (Hekman, 1995; Larrabee, 1993; Puka, 1991).

Research examining the charge that Kohlberg's system produces lower scores for females has found few gender differences in studies using Kohlberg's moral dilemmas (Jadack et al., 1995; Thoma, 1986; Walker, 1991, 1995). To the contrary, recent studies suggest that females may even score somewhat higher than males (Garmon et al., 1996; Wark & Krebs, 1996). It appears accurate that females are more likely to use a care orientation in resolving moral issues, especially real-life personal issues (Walker et al., 1987; Wark & Krebs, 1996), but both sexes typically use both orientations to some degree (Garrod, Beal, & Shin, 1990; Gilligan & Attanucci, 1988; Smetana, Killen, & Turiel, 1991; Walker, 1989; Walker et al., 1987). The gender difference may result primarily from the different types of moral dilemmas that males and females typically encounter. For example, one study found that when the moral dilemmas were restricted to a single issue—in this case, parenting problems—there was no difference in the proportions of mothers and fathers who adopted care or justice orientations (both sexes tended to adopt a care orientation) (Clopton & Sorell, 1997).

Moral reasoning appears to advance fastest when issues are discussed one stage above the child's own level. It is wise for parents to take this into account when reasoning with children, and adjust their arguments to the appropriate level.

Movement through Stages Finally, another aspect of Kohlberg's model that has been studied extensively involves two related assertions—that each stage represents a reorganization of the child's previous moral reasoning, and that this reorganization occurs when the child experiences cognitive conflict over a moral dilemma and cannot resolve it by reasoning at the current stage. If Kohlberg's model is correct, we would expect children to be most likely to experience such cognitive conflict when they are exposed to arguments at the level of reasoning just above their own.

Research on reorganization generally has supported Kohlberg's claims. Although children are better able to understand arguments at stages lower than their own, they tend to agree more with arguments at higher stages, *if they can understand them* (Boom & Molenaar, 1989; Carroll & Rest, 1981; Walker, deVries, & Bichard, 1984).

Much of the research on cognitive conflict has involved a method known as the **+1 stage technique** (Turiel, 1966; Walker, 1988). Research participants in these studies typically are asked to solve a moral dilemma and then are exposed to arguments that either agree or disagree with their own and that are either lower, higher, or at the same stage level as theirs. Kohlberg's theory predicts that the people who display the greatest change in moral reasoning will be those exposed to the most conflict and presented with reasoning just slightly more advanced than their own (that is, at +1 stage above). Although the findings of studies using the +1 stage technique have not been entirely consistent, for the most part they have supported this prediction (Matefy & Acksen, 1976; Norcini & Snyder, 1986; Walker, 1983; Walker & Richards, 1979).

Kohlberg's model has thus stood up fairly well under experimental testing. Children's moral reasoning does appear to progress through stages and to display the characteristics suggested by Kohlberg and other cognitive-developmental theorists. The role of moral reasoning in children's actual moral behavior, however, is not quite so clear, as we will see.

> **+1 stage technique**
> A method of investigating the hierarchical organization of moral stages; children are exposed to reasoning one stage above their own in order to maximize cognitive conflict and thus induce movement to the higher stage.

Evaluating Turiel's Model

Turiel's model has also been the focus of considerable research. As with the models of Piaget and Kohlberg, the evidence generally supports the basic elements of this theory (Smetana, 1994; Tisak, 1995).

The claims that moral reasoning involves several independent domains of social cognition and that children distinguish between them from an early age, have found support in many studies. For example, even preschool children generally believe that breaking a moral rule (such as stealing) is always wrong, whereas breaking a social convention (such as eating with your hands) depends on the setting and situation. Likewise, they believe that it is wrong to do something immoral whether or not an explicit rule about it exists; ignoring a social convention, however, is acceptable if there is no specific rule prohibiting it. Finally, when asked which is more wrong, a minor moral misdeed (stealing an eraser) versus a major social-conventional transgression (wearing pajamas to school), most children chose the former (Catron & Masters, 1993; Smetana & Braegers, 1990; Smetana et al., 1993; Tisak & Turiel, 1988). Nevertheless, it should be noted that some researchers believe that young children do not yet have the cognitive capabilities to make domain distinctions of this sort (Glassman & Zan, 1995).

Turiel's belief that children's moral reasoning will be influenced by the context in which it takes place similarly has much support (Turiel & Wainryb, 1994). For example, when presented as part of a story, children view the breaking of a moral rule as always wrong. However, when the same rule is broken within their real-life experience, children are more willing to consider other factors (such as motives or intentions) in determining the wrongness of the act (Smetana et al., 1993). Likewise, physical harm (pushing someone down) is viewed by children as always wrong, whereas psychological harm (calling someone stupid) is viewed as wrong when it occurs in real life, but as much more acceptable when it occurs as part of a game (Helwig, Hildebrandt, & Turiel, 1995).

Contextual influences are even more obvious when culture is involved. Although almost all cultures distinguish between moral and conventional rules, some important differences exist. Many Asian cultures, for example, attach a great deal of importance to everyday customs and traditions (such as are involved in food preparation, dress, or marriage and funeral practices), so much so that breaking one of these rules is viewed as seriously as killing or stealing (Shweder, Mahapatra, & Miller, 1987).

One reason that cultures differ in their moral concepts is that they often begin with different beliefs or assumptions. In India, for example, it is assumed that a strong connection exists between our world and the afterlife, so that events occurring here can produce consequences there. Widows in India thus are prohibited from eating fish because this presumably would offend the husband's spirit in the afterworld (Turiel et al., 1987). The important role of such assumptions was confirmed in a later study. When a group of Indian priests was presented with the same sorts of immoral acts, but had first been asked to suspend their belief in the earth-afterlife connection, the priests judged the acts to be more acceptable (Smetana, 1994).

Distributive Justice and Retributive Justice

We have been focusing on the ideas of Piaget, Kohlberg, and Turiel, but the moral concepts assessed by their methods are not the only areas of moral reasoning that have been of interest to psychologists. Here we briefly consider research on two other aspects of children's moral reasoning: distributive justice and retributive justice.

Distributive Justice The question of how to distribute a limited amount of resources among a group of deserving people—called *distributive justice* (Damon, 1983)—is usually assessed using a reward-allocation task. In the typical study, a group of children perform a task together for which they are to receive some sort of payment. One child is then asked to divide the pay among the participants. Usually the situation is designed so that the children have performed different amounts of work.

Children's reasoning regarding distributive justice appears to develop in several stages. Up until about 4 years of age, children's reward distribution is characterized by self-interest; they tend to take a large portion of the earnings for themselves, regardless of the amount of work they contributed (Lane & Coon, 1972; Nelson & Dweck, 1977). At 5 or 6 years of age, children begin to divide rewards according to an equality principle, with all children receiving the same share, whatever their input (Damon & Colby, 1987; Damon & Killen, 1982). By about 7 years of age, children start to use equity as the basis for reward allocation; children who did more work are given more of the reward, although not always in the correct proportions (Hook, 1982, 1983; Kourilsky & Kehret-Ward, 1984).

Children's allocation of rewards appears to be influenced not only by their cognitive development—for example, their understanding of proportions—but also by situational variables (Sigelman & Waitzman, 1991). For example, children distribute more reward to those whom they consider to be in greater need or whom they see as kind and helpful (Enright et al., 1984; Nisan, 1984). Also, if children believe they will interact again with someone who has done relatively little work, they tend to reward that person using the equality rule rather than the more advanced equity rule (Graziano, 1987).

Retributive Justice Children's concepts of justice have also been examined with a view toward determining what factors children use in assigning blame or responsibility—that is, their concept of *retributive justice*. Even young children appear to approach such problems in essentially the same way as adults.

When presented with a story about a character who broke a rule, both children and adults first examine whether any harm or damage was done. If none occurred, they typically do not pursue the issue of responsibility and justice. When damage is perceived to have occurred, people in both age groups then attempt to determine whether the story character was responsible. If no blame can be assigned to the character, punishment typically is not considered necessary. If, however, the character is deemed responsible for the harm, both children and adults proceed to the questions of whether punishment is warranted and, if so, how much. At both ages, then, they appear to follow a three-step line of reasoning: Harm? Responsibility? Punishment? (Shultz & Darley, 1991; Shultz & Wright, 1985; Shultz, Wright, & Schleifer, 1986).

Although their approach to punishment situations may be similar to that of adults, children *predict* that adults' approach will be different from their own. For example, when children were presented with several stories in which a character had bad intentions and produced a bad outcome, they rated the character's behavior negatively. When asked to predict how adults would evaluate the behavior, the children predicted that the adults would also view the behavior negatively but would focus more on the outcome of the bad behaviors than on the character's motives and would evaluate the character's behavior more harshly than they had. These predictions proved to be false when the children's parents were then also asked to rate the story characters (Saltzstein et al., 1987).

These findings indicate that children's moral reasoning in situations involving responsibility for damage does not represent a simple imitation of what they expect from adults. Furthermore, children's predictions about the harshness of adults' judgments may reflect their view of adults as the creators and enforcers of social rules.

Social and Family Influences on Moral Reasoning

We have seen that cognitive-developmental and social-learning theorists agree that social factors play a role in moral development, although they disagree as to the nature and importance of that role. In this section, we consider several of the most important forms of social influence on the development of moral reasoning.

Peer Interaction Both Piaget and Kohlberg believed that peer interactions play a major role in producing more sophisticated forms of moral thought. In their view, as children are forced to wrestle with the many moral conflicts encountered in everyday interactions with friends and playmates, they gradually ascend to new cognitive stages that enable them to confront such dilemmas with a more complex and effective style of reasoning.

Correlational studies generally have demonstrated a positive relation between aspects of a child's peer interactions (such as popularity) and the child's level of moral maturity (Brody & Shaffer, 1982; Enright & Satterfield, 1980; Higgins, Power, & Kohlberg, 1984). In one of the few experimental investigations of this issue, male

Both Piaget and Kohlberg believed that children's moral reasoning is strongly influenced by their interactions with peers.

and female adolescents were tested on several of Kohlberg's dilemmas and then assigned to same-sex pairs. To generate conflict and discussion, researchers made sure each pair was made up of individuals who had offered very different views on the moral dilemmas. In some of the pairs, both were at the same stage of reasoning; in others, they were less than one stage apart; and in others, they were one full stage apart. The pairs were then given additional dilemmas to resolve over a 2-month period. Finally, all research participants were again tested on a different set of Kohlberg's dilemmas.

In the pairs with adolescents at different levels, the lower-level person generally advanced more than the higher-level person. Greatest advancement occurred in the pairs whose members were only slightly different from one another. These data not only demonstrate the potential influence of peer interactions on moral reasoning, but also support the belief that arguments just above a subject's own stage are most effective in inducing movement to the next stage (Berkowitz, Gibbs, & Broughton, 1980).

Modeling   Children learn a good deal by observing others, and researchers have investigated whether this process extends to moral reasoning. It has been shown, for example, that parents tend to use higher stage levels of reasoning as their children grow older (Denney & Duffy, 1974), which might contribute to changes in the style of the children's reasoning. Parents also lower their level of moral reasoning when discussing a moral issue with a child, much as they lower their language level, using motherese with language-learning children (Walker & Taylor, 1991a).

Social-learning theorists contend that if modeling and imitation play a role in children's moral reasoning, there is no reason for moral development to follow an invariant sequence of stages. Rather, if a child who reasons at one level can be persuaded that a less sophisticated approach is somehow better, the child should regress to the more primitive form of reasoning (Perry & Bussey, 1984).

Several studies have reported that many children who are exposed to a peer or adult model who attempts to solve a moral dilemma using reasoning that is lower than the child's level of moral reasoning will subsequently solve other dilemmas using the same level of reasoning used by the model (Brody & Henderson, 1977; Harvey & Liebert, 1979; Saltzstein, Sanvitale, & Supraner, 1978). It is not clear, however, whether the children's reasoning is affected for more than a very brief time and whether they would have been as easily influenced in the natural environment.

Parents' Disciplinary Practices   How parents interact with their children regarding moral issues has been shown to affect the level of moral reasoning displayed by the children (Eisenberg & Murphy, 1995). For example, when discussing moral issues with a child, parents are most likely to promote movement to a higher level of moral thought by encouraging the child to consider more advanced moral reasoning, while at the same time respecting and supporting the child's current level of reasoning (Kruger, 1992; Walker & Taylor, 1991a).

Another way parents influence children's moral understanding is through discipline for misconduct. When parents punish children, they generally hope that children will not only avoid engaging in the inappropriate behaviors again, but also will gradually assume responsibility for enforcing the rules. As we saw in the previous chapter, the development of self-regulation often involves learning to control the desire to engage in forbidden behavior. And just as Vygotskians and others have argued, children seem to accomplish this by *internalizing* the rules and prohibitions presented by their parents, usually during disciplinary situations (Buzzelli, 1995; Hoffman, 1994; Tappan, 1997).

The effectiveness of discipline in promoting internalization of the parents' values and morals depends on a number of factors (Grusec & Goodnow, 1994). One involves the style of punishment parents employ. Three general classes of parental discipline have been identified (Hoffman, 1970, 1984b). *Power assertion* involves the use of commands, threats, and physical force. *Love withdrawal* refers to the use of verbal disapproval, ridicule, or the withholding of affection from the child. *Induction* involves reasoning with the child to explain why certain behaviors are prohibited and often encourages feelings of guilt in the child by pointing out how the misbehavior may have caused harm or distress to someone else.

Evidence from several studies indicates that American children who have been disciplined with an induction approach display the most advanced levels of moral reasoning; love-withdrawal techniques result in somewhat lower levels, and power assertion produces the least mature forms of reasoning (Boyes & Allen, 1993; Hart, 1988b; Weiss et al., 1992).

However, this pattern of results is less clear in research conducted in other countries and cultures. For example, in India, induction reasoning is more effective than other disciplinary practices only with older (adolescent) children in the upper classes (Parikh, 1980; Saraswathi & Sundaresan, 1980); in Israel, the effect occurs for fathers', but not mothers', disciplinary style (Eisikovits & Sagi, 1982); and in the Netherlands, mothers', but not fathers', use of induction is associated with higher levels of their children's moral reasoning (Janssens & Gerris, 1992). Thus, culture clearly plays a role in the socialization of children's moral reasoning, and generalizing the results of research conducted in the United States must be done with caution (Eisenberg & Murphy, 1995).

Another factor that affects how well discipline promotes internalization involves the child's temperament. Recent studies have identified *fearfulness* as an inborn trait that influences whether children will internalize their parents' rules

BOX 14.1

A STUDY IN MORAL CHARACTER: ARE THERE "GOOD KIDS" AND "BAD KIDS"?

Are there "good kids" and "bad kids," or does children's morality depend on the situation and circumstances in which they find themselves? This question formed the basis for a classic early study of children's character, conducted by Hugh Hartshorne and Mark May (1928–1930).

The question these researchers raised is really one of *cross-situational consistency*. We might state it this way: Does morality represent a consistent personality trait that each of us carries with us? Cognitive-developmental theorists, we have seen, expect cross-situational consistency to be high because they assume that children's moral behavior is guided by their current levels of moral reasoning. Environmental/learning theorists expect much less consistency, arguing that children's behavior is more likely to be influenced by the risks and rewards that exist in a given situation.

Hartshorne and May explored this problem by exposing over 10,000 children, ages 8 to 16, to situations that provided opportunities for dishonesty. The settings ranged from homes to schools to churches, and the behaviors of interest were various forms of lying, cheating, and stealing. Each situation was designed so that dishonest behavior would "pay off" for the child, but the apparent risk

of being detected varied; in reality, the researchers were always aware of whether the child was being honest. The children were also interviewed as to their attitudes regarding dishonesty.

The results seemed very straightforward at the time. The investigators reported almost no consistency across situations for the children they studied. The fact that a child stole in one context was not useful in predicting whether the child would cheat in another. And there was very little correspondence between children's verbal pronouncements of moral values and their actual behavior. Hartshorne and May thus concluded that children's moral behavior does not reflect a personality trait, but is *situation specific*, depending primarily on the circumstances at hand.

This conclusion has since been modified to some degree. A reanalysis of the project's data indicated that some degree of consistency did exist particularly for situations that were similar to one another (Burton, 1963, 1984). Nevertheless, it remained clear that the children observed in this classic study were, for the most part, willing to adjust their moral conduct to fit the demands of the moment.

(Kochanska, 1993, 1995, 1997). For fearful children, who are prone to being timid and anxious, gentle discipline and the avoidance of power tactics seem best to promote the development of conscience (internalization) in the child. For fearless children, the best disciplinary approach capitalizes on the child's positive motivation to accept the parents' values and so involves a cooperative and responsive approach by the adult. The goodness-of-fit concept discussed in Chapter 12 thus applies here as well. The type of discipline that is most effective with a particular child is the one that best "fits" with the child's personality and temperament (Kochanska & Thompson, 1997).

Moral Reasoning and Moral Conduct

A fundamental question that arises in the area of moral development is whether children's moral reasoning is related to their moral conduct. That is, does a child who displays a more sophisticated understanding of moral issues behave more appropriately than a child who reasons at a lower level (Burton, 1984; Kutnick, 1986)?

Cognitive-developmentalists contend that these elements should be consistent with each other as well as across situations. Kohlberg, for example, believed that moral thought and moral action should be consistent (although not perfectly so), and he claimed that the evidence shows that they are (Kohlberg, 1987; Kohlberg & Candee, 1984). Social-learning theorists make a different prediction. They argue that moral reasoning and conduct may show some correspondence but that it need not be very strong, because what children say and what they do involve somewhat independent processes (Bandura, 1991b; Liebert, 1984).

The evidence on this question has not supported Kohlberg's position. Studies based on Kohlberg's method have found only a modest relation between a child's level of moral reasoning and the child's moral behavior (Blasi, 1980, 1983; Rholes & Lane, 1985; Straughan, 1986). In most children, this relation simply does not hold.

Children's moral behavior is undoubtedly influenced by many factors; moral reasoning is just one of these. Rather than attempting to make global statements about children's moral reasoning and moral actions, therefore, many researchers have found that a more fruitful approach is to examine relations between specific cognitive processes and specific behaviors. We consider some of these studies in the sections that follow.

✓ *To Recap...*

Research generally supports Piaget's model but suggests that he somewhat underestimated younger children's moral reasoning. When, in the classic moral dilemmas, the story characters' motives are made salient, even preschoolers can use this information as a basis for moral evaluations.

Experimental studies generally support Kohlberg's contention that certain cognitive and perspective-taking abilities are prerequisite to the development of moral reasoning abilities. The data also are in line with his view that moral reasoning displays consistency across situations and that children proceed through the stages in an invariant order. The universality of the model is less well documented, and in some cultures Kohlberg's theory clearly does not apply. Some researchers have also questioned the universality of the model across genders. Kohlberg's belief that each stage represents a reorganization that results from cognitive conflict also has been supported by experimental data.

Turiel's domain theory likewise has found support in experimental studies. Research suggests that children do distinguish between moral and societal rules and from an early age. Their moral reasoning also appears to be influenced by contextual factors, including culture.

Children's allocation of rewards seems to follow a predictable sequence, moving from self-interest (up to age 4), to equality (ages 5 and 6), and then to equity (age 7 and older), but it is also influenced by situational variables. Children's reasoning about application of punishment uses much the same pattern found in adults: Was harm done? If so, was the person in question responsible? If so, is punishment warranted?

Interactions with peers, especially in situations of moral conflict, stimulate the development of moral reasoning. Children's level of reasoning can be regressed by use of modeling techniques, but the durability of the change is uncertain. Parental disciplinary techniques affect moral reasoning and the degree to which children internalize parents' standards. Induction is most effective in stimulating moral development and internalization among children in the United States. The temperamental trait of fearfulness in the child helps determine the type of discipline that promotes the development of conscience.

The relation between moral reasoning and moral behavior is a fundamental issue in moral development research. Kohlberg asserted that the two should be closely related, but this assertion has been largely unsupported.

Prosocial Behavior

Prosocial behavior
The aspect of moral conduct that includes socially desirable behaviors such as sharing, helping, and cooperating; often used interchangeably with *altruism* by modern researchers.

We turn now to moral conduct—how children act as opposed to how they think. Specifically, we examine **prosocial behavior**—those acts that society considers desirable and attempts to encourage in children. Three forms of prosocial behavior have been studied most extensively: sharing, cooperation, and helping (which includes comforting and caregiving) (Eisenberg & Fabes, 1998).

We said at the beginning of the chapter that altruism presented classical ethology with a paradox because altruistic behavior presumably only benefits someone else. Ethologists solved this problem by proposing several evolutionary mechanisms that make altruistic behaviors of value not only to the person being helped but also to the helper (that is, the helper's genes). Other psychologists have come to the similar conclusion that altruism in the purest sense probably does not exist—most, if not all, prosocial behaviors produce some form of positive consequence for the helper, even if it is only at the emotional level. Because of the similarities between altruism and prosocial behavior, the terms have come to be used interchangeably by modern researchers, and we follow that practice here.

Prosocial Behavior in Infancy

Babies obviously do not have a well-developed set of moral principles, but the roots of moral behavior nevertheless can be found in infancy (Emde et al., 1991).

Altruistic behaviors, in particular, are readily observable among infants. For example, babies cry when they hear the crying of other babies, but not when they hear their own tape-recorded crying—suggesting at least a primitive level of empathy (Martin & Clark, 1982). Sharing is also very common among infants. Babies as young as 1 year will often hand a toy or some of their food to their mother or to another child. These sorts of behaviors become more frequent by age 2, but begin to decline as children enter the preschool years—probably because children come to realize that sharing their possessions is not always in their best interest (Hay, 1994; Hay et al., 1995). Toddlers also can be observed to provide comforting and nurturing to someone in distress, including one of their toys (Rheingold, 1988; Rheingold & Emery, 1986), and they often are eager to help their parents perform everyday tasks, such as folding laundry and dusting furniture (Rheingold, 1982b).

One major project had mothers observe and record their infants' behavior at home every day over many months. The focus of this research concerned children's reactions to seeing someone in distress. To guarantee that enough of these situations occurred, the mothers provided some staged events, such as faking an injury (hurting an ankle) or displaying strong emotions (getting angry on the telephone). Hundreds of these episodes were recorded over the course of the project, and in a large proportion of them the children responded in a prosocial manner. Two general categories of reactions were observed. Younger infants primarily showed only empathic distress, such as crying. But many of the older toddlers actually attempted to help the victim, although the help was not always appropriate, as when one youngster tried to feed his cereal to his ailing father (Radke-Yarrow & Zahn-Waxler, 1984; Zahn-Waxler, Radke-Yarrow, et al., 1992).

Sharing can serve a variety of interpersonal functions for toddlers. It appears to be one way in which they initiate or maintain social interactions with adults or peers (Eckerman, Davis, & Didow, 1989; Hay et al., 1995). It also may be a means by which infants resolve conflicts among themselves, such as when the number of available toys is small (Caplan et al., 1991).

Sharing and helping behaviors are certainly not always observed in infants, however. Several studies suggest that at this age, such behaviors are likely to occur only when the infant has previously been involved in a give-and-take relationship with the other person and has experienced some "receiving" as well as "giving" (Hay & Murray, 1982; Levitt et al., 1985).

Age and Gender Differences in Prosocial Behavior

If children's prosocial behavior is influenced by advances in their cognitive and affective processes, we would expect altruism to increase with age. Many laboratory studies have found this to be the case—older children are more likely to share and help than are younger ones (e.g., Eisenberg, 1990; Eisenberg & Fabes, 1998; Froming, Allen, & Jensen, 1985; Midlarsky & Hannah, 1985). Nevertheless, the issue is a bit more complex than this.

Under some circumstances, no age differences are observed. In one study, for example, older children shared money they had just earned more readily than did younger children, but only when it was first made clear to them that (1) sharing is a good thing to do; (2) they were participating in an experiment on sharing; or (3) the experimenter was watching. In the absence of such information, the older children were no more generous than the younger ones (Zarbatany, Hartmann, & Gelfand, 1985). Similarly, another study found that younger children could be just as helpful as older children if it was first made clear to them that they had the knowledge and skills needed to provide assistance (Peterson, 1983). Finally, age differences often are not found when children's sharing and helping is observed in naturalistic, rather than laboratory, settings (Farver & Branstetter, 1994; Radke-Yarrow, Zahn-Waxler, & Chapman, 1983).

Older children have generally been found to cooperate more than younger ones, and here the difference appears to be more clearly based on differences in cognitive abilities. When participating in a task or game, older children can better determine the strategies that will benefit the majority of the other participants, whereas younger children typically can identify only the strategies that are good for themselves (Knight et al., 1987). Furthermore, older children are more flexible in adjusting their behavior to match their goals. For example, older children are able to shift between a competitive strategy that permits them to obtain the most points and a cooperative strategy that maximizes the points obtained by the children and their partners. Younger children cannot easily adjust their behavior in this way and tend to remain with their initial strategy (Schmidt, Ollendick, & Stanowicz, 1988).

No differences between males and females have been reported on any measure of prosocial behavior during infancy (Hay, 1994). The question of sex differences among school-age children, however, has produced mixed findings. When teachers and peers are asked to rate which school-age children are most helpful, generous, and comforting, they consistently rate girls higher (Shigetomi, Hartmann, & Gelfand, 1981; Zarbatany et al., 1985). Yet most studies indicate only a slight tendency for girls to be more altruistic (Eagly & Crowley, 1987; Eisenberg & Fabes, 1997) or to display more empathy (Farver & Branstetter, 1994; Lennon & Eisenberg, 1987).

Culture very likely plays a role in the socialization of some early sex differences in prosocial behavior. For example, among children in the United States, girls appear to be somewhat more nurturant than boys toward babies. Yet in cultures where male children are expected to take as much responsibility for infant care as female children—such as in Kenya and the Philippines—no sex differences in nurturance are observed (Whiting, 1983).

Although girls have the reputation of being more generous, research indicates that girls are only slightly more altruistic than boys.

Cognitive and Affective Determinants of Prosocial Behavior

We have so far seen that prosocial behaviors can take various forms and begin to appear at an early age. What factors determine when prosocial behaviors emerge and how much altruism a child will exhibit? And why are some children much more altruistic than others? In this section, we consider cognitive and emotional factors that may affect prosocial development.

Moral Reasoning   We have seen that cognitive-developmental psychologists believe that moral reasoning processes lie at the heart of moral development. Their models would predict, then, a positive relation between a child's moral reasoning and her altruistic behavior (Krebs & Van Hesteren, 1994).

Investigations of this issue have typically evaluated the child's level of moral reasoning through the use of *prosocial dilemmas.* These stories differ from those of Piaget and Kohlberg in that they place less emphasis on breaking rules or laws. Instead, the story character usually must decide whether to help someone, often at some personal expense. For example, one story requires a little girl to choose between helping a hurt child and being on time for a birthday party (Eisenberg, 1982).

Investigations comparing children's prosocial reasoning with their prosocial behavior have generally found a small positive relation (Eisenberg, 1986, 1987; Eisenberg et al., 1995). This finding is similar to findings pertaining to Kohlberg's justice reasoning dilemmas, which reveal only a modest relation between how children think about moral issues and how they act.

Perspective Taking   The ability to understand a situation from someone else's point of view is also basic to cognitive-developmental explanations of prosocial behavior. Perspective taking can be physical, social, or affective.

Physical perspective taking involves simply taking another's physical point of view. The best-known task for measuring this ability in children is Piaget's three-mountains task (Piaget & Inhelder, 1956), discussed in Chapter 8. Studies using this method have found only a small relation between physical perspective-taking abilities and altruistic behavior (Moore & Eisenberg, 1984; Underwood & Moore, 1982).

Research on social perspective taking—the ability to identify the thoughts and attitudes of someone else—has produced stronger results. For example, in several studies, children who were better at telling a story from another person's point of view were more often altruistic with peers (Chalmers & Townsend, 1990; Froming et al., 1985). There has been less research on children's affective perspective taking, which involves understanding (but not necessarily experiencing) the feelings and emotions of another person. It, too, displays a positive correlation with altruism (Garner, Jones, & Miner, 1994; Moore & Eisenberg, 1984).

Empathy   Empathy differs from affective perspective taking in that the empathic child not only identifies but also *feels* the emotions of the other person, although perhaps not as strongly (Barnett, 1987). The concept of empathy has been central to some theories of prosocial development, in particular to that of Martin Hoffman (1982, 1984a, 1991).

Hoffman believes that empathy is involved in altruistic behavior in two ways. First, the empathic child experiences emotional distress when observing another person in need. The child can often relieve this distress by helping or sharing with that person. Second, when a prosocial act produces joy or happiness in the other person, the empathic child can also experience these positive emotions.

Hoffman and others assume that the development of empathy is guided in part by biological processes (Eisenberg, 1986, 1989; Zahn-Waxler, Robinson, & Emde, 1992). As a species, humans are believed to be innately capable of emotionally responding to another person's distress. This ability is present in a primitive form during infancy (Ungerer et al., 1990)—although we have seen that, at this point, babies cannot clearly separate other people's feelings from their own. With increasing cognitive development, children come to understand better what others feel and why, and by 2 to 3 years of age, their first genuinely empathic responses occur. In later childhood, empathy develops fully, enabling children to generalize empathic responding to entire groups, such as the poor or oppressed.

Although biology may play an important role in the emergence of empathy, Hoffman and others feel that children's experiences influence how rapidly and completely it develops (Barnett, 1987; Hoffman, 1984b, 1987). For example, par-

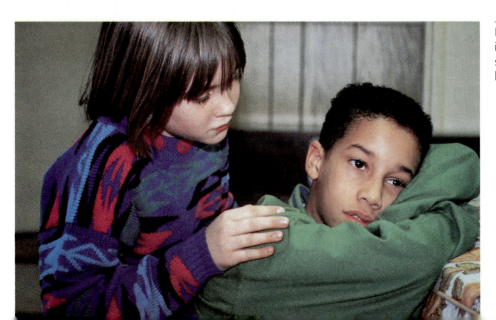

Empathy involves the ability not only to understand someone else's feelings, but also to share them.

ents who teach children to identify their own emotions and those of others may be facilitating empathic development. Similarly, discipline based on induction, in which parents point out how a child's misbehavior makes someone else feel, seems to promote the development of empathy (Krevans & Gibbs, 1996). And when parents frequently verbalize their own empathic responses, children are likely to pay more attention to these processes and thus achieve a greater understanding of how they operate (Eisenberg, Fabes, et al., 1992, 1993; Fabes, Eisenberg, & Miller, 1990).

The role of empathy in prosocial behavior has been studied more extensively than any other cognitive or affective variable (Batson & Oleson, 1991; Janssens & Gerris, 1992). In recent years, the assessment of empathy has focused on physiological responses, such as children's emotional arousal and facial expressions while viewing a videotape designed to induce feelings of sympathy for a story character. Children whose responses of this type are the greatest have been shown to be most likely to share or to display other prosocial behaviors when given the opportunity (Eisenberg & Fabes, 1998; Fabes et al., 1994; Miller et al., 1996). Some researchers have found this relation to be stronger in boys than in girls (Roberts & Strayer, 1996).

Social and Family Determinants of Prosocial Behavior

Children's willingness to share, help, and cooperate is, of course, also affected by social and situational factors. Social-learning theorists, in particular, believe that prosocial behaviors are influenced by the same sorts of learning processes that affect other social behaviors, including reinforcement and observational learning.

Reinforcement

Will children be more altruistic if they are reinforced for altruism? This straightforward question has been answered positively many times in laboratory studies, demonstrating clear effects of reward and praise on children's prosocial behaviors (Eisenberg & Murphy, 1995; Gelfand & Hartmann, 1982). Praise is especially effective in promoting altruism if it emphasizes that the child is a generous or helpful person ("You were a very nice girl for sharing your candy") (Mills & Grusec, 1989). Applied psychologists have used reward programs as a way of increasing prosocial behaviors in the classroom and other naturalistic settings (Barton, 1981; Kohler & Fowler, 1985; Serbin, Tonick, & Sternglanz, 1977).

But do reinforcement processes play a role in maintaining altruism under everyday circumstances, when no psychologist is involved? One study investigating preschool children's naturally occurring altruistic behavior found that peers often responded positively to this type of behavior, such as by smiling, thanking the child, or doing something nice in return (Eisenberg et al., 1981). Similar research conducted in home settings has indicated that mothers, like peers, often respond to altruistic behavior with some form of praise or verbal approval (Eisenberg, Fabes, et al., 1992; Mills & Grusec, 1988). And older siblings who are cooperative and helpful also tend to promote prosocial interactions among younger family members (Dunn & Munn, 1986).

Finally, even in the absence of external rewards or approval, reinforcement processes can still be in operation. Witnessing the joy experienced by someone we have just helped, for example, or sharing that person's relief from distress can reinforce our helping behavior. Whether pure altruism ever occurs remains a matter of debate, but there can be no doubt that much of children's prosocial behavior occurs because it rewards the giver as well as the receiver.

Modeling and the Media

Children's prosocial behavior is very much influenced by what they see others do (Eisenberg & Murphy, 1995). Laboratory studies have shown that children share more or are more helpful after observing a model performing similar behaviors (e.g., Eron & Huesmann, 1986; Lipscomb, McAllister, & Bregman, 1985; Radke-Yarrow & Zahn-Waxler, 1986). Not all models are imitated equally, however. Models who are seen as more powerful, competent, or important tend to be imitated more often (Eisenberg & Fabes, 1998).

Some psychologists have attempted to use modeling in applied settings to increase prosocial behavior. Children's educational television, for example, often includes moral themes and prosocial messages. Programs such as *Sesame Street*, *Barney and Friends*, and *Care Bears* are designed explicitly to encourage young children to help and cooperate (Huston & Wright, 1997). Research in field settings has shown that regular exposure to prosocial television can increase altruistic and socially desirable behaviors at all age levels (Friedrich-Cofer et al., 1979; Hearold, 1986; Stein & Friedrich, 1975).

✓ *To Recap...*

Prosocial, or altruistic, behaviors include sharing, cooperating, and helping. Even infants display some types of prosocial behavior. With age, prosocial behavior generally increases, although the relation is not a simple one. Typical experimental procedures may exaggerate differences in sharing and helping between younger and older children.

Although girls are generally rated as more altruistic by teachers and peers, the observed differences in actual behaviors of boys and girls are small.

Cognitive and affective factors influence prosocial behavior. Children's levels of moral reasoning, as measured by responses to prosocial dilemmas, display a small positive correlation with altruistic behavior. Physical, social, and affective perspective taking also correlate positively, although only modestly, with prosocial actions.

Empathy develops gradually through childhood and is believed to be the product of both innate processes and socialization. Parental child-rearing practices appear especially important. Physiological measures of empathy correlate positively with children's prosocial behavior.

Two environmental determinants clearly affect prosocial behavior. In both laboratory and classroom, systematically applied reinforcement increases altruism. Reinforcement also appears to operate in the natural environment, with peers and parents often providing social approval for altruistic acts. Modeling can increase prosocial responding in the laboratory. Television programs with prosocial content have also been demonstrated to increase children's altruism.

Aggression

At the opposite end of the spectrum from prosocial behavior is the antisocial behavior of **aggression**. Whether it takes the form of destroying a preschool playmate's block tower, teasing and taunting by a fourth grader, or fighting between teenage gangs, aggression is a common and important aspect of child development that has been studied extensively (Coie & Dodge, 1998; Loeber & Farrington, 1998; Pierce & Cohen, 1995).

Defining Aggression

Aggression can take many forms, and its scientific definition must include the elements common to all of them. But it has not been easy to settle on a definition that is both objective enough for research purposes—easy to observe and measure—and

Aggression
Behavior that is intended to cause harm to persons or property and that is not socially justifiable.

at the same time consistent with a commonsense understanding of what is and is not aggressive behavior.

Aggression might appear to be any behavior that hurts someone or damages property. But accidentally spilling hot coffee on a friend or his new carpet is not aggression, whereas throwing a brick at someone or her car, and missing, *is* aggression. So aggression seems to be based less on its *consequences* and more on the *intention* to cause harm. On the other hand, dentists sometimes cause pain that is not altogether accidental, and house wreckers intentionally damage property. Also, a person's intention is much more difficult for a researcher to observe and measure than is the behavior it produces.

These sorts of problems have led researchers to define aggression along these lines: *behavior that is intended to cause harm to persons or property and that is not socially justifiable.* Notice that by this definition, aggression is always based on a social judgment that takes into account both the individual's motives and the context in which the behavior occurs (Coie & Dodge, 1998; Parke & Slaby, 1983).

Aggression can be divided into types based on its form and function. For example, verbal aggression, involving name calling, teasing, threats, and so forth, can be distinguished from physical aggression, such as hitting, kicking, and biting. In addition, aggression aimed specifically at inflicting pain or harm is termed **hostile aggression** (or **retaliatory aggression**, if it is carried out in response to the aggression of someone else), whereas aggressive behavior whose purpose is to obtain something (e.g., shoving another child away from a desired toy) is termed **instrumental aggression** (Berkowitz, 1993). A form of aggression that has been studied extensively in recent years is **relational aggression**, whose purpose is to damage or manipulate social relationships, such as through rumor spreading, threats to withdraw friendship, or social exclusion (Crick, 1995; Crick & Grotpeter, 1995).

Age and Gender Differences in Aggression

The various types of aggression are worth distinguishing because they occur in different proportions among children of different ages and sexes. Most of our knowledge regarding aggression during the preschool years has been based on direct observation of peer interactions. Between the ages of 18 months and 5 years, there is no simple relation between children's ages and their overall aggression (Hay, 1984). There is some evidence, however, that physical and instrumental aggression are more prevalent at the younger ages, with verbal and hostile aggression becoming more common as children reach school age (McCabe & Lipscomb, 1988). Aggression in older children often is measured by use of teacher ratings or the *peer nomination* method (discussed again in Chapter 16), in which each child rates classmates. Ratings of children in first through fifth grades have indicated that overall levels of aggression gradually decrease (Coie & Dodge, 1998; Haapasalo & Tremblay, 1994).

Gender differences in aggression are well documented and begin early (Eagly & Steffen, 1986). Boys begin to display more aggression as preschoolers and continue to do so throughout the elementary-school years (Loeber & Hay, 1997). But beginning with the preschool years and extending into adolescence, girls display more relational aggression than boys do (Crick, Bigbee, & Howes, 1996; Crick, Casas, & Mosher, 1997). In the later elementary grades, another gender difference begins to become apparent. Aggression by boys toward other boys becomes increasingly physical in nature, but aggression by boys toward girls drops markedly. Aggression by girls remains primarily relational and is directed predominantly toward other girls (Cairns et al., 1989; Galen & Underwood, 1997).

Hostile (retaliatory) aggression
Aggression whose purpose is to cause pain or injury.

Instrumental aggression
Aggression whose purpose is to obtain something desired.

Relational aggression
Aggression designed to damage or disrupt social relationships.

In young males, aggression is often physical, whereas in young females it is often verbal.

Gender can also play a role in the measurement of aggression. Expectations based on gender influence how observers evaluate children's aggression. In one study, adults viewed a film of two preschoolers in snowsuits playing roughly in the snow. Some of the adults were told that the children were two boys, some that they were two girls, and some that they were a boy and a girl. Despite having viewed the same film, both male and female adults rated the "girls" as displaying more aggression than the "boys" (Condry & Ross, 1985). These results can be interpreted in a number of ways. For example, rough play may be seen as so inherent in little boys that it is viewed as a normal part of their behavior. In little girls, however, roughhousing is not expected and so may warrant a different label. Regardless of the explanation, the findings illustrate the social judgment aspect of defining aggression.

Biological Determinants of Aggression

Much of the research on children's aggression has been concerned with identifying its causes. Here we consider the determinants that have primarily a biological basis and then move on to social and cognitive influences.

An individual's level of aggression has proved to be remarkably stable over many years (Farrington, 1994; Loeber & Stouthamer-Loeber, 1998). Longitudinal research indicates that peer nominations of aggression at age 8 are excellent predictors of aggression and various other antisocial behaviors at age 30 (Eron, 1987; Eron et al., 1987). This degree of stability lends itself well to a genetic or biological explanation of the behavior. Hormones, inborn temperament styles, and dominance mechanisms are among the mechanisms that have been suggested.

Hormones   The hormones produced by our bodies are responsible for some of the physical and behavioral differences between males and females (a topic we discuss in more detail in Chapter 15). Injecting hormones from male laboratory animals into female animals causes the females to display more fighting and other forms of aggressive behavior (Svare, 1983). Research suggests that the hormone testosterone plays a role in human aggression (Archer, 1991; Coie & Dodge, 1998).

In a well-known Swedish study, 15- to 17-year-old boys were rated by peers for aggressive behavior and then tested for their levels of testosterone. The blood level of the hormone correlated significantly with peer ratings of both verbal and physical aggression—particularly for retaliatory aggression. The researchers explained this relation by noting that boys with higher levels of the hormone described themselves as being more irritable and impatient, perhaps making them especially susceptible to threats and provocations (Olweus et al, 1988). A number of other studies have also reported significant correlations between level of testosterone and measures of aggression (Dabbs, 1992; Dabbs & Morris, 1990; Sussman et al., 1987). It is not clear, however, whether testosterone acts directly on behavior or through its effects on neurotransmitters in the brain (Blackburn, 1993).

The influence of testosterone and other hormones may also occur through interactions with social factors. One theory is that testosterone affects the play patterns of boys and girls differently and that it is boys' preference for physical games and larger play groups that leads to their displaying more aggressive behavior (Archer, 1994).

Temperament   We saw in Chapter 12 that some babies are born with "difficult" response styles. They fuss, cry, and are more demanding than other infants of the same age. This personality dimension is quite stable across childhood (Thomas & Chess, 1986), prompting researchers to investigate whether it bears some relation to the development of aggressive behavior.

A team of researchers tested this hypothesis by asking a group of mothers to rate their 6-month-old infants on a temperament questionnaire that allowed the researchers to identify "difficult" babies. Over the course of the next 5 years, the same mothers periodically evaluated their children's aggressive behavior. As predicted, the early temperament ratings were quite good predictors of which children would display greater amounts of aggression (Bates et al., 1991). A more recent longitudinal study reported similar results extending into adolescence (Caspi et al., 1995; Henry et al., 1996).

Another study examined the question by asking identical and fraternal adult twins to describe how aggressive they had been as children. Identical twins reported a much higher correspondence than fraternal twins (Rushton et al., 1986). Both of these findings, of course, could have resulted from environmental influences interacting with certain inborn traits, but they suggest that at least some portion of aggressive behavior may be attributed to genetic factors (Cummings et al., 1986).

Dominance Another way in which nature factors may affect the development of aggression involves the evolutionary mechanisms described earlier. Unlike most other explanations of aggression—which treat it solely as undesirable behavior that is best eliminated or controlled—ethologists argue that aggression has been passed along through generations because it has value to the individual and to the species (Cairns, 1986).

The dominance relationships that characterize some other species—monkeys, for example—also appear to exist among young children. Observational studies of children in naturalistic settings suggest that intact social groups, such as classrooms or children in a neighborhood, often develop a dominance hierarchy (Ginsburg, 1980; Strayer & Noel, 1986). The more dominant children establish their position through overt fighting and physical force, but eventually they maintain control over less dominant children using only nonviolent threats and gestures. The strong resemblance of these groups to those found in other species supports the idea that aggression may have evolutionary origins (Fishbein, 1984; Sluckin, 1980).

Social and Family Determinants of Aggression

Social and situational factors are also very important determinants of aggressive behavior. One common argument against the ethologists' claim that aggression is innate in humans, for example, is that there are some cultures in which interpersonal conflict is very rare (Montague, 1968).

As might be expected, social-learning theorists believe that aggression is controlled largely by learning principles (Bandura, 1986, 1989, 1994). Their research indicates, for example, that gender differences in physical aggression may result because boys—by their own report—expect less disapproval for this sort of behavior and are less bothered by the disapproval when it occurs (Boldizar, Perry, & Perry, 1989; Perry, Perry, & Weiss, 1989). Environmental influences can also be illustrated by a consideration of two familiar contexts in which aggressive behavior develops: family interactions and the viewing of violence on television (Pearl, 1987).

Family Processes Children's aggression often stems from their interactions with parents and siblings. Parents of aggressive children have been found to deal with misbehavior more through power-assertion methods of discipline, using physical punishment, than through verbal explanation or reasoning (Chamberlain & Patterson, 1995; Rubin, Stewart, & Chen, 1995; Schwartz et al., 1997). For social-learning theorists, this finding suggests that two processes may be at work in these situations. First, the parents may be modeling aggressive behavior to their children, who go on to imitate what they see. And second, these parents may be interacting with their children in ways that actually promote aggression.

An example of the first of these processes can be found in a cross-cultural study of two neighboring communities in Mexico. In one village, the level of adult conflict and violence was very high, whereas the other village was unusually peaceful and nonviolent. As predicted, the behavior of the children in these communities paralleled that of the adults. In the violent village, children engaged in more frequent play fighting and real aggression, suggesting that they were imitating the behaviors they observed in their parents and other adults (Fry, 1988).

The other process is illustrated by a series of observational studies conducted by Gerald Patterson and his colleagues (Chamberlain & Patterson, 1995; Patterson, 1982; Patterson, Reid & Dishion, 1992; Snyder & Patterson, 1995). Patterson found that families of aggressive children commonly display a troublesome pattern of interactions, which he terms **coercive family process**. These households are char-

Coercive family process Gerald Patterson's term for the method by which some families control one another through aggression and other coercive means.

WHEN CHILDREN ARE EXPOSED TO REAL-LIFE VIOLENCE

Not all the violence children witness comes in the form of movies or television programs. Many children experience repeated violence firsthand in their everyday lives. Sometimes it occurs in the home among family members, perhaps in the form of spouse or child abuse (Kashani et al., 1992; Osofsky, 1995a). But increasingly, children around the world are exposed to political, ethnic, or community violence (Cairns, 1996; Leavitt & Fox, 1993). From the streets of Northern Ireland (Cairns, 1987), to the villages of South Africa (Straker, 1992), to the inner city of Chicago (Garbarino et al., 1992), children have been the unwitting victims of terrorism and bloodshed, sometimes on a daily basis.

What happens to children whose development takes place in the context of such violence? It is well documented that stress is an important risk factor for children's health and normal development (Garmezy & Rutter, 1983; Haggerty et al., 1994). This would suggest that living in a violent environment should increase the chances of negative outcomes for children. But another possibility is that children who are exposed repeatedly to violent events might develop psychological mechanisms that can protect or buffer them from the possible negative effects of these dangerous environments. Which model does the research evidence support? Most of the studies on this question have been conducted in only the last decade or so, leaving much more work to do. We can, however, consider what researchers know thus far.

Psychologists have typically approached this issue by identifying children who have been exposed to real-life violence and then comparing their development with that of children who have not had these direct experiences. Of greatest interest have been any subsequent psychological or behavioral problems, such as aggression, anxiety and phobias, depression, and the like. Typically, this information is gathered by interviewing parents or teachers or by having them complete a questionnaire regarding the child's behavior problems. The children themselves may be interviewed about their personal experiences and their feelings about the events taking place around them. Sometimes they are asked to draw pictures depicting where they live and what it is like to live there. These drawings frequently reveal children's perceptions of, and ideas about, the world in which they live.

Two examples illustrate the different approaches that are being used to gather data on this issue. In some cases, children are studied following a specific violent episode. One study compared the reactions of children living in Los Angeles at the time of the 1992 riots following the Rodney King trial to the reactions of children living in other parts of the country, whose only exposure to these events came from the news media (Farver & Frosch, 1996). Other research focuses on children whose exposure to violence has occurred over an extended period of time. An example of this type of research is a study of Palestinian children living in the Israeli-occupied territories two years after the start of the *Intifada*, or Palestinian Uprising, that began in December 1987 (Garbarino & Kostelny, 1996; Kostelny & Garbarino, 1994).

To this point, the overriding conclusion from these studies and others like them is that even when children are not physically injured by real-life violence, they are often invisible, or silent, victims of the traumatic events (Groves et al., 1993; Osofsky, 1995a, 1995b). Younger children, in par-

acterized by very few friendly, cooperative comments or behaviors and by a high rate of hostile and negative responses. Commonly, the parents spend a good deal of time scolding, berating, or threatening the children, while the children nag or disobey the parents and tease or frustrate one another.

In such environments, aggression is used as a means of stopping or escaping from these sorts of aversive experiences. For example, a little girl may tease and

Figure 14.2
Drawing by a 9-year-old Palestinian child, revealing feelings of victimization. Note the soldiers with guns standing over the small children near their house. From "Coping with the Consequences of Living in Danger: The Case of Palestinian Children and Youth" by K. Kostelny & J. Garbarino, 1994, *International Journal of Behavioral Development, 17,* 595–611.

ticular, seem to be more strongly affected in these situations. Common problems reveal evidence of fear and anxiety—such as withdrawal, constant crying and clinging, sleep disturbances, and bedwetting—with boys somewhat more vulnerable to these problems than girls. Such children also tend to display increased use of aggressive words, aggressive play, and a general preoccupation with aggressive themes.

Children's drawings, although sometimes reflecting themes of defiance and confrontation, have most often indicated children's fears and feelings of being helpless victims (see Figure 14.2 for

an example). Children who have a secure relationship with one or both parents generally fare the best in these environments, whereas any conflict or animosity within the family increases the likelihood that the children will be affected by the violence.

In short, there is presently little evidence that either short-term or chronic exposure to violence has any beneficial effects for children, especially at younger ages. Nevertheless, much more research attention needs to be given to children in these situations to understand better the potential problems they may face (Osofsky, 1995b; Richters, 1993).

taunt her brother, who punches her to make her stop, which leads his mother to spank him for punching his sister. Thus, both the children and parents use aggression to control one another and to get what they want.

Patterson refers to this pattern as coercion because the family members achieve their goals through threats, commands, and other coercive behaviors rather than through cooperative, prosocial means. Young boys who learn this style of interaction at home—and who fail to learn more positive interpersonal skills—also display aggression in other settings and often go on to delinquency and other serious forms of antisocial behavior (Conger et al., 1994; DeBaryshe, Patterson, & Capaldi, 1993; Patterson, 1995; Vuchinich, Bank, & Patterson, 1992). The relation between this sort of parenting and later aggression in young girls is not as clear, for reasons that are not yet understood (Keenan & Shaw, 1997; McFayden-Ketchum et al., 1996).

Violence on Television   No topic concerning childhood aggression has provoked as much interest as the possible effects of violence shown on television (Eron & Huesmann, 1986; Friedrich-Cofer & Huston, 1986; Gerbner et al., 1994; Hepburn, 1995; Sawin, 1990). And with good reason. Between the years 1973 and 1993, the average number of violent scenes on Saturday morning children's programs was 23 per hour; moreover, the average child spends more time viewing television than in any other activity except sleep—about 2.5 to 4 hours each day—and by the time he reaches age 21 has witnessed about 8,000 television murders (Huston & Wright, 1998; Liebert & Sprafkin, 1988).

Beginning with Bandura in the 1960s, researchers have repeatedly demonstrated that children can learn new forms of aggression, and can be stimulated to perform them, by viewing a violent film model (Bandura, 1973, 1983, 1994). But does the average child really become more aggressive simply as a result of watching a typical diet of current network programming? The answer, based on dozens of studies and reports, appears to be yes (Huesmann & Eron, 1986; Huesmann & Miller, 1994; Paik & Comstock, 1994). Moreover, the effects of violence can take several forms.

The most obvious effect is that children imitate the violent acts they see. They are especially likely to do so when the violence is performed by the "good guys" and also when the aggression successfully achieves its purpose. A somewhat less obvious effect is that television violence increases the likelihood of all other forms of aggression in children, even those that do not resemble the behavior of the television models. And the effects are long term—the amount of violence boys view at age 8 is a good predictor of their level of crime at age 30 (Huesmann & Miller, 1994). Violence on television can also make children more tolerant of aggression and less bothered by it (Parke & Slaby, 1983). Finally, the relation between violence and aggression appears to be circular: television violence stimulates aggression, and more aggressive children

Violence on television has been shown to be a common cause of children's aggression.

Reprinted by permission of NEA, Inc.

also tend to watch more violent television (Huesmann, Lagerspetz, & Eron, 1984). And in keeping with the sex differences noted earlier, boys watch more violent cartoons and action stories than do girls (Huston et al., 1990).

Cognitive Influences on Aggression

Any complete understanding of children's aggression must include the cognitive processes that control it. Much research in this area has involved the development of social cognition, or how children come to understand the social world in which they live (Crick & Dodge, 1994; Graham & Juvonen, 1998; Turiel, 1987).

Aggression is a subject with which most youngsters are familiar. From an early age, children can identify aggressive behavior and realize that it is considered undesirable. Even first graders show strong agreement on peer nominations of aggression, and they use this information to decide whom they would prefer as friends (Younger & Piccinin, 1989; Younger, Schwartzman, & Ledingham, 1985). By the age of 5, children can comprehend more complex forms of aggressive behavior, such as **displaced aggression**, in which a child who has been the object of aggression reacts by striking out at something else (Miller & DeMarie-Dreblow, 1990; Weiss & Miller, 1983).

Aggressive children (especially boys) show certain cognitive differences from their classmates. For example, their level of moral reasoning (Bear, 1989) and empathy (Cohen & Strayer, 1996) tend to be lower, and they are less likely to take into account a character's motives when making a moral judgment (Sanvitale et al., 1989). In addition, aggressive children often display a "self-protective" interpretation of their social world in that they tend to minimize the negative feelings that other children have toward them. This is especially true among minority children (Zabriski & Coie, 1996).

Aggressive children also have been found to differ in two other aspects of social cognition (Dodge & Crick, 1990). One of these is attributions. Kenneth Dodge and his associates, using an information-processing model, found that aggressive children have difficulty reading social cues in the environment (Crick & Dodge, 1994; Dodge & Crick, 1990; Quiggle et al., 1992). Their studies typically involve videotaped episodes in which one child is harmed or provoked by a peer whose intentions are unclear. In these situations, aggressive children are much more likely to attribute hostile or malicious motives to the provoker. And when cues are provided to suggest that the provoker's intentions are not hostile, aggressive children have more difficulty understanding and using these cues (Dodge & Crick, 1990; Dodge & Somberg, 1987). Thus, these children may be aggressive because they do not view the world in the same way that most children do (Waas, 1988; Waldman, 1996). Children whose aggression stems from these sorts of attributional problems are most likely to display hostile aggression (Crick & Dodge, 1996), defined earlier as aggression whose main purpose is to inflict harm.

Dodge believes that aggressive children also frequently have difficulty with another aspect of their social information-processing—deciding how to respond to a provocation from another child (Dodge & Crick, 1990). In such situations, these children are most likely to select an aggressive response as the best way to respond, apparently because they believe that this approach will produce the most positive outcomes. Aggressive children with this type of processing difficulty are most likely to display instrumental aggression, whose purpose, we have seen, is to obtain something (Crick & Dodge, 1996).

The studies described in this section, together with the research already discussed, indicate that aggression is a complex social behavior with biological, social,

Displaced aggression
Retaliatory aggression directed at a person or object other than the one against whom retaliation is desired.

and cognitive elements. This complexity has made the task of preventing or reducing the frequency of aggression a major challenge.

Development in Cultural Context
Does Being Aggressive Mean Being Rejected?

Aggression is considered a social problem primarily because it causes harm to others. But psychologists have also warned that aggressive children, by failing to acquire appropriate social skills, run the risk of being rejected by their peer group and becoming outcasts (Asher & Coie, 1990; Lochman & Wayland, 1994).

We will see in Chapter 16 that these concerns have some foundation. Aggressive children often have poor interpersonal skills, and aggression runs high among unpopular, rejected children (although the cause-and-effect relation probably operates in both directions). But does this mean that highly aggressive children never have friends? Or that they are never members of stable social groups?

These questions were addressed in a large-scale study of the social patterns of aggressive children (Cairns et al., 1988). To begin, the researchers identified a group of boys and girls in the fourth and seventh grades as very aggressive, based on reports from their teachers, principals, and counselors. Next, for comparison, the researchers selected a group of nonaggressive children who were similar in age, gender, race, and other related characteristics. The social patterns of the two groups were measured by a number of means, including interviews with classmates, ratings by teachers, and self-ratings.

The data from these measures were analyzed to answer several questions. First, did the children group themselves into social clusters, in which certain children spent a great deal of time together? If so, which children were members of these groups? Were any of the clusters made up predominantly of aggressive children? Finally, how often were aggressive children nominated as "best friends" by their classmates?

The results proved somewhat surprising. In the social clusters that were identified, aggressive individuals were just as likely to be members as those who were nonaggressive. Children high in aggression often tended to hang around together, forming their own clusters. And aggressive children had just as many peer nominations as best friend as did nonaggressive children. The best-friend relationships, however, involved aggressive children nominating one another and nonaggressive children nominating one another.

These findings, once again, demonstrate how studies of children in their natural environments often turn up unexpected results. The widely held belief that aggressive behavior automatically sentences a child to a life of social isolation is clearly overstated. Many aggressive children have a network of friends who are similar to themselves. Although these clusters may encourage and thus perpetuate antisocial behavior, they also appear to provide friendships and social support. Thus, although many aggressive children may fail to develop good interpersonal skills and may be rejected by their peers, some are socially competent enough to make and maintain friends.

Controlling Aggression

Parents, teachers, and public officials often look to developmental psychology for help in solving real-life problems. This has been very much the case with regard to reducing juvenile violence and aggression, a task in which legal and judicial methods have generally failed. But because researchers do not yet completely understand the mechanisms of antisocial behavior, attempts to control it through psychological or educational methods have been only partially successful (Kazdin, 1987; Tate, Reppucci, & Mulvey, 1995). We examine some of these methods next.

Catharsis   It was once believed that aggression is a means of venting steam and that it can thus be prevented by having the aggressive child channel energy into other behaviors or experience aggression vicariously. Hitting a punching bag or watching a wrestling match, then, could take the place of engaging in aggressive behaviors. Psychoanalytic theory refers to these substitute behaviors as forms of **catharsis**. The cathartic process has been used to defend the existence of violent television programs and aggression-related toys (Feshbach & Singer, 1971).

Catharsis
The psychoanalytic belief that the likelihood of aggression can be reduced by viewing aggression or by engaging in high-energy behavior.

Research evidence, however, does not support this theory. As we have seen, viewing violence on television increases rather than decreases the probability of aggression. And studies with both children and adults indicate that engaging in high-activity behaviors does not make aggression any less likely (Geen, 1983). Not surprisingly, methods aimed at curbing aggression through catharsis have generally proved ineffective (Parke & Slaby, 1983).

Parent Training   It is well established that parents' child-rearing methods are related to their children's aggression (Chamberlain & Patterson, 1995; Eisenberg & Murphy, 1995). One of the most straightforward and successful approaches to handling this source of aggression has been the use of parent training techniques (Kazdin, 1987; Reid, 1993). Drawing on principles of behavior modification, psychologists have trained parents in more effective ways of interacting with their children. Parents learn to reduce the use of negative remarks, such as threats and commands, and replace them with positive statements and verbal approval of children's prosocial behaviors. They are also trained in applying nonphysical punishment in a consistent and reasonable manner when discipline is required. The results of this form of intervention have often been dramatic in changing both the parents' and the children's behavior (Horne & Sayger, 1990; McCord & Tremblay, 1992). Similar techniques have been used to train teachers and other child-care workers (Kazdin, 1987).

Cognitive Methods   Another way to reduce aggression is to focus on cognitive processes, which tend to be different for aggressive children. This approach has been used with children ranging in age from preschoolers to adolescents (Gibbs, 1991).

One cognitive method focuses on the emotions that accompany behaviors. Aggression is often accompanied by anger. Laboratory studies with adults have shown that if this emotional response can be replaced with an incompatible response, such as empathy, aggression can be prevented or decreased (Baron, 1983). Similarly, programs for increasing children's empathy—by teaching them to take the perspective of the other child and to experience that child's emotional reactions—have found some success in reducing conflict and aggression (Feshbach & Feshbach, 1982; Gibbs, 1987).

A second cognitive approach involves preventing aggression through training in problem-solving techniques. This method teaches children to deal with problem situations more effectively by first generating and examining various strategies for confronting the problem and then following a systematic plan for dealing with it. With younger children, problem-solving training often is begun in a laboratory setting. The children first hear stories in which a character faces potential conflict and

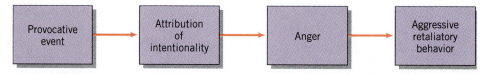

Figure 14.3
A model illustrating the roles of faulty attributions and anger in causing retaliatory aggres-
sion. Adapted from "Attributional and Emotional Determinants of Aggression among African-
American and Latino Young Adolescents" by S. Graham et al., 1992, *Developmental
Psychology, 28*, 731–740. Copyright © 1992 by the American Psychological Association.
Reprinted by permission.

then are trained to analyze the problem and develop constructive solutions.
Gradually, the children are encouraged to apply these new skills in real-life situations (Lochman et al., 1984; Shure, 1989). Similar programs have been used with
aggressive adolescents (Goldstein & Glick, 1994; Guerra & Slaby, 1990).

Applications
Understanding and Reducing Aggression in Inner-City Youth

In the United States, problems involving aggression have been prevalent among
inner-city youths during the past decade. It is generally accepted that these problems stem principally from sociocultural factors, including poverty, failure to complete high school, and family instability (Boone, 1991; Gibbs, 1988; Leadbeater &
Bishop, 1994; Staub, 1996).

A recent analysis has added faulty attributional processes as a contributor to the
aggressive behavior of these youths (Graham & Hochn, 1995; Graham & Juvonen,
1998; Graham, Hudley, & Williams, 1992). Like the attributional model of Dodge,
described earlier, this analysis also begins by suggesting that aggressive children are
more likely to interpret ambiguous, provocative actions by their peers (such as
bumping into them in the school hallway) as intentional and hostile. However, as
shown in Figure 14.3, this model adds a third step—emotional arousal, or anger—
which is thought to energize the aggressive, retaliatory behavior.

Using this model as a basis, the researchers developed a cognitive intervention
program designed to interrupt the sequence leading up to the aggression (Hudley
& Graham, 1993). Some earlier intervention programs had also assumed that anger
plays a role in causing aggression and so focused on methods of reducing the anger
(Bash & Camp, 1985; Goldstein & Glick, 1987). The present program, in contrast,
attacks the problem a step earlier, focusing on the attributions that are believed to
generate the anger.

The study involved urban African-American children in grades 4 to 6, who had
been selected on the basis of teacher and peer ratings of their aggression. Most of
the children had been rated high on aggression, but some had been rated low (so
that not all children selected to participate in the study were stigmatized as problem students). Each research participant was assigned to one of three groups: an
experimental group that received attribution training, an attention control group
that received training only in academic skills, and a second control group that
received no training.

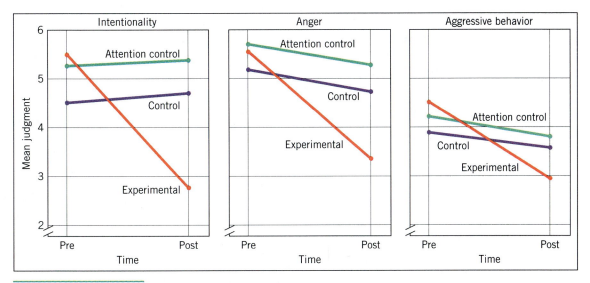

Figure 14.4
Results of an intervention study with African–American children. The Experimental group received attributional training and decreased the most on the three measures of interest. Adapted from "An Attributional Intervention to Reduce Peer-Directed Aggression among African–American Boys" by C. Hudley & S. Graham, 1993, *Child Development, 64,* 124–138. Copyright © 1993 by the Society for Research in Child Development. Reprinted by permission.

The attribution training involved teaching the children to recognize cues to another person's intentions (such as facial expressions), to encourage nonhostile attributions when the peer's actions were ambiguous (for example, "he probably did it by accident"), and to generate nonaggressive responses to the peer's behavior. The training continued for 6 weeks and included a variety of methods, such as storytelling, role-playing, videos, and group brainstorming.

Before and after the training, all research participants were given a series of assessments designed to determine how likely they were to (a) attribute hostile intentions in an ambiguous situation, (b) become angry in response to such attributions, and (c) respond with aggressive behavior. The data for those children initially rated high on aggression are shown in Figure 14.4. Obviously, the attributional training worked very well. On each of the three measures, children in the experimental group scored the lowest on the posttest that followed the training and showed by far the greatest change. These data suggest not only that attributions play a role in producing aggression toward peers in everyday classroom situations, but also that cognitive interventions designed to change these attributions can reduce such aggression.

The researchers caution, however, that other factors in the situation should not be overlooked. One is that not all aggression is directed toward peers and that this approach may not reduce problems involving vandalism, defiance of authority, theft, and so forth. Perhaps a more important point is that given the extremely difficult conditions under which many of these urban children live, attributing hostile intentions to peer provocations may often be accurate and retaliating with aggression may be a useful survival response in this setting.

✓ *To Recap...*

Aggression is often defined as behavior that is intended to cause harm and that is not socially justifiable. This definition always involves a social judgment. Aggression can be classified as verbal versus physical, as instrumental versus hostile or retaliatory, or as relational. To measure aggression, researchers may use direct observation or the peer-nomination method.

In preschoolers, physical and instrumental aggression gradually give way to verbal and hostile aggression. In school-age children, the overall level of aggression tends to decrease with age. Boys are more aggressive than girls, especially toward one another; girls display more relational aggression.

The fact that aggression is a very stable characteristic over the life span lends itself to a biological explanation of aggressive behavior. Biological explanations of aggression have linked it to blood levels of the hormone testosterone, to a "difficult" temperament during infancy, and to the evolutionary processes that operate in dominance relationships.

Situational factors are assumed to influence aggression by way of the social-learning principles of reinforcement, punishment, and observational learning. The families of aggressive children engage in an ongoing pattern of coercive interactions in which members control one another through forms of aggressive behavior. Violence on television also increases the likelihood of aggression in child viewers. The effects may include direct imitation of the violent behavior, an increase in overall aggression, and an increase in children's tolerance of aggression in others.

Aggressive children appear to be deficient in a number of cognitive areas, including moral reasoning and empathy. These children have difficulty interpreting social cues. They are more likely to attribute hostile motives to other children and to select responses involving aggression.

Various methods have been used in attempts to control children's aggression. Techniques based on the catharsis model have been of little value. Methods designed to teach parents more effective ways to discipline and interact with their children have proved very successful, as have cognitive approaches aimed at directly changing children's beliefs and attitudes.

Conclusion

In many respects, children's moral development is the same as any other aspect of their behavior. Hence, it is treated by developmental psychologists as simply one more topic of study. Yet issues of morality have an added element that makes them different.

It should be clear from this chapter that moral development can be studied scientifically. By viewing moral reasoning in terms of the development of rule following, psychologists can examine how this process changes with age and what factors influence it. Similarly, prosocial and antisocial behaviors can be conceptualized as forms of social behavior influenced by biological, cognitive, and environmental variables.

But although science will eventually answer many of the questions regarding moral development, it cannot answer all of them. Most moral issues—like those involving capital punishment, racial discrimination, and animal rights—are based on *values*. Values are both personal and societal, and they reflect the priorities that we attach to certain things in our lives. Each of us encounters moral decisions every day. And each of us participates in a society that is continually wrestling with moral struggles. The choices we make will sometimes be influenced by information that science has provided us, but science alone cannot dictate what we choose.

Can we develop a science of values? Those who have considered the question think it unlikely (Kurtines, Alvarez, Azmitia, 1990; Schwartz, 1990). The solutions to many of the moral issues we face may ultimately reside in the principles we develop as we grow from children to adults. Perhaps we will someday more clearly understand this process. But even if we do, the solutions still may not be obvious.

Visual Summary for Chapter 14:
Moral Development

Theories of Moral Development

Cognitive-Developmental Models → Cognitive developmentalists are most concerned with moral reasoning. Piaget proposed a 4-stage model which focused on the way children understand and follow rules. Kohlberg proposed a model that consists of three levels - preconventional, conventional, and postconventional - each composed of two stages. Turiel believes that children's moral reasoning involves several domains of social cognition and that even very young children can distinguish issues in the moral and societal domains.

Environmental/Learning Theories → Social-learning theory is most concerned with moral conduct, explaining moral behavior with reference to reinforcement and punishment principles, along with observational learning processes and self-regulation.

The Ethological Perspective → Sociobiologists have been interested in explaining altruistic behavior, while ethologists have been especially interested in aggression.

Moral Reasoning

Evaluating Piaget's Model → Research generally supports Piaget's model, but suggests that he somewhat underestimated younger children's moral reasoning. When motives are made salient, even preschoolers can use this information as a basis for moral evaluations.

Evaluating Kohlberg's Model → Research generally supports Kohlberg's model, but raises questions about the universality of the model. There are cultures where Kohlberg's theory clearly does not apply. Some researchers have also questioned the universality of the model across genders.

Evaluating Turiel's Model → Experimental studies support Turiel's domain theory. Research suggests that children from an early age distinguish between moral and societal rules. Their moral reasoning also appears to be influenced by contextual factors, including culture.

Other Forms of Justice → Children's allocation of rewards follows a predictable sequence, moving from self-interest (up to age 4), to equality (ages 5 and 6), and then to equity (age 7 and older). Children's reasoning about punishment uses much the same pattern found in adults: Was harm done? If so, is punishment warranted?

Social and Family Influences on Moral Reasoning → Interactions with peers stimulate the development of moral reasoning. Parental discipline techniques also affect moral reasoning and internalization of parents' standards. The temperamental trait of fearfulness helps determine the type of discipline that promotes the development of conscience.

Moral Reasoning and Moral Conduct → The relation between moral reasoning and moral behavior is a fundamental issue in moral development research. Kohlberg asserted that the two should be closely related, but this assertion has not been strongly supported.

Prosocial Behavior

Age and Gender Differences in Prosocial Behavior → *Even infants display some types of prosocial behavior, such as empathic crying and sharing. With age, prosocial behavior generally increases. Girls are generally rated as more altruistic by teachers and peers; however, differences in actual behaviors of boys and girls are small.*

Determinants of Prosocial Behavior → *Cognitive and affective factors influence prosocial behavior. Level of moral reasoning, as well as physical, social, and affective perspective-taking, correlate modestly with prosocial actions. Empathy correlates positively with children's prosocial behavior. Reinforcement and modeling have been found clearly to affect prosocial behavior, both in the laboratory and in the natural environment.*

Aggression

Age and Gender Differences in Aggression → *In preschoolers, physical and instrumental aggression decrease relative to verbal and hostile aggression. In school-age children, the overall level of aggression tends to decrease with age. Males are more aggressive than females, especially toward one another; females display more relational aggression.*

Biological Determinants of Aggression → *Biological explanations have linked aggression to blood levels of testosterone, to "difficult" temperament during infancy, and to evolutionary processes that operate in dominance relationships.*

Social and Family Determinants of Aggression → *Situational factors influence aggression by way of reinforcement, punishment, and observational learning. The families of aggressive children engage in an ongoing pattern of coercive interactions in which members control one another through forms of aggressive behavior. Violence on television also increases the likelihood of aggression.*

Cognitive Influences on Aggression → *Aggressive children appear deficient in a number of cognitive areas, including moral reasoning and empathy. They have difficulty interpreting social cues, and are more likely to attribute hostile motives to other children and to choose responses involving aggression.*

Controlling Aggresion → *Various methods have been used in attempts to control children's aggression. Teaching parents effective ways to discipline and interact with their children has been very successful, as have cognitive approaches aimed at directly changing children's beliefs and attitudes.*

Chapter *15*

Gender-Role Development and Sex Differences

In 1963, during what was supposed to be a routine circumcision, a baby boy's penis was accidentally damaged beyond repair. Rather than have him go through life in this condition, doctors at the renowned Johns Hopkins Medical School recommended to the boy's parents that he be transformed into a female—a process that would involve castrating him and then surgically constructing female genitalia (followed in later years by hormone treatments). In the hope of giving their baby the best chance for a normal life, the parents agreed to the surgery and went on to raise the child as their daughter, assured by the doctors that he would remain unaware of his original biology (Money, 1975).

As it turned out, the doctors were very wrong. From early on, the infant displayed more interest in toys and activities commonly preferred by boys. Across the childhood years, he continually felt uncomfortable in the female role and increasingly suspected that something was not right. His tomboy looks and mannerisms were clearly evident to other children, whose teasing and tormenting eventually led him, at age 14, to consider suicide. At this point his father finally confessed the truth of his gender, which the boy reports was a moment of great relief and self-understanding. Several operations later, the young man's original gender was restored and he resumed his life as a male (Diamond & Sigmundson, 1997).

If there is a moral to this unusual story, it might be that things are often more complex than they appear. Developmental psychologists have certainly discovered that such is the case for gender-role development. Contrary to what the medical experts believed in the 1960s, we cannot totally ignore our biology and simply select our gender arbitrarily. Nature is hardly fooled by a change of clothing. Yet, as we will see shortly, biology also is not the whole story. As with every other aspect of human development, children's genes and hormones interact in complex ways with their environments, experiences, and socialization to produce boys and girls, men and women. In this chapter we examine the fascinating topic of gender roles—how they develop, what they mean, and why they have attracted so much scientific attention.

Men and women typically differ in a number of ways—such as in physical appearance, dress, personality styles, occupational preferences, parenting roles, and certain talents and abilities—not only in Western society but in most cultures around the world. Many such differences can be traced to childhood and even infancy. What is the source of these sex-related characteristics, and how do they emerge?

During the first half of this century, most psychologists believed that after an infant had come into the world as either a boy or a girl, the child's gender-role development simply followed, more or less routinely, from there. Most sex differences in behavior were thought to have their roots in inborn factors, with the environment playing only a minor role.

The rise of the women's movement in the United States during the 1960s had an important effect on scientific thinking on this issue. As many of society's legal and cultural barriers to women were being challenged, so, too, were many scientific ideas regarding gender-role acquisition and behavior. Some researchers began to question whether many of the traditional gender differences found in our culture are really inevitable products of biology. Perhaps, instead, they are partially or totally created by the social environment. This newer point of view resulted in an explosion of scientific research and debate, which continues today and which has reexamined many previous beliefs and assumptions about sex differences (Bem, 1993; Eagly, 1995; Jacklin & Reynolds, 1993; Ruble & Martin, 1998).

In this chapter, we present a view of children's gender-role development that has resulted not only from changes in societal attitudes, but also from important advances in research methodology (Bigler, 1997; Fagot, 1982; Jacklin, 1981). Biological differences remain a major factor. But a growing understanding of cognitive and social influences and their interactions at different points in development gives us a much clearer picture of how this aspect of development unfolds.

Theories of Gender-Role Development

Before we go on to examine the major developmental theories, we should clarify the terminology we will be using throughout the chapter. When to use the label **gender** rather than **sex** has been a matter of some debate among psychologists (Deaux, 1993; Ruble & Martin, 1998). We use them interchangeably to refer to an individual's biological maleness or femaleness. The biological process through which these physical differences emerge is called **sex differentiation**. When we refer to a **sex difference**, however, we are saying simply that males and females differ on the particular personality trait or psychological characteristic under discussion; we are not assuming anything about the biological or environmental origins of that difference.

The term **gender role** (or **sex-role stereotype**) refers to a pattern or set of behaviors considered appropriate for males or females within a particular culture (Deaux, 1993; Gentile, 1993). In most cultures, for example, the male gender role is characterized by such traits as leadership, independence, and aggressiveness, whereas females are expected to be nurturant, dependent, and sensitive (Williams & Best, 1990). **Sex typing** is the process by which children develop the behaviors and attitudes considered appropriate for their gender. This process is assumed to involve a combination of biological, cognitive, and social mechanisms (Huston, 1983, 1985; Serbin, Powlishta, & Gulko, 1993).

The study of gender roles has covered many different questions and issues. And as usual, theorists from the three major traditions have had different things to say about the nature and causes of this aspect of development.

Ethological and Biological Explanations

The most traditional approach holds that evolutionary and biological processes are principally responsible for sex differences and gender-role development (Archer, 1996; Bjorklund & Kipp, 1996; Buss, 1995; Kendrick & Trost, 1993). There is no doubt, of course, that biological sex differences exist. Certainly, males and females have anatomical differences, and they also play very different roles in sexual reproduction—this is true for almost all other species as well. Among species most closely related to our own (such as primates and other mammals), males and females display clear differences in social behavior that undoubtedly have a genetic basis. Certain aspects of hormonal and brain functioning, which we consider later in the chapter, also appear to differ for males and females (Hines & Green, 1991; Kimura & Hampson, 1993, 1994).

The existence of such marked biological differences has led some theorists to suspect that most other aspects of gender-role behavior also are guided primarily by

Sex (gender)
An individual's biological maleness or femaleness.

Sex differentiation
The process through which biological sex differences emerge.

Sex difference
A behavior or characteristic in which males and females usually differ as a result of biological or environmental factors.

Gender role (sex-role stereotype)
A pattern of behaviors that is considered appropriate for males or females by the culture in which they live.

Sex typing
The process by which children develop the sex role considered by their culture to be appropriate for their gender.

inborn processes. For example, some ethologists and sociobiologists argue that sex differences in social behavior—such as females' being more nurturant toward the young and males' being more exploratory and aggressive—may have evolved because they are valuable to the survival of the species (Archer, 1996; Buss, 1995). Similar arguments have been made for certain sex differences in cognitive abilities (Geary, 1996; MacDonald, 1988c; Silverman & Eals, 1992).

Some proposals within this tradition, however, may be described as *biosocial* models (Ehrhardt, 1985; Gladue, 1994; Hood et al., 1987). The biosocial approach suggests that biological elements—namely, genes and hormones—set the process of sex differentiation in motion but that environmental conditions complete and maintain this process. One model, for example, refers to the "nature–critical period–nurture" principle. This principle holds that biological and social factors work together to produce sex differentiation, but only if they occur during specific developmental periods (Money, 1991, 1993; Money & Annecillo, 1987).

The idea that nature and nurture interact in gender-role development is not unique to biosocial models. It characterizes both the cognitive-developmental and social-learning theories as well. The differences among these approaches lie mainly in what mechanisms are believed to be involved and how much emphasis is placed on biological versus socialization influences.

Cognitive-Developmental Models

The cognitive approach to gender-role development focuses on the child's ability to understand the concepts of male and female and to identify with one of them. The emphasis, as always, is on the child's increasing knowledge regarding gender and gender roles and how this knowledge translates into the sex-typed behaviors that we commonly observe (Liben & Signorella, 1987; Martin, 1993).

Gender identity
Knowledge of one's own gender.

Gender stability
Understanding that one's gender will remain the same throughout life.

Gender consistency
Understanding that one's gender cannot be changed by superficial changes in clothing, occupation, etc.

Gender constancy
Understanding that one's gender is a fixed part of the self; it includes gender identity, gender stability, and gender consistency.

Gender schema
A cognitive structure used to organize information regarding one's gender.

A Stage Model   The early cognitive-developmental account of this process was based on a three-stage model of development. First, children develop **gender identity**—the ability to categorize themselves as male or female. This self-classification is followed by the emergence of **gender stability**—an awareness that all boys grow up to be men and all girls become women. Finally, children develop **gender consistency**—the recognition that an individual's gender is permanent and cannot change simply with changes in dress or behavior. Taken together, these three cognitive stages represent the child's understanding of **gender constancy**—the knowledge that our gender is an integral and fixed part of ourselves (Kohlberg & Ullian, 1974; Slaby & Frey, 1975).

As is typical of stage theories, the stages are assumed to be universal for all cultures, and all children are assumed to pass through them in an invariant order. More important, these changes in cognitive sophistication and awareness are thought to be the underlying causes of the changes in the child's gender-role behavior. That is, this model predicts that children will not show sex-typed behaviors until they have attained a clear understanding of gender constancy.

Information-Processing Models   Newer cognitive-developmental accounts of sex-role development have been based on the information-processing concepts of the gender schema and the gender script. We saw in Chapter 13 that children develop self-schemas, which are cognitive self-portraits of their personal characteristics. A **gender schema** is a cognitive representation of the characteristics associated with being either male or female.

The gender-schema model proposes that early in life, a child develops schemas for "boy" and "girl" (Bem, 1981, 1987; Liben & Signorella, 1987; Martin & Halverson,

Gender stability refers to the understanding that boys grow up to be men and girls grow up to be women.

1987). These schemas result principally from two factors: the child's inborn tendency to organize and classify information from the environment; and our culture's heavy emphasis on providing gender-distinguishing cues (such as clothing, names, and occupations) that make these concepts easily identifiable. The child then adopts one of the schemas—boy or girl. The schema, in turn, affects the child in three ways.

First, it prompts the child to pay greater attention to information relevant to his or her own gender. A girl may notice television ads for new Barbie dolls, for example, whereas a boy may be more attuned to sportscasts giving last night's baseball scores. Second, it influences the child's self-regulated behavior. For instance, a girl may decide to play with Barbie dolls and a boy to play baseball. Third, the gender schema may lead the child to make certain inferences, as when the child assumes that the new "quarterback" on the street is a boy (Bem, 1993; Martin, 1993; Powlishta, 1995). This model predicts that gender-stereotyped behavior will appear when the child has developed a gender schema, which seems to occur at about the same point as gender stability (Martin, 1993; Martin, Wood, & Little, 1990).

Research support for this cognitive model is growing (Cross & Markus, 1993). In Chapter 13 we saw that children can recall information better when they see it as relevant to their self-schemas. Similar findings have been reported regarding gender-related materials—children show better recall for material relevant to their own gender (Bauer, 1993; Liben & Signorella, 1993; Welch-Ross & Schmidt, 1996). A related finding is that children recall information better when it is consistent with the gender schemas they have formed. For example, in several studies, children were shown a series of pictures or photographs, each depicting either a male or female performing a gender-stereotyped activity. The children later were shown two pictures and asked which one they had seen earlier. Children had more accurate memory for gender-consistent pictures (such as a woman ironing clothes) than for gender-inconsistent pictures (such as a man ironing clothes) (Bigler & Liben, 1990; Boston & Levy, 1991; Liben & Signorella, 1993).

A similar study extended this finding to personality traits. Children recalled more things about a female character if they were told she was shy (gender consis-

BOX 15.1

STUDYING GENDER ROLES IN CROSS-CULTURAL CONTEXT

Are the traditional gender roles we find in Western societies the inevitable products of our evolutionary past, as some sociobiologists would have us believe? Have females been genetically programmed to assume the stereotyped "feminine" roles and responsibilities in any culture, whereas males are biologically destined to display stereotypical "masculine" attitudes and behaviors? This issue, which forms the basis of modern research on gender, was investigated many years ago in a classic cross-cultural study.

The research was conducted in the 1930s by Margaret Mead, a renowned anthropologist and writer. In the course of studying cultures in the South Pacific, Mead became interested in three tribes on the island of New Guinea. Although the tribes lived within 100 miles of one another, their cultures and social structures were remarkably different.

The Arapesh were peaceful mountain dwellers. In their culture, few role distinctions existed between males and females. Instead, all tribal members displayed a traditionally feminine personality. Both mothers and fathers were gentle, nurturant, and highly involved in rearing their children. The atmosphere of the society was cooperative with an emphasis on communal, rather than individual, goals and welfare.

The Mundugumor, in contrast, were fierce, cannibalistic warriors. In this tribe, too, few distinctions could be found between the roles of males and females. However, Mead described the personality style of this tribe as stereotypically masculine. Men and women fought and hunted side by side. Child rearing was given only minimal attention. The tribe had considerable wealth and resources, so little cooperation among families was required or observed. Although the society had many rules, tribal members frequently broke them, and disputes were common, leading to a general atmosphere of hostility and suspicion.

Perhaps the most interesting people were the Tschambuli. In their culture, the traditional Western gender roles were reversed. Men focused

tent) than if she was outgoing (gender inconsistent); the reverse was found for male characters (McAninch et al., 1993). Adding further support to this model, these patterns of schema-related findings are clearest among children who display the greatest knowledge of traditional sex stereotypes (Carter & Levy, 1988; Levy, 1989) and who hold the strongest sex-stereotyped attitudes (List, Collins, & Westby, 1983; Signorella & Liben, 1984).

Gender script
A familiar routine or sequence of events that is typically associated with only one gender.

A **gender script** is a cognitive representation of a familiar routine or activity that is generally associated with only one gender. According to this model, a child acquires such a script as a whole and then gradually learns to use it in more flexible ways, such as by replacing elements of it with new objects or behaviors. The gender-script approach to gender-role development is, in a sense, the opposite of the gender-schema approach (Levy & Fivush, 1993). It holds that children first learn to behave in ways that follow predictable scripts for their gender, such as having a tea party (female) or building a fort (male). Once these scripts have become familiar, the children use their experiences as one basis for constructing cognitive schemas around the categories of "male" and "female." In this way, the sex-typed behavior is seen as inducing the creation of the cognitive structures rather than vice versa.

Environmental/Learning Approaches

Social-learning theorists view gender roles as primarily learned patterns of behavior that are acquired through experience (Lott & Maluso, 1993). According to this their energies on artistic activities, including music, dance, and frequent ceremonies of all sorts. They paid great attention to their physical appearance, wearing makeup, elaborate costumes, and exotic hairstyles. In contrast, the women held most of the social and economic power. They took responsibility for obtaining food—mainly by fishing and trapping—as well as the other goods necessary for the family's survival. They also controlled the family's resources, which men could spend only with their permission. At the community level, the women served as the managers and administrators, seeing to it that the day-to-day affairs of the tribe were attended to.

Mead summarized the three tribes in this way: "The Arapesh ideal is the mild, responsive man married to the mild, responsive woman; the Mundugumor ideal is the violent, aggressive man married to the violent, aggressive woman.... In the Tschambuli we found a genuine reversal of the sex attitudes of our own culture, with the woman the dominant, impersonal, managing partner, the man the less responsible and the emotionally dependent person" (1935, p. 279).

Mead concluded from her observations that there is no inevitable relation between one's biological sex and the role one plays in a society. Our traditional gender roles, she contended, are culturally determined and socialized into our children. As we have seen, this conclusion proved to be years ahead of its time and foreshadowed much of what would be asserted by social activists and investigated by behavioral scientists 30 years later. Mead's overall view of human development, in fact, puts a major emphasis on culture as a socializing agent:

"We are forced to conclude that human nature is almost unbelievably malleable.... the differences between individuals who are members of different cultures, like the differences between individuals within a culture, are almost entirely to be laid to differences in conditioning, especially during early childhood, and the form of this conditioning is culturally determined" (p. 280).

This research has not escaped criticism, however. Some critics have suggested that Mead's data-collection methods were faulty and that her conclusions were inaccurate (Caton, 1990; Daly & Wilson, 1983). Nevertheless, her work drew attention to the important role that culture plays in human development, and it challenged the view that many of the social behaviors witnessed in Western society are the inevitable products of our genetic heritage.

approach, many sex-typed behaviors are products of the same learning principles that govern other social behaviors, including reinforcement processes, observational learning, and self-regulation (Bandura, 1989, 1991; Bussey & Bandura, 1992). Little boys, for example, are more likely to behave in traditionally masculine ways because they receive social approval for this type of behavior and disapproval when they exhibit traditionally feminine behavior or preferences. They also observe and imitate models in their environments—ranging from parents to classmates to television characters—who display gender-related behaviors. And, by learning to anticipate how others will respond to their behavior, they gradually internalize standards regarding what are appropriate and inappropriate gender behaviors and then self-regulate their behavior to conform to these standards.

Social-learning theorists do not deny that biological distinctions separate males and females, but they argue that many of the sex differences in children's social behavior and cognitive abilities are not inevitable results of their genetic makeup. Nor do they deny that children develop a cognitive understanding of different gender roles. But this understanding, they believe, is not necessarily the cause of the sex differences we observe in behavior, especially during early childhood (Bandura, 1991).

One implication of the social-learning approach has to do with the possibility for change. If sex-typed behaviors are learned, they can be unlearned or modified by changes in the child's environment or experiences. Psychologists who prefer a biological model, in contrast, do not generally believe that most sex differences can, or should, be changed.

✔ To Recap...

The biological analysis of gender-role development has looked to genetic and structural differences as the most likely causes of sex differences in behavior. Current theories, referred to as biosocial models, incorporate both biological and socialization processes.

The cognitive-developmental tradition has generated two theoretical approaches to gender-role development. The older is a stage model, in which children's understanding of gender-role issues proceeds through three stages: gender identity, gender stability, and gender consistency. Newer approaches involve information-processing models based on the concepts of the gender schema and the gender script. The gender schema is a cognitive representation of gender believed to help children organize gender-related information, regulate their gender-role behavior, and make inferences regarding gender-role issues. Both the gender-schema model and the stage model predict that children will not display sex-typed behavior until they have attained the appropriate cognitive level of development. In contrast, the gender-script model proposes that gender scripts are used as models for behavior, which in turn help induce the construction of gender schemas.

Social-learning theory views gender-role behaviors as simply another class of social responses acquired and maintained by learning principles, including reinforcement, modeling, and self-regulation. Sex differences in this view are not inevitable and may change with environmental conditions.

Sex Typing and the Socialization of Gender Differences

Of all the questions concerning gender-role development, the most intriguing and perhaps the most fundamental involves sex typing. Why do little girls and boys typically adopt the stereotyped behaviors and preferences of their gender? Most developmentalists would agree that sex typing involves biological, cognitive, and socialization processes, all operating together in the growing child (Jacklin & Reynolds, 1993; Ruble & Martin, 1998; Serbin et al., 1993). The real question, then, involves how we can identify these processes in more detail and understand precisely how they interact. In this section, we examine the role of socialization processes, which social-learning theorists contend are most influential in producing sex typing. We begin very early in development.

Early Sex Differences

We turn first to sex differences among infants and preschoolers. Differences here are especially relevant to the nature–nurture issue, because genetic influences can occur even before birth, whereas cognitive and socialization factors would seem to require some time to produce their effects.

Infancy   At birth, the most obvious sex differences involve the sexual anatomy. But several other biological differences are apparent in newborns as well. The female newborn generally is healthier and more developmentally advanced than the male, despite being somewhat smaller and lighter. Although she is less muscular and somewhat more sensitive to pain, she is better coordinated neurologically and physically (Garai & Scheinfeld, 1968; Tanner, 1974). Male and female new-borns also show somewhat different physiological reactions to minor stress (when administered the Brazelton scale, described in Chapter 6) (Davis & Emory, 1995).

Few clear differences in behavior have been demonstrated between male and female newborns (Phillips, King, & Dubois, 1978). During the first weeks of life, females maintain greater eye contact (Hittleman & Dickes, 1979); males spend more time awake and display more motor activity (Eaton & Enns, 1986; Feldman, Brody, & Miller, 1980). Male fetuses are more active in the womb as well (DiPietro et al., 1996). Sex differences are also apparent in some early lower-body reflexes (such as foot grasp and Babinski): females produce stronger reflexes on the right side; males produce stronger reflexes on the left side (Grattan et al., 1992). Similarly, at 5 months of age, females are more likely to reach for objects with their right hands, whereas males show no preference (Humphrey & Humphrey, 1987). These differences may be related to brain laterality, which we described in Chapter 6 and discuss again later in the chapter.

During the first 2 years, additional differences begin to emerge. Females generally are more vocal and begin to use language earlier (Harris, 1977). During this period, males are more likely to show illness, disease, and abnormalities of various kinds (Lahey et al., 1980).

It appears that a number of anatomical and physiological differences, along with a few behavioral distinctions, separate the sexes during infancy. But for the most part, the major gender distinctions that are so clear later in childhood do not yet exist in the newborn and young infant.

Preschool Period

Beginning at about 2 years of age, clear and pervasive sex differences in behaviors and activity preferences emerge. These differences very closely follow traditional gender stereotypes. Males show more interest in blocks, transportation toys (such as trucks and airplanes), and objects that can be manipulated. They also engage in more large-motor activities, including rough-and-tumble play, which tend to include more physical aggression (O'Brien & Huston, 1985; Roopnarine, 1984). Different socialization patterns also become evident in early childhood, with males spending more time with peers and nonfamily members than do females (Feiring & Lewis, 1987).

Girls prefer doll play, dress-up, artwork, and domestic activities such as sewing and cooking. They also prefer more sedentary activities, such as reading and drawing, over more vigorous ones. However, whereas males tend to stick to a rather narrowly defined group of toys and games, females display a wider range of interests and are more likely than males to engage in activities preferred by the opposite sex (Bussey & Bandura, 1992; Eisenberg, Tryon, & Cameron, 1984; Fagot & Leinbach, 1983). This asymmetrical pattern of sex typing is important and will appear again at other points in our discussion.

During this period **gender segregation** (also called **sex cleavage**) first emerges (Leaper, 1994; Moller & Serbin, 1996). This is the commonly observed pattern of children's playing in same-sex groups and sometimes strenuously avoiding contact with members of the other sex (Hayden-Thomson, Rubin, & Hymel, 1987; Maccoby & Jacklin, 1987; Sroufe et al., 1993). Girls generally exhibit this form of social grouping earlier than boys, but in both sexes, once it appears, it remains very strong throughout most of childhood (LaFreniere, Strayer, & Gauthier, 1984; Powlishta, Serbin, & Moller, 1993; Thorne, 1986). Furthermore, girls' groups and boys' groups differ in several ways. Boys play in larger groups, whereas girls generally limit their group size to two or three. Boys tend to play in public places away from adult obser-

Gender segregation (sex cleavage)
The tendency for male and female children to play in same-sex groups.

During the preschool period, boys and girls develop clear differences in their toy and activity preferences.

vation, whereas girls tend to stay closer to adults. And social interaction among boys often involves issues of dominance and leadership, whereas girls' interactions stress turn taking and equal participation by group members (Benenson, 1993; Benenson, Apostolerisa & Parnass, 1997; Maccoby, 1990, 1995).

If these early sex differences are primarily the products of socialization, rather than biology, then there should be evidence that male and female children are raised and treated differently by the people in their world. We turn next to the research that has examined this possibility.

Differential Treatment of Males and Females

Typically, parents anxiously await the news of whether their newborn baby is a boy or a girl. The very high interest in this characteristic—as opposed to the baby's length or blood type, for example—provides an important hint of what is to come. From the moment the child receives a gender label, he or she is in many ways treated according to that label (Block, 1983; Stern & Karraker, 1989). Let us consider some of what researchers have learned about the differential treatment of the sexes during the early childhood years.

Infancy   Even before newborns leave the hospital, parents use very different terms to describe their little boys (e.g., "firmer," "better coordinated," "stronger") (Rubin, Provenzano, & Luria, 1974), and most of the conversation centers on the baby's gender (Woolett, White, & Lyon, 1982). Once newborns arrive at home, many features of their environments are often based entirely on their gender, such as whether their nurseries are pink or blue, whether their toys are dolls or trucks, and whether their clothes have ruffles (Pomerleau et al., 1990; Shakin, Shakin, & Sternglanz, 1985). Children's names and hairstyles, of course, also typically correspond to their gender.

Society makes distinctions between males and females right from infancy.

More important differences in treatment involve how the parents interact with their babies. Boys receive more encouragement to crawl and walk, as well as more overall physical stimulation (Frisch, 1977; MacDonald & Parke, 1986). Girls usually experience a richer language environment. Mothers vocalize more to them, imitate their vocalizations more, and generally maintain a higher level of mother–infant vocal exchange (Leaper, Anderson, & Sanders, 1998; Wasserman & Lewis, 1985). Finally, when interacting with their infants, parents are more likely to encourage play with a toy that is neutral or that is considered to match the child's sex than to select one that is traditionally viewed as appropriate for the other sex (Caldera, Huston, & O'Brien, 1989; Eisenberg et al., 1985).

Although children display few sex differences in behavior before 2 years of age, differential treatment by parents and other adults during this early period may begin to promote the differences that will soon appear. An example can be seen in a study of children's communication styles. One-year-old infants were observed in a child-care center as they interacted with their teachers. One measure of interest was the frequency of assertive behaviors, defined as grabbing for objects, kicking, pushing, and the like. At this age, boys and girls exhibited an equal number of assertive behaviors. Teachers, however, were likely to respond in some way when a boy was involved but to ignore the behavior if performed by a girl. One year later, the children were observed again in the same setting. Boys now displayed more assertive behaviors than girls (Fagot et al., 1985). These findings suggest, although they do not prove, that the later difference in assertiveness resulted from the greater attention given to the little boys for these behaviors.

Preschool Period   After 2 years of age, differential reactions to males and females become more pronounced. Parents are likely to respond favorably to their children for gender-appropriate play and activities and to respond negatively to behaviors considered characteristic of the other sex (Fagot & Leinbach, 1987;

Lytton & Romney, 1991). This difference is also apparent in the toys parents provide for their children. A simple examination of children's rooms and toy collections usually reveals that they have been furnished mainly with sex-stereotyped games and activities (Lewis, 1987a; Rheingold & Cook, 1975). A similar situation exists for the Christmas presents parents give to their children, although girls often receive at least some toys appropriate for males, whereas boys are unlikely to be given any presents considered appropriate for females (Robinson & Morris, 1986).

For some children, nursery school or day care is the next step into the social world. Studies have shown that teachers, too, react differently to the two sexes. Boys receive criticism and disapproval for engaging in cross-sex activities more often than girls (Etaugh, Collins, & Gerson, 1975; Fagot, 1977). In addition, other children begin to respond similarly, typically showing disapproval to males who perform female activities but not to girls whose interests are "boyish" (Carter & McCloskey, 1984; Lamb & Roopnarine, 1979).

What effects on gender-role development might we expect from these reactions by parents, teachers, and peers? Because girls meet with little disapproval when they engage in masculine activities, their range of acceptable behaviors should be reasonably large. Males, however, cannot stray from the traditional masculine behaviors without negative consequences. Their range of gender-appropriate behaviors should thus be more restricted. These patterns, of course, are precisely what we described earlier for even younger children—being a tomboy is at least tolerated, but being a sissy is not (Feinman, 1981; Martin, 1990).

The evidence regarding early differential treatment of males and females thus offers support for the important role of reinforcement and punishment processes in children's sex typing. Socialization influences, as we have seen, can also occur through the process of observational learning.

Modeling: Gender-Role Information from the Environment

In previous chapters we have shown that various aspects of children's social behavior can be acquired and maintained through modeling and imitation. Psychologists have therefore investigated whether sex typing might not also result from the observation of models displaying gender-stereotyped behaviors, preferences, and attitudes (Lott & Maluso, 1993).

Laboratory studies have revealed that this is indeed possible, and some interesting relations have been found. Child observers focus more attention on models of the same sex, and they also recall and imitate these models' behavior to a greater degree (Bussey & Bandura, 1984; Perry & Bussey, 1979). In addition, children are sensitive to the gender appropriateness of the model's activity. If a male child, for example, believes that a behavior is "female," he is unlikely to imitate it even if it is modeled by a male (Masters et al., 1979; Raskin & Israel, 1981). An important sex difference emerges with respect to modeling, however. Boys imitate adult males and tend to avoid imitating behaviors modeled by adult females. In contrast, although girls prefer to imitate adult women, they will also imitate adult men (Bussey & Perry, 1982). This cross-sex imitation by girls may reflect their perception that our culture invests males with higher status and greater rewards (Williams, 1987). And it probably contributes to the fact that, as we have seen, the female gender role appears to be less restricted than that of the male.

Children, then, do imitate sex-typed behaviors in the laboratory. But what about the modeling children are exposed to in real life? Does it support traditional sex stereotypes?

Modeling is an important process through which children become sex-typed.

Modeling (like so many things) begins at home. In many U.S. households, children see their mothers and fathers engaged daily in traditional gender-role behaviors and activities (such as mothers cooking and fathers repairing). And, as they get older, children often spend more time in joint activities with the parent of the same sex (Crouter, Manke, & McHale, 1995). In homes in which parents perform nontraditional jobs and chores, children tend to be less sex stereotyped (Serbin et al., 1993). But even these children will likely be exposed to neighbors, relatives, classmates, and friends whose behaviors are consistent with gender stereotypes. So real-life models of traditional gender roles are abundant.

The mass media are another important source of information for children. Television, in particular, communicates to youngsters a great deal about social practices and behavior (Berry & Asamen, 1993; Gunter, 1995). Analyses of the contents of both network programs and commercials—in the United States and around the world—indicate that television has generally portrayed characters in very traditional gender roles (Craig, 1992; Furnam, Abramsky, & Gunter, 1997; Furnam & Bitar, 1993; Gilly, 1988; Loudal, 1989; Mazella et al., 1992; Signorielli, 1993). This is especially the case for children's cartoons (Thompson & Zerbinos, 1995, 1997). Perhaps it should not be surprising that children who are the heaviest television viewers also hold the most stereotyped perceptions of male and female sex roles (Luecke-Aleksa et al., 1995; McGhee & Frueh, 1980; Signorella, Bigler, & Liben, 1993).

Newspaper comics have also been analyzed for their gender-stereotyped messages. Some have clearly changed with the times. In the comic strip *Blondie*, for example, the wife recently took a job after years of being at home, and in *For Better or for Worse*, a gay character has joined the strip. Nevertheless, males most often continue to be portrayed in career situations outside the home, whereas females are shown performing domestic chores or caring for children inside the home (Brabant & Mooney, 1986, 1997; Chavez, 1985).

Finally, children's storybooks and schoolbooks represent another possible source of sex typing through modeling. Examination of recent children's books suggests that some efforts have been made to minimize sex stereotyping and to portray both males and females in a wide array of social roles (Purcell & Stewart, 1990; Turner-Bowker, 1996). But what writers try to do, mothers sometimes undo. One study, for example, reported on how mothers read picture books to their preschool children. Even when they read books that presented some of the characters (usually animals) as gender neutral, mothers referred to these characters as "he" about 95% of the time (DeLoache, Cassidy, & Carpenter, 1987).

Fathers and Sex Typing

Most young children spend a good deal more time with their mothers than with their fathers. We might expect, then, that the mother is the parent primarily responsible for the child's gender-role development. Research indicates, however, that fathers may also play a very important part in this process (Lamb, 1986; Parke, 1995, 1996).

We saw in Chapter 12 that fathers and mothers interact differently with their children. For example, fathers are more likely to play with the child, whereas mothers tend to provide caregiving. Fathers also are more likely to engage in physical play with the child—especially with a boy—whereas mothers more often engage in pretend play with the child (Jacklin, DiPietro, & Maccoby, 1984; Lindsey, Mize, & Pettit, 1997; MacDonald & Parke, 1986).

The age of the father seems to be a factor as well. Older fathers' play usually involves more verbal interactions with the child; younger fathers' play involves more physical stimulation (MacDonald & Parke, 1986; Neville & Parke, 1997). Older fathers also tend to be more affectionate toward their infant children than are younger fathers (Volling & Belsky, 1991).

In the area of gender-role socialization, fathers differ from mothers in important ways; the differences, however, are strongest during infancy and the preschool period (Fagot & Hagan, 1991; Lytton & Romney, 1991; Russell & Saebel, 1997). Fathers appear to be more concerned both that their male child be masculine and that their female child be feminine, whereas mothers tend to treat their sons and daughters alike (Fisher-Thompson, 1990; Jacklin et al., 1984; Turner & Gervai, 1995). These more rigid attitudes are expressed in fathers' descriptions of what constitutes appropriate gender-role behaviors as well as in their actual interactions with their sons and daughters (Bronstein, 1994; Lindsey et al., 1997; McGillicuddy-DeLisi, 1988; Siegal, 1987).

The fact that fathers may have greater concern for children's gender-related activities does not necessarily mean that they exert an influence on these activities. How can we determine the father's effects on the child's gender-role development? One approach, using a correlational method, suggests that fathers who hold more sex-stereotyped views have children who learn gender distinctions at an earlier age (Fagot, Leinbach, & O'Boyle, 1992; McHale et al., 1990). Another research approach, discussed later in the chapter, has examined the effects on children of being raised without a father.

There is thus much evidence for the role of socialization processes in sex typing (Jacklin & Reynolds, 1993). Boys and girls clearly are treated differently, in both obvious and subtle ways. But we will see next that the processes proposed by cognitive-developmental theorists are also involved in children's sex typing.

✔ To Recap...

Sex typing is a fundamental aspect of gender-role development. Sex typing is minimal in newborns and infants younger than about 2 years of age. Preschoolers older than about 2 years, however, display traditional sex-stereotyped toy and activity preferences. Boys show a narrower range of interests than girls, who more often engage in cross-sex activities. Gender segregation begins during this period and remains strong throughout childhood.

From birth, children's treatment is influenced by their gender. Newborns are immediately exposed to traditional cultural distinctions, and parents and other adults interact with male and female babies in stereotyped ways. In the preschool period, differential treatment of the sexes becomes even more pronounced. Parents provide children with gender-appropriate toys and encourage sex-stereotyped behaviors and interests. Nursery school and day-care teachers, as well as peers, dispense social approval and disapproval for gender-stereotyped behavior. Girls are permitted greater latitude, however, whereas boys receive criticism for straying from the more narrowly defined male role.

Modeling may also be a mechanism of sex typing. Laboratory studies report that children focus more attention on same-sex models and more often imitate their behavior. Here again, though, females display more cross-sex imitation. Real-life models of traditional gender roles are common in the everyday lives of most children. Television programs and commercials, cartoons, and newspaper comic strips also portray characters in sex-stereotyped roles.

Fathers, especially younger ones, provide infants more physical stimulation and play. Fathers appear to be more concerned than mothers with maintaining traditional gender-role behavior in their children. Children of fathers who make more sex-stereotyped distinctions learn these distinctions earlier.

Understanding Gender Roles and Stereotypes

We have reviewed considerable evidence that socialization processes are involved in sex typing. In this section, we turn to the cognitive processes that influence gender-role development. Of particular interest is the developing child's increasing understanding of gender roles and stereotypes.

Awareness of Gender Roles

A fundamental question regarding cognitive influences concerns when children first become aware of gender-related issues. This awareness involves a developing understanding of one's gender as well as an understanding of the gender-role characteristics and expectations of others (Martin, 1994; Signorella et al., 1993; Stangor & Ruble, 1987).

The ability to discriminate the categories of male and female develops remarkably early. By 2 months of age, infants can discriminate male and female voices (Jusczyk, Pisoni, & Mullenix, 1992); by 5 months of age, some can learn to respond differently to pictures of men and women (Leinbach & Fagot, 1993); and by 9 months, babies can match female voices to female faces (Poulin-Dubois et al., 1994).

We have already introduced the stage model of gender constancy, which includes gender identity ("I am a boy/girl"), gender stability ("I will grow up to be a man/woman"), and gender consistency ("I cannot change my sex") (Kohlberg & Ullian, 1974; Slaby & Frey, 1975). Data from a number of studies have confirmed this theoretical progression. By 3 years of age, almost all children display gender identity. Gender stability follows at about 4 years of age, and gender consistency at about 5. Males and females progress through these stages at approximately the same rate (Bem, 1989; Fagot, 1985; Martin & Little, 1990). This progression has been demonstrated in a variety of cultures, although children in many non-Western cultures appear to proceed through the stages more slowly (Munroe, Shimmin, & Munroe, 1984).

Gender-role knowledge
Understanding that a certain toy, activity, or personal characteristic is considered more appropriate for one sex than the other.

Other cognitive aspects of gender roles have also been investigated. The awareness that "male" and "female" are separate categories and that certain characteristics, objects, and activities are typically associated with each is termed **gender-role knowledge** (Fagot & Leinbach, 1993; Martin, 1993). By about 2 years of age, children can reliably sort pictures of males and females and their accessories (clothes, tools, and appliances) into separate piles and accurately point to pictures of things for males and things for females—two tasks commonly used to assess children's gender-role knowledge (Fagot, Leinbach, & Hagan, 1986; O'Brien & Huston, 1985).

Children do not accurately label sex-stereotyped toys until about a year later (Weinraub & Brown, 1983; Weinraub et al., 1984). Four-year-olds associate certain colors with males (blue, brown, and maroon) and females (pink and lavender) as adults do (Picariello, Greenberg, & Pillemer, 1990), but knowledge about sex-stereotyped social behavior does not emerge consistently until age 5. Before that age, few children categorize behavioral traits such as aggression, dominance, kindness, or emotionality as more masculine or feminine. This sort of classifying increases only gradually over childhood (Best & Williams, 1993; Serbin et al., 1993; Signorella et al., 1993). Finally, as we saw earlier, children tend to both learn and remember the characteristics of their own gender stereotype before those of the opposite-sex stereotype (Bauer, 1993; Boston & Levy, 1991; Welch-Ross & Schmidt, 1996).

Another kind of gender awareness involves an understanding of the rigidity of gender-role stereotypes. During the preschool years, most children view gender roles in inflexible, absolutist terms (consistent with preoperational thinking) and consider cross-sex behaviors to be serious violations of social standards. This attitude is stronger in males, however, perhaps relating to their narrower view of gender-appropriate activities (Levy, Taylor, & Gelman, 1995; Lobel & Menashri, 1993; Smetana, 1986). By middle childhood, children generally have begun to view gender roles as socially determined rules and conventions that can be approached somewhat flexibly and broken without major consequences (Serbin et al., 1993; Stoddart & Turiel, 1985)—a finding supported by longitudinal research with German children (Trautner, 1992).

One study presented children with a story of a baby who had been raised on an island with only members of the opposite sex. When asked which gender characteristics the baby would eventually display, children younger than age 9 or 10 predicted that the baby's biological sex would determine its later characteristics. Children above that age, in contrast, believed that the baby would be more influenced by the social environment and so would adopt the characteristics of the opposite sex (Taylor, 1996).

The transition to junior high school appears to increase adolescents' flexibility toward the roles of males and females. This may occur because the fairly dramatic change in setting and routine forces young adolescents to rethink many of their previous ideas (Katz & Ksansnak, 1994; Ruble, 1994). Nevertheless, across the junior high and high school years, gender stereotypes become increasingly rigid again (Alfieri, Ruble, & Higgins, 1996).

Gender Awareness and the Emergence of Sex-Typed Behavior

We have seen that some forms of gender knowledge are present relatively early in childhood. But how does this knowledge relate to sex-typed behavior?

Recall that cognitive-developmentalists view the understanding of gender roles as the fundamental process in sex typing. Once a child develops an awareness of being male, for example, he presumably becomes motivated to behave like a male, and he seeks information from his social environment to learn how this is done (Kohlberg & Ullian, 1974; Martin & Halverson, 1987).

This analysis leads to three predictions (Huston, 1985). First, the emergence of gender constancy or accurate gender-role knowledge should *precede* the corresponding sex-typed behavior. For example, children should believe that trucks are for boys and dolls are for girls *before* they display a gender-related preference for these toys. Second, gender-role knowledge should correlate with gender-role behavior. That is, at least during early childhood, the more developed the child's understanding of gender roles, the more sex-typed that child's behavior should be. And third, if we can alter a child's gender-related cognitions—for example, by providing information that reduces sex stereotyping of occupations or abilities—we should see changes in corresponding sex-typed behaviors and preferences. Let us consider the evidence available on each of the three predictions.

Numerous studies have shown that preference for sex-typed activities does not clearly depend on the emergence of gender-role knowledge, gender identity, or gender constancy (Blakemore, LaRue, & Olejnik, 1979; Bussey & Bandura, 1992; Carter & Levy, 1988; Fagot et al., 1986; Lobel & Menashri, 1993; Perry, White, & Perry, 1984). Many 2-year-olds exhibit preferences for sex-typed toys, for example, but cannot yet identify those toys as being more appropriate or typical for girls or boys. It has also been found that gender constancy is not a prerequisite for imitation of same-sex models (Bussey & Bandura, 1984, 1992). And gender knowledge does not appear to be clearly related to the degree of sex stereotyping in children's attitudes (Serbin & Sprafkin, 1986).

The second prediction—that gender-role knowledge should correlate with gender-role behavior—has not been studied extensively. The available evidence, however, does not show a strong relation between levels of cognitive awareness and sex-typed preferences or behavior in young children (Hort, Leinbach, & Fagot, 1991; Levy & Carter, 1989)—although level of gender knowledge does influence how well children can recall gender-related information (Carter & Levy, 1988; Levy, 1989).

Finally, attempts to change sex-typed behaviors by changing gender-role cognitions have produced both positive and negative results, but the long-term success of the interventions remains to be determined.

Without doubt, children's understanding and acceptance of gender-role stereotypes exerts considerable influence on their behavior from middle childhood onward (Galambos, Almeida, & Petersen, 1990; Serbin et al., 1993; Signorella, 1987). But it seems fair to conclude that a sophisticated understanding of gender and gender roles is not critical to the *appearance* of sex-typed activities and preferences. Socialization processes, therefore, probably play the major role (Fagot & Leinbach, 1993; Ruble & Martin, 1998; Serbin et al., 1993).

Effects of Sex-Typed Labeling

Gender-related cognitions affect behavior in one very important way—through the influence of the gender labels that are attached to objects and activities. It appears that children first attempt to determine whether a toy is "for boys" or "for girls." They then compare this information with their own sex and, if it matches, they accept the toy, but if it does not match, they reject it (Martin, Eisenbud, & Rose, 1995; Martin & Halverson, 1981). Younger children—those who do not yet display gender constancy—may play with a cross-sex toy if it is especially attractive. But older children, and especially boys, will tend to choose an own-sex toy, even if it is less attractive than an available opposite-sex toy (Frey & Ruble, 1992; Martin et al., 1995).

A second effect of sex-typed labels is their influence on children's performance of the labeled activity. In one study, children were presented with unfamiliar objects and told that they were things boys liked or things girls liked. Not only did children later have better recall of the objects labeled as appropriate to their sex, but they spent more time handling and exploring them (Bradbard et al., 1986). Moreover, other research has shown that in skill tasks, such as dropping marbles into a container or solving shape puzzles, children's performance was better when the task was labeled as an activity appropriate to their gender (Gold & Berger, 1978; Montemayor, 1974).

These findings illustrate the powerful role that gender labels may play in perpetuating sex differences in preferences and abilities. Once children decide that an activity is more appropriate for the other sex (for example, that "math is for boys"), their performance on the activity may suffer. In this way, the gender label serves to maintain both the stereotype and the sex difference (Carter & Levy, 1988; Levy & Carter, 1989).

✓ *To Recap...*

Cognitive issues in gender-role development include children's awareness of gender and gender roles, the relation between gender-role knowledge and emerging sex-typed behaviors, and the effects of sex-typed labeling.

Awareness of gender roles involves knowledge of both one's own gender and the gender-role characteristics and expectations of others. Even young infants can learn to discriminate the categories of male and female. More sophisticated gender awareness develops in three stages: gender identity (at about 3 years of age), gender stability (at about 4 years), and gender consistency (at about 5 years).

Gender-role knowledge involves awareness of the concepts of male and female and their culturally defined stereotypes. Children generally understand the basic male–female concept by age 2. Gender labeling of toys appears at age 3, and an awareness of sex-typed personality traits at about age 5. As children get older, they increasingly view gender roles as socially determined, and their attitudes toward violations become more tolerant and flexible.

Cognitive-developmental theory holds that the various forms of gender knowledge precede the corresponding sex-typed behaviors. Research generally fails to support this view, though a few studies have found relations between gender-role cognitions and aspects of sex-typed behavior.

Sex-typed labels affect childrens' behavior. When activities or objects are seen as being for one gender or the other, children prefer the same-sex activities and avoid the cross-sex ones. Children also tend to perform better on same-sex-labeled activities than on those with cross-sex labels.

Family Influences on Gender-Role Development

Gender-role development, like all aspects of children's development, takes place in a social context that influences it in important ways. The most influential of these contexts is the family. Many studies have been devoted to identifying those characteristics of families that affect children's gender-role development and sex-typed behavior. In this section we examine several of the most important ones.

Parental Attitudes and Child-Rearing Methods

Parents' gender-related beliefs and behaviors have long been assumed to exert a good deal of influence on their children's sex typing (Block, 1983; Huston, 1983). As we have seen, the nature of this influence may take several forms. One is based on modeling. The attitudes parents express, the kinds of household chores each engages in, whether the mother works and what she does—all may affect children's understanding and adoption of gender roles. A more direct source of influence involves the gender-role activities and behaviors that parents encourage and approve of in their children. The toys they buy, the teams or organizations they have their children join, the rules they establish for dress and social conduct, and many other specific child-rearing practices can directly shape the sorts of sex-typed behaviors in which their children will engage (Katz, 1986, 1987).

One fruitful approach to studying this question involved looking at the sex typing and gender knowledge of children raised by counterculture parents (Eiduson et al., 1982; Weisner & Eiduson, 1986). During the 1960s and early 1970s, the peace movement spawned a subculture of parents who challenged many of society's traditional social and political views. One aspect of this challenge was a belief in egalitarian gender roles, with males and females assumed to have equal abilities and to deserve equal opportunities and responsibilities. Many counterculture parents not only expressed these attitudes but put them into practice in their family interactions and lifestyles. If socialization by parents can influence children's gender-role knowledge and sex-typed behavior, relatively clear effects should have emerged within counterculture families.

The results of this research were interesting (Weisner & Wilson-Mitchell, 1990). Children of counterculture parents indeed showed less sex stereotyping, for example, in their beliefs regarding occupations, in their own occupational preferences, and in the degree to which they associated specific objects with a given sex. That is, at the cognitive level, they espoused beliefs and attitudes similar to those of their parents. But when toy and activity preferences were assessed, these children displayed much the same gender stereotyping as seen in children from more conventional families. One explanation for these findings is that the counterculture parents differed from conventional parents primarily in terms of the attitudes they modeled—what they said and how they lived. Their actual interactions with their children involving gender-related behaviors and activities, however, turned out not to be very different from those of conventional parents (Eiduson, 1980; Weitzman, Birns, & Friend, 1985). Hence, the relation between parents' socialization practices and their children's sex typing is not as clearly testable among counterculture families as we might have expected.

The role of parents as gender-role socializers, of course, must be viewed within the larger social context. Parents are simply one of the many socializing agents to which growing children are exposed. And though they may be the strongest influence, a great deal of pressure to conform to societal gender stereotypes is continually being exerted on children by peers, siblings, teachers, and the media.

Socioeconomic Status

It is commonly believed that parents in higher social classes, perhaps because they tend to be more worldly and better educated, rear their children in less gender-stereotyped ways and thus have children who display less rigid sex typing. The research evidence only partly supports this belief (Katz, 1987). Although older children and adolescents tend to display less traditional attitudes and preferences if their families are of higher socioeconomic status (Canter & Ageton, 1984; Emmerich & Shepard, 1982; Serbin et al., 1993), this relation is not as clear among younger children (Cummings & Taebel, 1980). The absence of a simple and strong relation here is probably not surprising, however, since social class is such a broad dimension on which to classify families.

Development in Family Context
Growing Up in a Single-Parent Household

Gender-role development has traditionally been studied in the context of two-parent families. But many children are not raised in such families. It is estimated that about 60% of the children born in the 1990s will spend some portion of their lives in a single-parent environment, primarily as a result of divorce (Hetherington, Bridges, & Insabella, 1998). Is gender-role development different for these children? And does divorce have different effects on boys and girls?

The answer to both questions is yes. Divorce can have a number of harmful effects on children's development, including on gender-role development. The nature and severity of these problems, however, depend on a variety of factors (Hetherington & Stanley-Hagan, 1995; Hetherington, et al., 1998).

In about 86% of divorces, mothers end up with custody of the children. Eventually, approximately 66% of these mothers (75% of fathers) remarry. But during the period immediately following divorce, children frequently experience problems of various sorts (Hetherington & Jodl, 1994; Hetherington et al., 1992). These problems often differ from one sibling to another (Monahan et al., 1993), so it may not be surprising that they also differ for males and females.

Boys generally react more negatively to divorce than do girls. Most often their problems involve conduct disorders at home and at school. Aggression and noncompliance sometimes persist for several years after the parents' divorce. Gender-role development can also be affected in boys living in households without fathers, especially if the parents were divorced during the boys' infancy or early childhood (Adams, Milner, & Schrepf, 1984). These boys typically exhibit fewer male sex-typed behaviors and attitudes than are exhibited by boys living in intact families (Serbin et al., 1993; Stevenson & Black, 1988). If separation occurs later, and particularly if an alternative male—such as an older brother—is available, the effects often are less obvious. When boys remain in the custody of their fathers, they generally show still fewer of these effects (Furstenberg & Cherlin, 1991; Hanson, 1988).

Although most researchers agree that girls react less negatively to divorce, some problems may nevertheless occur (Lee et al., 1994; Maccoby et al., 1993). The immediate emotional upheaval that follows the parents' divorce usually seems to disappear more quickly for girls, often within the first 2 years. But longer-term problems, such as dropping out of high school or college, are more frequent in these women (McLanahan & Sandefur, 1994). Among girls whose fathers are absent, very little gender-role disruption occurs before adolescence (Stevenson & Black, 1988). During the teenage years, however, several patterns of problem behavior may emerge. These girls tend to have more difficulty interacting with males of their own age. Some become shy and withdrawn, whereas others display overly outgoing and attention-seeking behavior (Newcomer & Udry, 1987; Wallerstein, Corbin, & Lewis, 1988).

The custodial parents' remarriage often intensifies children's problems, particularly in females (Hetherington & Stanley-Hagan, 1995; Lee et al., 1994). Adolescent girls who are close to their mothers may have difficulty adjusting to the introduction of a stepfather. Their relationships with their mothers frequently become hostile and antagonistic, and they tend to remain distant from their stepfathers. Boys, however, sometimes benefit from the addition of a stepfather, although usually only after a period of time (Hetherington, 1993).

The long-term effects of divorce need not be negative. Many children eventually adapt to the new family situation, whether it involves living with a single parent or with a new stepparent. Not all the factors that ease these transitions are known, but a predictable, structured environment—both at home and at school—and authoritative parenting appear to be major contributors to successful coping (Hetherington et al., 1998; Zill, Morrison, & Coiro, 1993).

Maternal Employment

We discussed the effects of maternal employment on infant–caregiver attachment in Chapter 12. Other research indicates that when mothers work outside the home, their children's gender-role development tends to be affected. Children of employed mothers are less sex-stereotyped in their attitudes, preferences, and behaviors than are the children of mothers who stay at home (Katz & Boswell, 1986; Levy, 1989; MacKinnon, Stoneman, & Brody, 1984; Signorella et al., 1993). This effect appears to be especially true for males and for younger children (Katz, 1987). Once again, the processes at work here are a matter of speculation.

Children of working mothers often spend time in day-care centers. Perhaps the staff in these centers tend to treat children in less sex-stereotyped ways or to encourage more cross-sex activities. It is also possible that mothers in the workforce maintain less traditional attitudes regarding gender roles than do mothers who stay at home, and so they tend to rear their children in less stereotyped ways. In either case, as children get older, the effects of maternal employment on sex typing become increasingly less evident.

✓ To Recap…

The family is the most influential social context in which sex typing occurs. Various characteristics of the family affect children's gender-role knowledge and behavior. Gender-related attitudes and behaviors displayed by parents influence children's sex-typed beliefs and behaviors. The clearest evidence involves a similarity in parent and child attitudes. Families from higher socioeconomic levels tend to have children who are less sex-typed in their behaviors and beliefs. This effect is strongest among older children and adolescents. Finally, the children of mothers who are employed display less sex-typed attitudes and behavior than do the children of mothers who stay at home. This effect is particularly strong among males and younger children, and it decreases with age.

Some Common Sex Differences

The toy and activity differences that distinguish boys and girls during early childhood are not the only differences commonly observed in growing children (Maccoby & Jacklin, 1974). Although some of the sex differences we will consider in this section are small, and all of them represent only the *average* difference across all males and females, they nevertheless remain to be explained.

Cognitive Differences

We begin with differences in cognition and related processes. Some appear early; others do not emerge until later. In all cases, the nature–nurture debate remains very much alive as researchers seek the sources of these differences in both biological and environmental variables.

Language and Verbal Abilities

There is little doubt that young females have greater abilities than do young males in some kinds of verbal skills (Feingold, 1992, 1993; Wentzel, 1988). Female infants produce more sounds at an earlier age than do males (Harris, 1977); they use words sooner; and the size of their early vocabularies is much larger (Nelson, 1973). On a variety of measures of grammar and language complexity (such as sentence length, use of pronouns, use of conjunctions, and so on), girls begin to show a marked superiority at about 2 years of age, and the differences continue through adolescence (Koenigsknecht & Friedman, 1976; Schacter et al., 1978). Comprehension abilities (such as understanding the meanings of words), however, do not favor females as strongly (Harris, 1977).

Recall that research indicates that mothers provide a richer language environment for their infant daughters than for their sons. These and related findings suggest that socialization factors may play a role in this sex difference. But most psychologists agree that a biological basis for early female verbal superiority probably also exists.

The sex differences in this area diminish with age. By late adolescence, females no longer display an obvious superiority in verbal abilities (Hyde & Linn, 1988).

Quantitative Abilities

The ability to deal with numbers and mathematical concepts reveals an interesting pattern of sex differences. Girls usually begin counting and using numbers before boys. Throughout the elementary-school years and junior high school, girls are better at computational problems, whereas boys do better with math reasoning problems (Fennema & Tartre, 1985; Marshall, 1984). During this period, girls also tend to get higher grades (Kimball, 1989). By high school, however, boys begin to perform better, especially at the higher levels of ability (Benbow, 1992; Gallagher & De Lisi, 1994; Hedges & Nowell, 1995). Some psychologists believe this advantage is genetic (Geary, 1996; Thomas, 1993). But it may derive, in part, from males' use of more effective strategies (Byrnes & Takahira, 1993) and their lower levels of anxiety (Duffy, Gunther, & Walters, 1997) when approaching mathematics problems.

It also has been suggested that the sex differences come about to some degree because girls view math as a male activity (and therefore have less interest in it) and because parents and teachers offer greater encouragement to males in this area. Some studies support this analysis (Catsambis, 1994; Eccles & Midgley, 1990; Jacobs, 1991; Lummis & Stevenson, 1990), but others do not (Raymond & Benbow, 1986). In this area, too, biological and socialization factors probably combine to produce the observed differences (Casey et al., 1995; Chipman, Brush, & Wilson, 1985).

In a related area, researchers have found that boys are more likely than girls to use computers in their schoolwork and play. They also express a more positive attitude toward computers and are more likely to enroll in computer courses or attend computer camp (Chen, 1985; Hess & Miura, 1985). These findings do not mean that males are better at using computers than females. They do suggest, however, the beginning of a stereotype that computers are for males. Females who accept this stereotype may shy away from computers, and so their performance may lag behind. In this way, a new, and perhaps avoidable, gender difference may be created (Lockheed, 1985).

Spatial Abilities

One area in which males repeatedly have been found to outperform females is in tasks involving spatial abilities (Feingold, 1993; Halpern, 1992). Researchers have studied spatial skills using a number of tasks and tech-

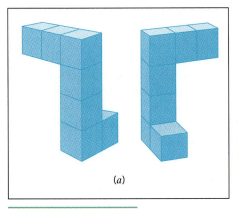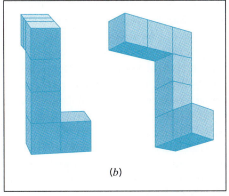

(a)   (b)

Figure 15.1
A mental–rotation task in which the subject must decide whether the two objects are the same (as in *a*) or different (as in *b*).

niques, with some producing larger and clearer differences than others (Horan & Rosser, 1984; Voyer, Voyer, & Bryden, 1995).

One type of task on which males and females differ markedly involves mental rotation (Linn & Petersen, 1985; Masters & Sanders, 1993). An example of a mental-rotation task appears in Figure 15.1. Another task at which females generally have more difficulty than males is the water-level task, shown in Figure 15.2 (Vasta & Liben, 1996). Some sex differences in spatial abilities are present during early and middle childhood (Herman & Siegel, 1978; Vasta & Green, 1982), but the differences tend to increase in adolescence and adulthood (Johnson & Meade, 1987; Voyer et al., 1995).

Biological explanations of these sex differences have involved several processes. The pattern of differences corresponds reasonably well with what would be predicted by a genetic model if spatial ability were controlled by a recessive gene carried on the X chromosome (McGee, 1982; Thomas, 1983). Some research also points to differences in the way the left and right hemispheres of the brain are organized in males and females (Bryden, 1982; McGlone, 1980). A later section discusses these biological processes and the roles they may play in sex differentiation.

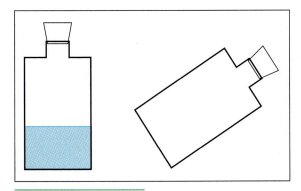

Figure 15.2
A water-level task in which the subject is asked to predict how the water will look when the bottle is tilted.

For now, we simply note that neither of these explanations has escaped major criticism (Caplan, MacPherson, & Tobin, 1985), and neither can account for all the findings in this area (Newcombe & Dubas, 1992).

Socialization analyses have been proposed as well. Some theorists believe that little girls are discouraged from engaging in activities that promote the development of spatial skills (such as playing with blocks and mechanical toys) because they are male-stereotyped activities. Thus, boys improve in these skills as girls fall behind—which, as we have seen, is consistent with the data (Baenninger & Newcombe, 1989; Newcombe & Dubas, 1992; Tracy, 1987).

In all likelihood, this sex difference, like many others, has both nature and nurture components. Males probably do have a biological advantage in some spatial skills, owing perhaps to one or both of the proposed biological mechanisms. But the effects of experience cannot be dismissed, and such effects may maintain or even magnify inherent differences in spatial abilities.

Complex Processes   Boys and girls do not appear to display major differences in traditional aspects of cognition, such as memory, reasoning, and problem solving. Those differences that have been found may actually reflect differences in the areas we have already discussed. Some research, for example, indicates that females are better at using organizational strategies to help them in memory tasks (Cox & Waters, 1986; Waters, 1981; Waters & Schreiber, 1991). They also exhibit better recall in tasks that involve verbal material rather than spatial location (Kail & Siegel, 1977). These findings, however, may reflect females' superior verbal abilities rather than superiority in the memory processes themselves.

Social and Personality Differences

Sex differences exist in some areas of social and personality functioning (Eagly, 1987). Most of these differences have been discussed in earlier chapters and so will be described here only briefly.

Activity and Exploration   Some evidence suggests that boys are more active and like to explore and manipulate more than do girls (Eaton & Enns, 1986; Eaton & Yu, 1989). Boys also spend more time playing outdoors, use considerably more physical space, and engage more frequently in rough-and-tumble play (DiPietro, 1981; Lindsey et al., 1997; Maccoby, 1990, 1995).

As infants, males and females are about equally likely to explore a new object, although males are more likely to touch the object, whereas females tend to explore it visually (Mayes, Carter, & Stubbe, 1993). But an interesting sex difference emerges with respect to the type of parental behavior that encourages infant exploration. Children's willingness to go off on their own can be predicted from how the caregiver reacts when the child is playing alone. Boys become more independent when their mothers do not interfere with their play and permit them to remain by themselves. Daughters treated in this manner, however, respond in the opposite way; they become less likely to explore and more likely to stay close to their mothers. Only when caregivers frequently join in the solitary play of their daughters do these children increase their independent exploration—even then, however, female infants are more likely to check in with the mother or seek her contact while exploring (Martin, 1981; Martin, Maccoby, & Jacklin, 1981; Mayes et al., 1993). Perhaps related to this finding, one study of social referencing found that changes in caregivers' facial expressions influenced how closely their infant daughters would approach an unfamiliar object but had no effect on their infant sons (Rosen, Adamson, & Bakeman, 1992).

Infants' willingness to explore their environments is related to their gender and to how their mothers interact with them.

The reasons for the sex differences in exploratory behavior remain unclear. Some research suggests that mothers interact with their male babies in ways that encourage autonomy and independence, whereas they tend to encourage more interpersonal closeness in their female babies (Robinson, Little, & Biringen, 1993). But it also is possible that males may be biologically more predisposed to explore than females, who need more encouragement to venture out.

Display of Emotions   We saw in Chapter 12 that children are socialized to believe that certain emotions should be either displayed or withheld, depending on the social circumstances. A common example is that boys are not expected to cry, even when experiencing pain or sadness.

Several studies have reported gender differences involving such display rules using a technique called the *disappointing gift* procedure (Saarni, 1984). Research participants are given a gift with which they will clearly be disappointed, and their emotional reactions are observed. Girls tend to be much better at hiding their negative emotions—that is, at following the display rule that a person should look pleased when receiving a gift from someone. Boys are not only more likely to show disappointment in this situation, but are less capable of hiding it even when given incentives to do so (Cole, 1986; Davis, 1995).

Social Influence   The two sexes react differently in situations involving social influence (Maccoby, 1990, 1995; Pettit et al., 1990; Serbin et al., 1994). When attempting to resolve a conflict or influence others to do something, boys take a more heavy-handed approach, often using threats or physical force. Girls are more likely to use verbal persuasion or to abandon the conflict altogether (Miller, Danaher, & Forbes, 1986; Sheldon, 1990, 1992). Similarly, in stories written by boys, conflict is more often resolved through the use of violence, whereas conflict resolution in girls' stories usually involves reasoning and compromise (Pierce & Edwards, 1988).

Prosocial Behavior   We saw in the previous chapter that females are generally rated as more generous, helpful, and cooperative than boys by their teachers and peers (Shigetomi, Hartmann, & Gelfand, 1981; Zarbatany et al., 1985). Some evidence does suggest that females have better affective perspective-taking abilities and experience more empathy (Dodge & Feldman, 1990; Zahn-Waxler, Robinson, & Emde, 1992; Zahn-Waxler et al., 1992). But when researchers have examined children's actual behavior, they have found few sex differences (Eagly & Crowley, 1987; Eisenberg, Martin, & Fabes, 1996), so if a difference exists in this area, it is very small.

Aggression   Perhaps the clearest and largest sex difference in behavior is that males generally display more aggression than do females—especially the more violent varieties. For example, FBI statistics indicate that in the United States, males commit about 88% of the murders and 87% of the aggravated assaults. Most other countries and cultures report similar statistics (Kenrick & Trost, 1993).

When less violent forms of aggression are considered, however, the situation becomes more complex (Crowell, 1987; Eagly & Steffen, 1986; Hyde, 1984, 1986). Preschool and elementary-school males display more physical aggression, such as kicking, pinching, and hitting, than do females of the same age; they are also rated as more aggressive by their peers (Eron et al., 1983; McCabe & Lipscomb, 1988). Females are more likely to use relational and social forms of aggression (Crick & Grotpeter, 1995). As indicated in Chapter 14, however, these findings need to be considered with caution, since observers' ratings of aggression tend to be influenced by the gender of the child (Condry & Ross, 1985; Lyons & Serbin, 1986).

One source of the sex differences in aggression may lie in cognitive differences between boys and girls. As we also saw in the previous chapter, aggressive children are more likely to make hostile attributions in response to ambiguous events than are nonaggressive children. One study found that when girls experience such events they are more likely than boys either to interpret them in a positive way or to walk away from them. Boys, in contrast, tend to respond to ambiguous provocations with retaliatory aggression (Dodge & Feldman, 1990).

Development in School Context
Do Schools Cheat Girls?

We have seen in earlier chapters that adolescence is a time when children undergo marked physical, cognitive, and social changes. Gender-role development is no exception. With the onset of puberty and an increase in self-consciousness, both males and females become more aware of gender-role expectations and strive harder to adhere to them (Hill & Lynch, 1983). As a result, some sex differences tend to increase during adolescence.

Many researchers are coming to believe that schools inadvertently contribute to this process (Huston & Alvarez, 1990). For example, a recent report entitled *How Schools Shortchange Women* (American Association of University Women, 1992) and a book called *Failing at Fairness: How America's Schools Cheat Girls* (Sadker & Sadker, 1994) both arrive at the conclusion that in school, girls are at a disadvantage in how they are viewed, how they are treated, and what is expected of them. These problems are especially evident in the typical junior high school, where many aspects of the educational environment clearly seem to favor boys.

One such aspect is the nature of the courses that students take. As children move beyond the elementary grades, schools place more emphasis on math and science. Children in the elementary grades generally view these courses as equally appropriate for either gender. But older students increasingly rate math and science as more appropriate for males (Wilder, Mackie, & Cooper, 1985), and girls' attitudes toward these subjects become less positive as they progress toward high school (Tittle, 1986). As noted earlier, attitudes toward computer work follow a similar course, a trend that may be especially troublesome given the increasing emphasis schools are placing on computer skills (Chen, 1985; Lockheed, 1985).

A second major issue involves the relation between school structure and students' learning styles. Studies have shown that males and females approach schoolwork in different ways. Girls generally favor familiar activities in which teachers or other adults are involved. Boys, on the other hand, tend to prefer tasks that are new and challenging, on which they can work independently (Dweck, 1986; Huston et al., 1986).

Some researchers believe that beginning at the junior high level, schools provide a more "masculine" learning environment (Chipman et al., 1985; LaTorre et al., 1983). Independent learning appears to be particularly suited to math and science courses. In addition, work in these areas often jumps quickly from familiar concepts to new ones. Thus, boys are more likely to make the transition to such courses more easily than are girls.

When we also consider that adolescent females tend to experience greater self-consciousness and lower self-esteem than adolescent males, we might well conclude

Studies suggest that beginning in junior high, the typical school environment is better suited to males than to females.

that junior high school is a more hospitable environment for young males and a more intimidating one for young females.

✓ *To Recap...*

Sex differences in some cognitive and social areas persist well beyond early childhood. In the cognitive area, females outperform males in rate of language acquisition and in overall verbal abilities, although these differences disappear by late adolescence. The fact that mothers more often interact verbally with their infant daughters may combine with biological factors to produce this difference. Although females begin counting earlier and solve computational problems better during middle childhood, male superiority in math, especially in math reasoning, becomes apparent during adolescence. Both socialization and biological variables are assumed to be involved. Males also display superior performance on many spatial tasks, a sex difference that increases into adulthood. Neither biological nor socialization explanations of this difference have proved conclusive. Sex differences in complex processes, such as memory, also have been reported but may simply reflect differences in verbal and math abilities.

In the area of social and personality differences, males are more physically active, use more space, and display more rough-and-tumble play than females. Male infants are more likely to explore by touch and if left alone; female infants are more likely to explore visually and if given support and encouragement. Social influence by boys often involves threats and physical force; girls use verbal persuasion and reasoning. Girls also have a reputation for being more altruistic, helpful, and cooperative, but few sex differences in these behaviors have actually been observed. Males display more physical aggression during childhood, whereas females display more social and relational aggression.

Biological Influences on Gender-Role Development

We turn once again to the biological component of gender-role development, which includes the genetic, structural, and physiological processes that distinguish males and females. As these mechanisms have become better understood in recent years, it has become increasingly clear that they interact in important ways with cognitive and socialization influences.

Like most other species, humans exhibit **sexual dimorphism**—that is, the male and female are biologically different for the purpose of reproduction. The process through which these biological differences emerge is called *sex differentiation.* Many of the biological influences on gender-role development appear to result from nature's preparing the individual in this way to participate in the reproduction process.

Sexual dimorphism
The existence in most species of biological differences between males and females for the purpose of reproduction.

Genetic Influences

As noted in Chapter 4, human body cells contain 46 chromosomes, which carry the genetic material that makes us who we are. These chromosomes consist of 22 matched pairs plus an additional pair of sex chromosomes. In the female, both sex chromosomes are called Xs; in the male, one chromosome is called X and the other Y. The chromosomes of the human female thus are designated 46,XX; those of the male, 46,XY. Human gametes, however, contain only half as many chromosomes as the body cells. In females, the ovum contains 22 chromosomes plus an X chromosome; in males, each sperm contains 22 chromosomes plus either an X or a Y.

During fertilization, then, the mother contributes 22 chromosomes and an X, and the father contributes 22 chromosomes and either an X or a Y. Thus, at the moment of conception, the child becomes genetically male or female, with the father determining the sex of the baby. But the process of sex differentiation has only just begun.

The X chromosome is relatively large and contains many genes that direct growth and functioning. The Y chromosome is about one quarter the size, with much less genetic material. The sex chromosomes have no influence at all on the fertilized zygote for about 6 weeks. At that point, if the embryo is genetically male (XY), the Y chromosome causes a portion of the embryo to become the male gonadal structure—the **testes**. Once this is accomplished, the Y chromosome does not appear to play any further role in the process of sex differentiation. If the embryo is genetically female (XX), the sex chromosomes produce no change at 6 weeks. At 10 to 12 weeks, however, one X chromosome causes a portion of the embryo to become female gonads—the **ovaries**. From this point on, sex differentiation is guided primarily by the hormones produced by the testes and the ovaries.

Chromosomal Abnormalities The process just described occasionally does not work as it should. When this happens, the embryo may have an unusual arrangement of sex chromosomes.

One such abnormality occurs when an ovum is fertilized by a sperm that carries no sex chromosome at all or when the sperm provides an X and the ovum has no sex chromosome. In either case, the resulting embryo has only an X and is designated 45,XO. Most of these embryos fail to develop in the uterus and are aborted by the mother's body without her even being aware that conception had occurred. But in the few cases in which the fetus develops completely, the child displays a variety of abnormalities referred to as **Turner's syndrome**. At birth, the baby is female in appearance, but the ovaries have already disappeared and do not produce the hormones necessary for the sex differentiation process to continue. As a result, women with Turner's syndrome do not develop breasts or menstruate unless they are given hormone therapy. Physically, they typically are short and have an unusual neck and chest structure. They have been described as having ultrafeminine personalities, and their cognitive abilities are consistent with this orientation—very high in verbal abilities and well below average in spatial skills (El Abd, Turk, & Hill, 1995; Rovet, 1991).

Another chromosomal problem occurs when an egg carrying two X chromosomes is fertilized by a sperm carrying a Y chromosome. In this case, a 47,XXY child is produced, with characteristics referred to as **Klinefelter's syndrome**. The presence of the Y chromosome causes the child to have a male appearance, but he is somewhat feminized, because his male hormone levels are low. Men with Klinefelter's syndrome have long arms, very little body hair, an underdeveloped penis, and sometimes overdeveloped breasts. They often are somewhat timid and unassertive in their interpersonal interactions (Mandoki et al., 1991).

A third chromosomal abnormality occurs when the sperm provides two Y chromosomes. The 47,XYY males produced when this occurs are perhaps the opposite of the 45,XO females in that they have large body builds and very masculine personality characteristics (Owen, 1972, 1979). There has been some controversy over whether these men are more likely than others to become criminals or to display antisocial behavior. Even if so, social factors probably are responsible (Delozier & Engel, 1982; Ratcliffe & Field, 1982).

Sex-Linked Traits Some genes are found only on the sex chromosomes and thus are called **sex-linked genes** or, more commonly, **X-linked genes**, because they

---

Testes
The male gonadal structure that produces the sperm.

Ovaries
The female gonadal structure that produces the ovum.

Turner's syndrome
A chromosomal disorder of females in which one X chromosome is absent; women with the syndrome have no ovaries, do not menstruate, are short in stature, and display ultrafeminine personality characteristics.

Klinefelter's syndrome (XXY)
A chromosomal disorder of males in which an extra X chromosome is present; men with the syndrome have long arms, little body hair, an underdeveloped penis, and somewhat feminine personality characteristics.

Sex-linked (X-linked) genes
Genes found only on the sex chromosomes, most often the X chromosome.

almost always occur on the X chromosome. If a child inherits an X-linked trait carried by a recessive gene from one parent, the trait only becomes apparent if the corresponding gene from the other parent is also recessive or if there is no corresponding gene on the other parent's sex chromosome. Thus, when a girl inherits a recessive X-linked trait from one parent, it usually is blocked by a dominant gene on the X chromosome donated by the other parent. For this reason, most recessive X-linked traits are not expressed in women. Typically, when a boy inherits a recessive X-linked trait from his mother, no matching gene is present on the Y chromosome because the Y chromosome carries so few genes. In such cases, the trait is expressed. Thus, recessive X-linked traits are much more common in males.

An example of a disorder caused by an X-linked gene is **fragile X syndrome** (Dykens, Hodapp, & Leckman, 1994; Hagerman, 1996). This genetic abnormality only became clearly understood in the 1980s, and the gene itself was not identified until 1991. The disorder is the most common inherited cause of mental retardation. The large majority of males who carry the gene display symptoms that include physical characteristics (such as a long face and large ears), difficulties with language and cognitive abilities, and many behaviors commonly found in children with autism and children with attention deficit/hyperactivity disorder. In contrast, only about 30% of females who carry the gene on one X chromosome show clear evidence of the syndrome.

About 70 traits are sex linked. Most of them are either dangerous (e.g., muscular dystrophy, hemophilia, and some forms of diabetes) or troublesome (e.g., poor night vision and color blindness). As indicated earlier, some researchers believe that spatial abilities may be a recessive X-linked trait, but the evidence for this is mixed (Boles, 1980; Thomas, 1983).

Sex-Limited Traits   Some genes that are not carried on the sex chromosomes may also affect males and females differently. Usually, this occurs when the expression of a trait requires the presence of certain levels of sex hormones. Such traits are called **sex-limited traits**. The gene for baldness, for example, may be carried by either men or women, but the characteristic appears primarily in men because high levels of male hormones are needed for it to be expressed.

Hormonal Influences

A major step in sex differentiation begins when the newly formed embryonic gonads begin to secrete hormones of different types. Up until about the 3rd month of gestation, the internal sex organs of the fetus can become either male or female. When a Y chromosome causes testes to develop in the embryo, these glands secrete hormones called **androgens**, which cause the male internal reproductive organs to grow (and they also secrete a chemical that causes the female organs to shrink). At 5 months, if androgens are present, the external sex organs also develop as male, producing a penis and scrotal sac. If androgens are not present at 3 months, the internal sex organs, and later the external sex organs, develop as female. No special hormone is needed for this to occur. The hormones produced mainly by the ovaries, **estrogen** and **progesterone**, do not play their principal role in sex differentiation until puberty.

Somewhere between 3 and 8 months after conception, sex hormones are believed to affect the development and organization of the fetal brain (Collaer & Hines, 1995; McEwen, 1987). The two major types of organizing effects involve hormonal regulation (how often the body releases various hormones) and brain lateralization.

Fragile X syndrome
An X-linked genetic disorder, most often expressed in males, producing retarded intellectual development, language and behavior problems, and identifiable physical characteristics.

Sex-limited traits
Genes that affect males and females differently but that are not carried on the sex chromosomes.

Androgens
Hormones that have masculinizing effects and are more abundant in males.

Estrogens and progesterone
Hormones that have feminizing effects and are more abundant in females.

Hormonal Regulation and Abnormalities In adult humans, the *pituitary gland* controls the production of hormones by the gonads. One effect of these hormones is to activate certain social behaviors, including aggression, maternal behaviors, and sexual activity. Some theorists believe that sex differences in these and other social behaviors may be largely controlled by such hormones (Ehrhardt, 1985; Hines & Green, 1991).

In support of this idea, researchers have given pregnant hamsters or monkeys extra doses of testosterone (a type of androgen), for example, and found that the female offspring tended to be more aggressive, dominant, and exploratory—characteristics more common in males of the species (Hines, 1982; Money & Annecillo, 1987). These sorts of studies, of course, cannot be conducted with humans, so we must use other methods of research, such as studying individuals who have hormonal irregularities.

As with chromosomes, hormonal processes sometimes go awry. Two such hormonal abnormalities are **congenital adrenal hyperplasia (CAH)**, in which too much androgen is produced during pregnancy, and **androgen insensitivity**, in which the fetus cannot respond to the presence of the masculinizing hormone.

CAH usually results from an inherited enzyme deficiency that causes the adrenal glands to produce androgens, regardless of the presence or absence of testes (Berenbaum, 1990; White, New, & Dupont, 1987). This problem typically begins after the internal sex organs have been formed but before the external sex organs appear. If the fetus is genetically female (XX), she will have ovaries and normal internal sex organs, but the excessive androgen will cause the external organs to develop in a masculine direction. Often the clitoris will be very large, resembling a penis, and sometimes a scrotal sac will develop (but it will be empty, because there are no testes).

Congenital adrenal hyperplasia (CAH)
A hormonal disorder caused by an overproduction of androgens during pregnancy. Afflicted females have large genitals and display male personality characteristics; afflicted males tend to be slightly more masculine in their interests and interactions.

Androgen insensitivity
A genetic disorder in which the fetus does not respond to masculinizing hormones. Affected individuals (XX or XY) usually are feminine in appearance and interests.

In a number of reported cases, such females have been mistaken at birth for males and raised as boys (Money & Annecillo, 1987). In most cases, however, the problem is discovered at birth and corrected by surgically changing the external sex organs and by administering drugs to reduce the high levels of androgens. Although these procedures return the girls to biological normality, the early androgen exposure appears to have some long-term effects. Many of these girls become "tomboys," preferring rough outdoor play and traditional male-stereotyped toys, while having little interest in dolls, jewelry, or activities typical of young females. At adolescence, the spatial abilities of CAH females are typically markedly better than those of normal females. The males who have received the extra dose of androgens react less dramatically. These boys are somewhat more inclined toward intense physical activity than are normal boys, but they do not appear to be more aggressive or antisocial (Berenbaum & Hines, 1992; Berenbaum & Snyder, 1995; Hines & Kaufman, 1994).

Androgen insensitivity is a genetic defect in males that prevents the body cells from responding to androgens. The testes of an XY fetus will produce hormones, but neither internal nor external male sex organs will develop. The substance that usually shrinks the potential female internal sex organs will be effective, however, leaving the fetus with neither a uterus nor an internal male system. The external organs will develop as female. Studies have shown that androgen-insensitive individuals are generally feminine in appearance, preferences, and abilities (Ehrhardt & Meyer-Bahlburg, 1981; Money & Ehrhardt, 1972).

Taken together, evidence from animals and humans suggests that fetal sex hormones play an important part in producing differences between males and females. But hormonal processes are complex, and scientists still do not understand exactly how they interact with socialization processes.

Brain Lateralization

The human brain is divided into left and right hemispheres that perform different functions, which we saw in Chapter 6 is termed **brain lateralization** (Molfese & Segalowitz, 1989). The left half both controls and receives information from the right side of the body, including the right ear, hand, and foot and the right visual field of each eye. The right hemisphere controls and receives information from the left side. The left hemisphere is primarily responsible for language and speech processes, whereas the right side appears to be more involved with quantitative and spatial abilities (Springer & Deutsch, 1989).

Because the division of these functions corresponds to the cognitive sex differences we discussed earlier, some psychologists believe that differences in brain laterality may be important for understanding certain differences in male and female behavior (Levy, 1981; Witelson & Kigar, 1989). Of particular interest are data suggesting that males are *more* lateralized—that is, their left and right hemispheres function more independently—than are females (Bryden, 1982; McGlone, 1980). As noted, this difference may result from the actions of fetal androgens that operate selectively on males (Finegan, Niccols, & Sitarenios, 1992; Jacklin, Wilcox, & Maccoby, 1988).

Studies of language and verbal abilities provide some support for the idea that brain lateralization plays a role in gender differences. For example, sex differences in hemisphere specialization have been found in both 3- and 6-month-old infants. When they responded to recordings of a voice speaking, female infants showed stronger brain-wave reactions to right-ear (left-hemisphere) presentations, whereas male infants showed stronger reactions to left-ear (right-hemisphere) presentations (Shucard & Shucard, 1990; Shucard et al., 1981). At 2 and 3 years of age, both sexes begin to process verbal stimuli (such as spoken words) through the right ear and nonverbal stimuli (such as music) through the left ear (Harper & Kraft, 1986; Kamptner, Kraft, & Harper, 1984). But at this point, males begin to show evidence of greater lateralization than females—for example, performing much better in response to verbal stimuli presented in the right ear than the left ear but showing the opposite tendency for nonverbal stimuli (Kraft, 1984).

Other research has reported that verbal abilities in males whose left hemispheres have been damaged (such as through strokes or tumors) are much more impaired than are those in females with a similar degree of damage in that area (McGlone, 1980; Sasanuma, 1980). These results suggest that language functioning in females is more equally spread between the two hemispheres.

The role of brain lateralization in spatial abilities has also been examined in a study of children's haptic (touch) performance. Children in the study first felt a pair of hidden shapes, one with each hand, for 10 seconds. They were then asked to pick out the two shapes from a visual display. For boys, left-hand (right-hemisphere) performance was better than right-hand performance. For girls, left- and right-hand performance were equal (Witelson, 1976).

The evidence that males seem to be more lateralized than females does not, in itself, provide a simple explanation of verbal and spatial sex differences. It does, however, suggest that some sex differences may literally exist in our brains.

Brain lateralization
The organization of the human brain into left and right hemispheres that perform different functions.

✓ *To Recap…*

In humans, the male and female are different for the purpose of reproduction, a characteristic called sexual dimorphism. The process through which these differences emerge is called sex differentiation.

Human body cells possess 46 chromosomes, including two sex chromosomes. In females, both sex chromosomes are Xs (46,XX); in males, one is X and the other, Y (46,XY). The sex chromosomes of the embryo cause the development of either testes or ovaries. Chromosomal abnormalities can produce individuals with unusual sex chromosome arrangements, such as Turner's syndrome (XO), Klinefelter's syndrome (XXY), and 47,XYY syndrome.

Traits carried by genes found only on the sex chromosomes (usually on an X) are called sex-linked or X-linked traits. They are usually recessive and often dangerous. X-linked traits almost always are found in men, in whom the Y chromosome fails to block the expression of the recessive problem gene.

Sex-limited traits are carried by genes that are not on the sex chromosomes but that require male or female sex hormones for their expression.

The principal fetal hormones are androgens in males and progesterone and estrogens in females. The production of androgens by the testes is necessary for the embryo to develop as male. Androgens also affect the organization of the fetal brain. Hormonal abnormalities in humans illustrate the role of hormones in gender-related behaviors. Congenital adrenal hyperplasia (CAH) results from the overproduction of androgens during gestation. Even with treatment, the personalities of CAH females remain masculinized. CAH males are much less affected. Androgen insensitivity involves a failure of the body cells to respond to androgens. The personalities of androgen-insensitive males are feminized.

Brain lateralization refers to the specialization in function of the brain hemispheres; each controls and receives input from the opposite side of the body. The right hemisphere is principally involved with quantitative and spatial abilities, and the left hemisphere is more involved with verbal abilities. Males appear to be more lateralized than females. This sex difference may be related to behavioral sex differences on verbal and spatial tasks.

Sexual Orientation

Sexual orientation
A person's sexual preference. Heterosexuals are attracted to members of the opposite sex and homosexuals are attracted to members of the same sex.

Most children begin to experience feelings of sexual desire and attraction during late childhood and preadolescence. The term **sexual orientation** involves the objects of that attraction, who are usually, but not always, members of the opposite sex.

In the United States, it is estimated that 5% to 10% of adults are lesbian, gay, or bisexual (Billy et al., 1993; Fay et al., 1989; Patterson, 1995c). Same-sex attraction and relations have undoubtedly existed throughout history, but only recently have large numbers of individuals explicitly identified themselves with one of these minority sexual orientations (D'Emilio, 1983; Faderman, 1991). In 1973, both the American Psychological Association and the American Psychiatric Association declared that homosexuality was normal and not evidence of psychopathology. With the gradual lessening of the prejudice and social stigma attached to this lifestyle, and with the increasing legal and political power of this community, the visible population of nonheterosexuals is growing.

The rise of this social movement has generated many interesting and provocative questions. For developmental psychologists, some important issues include: (1) the roles that biology and socialization play in sexual orientation, (2) whether sexual orientation is fixed and unalterable, or fluid and changeable, and (3) how children develop when they are raised in households with same-sex parents. These and related questions are also of interest to the courts—which have had to render many legal decisions regarding adoption, child custody, marriage, and so on—as well as to policy makers, who write laws and regulations governing these areas (D'Augelli & Patterson, 1995; Harvard Law Review, 1989).

Origins of Sexual Orientation

How does one's sexual orientation arise? On this topic, the nature–nurture question has perhaps been the most fundamental issue (Gladue, 1994). At the one extreme, some suspect that our sexual preference is genetically based and thus completely determined at birth. At the other extreme are those who believe that one's sexual orientation is socially determined and, in essence, chosen as the preferred lifestyle. Both possibilities, of course, could be correct, with some homosexuality being genetic and some social in origin.

Many researchers, however, favor interactional models—for example, our genes may predispose us toward either a same- or opposite-sex attraction, but our social environment may need to be supportive for us to move in that direction. And not all the presumed biological influences involve genetics—factors such as prenatal problems with the mother's immune system or her level of stress have also been suggested. In short, science at this point has more questions than answers regarding the origins of sexual orientation.

Some Intriguing Findings

Let us consider a few things that science does know. One frequently cited statistic is that about two-thirds of gay and lesbian adults recall their childhood play and interests to have involved activities more common for children of the opposite sex (Bailey & Zucker, 1995). Such *retrospective* studies sometimes also involve the recollections of parents or other family members (Bailey, Miller, & Willerman, 1993).

Similar reports have come from *prospective* studies of children displaying **gender identity disorder (GID)**. As used here, *gender identity* refers to more than just the child's ability to correctly identify his own sex; it also involves the child's personal sense of the sex to which he belongs. Children with this syndrome (most often boys) early on display evidence of being uncomfortable with their biological sex and preferring to dress and act like members of the opposite sex (Money, 1994; Zucker, 1992). Interestingly, many of the boys with this disorder are rated as very attractive (Zucker, Wild, et al., 1993). Researchers have followed the development of these children and discovered that a high percentage develop a homosexual orientation at adolescence and later (Bailey & Zucker, 1995; Green, 1974, 1987). The results from both retrospective and prospective studies thus suggest that sexual orientation usually forms early. Note, however, that the findings could be explained by either a biological or social model, and both have been proposed (Zucker & Bradley, 1995).

Another finding, which also could have either nature or nurture roots, is that homosexual boys tend to have more brothers and also a later birth order than heterosexual boys (Blanchard & Bogaert, 1996; Blanchard & Zucker, 1994). When homosexuality was considered a psychological disorder, many social theories were proposed to interpret these data. Currently, however, no theory provides a compelling explanation for them (Blanchard et al., 1995).

Two more reliable findings are that (1) identical (MZ) twins are more likely to both be homosexual than are fraternal twins (DZ) (Bailey & Pillard, 1991; Whitam, Diamond, & Martin, 1993), and (2) gay men have a higher proportion of brothers who are gay than do heterosexual men (Bailey, Willerman, & Parks, 1991). These results would seem to implicate genetic processes in the development of sexual orientation. However, genetic models cannot completely account for all the data in either case (Bailey et al., 1993).

Research on the origins of sexual orientation thus is generating important facts and information for which any successful theory will need to account. Identifying

Gender identity disorder (GID)

A disorder in which children, most often males, appear uncomfortable with their biological sex and display behavior more typical of the opposite sex.

FROM EXOTIC TO EROTIC: A DEVELOPMENTAL THEORY OF SEXUAL ORIENTATION

A new and sure-to-be-controversial theory of sexual orientation has been proposed by Daryl Bem, an eminent social psychologist at Cornell University (Bem, 1996). Departing from recent biologically-based models, Bem believes that children's perceptions, feelings, and experiences are important factors in their development of *either* a heterosexual or a homosexual orientation. The core process in Bem's analysis is captured by his shorthand label, EBE theory—meaning "exotic becomes erotic."

According to the model, children's early gender-related behaviors and interests ultimately determine whether they develop a same- or opposite-sex attraction. Children who are *gender-conforming*—meaning, they prefer toys and activities commonly associated with their gender and they prefer to interact with children of the same sex—go on to develop heterosexual lifestyles. Children who are *gender-nonconforming*—meaning they have nontypical (opposite) preferences for toys and playmates—develop homosexual orientations. We have seen that most gays and lesbians do recall nonconforming play and playmate preferences during childhood, whereas heterosexuals report more traditional experiences (Bailey & Zucker, 1995).

Where do these early behavior styles come from? In contrast to most current thinking, Bem does not believe they are the direct products of either genes or prenatal hormones. These biological mechanisms, he argues, produce only temperamental characteristics in the child, such as aggression and activity level, and these characteristics presumably influence whether the child will prefer male-typical or female-typical play and peers.

Thus, aggressive, high-energy children—usually male, but occasionally female—will gravitate toward rough-and-tumble, large-motor games (e.g., football, wrestling) and congregate with children displaying the same interests. Children with the opposite temperamental characteristics (usually, but not always, females) will have female-typical play and playmate preferences.

Why do the gender-conforming children become heterosexual and the gender-nonconforming children become homosexual? EBE theory proposes that while children prefer being with children having similar interests, they perceive children in the other group as different, unfamiliar, and what Bem terms *exotic*. These feelings—which gender-conforming children have toward members of the opposite sex but which gender-nonconforming children have toward members of the same sex—gradually become stronger, leading to heightened arousal in the presence of these children. Sometimes this occurs as the result of specific experiences. A girl who has been victimized by boys, for example, may feel frightened; or a boy with female-typical interests who has been teased by the other boys may feel ashamed.

At this point the model's unique EBE process occurs. Bem believes that the strong emotional arousal felt toward children in the other group is transformed into feelings of sexual and romantic attraction. Or, put more simply, children previously viewed as unfamiliar and exotic now become appealing and erotic. Bem credits this transformation to a collection of psychological processes—cognitive, physiological, evolutionary, and conditioning—that are too complex to detail here. But the result of the EBE process is the creation of the individual's sexual orientation.

In the more common case of heterosexuals, a boy who, for example, previously found girls "yucky" suddenly finds them sexually arousing; and a girl whose feelings toward boys involved fear and intimidation begins to find them romantically attractive. In the case of homosexuals, the boy who, for example, is sensitive and prefers fine-motor activities has his strong feelings of alienation and rejection from other boys transformed into feelings of physical attraction to them, as does the girl whose preferences for male-typical activities has led her to feel different and uncomfortable with other girls.

Bem admits that the theory is still speculative and in need of research support, but its creative interweaving of biological and social processes, along with its attempt to explain both the heterosexual and homosexual orientations, offers a fascinating account of this aspect of gender-role development.

the nature and nurture factors at work in this area of development becomes an important next step.

Biological Processes   Much of the biological focus regarding sexual orientation has involved prenatal hormones (Byne & Parsons, 1993; Ellis & Ames, 1987; Meyer-Bahlberg et al., 1995). As we saw earlier, hormones produced by the newly formed testes masculinize the fetus, which includes both the development of the reproductive organs and the organization of the fetal brain. Some researchers believe that sexual orientation is established during this process (Meyer-Bahlberg, 1993; Reinisch, Ziemba-Davis, & Sanders, 1991).

Support for this hypothesis can be found in individuals who exhibit hormonal disorders, two of which were discussed earlier. Whether a person is chromosomally male (XY) or female (XX), hormonal imbalances—such as those caused by CAH and androgen insensitivity—can affect the individual's gender-related behavior, personality traits, and sexual preferences (Dittmann et al., 1990). It is not known, however, whether the processes occurring in these individuals relate in any way to the hormonal processes of gays and lesbians unaffected by these disorders.

Additional evidence comes from a recent study examining the effects of prenatal exposure to the drug DES. This synthetic hormone, now banned because of serious side effects, had been widely prescribed to pregnant women who were at risk for miscarriage. The researchers suspected that the drug may have affected the sexual development of many of the fetuses, either by increasing production of masculinizing androgens or by interfering with fetal brain development and organization. To test this possibility, a group of adult women who had been exposed to DES during their fetal development were compared with women of similar age and medical history who had not been exposed to the drug. As predicted, women in the DES-exposure group scored higher on measures of same-sex and bisexual orientation (Meyer-Bahlberg et al., 1995).

Other evidence supporting a biological basis for homosexuality comes from postmortem examinations of the brains of gay and heterosexual men and women. Certain brain structures reliably differ in size between men and women; in gay men these structures are closer in size to those of women (Allen & Gorski, 1992; LeVay, 1991, 1993; Swaab, Gooren, & Hofman, 1992). Similarly, research has found that gay men's performance on various neuropsychological tasks—such as measures of spatial ability—also more closely resembles the performance of women than of other men (Gladue et al., 1990; McCormick & Witelson, 1991). Such correlational findings are consistent with a biological basis for homosexuality, but they are by no means definitive.

Social Explanations   On the nurture side, researchers have attempted to identify social processes that affect the development of sexual orientation. Much of this work has been done in relation to gender identity disorder, assumed by many to be a precursor of homosexuality (Bailey et al., 1995).

The story at the beginning of the chapter described the case of a boy who was reared as a girl until adolescence. Many similar cases, involving both males and females, have been reported in the scientific literature. Much of the earlier data suggested that it was the gender to which the child was *assigned*, rather than his or her biological sex, that guided the child's sex-typed behavior and preferences (Money, Devore, & Norman, 1986; Money & Ehrhardt, 1972). Although it is now obvious that sexual identity and orientation are not quite so simplistic, for many children, sex reassignment appears to have been successful. Thus, some evidence for the role of child rearing in gender identity can be found in these reports (Zucker & Bradley, 1995).

Other research has examined the role that parents' sex preferences may play in a child's gender identity. For example, are boys with GID more likely to have parents who were hoping for a girl? The evidence for this relationship is not strong, but there is reason to believe that a parent's disappointment at having a child of the non-preferred sex may exert some pressure in these cases (Zucker, Bradley, & Ipp, 1993).

We saw earlier in the chapter that children's sex-typed behavior seems to be influenced by social reinforcement and punishment from both adults and peers. Could these processes be involved in the development of children's gender identity? In fact, some studies have reported that mothers of boys with GID were more encouraging of feminine behavior and less encouraging of masculine behavior than were mothers in the control group (Green, 1987; Roberts et al., 1987; Zucker & Bradley, 1995).

Finally, some researchers have found that parents of children (especially females) with GID were more likely to display various types of psychopathology, such as depression (Marantz & Coates, 1991; Zucker & Bradley, 1995). Again, correlational findings such as these can be explained in a variety of ways, with social and child-rearing processes among them.

Gay and Lesbian Families

As gays and lesbians become increasingly more open in their lifestyles, marriage and parenthood have become commonplace in this community. Parenthood can involve a number of different approaches. Some lesbian couples become parents through donor insemination, whereas some gay couples recruit a surrogate mother to bear the child. Many states now permit gay and lesbian couples to adopt children. In some cases, one partner retains custody of a child from a prior heterosexual marriage (Patterson, 1994b).

One consequence of these different approaches is that the resulting biological relationships among family members tend to vary more than they do in heterosexual families. Children of gay and lesbian couples most often live with only one biological parent, and sometimes with none (Patterson, 1995b). These families also usually do not follow the traditional divisions of labor in occupations and household responsibilities, which tend to be shared more equally between partners (Patterson, 1995a).

Lesbian and gay parents thus differ from heterosexual parents in both obvious and subtle ways, raising many important questions. One fundamental question has been whether children raised by lesbian or gay couples generally develop in a normal and healthy way, or are at greater risk for social, emotional, and behavior problems. Although research on this issue is relatively new and not extensive, the best evidence to date suggests that these children face no greater developmental risks than do comparable children from heterosexual couples (Flaks et al., 1995; Patterson, 1992, 1994a). As with all families, the psychological adjustment of these children relates to the child-rearing skills of the parents and to the quality of the relationship between them (Patterson, 1995a, 1995b).

A second issue involves the gender-role development and sexual orientation of these children. Are children of gays and lesbians more likely to be homosexual themselves? Note that if this were true, it would be possible to learn something about the relative contributions of nature and nurture to sexual orientation. That is, if genetics played a role, children biologically related to one parent of a homosexual couple should be more likely to display a homosexual orientation than children with no biological connection to the parents (adopted children). And if modeling and imitation processes were at work here, no differences would be expected between children with a biological connection and those without, but higher rates of homosexuality should emerge from these nontraditional couples than from heterosexual parents.

There is even less research available on this issue, but it all tends to point to the same conclusion: children raised by gay or lesbian parents are no more likely to become homosexuals than are children of heterosexual parents (Gottman, 1990; Patterson, 1992, 1994a). One recent study found that about 9% of the sons of gay and bisexual men became nonheterosexuals—about the same proportion as in the entire population (Bailey et al., 1995).

Research into families headed by nonheterosexuals has only just begun, and the coming years should produce a great deal more information about this growing segment of the population. Following the children of such parents into adulthood and then observing their parenting practices, for example, could shed new light on the nature and nurture processes operating in this area.

✓ *To Recap...*

Psychologists have become increasingly interested in the origins of sexual orientation—one's sexual preference for members of the same or opposite sex—as a result of the increasing visibility of the gay and lesbian community.

The nature–nurture issue has been prominent in the research and theorizing in this area. Studies have found that children displaying gender identity disorder (GID)—in which the child rejects his own biological sex and adopts characteristics of the opposite sex—very often become homosexuals at adolescence. Support for a biological basis for sexual orientation comes from research on genetics, prenatal hormones and related disorders, and similarities in the brain structures and psychoneurological performance of women and gay men. Social processes of potential influence include parents' gender preferences, social approval and disapproval for sex-typed behaviors, and psychological disorders in the parents.

Gay and lesbian families have become more common, raising important questions for psychologists and policy makers. Current evidence suggests no detrimental effects in the development of children raised by nonheterosexual couples. Nor are these children any more likely to adopt nonheterosexual orientations and lifestyles.

Androgyny

Two assumptions have guided much of the research on gender-role development conducted during the past 2 decades. The first is that many observed sex differences are not inevitable. We have seen that a substantial amount of evidence is consistent with this contention. The second is that many of the sex differences that exist should be reduced or eliminated. Here the evidence and arguments are a bit more complicated (Katz, 1986).

When we examine the personality traits or characteristics traditionally considered desirable for males or females, we find two distinct clusters (Guisinger & Blatt, 1994). The masculine gender role includes principally what have been called *instrumental* characteristics, such as independence, ambition, and self-confidence. The feminine gender role is predominantly characterized by *expressive* traits, including compassion, sensitivity, and warmth. The early view in psychology was that these

Androgyny
A personality type composed of desirable characteristics of the masculine and feminine personality types.

masculine and feminine clusters represented opposite ends of a continuum. This view further held that our psychological well-being is maximized when we adopt the cluster of personality traits that matches our gender.

The modern challenge to these views is based on the concept of **androgyny** (Cook, 1985, 1987). According to this concept, masculine and feminine traits are not opposite ends of one dimension, but two separate dimensions. An individual thus may possess attributes from each. More importantly, the most psychologically healthy individuals are believed to be androgynous—that is, to possess a blend of desirable traits from both the masculine and the feminine cluster. These androgynous personality types can be, for example, bold yet kind, self-assured yet humble, assertive yet nurturing, and so forth. The presumed benefit of this blending is flexibility. The androgynous person should possess a wider range of available responses that can be brought to bear in a variety of situations (Bem, 1985; Spence, 1985).

Several instruments have been developed to assess androgyny. The two most popular are the Bem Sex-Role Inventory (Bem, 1974, 1979) and the Personal Attributes Questionnaire (Spence & Helmreich, 1978). These instruments list socially desirable traits or attributes, some instrumental and some expressive. Respondents are asked to rate themselves on each one. An overall gender-role rating can then be calculated and the individual classified as masculine, feminine, or androgynous.

As suggested earlier, proponents of the androgyny concept contend that androgynous individuals should exhibit more flexibility and better psychological adjustment than people with either strongly masculine or strongly feminine personalities. Although the results of some studies have been consistent with this view (Bem, 1975; Spence, Helmreich, & Holahan, 1979), the evidence has not been overwhelming (Long, 1989; Orlofsky & O'Heron, 1987).

Children with androgynous personalities presumably possess a wider range of abilities and interests.

Recent studies have focused on the individual components of androgyny—that is, the desirable traits from the instrumental and expressive clusters—to see whether one component is primarily responsible for the individual's level of psychological well-being. Some research has found that individuals are better adjusted when they rate high on the instrumental cluster (Markstrom-Adams, 1989; Whitely, 1985), whereas other research reports that the benefits derive mainly from the expressive cluster (Stake, 1997).

These last findings, however, need not force us to abandon androgyny as a useful concept or a desirable condition. It is always possible that the concept is sound but that our instruments are not accurately measuring the process. Nor should we assume that both masculine and feminine characteristics are not valuable for success or happiness in our culture. Traits from each cluster may operate in subtle ways in certain situations, which researchers simply may not yet have identified. More work is needed in this area.

Conclusion

Far from being simple and straightforward, as psychologists once thought, gender-role development appears to be a complex and delicate process. As in other areas of development, biological, cognitive, and environmental factors all play important parts in guiding the child's progress toward a sexual identity.

Importantly, research in this area reveals the intimate relations between scientific investigation and the social environment in which research is conducted. Recall that the explosion of research on gender roles that occurred in the 1970s grew primarily out of a political and sociological movement rather than a scientific one. It is likely that the earlier theoretical notions would eventually have been challenged anyway, but it is doubtful that as much attention would have been focused on this topic had it not been for the formation of women's studies departments in colleges, the debate over the Equal Rights Amendment, the creation of affirmative action programs, and so on. In some sense, then, society often dictates to scientists what needs to be studied.

Such pressure can pose problems for the research community. Even now, though some of the myths of gender-role development have been discarded and new views are replacing the old, many of the most important questions remain unanswered. Yet parents are clamoring to know what are the best methods for raising their children in nonsexist ways, educators want to know whether males and females require different types of instruction, courts are seeking answers to questions concerning same-sex parenting, employers want to know whether both sexes really can do any job equally well, and so forth.

Most psychologists are reluctant to provide firm answers to these questions at this point. For now, what we can say with some certainty is that the child's gender-role development does not occur automatically and that it is sensitive to how parents, teachers, peers, and the culture respond to the child. But the next step—prescribing the best rearing and teaching practices—remains a controversial and difficult business.

Visual Summary for Chapter 15:
Gender–Role Development and Sex Differences

Theories of Gender–Role Development

Ethological and Biological Explanations	→	The biological analysis of gender-role development has looked to genetic and structural differences as causes of sex differences in behavior. Current biosocial models incorporate both biological and socialization processes.
Cognitive-Developmental Models	→	Cognitive-developmental models include a stage model of children's understanding gender-role issues, as well as information-processing models based on the concepts of the gender schema and gender script.
Environmental/ Learning Models	→	Social-learning theory views gender-role behaviors as simply another class of responses acquired and maintained by learning principles. Sex differences are not viewed as inevitable and may change with environmental conditions.

Sex Typing and the Socialization of Gender Differences

Early Sex Differences	→	Preschoolers display sex-stereotyped preference, with boys showing a narrower range of interests than girls. Gender segregation begins during the preschool period.
Differential Treatment of Males and Females	→	Parents and other adults interact with male and female babies in stereotyped ways. Differential treatment of the sexes is even more pronounced in the preschool period. Parents, teachers, and peers dispense social approval and disapproval for gender- stereotyped behavior. Boys are more likely than girls to receive criticism for straying from gender-stereotyped roles.
Modeling	→	Children, especially boys, focus more attention on same-sex models and more often imitate their behavior. Real-life models of traditional gender roles are common in the everyday lives of children.
Fathers and Sex Typing	→	Fathers are more concerned than mothers with maintaining children's gender-role behavior. Children of fathers who make more sex-stereotyped distinctions learn these distinctions earlier.

Understanding Gender Roles and Stereotypes

Gender Awareness and the Emergence of Sex-Typed Behavior	→	Gender-role knowledge involves awareness of the concepts of male and female and their culturally defined stereotypes. Children generally understand the basic male-female concept by age 2. Gender labeling of toys appears at age 3, and awareness of sex-typed personality traits at about age 5. As children get older, they increasingly view gender roles as socially determined, and their attitudes towards violations become more flexible.
Effects of Sex-Typed Labeling	→	When activities or objects are seen as being for one gender or the other, children prefer same-sex activities. They also perform better on same-sex than on cross-sex activities.

Family Influences on Gender-Role Development

Parental Attitudes and Child-Rearing Methods 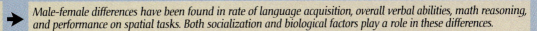 Parents' gender-related attitudes and behaviors influence children's sex-typed beliefs and behaviors. The clearest evidence involves a similarity in parent-child attitudes.

Socioeconomic Status ➡ Families from higher socioeconomic levels tend to have children who are less sex-typed in behavior and belief.

Maternal Employment ➡ Mothers who work have children who are less sex-typed in attitudes and behavior.

Some Common Sex Differences

Cognitive Differences ➡ Male-female differences have been found in rate of language acquisition, overall verbal abilities, math reasoning, and performance on spatial tasks. Both socialization and biological factors play a role in these differences.

Social and Personality Differences ➡ Boys are more active and display more rough-and-tumble play. Male infants are more likely to explore by touch; female infants explore visually. Social influence by boys often involves threats and force; girls use verbal persuasion. Boys display more physical aggression; girls display more social aggression.

Biological Influences on Gender-Role Development

Genetic Influences ➡ Unusual sex chromosome arrangements include Turner's syndrome (XO), Klinefelter's syndrome (XXY), and 47 XYY syndrome. Sex-linked traits carried by genes found only on the X chromosome are almost always found in men. Sex-limited traits are carried by genes not on the sex chromosomes, but require sex hormones for their expression.

Hormonal Influences ➡ Congenital Adrenal Hyperplasia (CAH) results from an overproduction of androgens during gestation. The personalities of CAH females are masculinized. Androgen insensitivity involves a failure to respond to androgens. The personalities of androgen insensitivity males are feminized.

Brain Lateralization ➡ The right hemisphere is largely involved with quantitative and spatial abilities. The left hemisphere is more involved with verbal abilities. Males appear to be more lateralized than females, a sex difference that may be related to behavioral sex differences on verbal and spatial tasks.

Sexual Orientation

Origins of Sexual Orientation Research suggests that both biological and social factors may play a role in determining sexual orientation. Many researchers favor models stressing the interaction between nature and nurture.

Gay and Lesbian Families Gay and lesbian families have become more common. Current evidence suggests no detrimental effects in the development of children raised by nonheterosexual couples, nor are these children any more likely to adopt nonheterosexual orientations and lifestyles.

Androgyny

According to the notion of androgyny, masculine and feminine traits are two separate dimensions. Androgynous individuals possess attributes from each, which some theorists argue is associated with more flexibility and better adjustment.

Chapter 16

Peer Relations

Everyone is familiar with "peer pressure"—it's an explanation frequently offered for why young teens, in particular, smoke, drink alcohol, use illegal drugs, join gangs, and engage in various other activities that adults would rather they avoided. There is no doubt that peer pressure can sometimes lead to self-destructive behaviors. But it can have positive effects as well.

An example is offered by an organization founded in 1981 as Students Against Driving Drunk (SADD). The organization's goal was straightforward: to use positive peer pressure to keep teenagers from drinking and driving, a leading cause of death among teens and young adults. By 1997, the group had 25,000 chapters in middle schools, high schools, and colleges in the United States and some other countries as well. Chapters vary in what they do—they might bring in speakers, monitor court cases, or sponsor parties. Most importantly, though, chapter members support each other's commitment not to drive after drinking and not to let their friends drive in that condition.

Does the approach work? It seems to have had a fair amount of success. The number of alcohol-related traffic deaths among 15- to 20-year-olds dropped 60% between 1981 and 1997, and federal officials credited SADD with helping to bring about this decrease. Indeed, encouraged by their success in the drinking-and-driving area, the national leaders of SADD announced in 1997 that the organization would broaden its mission to include teen suicide, drug abuse, rape, gang violence, and other problems. The organization's name has been changed accordingly, to Students Against Destructive Decisions.

How well SADD can carry out its broadened agenda remains to be seen. It is clear, however, that peer pressure can indeed be a powerful tool—in some cases in a positive direction and in some cases with much more negative results. The question of how and why peers influence each other is one of the many topics we address in this chapter.

Any visitor to a day-care center, playground, or park can readily see that children interact with other children from early in life. And the importance of peers is not limited to one culture. Societies around the world promote contact among children, in some cases more strongly than do North American societies (Draper & Harpending, 1988). As one psychologist wrote, "None of the world's cultures rears its children solely through interaction with adults" (Hartup, 1983, p. 104).

Nevertheless, until fairly recently the study of children's social development concentrated largely on relations within the family. This focus is understandable. The family is clearly important and is stressed in every theory of socialization. However, in recent years the interest in families has begun to be supplemented by research directed toward the role of peers. After years of relative neglect, the subject of peer relations has emerged as one of the hot topics in child psychology.

We touched on the role of peers in development at several points in the preceding chapters. The topic of peer relations is important enough, however, to merit a focus of its own, and that is the purpose of the present chapter. Two general questions will be of interest. One is how children relate to other children—that is, peers as objects or targets of the child's social behaviors. The other is how interaction with peers affects the child's development—that is, peers as sources of developmental change.

Theories of Peer Relations

The three major theoretical traditions have addressed somewhat different aspects of children's peer relations. To a great extent, therefore, the pictures they provide complement rather than contradict one another.

Cognitive-Developmental Theory

Cognitive-developmental theorists discuss peers in both of the senses just identified—as objects of behavior and as sources of change. An example of the latter is Piaget's (1932) theory of how peers contribute to changes in moral reasoning, discussed in Chapter 14. In Piaget's view, the child, lacking the power and authority of the adult, conforms to what he perceives to be the adult's views. The result is moral realism, characterized by a rigid conception of right and wrong. When the child interacts with peers, however, the relation is much more one of equals, and there is a continual need for cooperating, negotiating, and taking the point of view of the other. Interaction with peers, therefore, leads to the ability to consider different perspectives, an ability central to the more advanced form of reasoning known as moral relativism. More generally, interaction with peers is important in breaking down the child's egocentrism and encouraging more mature forms of thought.

Peers are also important in Kohlberg's (1987) theory of moral development. As in Piaget's theory, movement through Kohlberg's stages results partly from biological maturation. Achieving a new stage, however, requires not only a sufficient level of maturation, but also experience with moral issues. Kohlberg especially stresses experiences in which the child encounters different points of view and thus is forced to consider and integrate different perspectives. Such experiences of cognitive conflict may be especially likely in the give-and-take of the peer group.

As we saw in Chapter 10, peers also play a role in Vygotsky's theory (Tudge & Rogoff, 1989). Just as children benefit from interactions with a parent or teacher, they may also be helped to achieve new levels of understanding when they interact with a more competent peer.

In addition to their role in promoting cognitive change, peers are important as objects of the child's thought. Thinking about other children falls under the heading of *social cognition*—the child's understanding of the social and interpersonal world. Of course, peers are not the only targets for social cognition; children think about adults, about social institutions, and about themselves. But peers are undoubtedly frequent objects of social cognition for most children from early in life.

Piaget's discussions of social cognition (Piaget, 1950, 1967) stress its similarities to the child's reasoning about the physical world. Young children's egocentrism, for example, colors both their logical reasoning and their thinking about other people. More generally, the limitations of preoperational thought find their way into the child's attempts to make sense of other people (Flavell et al., 1993). And as these limitations are overcome, the child enters new stages of social reasoning. The idea that social cognition, like physical cognition, develops in stages is found in a number of models of social-cognitive development (Damon, 1977, 1980; Selman, 1980).

In addition to these similarities between physical and social cognition, there also are some important differences between the two forms of understanding (Damon, 1981; Hoffman, 1981). A primary difference is that other people, unlike

inanimate objects, are themselves conscious, thinking beings, capable of spontaneous and intentional behavior. Furthermore, our relations with other people
involve not just action but *interaction,* and such interaction requires mutual coordination of intention and action. Because of these complexities, understanding other
people, including peers, can present challenges that go beyond those posed by the
physical world.

Children's understanding of other children is an interesting topic in itself. But
it is also important because of its possible effects on the child's social behavior. A
basic principle of the cognitive-developmental approach is that the child's cognitive
level is an important determinant of the child's behavior, including behavior
toward other people. Thus, the cognitive theorist would expect older children to
show more complex and mature forms of social behavior because of their greater
cognitive maturity. And within an age group, the theorist would expect children
who are advanced in their level of social reasoning to be advanced in their social
behavior as well. We will consider shortly how well these expectations are borne out
by research.

The Environmental/Learning Approach

We have seen that social-learning theory attempts to identify basic learning principles that apply across a range of situations, age groups, and types of behavior. It
should come as no surprise, then, to learn that the social-learning concepts already
stressed are also important for the topic of peer relations.

Peers can affect a child's behavior and development in several ways. One way is
through peer reinforcement and punishment. Peers provide many reinforcing or
punishing consequences as a child develops—attention, praise, acquiescence to the
child's wishes, sharing or refusing to share, criticism, disapproval. Many of these consequences are, to be sure, unintended, but they may function as reinforcers or punishers nonetheless. Peers are also important as models of behavior. As discussed in
Chapter 2, Bandura (1986, 1989) places a heavy emphasis on the various ways in
which exposure to models can affect a child's behavior. Finally, peers contribute to
the development of self-efficacy—children's conceptions of which behaviors they are
capable of performing. One source of self-efficacy judgments is the child's observation of the behavior of others, and peers are clearly a natural comparison group.

Of course, none of the roles just cited is unique to peers. But peers may be
especially important sources of such effects, especially as children grow older. The
sheer amount of time spent with peers guarantees that any child will be exposed frequently to the behavior of other children and will experience frequent consequences from other children as the result of his behavior. Furthermore, the importance, for most children, of being accepted by other children guarantees that peers
will be effective agents of reinforcement and punishment as well as potent models
for a wide range of behaviors. And, of course, the behaviors that peers model and
reinforce may differ from the behaviors that adults try to promote.

Interaction with peers also provides a good example of Bandura's (1978) principle of reciprocal determinism. Recall that the model of reciprocal determinism
attempts to capture the interplay among three factors: the person, the person's
behavior, and the environment (see Figure 2.2). Each of these factors influences
the others when children interact. Characteristics of the child (such as cognitive
level) affect the behaviors directed toward other children. Characteristics of the
environment also affect behavior. We will see, for example, that children may
behave differently in small groups than in large groups, and with friends than with
nonfriends.

The environment is in turn affected by the child and the child's behaviors. Particular behaviors may change group size by attracting or repelling other children, and general characteristics of the child certainly affect the probability that friends will be available to play with. Finally, the child's behavior affects characteristics of the child. The success or failure of various efforts with peers, for example, may affect feelings of self-efficacy, which in turn will affect future behavior toward peers.

Ethological Theory

The ethological approach brings several emphases to the study of peer relations (Attili, 1990; Hinde, 1983; Miller, 1993). Theoretically, there is the familiar emphasis on the innate basis for behavior, a basis established during the evolutionary history of the species. Many of the social behaviors that children show, including behaviors toward other children, are assumed to have been selected during evolution because of their adaptive value. We have already seen this argument applied to two important classes of social behavior: altruism and aggression. Ethologists do not claim that such behaviors are totally under genetic control, because experience is clearly necessary for their emergence. But they do claim that there is an important genetic component (Zahn-Waxler, Cummings, & Iannotti, 1986).

A second emphasis concerns the value of comparative study. Ethology began as the study of animal behavior, and ethologists always look for informative comparisons across different species. Relations with peers are important in the development of a number of species, including all nonhuman primates (Suomi & Harlow, 1975). Furthermore, the ways in which peers relate show interesting similarities across species. The study of other species can therefore provide clues as to the nature and importance of peer relations in human development.

Let us consider an example that will illustrate both of the points just made. We have seen that ethologists believe that the tendency to be aggressive was selected for during evolution. But unchecked aggression is not adaptive for a species; evolution must also produce controls on aggression. One form of control found in a number of species is known as a *dominance hierarchy*. Recall from Chapter 14 that a dominance hierarchy is a kind of pecking order that determines who wins out over whom in social disputes. Over time, the members of a group come to realize, and to acknowledge in their behavior, that A dominates B, B dominates C, and so on. Some degree of aggression, or at least of rough-and-tumble play, may be necessary as the hierarchy is developing. Once it is established, however, disputes can be resolved simply through members' knowledge of their relative status and thus without use of force. This reduction in actual aggression represents the adaptive value of dominance hierarchies. Other evidence for an evolutionary basis to dominance hierarchies includes their universality within a species as well as their similar form across species.

As we saw in Chapter 14, children also form dominance hierarchies. Such hierarchies are evident in the preschool, once children have had sufficient experience to sort out the relative ordering (LaFreniere & Charlesworth, 1983; Strayer & Strayer, 1976). And although their exact form may be different, dominance hierarchies are also apparent among groups of well-acquainted adolescents (Savin-Williams, 1987). That such hierarchies are effective in minimizing actual aggression is shown by one study of adolescents at a summer camp. Of 7000 dominance encounters, only 1% resulted in fights (Savin-Williams, 1979).

Note again that the biological emphasis in ethological theorizing does not rule out the contribution of other factors. Experience is important in the formation of a hierarchy. Children cannot learn the standing of particular peers until they have experience with those peers. Cognitive abilities also enter in as the child weighs various cues and makes decisions about dominance. What ethological theory adds is the belief that there is a biologically based tendency, set by evolution, to utilize experience in this way.

The work on dominance can also serve to introduce a final ethological theme—the importance of naturalistic observation. Ethologists learn about dominance by observing how children interact in their natural settings—nursery schools for 3- and 4-year-olds, summer camps or boarding schools for adolescents. More generally, the ethological approach has always emphasized the need to study the natural behaviors of organisms in their natural settings (Eibl-Eibesfeldt, 1989; Strayer, 1980). Although the value of the naturalistic approach is now generally accepted, ethologists deserve credit for being among its first and most forceful advocates.

✓ To Recap...

The three major theoretical perspectives in child psychology offer their own distinct views on peer relations. In the cognitive-developmental approach, peers are important as an impetus for cognitive change. Both Piaget and Kohlberg stress cognitive conflict with peers as one source of the ability to consider different points of view, whereas Vygotsky's theory emphasizes the instructional role played by more competent peers. Peers are also important as objects of thought, a topic that falls under the heading of social cognition. Cognitive-developmental theorists maintain that how children think about their peers is one determinant of how they behave toward peers.

According to the social-learning approach, peers contribute to the socialization of the child in three main ways. Peers reinforce or punish certain behaviors and thereby increase or decrease their likelihood. Peers serve as models who may influence the child's subsequent behavior. Finally, peers are one source for self-efficacy judgments. Interactions among peers provide a good example of reciprocal determinism, or the mutual influences among person, behavior, and situation.

Ethological approaches reflect the assumption that behaviors toward peers (such as altruism and aggression) have an innate basis that reflects the evolutionary history of the species. Peer relations are important for a number of species, and comparative study is therefore a valuable guide in assessing their role in human development. Finally, ethologists stress the value of naturalistic observation of behavior, including behavior with peers.

Typical Peer Relations

How do children interact with one another? To answer this question, we first consider how peer relations change as children grow older—that is, the developmental aspect of peer relations. In the next section of the chapter we will explore situational and cognitive factors that can affect the nature of children's interactions.

The most obvious developmental change in peer relations is an increase in amount. As children grow older, they spend more and more time with peers and relatively less time with adults, including their parents. In one study the proportion of time children spent with other children increased from approximately 30% at ages 1 and 2 to almost 60% by age 11. Conversely, time spent with adults dropped from 55% at ages 1 and 2 to less than 10% at age 11 (Ellis, Rogoff, & Cromer, 1981).

The change in the amount of time spent with peers is a backdrop to the issue we now address—changes in the nature or quality of children's relations with their peers. Here, too, changes with age are dramatic.

Infancy

Unlike older children, infants cannot spontaneously seek out their peers for companionship or pleasure. If infants find themselves together, it is because adults have placed them together. Adults often do place babies together, however, and the likelihood of such contact is increasing as more and more mothers enter the labor force (NICHD Early Child Care Research Network, 1997). Three or four infants may be cared for in the home of one mother, or half a dozen or so may occupy the infant room of a day-care center. Even infants who do not have such experiences may be brought together by researchers for the purposes of study, a procedure that has been labeled the "baby party" technique (Perry & Bussey, 1984).

Interest in other children emerges quite early. Infants as young as 6 months look at, vocalize to, smile at, and touch other infants (Hay, 1985; Hay, Nash, & Pedersen, 1983). Such behaviors are, to be sure, limited in both frequency and complexity. They also have been characterized as *object-centered*, because infants' early interactions often center on some toy of mutual interest. Indeed, toys remain an important context for interaction throughout infancy.

Relations with peers change in various ways as babies develop (Brownell, 1990; Brownell & Brown, 1992; Howes, 1987). Initially simple and discrete behaviors, such as a touch, begin to be coordinated into more complex combinations, such as a touch in conjunction with a smile, perhaps followed by a vocalization. Reciprocity becomes more and more likely as one-way social acts evolve into more truly social interchanges. Thus, a social overture from Baby 1, such as the offer of a toy, elicits an appropriate response from Baby 2, which in turn elicits a further response from Baby 1. Bouts of mutual imitation develop, in which babies both imitate their partner and take pleasure in being imitated themselves (Howes, 1992). Positive emotional responses become more marked as infants begin to derive obvious enjoyment from the company and the behavior of their peers. Unfortunately, negative responses also become more evident, especially in disputes over toys. Nevertheless, most social interchanges among infants are positive. And the cognitive level of a child's play is generally higher when peers are present than when they are not (Rubenstein & Howes, 1976).

Experience with peers has a definite effect on how infants interact. Specific experience is important; like any of us, babies are more likely to be sociable with acquaintances than with a peer whom they have never seen before (Field & Roopnarine, 1982). General experience also contributes; infants with a relatively extended history of peer interaction are more likely to initiate contact with new peers (Becker, 1977). The conclusion that experience affects peer relations is, in fact, a general one that should be kept in mind as we review developmental changes beyond infancy. In addition to differences based on age, there are always individual differences in how children of the same age relate, and past experience is one source of these differences.

For many children, interaction with peers begins very early in life.

The Preschool Period

The years between 2 and 5 are a time of expanding peer relations. Developmental trends first evident during infancy continue, and new forms of social interaction and social competence emerge. Although relations within the family remain critical, for most preschoolers peers begin to constitute a second important social system.

We have already seen numerous differences between what infants can do and what preschoolers can do. It should be no surprise to learn that peer relations also differ between the two periods. The preschooler occupies a larger social world than

Table 16.1
Types of Play Classified According to Cognitive Level

Type	Description	Examples
Functional	Simple, repetitive muscular movements performed with or without objects	Shaking a rattle; jumping up and down
Constructive	Manipulation of objects with intention of creating something	Building a tower of blocks; cutting and pasting pictures
Pretend (or dramatic)	Use of an object or person to symbolize something that it is not	Pretending that a log is a boat; playing Batman and Robin with a friend
Games with rules	Playing games in accordance with prearranged rules and limits	Playing hopscotch; playing checkers

Source: Based on information from *The Effects of Sociodramatic Play on Disadvantaged Preschool Children* by S. Smilansky, 1968, New York: John Wiley & Sons.

the infant, with a greater number and variety of playmates (Howes, 1983, 1987). The preschooler's social world is also more differentiated—that is, the child can direct different behaviors to different social objects and form somewhat different relations with different peers (Ross & Lollis, 1989). The complexity of social interactions increases as symbolic forms of behavior begin to predominate over physical ones. The same goal that was once accomplished with a pull or a shove can now be achieved (at least sometimes) with a verbal request. Children also become more skilled at adjusting such communications to the different needs of different listeners (Garvey, 1986; Shatz & Gelman, 1973), and the first truly collaborative problem solving emerges (Brownell & Carriger, 1990; Cooper, 1980).

Of course, none of these developments is instantaneous—skill in interacting with peers increases gradually in the years between 2 and 5, and indeed for some time afterward. The preschooler's social competence is impressive compared with that of the infant, but there is still a long way to go.

Much of the research concerned with peer relations during the preschool years has focused on children's play. One common approach to categorizing play is shown in Table 16.1. As you can see, the categories vary in the cognitive complexity of the play, ranging from the simple motor exercise of functional play to the give-and-take intricacies of games with rules. As would be expected, children of different ages are likely to engage in different types of play. Functional play emerges early and predominates during the infant and toddler years, whereas games with rules are infrequent among children younger than grade-school age (Rubin, Fein, & Vandenberg, 1983).

Pretend play
A form of play in which children use an object or person as a symbol to stand for something else.

The category of **pretend play** has been of special interest to investigators of preschool development. Studies have demonstrated that both the frequency and the complexity of pretend play increase across the preschool years. Such research also suggests that pretend play can have beneficial effects on both the child's cognitive development and the child's relations with peers (Fisher, 1992; Stambak & Sinclair, 1993).

Another popular approach to categorizing play is shown in Table 16.2. Here, the focus is on the social organization rather than the cognitive level of the child's play. The usual assumption has been that the various types of play develop in the order shown in the table. Thus, 2-year-olds are most likely to be found in solitary or

Table 16.2
Types of Play Classified According to Social Level

Type	*Description*
Onlooker	Watching others play without participating oneself
Solitary	Playing alone and independently, with no attempt to get close to other children
Parallel	Playing alongside other children and with similar materials but with no real interaction or cooperation
Associative	Playing with other children in some common activity but without division of labor or subordination to some overall group goal
Cooperative	Playing in a group that is organized for the purpose of carrying out some activity or attaining some goal, with coordination of individual members' behavior in pursuit of the common goal

Source: Based on information from "Social Participation among Preschool Children" by M. B. Parten, 1932, *Journal of Abnormal and Social Psychology, 27,* pp. 243–269.

onlooker behavior; in 5- and 6-year-olds, cooperative and associative play are common. A particularly interesting category is that of **parallel play**, in which two or more children play next to each other, using the same sorts of materials and perhaps even talking, yet without any genuine interaction. Anyone who has watched groups of 3- and 4-year-olds can verify that such "semisocial" play is common.

The categories listed in Table 16.2 were developed more than 60 years ago (Parten, 1932). Although recent research verifies that children today show the same general patterns of play, such research also suggests some qualifications and complexities in the developmental picture (Howes & Matheson, 1992; Rubin, Bukowski, & Parker, 1998). Not all children progress in the order shown in the table; a child might move directly from solitary behavior to cooperative play, for example, without an intervening phase of parallel play (Smith, 1978). Nor do the early categories of play necessarily disappear as children grow older; solitary and parallel play are still common among 4- and 5-year-olds (Tieszen, 1979). What does change with age is the cognitive maturity of the play. The nonsocial play of 2- and 3-year-olds consists mainly of various kinds of functional play (see Table 16.1). Older children are more likely to embed even their nonsocial play in a constructive

Parallel play
A form of play in which children play next to each other and with similar materials but with no real interaction or cooperation.

Children's play undergoes characteristic changes across the preschool and grade-school years (see Table 16-2). For very young children, the onlooker role is a common one.

Solitary play is common prior to the onset of social play.

or dramatic context (Rubin, Watson, & Jambor, 1978). Because of this interplay of cognitive and social factors, modern scales to assess play typically include both cognitive and social dimensions (Howes, Unger, & Seidner, 1989; Rubin, 1989).

Development in Cultural Context
Cross-Cultural Variations in Early Play

Play appears to be a universal feature of childhood around the world. Exactly how children play, however, can vary from one cultural setting to another.

Consider the vignettes in Table 16.3. The first will surely have a familiar sound to anyone who has spent much time in a preschool in the United States. Fantasy characters, action, danger, heroics—all are common elements in the pretend play of Western preschoolers. Also familiar is the assertive and somewhat self-centered nature of the interaction. Each child talks primarily about his own activities; disagreements are frequent; and commands and contradictions outnumber questions and requests.

The second vignette is also characterized by rich imagination and plentiful action. The interplay between the children, however, has a somewhat different quality. Requests are now more likely than commands; tag questions ("right?" "isn't he?") and other indices of agreement are common; and there is more attempt to coordinate the action in ways agreeable to both parties.

The examples in the table are drawn from a study by Farver and Shin (1997). The children in both cases are American, but those in the second vignette come from Korean-American families who have recently emigrated to the United States and for whom traditional Korean values and practices are still very important. A number of emphases characterize both the home lives of these children and the predominantly Korean-American preschools they attend: a concern with family and respect for others, an emphasis on harmony and avoidance of conflict, and a reluctance to talk about the self or to force one's opinions on others. The nature of the

Table 16.3
Cultural Differences in Play: A Contrast between Korean-American and Anglo-American
Children

Typical Anglo-American Sequence

A: Where's the king?

B: I need the dragon. Where's the dragon?

A: I'm having that. (*A takes the dragon from B*) And I am your king! Do not obey the bad king! (*High voice*) And here was the queen. Miss Lunchmea, tell them what you want to say. (*Low voice*) We shall never hurt the people. (*High voice speaking for the queen figure*)

B: I want this one. (*Taking the dragon from A*) Help! Help! Help! (*High voice*) The dragon is getting her! (*Low voice*)

A: I'll save you! (*High voice; tries to take the dragon from B*)

B: No! No! Help! Help! (*High voice*) I want to be the dragon now. (*Regular voice*)

A: No! The dragon's the queen now. You have this horse now. (*Hands B the horse*)

B: I'm the horse hero now! and I'll save everyone.

A: No, I'm the hero of you. I'm the hero of you 'cause I'm so cute.

B: Well, I'm not playing then. (*B gets up to leave the play*)

Typical Korean-American Sequence

A: Let's play here. He is a king, isn't he? (*Picks up the king figure and shows it to B*)

B: Yes. Let's put him here. (*Puts king figure on the "bed"*)

A: He is the bad buy, isn't he? (*Picks up the knight figure, shows B*)

B: Yes, but the good guy caught and killed him, right?

A: Right, the bad guy will die here. (*Puts the knight in the castle/dungeon/jail*)

B: Yes, let's go to sleep now.

A: The good guy caught him, right?

B: Yes, the good guy caught him, so he died.

A: So the jail is broken open.

B: Right. And everybody died…the sun died, too.

Source: From "Social Pretend Play in Korean- and Anglo-American Preschoolers" by J. A. Farver and Y. L. Shin, 1997, *Child Development, 68,* p. 552. Copyright © 1997 by the Society for Research in Child Development. Reprinted by permission.

children's play reflects these emphases, both in the themes that are selected (much play concerned with family life and everyday activities, in contrast to the adventure motifs that dominate the Anglo-American children's play) and the manner in which the children interact.

The cultural differences illustrated in Table 16.3 are fairly subtle. More dramatic contrasts emerge when we examine a wider range of cultural settings. In the Marquesas Islands of Polynesia, for example, children between ages 2 and 5 are often left to care for themselves while their older siblings attend nearby schools. These children therefore have a degree of independence at an early age that is unusual in most cultures—a situation made even more challenging by the demanding nature of the physical terrain within which their play occurs (near an ocean with strong surf and sharp rocks, and a valley with steep and slippery walls).

The kinds of play that develop reflect these circumstances, as well as the values of the adult society toward which the children are developing. From the time that children first enter the play group, there is an emphasis on self-reliance and emotional control, and older children use various techniques (teasing, hazing) to instill the necessary toughness in their younger playmates. There is an emphasis as well on staying together, and play in large groups (as opposed to solitary or dyadic play) is much more common than it is among American children of the same age. Furthermore, the children's group play shows characteristics (e.g., organized roles, a sense of solidarity) that typically emerge only several years later in the play of Western children, as we will see (Martini, 1994).

Both the physical environment and the social setting contribute to the distinctive nature of play in the Marquesas Islands. More generally, social context proves to be an important source of variations in play across different cultures. The Marquesas example provides a striking demonstration of play largely in the absence of adult guidance or supervision. In contrast, in the United States and other Western societies, parents often take an active role in their children's early pretend play, initiating play episodes and guiding the child to more complex forms of pretense (Haight & Miller, 1993). In some cultures, older siblings assume a major caregiving role; in these cases many forms of play develop under the tutelage of a sibling (Zukow, 1989). We see, once again, a mixture of the normative and the idiographic. The tendency to play and many of its qualities appear to be universal; its specific content and context, however, may vary from one culture to another.

As noted, the preschool years are a time of expanding peer interaction, especially for children who attend a nursery school or day-care center. This period is a good one, therefore, for a first look at the processes stressed in social-learning accounts of peer relations.

One important process is modeling. Children clearly imitate other children in preschool settings; one study reports an average of 13 imitative acts per child per hour (Abramovitch & Grusec, 1978). A variety of behaviors have been shown to be susceptible to the effects of preschool peer models, including compliance with adult instructions (Ross, 1971), sharing (Elliott & Vasta, 1970), social participation (O'Connor, 1969), and problem solving (Morrison & Kuhn, 1983). Indeed, as we noted in our discussion of infancy, some capacity for imitative learning emerges even before the usual age for preschool attendance. Recent research has shown simple forms of peer imitation in children as young as 15 to 20 months (Asendorpf & Baudonniere, 1993; Eckerman, 1993; Hanna & Meltzoff, 1993).

Reinforcement, too, occurs frequently in the preschool (Charlesworth & Hartup, 1967; Furman & Gavin, 1989). Among the reinforcers children deliver are help giving, praise, smiling or laughing, affection, and compliance. Preschool children also deliver punishment to one another; examples include noncompliance, blaming, disapproval, physical attack, and ignoring. That such behaviors do function as reinforcements or punishments is suggested by children's reactions to them; reinforcers tend to elicit positive responses in their recipients, whereas punishments tend to elicit negative ones (Furman & Masters, 1980). The reinforcing or punishing nature of such events is also verified by their effects on subsequent behavior. Children are most likely to repeat a response that results in reinforcement and least likely to repeat one that results in punishment (Hartup, 1983); they are also most likely to continue to play with peers from whom they generally receive positive consequences (Snyder et al., 1996). Among the aspects of social development that have been shown to be responsive to peer consequences in the preschool are gender-typed behaviors (Lamb, Easterbrooks, & Holden, 1980), modes of initiating interaction (Leiter, 1977), and aggression (Patterson, Littman, & Bricker, 1967).

We noted earlier that children's reinforcement of their peers is often unintentional. The same is true, of course, for many instances of modeling. These process-

Parallel play is a familiar sight among preschoolers.

The appearance of associative play marks an advance in the social organization of the child's play.

The most advanced form of social play is found in the cooperation and coordination of cooperative play.

es are not necessarily inadvertent, however, even in children as young as preschool age. Research indicates that preschool children often use imitation of peers as a technique to win friends or to enter ongoing groups (Grusec & Abramovitch, 1982)—a successful technique, in that imitation is generally responded to positively. And anyone who has spent much time around young children is familiar with their deliberate manipulation of reinforcement through such promises as "I'll be your friend if…" and the corresponding threat "I won't be your friend unless…"

Later Childhood and Adolescence

As children develop, their play continues to evolve through the hierarchies shown in Tables 16.1 and 16.2. By age 8 or 9, children have become enthusiastic participants in games with rules, as any visit to a school playground or toy store will readily verify (Eifermann, 1971). By middle childhood, children's play is also more likely to fall within the most advanced of the categories in Table 16.2—cooperative play.

These changes in both the cognitive level and the social organization of play in turn relate to more general factors in the child's development. Increased experience with peers clearly plays a role as children spend more and more time with a wider variety of children. Advances in cognitive level also contribute. In particular, gains in perspective-taking skills during middle childhood may underlie both the newfound facility at games with rules and the general ability to interact cooperatively.

One of the most striking developmental changes in peer relations is the increased importance of groups as a context for peer interaction. For psychologists, the term **group** describes something more than just a collection of individuals. Hartup (1983) suggests the following criteria for determining that a group exists: "social interaction occurs regularly, values are shared over and above those maintained in society at large, individual members have a sense of belonging, and a structure exists to support the attitudes that members should have toward one another" (p. 144).

Preschool children occasionally interact in ways that seem to fit this definition. The same four boys, for example, may play together in similar ways every day, demonstrating clear leader-and-follower roles in their play as well as a clear sense of "we" versus "they" in their relations with those outside their group. Indeed, children as young as 2 may show some of the criteria of group formation (Lakin, Lakin, & Constanzo, 1979). Nevertheless, it is during the grade-school years that membership in groups assumes a clear significance in the lives of most children. Some such groups are formal ones with a substantial degree of adult input, such as Brownies, Cub Scouts, 4-H, and Little League. Other groups are more informal, child-created, and child-directed, reflecting mutual interests of the group members. The culmination of this developmental progression can be seen in the **cliques** to which many adolescents belong—groups of perhaps 5 to 10 friends who interact frequently and whose shared interests and behavior patterns set them apart from both their peers and the adult world.

How does membership in a group affect peer relations? A classic study of this question is the Robbers Cave Experiment (Sherif et al., 1961). For this study, 22 fifth-grade boys, initially unacquainted, were recruited to attend one of two summer camps. In each camp, the boys engaged in typical activities—hiking, sports, crafts, and the like. Thanks to the manipulation of the experimenters, they also coped with various unexpected challenges—for example, preparing a meal when the staff had failed to do so. In both camps, divisions of labor and cooperative problem solving ensued, both in response to immediate crises and with respect to longer-term group organization and group goals. Leaders and followers emerged. And both camps adopted names—Rattlers in one case, Eagles in the other.

Group
A collection of individuals who interact regularly in a consistent, structured fashion and who share values and a sense of belonging to the group.

Clique
A kind of group typical in adolescence, consisting usually of 5 to 10 members whose shared interests and behavior patterns set them apart from their peers.

Initially, neither group was aware of the other. After 5 days, however, the experimenters arranged for the two groups to meet "accidentally." A series of competitions (baseball, tug-of-war, and so on) followed, engineered so that neither group enjoyed more success than the other. The immediate effects of the competitions on group cohesiveness were detrimental; bickering followed any defeat, and the leader of one group was actually overthrown. Over time, however, the between-group competitions led to a heightened sense of within-group—"us" as opposed to "them"—solidarity. At the same time, the rivalry between groups escalated, eventually reaching the point of physical violence. Only through cooperative efforts to solve further experimentally engineered crises (for example, a nonfunctioning water supply on a hot day) did the two groups begin to resolve their conflict and develop between-group friendships.

The Robbers Cave experiment suggests several conclusions about children's groups that are verified by more recent research (Fine, 1987; Hartup, 1992c). Most generally, it is clear that children tend to form groups based on common interests and goals and that groups serve as a source of self-identity and gratification. Groups are organized, with rules and norms that must be adhered to and divisions of the members into leaders and followers. Work in support of common goals is one source of group cohesiveness; competition with other groups is another source. Between-group rivalry is clearly the most worrisome aspect of group functioning, since attitudes and behaviors toward outsiders may become quite negative. More positively, the same factors that promote within-group cohesion—in particular, working toward a common goal—can also serve to reduce between-group hostility. These conclusions are not limited to children, but apply to adults' groups as well. At the most far-reaching level, they have implications for relations between ethnic groups and between nations (Hartup, 1983). (In Box 16.1 we consider a classic study of a group-oriented method of socialization.)

The Robbers Cave experiment is a classic study of group formation. M. Sherif, O.J. Harvey, B. Jack White, William R. Hood, Carolyn W. Sherif, photograph p. 103 from the Robbers Cave Experiment, © 1988 by Muzafer Sherif, Wesleyan University Press reprinted by permission of the University Press of New England.

TWO WORLDS OF CHILDHOOD: A SOVIET–AMERICAN COMPARISON

In every culture, peers play certain roles—reinforcing and punishing particular actions, serving as models for a wide range of behaviors, providing standards for social comparisons and for judgments of self-efficacy, and establishing group norms and practices to which other children must adhere. Furthermore, adults in every culture make deliberate use of the power of peers—citing particular peers as models of good behavior, pointing out the consequences of the child's behavior for the peer group as a whole, and so forth. In most instances, this sort of peer-based socialization is casual and unsystematic—just one of many ways in which perceptive parents and teachers attempt to instill desired behavior. But what would happen if a society as a whole decided to make the peer group a major vehicle of socialization?

A classic study by Urie Bronfenbrenner (1962, 1970) sought to answer this question. Bronfenbrenner's test case was the Soviet Union of the 1950s and 1960s. Child-rearing methods in the Soviet Union during this time placed a heavy emphasis on various collectives, or organized peer groups, to which children belonged as they grew up. For many children, collective upbringing began with enrollment in infant nurseries and public preschools. For all children, collectives of various levels and sizes were important throughout the school years—the classroom as a whole; the individual rows, or "links," within the classroom; and the broader Communist youth groups to which virtually all children belonged and of which each classroom was a unit. Between the ages of 10 and 15, the youth group was the Pioneers. Figure 16.1 shows examples of posters that were used to illustrate some of the laws of the Pioneers.

This kind of social structure guarantees an important role for peers, simply because children spend so much time with other children from early in life. The Soviet emphasis on peers, however, went well beyond simple proximity. For Soviet children the collective, rather than the individual child, was the primary unit for achievement and for evaluation. The frequent school competitions, for example, were always structured in terms of the collective: the best row within a class, the best class within a school, the best school within a district. The rewards for success in such competitions—for example, large "Who Is Best?" charts displayed throughout the school—listed not the winning children but the winning groups. Because any one child's success was tied to that of the group, children had a clear incentive for monitoring and regulating their peers' behavior, as well as a clear reason for being responsive themselves to suggestions or criticisms from the group. That such criticisms would be forthcoming was ensured by the designation of some children as "monitors" whose job was to help the teacher maintain order and elicit optimal performance. As the following examples from a third-grade monitor illustrate, the monitors were quite willing to be critical: "Today Valodya did the wrong problem. Masha didn't write neatly and forgot to underline the right words in her lesson; Alyosha had a dirty shirt collar" (Bronfenbrenner, 1970, p. 60).

How does such socialization affect children's development? In attempting to answer this question, Bronfenbrenner drew on two sources of evidence: informal observations of the behavior of Soviet children in a variety of settings, and controlled experiments comparing the responses of Soviet children to those of children from the

Conformity to Peers

The work on groups raises the general question of peers' influence on a child's development. To many adults, the importance of peer-group membership for the grade-schooler or adolescent raises the disturbing possibility that peers may come to outweigh parents as a source of behaviors and values. What do we know about

Figure 16.1
Posters illustrating the laws of the Pioneers, a Communist youth group to which many children in the Soviet Union belonged during the 1950s and 1960s. The caption for the first poster reads, "A Pioneer is an example to all children"; that for the second poster reads, "A Pioneer tells the truth and treasures the honor of his unit." From *Two Worlds of Childhood* (pp. 45, 48) by U. Bronfenbrenner, 1970, New York: Russell Sage Foundation.

United States and other Western countries. Both kinds of evidence led to the same conclusion. Soviet children appeared in general to be well mannered, hardworking, obedient, and respectful of others, both peers and adults. Naturally occurring instances of antisocial behavior were rare among the Soviet youths, and Soviet children were also less likely than their Western counterparts to act antisocially or immorally when given a chance to do so in experimental settings (for example, to cheat on a test). One Soviet-American experimental comparison proved especially instructive with respect to the role of the peer group. When told that classmates would be informed of any misconduct, Soviet children became even less likely to behave antisocially. American children, in contrast, became more likely.

Bronfenbrenner's general conclusion was that the Soviet system of socialization appeared to accomplish its goal, namely, production of well-behaved and responsible citizens who would conform to the dictates of Soviet society. He also noted, however, that by the late 1960s cracks were becoming evident in the socialization edifice, and various forms of dissatisfaction were creeping in. And as the recent events in the former Soviet Union make clear, even a group-oriented and conformity-based method of socialization does not remove the possibility of individual initiative and social change.

the influence of peers in general and about the relative influence of peers and parents in particular?

The issue of peer influence turns out to be one of those "it depends" issues (Berndt, 1989a; Newman, 1982). Peers can clearly be an important source of values. But how important they are depends on a number of factors. Peer influence varies with age, reaching a peak, at least by some measures, in early adolescence and declining thereafter (Berndt, 1979; Constanzo, 1970). Peer influence varies from child to child (Berndt, 1996b). And peer influence, as well as the relative importance of peers and parents, varies from one area of life to another. In areas such as clothing, music, and choice of friends, peers are often more important than parents, especially by adolescence. In areas such as academic planning and occupational aspirations, however, parents usually have the dominant voice (Berndt, Miller, & Park, 1989; Sebald, 1989).

This discussion is not meant to imply that peers are never a negative influence. In particular cases, they clearly can be—in problem areas as serious as smoking (Urberg, Degirmenciouglu, & Pilgrim, 1997), drug use (Dinges & Oetting, 1993; Mounts & Steinberg, 1995), delinquency (Jessor & Jessor, 1977), and gang violence (a topic that we address in the Applications section). Despite these cautionary points, it is important to remember that membership in groups, in addition simply to being enjoyable for children, promotes a number of social skills that will remain valuable throughout life. Furthermore, surveys reveal that the common perception of a clash in values between peers and parents is overstated; on most questions, peers and parents are more similar than different in their views (Brown, 1990; Newman, 1982). Finally, decisions about many issues, especially by adolescence, are not a matter simply of acquiescence to either peers or parents; rather, individuals may arrive at positions of their own that do not mirror those of any outside group (Savin-Williams & Berndt, 1990). Thus, one legacy of effective socialization, including membership in peer groups, may be a healthy capacity for independent thought.

Applications
Controlling Gang Violence

In 1990 the number of gang homicides in Los Angeles reached an all-time high of 329. This figure represented 34% of the homicides in the city that year. Homicide is now the leading cause of death among African-American youths in the United States and the second leading cause of death (after automobile accidents) for Caucasian youths.

It is difficult to determine how many gangs and gang members there are, given the diversity of ways in which *gang* has been defined. By one estimate, however, in the approximately 800 cities in the United States there are about 10,000 gangs and perhaps as many as a half-million gang members (Klein, 1995).

Attempts to control the violent activities of teenage gangs have a long and mostly unsuccessful history (Covey, Menard, & Franzese, 1997). In 1987 the Office of Juvenile Justice and Delinquency Prevention established the National Youth Gang Suppression and Intervention Program (Spergel, Chance, & Curry, 1990; Spergel & Curry, 1993). The mandate of the National Program was to coordinate information about gang activities and intervention efforts from 45 communities around the United States. The ultimate goal was to use such information to develop and disseminate effective intervention programs.

How have communities attempted to combat teenage violence? The National Program identified five strategies. Most common (44% of cases) was *suppression*—an emphasis on tactics such as surveillance, arrest, and imprisonment. The next most common policy (31.5%) was *social intervention*—an emphasis on crisis intervention, treatment for the youths and their families, and referral to social services. With *orga-*

nizational development (10.9% of cases), the primary strategy was the creation of special units for handling the problem, such as new police units and special youth agency crisis programs. *Community mobilization* (8.9%) focused on improved communication and joint policy and program development among various community agencies. Finally, the least common strategy (4.8%) was *social opportunities*—the provision of basic or remedial education, training, work incentives, and jobs.

How well do such strategies work? Answering this question is not easy. Intervention projects seldom take the form of neat, well-controlled experiments, and obtaining clear indications of their success or failure can be difficult. The evaluative component of the National Program relied on two main sources of data: evaluations from various members of the juvenile justice system (such as police officers, judges, and church leaders) and objective data concerning changes in gang activity over time (number of gangs, number of gang members, number of gang homicides, and so on).

In part, the conclusions from both sorts of data confirmed the caution and pessimism of previous reviews: In only 8 of the 45 cities was there evidence of improvement in the gang situation over time. More positively, the survey did provide information about differences in the effectiveness of the five intervention strategies. The authors summarized their conclusions as follows: "Community mobilization was the factor that most powerfully predicted a decline in the gang problem. The provision of basic social opportunities to gang youth, that is, education and employment, was also very important in cities with chronic gang problems" (Spergel et al., 1990, p. 3).

Because of the complexities noted, the results from the National Program must be regarded as tentative. Indeed, not all reviews have reached the same conclusions (Lundman, 1984). Nevertheless, the National Program does represent an ambitious and promising attempt to provide a scientific grounding for efforts to address one of the nation's most pressing social problems. And it does send a disquieting message in the conjunction of two of its findings: The most effective intervention strategies were also the ones that were least often employed.

✔ To Recap...

Children's peer relations undergo dramatic changes with development. Infants as young as 6 months show interest in and positive behaviors toward other babies, and as infants develop, their interactions with peers become more frequent, more complex, and more reciprocal. Such interactions are affected not only by age but by experience, a point that remains true throughout childhood.

During the preschool years, peer interactions continue to grow in frequency and complexity. Relations with peers become more differentiated, and symbolic forms of interaction begin to predominate over physical ones. Play increases in both cognitive level and social organization as cooperative play becomes increasingly likely. As they interact more and more, children become important socializing agents for one another, especially by delivering reinforcements and punishments for particular behaviors and by serving as models.

Development during the grade-school years is in part a continuation of trends present earlier. In addition, groups, both formal and informal, begin to assume a prominent role. Studies of children's groups reveal the importance of common interests and goals for group formation, as well as the importance of organization and agreed-upon norms for effective group functioning. Although the peer group can be an influential source of values and behavior, parents remain influential as well, and on most issues the views of peers and of parents are more similar than different.

Contributors to Peer Relations

Situational Factors

Children's age is one determinant of how they interact. The situation in which they find themselves is another. Situational factors are of particular importance in social-learning theory. Social-learning theorists believe that behaviors are always learned within particular situations and that the immediate situation therefore is always an important determinant of how children behave. It follows that children's behavior may vary from one situation to another. The same child who is a model of decorum at home, for example, may be the terror of the playground at nursery school. Understanding behavior, then—including behavior with peers—requires knowledge of the setting in which the behavior occurs.

Space and Resources   Research has identified a variety of situational factors that can affect behavior in both animals and humans. One such factor is crowding. When many organisms are packed into a small space, negative consequences often result, including increased aggression, heightened emotional arousal, and decreased problem solving. Such effects have been demonstrated in species ranging from rats (Calhoun, 1962) to adult humans (Epstein, 1981).

Crowding can also affect children. In one study, 4th-, 8th-, and 11th-grade children spent 30 minutes together under one of two conditions: four children in a 20- by 24-foot space, or four children in a 5- by 8-foot space. Children in the latter condition showed greater physiological arousal and reported more discomfort and annoyance. When later asked to choose a game to play together, they were more likely to choose competitive rather than cooperative options (Aiello, Nicosia, & Thompson, 1979). Other studies have demonstrated effects of more extended periods of crowding under naturalistic circumstances, such as in the preschool (Liddell & Kruger, 1987, 1989). Children have been found, for example, to engage in less cooperative play in crowded classrooms than in less crowded ones. More fights occur on small playgrounds than on large ones (Ginsburg, 1975).

The resources available can also affect how children interact. As we saw, toys often facilitate peer interaction, especially for young children. On the other hand, a scarcity of toys sometimes leads to an increase in play with peers, presumably because the environment presents the child with fewer interesting alternatives (Vandell, Wilson, & Buchanan, 1980). The nature of the toys or other resources also plays a role. Not surprisingly, solitary and parallel play are most common in the art and book corners and other "quiet" areas within a school. Conversely, the doll area is a likely setting for cooperative and dramatic play (Rubin, 1977). Outdoor settings and areas encouraging large-muscle activity (running, throwing, etc.) are also associated with more cooperative play, along, of course, with a general increase in the energy level and physical nature of the play (Hartup, 1983).

Familiarity   It has long been known that the familiarity of the setting can affect how young children interact with adults, both their own parents and strangers. Familiarity also influences interactions with peers. Infants are more likely to direct social behaviors toward fellow infants when they are in their own homes than when they are in the other babies' homes (Becker, 1977). Comparable effects have been found for preschool children. In one study, 32 sets of two initially unacquainted preschoolers were observed playing together twice, first in the experimenter's home and then in the home of one of the children. Based on the sessions in the experimenter's home, one member of each pair was identified as relatively sociable and the other as relatively shy. During the second session all 16 of the initially sociable children who were observed at home remained socially dominant. But 15 of the 16 "shy" children became socially dominant when observed in *their* homes. The greater social activity included both a higher frequency of positive behaviors, such as initiating play, and a higher frequency of negative behaviors, such as aggression (Jeffers & Lore, 1979).

As the researchers note, parents are often surprised when told that the outgoing child they know is timid or withdrawn at school. Studies such as this suggest that the child's behavior may in fact be different at home from what it is in other settings. And they carry a message for parents of a shy child: Arranging opportunities to play with peers in the familiar home setting may help to break down the shyness and increase social confidence.

Another way to examine familiarity is in terms not of the physical environment but of the people in it. We have seen that babies behave differently with familiar playmates than with strangers. Acquaintanceship also affects interaction in older children. Social interaction is both more frequent and more positive with familiar peers than with unfamiliar ones. The cognitive level of play increases with familiar peers; cooperative and associative play become more common and solitary and onlooker behavior less common (Doyle, Connolly, & Rivest, 1980). Collaborative problem solving proceeds more smoothly and efficiently among familiar peers than among unfamiliar ones (Brody, Graziano, & Musser, 1983). Finally, as they become acquainted, children become more likely to exhibit behaviors that may be the precursors of friendship, such as sharing information about the self (Furman, 1987).

Group Size   Group size is both a dependent variable and an independent variable in the study of peer relations. It is dependent in the sense that it is one of the outcomes we can study: What size play groups do children prefer? The answer varies some with age. Toddlers and preschoolers play most often in groups of two. Even when more children are present, social behaviors in this age group often involve only two children at a time (Bronson, 1981). Older children are more likely to interact with several peers simultaneously, although one-on-one interaction remains important (Hartup, 1992c). Recall that there is also a gender difference in this aspect of development: Boys, on average, play in larger groups than do girls (Benenson, Apostoleris, & Parnass, 1997; Waldrop & Halverson, 1975).

Group size can also be examined as an independent variable that may affect the quality of children's interactions. It is a variable that is hard to study in isolation, because the number of children in a group often varies with other factors, such as the amount of space per child and the number of available adults. At least sometimes, however, smaller numbers seem to be better than larger numbers. For example, children have been observed to engage in more conversational interchanges (Howes & Rubenstein, 1979), to ask more questions of adults (Torrance, 1970), and to show more imaginative play (Smith & Connolly, 1981) in small groups than in large groups. Note that these findings are of practical as well as theoretical importance. They have implications, for example, for policies concerning classroom size and the number of children in day-care groups (Howes, Phillips, & Whitebook, 1992).

Cognitive Contributions

We turn now to the role that cognitive development plays in peer relations. As the name suggests, cognitive factors are stressed most heavily in the cognitive-developmental approach. But any theoretical perspective must allow some role for cognitive factors. It seems obvious that how children think about peers must affect their behavior toward peers. The question is exactly how these factors contribute.

A reasonable first step is to ask which cognitive factors might be important. The most popular candidate has been perspective taking. The ability to adopt the perspective of another—to figure out what someone else feels, thinks, wishes, or the like—seems clearly relevant to the ability to interact with others. More broadly, researchers have stressed various aspects of social cognition—the child's thoughts and level of reasoning with respect to other people. How, for example, do children reason about the causes of other people's behavior, or about the morality of various behaviors, or about the nature of friendship (Shantz, 1983)? Finally, some investigators have moved closer to actual social interaction by focusing on **social problem-solving skills**, the skills needed to resolve social dilemmas (Rubin & Krasnor, 1986; Rubin & Rose-Krasnor, 1992). An example of an approach to assessing social problem-solving skills is shown in Table 16.4. As you can see, the dilemmas in this case involve sharing resources and initiating friendship. Models of the skills needed to solve such problems have often been grounded in information-processing conceptions of the components—such as attention, representation, and memory—of problem solving in general (Dodge, 1986).

Skills such as those assessed by the tasks in Table 16.4 improve with age—as, of course, do perspective-taking and information-processing abilities more generally. The parallel changes with age in cognitive skills and peer relations are compatible with the idea that cognitive advances lead to social advances—as children can do

Social problem-solving skills
Skills needed to resolve social dilemmas.

Table 16.4
Examples of Items Used to Assess Children's Social Problem-Solving Skills

Stimulus	Narration	Questions
Picture of one girl swinging and another girl standing nearby	This girl's name is Laurie, and this is Kathy. Laurie is five years old. Kathy is seven years old. Kathy is older than Laurie. Kathy has been on the swing for a long, long time. Laurie would really like to play on the swing.	What do you think Laurie could say or do so that she could play on the swing? If that didn't work, what else could Laurie do or say so that she could play on the swing? What do you think you would do or say if you wanted to play on the swing?
Picture of a boy riding a tricycle and a girl standing nearby	This boy's name is Bert and this girl's name is Erika. They are both five years old. Bert, the boy, has been on the tricycle for a long, long time. Erika, the girl, would like to ride the tricycle.	What do you think Erika could say or do so that she could ride the tricycle? If that didn't work, what else could Erika do or say so that she could have the tricycle? What do you think you would do or say if you wanted to ride on the tricycle?
Picture of a school setting with two girls sitting near each other	This girl's name is Kim and this is Jenny. Kim and Jenny are both five years old. They are both the same age. Kim and Jenny are in the same class as school, but this is Jenny's first day at the school. Jenny is a new girl in the class. Kim would like to get to know Jenny better.	What do you think Kim could say or do to get to know Jenny? If that didn't work, what else could Kim do or say to get to know Jenny? What do you think you would do or say to get to know Jenny?

Source: Excerpted from *The Social Problem-Solving Test–Revised* (pp. 3,4) by K. H. Rubin, 1988, Waterloo, Ontario: University of Waterloo. Copyright © 1988 by K. H. Rubin. Reprinted by permission.

more cognitively, they also can do more socially. This kind of evidence, however, is very indirect. Stronger support for the role of cognitive factors in peer relations would come from two further sorts of data. If the cognitive-developmental position is correct, we would expect to find cognitive-social links *within* an age group—children who are advanced in the relevant cognitive abilities should also be advanced in their peer relations. We would also expect that teaching children relevant cognitive skills would lead to advances in their social behavior as well.

Correlations within Age Groups   In a correlational study, a researcher measures two aspects of development simultaneously to see whether they are related. A researcher investigating the relationship of peer interaction and cognitive skills would direct one measure to some aspect of peer relations (such as the frequency of cooperative play) and the other to the presumed cognitive prerequisite (such as perspective taking). Support for the importance of cognitive factors would come from a significant positive correlation between cognitive ability and social development.

Many studies have looked for such correlations. The general conclusion has been that there *is* a positive relation between level of cognitive development and level of peer relations. Perspective taking has been the most frequently examined cognitive variable, and a variety of forms of perspective taking have been shown to relate to how children interact (Kurdek, 1978). Measures of communication skill, both in speaking and listening, also relate positively to peer interaction (Gottman, Gonso, & Rasmussen, 1975). So do various measures of social cognition—for example, level of moral judgment (Blasi, 1980) and attributions concerning the intentions underlying behavior (Dodge, Murphy, & Buchsbaum, 1984). And so do measures of the kind of social problem-solving skills described in Table 16.4 (Rubin & Krasnor, 1986; Yeates, Schultz, & Selman, 1991). Among the aspects of peer relations that have been found to relate to cognitive development are play (Rubin & Maioni, 1975), prosocial behavior (Wentzel & Erdley, 1993), and aggression (Rubin, Bream, & Rose-Krasnor, 1991).

Although the evidence for cognitive-social links is generally positive, several cautions should be noted. First, not all the evidence is positive; a number of studies have reported no relation between cognitive ability and behavior with peers (Shantz, 1983). Furthermore, when significant relations do emerge, they usually are not very large. Thus, cognitive measures account for only a modest amount of the variation in the way children behave with peers. This conclusion is perhaps not surprising. No study, after all, assesses every aspect of cognitive development that might be relevant. And no one would claim that cognitive level is the *sole* determinant of peer relations. At best, it is one contributor.

One final caution concerns the conclusions that can be drawn from a significant correlation. As we discussed in Chapter 3, correlational data do not permit clear cause-and-effect conclusions. Simply knowing, for example, that perspective taking is correlated with cooperation does not allow us to conclude that perspective taking *causes* cooperation. To determine causality with certainty, we need an experimental design in which one of the variables can be experimentally manipulated. This brings us to the next source of evidence.

Training   If cognitive advances underlie social advances, then we would expect teaching children relevant cognitive skills to lead to changes in their social behavior as well. Consider the hypothesized link between perspective taking and cooperation. If a causal relation exists, then training children in perspective taking should also produce gains in cooperation.

In general, the results from training studies are compatible with those from correlational research. Not all training studies produce positive results, and the effects that do occur are generally modest in magnitude. Nevertheless, most of the evidence suggests that training in relevant cognitive skills does have some effect on how children behave with peers. Training in perspective taking, for example, has been shown to lead to decreased aggression (Chandler, 1973) and increased helpfulness and cooperation (Iannotti, 1978). Teaching children social problem-solving skills has been shown to result in improvements in prosocial behavior and general social adjustment (Weissberg, 1985).

Training studies of this sort are not only of scientific interest. Such interventions are also one way to attempt to help children who are having difficulties in social adjustment. We consequently return to training studies later, in our discussion of problems in peer relations.

✓ *To Recap...*

Situational factors influence how peers interact. Aspects of the physical environment— such as the familiarity of the setting, the amount of space per child, and the nature of the available resources—can be important. The social environment also plays a role; for example, the number and familiarity of the other children present can affect children's behavior with peers.

A factor stressed especially in the cognitive-developmental approach to peer relations is the cognitive level of the child. Cognitive level is by no means a perfect predictor of peer interaction; cognitive-social relations are only sometimes found, and when they do occur, they are modest in magnitude. Nevertheless, evidence from both correlational research and experimental training studies suggests that cognitive factors do contribute to peer relations.

Friendship

According to the dictionary, the word *peer* means "equal." Clearly, however, some peers (to borrow from George Orwell's *Animal Farm*) are more equal than others. Relations among peers, like peers themselves, differ. In this section, we focus on the most important peer relationship—friendship. We begin by considering what children themselves mean by the word *friend*. We then examine how friendships are formed and how friendship influences children's behavior and development.

Conceptions of Friendship

Consider the following answers in response to the question "What is a friend?"

> *"A friend is a person you like. You play around with them."*
>
> *"Friends don't snatch or act snobby, and they don't argue or disagree. If you're nice to them, they'll be nice to you."*
>
> *"A person who helps you do things. When you need something, they get it. You do the same for them."*
>
> *"Someone you can share things with and who shares things with you. Not material things; feelings. When you feel sad, she feels sad. They understand you."*
>
> *"A stable, affective, dyadic relationship marked by preference, reciprocity, and shared positive affect."*

It does not take much psychological insight to guess that these answers were given by respondents of different ages—or to figure out which is the definition offered by professional researchers. The first four answers (drawn from studies by Rubin, 1980, and Youniss and Volpe, 1978) came from children ranging in age from 6 to 13. The last (from Howes, 1987, p. 253) is typical of how psychologists define **friendship**.

Despite their diversity, the different definitions do share some common elements. All agree that there is something special about a friend that does not apply to peers in general. All state or imply that friendship is not just any sort of relationship, but a relationship of affection—friends like each other. And all acknowledge that friendship is a two-way, reciprocal process. One child may like another child, but liking alone does not make one a friend. For friendship to exist, the affection must be returned.

As the examples indicate, the presence of these common elements does not rule out the possibility that children's reasoning about friendship might change with age. At a general level, a description of the changes that occur should sound familiar, because such changes parallel more general advances in the way children think about the world (Berndt, 1988; Rawlins, 1992). Young children's thinking about friendship tends to focus on concrete, external attributes—a friend is someone who is fun to play with and who shares things. Older children are more capable of penetrating beneath the surface to take into account more abstract aspects of friendship, such as caring for another person. For young children, friendship is often a momentary state dependent on specific acts just performed or about to be performed. Older children are more likely to see friendship as an enduring relationship that persists across time and even in the face of occasional conflicts. Finally, although even young children realize the importance of mutual liking between friends, qualities such as loyalty and intimacy do not become central in children's thinking about friendship until late childhood or adolescence.

The kinds of findings just sketched have led to the formation of several stage models of conceptions of friendship (Damon, 1977; Keller & Wood, 1989; Selman, 1980; Youniss & Volpe, 1978). Whether changes in how children think about friendship are best conceptualized in terms of stages is still a subject of dispute (Hartup, 1992b). Nevertheless, such models provide interesting attempts to capture the major transformations in children's thinking. Table 16.5 provides an example of how one stage model conceptualizes understanding of friendship.

Determinants of Friendship

How do children become friends? The studies just considered are one relevant source of evidence, for they tell us what children themselves say is important to look for in a friend. Other common ways to study the determinants of friendship are to interview parents about their children's friends (e.g., Hayes, Gershman, & Bolin, 1980) and to observe children as they become acquainted over time (e.g., Gottman, 1983). Here we consider two general questions about determinants: which children become friends, and how friendships are formed.

Friendship Selection Friends are not selected randomly. As children develop, they are exposed to many different people, but only a few of these potential friends ever become actual friends. On what basis are these selections made?

Studies of friendship formation show a rare unanimity in agreeing that one general factor is central to most friendship choices (Aboud & Mendelson, 1996; Hartup & Stevens, 1997). This factor is similarity. Children tend to pick friends who

Friendship
An enduring relationship between two individuals, characterized by loyalty, intimacy, and mutual affection.

Table 16.5
A Stage Model of Conceptions of Friendship

Stage Level	Description	Typical Statements
Level 1 (approximately 5 to 7)	Friends are associates who are nice to me and who are fun to play with. Friendship is a temporary relationship, easily established and easily terminated.	"He's my friend because he plays with me and gives me lots of toys." "She likes me because I let her come to my house and play with me."
Level 2 (approximately 8 to 10)	Friends are people who help each other in a relationship of reciprocal trust. The friend is liked because of certain dispositions or traits and not merely because of frequent play contacts.	"A friend is someone who helps you, like if you fall down on your bike." "You do a lot for them and they do a lot for you and you can trust them."
Level 3 (approximately 11)	Friends are people who understand each other and share their innermost thoughts and feelings. Friendship is a long-term relationship based on compatibility of interest and personality.	"Someone you can talk to and tell your problems to and they understand you." "You like the same kinds of things and you can say what you want around each other."

Source: Based on information from *The Social World of the Child* by W. Damon, 1977, San Francisco: Josey-Bass.

are similar to themselves. Similarity is not the only criterion used; children may sometimes seek out friends who are more popular than they (Hirsch & Renders, 1986) or who have a higher socioeconomic status (Epstein, 1983). Nevertheless, similarity seems to be a major contributor to most friendship selections.

Various kinds of similarity are important. One is similarity in age. Friendships are most common among children who are close in age. Mixed-age friendships are found, of course, especially when children move outside the same-age groupings imposed by school (Epstein, 1989). Even when not constrained by adults, however, most children tend to pick friends who are about the same age (Berndt, 1988).

Similarity in gender is also important. As we saw in Chapter 15, a preference for same-sex friends emerges in the preschool years and becomes quite strong by mid-

The most important peer relationship is that of friendship.

dle childhood. Indeed, throughout much of childhood, gender is a better predictor of friendship choices than age (Epstein, 1986). By adolescence, of course, cross-sex romantic relationships have begun to emerge (Shulman & Collins, 1997); even here, however, same-sex friendships continue to predominate (Hartup, 1993).

Finally, still another contributor to friendship choices is similarity in race. As with gender, a preference for same-race friends is evident as early as preschool and generally increases with age (Fishbein & Imai, 1993). It should be noted, however, that the strength of this tendency depends on a number of factors, including the degree of integration in both the school system and the neighborhood (Epstein, 1986). Furthermore, the preference for same-race friends does not mean that all friendships are of this sort; 80 to 90% of adolescents report having at least one cross-race friend (DuBois & Hirsch, 1990; Patchens, 1982). Most also report, however, that they see such friends only at school and not in other contexts.

Although the variables of age, gender, and race are important, they do not completely explain friendship selection. Most children encounter many peers who are similar to them in age, gender, and race, yet only some of these peers are selected as friends. What seems to be important in addition to general similarity to a peer is specific similarity in behaviors and interests—what psychologists call **behavioral homophyly**. In short, one reason that children become friends is that they like to do the same sorts of things.

This pattern is evident as early as the preschool period (Rubin et al., 1994), and it eventually extends to various settings in which children find themselves. Among older children, friends tend to be similar in their orientation toward school; they show correlations, for example, in educational aspirations and achievement test scores (Ide et al., 1981). They also tend to be similar in what Berndt (1988) labels their "orientation toward children's culture," or what they like to do outside of school (music, sports, games, and so on). And they tend to be similar in general behavior patterns and personality—for example, in the tendency to be shy or aggressive (Kupersmidt, DeRosier, & Patterson, 1995; Poulin et al., 1997).

Although the relation between similarity and friendship is well established, the causal basis for the relation is less clear. There are two possibilities. Do children become friends because they have similar interests and preferences or do children develop similar interests and preferences because they are friends? Answering this question requires longitudinal study, in which patterns of similarity can be traced over time. Such studies suggest that the cause and effect flow in both directions (Epstein, 1989; Hartup, 1996a). Children who later become friends are more similar initially than are children who do not become friends, indicating that similarity is indeed a determinant of friendship selection. But children who are friends become more similar over time, indicating that friendship also promotes further similarity.

A final issue with respect to friendship choices concerns their stability. Do children tend to keep the same friends over time, or is childhood friendship a more transient phenomenon? As is often the case regarding questions about stability, the answer depends on a number of factors (Berndt, 1988; Epstein, 1986). One is age. Young children's friendship choices are often only moderately stable, at best, over time—a finding in keeping with the ways in which young children reason about friendship. The stability of friendship increases as children get older. Another important factor is the stability of the environment. Fluctuations in friendship are most likely when children experience changes in their environment, as when they move to a new school. Conversely, friendships may remain quite stable when children remain together in the same setting.

Behavioral homophyly
Similarity between peers in behaviors and interests. Such similarity is one determinant of friendship selection.

Friendship Formation   Consider the following exchange:

> *Interviewer: Is it easy or hard to make friends?*
> *Child [4 years old]: Hard, because sometimes if you wave to the other person, they might not see you wave, so it's hard to get that friend.*
> *Interviewer: What if they see you?*
> *Child: Then it's easy. (Selman & Jaquette, 1977, p. 18)*

For some children, making friends may indeed be (or at least seem) this easy. Generally, however, the process is more complicated. A study by John Gottman (1983) provides an exceptionally detailed account of how children become friends.

The participants in Gottman's research were children between the ages of 3 and 9, none of whom knew one another at the start of the study. Pairs of same-aged children were randomly formed, and each pair then met in the home of one of the children for three play sessions across a period of 4 weeks. The questions were whether the children would become friends and, if so, what processes led to friendship formation. The answer to the first question was provided by the mothers' responses to a questionnaire concerned with whether, and how strongly, their children had become friends with their new playmates. The answer to the second question came from observations of the children's behavior during the play sessions. These sessions were tape-recorded, and the children's conversations were later coded for a variety of aspects of social interaction.

Gottman found that some of the children did indeed become friends, whereas others did not. What aspects of the interaction differentiated the two groups? Several processes proved important. Children who became friends were more successful at establishing a *common-ground activity*—that is, agreeing on what to do—than were children who did not become friends. Eventual friends showed greater *communication clarity* and were more successful at *exchanging information* than were nonfriends. Eventual friends were more skillful at *resolving conflict*—an important skill, for conflict is frequent in young children's interactions. And eventual friends were more likely to engage in *self-disclosure*, or sharing of personal information about oneself.

Considering its importance, the topic of friendship formation has received surprisingly little study (perhaps because of the difficulty of such study—it took several years to analyze the tapes in Gottman's research!). Nevertheless, the available evidence supports Gottman's conclusion that processes such as exchange of information and resolution of conflict are central to friendship formation (Grusec & Lytton, 1988). As we will see, processes of this sort do not disappear once a friendship has been formed. The same kinds of skills that help to build a friendship are also central to the ways in which friends interact with each other.

Behavior with Friends

That behavior is different with friends than with nonfriends seems almost part of the definition of friendship. But exactly how does behavior differ as a function of friendship? Some differences are obvious. Children spend more time with friends than with nonfriends, and they typically derive more pleasure from interacting with friends (Newcomb & Bagwell, 1995). Friends, clearly, are fun to be with. In this section we focus on several further areas of possible differences between friends and nonfriends.

Prosocial Behavior   As we saw in Chapter 14, the term *prosocial behavior* refers to forms of conduct that society considers desirable and whose development is thus encouraged in children. Examples of prosocial behavior include helping someone in need, comforting someone in distress, and sharing with others. It seems reasonable to expect that such clearly positive behaviors will be more likely with friends than with peers in general.

For the most part, this commonsense prediction is borne out by research. Children share more with friends than with classmates who are merely acquaintances (Jones, 1985). Cooperation in carrying out some common task is generally greater among friends than nonfriends, as is equity in dividing any rewards that are obtained (Berndt, 1981). Even as early as the preschool years, children may cooperate and share more with friends than with nonfriends (Birch & Billman, 1986; Matsumoto et al., 1986), and they are more likely to offer help to a friend in distress than to a mere acquaintance (Costin & Jones, 1992). Preschoolers also deliver reinforcements more often to friends than to peers in general (Masters & Furman, 1981).

Despite this positive evidence, not all studies find that prosocial behaviors are more likely with friends. Berndt (1986b) summarizes a series of studies in which elementary-school children actually shared less with friends than with acquaintances. According to Berndt, the critical element may be the presence of perceived competition with the friend. Research indicates that children believe friends should be equal (Tesser, 1984). Sharing too freely threatens this principle, because it may result in the friend "winning the contest" by ending up with the greater amount. Allowing a nonfriend to "win" is less threatening; hence, children are more willing to share with nonfriends. Anyone who has watched best friends compete in some contest (or can think back to his own such experiences) will probably agree that there is an especially strong resistance to being bested by a friend. By adolescence, this "can't let him beat me" attitude has diminished, and sharing is more likely with friends even under competitive conditions.

Conflict We turn next to a less positive side of peer interaction. The definition psychologists give to *conflict* is a broad one: Conflict occurs "when one person does something to which a second person objects" (D. F. Hay, 1984, p. 2). The core notion is thus one of opposition between individuals, a notion conveyed by words such as *refusing, denying, objecting,* and *disagreeing* (Hartup, 1992a).

Defined this broadly, conflict is clearly a frequent component of peer interaction (Shantz & Hartup, 1995). It is also a frequent component of interaction between friends; indeed, conflicts probably occur most often among friends (Shantz, 1987). This situation results, in part, simply because friends spend so much time together. But it also reflects the freedom and security that friends feel with one another, and thus their ability to criticize and to disagree without threatening the relationship (Hartup et al., 1993).

The important difference between friends and nonfriends, therefore, is not the probability of conflict, but the ways in which conflict is handled (Laursen, 1993; Laursen, Hartup, & Koplas, 1996; Vespo & Caplan, 1993). Although exceptions certainly occur, conflicts are generally less heated among friends than among nonfriends. Friends use what Hartup (1992a) refers to as "softer" modes of managing conflict than do nonfriends: They are more likely to attempt to reason with the other person and less likely to get into extended chains of disagreement. They are also more likely to resolve the conflict in an equitable, mutually satisfactory way. And they are more likely to let bygones be bygones and to continue playing together following the conflict. We saw that the ability to resolve conflicts satisfactorily plays a role in forming a friendship. The findings just mentioned indicate that such

Occasional conflicts are an inevitable part of friendship. But friends are skilled at defusing conflict and restoring positive relations.

skills are also important for maintaining a friendship. Indeed, the ability to overcome conflict and remain close can be seen as one definition of the term *friendship.*

Collaborative Problem Solving   We tend to think of peer interaction in terms of play and recreation—games on the playground, outings to the mall, or perhaps simply sitting and talking. But peers also interact in more cognitive contexts, pooling resources and coordinating efforts when there is some problem to be solved. Some such collaborations are formal endeavors engineered by teachers in school; others are spontaneous outgrowths of children's natural activities with peers (figuring out the rules to a game, building a scale model, etc.). Recall that both Piaget and Vygotsky emphasized such peer interchanges as an important source of cognitive progress.

Children are generally most comfortable and assured when with friends, and friends clearly know one another better than do nonfriends. We might expect, then, that collaborative problem solving will proceed more effectively among friends than among children in general. And such, with some exceptions, is the case (Newcomb & Bagwell, 1995). Here we consider two examples.

Azmitia and Montgomery (1993) presented scientific reasoning tasks, similar to those used by Piaget to study formal operations, to pairs of 11-year-old children. The pairs consisted either of acquaintances drawn from the same classroom or of close friends. Children in both types of pairs benefited from the chance to work together—a finding compatible with theories such as Piaget's and Vygotsky's that stress the value of peer interaction. But friends benefited more. Friends, on average, adopted a more truly collaborative style of problem solving than did acquaintances; they were more likely, for example, to offer justifications for their suggestions, as well as to be responsive to their partner's ideas. Friends also were more successful at solving the most difficult versions of the problems.

A study by Hartup and colleagues (Hartup, 1996b; Hartup et al., 1995) demonstrated similar benefits from friendship on a quite different task. The 10-year-olds in their study first learned about the rain forest during a 6-week unit in school. They then composed stories about the rain forest, on a computer, under three conditions: alone, working with an acquaintance, or working with a best friend. Friends did not talk more, in general, than did nonfriends as they worked on the stories, but the nature of the talk varied across the types of pairing. As in the Azmitia and Montgomery (1993) study, friends' conversations were more other-oriented and reciprocal; they were more likely to respond carefully to each other's suggestions, to explain their own proposed ideas, and to agree rather than disagree as they worked. They were also more likely to remain focused on the problem at hand; nonfriends, in contrast, had a higher proportion of "off task" behavior. And, like the friend pairs in the Azmitia and Montgomery study, they were more successful at the task—by various measures, the stories produced by friends were judged to be of higher quality than the stories produced either by acquaintances or by children working alone.

Note that studies such as these have potential applied value within the school setting. The findings do not mean, clearly, that teachers should group children solely on the basis of friendship—having children work with a variety of peers can be beneficial both socially and cognitively. But they do suggest that some forms of collaborative learning may proceed especially well when children are allowed to work with friends.

Intimacy   The idea that intimacy is central to friendship is expressed clearly in the fourth of the quotations that opened the section on conceptions of friendship: A friend is someone with whom to share one's innermost thoughts and feelings.

The quotation that expressed this view came from a 13-year-old, and it is usually not until late childhood or adolescence that the emphasis on intimacy in children's talk about friendship emerges.

Do friends in fact interact in more intimate ways than do nonfriends? Children's own statements about friendship provide one source of evidence. If a girl says she shares things with her best friend that she can share with no one else, there seems little reason to doubt the accuracy of her statement. In one series of studies, statements of this sort were absent among kindergarteners, but were offered by approximately 40% of the sixth-grade participants (Berndt, 1986a).

Researchers have also attempted to probe the intimacy of friendships by direct observation of how friends interact. With this approach, however, we run into an obvious methodological problem: The presence of the observer may change the behavior being observed. It seems unrealistic to think that friends will share intimate secrets when they know that their conversation is being tape-recorded! In fact, some studies of this sort have reported few, if any, differences in the intimacy of conversations between friends and between nonfriends (Berndt & Hanna, 1995; Mettetal, 1983).

Some differences do emerge, however, when observations are made in more natural settings. Children who are friends or are in the process of becoming friends are more likely than nonfriends to talk about feelings and to engage in various forms of self-disclosure (Gottman, 1983). Because this difference emerges as early as the preschool years, these data suggest that intimacy may be a characteristic of friendship long before children begin to talk about intimacy as being important. On the other hand, the frequency of such intimate disclosures does increase as children grow older (Berndt & Perry, 1990; Buhrmester & Prager, 1995; Rotenberg & Sliz, 1988). And the importance of intimacy as a determinant of the quality of friendship is greater for adolescents than for younger children (Buhrmester, 1990; Hartup, 1993). It is worth noting that in addition to age differences there are gender differences in this aspect of friendship: Girls' friendships are characterized by a higher degree of intimacy than are those of boys (Buhrmester, 1996; Jones & Dembo, 1989). This difference begins to emerge by middle childhood and increases into adolescence.

Effects of Friendship

Friendship, as we have seen, can have a number of positive effects on the ways in which children interact—effects, for example, on the likelihood of prosocial forms of behavior or on the success of collaborative problem solving. The effects that we have discussed, however, have all been fairly immediate and short-term. In this section we turn to the more long-term impact of childhood friendship. Do children with many friends develop differently than children with few or no friends? Do children with high-quality friendships differ in their development from children whose friendships are less satisfactory?

Both common sense and the studies already discussed suggest that the answer to these questions should be positive. And research on the long-term consequences of friendship in fact confirms the commonsense expectation. Here we consider three of the benefits of growing up with friends.

Self-Esteem One effect of friendship is on the child's self-esteem. We saw in Chapter 13 that children vary in how positive they feel about different aspects of their lives (academic abilities, physical prowess, etc.). We saw also that the successes or failures a child experiences in a particular domain are one determinant of these feelings of self-worth. The specific example discussed was academic self-concept; as we would expect, children who do well in school tend to feel better about their academic competence than children who do less well.

Children's success in the peer group also affects self-esteem. The primary measure used in this research is the Self-Perception Profile for Children, which we described in Chapter 13 (see p. 503). On average, children with relatively satisfactory friendships have more positive scores on the Self-Perception Profile than do children who lack such friendships (Berndt & Keefe, 1995; Keefe & Berndt, 1996). As we might expect, the greatest differences tend to be on the Social Acceptance subscale, but the effects are not limited to perceptions of peer relations. Global self-worth—the most general index of self-evaluation—also tends to be higher in children who have satisfactory friendships.

At several points in this chapter we have discussed the issue of the direction of cause and effect when two measures correlate. It may have occurred to you that the same question arises here. It seems very likely that friendship does contribute to self-esteem, as we have been arguing. But it is also possible that the correlation comes about because children with high self-esteem are more successful at making and keeping friends. Very probably, both causal directions contribute to the relationship (Berndt, 1996a).

Adjustment to School

School is one of the main contexts in which children interact with friends. It is reasonable to predict, therefore, that the presence or absence of friends should influence how well children adjust to school.

Friendship does in fact affect adjustment to school in several ways at several points in development. The initial effects are evident quite early, at the point when children begin formal schooling. Children who have several good friends when they start kindergarten are happier in school than are children who lack such friendships; they develop more positive attitudes toward school; and they show greater gains in performance across the school year. Conversely, being rejected by peers is associated with unfavorable attitudes and poorer school performance (Ladd, 1990; Ladd & Coleman, 1997; Ladd, Kochenderfer, & Coleman, 1996).

Friendship remains important as children progress through school. Indeed, a recent review concluded that the "best and most predictive outcomes" of problems in the peer group are school related (Rubin et al., 1998). Throughout grade school and high school, children who lack friends are less well-adjusted in the classroom, show higher rates of absenteeism, and are more at risk for being retained at a grade (Coie et al., 1992; DeRosier, Kupersmidt, & Patterson, 1994). They are also less likely to complete school; across studies, socially unsuccessful children have been found to be two to eight times more likely to drop out of school than are children in general (Parker & Asher, 1987). Of course, friendship is not the only determinant of how children fare in school. But it does seem to be one contributor.

Social Support

Perhaps the most general benefit of friendship is that it provides social support. The term **social support** refers to resources provided by other people in times of uncertainty or stress. We all need such support on occasion, even if the help is simply in the form of someone's "being there" during a difficult time. Research with adults has shown that success in obtaining support is an important determinant of people's ability to cope with stress (Cohen & Wills, 1985).

Social support is also important in the lives of children (Bryant, 1985; Reid et al., 1989). The supports that children need can take a variety of forms, depending on the particular situation. One important category is *emotional support*—behaviors of others that offer needed comfort or reassurance and in general enhance the self-

Social support
Resources (both tangible and intangible) provided by other people in times of uncertainty or stress.

esteem of the recipient. Providing reassurance after a potentially embarrassing failure is a form of emotional support, as is lending a sympathetic ear when a friend has frustrations to vent. Other forms of support include *instrumental support* (provision of tangible resources to help solve practical tasks), *informational support* (provision of information or advice about how to cope with problems), and *companionship support* (sharing of activities and experiences).

Just as they can take many forms, supports can come from many sources. As we would expect, parents tend to be the most important sources of support for most children. A variety of other sources can also be important, however, including peers, siblings, grandparents, teachers, and even pets. Among peers, friends, not surprisingly, typically rank highest. In one study, friends were judged second only to parents as sources of emotional support, and friends headed the list when children were in need of companionship (Reid et al., 1989). Furthermore, the value of friends as sources of support increases as children grow older (Berndt, 1989b; Denton & Zarbatany, 1996). Older children, as we have seen, emphasize such qualities as intimacy and trust in their thinking about friendship and in their behavior with friends. It is not surprising, then, that development brings an increased tendency to turn to friends in times of need.

We noted that adults benefit from the social support they receive in times of need. So do children. Children with a relatively strong system of social support have been found to score better on various measures of social adjustment and academic performance than children to whom support is less available (Dubow et al., 1991; Levitt, Guacci-Franco, & Levitt, 1993). As with self-esteem, the causal basis for this relation probably goes in both directions. Children who are well-adjusted may be most successful at obtaining support; at the same time, securing support in times of need—including support from friends—may well contribute to social adjustment.

✓ *To Recap...*

A particularly important peer relation is friendship. Children themselves agree with this assessment—from the preschool years on, children talk about friends as being different from peers in general. Children reason about friendship in increasingly sophisticated ways as they develop. Young children tend to think of friends in concrete terms as sources of immediate pleasure; older children are more likely to see friendship as an enduring relationship characterized by attributes such as intimacy and loyalty.

Children tend to pick friends who are similar to themselves. Similarities in age, gender, and race have all been shown to influence selection. Similarities of a more behavioral sort also play a role. Friends tend to be similar in academic orientation, and they often share the same outside-of-school interests. Studies of friendship formation suggest that a variety of processes contribute, including exchange of information, self-disclosure, and successful resolution of conflict.

Behavior with friends differs from that with nonfriends in a number of ways. Prosocial behaviors, such as sharing and helping, are generally more common with friends. Although conflict does not disappear once a friendship has been formed, resolution of conflict is usually more successful among friends than among nonfriends. Collaborative problem solving proceeds more smoothly and effectively when friends work together than for peers in general. Finally, sharing of intimate information is more likely among friends, and the importance of intimacy for friendship increases as children get older.

Friendship can have long-term as well as immediate benefits. Among the aspects of development that are influenced by the quality of friendships are self-esteem, adjustment to school, and availability of social support in times of need.

Popularity and Problems

Our emphasis thus far has been on general processes in peer relations and general changes that accompany development. But peer relations do not follow a single general pattern. For some children, life in the peer group is a good deal more enjoyable and fulfilling than it is for others. In this section, our focus shifts to individual differences in the quality of peer relations. We begin with the more positive side and the question of popularity. We then move on to the various kinds of problems with peer relations that some children develop.

Popularity

Before we can explore the sources of differences in peer relations, we must know what the differences are. A first question, therefore, concerns measurement. How can we determine which children are doing well in the peer group and which children are not?

Measuring Popularity   The most common approach to assessing popularity has been to ask children themselves, the assumption being that a child's peers should be the best judges of that child's standing among peers. Such peer-based evaluations of social standing are referred to as **sociometric techniques** (Asher & Hymel, 1981; Terry & Coie, 1991).

Sociometric techniques
Procedures for assessing children's social status based on evaluations by the peer group. Sociometric techniques may involve ratings of degree of liking, nominations of liked or disliked peers, or forced-choice judgments between pairs of peers.

Researchers have used a variety of specific sociometric approaches (and conclusions vary to some extent depending on the approach used). In the *nomination technique*, the child is asked to name some specific number of well-liked peers—for example, "Tell me the names of three kids in the class you especially like." The technique can also be directed to negative relations—"Tell me the names of three kids in the class you don't like very much." In the *rating-scale technique*, the child is asked to rate each of her classmates along the dimension of interest. The child might be asked, for example, to rate each classmate on a 5-point scale ranging from "really like to play with" to "really don't like to play with." Finally, in the *paired-comparison technique*, the child is presented with the names of two classmates at a time and asked to pick the one that he likes better. Because all pairs are eventually presented, the technique yields an overall measure of liking for each target child.

What is the evidence that sociometric measures yield a valid picture of a child's social standing? In a sense, this question might seem a silly one to ask. If a child is rated as "liked" by everyone in the class, what better measure of popularity might we hope to find? Sociometric techniques, after all, focus directly on what we are trying to determine—what the peer group thinks of the child. Nevertheless, the uncertainty of verbal-report measures with children, especially young children, makes it necessary to ask whether such techniques correlate with other ways of assessing a child's social standing.

The answer is that they do. Sociometric scores correlate with teacher ratings of popularity or social competence—that is, the children who are identified by their peers as well liked also tend to be the ones whom teachers identify as popular (Green et al., 1980). Sociometric scores also correlate with direct observations of children's social interactions (Bukowski & Hoza, 1989). Even sociometric assessments by children as young as preschool age show correlations with such external measures and thus some evidence of validity (Denham & McKinley, 1993; Hymel, 1983).

Determinants of Popularity   However it is measured, *popularity* is easy to define. A popular child is one who is well liked by his peers. In terms of sociometric techniques, such children receive high ratings and are the objects of many positive and few, if any, negative choices. These children are sometimes referred to as the stars in sociometric classification systems (Gronlund, 1959). But what underlies such star status?

Some examinations of this question have focused on relatively indirect predictors of popularity. Birth order, for example, has been found to relate to popularity. Last-born children tend to be more popular than middle-born or firstborn children (Miller & Maruyama, 1976). (It should be recognized, of course, that there are plenty of exceptions to this and to all of the other on-the-average findings that we present.) Hartup (1983) suggests an explanation for this finding. Last-born children may have the greatest need to develop interpersonal skills within the family (such as tolerance and persuasiveness), and these skills continue to serve them when they interact with peers.

Intellectual ability also relates to popularity. Both IQ scores (Czeschlik & Rost, 1995; Roff, Sells, & Golden, 1972) and measures of academic performance (Green et al., 1980) have been found to correlate with sociometric ratings. Finally, physical attractiveness shows a relation. On the average, relatively attractive children (as rated either by adults or by children themselves) are more popular than are relatively unattractive children (Dion & Berscheid, 1974; Langlois, 1986).

It is perhaps not surprising that intellectual ability correlates with popularity, given the importance of the school as a context for observation of peers. But why should physical attractiveness relate to popularity? Although no one knows for sure, an intriguing suggestion is that attractive and unattractive children may actually behave differently. In one study, 5-year-olds rated as unattractive showed more aggression and were more boisterous in their play than their more attractive counterparts (Langlois & Downs, 1979). Thus, part of the reason for the unattractive child's social problems may lie in the child's behavior. On the other hand, there is also ample evidence that both adults and children in U.S. society tend to hold a "beauty is good" stereotype, evaluating attractive individuals positively even in the absence of objective evidence (Ritts, Patterson, & Tubbs, 1992). Such stereotypes, moreover, may begin to operate very early. A recent study found that mothers of relatively attractive newborns responded more positively to their babies than did mothers whose infants were less attractive (Langlois et al., 1995). Thus, part of the basis for the unattractive child's difficulties may stem from stereotyped expectations about what attractive and unattractive people are like.

In Chapter 2 we introduced the concept of the *transactional* nature of developmental change in the discussion of Bronfenbrenner's ecological approach. The relation between physical attractiveness and popularity provides a nice example of how the transactional model may apply. The proposed sequence is as follows: The expectations that others hold about unattractive children affect both their evaluations of such children and their treatment of them; this treatment, in turn, affects the way in which unattractive children behave; and the unattractive children's behavior then combines with the stereotypes to yield the negative social evaluations that such children receive.

As noted, the research we have considered thus far has concerned relatively indirect predictors of popularity. We turn next to direct measures of behavior. Presumably, popular children become popular because they behave in ways that other children find attractive. What do we know about behavioral contributors to popularity?

In general, the behavioral correlates of popularity are not at all surprising. Popular children tend to be friendly, socially visible, outgoing in their behavior, and reinforcing in their interactions with others (Newcomb, Bukowski, & Pattee, 1993). At a more specific level, three sets of skills seem to be especially important for popularity (Asher, Renshaw, & Hymel, 1982). Popular children are skilled at *initiating interaction* with other children. They enter ongoing groups smoothly and set about making friends in a carefully paced but confident manner, not forcing themselves on other children but also not giving up at the slightest rebuff. Popular children are also skilled at *maintaining interaction*. They reinforce other children, show sensitivity to the needs and wishes of others, and communicate effectively in the role of both speaker and listener. Finally, popular children are skilled at *resolving conflict*. The popular child knows how to defuse touchy situations in ways agreeable to all parties, using reasoning rather than force and drawing on general principles of fairness and general rules for how people should interact.

This list of contributors to popularity should sound familiar. The kinds of social skills that help make a child popular are the same sorts of skills that we saw are important for forming and maintaining friendships. The concurrence is what we would expect—popular children are children who have the qualities desirable in a friend.

Problems in Peer Relations

Popularity is the bright side of the sociometric picture. But not everyone is popular, and not everyone develops satisfactory friendships. Problems in peer relations are a topic not only of scientific interest, but also of great practical importance in the lives of many children.

Measuring Problems   The techniques used to assess problems in children's relations with their peers are the same as those used to measure popularity. Indeed, the two constructs are often measured at the same time in the same sample; after all, not everyone can be a star, and some children will come out at the negative end in any assessment of social standing. Sociometric techniques are therefore again prominent. Teacher assessments and direct observations of behavior are also sometimes used (Schneider, Rubin, & Ledingham, 1985).

Much debate in the study of social problems has concerned not the initial assessments, but how to classify children based on these assessments. Popularity, as we saw, is easy to define. Problems, however, can take many forms, and different investigators have proposed different classification systems (Asher & Coie, 1990; Newcomb et al., 1993).

One often used system distinguishes rejected children, neglected children, and controversial children. The **rejected child** receives few positive but many negative nominations from her peers. The rejected child seems to be actively disliked. The **neglected child**, in contrast, receives few nominations of any sort, positive or negative, from peers. The neglected child seems to be less disliked than ignored. Finally, the **controversial child**, as the name suggests, receives a mixed evaluation from the peer group, earning both many positive and many negative nominations. The rejected-neglected-controversial distinction has been the focus of much research, and so we begin by reviewing findings concerning these three groups. As we go, however, we also note some qualifications to the general conclusions, as not all children with problems fall clearly into one of these categories.

Determinants of Problems   We have already discussed the kinds of social skills that seem to underlie popularity. This work gives us a start toward understanding the source of problems in peer relations. Children who develop problems fall well short of the level of social skills that popular children show. But rejected children and neglected children fall short in somewhat different ways.

Studies of the behavior of rejected children suggest several ways in which the rejected child's behavior may contribute to his social difficulties (Cillessen et al.,

Rejected child
A child who receives few positive and many negative nominations in sociometric assessments by peers. Such children seem to be disliked by the peer group.

Neglected child
A child who receives few nominations of any sort, positive or negative, in sociometric assessments by peers. Such children seem to be ignored by the peer group.

Controversial child
A child who receives both many positive and many negative nominations in sociometric assessments by peers.

1992; Coie, Dodge, & Kupersmidt, 1990; Rubin et al., 1998). Probably the most consistent correlate of peer rejection is aggression. Peers report, and behavioral observations confirm, that many rejected children are well above average in levels of aggression. More generally, rejected children often show behavior that is antisocial, inappropriate to the situation at hand, and disruptive of ongoing group activities. Their attempts to enter new groups or to make new friends tend to be especially maladroit, consisting of overly intrusive and even bizarre overtures whose outcome, predictably, is exactly the opposite of their intent (Putallaz & Wasserman, 1990).

The picture for neglected children is different (Coie & Kupersmidt, 1983). Neglected children are often perceived by their peers as being shy. This perception is not surprising, in that neglected children are less talkative and less socially active than are other children. Compared with most children, neglected children make fewer and more hesitant attempts to enter groups and to make new friends. They also tend to give up quickly when their tentative and not very skilled efforts do not meet with success.

As befits their in-between sociometric status, controversial children typically show a mixture of positive and negative social behaviors (Newcomb et al., 1993). Like rejected children, controversial children tend to rank high on measures of aggression. But, like popular children, they also tend to score high on measures of sociability.

The patterns just described reflect typical, on average differences among groups of children. As such, they do not apply to all rejected or neglected children. Only some neglected children, for example, show the shy behavioral style described; others are indistinguishable in their behaviors from sociometrically average children (Rubin, LeMare, & Lollis, 1990). Similarly, only some rejected children seem to earn their status through high aggression and lack of control; for others, social withdrawal appears to be a more important contributor (French, 1988, 1990). Some researchers have argued, in fact, that **social withdrawal**—that is, self-imposed isolation from the peer group—can be an important problem in itself, even in the absence of rejection or neglect (Asendorpf, 1990; Rubin, 1993).

Social withdrawal
Self-imposed isolation from the peer group.

Finally, not all unpopular children are totally lacking in friends. As we saw in Chapter 14, aggressive, rejected children, in particular, may have a small set of close, long-term friends. These children are not generally liked by the peer group, however, and the friends they do have are often other aggressive children who are more likely to maintain than to moderate their antisocial behavior (Cairns et al., 1988).

The response of peers can be important more generally to the problems of the unpopular child. Children develop reputations within the peer group (fools around in class, hits other kids, never wants to play). Research reveals that these reputations are to some extent self-perpetuating—that is, the unpopular child's behavior may be interpreted in negative ways by peers, even when the behavior does not fit the expectation (Hymel, Wagner, & Butler, 1990). Clearly, such effects make the task of winning peer acceptance even more difficult.

The message from this discussion is that problems in peer relations can take many forms and can have many sources. Is it possible, despite this diversity, that the various problems have a common underlying core? The common element that has been most often proposed is a cognitive one. Earlier we reviewed evidence indicating that social-cognitive skills are important for successful peer relations. Perhaps children with social problems acquire their status because they lack such skills. Simply put, such children do not know how to make or maintain friends.

Research to investigate the hypothesis that cognitive deficits underlie social problems is similar to the research discussed earlier in the chapter under the heading Cognitive Contributions. Again, the findings are mixed. Not all studies find relations between cognitive and social skills, and when relations do emerge, they are seldom large (Crick & Dodge, 1994; Dodge & Feldman, 1990). It is clear that cognitive deficits are at best only one contributor to problems in peer relations. A variety of studies suggest, however, that cognitive problems do indeed contribute. Unpopular children are often lower in perspective-taking skills than are their more popular peers (Jennings, 1975). Rejected children have difficulty in judging the intentions behind the behavior of others, a deficiency that may contribute to their high levels of aggression (Dodge, 1986; Quiggle et al., 1992). And both rejected and neglected children show deficits in the kind of social problem-solving skills illustrated in Table 16.4 (Rubin & Krasnor, 1986; Rubin & Rose-Krasnor, 1992). This finding makes sense, because the kinds of solutions such dilemmas call for are precisely the behaviors that rejected and neglected children fail to show.

Studies of socially withdrawn children add an interesting qualification to conclusions concerning the cognitive bases for social problems. Despite their social timidity, withdrawn children typically do quite well on social problem-solving measures such as the items in Table 16.4 (Stewart & Rubin, 1995). These children, then, do not seem to have any cognitive deficits; they know what to do to win friends and to interact successfully. Their problem comes in acting on their knowledge—in actually carrying out the strategies that could help them be more successful in the peer group.

Development in Cultural Context
Cross-Cultural Studies of Sociometric Status

As with many topics in developmental psychology, most of what we know about the bases for children's sociometric standing comes from research in a narrow range of cultural settings. For example, in their 1993 review of the contributors to sociometric status, Newcomb and colleagues summarized results from 41 studies, 39 of which had been carried out in North America.

Fortunately, this situation is changing. Recent years have seen the extension of sociometric research to a number of new settings beyond the United States and Canada. The picture that emerges from these studies is in some respects similar to what is found with North American samples and in some respects different.

Let us first consider a major similarity. In North American samples, one of the strongest and most consistent predictors of peer rejection is aggression. This finding has proved to be general across a range of cultures. Similar aggression-rejection links have now been demonstrated in China (Chen & Rubin, 1994; Chen, Rubin, & Li, 1995), Italy (Attili, Vermigli, & Schneider, 1997; Tomada & Schneider, 1997), the Netherlands (Cillessen et al., 1992), and Costa Rica (Kupersmidt & Trejos, 1987). These findings confirm what most of us would predict: Hitting other children is not an effective way to win friends or earn group approval, whatever the specific cultural setting in which the child is developing.

On the other hand, not all findings from North American samples have proved to be generalizable to other cultures. Recall that American children who are shy and reserved in their interactions with peers are at risk of being neglected by the peer group. In China, however, there is no association between a reserved pattern of behavior and neglect. To the contrary, Chinese children who are quiet and nonassertive tend to be above average in popularity. They also are rated by their teachers as especially competent, and they hold a disproportionate number of honorship and leadership positions within the school (Chen et al., 1992; Chen, Rubin, & Sun, 1992).

Why might a similar behavior pattern lead to such different outcomes in different cultures? The most likely answer concerns cultural values and expectations. In China, a cautious, self-restrained style of interpersonal interaction is regarded as a sign of competence and maturity (Ho, 1986). Adults therefore encourage such a behavior pattern in children, and children themselves come to value it and to reward it in their peers.

In a sense, then, the comparison of Chinese and American children reveals similarity as well as difference. In any culture there are expectations about appropriate forms of behavior—expectations held by children as well as adults. Children whose behavior is in accord with cultural values and expectations are the ones who are most likely to find acceptance in the peer group.

Applications
Interventions to Help Children with Problems

We turn next to an issue of considerable pragmatic importance. Can children with problems in peer relations be helped by intervention programs designed to improve their success with peers?

Before we attempt intervention, it is important to ask about the stability of such problems. Perhaps children who have difficulties in relating to peers early in childhood will simply outgrow their problem as they get older—become less shy or less aggressive, for example. If so, there may be little point in intervening.

Longitudinal studies indicate that children with problems do *not* automatically outgrow them (Coie et al., 1992; Rubin, 1993). Some, of course, do; early peer status is no more perfectly predictive of later development than is any other early childhood measure. For many children, however, early rejection or neglect or withdrawal does predict continuing rejection or neglect or withdrawal. The category of rejection is especially stable over time. And rejected children are the ones who are at greatest risk for a number of problems later in life, including juvenile delinquency, dropping out of school, and mental illness (Coie & Cillessen, 1993; Parker et al., 1995). Although less is known about the long-term consequences of early social withdrawal, recent evidence suggests that withdrawn children are also at risk for later problems (Rubin & Asendorpf, 1993).

A variety of intervention approaches have been tried (LaGreca, 1993; Ramsey, 1991; Schneider et al., 1985). Some are grounded in social-learning theory. Modeling, for example, has been used in an attempt to increase social skills and social acceptance (Schunk, 1987). Shaping of desirable social behaviors through reinforcement has also been explored (O'Connor, 1972). Other approaches have their origins in cognitive-developmental theory. Included in this category are attempts to improve peer relations through teaching perspective-taking skills (Chandler, 1973) and through training in social problem-solving abilities (Pepler, King, & Byrd, 1991; Urbain & Kendell, 1980). Still other programs are more eclectic, encompassing a number of different training techniques in an effort to promote the needed social skills (Mize & Ladd, 1990).

A particularly interesting form of intervention is labeled **peer-mediated intervention** (Odom & Strain, 1984). This approach focuses not only on the target child, but also on the group of peers with whom the child interacts. The attempt is to utilize responses from these other children (for example, offers to play, praise for desirable behavior) to promote more effective social behaviors in the target child.

Peer-mediated intervention Form of intervention for children with sociometric problems in which responses of the peer group are utilized to elicit more effective social behaviors from the target children.

Intervention efforts do have beneficial effects (Asher, Parker, & Walker, 1996; Erwin, 1993; Schneider & Byrne, 1985). All of the approaches we have mentioned have yielded positive results in terms of both the social skills being taught and subsequent sociometric status. These effects are, to be sure, limited in various ways. Not all children benefit from intervention, and at present we know little about the long-term impact of such programs. Nevertheless, the picture is encouraging. Especially heartening is the fact that rejected children, who may be most at risk for later problems, can be helped through intervention to improve their social status (Asher, 1985). It is interesting to note that one technique that has proved especially effective with such children is training in academic skills (Coie & Krehbiel, 1984). Apparently, the improvement in the rejected child's academic performance has a beneficial impact on the child's self-concept and general classroom behavior, changes that in turn affect how the peer group evaluates the child.

✔ *To Recap...*

Children show important individual differences in the quality of their peer relations. Typically, such differences have been assessed through sociometric techniques—judgments offered by the child's peers. Children are defined as popular if they are the objects of many positive and few negative judgments.

Studies of the determinants of popularity have explored both relatively indirect predictors and more direct behavioral correlates. Variables in the first category that correlate (although far from perfectly) with popularity include birth order, intellectual ability, and physical attractiveness. The behavioral skills that seem to distinguish popular from less popular children are of three sorts: skill in initiating interaction, skill in maintaining interaction, and skill in resolving conflict.

Sociometric assessments also identify children with problems in peer relations. The rejected child receives few positive but many negative nominations from the peer group, whereas the controversial child receives many choices in both categories and the neglected child receives few nominations of any sort. Both rejected and neglected children show deficits in social skills, although their behavioral problems take different forms. Many (although not all) rejected children are characterized by aggressive, antisocial, and inappropriate behavior, whereas many (although again not all) neglected children are characterized by shy and withdrawn behavior.

The Family

For most children, the family and the peer group are the two most important microsystems within which development occurs. In this final section of the chapter we consider how these two major social worlds relate. We begin by examining how children's relations with their siblings compare with their peer relations. We then explore the contribution of parents to children's peer relations.

Siblings and Peers

Much like the topic of peer relations, the topic of siblings has enjoyed a resurgence of research interest in recent years (Brody, 1996, 1998; Brody & Stoneman, 1995; Dunn, 1996; Mendelson, 1990). We focus here on two questions: How do sibling relations compare with peer relations? And how does experience with siblings contribute to behavior with peers?

There are both obvious similarities and obvious differences in children's relations with their siblings and their relations with their peers, especially with their friends. On the one hand, both sibships and friendships are intimate, long-lasting relationships that are the context for frequent and varied interactions—usually positive in tone, but including moments of conflict and rivalry as well. Both relationships involve partners who are close in age, and hence interactions are likely to be more egalitarian and symmetrical than are interactions with adults, such as parents or teachers.

On the other hand, siblings (unless they are twins) are not identical in age, and the younger-older contrast introduces a basic asymmetry not necessarily found with friends. Furthermore, siblings, unlike friends, are not together by choice and do not have the option of terminating the relationship if negative aspects begin to outweigh positive ones. As one researcher put it, "Siblings do not choose each other, very often do not trust or even like each other, and may be competing strongly for parental affection and interest; the sources of conflict and hostility in this relationship are likely to be very different from those leading to tension in a friendship" (Dunn, 1992, p. 7).

This analysis suggests that we should expect some similarity, but hardly perfect similarity, between sibling relations and peer relations. And this, in fact, is what research shows. Let us first consider some similarities. Siblings clearly can perform the same roles and fulfill the same needs that we have seen are important among friends—as objects of pleasure or companionship, for instance, or as sources of affection, or as confidants for intimate interchanges (Buhrmester, 1992). Less positively, siblings, like friends, may also sometimes be targets for hostility and conflict; especially among younger children, conflicts among siblings are a depressingly familiar experience for many parents (Dunn, 1993). Some conflict is inevitable in any long-term, intimate relationship, and sibships, like friendships, are no exception to this rule.

Along with these general similarities in sibling and peer relations come differences. Some differences follow from the differences in age between siblings and the contrasting roles played by the younger and older child. Older siblings usually take the lead in dealings with their younger siblings, initiating both more positive and more negative actions and generally directing the course of the interaction; younger siblings, in turn, are more likely to give in to and to imitate their older partner (Teti, 1992). Such asymmetry does lessen with age, however, and by adolescence the relations between siblings are typically more egalitarian; now the younger sibling is sometimes the dominant member, and now the younger sibling can be the one who provides nurturance or help (Buhrmester & Furman, 1990).

Another change that is evident by adolescence—and another contrast between siblings and friends—is a decline in the relative importance of siblings as sources of

Both conflict and cooperation are frequent components of sibling interaction.

intimacy or help. As friends come to play these roles more often, children have less need to turn to their siblings for emotional or instrumental support (Buhrmester & Furman, 1990).

Finally, the domain of conflict reveals differences as well as similarities between sibling relations and peer relations. Although conflicts occur in both relationships, they tend to be more frequent between siblings than between friends (Buhrmester, 1992), and they also take somewhat different forms in the two contexts. Children are less likely to reason with siblings than with friends, less likely to attempt to take the sibling's point of view, and more likely to judge perceived transgressions negatively when the perpetrator is a sibling (Dunn, 1993; Slomkowski & Dunn, 1993). This more negative quality of sibling conflicts may reflect the forced, "not chosen" nature of the sibling relationship.

Our discussion thus far has concerned general similarities or differences between sibling relations and peer relations. But it is also important to ask about *within-child* links between the two social worlds. Does a particular child tend to show the same sorts of behaviors with peers as with siblings? And does the overall quality of a child's peer relations mirror the quality of relations with siblings?

The answer, once again, turns out to be "sometimes but not always" (Dunn & McGuire, 1992). Research makes clear that there is no simple, direct carryover of relations forged with siblings to relations with peers. Indeed, some examinations of the issue report little if any association between how children behave with siblings and how they behave with peers (Abramovitch et al., 1986; Volling, Youngblade, & Belsky, 1997). Such findings demonstrate, once again, the importance of context for children's behavior—what we see in one social context does not necessarily hold true when we move to a different context.

In other studies, sibling-peer connections do emerge, but they are seldom strong. As we might expect, links tend to be greater with friendship (another intense, dyadic relationship) than with peer relations in general (Stocker & Dunn, 1990). In some cases the direction of the relation is positive. For example, studies have shown positive correlations between cooperation with siblings and cooperation with friends (Stocker & Mantz-Simmons, 1993), as well as between aggression with siblings and aggression toward peers (Vandell et al., 1990). In other cases the direction is negative. For example, children with relatively hostile sibling relations sometimes form especially close friendships (Stocker & Dunn, 1990); similarly, children who are unpopular with peers may rank high on affection and companionship with their siblings (East & Rook, 1992). What seems to be happening in these cases is a kind of compensation: When one component of children's social world is unsatisfactory, they may try especially hard to obtain pleasure and support from other components.

A general conclusion to take away from these studies is that growing up with siblings can affect a number of aspects of children's development, including their behavior with peers. The links between siblings and peers are neither simple nor inevitable, however, and in any case experience with siblings is just one contributor to how children fare with peers. We turn next to another potentially important contributor: parents' child-rearing practices.

Parents and Peers

The question to be examined now is one of interest to any parent: What do parents do that helps or hinders their children's success with peers? The answer, we will see, is that parents do a variety of things that can be important (Ladd & Lesieur, 1995; Parke & Ladd, 1992; Putallaz & Heflin, 1990).

Parents' contribution to peer relations can begin very early in life, before most children have even begun to interact with peers. As we saw in Chapter 12, infants differ in the security of the attachments they form with the caregiver, and these differences in turn relate to the sensitivity and responsiveness of caregiving practices. As we also saw, secure attachment in infancy is associated with a number of positive outcomes in later childhood, including various aspects of peer relations. Children who were securely attached as infants tend to do well on measures of social competence and popularity later in childhood (Elicker, Englund, & Sroufe, 1992; Fagot, 1997; LaFreniere & Sroufe, 1985). Security of attachment is also related to quality of friendships; children with a history of secure attachment tend to form more harmonious and well-balanced friendships than do children with a history of less satisfactory attachments (Kerns, 1996; Youngblade & Belsky, 1992). Although most studies to date have examined outcomes in preschool or grade-school children, recent research indicates that some links between infant attachment and social competence are evident even in adolescence (Englund, Reed, & Sroufe, 1993).

Parents may also contribute to the development of the forms of play that occupy such a central position in children's early interactions with their peers. Before they embark on pretend or dramatic play with peers, many children have spent dozens of hours engaged in such play with their mothers and fathers at home. Observational studies verify that joint pretend play is a frequent activity in many households and that parents (mothers, in particular, in these studies) often assume a directive role in such play (Haight & Miller, 1993; O'Reilly & Bornstein, 1993). Recall, though, that there are cultural (and, we should add, individual) differences here—not all parents take an active part in their children's play.

Parents' involvement in early play represents a relatively indirect contribution to eventual peer relations. Parents may also take a more direct role in promoting and managing their children's encounters with peers. Ladd (1992) identified four ways in which parents may influence the frequency and nature of peer interactions: (a) as designers of the child's environment, parents make choices that affect the availability of peers and the settings (such as a safe versus a hazardous neighborhood) within which peer interactions take place; (b) as mediators, parents arrange peer contacts for their children and regulate their choice of play partners; (c) as supervisors, parents monitor their children's peer interactions and offer guidance

Parents are important contributors to the emergence of play and to the development of peer relations. But the kinds of experiences that parents provide may vary across different cultural settings.

and support; and finally, (d) as consultants, parents provide more general advice and emotional support with respect to peer relations, especially in response to questions and concerns from the child.

Research indicates that parents vary in the frequency and the skill with which they perform these various roles and that these variations in parental behavior in turn relate to variations in children's peer relations (Ladd & Coleman, 1993; Ladd, Profilet, & Hart, 1992; Lollis, Ross, & Tate, 1992). It has been found, for example, that peer acceptance in the preschool is related to the extent to which parents initiate play opportunities for their children (Ladd & Hart, 1992). Play among children, especially toddlers or preschoolers, proceeds more smoothly and happily when a parent is present to facilitate and direct (Bhavnagri & Parke, 1991). And play opportunities are more frequent and friendship networks larger when children grow up in safe neighborhoods with closely spaced houses than when conditions are less conducive to peer interaction (Medrich et al., 1982).

Although these kinds of direct management can undoubtedly be important, most attempts to identify the parental contribution to peer relations have focused on general childrearing strategies that either nurture or fail to nurture the social skills necessary for success with peers. Several dimensions emerge as important (Cassidy et al., 1992; Parke et al., 1992). One consistent correlate of sociometric status and social skills is parental warmth (MacDonald, 1992). Children who come from homes that are characterized by high levels of warmth, nurturance, and emotional expressiveness tend to do well in the peer group; conversely, children whose home lives are less harmonious are at risk for peer problems as well. The extreme of the latter situation arises in cases of physical abuse or neglect. Children who have been abused show special difficulty in responding appropriately when peers exhibit signs of distress (Klimes-Dougan & Kistner, 1990). Children who have been maltreated also show heightened levels of aggressiveness and social withdrawal (Mueller & Silverman, 1989). Not surprisingly, abused children tend to fare poorly on sociometric measures, and their unskilled behavior with peers often perpetuates their difficulties (Cicchetti et al., 1992; Salzinger et al., 1993).

The parent's methods of controlling and disciplining the child can also be important (Dekovic & Janssens, 1992; Dishion, 1990; Hart et al., 1992). Parents of popular children tend to be intermediate in the degree of control they exert, neither rigidly directing the child's every action nor allowing too much leeway because of lack of time or interest. These parents are involved in the lives of their children, but the goal of their socialization seems to be to promote autonomy and not merely immediate compliance. When discipline becomes necessary, parents of popular children tend to prefer verbal rather than physical methods, reasoning with the child and negotiating rather than imposing solutions. In contrast, techniques of power assertion (threats and physical punishment) are likely to characterize the home lives of children with peer problems.

As Putallaz and Heflin (1990) have noted, these conclusions about the contribution of parents to peer relations should not sound new or surprising. They fit with general conclusions about the effects of parental practices on children's social development. They are reminiscent, therefore, of evidence that we discussed in the preceding chapters with regard to parents' contributions to their children's prosocial behavior, or level of aggressiveness, or self-concept. The main way in which parents affect their children's success with peers is by promoting (or failing to promote) attributes that are important to peer interaction.

The conclusions also fit with what we would expect from theory. Support for cognitive-developmental positions is evident in the value of rational, cognitively oriented techniques of control and discipline. Support for social-learning theory can be seen in the clear role of parental reinforcements and parental models in fostering social skills. Indeed, the importance of parents as models is perhaps the clearest conclusion to be drawn from studies of the family's contribution to peer relations. Parents who are warm and friendly and effective with others have children who are warm and friendly and effective with others.

✓ *To Recap...*

Experiences within the family are one contributor to children's behavior with friends. Siblings are in many respects similar to peers as social objects, and sibling relations show many of the characteristics important in relations with peers, especially friends. Sibships and friendships are different in some respects, however, and specific qualities of sibling relations are only sometimes reflected in relations with peers.

Parents can contribute to their children's behavior with peers in a number of ways. Secure attachment to the parent during infancy is associated with positive peer relations in later childhood. Parents' participation in early pretend play may facilitate the emergence of play with peers. Both the frequency and the nature of peer interactions may be affected by various parental actions, ranging from choice of neighborhood to direct initiation and management of peer encounters. Finally, parents' child-rearing practices can help instill the social skills necessary for success in the peer group. Among the parental practices that can be beneficial are creation of a warm and supportive family atmosphere, use of cognitively oriented techniques of discipline, and provision of models of socially appropriate actions in the parents' own behavior.

Conclusion

The topic of peer relations is a good one with which to conclude our survey of the modern science of child psychology, because in considering how peers relate to and affect each other we can see again many of the themes and issues that we have encountered throughout this book. The influence of the three major theoretical perspectives is again evident. Indeed, much of the contemporary interest in peer relations can be traced to the emergence of the cognitive-developmental, social-learning, and ethological positions. Issues that are fundamental to child psychology in general, such as the nature–nurture debate and the continuity of early and later development, are also central to the study of peer relations. And the methodological approaches that characterize child psychology are all represented in the study of peer relations: laboratory studies, naturalistic observations, questionnaires and interviews, experimental and correlational designs.

The topic is representative in another respect as well. The advances in our understanding of peer relations in just the last dozen or so years have been truly remarkable. We know much more than we used to, for example, about the ways in which peers influence one another, and about the importance of friendship in children's development, and about links between cognitive abilities and social abilities. We have also made great progress with respect to the pragmatically important question of how to identify and help children who are having problems with peers. At the same time, there is still much to be learned about almost every topic we have considered. The power of the scientific approach is verified daily in the study of child psychology. But the mysteries of human development yield their secrets slowly.

Visual Summary for Chapter 16:

Peer Relations

Theories of Peer Relations

Cognitive-Developmental Theory	➡	Peers are an important impetus for cognitive change.	➡	Piaget and Kohlberg stressed the importance of cognitive conflict with peers. Vygotsky stressed the instructional role played by more competent peers.
Environmental/Learning Approach	➡	Peers contribute to the socializing of the child.	➡	Peers are reinforcers/punishers of behavior, serve as models of behavior, and are one source for self-efficacy judgments.
Ethological Theory	➡	Behavior toward peers has an innate basis that reflects the evolutionary development of a species.	➡	Peer relations are important for learning such things as one's place in the dominance hierarchy, controls on aggression, and so on.

Typical Peer Relations

Infancy	➡	Infants as young as 6 months show interest in and positive behavior toward other infants. With age, interactions become more frequent, more complex, and more reciprocal.
Preschool	➡	Play increases in both cognitive level and social organization. Symbolic forms of interaction begin to predominate over physical forms. Children become important socializing agents for each other.
Later Childhood and Adolescence	➡	Groups assume a prominent role. Common interests and goals, as well as organization and agreed-upon norms, are important for group functioning.
Conformity to Peers	➡	Although the peer group can be an influential source of values and behavior, parents remain influential as well, and on most issues the views of peers and of parents are more similar than different.

Contributors to Peer Relations

Situational Factors	➡	Aspects of the physical environment, such as familiarity of the setting, amount of space, and nature of available resources, can be important. Aspects of the social environment, such as number and familiarity of other children present, can affect children's behavior with peers.
Cognitive Contributions	➡	Cognitive level of the child is stressed especially in cognitive-developmental approaches to peer relations. Cognitive level is by no means a perfect predictor of peer interaction; cognitive-social relations are only sometimes found, and when they do occur, they are modest in magnitude. Nevertheless, evidence from both correlational and experimental training studies suggests that cognitive factors do contribute to peer relations.

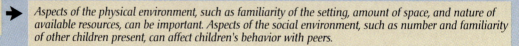

Friendship

Conceptions of Friendship	→ Young children think of friends in concrete terms as sources of immediate pleasure. Older children think of friends in terms of enduring relationships characterized by intimacy and loyalty.
Friendship Selection	→ Friends share similarities in terms of age, gender, race, interests, and academic orientation.
Friendship Formation	→ Contributors to friendship formation include exchange of information, self-disclosure, and successful resolution of conflict.
Behavior with Friends	→ Among friends, prosocial behavior is more frequent, conflict is less intense and better resolved, and intimacy is more common.
Effects of Friendship	→ Friendship can have long-term as well as immediate benefits. Among the aspects of development influenced by friendship are self-esteem, adjustment to school, and availability of social support in times of need.

Popularity and Problems

	Sociometric Choices	Characteristic Behavior
Popular Child	→ Many positive, few negative choices. Actively liked by peers.	→ Skilled in initiating interaction, maintaining interaction, and resolving conflict.
Rejected Child	→ Few positive, many negative choices. Actively disliked by peers.	→ May display antisocial, disruptive, inappropriate, aggressive behavior.
Neglected Child	→ Few positive, few negative choices. Ignored by peers.	→ May be shy and withdrawn.
Controversial Child	→ Many positive, many negative choices.	→ May display both aggressive and sociable behaviors.

Family

Siblings and Peers

Similarities	→ Sibling relationships, like peer relationships, are enduring and offer companionship, affection, and intimacy, but also have the potential for hostility and conflict.
Differences	→ Age differences among siblings may result in less symmetrical relationships than with peers. Conflict may be greater among siblings. With age, siblings may play less of a role than peers as sources of emotional and instrumental support.

Parents and Peers

Early Contributions	→ Secure attachment in infancy is associated with positive peer relations. Parents' participation in early pretend play facilitates the emergence of play with peers.
Direct Involvement	→ Parents may influence their children's peer relations by serving as designers, mediators, supervisors, and consultants.
Child Rearing	→ Family warmth, nurturance, discipline methods, and modeling of socially appropriate behavior all contribute to peer relations.

AB error Infants' tendency to search in the original location in which an object was found rather than in its most recent hiding place. A characteristic of stage 4 of object permanence.

Academic self-concept The part of self-esteem involving children's perceptions of their academic abilities.

Accommodation Changing existing cognitive structures to fit with new experiences. One of the two components of adaptation in Piaget's theory.

Adaptation The tendency to fit with the environment in ways that promote survival. One of the two biologically based functions stressed in Piaget's theory.

Adult Attachment Interview (AAI) An instrument used to assess an adult's childhood recollections of the attachment relationship with the primary caregiver.

Affect The outward expression of emotions through facial expressions, gestures, intonation, and the like.

Aggression Behavior that is intended to cause harm to persons or property and that is not socially justifiable.

Alleles Genes for the same trait located in the same place on a pair of chromosomes.

Amniocentesis A procedure for collecting cells that lie in the amniotic fluid surrounding the fetus. A needle is passed through the mother's abdominal wall into the amniotic sac to gather discarded fetal cells. These cells can be examined for chromosomal and genetic defects.

Amniotic sac A fluid-containing watertight membrane that surrounds and protects the embryo and fetus.

Androgen insensitivity A genetic disorder in which the fetus does not respond to masculinizing hormones. Affected individuals (XX or XY) usually are feminine in appearance and interests.

Androgens Hormones that have masculinizing effects and are more abundant in males.

Androgyny A personality type composed of desirable characteristics of the masculine and feminine personality types.

Anorexia nervosa A severe eating disorder, usually involving excessive weight loss through self-starvation, most often found in teenage girls.

Anoxia A deficit of oxygen to the cells, which can produce brain or other tissue damage.

Appearance–reality distinction Distinction between how objects appear and what they really are. Understanding the distinction implies an ability to judge both appearance and reality correctly when the two diverge.

Assimilation Interpreting new experiences in terms of existing cognitive structures. One of the two components of adaptation in Piaget's theory.

At risk Describes babies who have a higher likelihood than other babies of experiencing developmental problems.

Attachment Q-Set A method of assessing attachment in which cards bearing descriptions of the child's interactions with the caregiver are sorted into categories to create a profile of the child.

Attention-deficit hyperactivity disorder (ADHD) A developmental disorder characterized by difficulty in sustaining attention, hyperactivity, and impulsive and uncontrolled behavior.

Attention The selection of particular sensory input for perceptual and cognitive processing and the exclusion of competing input.

Autobiographical memory Specific, personal, and long-lasting memory regarding the self.

Automatization An increase in the efficiency with which cognitive operations are executed as a result of practice. A mechanism of change in information-processing theories.

Autosomes The 22 pairs of human chromosomes, other than the sex chromosomes

Axon A long fiber extending from the cell body in a neuron; conducts activity from the cell.

Babbling drift A hypothesis that infants' babbling gradually gravitates toward the language they are hearing and soon will speak.

Behavior analysis B. F. Skinner's environmental/learning theory, which emphasizes the role of operant learning in changing observable behaviors.

Behavior genetics The field of study that explores the role of genes in producing individual differences in behavior and development.

Behavioral homophyly Similarity between peers in behaviors and interests. Such similarity is one determinant of friendship selection.

Behaviorism A theory of psychology, first advanced by John B. Watson, that human development results primarily from conditioning and learning processes.

Bioecological theory Theory of intelligence that emphasizes the interplay of domain-specific knowledge and basic cognitive processes in the generation of intelligent behavior.

Bone age The degree of maturation of an individual as indicated by the extent of hardening of the bones.

Brain lateralization The organization of the human brain into left and right hemispheres that perform different functions.

Brain stem The lower part of the brain, closest to the spinal cord; includes the cerebellum, which is important for maintaining balance and coordination.

Brightness constancy The experience that the brightness of an object remains the same even though the amount of light it reflects back to the eye changes (because of shadows or changes in the illuminating light).

Bulimia A disorder of food binging and sometimes purging by self-induced vomiting, typically observed in teenage girls.

Cartesian dualism René Descartes's idea that the mind and body are separate, which helped clear the way for the scientific study of human development.

Case study A research method that involves only a single individual, often with a focus on a clinical issue.

Categorical perception The ability to detect differences in speech sounds that correspond to differences in meaning; the ability to discriminate phonemic boundaries.

Categorical self The "Me" component of the self, which involves one's objective personal characteristics.

Catharsis The psychoanalytic belief that the likelihood of aggression can be reduced by viewing aggression or by engaging in high-energy behavior.

Centration Piaget's term for the young child's tendency to focus on only one aspect of a problem at a time, a perceptually biased form of responding that often results in incorrect judgments.

Cephalocaudal Literally, head to tail. This principle of development refers to the tendency of body parts to mature in a head-to-foot progression.

Cerebral cortex The thin sheet of gray matter that covers the brain.

Cerebrum The highest brain center; includes both hemispheres of the brain and the interconnections between them.

Cesarean section Surgical delivery of the fetus directly from the uterus; performed when normal delivery is prohibited.

Chorionic villus sampling (CVS) A procedure for gathering fetal cells earlier in pregnancy than is possible through amniocentesis. A tube is passed through the vagina and cervix so that fetal cells can be gathered at the site of the developing placenta.

Chromosomes Chemical strands in the cell nucleus that contain the genes. The nucleus of each human cell has 46 chromosomes, with the exception of the gametes, which have 23.

Chronosystem Bronfenbrenner's term for the passage of time as a context for studying human development.

Clarification question A response that indicates that a listener did not understand a statement.

Class inclusion The knowledge that a subclass cannot be larger than the superordinate class that includes it. In Piaget's theory, a concrete operational achievement.

Clinical method Piaget's principal research method, which involved a semistructured interview with questions designed to probe children's understanding of various concepts.

Clique A kind of group typical in adolescence, consisting usually of 5 to 10 members whose shared interests and behavior patterns set them apart from their peers.

Codominance The case in which alleles are both dominant and each is completely expressed in the phenotype.

Coercive family process Gerald Patterson's term for the method by which some families control one another

through aggression and other coercive means.

Cognition Higher-order mental processes, such as reasoning and problem solving, through which humans attempt to understand the world.

Cohort effect A problem sometimes found in cross-sectional research in which people of a given age are affected by factors unique to their generation.

Coining Children's creation of new words to label objects or events for which the correct label is not known.

Color constancy The experience that the color of an object remains the same even though the wavelengths it reflects back to the eye change (because of changes in the color of the illuminating light).

Comparative research Research conducted with nonhuman species to provide information relevant to human development.

Competence Self-evaluation that includes both what one would like to achieve and one's confidence in being able to achieve it.

Competition model A proposed strategy children use for learning grammar in which they weight possible cues in terms of availability and reliability.

Computer simulation Programming a computer to perform a cognitive task in the same way that humans are thought to perform it. An information-processing method for testing theories of underlying process.

Concept A mental grouping of different items into a single category on the basis of some unifying similarity or set of similarities.

Conception The combining of the genetic material from a male gamete (sperm) and a female gamete (ovum); fertilization.

Concrete operations Form of intelligence in which mental operations make logical problem solving with concrete objects possible. The third of Piaget's periods, extending from about 6 to 11 years of age.

Conditioned reflex method John B. Watson's name for the Pavlovian conditioning process in which reflexive responses can be conditioned to stimuli in the environment.

Conditioned stimulus (CS) A neutral stimulus that comes to elicit a response

(UCR) through a conditioning process in which it is consistently paired with another stimulus (UCS) that naturally evokes the response.

Congenital adrenal hyperplasia (CAH) A hormonal disorder caused by an overproduction of androgens during pregnancy. Afflicted females have large genitals and display male personality characteristics; afflicted males tend to be slightly more masculine in their interests and interactions.

Congenitally organized behavior Early behaviors of newborns that do not require specific external stimulation and that show more adaptability than simple reflexes.

Conservation The knowledge that the quantitative properties of an object or collection of objects are not changed by a change in appearance. In Piaget's theory, a concrete operational achievement.

Constraints Implicit assumptions about word meanings that are hypothesized to narrow down the possibilities children must consider and hence to facilitate the task of word learning.

Constructive memory Effects of the general knowledge system on how information is interpreted and thus remembered.

Constructivism Piaget's belief that children actively create knowledge rather than passively receive it from the environment.

Continuity versus discontinuity debate The scientific controversy regarding whether development is constant and connected (continuous) or uneven and disconnected (discontinuous).

Controversial child A child who receives both many positive and many negative nominations in sociometric assessments by peers.

Conventional level Kohlberg's third and fourth stages of moral development. Moral reasoning is based on the view that a social system must be based on laws and regulations.

Cooing A stage in the preverbal period, beginning at about 2 months, when babies primarily produce one-syllable vowel sounds.

Correlation The relation between two variables, described in terms of direction and strength.

Correlation coefficient (*r*) A number between +1.00 and −1.00 that indicates the direction and strength of a correlation between two variables.

Cross-cultural studies Research designed to determine the influence of culture on some aspect of development and in which culture typically serves as an independent variable.

Crossing over The exchange of genetic material between pairs of chromosomes during meiosis.

Cross-sectional design A research method in which people of different ages are studied simultaneously to examine the effects of age on some aspect of behavior.

Cross-sequential design A research method combining longitudinal and cross-sectional designs.

Cultural compatibility hypothesis The hypothesis that schooling will be most effective when methods of instruction are compatible with the child's cultural background.

Cultural relativism The idea that certain behaviors or patterns of development vary from one culture to another.

Deep structure Chomsky's term for the inborn knowledge humans possess about the properties of language.

Defensive reflex A natural reaction to novel stimuli that tends to protect the organism from further stimulation and that may include orientation of the stimulus receptors away from the stimulus source and a variety of physiological changes.

Deferred imitation Imitation of a model observed some time in the past.

Delay-of-gratification technique An experimental procedure for studying children's ability to postpone a smaller, immediate reward in order to obtain a larger, delayed one.

Dendrite One of a net of short fibers extending out from the cell body in a neuron; receives activity from nearby cells and conducts that activity to the cell body.

Deoxyribonucleic acid (DNA) A stairlike, double-helix molecule that carries genetic information on chromosomes.

Dependent variable The variable that is predicted to be affected by an experimental manipulation. In psychology, usually some aspect of behavior.

Descriptive research Research based solely on observations, with no attempt to determine systematic relations among the variables.

Developmental pacing The rate at which spurts and plateaus occur in an individual's physical and mental development.

Developmental psychology The branch of psychology devoted to the study of changes in behavior and abilities over the course of development.

Dialectical process The process in Vygotsky's theory whereby children learn through problem-solving experiences shared with others.

Dialogic reading Form of joint picture-book reading in which the adult uses open-ended questions and other prompts to encourage the child to tell the story, with the goal of promoting linguistic skills.

Discourse Language used in social interactions; conversation.

Dishabituation The recovery of a habituated response that results from a change in the eliciting stimulus.

Displaced aggression Retaliatory aggression directed at a person or object other than the one against whom retaliation is desired.

Display rules The expectations and attitudes a society holds toward the expression of affect.

Dominance hierarchy A structured social group in which members higher on the dominance ladder control those who are lower, initially through aggression and conflict, but eventually simply through threats.

Down syndrome A chromosomal disorder caused by an extra chromosome. Its effects include mental retardation and a characteristic physical appearance.

Dynamic assessment Method of assessing children's abilities derived from Vygotsky's concept of the zone of proximal development. Measures the child's ability to benefit from adult-provided assistance, typically in a test-train-retest design.

Dynamic systems Thelen's model of the development of motor skills, in which infants who are motivated to accomplish a task create a new motor behavior from their available physical abilities

EAS model Plomin and Buss's theory of temperament, which holds that temperament can be measured along the dimensions of emotionality, activity, and sociability.

Ecological approach An approach to studying development that focuses on individuals within their environmental contexts.

Egocentrism In infancy, an inability to distinguish the self (e.g., one's actions or perceptions) from the outer world. In later childhood, an inability to distinguish one's own perspective (e.g., visual experience, thoughts, feelings) from that of others.

Electroencephalograph (EEG) An instrument that measures brain activity by sensing minute electrical changes at the top of the skull.

Embryo The developing organism from the third week, when implantation is complete, through the eighth week after conception.

Emotion An internal reaction or feeling, which may be either positive (such as joy) or negative (such as anger), and may reflect a readiness for action.

Encoding Attending to and forming internal representations of certain features of the environment. A mechanism of change in information-processing theories.

Epigenetic principle According to Erikson, the genetic process that guides personality formation through its stages of development.

Equilibration Piaget's term for the biological process of self-regulation that propels the cognitive system to higher and higher forms of equilibrium.

Equilibrium A characteristic of a cognitive system in which assimilation and accommodation are in balance, thus permitting adaptive, nondistorted responses to the world.

Erogenous zones According to Freud's theory of psychosexual development, the areas of the body where the libido resides during successive stages of development. The child seeks physical pleasure in the erogenous zone at which the libido is located.

Estrogens and progesterone Hormones that have feminizing effects and are more abundant in females.

Ethology The study of development from an evolutionary perspective.

Evaluative self-reactions Bandura's term for consequences people apply to themselves as a result of meeting or failing to meet their personal standards.

Existential self The "I" component

of the self, which is concerned with the subjective experience of existing.

Exosystem Social systems that can affect children but in which they do not participate directly. Bronfenbrenner's third layer of context.

Expansion A repetition of speech in which errors are corrected and statements are elaborated.

Expertise Organized factual knowledge with respect to some content domain.

Expressive style Vocabulary acquired during the naming explosion that emphasizes the pragmatic functions of language.

False belief The realization that people can hold beliefs that are not true. Such understanding, which is typically acquired during the preoperational period, provides evidence of the ability to distinguish the mental from the nonmental.

False self behavior Behaving in a way that is knowingly different from how one's true self would behave.

Fast-mapping A process in which children acquire the meaning of a word after a brief exposure.

Fetal alcohol syndrome A set of features in the infant caused by the mother's use of alcohol during pregnancy; typically includes facial malformations and other physical and mental disabilities.

Fetal distress A condition of abnormal stress in the fetus, reflected during the birth process in an abnormal fetal heart rate.

Fetus The developing organism from the ninth week to the thirty-eighth week after conception.

Forbidden-toy technique An experimental procedure for studying children's resistance to temptation in which the child is left alone with an attractive toy and instructed not to play with it.

Formal operations Form of intelligence in which higher-level mental operations make possible logical reasoning with respect to abstract and hypothetical events and not merely concrete objects. The fourth of Piaget's periods, beginning at about 11 years of age.

Fragile X syndrome An X-linked genetic disorder, most often expressed in males, producing retarded intellectual development, language and behavior problems, and identifiable physical characteristics.

Fraternal (dizygotic [DZ]) twins Twins who develop from separately fertilized ova and who thus are no more genetically similar than are other siblings.

Friendship An enduring relationship between two individuals, characterized by loyalty, intimacy, and mutual affection.

Functionalist model A theory of language development that stresses the uses of language and the context in which it develops.

g General intelligence; g is assumed to determine performance on a wide range of intellectual measures.

Gender consistency Understanding that one's gender cannot be changed by superficial changes in clothing, occupation, etc.

Gender constancy Understanding that one's gender is a fixed part of the self; it includes gender identity, gender stability, and gender consistency.

Gender identity disorder (GID) A disorder in which children, most often males, appear uncomfortable with their biological sex and display behavior more typical of the opposite sex.

Gender identity Knowledge of one's own gender.

Gender role (sex-role stereotype) A pattern of behaviors that is considered appropriate for males or females by the culture in which they live.

Gender schema A cognitive structure used to organize information regarding one's gender.

Gender script A familiar routine or sequence of events that is typically associated with only one gender.

Gender segregation (sex cleavage) The tendency for male and female children to play in same-sex groups.

Gender stability Understanding that one's gender will remain the same throughout life.

Gender-role knowledge Understanding that a certain toy, activity, or personal characteristic is considered more appropriate for one sex than the other.

Gene A segment of DNA on the chromosome. The basic unit of inheritance.

Genetic counseling The practice of advising prospective parents about genetic diseases and the likelihood that they might pass on defective genetic traits to their offspring.

Genetic epistemology Jean Piaget's term

for the study of children's knowledge and how it changes with development.

Genotype The arrangement of genes underlying a trait.

Goodness of fit A concept describing the relation between a baby's temperament and her social and environmental surroundings.

Grammar The study of the structural properties of language, including syntax, inflection, and intonation.

Group A collection of individuals who interact regularly in a consistent, structured fashion and who share values and a sense of belonging to the group.

Habituation The decline or disappearance of a reflex response as a result of repeated elicitation. The simplest type of learning.

Haptic perception The perceptual experience that results from active exploration of objects by touch.

Heritability The proportion of variance in a trait (such as IQ) that can be attributed to genetic variance in the sample being studied.

Hierarchical model of intelligence A model of the structure of intelligence in which intellectual abilities are seen as being organized hierarchically, with broad, general abilities at the top of the hierarchy and more specific skills nested underneath.

Holophrase A single word used to express a larger idea; common during the second year of life.

HOME (Home Observation for Measurement of the Environment) An instrument for assessing the quality of the early home environment. Included are dimensions such as maternal involvement and variety of play materials.

Hostile (retaliatory) aggression Aggression whose purpose is to cause pain or injury.

Huntington's chorea An inherited disease in which the nervous system suddenly deteriorates, resulting in uncontrollable muscular movements and disordered brain function. The disease typically strikes people between about 30 and 40 years of age and ultimately causes death.

Hypothesis A predicted relation between a phenomenon and a factor assumed to affect it that is not yet supported by a great deal of evidence. Hypotheses are tested in experimental investigations.

Hypothetical-deductive reasoning A form

of problem solving characterized by the ability to generate and test hypotheses and draw logical conclusions from the results of the tests. In Piaget's theory, a formal operational achievement.

Identical (monozygotic [MZ]) twins Twins who develop from a single fertilized ovum and thus inherit identical genetic material.

Identification The Freudian process through which the child adopts the characteristics of the same-sex parent during the phallic stage.

Identity In Erikson's theory, the component of personality that develops across the eight stages of life and that motivates progress through the stages.

Imitation Behavior of an observer that results from and is similar to the behavior of a model.

Immanent justice Literally, inherent justice; refers to the expectation of children in Piaget's stage of moral realism that punishment must follow any rule violation, including those that appear to go undetected.

Imprinting A biological process in some species in which the young acquire an emotional attachment to the mother through following.

Incomplete dominance The case in which a dominant gene does not completely suppress the effect of a recessive gene, which is then somewhat expressed in the phenotype.

Independent variable The variable in an experiment that is systematically manipulated.

Infantile amnesia The inability to remember experiences from the first 2 or 3 years of life.

Inflections The aspect of grammar that involves adding endings to words to modify their meaning.

Inhibition Kagan's proposed temperamental response style characterizing infants who react to unfamiliar events and people with timidity and avoidance.

Innate releasing mechanism A stimulus that triggers an innate sequence or pattern of behaviors.

Institutionalization studies Examinations of the effects of naturally occurring deprivation (such as in certain kinds of orphanage rearing) on children's development.

Instrumental aggression Aggression whose purpose is to obtain something desired.

Intentional behavior In Piaget's theory, behavior in which the goal exists prior to the action selected to achieve it; made possible by the ability to separate means and end.

Interactional synchrony The smooth intermeshing of behaviors between mother and baby.

Interactionist perspective The theory that human development results from the combination of nature and nurture factors.

Internal working model An infant's and a caregiver's cognitive conception of each other, which they use to form expectations and predictions.

Internalization Vygotsky's term for the child's incorporation, primarily through language, of bodies of knowledge and tools of thought from the culture.

Invariants Aspects of the world that remain the same even though other aspects have changed. In Piaget's theory, different forms of invariants are understood at different stages of development.

Joint attention Using cues (such as direction of gaze) to identify and share the attentional focus of another.

Kin selection A proposed mechanism by which an individual's altruistic behavior toward a kin member increases the likelihood of the survival of genes similar to those of the individual.

Kinetic cues Visual cues that indicate the relative distances of objects through movement either of the objects or of the observer.

Klinefelter's syndrome (XXY) A chromosomal disorder of males in which an extra X chromosome is present; men with the syndrome have long arms, little body hair, an underdeveloped penis, and somewhat feminine personality characteristics.

Language acquisition device (LAD) Chomsky's proposed brain mechanism for analyzing speech input; the mechanism that allows young children to acquire quickly the language to which they are exposed.

Language acquisition support system (LASS) Bruner's proposed process by which parents provide children assistance in learning language.

Law (principle) A predicted relation between a phenomenon and a factor assumed to affect it that is supported by a good deal of scientific evidence.

Learnability theory A nativistic theory of language acquisition that uses mathematical models to determine the kinds of evidence necessary to learn grammatical rules.

Learning A relatively permanent change in behavior that results from practice or experience.

Lexical contrast theory A theory of semantic development holding that (1) children automatically assume that a new word has a meaning different from that of any other word they know and (2) children always choose word meanings that are generally accepted over more individualized meanings.

Lexicon A vocabulary, or repertoire of words.

Libido Sigmund Freud's term for the sexual energy that he believed is possessed by all children from birth and then moves to different locations on the body over the course of development.

Locomotion The movement of a person through space. Psychologists have been most interested in movements that individuals control themselves, such as walking and crawling.

Longitudinal design A research method in which the same individuals are studied repeatedly over time.

Looking-glass self The conception of the self based on how one thinks others see him or her.

Macrosystem The culture or subculture in which the child lives. Bronfenbrenner's fourth layer of context.

Mastery motivation An inborn desire to affect or control one's environment.

Maternal bonding The mother's emotional attachment to the child, which appears shortly after birth and which some theorists believe develops through early contact during a sensitive period.

Maternal separation anxiety Strong negative emotional reactions experienced by some mothers when separated from their children.

Maturation The biological processes assumed by some theorists to be primarily responsible for human development.

Meiosis The process by which germ cells produce four gametes (sperm or ovum), each with half the number of chromosomes of the parent cell.

Mesosystem The interrelationships among the child's microsystems. The second of Bronfenbrenner's layers of context.

Metamemory Knowledge about memory.

Microanalysis A research technique for studying dyadic interactions, in which two individuals are simultaneously videotaped with different cameras, and then the tapes are examined side by side.

Microgenetic method A research method in which a small number of individuals are observed repeatedly in order to study an expected change in a developmental process.

Microsystem The environmental system closest to the child, such as the family or school. The first of Bronfenbrenner's layers of context.

Midbrain A part of the brain that lies above the brain stem; serves as a relay station and as a control area for breathing and swallowing and houses part of the auditory and visual systems.

Mitosis The process by which body cells reproduce, resulting in two identical cells.

Mnemonic strategies Techniques (such as rehearsal or organization) that people use in an attempt to remember something.

Modal action pattern A sequence of behaviors elicited by a specific stimulus.

Moral conduct The aspect of children's moral development concerned with behavior.

Moral dilemmas Stories used by Piaget and others to assess children's levels of moral reasoning.

Moral realism Piaget's second stage of moral development, in which children's reasoning is based on objective and physical aspects of a situation and is often inflexible.

Moral reasoning The aspect of children's moral development concerned with knowledge and understanding of moral issues and principles.

Moral relativism Piaget's third stage of moral development, in which children view rules as agreements that can be altered and consider people's motives or intentions when evaluating their moral conduct.

Moral rules Rules used by a society to protect individuals and to guarantee their rights.

Moro reflex The infant's response to loss of head support or to a loud sound, con-

sisting of thrusting the arms and fingers outward, followed by clenching the fists and making a grasping motion of the arms across the chest.

Motherese Simplified speech directed at very young children by adults and older children.

Motion parallax An observer's experience that a closer object moves across the field of view faster than a more distant object when both objects are moving at the same speed or when the objects are stationary and the observer moves.

Myelin A sheath of fatty material that surrounds and insulates the axon, resulting in speedier transmission of neural activity.

Naming explosion A period of language development, beginning at about 18 months, when children suddenly begin to acquire words (especially labels) at a high rate.

Nativism The theory that human development results principally from inborn processes that guide the emergence of behaviors in a predictable manner.

Nativistic theory A theory of language development, originated by Chomsky, that stresses innate mechanisms separate from cognitive processes.

Natural selection An evolutionary process proposed by Charles Darwin in which characteristics of an individual that increase its chances of survival are more likely to be passed along to future generations.

Nature versus nurture debate The scientific controversy regarding whether the primary source of developmental change rests in biological (nature) factors or in environmental and experiential (nurture) factors.

Negative correlation A correlation in which two variables change in opposite directions.

Negative reinforcer A consequence that makes the behavior it follows more likely through the removal of something unpleasant.

Neglected child A child who receives few nominations of any sort, positive or negative, in sociometric assessments by peers. Such children seem to be ignored by the peer group.

Neuron A nerve cell, consisting of a cell body, axon, and dendrites. Neurons transmit activity from one part of the nervous system to another.

Neurotransmitter A chemical that transmits electrical activity from one neuron across the synapse to another neuron.

New York Longitudinal Study (NYLS) A well-known longitudinal project conducted by Thomas and Chess to study infant temperament and its implications for later psychological adjustment.

Nonshared environment A concept used in behavior genetics to refer to presumed aspects of the environment that children experience differently.

Normative versus idiographic development The question of whether research should focus on identifying commonalities in human development (normative development) or on the causes of individual differences (idiographic development).

Norms A timetable of age ranges indicating when normal growth and developmental milestones are typically reached.

Obesity A condition of excess fat storage; often defined as weight more than 20% over a standardized, ideal weight.

Object permanence The knowledge that objects have a permanent existence that is independent of our perceptual contact with them. In Piaget's theory, a major achievement of the sensorimotor period.

Objective responsibility Responsibility assigned solely in terms of an action's objective and physical consequences. Children in Piaget's stage of moral realism evaluate situations using this concept.

Objectivity A characteristic of scientific research; it requires that the procedures and subject matter of investigations should be formulated so that they could, in principle, be agreed on by everyone.

Observational learning A form of learning in which an observer's behavior changes as a result of observing a model.

Operant behaviors Voluntary behaviors controlled by their consequences. The larger category of human behaviors.

Operant learning A form of learning in which the likelihood of an operant behavior changes as a result of its reinforcing or punishing consequences.

Operating principle A hypothetical innate strategy for analyzing language input and discovering grammatical structure.

Operating space In Case's theory, the resources necessary to carry out cognitive operations.

Operations Piaget's term for the various forms of mental action through which older children solve problems and reason logically.

Organization The tendency to integrate knowledge into interrelated cognitive structures. One of the two biologically based functions stressed in Piaget's theory.

Orienting reflex A natural reaction to novel stimuli that enhances stimulus processing and includes orientation of the eyes and ears to optimize stimulus reception, inhibition of ongoing activity, and a variety of physiological changes.

Ovaries The female gonadal structure that produces the ovum.

Overextension An early language error in which children use labels they already know for things whose names they do not yet know.

Overregularization An early structural language error in which children apply inflectional rules to irregular forms (e.g., adding -ed to say).

Palmar reflex The infant's finger grasp of an object that stimulates the palm of the hand.

Paradox of altruism The logical dilemma faced by ethological theorists who try to reconcile self-sacrificial behavior with the concepts of natural selection and survival of the fittest.

Parallel play A form of play in which children play next to each other and with similar materials but with no real interaction or cooperation.

Peer-mediated intervention Form of intervention for children with sociometric problems in which responses of the peer group are utilized to elicit more effective social behaviors from the target children.

Perception The interpretation of sensory stimulation based on experience.

Perinatal period The events and environment surrounding the birth process.

Periods Piaget's term for the four general stages into which his theory divides development. Each period is a qualitatively distinct form of functioning that characterizes a wide range of cognitive activities.

Peripheral vision The perception of visual input outside the area on which the individual is fixating.

Personal agency The understanding that one can be the cause of events.

Phenotype The characteristic of a trait that is expressed or observable.

Phenylketonuria (PKU) An inherited metabolic disease caused by a recessive gene. It can produce severe mental retardation if dietary intake of phenylalanine is not controlled for the first several years of life.

Phoneme A sound contrast that changes meaning.

Phonemics The branch of phonology that deals with the relation between speech sounds and meaning.

Phonetics The branch of phonology that deals with articulation skills.

Phonics An approach to reading instruction that stresses letter–sound correspondences and the build-up of words from individual units.

Phonological awareness The realization that letters correspond to sounds and the ability to perform specific letter-to-sound translations.

Phonology The study of speech sounds.

Pictorial cues Visual cues that indicate the relative distances of objects through static, picturelike information—for example, interposition of one object in front of another.

Placenta An organ that forms where the embryo attaches to the uterus. This organ exchanges nutrients, oxygen, and wastes between the embryo or fetus and the mother through a very thin membrane that does not allow the passage of blood.

Polygenic inheritance The case in which a trait is determined by a number of genes.

Positive correlation A correlation in which two variables change in the same direction.

Positive reinforcer A consequence that makes the behavior it follows more likely through the presentation of something pleasant.

Postconventional level Kohlberg's final stages of moral development. Moral reasoning is based on the assumption that the value, dignity, and rights of each individual person must be maintained.

Postural development The increasing ability of the baby to control parts of the body, especially the head and the trunk.

Pragmatics The study of the social uses of language.

Preconventional level Kohlberg's first two stages of moral development. Moral reasoning is based on the assumption that individuals must serve their own needs.

Prehension The ability to grasp and manipulate objects with the hands.

Preoperational Form of intelligence in which symbols and mental actions begin to replace objects and overt behaviors. The second of Piaget's periods, extending from about 2 to about 6 years old.

Pretend play A form of play in which children use an object or person as a symbol to stand for something else.

Preterm Describes babies born before the end of the normal gestation period.

Primary caregiver The person, usually the mother, with whom the infant develops the major attachment relationship.

Principle of mutual exclusivity A proposed principle of semantic development stating that children assume that an object can have only one name.

Private speech Speech children produce and direct toward themselves during a problem-solving activity.

Production deficiency The failure to generate a mnemonic strategy spontaneously.

Productivity The property of language that permits humans to produce and comprehend an infinite number of statements.

Progressive decentering Piaget's term for the gradual decline in egocentrism that occurs across development.

Prosocial behavior The aspect of moral conduct that includes socially desirable behaviors such as sharing, helping, and cooperating; often used interchangeably with *altruism* by modern researchers.

Proximal processes Bronfenbrenner and Ceci's term for interactions between the child and aspects of the microsystem that have positive effects on psychological functioning and that help to maximize expression of the child's genetic potential.

Proximodistal Literally, near to far. This principle of development refers to the tendency of body parts to develop in a trunk-to-extremities direction.

Psychometric An approach to the study of intelligence that emphasizes the use of standardized tests to identify individual differences among people.

Psychoteratology The study of the harmful effects of teratogens through the use of behavioral measures, such as learning ability.

Puberty The period in which chemical and physical changes in the body occur that enable sexual reproduction.

Punisher A consequence that makes the behavior it follows less likely, either through the presentation of something unpleasant or the removal of something desirable.

Qualitative identity The knowledge that the qualitative nature of something is not changed by a change in its appearance. In Piaget's theory, a preoperational achievement.

Rapid eye movement (REM) sleep A stage of irregular sleep in which the eyes move rapidly while the eyelids are closed.

Reaction range In Gottesman's model, the term for the range of ability or skill that is set by the genes.

Reactivation The preservation of the memory for an event through reencounter with at least some portion of the event in the interval between initial experience and memory test.

Recall memory The retrieval of some past stimulus or event that is not perceptually present.

Recapitulation theory An early biological notion, later adopted by psychologist G. Stanley Hall, that the development of the individual repeats the development of the species.

Recast A response to speech that restates it using a different structure.

Reciprocal altruism A proposed mechanism by which an individual's altruistic behavior toward members of the social group may promote the survival of the individual's genes through reciprocation by others or may ensure the survival of similar genes.

Reciprocal determinism Albert Bandura's proposed process describing the interaction of a person's characteristics and abilities (P), behavior (B), and environment (E).

Recognition memory The realization that some perceptually present stimulus or event has been encountered before.

Reduplicated babbling A stage in the preverbal period, beginning at about 6 months, when infants produce strings of identical sounds, such as *dadada*.

Referential style Vocabulary acquired during the naming explosion that involves a large proportion of nouns and object labels.

Reflex A biological relation in which a specific stimulus reliably elicits a specific response.

Rejected child A child who receives few positive and many negative nominations in sociometric assessments by peers. Such children seem to be disliked by the peer group.

Relational aggression Aggression designed to damage or disrupt social relationships.

Reliability The consistency or repeatability of a measuring instrument. A necessary property of a standardized test.

Representation The use of symbols to picture and act on the world internally.

Repression Freud's term for the process through which desires or motivations are driven into the unconscious, as typically occurs during the phallic stage.

Respondent behaviors Responses based on reflexes, which are controlled by specific eliciting stimuli. The smaller category of human behaviors.

Respondent (classical) conditioning A form of learning, involving reflexes, in which a neutral stimulus acquires the power to elicit a reflexive response (UCR) as a result of being associated (paired) with the naturally eliciting stimulus (UCS). The neutral stimulus then becomes a conditioned stimulus (CS).

Respondent extinction A process related to respondent conditioning in which the conditioned stimulus (CS) gradually loses its power to elicit the response as a result of no longer being paired with the unconditioned stimulus (UCS).

Response inhibition The absence of a particular response that has just been modeled; often the result of vicarious punishment.

Reversal-replication (ABAB) design An experimental design in which the independent variable is systematically presented and removed several times. Can be used in studies involving very few research participants.

Reversibility Piaget's term for the power of operations to correct for potential disturbances and thus arrive at correct solutions to problems.

Rooting reflex The turning of the infant's head toward the cheek at which touch stimulation is applied, followed by opening of the mouth.

Rules Procedures for acting on the environment and solving problems.

Scaffolding A method of teaching in which the adult adjusts the level of help provided in relation to the child's level of performance, the goal being to encourage independent performance.

Scatter diagram A graphic illustration of a correlation between two variables.

Schemes Piaget's term for the cognitive structures of infancy. A scheme consists of a set of skilled, flexible action patterns through which the child understands the world.

Scientific method The system of rules used by scientists to conduct and evaluate their research.

Script A representation of the typical sequence of actions and events in some familiar context.

Selective attention Concentration on a stimulus or event with attendant disregard for other stimuli or events.

Self-consciousness A concern about the opinions others hold about one.

Self-efficacy Bandura's term for people's ability to succeed at various tasks, as judged by the people themselves.

Self-esteem (self-worth) A person's evaluation of the self, and the affective reactions to that evaluation.

Self-evaluation The part of the self-system concerned with children's opinions of themselves and their abilities.

Self-knowledge (self-awareness) The part of the self-system concerned with children's knowledge about themselves.

Self-regulation The part of the self-system concerned with self-control.

Self-schema An internal cognitive portrait of the self used to organize information about the self.

Self-system The set of interrelated processes—self-knowledge, self-evaluation, and self-regulation—that make up the self.

Semantic bootstrapping A proposed mechanism of grammatical development in which children use semantic cues to infer aspects of grammar.

Semantics The study of how children acquire words and their meanings.

Sensation The experience resulting from the stimulation of a sense organ.

Sensitive period A period of development during which certain behaviors are more easily learned.

Sensorimotor schemes Skilled and generalizable action patterns by which infants act on and understand the world. In Piaget's theory, the cognitive structures of infancy.

Sensorimotor Form of intelligence in which knowledge is based on physical interactions with people and objects. The first of Piaget's periods, extending from birth to about 2 years.

Separation protest Crying and searching by infants separated from their mothers; an indication of the formation of the attachment bond.

Seriation The ability to order stimuli along some quantitative dimension, such as length. In Piaget's theory, a concrete operational achievement.

Sex chromosomes The pair of human chromosomes that determines one's sex. Females have two X chromosomes, males have an X and a Y.

Sex difference A behavior or characteristic in which males and females usually differ as a result of biological or environmental factors.

Sex differentiation The process through which biological sex differences emerge.

Sex (gender) An individual's biological maleness or femaleness.

Sex typing The process by which children develop the sex role considered by their culture to be appropriate for their gender.

Sex-limited traits Genes that affect males and females differently but that are not carried on the sex chromosomes.

Sex-linked (X-linked) genes Genes found only on the sex chromosomes, most often the X chromosome.

Sexual dimorphism The existence in most species of biological differences between males and females for the purpose of reproduction.

Sexual orientation A person's sexual preference. Heterosexuals are attracted to members of the opposite sex and homosexuals are attracted to members of the same sex.

Shape constancy The experience that the physical shape of an object remains the same even though the shape of its projected image on the eye varies.

Short-term storage space In Case's theory, the resources necessary to store results from previous cognitive operations while carrying out new ones.

Sickle-cell anemia (SCA) An inherited blood disease caused by a recessive gene. The red blood cells assume a sickle shape and do not distribute oxygen efficiently to the cells of the body.

Size constancy The experience that the physical size of an object remains the same even though the size of its projected image on the eye varies.

Small for gestational age (SGA) Describes babies born at a weight in the bottom 10% of babies of a particular gestational age.

Social cognition Knowledge of the social world and interpersonal relationships.

Social comparison Comparing one's abilities to those of others.

Social conventions Rules used by a society to govern everyday behavior and to maintain order.

Social problem-solving skills Skills needed to resolve social dilemmas.

Social referencing Using information gained from other people to regulate one's own behavior.

Social referential communication A form of communication in which a speaker sends a message that is comprehended by a listener.

Social support Resources (both tangible and intangible) provided by other people in times of uncertainty or stress.

Social withdrawal Self-imposed isolation from the peer group.

Socialization The process through which society molds the child's beliefs, expectations, and behavior.

Social-learning theory A form of environmental/learning theory that adds observational learning to respondent and operant learning as a process through which children's behavior changes.

Sociobiology A branch of biology that attempts to discover the evolutionary origins of social behavior.

Sociogenesis The process of acquiring knowledge or skills through social interactions.

Sociometric techniques Procedures for assessing children's social status based on evaluations by the peer group. Sociometric techniques may involve ratings of degree of liking, nominations of liked or disliked peers, or forced-choice judgments between pairs of peers.

Speech act An instance of speech used to perform pragmatic functions, such as requesting or complaining.

+1 stage technique A method of investigating the hierarchical organization of moral stages; children are exposed to reasoning one stage above their own in order to maximize cognitive conflict and thus induce movement to the higher stage.

Stepping reflex The infant's response to pressure on the soles of the feet, consisting of stepping (flexing) movements.

Stimulus generalization A process related to respondent conditioning in which stimuli that are similar to the conditioned stimulus (CS) also acquire the power to elicit the response.

Strange Situation procedure Ainsworth's laboratory procedure for assessing the strength of the attachment relationship by observing the infant's reactions to a series of structured episodes involving the mother and a stranger.

Strategy construction The creation of strategies for processing and remembering information. A mechanism of change in information-processing theories.

Strategy selection Progressively greater use of relatively effective strategies in comparison to relatively ineffective ones. A mechanism of change in information-processing theories.

Study strategies Mnemonic strategies (such as outlining and note taking) that students use in an attempt to remember school material.

Surface structure Chomsky's term for the way words and phrases are arranged in spoken languages.

Symbolic function The ability to use one thing (such as a mental image or word) as a symbol to represent something else.

Symbolic play Form of play in which the child uses one thing in deliberate pretense to stand for something else.

Synapse The small space between neurons across which neural activity is communicated from one cell to another.

Syntactic bootstrapping A proposed mechanism of semantic development in which children use syntactic cues to infer the meanings of words.

Syntax The aspect of grammar that involves word order.

Tabula rasa Latin phrase, meaning "blank slate," used to describe the newborn's mind as entirely empty of inborn abilities, interests, or ideas.

Tay-Sachs disease An inherited disease in which the lack of an enzyme that breaks down fats in brain cells causes progressive brain deterioration. Affected children usually die by the age of 6.

Telegraphic speech Speech from which unnecessary function words (e.g., *in, the, with*) are omitted; common during early language learning.

Temperament The aspect of personality studied in infants, which includes their emotional expres-siveness and respon-siveness to stimulation.

Teratogen An agent that can cause abnormal development in the fetus.

Testes The male gonadal structure that produces the sperm.

Theory of mind Thoughts and beliefs concerning the mental world.

Theory A broad set of statements describing the relation between a phenomenon and the factors assumed to affect it.

Tonic neck reflex The infant's postural change when the head is turned to the side, consisting of extension of the arm on that side and clenching of the other arm in what looks like a fencer's position.

Tools of intellectual adaptation Vygotsky's term for the techniques of thinking and problem solving that children internalize from their culture.

Transactional influence A bidirectional, or reciprocal, relationship in which individuals influence one another's behaviors.

Transformational grammar A set of rules developed by the LAD to translate a language's surface structure to a deep structure that the child can innately understand.

Transitivity The ability to combine relations logically to deduce necessary con-

clusions—for example, if A > B and B > C, then A > C. In Piaget's theory, a concrete operational achievement.

Turner's syndrome A chromosomal disorder of females in which one X chromosome is absent; women with the syndrome have no ovaries, do not menstruate, are short in stature, and display ultrafeminine personality characteristics.

Ultrasound imaging A noninvasive procedure for detecting physical defects in the fetus. A device that produces sound-like waves of energy is moved over the pregnant woman's abdomen, and reflections of these waves form an image of the fetus.

Umbilical cord A soft cable of tissue and blood vessels that connects the fetus to the placenta.

Unconditioned response (UCR) The response portion of a reflex, which is reliably elicited by a stimulus (UCS).

Unconditioned stimulus (UCS) The stimulus portion of a reflex, which reliably elicits a respondent behavior (UCR).

Underextension A language error in which children fail to apply labels they know to things for which the labels are appropriate.

Universals of development Aspects of development or behavior that are common to children everywhere.

Utilization deficiency The failure of a recently developed mnemonic strategy to facilitate recall.

Validity The accuracy with which a measuring instrument assesses the attribute that it is designed to measure. A necessary property of a standardized test.

Variable Any factor that can take on different values along a dimension.

Vestibular sensitivity The perceptual experience that results from motion of the body and the pull of gravity.

Vicarious punishment Punishing consequences experienced when viewing a model that affect an observer similarly.

Vicarious reinforcement Reinforcing consequences experienced when viewing a model that affect an observer similarly.

Visual accommodation The automatic adjustment of the lens of the eye to produce a focused image of an object on the light-sensitive tissue at the back of the eye.

Visual acuity The clarity with which visual images can be perceived.

Visual self-recognition The ability to recognize oneself; often studied in babies by having them look into mirrors.

Wariness of strangers A general fear of unfamiliar people that appears in many infants at around 8 months of age and indicates the formation of the attachment bond.

Whole-word An approach to reading instruction that stresses learning and visual retrieval of entire words.

47,XYY syndrome A chromosomal disorder of males in which an extra Y chromosome is present; men with the syndrome have large body builds and very masculine personality characteristics.

Zeitgeist The spirit of the times, or the ideas shared by most scientists during a given period.

Zone of proximal development Vygotsky's term for the difference between what children can do by themselves and what they can do with help from an adult.

Zygote A fertilized ovum.

ABBEDUTO, L., DAVIES, B., & FURMAN, L. (1998). The development of speech act comprehension in mentally retarded individuals and nonretarded children. *Child Development, 59,* 1460–1472.

ABEL, E. L. (1980). Fetal alcohol syndrome: Behavioral teratology. *Psychological Bulletin, 87,* 29–50.

ABEL, E. L. (1981). Behavioral teratology of alcohol. *Psychological Bulletin, 90,* 564–581.

ABOUD, F. E. (1985). Children's application of attribution principles to social comparisons. *Child Development, 56,* 682–688.

ABOUD, F. E., & MENDELSON, M. J. (1996). Determinants of friendship selection and quality: Links to child-mother attachment. In W. M. Bukowski, A. F. Newcomb, & W. W. Hartup (Eds.), *The company they keep: Friendship in childhood and adolescence.* New York: Cambridge University Press.

ABRAMOVITCH, R., & GRUSEC, J. E. (1978). Peer imitation in a natural setting. *Child Development, 49,* 60–65.

ABRAMOVITCH, R., CORTER, C., PEPLER, D. J., & STANHOPE, L. (1986). Sibling and peer interaction: A final follow-up and a comparison. *Child Development, 57,* 217–229.

ACKERMAN, B. P. (1993). Children's understanding of the speaker's meaning in referential communication. *Journal of Experimental Child Psychology, 55,* 56–86.

ACKERMAN, B. P., & SILVER, S. (1990). Children's understanding of private keys in referential communication. *Journal of Experimental Child Psychology, 50,* 217–242.

ACKERMAN, B. P., SZYMANSKI, J., & SILVER, D. (1990). Children's use of common ground in interpreting ambiguous referential utterances. *Developmental Psychology, 26,* 234–245.

ACREDOLO, L. P. (1978). Development of spatial orientation in infancy. *Developmental Psychology, 14,* 224–234.

ACREDOLO, L. P. (1985). Coordinating perspectives on infant spatial orientation. In R. Cohen (Ed.), *The development of spatial cognition.* Hillsdale, NJ: Erlbaum.

ACREDOLO, L. P., & GOODWYN, S. W. (1988). Symbolic gesturing in normal infants. *Child Development, 59,* 450–466.

ACREDOLO, L. P., & GOODWYN, S. W. (1990). Development of communicative gesturing. In R. Vasta (Ed.), *Annals of child development* (Vol. 7). Greenwich, CT: JAI Press.

ADAMS, G. R., ABRAHAM, K. G., & MARKSTROM, C. A. (1987). The relations among identity development, self-consciousness, and self-focusing during middle and late adolescence. *Developmental Psychology, 23,* 292–297.

ADAMS, M. J. (1990). *Beginning to read: Thinking and learning about print.* Cambridge: MIT Press.

ADAMS, M. J. (1990). *Learning to read: Thinking and learning about print.* Cambridge: MIT Press.

ADAMS, M. J., TREIMAN, R., & PRESSLEY, M. (1998). Reading, writing, and literacy. In W. Damon (Series Ed.) & I. E. Sigel & K. A. Renninger (Vol. Eds.), *Handbook of child psychology: Vol. 4. Child psychology in practice* (5th ed.). New York: Wiley.

ADAMS, P. L., MILNER, J. R., & SCHREPF, N. A. (1984). *Fatherless children.* New York: Wiley.

ADAMS, R. J. (1989). Newborns' discrimination among mid- and long-wavelength stimuli. *Journal of Experimental Child Psychology, 47,* 30–141.

ADAMS, R. J. (1995). Further exploration of human neonatal chromatic-achromatic distinction. *Journal of Experimental Child Psychology, 60,* 344–360.

ADAMSON, L. B. (1995). *Communication development during infancy.* Madison, WI: Brown & Benchmark.

ADAMSON, L. B., & BAKEMAN, R. (1991). The development of shared attention during infancy. In R. Vasta (Ed.), *Annals of child development* (Vol. 8). London: Kingsley.

AIELLO, J. R., NICOSIA, G., & THOMPSON, D. E. (1979). Physiological, social, and behavioral consequences of crowding on children and adolescents. *Child Development, 50,* 195–202.

AINSWORTH, M. D. S. (1983). Patterns of infant–mother attachment as related to maternal care: Their early history and their contribution to continuity. In D. Magnusson & V. Allen (Eds.), *Human development: An interactional perspective.* New York: Academic Press.

AINSWORTH, M. D. S. (1992). A consideration of social referencing in the context of attachment theory and research. In S. Feinman (Ed.), *Social referencing and the social construction of reality in infancy.* New York: Plenum.

AINSWORTH, M. D. S., & BOWLBY, J. (1991). An ethological approach to personality development. *American Psychologist, 46,* 331–341.

AINSWORTH, M. D. S., & WITTIG, B. A. (1969). Attachment and exploratory behavior of one-year-olds in a strange situation. In B. M. Foss (Ed.), *Determinants of infant behavior* (Vol. 4). London: Methuen.

AINSWORTH, M. D. S., BLEHAR, M. C., WATERS, E., & WALL, S. (1978). *Patterns of attachment: A psychological study of the strange situation.* Hillsdale, NJ: Erlbaum.

ALESSANDRI, S. M. (1992). Effects of maternal work status in single-parent families on children's perception of self and family and school achievement. *Journal of Experimental Child Psychology, 54,* 417–433.

ALFIERI, T., RUBLE, D. N., & HIGGINS, E. T. (1996). Gender stereotypes during adolescence: Developmental changes and the transition to junior high school. *Developmental Psychology, 32,* 1129–1137.

ALIBALI, M. W., FLEVARES, L. M., & GOLDIN-MEADOW, S. (1997). Assessing knowledge conveyed in gesture: Do teachers have the upper hand? *Journal of Educational Psychology, 89,* 183–193.

ALLEN, L. S., & GORSKI, R. A. (1992). Sexual orientation and the size of the anterior commissure in the human brain. *Proceedings of the National Academy of Sciences, USA, 89,* 7199–7202.

ALLEY, T. R. (1983). Infantile head shape as an elicitor of adult protection. *Merrill-Palmer Quarterly, 29,* 411–427.

ALS, H., DUFFY, F. H., & McANULTY, G. B. (1988). Behavioral differences between preterm and full-term newborns as measured with the APIB System Scores: I. *Infant Behavior and Development, 11,* 305–318.

ALTMAN, L. (1993, July 7). World Bank reports health gains for poor. *New York Times,* p. A6.

AMERICAN ASSOCIATION OF UNIVERSITY WOMEN. (1992). *How schools shortchange women.* Wellesley, MA: American Association of University Women and National Education Association.

AMERICAN PSYCHIATRIC ASSOCIATION. (1994). *Diagnostic and statistical manual of mental disorders* (4th ed.). Washington, DC: Author.

ANDERSON, D. R., LORCH, E. P., FIELD, D. E., COLLINS, P. A., & NATHAN, J. G. (1986). Television viewing at home: Age trends in visual attention and time with T.V. *Child Development, 57,* 1024–1033.

ANDERSON, E., HETHERINGTON, E. M., CLINGEMPEEL, W. G. (1989). Transformations in family relations at puberty: Effects of family context. *Journal of Early Adolescence, 9,* 310–334.

ANDERSON, G. M., & ALLISON, D. J. (1990). Intrauterine growth retardation and the routine use of ultrasound. In R. B. Goldbloom & R. S. Lawrence (Eds.), *Preventing disease: Beyond the rhetoric.* New York: Springer-Verlag.

ANDERSSON, B.-E. (1992). Effects of day-care on cognitive and socio-emotional competence of thirteen-year-old Swedish schoolchildren. *Child Development, 63,* 20–36.

ANGLIN, J. M. (1993). Vocabulary development: A morphological analysis. *Monographs of the Society for Research in Child Development, 58*(10, Serial No. 238).

ANGOFF, W. H. (1988). The nature–nurture debate, aptitudes, and group differences. *American Psychologist, 43,* 713–720.

ANISFELD, E., CASPER, V., NOZYCE, M., & CUNNINGHAM, N. (1990). Does infant carrying promote attachment? An experimental study of the effects of increased physical contact on the development of attachment. *Child Development, 61,* 1617–1627.

ANISFELD, M. (1991). Neonatal imitation. *Developmental Review, 11,* 60–97.

ANISFELD, M. (1996). Only tongue protrusion modeling is matched by neonates. *Developmental Review, 16,* 149–161.

ANTELL, S. E., & KEATING, D. P. (1983). Perception of numerical invariance in neonates. *Child Development, 54,* 695–701.

ANTONINI, A., & STRYKER, M. P. (1993). Rapid remodeling of axonal arbors in the visual cortex. *Science, 260,* 1819–1821.

APGAR, V. (1953). A proposal for a new method of evaluation of the newborn infant. *Current Researches in Anesthesia and Analgesia, 32,* 260–267.

APPEL, L. F., COOPER, R. G., McCARRELL, N., SIMS-KNIGHT, J., YUSSEN, S. R., & FLAVELL, J. H. (1972). The development of the distinction between perceiving and memorizing. *Child Development, 43,* 1365–1381.

APPLEY, M. (1986). G. Stanley Hall: Vow on Mount Owen. In S. H. Hulse & B. F. Green (Eds.), *One hundred years of psychological research in America.* Baltimore: Johns Hopkins University Press.

ARBUTHNOT, J., SPARLING, Y., FAUST, D., & KEE, W. (1983). Logical and moral development in preadolescent children. *Psychological Reports, 52,* 209–210.

ARCHER, J. (1991). The influence of testosterone on human aggression. *British Journal of Psychology, 82,* 1–28.

ARCHER, J. (1992). *Ethology and human development.* London: Harvester Wheatsheaf and Barnes & Noble.

ARCHER, J. (1994). Testosterone and aggression: A theoretical review. *Journal of Offender Rehabilitation, 21,* 3–39.

ARCHER, J. (1996). Sex differences in social behavior: Are the social role and evolutionary explanations compatible? *American Psychologist, 51,* 909–917.

ARIES, P. (1962). *Centuries of childhood: A social history of family life.* New York: Knopf.

ASENDORPF, J. B. (1990). Beyond social withdrawal: Shyness, unsociability, and peer avoidance. *Human Development, 33,* 250–259.

ASENDORPF, J. B. (1990). Development of inhibition during childhood: Evidence for situational specificity and a two-factor model. *Developmental Psychology, 26,* 721–730.

ASENDORPF, J. B. (1994). The malleability of behavioral inhibition: A study of individual developmental functions. *Developmental Psychology, 30,* 912–919.

ASENDORPF, J. B., & BAUDONNIERE, P. (1993). Self-awareness and other-awareness: Mirror self-recognition and synchronic imitation among unfamiliar peers. *Developmental Psychology, 29,* 88–95.

ASENDORPF, J. B., WARKENTIN, V., & BAUDONNIERE, P. (1996). Self-awareness and other-awareness II: Mirror-self recognition, social contingency awareness, and synchronic imitation. *Developmental Psychology, 32,* 313–321.

ASHCRAFT, M. H. (1990). Strategic processing in children's mental arithmetic: A review and proposal. In D. F. Bjorklund (Ed.), *Children's strategies: Contemporary views of cognitive development.* Hillsdale, NJ: Erlbaum.

ASHER, S. R. (1985). An evolving paradigm in social skill training research with children. In B. H. Schneider, K. H. Rubin, & J. E. Ledingham (Eds.), *Children's peer relations: Issues in assessment and intervention.* New York: Springer-Verlag.

ASHER, S. R., & COIE, J. D. (Eds.). (1990). *Peer rejection in childhood.* New York: Cambridge University Press.

ASHER, S. R., & HYMEL, S. (1981). Children's social competence in peer relations: Sociometric and behavioral assessment. In J. D. Wine & M. D. Smye (Eds.), *Social competence.* New York: Guilford.

ASHER, S. R., PARKER, J. G., & WALKER, D. L. (1996). Distinguishing friendship from acceptance: Implications for intervention and assessment. In W. M. Bukowski, A. F. Newcomb, & W. W. Hartup (Eds.), *The company they keep: Friendship in childhood and adolescence.* New York: Cambridge University Press.

ASHER, S. R., RENSHAW, P. D., & HYMEL, S. (1982). Peer relations and the development of social skills. In S. G. Moore (Ed.), *The young child: Reviews of research* (Vol. 3). Washington, DC: National Association for the Education of Young Children.

ASHMEAD, D. H., & PERLMUTTER, M. (1980). Infant memory in everyday life. In M. Perlmutter (Ed.), *New directions for child development: No. 10. Children's memory.* San Francisco: Jossey-Bass.

ASHMEAD, D. H., DAVIS, D. L., WHALEN, T., & ODOM, R. D. (1991). Sound localization and sensitivity to interaural time differences in human infants. *Child Development, 62,* 1211–1226.

ASLIN, R. N., & SHEA, S. L. (1990). Velocity thresholds in human infants: Implications for the perception of motion. *Developmental Psychology, 26,* 589–598.

ASLIN, R. N., JUSCZYK, P. W., & PISONI, D. B. (1998). Speech and auditory processing during infancy: Constraints on and precursors to language. In W. Damon (Series Ed.) & D. Kuhn & R. S. Siegler (Vol. Eds.), *Handbook of child psychology: Vol. 2. Cognition, perception, and language* (5th ed.). New York: Wiley.

ASLIN, R. N., PISONI, D. B., & JUSCZYK, P. W. (1983). Auditory development and speech perception in infancy. In P. H. Mussen (Series Ed.) & M. M. Haith & J. J. Campos (Vol. Eds.), *Handbook of child psychology: Vol. 2. Infancy and developmental psychobiology.* New York: Wiley.

ASTINGSON, J. W. (1988). Children's production of commissive speech acts. *Journal of Child Language, 15,* 411–423.

ASTINGTON, J. W. (1993). *The child's discovery of the mind.* Cambridge, MA: Harvard University Press.

ATTILI, G. (1990). Successful and disconfirmed children in the peer group: Indices of social competence within an evolutionary perspective. *Human Development, 33,* 238–249.

ATTILI, G., VERMIGLI, P., & SCHNEIDER, B. H. (1997). Peer acceptance and friendship patterns within a cross-cultural perspective. *International Journal of Behavioral Development, 21,* 277–288.

AZMITIA, M., & MONTGOMERY, R. (1993). Friendship, transactive dialogues, and the development of scientific reasoning. *Social Development, 2,* 202–221.

BACHU, A. (1995). *Fertility of American women: June, 1994* (U.S. Bureau of the Census Current Population Report No. P20–482). Washington, DC: U.S. Government Printing Office.

BAENNINGER, M., & NEWCOMBE, N. (1989). The role of experience in spatial test performance: A meta-analysis. *Sex Roles, 20,* 327–344.

BAHRICK, L. E. (1983). Infants' perception of substance and temporal synchrony in multimodal events. *Infant Behavior and Development, 6,* 429–451.

BAHRICK, L. E. (1992). Infants' perceptual differentiation of amodal and modality-specific audio-visual relations. *Journal of Experimental Child Psychology, 53,* 180–199.

BAHRICK, L. E. (1995). Intermodal origins of self-perception. In P. Rochat (Ed.), *The self in infancy: Theory and research.* Amsterdam: Elsevier.

BAHRICK, L. E., & PICKENS, J. N. (1994). Amodal relations: The basis for intermodal perception and learning in infancy. In D. J. Lewkowicz & R. Lickliter (Eds.), *The development of intersensory perception: Comparative perspectives.* Hillsdale, NJ: Erlbaum.

BAHRICK, L. E., & PICKENS, J. N. (1995). Infant memory for object motion across a period of three months: Implications for a four-phase attention function. *Journal of Experimental Child Psychology, 59,* 343–371.

BAILEY, J. M., & PILLARD, R. C. (1991). A genetic study of male sexual orientation. *Archives of General Psychiatry, 48,* 1089–1096.

BAILEY, J. M., & ZUCKER, K. J. (1995). Childhood sex-typed behavior and sexual orientation: A conceptual analysis and quantitative review. *Developmental Psychology, 31,* 43–55.

BAILEY, J. M., BOBROW, D., WOLFE, M., & MIKACH, S. (1995). Sexual orientation of adult sons of gay fathers. *Developmental Psychology, 31,* 124–129.

BAILEY, J. M., MILLER, J. S., & WILLERMAN, L. (1993). Maternally rated childhood gender nonconformity in homosexuals and heterosexuals. *Archives of Sexual Behavior, 22,* 461–469.

BAILEY, J. M., WILLERMAN, L., & PARKS, C. (1991). A test of the maternal stress theory of human male homosexuality. *Archives of Sexual Behavior, 20,* 277–293.

BAILEY, S. M., & GARN, S. M. (1986). The genetics of maturation. In F. Falkner & J. M.

Tanner (Eds.), *Human growth: A comprehensive treatise.* New York: Plenum.

BAILLARGEON, R. (1986). Representing the existence and the location of hidden objects: Object permanence in 6- and 8-month-old infants. *Cognition, 23,* 21–41.

BAILLARGEON, R. (1987a). Object permanence in $3\frac{1}{2}$- and $4\frac{1}{2}$-month-old infants. *Developmental Psychology, 23,* 655–664.

BAILLARGEON, R. (1987b). Young infants' reasoning about the physical and spatial properties of a hidden object. *Cognitive Development, 2,* 179–200.

BAILLARGEON, R. (1993). The object concept revisited: New directions in the investigation of infants' physical knowledge. In H. W. Reese (Ed.), *Advances in child development and behavior* (Vol. 23). New York: Academic Press.

BAILLARGEON, R. (1994). How do infants learn about the physical world? *Current Directions in Psychological Science, 3,* 133–140.

BAILLARGEON, R. (1995). A model of physical reasoning in infancy. In C. K. Rovee-Collier & L. P. Lipsitt (Eds.), *Advances in infancy research* (Vol. 9). Norwood, NJ: Ablex.

BAILLARGEON, R., KOTOVSKY, L., & NEEDHAM, A. (1995). The acquisition of physical knowledge in infancy. In D. Sperber, D. Premack, & A. J. Premack (Eds.), *Causal cognition: A multidisciplinary debate.* New York: Clarendon Press.

BAKER, L., SONNENSCHEIN, S., SERPELL, R., FERNANDEZ-FEIN, S., & SCHER, D. (1994). *Contexts of emergent literacy: Everyday home experiences of urban pre-kindergarten children.* (Reading Research Report No. 24). National Reading Research Center, University of Georgia and University of Maryland.

BAKER-WARD, L., ORNSTEIN, P. A., & HOLDEN, D. J. (1984). The expression of memorization in early childhood. *Journal of Experimental Child Psychology, 37,* 555–575.

BALABAN, M. T. (1995). Affective influences on startle in five-month-old infants: Reactions to facial expressions of emotion. *Child Development, 66,* 28–36.

BALDWIN D. A. (1991). Infants' contributions to the achievement of joint reference. *Child Development, 63,* 875–890.

BALDWIN, D. A. (1995). Understanding the link between joint attention and language. In C. Moore & P. J. Dunham (Eds.), *Joint attention: Its origins and role in development.* Hillsdale, NJ: Erlbaum.

BALDWIN, D. A., & MOSES, L. J. (1994). Early understanding of referential intent and attentional focus: Evidence from language and emotion. In C. Lewis & P. Mitchell (Eds.), *Children's early understanding of mind.* Hillsdale, NJ: Erlbaum.

BALDWIN, D. A., & MOSES, L. J. (1996). The ontogeny of social information gathering. *Child Development, 67,* 1915–1939.

BALÁZS, R., JORDAN, T., LEWIS, P. D., & PATEL, A. J. (1986). Undernutrition and brain development. In F. Falkner & J. M. Tanner (Eds.), *Human growth: A comprehensive treatise.* New York: Plenum.

BANDURA, A. (1965). Influence of models' reinforcement contingencies on the acquisition of imitative responses. *Journal of Personality and Social Psychology, 1,* 589–595.

BANDURA, A. (1973). *Aggression: A social learning analysis.* Englewood Cliffs, NJ: Prentice-Hall.

BANDURA, A. (1977). *Social learning theory.* Englewood Cliffs, NJ: Prentice Hall.

BANDURA, A. (1978). The self system in reciprocal determinism. *American Psychologist, 33,* 344–358.

BANDURA, A. (1983). Psychological mechanisms of aggression. In R. G. Geen & E. I. Donnerstein (Eds.), *Aggression: Theoretical and empirical reviews* (Vol. 1). New York: Academic Press.

BANDURA, A. (1986). *Social foundations of thought and action: A social cognitive theory.* Englewood Cliffs, NJ: Prentice-Hall.

BANDURA, A. (1989). Social cognitive theory. In R. Vasta (Ed.), *Annals of child development* (Vol. 6). Greenwich, CT: JAI Press.

BANDURA, A. (1991a). Self-regulation of motivation through anticipatory and self-regulatory mechanisms. In R. A. Dienstbier (Ed.), *Perspectives on motivation: Nebraska symposium on motivation* (Vol. 38). Lincoln: University of Nebraska Press.

BANDURA, A. (1991b). Social cognitive theory of moral thought and action. In W. M. Kurtines & J. L. Gewirtz (Eds.), *Handbook of moral behavior and development: Vol. 1. Theory.* Hillsdale, NJ: Erlbaum.

BANDURA, A. (1992). Social cognitive theory. In R. Vasta (Ed.), *Six theories of child development: Revised formulations and current issues.* London: Kingsley.

BANDURA, A. (1994). Social cognitive theory of mass communication. In J. Bryant & D. Zillman (Eds.), *Media effects: Advances in theory and research.* Hillsdale, NJ: Erlbaum.

BANDURA, A. (1997). *Self-efficacy: The exercise of control.* New York: W. H. Freeman.

BANDURA, A., & SCHUNK, D. H. (1981). Cultivating competence, self-efficacy, and intrinsic interest through proximal self-motivation. *Journal of Personality and Social Psychology, 41,* 586–598.

BANKS, M. S., & GINSBURG, A. P. (1985). Infant visual preferences: A review and new theoretical treatment. In H. W. Reese (Ed.), *Advances in child development and behavior* (Vol. 19). Orlando, FL: Academic Press.

BANKS, M. S., & SALAPATEK, P. (1983). Infant visual perception. In P. H. Mussen (Series Ed.) & M. M. Haith & J. J. Campos (Vol. Eds.), *Handbook of child psychology: Vol. 2. Infancy and developmental psychobiology.* New York: Wiley.

BARD, C., HAY, L., & FLEURY, M. (1990). Timing and accuracy of visually directed movements in children: Control of direction and amplitude components. *Journal of Experimental Child Psychology, 50,* 102–118.

BARGLOW, P., VAUGHN, B. E., & MOLITOR, N. (1987). Effects of maternal absence due to employment on the quality of infant–mother attachment. *Child Development, 58,* 45–954.

BARINGA, M. (1993). Death gives birth to the nervous system. But how? *Science, 259,* 762–763.

BARKER, R. G., & WRIGHT, H. F. (1951). *One boy's day: A specimen record of behavior.* New York: Harper & Row.

BARKER, R. G., & WRIGHT, H. F. (1955). *Midwest and its children.* New York: Harper & Row.

BARKLEY, R. A. (1990). *Attention-deficit hyperactivity disorder: A handbook for diagnosis and treatment.* New York: Guilford.

BARNARD, K. E., BEE, H. L., & HAMMOND, M. A. (1984). Home environment and cognitive development in a healthy, low-risk sample: The Seattle study. In A. W. Gottfried (Ed.), *Home environment and early cognitive development.* New York: Academic Press.

BARNARD, K. E., BEE, H. L., & HAMMOND, M. A. (1984a). Developmental changes in maternal interactions with term and preterm infants. *International Journal of Behavior and Development, 7,* 101–113.

BARNARD, K. E., MORISSET, C. E., & SPIEKER, S. (1993). Preventive interventions: Enhancing parent–infant relationships. In C. H. Zeanah, Jr. (Ed.), *Handbook of infant mental development.* New York: Guilford.

BARNETT, C. R., LEIDERMAN, P. H., GROBSTEIN, R., & KLAUS, M. H. (1970). Neonatal separation: The maternal side of interactional deprivation. *Pediatrics, 45,* 197–205.

BARNETT, M. A. (1987). Empathy and related responses in children. In N. Eisenberg & J. Strayer (Eds.), *Empathy and its development.* New York: Cambridge University Press.

BARNETT, W. S. (1995). Long-term effects of early childhood programs on cognitive and school outcomes. In The Center for the Future of Children (Ed.), *The future of children.* Los Altos, CA: The David and Lucile Packard Foundation.

BARON, R. A. (1983). The control of human aggression: A strategy based on incompatible responses. In R. G. Geen & E. I. Donnerstein (Eds.), *Aggression: Theoretical and empirical reviews* (Vol. 2). New York: Academic Press.

BARON-COHEN, S. (1995). *Mindblindness: An essay on autism and theory of mind.* Cambridge: MIT Press.

BARONE, D. (1993). Wednesday's child: Literacy development of children prenatally exposed to crack or cocaine. *Research in the Teaching of English, 27,* 7–45.

BARRERA, M., & MAURER, D. (1981). The perception of facial expressions by the three-month-old. *Child Development, 52,* 203–206.

BARTON, E. J. (1981). Developing sharing: An analysis of modeling and other behavioral techniques. *Behavior Modification, 5,* 386–398.

BASH, M. A. S., & CAMP, B. W. (1985). *Think aloud: Classroom program.* Champaign, IL: Research Press.

BATES, E. (1990). Language about me and you: Pronominal reference and the emerging concept of self. In D. Cicchetti & M. Beeghly (Eds.), *The self in transition: Infancy to childhood.* Chicago: University of Chicago Press.

BATES, E., CAMAIONI, L., & VOLTERRA, V. (1975). The acquisition of performatives prior to speech. *Merrill-Palmer Quarterly, 21,* 205–226.

BATES, E., & CARNEVALE, G. F. (1993). New directions in research on language development. *Developmental Review, 13,* 436–470.

BATES, E., & MacWHINNEY, B. (1982). Functionalist approaches to grammar. In E. Wanner & L. Gleitman (Eds.), *Language acquisition: The state of the art.* New York: Cambridge University Press.

BATES, E., & MacWHINNEY, B. (1987). Competition, variation, language learning. In B. MacWhinney (Ed.), *Mechanisms of language acquisition.* Hillsdale, NJ: Erlbaum.

BATES, E., O'CONNELL, B., & SHORE, C. (1987). Language and communication in infancy. In J. D. Osofsky (Ed.), *Handbook of infant development* (2nd ed.). New York: Wiley.

BATES, J. E. (1987). Temperament in infancy. In J. D. Osofsky (Ed.), *Handbook of infant development* (2nd ed.). New York: Wiley.

BATES, J. E. (1990). Conceptual and empirical linkages between temperament and behavior problems: A commentary on the Sanson, Prior, and Kyrios study. *Merrill-Palmer Quarterly, 36,* 193–199.

BATES, J. E., & BAYLES, K. (1984). Objective and subjective components in mothers' perceptions of their children from age 6 months to 3 years. *Merrill-Palmer Quarterly, 30,* 111–130.

BATES, J. E., BAYLES, K., BENNETT, D. S., RIDGE, B., & BROWN, M. M. (1991). Origins of externalizing behavior problems at eight years of age. In D. Pepler & K. Rubin (Eds.), *Development and treatment of childhood aggression.* Hillsdale, NJ: Erlbaum.

BATES, J. E., & WACHS, T. D. (1994). *Temperament: Individual differences at the interface of biology and behavior.* Washington, DC: American Psychological Association.

BATES, J. E., WACHS, T. D., & EMDE R. N. (1994). Toward practical uses for biological concepts of temperament. In J. E. Bates & T. D. Wachs (Eds.), *Temperament: Individual differences at the interface of biology and behavior.* Washington, DC: American Psychological Association.

BATSON, C. D., & OLESON, K. C. (1991). Current status of the empathy-altruism hypothesis. In M. S. Clark (Ed.), *Review of personality and social psychology: Prosocial behavior.* Newbury Park, CA: Sage.

BAUER, P. J. (1992). Holding it all together: How enabling relations facilitate young children's event recall. *Cognitive Development, 7,* 1–28.

BAUER, P. J. (1993). Identifying subsystems of autobiographical memory: Commentary on Nelson. In C. A. Nelson (Ed.), *Minnesota symposia on child psychology: Vol. 26. Memory and affect in development.* Hillsdale, NJ: Erlbaum.

BAUER, P. J. (1993). Memory for gender-consistent and gender-inconsistent event sequences by twenty-five-month-old children. *Child Development, 64,* 285–297.

BAUER, P. J., & FIVUSH, R. (1992). Constructing event representations: Building on a foundation of variation and enabling relations. *Cognitive Development, 2,* 381–401.

BAUER, P. J., & MANDLER, J. M. (1992). Putting the horse before the cart: The use of temporal order in recall of events by one-year-old children. *Developmental Psychology, 28,* 441–452.

BAUER, P. J., & TRAVIS, L. L. (1993). The fabric of an event: Different sources of temporal invariance differentially affect 24-month-olds' recall. *Cognitive Development, 8,* 319–341.

BAUER, P. J., HERTSGAARD, L. A., & DOW, G. A. (1994). After 8 months have passed: Long-term recall of events by 1- to 2-year-old children. *Memory, 2,* 353–382.

BAUERFELD, S. L., & LACHENMEYER, J. R. (1992). Prenatal nutritional status and intellectual development: Critical review and evaluation. In B. B. Lahey & A. E. Kazdin (Eds.), *Advances in clinical child psychology* (Vol. 14). New York: Plenum.

BAUMRIND, D. (1971). Current patterns of parental authority. *Developmental Psychology Monograph, 4,* 1–103.

BAUMRIND, D. (1989). Rearing competent children. In W. Damon (Ed.), *Child development today and tomorrow.* San Francisco: Jossey-Bass.

BAUMRIND, D. (1991). The influence of parenting style on adolescent competence and substance abuse. *Journal of Early Adolescence, 11,* 56–95.

BAYLEY, N. (1970). Development of mental abilities. In P. H. Mussen (Ed.), *Carmichael's manual of child psychology* (3rd ed., Vol. 1). New York: Wiley.

BAYLEY, N. (1993). *Bayley Scales of Infant Development: Birth to Two Years* (2nd ed.). New York: The Psychological Corporation.

BEAR, G. G. (1989). Sociomoral reasoning and antisocial behaviors among normal sixth graders. *Merrill-Palmer Quarterly, 35,* 181–196.

BEAUCHAMP, D. K., COWART, B. J., MENNELLA, J. A., & MARSH, R. R. (1994). Infant salt taste: Developmental, methodological, and contextual factors. *Developmental Psychobiology, 27,* 353–365.

BECKER, J. (1993). Young children's numerical use of number words: Counting in many-to-one situations. *Developmental Psychology, 29,* 458–465.

BECKER, J. (1994). "Sneak-shoes," "sworders," and "nose-beards": A case study of lexical innovation. *First Language, 14,* 195–211.

BECKER, J. M. F. (1977). A learning analysis of the development of peer-oriented behavior in nine-month-old infants. *Developmental Psychology, 13,* 481–491.

BECKWITH, L., & PARMELEE, A. (1986). EEG patterns of preterm infants, home environment, and later IQ. *Child Development, 57,* 777–789.

BEDARD, J., & CHI, M. T. H. (1992). Expertise. *Current Directions in Psychological Science, 1,* 135–139.

BEEBE, B., ALSON, D., JAFFE, J., FELDSTEIN, S., & CROWN, C. (1988). Vocal congruence in mother–infant play. *Journal of Psycholinguistic Research, 17,* 245–259.

BEEBE, T. P., JR., WILSON, T. E., OGLETREE, D. F., KATZ, J. E., BALHORN, R., SALMERON, M. D., & SIERHAUS, W. J. (1989). Direct observation of native DNA structures with the scanning tun-neling microscope. *Science, 243,* 370–372.

BEHREND, D. A. (1988). Overextensions in early language comprehension: Evidence from a signal detection approach. *Journal of Child Language, 15,* 63–75.

BEHREND, D. A., ROSENGREN, K. S., & PERLMUTTER, M. (1992). The relation between private speech and parental interactive style. In R. M. Diaz & L. E. Berk (Eds.), *Private speech: From social interaction to self-regulation.* Hillsdale, NJ: Erlbaum.

BEHRMAN, R. E., & VAUGHAN, V. C., III. (1987). *Nelson textbook of pediatrics* (3rd ed.). Philadelphia: Saunders.

BEIER, E. G. (1991). Freud: Three contributions. In G. A. Kimble, M. Wertheimer, & C. L. White (Eds.), *Portraits of pioneers in psychology.* Hillsdale, NJ: Erlbaum.

BEILIN, H. (1978). Inducing conservation through training. In G. Steiner (Ed.), *Psychology of the 20th century: Vol. 7. Piaget and beyond.* Zurich: Kindler.

BEILIN, H. (1989). Piagetian theory. In R. Vasta (Ed.), *Annals of child development* (Vol. 6). Greenwich, CT: JAI Press.

BEILIN, H. (1992). Piaget's new theory. In H. Beilin & P. B. Pufall (Eds.), *Piaget's theory: Prospects and possibilities.* Hillsdale, NJ: Erlbaum.

BEILIN, H. (1992a). Piaget's enduring contribution to developmental psychology. *Developmental Psychology, 28,* 191–204.

BEILIN, H. (1992b). Piaget's new theory. In H. Beilin & P. B. Pufall (Eds.), *Piaget's theory: Prospects and possibilities.* Hillsdale, NJ: Erlbaum.

BELLINGER, D., LEVITON, A., NEEDLEMAN, H. L., WATERNAUX, C., & RABINOWITZ, M. (1986). Low-level lead exposure and infant development in the first year. *Neurobehavioral Toxicology and Teratology, 8,* 151–161.

BELSEY, E. M., ROSENBLATT, D. B., LIEBER-MAN, B. A., REDSHAW, M., CALDWELL, J., NOTARIANNI, L., SMITH, R. L., & BEARD, R. W. (1981). The influence of maternal analgesia on neonatal behavior: I. Pethidine. *British Journal of Obstetrics and Gynecology, 887,* 398–406.

BELSKY, J. (1988). The "effects" of infant day care reconsidered. *Early Childhood Research Quarterly, 3,* 235–272.

BELSKY, J. (1996). Parent, infant, and social-contextual antecedents of father–son attachment security. *Developmental Psychology, 32,* 905–913.

BELSKY, J., & ROVINE, M. (1988). Nonmaternal care in the first year of life and infant–parent attachment security. *Child Development, 59,* 157–167.

BELSKY, J., FISH, M., & ISABELLA, R. (1991). Continuity and discontinuity in infant negative and positive emotionality: Family antecedents and attachment consequences. *Developmental Psychology, 27,* 421–431.

BELSKY, J., GILSTRAP, B., & ROVINE, M. (1984). The Pennsylvania Infant and Family Development Project: I. Stability and change in mother–infant and father–infant interaction in a family setting at one, three, and nine months. *Child Development, 55,* 692–705.

BELSKY, J., ROSENBERGER, K., & CRNIC, K. (1995). The origins of attachment security: "Classical" and contextual determinants. In S. Goldberg, R. Muir, & J. Kerr (Eds.), *Attachment theory: Social, developmental, and clinical perspectives.* Hillsdale, NJ: The Analytic Press.

BELSKY, J., ROVINE, M., & TAYLOR, D. G. (1984). The Pennsylvania Infant and Family Development Project; III. The origins of individual differences in infant–mother attachment: Maternal and infant contributions. *Child Development, 55,* 718–728.

BELSKY, J., STEINBERG, L., & DRAPER, P. (1991). Childhood experience, interpersonal development, and reproductive strategy: An evolutionary theory of socialization. *Child Development, 62,* 647–670.

BEM, D. J. (1996). Exotic becomes erotic: A developmental theory of sexual orientation. *Psychological Review, 103,* 320–335.

BEM, S. L. (1974). The measurement of psychological androgyny. *Journal of Consulting and Clinical Psychology, 42,* 155–162.

BEM, S. L. (1975). Sex role adaptability: One consequence of psychological androgyny. *Journal of Personality and Social Psychology, 31,* 634–643.

BEM, S. L. (1979). Theory and measurement of androgyny: A reply to the Pedhazur-Tetenbaum and Locksley-Colten critiques. *Journal of Personality and Social Psychology, 37,* 1047–1054.

BEM, S. L. (1981). Gender schema theory: A cognitive account of sex-typing. *Psychological Review, 88,* 354–364.

BEM, S. L. (1985). Androgyny and gender schema theory. In T. B. Sonderegger (Ed.), *Nebraska symposium on motivation: Psychology and gender* (Vol. 32). Lincoln: University of Nebraska Press.

BEM, S. L. (1987). Masculinity and femininity exist only in the mind of the perceiver. In J. M. Reinisch, L. A. Rosenblum, & S. A. Sanders (Eds.), *Masculinity/femininity: Basic perspectives.* New York: Oxford University Press.

BEM, S. L. (1989). Genital knowledge and gender constancy in preschool children. *Child Development, 60,* 649–662.

BEM, S. L. (1993). *The lenses of gender: Transforming the debate on sexual inequality.* New Haven, CT: Yale University Press.

BENASICH, A. A., & BROOKS-GUNN, J. (1996). Maternal attitudes and knowledge of child-rearing: Associations with family and child outcomes. *Child Development, 67,* 1186–1205.

BENASICH, A. A., BROOKS-GUNN, J., & CLEWELL, B. C. (1992). How do mothers benefit from early intervention programs? *Journal of Applied Developmental Psychology, 13,* 311–362.

BENBOW, C. (1992). Academic achievement in mathematics and science of students between ages 13 and 23: Are there differences among students in the top one percent of mathematics ability? *Journal of Educational Psychology, 84,* 51–61.

BENEDICT, H. (1979). Early lexical development: Comprehension and production. *Journal of Child Language, 6,* 183–200.

BENENSON, J. F. (1993). Greater preference among females than males for dyadic interaction in early childhood. *Child Development, 64,* 544–555.

BENENSON, J. F., & DWECK, C. S. (1986). The development of trait explanations and self-evaluations in the academic and social domains. *Child Development, 57,* 1179–1187.

BENENSON, J. F., APOSTOLERIS, N. H., & PARNASS, J. (1997). Age and sex differences in dyadic and group interaction. *Developmental Psychology, 33,* 538–543.

BENOIT, D. (1993). Failure to thrive and feeding disorders. In C. H. Zeanah, Jr. (Ed.), *Handbook of infant mental development.* New York: Guilford.

BENSON, J. B. (1990). The significance and development of crawling in human infancy. In J. E. Clark & J. H. Humphrey (Eds.), *Advances in motor development research* (Vol. 3). New York: AMS Press.

BENSON, J. B., & UZGIRIS, I. C. (1985). Effects of self-initiated locomotion on infant search activity. *Developmental Psychology, 21,* 923–931.

BERENBAUM, S. A. (1990). Congenital adrenal hyperplasia: Intellectual and psychosexual functioning. In C. Holmes (Ed.), *Psychoneuroendocrinology: Brain, behavior, and hormonal interactions.* New York: Springer-Verlag.

BERENBAUM, S. A., & HINES, M. (1992). Early androgens are related to sex-typed toy preferences. *Psychological Science, 3,* 203–206.

BERENBAUM, S. A., & SNYDER, E. (1995). Early hormonal influences on childhood sex-typed activity and playmate preferences: Implications for the development of sexual orientation. *Developmental Psychology, 31,* 31–42.

BERG, W. K., & BERG, K. M. (1987). Psychophysiological development in infancy. In J. Osofsky (Ed.), *Handbook of infant development* (2nd ed.). New York: Wiley.

BERK, L. E. (1994). Why children talk to themselves. *Scientific American, 271,* 78–83.

BERK, L. E., & SPUHL, S. T. (1995). Maternal interaction, private speech, and task performance in preschool children. *Early Childhood Research Quarterly, 10,* 145–169.

BERKO, J. (1958). The child's learning of English morphology. *Word, 14,* 150–177.

BERKOWITZ, L. (1993). *Aggression: Its causes, consequences, and control.* New York: Academic Press.

BERKOWITZ, M. W., GIBBS, J. C., & BROUGHTON, J. M. (1980). The relation of moral judgment stage disparity to developmental effects of peer dialogues. *Merrill-Palmer Quarterly, 26,* 341–357.

BERNDT, T. J. (1979). Developmental changes in conformity to peers and parents. *Developmental Psychology, 15,* 608–616.

BERNDT, T. J. (1981). Age changes and changes over time in prosocial intentions and behavior between friends. *Developmental Psychology, 17,* 408–416.

BERNDT, T. J. (1986a). Children's comments about their friendships. In M. Perlmutter (Ed.), *Minnesota symposia on child psychology: Vol. 18. Cognitive perspectives on children's social and behavioral development.* Hillsdale, NJ: Erlbaum.

BERNDT, T. J. (1986b). Sharing between friends: Contexts and consequences. In E. C. Mueller & C. R. Cooper (Eds.), *Process and outcome in peer relationships.* New York: Academic Press.

BERNDT, T. J. (1988). The nature and significance of children's friendships. In R. Vasta (Ed.), *Annals of child development* (Vol. 5). Greenwich, CT: JAI Press.

BERNDT, T. J. (1989a). Friendships in childhood and adolescence. In W. Damon (Ed.), *Child development today and tomorrow.* San Francisco: Jossey-Bass.

BERNDT, T. J. (1989b). Obtaining support from friends during childhood and adolescence. In D. Belle (Ed.), *Children's social networks and social supports.* New York: Wiley.

BERNDT, T. J. (1996a). Exploring the effects of friendship quality. In W. M. Bukowski, A. F. Newcomb, & W. W. Hartup (Eds.), *The company they keep: Friendship in childhood and adolescence.* New York: Cambridge University Press.

BERNDT, T. J. (1996b). Transitions in friendship and friends' influence. In J. A. Graber, J. Brooks-Gunn, & A. C. Petersen (Eds.), *Transi-*

tions through adolescence: Interpersonal domains and context. Mahwah, NJ: Erlbaum

BERNDT, T. J., & HANNA, N. A. (1995). Intimacy and self-disclosure in friendships. In K. J. Rotenberg (Ed.), *Disclosure processes in children and adolescents.* New York: Cambridge University Press.

BERNDT, T. J., & KEEFE, K. (1995). Friends' influence on adolescents' adjustment to school. *Child Development, 66,* 1312–1329.

BERNDT, T. J., & PERRY, T. B. (1990). Distinctive features and effects of adolescent friendships. In R. Montemayor, G. R. Adams, & T. P. Gullotta (Eds.), *From childhood to adolescence: A transitional period?* London: Sage.

BERNDT, T. J., MILLER, K. E., & PARK, K. (1989). Adolescents' perceptions of friends' and parents' influence on aspects of their school adjustment. *Journal of Early Adolescence, 9,* 419–435.

BERNIER, J. G., & SIEGEL, D. H. (1994). Attention-deficit hyperactivity disorder: A family ecological systems perspective. *Families in Society, 75,* 142–150.

BERRY, G., & ASAMEN, J. K. (Eds.). (1993). *Children and television: Images in a changing sociocultural world.* Newbury Park, CA: Sage.

BERSOFF, D. M., & MILLER, J. G. (1993). Culture, context, and the development of moral accountability judgments. *Developmental Psychology, 29,* 664–676.

BERTENTHAL, B. I. (1996). Origins and early development of perception, action, and representation. *Annual Review of Psychology, 47,* 431–459.

BERTENTHAL, B. I., & BAI, D. L. (1989). Infants' sensitivity to optical flow for controlling posture. *Developmental Psychology, 25,* 936–945.

BERTENTHAL, B. I., & CLIFTON, R. K. (1998). Perception and action. In W. Damon (Series Ed.) & D. Kuhn & R. S. Siegler (Vol. Eds.), *Handbook of child psychology: Vol. 2. Cognition, perception, and language* (5th ed.). New York: Wiley.

BERTENTHAL, B. I., & FISCHER, K. W. (1978). Development of self-recognition in the infant. *Developmental Psychology, 11,* 44–50.

BERTENTHAL, B. I., CAMPOS, J. J., & BARRETT, K. (1984). Self-produced locomotion: An organizer of emotional, cognitive, and social development in infancy. In R. Emde & R. Harmon (Eds.), *Continuities and discontinuities in development.* New York: Plenum.

BERTENTHAL, B. I., CAMPOS, J. J., & HAITH, M. M. (1980). Development of visual organization: The perception of subjective contours. *Child Development, 51,* 1072–1080.

BERTENTHAL, B. I., CAMPOS, J. J., & KERMOIAN, R. (1994). An epigenetic perspective on the development of self-produced locomotion and its consequences. *Current Directions in Psychological Science, 3,* 140–145.

BEST, C. T. (1995). Learning to perceive the sound pattern of English. In C. Rovee-Collier

& L. P. Lipsitt (Eds.), *Advances in infancy research* (Vol. 9). Norwood, NJ: Ablex.

BEST, D. L., & WILLIAMS, J. E. (1993). A cross-cultural viewpoint. In A. E. Beall & R. J. Sternberg (Eds.), *The psychology of gender.* New York: Guilford.

BHAVNAGRI, N., & PARKE, R. D. (1991). Parents as direct facilitators of children's peer relationships: Effects of age of child and sex of parent. *Journal of Social and Personal Relationships, 8,* 423–440.

BIALYSTOK, E., & CUMMINS, J. (1991). Language, cognition, and education of bilingual children. In E. Bialystok (Ed.), *Language processing in bilingual children.* Cambridge: Cambridge University Press.

BICKERTON, D. (1984). The language bioprogram hypothesis. *Behavioral and Brain Sciences, 7,* 173–187.

BIERNAT, M., & WORTMAN, C. (1991). Sharing of home responsibilities between professionally employed women and their husbands. *Journal of Personality and Social Psychology, 60,* 844–860.

BIGELOW, A. E. (1981). The correspondence between self- and image movement as a cue to self-recognition for young children. *Journal of Genetic Psychology, 139,* 11–26.

BIGLER, R. S. (1997). Conceptual and methodological issues in the measurement of children's sex typing. *Psychology of Women Quarterly, 21,* 53–69.

BIGLER, R. S., & LIBEN, L. S. (1990). The role of attitudes and interventions in gender-schematic processing. *Child Development, 61,* 1440–1452.

BIGLER, R. S., & LIBEN, L. S. (1993). A cognitive-developmental approach to social stereotyping and reconstructive memory in Euro-American children. *Child Development, 64,* 1507–1518.

BIJOU, S. W. (1995). *Behavior analysis of child development.* Reno, NV: Context Press.

BILLY, J. O. G., TANFER, K., GRADY, W. R., & KLEPINGER, D. H. (1993). The sexual behavior of men in the United States. *Family Planning Perspectives, 25,* 52–60.

BINSACCA, D. B., ELLIS, J., MARTIN, D. G., & PETITTI, D. B. (1987). Factors associated with low birthweight in an inner-city population: The role of financial problems. *American Journal of Public Health, 77,* 505–506.

BIOLOGICAL SYSTEMS. (1988, June 10). *Science,* p. 1383.

BIRCH, L. L., & BILLMAN, J. (1986). Preschool children's food sharing with friends and acquaintances. *Child Development, 57,* 387–395.

BIRNHOLZ, J. C., & BENACERRAF, B. R. (1983). The development of human fetal hearing. *Science, 222,* 516–518.

BISANZ, J., & LeFEVRE, J. (1990). Strategic and nonstrategic processing in the development of mathematical cognition. In D. F.

Bjorklund (Ed.), *Children's strategies: Contemporary views of cognitive development.* Hillsdale, NJ: Erlbaum.

BIVENS, J. A., & BERK, L. E. (1990). A longitudinal study of the development of elementary school children's private speech. *Merrill-Palmer Quarterly, 36,* 443–463.

BJORKLUND, D. F. (1987). How age changes in knowledge base contri-bute to the development of children's memory: An interpretive review. *Developmental Review, 7,* 93–130.

BJORKLUND, D. F. (Ed.). (1990). *Children's strategies: Contemporary views of cognitive development.* Hillsdale, NJ: Erlbaum.

BJORKLUND, D. F. (1995). *Children's thinking* (2nd ed.). Pacific Grove, CA: Brooks/Cole.

BJORKLUND, D. F. (1997). In search of a metatheory for cognitive development (or, Piaget is dead and I don't feel so good myself). *Child Development, 68,* 144–148.

BJORKLUND, D. F., & COYLE, T. R. (1995). Utilization deficiencies in the development of memory strategies. In F. E. Weinert & W. Schneider (Eds.), *Memory performance and competencies: Issues in growth and development.* Mahwah, NJ: Erlbaum.

BJORKLUND, D. F., & KIPP, K. (1996). Parental investment theory and gender differences in the evolution of inhibition mechanisms. *Psychological Bulletin, 120,* 163–188.

BJORKLUND, D. F., & SCHNEIDER, W. (1996). The interaction of knowledge, aptitude, and strategies in children's memory performance. In H. W. Reese (Ed.), *Advances in child development and behavior* (Vol. 26). San Diego: Academic Press.

BJORKLUND, D. F., MUIR-BROADDUS, J. E., & SCHNEIDER, W. (1990). The role of knowledge in the development of strategies. In D. F. Bjorklund (Ed.), *Children's strategies: Contemporary views of cognitive development.* Hillsdale, NJ: Erlbaum.

BLACKBURN, R. (1993). *The psychology of criminal conduct.* Chichester, England: Wiley.

BLAKE, J., & BOYSSON-BARDIES, B. (1992). Patterns in babbling: A cross-linguistic study. *Journal of Child Language, 19,* 51–74.

BLAKEMORE, J. E. O., LaRUE, A. A., & OLEJNIK, A. B. (1979). Sex-appropriate toy preferences and the ability to conceptualize toys as sex-role related. *Developmental Psychology, 15,* 339–340.

BLANCHARD, R., & BOGAERT, A. F. (1996). Homosexuality in men and number of older brothers. *American Journal of Psychiatry, 153,* 27–31.

BLANCHARD, R., & ZUCKER, K. J. (1994). Re-analysis of Bell, Weinberg, and Hammersmith's data on birth order, sibling sex ratio, and parental age in homosexual men. *American Journal of Psychiatry, 151,* 1375–1376.

BLANCARD, R., ZUCKER, K. J., BRADLEY, S. J., & HUME, C. S. (1995). Birth order and sibling sex ratio in homosexual male adolescents and probably prehomosexual feminine boys. *Developmental Psychology, 31,* 22–30.

BLASI, A. (1980). Bridging moral cognition and moral action: A critical review of the literature. *Psychological Bulletin, 88,*1–45.

BLASI, A. (1983). Moral cognition and moral action: A theoretical perspective. *Developmental Review, 3,* 178–210.

BLASI, A., & GLODIS, K. (1995). The development of identity: A critical analysis from the perspective of the self as subject. *Developmental Review, 15,* 404–433.

BLASS, E. M., & SMITH, B. A. (1992). Differential effects of sucrose, fructose, glucose, and lactose. *Developmental Psychology, 28,* 804–810.

BLASS, E. M., GANCHROW, J. R., & STEINER, J. E. (1984). Classical conditioning in newborn humans 2–48 hours of age. *Infant Behavior and Development, 7,* 223–235.

BLOCK, J., & ROBINS, R. W. (1993). A longitudinal study of consistency and change in self-esteem from early adolescence to early adulthood. *Child Development, 64,* 909–923.

BLOCK, J. H. (1983). Differential premises arising from differential socialization of the sexes: Some conjectures. *Child Development, 54,* 1335–1354.

BLOOM, L. (1973). *One word at a time.* The Hague, Netherlands: Mouton.

BLOOM, L. (1993, Winter). Word learning. *SRCD Newsletter,* pp. 1–13.

BLOOM, L. (1998). Language acquisition in developmental contexts. In W. Damon (Series Ed.) & D. Kuhn & R. S. Siegler (Vol. Eds.), *Handbook of child psychology: Vol. 2. Cognition, perception, and language* (5th ed.). New York: Wiley.

BLOOM, L., HOOD, L., & LIGHTBROWN, P. (1974). Imitation in language development: If, when, and why. *Cognitive Psychology, 6,* 380–420.

BLOOM, L., LIGHTBROWN, P., & HOOD, L. (1975). Structure and variation in child language. *Monographs of the Society for Research in Child Development, 40* (2, Serial No. 160).

BLOOM, L., MARGULIS, C., TINKER, E., & FUJITA, N. (1996). Early conversations and word learning: Contributions from child and adult. *Child Development, 67,* 3154–3175.

BLOOM, P. (1996). Controversies in language acquisition: Word learning and the part of speech. In R. Gelman & T. Au (Eds.), *Perceptual and cognitive development.* San Diego: Academic Press.

BLOUNT, B. G. (1982). The ontogeny of emotions and their vocal expression in infants. In S. A. Kuczaj (Ed.), *Language development* (Vol. 2). Hillsdale, NJ: Erlbaum.

BLURTON-JONES, N. (1972). *Ethological studies of child behavior.* Cambridge: Cambridge University Press.

BLYTH, D. A., SIMMONS, R. G., & CARLTON-FORD, S. (1983). The adjustment of early adolescents to school transitions. *Journal of Early Adolescence, 3,* 105–120.

BOCCIA, M., & CAMPOS, J. J. (1989). Maternal emotional signals, social referencing, and infants' reactions to strangers. In N. Eisenberg (Ed.), *New directions for child development* (Vol. 44). San Francisco: Jossey-Bass.

BODROVA, E., & LEONG, D. J. (1996). *Tools of the mind: The Vygotskian approach to early childhood education.* Englewood Cliffs, NJ: Merrill.

BOGGIANO, A. K., MAIN, D. S., & KATZ, P. A. (1988). Children's preference for challenge: The role of perceived competence and control. *Journal of Personality and Social Psychology, 54,* 134–141.

BOHANNON, J. N., III, & STANOWICZ, L. (1988). The issue of negative evidence: Adult responses to children's language errors. *Developmental Psychology, 24,* 684–689.

BOHANNON, J. N., III, PADGETT, R. J., NELSON, K. E., & MARK, M. (1996). Useful evidence on negative evidence. *Developmental Psychology, 32,* 551–555.

BOISMER, J. D. (1977). Visual stimulation and wake–sleep behavior in human neonates. *Developmental Psychology, 10,* 219–227.

BOLDIZAR, J. P., PERRY, D. G., & PERRY, L. C. (1989). Outcome values and aggression. *Child Development, 60,* 571–579.

BOLES, D. B. (1980). X-linkage of spatial ability: A critical review. *Child Development, 51,* 625–635.

BOLLES, R. C., & BEECHER, M. D. (Eds.). (1988). *Evolution and learning.* Hillsdale, NJ: Erlbaum.

BOOM, J., & MOLENAAR, P. C. M. (1989). A developmental model of hierarchical stage structure in objective moral judgments. *Developmental Review, 9,* 133–145.

BOONE, S. L. (1991). Aggression in African-American boys: A discriminant analysis. *Genetic, Social, and General Psychology Monographs, 117,* 205–228.

BORKE, H. (1975). Piaget's mountains revisited: Changes in the egocentric landscape. *Developmental Psychology, 11,* 240–243.

BORNSTEIN, M. H. (Ed.). (1987). *Sensitive periods in development: Interdisciplinary perspectives.* Hillsdale, NJ: Erlbaum.

BORNSTEIN, M. H. (Ed.). (1991). *Cultural approaches to parenting.* Hillsdale, NJ: Erlbaum.

BORNSTEIN, M. H, & SIGMAN, M. D. (1986). Continuity in mental development from infancy. *Child Development, 57,* 251–274.

BORNSTEIN, M. H., & TAMIS-LeMONDA, C. S. (1990). Activities and interactions of mothers and their firstborn infants in the first six months of life: Covariation, stability, continuity, correspondence, and prediction. *Child Development, 61,* 1206–1217.

BORSTELMANN, L. J. (1983). Children before psychology: Ideas about children from antiquity to the later 1800s. In W. Kessen (Ed.), *Handbook of child psychology: Vol. 1. History, theory, and methods.* New York: Wiley.

BOSTON, M. B., & LEVY, G. D. (1991). Changes and differences in preschoolers' understanding of gender scripts. *Cognitive Psychology, 6,* 417–432.

BOTTOMS, B. L., & GOODMAN, G. S. (Eds.). (1996). *International perspectives on child abuse and children's testimony: Psychological research and law.* Thousand Oaks, CA: Sage.

BOTTOMS, B. L., GOODMAN, G. S., SCHWARTZ-KENNEY, B. M., SACHSEN-MAIER, T., & THOMAS, S. (1990, March). *Keeping secrets: Implications for children's testimony.* Paper presented at the American Psychology and Law Society Meeting, Williamsburg, VA.

BOUCHARD, T. J., JR. (1997). IQ similarity in twins reared apart: Findings and responses to critics. In R. J. Sternberg & E. L. Grigorenko (Eds.), *Intelligence, heredity, and environment.* New York: Cambridge University Press.

BOUCHARD, T. J., JR., & McGUE, M. (1981). Familial studies of in-telligence: A review. *Science, 212,* 1055–1059.

BOUCHARD, T. J., JR., LYKKEN, D. T., McGUE, M., SEGAL, N. L., & TELLEGEN, A. (1990). Sources of human psychological differences: The Minnesota Study of Twins Reared Apart. *Science, 250,* 223–228.

BOUCHARD, T. J., JR., LYKKEN, D. T., TELLEGEN, A., & McGUE, M. (1996). Genes, drives, environment and experience: EPD theory—revised. In C. Benbow & D. Lubinski (Eds.), *From psychometrics to giftedness: Essays in honor of Julian Stanley.* Baltimore: Johns Hopkins University Press.

BOWERMAN, M. (1975). Cross-linguistic similarities at two stages of syntactic development. In E. H. Lenneberg & E. E. Lenneberg (Eds.), *Foundations of language: A multidisciplinary approach.* New York: Academic Press.

BOWERMAN, M. (1976). Semantic factors in the acquisition of rules for word use and sentence construction. In D. M. Morehead & A. E. Morehead (Eds.), *Normal and deficient child language.* Baltimore: University Park Press.

BOWERMAN, M. (1981). Language development. In H. C. Triandis & A. Heron (Eds.), *Handbook of cross-cultural psychology: Vol. 4. Developmental psychology.* Boston: Allyn & Bacon.

BOWERMAN, M. (1982). Reorganizational processes in lexical and syntactic development. In E. Wanner & L. R. Gleitman (Eds.), *Language acquisition: The state of the art.* New York: Cambridge University Press.

BOWERMAN M. (1988). Inducing the latent structure of language. In F. S. Kessel (Ed.), *The development of language and language researchers: Essays in honor of Roger Brown.* Hillsdale, NJ: Erlbaum.

BOWLBY, J. (1969). *Attachment and loss: Vol. 1. Attachment.* New York: Basic Books.

BOWLBY, J. (1973). *Attachment and loss: Vol. 2. Separation.* New York: Basic Books.

BOWLBY, J. (1980). *Attachment and loss: Vol. 3. Loss.* New York: Basic Books.

BOWLBY, J. (1982). *Attachment and loss: Vol. 1. Attachment* (2nd ed.). New York: Basic Books. (Original work published 1969).

BOWLBY, J. (1988). *A secure base: Parent–child attachment and healthy human development.* New York: Basic Books.

BOYES, M. C., & ALLEN, S. G. (1993). Styles of parent–child interaction and moral reasoning in adolescence. *Merrill-Palmer Quarterly, 39,* 551–570.

BRABANT, S., & MOONEY, L. (1986). Sex role stereotyping in the Sunday comics: Ten years later. *Sex Roles, 14,* 141–148.

BRABANT, S., & MOONEY, L. A. (1997). Sex role stereotyping in the Sunday comics: A twenty year update. *Sex Roles, 37,* 269–281.

BRACKBILL, Y., ADAMS, G., CROWELL, D. H., & GRAY, M. L. (1966). Arousal level in neonates and preschool children under continuous auditory stimulation. *Journal of Experimental Child Psychology, 4,* 178–188.

BRACKEN, B. A. (Ed.). (1996). *Handbook of self-concept: Developmental, social, and clinical considerations.* New York: Wiley.

BRADBARD, M. R., MARTIN, C. L., ENDSLEY, R. C., & HALVERSON, C. F. (1986). Influence of sex stereotypes on children's exploration and memory: A competence versus performance distinction. *Developmental Psychology, 22,* 481–486.

BRADDICK, O., & ATKINSON, J. (1988). Sensory selectivity, attentional control, and cross-channel integration in early visual development. In A. Yonas (Ed.), *Minnesota symposia on child psychology: Vol. 20. Perceptual development in infancy.* Hillsdale, NJ: Erlbaum.

BRADLEY, R. H. (1994). The HOME Inventory: Review and reflections. In H. W. Reese (Ed.), *Advances in child development and behavior* (Vol. 25). San Diego: Academic Press.

BRADLEY, R. H., & CALDWELL, B. M. (1984a). 174 children: A study of the relationship between home environment and cognitive development during the first 5 years. In A. W. Gottfried (Ed.), *Home environment and early cognitive development.* New York: Academic Press.

BRADLEY, R. H., & CALDWELL, B. M. (1984b). The relation of infants' home environments to achievement test performance in first grade: A follow-up study. *Child Development, 55,* 803–809.

BRAINE, M. D. S. (1976). Children's first word combinations. *Monographs of the Society for Research in Child Development, 41* (1, Serial No. 164).

BRAINE, M. D. S., & RUMAINE, B. (1983). Logical reasoning. In P. H. Mussen (Series Ed.) & J. H. Flavell & E. M. Markman (Vol. Eds.), *Handbook of child psychology: Vol. 3. Cognitive development.* New York: Wiley.

BRANDT, M. M., & STRATTNER-GREGORY, M. J. (1980). Effect of highlighting intention on intentionality and restitutive justice. *Developmental Psychology, 16,* 147–148.

BRANIGAN, G. (1979). Some reasons why successive single word utterances are not. *Journal of Child Language, 6,* 411–421.

BRAUNGART, J. M., FULKER, D. W., & PLOMIN, R. (1992). Genetic mediation of the home environment during infancy: A sibling adoption study of the HOME. *Developmental Psychology, 28,* 1048–1055.

BRAUNGART, J. M., PLOMIN, R., DeFRIES, J. C., & FULKER, D. W. (1992). Genetic influence on tester-rated infant temperament as assessed by Bayley's Infant Behavior Record: Non-adoptive and adoptive siblings and twins. *Developmental Psychology, 28,* 40–47.

BRAZELTON, T. B. (1982). Joint regulation of neonate-parent behavior. In E. Z. Tronick (Ed.), *Social interchange in infancy: Affect, cognition, and communication.* Baltimore: University Park Press.

BRAZELTON, T. B., & YOGMAN, M. W. (Eds.). (1986). *Affective development in infancy.* Norwood, NJ: Ablex.

BRAZELTON, T. B., NUGENT, J. K., & LESTER, B. M. (1987). Neonatal behavioral assessment scale. In J. D. Osofsky (Ed.), *Handbook of infant development* (2nd ed.). New York: Wiley.

BREINER, S. J. (1990). *Slaughter of the innocents: Child abuse through the ages.* New York: Plenum.

BREMNER, J. G. (1996). *Infancy.* Cambridge, MA: Blackwell.

BRETHERTON, I. (1987). New perspectives on attachment relations: Security, communication, and internal working models. In J. D. Osofsky (Ed.), *Handbook of infant development* (2nd ed.). New York: Wiley.

BRETHERTON, I. (1988). How to do things with one word: The ontogenesis of intentional message making in infancy. In M. D. Smith & J. L. Locke (Eds.), *The emergent lexicon.* San Diego: Academic Press.

BRETHERTON, I. (1993). From dialogue to internal working models: The co-construction of self in relationships. In C. A. Nelson (Ed.), *Minnesota symposium on child development: Vol. 26. Memory and affect in development.* Hillsdale, NJ: Erlbaum.

BRETHERTON, I. (1995). The origins of attachment theory: John Bowlby and Mary Ainsworth. In S. Goldberg, R. Muir, & J. Kerr (Eds.), *Attachment theory: Social, developmental, and clinical perspectives.* Hillsdale, NJ: The Analytic Press.

BRETHERTON, I., & BEEGHLY, M. (1982). Talking about internal states: The acquisition of an explicit theory of mind. *Developmental Psychology, 18,* 906–921.

BRETHERTON, I., & WATSON, M. W. (Eds.). (1990). *New directions for child development: No. 48. Children's perspectives on the family.* San Francisco: Jossey-Bass.

BREWER, W. F., HERDRICH, D. J., & VOSNIADOU, S. (1987, January). *A cross-cultural study of children's development of cosmological models: Samoan and American data.* Paper presented at the Third International Conference on Thinking, Honolulu.

BRIDGES, A. (1986). Actions and things: What adults talk about to 1-year-olds. In S. A. Kuczaj & M. D. Barrett (Eds.), *The development of word meaning.* New York: Springer-Verlag.

BRIDGES, L. J., CONNELL, J. P., & BELSKY, J. (1988). Similarities and differences in infant–mother and infant–father interaction in the Strange Situation: A component process analysis. *Developmental Psychology, 24,* 92–100.

BROBERG, A. G., WESSELS, H., LAMB, M. E., & HWANG, C. P. (1997). Effects of day care on the development of cognitive abilities in 8-year-olds: A longitudinal study. *Developmental Psychology, 33,* 62–69.

BROBERG, A., LAMB, M. E., & HWANG, P. (1990). Inhibition: Its stability and correlates in sixteen- to forty-month-old children. *Child Development, 61,* 1153–1163.

BRODY, G. H. (1998). Sibling relationship quality: Its causes and consequences. *Annual Review of Psychology, 49,* 1–24.

BRODY, G. H. (Ed.). (1996). *Sibling relationships: Their causes and consequences.* Norwood, NJ: Ablex.

BRODY, G. H., & HENDERSON, R. W. (1977). Effects of multiple model variations and rationale provision on the moral judgments and explanations of young children. *Child Development, 48,* 1117–1120.

BRODY, G. H., & SHAFFER, D. R. (1982). Contributions of parents and peers to children's moral socialization. *Developmental Review, 2,* 31–75.

BRODY, G. H., & STONEMAN, Z. (1995). Sibling relationships in middle childhood. In R. Vasta (Ed.), *Annals of child development* (Vol. 11). London: Kingsley.

BRODY, G. H., GRAZIANO, W. G., & MUSSER, L. M. (1983). Familiarity and children's behavior in same-age and mixed-age peer groups. *Developmental Psychology, 19,* 568–576.

BRODY, N. (1997). Intelligence, schooling, and society. *American Psychologist, 52,* 1046–1050.

BRODZINSKY, D. M., LANG, R., & SMITH, D. W. (1995). Parenting adopted children. In M. H. Bornstein (Ed.), *Handbook of parenting: Vol. 3. Status and social conditions of parenting.* Mahwah, NJ: Erlbaum.

BRONFENBRENNER, U. (1962). Soviet methods of character education: Some implications for research. *Religious Education, 57,* 545–561.

BRONFENBRENNER, U. (1970). *Two worlds of childhood: U.S. and U.S.S.R.* New York: Russell Sage Foundation.

BRONFENBRENNER, U. (1979). *The ecology of human development: Experiments by nature and design.* Cambridge: Harvard University Press.

BRONFENBRENNER, U. (1989). Ecological systems theory. In R. Vasta (Ed.), *Annals of child development* (Vol. 6). Greenwich, CT: JAI Press.

BRONFENBRENNER, U. (1992). Ecological

systems theory. In R. Vasta (Ed.), *Six theories of child development: Revised formulations and current issues*. London: Kingsley.

BRONFENBRENNER, U., & CECI, S. J. (1994). Nature–nurture reconceptualized in developmental perspective: A bioecological model. *Psychological Review, 101,* 568–586.

BRONFENBRENNER, U., & MORRIS, P. A. (1998). The ecology of developmental processes. In W. Damon (Ed.), *Handbook of child psychology: Vol. 1. Theoretical models of human development*. New York: Wiley.

BRONSON, W. C. (1981). *Toddlers' behaviors with agemates: Issues of interaction, cognition, and affect*. Norwood, NJ: Ablex.

BRONSTEIN, P. (1994). Differences in mothers' and fathers' behaviors toward children: A cross-cultural comparison. *Developmental Psychology, 20,* 995–1003.

BROOKE, J. (1991, June 15). Signs of life in Brazil's industrial valley of death. *New York Times International*, p. 2.

BROOKS-GUNN, J. (1987). Pubertal processes and girls' psychological adaptation. In R. M. Lerner & T. L. Foch (Eds.), *Biological psychosocial interactions in early adolescence*. Hillsdale, NJ: Erlbaum.

BROOKS-GUNN, J. (1991). Maturational timing variations in adolescent girls, consequences of. In R. M. Lerner, A. C. Petersen, & J. Brooks-Gunn (Eds.), *Encyclopedia of adolescence* (Vol. 2). New York: Garland.

BROOKS-GUNN, J., & CHASE-LANSDALE, P. L. (1995). Adolescent parenthood. In M. H. Bornstein (Ed.), *Handbook of parenting: Vol. 3. Status and social conditions of parenting*. Mahwah, NJ: Erlbaum.

BROOKS-GUNN, J., & LEWIS, M. (1984). The development of early visual self-recognition. *Developmental Review, 4,* 215–239.

BROOKS-GUNN, J., & REITER, E. O. (1990). The role of pubertal processes. In S. S. Feldman & G. R. Elliott (Eds.), *At the threshold: The developing adolescent*. Cambridge: Harvard University Press.

BROOKS-GUNN, J., KLEBANOV, P. K., LIAW, F., & SPIKER, D. (1993). Enhancing the development of low-birthweight premature infants: Changes in cognition and behavior over the first three years. *Child Development, 64,* 736–753.

BROOKS-GUNN, J., KLEBANOV, P., LIAW, F., & DUNCAN, G. (1995). Toward an understanding of the effects of poverty upon children. In H. E. Fitzgerald, B. M. Lester, & B. Zuckerman (Eds.), *Children of pov-erty: Research, health, and policy issues*. New York: Garland.

BROWN, A. L., & CAMPIONE, J. C. (1990). Communities of learning and thinking, or a context by any other name. In D. Kuhn (Ed.), *Developmental perspectives on teaching and learning thinking skills*. Basel, Switzerland: Karger.

BROWN, A. L., & FERRARA, R. A. (1985). Diagnosing zones of proximal development. In J. V. Wertsch (Ed.), *Culture, communication, and cognition: Vygotskian perspectives*. Cambridge: Cambridge University Press.

BROWN, A. L., PALINCSAR, A. S., & ARMBRUSTER, B. B. (1984). Instructing comprehension-fostering activities in interactive learning situations. In H. Mandl, N. L. Stein, & T. Trabasso (Eds.), *Learning and comprehension of text*. Hillsdale, NJ: Erlbaum.

BROWN, B. B. (1990). Peer groups and peer cultures. In S. S. Feldman & G. R. Elliott (Eds.), *At the threshold: The developing adolescent*. Cambridge: Harvard University Press.

BROWN, K. W., & GOTTFRIED, A. W. (1986). Development of cross-modal transfer in early infancy. In L. P. Lipsitt & C. K. Rovee-Collier (Eds.), *Advances in infancy research* (Vol. 4). Norwood, NJ: Ablex.

BROWN, R. (1958a). How shall a thing be called? *Psychological Review, 65,* 14–21.

BROWN, R. (1958b). *Words and things*. Glencoe, IL: Free Press.

BROWN, R. (1973). *A first language: The early stages*. Cambridge: Harvard University Press.

BROWN, R., & HANLON, C. (1970). Derivational complexity and order of acquisition in child speech. In J. R. Hayes (Ed.), *Cognition and the development of language*. New York: Wiley.

BROWNELL, C. A. (1990). Peer social skills in toddlers: Competencies and constraints illustrated by same-age and mixed-age interaction. *Child Development, 61,* 838–848.

BROWNELL, C. A., & BROWN, E. (1992). Peers and play in infants and toddlers. In V. B. Van Hasselt & M. Hersen (Eds.), *Handbook of social development*. New York: Plenum.

BROWNELL, C. A., & CARRIGER, M. S. (1990). Changes in cooperation and self-other differentiation during the second year. *Child Development, 61,* 1164–1174.

BROWNELL, C. A., & STRAUSS, M. A. (1984). Infant stimulation and development: Conceptual and empirical considerations. *Journal of Children in Contemporary Society, 6,* 109–130.

BRUNER, J. (1979). Learning how to do things with words. In D. Aaronson & R. W. Rieber (Eds.), *Psycholinguistic research: Implications and applications*. Hillsdale, NJ: Erlbaum.

BRUNER, J. (1983). *Child's talk: Learning to use language*. New York: Norton.

BRUNER, J., & GOODMAN, C. C. (1947). Value and need as organizing factors in perception. *Journal of Abnormal and Social Psychology, 42,* 33–44.

BRUNER, J., GOODNOW, J. J., & AUSTIN, G. A. (1956). *A study of thinking*. New York: Wiley.

BRUNER, J., ROY, C., & RATNER, N. (1982). The beginnings of request. In K. E. Nelson (Ed.), *Children's language* (Vol. 3). Hillsdale, NJ: Erlbaum.

BRYANT, B. K. (1985). The Neighborhood Walk: Sources of support in middle childhood. *Monographs of the Society for Research in Child Development, 50* (3, Serial No. 210).

BRYDEN, M. P. (1982). *Laterality: Functional asymmetry in the intact brain*. New York: Academic Press.

BUCHER, B., & SCHNEIDER, R. E. (1973). Acquisition and generalization of conservation by pre-schoolers, using operant training. *Journal of Experimental Child Psychology, 16,* 187–204.

BUDWIG, N. (1995). *A developmental-functionalist approach to child language*. Mahwah, NJ: Erlbaum.

BUGENTHAL, D. B., & GOODNOW, J. J. (1998). Socialization processes. In W. Damon (Ed.), *Handbook of child psychology: Vol. 3. Social, emotional, and personality development*. New York: Wiley.

BUHRMESTER, D. (1990). Intimacy of friendship, interpersonal competence, and adjustment during preadolescence and adolescence. *Child Development, 61,* 1101–1111.

BUHRMESTER, D. (1992). The developmental courses of sibling and peer relationships. In F. Boer & J. Dunn (Eds.), *Children's sibling relationships: Developmental and clinical issues*. Hillsdale, NJ: Erlbaum.

BUHRMESTER, D. (1996). Need fulfillment, interpersonal competence, and the developmental contexts of early adolescent friendship. In W. M. Bukowski, A. F. Newcomb, & W. W. Hartup (Eds.), *The company they keep: Friendship in childhood and adolescence*. New York: Cambridge University Press.

BUHRMESTER, D., & FURMAN, W. (1990). Perceptions of sibling relationships during middle childhood and adolescence. *Child Development, 61,* 1387–1398.

BUHRMESTER, D., & PRAGER, K. (1995). Patterns and functions of self-disclosure during childhood and adolescence. In K. J. Rotenberg (Ed.), *Disclosure processes in children and adolescents*. New York: Cambridge University Press.

BUKOWSKI, W. M., & HOZA, B. (1989). Popularity and friendship: Issues in theory, measurement, and outcome. In T. J. Berndt & G. W. Ladd (Eds.), *Peer relationships in child development*. New York: Wiley.

BULLOCK, M., & LUTKENHAUS, P. (1988). The development of volitional behavior in the toddler years. *Child Development, 59,* 664–674.

BULLOCK, M., & LUTKENHAUS, P. (1990). Who am I? Self-understanding in toddlers. *Merrill-Palmer Quarterly, 36,* 217–238.

BURHANS, K. K., & DWECK, C. S. (1995). Helplessness in early childhood: The role of contingent worth. *Child Development, 66,* 1719–1738.

BURTON, R. V. (1963). The generality of honesty reconsidered. *Psychological Review, 70,* 481–499.

BURTON, R. V. (1984). A paradox in theories and research in moral development. In W. M. Kurtines & J. L. Gewirtz (Eds.), *Morality, moral behavior, and moral development*. New York: Wiley.

BUSHNELL, E. W. (1982). Visual-tactual knowledge in 8-, 9-, and 11-month-old infants. *Infant Behavior and Development, 5,* 63–75.

BUSHNELL, E. W. (1994). A dual-processing approach to cross-modal matching: Implications for development. In D. J. Lewkowicz & R. Lickliter (Eds.), *The development of intersensory perception: Comparative perspectives.* Hillsdale, NJ: Erlbaum.

BUSHNELL, I. W. R., SAI, F., & MULLIN, J. T. (1989). Neonatal recognition of the mother's face. *British Journal of Developmental Psychology, 7,* 3–15.

BUSS, A. H., & PLOMIN, R. (1984). *Temperament: Early developing personality traits.* Hillsdale, NJ: Erlbaum.

BUSS, A. H., & PLOMIN, R. (1986). The EAS approach to temperament. In R. Plomin & J. Dunn (Eds.), *The study of temperament: Changes, continuities and challenges.* Hillsdale, NJ: Erlbaum.

BUSS, D. M. (1995). Psychological sex differences: Origins through sexual selection. *American Psychologist, 50,* 164–168.

BUSSEY, K., & BANDURA, A. (1984). Gender constancy, social power, and sex-linked modeling. *Journal of Personality and Social Psychology, 47,* 1292–1302.

BUSSEY, K., & BANDURA, A. (1992). Self-regulatory mechanisms governing gender development. *Child Development, 63,* 1236–1250.

BUSSEY, K., & PERRY, D. G. (1982). Same-sex imitation: The avoidance of cross-sex models or the acceptance of same-sex models? *Sex Roles, 8,* 773–784.

BUTLER, R. (1990). The effects of mastery and competitive conditions on self-assessment at different ages. *Child Development, 61,* 201–210.

BUTLER, R. (1992). What young people want to know when: The effects of mastery and ability on social information seeking. *Journal of Social and Personality Psychology, 62,* 934–943.

BUTLER, R., & RUZANY, N. (1993). Age and socialization effects on the development of social comparison motives and normative ability assessment in kibbutz and urban children. *Child Development, 64,* 532–543.

BUTTERWORTH, G. (1990). Self-perception in infancy. In D. Cicchetti & M. Beeghly (Eds.), *The self in transition: Infancy to childhood.* Chicago: University of Chicago Press.

BUTTERWORTH, G. (1995). Origins of mind in perception and action. In C. Moore & P. J. Dunham (Eds.), *Joint attention: Its origins and role in development.* Hillsdale, NJ: Erlbaum.

BUTTERWORTH, G. (1995). The self as an object of consciousness in infancy. In P. Rochat (Ed.), *The self in infancy: Theory and research.* Amsterdam: Elsevier.

BUZZELLI, C. A. (1995). Teacher-child discourse in the early childhood classroom: A dialogic model of self-regulation and moral development. In S. Reifel (Ed.), *Advances in early education and day care.* (Vol. 7). Greenwich, CT: JAI Press.

BYNE, W., & PARSONS, B. (1993). Human sexual orientation: The biologic theories reappraised. *Archives of General Psychiatry, 50,* 228–239.

BYRNE, B. M. (1996). Academic self-concept: Its structure, measurement, and relation to academic achievement. In B. A. Bracken (Ed.), *Handbook of self-concept: Developmental, social, and clinical considerations.* New York: Wiley.

BYRNES, J. B., & TAKAHIRA, S. (1993). Explaining gender differences on SAT-math items. *Developmental Psychology, 29,* 805–810.

BYRNES, J. P. (1988). Formal operations: A systematic reformulation. *Developmental Review, 8,* 66–87.

CAIN, K. M., & DWECK, C. S. (1995). The relation between motivational patterns and achievement cognitions through the elementary years. *Merrill-Palmer Quarterly, 41,* 25–52.

CAIRNS, E. (1987). *Caught in crossfire: Children and the Northern Ireland conflict.* Belfast, Northern Ireland: Appletree Press.

CAIRNS, E. (1996). *Children and political violence.* Oxford, England: Blackwell.

CAIRNS, R. B. (1986). An evolutionary and developmental perspective on aggressive patterns. In C. Zahn-Waxler, E. M. Cummings, & R. Iannotti (Eds.), *Altruism and aggression: Biological and social origins.* Cambridge: Cambridge University Press.

CAIRNS, R. B. (1998). The making of developmental psychology. In W. Damon (Ed.), *Handbook of child psychology: Vol. 1. Theoretical models of human development.* New York: Wiley.

CAIRNS, R. B., & CAIRNS, B. D. (1988). The sociogenesis of self concepts. In N. Bolger, A. Caspi, G. Downey, & M. Moorehouse (Eds.), *Persons in context: Developmental processes.* New York: Cambridge University Press.

CAIRNS, R. B., CAIRNS, B. D., NECKERMAN, H. J., FERGUSON, L. L., & GARIEPY, J. (1989). Growth and aggression: I. Childhood to early adolescence. *Developmental Psychology, 25,* 320–330.

CAIRNS, R. B., CAIRNS, B. D., NECKERMAN, H. J., GEST, S. D., & GARIEPY, J. (1988). Social networks and aggressive behavior: Peer support or peer rejection? *Developmental Psychology, 24,* 815–823.

CALDERA, Y. M., HUSTON, A. C., & O'BRIEN, M. (1989). Social interactions and play patterns of parents and toddlers with feminine, masculine, and neutral toys. *Child Development, 60,* 70–76.

CALDWELL, B. M. (1964). The effects of infant care. In M. L. Hoffman & L. W. Hoffman (Eds.), *Review of child development research* (Vol. 1). New York: Russell Sage Foundation.

CALDWELL, B. M., & BRADLEY, R. (1979). *Home Observation for Measurement of the Environment.* Unpublished manuscript, University of Arkansas.

CALHOUN, J. B. (1962). Population density and social pathology. *Scientific American, 206,* 139–148.

CALKINS, S. D., & FOX, N. A. (1992). The relations among infant temperament, security of attachment, and behavioral inhibition at twenty-four months. *Child Development, 63,* 1456–1472.

CALLANAN, M. A. (1985). How parents label objects for young children: The role of input in the acquisition of category hierarchies. *Child Development, 56,* 508–523.

CAMARATA, S., & LEONARD, L. B. (1986). Young children pronounce object words more accurately than action words. *Journal of Child Language, 13,* 51–65.

CAMPBELL, R. L., & CHRISTOPHER, J. C. (1996). Moral development theory: A critique of its Kantian presuppositions. *Developmental Review, 16,* 1–47.

CAMPOS, J. J., BERTENTHAL, B. I., & KERMOIAN, R. (1992). Early experience and emotional development: The emergence of wariness of heights. *Psychological Science, 3,* 61–64.

CAMPOS, J. J., HIATT, S., RAMSAY, D., HENDERSON, C., & SVEJDA, M. (1978). The emergence of fear on the visual cliff. In M. Lewis & L. Rosenblum (Eds.), *The origins of affect.* New York: Plenum

CAMPOS, J., MUMME, D., KERMOIAN, R., & CAMPOS, R. (1994). A functionalist perspective on the nature of emotion. In N. Fox (Ed.), *The development of emotion regulation: Biological and behavioral considerations. Monographs of the Society for Research in Child Development, 59*(2–3, Serial No. 240).

CAMPOS, R. G. (1989). Soothing pain-elicited distress in infants with swaddling and pacifiers. *Child Development, 60,* 781–792.

CAMRAS, L. A., MALATESTA, C. Z., & IZARD, C. E. (1991). The development of facial expressions in infancy. In R. Felman & B. Rime (Eds.), *Fundamentals of nonverbal behavior.* Cambridge: Cambridge University Press.

CAMRAS, L., OSTER, L. A., CAMPOS, J. J., MIYAKE, K., & BRADSHAW, D. (1992). Japanese and American infants' responses to arm restraint. *Developmental Psychology, 28,* 578–583.

CANTER, R. J., & AGETON, S. S. (1984). The epidemiology of adolescent sex-role attitudes. *Sex Roles, 11,* 657–676.

CAPECCHI, M. R. (1994, March). Targeted gene replacement. *Scientific American,* pp. 52–59.

CAPLAN, M., VESPO, J. E., PEDERSEN, J., & HAY, D. F. (1991). Conflict and its resolution in small groups of one- and two-year-olds. *Child Development, 62,* 1513–1524.

CAPLAN, P. J., MacPHERSON, G. M., & TOBIN, P. (1985). Do sex-related differences in spatial abilities exist? A multilevel critique with new data. *American Psychologist, 40,* 786–799.

CAPRON, C., & DUYME, M. (1989). Assessment of effects of socio-economic status on IQ in a full cross-fostering study. *Nature, 340,* 552–554.

CARDON, L. R. (1994). Specific cognitive abilities. In J. C. DeFries, R. Plomin, & D. W. Fulker (Eds.), *Nature and nurture during middle childhood*. Oxford, England: Blackwell.

CAREY, S. (1977). The child as word learner. In M. Halle, J. Bresnan, & G. A. Miller (Eds.), *Linguistic theory and psychological reality*. Cambridge: MIT Press.

CAREY, S. (1985). *Conceptual change in childhood*. Cambridge: MIT Press.

CAREY, W. B., & McDEVITT, S. C. (1978). Revision of the Infant Temperament Questionnaire. *Pediatrics, 61,* 735–739.

CARLSON, M., & EARLS, F. (1997). Psychological and neuroendocrinological sequelae of early social deprivation in institutionalized children in Romania. In C. S. Carter, I. I. Lederhendler, & B. Kirkpatrick (Eds.), *The integrative neurobiology of affiliation*. New York: New York Academy of Sciences.

CARLSON, V., CICCHETTI, D., BARNETT, D., & BRAUNWALD, K. G. (1989). Finding order in disorganization: Lessons from research on maltreated infants' attachments to their caregivers. In D. Cicchetti & V. Carlson (Eds.), *Child maltreatment: Theory and research on the causes and consequences of child abuse and neglect.* New York: Cambridge University Press.

CARNEGIE TASK FORCE. (1994). *Starting points: Meeting the needs of our youngest children.* New York: Carnegie Corporation of New York.

CARON, A. J., CARON, R. F., & MacLEAN, D. J. (1988). Infant discrimination of naturalistic emotional expressions: The role of face and voice. *Child Development, 59,* 604–616.

CARPENDALE, J. I. M., & KREBS, D. L. (1995). Variations in moral judgment as a function of type of dilemma and moral choice. *Journal of Personality, 63,* 289–313.

CARR, M., KURTZ, B. E., SCHNEIDER, W., TURNER, L. A., & BORKOWSKI, J. G. (1989). Strategy acquisition and transfer among American and German children: Environmental influences on meta-cognitive development. *Developmental Psychology, 25,* 765–771.

CARRAHER, T. N., CARRAHER, D. W., & SCHLIEMANN, A. D. (1985). Mathematics in the streets and schools. *British Journal of Developmental Psychology, 3,* 21–29.

CARROLL, J. L., & REST, J. R. (1981). Development in moral judgment as indicated by rejection of lower-style statements. *Journal of Research in Personality, 15,* 538–544.

CARTER, D. B., & LEVY, G. D. (1988). Cognitive aspects of early sex-role development: The influence of gender schemas on preschoolers' memories and preferences for sex-typed toys and activities. *Child Development, 59,* 782–792.

CARTER, D. B., & McCLOSKEY, L. A. (1984). Peers and maintenance of sex-typed behavior: The development of children's conceptions of cross-gender behavior in their peers. *Social Cognition, 2,* 294–314.

CASE, R. (1985). *Intellectual development.* New York. Academic Press.

CASE, R. (1991). Stages in the development of the young child's first sense of self. *Developmental Review, 11,* 210–230.

CASE, R. (1992). *The mind's staircase: Exploring the conceptual underpinnings of children's thought and knowledge.* Hillsdale, NJ: Erlbaum.

CASE, R., & OKAMOTO, Y. (1996). The role of central conceptual structures in the development of children's thought. *Monographs of the Society for Research in Child Development, 61* (1–2, Serial No. 246).

CASEY, M. B., NUTTAL, R., PEZARIS, E., & BENBOW, C. P. (1995). The influence of spatial ability on gender differences in mathematics college entrance test scores across diverse samples. *Developmental Psychology, 31,* 697–705.

CASPI, A. (1998). Personality development across the life span. In W. Damon (Ed.), *Handbook of child psychology: Vol. 3. Social, emotional, and personality development.* New York: Wiley.

CASPI, A., & ELDER, G. H., JR. (1988). Childhood precursors of the life course: Early personality and life disadvantage. In E. M. Hetherington, R. M. Lerner, & M. Perlmutter (Eds.), *Child development in a life-span perspective.* Hillsdale, NJ: Erlbaum.

CASPI, A., ELDER, G. H., JR., & BEM, D. J. (1987). Moving against the world: Life-course patterns of explosive children. *Developmental Psychology, 23,* 308–313.

CASPI, A., ELDER, G. H., JR., & BEM, D. J. (1988). Moving away from the world: Life-course patterns of shy children. *Developmental Psychology, 24,* 824–831.

CASPI, A., HENRY, B., McGEE, R. O., MOFFITT, T. E., & SILVA, P. A. (1995). Temperamental origins of child and adolescent behavior problems: From age 3 to age 15. *Child Development, 66,* 55–68.

CASPI, A., MOFFITT, T. E., NEWMAN, D. L., & SILVA, P. A. (1996). Behavioral observations at age 3 predict adult psychiatric disorders: Longitudinal evidence from a birth cohort. *Archives of General Psychiatry, 53,* 1033–1039.

CASSIDY, J. (1988). Child–mother attachment and the self in six-year-olds. *Child Development, 59,* 121–134.

CASSIDY, J., KIRSH, S. J., SCOLTON, K. L., & PARKE, R. D. (1996). Attachment and representations of peer relationships. *Developmental Psychology, 32,* 892–904.

CASSIDY, J., PARKE, R. D., BUTKOVSKY, L., & BRAUNGART, J. M. (1992). Family-peer connections: The roles of emotional expressiveness within the family and children's understanding of emotions. *Child Development, 63,* 603–618.

CATON, H. (1990). *The Samoa reader.* Lanham, MD: University Press of America.

CATRON, T. F., & MASTERS, J. C. (1993). Mothers' and children's conceptualizations of corporal punishment. *Child Development, 64,* 1815–1828.

CATSAMBIS, S. (1994). The path to math: Gender and racial-ethnic differences in mathematics participation from middle school to high school. *Sociology of Education, 67,* 199–215.

CAUGHY, M. O. (1996). Health and environmental effects on the academic readiness of school-age children. *Developmental Psychology, 32,* 515–522.

CAVANAUGH, J. C., & PERLMUTTER, M. (1982). Metamemory: A critical examination. *Child Development, 53,* 11–28.

CECI, S. J. (1990). *On intelligence . . . more or less: A bioecological theory.* Englewood Cliffs, NJ: Prentice Hall.

CECI, S. J. (1991). How much does schooling influence general intelligence and its cognitive components? A reassessment of the evidence. *Developmental Psychology, 27,* 703–722.

CECI, S. J. (1992, September/October). Schooling and intelligence. *Psychological Science Agenda,* pp. 7–9.

CECI, S. J. (1993). Contextual trends in intellectual development. *Developmental Review, 13,* 403–435.

CECI, S. J. (1996). *On intelligence: A bioecological treatise on intellectual development* (expanded ed.). Cambridge: Harvard University Press.

CECI, S. J., & BRUCK, M. (1993). Suggestibility of the child witness: A historical review and synthesis. *Psychological Bulletin, 113,* 403–439.

CECI, S. J., & BRUCK, M. (1995). *Jeopardy in the courtroom: A scientific analysis of children's testimony.* Washington, DC: American Psychological Association.

CECI, S. J., & BRUCK, M. (1998). Children's testimony. In W. Damon (Series Ed.) & I. E. Sigel & K. A. Renninger (Vol. Eds.), *Handbook of child psychology: Vol. 4. Child psychology in practice* (5th ed.). New York: Wiley.

CECI, S. J., & LIKER, L. K. (1986). A day at the races: A study of IQ, expertise, and cognitive complexity. *Journal of Experimental Psychology: General, 115,* 255–266.

CECI, S. J., & WILLIAMS, W. M. (1997). Schooling, intelligence, and income. *American Psychologist, 52,* 1051–1058.

CECI, S. J., LEICHTMAN, M., & WHITE, T. (in press). Interviewing preschoolers: Remembrance of things planted. In D. P. Peters (Ed.), *The child witness in context: Cognitive, social, and legal perspectives.* Dordrecht, Holland: Kluwer.

CHALL, J. S. (1983). *Learning to read: The great debate* (updated ed.). New York: McGraw-Hill.

CHALMERS, J. B., & TOWNSEND, M. A. R. (1990). The effects of training in social perspective taking on socially maladjusted girls. *Child Development, 61,* 178–190.

CHAMBERLAIN, P., & PATTERSON, G. R. (1995). Discipline and child compliance in parenting. In M. H. Bornstein (Ed.), *Handbook of parenting: Vol. 4. Applied and practical parenting.* Mahwah, NJ: Erlbaum.

CHANDLER, M. J. (1973). Egocentrism and antisocial behavior: The assessment and training of social perspective-taking skills. *Developmental Psychology, 9,* 326–332.

CHANDLER, M. J., & LALONDE, C. (1996). Shifting to an interpretive theory of mind: 5-to-7-year-olds' changing conceptions of mental life. In A. J. Sameroff & M. M. Haith (Eds.), *The five to seven year shift: The age of reason and responsibility.* Chicago: University of Chicago Press.

CHANDLER, M. J., GREENSPAN, S., & BARENBOIM, C. (1973). Judgments of intentionality in response to videotaped and verbally presented moral dilemmas: The medium is the message. *Child Development, 44,* 315–320.

CHAPMAN, M. (1988). *Constructive evolution: Origins and development of Piaget's thought.* Cambridge: Cambridge University Press.

CHAPMAN, M. (1992). Equilibration and the dialectics of organization. In H. Beilin & P. B. Pufall (Eds.), *Piaget's theory: Prospects and possibilities.* Hillsdale, NJ: Erlbaum.

CHARLESWORTH, R., & HARTUP, W. W. (1967). Positive social reinforcement in the nursery school peer group. *Child Development, 38,* 993–1002.

CHARLESWORTH, W. R. (1978). Ethology: Its relevance for observational studies of human adaptation. In G. P. Sackett (Ed.), *Observing behavior* (Vol. 1). Baltimore: University Park Press.

CHARLESWORTH, W. R. (1983). An ethological approach to cognitive development. In C. J. Brainerd (Ed.), *Recent advances in cognitive-developmental theory: Progress in cognitive development research.* New York: Springer-Verlag.

CHARLESWORTH, W. R. (1992). Darwin and developmental psychology: Past and present. *Developmental Psychology, 28,* 5–16.

CHARLESWORTH, W. R. (1995). An evolutionary approach to cognition and learning. In C. A. Nelson (Ed.), *Minnesota symposia on child psychology: Vol. 28. Basic and applied perspectives on learning, cognition, and development.* Mahwah, NJ: Erlbaum.

CHASNOFF, I. J., SCHNOLL, S. H., BURNS, W. J., & BURNS, K. (1984). Maternal narcotic substance abuse during pregnancy: Effects on infant development. *Neurobehavioral Toxicology and Teratology, 6,* 277–280.

CHAVEZ, D. (1985). Perpetuation of gender inequality: A content analysis of comic strips. *Sex Roles, 13,* 93–102.

CHEN, C., & STEVENSON, H. W. (1995). Motivation and mathematics achievement: A comparative study of Asian-American, Caucasian-American, and East Asian high school students. *Child Development, 66,* 1215–1234.

CHEN, M. (1985). Gender differences in adolescents' use of and attitudes toward computers. In M. McLaughlin (Ed.), *Communication yearbook* (Vol. 10). Beverly Hills, CA: Sage.

CHEN, X., & RUBIN, K. H. (1994). Family conditions, parental acceptance, and social competence and aggression in Chinese children. *Social Development, 3,* 269–290.

CHEN, X., RUBIN, K. H., & LI, Z. (1995). Social functioning and adjustment in Chinese children: A longitudinal study. *Developmental Psychology, 31,* 531–539.

CHEN, X., RUBIN, K. H., & SUN, Y. (1992). Social reputation and peer relationships in Chinese and Canadian children: A cross-cultural study. *Child Development, 63,* 1336–1343.

CHERNY, S. S. (1994). Home environmental influences on general cognitive ability. In J. C. DeFries, R. Plomin, & D. W. Fulker (Eds.), *Nature and nurture during middle childhood.* Cambridge, MA: Blackwell.

CHERNY, S. S., & CARDON, L. R. (1994). General cognitive ability. In J. C. DeFries, R. Plomin, & D. W. Fulker (Eds.), *Nature and nurture during middle childhood.* Oxford, England: Blackwell.

CHERNY, S. S., FULKER, D. W., CORLEY, R. P., PLOMIN, R., & DeFRIES, J. C. (1994). Continuity and change in infant shyness from 14 to 20 months. *Behavior Genetics, 24,* 365–379.

CHERNY, S. S., FULKER, D. W., EMDE, R. N., ROBINSON, J., CORLEY, R. P., REZNICK, J. S., PLOMIN, R., & DeFRIES, J. C. (1994). A developmental-genetic analysis of continuity and change in the Bayley mental development index from 14 to 24 months: The MacArthur Longitudinal Twin Study. *Psychological Science, 5,* 354–360.

CHERRY, L., & LEWIS, M. (1976). Mothers and two-year-olds. A study of sex differentiated aspects of verbal interaction. *Developmental Psychology, 12,* 278–282.

CHESS, S., & THOMAS, A. (1987). *Origins and evolution of behavior disorders: From infancy to early adult life.* Cambridge: Harvard University Press.

CHI, M. T. H. (1978). Knowledge structures and memory development. In R. S. Siegler (Ed.), *Children's thinking: What develops?* Hillsdale, NJ: Erlbaum.

CHI, M. T. H., & KOESKE, R. D. (1983). Network representation of a child's dinosaur knowledge. *Developmental Psychology, 19,* 29–39.

CHI, M. T. H., GLASER, R., & FARR, M. J. (Eds.). (1988). *The nature of expertise.* Hillsdale, NJ: Erlbaum.

CHIPMAN, S. F., BRUSH, L., & WILSON, D. (Eds.). (1985). *Women and mathematics: Balancing the equation.* Hillsdale, NJ: Erlbaum.

CHOI, S. (1997). Language-specific input and early semantic development: Evidence from children learning Korean. In D. I. Slobin (Ed.), *The crosslinguisitic study of language acquisition: Vol. 5. Expanding the contexts.* Mahwah, NJ: Erlbaum.

CHOI, S., & GOPNIK, A. (1995). Early acquisition of verbs in Korean: A cross-linguistic study. *Journal of Child Language, 22,* 497–530.

CHOMITZ, V. R., CHEUNG, L., & LIEBERMAN, E. (1995). The role of lifestyle in preventing low birth weight. *The future of children*

(Vol. 5, No. 1). Los Angeles: Packard Foundation.

CHOMSKY, N. (1959). A review of B. F. Skinner's *Verbal Behavior. Language, 35,* 26–58.

CHOMSKY, N. (1965). *Aspects of the theory of syntax.* Cambridge: MIT Press.

CHOMSKY, N. (1995). *The minimalist program.* Cambridge: MIT Press.

CHURCH, R. B., & GOLDIN-MEADOW, S. (1986). The mismatch between gesture and speech as an index of transitional knowledge. *Cognition, 23,* 43–71.

CICCHETTI, D. (1991). Fractures in the crystal: Developmental psychopathology and the emergence of self. *Developmental Review, 11,* 271–287.

CICCHETTI, D., & CARLSON, V. (Eds.). (1989). *Child maltreatment: Theory and research on the causes and consequences of child abuse and neglect.* New York: Cambridge University Press.

CICCHETTI, D., BEEGHLY, M., CARLSON, V., & TOTH, S. (1990). The emergence of self in atypical populations. In D. Cicchetti & M. Beegly (Eds.), *The self in transition: Infancy to childhood.* Chicago: University of Chicago Press.

CICCHETTI, D., LYNCH, M., SHONK, S., & MANLY, J. T. (1992). An organizational perspective on peer relations in maltreated children. In R. D. Parke & G. W. Ladd (Eds.), *Family-peer relationships: Modes of linkage.* Hillsdale, NJ: Erlbaum.

CILLESSEN, A. H. N., VAN IJZENDOORN, H. W., VAN LIESHOUT, C. F. M., & HARTUP, W. W. (1992). Heterogeneity among peer-rejected boys: Subtypes and stabilities. *Child Development, 63,* 893–905.

CLARKE, A. M., & CLARKE, A. D. B. (1976). *Early experience: Myth and evidence.* New York: Free Press.

CLARK, E. V. (1982). The young word-maker: A case study of innovation in the child's lexicon. In E. Wanner & L. R. Gleitman (Eds.), *Language acquisition: The state of the art.* Cambridge: Cambridge University Press.

CLARK, E. V. (1983). Meanings and concepts. In P. H. Mussen (Series Ed.) & J. H. Flavell & E. M. Markman (Vol. Eds.), *Handbook of child psychology: Vol. 3. Cognitive development.* New York: Wiley.

CLARK, E. V. (1987). The principle of contrast: A constraint on language acquisition. In B. MacWhinney (Ed.), *Mechanisms of language acquisition.* Hillsdale, NJ: Erlbaum.

CLARK, E. V. (1993). *The lexicon in acquisition.* New York: Cambridge University Press.

CLARK, R. (1977). What's the use of imitation? *Journal of Child Language, 4,* 341–358.

CLARK, R., HYDE, J. S., ESSEX, M. J., & KLEIN, M. H. (1997). Length of maternity leave and quality of mother-infant interactions. *Child Development, 68,* 364–383.

CLARKE, S., & TAFFEL, S. (1995). Changes in

cesarean delivery in the United States, 1988 and 1993. *Birth, 22,* 63–67.

CLARKE-STEWART, K. A. (1989). Infant day care: Maligned or malignant? *American Psychologist, 44,* 266–273.

CLARKE-STEWART, K. A., GRUBER, C. P., & FITZGERALD, L. M. (1994). *Children at home and in day care.* Hillsdale, NJ: Erlbaum.

CLEWELL, W. H., JOHNSON, M. L., MEIER, P. R., NEWKIRK, J. B., ZIDE, S. L., HENDEE, R. W., BOWES, W. A., JR., HECHT, F., O'KEEFE, D., HENRY, G. P., & SHIKES, R. H. (1982). A surgical approach to the treatment of fetal hydrocephalus. *New England Journal of Medicine, 306,* 1320–1325.

CLIFTON, R. K., GWIAZDA, J., BAUER, J. A., CLARKSON, M. G., & HELD, R. M. (1988). Growth in head size during infancy: Implications for sound localization. *Developmental Psychology, 24,* 477–483.

CLINGEMPEEL, W. G., COLYAR, J. J., BRAND, E., & HETHERINGTON, E. M. (1992). Children's relations with maternal grandparents: A longitudinal study of family structure and pubertal status effects. *Child Development, 63,* 1404–1422.

CLOPTON, N. A., & SORELL, G. T. (1997). Gender differences in moral reasoning: Stable or situational? *Psychology of Women Quarterly, 17,* 85–101.

CLUMECK, H. V. (1980). The acquisition of tone. In G. H. Yeni-Komshian, J. Kavanagh, & C. A. Ferguson (Eds.), *Child phonology: Vol. 1. Production.* New York: Academic Press.

COHEN, D. (1979). *J. B. Watson: The founder of behaviorism.* London: Routledge & Kegan Paul.

COHEN, D., & STRAYER, J. (1996). Empathy in conduct-disordered and comparison youth. *Developmental Psychology, 32,* 988–998.

COHEN, S., & WILLS, T. A. (1985). Stress, social support, and the buffering hypothesis. *Psychological Bulletin, 98,* 310–357.

COHEN, S. E. (1974). Developmental differences in infants' attentional responses to face–voice incongruity of mother and stranger. *Child Development, 45,* 1155–1158.

COHN, D. A., COWAN, P. A., COWAN, C. P., & PEARSON, J. (1992). Mothers' and fathers' working models of childhood attachment relationships, parenting styles, and child behavior. *Development and Psychopathology, 4,* 417–431.

COHN, J. F., & TRONICK, E. Z. (1983). Three-month-old infants' reaction to simulated maternal depression. *Child Development, 54,* 185–193.

COHN, J. F., CAMPBELL, S. B., MATIAS, R., & HOPKINS, J. (1990). Face-to-face interactions of postpartum depressed and nondepressed mother-infant pairs at 2 months. *Developmental Psychology, 26,* 15–23.

COIE, J. D., & CILLESSEN, A. H. N. (1993). Peer rejection: Origins and effects on children's development. *Current Directions in Psychological Science, 2,* 89–92.

COIE, J. D., & DODGE, K. A. (1998). Aggression and antisocial behavior. In W. Damon (Ed.), *Handbook of child psychology: Vol. 3. Social, emotional, and personality development.* New York: Wiley.

COIE, J. D., & KREHBIEL, G. (1984). Effects of academic tutoring on the social status of low-achieving, socially rejected children. *Child Development, 55,* 1465–1478.

COIE, J. D., & KUPERSMIDT, J. (1983). A behavioral analysis of emerging social status in boys' groups. *Child Development, 54,* 1400–1416.

COIE, J. D., DODGE, K. A., & KUPERSMIDT, J. B. (1990). Peer group behavior and social status. In S. R. Asher & J. D. Coie (Eds.), *Peer rejection in childhood.* New York: Cambridge University Press.

COIE, J. D., LOCHMAN, J. E., TERRY, R., & HYMAN, C. (1992). Predicting early adolescent disorder from childhood aggression and peer rejection. *Journal of Consulting and Clinical Psychology, 60,* 783–792.

COLBY, A., & KOHLBERG, L. (1987). *The measurement of moral judgment* (Vols. 1–2). New York: Cambridge University Press.

COLE, M. (1998). Culture and schooling. In W. Damon (Series Ed.) & I. E. Sigel & K. A. Renninger (Vol. Eds.), *Handbook of child psychology: Vol. 4. Child psychology in practice* (5th ed.). New York: Wiley.

COLE, P. M. (1986). Children's spontaneous control of facial expression. *Child Development, 57,* 1309–1321.

COLEMAN, W. (1971). *Biology in the nineteenth century: Problems of form, function, and transformation.* New York: Wiley.

COLLAER, M. L., & HINES, M. (1995). Human behavioral sex differences: A role for gonadal hormones during early development? *Psychological Bulletin, 118,* 55–107.

COLLIS, G. M. (1985). On the origins of turn-taking: Alternation and meaning. In M. D. Barrett (Ed.), *Children's single-word speech.* New York: Wiley.

COLOMBO, J. (1993). *Infant cognition: Predicting later intellectual functioning.* Thousand Oaks, CA: Sage.

COLOMBO, J., & BUNDY, R. S. (1981). A method for the measurement of infant auditory selectivity. *Infant Behavior and Development, 4,* 219–223.

COMMONS, M. L., MILLER, P. M., & KUHN, D. (1982). The relation between formal operational reasoning and academic course selection and performance among college freshmen and sophomores. *Journal of Applied Developmental Psychology, 3,* 1–10.

CONDRY, J. C., & ROSS, D. F. (1985). Sex and aggression: The influence of gender label on the perception of aggression in children. *Child Development, 56,* 225–233.

CONGER, D., & ELDER, G. H., JR. (1994). *Families in troubled times.* Hawthorne, NY: Aldine de Gruyter.

CONGER, R. D., GE, X., ELDER, G. H., LORENZ, F. O., & SIMONS, R. L. (1994). Economic stress, coercive family process, and developmental problems of adolescents. *Child Development, 65,* 541–561.

CONNELL, J. P., & ILARDI, B. C. (1987.) Self-system concomitants of discrepancies between children's and teachers' evaluations of academic competence. *Child Development, 58,* 1297–1307.

CONNELL, J. P., & WELLBORN, J. G. (1991). Competence, autonomy, and relatedness: A motivational analysis of self-system processes. In M. R. Gunnar & L. A. Sroufe (Eds.), *Minnesota symposium on child development: Vol. 23. Self processes and development.* Hillsdale, NJ: Erlbaum.

CONSORTIUM FOR LONGITUDINAL STUDIES. (1983). *As the twig is bent . . . lasting effects of preschool programs.* Hillsdale, NJ: Erlbaum.

CONSTANZO, P. R. (1970). Conformity development as a function of self-blame. *Journal of Personality and Social Psychology, 14,* 366–374.

CONTI, D. J., & CAMRAS, L. A. (1984). Children's understanding of conversational principles. *Journal of Experimental Child Psychology, 38,* 456–463.

COOK, E. P. (1985). *Psychological androgyny.* New York: Pergamon.

COOK, E. P. (1987). Psychological androgyny: A review of the research. *The Counseling Psychologist, 15,* 471–513.

COOLEY, C. H. (1902). *Human nature and the social order.* New York: Charles Scribner's Sons.

COOPER, C. R. (1980). Development of collaborative problem solving among preschool children. *Developmental Psychology, 16,* 433–440.

COOPER, N. G. (Ed.). (1994). *The human genome project: Deciphering the blueprint of heredity.* Mill Valley, CA: University Science Books.

COOPER, R. G. (1984). Early number development: Discovering number space with addition and subtraction. In C. Sophian (Ed.), *Origins of cognitive skills.* Hillsdale, NJ: Erlbaum.

COOPER, R. P., & ASLIN, R. N. (1989). The language environment of the young infant: Implications for early perceptual development. *Canadian Journal of Psychology, 43,* 247–265.

COOPER, R. P., & ASLIN, R. N. (1990). Preference for infant-directed speech in the first month after birth. *Child Development, 61,* 1584–1595.

COOPER, R. P., & ASLIN, R. N. (1994). Developmental differences in infant attention to the spectral properties of infant-directed speech. *Child Development, 65,* 1663–1677.

CORINA, D. P., VAID, J., & BELLUGI, U. (1992). The linguistic basis of left hemisphere specialization. *Science, 255,* 1258–1260.

CORNELIUS, M., TAYLOR, P., GEVA, D., & DAY, N. (1995). Prenatal tobacco exposure and marijuana use among adolescents: Effects on offspring gestational age, growth, and morphology. *Pediatrics, 95,* 738–743.

COSTER, W. J., GERSTEN, M. S., BEEGHLY, M., & CICCHETTI, D. (1989). Communicative functioning in maltreated toddlers. *Developmental Psychology, 25,* 1020–1029.

COSTIN, S. E., & JONES, D. C. (1992). Friendship as a facilitator of emotional responsiveness and prosocial interventions among young children. *Developmental Psychology, 28,* 941–947.

COVEY, H. C., MENARD, S., & FRANZESE, R. J. (1997). *Juvenile gangs* (2nd ed.). Springfield, IL: Charles C. Thomas.

COWAN, C. P., & COWAN, P. A. (1992). *When partners become parents.* New York: Basic Books.

COWAN, P. A. (1978). *Piaget: With feeling.* New York: Holt, Rinehart & Winston.

COWAN, P. A., & McHALE, J. P. (1997). *New directions for child psychology: Family-level dynamics and children's development.* San Francisco: Jossey-Bass.

COWAN, P. A., POWELL, D., & COWAN, C. P. (1998). Parenting interventions: A family systems perspective. In W. Damon (Ed.), *Handbook of child psychology: Vol 4. Child psychology in practice.* New York: Wiley.

COX, B. D., & LIGHTFOOT, C. (Eds.). (1997). *Sociogenetic perspectives on internalization.* Mahwah, NJ: Erlbaum.

COX, D., & WATERS, H. S. (1986). Sex differences in the use of organization strategies: A developmental analysis. *Journal of Experimental Child Psychology, 41,* 18–37.

COX, M. J., OWEN, M. T., HENDERSON, V. K., & MARGAND, N. A. (1992). Prediction of infant–father and infant–mother attachment. *Developmental Psychology, 28,* 474–483.

COYLE, T. R., & BJORKLUND, D. F. (1997). Age differences in, and consequences of, multiple- and variable-strategy use on a multitrial sort-recall task. *Developmental Psychology, 33,* 372–380.

COZBY, P. C., BROWN, K. W., WORDEN, P. E., & KEE, D. W. (1998). *Research methods in human development* (2nd ed.). Mountain View, CA: Mayfield.

CRAIG, R. S. (1992). The effect of television's daily part in gender portrayals in television commercials: A continuing analysis. *Sex Roles, 26,* 197–211.

CRAIN-THORESON, C., & DALE, P. S. (1992). Do early talkers become early readers? Linguistic precocity, preschool language, and emergent literacy. *Developmental Psychology, 28,* 421–429.

CRAVENS, H. (1992). A scientific project locked in time: The Terman genetic studies of genius, 1920s–1950s. *American Psychologist, 47,* 183–189.

CRICK, N. R. (1995). Relational aggression: The role of intent attributions, feelings of distress, and provocation type. *Development and Psychopathology, 7,* 313–322.

CRICK, N. R., & DODGE, K. A. (1994). A review and reformulation of social information-processing mechanisms in children's social adjustment. *Psychological Bulletin, 115,* 74–101.

CRICK, N. R., & DODGE, K. A. (1996). Social information-processing mechanisms in reactive and proactive aggression. *Child Development, 67,* 993–1002.

CRICK, N. R., & GROTPETER, J. K. (1995). Relational aggression, gender, and social-psychological adjustment. *Child-Development, 66,* 710–722.

CRICK, N. R., BIGBEE, M. A., & HOWES, C. (1996). Gender differences in children's normative beliefs about aggression: How do I hurt thee? Let me count the ways. *Child Development, 67,* 1003–1014.

CRICK, N. R., CASAS, J. F., & MOSHER, M. (1997). Relational and overt aggression in preschool. *Developmental Psychology, 33,* 579–588.

CRITTENDEN, P. M., & AINSWORTH, M. D. S. (1989). Child maltreatment and attachment theory. In D. Cicchetti & V. Carlson (Eds.), *Child maltreatment: Theory and research on the causes and consequences of child abuse and neglect.* New York: Cambridge University Press.

CROCKETT, L. J., & PETERSEN, A. C. (1987). Pubertal status and psychosocial development: Findings from the early adolescence study. In R. M. Lerner & T. L. Foch (Eds.), *Biological psychosocial interactions in early adolescence.* Hillsdale, NJ: Erlbaum.

CROOK, C. K. (1979). The organization and control of infant sucking. In H. W. Reese & L. P. Lipsitt (Eds.), *Advances in child development and behavior* (Vol. 14). New York: Academic Press.

CROSS, S. E., & MARKUS, H. R. (1993). Gender in thought, belief, and action: A cognitive approach. In A. E. Beall & R. J. Sternberg (Eds.), *The psychology of gender.* New York: Guilford.

CROUCHMAN, M. (1985). What mothers know about their newborns' visual skills. *Developmental Medicine and Child Neurology, 27,* 455–460.

CROUTER, A. C., MANKE, B. A., & MCHALE, S. M. (1995). The family context of gender intensification in early adolescence. *Child Development, 66,* 317–329.

CROWELL, D. H. (1987). Childhood aggression and violence: Contemporary issues. In D. H. Crowell, I. M. Evans, & C. R. O'Donnell (Eds.), *Childhood aggression and violence: Sources of influence, prevention, and control.* New York: Plenum.

CROWELL, J. A., & FELDMAN, S. S. (1991). Mothers' working models of attachment relationships and mother and child behavior during separation and reunion. *Developmental Psychology, 27,* 597–605.

CUMMINGS, E. M., HOLLENBECK, B., IANNOTTI, R., RADKE-YARROW, M., & ZAHN-WAXLER, C. (1986). Early organization of al-truism and aggression: Developmental patterns and individual differences. In C. Zahn-Waxler, E. M. Cummings, & R. Iannotti (Eds.), *Altruism and aggression: Biological and social origins.* New York: Cambridge University Press.

CUMMINGS, S., & TAEBEL, D. (1980). Sex inequality and the reproduction consciousness: An analysis of sex-role stereotyping among children. *Sex Roles, 6,* 631–644.

CUMMINS, J. (1991). Interdependence of first- and second-language proficiency in bilingual children. In E. Bialystok (Ed.), *Language processing in bilingual children.* Cambridge: Cambridge University Press.

CUNNINGHAM, F. G., MacDONALD, P. C., & GANT, N. F. (1989). *Williams obstetrics* (18th ed.). London: Appleton & Lange.

CURTISS, S. (1977). *Genie: A psycholinguistic study of a modern day "wild child."* New York: Academic Press.

CZESCHLIK, T., & ROST, D. H. (1995). Sociometric types and children's intelligence. *British Journal of Developmental Psychology, 13,* 177–189.

DABBS, J. M., JR. (1992). Testosterone measurements in social and clinical psychology. *Journal of Social and Clinical Psychology, 11,* 302–321.

DABBS, J. M., JR., & MORRIS, R. (1990). Testosterone, social class, and antisocial behavior in a sample of 4,462 men. *Psychological Science, 1,* 209–211.

DALY, M., & WILSON, M. (1983). *Sex, evolution, and behavior* (2nd ed.). Boston: PWS.

DAMON, W. (1977). *The social world of the child.* San Francisco: Jossey-Bass.

DAMON, W. (1980). Patterns of change in children's social reasoning: A two-year longitudinal study. *Child Development, 51,* 1010–1017.

DAMON, W. (1981). Exploring children's social cognition on two fronts. In J. H. Flavell & L. Ross (Eds.), *Social cognitive development.* Cambridge: Cambridge University Press.

DAMON, W. (1983). *Social and personality development.* New York: Norton.

DAMON, W., & COLBY, A. (1987). Social influence and moral change. In W. M. Kurtines & J. L. Gewirtz (Eds.), *Moral development through social interaction.* New York: Wiley.

DAMON, W., & HART, D. (1988). *Self-understanding in childhood and adolescence.* New York: Cambridge University Press.

DAMON, W., & HART, D. (1992). Self-understanding and its role in social and moral development. In M. H. Bornstein & M. E. Lamb (Eds.), *Developmental psychology: An advanced textbook* (3rd ed.). Hillsdale, NJ: Erlbaum.

DAMON, W., & KILLEN, M. (1982). Peer interaction and the process of change in children's moral reasoning. *Merrill-Palmer Quarterly, 28,* 347–367.

DANDY, E. B. (1991). *Black communications: Breaking down the barriers.* Chicago: African American Images.

DANEMAN, M., & CASE, R. (1981). Syntactic form, semantic complexity, and short-term memory: Influences on children's acquisition of new linguistic structures. *Developmental Psychology, 17,* 367–378.

DANNEMILLER, J. L. (1985). The early phase of dark adaptation in human infants. *Vision Research, 25,* 207–212.

DANNEMILLER, J. L., & HANKO, S. A. (1987). A test of color constancy in 4-month-old infants. *Journal of Experimental Child Psychology, 44,* 255–267.

DANNER, F. W., & DAY, M. C. (1977). Eliciting formal operations. *Child Development, 48,* 1600–1606.

DARWIN, C. (1872). *The expression of emotions in man and animals.* London: Murray.

DARWIN, C. (1877). A biographical sketch of an infant. *Mind, 2,* 285–294.

DASEN, P. R. (1975). Concrete operational development in three cultures. *Journal of Cross-Cultural Psychology, 6,* 156–172.

D'AUGELLI, A. R., & PATTERSON, C. J. (Eds.). (1995). *Lesbian, gay, and bisexual identities over the lifespan: Psychological perspectives.* New York: Oxford University Press.

DAVIDSON, D. (1996). The role of schemata in children's memory. In H. W. Reese (Ed.), *Advances in child development and behavior* (Vol. 26). San Diego: Academic Press.

DAVIDSON, D., & HOE, S. (1993). Children's recall and recognition memory for typical and atypical actions in script-based stories. *Journal of Experimental Child Psychology, 55,* 104–126.

DAVIDSON, D., CAMERON, P., & JERGOVIC, D. (1995). The effects of children's stereotypes on their memory for elderly individuals. *Merrill-Palmer Quarterly, 41,* 70–90.

DAVIS, K. (1947). Final note on a case of extreme isolation. *American Journal of Sociology, 45,* 554–565.

DAVIS, M., & EMORY, E. (1995). Sex differences in neonatal stress reactivity. *Child Development, 66,* 14–27.

DAVIS, T. L. (1995). Gender differences in masking negative emotions: Ability or motivation? *Developmental Psychology, 31,* 660–667.

DAWKINS, R. (1976). *The selfish gene.* New York: Oxford University Press.

DAY, M. C. (1975). Developmental trends in visual scanning. In H. W. Reese (Ed.), *Advances in child development and behavior* (Vol. 10). New York: Academic Press.

DAY, R. H. (1987). Visual size constancy in infancy. In B. E. McKenzie & R. H. Day (Eds.), *Perceptual development in early infancy: Problems and issues.* Hillsdale, NJ: Erlbaum.

DEARY, I. J. (1995). Auditory inspection time and intelligence: What is the causal direction? *Developmental Psychology, 31,* 237–250.

DEATER-DECKARD, K., SCARR, S., McCARTNEY, K., & EISENBERG, M. (1994). Pater-

nal separation anxiety: Relationships with parenting stress, child-rearing attitudes, and maternal anxieties. *Psychological Science, 5,* 341–346.

DEAUX, K. (1993). Sorry, wrong number—A reply to Gentile's call. Sex or gender? *Psychological Science, 4,* 125–126.

DEBARYSHE, B. D., PATTERSON, G. R., & CAPALDI, D. M. (1993). Performance model for academic achievement in early adolescent boys. *Developmental Psychology, 29,* 795–804.

DeCASPER, A. J., & FIFER, W. P. (1980). Of human bonding: Newborns prefer their mothers' voices. *Science, 208,* 1174–1176.

DeCASPER, A. J., LECANUET, J.-P., BUSNEL, M.-C., GRANIER-DEFERRE, C., & MAUGEAIS, R. (1994). Fetal reactions to recurrent maternal speech. *Infant Behavior and Development, 17,* 159–164.

DeCASPER, A. J., & PRESCOTT, P. A. (1984). Human newborns' perception of male voices: Preference, discrimination, and reinforcing value. *Developmental Psychobiology, 17,* 481–491.

DeCASPER, A. J., & SPENCE, M. J. (1986). Newborns prefer a familiar story over an unfamiliar one. *Infant Behavior and Development, 9,* 133–150.

DeCASPER, A. J., & SPENCE, M. J. (1991). Auditory mediated behavior during the perinatal period: A cognitive view. In M. J. S. Weiss & P. R. Zelazo (Eds.), *Newborn attention: Biological constraints and the influence of experience.* Norwood, NJ: Ablex.

DE COOKE, P. A., & BROWNELL, C. A. (1995). Young children's help-seeking in mastery-oriented contexts. *Merrill-Palmer Quarterly, 41,* 229–246.

DeFRIES, J. C., PLOMIN, R., & FULKER, D. W. (Eds.). (1994). *Nature and nurture during middle childhood* (Chapter 2). Cambridge, MA: Blackwell.

DEL CARMEN, R., PEDERSEN, F. A., HUFFMAN, L. C., & BRYAN, Y. E. (1993). Dyadic distress management predicts subsequent security of attachment. *Infant Behavior and Development, 16,* 131–147.

DEKAY, W. T., & BUSS, D. M. (1992). Human nature, individual differences, and the importance of context: Perspectives from an evolutionary psychology. *Current Directions in Psychological Science, 1,* 184–189.

DEKOVIC, M., & JANSSENS, J. M. A. M. (1992). Parents' childrearing style and child's sociometric status. *Developmental Psychology, 28,* 925–932.

DE LISI, R., & STAUDT, J. (1980). Individual differences in college students' performance on formal operations tasks. *Journal of Applied Developmental Psychology, 1,* 201–208.

DeLOACHE, J. S., CASSIDY, D. J., & CARPENTER, C. J. (1987). The three bears are all boys: Mothers' gender labeling of neutral picture book characters. *Sex Roles, 17,* 163–178.

DeLOACHE, J. S., MILLER, K. F., & PIER-

ROUTSAKSOS, S. L. (1998). Reasoning and problem solving. In W. Damon (Series Ed.) & D. Kuhn & R. S. Siegler (Vol. Eds.), *Handbook of child psychology: Vol. 2. Cognition, perception, and language* (5th ed.). New York: Wiley.

DELOZIER, C. D., & ENGEL, E. (1982). Sexual differentiation as a model for genetic and environmental interaction affecting physical and psychological development. In W. R. Gove & G. R. Carpenter (Eds.), *The fundamental connection between nature and nurture: A review of the evidence.* Lexington, MA: Lexington.

DEMETRAS, M. J., POST, K. N., & SNOW, C. E. (1986). Feedback to first language learners: The role of repetitions and clarification questions. *Journal of Child Language, 13,* 275–292.

DEMETRIOU, A., SHAYER, M., & EFKLIDES, A. (Eds.). (1993). *Neo-Piagetian theories of cognitive development.* New York: Routledge.

D'EMILIO, J. (1983). *Sexual politics, sexual communities: The making of a homosexual minority in the United States, 1940–1970.* Chicago: University of Chicago Press.

DEMOS, V. (1986). Crying in early infancy: An illustration of the motivational function of affect. In T. B. Brazelton & M. Yogman (Eds.), *Affect and early infancy.* Norwood, NJ: Ablex.

DENENBERG, V., & THOMAN, E. (1981). Evidence for a functional role for active (REM) sleep in infancy. *Sleep, 4,* 185–191.

DENHAM, S. A., & McKINLEY, M. (1993). Sociometric nominations of preschoolers: A psychometric analysis. *Early Education and Development, 4,* 109–122.

DENHAM, S. A., ZOLLER, D., & COUCHOUD, E. A. (1994). Socialization of preschoolers' emotion understanding. *Developmental Psychology, 30,* 928–936.

DENNEY, N. W., & DUFFY, D. M. (1974). Possible environmental causes of stages in moral reasoning. *Journal of Genetic Psychology, 125,* 277–284.

DENNIS, W. (1960). Causes of retardation among institutional children: Iran. *Journal of Genetic Psychology, 96,* 47–59.

DENNIS, W. (1973). *Children of the creche.* New York: Appleton-Century-Crofts.

DENNIS, W., & NAJARIAN, P. (1957). Infant development under environmental handicap. *Psychological Monographs, 71* (7, Whole No. 436).

DENTON, K., & ZARBATANY, L. (1996). Age differences in support processes in conversations between friends. *Child Development, 67,* 1360–1373.

DE RIBAUPIERRE, A., RIEBEN, L., & LAUTREY, J. (1991). Developmental change and individual differences: A longitudinal study using Piagetian tasks. *Genetic, Social, and General Psychology Monographs, 117,* 285–311.

DeROSIER, M., KUPERSMIDT, J., & PATTERSON, C. (1994). Children's academic and behavioral adjustment as a function of the chronicity and proximity of peer rejection. *Child Development, 65,* 1799–1813.

DeVILLIERS, J. G. (1980). The process of rule learning in child speech: A new look. In K. E. Nelson (Ed.), *Children's language* (Vol. 2). New York: Gardner.

DeVRIES, R. (1969). Constancy of generic identity in the years three to six. *Monographs of the Society for Research in Child Development, 34,* (3, Serial No. 127).

DeVRIES, R. (1991). The cognitive-developmental paradigm. In W. M. Kurtines & J. L. Gewirtz (Eds.), *Handbook of moral behavior and development: Vol. 1. Theory.* Hillsdale, NJ: Erlbaum.

DeVRIES, M. W., & SAMEROFF, A. J. (1984). Culture and temperament: Influences on infant temperament in three East African societies. *American Journal of Orthopsychiatry, 54,* 83–96.

DEVRIES, R., & ZAN, B. (1994). *Moral classrooms, moral children: Creating a constructivist atmosphere in early education.* New York: Teachers College Press.

De WAAL, F. (1996). *Good natured: The origins of right and wrong in humans and other animals.* Cambridge: Harvard University Press.

De WOLFF, M. S., & VAN IJZENDOORN, M. H. (1997). Sensitivity and attachment: A meta-analysis on parental antecedents of infant attachment. *Child Development, 68,* 571–591.

DIAMOND, A. (1991). Frontal lobe involvement in cognitive changes during the first year of life. In K. Gibson, M. Konner, & A. Petersen (Eds.), *Brain and behavioral development.* New York: Aldine de Gruyter.

DIAMOND, M., & SIGMUNDSON, K. (1997). Sex reassignment at birth: Long-term review and clinical implications. *Archives of Pediatric Adolescent Medicine, 151,* 298–304.

DIAZ, R. M. (1983). Thought and two languages: The impact of bilingualism on cognitive development. *Review of Research in Education, 10,* 23–54.

DIAZ, R. M. (1985). Bilingual cognitive development: Addressing three gaps in current research. *Child Development, 56,* 1376–1388.

DIAZ, R. M., & BERK, L. E. (Eds.). (1992). *Private speech: From social interaction to self-regulation.* Hillsdale, NJ: Erlbaum.

DIAZ, R. M., NEAL, C. J., & VACHIO, A. (1991). Maternal teaching in the zone of proximal development: A comparison of low- and high-risk dyads. *Merrill-Palmer Quarterly, 37,* 83–108.

DICK-READ, G. (1933). *Natural childbirth.* New York: Dell.

DICK-READ, G. (1944). *Childbirth without fear.* New York: Dell.

DIEN, D. S. F. (1982). A Chinese perspective on Kohlberg's theory of moral development. *Developmental Review, 2,* 331–341.

DIENER, C. I., & DWECK, C. S. (1978). An analysis of learned helplessness: Continuous

changes in performance, strategy, and achievement cognitions following failure. *Journal of Personality and Social Psychology, 36,* 451–462.

DIENER, C. I., & DWECK, C. S. (1980). An analysis of learned helplessness: II. The processing of success. *Journal of Personality and Social Psychology, 39,* 940–952.

DIENER, M. L., GOLDSTEIN, L. H., & MANGELSDORF, S. C. (1995). The role of prenatal expectations in parents' reports of infant temperament. *Merrill-Palmer Quarterly, 41,* 172–190.

DINGES, M. M., & OETTING, E. R. (1993). Similarity in drug use patterns between adolescents and their friends. *Adolescence, 28,* 253–266.

DION, K. K., & BERSCHEID, E. (1974). Physical attractiveness and peer perception among children. *Sociometry, 37,* 1–12.

DiPIETRO, J. A. (1981). Rough and tumble play: A function of gender. *Developmental Psychology, 17,* 50–58.

DiPIETRO, J. A., HODGSON, D. M., COSTIGAN, K. A., HILTON, S. C., & JOHNSON, T. R. B. (1996). Fetal neurobehavioral development. *Child Development, 67,* 2553–2567.

DiPIETRO, J. A., HODGSON, D. M., COSTIGAN, K. A., & JOHNSON, T. R. B. (1996). Fetal antecedent of infant temperament. *Child Development, 67,* 2568–2583.

DiPIETRO, J. A., SUESS, P. E., WHEELER, J. S., SMOUSE, P. H., & NEWLIN, D. B. (1995). Reactivity and regulation in cocaine-exposed neonates. *Infant Behavior and Development, 18,* 407–414.

DISHION, T. J. (1990). The family ecology of boys' peer relations in middle childhood. *Child Development, 61,* 874–892.

DITTMANN, R. W., KAPPES, M. H., KAPPES, M. E., BORGER, D., MEYER-BAHLBERG, H. F. L., STEGNER, H., WILLIG, R. H., & WALLIS, H. (1990). Congenital adrenal hyperplasia: II. Gender-related behavior and attitudes in female patients and sisters. *Psychoneuroendocrinology, 15,* 410–420.

DLUGOSZ, L., & BRACKEN, M. B. (1992). Reproductive effects of caffeine: A review and theoretical analysis. *Epidemiological Review, 14,* 83–100.

DODGE, K. A. (1986). A social information processing model of social competence in children. In M. Perlmutter (Ed.), *Minnesota symposia on child psychology: Vol. 18. Cognitive perspectives on children's social and behavioral development.* Hillsdale, NJ: Erlbaum.

DODGE, K. A., & CRICK, N. R. (1990). Social-information processing bases of aggressive behavior in children. *Personality and Social Psychology Bulletin, 16,* 8–22.

DODGE, K. A., & FELDMAN, E. (1990). Issues in social cognition and sociometric status. In S. R. Asher & J. D. Coie (Eds.), *Peer rejection in childhood.* Cambridge: Cambridge University Press.

DODGE, K. A., & SOMBERG, D. R. (1987). Hostile attributional biases among aggressive boys are exacerbated under conditions of threats to the self. *Child Development, 58,* 213–224.

DODGE, K. A., MURPHY, R. R., & BUCHSBAUM, K. (1984). The assessment of intention-cue detection skills in children: Implications for developmental psychopathology. *Child Development, 55,* 163–173.

DONALDSON, M. (1982). Conservation: What is the question? *British Journal of Psychology, 73,* 199–207.

DORE, J. (1976). Children's illocutionary acts. In R. Freedle (Ed.), *Comprehension and production.* Hillsdale, NJ: Erlbaum.

DORE, J. (1985). Holophrases revisited: Their "logical" development during dialog. In M. D. Barrett (Ed.), *Children's single-word speech.* New York: Wiley.

DORNBUSCH, S. M., GLASGOW, K. L., & LIN, I.-C. (1996). The social structure of schooling. *Annual Review of Psychology, 47,* 401–429.

DORNBUSCH, S. M., RITTER, P. L., LEIDERMAN, P. H., ROBERTS, D. F., & FRALEIGH, M. J. (1985). The relation of parenting style to adolescent school performance. *Child Development, 58,* 1244–1257.

DOUGHERTY, T., & HAITH, M. M. (1993, March). *Processing speed in infants and children: A component of IQ?* Paper presented at the meeting of the Society for Research in Child Development, New Orleans.

DOUGHERTY, T. M., & HAITH, M. M. (1997). Infant expectations and reaction time as predictors of childhood speed of processing and IQ. *Developmental Psychology, 33,* 146–155.

DOWLING, M., & BENDELL, D. (1988). Characteristics of small-for-gestational-age infants. *Infant Behavior and Development, 11,* 77.

DOYLE, A., CONNOLLY, J., & RIVEST, L. (1980). The effect of playmate familiarity on the social interactions of young children. *Child Development, 51,* 217–223.

DRAPER, P., & HARPENDING, H. (1988). A sociobiological perspective on the development of human reproductive strategies. In K. B. MacDonald (Ed.), *Sociobiological perspectives on human development.* New York: Springer-Verlag.

DREHER, M. C., & HAYES, J. S. (1993). Triangulation in cross-cultural research of child development in Jamaica. *Western Journal of Nursing Research, 15,* 216–229.

DREHER, M. C., NUGENT, K., & HUDGINS, R. (1994). Prenatal marijuana exposure and neonatal outcomes in Jamaica: An ethnographic study. *Pediatrics, 93,* 254–260.

DROTAR, D. K., ECKERLE, D., SATOLA, J., PALLOTTA, J., & WYATT, B. (1990). Maternal interactional behavior with nonorganic failure-to-thrive infants: A case comparison study. *Child Abuse and Neglect, 14,* 41–51.

DuBOIS, D. L., & HIRSCH, B. J. (1990). School and neighborhood friendship patterns of blacks and whites in early adolescence. *Child Development, 61,* 524–536.

DUBOW, E. F., TISAK, J., CAUSEY, D., HRYSHKO, A., & REID, G. (1991). A two-year longitudinal study of stressful life events, social support, and social problem-solving skills: Contributions to children's behavioral and academic adjustment. *Child Development, 62,* 583–599.

DUCKWORTH, E. (1987). *The having of wonderful ideas and other essays on teaching and learning.* New York: Teachers College Press.

DUDLEY, M., GYLER, L., BLINK-HORN, S., & BARNETT, B. (1993). Psychosocial interventions for very low birthweight infants: Their scope and efficacy. *Australian and New Zealand Journal of Psychiatry, 27,* 74–83.

DUFFY, F. H., ALS, H., & McANULTY, G. B. (1990). Behavioral and electrophysiological evidence for gestational age effects in healthy preterm and full-term infants studied two weeks after expected due date. *Child Development, 61,* 1271–1286.

DUFFY, J., GUNTHER, G., & WALTERS, L. (1997). Gender and mathematical problem solving. *Sex Roles, 37,* 477–494.

DUFRESNE, A., & KOBASIGAWA, A. (1989). Children's spontaneous allocation of study time: Differential and sufficient aspects. *Journal of Experimental Child Psychology, 47,* 274–296.

DUNCAN, G. J., BROOKS-GUNN, J., & KLEBANOV, P. K. (1994). Economic deprivation and early childhood development. *Child Development, 65,* 296–318.

DUNHAM, P., & DUNHAM, F. (1992). Lexical development during middle infancy: A mutually driven infant-caregiver process. *Developmental Psychology, 28,* 414–420.

DUNN, J. (1992). Sisters and brothers: Current issues in developmental research. In F. Boer & J. Dunn (Eds.), *Children's sibling relationships: Developmental and clinical issues.* Hillsdale, NJ: Erlbaum.

DUNN, J. (1993). *Young children's close relationships.* Newbury Park, CA: Sage.

DUNN, J. (1994). Sibling relationships and perceived self-competence: Patterns of stability between childhood and early adolescence. In A. Sameroff & M. M. Haith (Eds.), *Reason and responsibility: The passage through childhood.* Chicago: University of Chicago Press.

DUNN, J. (1996). Sibling relationships and perceived self-competence: Patterns of stability between childhood and early adolescence. In A. J. Sameroff & M. M. Haith (Eds.), *The five to seven year shift: The age of reason and responsibility.* Chicago: University of Chicago Press.

DUNN, J., & KENDRICK, C. (1982). The speech of two- and three-year-olds to infant siblings: "Baby talk" and the context of communication. *Journal of Child Language, 9,* 579–595.

DUNN, J., & McGUIRE, S. (1992). Sibling and peer relationships in childhood. *Journal of Child Psychology and Psychiatry and Allied Disciplines, 33,* 67–105.

DUNN, J., & McGUIRE, S. (1994). Young children's nonshared experiences: A summary of studies in Cambridge and Colorado. In E. M. Hetherington, D. Reiss, & R. Plo-min (Eds.), *Separate social worlds of siblings: The impact of nonshared environment on development.* Hillsdale, NJ: Erlbaum.

DUNN, J., & MUNN, P. (1986). Siblings and the development of prosocial behaviors. *International Journal of Behavioral Development, 9,* 265–284.

DUSEK, J. B., & JOSEPH, G. (1983). The bases of teacher expectancies: A meta-analysis. *Journal of Educational Psychology, 75,* 327–346.

DWECK, C. S. (1975). The role of expectations and attributions in the alleviation of learned helplessness. *Journal of Personality and Social Psychology, 31,* 674–685.

DWECK, C. S. (1986). Motivational processes affecting learning. *American Psychologist, 41,* 1040–1048.

DWECK, C. S. (1991). Self-theories and goals: Their role in motivation, personality, and development. In R. A. Dienstbier (Ed.), *Nebraska Symposia on Motivation* (Vol. 38). Lincoln: University of Nebraska Press.

DWECK, C. S., & GILLIARD, D. (1975). Expectancy statements as determinants of reaction to failure: Sex differences in persistence and expectancy change. *Journal of Personality and Social Psychology, 32,* 1077–1084.

DWECK, C. S., & GOETZ, T. E. (1980). Attributions and learned helplessness. In J. H. Harvey, W. Ickles, & R. F. Kidd (Eds.), *New directions in attribution research* (Vol. 2). Hillsdale, NJ: Erlbaum.

DWECK, C. S., & LEGGETT, E. L. (1988). A social-cognitive approach to motivation and personality. *Psychological Review, 95,* 256–273.

DWECK, C. S., & REPPUCCI, N. D. (1973). Learned helplessness and reinforcement responsibility in children. *Journal of Personality and Social Psychology, 25,* 109–116.

DWECK, C. S., DAVIDSON, W., NELSON, S., & ENNA, B. (1978). Sex differences in learned helplessness: II. The contingencies of evaluative feedback in the classroom, and III. An experimental analysis. *Developmental Psychology, 14,* 268–276.

DWYER, T., & PONSONBY, A. (1995). SIDS epidemiology and incidence. *Pediatric Annals, 24,* 350–356.

DYKENS, E. M., HODAPP, R. M., & LECKMAN, J. F. (1994). *Behavior and development in fragile X syndrome.* London: Sage.

EAGLY, A. H. (1987). *Sex differences: A social-role interpretation.* Hillsdale, NJ: Erlbaum.

EAGLY, A. H. (1995). The science and politics of comparing women and men. *American Psychologist, 50,* 145–158.

EAGLY, A. H., & CROWLEY, M. (1987). Gender and helping behavior: A meta-analytic review of the social psychological literature. *Psychological Bulletin, 100,* 283–308.

EAGLY, A. H., & STEFFEN, V. J. (1986). Gender and aggressive behavior: A meta-analytic review of the social psychological literature. *Psychological Bulletin, 100,* 309–330.

EAST, P. L., & ROOK, K. S. (1992). Compensatory patterns of support among children's peer relationships: A test using school friends, nonschool friends, and siblings. *Developmental Psychology, 28,* 163–172.

EASTERBROOKS, M. A., & GOLDBERG, W. A. (1984). Toddler development in the family: Impact of father involvement and parenting characteristics. *Child Development, 55,* 740–752.

EATON, W. O. (1994). Temperament, development, and the Five-Factor Model: Lessons from activity level. In C. F. Halverson, Jr., G. A. Kohnstamm, & R. P. Martin (Eds.), *The developed structure of temperament and personality from infancy to adulthood.* Hillsdale, NJ: Erlbaum.

EATON, W. O., & ENNS, L. R. (1986). Sex differences in human motor activity level. *Psychological Bulletin, 100,* 19–28.

EATON, W. O., & SAUDINO, K. J. (1992). Prenatal activity level as a temperament dimension? Individual differences and the developmental functions in fetal movement. *Infant Behavior and Development, 15,* 57–70.

EATON, W. O., & YU, A. P. (1989). Are sex differences in child motor activity level a function of sex differences in maturational status? *Child Development, 60,* 1005–1011.

ECCLES, J. S., & MIDGLEY, C. (1990). Changes in academic motivation and self-perception during early adolescence. In R. Montemayor, G. R. Adams, & T. P. Gullotta (Eds.), *From childhood to adolescence: A transitional period?* Newbury Park, CA: Sage.

ECCLES, J. S., MIDGLEY, C., & ADLER, T. (1984). Grade-related changes in the school environment: Effects on achievement motivation. In J. G. Nicholls (Ed.), *The development of achievement motivation.* Greenwich, CT: JAI Press.

ECCLES, J. S., MIDGLEY, C., WIGFIELD, A., BUCHANAN, C. M., REUMAN, D., FLANAGAN, C., & MACIVER, D. (1993). Development during adolescence: The impact of stage-environment fit on young adolescents' experiences in schools and in families. *American Psychologist, 48,* 90–101.

ECCLES, J., WIGFIELD, A., HAROLD, R. D., & BLUMENFELD, P. (1993). Age and gender differences in children's self- and task perceptions during elementary school. *Child Development, 64,* 830–847.

ECKERMAN, C. O. (1993). Imitation and toddlers' achievement of co-ordinated action with others. In J. Nadel & L. Camaioni (Eds.), *New perspectives in early communicative development.* New York: Routledge.

ECKERMAN, C. O., DAVIS, C. C., & DIDOW, S. (1989). Toddlers' emerging ways of achieving social coordinations with a peer. *Child Development, 60,* 440–453.

ECKERMAN, C. O., & STEIN, M. R. (1990). How imitation begets imitation and toddlers' generation of games. *Developmental Psychology, 26,* 370–378.

ECKSTEIN, S., & SHEMESH, M. (1992). The rate of acquisition of formal operational schemata in adolescence: A secondary analysis. *Journal of Research in Science Teaching, 29,* 441–451.

EDELMAN, G. M. (1993). Neural Darwinism: Selection and reentrant signaling in higher brain function. *Neuron, 10,* 115–125.

EDER, R. A. (1989). The emergent personologist: The structure and content of 3 1/2-, 5 1/2-, and 7 1/2-year-olds' concepts of themselves and others. *Child Development, 60,* 1218–1228.

EDER, R. A. (1990). Uncovering young children's psychological selves: Individual and developmental differences. *Child Development, 61,* 849–863.

EDWARDS, C. P. (1986). Cross-cultural research on Kohlberg's stages: The basis for consensus. In S. Modgil & C. Modgil (Eds.), *Lawrence Kohlberg: Consensus and controversy.* Philadelphia: Falmer.

EGELAND, B., & FARBER, E. (1984). Infant–mother attachment: Factors related to its development and changes over time. *Child Development, 55,* 753–771.

EGELAND, B., & HEISTER, M. (1995). The long-term consequences of infant day-care and mother–infant attachment. *Child Development, 66,* 474–485.

EHRHARDT, A. A. (1985). The psychobiology of gender. In A. S. Rossi (Ed.), *Gender and the life course.* New York: Aldine.

EHRHARDT, A. A., & MEYER-BAHLBURG, H. F. L. (1981). Effects of prenatal sex hormones on gender-related behavior. *Science, 211,* 1312–1318.

EIBL-EIBESFELDT, I. (1989). *Human ethology.* Hawthorne, NY: Aldine de Gruyter.

EICHORN, D. (1970). Physiological development. In P. H. Mussen (Ed.), *Carmichael's Manual of Child Psychology* (3rd ed.). New York: Wiley.

EICHORN, D. (1979). Physical development: Current foci of research. In J. D. Osofsky (Ed.), *Handbook of infant development.* New York: Wiley.

EIDUSON, B. T. (1980). Changing sex roles in alternative family styles: Implications for young children. In E. J. Anthony & C. Chiland (Eds.), *The child in his family: Preventive child psychiatry in an age of transition* (Vol. 6). New York: Wiley.

EIDUSON, B. T., KORNFEIN, M., ZIMMERMAN, I. L., & WEISNER, T. S. (1982). Comparative socialization practices in alternative family settings. In M. E. Lamb (Ed.), *Nontraditional families.* New York: Plenum.

EIFERMANN, R. R. (1971). Social play in childhood. In R. E. Herron & B. Sutton-Smith (Eds.), *Child's play.* New York: Wiley.

EILERS, R. E., & OLLER, D. K. (1988). Precursors to speech: What is innate and what is acquired? In R. Vasta (Ed.), *Annals of child development* (Vol. 5). Greenwich, CT: JAI Press.

EIMAS, P. D. (1975). Auditory and phonetic coding of the cues for speech: Discrimination of the [r-l] distinction by young infants. *Perception and Psychophysics, 18,* 341–347.

EISENBERG, N. (1982). The development of reasoning regarding prosocial behavior. In N. Eisenberg (Ed.), *The development of prosocial behavior.* New York: Academic Press.

EISENBERG, N. (1986). *Altruistic emotion, cognition, and behavior.* Hillsdale, NJ: Erlbaum.

EISENBERG, N. (1987). The relation of altruism and other moral behaviors to moral cognition: Methodological and conceptual issues. In N. Eisenberg & J. Strayer (Eds.), *Empathy and its development.* New York: Cambridge University Press.

EISENBERG, N. (1989). Empathy and sympathy. In W. Damon (Ed.), *Child development today and tomorrow.* San Francisco: Jossey-Bass.

EISENBERG, N. (1990). Prosocial development in early and mid-adolescence. In R. Montemayor, G. R. Adams, & T. P. Gullotta (Eds.), *From childhood to adolescence: A transitional period?* Newbury Park, CA: Sage.

EISENBERG, N., & FABES, R. A. (1991). Prosocial behavior and empathy: A multimethod, developmental perspective. In P. Clark (Ed.), *Review of personality and social psychology.* Newbury Park, CA: Sage.

EISENBERG, N., & FABES, R. A. (1998). Prosocial development. In W. Damon (Ed.), *Handbook of child psychology: Vol. 3. Social, emotional, and personality development.* New York: Wiley.

EISENBERG, N., & MURPHY, B. (1995). Parenting and children's moral development. In M. H. Bornstein (Ed.), *Handbook of parenting: Vol. 4. Applied and practical parenting.* Mahwah, NJ: Erlbaum.

EISENBERG, N., CAMERSON, E., TRYON, K., & DODEZ, R. (1981). Socialization of prosocial behavior in the preschool classroom. *Developmental Psychology, 17,* 773–782.

EISENBERG, N., CARLO, G., MURPHY, B., & VAN COURT, P. (1995). Prosocial development in late adolescence: A longitudinal study. *Child Development, 66,* 1179–1197.

EISENBERG, N., FABES, R. A., CARLO, G., SPEER, A. L., SWITZER, G., KARBON, M., & TROYER, D. (1993). The relations of empathy-related and maternal practices to children's comforting behavior. *Journal of Experimental Child Psychology, 55,* 131–150.

EISENBERG, N., MARTIN, C. L., & FABES, R. A. (1996). Gender development and gender effects. In D. C. Berliner & R. C. Calfee (Eds.), *The handbook of educational psychology.* New York: Simon & Schuster.

EISENBERG, N., TRYON, K., & CAMERON, E. (1984). The relation of preschoolers' peer interaction to their sex-typed toy choices. *Child Development, 55,* 1044–1050.

EISENBERG, N., WOLCHIK, S. A., HERNANDEZ, R., & PASTERNACK, J. F. (1985). Parental socialization of young children's play: A short-term longitudinal study. *Child Development, 56,* 1506–1513.

EISENBERG, R. B. (1976). *Auditory competence in early life.* Baltimore: University Park Press.

EISIKOVITS, Z., & SAGI, A. (1982). Moral development and discipline encountered in delinquent and nondelinquent adolescents. *Journal of Youth and Adolescence, 11,* 217–246.

EKMAN, P. (1993). Facial expression and emotion. *American Psychologist, 48,* 384–392.

EL ABD, S., TURK, J., & HILL, P. (1995). Annotation: Psychological characteristics of Turner syndrome. *Journal of Child Psychology and Psychiatry, 36,* 1109–1125.

ELARDO, R., & BRADLEY, R. H. (1981). The Home Observation for Measurement of the Environment (HOME) scale: A review of research. *Developmental Review, 1,* 113–145.

ELDER, G. H., JR. (1998). The life course and human development. In W. Damon (Ed.), *Handbook of child psychology: Vol. 1. Theoretical models of human development.* New York: Wiley.

ELDER, G. H., JR., & CASPI, A. (1988). Human development and social change: An emerging perspective on the life course. In N. Bolger, A. Caspi, G. Downey, & M. Moorehouse (Eds.), *Persons in context: Developmental processes.* New York: Cambridge University Press.

ELDER, G. H., JR., CASPI, A., & DOWNEY, G. (1986). Problem behavior and family relationships: Life course and intergenerational themes. In A. B. Sorensen, F. E. Weinert, & L. R. Sherrod (Eds.), *Human development and the life course: Multidisciplinary perspectives.* Hillsdale, NJ: Erlbaum.

ELDER, G. H., JR., SHANAHAN, M., & CLIPP, E. C. (1994). When war comes to men's lives: Life course patterns in family, work, and health. *Psychology and Aging, 9,* 5–16.

ELICKER, J., ENGLUND, M., & SROUFE, L. A. (1992). Predicting peer competence and peer relationships in childhood from early parent–child relationships. In R. D. Parke & G. W. Ladd (Eds.), *Family-peer relationships: Modes of linkage.* Hillsdale, NJ: Erlbaum.

ELKIND, D. (1980). Strategic interactions in early adolescence. In J. Adelson (Ed.), *Handbook of adolescent psychology.* New York: Wiley.

ELKINS, I. J., McGUE, M., & IACONO, W. G. (1997). Genetic and environmental influences on parent-son relationships: Evidence for increasing genetic influence during adolescence. *Developmental Psychology, 33,* 351–363.

ELLIOTT, R., & VASTA, R. (1970). The modeling of sharing: Effects associated with vicarious reinforcement, symbolization, age, and generalization. *Journal of Experimental Child Psychology, 10,* 8–15.

ELLIS, L., & AMES, M. A. (1987). Neurohormonal functioning and sexual orientation: A theory of homosexuality-heterosexuality. *Psychological Bulletin, 101,* 233–258.

ELLIS, S. (1997). Strategy choice in sociocultural context. *Developmental Review, 17,* 490–524.

ELLIS, S., ROGOFF, B., & CROMER, C. C. (1981). Age segregation in children's social interactions. *Developmental Psychology, 17,* 399–407.

ELLSWORTH, C. P., MUIR, D. W., & HAINS, S. M. J. (1993). Social competence and person-object differentiation: An analysis of the still-face effect. *Developmental Psychology, 29,* 63–73.

ELMER-DeWITT, P. (1994, January 17). The genetic revolution. *Time,* pp. 46–53.

EMDE, R. N. (1992). Individual meaning and increasing complexity: Contributions of Sigmund Freud and René Spitz to developmental psychology. *American Psychologist, 28,* 347–359.

EMDE, R. N., & HARMON, R. J. (Eds.). (1984). *Continuities and discontinuities in development.* New York: Plenum.

EMDE, R. N., BIRINGEN, Z., CLYMAN, R. B., & OPPENHEIM, D. (1991). The moral sense of infancy: Affective core and procedural knowledge. *Developmental Review, 11,* 251–270.

EMDE, R. N., GAENSBAUER, T. J., & HARMON, R. J. (1976). Emotional expression in infancy: A biobehavioral study. *Psychological Issues Monograph Series, 10* (Whole No. 37). New York: International Universities Press.

EMDE, R. N., PLOMIN, R., ROBINSON, J., CORLEY, R., DeFRIES, J., FULKER, D. W., REZNICK, J. S., CAMPOS, J., KAGAN, J., & ZAHN-WAXLER, C. (1992). Temperament, emotion, and cognition at fourteen months: The MacArthur Longitudinal Twin Study. *Child Development, 63,* 1437–1455.

EMDE, R. N., SWEDBERG, J., & SUZUKI, B. (1975). Human wakefulness and biological rhythms after birth. *Archives of General Psychiatry, 32,* 780–783.

EMERY, R. E., & LAUMANN-BILLINGS, L. (1998). An overview of the nature, causes, and consequences of abusive family relationships: Toward differentiating maltreatment and violence. *American Psychologist, 53,* 121–135.

EMMERICH, W., & SHEPARD, K. (1982). Development of sex-differentiated preferences during late childhood and adolescence. *Developmental Psychology, 18,* 406–417.

ENGLUND, M. M., REED, T., & SROUFE, L. A. (March, 1993). *Continuity of social competence from infancy to adolescence.* Paper presented at the meeting of the Society for Research in Child Development, New Orleans.

ENNIS, R. H. (1976). An alternative to Piaget's conceptualization of logical competence. *Child Development, 47,* 903–919.

ENNOURI, K., & BLOCH, H. (1996). Visual control of hand approach movements in newborns. *British Journal of Developmental Psychology, 14,* 327–338.

ENRIGHT, R. D., & SATTERFIELD, S. J. (1980). An ecological validation of social cognitive development. *Child Development, 51,* 156–161.

ENRIGHT, R. D., BJERSTEDT, A., ENRIGHT, W. F., LEVY, V. M., LAPSLEY, D. K., BUSS, R. R., HARWELL, M., & ZINDLER, M. (1984). Distributive justice development: Cross-cultural, contextual, and longitudinal evaluations. *Child Development, 55,* 1737–1751.

ENTWISTLE, D. R., ALEXANDER, K. L., PALLAS, A. M., & CADIGAN, D. (1987). The emergent academic self-image of first-graders: Its response to social structure. *Child Development, 58,* 1190–1206.

EPSTEIN, J. L. (1983). Selections of friends in differently organized schools and classrooms. In J. L. Epstein & M. Karweit (Eds.), *Friends in school.* New York: Academic Press.

EPSTEIN, J. L. (1986). Friendship selection: Developmental and environmental influences. In E. C. Mueller & C. R. Cooper (Eds.), *Process and outcome in peer relationships.* New York: Academic Press.

EPSTEIN, J. L. (1989). The selection of friends: Changes across the grades and in different school environments. In T. J. Berndt & G. W. Ladd (Eds.), *Peer relationships in child development.* New York: Wiley.

EPSTEIN, Y. M. (1981). Crowding stress and human behavior. *Journal of Social Issues, 37,* 126–144.

ERICKSON, M. F., SROUFE, L. A., & EGELAND, B. (1985). The relationship between quality of attachment and behavior problems in pre-school in a high-risk sample. In I. Bretherton & E. Waters (Eds.), Growing points of attachment theory and research. *Monographs of the Society for Research in Child Development, 50* (1–2, Serial No. 209).

ERON, L. D. (1987). The development of aggressive behavior from the perspective of a developing behaviorism. *American Psychologist, 42,* 435–442.

ERON, L. D., & HUESMANN, L. R. (1986). The role of television in the development of prosocial and antisocial behavior. In D. Olweus, J. Block, & M. Radke-Yarrow (Eds.), *Development of antisocial and prosocial behavior.* Orlando, FL: Academic Press.

ERON, L. D., HUESMANN, L. R., BRICE, P., FISCHER, P., & MERMELSTEIN, R. (1983). Age trends in the development of aggression, sex typing, and related television habits. *Developmental Psychology, 19,* 71–77.

ERON, L. D., HUESMANN, L. R., DUBOW, E., ROMANOFF, R., & YARMEL, R. W. (1987). Aggression and its correlates over 22 years. In D. H. Crowell, I. M. Evans, & C. R. O'Donnell (Eds.), *Childhood aggression and violence: Sources of influence, prevention, and control.* New York: Plenum.

ERVIN, S. M. (1964). Imitation and structural change in children's language. In E. H. Lenneberg (Ed.), *New directions in the study of language.* Cambridge: MIT Press.

ERWIN, P. (1993). *Friendship and peer relations in children.* Chichester, England: Wiley.

ESKANAZI, B. (1993). Caffeine during pregnancy: Grounds for concern? *Journal of the American Medical Association, 270,* 2973–2974.

ETAUGH, C., COLLINS, G., & GERSON, A. (1975). Reinforcement of sex-typed behaviors of two-year-old children in a nursery school setting. *Developmental Psychology, 11,* 255.

ETZEL, B. C., & GEWIRTZ, J. L. (1967). Experimental modification of caretaker-maintained high rate operant crying in a 6- and a 20-week old infant (*Infans tyrannotearus*): Extinction of crying with reinforcement of eye contact and smiling *Journal of Experimental Child Psychology, 5,* 303–317.

EUROPEAN COLLABORATIVE STUDY. (1991). Children born to women with HIV-1 infection: Natural history and risk of transmission. *Lancet, 337,* 253–260.

EVELYTH, P. B. (1986). Population differences in growth. In F. Falkner & J. M. Tanner (Eds.), *Human growth: A comprehensive treatise.* New York: Plenum.

EYER, D. E. (1992). *Mother–infant bonding: A scientific fiction.* New Haven, CT: Yale University Press.

FABES, R. A., EISENBERG, N., KARBON, M., TROYER, D., & SWITZER, G. (1994). The relations of children's emotion regulation to their vicarious emotional responses and comforting behavior. *Child Development, 65,* 1678–1693.

FABES, R. A., EISENBERG, N., & MILLER, P. A. (1990). Maternal correlates of children's vicarious emotional responsiveness. *Developmental Psychology, 26,* 639–648.

FABRICIUS, W. V., & CAVALIER, L. (1989). The role of causal theories about memory in young children's memory strategy choice. *Child Development, 60,* 298–308.

FABRICIUS, W. V., & STEFFE, L. (1989, April). *Considering all possible combinations: The early beginnings of a formal operational skill.* Paper presented at the meeting of the Society for Research in Child Development, Kansas City, MO.

FADERMAN, L. (1991). *Odd girls and twilight lovers: A history of lesbian life in twentieth-century America.* New York: Columbia University Press.

FADIMAN, A. (1983, April). The unborn patient. *Life,* pp. 38–44.

FAGAN, J. F., III. (1973). Infants' delayed recognition memory and forgetting. *Journal of Experimental Child Psychology, 16,* 424–450.

FAGAN, J. F., III. (1992). Intelligence: A theoretical viewpoint. *Current Directions in Psychological Science, 1,* 82–86.

FAGAN, J. F., III, & DETTERMAN, D. H. (1992). The Fagan Test of Infant Intelligence: A technical summary. *Journal of Applied Developmental Psychology, 13,* 173–193.

FAGAN, J. F., III, & SHEPHERD, P. A. (1986). *The Fagan Test of Infant Intelligence: Training manual.* Cleveland, OH: Infantest Corporation.

FAGOT, B. I. (1977). Consequences of moderate cross-gender behavior in preschool children. *Child Development, 48,* 902–907.

FAGOT, B. I. (1982). Sex role development. In R. Vasta (Ed.), *Strategies and techniques of child study.* New York: Academic Press.

FAGOT, B. I. (1985). Stages in thinking about early sex role development. *Developmental Review, 5,* 83–98.

FAGOT, B. I. (1997), Attachment, parenting, and peer interactions of toddler children. *Developmental Psychology, 33,* 489–499.

FAGOT, B. I., & GAUVAIN, M. (1997). Mother-child problem solving: Continuity through the early childhood years. *Developmental Psychology, 33,* 480–488.

FAGOT, B. I., & HAGAN, R. (1991). Observations of parent reactions to sex-stereotyped behaviors: Age and sex effects. *Child Development, 62,* 617–628.

FAGOT, B. I., & LEINBACH, M. D. (1987). Socialization of sex roles within the family. In D. B. Carter (Ed.),*Current conceptions of sex roles and sex typing: Theory and research.* New York: Praeger.

FAGOT, B. I., & LEINBACH, M. D. (1993). Gender-role development in young children: From discrimination to labeling. *Developmental Review, 13,* 205–224.

FAGOT, B. I., HAGAN, R., LEINBACH, M. D., & KRONSBERG, S. (1985). Differential reactions to assertive and communicative acts of toddler boys and girls. *Child Development, 56,* 1499–1505.

FAGOT, B. I., LEINBACH, M. D., & HAGAN, R. (1986). Gender labeling and the adoption of sex-typed behaviors. *Developmental Psychology, 22,* 440–443.

FAGOT, B. I., LEINBACH, M. D., & O'BOYLE, C. (1992). Gender labeling, gender stereotyping, and parenting behaviors. *Developmental Psychology, 28,* 225–230.

FALBO, T., & POSTON, D. L., JR. (1993). The academic, personality, and physical outcomes of only children in China. *Child Development, 64,* 18–35.

FANTUZZO, J. W., MCDERMOTT, P. A., MANZ, P. H., HAMPTON, V. R., & BURDICK, N. A. (1996). The Pictorial Scale of Perceived Competence and Social Acceptance: Does it work with low-income urban children? *Child Development, 67,* 1071–1084.

FANTZ, R. L. (1961). The origin of form perception. *Scientific American, 204,* 66–72.

FANTZ, R. L. (1963). Pattern vision in newborn infants. *Science, 140,* 296–297.

FARBER, S. L. (1981). *Identical twins reared apart: A reanalysis.* New York: Basic Books.

FARRAR M. J. (1990). Discourse and the acquisition of grammatical morphemes. *Journal of Child Language, 17,* 607–624.

FARRAR, M. J. (1992). Negative evidence and grammatical morpheme acquisition. *Developmental Psychology, 28,* 90–98.

FARRAR, M. J., & GOODMAN, G. S. (1990). Developmental differences in the relation between scripts and episodic memory: Do they exist? In R. Fivush & J. Hudson (Eds.), *Knowing and remembering in young children.* New York: Cambridge University Press.

FARRAR, M. J., & GOODMAN, G. S. (1992). Developmental changes in event memory. *Child Development, 63,* 173–187.

FARRINGTON, D. P. (1994). Childhood, adolescent, and adult features of violent males. In L. R. Huesmann (Ed.), *Aggressive behavior: Current perspectives.* New York: Plenum.

FARVER, J. M., & BRANSTETTER, W. H. (1994). Preschoolers' prosocial responses to their peers' distress. *Developmental Psychology, 30,* 334–341.

FARVER, J. M., & FROSCH, D. L. (1996). L.A. stories: Aggression in preschoolers' spontaneous narratives after the riots of 1992. *Child Development, 67,* 19–32.

FARVER, J. M., & SHIN, Y. L. (1997). Social pretend play in Korean- and Anglo-American pre-schoolers. *Child Development, 68,* 544–556.

FAY, R. E., TURNER, C. F., KLASSEN, A. D., & GAGNON, J. H. (1989). Prevalence and patterns of same-gender contact among men. *Science, 243,* 338–348.

FEIN, G. G., SCHWARTZ, P. M., JACOBSON, S. W., & JACOBSON, J. L. (1983). Environmental toxin and behavioral development: A new role for psychological research. *American Psychologist, 38,* 1198–1205.

FEINGOLD, A. (1992). Sex differences in variability in intellectual abilities: A new look at an old controversy. *Review of Educational Research, 62,* 61–84.

FEINGOLD, A. (1993). Cognitive gender differences: A developmental perspective. *Sex Roles, 29,* 91–112.

FEINMAN, S. (1981). Why is cross-sex role behavior more approved for girls than for boys? *Sex Roles, 7,* 289–300.

FEINMAN, S., ROBERTS, D., HSIEH, K., SAWYER, D., & SWANSON, D. (1992). A critical review of social referencing in infancy. In S. Feinman (Ed.), *Social referencing and the social construction of reality in infancy.* New York: Plenum.

FEIRING, C., & LEWIS, M. (1987). The child's social network: Sex differences from three to six years. *Sex Roles, 17,* 621–636.

FELDLAUFER, H., MIDGLEY, C., & ECCLES, J. S. (1988). Student, teacher, and observer perceptions of the classroom environment before and after the transition to junior high school. *Journal of Early Adolescence, 8,* 133–156.

FELDMAN, J. F., BRODY, N., & MILLER, S. A. (1980). Sex differences in non-elicited neonatal behaviors. *Merrill-Palmer Quarterly, 26,* 63–73.

FENNEMA, E., & TARTRE, L. A. (1985). The use of spatial visualization in mathematics by girls and boys. *Journal for Research in Mathematics Education, 16,* 184–206.

FENSON, L., DALE, P. S., REZNICK, J. S., BATES E., THAL, D. J., & PETHICK, S. J. (1994). Variability in early communicative development. *Monographs of the Society for Research in Child Development, 59* (5, Serial No. 242).

FERGUSON, C. A. (1983). Reduplication in child phonology. *Journal of Child Language, 10,* 239–243.

FERGUSON, L. R. (1970). Dependency motivation in socialization. In R. A. Hoppe, G. A. Milton, & E. C. Simmel (Eds.), *Early experience and the process of socialization.* New York: Academic Press.

FERGUSON, T. J., & RULE, B. G. (1988). Children's evaluations of retaliatory aggression. *Child Development, 59,* 961–968.

FERNALD, A. (1991). Prosody in speech to children: Prelinguistic and linguistic functions. In R. Vasta (Ed.), *Annals of child development* (Vol. 8). London: Kingsley.

FERNALD, A. (1993). Approval and disapproval: Infant responsiveness to vocal affect in familiar and unfamiliar languages. *Child Development, 64,* 657–674.

FERNALD, A., & MORIKAWA, H. (1993). Common themes and cultural variations in Japanese and American mothers' speech to infants. *Child Development, 64,* 637–656.

FERNALD, A., & O'NEILL, D. K. (1993). Peek-aboo across cultures: How mothers and infants play with voices, faces, and expectations. In K. MacDonald (Ed.), *Parent-child play.* Albany: State University of New York Press.

FERRIERA, A. J. (1969). *Prenatal environment.* Springfield, IL: Charles C. Thomas.

FESHBACH, N. D., & FESHBACH, S. (1982). Empathy training and the regulation of aggression: Potentialities and limitations. *Academic Psychology Bulletin, 4,* 399–413.

FESHBACH, S., & SINGER, R. D. (1971). *Television and aggression: An experimental field study.* San Francisco: Jossey-Bass.

FEUERSTEIN, R. (1979). *The dynamic assessment of retarded performers.* Baltimore: University Park Press.

FIELD, D. (1987). A review of preschool conservation training: An analysis of analyses. *Developmental Review, 7,* 210–251.

FIELD, T. (1995). Massage therapy for infants and children. *Developmental and Behavioral Pediatrics, 16,* 105–111.

FIELD, T. M. (1987). Affective and interactive disturbances in infants. In J. D. Osofsky (Ed.), *Handbook of infant development* (2nd ed.). New York: Wiley.

FIELD, T. M., & ROOPNARINE, J. L. (1982). Infant-peer interactions. In T. M. Field, A. Huston, H. C. Quay, L. Troll, & G. E. Finley (Eds.), *Review of human development.* New York: Wiley.

FIELD, T. M., & WALDEN, T. A. (1982). Production and perception of facial expressions in infancy and early childhood. In H. W. Reese & L. P. Lipsitt (Eds.), *Advances in child development and behavior* (Vol. 16). New York: Academic Press.

FIELD, T. M., COHEN, D., GARCIA, R., & GREENBERG, R. (1985). Mother–stranger face discrimination by the newborn. *Infant Behavior and Development, 7,* 19–25.

FIELD, T. M., HEALY, B., GOLDSTEIN, S., & GUTHERTZ, M. (1990). Behavior-state matching and synchrony in mother–infant interactions of nondepressed versus depressed dyads. *Developmental Psychology, 26,* 7–14.

FIFER, W. P., & MOON, C. M. (1995). The effects of fetal experience with sound. In J.-P. Lecanuet, W. P. Fifer, N. A. Krasnegor, & W. P. Smotherman (Eds.), *Fetal development: A psychobiological perspective.* Hillsdale, NJ: Erlbaum.

FINE, G. A. (1987). *With the boys: Little League baseball and preadolescent culture.* Chicago: University of Chicago Press.

FINEGAN, J. K., NICCOLS, G. A., & SITARENIOS, G. (1992). Relations between prenatal testosterone levels and cognitive abilities at 4 years. *Developmental Psychology, 28,* 1075–1089.

FINLAY, D., & IVINSKIS, A. (1987). Cardiac change responses and attentional mechanisms in infants. In B. E. McKenzie & R. H. Day (Eds.), *Perceptual development in early infancy: Problems and issues.* Hillsdale, NJ: Erlbaum.

FINNEGAN, L. P., & FEHR, K. O. (1980). The effects of opiates, sedative-hypnotics, amphetamines, cannabis, and other psychoactive drugs on the fetus and newborn. In O. J. Kalant (Ed.), *Research advances in alcohol and drug problems: Vol. 5. Alcohol and drug problems in women.* New York: Plenum.

FIREMAN, G., & BEILIN, H. (1990, May). *Preformationism and Piaget's stage concept.* Paper presented at the meeting of the Jean Piaget Society, Philadelphia.

FIRSCH, R. E. (1984). Fatness, puberty, and fertility. In J. Brooks-Gunn & A. C. Petersen (Eds.), *Girls at puberty: Biological, psychological, and social perspectives.* New York: Plenum.

FISCHER, K. W. (1980). A theory of cognitive development: The control and construction of hierarchies of skills. *Psychological Review, 87,* 477–531.

FISCHER, M., & LEITENBERG, H. (1986). Optimism and pessimism in elementary school-aged children. *Child Development, 57,* 241–248.

FISHBEIN, H. D. (1984). *The psychology of infancy and childhood: Evolutionary and cross-cultural perspectives.* Hillsdale, NJ: Erlbaum.

FISHBEIN, H. D., & IMAI, S. (1993). Preschoolers select playmates on the basis of gender and race. *Journal of Applied Developmental Psychology, 14,* 303–316.

FISHER, C. B., & LERNER, R. M. (Eds.). (1994). *Applied developmental psychology.* New York: McGraw-Hill.

FISHER, C. B., & TRYON, W. W. (1990). *Ethics in applied developmental psychology: Emerging issues in an emerging field.* Norwood, NJ: Ablex.

FISHER, E. P. (1992). The impact of play on development: A meta-analysis. *Play and Culture, 5,* 159–181.

FISHER-THOMPSON, D. (1990). Adult gender typing of children's toys. *Sex Roles, 23,* 291–303.

FIVUSH, R. (1991). The social construction of personal narratives. *Merrill-Palmer Quarterly, 37,* 59–82.

FIVUSH, R. (1993). Emotional content of parent–child conversations about the past. In C. A. Nelson (Ed.), *Minnesota symposia on child psychology: Vol. 26. Memory and affect in development.* Hillsdale, NJ: Erlbaum.

FIVUSH, R. (1994). Constructing narrative, emotion, and self in parent-child conversations about the past. In U. Neisser & R. Fivush (Eds.), *The remembering self: Construction and accuracy in the self-narrative.* New York: Cambridge University Press.

FIVUSH, R., & KUEBLI, J. (1997). Making everyday events emotional: The construal of emotion in parent–child conversations about the past. In N. L. Stein, P. A. Ornstein, B. Tversky, & C. J. Brainerd (Eds.), *Memory for everyday and emotional events.* Mahwah, NJ: Erlbaum.

FIVUSH, R., HADEN, C., & REESE, E. (1996). Remembering, recounting, and reminiscing: The development of autobiographical memory in social context. In D. C. Rubin (Ed.), *Remembering our past: Studies in autobiographical memory.* New York: Cambridge University Press.

FIVUSH, R., KUEBLI, J., & CLUBB, P. A. (1992). The structure of events and event representations: A developmental analysis. *Child Development, 63,* 188–201.

FLAKS, D. K., FICHER, I., MASTERPASQUA, F., & JOSEPH, G. (1995). Lesbians choosing motherhood: A comparative study of lesbian and heterosexual parents and their children. *Developmental Psychology, 31,* 105–114.

FLAVELL, J. H. (1963). *The developmental psychology of Jean Piaget.* Princeton, NJ: Van Nostrand.

FLAVELL, J. H. (1970). Developmental studies of mediated memory. In H. W. Reese & L. P. Lipsitt (Eds.), *Advances in child development and behavior* (Vol. 5). New York: Academic Press.

FLAVELL, J. H. (1971). First discussant's comments: What is memory development the development of? *Human Development, 14,* 272–278.

FLAVELL, J. H. (1985). *Cognitive development* (2nd ed.). Englewood Cliffs, NJ: Prentice Hall.

FLAVELL, J. H. (1986). The development of children's knowledge about the appearance–reality distinction. *American Psychologist, 41,* 418–425.

FLAVELL, J. H. (1992a). Cognitive development: Past, present, and future. *Developmental Psychology, 28,* 998–1005.

FLAVELL, J. H. (1992b). Perspectives on perspective taking. In H. Beilin & P. B. Pufall (Eds.), *Piaget's theory: Prospects and possibilities.* Hillsdale, NJ: Erlbaum.

FLAVELL, J. H., & MILLER, P. H. (1998). Social cognition. In W. Damon (Series Ed.) & D. Kuhn & R. S. Siegler (Vol. Eds.), *Handbook*

of child psychology: Vol. 2. Cognition, perception, and language (5th ed.). New York: Wiley.

FLAVELL, J. H., BEACH, D. H., & CHINSKY, J. M. (1966). Spontaneous verbal rehearsal in a memory task as a function of age. *Child Development, 37,* 283–299.

FLAVELL, J. H., FLAVELL, E. R., & GREEN, F. L. (1983). Development of the appearance–reality distinction. *Cognitive Psychology 15,* 95–120.

FLAVELL, J. H., FRIEDRICHS, A., & HOYT, J. (1970). Developmental changes in memorization processes. *Cognitive Psychology, 1,* 324–340.

FLAVELL, J. H., GREEN, F. L., & FLAVELL, E. R. (1989). Young children's ability to differentiate appearance–reality and Level 2 perspectives in the tactile modality. *Child Development, 60,* 201–213.

FLAVELL, J. H., LINDBERG, N. A., GREEN, F. L., & FLAVELL, E. R. (1992). The development of children's understanding of the appearance–reality distinction between how people look and what they are really like. *Merrill-Palmer Quarterly, 38,* 513–524.

FLAVELL, J. H., MILLER, P. H., & MILLER, S. A. (1993). *Cognitive development* (3rd ed.). Englewood Cliffs, NJ: Prentice Hall.

FLAVELL, J. H., & MILLER, P. H. (1997). Social cognition. In D. Kuhn & R. Siegler (Eds.), *Handbook of child psychology: Vol. 2. cognition, perception, and language.* New York: Wiley.

FLAVELL, J. H., SHIPSTEAD, S. G., & CROFT, K. (1980). What young children think you see when their eyes are closed. *Cognition, 8,* 369–387.

FLAVELL, J. H., ZHANG, H.-D., ZOU, H., DONG, Q., & QI, S. (1983). A comparison between the development of the appearance–reality distinction in the People's Republic of China and the United States. *Cognitive Psychology, 15,* 459–466.

FLEMING, P., BLAIR, P., BACON, C., BENSLEY, D., SMITH, I., TAYLOR, E., BERRY, J., GOLDING, J., & TRIPP, J. (1996). Environments of infants during sleep and risk of the sudden infant death syndrome: Results of 1993–5 case-control study for confidential inquiry into still-births and deaths in infancy. *British Medical Journal, 313,* 191–195.

FLETCHER, A. C., DARLING, N. E., STEINBERG, L., & DORNBUSCH, S. M. (1995). The company they keep: Relation of adolescents' adjustment and behavior to their friends' perceptions of authoritative parenting in the social network. *Developmental Psychology, 31,* 300–310.

FLYNN, J. R. (1987). Massive IQ gains in 14 nations: What IQ tests really measure. *Psychological Bulletin, 101,* 171–191.

FOGEL, A., & THELEN, E. (1987). Development of early expressive and communicative action: Reinterpreting the evidence from a dynamic systems perspective. *Developmental Psychology, 23,* 747–761.

FOGELMAN, K. (1980). Smoking in pregnancy and subsequent development of the child. *Child Care, Health and Development, 6,* 233–249.

FOGLE, S. (1992). Pretty BABI: Blastomere screen detects CF gene. *Journal of NIH Research, 4,* 46.

FORMAN, E. A. (1992). Discourse, intersubjectivity, and the development of peer collaboration: A Vygotskian approach. In L. T. Winegar & J. Valsiner (Eds.), *Children's development within social context: Vol. 1. Metatheory and theory.* Hillsdale, NJ: Erlbaum.

FORSLUND, M., & BJERRE, I. (1983). Neurological assessment of preterm infants at term conceptional age in comparison with normal full-term infants. *Early Human Development, 8,* 195–208.

FOX, N. A. (Ed.) (1994). The development of emotion regulation: Biological and behavioral considerations. *Monographs of the Society for Research in Child Development, 59*(2–3, Serial No. 240).

FOX, N. A., KIMMERLY, N. L., & SCHAFER, W. D. (1991). Attachment to mother/attachment to father: A meta-analysis. *Child Development, 62,* 210–225.

FRANCIS, P. L., SELF, P. A., & HOROWITZ, F. D. (1987). The behavioral assessment of the neonate: An overview. In J. D. Osofsky (Ed.), *Handbook of infant development* (2nd ed.). New York: Wiley.

FRANKEL, K. A., & BATES, J. E. (1990). Mother–toddler problem solving: Antecedents of attachment, home behavior, and temperament. *Child Development, 61,* 810–819.

FRASER, S. (Ed.). (1995). *The Bell Curve wars: Race, intelligence, and the future of America.* New York: Basic Books.

FRAUENGLASS, M. H., & DIAZ, R. M. (1985). Self-regulatory functions of children's speech: A critical analysis of recent challenges to Vygotsky's theory. *Developmental Psychology, 21,* 357–364.

FREDA, M. C., ANDERSON, F. H., DAMUS, K., PROUST, D., BRUSTMAN, L., & MERKATZ, I. R. (1990). Lifestyle for inner city women at high risk for preterm birth. *Journal of Advanced Nursing, 15,* 364–372.

FREEBURG, T. J., & LIPPMAN, M. Z. (1986). Factors influencing discrimination of infant cries. *Journal of Child Language, 13,*3–13.

FREEDLAND, R. L., & BERTENTHAL, B. I. (1994). Developmental stages in interlimb coordination: Transition to hands-and-knees crawling. *Psychological Science, 5,* 26–32.

FRENCH, D. C. (1988). Heterogeneity of peer-rejected boys: Aggressive and nonaggressive subtypes. *Child Development, 59,* 976–985.

FRENCH, D. C. (1990). Heterogeneity of peer rejected girls. *Child Development, 61,* 2028–2031.

FREUND, L. S. (1990). Maternal regulation of children's problem-solving behavior and its impact on children's performance. *Child Development, 61,* 113–126.

FREY, K. S., & RUBLE, D. N. (1987). What children say about classroom performance: Sex and grade differences in perceived competence. *Child Development, 58,* 1066–1078.

FREY, K. S., & RUBLE, D. N. (1992). Gender constancy and the "cost" of sex-typed behavior: A test of the conflict hypothesis. *Developmental Psychology, 28,* 714–721.

FRIED, P. A., O'CONNELL, C. M., & WATKINSON, M. A. (1992). Sixty- and 72-month follow-up of children prenatally exposed to marijuana, cigarettes, and alcohol: Cognitive and language assessment. *Developmental and Behavioral Pediatrics, 13,* 383–391.

FRIED, P. A., WATKINSON, B., & GRAY, R. (1992). A follow-up study of attentional behavior in 6-year-old children exposed prenatally to marijuana, cigarettes, and alcohol. *Neuro-toxicology and Teratology, 14,* 299–311.

FRIEDMAN, H. S., TUCKER, J. S., SCHWARTZ, J. E., TOMLINSON-KEASEY, C., MARTIN, L. R., WINGARD, D. L., & CRIQUI, M. H. (1995). Psychosocial and behavioral predictors of longevity: The aging and death of the "Termites." *American Psychologist, 50,* 69–78.

FRIEDMAN, J. M. (1981). Genetic disease in the offspring of older fathers. *Obstetrics and Gynecology, 57,* 745–749.

FRIEDRICH-COFER, L. K., & HUSTON, A. C. (1986). Television violence and aggression: The debate continues. *Psychological Bulletin, 100,* 364–371.

FRIEDRICH-COFER, L. K., HUSTON-STEIN, A., KIPNIS, D. M., SUSMAN, E. J., & CLEWETT, A. S. (1979). Environmental enhancement of prosocial television content: Effects on interpersonal behavior, imaginative play, and self-regulation in a natural setting. *Developmental Psychology, 15,* 637–646.

FRISCH, H. L. (1977). Sex stereotypes in adult–infant play. *Child Development, 48,* 1671–1675.

FRITH, U. (1989). *Autism: Explaining the enigma.* Oxford, England: Basil Blackwell.

FRODI, A. M., LAMB, M. E., LEAVITT, L. A., & DONOVAN, W. L. (1978). Fathers' and mothers' responses to infant smiles and cries. *Infant Behavior and Development, 1,* 187–198.

FROMING, W. J., ALLEN, L., & JENSEN, R. (1985). Altruism, role-taking, and self-awareness: The acquisition of norms governing altruistic behavior. *Child Development, 56,* 1223–1228.

FROMKIN, V., & RODMAN, R. (1988). *An introduction to language* (4th ed.). New York: Holt, Rinehart, and Winston.

FRY, D. P. (1988). Intercommunity differences in aggression among Zapotec children. *Child Development, 59,* 1008–1019.

FUKAHARA, H., SHIMURA, Y., & YAMANOUCHI, I. (1988, November). *The transmission of ambient noise and self-produced sound into the human body.* Poster presented at the second joint meeting of the Acoustical Society of America and the Acoustical Society of Japan, Honolulu.

FULLARD, W., & REILING, A. M. (1976). An investigation of Lorenz's "babyness." *Child Development, 47,* 1191–1193.

FULLARD, W., MCDEVITT, S. C., & CAREY, W. B. (1984). Assessing temperament in one to three year old children. *Journal of Pediatric Psychology, 9,* 205–217.

FULLER, B. (1987). Defining school quality. In J. Hannway & M. Lockhead (Eds.), *The contribution of social sciences to educational policy and practice: 1965–1985.* Berkeley, CA: McCuthan.

FURMAN, W. (1987). Acquaintanceship in middle childhood. *Developmental Psychology, 23,* 563–570.

FURMAN, W., & GAVIN, L. A. (1989). Peers' influence on adjustment and development. In T. J. Berndt & G. W. Ladd (Eds.), *Peer relationships in child development.* New York: Wiley.

FURMAN, W., & MASTERS, J. C. (1980). Affective consequences of social reinforcement, punishment, and neutral behavior. *Developmental Psychology, 16,* 100–104.

FURNAM, A., & BITAR, N. (1993). The stereotyped portrayal of men and women in British television advertisements. *Sex Roles, 29,* 297–310.

FURNAM, A., ABRAMSKY, S., & GUNTER, B. (1997). A cross-cultural content analysis of children's television advertisements. *Sex Roles, 37,* 91–99.

FURROW, D., BAILLIE, C., McCLAREN, J., & MOORE, C. (1993). A further look at the motherese hypothesis: A reply to Gleitman, Newport, and Gleitman. *Journal of Child Language, 20,* 363–375.

FURROW, D., NELSON, K., & BENEDICT, H. (1979). Mothers' speech to children and syntactic development: Some simple relationships. *Journal of Child Language, 6,* 423–442.

FURSTENBERG, F. F., JR., & CHERLIN, A. J. (1991). *Divided families.* Cambridge: Harvard University Press.

GALAMBOS, N. L., ALMEIDA, D. M., & PETERSEN, A. C. (1990). Masculinity, femininity, and sex role attitudes in early adolescence: Exploring gender intensification. *Child Development, 61,* 1905–1914.

GALEN, B. R., & UNDERWOOD, M. K. (1997). A developmental investigation of social aggression among children. *Developmental Psychology, 33,* 589–600.

GALLAGHER, A. M., & DE LISI, R. (1994). Gender differences in Scholastic Aptitude Test—mathematics problem solving among high-ability students. *Journal of Educational Psychology, 86,* 204–211.

GALLAHUE, D. L. (1989). *Understanding motor development* (2nd ed.). Carmel, IN: Benchmark Press.

GALPERT, L., & DOCKRELL, J. (1995). Is understanding the experimenter's intention the clue to conservation ability? *International Journal of Behavioral Development, 18,* 505–517.

GARAI, J. E., & SCHEINFELD, A. (1968). Sex differences in mental and behavioral traits. *Genetic Psychology Monographs, 77,* 169–299.

GARBARINO, J., & ABRAMOWITZ, R. H. (1992). The family as a social system. In J. Garbarino (Ed.), *Children and families in the social environment* (2nd ed.). New York: Aldine de Gruyter.

GARBARINO, J., & KOSTELNY, K. (1995). Parenting and public policy. In M. H. Bornstein (Ed.), *Handbook of parenting: Vol. 3. Status and social conditions of parenting.* Mahwah, NJ: Erlbaum.

GARBARINO, J., & KOSTELNY, K. (1996). The effects of political violence on Palestinian children's behavior problems: A risk accumulation model. *Child Development, 67,* 33–45.

GARBARINO, J., DUBROW, N., KOSTELNY, K., & PARDO, C. (1992). *Children in danger: Coping with the consequences of community violence.* San Francisco: Jossey-Bass.

GARBARINO, J., GABOURY, M. T., & PLANTZ, M. C. (1992). Social policy, children, and their families. In J. Garbarino (Ed.), *Children and families in the social environment* (2nd ed.). New York: Aldine de Gruyter.

GARDEN, R. A. (1987). The second IEA mathematics study. *Comparative Education Review, 31,* 47–68.

GARDNER, H. (1983). *Frames of mind: The theory of multiple intelligences.* New York: Basic Books.

GARDNER, H. (1993). *Multiple intelligences.* New York: Basic Books.

GARDNER, H. (1995). Reflections on multiple intelligences: Myths and messages. *Phi Delta Kappan, 77*(2).

GARDNER, J. M., KARMEL, B. Z., & MAGNANO, C. L. (1992). Arousal/visual preference interactions in high-risk neonates. *Developmental Psychology, 28,* 821–830.

GARMEZY, N., & RUTTER, M. (Eds.). (1983). *Stress, coping, and development in children.* New York: McGraw-Hill.

GARMON, L. C., BASINGER, K. S., GREGG, V. R., & GIBBS, J. C. (1996). Gender differences in stage and expression of moral judgment. *Merrill-Palmer Quarterly, 42,* 418–437.

GARNER, P. W., JONES, D. C., & MINER, J. L. (1994). Social competence among low-income pre-schoolers: Emotion socialization practices and social cognitive correlates. *Child Development, 65,* 622–637.

GARNER, R. (1990). Children's use of strategies in reading. In D. F. Bjorklund (Ed.), *Children's strategies: Contemporary views of cognitive development.* Hillsdale, NJ: Erlbaum.

GARRISON, W. T., & EARLS, F. J. (1987). *Temperament and child psychopathology.* Newbury Park, CA: Sage.

GARROD, A., BEAL, C., & SHIN, P. (1990). The development of moral orientation in elementary school children. *Sex Roles, 22,* 13–26.

GARVEY, C. (1986). Peer relations and the growth of communication. In E. C. Mueller &

C. R. Cooper (Eds.), *Process and outcome in peer relationships.* New York: Academic Press.

GAUVAIN, M., & FAGOT, B. I. (1995). Child temperament as a mediator of mother-toddler problem solving. *Social Development, 4,* 257–278.

GE, X., CONGER, R. D., CADORET, R. J., NEIDERHISER, J. M., YATES, W., TROUGHTON, E., & STEWART, M. A. (1996). The developmental interface between nature and nurture: A mutual in-fluence model of child antisocial behavior and parents' behaviors. *Developmental Psychology, 32,* 574–589.

GEARY, D. C. (1995a). *Children's mathematical development.* Washington, DC: American Psychological Association.

GEARY, D. C. (1995b). Reflections of evolution and culture in children's cognition. *American Psychologist, 50,* 24–37.

GEARY, D. C. (1996). International differences in mathematical achievement: Their nature, courses, and consequences. *Current Directions in Psychological Science, 5,* 133–137.

GEARY, D. C. (1996). Sexual selection and sex differences in mathematical abilities. *Behavioral and Brain Sciences, 19,* 229–284.

GEARY, D. C., FAN, L., & BOW-THOMAS, C. C. (1992). Numerical cognition: Loci of ability differences comparing children from China and the United States. *Psychological Science, 3,* 180–185.

GEEN, R. G. (1983). Aggression and television violence. In R. G. Geen & E. I. Donnerstein (Eds.), *Aggression: Theoretical and empirical reviews* (Vol. 2). New York: Academic Press.

GELFAND, D. M., & HARTMANN, D. P. (1982). Response consequences and attributions: Two contributors to prosocial behavior. In N. Eisenberg (Ed.), *The development of prosocial behavior.* New York: Academic Press.

GELMAN, R. (1982). Basic numerical abilities. In R. J. Sternberg (Ed.), *Advances in the psychology of human intelligence* (Vol. 1). Hillsdale, NJ: Erlbaum.

GELMAN, R. (1991). Epigenetic foundations of knowledge structures: Initial and transcendent constructions. In S. Carey & R. Gelman (Eds.), *The epigenesis of mind.* Hillsdale, NJ: Erlbaum.

GELMAN, R., & BAILLARGEON, R. (1983). A review of some Piagetian concepts. In P. H. Mussen (Series Ed.) & J. H. Flavell & E. M. Markman (Vol. Eds.), *Handbook of child psychology: Vol. 3. Cognitive development.* New York: Wiley.

GELMAN, R., & GALLISTEL, C. R. (1978). *The child's understanding of number.* Cambridge: Harvard University Press.

GELMAN, S. A. (1996). Concepts and theories. In R. Gelman & T. Au (Eds.), *Perceptual and cognitive development.* San Diego: Academic Press.

GELMAN, S. A., & COLEY, J. D. (1990). The importance of knowing a dodo is a bird: Categories and inferences in 2-year-old children. *Developmental Psychology, 26,* 796–804.

GELMAN, S. A., & MARKMAN, E. M. (1986). Categories and induction in young children. *Cognition, 23,* 183–209.

GELMAN, S. A., & MARKMAN, E. M. (1987). Young children's inductions from natural kinds: The role of categories and appearances. *Child Development, 58,* 1532–1541.

GELMAN, S. A., WILCOX, S. A., & CLARK, E. V. (1989). Conceptual and lexical hierarchies in young children. *Cognitive Development, 4,* 309–326.

GENESEE, F. (Ed.). (1994). *Educating second language children.* New York: Cambridge University Press.

GENESEE, F. (1989). Early bilingual development: One language or two? *Journal of Child Language, 16,* 161–179.

GENTILE, D. A. (1993). Just what are sex and gender anyway? *Psychological Science, 4,* 120–124.

GENTNER, D. (1982). Why nouns are learned before verbs: Linguistic relativity versus natural partitioning. In S. A. Kuczaj (Ed.), *Language development* (Vol. 2). Hillsdale, NJ: Erlbaum.

GEORGE, C., & SOLOMON, J. (1989). Internal working models of parenting and security of attachment at age six. *Infant Mental Health Journal, 10,* 222–237.

GEORGE, C., KAPLAN, N., & MAIN, M. (1985). *The Adult Attachment Interview.* Unpublished manuscript, University of California, Department of Psychology, Berkeley.

GERBNER, G., GROSS, L., MORGAN, M., & SIGNORELLI, N. (1994). Growing up with television: The cultivation perspective. In J. Bryant & D. Zillman (Eds.), *Media effects: Advances in theory and research.* Hillsdale, NJ: Erlbaum.

GERGEN, K. J. (1994). Mind, text, and society: Self-memory in social context. In U. Neisser & R. Fivush (Eds.), *The remembering self: Construction and accuracy in the self-narrative.* New York: Cambridge University Press.

GERSHKOFF-STOWE, L., & SMITH, L. B. (1991, April). *Changes in pointing and labeling during the naming explosion.* Poster session presented at the Meeting of the Society for Research in Child Development, Seattle, WA.

GESELL, A. (1954). The ontogeneses of infant behavior. In L. Carmichael (Ed.), *Manual of child psychology* (2nd ed.). New York: Wiley.

GESELL, A., & ILG, F. L. (1943). *Infant and child in the culture of today.* New York: Harper.

GESELL, A., & THOMPSON, H. (1929). Learning and growth in identical infant twins: An experimental study by the method of co-twin control. *Genetic Psychological Monographs, 6,* 1–24.

GESELL, A., & THOMPSON, H. (1938). *The psychology of early growth.* New York: Macmillan.

GEWIRTZ, J. L. (1991). Social influence on child and parent via stimulation and operant learning mechanisms. In M. Lewis & S. Feinman (Eds.), *Social influences and socialization in infancy.* New York: Plenum.

GEWIRTZ, J. L., & BOYD, E. F. (1976). Mother–infant interaction and its study. In H. W. Reese (Ed.), *Advances in child development and behaviors* (Vol. 11). New York: Academic Press.

GEWIRTZ, J. L., & BOYD, E. F. (1977). Experiments on mother–infant interaction underlying mutual attachment acquisition: The infant conditions the mother. In T. Alloway, P. Pliner, & L. Kramer (Eds.), *Advances in the study of communication and affect: Vol. 3. Attachment behavior.* New York: Plenum.

GEWIRTZ, J. L., & PELAEZ-NOGUERAS, M. (1991a). The attachment metaphor and the conditioning of infant separation protests. In J. L. Gewirtz & W. M. Kurtines (Eds.), *Intersections with attachment.* Hillsdale, NJ: Erlbaum.

GEWIRTZ, J. L., & PELAEZ-NOGUERAS, M. (1991b). Proximal mechanisms underlying the acquisition of moral behavior patterns. In W. M. Kurtines & J. L. Gewirtz (Eds.), *Handbook of moral behavior and development: Vol. 1. Theory.* Hillsdale, NJ: Erlbaum.

GEWIRTZ, J. L., & PELAEZ-NOGUERAS, M. (1992a). B. F. Skinner's legacy to human infant behavior and development. *American Psychologist, 47,* 1411–1422.

GEWIRTZ, J. L., & PELAEZ-NOGUERAS, M. (1992b). Social referencing as a learned process. In S. Feinman (Ed.), *Social referencing and the social construction of reality in infancy.* New York: Plenum.

GHATALA, E. S., LEVIN, J. R., PRESSLEY, M., & LODICO, M. G. (1985). Training cognitive strategy monitoring in children. *American Educational Research Journal, 22,* 199–216.

GIANINO, A., & TRONICK, E. Z. (1988). The mutual regulation model: The infant's self and interactive regulation coping and defense. In T. Field, P. McCabe, & N. Schneiderman (Eds.), *Stress and coping.* Hillsdale, NJ: Erlbaum.

GIBBS, J. C. (1987). Social processes in delinquency: The need to facilitate empathy as well as sociomoral reasoning. In W. M. Kurtines & J. L. Gewirtz (Eds.), *Moral development through social interaction.* New York: Wiley.

GIBBS, J. C. (1991). Sociomoral developmental delay and cognitive distortion: Implications for the treatment of antisocial youth. In W. M. Kurtines & J. L. Gewirtz (Eds.), *Handbook of moral behavior and development: Vol. 3. Application.* Hillsdale, NJ: Erlbaum.

GIBBS, J. C., & SCHNELL, S. V. (1985). Moral judgment "versus" socialization: A critique. *American Psychologist, 40,* 1071–1080.

GIBBS, J. T. (Ed.). (1988). *Young, black, and male in America: An endangered species.* Dover, MA: Auburn House.

GIBSON, E. J. (1969). *Principles of perceptual learning and development.* New York: Appleton-Century-Crofts.

GIBSON, E. J. (1988). Exploratory behavior in the development of perceiving, acting, and the acquiring of knowledge. *Annual Review of Psychology, 39,* 1–41.

GIBSON, E. J. (1993). Ontogenesis of the perceived self. In U. Neisser (Ed.), *The perceived self: Ecological and interpersonal sources of self-knowledge.* Cambridge, MA: Cambridge University Press.

GIBSON, E. J., & WALK, R. D. (1960). The "visual cliff." *Scientific American, 202,* 64–71.

GIBSON, E. J., & WALKER, A. (1984). Development of knowledge of visual-tactual affordances of substance. *Child Development, 55,* 453–460.

GIBSON, J. J. (1966). *The senses considered as perceptual systems.* Boston: Houghton Mifflin.

GILLIGAN, C. (1982). *In a different voice: Psychological theory and women's development.* Cambridge: Harvard University Press.

GILLIGAN, C., & ATTANUCCI, J. (1988). Two moral orientations: Gender differences and similarities. *Merrill-Palmer Quarterly, 34,* 223–237.

GILLY, M. (1988). Gender roles in advertising: A comparison of television advertisements in Australia, Mexico, and the United States. *Journal of Marketing, 52,* 75–85.

GINSBURG, H. J. (1975, April). *Variations of aggressive interaction among male elementary school children as a function of spatial density.* Paper presented at the meeting of the Society for Research in Child Development, Denver, CO.

GINSBURG, H. J. (1980). Playground as laboratory: Naturalistic studies of appeasement, altruism, and the Omega child. In D. R. Omark, F. F. Strayer, & D. G. Freedman (Eds.), *Dominance relations: An ethological view of human conflict and social interaction.* New York: Garland.

GINSBURG, H., & OPPER, S. (1988). *Piaget's theory of intellectual development* (3rd ed.). Englewood Cliffs, NJ: Prentice Hall.

GINSBURG, H. P., KLEIN, A., & STARKEY, P. (1998). The development of children's mathematical thinking: Theory, research, and practice. In W. Damon (Series Ed.) & I. E. Sigel, & K. A. Renninger (Vol. Eds.), *Handbook of child psychology: Vol. 4. Child psychology in practice* (5th ed.). New York: Wiley.

GLADUE, B. A. (1994). The biopsychology of sexual orientation. *Current Directions in Psychological Science, 3,* 150–154.

GLADUE, B. A., BEATTY, W. W., LARSON, J., & STATON, R. D. (1990). Sexual orientation and spatial ability in men and women. *Psychobiology, 18,* 101–108.

GLASSMAN, M. (1994). All things being equal: The two roads of Piaget and Vygotsky. *Developmental Review, 114,* 186–214.

GLASSMAN, M., & ZAN, B. (1995). Moral activity and domain theory: An alternative interpretation of research with young children. *Developmental Review, 15,* 434–457.

GLEASON, J. B., & WEINTRAUB, S. (1978). Input and the acquisition of communicative competence. In K. E. Nelson (Ed.), *Children's language* (Vol. 1). New York: Gardner.

GLEITMAN, L. R. (1990). The structural sources of word meaning. *Language Acquisition, 1,* 3–55.

GLEITMAN, L. R., NEWPORT, E. L., & GLEITMAN, H. (1984). The current status of the motherese hypothesis. *Journal of Child Language, 11,* 43–79.

GLENN, S. M., CUNNINGHAM, C. C., & JOYCE P. F. (1981). A study of auditory preferences in nonhandicapped infants and infants with Down's syndrome. *Child Development, 52,* 1303–1307.

GODDARD, M., DURKIN, K., & RUTTER, D. R. (1985). The semantic focus of maternal speech: A comment on Ninio and Bruner (1978). *Journal of Child Language, 12,* 209–213.

GOLD, D., & BERGER, C. (1978). Problem-solving performance of young boys and girls as a function of task appropriateness and sex identity. *Sex Roles, 4,* 183–193.

GOLDBERG, S. (1983). Parent–infant bonding: Another look. *Child Development, 54,* 1355–1382.

GOLDFIELD, B. A. (1993). Noun bias in maternal speech to one-year-olds. *Journal of Child Language, 20,* 85–99.

GOLDFIELD, B. A., & REZNICK, J. S. (1990). Early lexical acquisition: Rate, content, and the vocabulary spurt. *Journal of Child Language, 17,* 171–183.

GOLDIN-MEADOW, S., & MYLANDER, C. (1984). Gestural communication in deaf children: The effects and noneffects of parental input on early language development. *Monographs of the Society for Research in Child Development, 49* (3–4, Serial No. 207).

GOLDIN-MEADOW, S., ALIBALI, M. W., & CHURCH, R. B. (1993). Transitions in concept acquisition: Using the hand to read the mind. *Psychological Review, 100,* 279–297.

GOLDIN-MEADOW, S., WEIN, D., & CHANG, C. (1992). Assessing knowledge through gesture: Using children's hands to read their minds. *Cognition and Instruction, 9,* 201–219.

GOLDMAN, A. S. (1980). Critical periods of prenatal toxic insults. In R. H. Schwartz & S. J. Yaffe (Eds.), *Drug and chemical risks to the fetus and newborn.* New York: Alan R. Liss.

GOLDSMITH, H. H., BUSS, A. H., PLOMIN, R., ROTHBART, M. K., THOMAS, A., CHESS, S., HINDE, R. A., & McCALL, R. B. (1987). Roundtable: What is temperament? Four approaches. *Child Development, 58,* 505–529.

GOLDSMITH, H. H., BUSS, K. A., & LEMERY, K. S. (1997). Toddler and childhood temperament: Expanded content, stronger genetic evidence, new evidence for the importance of environment. *Developmental Psychology, 33,* 891–905.

GOLDSMITH, H. H., & HARMAN, C. (1994). Temperament and attachment: Individuals and relationships. *Current Directions in Psychological Science, 3,* 53–57.

GOLDSMITH, H. H., & ROTHBART, M. K. (1991) Contemporary instruments for assessing early temperament by questionnaire and in the laboratory. In J. Strelau & A. Angleitner

(Eds.), *Explorations in temperament: International perspectives on theory and measurement.* New York: Plenum.

GOLDSTEIN, A. P., & GLICK, B. (1987). *Aggression replacement training: A comprehensive intervention for aggressive youth.* Champaign, IL: Research Press.

GOLDSTEIN, A. P., & GLICK, B. (1994). Aggression replacement training: Curriculum and evaluation. *Simulation and Gaming, 25,* 9–26.

GOLINKOFF, R. M., HIRSH-PASEK, K., CAULEY, K., & GORDON, L. (1987). The eyes have it: Lexical and syntactic comprehension in a new paradigm. *Journal of Child Language, 14,* 23–45.

GOLOMBOK, S., COOK, R., BISH, A., & MURRAY, C. (1995). Families created by the new reproductive technologies: Quality of parenting and social and emotional development of the children. *Child Development, 66,* 285–298.

GOOD, T. L. (1993). Teacher expectations. In L. Anderson (Ed.), *International encyclopedia of education* (2nd ed.). Oxford, England: Pergamon.

GOOD, T. L., & BROPHY, J. E. (1997). *Looking in classrooms* (7th ed.). New York: Longman.

GOODMAN, G. S., HIRSCHMANN, J. E., HEPPS, D., & RUDY, L. (1991). Children's memory for stressful events. *Merrill-Palmer Quarterly, 37,* 109–158.

GOODMAN, G. S., PYLE TAUB, E., JONES, D. P. H., ENGLAND, P., PORT, L. K., RUDY, L., & PRADO, L. (1992). Testifying in criminal court. *Monographs of the Society for Research in Child Development, 57* (5, Serial No. 229).

GOODMAN, G. S., & QUAS, J. A. (1997). Trauma and memory: Individual differences in children's recounting of a stressful experience. In N. L. Stein, P. A. Ornstein, B. Tversky, & C. Brainerd (Eds.), *Memory for everyday and emotional events.* Mahwah, NJ: Erlbaum.

GOODMAN, G. S., & TOBEY, A. E. (1994). Memory development within the context of child sexual abuse investigations. In C. B. Fisher & R. M. Lerner (Eds.), *Applied developmental psychology.* New York: McGraw-Hill.

GOODMAN, R., & STEVENSON, J. (1989). A twin study of hyperactivity: II. The aetiological role of genes, family relationships, and perinatal adversity. *Journal of Child Psychology and Psychiatry, 30,* 691–709.

GOODNOW, J. J. (1988). Children, families, and communities: Ways of viewing their relationships to each other. In N. Bolger, A. Caspi, G. Downey, & M. Moorehouse (Eds.), *Persons in context.* New York: Cambridge University Press.

GOODNOW, J. J., & COLLINS, W. A. (1990). *Development according to parents: The nature, sources, and consequences of parents' ideas.* Hillsdale, NJ: Erlbaum.

GOODZ, N. S. (1989). Parental language mixing in bilingual families. *Journal of Infant Mental Health, 10,* 25–34.

GOOSENS, F. A., & VAN IJZENDOORN, M. H. (1990). Quality of infants' attachments to professional caregivers: Relation to infant–parent attachment and day-care characteristics. *Child Development, 61,* 832–837.

GOPNIK, A., & MELTZOFF, A. N. (1987). Early semantic developments and their relationship to object permanence, means–ends understanding and categorization. In K. Nelson & A. VanKleek (Eds.), *Children's language* (Vol. 6). Hillsdale, NJ: Erlbaum.

GOPNIK, A., & MELTZOFF, A. N. (1992). Categorization and mapping: Basic-level sorting in eighteen-month-olds and its relation to language. *Child Development, 63,* 1091–1103.

GOPNIK, A., & MELTZOFF, A. N. (1996). *Words, thoughts, and theories.* Cambridge: MIT Press.

GOPNIK, A., & MELTZOFF, A. N. (1997). *Words, thoughts, and theories.* Cambridge: MIT Press.

GORMAN, K. S., & POLLITT, E. (1992). Relationship between weight and body proportionality at birth, growth during the first year of life, and cognitive development at 36, 48, and 60 months. *Infant Behavior and Development, 15,* 279–296.

GOSWAMI, U. (1995). Transitive relational mappings in three- and four-year-olds: The analogy of Goldilocks and the three bears. *Child Development, 66,* 877–892.

GOSWAMI, U., & BRYANT, P. (1990). *Phonological skills and learning to read.* Hove, England: Erlbaum.

GOTLIB, I. H., & HAMMEN, C. L. (1992). *Psychological aspects of depression: Toward a cognitive-interpersonal integration.* New York: Wiley.

GOTLIEB, S. J., BAISINI, F. J., & BRAY, N. W. (1988). Visual recognition memory in IVGR and normal birthweight infants. *Infant Behavior and Development, 11,* 223–228.

GOTTESMAN, I. I. (1974). Developmental genetics and ontogenetic psychology: Overdue detente and propositions from a matchmaker. In A. Pick (Ed.), *Minnesota symposium on child psychology.* Minneapolis: University of Minnesota Press.

GOTTESMAN, I. I., & SHIELDS, J. (1982). *Schizophrenia.* Cambridge: Cambridge University Press.

GOTTFRIED, A. W. (Ed.). (1984a). *Home environment and early cognitive development.* New York: Academic Press.

GOTTFRIED, A. W. (1984b). Home environment and early cognitive development: Integration, meta-analyses, and conclusions. In A. W. Gottfried (Ed.), *Home environment and early cognitive development.* New York: Academic Press.

GOTTMAN, J. M. (1983). How children become friends. *Monographs of the Society for Research in Child Development, 48* (3, Serial No. 201).

GOTTMAN, J. M., GONSO, J., & RASMUSSEN, B. (1975). Social interaction, social competence, and friendship in children. *Child Development, 46,* 709–718.

GOTTMAN, J. S. (1990). Children of gay and lesbian parents. In F. W. Bozett & M. B. Sussman (Eds.), *Homosexuality and family relations.* New York: Harrington Park Press.

GRABER, J. A., BROOKS-GUNN, J., PAIKOFF, R. L., & WARREN, M. P. (1994). Prediction of eating problems: An 8-year study of adolescent girls. *Developmental Psychology, 30,* 823–834.

GRAHAM, F. K., & CLIFTON, R. K. (1966). Heart-rate change as a component of the orienting response. *Psychological Bulletin, 65,* 305–320.

GRAHAM, S., & HOCHN, S. (1995). Children's understanding of aggression and withdrawal as social stigmas: An attributional analysis. *Child Development, 66,* 1143–1161.

GRAHAM, S., & HUDLEY, C. (1994). Attributions of aggressive and nonaggressive African-American male early adolescents: A study of construct accessibility. *Developmental Psychology, 30,* 365–373.

GRAHAM, S., & JUVONEN, J. (1998). A social cognitive perspective on peer aggression and victimization. In R. Vasta (Ed.), *Annals of child development.* (Vol. 13). London: Kingsley.

GRAHAM, S., HUDLEY, C., & WILLIAMS, E. (1992). Attributional and emotional determinants of aggression among African-American and Latino young adolescents. *Developmental Psychology, 28,* 731–740.

GRALINSKI, J. H., & KOPP, C. B. (1993). Everyday rules for behavior: Mothers' requests to young children. *Developmental Psychology, 29,* 573–584.

GRATTAN, M. P., De VOS, E., LEVY, J., & McCLINTOCK, M. K. (1992). Asymmetric action in the human newborn: Sex differences in patterns of organization. *Child Development, 62,* 273–289.

GRAY, S. W., & RAMSEY, B. K. (1982). The Early Training Project: A life-span view. *Human Development, 25,* 48–57.

GRAY, S. W., RAMSEY, B. K., & KLAUS, R. A. (1982). *From 3 to 20: The early training project.* Baltimore: University Park Press.

GRAY, W. M. (1990). Formal operational thought. In W. F. Overton (Ed.), *Reasoning, necessity, and logic: Developmental perspectives.* Hillsdale, NJ: Erlbaum.

GRAY, W. M., & HUDSON, L. M. (1984). Formal operations and the imaginary audience. *Developmental Psychology, 20,* 619–627.

GRAZIANO, W. G. (1987). Lost in thought at the choice point: Cognition, context, and equity. In J. C. Masters & W. P. Smith (Eds.), *Social comparison, social justice, and relative deprivation.* Hillsdale, NJ: Erlbaum.

GREEN, J. A., JONES, L. E., & GUSTAFSON, G. E. (1987). Perception of cries by parents and nonparents: Relation to cry acoustics. *Developmental Psychology, 23,* 370–382.

GREEN, K. D., FOREHAND, R., BECK, S. J., & VOSK, B. (1980). An assessment of the relationship among measures of children's social competence and children's academic achievement. *Child Development, 51,* 1149–1156.

GREEN, R. (1974). *Sexual identity conflict in children and adults.* New York: Basic Books.

GREEN, R. (1987). *The "sissy boy syndrome" and the development of homosexuality.* New Haven, CT: Yale University Press.

GREENFIELD, P. M. (1966). On culture and conservation. In J. S. Bruner, R. R. Olver, & P. M. Greenfield (Eds.), *Studies in cognitive growth.* New York: Wiley.

GREENLEAF, B. K. (1978). *Children through the ages: A history of childhood.* New York: McGraw-Hill.

GREENOUGH, W. T., & BLACK, J. E. (1992). Induction of brain structure by experience: Substrates for cognitive development. In M. R. Gunnar & C. A. Nelson (Eds.), *Minnesota symposia on child psychology: Vol. 24. Developmental behavioral neuroscience.* Hillsdale, NJ: Erlbaum.

GREENOUGH, W. T., BLACK, J. E., & WALLACE, C. S. (1987). Experience and brain development. *Child Development, 58,* 539–559.

GREENWALD, A., & PRATKANIS, A. (1984). The self. In R. Wyer & T. Srull (Eds.), *Handbook of social cognition* (Vol. 3). Hillsdale, NJ: Erlbaum.

GREGORY, R. (1978). *Eye and brain: The psychology of seeing* (3rd ed.). New York: McGraw Hill.

GRIFFITHS, P. (1985). The communicative functions of children's single-word speech. In M. D. Barrett (Ed.), *Children's single-word speech.* New York: Wiley.

GRIMSHAW, J. (1981). Form, function, and the language-acquisition device. In C. L. Baker & J. J. McCarthy (Eds.), *The logical problem of language acquisition.* Cambridge: MIT Press.

GRINDER, R. E. (1967). *A history of genetic psychology: The first science of human development.* New York: Wiley.

GROLNICK, W., BRIDGES, L. J., & CONNELL, J. P. (1996). Emotion regulation in two-year-olds: Strategies and emotional expression in four contexts. *Child Development, 67,* 928–941.

GRONAU, R. C., & WAAS, G. A. (1997). Delay of gratification and cue utilization: An examination of children's social information processing. *Merrill-Palmer Quarterly, 43,* 305–322.

GRONLUND, N. (1959). *Sociometry in the classroom.* New York: Harper.

GROOME, L. J., SWIBER, M. J., ATTERBURY, J. L., BENTZ, L. S., & HOLLAND, S. B. (1997). Similarities and differences in behavioral state organization during sleep periods in the perinatal infant before and after birth. *Child Development, 68,* 1–11.

GROSSMAN, K. E. (1995). The evolution and history of attachment research and theory. In S. Goldberg, R. Muir, & J. Kerr (Eds.), *Attachment theory: Social, developmental, and clinical perspectives.* Hillsdale, NJ: The Analytic Press.

GROSSMANN, K. E., & GROSSMANN, K. (1990). The wider concept of attachment in cross-cultural research. *Human Development, 33,* 31–47.

GROSSMANN, K., GROSSMANN, K. E., SPANGLER, G., SUESS, G., & UNZNER, L. (1985). Maternal sensitivity and newborns' orientation responses as related to quality of attachment in northern Germany. In I. Bretherton & E. Waters (Eds.), Growing points of attachment theory and research. *Monographs of the Society for Research in Child Development, 50*(1–2, Serial No. 209).

GROTEVANT, H. D. (1989). Child development within the family context. In W. Damon (Ed.), *Child development today and tomorrow.* San Francisco: Jossey-Bass.

GROVES, B., ZUCKERMAN, B., MARANS, S., & COHEN, D. (1993). Silent victims: Children who witness violence. *Journal of the American Medical Association, 269,* 262–264.

GRUENEICH, R. (1982). Issues in the developmental study of how children use intention and consequence information to make moral evaluations. *Child Development, 53,* 29–43.

GRUSEC, J. E. (1992). Social learning theory and developmental psychology: The legacy of Robert Sears and Albert Bandura. *Developmental Psychology, 28,* 776–786.

GRUSEC, J. E., & ABRAMOVITCH, R. (1982). Imitation of peers and adults in a natural setting: A functional analysis. *Child Development, 53,* 636–642.

GRUSEC, J. E., & GOODNOW, J. J. (1994). Impact of parental discipline methods on the child's internalization of values: A reconceptualization of current points of view. *Developmental Psychology, 30,* 4–19.

GRUSEC, J. E., & LYTTON, H. (1988). *Social development: History, theory, and research.* New York: Springer-Verlag.

GRUSEC, J. E., KUCZYNSKI, L., RUSHTON, J. P., & SIMUTIS, Z. M. (1979). Learning resistance to temptation through observation. *Developmental Psychology, 15,* 233–240.

GUERIN, D. W., & GOTTFRIED, A. W. (1994). Developmental stability and change in parent reports of temperament: A ten-year longitudinal investigation from infancy through preadolescence. *Merrill-Palmer Quarterly, 40,* 334–355.

GUERRA, N. G., & SLABY, R. G. (1990). Cognitive mediators of aggression in adolescent offenders: 2. Intervention. *Developmental Psychology, 26,* 269–277.

GUILFORD, J. P. (1988). Some changes in the structure-of-the-intellect model. *Educational and Psychological Measurement, 48,* 1–4.

GUILLEMIN, J. (1993). Cesarean birth: Social and political aspects. In B. K. Rothman (Ed.), *Encyclopedia of childbearing.* Phoenix, AZ: Oryx Press.

GUISINGER, S., & BLATT, S. J. (1994). Individuality and relatedness. *American Psychologist, 49,* 104–111.

GUNNAR, M. R., FISCH, R. O., & MALONE, S. (1984). The effects of a pacifying stimulus on behavioral and adrenocortical responses to circumcision in the newborn. *Journal of the American Academy of Child Psychiatry, 23,* 34–38.

GUNNAR, M. R., MALONE, S., VANCE, G., & FISCH, R. O. (1985). Coping with aversive stimulation in the neonatal period: Quiet sleep and plasma cortisol levels during recovery from circumcision. *Child Development, 56,* 824–834.

GUNTER, B. (1995). *Television and gender representation.* London: John Libbey.

GUNTHEROTH, W. (1995). *Crib death: The sudden infant death syndrome* (3rd ed.). Armonk, NY: Futura.

GURMAN BARD, E., & ANDERSON, A. (1983). The unintelligibility of speech to children. *Journal of Child Language, 10,* 265–292.

GURUCHARRI, C., & SELMAN, R. L. (1982). The development of interpersonal understanding during childhood, preadolescence, and adolescence: A longitudinal follow-up study. *Child Development, 53,* 924–927.

GUSTAFSON, G. E., & HARRIS, K. L. (1990). Women's responses to young infants' cries. *Developmental Psychology, 26,* 144–152.

HAAPASALO, J., & TREMBLAY, R. E. (1994). Physically aggressive boys from age 6 to 12: Family background, parenting behavior, and prediction of delinquency. *Journal of Consulting and Clinical Psychology, 62,* 1044–1052.

HACK, M., KLEIN, N. K., & TAYLOR, H. G. (1995). Long-term developmental outcomes of low birth weight infants. *The future of children* (Vol. 5, No. 1). Los Angeles: Packard Foundation.

HADJISTAVROPOULOS, H. D., CRAIG, K. D., GRUNAU, R. V. E., & JOHNSTON, C. C. (1994). Judging pain in newborns: Facial and cry determinants. *Journal of Pediatric Psychology, 19,* 485–491.

HAECKEL, E. (1977). Last words on evolution. In D. N. Robinson (Ed.), *Significant contributions to the history of psychology: 1750–1920.* Washington, DC: University Publications of America. (Original work published 1906).

HAGEN, J.W., & HALE, G. A. (1973). The development of attention in children. In A. D. Pick (Ed.), *Minnesota symposia on child psychology* (Vol. 7). Minneapolis: University of Minnesota Press.

HAGERMAN, R. J. (1996). Biomedical advances in developmental psychology: The case of Fragile X syndrome. *Developmental Psychology, 32,* 416–424.

HAGGERTY, R., GARMEZY, N., RUTTER, M., & SHERROD, L. R. (Eds.). (1994). *Stress, risk and resilience in children and adolescents: Processes, mechanisms, and interventions.* New York: Cambridge University Press.

HAIGHT, W., & MILLER, P. J. (1993). *Pretending at home.* Albany, NY: SUNY Press.

HAINLINE, L., & ABRAMOV, I. (1992). Assessing visual development: Is infant vision good enough? In C. Rovee-Collier & L. P. Lipsitt (Eds.), *Advances in infancy research* (Vol. 7). Norwood, NJ: Ablex.

HAITH, M. M. (1966). The response of the human newborn to visual movement. *Journal of Experimental Child Psychology, 3,* 235–243.

HAITH, M. M. (1980). *Rules that babies look by.* Hillsdale, NJ: Erlbaum.

HAITH, M. M. (1986). Sensory and perceptual processes in early infancy. *Journal of Pediatrics, 109,* 158–171.

HAITH, M. M. (1991). Gratuity, perception-action integration and future orientation in infant vision. In F. Kessel, A. Sameroff, & M. Bornstein (Eds.), *The past as prologue in developmental psychology: Essays in honor of William Kessen.* Hillsdale, NJ: Erlbaum.

HAITH, M. M. (1993). Preparing for the 21st century: Some goals and challenges for studies of infant sensory and perceptual development. *Developmental Review, 13,* 354–371.

HAITH, M. M. (1994). Visual expectations as the first step toward the development of future-oriented processes. In M. M. Haith, J. B. Benson, R. J. Roberts, Jr., & B. F. Pennington (Eds.), *The development of future-oriented processes.* Chicago: University of Chicago Press.

HAITH, M. M., & BENSON, J. B. (1998). Infant cognition. In W. Damon (Series Ed.) & D. Kuhn & R. S. Siegler (Vol. Eds.), *Handbook of child psychology: Vol. 2. Cognition, perception, and language* (5th ed.). New York: Wiley.

HAITH, M. M., BENSON, J. B., ROBERTS, R. J., JR., & PENNINGTON, B. F. (Eds.). (1994). *The development of future-oriented processes.* Chicago: University of Chicago Press.

HAITH, M. M., BERGMAN, T., & MOORE, M. J. (1977). Eye contact and face scanning in early infancy. *Science, 198,* 853–855.

HAITH, M. M., WENTWORTH, N., & CANFIELD, R. L. (1993). The formation of expectations in early infancy. In C. Rovee-Collier & L. P. Lipsitt (Eds.), *Advances in infancy research* (Vol. 8). Norwood, NJ: Ablex.

HALFORD, G. S. (1989). Reflections on 25 years of Piagetian cognitive developmental psychology, 1963–1988. *Human Development, 32,* 325–357.

HALFORD, G. S. (1993). *Children's understanding: The development of mental models.* Hillsdale, NJ: Erlbaum.

HALL, G. S. (1904). *Adolescence: Its psychology and its relations to physiology, anthropology, sociology, sex, crime, religion, and education* (2 vols.). New York: Appleton.

HALPERN, D. F. (1992). *Sex differences in cognitive abilities* (2nd ed.). Hillsdale, NJ: Erlbaum.

HALPERN, L. F., MacLEAN, JR., W. E., & BAUMEISTER, A. A. (1995). Infant sleep-wake characteristics: Relation to neurological status and the prediction of developmental outcome. *Developmental Review, 15,* 255–291.

HALPERN, R. (1993). Poverty and infant development. In C. H. Zeanah, Jr. (Ed.), *Handbook*

of infant mental development. New York: Guilford.

HAMER, D. H., HU, S., MAGNUSON, V. L., HU, N., & PATTATUCCI, A. M. L. (1993). A linkage between DNA markers on the X chromosome and male sexual orientations. *Science, 261,* 321–327.

HAMMEN, C., & ZUPAN, B. A. (1984). Self-schemas, depression, and the processing of personal information in children. *Journal of Experimental Child Psychology, 37,* 598–608.

HAMPSON, I., & NELSON, K. (1993). The relation of maternal language to variation in rate and style of language acquisition. *Journal of Child Language, 20,* 313–342.

HANDYSIDE, A. H., LESKO, J. G., TARÍN, J. J., WINSTON, R. M. L., & HUGHES, M. R. (1992). Birth of a normal girl after in vitro fertilization and preimplantation diagnostic testing for cystic fibrosis. *New England Journal of Medicine, 327,* 905–909.

HANNA, E., & MELTZOFF, A. N. (1993). Peer imitation by toddlers in laboratory, home, and day-care contexts: Implications for social learning and memory. *Developmental Psychology, 29,* 701–710.

HANSON, S. M. H. (1988). Divorced fathers with custody. In P. Bronstein & C. P. Cowan (Eds.), *Fatherhood today: Men's changing role in the family.* New York: Wiley.

HARDING, C. G. (1983). Setting the stage for language acquisition: Communication development in the first year. In R. M. Golinkoff (Ed.), *The transition from prelinguistic to linguistic communication.* Hillsdale, NJ: Erlbaum.

HARKNESS, S., & SUPER, C. M. (1987). The use of cross-cultural research in child development. In R. Vasta (Ed.), *Annals of child development* (Vol. 4). Greenwich, CT: JAI Press.

HARLOW, H. F., & HARLOW, M. K. (1966). Learning to love. *American Scientist, 54,* 244–272.

HARPER, L., & KRAFT, R. H. (1986). Lateralization of receptive language in pre-schoolers: Test–retest reliability in a dichotic listening task. *Developmental Psychology, 22,* 553–556.

HARPER, P. S. (1981). *Practical genetic counseling.* Baltimore: University Park Press.

HARRIS, L. J. (1977). Sex differences in the growth and use of language. In E. Donelson & J. E. Gullahorn (Eds.), *Women: A psychological perspective.* New York: Wiley.

HARRIS, M., BARRETT, M., JONES, D., & BROOKES, S. (1988). Linguistic input and early word meaning. *Journal of Child Language, 15,* 77–94.

HARRIS, M., JONES, D., & GRANT, J. (1983). The nonverbal context of mothers' speech to infants. *First Language, 4,* 21–30.

HARRIS, P. L. (1983). Infant cognition. In P. H. Mussen (Series Ed.) & M. M. Haith & J. J. Campos (Vol. Eds.), *Handbook of child psychology: Vol. 2. Infancy and developmental psychobiology.* New York: Wiley.

HARRIS, P. L. (1989). Object permanence in infancy. In A. Slater & G. Bremner (Eds.), *Infant development.* Hillsdale, NJ: Erlbaum.

HART, C. H., DeWOLF, D. M., WOZNIAK, P., & BURTS, D. C. (1992). Maternal and paternal disciplinary styles: Relations with preschoolers' playground behavioral orientations and peer status. *Child Development, 63,* 879–892.

HART, D. (1988a). The development of personal identity in adolescence: A philosophical dilemma approach. *Merrill-Palmer Quarterly, 34,* 105–114.

HART, D. (1988b). A longitudinal study of adolescents' socialization and identification as predictors of adult moral judgment development. *Merrill-Palmer Quarterly, 34,* 245–260.

HART, D., & DAMON, W. (1985). Contrasts between understanding self and understanding others. In R. L. Leahy (Ed.), *The development of the self.* Orlando, FL: Academic Press.

HART, D., & FEGLEY, S. (1995). Prosocial behavior and caring in adolescence: Relations to self-understanding and social judgment. *Child Development, 66,* 1346–1359.

HART, D., & FEGLEY, S. (1997). Children's self-awareness and self-understanding in cultural context. In U. Neisser & D. A. Jopling (Ed.), *The conceptual self in context: Culture, experience, and self-understanding.* New York: Cambridge University Press.

HART, D., & YATES, M. (1996). The interrelation of self and identity in adolescence: A developmental account. In R. Vasta (Ed.), *Annals of child development* (Vol. 12). London: Kingsley.

HART, D., YATES, M., FEGLEY, S., & WILSON, G. (1995). Moral commitment among inner-city adolescents. In M. Killen & D. Hart (Eds.), *Morality in everyday life: Developmental perspectives.* New York: Cambridge University Press.

HART, S. N. (1991). From property to person status: Historical perspective on children's rights. *American Psychologist, 46,* 53–59.

HARTER, S. (1981). A new self-report scale of intrinsic versus extrinsic orientation in the classroom: Motivational and informational components. *Developmental Psychology, 17,* 300–312.

HARTER, S. (1982). A developmental perspective on some parameters of self-regulation in children. In P. Karoly & F. H. Kanfer (Eds.), *Self-management and behavior change: From theory to practice.* New York: Pergamon.

HARTER, S. (1983). Developmental perspectives on the self-system. In E. M. Hetherington (Ed.), *Handbook of child psychology: Vol. 4. Socialization, personality, and social development.* New York: Wiley.

HARTER, S. (1985). Competence as a dimension of self-evaluation: Toward a comprehensive model of self-worth. In R. L. Leahy (Ed.), *The development of the self.* Orlando, FL: Academic Press.

HARTER, S. (1986). Processes underlying the construction, maintenance, and enhancement of the self-concept in children. In J. Suls &

A. Greenwald (Eds.), *Psychological perspectives on the self* (Vol. 3). Hillsdale, NJ: Erlbaum.

HARTER, S. (1987). The determinants and mediational role of global self-worth in children. In N. Eisenberg (Ed.), *Contemporary topics in developmental psychology*. New York: Wiley.

HARTER, S. (1988). Developmental processes in the construction of the self. In T. D. Yawkey & J. E. Johnson (Eds.), *Integrative processes and socialization: Early to middle childhood*. Hillsdale, NJ: Erlbaum.

HARTER, S. (1990). Causes, correlates and the functional role of self-worth: A life-span perspective. In R. J. Sternberg & J. Kolligian (Eds.), *Competence considered*. New Haven, CT: Yale University Press.

HARTER, S. (1994). Developmental changes in self-understanding across the 5 to 7 shift. In A. Sameroff & M. M. Haith (Eds.), *Reason and responsibility: The passage through childhoood*. Chicago: University of Chicago Press.

HARTER, S. (1998). The development of self-representations. In W. Damon (Ed.), *Handbook of child psychology: Vol. 3. Social, emotional, & personality development*. New York: Wiley.

HARTER, S., & CONNELL, J. P. (1984). A model of the relationship among children's academic achievement and their self-perceptions of competence, control, and motivational orientation. In J. Nicholls (Ed.), *The development of achievement motivation*. Greenwich, CT: JAI Press.

HARTER, S., & MONSOUR, A. (1992). Developmental analysis of conflict caused by opposing attributes in the adolescent self-portrait. *Developmental Psychology, 28*, 251–260.

HARTER, S., & PIKE, R. (1984). The Pictorial Scale of Perceived Competence and Social Acceptance for Young Children. *Child Development, 55*, 1969–1982.

HARTER, S., MAROLD, D. B., WHITESELL, N. R., & COBBS, G. (1996). A model of the effects of perceived parent and peer support on adolescent false self behavior. *Child Development, 67*, 360–374.

HARTIG, M., & KANFER, F. H. (1973). The role of verbal self-instructions in children's resistance to temptation. *Journal of Personality and Social Psychology, 25*, 259–267.

HARTSHORNE, H., & MAY, M. S. (1928–1930). *Studies in the nature of character* (3 vols.). New York: Macmillan.

HARTUP, W. W. (1983). Peer relations. In P. H. Mussen (Series Ed.) & J. H. Flavell & E. M. Hetherington (Vol. Eds.), *Handbook of child psychology: Vol. 4. Socialization, personality, and social development*. New York: Wiley.

HARTUP, W. W. (1992a). Conflict and friendship relations. In C. U. Shantz & W. W. Hartup (Eds.), *Conflict in child and adolescent development*. Cambridge: Cambridge University Press.

HARTUP, W. W. (1992b). Friendships and their developmental significance. In H. McGurk (Ed.), *Childhood social development: Contemporary perspectives*. Hillsdale, NJ: Erlbaum.

HARTUP, W. W. (1992c). Peer relations in early and middle childhood. In V. B. Van Hasselt & M. Hersen (Eds.), *Handbook of social development*. New York: Plenum.

HARTUP, W. W. (1993). Adolescents and their friends. In B. Laursen (Ed.), *New directions for child development: No. 60. Close friendships in adolescence*. San Francisco: Jossey-Bass.

HARTUP, W. W. (1996a). The company they keep: Friendships and their developmental significance. *Child Development, 67*, 1–13.

HARTUP, W. W. (1996b). Cooperation, close relationships, and cognitive development. In W. M. Bukowski, A. F. Newcomb, & W. W. Hartup (Eds.), *The company they keep: Friendship in childhood and adolescence*. New York: Cambridge University Press.

HARTUP, W. W., & STEVENS, N. (1997). Friendships and adaptation in the life course. *Psychological Bulletin, 121*, 355–370.

HARTUP, W. W., DAIUTE, C., ZAJAC, R., & SHALL, W. (1995). *Collaboration in creative writing by friends and nonfriends*. Unpublished manuscript, University of Minnesota, Minneapolis.

HARTUP, W. W., FRENCH, D. C., LAURSEN, B., JOHNSON, M. K., & OGAWA, J. R. (1993). Conflict and friendship relations in middle childhood: Behavior in a closed-field situation. *Child Development, 64*, 445–454.

HARVARD LAW REVIEW. (1989). *Sexual orientation and the law*. Cambridge: Harvard University Press.

HARVEY, S. E., & LIEBERT, R. M. (1979). Abstraction, inference, and acceptance in children's processing of an adult model's moral judgments. *Developmental Psychology, 15*, 552–558.

HARWOOD, R. L. (1992). The influence of culturally derived values on Anglo and Puerto Rican mothers' perceptions of attachment behavior. *Child Development, 63*, 822–839.

HARWOOD, R. L., & MILLER, J. G. (1991). Perceptions of attachment behavior: A comparison of Anglo and Puerto Rican mothers. *Merrill-Palmer Quarterly, 37*, 583–599.

HARWOOD, R. L., MILLER, J. G., & IRIZARRY, N. L. (1995). *Culture and attachment*. New York: Guilford.

HASSELHORN, M. (1992). Task dependency and the role of category typicality and metamemory in the development of an organizational strategy. *Child Development, 63*, 202–214.

HATANO, G. (1990). Commentary: Toward the cultural psychology of mathematical cognition. *Monographs of the Society for Research in Child Development, 55* (1–2, Serial No. 221).

HATTIE, J., & MARSH, H. W. (1996). Future directions in self-concept research. In B. A. Bracken (Ed.), *Handbook of self-concept: Developmental, social, and clinical considerations*. New York: Wiley.

HAVILAND, J. M., & LELWICA, M. (1987). The induced affect response: 10-week-old infants' response to three emotion expressions. *Developmental Psychology, 23*, 97–104.

HAWKINS, J., PEA, R. D., GLICK, J., & SCRIBNER, S. (1984). "Merds that laugh don't like mushrooms": Evidence for deductive reasoning in preschoolers. *Developmental Psychology, 20*, 584–594.

HAWLEY, T. L., & DISNEY, E. R. (1992). Crack's children: The consequences of maternal cocaine abuse. Social Policy Report. *Society for Research in Child Development, 6*, 1–23.

HAY, D. F. (1984). Social conflict in early childhood. In G. J. Whitehurst (Ed.), *Annals of child development* (Vol. 1). Greenwich, CT: JAI Press.

HAY, D. F. (1985). Learning to form relationships in infancy: Parallel attainments with parents and peers. *Developmental Review, 5*, 122–161.

HAY, D. F. (1986). Learning to be social: Some comments on Schaffer's *The child's entry into a social world*. *Developmental Review, 6*, 107–114.

HAY, D. F. (1994). Prosocial development. *Journal of Child Psychology and Psychiatry, 35*, 29–71.

HAY, D. F., & MURRAY, P. (1982). Giving and requesting: Social facilitation of infants' offers to adults. *Infant Behavior and Development, 5*, 301–310.

HAY, D. F., CASTLE, J., STIMSOM, C., & DAVIES, L. (1995). The social construction of character in toddlerhood. In M. Killen & D. Hart (Eds.), *Morality in everyday life*. New York: Cambridge University Press.

HAY, D. F., MURRAY, P., CECIRE, S., & NASH, A. (1985). Social learning of social behavior in early life. *Child Development, 56*, 43–57.

HAY, D. F., NASH, A., & PEDERSEN, J. (1983). Interaction between six-month-old peers. *Child Development, 54*, 557–562.

HAY, L. (1984). Discontinuity in the development of motor control in children. In W. Prinz & A. F. Sanders (Eds.), *Cognition and motor processes*. Berlin: Springer-Verlag.

HAYDEN-THOMSON, L., RUBIN, K. H., & HYMEL, S. (1987). Sex preferences in sociometric choices. *Developmental Psychology, 23*, 558–562.

HAYES, D. S., GERSHMAN, E., & BOLIN, L. J. (1980). Friends and enemies: Cognitive bases for preschool children's unilateral and reciprocal relationships. *Child Development, 51*, 1276–1279.

HAYES, J. S., LAMPART, R., DREHER, M. C., & MORGAN, L. (1991). Five-year follow-up of rural Jamaican children whose mothers used marijuana during pregnancy. *W. I. Medical Journal, 40*, 120–123.

HAYNE, H. (1996). Categorization in infancy. In C. Rovee-Collier & L. P. Lipsitt (Eds.), *Advances in infancy research* (Vol. 10). Norwood, NJ: Ablex.

HAYNES, H., WHITE, B. L., & HELD, R. (1965). Visual accommodation in human infants. *Science, 148*, 528–530.

HAZEN, N. L., & DURRETT, M. E. (1982). Relationship of security of attachment to exploration and cognitive mapping abilities in 2-year-olds. *Developmental Psychology, 18,* 751–759.

HEAROLD, S. (1986). A synthesis of 1043 effects of television on social behavior. In G. Comstock (Ed.), *Public communication and behavior* (Vol. 1). Orlando, FL: Academic Press.

HEATH, S. B. (1983). *Ways with words: Language, life, and work in communities and classrooms.* New York: Cambridge University Press.

HEBB, D. O. (1949). *The organization of behavior.* New York: Wiley.

HEDGES, L. V., & NOWELL, A. (1995). Sex differences in mental test scores, variability, and numbers of high-scoring individuals. *Science, 269,* 41–45.

HEIBECK, T., & MARKMAN, E. M. (1987). Word learning in children: An examination of fast mapping. *Child Development, 58,* 1021–1034.

HEIMANN, M., NELSON, K. E., & SCHALLER, J. (1989). Neonatal imitation of tongue protrusion and mouth opening: Methodological aspects and evidence of early individual differences. *Scandinavian Journal of Psychology, 30,* 90–101.

HEKMAN, S. J. (1995). *Moral voices, moral selves: Carol Gilligan and feminist moral theory.* University Park: The University of Pennsylvania Press.

HELLER, J. (1987). What do we know about the risk of caffeine consumption in pregnancy? *British Journal of Addiction, 82,* 885–889.

HELWIG, C. C., HILDEBRANDT, C., & TURIEL, E. (1995). Children's judgments about psychological harm in social context. *Child Development, 66,* 1680–1693.

HENRY, B., CASPI, A., MOFFITT, T. E., & SILVA, P. A. (1996). Temperamental and familial predictors of violent and nonviolent criminal convictions: Age 3 to age 18. *Developmental Psychology, 32,* 614–623.

HEPBURN, M. A. (1995). TV violence: Myth and reality. *Social Education, 59,* 309–311.

HERMAN, J. F., & SIEGEL, A. W. (1978). The development of cognitive mapping of the large-scale environment. *Journal of Experimental Child Psychology, 26,* 389–406.

HERRNSTEIN, R. J. (1971, September). I.Q. *Atlantic Monthly,* pp. 43–64.

HERRNSTEIN, R. J. (1973). *IQ in the meritocracy.* Boston: Little, Brown.

HERRNSTEIN, R. J., & MURRAY, C. (1994). *The bell curve: Intelligence and class structure in American life.* New York: Free Press.

HERSHENSON, M. (1964). Visual discrimination in the human newborn. *Journal of Comparative and Physiological Psychology, 58,* 270–276.

HESS, E. K., & PETROVICH. S. (1991). Ethology and attachment: A historical perspective. In J. L. Gewirtz & W. M. Kurtines (Eds.), *Intersections with attachment.* Hillsdale, NJ: Erlbaum.

HESS, R. D., & MIURA, I. T. (1985). Gender differences in enrollment in computer-camps and classes. *Sex Roles, 13,* 193–203.

HETHERINGTON, E. M. (1993). An overview of the Virginia Longitudinal Study of Divorce and Remarriage: A focus on early adolescence. *Journal of Family Psychology, 7,* 39–56.

HETHERINGTON, E. M., & JODL, K. M. (1994). Stepfamilies as settings for child development. In A. Booth & J. Dunn (Eds.), *Stepfamilies: Who benefits? Who does not?* Hillsdale, NJ: Erlbaum.

HETHERINGTON, E. M., & STANLEY-HAGAN, M. M. (1995). Parenting in divorced and remarried families. In M. H. Bornstein (Ed.), *Handbook of parenting: Vol. 3. Status and social conditions of parenting.* Mahwah, NJ: Erlbaum.

HETHERINGTON, E. M., BRIDGES, M., & INSABELLA, G. M. (1998). What matters? What does not? Five perspectives on the association between marital transitions and children's adjustment. *American Psychologist, 53,* 167–184.

HETHERINGTON, E. M., CLING-EMPEEL, W. G., ANDERSON, E. R., DEAL, J. E., STANLEY-HAGAN, M., HOLLIER, E. A., & LINDNER, M. S. (1992). Coping with marital transitions: A family perspective. *Monographs of the Society for Research in Child Development, 57* (2–3, Serial No. 227).

HETHERINGTON, E. M., REISS, D., & PLOMIN, R. (Eds.). (1994). *Separate social worlds of siblings: The impact of nonshared environment on development.* Hillsdale, NJ: Erlbaum.

HEWLETT, B. S. (Ed.). (1992). *Father–child relations: Cultural and biosocial contexts.* New York: Aldine de Gruyter.

HICKMANN, M. (1986). Psychosocial aspects of language acquisition. In P. Fletcher & M. Garman (Eds.), *Language acquisition: Studies in first language acquisition* (2nd ed.). New York: Cambridge University Press.

HICKS, D. (1996). *Discourse, learning, and schooling.* New York: Cambridge University Press.

HIGGINS, A., POWER, C., & KOHLBERG, L. (1984). The relationship of moral atmosphere to judgments of responsibility. In W. M. Kurtines & J. L. Gewirtz (Eds.), *Morality, moral behavior, and moral development.* New York: Wiley.

HIGGINS, E. T. (1991). Development of self-regulatory and self-evaluative processes: Costs, benefits, and tradeoffs. In M. R. Gunnar & L. A. Sroufe (Eds.), *Minnesota symposia on child development:* Vol. 23. *Self processes and development.* Hillsdale, NJ: Erlbaum.

HILGARD, E. R. (1987). *Psychology in America: A historical survey.* San Diego: Harcourt Brace Jovanovich.

HILL, J. P., & LYNCH, M. E. (1983). The intensification of gender-related role expectations during early adolescence. In J. Brooks-Gunn & A. C. Petersen (Eds.), *Girls at puberty: Biological and psychological perspectives.* New York: Plenum.

HINDE, R. A. (1983). Ethology and child development. In P. H. Mussen (Series Ed.) & M. M. Haith & J. J. Campos (Vol. Eds.), *Handbook of child psychology: Vol. 2. Infancy and developmental psychobiology.* New York: Wiley.

HINDE, R. A. (1986). Some implications of evolutionary theory and comparative data for the study of human prosocial and aggressive behavior. In D. Olweus, J. Block, & M. Radke-Yarrow (Eds.), *Development of antisocial and prosocial behavior.* New York: Academic Press.

HINES, M. (1982). Prenatal gonad hormones and sex differences in human behavior. *Psychological Bulletin, 92,* 56–80.

HINES, M., & GREEN, R. (1991). Human hormonal and neural correlates of sex-typed behaviors. *Review of Psychiatry, 10,* 536–555.

HINES, M., & KAUFMAN, F. R. (1994). Androgen and the development of human sex-typical behavior: Rough-and-tumble and sex of preferred playmates in children with congenital adrenal hyperplasia (CAH). *Child Development, 65,* 1042–1053.

HIRSCH, B. J., & RENDERS, R. J. (1986). The challenge of adolescent friendships: A study of Lisa and her friends. In S. E. Hobfolk (Ed.), *Stress, social support, and women.* Washington, DC: Hemisphere.

HIRSH-PASEK, K., & GOLINKOFF, R. M. (1996). *The origins of grammar: Evidence from early language comprehension.* Cambridge: MIT Press.

HIRSH-PASEK, K., TREIMAN, R., & SCHNEIDERMAN, M. (1984). Brown and Hanlon revisited: Mothers' sensitivity to ungrammatical forms. *Journal of Child Language, 11,* 81–88.

HITTLEMAN, J. H., & DICKES, R. (1979). Sex differences in neonatal eye contact time. *Merrill-Palmer Quarterly, 25,* 171–184.

HO, D. Y. F. (1986). Chinese patterns of socialization: A critical review. In M. H. Bond (Ed.), *The psychology of Chinese people.* New York: Oxford University Press.

HO, D. Y. F. (1987). Fatherhood in Chinese culture. In M. E. Lamb (Ed.), *The father's role: Cross-cultural perspectives.* Hillsdale, NJ: Erlbaum.

HOCK, E., & DEMEIS, D. K. (1990). Depression in mothers of infants: The role of maternal employment. *Developmental Psychology, 26,* 285–291.

HOCK, E., & SCHIRTZINGER, M. B. (1992). Maternal separation anxiety: Its developmental course and relation to maternal mental health. *Developmental Psychology, 63,* 93–102.

HODAPP, R. M., & GOLDFIELD, E. C. (1985). Self- and other regulation during the infancy period. *Developmental Review, 5,* 274–288.

HOEK, D., INGRAM, D., & GIBSON, D. (1986). Some possible causes of children's early word overextensions. *Journal of Child Language, 13,* 477–494.

HOFF-GINSBERG, E. (1990). Maternal speech and the child's development of syntax: A further look. *Journal of Child Language, 17,* 85–99.

HOFF-GINSBERG, E., & SHATZ, M. (1982). Linguistic input and the child's acquisition of language. *Psychological Bulletin, 92,* 3–26.

HOFFMAN, L. W. (1984). Work, family, and the socialization of the child. In R. D. Parke (Ed.), *The family: Review of child development research* (Vol. 7). Chicago: University of Chicago Press.

HOFFMAN, L. W. (1989). Effects of maternal employment in the two-parent family. *American Psychologist, 44,* 283–292.

HOFFMAN, M. L. (1970). Moral development. In P. H. Mussen (Ed.), *Carmichael's manual of child psychology* (3rd ed., Vol. 2). New York: Wiley.

HOFFMAN, M. L. (1981). Perspectives on the difference between understanding people and understanding things: The role of affect. In J. H. Flavell & L. Ross (Eds.), *Social cognitive development.* New York: Cambridge University Press.

HOFFMAN, M. L. (1982). Development of prosocial motivation: Empathy and guilt. In N. Eisenberg-Berg (Ed.), *Development of prosocial behavior.* New York: Academic Press.

HOFFMAN, M. L. (1984a). Empathy, its limitations, and its role in a comprehensive moral theory. In W. M. Kurtines & J. L. Gewirtz (Eds.), *Morality, moral behavior, and moral development.* New York: Wiley.

HOFFMAN, M. L. (1984b). Parent discipline, moral internalization, and development of prosocial motivation. In E. Staub, D. Bar-Tal, J. Karylowski, & J. Reykowski (Eds.), *Development and maintenance of prosocial behavior.* New York: Plenum.

HOFFMAN, M. L. (1987). The contribution of empathy to justice and moral judgment. In N. Eisenberg & J. Strayer (Eds.), *Empathy and its development.* New York: Cambridge University Press.

HOFFMAN, M. L. (1991). Empathy, social cognition, and moral action. In W. M. Kurtines & J. L. Gewirtz (Eds.), *Handbook of moral behavior and development: Vol. 1. Theory.* Hillsdale, NJ: Erlbaum.

HOFFMAN, M. L. (1994). Discipline and internalization. *Developmental Psychology, 30,* 26–28.

HOGGE, W. A. (1990). Teratology. In I. R. Merkatz & J. E. Thompson (Eds.), *New perspectives on prenatal care.* New York: Elsevier.

HOLDEN, C. (1986). High court says no to administration's Baby Doe rules. *Science, 232,* 1595–1596.

HOLMES, J. (1995). "Something there is that doesn't love a wall": John Bowlby, attachment theory, and psychoanalysis. In S. Goldberg, R. Muir, & J. Kerr (Eds.), *Attachment theory: Social, developmental, and clinical perspectives.* Hillsdale, NJ: The Analytic Press.

HOLSTEIN, C. (1976). Irreversible, stepwise sequence in the development of moral judgment: A longitudinal study of males and females. *Child Development, 47,* 51–61.

HOOD, K. E., DRAPER, P., CROCKETT, L. J., & PETERSEN, A. C. (1987). The ontogeny and phylogeny of sex differences in development: A biosocial synthesis. In D. B. Carter (Ed.), *Current conceptions of sex roles and sex-typing: Theory and research.* New York: Praeger.

HOOK, J. (1982). Development of equity and altruism in judgments of reward and damage allocation. *Developmental Psychology, 18,* 825–834.

HOOK, J. (1983). The development of children's equity judgments. In R. L. Leahy (Ed.), *The child's construction of social equality.* New York: Academic Press.

HOOKER, K., NESSELROADE, D. W., NESSELROADE, J. R., & LERNER, R. M. (1987). The structure of intraindividual temperament in the context of mother–child dyads: P-technique factor analyses of short-term change. *Developmental Psychology, 23,* 332–346.

HOPKINS, A. (1987). Prescribing in pregnancy: Epilepsy and anticonvulsant drugs. *British Medical Journal, 294,* 497–501.

HOPKINS, B. (1991). Facilitating early motor development: An intracultural study of West Indian mothers and their infants living in Britain. In J. K. Nugent, B. M. Lester, & T. B. Brazelton (Eds.), *The cultural context of infancy: Vol. 2. Multicultural and interdisciplinary approaches to parent–infant relations.* Norwood, NJ: Ablex.

HORAN, J. (1993, June). Eugenics revisited. *Scientific American,* pp. 122–131.

HORAN, R. F., & ROSSER, R. A. (1984). Multivariable analysis of spatial abilities by sex. *Developmental Review, 4,* 381–411.

HORN, J. M. (1983). The Texas Adoption Project: Adopted children and their intellectual resemblance to biological and adoptive parents. *Child Development, 54,* 268–275.

HORNE, A. M., & SAYGER, T. V. (1990). *Treating conduct and oppositional defiant disorders in children.* New York: Pergamon.

HORNIK, R., & GUNNAR, M. R. (1988). A descriptive analysis of infant social referencing. *Child Development, 59,* 626–634.

HOROWITZ, F. D. (1992). John B. Watson's legacy: Learning and environment. *Developmental Psychology, 28,* 360–367.

HORT, B. E., LEINBACH, M. D., & FAGOT, B. I. (1991). Is there coherence among the cognitive components of gender acquisition? *Sex Roles, 24,* 195–207.

HOWE, C. (1981). *Acquiring language in a conversational context.* Orlando, FL: Academic Press.

HOWE, M. L., & COURAGE, M. L. (1993). On resolving the enigma of infantile amnesia. *Psychological Bulletin, 113,* 305–326.

HOWE, M. L., & RABINOWITZ, F. M. (1990). Resource panacea? Or just another day in the developmental forest? *Developmental Review, 10,* 125–154.

HOWES, C. (1983). Patterns of friendship. *Child Development, 54,* 1041–1053.

HOWES, C. (1987). Social competence with peers in young children: Developmental sequences. *Developmental Review, 7,* 252–272.

HOWES, C. (1992). *The collaborative construction of pretend.* New York: SUNY Press.

HOWES, C. (1997). Children's experiences in center-based child care as a function of teacher background and adult:child ratio. *Merrill-Palmer Quarterly, 43,* 404–425.

HOWES, C., & HAMILTON, C. E. (1992). Children's relationships with caregivers: Mothers and child care teachers. *Child Development, 63,* 859–866.

HOWES, C., & MATHESON, C. C. (1992). Sequences in the development of competent play with peers: Social and social pretend play. *Developmental Psychology, 28,* 961–974.

HOWES, C., & RUBENSTEIN, J. L. (1979). *Influences on toddler peer behavior in two types of daycare.* Unpublished manuscript, Harvard University, Cambridge.

HOWES, C., PHILLIPS, D. A., & WHITEBOOK, M. (1992). Thresholds of quality: Implications for the social development of children in center-based child care. *Child Development, 63,* 449–460.

HOWES, C., UNGER, O., & SEIDNER, L. B. (1989). Social pretend play in toddlers. Parallels with social play and with solitary pretend. *Child Development, 60,* 77–84.

HOY, E. A., BILL, J. M., & SYKES, D. H. (1988). Very low birthweight: A long-term developmental impairment? *International Journal of Behavioral Development, 11,* 37–67.

HSU, L. K. G. (1990). *Eating disorders.* New York: Guilford.

HUDLEY, C., & GRAHAM, S. (1993). An attributional intervention to reduce peer-directed aggression among African-American boys. *Child Development, 64,* 124–138.

HUDSON, J. A. (1990). The emergence of autobiographical memory in mother–child conversation. In R. Fivush & J. A. Hudson (Eds.), *Knowing and remembering in young children.* Hillsdale, NJ: Erlbaum.

HUDSON, J. A., & NELSON, K. (1983). Effects of script structure on children's story recall. *Developmental Psychology, 19,* 625–635.

HUESMANN, L. R., & ERON, L. D. (1986). *Television and the aggressive child: A cross-national perspective.* Hillsdale, NJ: Erlbaum.

HUESMANN, L. R., & MILLER, L. S. (1994). Long-term effects of repeated exposure to media violence in childhood. In L. R. Huesmann (Ed.), *Aggressive behavior: Current perspectives.* New York: Plenum.

HUESMANN, L. R., LAGERSPETZ, K., & ERON, L. D. (1984). Intervening variables in the television violence–aggression relation: Evidence from two countries. *Developmental Psychology, 20,* 746–775.

HUMPHREY, D. E., & HUMPHREY, G. K. (1987). Sex differences in infant reaching. *Neurophysiologia, 25,* 971–975.

HUNT, E., STREISSGUTH, A. P., KERR, B., & OLSON, H. C. (1995). Mother's alcohol consumption during pregnancy: Effects on spatial-visual reasoning in 14-year-old children. *Psychological Science, 6,* 339–342.

HUNT, J. McV. (1961). *Intelligence and experience.* New York: Ronald Press.

HUNTER, J. E., & HUNTER, R. F. (1984). Validity and utility of alternative predictors of job performance. *Psychological Bulletin, 96,* 72–98.

HUR, Y., & BOUCHARD, T. J., JR. (1995). Genetic influences on perceptions of family environment: A reared apart twin study. *Child Development, 66,* 330–345.

HUSTON, A. C. (1983). Sex-typing. In E. M. Hetherington (Ed.), *Handbook of child psychology: Vol. 4. Socialization, personality, and social development.* New York: Wiley.

HUSTON, A. C. (1985). The development of sex typing: Themes from recent research. *Developmental Review, 5,* 1–17.

HUSTON, A. C., & ALVAREZ, M. M. (1990). The socialization context of gender role development in early adolescence. In R. Montemayor, G. R. Adams, & T. P. Gullotta (Eds.), *From childhood to adolescence: A transitional period?* Newbury Park, CA: Sage.

HUSTON, A. C., & WRIGHT, J. C. (1998). Mass media and children's development. In W. Damon (Ed.), *Handbook of child psychology: Vol. 4. Child psychology in practice.* New York: Wiley.

HUSTON, A. C., CARPENTER, J. C., ATWATER, J. B., & JOHNSON, L. M. (1986). Gender, adult structuring of activities, and social behavior in middle childhood. *Child Development, 57,* 1200–1209.

HUSTON, A. C., WRIGHT, J. C., RICE, M. L., KERKMAN, D., & St. PETERS, H. (1990). Development of television viewing patterns in early childhood: A longitudinal analysis. *Developmental Psychology, 26,* 409–420.

HUTCHINS, E. (1983). Understanding Micronesian navigation. In D. Gentner & A. Stevens (Eds.), *Mental models.* Hillsdale, NJ: Erlbaum.

HUTTENLOCHER, J., HAIGHT, W., BRYK, A., SELTZER, M., & LYONS, T. (1991). Early vocabulary growth: Relation to language input and gender. *Developmental Psychology, 27,* 236–248.

HUTTENLOCHER, J., SMILEY, P., & CHARNEY, R. (1983). Emergence of action categories in the child: Evidence from verb meanings. *Psychological Review, 90,* 72–93.

HUTTENLOCHER, P. R. (1990). Morphometric study of human cerebral cortex development. *Neuropsychologia, 28,* 517–527.

HYDE, J. S. (1984). How large are gender differences in aggression? A developmental meta-analysis. *Developmental Psychology, 20,* 722–736.

HYDE, J. S. (1986). Gender differences in aggression. In J. S. Hyde & M. C. Linn (Eds.), *The psychology of gender differences: Advances through meta-analysis.* Baltimore: Johns Hopkins University Press.

HYDE, J. S., & LINN, M. C. (1988). Gender differences in verbal ability: A meta-analysis. *Psychological Bulletin, 104,* 53–69.

HYLTENSTAM, K., & OBLER, L. (Eds.). (1989). *Bilingualism across the lifespan: Aspects of acquisition, maturity, and loss.* Cambridge: Cambridge University Press.

HYMEL, S. (1983). Preschool children's peer relations: Issues in sociometric assessment. *Merrill-Palmer Quarterly, 29,* 237–260.

HYMEL, S., WAGNER, E., & BUTLER, L. J. (1990). Reputational bias: View from the peer group. In S. R. Asher & J. D. Coie (Eds.), *Peer rejection in childhood.* New York: Cambridge University Press.

IANNOTTI, R. (1978). Effect of role-taking experiences on role taking, empathy, altruism, and aggression. *Developmental Psychology, 14,* 119–124.

IDE, J. K., PARKERSON, J., HAERTEL, G. D., & WALBERG, H. J. (1981). Peer group influence on educational outcomes: A quantitative synthesis. *Journal of Educational Psychology, 73,* 472–484.

INAGAKI, K., & HATANO, G. (1987). Young children's spontaneous personification as analogy. *Child Development, 58,* 1013–1020.

INAGAKI, K., & SUGIYAMA, K. (1988). Attributing human characteristics: Developmental changes in over- and underattribution. *Cognitive Development, 3,* 55–70.

INFANTE-RIVARD, C., FERNANDEZ, A., GAUTHIER, R., & RIVARD, C. (1993). Fetal loss associated with caffeine intake before and during pregnancy. *Journal of the American Medical Association, 270,* 2940–2943.

INHELDER, B., & PIAGET, J. (1958). *The growth of logical thinking from childhood to adolescence.* New York: Basic Books.

INHELDER, B., & PIAGET, J. (1964). *The early growth of logic in the child.* New York: Norton.

ISABELLA, R. A. (1993). Origins of attachment: Maternal interactive behavior across the first year. *Child Development, 64,* 605–621.

ISABELLA, R. A. (1994). The origins of infant–mother attachment: Maternal behavior and infant development. In R. Vasta (Ed.), *Annals of child development* (Vol. 10). London: Kingsley.

ISABELLA, R. A., & BELSKY, J. (1991). Interactional synchrony and the origins of infant–mother attachment: A replication study. *Child Development, 62,* 373–384.

ISABELLA, R. A., BELSKY, J., & VON EYE, A. (1989). Origins of infant–mother attachment: An examination of interactional synchrony during the infant's first year. *Developmental Psychology, 25,* 12–21.

ISTVAN, J. (1986). Stress, anxiety, and birth outcomes: A critical review of the evidence. *Psychological Bulletin, 100,* 331–348.

IZARD, C. (1989). *The maximally discriminative facial movement coding system (MAX)* (rev. ed.). Newark: University of Delaware, Information Technologies and University Media Services.

IZARD, C. (1993). Organizational and motivational functions of discrete emotions. In M. Lewis & J. Haviland (Eds.), *Handbook of emotions.* New York: Guilford.

IZARD, C. (1995). Innate and universal facial expressions: Evidence from developmental and cross-cultural research. *Psychological Bulletin, 115,* 288–299.

IZARD, C. E., FANTAUZZO, C. A., CASTLE, J. M., HAYNES, O. M., RAYIAS, M. F., & PUTNAM, P. H. (1995). The ontogeny and significance of infants' facial expressions in the first 9 months of life. *Developmental Psychology, 31,* 997–1013.

JACKLIN, C. N. (1981). Methodological issues in the study of sex-related differences. *Developmental Review, 1,* 266–273.

JACKLIN, C. N., & REYNOLDS, C. (1993). Gender and childhood socialization. In A. E. Beall & R. J. Sternberg (Eds.), *The psychology of gender.* New York: Guilford.

JACKLIN, C. N., DiPIETRO, J. A., & MacCOBY, E. E. (1984). Sex-typing behavior and sex-typing pressure in child/parent interactions. *Archives of Sexual Behavior, 13,* 413–425.

JACKLIN, C. N., WILCOX, K. T., & MacCOBY, E. E. (1988). Neonatal sex steroid hormones and intellectual abilities of six year old boys and girls. *Developmental Psychobiology, 21,* 567–574.

JACKSON, J. F. (1993). Multiple caregiving among African Americans and infant attachment: The need for an emic approach. *Human Development, 36,* 87–102.

JACOBS, J. E. (1991). Influence of gender stereotypes on parent and child mathematics attitudes. *Journal of Educational Psychology, 83,* 518–527.

JACOBSEN, T., EDELSTEIN, W., & HOFMANN, V. (1994). A longitudinal study of the relation between representations of attachment in childhood and cognitive functioning in childhood and adolescence. *Developmental Psychology, 30,* 112–124.

JACOBSON, J. L., & JACOBSON, S. W. (1988). New methodologies for assessing the effects of prenatal toxic exposure on cognitive functioning in humans. In M. Evans (Ed.), *Toxic contaminants and ecosystem health: A Great Lakes focus.* New York: Wiley.

JACOBSON, J. L., JACOBSON, S. W., PADGETT, R. J., BRUMITT, G. A., & BILLINGS, R. L. (1992). Effects of prenatal PCB exposure on cognitive processing efficiency and sustained attention. *Developmental Psychology, 28,* 297–306.

JACOBSON, S., FEIN, G. G., JACOBSON, J. L., SCHWARTZ, P. M., & DOWLER, J. K. (1985). The effect of intrauterine PCB exposure on visual recognition memory. *Child Development, 56,* 853–860.

JACOBVITZ, D., & SROUFE, L. A. (1987). The early caregiver-child relationship and attention-deficit disorder with hyperactivity in kindergarten: A prospective study. *Child Development, 58,* 1496–1504.

JADACK, R. A., HYDE, J. S., MOORE, C. F., & KELLER, M. L. (1995). Moral reasoning about sexually transmitted diseases. *Child Development, 66,* 167–177.

JAEGER, E., & WEINRAUB, M. (1990). Early nonmaternal care and infant attachment: In search of process. In K. McCartney (Ed.), *New directions for child development: No. 49. Child care and maternal employment: A social ecology approach.* San Francisco: Jossey-Bass.

JAMES, W. (1890). *Principles of psychology.* New York: Holt.

JAMES, W. (1892). *Psychology: The briefer course.* New York: Holt.

JAMISON, W. (1977). Developmental inter-relationships among concrete operational tasks: An investigation of Piaget's stage concept. *Journal of Experimental Child Psychology, 24,* 235–253.

JANKOWIAK, W. (1992). Father–child relations in urban China. In B. S. Hewlett (Ed.), *Father–child relations: Cultural and biosocial contexts.* New York: Aldine de Gruyter.

JANSSENS, J. M. A. M., & GERRIS, J. R. M. (1992). Child rearing, empathy, and prosocial development. In J. M. A. M. Janssens & J. R. M. Gerris (Eds.), *Child rearing: Influence on prosocial and moral development.* Amsterdam: Swets & Zeitlinger.

JAROFF, L. (1989, March 20). The gene hunt. *Time,* pp. 62–67.

JEFFERS, V. W., & LORE, R. K. (1979). Let's play at my house: Effects of the home environment on the social behavior of children. *Child Development, 50,* 837–841.

JEFFREYS, A. J., BROOKFIELD, J. F. Y., & SEMEONOFF, R. (1992). Positive identification of an immigration test-case using human DNA fingerprints. *Journal of NIH Research, 4,* 81–87.

JENCKS, C. (1972). *Inequality.* New York: Basic Books.

JENKINS, J. M., & ASTINGTON, J. W. (1996). Cognitive factors and family structure associated with theory of mind development in young children. *Developmental Psychology, 32,* 70–78.

JENNINGS, K. D. (1975). People versus object orientation, social behavior, and intellectual abilities in preschool children. *Developmental Psychology, 11,* 511–519.

JENNINGS, K. D. (1991). Early development of mastery motivation and its relation to the self-concept. In M. Bullock (Ed.), *The development of intentional action: Cognitive, motivational, and interactive-process.* Basel, Switzerland: Karger.

JENSEN, A. R. (1969). How much can we boost IQ and scholastic achievement? *Harvard Educational Review, 39,* 1–123.

JENSEN, A. R. (1972). *Genetics and education.* New York: Harper & Row.

JENSEN, A. R. (1973). *Educability and group differences.* New York: Harper & Row.

JENSEN, A. R. (1980). *Bias in mental testing.* New York: Free Press.

JENSEN, A. R. (1981). *Straight talk about mental tests.* New York: Free Press.

JERISON, H. J. (1982). The evolution of biological intelligence. In R. J. Sternberg (Ed.), *Handbook of human intelligence.* New York: Cambridge University Press.

JESSOR, R., & JESSOR, S. L. (1977). *Problem behavior and psychosocial development.* New York: Academic Press.

JOHNSON, D. B. (1983). Self-recognition in infants. *Infant Behavior and Development, 6,* 211–222.

JOHNSON, E. S., & MEADE, A. C. (1987). Developmental patterns of spatial ability: An early sex difference. *Child Development, 58,* 725–740.

JOHNSON, J. (1991). Constructive processes in bilingualism and their cognitive growth effects. In E. Bialystok (Ed.), *Language processing in bilingual children.* Cambridge: Cambridge University Press.

JOHNSON, M. H., & MORTON, J. (1991). *Biology and cognitive development: The case of face recognition.* Cambridge, MA: Blackwell.

JOHNSON, M. H., DZIURAWIEC, S., ELLIS, H., & MORTON, J. (1991). Newborns' preferential tracking of facelike stimuli and its subsequent decline. *Cognition, 40,* 1–19.

JOHNSON, S. P. (1997). Young infants' perception of object unity: Implications for development of attentional and cognitive skills. *Current Directions in Psychological Science, 6,* 5–11.

JOHNSON, S. P., & ASLIN, R. N. (1995). Perception of object unity in 2-month-old infants. *Developmental Psychology, 31,* 739–745.

JOHNSTON, J. R. (1986). Cognitive prerequisites: The evidence from children learning English. In D. I. Slobin (Ed.), *The crosslinguistic study of language acquisition: Vol. 2. Theoretical issues.* Hillsdale, NJ: Erlbaum.

JONES, C., & ADAMSON, L. B. (1987). Language use in mother–child and mother–child–sibling interactions. *Child Development, 58,* 356–366.

JONES, C., & LOPEZ, R. (1990). Drug abuse and pregnancy. In I. R. Merkatz & J. E. Thompson (Eds.), *New perspectives on prenatal care.* New York: Elsevier.

JONES, D. C. (1985). Persuasive appeals and responses to appeals among friends and acquaintances. *Child Development, 56,* 757–763.

JONES, E. F., & NELSON-LE GALL, S. (1995). The influence of personal effort cues on children's judgments of morality and disposition. *Merrill-Palmer Quarterly, 41,* 53–69.

JONES, G. E., & DEMBO, M. H. (1989). Age and sex role differences in intimate friendships during childhood and adolescence. *Merrill-Palmer Quarterly, 35,* 445–462.

JONES, K. L., JOHNSON, K. A., & CHAMBERS, C. C. (1992). Pregnancy outcome in women treated with phenobarbital monotherapy. *Teratology, 45,* 452–453.

JONES, K. L., LACRO, R. V., JOHNSON, K. A., & ADAMS, J. (1988). Pregnancy outcome in women treated with Tegretol. *Teratology, 37,* 468–469.

JONES, K. L., SMITH, D. W., ULLELAND, C. N., & STREISSGUTH, A. P. (1973). Pattern of malformation in offspring of chronic alcoholic mothers. *Lancet, 1,* 1267–1271.

JONES, M. C. (1924). A laboratory study of fear: The case of Peter. *Pedagogical Seminary, 31,* 308–315.

JONES, S. S. (1996). Imitation or exploration? Young infants' matching of adults' oral gestures. *Child Development, 67,* 1952–1969.

JONES, S. S., COLLINS, K., & HONG, H. (1991). An audience effect on smile production in 10-month-old infants. *Psychological Science, 2,* 45–49.

JOOS, S. K., POLLITT, E., MUELLER, W. H., & ALBRIGHT, D. L. (1983). The Bacon Chow study: Maternal nutritional supplementation and infant behavioral development. *Child Development, 54,* 669–676.

JUSCZYK, P. W. (1997). *The discovery of spoken language.* Cambridge: MIT Press.

JUSCZYK, P. W., CUTLER, A., & REDANZ, N. J. (1993). Infants' preference for the predominant stress patterns of English words. *Child Development, 64,* 675–687.

JUSCZYK, P. W., PISONI, D. B., & MULLENIX, J. (1992). Some consequences of stimulus variability on speech processing by two-month-old infants. *Cognition, 43,* 253–291.

KABACK, M. M. (1982). Screening for reproductive counseling: Social, ethical, and medicolegal issues in the Tay-Sachs disease experience. In *Human genetics: Part B. Medical aspects.* New York: Alan R. Liss.

KAGAN, J. (1970). Attention and psychological change in the young child. *Science, 170,* 826–832.

KAGAN, J. (1991). The theoretical utility of constructs for self. *Developmental Review, 11,* 244–250.

KAGAN, J. (1994). *Galen's prophecy.* New York: Basic Books.

KAGAN, J. (1997). Temperament and the reactions to unfamiliarity. *Child Development, 68,* 139–143.

KAGAN, J., ARCUS, D., SNIDMAN, N., YUFENG, W., HENDLER, J., & GREENE, S. (1994). Reactivity in infants: A cross-national comparison. *Developmental Psychology, 30,* 342–345.

KAGAN, J., KEARSLEY, R., & ZELAZO, P. (1978). *Infancy.* Cambridge: Harvard University Press.

KAGAN, J., REZNICK, J. S., & GIBBONS, J. (1989). Inhibited and uninhibited types of children. *Child Development, 60,* 838–845.

KAGAN, J., REZNICK, J. S., & SNIDMAN, N. (1987). The physiology and psychology of behavioral inhibition. *Child Development, 58,* 1459–1473.

KAGAN, J., REZNICK, J. S., & SNIDMAN, N. (1988). Biological bases of childhood shyness. *Science, 240,* 167–171.

KAGAN, J., REZNICK, J. S., SNIDMAN, N., GIBBONS, J., & JOHNSON, M. O. (1988). Childhood derivatives of inhibition and lack of inhibition to the unfamiliar. *Child Development, 59,* 1580–1589.

KAGAN, J., SNIDMAN, N., & ARCUS, D. M. (1992). Initial reactions to unfamiliarity. *Current Directions in Psychological Science, 1,* 171–174.

KAGAN, J., SNIDMAN, N., & ARCUS, D. (1993). On the temperamental categories of inhibited and uninhibited children. In H. Rubin & J. B. Asendorpf (Eds.), *Social withdrawal, inhibition, and shyness.* Hillsdale, NJ: Erlbaum.

KAIL, R. (1991). Developmental change in speed of processing during childhood and adolescence. *Psychological Bulletin, 109,* 490–501.

KAIL, R. (1995). Processing speed, memory, and cognition. In F. E. Weinert & W. Schneider (Eds.), *Memory performance and competencies: Issues in growth and development.* Mahwah, NJ: Erlbaum.

KAIL, R., & BISANZ, J. (1982). Cognitive development: An information-processing perspective. In R. Vasta (Ed.), *Strategies and techniques of child study.* New York: Academic Press.

KAIL, R., & BISANZ, J. (1992). The information-processing perspective on cognitive development in childhood and adolescence. In R. J. Sternberg & C. A. Berg (Eds.), *Intellectual development.* New York: Cambridge University Press.

KAIL, R., & PELLEGRINO, J. W. (1985). *Human intelligence: Perspectives and prospects.* New York: W. H. Freeman.

KAIL, R., & SIEGEL, A. W. (1977). Sex differences in retention of verbal and spatial characteristics of stimuli. *Journal of Experimental Child Psychology, 23,* 341–347.

KAITZ, M., GOOD, A., ROKEM, A. M., & EIDELMAN, A. I. (1987). Mothers' recognition of their newborns by olfactory cues. *Developmental Psychology, 20,* 587–591.

KAITZ, M., LAPIDOT, P., BRONNER, R., & EIDELMAN, A. I. (1992). Parturient women can recognize their infants by touch. *Developmental Psychology, 28,* 35–39.

KAITZ, M., MEIROV, H., LANDMAN, I., & EIDELMAN, A. I. (1993). Infant recognition by tactile cues. *Infant Behavior and Development, 16,* 333–341.

KAITZ, M., SHIRI, S., DANZIGER, S., HERSHKO, Z., & EIDELMAN, A. I. (1993). Fathers can also recognize their newborns by touch. *Infant Behavior and Development, 17,* 205–207.

KAMII, C., & DEVRIES, R. (1993). *Physical knowledge in preschool education: Implications of Piaget's theory* (rev. ed.). New York: Teachers College Press.

KAMIN, L. (1974). *The science and politics of IQ.* Hillsdale, NJ: Erlbaum.

KAMPTNER, L., KRAFT, R. H., & HARPER, L. V. (1984). Lateral specialization and social-verbal development in preschool children. *Brain and Cognition, 3,* 42–50.

KANDEL, E. R., & O'DELL, T. J. (1992). Are adult mechanisms also used for development? *Science, 258,* 243–245.

KARMEL, B. Z., & MAISEL, E. B. (1975). A neuronal activity model for infant visual attention. In L. B. Cohen & P. Salapatek (Eds.), *Infant perception: From sensation to cognition: Vol. 1. Basic visual processes.* New York: Academic Press.

KARMILOFF-SMITH, A. (1995). Annotation: The extraordinary cognitive journey from foetus through infancy. *Journal of Child Psychology and Psychiatry and Allied Disciplines, 36,* 1293–1313.

KARNIOL, R. (1978). Children's use of intention cues in evaluating behavior. *Psychological Bulletin, 85,* 76–85.

KARNIOL, R., & MILLER, D. T. (1981). The development of self-control in children. In S. S. Brehm, S. M. Kassin, & F. X. Gibbons (Eds.), *Developmental social psychology: Theory and research.* New York: Oxford University Press.

KARSON, E. M., POLVINO, W., & ANDERSON, W. F. (1992). Pros-pects for human gene therapy. *Journal of Reproductive Medicine, 37,* 508–514.

KASHANI, J., DANIEL, A. E., DANDOY, A. C., & HOLCOMB, W. R. (1992). Family violence: Impact on children. *Journal of the American Academy of Child and Adolescent Psychiatry, 31,* 181–182.

KATZ, P. A. (1986). Modification of children's gender stereotyped behavior: General issues and research considerations. *Sex Roles, 14,* 591–602.

KATZ, P. A. (1987). Variations in family constellation: Effects of gender schemata. In L. S. Liben & M. L. Signorella (Eds.), *New directions for child development: Vol. 38. Children's gender schemata.* San Francisco: Jossey-Bass.

KATZ, P. A., & BOSWELL, S. L. (1986). Flexibility and traditionality in children's gender roles. *Genetic, Social, and General Psychology Monographs, 112,* 105–147.

KATZ, P. A., & KSANSNAK, K. R. (1994). Developmental aspects of gender role flexibility and traditionality in middle childhood and adolescence. *Developmental Psychology, 30,* 272–282.

KAUFMAN, A. S., & KAUFMAN, N. L. (1983). *Kaufman Assessment Battery for Children.* Circle Pines, MN: American Guidance Service.

KAWASAKI, C., NUGENT, J. K., MIYASHITA, H., MIYAHARA, H., & BRAZELTON, T. B. (1994). The cultural organization of infants' sleep. *Children's Environments, 11,* 135–141.

KAY, D. A., & ANGLIN, J. M. (1982). Overextension and underextension in the child's expressive and receptive speech. *Journal of Child Language, 9,* 83–98.

KAYE, K. (1982). *The mental and social life of babies.* Chicago: University of Chicago Press.

KAYE, K. L., & BOWER, T. G. R. (1994). Learning and intermodal transfer of information in newborns. *Psychological Science, 5,* 286–288.

KAZDIN, A. E. (1987). *Conduct disorders in childhood and adolescence.* Newbury Park, CA: Sage.

KEARSLEY, R. B. (1973). The newborn's response to auditory stimulation: A demonstration of orienting and defensive behavior. *Child Development, 44,* 582–590.

KEATING, D. P. (1988). Byrnes' reformulation of Piaget's formal operations: Is what's left what's right? Commentary. *Developmental Review, 8,* 376–384.

KEATING, D. P. (1996). Central conceptual structures: Seeking developmental integration. *Monographs of the Society for Research in Child Development, 61* (1–2, Serial No. 246).

KEE, D. W., & GUTTENTAG, R. (1994). Resource requirements of knowledge access and recall benefits of associative strategies. *Journal of Experimental Child Psychology, 57,* 211–223.

KEEFE, K., & BERNDT, T. J. (1996). Relations of friendship quality to self-esteem in early adolescence. *Journal of Early Adolescence, 16,* 110–129.

KEEFE, M. R. (1987). Comparison of neonatal nighttime sleep–wake patterns in nursery versus rooming-in environments. *Nursing Research, 36,* 140–144.

KEENAN, K., & SHAW, D. (1997). Developmental and social influences on young girls' early problem behavior. *Psychological Bulletin, 121,* 95–113.

KEIL, F. C. (1998). Cognitive science and the origins of thought and knowledge. In W. Damon (Ed.), *Handbook of child psychology: Vol. 1. Theoretical models of human development.* New York: Wiley.

KEITH, L. K., & BRACKEN, B. A. (1996). Self-concept instrumentation: A historical and evaluative review. In B. A. Bracken (Ed.), *Handbook of self-concept: Developmental, social, and clinical considerations.* New York: Wiley.

KELLER, H., & SCHOLMERICH, A. (1987). Infant vocalizations and parental reactions during the first four months of life. *Developmental Psychology, 23,* 62–67.

KELLER, M., & WOOD, P. (1989). Development of friendship reasoning: A study of interindividual differences in intraindividual change. *Developmental Psychology, 25,* 820–826.

KELLMAN, P. J. (1996). The origins of object perception. In R. Gelman & T. Au (Eds.), *Perceptual and cognitive development.* San Diego: Academic Press.

KELLMAN, P. J., & BANKS, M. S. (1998). Infant visual perception. In W. Damon (Series Ed.) & D. Kuhn & R. S. Siegler (Vol. Eds.), *Handbook of child psychology: Vol. 2. Cognition, perception, and language* (5th ed.). New York: Wiley.

KELLMAN, P. J., & SPELKE, E. S. (1983). Perception of partly occluded objects in infancy. *Cognitive Psychology, 15,* 483–524.

KEMLER NELSON, D. G., HIRSH-PASEK, K., JUSCZYK, P., & CASSIDY, K. W. (1989). How the prosodic cues in motherese might assist language learning. *Journal of Child Language, 16,* 55–68.

KENDALL, P. C., & BRASWELL, L. (1985). *Cognitive-behavioral therapy for impulsive children.* New York: Guilford.

KENDRICK, D. T., & TROST, M. R. (1993). The evolutionary perspective. In A. E. Beall & R. J. Sternberg (Eds.), *The psychology of gender.* New York: Guilford.

KENT, R. D., & BAUER, H. R. (1985). Vocalizations of one-year-olds. *Journal of Child Language, 12,* 491–526.

KERNS, K. A. (1994). A longitudinal examination of links between mother-child attachment and children's friendships in early childhood. *Journal of Social and Personal Relationships, 11,* 379–381.

KERNS, K. A. (1996). Individual differences in friendship quality: Links to child-mother attachment. In W. M. Bukowski, A. F. Newcomb, & W. W. Hartup (Eds.), *The company they keep: Friendship in childhood and adolescence.* New York: Cambridge University Press.

KERR, M., LAMBERT, W. W., & BEM, D. J. (1996). Life course sequelae of childhood shyness in Sweden: Comparison with the United States. *Developmental Psychology, 32,* 1100–1105.

KERR, M., LAMBERT, W. W., STATTIN, H., & KLACKENBERG-LARSSON, I. (1994). Stability of inhibition in a Swedish longitudinal sample. *Child Development, 65,* 138–146.

KIMBALL, M. M. (1989). A new perspective on women's math achievement. *Psychological Bulletin, 105,* 198–214.

KIMURA, D., & HAMPSON, E. (1994). Cognitive pattern in men and women is influenced by fluctuations in sex hormones. *Current Directions in Psychological Science, 3,* 57–61.

KIMURA, D., & HAMPSON, E. (1993). Neural and hormonal mechanisms mediating sex differences in cognition. In P. A. Vernon (Ed.), *Biological approaches to the study of human intelligence.* Norwood, NJ: Ablex.

KISER, L. J., BATES, J. E., MASLIN, C. A., & BAYLES, K. (1986). Mother–infant play at six months as a predictor of attachment security at thirteen months. *Journal of the American Academy of Child Psychiatry, 25,* 68–75.

KISILEVSKY, B. S., & MUIR, D. W. (1984). Neonatal habituation and dishabituation to tactile stimulation during sleep. *Developmental Psychology, 20,* 367–373.

KLAHR, D., & MacWHINNEY, B. (1998). Information processing. In W. Damon (Series Ed.) & D. Kuhn & R. S. Siegler (Vol. Eds.), *Handbook of child psychology: Vol. 2. Cognition, perception, and language* (5th ed.). New York: Wiley.

KLAHR, D., & ROBINSON, M. (1981). Formal assessment of problem solving and planning

processes in preschool children. *Cognitive Psychology, 13,* 113–148.

KLAUS, M. H., & KENNELL, J. H. (1976). *Maternal–infant bonding.* St. Louis: Mosby.

KLAUS, M. H., KENNELL, J. H., & KLAUS, P. H. (1995). *Bonding: Building the foundations of secure attachment and independence.* Reading, MA: Addison-Wesley.

KLEIN, M. W. (1995). Street gang cycles. In J. Q. Wilson & J. Petersilia (Eds.), *Crime.* San Francisco: Institute for Contemporary Studies.

KLEMCHUK, H. P., BOND, L. A., & HOWELL, D. C. (1990). Coherence and correlates of level 1 perspective taking in young children. *Merrill-Palmer Quarterly, 36,* 369–387.

KLIMES-DOUGAN, B., & KISTNER, J. (1990). Physically abused pre-schoolers' responses to peers' distress. *Developmental Psychology, 26,* 599–602.

KLINNERT, M. D., CAMPOS, J. J., SORCE, J. F., EMDE, R. N., & SVEJDA, M. (1983). Emotions as behavior regulators: Social referencing in infancy. In R. Plutchik & H. Kellerman (Eds.), *Emotions in early development: Vol. 2. The emotions.* New York: Academic Press.

KLINNERT, M. D., SORCE, J. F., EMDE, R. N., STENBERG, C., & GAENSBAURER, T. (1984). Continuities and change in early emotional life: Maternal perceptions of surprise, fear, and anger. In R. N. Emde & R. J. Harmon (Eds.), *Continuities and discontinuities in development.* New York: Plenum.

KNIGHT, G. P., BERNING, A. L., WILSON, S. L., & CHAO, C. (1987). The effects of information-processing demands and social-situational factors on the social decision making of children. *Journal of Experimental Child Psychology, 43,* 244–259.

KOCH, R., & De La CRUZ, F. (1991). The danger of birth defects in the children of women with phenylketonuria. *Journal of NIH Research, 3,* 61–63.

KOCHANSKA, G. (1993). Toward a synthesis of parental socialization and child temperament in early development of conscience. *Child Development, 64,* 325–347.

KOCHANSKA, G. (1995). Children's temperament, mothers' discipline, and security of attachment: Multiple pathways to emerging internalization. *Child Development, 66,* 597–615.

KOCHANSKA, G. (1997). Multiple pathways to conscience for children with different temperaments: From toddlerhood to age 5. *Developmental Psychology, 33,* 228–240.

KOCHANSKA, G., & THOMPSON, R. A. (1997). The emergence and development of conscience in toddlerhood and early childhood. In J. E. Grusec & L. Kuczynski (Eds.), *Handbook of parenting and the transmission of values.* New York: Wiley.

KOCHANSKA, G., MURRAY, K., & COY, K. C. (1997). Inhibitory control as a contributor to conscience in childhood: From toddler to

early school age. *Child Development, 68,* 263–277.

KOENIGSKNECHT, R. A., & FRIEDMAN, P. (1976). Syntax development in boys and girls. *Child Development, 47,* 1109–1115.

KOHLBERG, L. (1969). Stage and sequence: The cognitive-developmental approach to socialization. In D. A. Goslin (Ed.), *Handbook of socialization theory and research.* Chicago: Rand McNally.

KOHLBERG, L. (1984). *The psychology of moral development: The nature and validity of moral stages.* San Francisco: Harper & Row.

KOHLBERG, L. (1986). A current statement on some theoretical issues. In S. Modgil & C. Modgil (Eds.), *Lawrence Kohlberg: Consensus and controversy.* Philadelphia: Falmer.

KOHLBERG, L. (1987). The development of moral judgment and moral action. In L. Kohlberg (Ed.), *Child psychology and childhood education: A cognitive-developmental view.* New York: Longman.

KOHLBERG, L., & CANDEE, D. (1984). The relationship of moral judgment to moral action. In W. M. Kurtines & J. L. Gewirtz (Eds.), *Morality, moral behavior, and moral development.* New York: Wiley.

KOHLBERG, L., & KRAMER, R. (1969). Continuities and discontinuities in childhood and adult moral development. *Human Development, 12,* 93–120.

KOHLBERG, L., & ULLIAN, D. Z. (1974). Stages in the development of psychosexual concepts and attitudes. In R. C. Friedman, R. M. Richart, & R. L. VandeWiele (Eds.), *Sex differences in behavior.* New York: Wiley.

KOHLBERG, L., LEVINE, C., & HEWER, A. (1983). *Moral stages: A current formulation and a response to critics.* Basel, Switzerland: Karger.

KOHLBERG, L., YAEGER, J., & HJERTHOLM, E. (1968). Private speech: Four studies and a review of theories. *Child Development, 39,* 817–826.

KOHLER, F. W., & FOWLER, S. A. (1985). Training prosocial behaviors to young children: An analysis of reciprocity with untrained peers. *Journal of Applied Behavior Analysis, 18,* 187–200.

KOLB, B. (1989). Brain development, plasticity, and behavior. *American Psychologist, 44,* 1203–1212.

KONNER, M. J. (1976). Maternal care, infant behavior and development among the Kung. In R. B. Lee & I. DeVore (Eds.), *Kalahari hunter-gatherers.* Cambridge: Harvard University Press.

KOPP, C. B. (1991). Young children's progression to self-regulation: In M. Bullock (Ed.), *The development of intentional action: Cognitive, motivational, and interactive process.* Basel, Switzerland: Karger.

KOPP, C. B., & KALER, S. R. (1989). Risk in infancy: Origins and implications. *American Psychologist, 44,* 224–230.

KORN, S. J. (1984). Continuities and discontinuities in difficult/easy temperament: Infancy to young adulthood. *Merrill-Palmer Quarterly, 30,* 189–199.

KORNER, A. F., & THOMAN, E. (1970). Visual alertness in neonates as evoked by maternal care. *Journal of Experimental Child Psychology, 10,* 67–78.

KORNHABER, M. (1994). *The theory of multiple intelligences: Why and how schools use it.* Cambridge: Harvard Graduate School of Education.

KORNHABER, M., KRECHEVSKY, M., & GARDNER, H. (1990). Engaging intelligence. *Educational Psychologist, 25,* 177–199.

KOSTELNY, K., & GARBARINO, J. (1994). Coping with the consequences of living in danger: The case of Palestinian children and youth. *International Journal of Behavioral Development, 17,* 595–611.

KOURILSKY, M., & KEHRET-WARD, T. (1984). Kindergartners' attitudes toward distributive justice: Experiential mediators. *Merrill-Palmer Quarterly, 30,* 49–64.

KOZOL, J. (1991). *Savage inequalities: Children in America's schools.* New York: Crown.

KOZULIN, A. (1990). *Vygotsky's psychology.* Cambridge: Harvard University Press.

KRAFT, R. H. (1984). Lateral specialization and verbal/spatial ability in preschool children: Age, sex, and familial handedness differences. *Neuropsychologia, 22,* 319–335.

KREBS, D. (1987). The challenge of altruism in biology and psychology. In C. Crawford, M. Smith, & D. Krebs (Eds.), *Sociobiology and psychology: Ideas, issues, and applications.* Hillsdale, NJ: Erlbaum.

KREBS, D., DENTON, K., & HIGGINS, N. C. (1987). On the evolution of self-knowledge and self-deception. In K. B. MacDonald (Ed.), *Sociobiological perspectives on human development.* New York: Springer-Verlag.

KREBS, D. L., & GILLMORE, J. (1982). The relationship and the first stages of cognitive development, role-taking abilities, and moral development. *Child Development, 53,* 877–886.

KREBS, D. L., & VAN HESTEREN, F. (1994). The development of altruism: Toward an integrative model. *Developmental Review, 14,* 103–158.

KREIPE, R. E., & STRAUSS, J. (1989). Adolescent medical disorders, behavior and development. In G. R. Adams, R. Montemayor, & T. P. Gullotta (Eds.), *Biology of adolescent behavior and development.* Newbury Park, CA: Sage.

KREITLER, S., & KREITLER, H. (1989). Horizontal decalage: A problem and its solution. *Cognitive Development, 4,* 89–119.

KREUTZER, M. A., LEONARD, C., & FLAVELL, J. H. (1975). An interview study of children's knowledge about memory. *Monographs of the Society for Research in Child Development, 40* (1, Serial No. 159).

KREVANS, J., & GIBBS, J. C. (1996). Parents' use of inductive discipline: Relations to children's empathy and prosocial behavior. *Child Development, 67,* 3263–3277.

KRISTOF, N. D. (1993, July 21). Ultrasound undertaker: China's peasants find new way to avoid unwanted daughters. *The Denver Post,* p. 2A.

KROLL, J. (1977). The concept of childhood in the middle ages. *Journal of the History of Behavioral Sciences, 13,* 384–393.

KROPP, J. P., & HAYNES, O. M. (1987). Abusive and nonabusive mothers' ability to identify general and specific emotion signals of infants. *Child Development, 58,* 187–190.

KRUGER, A. C. (1992). The effect of peer and adult-child transactive discussions on moral reasoning. *Merrill-Palmer Quarterly, 38,* 191–211.

KUCHUK, A., VIBBERT, M., & BORNSTEIN, M. H. (1986). The perception of smiling and its experiential correlates in three-month-old infants. *Child Development, 57,* 1054–1061.

KUCZAJ, S. A. (1977). The acquisition of regular and irregular past tense forms. *Journal of Verbal Learning and Verbal Behavior, 16,* 589–600.

KUCZAJ, S. A. (1982). Language play and language acquisition. In H. W. Reese (Ed.), *Advances in child development and behavior* (Vol. 17). New York: Academic Press.

KUHL, P. K. (1991). Perception, cognition, and the ontogenetic and phylogenetic emergence of human speech. In S. Brauth, W. Hall, & R. Dooling (Eds.), *Plasticity of development.* Cambridge: MIT Press/Bradford Books.

KUHL, P. K. (1993). Early linguistic experience and phonetic perception: Implications for theories of developmental speech perception. *Journal of Phonetics, 21,* 125–139.

KUHL, P. K., & MELTZOFF, A. N. (1988). Speech as an intermodal object of perception. In A. Yonas (Ed.), *Minnesota symposia on child psychology: Vol. 20. Perceptual development in infancy.* Hillsdale, NJ: Erlbaum.

KUHN, D. (1991). *The skills of argument.* New York: Cambridge University Press.

KUHN, D. (1992a). Cognitive development. In M. H. Bornstein & M. E. Lamb (Eds.), *Developmental psychology: An advanced textbook* (3rd ed.). Hillsdale, NJ: Erlbaum.

KUHN, D. (1992b). Piaget's child as scientist. In H. Beilin & P. B. Pufall (Eds.), *Piaget's theory: Prospects and possibilities.* Hillsdale, NJ: Erlbaum.

KUHN, D. (1995). Microgenetic study of change: What has it told us? *Psychological Science, 6,* 133–139.

KUHN, D., HO, V., & ADAMS, C. (1979). Formal reasoning among pre- and late-adolescents. *Child Development, 50,* 1128–1135.

KUHN, D., LANGER, J., KOHLBERG, L., & HAAN, N. S. (1977). The development of formal operations in logical and moral judgment. *Genetic Psychology Monographs, 95,* 97–188.

KULIN, II. E. (1991). Puberty, hypothalamic-pituitary changes of. In R. M. Lerner, A. C. Peterson, & J. Brooks-Gunn (Eds.), *Encyclopedia of adolescence* (Vol. 2). New York: Garland.

KUPERSMIDT, J. B., & TREJOS, L. (1987, April). *Behavioral correlates of sociometric status among Costa Rican children.* Paper presented at the meeting of the Society for Research in Child Development, Baltimore.

KUPERSMIDT J. B., DeROSIER, M. E., & PATTERSON, C. P. (1995). Similarity as the basis for children's friendships: The roles of sociometric status, aggressive and withdrawn behavior, academic achievement, and demographic characteristics. *Journal of Social and Personal Relationships, 12,* 439–452.

KURDEK, L. A. (1978). Perspective taking as the cognitive basis of children's moral development: A review of the literature. *Merrill-Palmer Quarterly, 34,* 3–28.

KURTINES, W. M., & GRIEF, E. B. (1974). The development of moral thought: Review and evaluation of Kohlberg's approach. *Psychological Bulletin, 81,* 453–470.

KURTINES, W. M., ALVAREZ, M., & AZMITIA, M. (1990). Science and morality: The role of values in science and the study of moral phenomena. *Psychological Bulletin, 107,* 283–295.

KURTZ, B. E., & BORKOWSKI, J. G. (1987). Development of strategic skills in impulsive and reflective children: A longitudinal study of metacognition. *Journal of Experimental Child Psychology, 43,* 129–148.

KURTZ, B. E., SCHNEIDER, W., CARR, M., & RELLINGER, E. (1990). Strategy instruction and attributional beliefs in West Germany and the United States: Do teachers foster metacognitive development? *Contemporary Educational Psychology, 15,* 268–283.

KUTNICK, P. (1986). The relationship of moral judgment and moral action: Kohlberg's theory, criticism and revision. In S. Modgil & C. Modgil (Eds.), *Lawrence Kohlberg: Consensus and controversy.* Philadelphia: Falmer.

LABORATORY OF COMPARATIVE HUMAN COGNITION. (1983). Culture and cognitive development. In P. H. Mussen (Series Ed.) & W. Kessen (Vol. Ed.), *Handbook of child psychology: Vol. 1. History, theory, and methods.* New York: Wiley.

LABOV, W. (1997). Testimony before the United States Senate Subcommittee on Appropriations.

LADD, G. W. (1990). Having friends, keeping friends, making friends, and being liked by peers in the classroom: Predictors of children's early school adjustment? *Child Development, 61,* 1081–1100.

LADD, G. W. (1992). Themes and theories: Perspectives on processes in family-peer relationships. In R. D. Parke & G. W. Ladd (Eds.), *Family-peer relationships: Modes of linkage.* Hillsdale, NJ: Erlbaum.

LADD, G. W., & COLEMAN, C. C. (1997). Children's classroom peer relationships and early school attitudes: Concurrent and longitudinal associations. *Early Education and Development, 8,* 51–66.

LADD, G. W., & COLEMAN, C. (1993). Young children's peer relationships: Forms, features, and functions. In B. Spodek (Ed.), *Handbook of research on the education of young children* (2nd ed.). New York: Macmillan.

LADD, G. W., & HART, C. H. (1992). Creating informal play opportunities: Are parents' and pre-schoolers' initiations related to children's competence with peers? *Developmental Psychology, 28,* 1179–1187.

LADD, G. W., & LESIEUR, K. D. (1995). Parents and children's peer relationships. In M. H. Bornstein (Ed.), *Handbook of parenting: Vol. 4. Applied and practical parenting.* Mahwah, NJ: Erlbaum.

LADD, G. W., KOCHENDERFER, B. J., & COLEMAN, C. C. (1996). Friendship quality as a predictor of young children's early school adjustment. *Child Development, 67,* 1103–1118.

LADD, G. W., PROFILET, S. M., & HART, C. H. (1992). Parents' management of children's peer relations: Facilitating and supervising children's activities in the peer culture. In R. D. Parke & G. W. Ladd (Eds.), *Family–peer relationships: Modes of linkage.* Hillsdale, NJ: Erlbaum.

LaFRENIERE, P., & CHARLESWORTH, W. R. (1983). Dominance, attention, and affiliation in a preschool group: A nine-month longitudinal study. *Ethology and Sociobiology, 4,* 55–67.

LaFRENIERE, P., & SROUFE, L. A. (1985). Profiles of peer competence in the preschool: Interrelations between measures, influence of social ecology, and relation to attachment history. *Developmental Psychology, 21,* 56–69.

LaFRENIERE, P., STRAYER, F. F., & GAUTHIER, R. (1984). The emergence of same-sex affiliative preferences among preschool peers: A developmental/ethological perspective. *Child Development, 55,* 1958–1965.

LAGASSE, L. L., GRUBER, C. P., & LIPSITT, L. P. (1989). The infantile expression of avidity in relation to later assessments of inhibition and attachment. In J. S. Reznick (Ed.), *Perspectives on behavioral inhibition.* Chicago: University of Chicago Press.

LaGRECA, A. M. (1993). Social skills training with children: Where do we go from here? *Journal of Clinical Child Psychology, 22,* 288–298.

LAHEY, B. B., HAMMER, D., CRUMRINE, P. L., & FOREHAND, R. L. (1980). Birth order X sex interactions in child behavior problems. *Developmental Psychology, 16,* 608–615.

LAKIN, M., LAKIN, M. G., & CONSTANZO, P. R. (1979). Group processes in early childhood: A dimension of human development. *International Journal of Behavioral Development, 2,* 171–183.

LAMAZE, F. (1970). *Painless childbirth: Psychoprophylactic method.* Chicago: Henry Regnery.

LAMB, M. E. (1986). The changing roles of fathers. In M. E. Lamb (Ed.), *The father's role: Applied perspectives.* New York: Wiley.

LAMB, M. E. (1998). Nonparental child care: Context, quality, correlates, and consequences. In I. E. Sigel & K. A. Renninger (Eds.), *Handbook of child psychology: Vol. 4. Child psychology in practice.* New York: Wiley.

LAMB, M. E., & HWANG, C. (1982). Maternal attachment and mother–neonate bonding: A critical review. In M. E. Lamb & A. L. Brown (Eds.), *Advances in developmental psychology* (Vol. 2). Hillsdale, NJ: Erlbaum.

LAMB, M. E., & ROOPNARINE, J. L. (1979). Peer influences on sex-role development in preschoolers. *Child Development, 50,* 1219–1222.

LAMB, M. E., & STERNBERG, K. J. (1998). Child care in context: The role and impact of early nonparental child care. In W. Damon (Ed.), *Handbook of child psychology: Vol. 4. Child psychology in practice.* New York: Wiley.

LAMB, M. E., EASTERBROOKS, M. A., & HOLDEN, G. W. (1980). Reinforcement and punishment among preschoolers: Characteristics, effects, and correlates. *Child Development, 51,* 1230–1236.

LAMB, M. E., KETTERLINUS, R. D., & FRACASSO, M. P. (1992). Parent–child relationships. In M. H. Bornstein & M. E. Lamb (Eds.), *Developmental psychology: An advanced textbook* (3rd ed.). Hillsdale, NJ: Erlbaum.

LAMB, M. E., MORRISON, D. C., & MALKIN, C. M. (1987). The development of infant social expectations in face-to-face interaction: A longitudinal study. *Merrill-Palmer Quarterly, 33,* 241–254.

LAMB, M. E., STERNBERG, K., & PRODROMIDIS, M. (1992). Nonmaternal care and the security of infant–mother attachment: A reanalysis of the data. *Infant Behavior and Development, 15,* 71–83.

LAMB, M. E., THOMPSON, R. A., & FRODI, A. M. (1982). Early social development. In R. Vasta (Ed.), *Strategies and techniques of child study.* New York: Academic Press.

LAMBORN, S. D., MOUNTS, N. S., STEINBERG, L., & DORNBUSCH, S. M. (1991). Patterns of competence and adjustment among adolescents from authoritative, authoritarian, indulgent, and neglectful families. *Child Development, 62,* 1049–1065.

LANDAU, B. (1991). Spatial representation of objects in the young blind child. *Cognition, 38,* 145–178.

LANE, I. M., & COON, R. C. (1972). Reward allocation in preschool children. *Child Development, 43,* 1382–1389.

LANGER, O. (1990). Critical issues in diabetes and pregnancy. In I. R. Merkatz & J. E. Thompson (Eds.), *New perspectives on prenatal care.* New York: Elsevier.

LANGER, W. L. (1974). Infanticide: A historical survey. *History of Childhood Quarterly, 1,* 53–365.

LANGLOIS, J. H. (1986). From the eye of the beholder to behavioral reality: Development of social behaviors and social relations as a function of physical attractiveness. In C. P. Herman, M. P. Zanna, & E. T. Higgins (Eds.), *Physical appearance, stigma, and social behavior.* Hillsdale, NJ: Erlbaum.

LANGLOIS, J. H., & DOWNS, A. C. (1979). Peer relations as a function of physical attractiveness: The eye of the beholder or behavioral reality? *Child Development, 50,* 409–418.

LANGLOIS, J. H., RITTER, J. M., CASEY, R. J., & SAWIN, D. B. (1995). Infant attractiveness predicts maternal behaviors and attitudes. *Developmental Psychology, 31,* 464–472.

LANZA, E. (1992). Can bilingual two-year-olds code-switch? *Journal of Child Language, 19,* 633–658.

LAPSLEY, D. K., & QUINTANA, S. M. (1985). Integrative themes in social and developmental theories of self. In J. B. Pryor & J. D. Day (Eds.), *The development of social cognition.* New York: Springer-Verlag.

LARGO, R. H., MOLINARI, L., WEBER, M., PINTO, L. C., & DUC, G. (1985). Early development of locomotion: Significance of prematurity, cerebral palsy and sex. *Developmental Medicine and Child Neurology, 27,* 183–191.

LARNER, M., HALPERN, R., & HARKAVY, O. (Eds.). (1992). *Fair start for children: Lessons learned from seven demonstration projects.* New Haven, CT: Yale University Press.

LARRABEE, M. J. (Ed.). (1993). *An ethic of care: Feminist and interdisciplinary perspectives.* New York: Routledge.

LARSEN, S. F. (1992). Potential flashbulbs: Memories of ordinary news as the baseline. In E. Winograd & U. Neisser (Eds.), *Affect and accuracy in recall: Studies of flashbulb memories.* New York: Cambridge University Press.

LARSSON, G., BOHLIN, A. B., & TUNELL, R. (1985). Prospective study of children exposed to variable amounts of alcohol in utero. *Archives of Disease in Childhood, 60,* 316–321.

LATORRE, R. A., YU, L., FORTIN, L., & MARRACHE, M. (1983). Gender-role adoption and sex as academic and psychological risk factors. *Sex Roles, 9,* 1127–1136.

LAURSEN, B. (1993). Conflict management among close peers. In B. Laursen (Ed.), *New directions for child development: No. 60. Close friendships in adolescence.* San Francisco: Jossey-Bass.

LAURSEN, B., HARTUP, W. W., & KOPLAS, A. L. (1996). Towards understanding peer conflict. *Merrill-Palmer Quarterly, 42,* 76–102.

LAZAR, I., & DARLINGTON, R. (1982). Lasting effects of early education: A report from the Consortium for Longitudinal Studies. *Monographs of the Society for Research in Child Development, 47* (2–3, Serial No. 195).

LEADBEATER, B. J., & BISHOP, S. J. (1994). Predictors of behavior problems in preschool children of inner-city Afro-American and Puerto Rican adolescent mothers. *Child Development, 65,* 638–648.

LEAPER, C. (Ed.). (1994). *Childhood gender segregation: Causes and consequences.* San Francisco: Jossey-Bass.

LEAPER, C., ANDERSON, K. J., & SANDERS, P. (1998). Moderators of gender effects on parents' talk to their children: A meta-analysis. *Developmental Psychology, 34,* 3–27.

LEAVITT, L., & FOX, N. (Eds.). (1993). *Psychological effects of war and violence on children.* Hillsdale, NJ: Erlbaum.

LEBOYER, F. (1975). *Birth without violence.* New York: Knopf.

LEE, C., & BATES, J. E. (1985). Mother–child interaction at the age of two years and perceived difficult temperament. *Child Development, 56,* 1314–1325.

LEE, D. N., & ARONSON, E. (1974). Visual proprioceptive control of standing in human infants. *Perception and Psychophysics, 15,* 529–532.

LEE, V. E., BROOKS-GUNN, J., SCHNUR, E., & LIAW, F.-R. (1990). Are Head Start effects sustained? A longitudinal follow-up comparison of disadvantaged children attending Head Start, no preschool, and other preschool programs. *Child Development, 61,* 495–507.

LEE, V. E., BURKHAM, D. T., ZIMILES, H., & LADEWSKI, J. (1994). Family structure and its effect on behavioral and emotional problems in young adolescents. *Journal of Research on Adolescence, 4,* 405–437.

LEGER, D. W., THOMPSON, R. A., MERRITT, J. A., & BENZ, J. J. (1996). Adult perception of emotion intensity in human infant cries: Effects of infant age and cry acoustics. *Child Development, 67,* 3238–3249.

LEGERSTEE, M., ANDERSON, D., & SCHAFFER, A. (1998). Five- and eight-month-old infants recognize their faces and voices as familiar and social stimuli. *Child Development, 69,* 37–50.

LEI, T., & CHENG, S. (1989). A little but special light on the universality of moral judgment development. In L. Kohlberg, D. Candee, & A. Colby (Eds.), *Rethinking moral development.* Cambridge: Harvard University Press.

LEIDERMAN, P. H., & SEASHORE, M. J. (1975). Mother–infant separation: Some delayed consequences. In *Parent-infant interaction* (CIBA Foundation Symposium No. 33). New York: Elsevier.

LEIJON, I. (1980). Neurology and behavior of newborn infants delivered by vacuum extraction of maternal indication. *Acta Paediatrica Scandinavica, 69,* 626–631.

LEINBACH, M. D., & FAGOT, B. I. (1993). Categorical habituation to male and female faces: Gender schematic processing in infancy. *Infant Behavior and Development, 16,* 317–332.

LEITER, M. P. (1977). A study of reciprocity in preschool play groups. *Child Development, 48,* 1288–1295.

LEMPERS, J. D., FLAVELL, E. R., & FLAVELL, J. H. (1977). The development in very young children of tacit knowledge concerning visual perception. *Genetic Psychology Monographs, 95,* 3–53.

LEMPERT, H. (1984). Topic as starting point for syntax. *Monographs of the Society for Research in Child Development, 49* (5, Serial No. 208).

LENNEBERG, E. H. (1967). *Biological foundations of language.* New York: Wiley.

LENNON, R., & EISENBERG, N. (1987). Gender and age differences in empathy and sympathy. In N. Eisenberg & J. Strayer (Eds.), *Empathy and its determinants.* New York: Cambridge University Press.

LEON, G. R. (1991). Bulimia nervosa in adolescence. In R. M. Lerner, A. C. Petersen, & J. Brooks-Gunn (Eds.), *Encyclopedia of adolescence.* New York: Garland.

LEON, M. (1982). Rules in children's moral judgments: Integration of intent, damage, and rationale information. *Developmental Psychology, 18,* 835–842.

LEPPERT, P. C., NAMEROW, P. B., & BARKER, D. (1986). Pregnancy outcomes among adolescent and older women receiving comprehensive prenatal care. *Journal of Adolescent Health Care, 7,* 112–117.

LERNER, R. M. (1982). Children and adolescents as producers of their own development. *Developmental Review, 2,* 342–370.

LERNER, R. M., & VON EYE, A. (1992). Sociobiology and human development: Arguments and evidence. *Human Development, 35,* 12–33.

LERNER, R. M., CASTELLINO, D. R., TERRY, P. A., VILLARRUEL, F. A., & McKINNEY, M. H. (1995). Developmental contextual perspective on parenting. In M. H. Bornstein (Ed.), *Handbook of parenting: Vol. 2. Biology and ecology of parenting.* Mahwah, NJ: Erlbaum.

LERNER, R. M., LERNER, J. V., & TUBMAN, J. (1989). Organismic and contextual bases of development in adolescence: A developmental contextual view. In G. R. Adams, R. Montemayor, & T. P. Gullotta (Eds.), *Biology of adolescent behavior and development.* Newbury Park, CA: Sage.

LESLIE, A. M., & KEEBLE, S. (1987). Do six-month-olds perceive causality? *Cognition, 25,* 265–288.

LESTER, B. M., HOFFMAN, J., & BRAZELTON, T. B. (1985). The rhythmic structure of mother–infant interaction in term and preterm infants. *Child Development, 56,* 15–27.

LESTER, B. M. (1976). Spectrum analysis of the cry sounds of well-nourished and malnourished infants. *Child Development, 47,* 237–241.

LESTER, B. M. (1984). A biosocial model of infant crying. In L. P. Lipsitt (Ed.), *Advances in infancy research* (Vol. 3). Norwood, NJ: Ablex.

LEUNG, E. H. L., & RHEINGOLD, H. L. (1981). Development of pointing as a social gesture. *Developmental Psychology, 17,* 215–220.

LEVAY, S. (1991). A difference in hypothalamic structure between heterosexual and homosexual men. *Science, 253,* 1034–1037.

LEVAY, S. (1993). *The sexual brain.* Cambridge: MIT Press.

LEVIN, M. (1994). Comment on the Minnesota Transracial Adoption Study. *Intelligence, 19,* 13–20.

LEVIT, A. G., & UTMAN, J. G. A. (1992). From babbling towards the sound systems of English and French: A longitudinal two-case study. *Journal of Child Language, 19,* 19–49.

LEVITT, M. J., GUACCI-FRANCO, N., & LEVITT, J. L. (1993). Convoys of social support in childhood and early adolescence: Structure and function. *Developmental Psychology, 29,* 811–818.

LEVITT, M. J., WEBER, R. A., CLARK, M. C., & MCDONNELL, P. (1985). Reciprocity of exchange in toddler sharing behavior. *Developmental Psychology, 21,* 122–123.

LEVY, G. D. (1989). Developmental and individual differences in preschoolers' recognition memories: The influences of gender schematization and verbal labeling of information. *Sex Roles, 21,* 305–324.

LEVY, G. D., & CARTER, D. B. (1989). Gender schema, gender constancy, and gender-role knowledge: The roles of cognitive factors in preschoolers' gender-role stereotype attributions. *Developmental Psychology, 25,* 444–449.

LEVY, G. D., & FIVUSH, R. (1993). Scripts and gender: A new approach for examining gender-role development. *Developmental Psychology, 13,* 126–146.

LEVY, G. D., TAYLOR, M. G., & GELMAN, S. A. (1995). Traditional and evaluative aspects of flexibility in gender roles, social conventions, moral rules, and physical laws. *Child Development, 66,* 515–531.

LEVY, J. (1981). Lateralization and its implications for variation in development. In E. S. Gollin (Ed.), *Developmental plasticity.* New York: Academic Press.

LEWIS, M. (1981). Self-knowledge: A social cognitive perspective on gender identity and sex-role development. In M. E. Lamb & L. R. Sherrod (Eds.), *Infant social cognition: Empirical and theoretical considerations.* Hillsdale, NJ: Erlbaum.

LEWIS, M. (1987a). Early sex role behavior and school age adjustment. In J. M. Reinisch, L. A. Rosenblum, & S. A. Sanders (Eds.), *Masculinity/femininity: Basic perspectives.* New York: Oxford University Press.

LEWIS, M. (1987b). Social development in infancy and early childhood. In J. D. Osofsky (Ed.), *Handbook of infant development* (2nd ed.). New York: Wiley.

LEWIS, M. (1993). Early socioemotional predictors of cognitive competence at 4 years. *Developmental Psychology, 29,* 1036–1045.

LEWIS, M. (1993). Self-conscious emotions: Embarrassment, pride, shame, and guilt. In M. Lewis & J. Haviland (Eds.), *The handbook of emotions.* New York: Guilford.

LEWIS, M. (1994). Myself and me. In S. T. Parker, R. W. Mitchell, & M. L. Boccia (Eds.), *Self-awareness in animals and humans: Developmental perspectives.* New York: Cambridge University Press.

LEWIS, M. (1995a). Aspects of the self: From systems to ideas. In P. Rochat (Ed.), *The self in early infancy: Theory and research.* North Holland, Netherlands: Elsevier.

LEWIS, M. (1995b). Embarrassment: The emotion of self-exposure and evaluation. In J. Tangney & K. Fischer (Eds.), *Self-conscious emotions: The psychology of shame, guilt, embarassment, and pride.* New York: Guilford.

LEWIS, M., & BROOKS-GUNN, J. (1979). *Social cognition and the acquisition of self.* New York: Plenum.

LEWIS, M., & RAMSEY, D. S. (1997). Stress reactivity and self-recognition. *Child Development, 68,* 621–629.

LEWIS, M., ALESSANDRI, S. M., & SULLIVAN, M. W. (1990). Violation of expectancy, loss of control, and anger expression in young infants. *Developmental Psychology, 26,* 745–751.

LEWIS, M., FEIRING, C., McGUFFOG, C., & JASKIR, J. (1984). Predicting psychopathology in six-year-olds from early social relations. *Child Development, 55,* 123–136.

LEWIS, M., RAMSEY, D. S., & KAWAKAMI, K. (1993). Differences between Japanese infants and Caucasian-American infants in behavioral and cortisol response to inoculation. *Child Development, 64,* 1722–1731.

LEWKOWICZ, D. J., & LICKLITER, R. (Eds.) (1994). *The development of intersensory perception: Comparative perspectives.* Hillsdale, NJ: Erlbaum.

LEYENDECKER, B., & SCHOLMERICH, A. (1991). An ecological perspective on infant development. In M. E. Lamb & H. Keller (Eds.), *Infant development: Perspectives from German-speaking countries.* Hillsdale, NJ: Erlbaum.

LIBEN, L. S., & SIGNORELLA, M. L. (Eds.). (1987). *New directions for child development: No. 38. Children's gender schemata.* San Francisco: Jossey-Bass.

LIDDELL, C., & KRUGER, P. (1987). Activity and social behavior in a South African township nursery: Some effects of crowding. *Merrill-Palmer Quarterly, 33,* 195–211.

LIDDELL, C., & KRUGER, P. (1989). Activity and social behavior in a crowded South African nursery: A follow-up study on the effects of crowding at home. *Merrill-Palmer Quarterly, 35,* 209–226.

LIDZ, C. S. (1992). Dynamic assessment: Some thoughts on the model, the medium, and the message. *Learning and Individual Differences, 4,* 125–136.

LIEBERT, R. M. (1984). What develops in moral development? In W. M. Kurtines & J. L. Gewirtz (Eds.), *Morality, moral behavior, and moral development.* New York: Wiley.

LIEBERT, R. M., & SPRAFKIN, J. (1988). *The early window: Effects of television on children and youth* (3rd ed.). New York: Pergamon.

LINDBERG, M. A. (1980). Is knowledge base development a necessary and sufficient condition for memory development? *Journal of Experimental Child Psychology, 30,* 401–410.

LINDSEY, E. W., MIZE, J., & PETTIT, G. S. (1997). Differential play patterns of mothers and fathers of sons and daughters: Implications for children's gender role development. *Sex Roles, 17,* 643–661.

LINN, M. C., & PETERSEN, A. C. (1985). Emergence and characterization of sex differences in spatial ability: A meta-analysis. *Child Development, 56,* 1479–1498.

LIPSCOMB, T. J., MCALLISTER, H. A., & BREGMAN, N. J. (1985). A developmental inquiry into the effects of multiple models on children's generosity. *Merrill-Palmer Quarterly, 31,* 335–344.

LIPSITT, L. P. (1977). Taste in human neonates: Its effect on sucking and heart rate. In J. M. Weiffenbach (Ed.), *Taste and development: The genesis of sweet preference.* Washington, DC: U.S. Government Printing Office.

LIPSITT, L. P. (1990). Learning and memory in infants. *Merrill-Palmer Quarterly, 36,* 53–66.

LIPSITT, L. P. (1992). Discussion: The Bayley Scales of Infant Development: Issues of prediction and outcome revisited. In C. Rovee-Collier & L. P. Lipsitt (Eds.), *Advances in infancy research* (Vol. 7). Norwood, NJ: Ablex.

LIPSITT, L. P., ENGEN, T., & KAYE, H. (1963). Developmental changes in the olfactory threshold of the neonate. *Child Development, 34,* 371–376.

LIST, J. A., COLLINS, W. A., & WESTBY, S. D. (1983). Comprehension and inferences from traditional and nontraditional sex-role portrayals on television. *Child Development, 54,* 1579–1587.

LOBEL, M., DUNKEL-SCHETTER, C., & SCRIMSHAW, S. C. M. (1992). Prenatal maternal stress and prematurity: A prospective study of socioeconomically disadvantaged women. *Health Psychology, 11*(1), 32–40.

LOBEL, T. E., & MENASHRI, J. (1993). Relations of conceptions of gender-role transgressions and gender constancy to gender-typed toy preferences. *Developmental Psychology, 29,* 150–155.

LOCHMAN, J. E., & WAYLAND, K. (1994). Aggression, social acceptance and race as predictors of negative adolescent outcomes. *Journal of the American Academy of Child and Adolescent Psychiatry, 33,* 1026–1035.

LOCHMAN, J. E., BURCH, P. P., CURRY, J. F., & LAMPRON, L. B. (1984). Treatment and generalization effects of cognitive-behavioral and goal-setting interventions with aggressive boys. *Journal of Consulting and Clinical Psychology, 52,* 915–916.

LOCKE, J. (1824). *An essay concerning human understanding.* New York: Seaman. (Original work published 1694).

LOCKE, J. L. (1989). Babbling and early speech: Continuity and individual differences. *First Language, 9,* 191–206.

LOCKE, J. L. (1993). *The child's path to spoken language.* Cambridge: Harvard University Press.

LOCKE, J. L., & PEARSON, D. M. (1990). Linguistic significance of babbling: Evidence from a tracheostomized infant. *Journal of Child Language, 17,* 1–16.

LOCKHEED, M. (1985). Women, girls, and computers: A first look at the evidence. *Sex Roles, 13,* 115–122.

LOCKMAN, J. J. (1984). The development of detour ability during infancy. *Child Development, 55,* 482–491.

LOEBER, R., & FARRINGTON, D. P. (Eds.). (1998). *Serious and violent juvenile offenders: Risk factors and successful interventions.* Thousand Oaks, CA: Sage.

LOEBER, R., & HAY, D. F. (1997). Key issues in the development of aggression and violence from childhood to early adulthood. *Annual Review of Psychology, 48,* 371–410.

LOEBER, R., & STOUTHAMER-LOEBER, M. (1998). Development of juvenile aggression and violence: Some common misconceptions and controversies. *American Psychologist, 53,* 242–259.

LOEHLIN, J. C., LINDZEY, G., & SPUHLER, J. N. (1975). *Race differences in intelligence.* San Francisco: W. H. Freeman.

LOLLIS, S. P., ROSS, H. S., & TATE, E. (1992). Parents' regulation of children's peer interactions: Direct influences. In R. D. Parke & G. W. Ladd (Eds.), *Family-peer relationships: Modes of linkage.* Hillsdale, NJ: Erlbaum.

LONG, B. C. (1989). Sex-role orientation, coping strategies, and self-efficacy of women in traditional and nontraditional occupations. *Psychology of Women Quarterly, 13,* 307–324.

LONIGAN, C. J., & WHITEHURST, G. J. (in press). Examination of the relative influence of parent and teacher involvement in a shared-reading intervention for preschool children from low-income backgrounds. *Early Childhood Research Quarterly.*

LORE, R. K., & SCHULTZ, L. A. (1993). Control of human aggression: A comparative perspective. *American Psychologist, 48,* 16–25.

LORENZ, K. Z. (1937). The companion in the bird's world. *Auk, 54,* 245–273.

LORENZ, K. Z. (1950). Innate behaviour patterns. *Symposia for the Society of Experimental Biology, 4,* 211–268.

LORENZ, K. Z. (1981). *The foundations of ethology.* New York: Springer-Verlag.

LOTT, B., & MALUSO, D. (1993). The social learning of gender. In A. E. Beall & R. J. Sternberg (Eds.), *The psychology of gender.* New York: Guilford.

LOUDAL, L. T. (1989). Sex role messages in television commercials: An update. *Sex Roles, 21,* 715–724.

LOUNSBURY, M. L., & BATES, J. E. (1982). The cries of infants of differing levels of perceived temperamental difficultness: Acoustic properties and effects on listeners. *Child Development, 53,* 677–686.

LOURENCO, O., & MACHADO, A. (1996). In defense of Piaget's theory: A reply to 10 common criticisms. *Psychological Review, 103,* 143–164.

LOVELAND, K. A. (1986). Discovering the affordances of a reflecting surface. *Developmental Review, 6,* 1–24.

LOWREY, G. H. (1978). *Growth and development of children* (7th ed.). Chicago: Year Book Medical Publishers.

LOZOFF, B., WOLFF, A., & DAVIS, N. (1984). Cosleeping in urban families with young children in the United States. *Pediatrics, 74,* 171–182.

LUDEMANN, P. M. (1991). Generalized discrimination of positive facial expressions by seven- and ten-month-old infants. *Child Development, 62,* 55–67.

LUECKE-ALEKSA, D., ANDERSON, D. R., COLLINS, P. A., & SCHMITT, K. L. (1995). Gender constancy and television viewing. *Developmental Psychology, 31,* 773–780.

LUMMIS, M., & STEVENSON, H. W. (1990). Gender differences in beliefs and achievement: A cross-cultural study. *Developmental Psychology, 26,* 254–263.

LUNDMAN, R. J. (1984). *Prevention and control of juvenile delinquency.* New York: Oxford University Press.

LURIA, A. R. (1961). *The role of speech in the regulation of normal and abnormal behavior.* New York: Liveright.

LURIA, A. R. (1982). *Language and cognition.* New York: Wiley.

LUSTER, T., & DENBOW, E. (1992). Home environment and maternal intelligence as predictors of verbal intelligence: A comparison of preschool and school-age children. *Merrill-Palmer Quarterly, 38,* 151–175.

LYNCH, M. P., & EILERS, R. E. (1992). A study of perceptual development for musical tuning. *Perception and Psychophysics, 52,* 599–608.

LYNCH, M. P., EILERS, R. E., OLLER, K. D., & URBANO, R. C. (1990). Innateness, experience, and music perception. *Psychological Science, 1,* 272–276.

LYNCH, M. P., SHORT, L. B., & CHUA, R. (1995). Contributions of experience to the development of musical processing in infancy. *Developmental Psychobiology, 28,* 377–398.

LYON, T. D., & FLAVELL, J. H. (1993). Young children's understanding of forgetting over time. *Child Development, 64,* 789–800.

LYONS, J. A., & SERBIN, L. A. (1986). Observer bias in scoring boys' and girls' aggression. *Sex Roles, 14,* 301–313.

LYONS-RUTH, K., ALPERN, L., & REPACHOLI, B. (1993). Disorganized infant attachment classification and maternal psychosocial problems as predictors of hostile-aggressive behavior in the pre-school classroom. *Child Development, 64,* 572–585.

LYONS-RUTH, K., CONNELL, D. B., & ZOLL, D. (1989). Patterns of maternal behavior among infants at risk for abuse: Relations with infant attachment behavior and infant development at 12 months of age. In D. Cicchetti & V. Carlson (Eds.), *Child maltreatment: Theory and research on the causes and consequences of child abuse and neglect.* New York: Cambridge University Press.

LYTTON, H. (1977). Do parents create, or respond to, differences in twins? *Developmental Psychology, 13,* 456–459.

LYTTON, H. (1980). *Parent–child interaction: The socialization process observed in twin and singleton families.* New York: Plenum.

LYTTON, H., & ROMNEY, D. M. (1991). Parents' sex-related differential socialization of boys and girls: A meta-analysis. *Psychological Bulletin, 109,* 267–296.

MACCOBY, E. E. (1978). *The two sexes: Growing up apart, coming together.* Cambridge, MA: Harvard University Press.

MACCOBY, E. E. (1990). Gender and relationships: A developmental account. *American Psychologist, 45,* 513–521.

MACCOBY, E. E. (1992). The role of parents in the socialization of children: An historical overview. *Developmental Psychology, 28,* 1006–1017.

MACCOBY, E. E. (1995). The two sexes and their social systems. In P. Moen, G. H. Elder, Jr., & K. Luscher (Eds.), *Examining lives in context: Perspectives on the ecology of human development.* Washington, DC: American Psychological Association.

MACCOBY, E. E. (1998). *The two sexes: Growing up apart, coming together.* Cambridge, MA: Harvard University Press.

MACCOBY, E. E., & JACKLIN, C. N. (1974). *The psychology of sex differences.* Stanford, CA: Stanford University Press.

MACCOBY, E. E., & JACKLIN, C. N. (1987). Gender segregation. In H. W. Reese (Ed.), *Advances in child development and behavior* (Vol. 20). Orlando, FL: Academic Press.

MACCOBY, E. E., & MARTIN, J. A. (1983). Socialization in the context of the family: Parent–child interaction. In E. M. Hetherington (Ed.), *Handbook of child psychology: Vol. 4. Socialization, personality, and social development.* New York: Wiley.

MACCOBY, E. E., BUCHANAN, C. M., MNOOKIN, R. H., & DORNBUSCH, S. M. (1993). Post-divorce roles of mothers and fathers in the lives of their children. *Journal of Family Psychology, 7,* 1–15.

MacDONALD, K. B. (1988a). The interfaces between sociobiology and developmental psychology. In K. B. MacDonald (Ed.), *Sociobiological perspectives on human development.* New York: Springer-Verlag.

MacDONALD, K. B. (1988b). *Social and personality development: An evolutionary synthesis.* New York: Plenum.

MacDONALD, K. B. (1988c). Sociobiology and the cognitive-developmental tradition in moral development research. In K. B. MacDonald (Ed.), *Sociobiological perspectives on human development.* New York: Springer-Verlag.

MacDONALD, K. B. (1992). Warmth as a developmental construct: An evolutionary analysis. *Child Development, 63,* 753–773.

MacDONALD, K., & PARKE, R. D. (1986). Parent-child physical play: The effects of sex and age of children and parents. *Sex Roles, 15,* 367–378.

MacFARLANE, A. (1975). Olfaction in the development of social preferences in the human neonate. In *Parent–infant interaction* (CIBA Foundation Symposium No. 33). Amsterdam: Elsevier.

MacFARLANE, A. (1987). *The culture of capitalism.* Oxford, England: Basil Blackwell.

MacKENZIE, B. (1984). Explaining race differences in IQ: The logic, the methodology, and the evidence. *American Psychologist, 39,* 1214–1233.

MacKINNON, C. E., STONEMAN, Z., & BRODY, G. H. (1984). The impact of maternal employment and family form on children's sex-role stereotypes and mothers' traditional attitudes. *Journal of Divorce, 8,* 51–60.

MacWHINNEY, B. (1987). The competition model. In B. MacWhinney (Ed.), *Mechanisms of language acquisition.* Hillsdale, NJ: Erlbaum.

MacWHINNEY, B. (1991). *The CHILDES project: Tools for analyzing talk.* Hillsdale, NJ: Erlbaum.

MacWHINNEY, B. (1998). Models of the emergence of language. *Annual Review of Psychology, 49,* 199–227.

MacWHINNEY, B., & BATES, E. (1993). *The crosslinguistic study of sentence processing.* Cambridge: Cambridge University Press.

MacWHINNEY, B., & CHANG, F. (1995). Connectionism and language learning. In C. A. Nelson (Ed.), *Minnesota symposia on child psychology: Vol. 28. Basic and applied perspectives on learning, cognition, and development.* Mahwah, NJ: Erlbaum.

MacWHINNEY, B., & LEINBACH, J. (1991). Implementations are not conceptualizations: Revising the verb learning model. *Cognition, 40,* 121–157.

MAGNUSSON, D., BERGMAN, L. R., RUDIGER, G., & TORESTAD, B. (Eds.). (1991). *Problems and methods in longitudinal research: Stability and change.* Cambridge: Cambridge University Press.

MAIN, M. (1990). Cross-cultural studies of attachment organization: Recent studies, changing methodologies, and the concept of conditional strategies. *Human Development, 33,* 48–61.

MAIN M., & GOLDWYN, R. (1998). Adult attachment rating and classification systems. In M. Main (Ed.), *Assessing attachment through discourse, drawings, and reunion situations.* New York: Cambridge University Press.

MAIN, M., & SOLOMON, J. (1986). Discovery of a disorganized/disoriented attachment pattern. In T. B. Brazelton & M. W. Yogman

(Eds.), *Affective development in infancy*. Norwood, NJ: Ablex.

MAIN M., & SOLOMON, J. (1990). Procedures for identifying infants as disorganized/disoriented during the Ainsworth Strange Situation. In M. Greenberg, D. Cicchetti, & M. Cummings (Eds.), *Attachment during the preschool years*. Chicago: University of Chicago Press.

MAIN M., KAPLAN, N., & CASSIDY, J. (1985). Security in infancy, childhood and adulthood: A move to the level of representation. In I. Bretherton & E. Waters (Eds.), Growing points of attachment theory and research. *Monographs of the Society for Research in Child Development, 50*(1–2, Serial No. 209).

MALATESTA, C. Z., & HAVILAND, J. M. (1982). Learning display rules: The socialization of emotion expression in infancy. *Child Development, 53*, 991–1003.

MALATESTA, C. Z., CULVER, C., TESMAN, J. R., & SHEPARD, B. (1989). The development of emotion expression during the first two years of life. *Monographs of the Society for Research in Child Development, 54*(1–2, Serial No. 219).

MALATESTA, C. Z., GRIGORYEV, P., LAMB, C., ALBIN, M., & CULVER, C. (1986). Emotion socialization and expressive development in preterm and full term infants. *Child Development, 57*, 316–330.

MALATESTA, C. Z., IZARD, C. E., & CAMRAS, L. (1991). Conceptualizing early infant affect: Emotions as fact, fiction, or artifact? In K. Strongman (Ed.), *International review of studies on emotion*. New York: Wiley.

MALINA, R. M. (1990). Physical growth and performance during the transitional years (9–16). In R. Montemayor, G. R. Adams, & T. Gullotta (Eds.), *From childhood to adolescence: Vol. 2. Advances in adolescent development*. London: Sage.

MANDEL, D., KEMLER NELSON, D. G., & JUSCZYK, P. W. (1996). Infants remember the order of words in a spoken sentence. *Cognitive Development, 11*, 181–196.

MANDLER, J. M. (1983). Representation. In P. H. Mussen (Series Ed.) & J. H. Flavell & E. M. Markman (Vol. Eds.), *Handbook of child psychology: Vol. 3. Cognitive development*. New York: Wiley.

MANDLER, J. M. (1990). Recall of events by preverbal children. In A. Diamond (Ed.), *The development and neural bases of higher cognitive functions*. New York: New York Academy of Sciences.

MANDLER, J. M. (1998). Representation. In W. Damon (Series Ed.) & D. Kuhn & R. S. Siegler (Vol. Eds.), *Handbook of child psychology: Vol. 2. Cognition, perception, and language* (5th ed.). New York: Wiley.

MANDOKI, M. W., SUMMER, G. S., HOFFMAN, R. P., & RICONDA, D. L. (1991). A review of Klinefelter's syndrome in children and adolescents. *Journal of the American Academy of Child and Adolescent Psychiatry, 30*, 167–172.

MANGELSDORF, S. C., PLUNKETT, J. W., DEDRICK, C. F., BERLIN, M., MEISELS, S. J., McHALE, J. L., & DICHTELLMILLER, M. (1996). Attachment security in very low birth weight infants. *Developmental Psychology, 32*, 914–920.

MANNLE, S., & TOMASELLO, M. (1987). Fathers, siblings, and the Bridge Hypothesis. In K. E. Nelson & A. VanKleeck (Eds.), *Children's language* (Vol. 6). Hillsdale, NJ: Erlbaum.

MARANTZ, S., & COATES, S. (1991). Mothers of boys with gender identity disorder: A comparison of matched controls. *Journal of the American Academy of Child and Adolescent Psychiatry, 30*, 310–315.

MARATSOS, M. (1976). *Language development: The acquisition of language structure*. Morristown, NJ: General Learning Press.

MARATSOS, M. (1983). Some current issues in the study of the acquisition of grammar. In P. H. Mussen (Series Ed.) & J. H. Flavell & E. M. Markman (Vol. Eds.), *Handbook of child psychology: Vol. 3. Cognitive development*. New York: Wiley.

MARATSOS, M. (1988). The acquisition of formal word classes. In Y. Levy, I. M. Schlesinger, & M. D. S. Braine (Eds.), *Categories and processes in language acquisition*. Hillsdale, NJ: Erlbaum.

MARATSOS, M. (1998). The acquisition of grammar. In W. Damon (Series Ed.) & D. Kuhn & R. S. Siegler (Vol. Eds.), *Handbook of child psychology: Vol. 2. Cognition, perception, and language* (5th ed.). New York: Wiley.

MARCOVITCH, S., GOLDBERG, S., GOLD, A., & WASHINGTON, J. (1997). Determinants of behavioural problems in Romanian children adopted in Ontario. *International Journal of Behavioral Development, 20*, 17–31.

MARCUS, G. F. (1996). Why do children say "breaked"? *Current Directions in Psychological Science, 5*, 81–85.

MARCUS, G. F., PINKER, S., ULLMAN, M., HOLLANDER, M., ROSEN, T. J., & XU, F. (1992). Overregularization in language acquisition. *Monographs of the Society for Research in Child Development, 57* (4, Serial No. 228).

MARINI, Z., & CASE, R. (1989). Parallels in the development of preschoolers' knowledge about their physical and social worlds. *Merrill-Palmer Quarterly, 35*, 63–87.

MARINI, Z., & CASE, R. (1994). The development of abstract reasoning about the physical and social world. *Child Development, 65*, 147–159.

MARKMAN, E. M. (1989). *Categorization and naming in children: Problems of induction*. Cambridge: MIT Press.

MARKMAN, E. M. (1991). The whole object, taxonomic, and mutual exclusivity assumptions as initial constraints on word meanings. In S. A. Gelman & J. P. Byrnes (Eds.), *Perspectives on language and thought: Interrelations in development*. Cambridge: Cambridge University Press.

MARKSTROM-ADAMS, C. (1989). Androgyny and its relation to adolescent psychosocial well-being: A review of the literature. *Sex Roles, 21*, 325–340.

MARKUS, H. J., & NURIUS, P. S. (1984). Self-understanding and self-regulation in middle childhood. In W. A. Collins (Ed.), *Development during middle childhood: The years from six to twelve*. Washington, DC: National Academy Press.

MARKUS, H. J., CROSS, S., & WURF, E. (1990). The role of the self-system in competence. In R. J. Sternberg & J. Kolligan, Jr. (Eds.), *Competence considered*. New Haven: Yale University Press.

MARKUS, H. R., & KITAYAMA, S. (1991). Culture and self: Implications for cognition, emotion, and motivation. *Psychological Review, 98*, 224–253.

MARSH, H. W. (1993). Academic self-concept: Theory, measurement, and research. In J. Suls (Ed.), *Psychological perspectives on the self* (Vol. 4). Hillsdale, NJ: Erlbaum.

MARSHALL, S. P. (1984). Sex differences in children's mathematics achievement: Solving computations and story problems. *Journal of Educational Psychology, 76*, 194–204.

MARTIN, C. L. (1990). Attitudes and expectations about children with nontraditional and traditional gender roles. *Sex Roles, 22*, 151–165.

MARTIN, C. L. (1993). New directions for investigating children's gender knowledge. *Developmental Review, 13*, 184–204.

MARTIN, C. L. (1994). Cognitive influences on the development and maintenance of gender segregation. In B. Damon (Series Ed.) & C. Leaper (Vol. Ed.). *New directions for child development: The development of gender relationships*. San Francisco: Jossey-Bass.

MARTIN, C. L., & HALVERSON, C. F. (1981). A schematic-processing model of sex typing and stereotyping in children. *Child Development, 52*, 1119–1134.

MARTIN, C. L., & HALVERSON, C. F. (1983). The effects of sex-typing schemas on young children's memory. *Child Development, 54*, 563–574.

MARTIN, C. L., & HALVERSON, C. F. (1987). The roles of cognition in sex role acquisition. In D. B. Carter (Ed.), *Current conceptions of sex roles and sex typing*. New York: Praeger.

MARTIN, C. L., & LITTLE, J. K. (1990). The relation of gender understanding to children's sex-typed preferences and gender stereotypes. *Child Development, 61*, 1427–1439.

MARTIN, C. L., EISENBUD, L., & ROSE, H. (1995). Children's gender-based reasoning about toys. *Child Development, 66*, 1453–1471.

MARTIN, C. L., WOOD, C. H., & LITTLE, J. K. (1990). The development of gender stereotype components. *Child Development, 61*, 1891–1904.

MARTIN, G. B., & CLARK, R. D. (1982). Distress crying in neonates: Species and peer specificity. *Developmental Psychology, 18*, 3–9.

MARTIN, J. A. (1981). A longitudinal study of the consequences of early mother-infant interaction: A microanalytic approach. *Monographs of the Society for Research in Child Development, 46*(3, Serial No. 190).

MARTIN, J. A., MACCOBY, E. E., & JACKLIN, C. N. (1981). Mothers' responsiveness to interactive bidding and nonbidding in boys and girls. *Child Development, 52,* 1064–1067.

MARTIN, T. R., & BRACKEN, M. B. (1986). Association of low birth weight with passive smoke exposure in pregnancy. *American Journal of Epidemiology, 124,* 633–642.

MARTINI, M. (1994). Peer interactions in Polynesia: A view from the Marquesas. In J. L. Roopnarine, J. E. Johnson, & F. H. Hooper (Eds.), *Children's play in diverse cultures.* Albany, NY: SUNY Press.

MARTORANO, S. C. (1977). A developmental analysis of performance on Piaget's formal operational tasks. *Developmental Psychology, 13,* 666–672.

MASATAKA, N. (1993). Effects of contingent and noncontingent maternal stimulation on the social behavior of three- to four-month-old Japanese infants. *Journal of Child Language, 20,* 303–312.

MASATAKA, N. (1996). Perception of motherese in a signed language by 6-month-old deaf infants. *Developmental Psychology, 32,* 874–879.

MASSEY, C. M., & GELMAN, R. (1988). Preschoolers' ability to decide whether a photographed unfamiliar object can move itself. *Developmental Psychology, 24,* 307–317.

MASTERS, J. C., & FURMAN, W. (1981). Popularity, individual friendship selection, and specific peer interaction among children. *Developmental Psychology, 17,* 344–350.

MASTERS, J. C., FORD, M. E., AREND, R., GROTEVANT, H. D., & CLARK, L. V. (1979). Modeling and labeling as integrated determinants of children's sex-typed imitative behaviors. *Child Development, 50,* 364–371.

MASTERS, M. S., & SANDERS, B. (1993). Is the gender difference in mental rotation disappearing? *Behavior Genetics, 23,* 337–341.

MASUR, E. F. (1982). Mothers' responses to infants' object-related gestures: Influences on lexical development. *Journal of Child Language, 9,* 23–30.

MATAS, L., AREND, R., & SROUFE, L. A. (1978). Continuity of adaptation in the second year: The relationship between quality of attachment and later competence. *Child Development, 49,* 547–556.

MATEFY, R. E., & ACKSEN, B. A. (1976). The effect of role-playing discrepant positions on change in moral judgments and attitudes. *Journal of Genetic Psychology, 128,* 189–200.

MATHENY, A. P., JR. (1986). Stability and change of infant temperament: Contributions from infant, mother, and family environment. In G. Kohnstamm (Ed.), *Temperament discussed.* Berwyn, PA: Swets North America.

MATHENY, A. P., JR. (1989). Children's behavioral inhibition over age and across situations: Genetic similarity for a trait during change. Long-term stability and change in personality [Special issue]. *Journal of Personality, 57,* 215–235.

MATSUMOTO, D., HAAN, N., YABROVE, G., THEODOROU, P., & CARNEY, C. C. (1986). Pre-schoolers' moral actions and emotions in Prisoner's Dilemma. *Developmental Psychology, 22,* 663–670.

MAURER, D., & SALAPATEK, P. (1976). Developmental changes in the scanning of faces by young infants. *Child Development, 47,* 523–527.

MAYER, N. K., & TRONICK, E. Z. (1985). Mothers' turn-giving signals and infant turn-taking in mother–infant interaction. In T. M. Field & N. A. Fox (Eds.), *Social perception in infants.* Norwood, NJ: Ablex.

MAYES, L. C. (1992). Prenatal cocaine exposure and young children's development. *Annals, AAPSS, 521,* 11–27.

MAYES, L. C., CARTER, A. S., & STUBBE, D. (1993). Individual differences in exploratory behavior in the second year of life. *Infant Behavior and Development, 16,* 269–284.

MAYNARD SMITH, J. (1976). Group selection. *Quarterly Review of Biology, 51,* 277–283.

MAZZELLA, C., DURKIN, K., CERINI, E., & BURALLI, P. (1992). Sex-role stereotyping in Australian television advertisements. *Sex Roles, 26,* 243–259.

McANINCH, C. B., MANOLIS, M. B., MILICH, R., & HARRIS, M. J. (1993). Impression formation in children: Influence of gender and expectancy. *Child Development, 64,* 1492–1506.

McBRIDE -CHANG, C. (1995). What is phonological awareness? *Journal of Educational Psychology, 87,* 179–192.

McBRIDE, S. (1990). Maternal modulators of child care: The role of maternal separation anxiety. In K. McCartney (Ed.), *New directions for child development: No. 49. Child care and maternal employment: A social ecology approach.* San Francisco: Jossey-Bass.

McCABE, A., & LIPSCOMB, T. J. (1988). Sex differences in children's verbal aggression. *Merrill-Palmer Quarterly, 34,* 389–401.

McCABE, A., & LIPSCOMB, T. J. (1988). Sex differences in children's verbal aggression. *Merrill-Palmer Quarterly, 34,* 389–401.

McCABE, A. E. (1989). Differential language learning styles in young children: The importance of context. *Developmental Review, 9,* 1–20.

McCALL, R. B. (1977). Challenges to a science of developmental psychology. *Child Development, 48,* 333–344.

McCALL, R. B. (1981). Early predictors of later IQ: The search continues. *Intelligence, 5,* 141–148.

McCALL, R. B. (1994). What process mediates predictions of childhood IQ from infant habituation and recognition memory? Speculations on the roles of inhibition and rate of information processing. *Intelligence, 18,* 107–125.

McCALL, R. B., & CARRIGER, M. S. (1993). A meta-analysis of infant habituation and recognition memory as predictors of later IQ. *Child Development, 64,* 57–79.

McCALL, R. B., & MASH, C. W. (1994). Infant cognition and its relation to mature intelligence. In R. Vasta (Ed.), *Annals of child development* (Vol. 10). London: Kingsley.

McCALL, R. B., APPLEBAUM, M. I., & HOGARTY, P. S. (1973). Developmental changes in mental performance. *Monographs of the Society for Research in Child Development, 38* (3, Serial No. 150).

McCARTNEY, K. (Ed.). (1990). *New directions for child development: No. 49. Child care and maternal employment: A social ecology approach.* San Francisco: Jossey-Bass.

McCARTNEY, K., & NELSON, K. (1981). Children's use of scripts in story recall. *Discourse Processes, 4,* 59–70.

McCORD, J., & TREMBLAY, R. E. (1992). *Preventing antisocial behavior: Interventions from birth through adolescence.* New York: Guilford.

McCORMICK, C. M., & WITELSON, S. F. (1991). A cognitive profile of homosexual men compared to heterosexual men and women. *Psychoneuroendocrinology, 16,* 459–473.

McCOY, E. (1988). Childhood through the ages. In R. Finsterbusch (Ed.), *Sociology 88/89.* Guildford, CT: Dushkin.

McCUNE-NICOLICH, L. (1981). The cognitive bases of relational words in the single word period. *Journal of Child Language, 8,* 15–34.

McDANIEL, D., McKEE, C., & CAIRNS, H. S. (Eds.). (1997). *Methods for assessing children's syntax.* Cambridge: MIT Press.

McDONALD, J. L. (1997). Language acquisition: The acquisition of linguistic structure in normal and special populations. *Annual Review of Psychology, 48,* 215–241.

McDONOUGH, L., & MANDLER, J. M. (1994). Very long-term recall in infants: Infantile amnesia reconsidered. *Memory, 2,* 339–352.

McEWEN, B. S. (1987). Observations on brain sexual differentiation: A biochemist's view. In J. M. Reinisch, L. A. Rosenblum, & S. A. Sanders (Eds.), *Masculinity/femininity: Basic properties.* New York: Oxford University Press.

McFAYDEN-KETCHUM, S. A., BATES, J. E., DODGE, K. A., & PETTIT, G. S. (1996). Patterns of change in early childhood aggressive-disruptive behavior: Gender differences in predictions from early coercive and affectionate mother-child interactions. *Child Development, 67,* 2417–2433.

McGEE, L. M., & RICHGELS, D. J. (1990). *Literacy's beginnings: Supporting young readers and writers.* Boston: Allyn & Bacon.

McGEE, M. G. (1982). Spatial abilities: The influence of genetic factors. In M. Potegal (Ed.), *Spatial abilities: Development and physiological foundations.* New York: Academic Press.

McGHEE, P. E., & FRUEH, T. (1980). Television viewing and the learning of sex-role stereotypes. *Sex Roles, 6,* 179–188.

McGILLICUDDY-DE LISI, A. V. (1988). Sex differences in parental teaching behaviors. *Merrill-Palmer Quarterly, 34,* 147–162.

McGLONE, J. (1980). Sex differences in human brain asymmetry: Critical survey. *Behavioral and Brain Sciences, 3,* 215–227.

McGRAW, M. B. (1935). *Growth: A study of Johnny and Jimmy.* New York: Appleton-Century-Crofts.

McGRAW, M. B. (1940). Suspension grasp behavior of the human infant. *American Journal of the Disabled Child, 60,* 799–811.

McGUE, M., & LYKKEN, D. T. (1992). Genetic influences on risk of divorce. *Psychological Science, 3,* 368–373.

McGUE, M., BOUCHARD, T. J., JR., IACONO, W., & LYKKEN, D. T. (1993). Behavioral genetics of cognitive ability: A life-span perspective. In R. Plomin & G. McLearn (Eds.), *Nature, nurture, and psychology.* Washington, DC: American Psychological Association.

McGUE, M., BOUCHARD, T. J., JR., IACONO, W. G., & LYKKEN, D. T. (1993). Behavior genetics of cognitive ability: A life-span perspective. In R. Plomin & G. E. McClearn (Eds.), *Nature, nurture, and psychology.* Washington, DC: American Psychological Association.

McHALE, S. M., BARTKO, W. T., CROUTER, A. C., & PERRY-JENKINS, M. (1990). Children's housework and psychosocial functioning: The mediating effects of parents' sex-role behaviors and attitudes. *Child Development, 61,* 1413–1426.

McKNIGHT, C. C., CROSSWHITE, F. J., DOSSEY, J. A., KIFER, E., SWAFFORD, J. O., TRAVERS, K. J., & COONEY, T. J. (1987). *The uderachieving curriculum: Assessing U.S. school mathematics from an international perspective.* Champaign, IL: Stipes.

McKUSICK, V. A. (1994). *Mendelian inheritance in man* (11th ed.). Baltimore: Johns Hopkins University Press.

McLANAHAN, S., & SANDEFUR, G. (1994). *Growing up with a single parent: What hurts, what helps?* Cambridge: Harvard University Press.

McLAUGHLIN, B., WHITE, D., McDEVITT, T., & RASKIN, R. (1983). Mothers' and fathers' speech to their young children: Similar or different? *Journal of Child Language, 10,* 245–252.

McLOYD, V. C. (1998). Poverty. In W. Damon (Ed.), *Handbook of child psychology: Vol 4. Child psychology in practice.* New York: Wiley.

McNEILL, D. (1992). *Hand and mind: What gestures reveal about thought.* Chicago: University of Chicago Press.

MEAD, M. (1935). *Sex and temperament in three primitive societies.* New York: William Morrow.

MEAD, M., & NEWTON, N. (1967). Cultural patterning of perinatal behavior. In S. A. Richardson & A. F. Guttmacher (Eds.), *Childbearing: Its social and psychological factors.* Baltimore: Williams & Wilkins.

MEBERT, C. J. (1989). Stability and change in parents' perceptions of infant temperament: Early pregnancy to 13.5 months postpartum. *Infant Behavior and Development, 2,* 237–244.

MEBERT, C. J. (1991). Dimensions of subjectivity in parents' ratings of infant temperament. *Child Development, 62,* 352–361.

MEDOFF-COOPER, B., CAREY, W. B., & McDEVITT, S. C. (1993). The Early Infancy Temperament Questionnaire. *Journal of Developmental and Behavioral Pediatrics, 14,* 230–235.

MEDRICH, E. A., ROIZEN, J. A., RUBIN, V., & BUCKLEY, S. (1982). *The serious business of growing up: A study of children's lives outside school.* Berkeley: University of California Press.

MEHLER, J., BERTONCINI, J., BARRIERE, M., & JASSIK-GERSHENFELD, D. (1978). Infant recognition of mother's voice. *Perception, 7,* 491–497.

MEHLER, J., JUSCZYK, P. W., LAMBERTZ, G., HALSTED, N., BERTONCINI, J., & AMIEL-TISON, C. (1988). A precursor of language acquisition in young infants. *Cognition, 29,* 143–178.

MEICHENBAUM, D., & GOODMAN, S. (1979). Clinical use of private speech and critical questions about its study in natural settings. In G. Zivin (Ed.), *The development of self-regulation through private speech.* New York: Wiley.

MEIER, R. P., & NEWPORT, E. L. (1990). Out of the hands of babes: On a possible sign advantage in language acquisition. *Language, 66,* 1–23.

MELOT, A.-M., & CORROYER, D. (1992). Organization of metacognitive knowledge: A condition for strategy use in memorization. *European Journal of Psychology of Education, 7,* 23–38.

MELTZOFF, A. N. (1988). Infant imitation and memory: Nine-month-olds in immediate and defer-red tests. *Child Development, 59,* 217–225.

MELTZOFF, A. N. (1988a). Infant imitation after a 1-week delay: Long-term memory for novel and multiple stimuli. *Developmental Psychology, 24,* 470–476.

MELTZOFF, A. N. (1988b). Infant imitation and memory: Nine-month-olds in immediate and deferred tests. *Child Development, 59,* 217–225.

MELTZOFF, A. N. (1990). Foundations for developing a concept of self: The role of imitation in relating self to other and the value of social mirroring, social modeling, and self practice in infancy. In D. Cicchetti & M. Beeghly (Eds.), *The self in transition: Infancy to childhood.* Chicago: University of Chicago Press.

MELTZOFF, A. N., & BORTON, R. W. (1979). Intermodal matching by human neonates. *Nature, 282,* 403–404.

MELTZOFF, A. N., & MOORE, M. K. (1977). Imitation of facial and manual gestures by human neonates. *Science, 198,* 75–78.

MELTZOFF, A. N., & MOORE, M. K. (1983). Newborn infants imitate adult facial gestures. *Child Development, 54,* 702–709.

MELTZOFF, A. N., & MOORE, M. K. (1985). Cognitive foundations and social functions of imitation and intermodal representation in infancy. In J. Mehler & R. Fox (Eds.), *Neonate cognition: Beyond the blooming buzzing confusion.* Hillsdale, NJ: Erlbaum.

MELTZOFF, A. N., & MOORE, M. K. (1989). Imitation in newborn infants: Exploring the range of gestures imitated and the underlying mechanisms. *Developmental Psychology, 25,* 954–962.

MELTZOFF, A. N., & MOORE, M. K. (1994). Imitation, memory, and the representation of persons. *Infant Behavior and Development, 17,* 83–99.

MELTZOFF, A. N., & MOORE, M. K. (1995). A theory of the role of imitation in the emergence of self. In P. Rochat (Ed.), *The self in infancy: Theory and research.* Amsterdam: Elsevier.

MENARD, S. (1991). *Longitudinal research.* Newbury Park, CA: Sage.

MENDELSON, M. J. (1990). *Becoming a brother.* Cambridge: MIT Press.

MENIG-PETERSON, C. L. (1975). The modification of communicative behaviors in preschool-aged children as a function of the listener's perspective. *Child Development, 46,* 1015–1018.

MEREDITH, H. V. (1963). Change in the stature and body weight of North American boys during the last 80 years. In L. P. Lipsitt & C. C. Spiker (Eds.), *Advances in child development and behavior* (Vol. 1). New York: Academic Press.

MERRIMAN, W. E. (1997). CALLED: A model of early word learning. In R. Vasta (Ed.), *Annals of child development* (Vol. 13). London: Kingsley.

MERVIS, C. B. (1987). Child-basic object categories and early lexical development. In U. Neisser (Ed.), *Concepts and conceptual development: Ecological and intellectual factors in categorization.* New York: Cambridge University Press.

MESSER, D. J. (1980). The episodic structure of maternal speech to young children. *Journal of Child Language, 7,* 29–40.

MESSER, D. J., McCARTHY, M. E., McQUISTON, S., MacTURK, R. H., YARROW, L. J., & VIETZE, P. M. (1986). Relation between mastery motivation in infancy and competence in early childhood. *Developmental Psychology, 22,* 366–372.

METTETAL, G. (1983). Fantasy, gossip, and self-disclosure: Children's conversations with friends. In R. N. Bostrom (Ed.), *Communication yearbook* (Vol. 7). Beverly Hills, CA: Sage.

MEYER-BAHLBERG, H. F. L., EHRHARDT, A. A., ROSEN, L. R., GRUEN, R. S., VERIDIANO, N. P., VANN, F. H., & NEUWALDER, H. F. (1995). Prenatal estrogens and the development of homosexual orientation. *Developmental Psychology, 31,* 12–21.

MEYER-BAHLBERG, H. F. L. (1993). Psychobiologic research on homosexuality. *Child and Adolescent Psychiatric Clinics of North America, 2,* 489–500.

MICHAEL, J. (1984). Verbal behavior. *Journal of the Experimental Analysis of Behavior, 42,* 363–376.

MIDGLEY, C., FELDLAUFER, H., & ECCLES, J. (1988a). Student/teacher relations and attitudes towards mathematics before and after the transition to junior high school. *Child Development, 60,* 375–395.

MIDGLEY, C., FELDLAUFER, H., & ECCLES, J. (1988b). The transition to junior high school: Beliefs of pre- and post-transition teachers. *Journal of Youth and Adolescence, 17,* 543–562.

MIDLARSKY, E., & HANNAH, M. E. (1985). Competence, reticence, and helping by children and adolescents. *Developmental psychology, 21,* 534–541.

MILLER, L. T., & VERNON, P. A. (1997). Developmental changes in speed of information processing in young children. *Developmental Psychology, 23,* 549–554.

MILLER, N., & MARUYAMA, G. (1976). Ordinal position and peer popularity. *Journal of Personality and Social Psychology, 33,* 123–131.

MILLER, P. A., EISENBERG, N., FABES, R. A., & SHELL, R. (1996). Relations of moral reasoning and vicarious emotion to young children's prosocial behavior toward peers and adults. *Developmental Psychology, 32,* 210–219.

MILLER, P. H. (1990). The development of strategies of selective attention. In D. F. Bjorklund (Ed.), *Children's strategies: Contemporary views of cognitive development.* Hillsdale, NJ: Erlbaum.

MILLER, P. H. (1993). *Theories of developmental psychology* (3rd ed.). New York: W. H. Freeman.

MILLER, P. H., & DeMARIE-DREBLOW, D. (1990). Social-cognitive correlates of children's understanding of displaced aggression. *Journal of Experimental Child Psychology, 49,* 488–504.

MILLER, P. H., & SEIER, W. L. (1994). Strategy utilization deficiencies in children: When, where, and why? In H. W. Reese (Ed.), *Advances in child development and behavior* (Vol. 25). New York: Academic Press.

MILLER, P. J. (1994). Narrative practices: Their role in socialization and self-construction. In U. Neisser & R. Fivush (Eds.), *The remembering self: Construction and accuracy in the self-narrative.* New York: Cambridge University Press.

MILLER, P. M., DANAHER, D. L., & FORBES, D. (1986). Sex-related strategies for coping with interpersonal conflict in children aged five to seven. *Developmental Psychology, 22,* 543–548.

MILLER, S. A. (1976). Nonverbal assessment of Piagetian concepts. *Psychological Bulletin, 83,* 405–430.

MILLER, S. A. (1982). Cognitive development: A Piagetian perspective. In R. Vasta (Ed.), *Strategies and techniques of child study.* New York: Aca-demic Press.

MILLER, S. A. (1986). Certainty and necessity in the understanding of Piagetian concepts. *Developmental Psychology, 22,* 3–18.

MILLER, S. A. (1998). *Developmental research methods* (2nd ed.). Englewood Cliffs, NJ: Prentice-Hall.

MILLER, S. A., & DAVIS, T. L. (1992). Beliefs about children: A comparative study of mothers, teachers, peers, and self. *Child Development, 63,* 1251–1265.

MILLER, S. A., SHELTON, J., & FLAVELL, J. H. (1970). A test of Luria's hypothesis concerning the development of verbal self-regulation. *Child Development, 41,* 651–665.

MILLS, R. S. L., & GRUSEC, J. E. (1988). Socialization from the perspective of the parent–child relationship. In S. Duck (Ed.), *Handbook of personal relationships.* Chichester, England: Wiley.

MILLS, R. S. L., & GRUSEC, J. E. (1989). Cognitive, affective, and behavioral consequences of praising altruism. *Merrill-Palmer Quarterly, 35,* 299–326.

MINDE, K. (1993). Prematurity and illness in infancy: Implications for development and intervention. In C. H. Zeanah, Jr. (Ed.), *Handbook of infant mental development.* New York: Guilford.

MINUCHIN, P. (1985). Families and individual development: Provocations from the field of family therapy. *Child Development, 56,* 289–302.

MISCHEL, W., SHODA, Y., & PEAKE, P. K. (1988). The nature of adolescent competencies predicted by preschool delay of gratification. *Journal of Personality and Social Psychology, 54,* 687–696.

MISCHEL, W., SHODA, Y., & RODRIGUEZ, M. L. (1989). Delay of gratification in children. *Science, 244,* 933–938.

MITCHELL, P. (1996). *Introduction to theory of mind.* New York: Arnold.

MITZENHEIM, P. (1985). The importance of Rousseau's developmental thinking for child psychology. In G. Eckardt, W. G. Bringmann, & L. Sprung (Eds.), *Contributions to a history of developmental psychology.* Berlin: Mouton.

MIYAKE, K., CHEN, S. J., & CAMPOS, J. J. (1985). Infant temperament, mother's mode of interaction, and attachment in Japan: An interim report. In I. Bretherton & E. Waters (Eds.), Growing points of attachment theory and research. *Monographs of the Society for Research in Child Development, 50*(1–2, Serial No. 209).

MIYAWAKI, K., STRANGE, W., VERBRUGGE, R., LIBERMAN, A. M., JENKINS, J. J., & FUJIMURA, O. (1975). An effect of linguistic experience: The discrimination of the [r] and [l] by native speakers of Japanese and English. *Perception and Psychophysics, 18,* 331–340.

MIZE, J., & LADD, G. W. (1990). A cognitive-social learning approach to social skill training with low-status preschool children. *Developmental Psychology, 26,* 388–397.

MODGIL, S., & MODGIL, C. (1976). *Piagetian research: Compilation and commentary* (Vols. 1–8). Windsor, England: NFER.

MOELY, B. E., HART, S. S., SANTULLI, K. A., LEAL, L., JOHNSON, T., RAO, N., & BURNEY, L. (1986). How do teachers teach memory skills? *Educational Psychologist, 21,* 55–71.

MOELY, B. E., SANTULLI, K. A., & OBACH, M. S. (1995). Strategy instruction, metacognition, and motivation in the elementary school classroom. In F. E. Weinert & W. Schneider (Eds.), *Memory performance and competencies: Issues in growth and development.* Mahwah, NJ: Erlbaum.

MOEN, P., ELDER, G. H., JR., LUSCHER, K. (Eds.). (1995). *Examining lives in context: Perspectives on the ecology of human development.* Washington, DC: American Psychological Association.

MOERK, E. L. (1996). Input and learning processes in first language acquisition. In H. W. Reese (Ed.), *Advances in child development and behavior* (Vol. 26). San Diego: Academic Press.

MOFFITT, A. R. (1973). Intensity discrimination and cardiac reaction in young infants. *Developmental Psychology, 8,* 357–359.

MOFFITT, T. E., CASPI, A., HARKNESS, A. R., & SILVA, P. A. (1993). The natural history of change in intellectual performance: Who changes? How much? Is it meaningful? *Journal of Child Psychology and Psychiatry and Allied Disciplines, 34,* 455–506.

MOLFESE, D. L., & MOLFESE, V. J. (1979). Hemispheric and stimulus differences as reflected in the cortical responses of newborn infants to speech stimuli. *Developmental Psychology, 15,* 505–511.

MOLFESE, D. L., & SEGALOWITZ, S. J. (1989). *Brain lateralization in children: Developmental implications.* New York: Guilford.

MOLLER, L. C., & SERBIN, L. A. (1996). Antecedents of toddler gender segregation: Cognitive consonance, gender-typed toy preferences and behavioral compatibility. *Sex Roles, 26,* 331–353.

MONAHAN, S. C., BUCHANAN, C. M., MACCOBY, E. E., & DORNBUSCH, S. M. (1993). Sibling differences in divorced families. *Child Development, 64,* 152–168.

MONEY, J. (1975). Ablatio penis: Normal male infant sex-reassigned as a girl. *Archives of Sexual Behavior, 4,* 65–71.

MONEY, J. (1991). *Biographies of gender and hermaphroditism in paired comparisons.* Amsterdam: Elsevier.

MONEY, J. (1993). *The Adam principle. Genes, genitals, hormones, and gender: Selected readings in sexology.* Buffalo, NY: Prometheus Books.

MONEY, J. (1994). The concept of gender identity disorder in childhood and adolescence after 39 years. *Journal of Sex and Marital Therapy, 20,* 163–177.

MONEY, J. C., & ANNECILLO, C. (1987). Crucial period effect in psychoendocrinology: Two syndromes, abuse dwarfism and female (CVAH) hermaphroditism. In M. H. Bornstein (Ed.), *Sensitive periods in development: Interdisciplinary perspectives.* Hillsdale, NJ: Erlbaum.

MONEY, J. C., & EHRHARDT, A. A. (1972). *Man and woman, boy and girl.* Baltimore: Johns Hopkins University Press.

MONEY, J., DEVORE, H., & NORMAN, B. F. (1986). Gender identity and gender transposition: Longitudinal outcome study of 32 male hermaphrodites assigned as girls. *Journal of Sex and Marital Therapy, 12,* 165–181.

MONTAGUE, M. F. A. (1968). *Man and aggression.* New York: Oxford University Press.

MONTEMAYOR, R. (1974). Children's performance in a game and their attraction to it as a function of sex-typed labels. *Child Development, 45,* 152–156.

MONTGOMERY, D. E. (1993). Young children's understanding of interpretive diversity between different-age listeners. *Developmental Psychology, 29,* 337–345.

MOON, C., COOPER, R. P., & FIFER, W. P. (1993). Two-day-olds prefer their native language. *Infant Behavior and Development, 16,* 495–500.

MOORE, B. S., & EISENBERG, N. (1984). The development of altruism. In G. J. Whitehurst (Ed.), *Annals of child development* (Vol. 1). Greenwich, CT: JAI Press.

MOORE, L., HUGHES, J., & ROBINSON, M. (1992). A comparison of the social information-processing abilities of rejected and accepted hyperactive children. *Journal of Clinical Child Psychology, 21,* 123–131.

MORAN, G. F., & VINOVSKIS, M. A. (1985). The great care of godly parents: Early childhood in Puritan New England. In A. B. Smuts & J. W. Hagen (Eds.), History and research in child development. *Monographs of the Society for Research in Child Development, 50*(4–5, Serial No. 211).

MORAN, J. D., III, & McCULLERS, J. C. (1984). The effects of recency and story content on children's moral judgments. *Journal of Experimental Child Psychology, 38,* 447–455.

MORELL, V. (1993). The puzzle of the triple repeats. *Science, 260,* 1422–1423.

MORELLI, G., ROGOFF, B., OPPENHEIM, D., & GOLDSMITH, D. (1992). Cultural variations in infants' sleeping arrangements: Questions of independence. *Developmental Psychology, 28,* 604–613.

MORETTI, M. M., & HIGGINS, E. T. (1990). The development of self-esteem vulnerabilities: Social and cognitive factors in developmental psychopathology. In R. J. Sternberg & J. Kolligian, Jr. (Eds.), *Competence considered.* New Haven, CT: Yale University Press.

MORGAN, B., & GIBSON, K. R. (1991). Nutritional and environmental interactions in brain development. In K. R. Gibson and A. C. Petersen (Eds.), *Brain maturation and cognitive development.* New York: Aldine de Gruyter.

MORGAN, J. L. (1986). *From simple input to complex grammar.* Cambridge: MIT Press.

MORGAN, J. L., BONAMO, K. M., & TRAVIS, L. L. (1995). Negative evidence on negative evidence. *Developmental Psychology, 31,*180–197.

MORGANE, P. J., AUSTIN-LaFRANCE, R., BRONZINO, J., TONKISS, J., DIÁZ-CINTRA, S., CINTRA, L., KEMPER, T., & GALLER, J. R. (1993). Prenatal malnutrition and development of the brain. *Neuroscience and Biobehavioral Reviews, 17,* 91–128.

MORO, E. (1918). Das erste Trimenon. *Munch. med. Wschr., 65,* 1147–1150.

MORRISON, F. J., GRIFFITH, E. M., & ALBERTS, D. M. (1997). Nature–nurture in the classroom: Entrance age, school readiness, and learning in children. *Developmental Psychology, 33,* 254–262.

MORRISON, F. J., SMITH, L., & DOW-EHRENSBERGER, M. (1995). Education and cognitive development: A natural experiment. *Developmental Psychology, 31,* 789–799.

MORRISON, H., & KUHN, D. (1983). Cognitive aspects of preschoolers' peer imitation in a play situation. *Child Development, 54,* 1054–1063.

MORRONGIELLO, B. A., FENWICK, K. D., HILLIER, L., & CHANCE, G. (1994). Sound localization in newborn human infants. *Developmental Psychobiology, 27,* 519–538.

MORRONGIELLO, B. A. (1988). Infants' localization of sounds along two spatial dimensions: Horizontal and vertical axes. *Infant Behavior and Development, 11,* 127–143.

MORRONGIELLO, B. A. (1994). Effects of colocation on auditory-visual interactions and cross-modal perception in infants. In D. J. Lewkowicz & R. Lickliter (Eds.), *The development of intersensory perception: Comparative perspectives.* Hillsdale, NJ: Erlbaum.

MOSHMAN, D. (1998). Cognitive development beyond childhood. In W. Damon (Series Ed.) & D. Kuhn & R. S. Siegler (Vol. Eds.), *Handbook of child psychology: Vol. 2. Cognition, perception, and language* (5th ed.). New York: Wiley.

MOUNTEER, C. A. (1987). Roman childhood, 200 B.C. to A.D. 600. *Journal of Psychohistory, 14,* 233–254.

MOUNTS, N. S., & STEINBERG, L. (1995). An ecological analysis of peer influence on adolescent grade point average and drug use. *Developmental Psychology, 31,* 915–922.

MRAZEK, P. J. (1993). Maltreatment and infant development. In C. H. Zeanah, Jr. (Ed.), *Handbook of infant mental development.* New York: Guilford.

MUELLER, C. (1996). Multidisciplinary research of multimodal stimulation of premature infants: An integrative review of the literature. *Maternal-Child Nursing Journal, 24,* 18–31.

MUELLER, E., & SILVERMAN, N. (1989). Peer relations in maltreated children. In D. Cicchetti & V. Carlson (Eds.), *Child maltreatment: Theory and research on the causes and consequences of child abuse and neglect.* New York: Cambridge University Press.

MUELLER, W. H. (1986). The genetics of size and shape in children and adults. In F. Falkner & J. M. Tanner (Eds.), *Human growth: A comprehensive treatise* (2nd ed., Vol. 3). New York: Plenum.

MUIR, D., & CLIFTON, R. K. (1985). Infants' orientation to the location of sound sources. In G. Gottlieb & N. A. Krasnegor (Eds.), *Measurement of audition and vision in the first year of postnatal life: A methodological overview.* Norwood, NJ: Ablex.

MULLEN, M. K. (1994). Earliest recollections of childhood: A demographic analysis. *Cognition, 52,* 55–79.

MULLEN, M. K., & YI, S. (1995). The cultural context of talk about the past: Implications for the development of autobiographical memory. *Cognitive Development, 10,* 407–419.

MUMME, D. L., FERNALD, A., & HERRERA, C. (1996). Infants' responses to facial and vocal emotional signals in a social referencing paradigm. *Child Development, 67,* 3219–3237.

MUNAKATA, Y., McCLELLAND, J. L., JOHNSON, M. H., & SIEGLER, R. S. (1997). Rethinking infant knowledge: Toward an adaptive process account of successes and failures in object permanence tasks. *Psychological Review, 104,* 686–713.

MUNRO, D. J. (1977). *The concept of man in contemporary China.* Ann Arbor: University of Michigan Press.

MUNROE, R. H., SHIMMIN, H. S., & MUNROE, R. L. (1984). Gender understanding and sex role preference in four cultures. *Developmental Psychology, 20,* 673–682.

MURATA, P. J., McGLYNN, E. A., SIU, A. L., & BROOK, R. H. (1992). *Prenatal care.* Santa Monica, CA: Rand.

MURPHEY, D. A. (1992). Constructing the child: Relations between parents' beliefs and child outcomes. *Developmental Review, 12,* 199–232.

MURRAY, A. D., JOHNSON, J., & PETERS, J. (1990). Fine-tuning of utterance length to preverbal infants: Effects on later language development. *Journal of Child Language, 17,* 511–525.

MURRAY, F. B. (1982). Learning and development through social interaction and conflict: A challenge to social learning theory. In L. Liben (Ed.), *Piaget and the foundation of knowledge.* Hillsdale, NJ: Erlbaum.

MURRAY, L., FIORI-COWLEY, A., HOOPER, R., & COOPER, P. (1996). The impact of postnatal depression and associated adversity on early mother-infant interactions and later outcome. *Child Development, 67,* 2512–2526.

MWAMWENDA, T. S. (1992). Cognitive development in African children. *Genetic, Social, and General Psychology Monographs, 118,* 5–72.

MYERS, B. J. (1987). Mother–infant bonding as a critical period. In M. H. Bornstein (Ed.), *Sensitive periods in development: Interdisciplinary perspectives.* Hillsdale, NJ: Erlbaum.

NADEL, J., & FONTAINE, A. (1989). Communicating by imitation: A developmental and comparative approach to transitory social competence. In B. H. Schneider, G. Attili, J. Nadel, & R. P. Weissberg (Eds.), *Social competence in developmental perspective.* Dordrecht, Netherlands: Kluwer.

NAEYE, R. L., DIENER, M. M., & DELLINGER, W. S. (1969). Urban poverty: Effects on prenatal nutrition. *Science, 166,* 1026.

NAIGLES, L. G., & GELMAN, S. A. (1995). Overextensions in comprehension and production revisited: Preferential-looking in a study of dog, cat, and cow. *Journal of Child Language, 22,* 19–46.

NAKAHARA, T., UOZUMI, T., MONDEN, S., MUTTAGIN, Z., KURISU, K., ARITA, K., KUWABARA, S., OHAMA, K., KUMAGAI, M., & NAKAHARA, K. (1993). Prenatal diagnosis of open spina bifida by MRI and ultrasonography. *Brain and Development, 15,* 75–78.

NATHANIELSZ, P. W. (1995). The role of basic science in preventing low birth weight. *The future of children* (Vol. 5, No. 1). Los Angeles: Packard Foundation.

NATIONAL INSTITUTES OF HEALTH. (1993). The human genome: A race to the 3 billionth base. *Journal of NIH Research, 5,* 44.

NEEDHAM, J. (1959). *A history of embryology.* Cambridge: Cambridge University Press.

NEEDLEMAN, H. L., SCHELL, A. S., BELLINGER, D., LEVITON, A., & ALLDRED, E. N. (1990). The long-term effects of exposure to low doses of lead in childhood: An 11-year follow-up report. *New England Journal of Medicine, 322,* 83.

NEISSER, U., BOODOO, G., BOUCHARD, T. J., JR., BOYKIN, A. W., BRODY, N., CECI, S. J., HALPERN, D. F., LOEHLIN, J. C., PERLOFF, R., STERNBERG, R. J., & URBINA, S. (1996). Intelligence: Knowns and unknowns. *American Psychologist, 51,* 77–101.

NEISSER, U. (Ed.). (1993). *Ecological and interpersonal knowledge of self.* New York: Cambridge University Press.

NEISSER, U. (1995). Criteria for an ecological self. In P. Rochat (Ed.), *The self in infancy: Theory and research.* Amsterdam: Elsevier.

NELSON, C. A. (1987). The recognition of facial expressions in the first two years of life: Mechanisms of development. *Child Development, 58,* 889–909.

NELSON, C. A., & HOROWITZ, F. D. (1987). Visual motion perception in infancy: A review and synthesis. In P. Salapatek & L. Cohen (Eds.), *Handbook of infant perception: Vol. 2. From perception to cognition.* New York: Academic Press.

NELSON, K. (1973). Structure and strategy in learning to talk. *Monographs of the Society for Research in Child Development, 38*(1–2, Serial No. 149).

NELSON, K. (1985). *Making sense: The acquisition of shared meaning.* Orlando, FL: Academic Press.

NELSON, K. (1986). *Event knowledge: Structure and function in development.* Hillsdale, NJ: Erlbaum.

NELSON, K. (1988). Constraints on word learning? *Cognitive Development, 3,* 221–246.

NELSON, K. (1993a). Events, narratives, memory: What develops? In C. A. Nelson (Ed.), *Minnesota symposia on child psychology: Vol. 26. Memory and affect in development.* Hillsdale, NJ: Erlbaum.

NELSON, K. (1993b). The psychological and social origins of autobiographical memory. *Psychological Science, 4,* 7–14.

NELSON, K. (1996). *Language in cognitive development.* New York: Cambridge University Press.

NELSON, K., HAMPSON, J., & SHAW, L. K. (1993). Nouns in early lexicons: Evidence, explanations, and implications. *Journal of Child Language, 20,* 61–84.

NELSON, S. A. (1980). Factors influencing young children's use of motives and outcomes as moral criteria. *Child Development, 51,* 823–829.

NELSON, S. A., & DWECK, C. S. (1977). Motivation and competence as determinants of young children's reward allocation. *Developmental Psychology, 13,* 192–197.

NEVILLE, B., & PARKE, R. D. (1997). Waiting for paternity: Interpersonal and contextual implications of the timing of fatherhood. *Sex Roles, 37,* 45–59.

NEWCOMB, A. F., & BAGWELL, C. L. (1995). Children's friendship relations: A meta-analytic review. *Psychological Bulletin, 117,* 306–347.

NEWCOMB, A. F., BUKOWSKI, W. M., & PATTEE, L. (1993). Children's peer relations: A meta-analytic review of popular, rejected, neglected, controversial, and average sociometric status. *Psychological Bulletin, 113,* 99–128.

NEWCOMBE, N. (1989). The development of spatial perspective taking. In H. W. Reese (Ed.), *Advances in child development and behavior* (Vol. 22). San Diego: Academic Press.

NEWCOMBE, N., & DUBAS, J. S. (1992). A longitudinal study of predictors of spatial ability in adolescent females. *Child Development, 63,* 37–46.

NEWCOMER, S., & UDRY, J. R. (1987). Parental marital status effects on adolescent sexual behavior. *Journal of Marriage and the Family, 48,* 235–240.

NEWMAN, D. L., CASPI, A., MOFFITT, T. E., & SILVA, P. A. (1997). Antecedents of adult interpersonal functioning: Effects of individual differences in age 3 temperament. *Developmental Psychology, 33,* 206–217.

NEWMAN, P. R. (1982). The peer group. In B. B. Wolman (Ed.), *Handbook of developmental psychology.* Englewood Cliffs, NJ: Prentice-Hall.

NEWPORT, E. L. (1977). Motherese: The speech of mothers to young children. In N. J. Castellan, D. B. Pisoni, & G. Potts (Eds.), *Cognitive theory* (Vol. 2). Hillsdale, NJ: Erlbaum.

NEWPORT, E. L. (1991). Contrasting concepts of the critical period for language. In S. Carey & R. Gelman (Eds.), *The epigenesis of mind: Essays on biology and cognition.* Hillsdale, NJ: Erlbaum.

NICHD EARLY CHILD CARE RESEARCH NETWORK. (1997). Child care in the first year of life. *Merrill-Palmer Quarterly, 43,* 340–360.

NICHD EARLY CHILD CARE RESEARCH NETWORK. (1997). The effects of infant child care on infant-mother attachment security: Results of the NICHD study of early child care. *Child Development, 68,* 860–879.

NICHOLS, R. C. (1978). Heredity and environment: Major findings from twin studies of ability, personality, and interests. *Homo, 29,* 158–173.

NINIO, A. (1992). The relation of children's single-word utterances to single-word utterances in the input. *Journal of Child Language, 19,* 87–110.

NINIO, A., & BRUNER, J. (1978). The achievement and antecedents of labeling. *Journal of Child Language, 5,* 1–15.

NINIO, A., & SNOW, C. E. (1988). Language acquisition through language use: The functional sources of children's early utterances. In Y. Levy, I. M. Schlesinger, & M. D. S. Braine (Eds.), *Categories and processes in language acquisition.* Hillsdale, NJ: Erlbaum.

NINIO, A., & SNOW, C. E. (1996). *Pragmatic development.* Boulder, Co: Westview Press.

NINIO, A., & WHEELER, P. (1984). Functions of speech in mother–infant interaction. In L. Feagans, C. Garvey, & R. Golinkoff (Eds.), *The origins and growth of communication.* Norwood, NJ: Ablex.

NISAN, M. (1984). Distributive justice and social norms. *Child Development, 55,* 1020–1029.

NOLEN-HOEKSEMA, S., GIRGUS, J. S., & SELIGMAN, M. E. P. (1986). Learned helplessness in children: A longitudinal study of depression, achievement, and explanatory style. *Journal of Personality and Social Psychology, 51,* 435–442.

NORCINI, J. J., & SNYDER, S. S. (1986). Effects of modeling and cognitive induction on moral reasoning. In G. L. Sapp (Ed.), *Handbook of moral development: Models, processes, techniques, and research.* Birmingham, AL: Religious Education Press.

NOTTLEMAN, E. D. (1987). Competence and self-esteem during transition from childhood to adolescence. *Developmental Psychology, 23,* 441–450.

NOVICK, N., CAUCE, A. M., & GROVE, K. (1996). Competence self-concept. In B. A. Bracken (Ed.), *Handbook of self-concept: Developmental, social, and clinical considerations.* New York: Wiley.

NUNES, T., CARRAHER, D. W., & SCHLIEMANN, A. D. (1993). *Street mathematics and school mathematics.* New York: Cambridge University Press.

NUNNALLY, J. C. (1982). The study of human change: Measurement, research strategies, and methods of analysis. In B. B. Wolman (Ed.), *Handbook of developmental psychology.* Englewood Cliffs, NJ: Prentice Hall.

NUNNER-WINKLER, G., & SODIAN, B. (1988). Children's understanding of moral emotions. *Child Development, 59,* 1323–1338.

NYITI, R. M. (1982). The validity of "cultural differences explanations" for cross-cultural variation in the rate of Piagetian cognitive development. In D. A. Wagner & H. W. Stevenson (Eds.), *Cultural perspectives on child development.* San Francisco: W. H. Freeman.

OAKES, L. M., & COHEN, L. B. (1995). Infant causal perception. In C. K. Rovee-Collier & L. P. Lipsitt (Eds.), *Advances in infancy research* (Vol. 9). Norwood, NJ: Ablex.

O'BRIEN, M., & HUSTON, A. C. (1985). Development of sex-typed play behavior in toddlers. *Developmental Psychology, 21,* 866–871.

O'BRIEN, M., & NAGLE, K. (1987). Parents' speech to toddlers: The effect of play context. *Journal of Child Language, 14,* 269–279.

OCHS, E. (1982). Talking to children in western Samoa. *Language in Society, 11,* 77–104.

O'CONNOR, B. (1993). The home birth movement in the United States. *The Journal of Medicine and Philosophy, 18,* 147–174.

O'CONNOR, R. D. (1969). Modification of social withdrawal through symbolic modeling. *Journal of Applied Behavior Analysis, 2,* 15–22.

O'CONNOR, R. D. (1972). Relative efficacy of modeling, shaping, and the combined procedures for modification of social withdrawal. *Journal of Abnormal Psychology, 79,* 327–334.

ODOM, S. L., & STRAIN, P. S. (1984). Peer-mediated approaches to promoting children's social interaction: A review. *American Journal of Orthopsychiatry, 54,* 544–557.

OEHLER, J. M., & ECKERMAN, C. D. (1988). Regulatory effects of human speech and touch in premature infants prior to term age. *Infant Behavior and Development, 11,* 249.

OHLENDORF-MOFFAT, P. (1991, February). Surgery before birth. *Discover,* pp. 59–65.

OLLER, D. K., & EILERS, R. E. (1982). Similarity of babbling in Spanish- and English-learning babies. *Journal of Child Language, 9,* 565–577.

OLLER, D. K., & EILERS, R. E. (1988). The role of audition in infant babbling. *Child Development, 59,* 441–449.

OLSON, G. M., & SHERMAN, T. (1983). Attention, learning, and memory in infants. In P. H. Mussen (Series Ed.) & M. M. Haith & J. J. Campos (Vol. Eds.), *Handbook of child psychology: Vol. 2. Infancy and developmental psychobiology.* New York: Wiley.

OLSON, H. (1994). The effects of prenatal alcohol exposure on child development. *Infants and Young Children, 6,* 10–25.

OLSON, S. L., BATES, J. E., & KASKIE, B. (1992). Caregiver–infant interaction antecedents of children's school-age cognitive ability. *Merrill-Palmer Quarterly, 38,* 309–330.

OLVERA-EZZELL, N., POWER, T. G., & COUSINS, J. H. (1990). Maternal socialization of children's eating habits: Strategies used by obese Mexican-American mothers. *Child Development, 61,* 395–400.

OLWEUS, D., MATTISON, A., SCHALLING, D., & LOW, H. (1988). Circulating testosterone levels and aggression in adolescent males: A causal analysis. *Psychosomatic Medicine, 50,* 261–272.

OMARK, D. R., STRAYER, F. F., & FREEDMAN, D. G. (1980). *Dominance relations: An ethological view of human conflict and social interaction.* New York: Garland.

O'NEILL, D. K. (1996). Two-year-olds' sensitivity to a parent's knowledge state when making requests. *Child Development, 51,* 659–677.

O'NEILL, D. K., & GOPNIK, A. (1991). Young children's ability to identify the sources of their beliefs. *Developmental Psychology, 27,* 390–397.

O'NEILL, D. K., ASTINGTON, J. W., & FLAVELL, J. H. (1992). Young children's understanding of the role that sensory experiences play in knowledge acquisition. *Child Development, 63,* 474–490.

OOSTERWEGEL, A., & OPPENHEIMER, L. (1993). *The self-system: Developmental changes between and within self-concepts.* Hillsdale, NJ: Erlbaum.

O'REILLY, A. W., & BORNSTEIN, M. (1993). Caregiver–child interaction in play. In M. H. Bornstein & A. W. O'Reilly (Eds.), *New directions for child development: No. 59. The role of play in the development of thought.* San Francisco: Jossey-Bass.

ORLOFSKY, J. L., & O'HERON, C. A. (1987). Stereotypic and nonstereotypic sex-role trait and behavior orientations: Implications for personal adjustment. *Journal of Personality and Social Psychology, 52,* 1034–1042.

ORNSTEIN, P. A., NAUS, M. J., & LIBERTY, C. (1975). Rehearsal and organizational processes in children's memory. *Child Development, 46,* 818–830.

OSHERSON, D. N. (1990). *An invitation to cognitive science.* Cambridge: MIT Press.

OSOFSKY, J. (1995a). Children who witness domestic violence: The invisible victims. *Social Policy Report: Society for Research in Child Development, 18,* 1–16.

OSOFSKY, J. (1995b). The effects of exposure to violence on young children. *American Psychologist, 50,* 782–788.

OSTER, H., HEGLEY, D., & NAGEL, L. (1992). Adult judgments and fine-grained analysis of infant facial expressions: Testing the validity of a priori coding formulas. *Developmental Psychology, 28,* 1115–1131.

OWEN, D. R. (1972). The 47,XYY male: A review. *Psychological Bulletin, 78,* 209–233.

OWEN, D. R. (1979). Psychological studies in XYY men. In H. L. Vallet & I. H. Porter (Eds.), *Genetic mechanisms of sexual development.* New York: Academic Press.

PAGE, R. A. (1981). Longitudinal evidence for the sequentiality of Kohlberg's stages of moral judgment in adolescent males. *Journal of Genetic Psychology, 139,* 3–9.

PAIK, H., & COMSTOCK, G. (1994). The effects of television violence on antisocial behavior: A meta-analysis. *Communication Research, 21,* 516–546.

PAIKOFF, R. L., & BROOKS-GUNN, J. (1990). Physiological processes: What role do they play during the transition to adolescence? In R. Montemayor, G. R. Adams, & T. Gullotta (Eds.), *From childhood to adolescence: Vol. 2. Advances in adolescent development.* London: Sage.

PAINE, P., DOREA, J. G., PASQUALI, L., & MONTEIRO, A. M. (1992). Growth and cognition in Brazilian school children: A spontaneously occurring intervention. *International Journal of Child Development, 15,* 169–183.

PALCA, J. (1990). AIDS and the future. *Science, 248,* 1484.

PALINCSAR, A. S. (1992, April). *Beyond reciprocal teaching: A retrospective and prospective view.* Address presented at the meeting of the American Educational Research Association, San Francisco.

PALKOVITZ, R. (1984). Parental attitudes and fathers' interactions with their 5-month-old infants. *Developmental Psychology, 20,* 1054–1060.

PANETH, N. S. (1995). The problem of low birth weight. *The future of children* (Vol. 5. No. 1). Los Angeles: Packard Foundation.

PAREKH, V. C., PHERWANI, A., UDANI, P. M., & MUKKERJIE, S. (1970). Brain weight and head circumference in fetus, infant, and children of different nutritional and socioeconomic groups. *Indian Pediatrics, 7,* 347–358.

PARIKH, B. (1980). Development of moral judgment and its relation to family environment factors in Indian and American families. *Child Development, 51,* 1030–1039.

PARIS, S. G., & CROSS, D. R. (1988). The zone of proximal development: Virtues and pitfalls of a metaphorical representation of children's learning. *Genetic Epistemologist, 16*(1), 27–37.

PARIS, S. G., & LINDAUER, B. K. (1976). The role of inference in children's comprehension and memory for sentences. *Cognitive Psychology, 8,* 217–227.

PARIS, S. G., & OKA, E. R. (1986). Children's reading strategies, meta-cognition, and motivation. *Developmental Review, 6,* 25–56.

PARKE, R. D. (1977). Some effects of punishment on children's behavior—revisited. In E. M. Hetherington & R. D. Parke (Eds.), *Contemporary readings in child psychology.* New York: McGraw-Hill.

PARKE, R. D. (1994). Progress, paradigms, and unresolved problems: Recent advances in our understanding of children's emotions. *Merrill-Palmer Quarterly, 40,* 157–169.

PARKE, R. D. (1995). Fathers and families. In M. H. Bornstein (Ed.), *Handbook of parenting: Vol. 3. Status and social conditions of parenting.* Hillsdale, NJ: Erlbaum.

PARKE, R. D. (1995). Fathers and families. In M. H. Bornstein (Ed.), *Handbook of parenting: Vol. 3. Status and social conditions of parenting.* Mahwah, NJ: Erlbaum.

PARKE, R. D. (1996). *Fatherhood.* Cambridge: Harvard University Press.

PARKE, R. D., & BURIEL, R. (1998). Socialization in the family: Ethnic and ecological perspectives. In W. Damon (Ed.), *Handbook of child psychology: Vol. 3. Social, emotional, and personality development.* New York: Wiley.

PARKE, R. D., & LADD, G. W. (Eds.). (1992). *Family-peer relationships: Modes of linkage.* Hillsdale, NJ: Erlbaum.

PARKE, R. D., & SLABY, R. G. (1983). The development of aggression. In E. M. Hetherington (Ed.), *Handbook of child psychology: Vol. 4. Socialization, personality, and social development.* New York: Wiley.

PARKE, R. D., CASSIDY, J., BURKS, V. M., CARSON, J. L., & BOYUM, L. (1992). Familial contribution to peer competence among young children: The role of interactive and affective processes. In R. D. Parke & G. W. Ladd (Eds.), *Family-peer relationships: Modes of linkage.* Hillsdale, NJ: Erlbaum.

PARKER, J. G., & ASHER, S. R. (1987). Peer relations and later personal adjustment: Are low-accepted children at risk? *Psychological Bulletin, 102,* 357–389.

PARKER, J. G., RUBIN, K. H., PRICE, J. M., & DEROSIER, M. E. (1995). Peer relationships, child development, and adjustment: A developmental psychopathology perspective. In D. Cicchetti & D. J. Cohen (Eds.), *Developmental psychopathology: Vol. 2. Risk, disorder, and adaptation.* New York: Wiley.

PARMELEE, A. H., & GARBANATI, J. (1987). Clinical neurobehavioral aspects of state organization in newborn infants. In A. Kobayashi (Ed.), *Neonatal brain and behavior.* Nagoya, Japan: University of Nagoya Press.

PARMELEE, A. H., & SIGMAN, M. D. (1983). Perinatal brain development and behavior. In M. M. Haith & J. J. Campos (Eds.), *Handbook of child psychology: Vol. 2. Infancy and developmental psychobiology.* New York: Wiley.

PARMELEE, A. H., & SIGMAN, M. D. (1983). Perinatal brain development and behvior. In P. H. Mussen (Series Ed.) & M. M. Haith & J. J. Campos (Vol. Eds.), *Handbook of child psychology: Vol. 2. Infancy and developmental psychobiology.* New York: Wiley.

PARSONS, C. (1960). Inhelder and Piaget's "The growth of logical thinking": II. A logician's viewpoint. *British Journal of Psychology, 51,* 75–84.

PARTEN, M. B. (1932). Social participation among preschool children. *Journal of Abnormal and Social Psychology, 27,* 243–269.

PASCALIS, O., DE SCHONEN, S., MORTON, J., & DERUELLE, C. (1995). Mother's face recognition by neonates: A replication and an extension. *Infant Behavior and Development, 18,* 79–85.

PASCALIS, O., DE SCHONEN, S., MORTON, J., DERUELLE, C., & FABRE-GRENET, M. (1995). Mothers' face recognition by neonates: A replication and extension. *Infant Behavior and Development, 18,* 79–95.

PATCHENS, M. (1982). *Black-white contact in the schools: Its social and academic effects.* West Lafayette, IN: Purdue University Press.

PATTERSON, C. J. (1982). Self-control and self-regulation in childhood. In T. M. Field, A. Huston, H. C. Quay, L. Troll, & G. E. Finley (Eds.), *Review of human development.* New York: Wiley.

PATTERSON, C. J. (1992). Children of lesbian and gay parents. *Child Development, 63,* 1025–1042.

PATTERSON, C. J. (1994). Lesbian and gay families. *Current Directions in Psychological Science, 3,* 62–64.

PATTERSON, C. J. (1994a). Children of the lesbian baby boom: Behavioral adjustment, self-concepts, and sex-role identity. In B. Greene & G. Herek (Eds.), *Contemporary perspectives on lesbian and gay psychology: Theory, research, and application.* Beverly Hills, CA: Sage.

PATTERSON, C. J. (1994b). Lesbian and gay families. *Current Directions in Psychological Science, 3,* 62–64.

PATTERSON, C. J. (1995). Lesbian and gay parenthood. In M. H. Bornstein (Ed.), *Handbook of parenting: Vol. 3. Status and social conditions of parenting.* Mahwah, NJ: Erlbaum.

PATTERSON, C. J. (1995a). Families of the lesbian baby boom: Parents' division of labor and children's adjustment. *Developmental Psychology, 31,* 115–123.

PATTERSON, C. J. (1995b). Lesbian and gay parenthood. In M. H. Bornstein (Ed.), *Handbook of parenting: Vol. 3. Status and social conditions of parenting.* Mahwah, NJ: Erlbaum.

PATTERSON, C. J. (1995c). Sexual orientation and human development: An overview. *Developmental Psychology, 31,* 3–11.

PATTERSON, G. R. (1982). *Coercive family process.* Eugene, OR: Castalia.

PATTERSON, G. R. (1995). Coercion—A basis for early age of onset of arrest. In J. McCord (Ed.), *Coercion and punishment in long-term perspective.* New York: Cambridge University Press.

PATTERSON, G. R., LITTMAN, R. A., & BRICKER, W. (1967). Assertive behavior in children: A step toward a theory of aggression. *Monographs of the Society for Research in Child Development, 32* (5, Serial No. 113).

PATTERSON, G. R., REID, J. B., & DISHION, T. J. (1992). *Antisocial boys.* Eugene, OR: Castalia.

PAUL, R., & MILLER, D. (1995). Cesarean delivery: How to reduce the rate. *American Journal of Obstetrics and Gynecology, 172,* 1903–1911.

PAYNE, A. C., WHITEHURST, G. J., & ANGELL, A. A. (1994). The role of home literacy environment in the development of language ability in preschool children from low-income families. *Early Childhood Research Quarterly, 9,* 427–440.

PEARL, D. (1987). Familial, peer, and television influences on aggressive and violent behavior. In D. H. Crowell, I. M. Evans, & C. R. O'Donnell (Eds.), *Childhood aggression and violence: Sources of influence, prevention, and control.* New York: Plenum.

PECHEUX, M., LEPECQ, J., & SALZARULO, P. (1988). Oral activity and exploration in 1–2-month-old infants. *British Journal of Developmental Psychology, 6,* 245–256.

PEDERSON, D. R., & MORAN, G. (1995). A categorical description of infant-mother relationships in the home and its relation to Q-sort measures of infant-mother interaction. In E. Waters, B. E. Vaughn, G. Posada, & K. Kondo-Ikemura (Eds.), *Caregiving, cultural, and cognitive perspectives on secure-base behavior and working models. Monographs of the Society for Research in Child Development, 60* (2–3, Serial No. 244).

PEDERSON, D. R., & MORAN, G. (1996). Expressions of the attachment relationship outside of the Strange Situation. *Child Development, 67,* 915–927.

PEDERSON, D. R., & TER VRUGT, D. (1973). The influence of amplitude and frequency of vestibular stimulation on the activity of two-month-old infants. *Child Development, 44,* 122–128.

PEDERSON, N. L., FRIBERG, L., FLODERUS-MYRHED, B., McCLEARN, G. E., & PLOMIN, R. (1984). Swedish early-separated twins: Identification and characterization. *Acta Geneticae Medicae et Gemellogiae, 33,* 243–250.

PEDLOW, R., SANSON, A., PRIOR, M., & OBERKLAID, F. (1993). Stability of maternally reported temperament from infancy to 8 years. *Developmental Psychology, 29,* 998–1007.

PEGG, J. E., WERKER, J. F., & McLEOD, P. J. (1992). Preferences for infant-directed over adult-directed speech: Evidence from 7-week-old infants. *Infant Behavior and Development, 15,* 325–345.

PEIPER, A. (1963). *Cerebral function in infancy and adulthood.* New York: Consultants Bureau.

PELAEZ-NOGUERAS, M., FIELD, T., CIGALES, M., GONZALEZ, A., & CLASKY, S. (1994). Infants of depressed mothers show less "depressed" behavior with their nursery teachers. *Infant Mental Health Journal, 15,* 358–367.

PELHAM, W. E., & HINSHAW, S. P. (1992). Behavior intervention for attention-deficit hyperactivity disorder. In S. M. Turner, K. S. Calhoun, & H. E. Adams (Eds.), *Handbook of clinical behavior therapy* (2nd ed.). New York: Wiley.

PENNER, S. G. (1987). Parental responses to grammatical and ungrammatical child utterances. *Child Development, 58,* 376–384.

PEPLER, D. J., KING, G., & BYRD, W. (1991). A social-cognitively based social skills training program for aggressive children. In D. J. Pepler & K. H. Rubin (Eds.), *The development and treatment of childhood aggression.* Hillsdale, NJ: Erlbaum.

PERFETTI, C. A. (1991). The psychology, pedagogy, and politics of reading. *Psychological Science, 2,* 70–76.

PERNER, J., RUFFMAN, T. K., & LEEKAM, S. R. (1994). Theory of mind is contagious: You catch it from your sibs. *Child Development, 65,* 1228–1238.

PERRY, D. G., & BUSSEY, K. (1979). The social learning theory of sex differences: Imitation is alive and well. *Journal of Personality and Social Psychology, 37,* 1699–1712.

PERRY, D. G., & BUSSEY, K. (1984). *Social development.* Englewood Cliffs, NJ: Prentice Hall.

PERRY, D. G., & PERRY, L. C. (1983). Social learning, causal attribution, and moral internalization. In J. Bizanz, G. L. Bizanz, & R. Kail (Eds.), *Learning in children: Progress in cognitive development research.* New York: Springer-Verlag.

PERRY, D. G., PERRY, L. C., & WEISS, R. J. (1989). Sex differences in the consequences that children anticipate for aggression. *Developmental Psychology, 25,* 312–319.

PERRY, D. G., WHITE, A. J., & PERRY, L. C. (1984). Does early sex typing result from children's attempts to match their behavior to sex role stereotypes? *Child Development, 55,* 2114–2121.

PERRY, M., & ELDER, A. D. (1997). Knowledge in transition: Adults' developing understanding of a principle of physical causality. *Cognitive Development, 12,* 131–157.

PERRY, M., CHURCH, R. B., & GOLDIN-MEADOW, S. (1988). Transitional knowledge in the acquisition of concepts. *Cognitive Development, 3,* 359–400.

PERRY, M., WOOLLEY, J., & IFCHER, J. (1995). Adults' abilities to detect children's readiness to learn. *International Journal of Behavioral Development, 18,* 364–381.

PETERS, D. P. (1991). The influence of stress and arousal on the child witness. In J. Doris (Ed.), *The suggestibility of children's recollections.* Washington, DC: American Psychological Association.

PETERSEN, A. C. (1987). The nature of biological-psychosocial interactions: The sample case of early adolescence. In R. M. Lerner & T. L. Foch (Eds.), *Biological-psychosocial interactions in early adolescence.* Hillsdale, NJ: Erlbaum.

PETERSON, L. (1983). Role of donor competence, donor age, and peer presence on helping in an emergency. *Developmental Psychology, 19,* 873–880.

PETITTO, L. A., & MARENTETTE, P. F. (1991). Babbling in the manual mode: Evidence for the ontogeny of language. *Science, 251,* 1493–1496.

PETITTO, L. A. (1992). Modularity and constraints in early lexical acquisition: Evidence from children's early language and gesture. In M. R. Gunnar & M. Maratsos (Eds.), *Minnesota symposia on child psychology: Vol. 25. Modularity*

and constraints in language and cognition. Hillsdale, NJ: Erlbaum.

PETTIT, G. S., BAKSHI, A., DODGE, K. A., & COIE, J. D. (1990). The emergence of social dominance in young boys' play groups: Developmental differences and behavioral correlates. *Developmental Psychology, 26,* 1017–1025.

PHARES, V. (1992). Where's Poppa?: The relative lack of attention to the role of fathers in child and adolescent psychopathology. *American Psychologist, 47,* 656–664.

PHARES, V., & COMPAS, E. (1992). The role of fathers in child and adolescent psychopathology: Make room for daddy. *Psychological Bulletin, 111,* 387–412.

PHELPS, E., & DAMON, W. (1991). Peer collaboration as a context for cognitive growth. In L. T. Landsmann (Ed.), *Culture, schooling, and psychological development.* Norwood, NJ: Ablex.

PHILLIPS, D. A., & ZIMMERMAN, M. (1990). The developmental course of perceived competence and incompetence among competent children. In R. J. Sternberg & J. Kolligian (Eds.), *Competence considered.* New Haven, CT: Yale University Press.

PHILLIPS, D. A. (1984). The illusion of incompetence among academically competent children. *Child Development, 55,* 2000–2016.

PHILLIPS, D. A. (1987). Socialization of perceived academic competence among highly competent children. *Child Development, 58,* 1308–1320.

PHILLIPS, R. B., SHARMA, R., PREMACHANDRA, B. R., VAUGHN, A. J., & REYES-LEE, M. (1996). Intrauterine exposure to cocaine: Effect on neurobehavior of neonates. *Infant Behavior and Development, 19,* 71–81.

PHILLIPS, S., KING, S., & DUBOIS, L. (1978). Spontaneous activities of female versus male newborns. *Child Development, 49,* 590–597.

PIAGET, J. (1926). *The language and thought of the child.* New York: Harcourt Brace.

PIAGET, J. (1929). *The child's conception of the world.* London: Routledge & Kegan Paul.

PIAGET, J. (1932). *The moral judgment of the child.* London: Routledge & Kegan Paul.

PIAGET, J. (1950). *The psychology of intelligence.* New York: Harcourt Brace.

PIAGET, J. (1951). *Plays, dreams, and imitation in childhood.* New York: Norton.

PIAGET, J. (1952). *The origins of intelligence in children.* New York: International Universities Press.

PIAGET, J. (1954). *The construction of reality in the child.* New York: Basic Books.

PIAGET, J. (1957). Logique et equilibre dans les comportements du sujet. In L. Apostel, B. Mandelbrot, & J. Piaget (Eds.), *Etudes d'epistemologie genetique* (Vol. 2). Paris: Presses Universitaires de France.

PIAGET, J. (1964). Development and learning. In R. E. Ripple & V. N. Rockcastle (Eds.), *Piaget rediscovered.* Ithaca, NY: Cornell University Press.

PIAGET, J. (1967). *Six psychological studies.* New York: Random House.

PIAGET, J. (1968). *On the development of memory and identity.* Barre, MA: Clark University Press and Barre Publishers.

PIAGET, J. (1969). *The child's conception of time.* London: Routledge & Kegan Paul.

PIAGET, J. (1970). *The child's conception of movement and speed.* London: Routledge & Kegan Paul.

PIAGET, J. (1971). *Science of education and the psychology of the child.* New York: Viking.

PIAGET, J. (1972). Intellectual evolution from adolescence to adulthood. *Human Development, 15,* 1–12.

PIAGET, J. (1976). *To understand is to invent: The future of education.* New York: Penguin.

PIAGET, J. (1977). *The development of thought: Equilibration of cognitive structures.* New York: Viking.

PIAGET, J. (1979). Correspondence and transformation. In F. B. Murray (Ed.), *The impact of Piagetian theory.* Baltimore: University Park Press.

PIAGET, J. (1980). Recent studies in genetic epistemology. *Cashiers Foundation Archives, Jean Piaget, No. 1.*

PIAGET, J. (1983). Piaget's theory. In P. H. Mussen (Series Ed.) & W. Kessen (Vol. Ed.), *Handbook of child psychology: Vol. 1. History, theory, and methods.* New York: Wiley.

PIAGET, J., & INHELDER, B. (1956). *The child's conception of space.* London: Routledge & Kegan Paul.

PIAGET, J., & INHELDER, B. (1956). *The child's conception of space.* London: Routledge & Kegan Paul.

PIAGET, J., & INHELDER, B. (1969). *The psychology of the child.* New York: Basic Books.

PIAGET, J., & INHELDER, B. (1973). *Memory and intelligence.* New York: Basic Books.

PIAGET, J., & INHELDER, B. (1974). *The child's construction of quantities.* London: Routledge & Kegan Paul.

PIAGET, J., & SZEMINSKA, A. (1952). *The child's conception of number.* New York: Basic Books.

PIAGET, J., INHELDER, B., & SZEMINSKA, A. (1960). *The child's conception of geometry.* New York: Basic Books.

PICARIELLO, M. L., GREENBERG, D. N., & PILLEMER, D. B. (1990). Children's sex-related stereotyping of colors. *Child Development, 61,* 1453–1460.

PICK, H. L., JR., (1992). Eleanor J. Gibson: Learning to perceive and perceiving to learn. *Developmental Psychology, 28,* 787–794.

PICKENS, J., & FIELD, T. (1993). Facial expressivity in infants of depressed mothers. *Developmental Psychology, 29,* 986–988.

PIERCE, K., & EDWARDS, E. D. (1988). Children's construction of fantasy stories: Gender differences in conflict resolution strategies. *Sex Roles, 18,* 393–404.

PIERCE, K. A., & COHEN, R. (1995). Aggressors and their victims: Toward a contextual framework for understanding children's aggressor-victim relationships. *Developmental Review, 15,* 292–310.

PINE, J. M., LIEVEN, E. V. M., & ROWLAND, C. F. (1997). Stylistic variation at the "single-word stage": Relations between maternal speech characteristics and children's vocabulary composition and usage. *Child Development, 68,* 807–819.

PINKER, S. (1984). *Language learnability and language development.* Cambridge: Harvard University Press.

PINKER, S. (1987). The bootstrapping problem in language acquisition. In B. MacWhinney (Ed.), *Mechanisms of language acquisition.* Hillsdale, NJ: Erlbaum.

PINKER, S. (1989). *Learnability and cognition: The acquisition of argument structure.* Cambridge: MIT Press.

PINKER, S. (1994). *The language instinct: How the mind creates language.* New York: William Morrow.

PIPP, S. (1990). Sensorimotor and representational internal working models of self, other, and relationship: Mechanisms of connection and separation. In D. Cicchetti & M. Beeghly (Eds.), *The self in transition: Infancy to childhood.* Chicago: University of Chicago Press.

PIPP, S. (1993). Infants' knowledge of self, other, and relationship. In U. Neisser (Ed.), *Ecological and interpersonal knowledge of self.* New York: Cambridge University Press.

PIPP, S., EASTERBROOKS, M. A., & HARMON, R. J. (1992). The relation between attachment and knowledge of self and mother in one- to three-year-old infants. *Child Development, 63,* 738–750.

PIPP, S., FISCHER, K. W., & JENNINGS, S. (1987). Acquisition of self- and mother knowledge in infancy. *Developmental Psychology, 23,* 86–96.

PIPP-SIEGEL, S., & FOLTZ, C. (1997). Toddlers' acquisition of self/other knowledge: Ecological and interpersonal aspects of self and other. *Child Development, 68,* 69–79.

PLOMIN, R. (1990). *Nature and nurture.* Belmont, CA: Wadsworth.

PLOMIN, R. (1994). *Genes and experience: The interplay between nature and nurture.* Thousand Oaks, CA: Sage.

PLOMIN, R. (1995). Molecular genetics and psychology. *Current Directions in Psychological Science, 4,* 114–117.

PLOMIN, R., & DeFRIES, J. C. (1985). *Origins of individual differences in infancy: The Colorado Adoption Project.* Orlando, FL: Academic Press.

PLOMIN, R., & McCLEARN, G. E. (Eds.). (1993). *Nature, nurture, and psychology.* Washington, DC: American Psychological Association.

PLOMIN, R., & NEIDERHISER, J. M. (1992).

Genetics and experience. *Current Directions in Psychological Science, 1,* 160–164.

PLOMIN, R., DeFRIES, J. C., & FULKER, D. W. (1988). *Nature and nurture during infancy and early childhood.* Cambridge: Cambridge University Press.

PLOMIN, R., DeFRIES, J. C., McCLEARN, G. E., & RUTTER, M. (1997). *Behavioral genetics* (3rd ed.). New York: W. H. Freeman.

PLOMIN, R., EMDE, R. N., BRAUNGART, J. M., CAMPOS, J., CORLEY, R., FULKER, D. W., KAGAN, J., REZNICK, J. S., ROBINSON, J., ZAHN-WAXLER, C., & DeFRIES, J. C. (1993). Genetic change and continuity from fourteen to twenty months: The MacArthur Longitudinal Twin Study. *Child Development, 64,* 1354–1376.

PLOMIN, R., FULKER, D. W., CORLEY, R., & DeFRIES, J. C. (1997). Nature, nurture, and cognitive development from 1 to 16 years: A parent–offspring adoption study. *Psychological Science, 8,* 442–447.

PLOMIN, R., FULKER, D. W., CORLEY, R., & DeFRIES, J. C. (1997). Nature, nurture, and cognitive development from 1 to 16 years: A parent-offspring adoption study. *Psychological Science, 8,* 442–447.

PLOMIN, R., REISS, D., HETHERINGTON, E. M., & HOWE, G. W. (1994). Nature and nurture: Genetic contributions to measures of the family environment. *Developmental Psychology, 30,* 32–43.

PLUMERT, J. M. (1995). Relations between children's overestimation of their physical abilities and accident proneness. *Developmental Psychology, 31,* 866–876.

POLLITT, E., GOLUB, M., GORMAN, K., GRANTHAM-McGREGOR, S., LEVITSKY, D., SCHURCH, B., STRUPP, B., & WACHS, T. (1996). A reconceptualization of the effects of undernutrition on children's biological, psychosocial, and behavioral development. *Social Policy Report: Society for Research in Child Development, 10,* 1–31.

POLLITT, E., GORMAN, K., ENGLE, P., MARTORELL, R., & RIVERA, J. (1993). Early supplementary feeding and cognition: Effects over two decades. *Monographs of the Society for Research in Child Development, 58*(6, Serial No. 235).

POLLOCK, L. (1983). *Forgotten children: Parent–child relations from 1500 to 1900.* Cambridge: Cambridge University Press.

POLLOCK, L. (1987). *A lasting relationship: Parents and children over three centuries.* London: Fourth Estate.

POMERANTZ, E. M., RUBLE, D. N., FREY, K. S., & GREULICH, F. (1995). Meeting goals and confronting conflict: Children's changing perceptions of social comparison. *Child Development, 66,* 723–738.

POMERLEAU, A., BOLDUC, D., MALCUIT, G., & COSSETTE, L. (1990). Pink or blue: Environmental gender stereotypes in the first two years of life. *Sex Roles, 22,* 359–367.

PORTER, R. H., & LANEY, M. D. (1980).

Attachment theory and the concept of inclusive fitness. *Merrill-Palmer Quarterly, 26,* 35–51.

PORTER, R. H., BALOGH, R. D., & MAKIN, J. W. (1988). Olfactory influences on mother-infant interaction. In C. Rovee-Collier & L. P. Lipsitt (Eds.), *Advances in infancy research* (Vol. 5). Norwood, NJ: Ablex.

POSADA, G., WATERS, E., CROWELL, J. A., & LAY, K. (1995). Is it easier to use a secure mother as a secure base? Attachment Q-sort correlates of the Adult Attachment Interview. In E. Waters, B. E. Vaughn, G. Posada, & K. Kondo-Ikemura (Eds.), Caregiving, cultural, and cognitive perspectives on secure-base behavior and working models. *Monographs of the Society for Research in Child Development, 60*(2–3, Serial No. 244).

POSNER, M. C., PETERSEN, S. E., FOX, P. T., & RAICHLEY, M. E. (1988). Localization of cognitive operations in the human brain. *Science, 240,* 1627–1631.

POULIN, F., CILLESSEN, A. H. N., HUBBARD, J. A., COIE, J. D., DODGE, K. A., & SCHWARTZ, D. (1997). Children's friends and behavioral similarity in two social contexts. *Social Development, 6,* 224–236.

POULIN-DUBOIS, D., GRAHAM, S., & SIPPOLA, L. (1995). Early lexical development: The contribution of parental labeling and infants' categorization abilities. *Journal of Child Language, 22,* 325–343.

POULIN-DUBOIS, D., SERBIN, L. A., KENYON, B., & DERBYSHIRE, A. (1994). Infants' intermodal knowledge about gender. *Developmental Psychology, 30,* 436–442.

POULSON, C. L., & NUNES, L. R. P. (1988). The infant vocal-conditioning literature: A theoretical and methodological review. *Journal of Experimental Child Psychology, 46,* 438–450.

POVINELLI, D. J. (1995). The unduplicated self. In P. Rochat (Ed.), *The self in infancy: Theory and research.* Amsterdam: Elsevier.

POWELL, G. F., BRASEL, J. A., & BLIZZARD, R. M. (1967). Emotional deprivation and growth retardation simulating ideopathic hypopituitarism: I. Clinical evaluation of the syndrome. *New England Journal of Medicine, 276,* 1271–1278.

POWLISHTA, K. K. (1995). Intergroup processes in childhood: Social categorization and sex role development. *Developmental Psychology, 31,* 781–788.

POWLISHTA, K. K., SERBIN, L. A., & MOLLER, L. C. (1993). The stability of individual differences in gender typing: Implications for understanding gender segregation. *Sex Roles, 29,* 723–737.

PRADER, A., TANNER, J. M., & VON HARNACK, G. A. (1963). Catch up growth following illness or starvation. *Journal of Paediatrics, 62,* 646–659.

PRATT, M. W., KERIG, P., COWAN, P. A., & COWAN, C. P. (1988). Mothers and fathers teaching 3-year-olds: Authoritative parenting and adult scaffolding of young children's learning. *Developmental Psychology, 24,* 832–839.

PRECHTL, H. F. R. (1968). Neurological findings in newborn infants after pre- and paranatal complications. In J. H. P. Jonxis, H. K. A. Visser, & J. A. Troelstra (Eds.), *Aspects of prematurity and dysmaturity.* Springfield, IL: Charles C. Thomas.

PRECHTL, H. F. R. (1977). *The neurological examination of the full-term newborn infant* (2nd ed.). London: Heinemann.

PRECHTL, H. F. R., & BEINTEMA, D. (1964). *The neurological examination of the full-term newborn infant.* London: Heinemann.

PRESSLEY, M. (1992). How not to study strategy discovery. *American Psychologist, 47,* 1240–1241.

PRESSLEY, M., BORKOWSKI, J. G., & O'SULLIVAN, J. (1985). Children's metamemory and the teaching of memory strategies. In D. L. Forrest-Pressley, G. E. MacKinnon, & T. G. Waller (Eds.), *Metacognition, cognition, and human performance: Vol. 1. Theoretical perspectives.* New York: Academic Press.

PRESSLEY, M., FORREST-PRESSLEY, D., & ELLIOT-FAUST, D. J. (1988). What is strategy instructional enrichment and how to study it: Illustrations from research on children's prose memory and comprehension. In F. E. Weinert & M. Perlmutter (Eds.), *Memory development: Universal changes and individual differences.* Hillsdale, NJ: Erlbaum.

PRESSLEY, M., LEVIN, J. R., & BRYANT, S. L. (1983). Memory and strategy instruction during adolescence: When is explicit instruction needed? In M. Pressley & J. R. Levin (Eds.), *Cognitive strategy research: Psychological foundations.* New York: Springer-Verlag.

PRIEL, B., & de SCHONEN, S. (1986). Self-recognition: A study of a population without mirrors. *Journal of Experimental Child Psychology, 41,* 237–250.

PUKA, B. (1991). Interpretive experiments: Probing the care-justice debate in moral development. *Human Development, 34,* 61–80.

PULLYBANK, J., BISANZ, J., SCOTT, C., & CHAMPION, M. A. (1985). Developmental invariance in the effects of functional self-knowledge on memory. *Child Development, 56,* 1447–1454.

PURCELL, P., & STEWART, L. (1990). Dick and Jane in 1989. *Sex Roles, 22,* 177–185.

PUTALLAZ, M., & HEFLIN, A. H. (1990). Parent–child interaction. In S. R. Asher & J. D. Coie (Eds.), *Peer rejection in childhood.* New York: Cambridge University Press.

PUTALLAZ, M., & WASSERMAN, A. (1990). Children's entry behavior. In S. R. Asher & J. D. Coie (Eds.), *Peer rejection in childhood.* New York: Cambridge University Press.

PYE, C. (1986). One lexicon or two? An alternative interpretation of early bilingual speech. *Journal of Child Language, 13,* 591–593.

QUIGGLE, N. L., GARBER, J., PANAK, W. F., & DODGE, K. A. (1992). Social information

processing in aggressive and depressed children. *Child Development, 63,* 1305–1320.

QUINN, P. C., & EIMAS, P. D. (1996). Perceptual organization and categorization in young infants. In C. Rovee-Collier & L. P. Lipsitt (Eds.), *Advances in infancy research* (Vol. 10). Norwood, NJ: Ablex.

RACK, J. P., HULME, C., & SNOWLING, M. J. (1993). Learning to read: A theoretical synthesis. In H. W. Reese (Ed.), *Advances in child development and behavior* (Vol. 24). San Diego: Academic Press.

RADFORD, A. (1990). *Syntactic theory and the acquisition of English syntax: The nature of early child grammars of English.* Oxford, England: Blackwell.

RADKE-YARROW, M., & ZAHN-WAXLER, C. (1984). Roots, motives, and patterns in children's prosocial behavior. In E. Staub, D. Bar-Tal, J. Karylowski, & J. Reykowski (Eds.), *Development and maintenance of prosocial behavior.* New York: Plenum.

RADKE-YARROW, M., & ZAHN-WAXLER, C. (1986). The role of familial factors in the development of prosocial behavior: Research findings and questions. In D. Olweus, J. Block, & M. Radke-Yarrow (Eds.), *Development of antisocial and prosocial behavior.* Orlando, FL: Academic Press.

RADKE-YARROW, M., ZAHN-WAXLER, C., & CHAPMAN, M. (1983). Children's prosocial dispositions and behavior. In E. M. Hetherington (Ed.), *Handbook of child psychology: Vol. 4. Socialization, personality, and social development.* New York: Wiley.

RAFF, M. C., BARRES, B. A., BURNE, J. F., COLES, H. S., ISHIZAKI, Y., & JACOBSON, M. D. (1993). Programmed cell death and the control of cell survival: Lessons from the nervous system. *Science, 262,* 695–700.

RAKIC, P. (1988). Specification of cerebral cortical areas. *Science, 241,* 170–176.

RAMSEY, P. G. (1991). *Making friends in school: Promoting peer relationships in early childhood.* New York: Teachers College Press.

RAPOPORT, J. L., BUCHSBAUM, M. S., ZAHN, T. P., WEINGARTNER, H., LUDLOW, D., & MIKKELSON, E. J. (1978). Dextroamphetamine: Cognitive and behavioral effects in normal prepubertal boys. *Science, 199,* 560–563.

RASKIN, P. A., & ISRAEL, A. C. (1981). Sex-role imitation in children: Effects of sex of child, sex of model, and sex-role appropriateness of modeled behavior. *Sex Roles, 7,* 1067–1077.

RATCLIFFE, S. G., & FIELD, M. A. S. (1982). Emotional disorder in XYY children: Four case reports. *Journal of Child Psychology and Psychiatry, 23,* 401–406.

RATNER, N. B. (1988). Patterns of parental vocabulary selection in speech to very young children. *Journal of Child Language, 15,* 481–492.

RAVN, K. E., & GELMAN, S. A. (1984). Rule usage in children's understanding of "big" and "little." *Child Development, 55,* 2141–2150.

RAWLINS, W. K. (1992). *Friendship matters: Communication, dialectics, and the life course.* New York: Aldine de Gruyter.

RAYMOND, C. L., & BENBOW, C. P. (1986). Gender differences in mathematics: A function of parental support and student sex typing? *Developmental Psychology, 22,* 808–819.

RECHT, D. R., & LESLIE, L. (1988). Effect of prior knowledge on good and poor readers' memory of text. *Journal of Educational Psychology, 80,* 16–20.

REDLINGER, W. E., & PARK, T. (1980). Language mixing in young bilinguals. *Journal of Child Language, 7,* 337–352.

REES, J. M., & TRAHMS, C. M. (1989). Nutritional influences on physical growth and behavior in adolescence. In G. R. Adams, R. Montemayor, & T. P. Gullotta (Eds.), *Biology of adolescent behavior and development.* Newbury Park, CA: Sage.

REGALADO, M. G., SCHECHTMAN, V. L., DEL ANGEL, A. P., & BEAN, X. D. (1995). Sleep disorganization in cocaine-exposed neonates. *In-fant Behavior and Development, 18,* 319–327.

REID, J. B. (1993). Prevention of conduct disorder before and after school entry: Relating interventions to developmental findings. *Development and Psychopathology, 5,* 243–262.

REID, M., LANDESMAN, S., TREDER, R., & JACCARD, J. (1989). "My Family and Friends": Six- to twelve-year-old children's perceptions of social support. *Child Development, 60,* 896–910.

REINISCH, J. M., ZIEMBA-DAVIS, M., & SANDERS, S. A. (1991). Hormonal contributions to sexual dimorphic behavioral development in humans. *Psychoneuroendocrinology, 16,* 213–278.

REISMAN, J. E. (1987). Touch, motion and perception. In P. Salapatek & L. Cohen (Eds.), *Handbook of infant perception: Vol. 1. From sensation to perception.* New York: Academic Press.

REISSLAND, N. (1988). Neonatal imitation in the first hour of life: Observations in rural Nepal. *Developmental Psychology, 24,* 464–469.

RENNINGER, K. A. (1998). Developmental psychology and instruction: Issues from and for practice. In W. Damon (Series Ed.) & I. E. Sigel & K. A. Renninger (Vol. Eds.), *Handbook of child psychology: Vol. 4. Child psychology in practice* (5th ed.). New York: Wiley.

REPETTI, R. L. (1996). The effects of perceived daily social and academic failure experiences on school-age children's subsequent interactions with parents. *Child Development, 67,* 1467–1482.

RESCORLA, L. A. (1980). Overextension in early language development. *Journal of Child Language, 7,* 321–335.

RESCORLA, L. A. (1981). Category development in early language. *Journal of Child Language, 8,* 225–238.

REST, J. R. (1983). Morality. In J. H. Flavell & E. M. Markman (Eds.), *Handbook of child psy-*

chology: Vol. 3. Cognitive development. New York: Wiley.

REZNICK, J. S., GIBBONS, J. L., JOHNSON, M. O., & McDONOUGH, P. M. (1989). Behavioral inhibition in a normative sample. In J. S. Reznick (Ed.), *Perspectives on behavioral inhibition*. Chicago: University of Chicago Press.

REZNICK, J. S., KAGAN, J., SNIDMAN, N., GERSTEN, M., BAAK, K., & ROSENBERG, A. (1986). Inhibited and uninhibited behavior: A follow-up study. *Child Development, 51,* 660–680.

RHEINGOLD, H. L. (1982a). Ethics as an integral part of research in child development. In R. Vasta (Ed.), *Strategies and techniques of child study*. New York: Academic Press.

RHEINGOLD, H. L. (1982b). Little children's participation in the work of adults: A nascent prosocial behavior. *Child Development, 53,* 114–125.

RHEINGOLD, H. L. (1988). The infant as a member of society. *Acta Paediatrica Scandinavica, 77,* 9–20.

RHEINGOLD, H. L., & COOK, K. (1975). The contents of boys' and girls' rooms as an index of parents' behavior. *Child Development, 46,* 459–463.

RHEINGOLD, H. L., & EMERY, G. N. (1986). The nurturant acts of very young children. In D. Olweus, J. Block, & M. Radke-Yarrow (Eds.), *Development of antisocial and prosocial behavior*. Orlando, FL: Academic Press.

RHEINGOLD, H. L., HAY, D. F., & WEST, M. J. (1976). Sharing in the second year of life. *Child Development, 47,* 1148–1158.

RHOLES, W. S., & LANE, J. W. (1985). Consistency between cognitions and behavior: Cause and consequence of cognitive moral development. In J. B. Pryor & J. D. Day (Eds.), *The development of social cognition*. New York: Springer-Verlag.

RICCIO, C. A., HYND, G. W., COHEN, M. J., & GONZALEZ, J. J. (1993). Neurological basis of attention deficit hyperactivity disorder. *Exceptional Children, 60,* 118–124.

RICCIUTI, H. N. (1993). Nutrition and mental development. *Current Directions in Psychological Science, 2,* 43–46.

RICE, M. L. (1989). Children's language acquisition. *American Psychologist, 44,* 149–156.

RICE, M. L., & WOODSMALL, L. (1988). Lessons from television: Children's word learning when viewing. *Child Development, 59,* 420–429.

RICHARDS, D. S., FRENTZEN, B., GERHARDT, K. J., McCANN, M. E., & ABRAMS, R. M. (1992). Sound levels in the human uterus. *Obstetrics and Gynecology, 80,* 186–190.

RICHTERS, J. E. (1993). Community violence and children's development: Toward a research agenda for the 1990s. In D. Reiss, J. E. Richters, M. Radke-Yarrow, & D. Scharf,

(Eds.), *Children and violence*. New York: Guilford.

RIESE, M. L. (1987). Temperament stability between the neonatal period and 24 months. *Developmental Psychology, 23,* 216–222.

RIESER, J., YONAS, A., & WIKNER, K. (1976). Radial localization of odors by human newborns. *Child Development, 47,* 856–859.

RITTS, V., PATTERSON, M. L., & TUBBS, M. E. (1992). Expectations, impressions, and judgments of physically attractive students: A review. *Review of Educational Research, 62,* 413–426.

RIZZO, T. A., & CORSARO, W. A. (1988). Toward a better understanding of Vygotsky's process of internalization: Its role in the development of the concept of friendship. *Developmental Review, 8,* 219–237.

ROBERTS, C. W., GREEN, R., WILLIAMS, K., & GOODMAN, M. (1987). Boyhood gender identity development: A statistical contrast of two family groups. *Developmental Psychology, 23,* 544–557.

ROBERTS, L. (1990). To test or not to test? *Science, 247,* 17–19.

ROBERTS, R. J., BROWN, D., WIEBKE, S., & HAITH, M. M. (1991). A computer-automated laboratory for studying complex perception-action skills. *Behavior Research Methods and Instrumentation, 23,* 493–504.

ROBERTS, R. N., NELSON, R. O., & OLSON, T. W. (1987). Self-instruction: An analysis of the differential effects of instruction and reinforcement. *Journal of Applied Behavior Analysis, 20,* 235–242.

ROBINSON, C. C., & MORRIS, J. T. (1986). The gender-stereotyped nature of Christmas toys received by 36-, 48-, and 60-month old children: A comparison between nonrequested vs. requested toys. *Sex Roles, 15,* 21–32.

ROBINSON, E. J. (1981). The child's understanding of inadequate messages and communication failure: A problem of ignorance or egocentrism? In W. P. Dickson (Ed.), *Children's oral communication skills*. New York: Academic Press.

ROBINSON, J. L., REZNICK, J. S., KAGAN, J., & CORLEY, R. (1992). The heritability of inhibited and uninhibited behavior: A twin study. *Developmental Psychology, 28,* 1030–1037.

ROBINSON, J., LITTLE, C., & BIRINGEN, Z. (1993). Emotional communication in mother–toddler relationships: Evidence for early gender differentiation. *Merrill-Palmer Quarterly, 39,* 496–517.

ROCHAT, P. (Ed.). (1995). *The self in infancy: Theory and research.* Amsterdam: Elsevier.

ROCHAT, P. (1989). Object manipulation and exploration in 2- to 5-month-old infants. *Developmental Psychology, 25,* 871–884.

ROCHAT, P. (1993). Hand–mouth coordination in the newborn: Morphology, determinants, and early development of a basic act. In G. J. P. Savelsbergh (Ed.), *The development of coordination in infancy*. London: Elsevier.

ROCHAT, P., & MORGAN, R. (1995). Spatial determinants in the perception of self-produced leg movements by 3- to 5-month-old infants. *Developmental Psychology, 31,* 626–636.

RODE, S., CHANG, P., FISCH, R., & SROUFE, L. A. (1981). Attachment patterns of infants separated at birth. *Developmental Psychology, 17,* 188–191.

ROFF, M., SELLS, S. B., & GOLDEN, M. M. (1972). *Social adjustment and personality development in children.* Minneapolis: University of Minnesota Press.

ROGAN, W. J. (1982). PCB's and cola-colored babies: Japan, 1968, and Taiwan, 1979. *Teratology, 26,* 259–261.

ROGOFF, B. (1981). Schooling and the development of cognitive skills. In H. C. Triandis & A. Heron (Eds.), *Handbook of cross-cultural psychology: Vol. 4. Developmental psychology.* Boston: Allyn & Bacon.

ROGOFF, B. (1990). *Apprenticeship in thinking: Cognitive development in social context.* New York: Oxford University Press.

ROGOFF, B. (1991). The joint socialization of development by young children and adults. In M. Lewis & S. Feinman (Eds.), *Social influences and socialization in infancy*. New York: Plenum.

ROGOFF, B. (1998). Cognition as a collaborative process. In W. Damon (Series Ed.) & D. Kuhn & R. S. Siegler (Vol. Eds.), *Handbook of child psychology: Vol. 2. Cognition, perception, and language* (5th ed.). New York: Wiley.

ROGOFF, B., & MISTRY, J. (1990). The social and functional context of children's remembering. In R. Fivush & J. A. Hudson (Eds.), *Knowing and remembering in young children.* New York: Cambridge University Press.

ROGOFF, B., & WADDELL, K. J. (1982). Memory for information organized in a scene by children from two cultures. *Child Development, 53,* 1224–1228.

ROGOFF, B., MISTRY, J., GONCU, A., & MOSIER, C. (1991). Cultural variation in the role relations of toddlers and their families. In M. H. Bornstein (Ed.), *Cultural approaches to parenting.* Hillsdale, NJ: Erlbaum.

ROGOFF, B., MISTRY, J., GONCU, A., & MOSIER, C. (1993). Guided participation in cultural activity by toddlers and caregivers. *Monographs of the Society for Research in Child Development, 58* (Serial No. 236).

ROGOFF, B., MISTRY, J., RADZISZEWSKA, B., & GERMOND, J. (1992). Infants' instrumental social interaction with adults. In S. Feinman (Ed.), *Social referencing and the social construction of reality in infancy.* New York: Plenum.

ROGOSCH, F. A., CICCHETTI, D., SHIELDS, A., & TOTH, S. L. (1995). Parenting dysfunction in child maltreatment. In M. H. Bornstein

(Ed.), *Handbook of parenting: Vol. 4. Applied and practical parenting.* Mahwah, NJ: Erlbaum.

ROOPNARINE, J. L. (1984). Sex-typed socialization in mixed-age preschool classrooms. *Child Development, 55,* 1078–1084.

ROSALES-RUIZ, J., & BAER, D. M. (1996). A behavior-analytic view of development. In S. W. Bijou & E. Ribes (Eds.), *New directions in behavior development.* Reno, NV: Context Press.

ROSE, S. A. (1994). From hand to eye: Findings and issues in infant cross-modal transfer. In D. J. Lewkowicz & R. Lickliter (Eds.), *The development of intersensory perception: Comparative perspectives.* Hillsdale, NJ: Erlbaum.

ROSE, S. A., & FELDMAN, J. F. (1995). Prediction of IQ and specific cognitive abilities at 11 years from infancy measures. *Developmental Psychology, 31,* 685–696.

ROSE, S. A., & ORLIAN, E. K. (1991). Asymmetries in cross-modal transfer. *Child Development, 62,* 706–718.

ROSE, S. A., & RUFF, H. A. (1987). Cross-modal abilities in human infants. In J. D. Osofsky (Ed.), *Handbook of infant development* (2nd ed.). New York: Wiley.

ROSE, S. A., GOTTFRIED, A. W., & BRIDGER, W. H. (1981). Cross-modal transfer and information processing by the sense of touch in infancy. *Developmental Psychology, 17,* 90–98.

ROSEN, K. S., & ROTHBAUM, F. (1993). Quality of parental caregiving and security of attachment. *Developmental Psychology, 29,* 358–367.

ROSEN, W. D., ADAMSON, L. B., & BAKEMAN, R. (1992). An experimental investigation of infant social referencing: Mothers' messages and gender differences. *Developmental Psychology, 28,* 1172–1178.

ROSENBAUM, M. S., & DRABMAN, R. S. (1979). Self-control training in the classroom: Review and critique. *Journal of Applied Behavior Analysis, 12,* 467–485.

ROSENBERG, M. (1985). Self-concept and psychological well-being in adolescence. In R. L. Leahy (Ed.), *The development of the self.* Orlando, FL: Academic Press.

ROSENBERG, M. (1986a). *Conceiving the self.* Melbourne, FL: Krieger.

ROSENBERG, M. (1986b). Self-concept from middle childhood through adolescence. In J. Suls (Ed.), *Psychological perspectives on the self* (Vol. 3). Hillsdale, NJ: Erlbaum.

ROSENGREN, K. S., GELMAN, S. A., KALISH, C. W., & McCORMICK, M. (1991). As time goes by: Children's early understanding of growth in animals. *Child Development, 62,* 1302–1320.

ROSENSTEIN, D., & OSTER, H. (1988). Differential facial responses to four basic tastes in newborns. *Child Development, 59,* 1555–1568.

ROSENTHAL, R. (1976). *Experimenter effects in behavioral research* (enl. ed.). New York: Halsted Press.

ROSENTHAL, R., & JACOBSON, L. (1968). *Pygmalion in the classroom.* New York: Holt, Rinehart & Winston.

ROSENTHAL, R., & VANDELL, D. L. (1996). Quality of care at school-aged child-care programs: Regulatable features, observed experiences, child perspectives, and parent perspectives. *Child Development, 67,* 2434–2445.

ROSS, D. S. (1972). *G. Stanley Hall: The psychologist as prophet.* Chicago: University of Chicago Press.

ROSS, G. (1980). Categorization in 1- to 2-year-olds. *Developmental Psychology, 16,* 391–396.

ROSS, H. S., & LOLLIS, S. P. (1987). Communication within infant social games. *Developmental Psychology, 23,* 241–248.

ROSS, H. S., & LOLLIS, S. P. (1989). A social relations analysis of toddler peer relationships. *Child Development, 60,* 1082–1091.

ROSS, S. A. (1971). A test of the generality of the effects of deviant preschool models. *Developmental Psychology, 4,* 262–267.

ROSSO, P. (1990). *Nutrition and metabolism in pregnancy.* New York: Oxford University Press.

ROTENBERG, K. J. (1980). Children's use of intentionality in judgments of character and disposition. *Child Development, 51,* 282–284.

ROTENBERG, K. J., & SLIZ, D. (1988). Children's restrictive disclosure to friends. *Merrill-Palmer Quarterly, 34,* 203–215.

ROTHBART, M. K., & BATES, J. E. (1998). Temperament. In W. Damon (Ed.), *Handbook of child psychology: Vol. 3. Social, emotional, and personality development.* New York: Wiley.

ROTHBART, M. K., & GOLDSMITH, H. H. (1985). Three approaches to the study of infant temperament. *Developmental Review, 5,* 237–260.

ROTHBART, M. K., & POSNER, M. I. (1985). Temperament and the development of self-regulation. In L. C. Hartledge & C. F. Telzrow (Eds.), *The neuropsychology of individual differences: A developmental perspective.* New York: Plenum.

ROTHBART, M. K., & POSNER, M. I. (1985). Temperament and the development of self-regulation. In L. C. Hartledge & C. F. Telzrow (Eds.), *The neuropsychology of individual differences: A developmental perspective.* New York: Plenum.

ROTHBART, M. K., AHADI, S. A., & HERSHEY, K. L. (1994). Temperament and social behavior in childhood. *Merrill-Palmer Quarterly, 40,* 21–39.

ROTHBART, M. K., POSNER, M. I., & HERSHEY, K. L. (1995). Temperament, attention, and developmental psychopathology. In D. Cicchetti & D. J. Cohen (Eds.), *Manual of developmental psychopathology* (Vol. 1). New York: Wiley.

ROTMAN, B. (1977). *Jean Piaget: Psychologist of the real.* Hassocks, England: Harvester Press.

ROVEE-COLLIER, C. K. (1987). Learning and memory in infancy. In J. D. Osofsky (Ed.), *Handbook of infant development* (2nd ed.). New York: Wiley.

ROVEE-COLLIER, C. K., & BHATT, R. S. (1993). Evidence of long-term memory in infancy. In R. Vasta (Ed.), *Annals of child development* (Vol. 9). London: Kingsley.

ROVEE-COLLIER, C. K., & HAYNE, H. (1987). Reactivation of infant memory: Implications for cognitive development. In H. W. Reese (Ed.), *Advances in child development and behavior* (Vol. 20). New York: Academic Press.

ROVEE-COLLIER, C. K., & SHYI, G. (1992). A functional and cognitive analysis of infant long-term retention. In M. L. Howe, C. J. Brainerd, & V. F. Reyna (Eds.), *Development of long-term retention.* New York: Springer-Verlag.

ROVET, J. F. (1991). The cognitive and neuropsychological characteristics of females with Turner syndrome. In B. Bender & D. Berch (Eds.), *Sex chromosome abnormalities and behavior: Psychological studies.* Boulder, CO: Westview.

ROWE, I., & MARCIA, J. E. (1980). Ego identity status, formal operations, and moral development. *Journal of Youth and Adolescence, 9,* 87–99.

RUBENSTEIN, J., & HOWES, C. (1976). The effect of peers on toddler interaction with mother and toys. *Child Development, 47,* 597–605.

RUBIN, J. Z., PROVENZANO, F. J., & LURIA, Z. (1974). The eye of the beholder: Parents' views on sex of newborns. *American Journal of Orthopsychiatry, 44,* 512–519.

RUBIN, K. H. (1977). The social and cognitive value of preschool toys and activities. *Canadian Journal of Behavioral Science/Review of Canadian Science, 9,* 382–385.

RUBIN, K. H. (1989). *The Play Observation Scale (POS).* Unpublished manuscript. University of Waterloo, Waterloo, Ontario.

RUBIN, K. H. (1993). The Waterloo Longitudinal Project: Correlates and consequences of social withdrawal from childhood to adolescence. In K. H. Rubin & J. B. Asendorpf (Eds.), *Social withdrawal, inhibition, and shyness in childhood.* Hillsdale, NJ: Erlbaum.

RUBIN, K. H., & ASENDORPF, J. B. (Eds.). (1993). *Social withdrawal, inhibition, and shyness in childhood.* Hillsdale, NJ: Erlbaum.

RUBIN, K. H., & KRASNOR, L. R. (1986). Social-cognitive and social behavioral perspectives on problem solving. In M. Perlmutter (Ed.), *Minnesota symposia on child psychology: Vol. 19. Cognitive perspectives on children's social and behavioral development.* Hillsdale, NJ: Erlbaum.

RUBIN, K. H., & MAIONI, T. L. (1975). Play preference and its relationship to egocentrism, popularity and classification skills in preschoolers. *Merrill-Palmer Quarterly, 21,* 171–179.

RUBIN, K. H., & ROSE-KRASNOR, L. (1992). Interpersonal problem solving and social competence in children. In W. B. Van Hasselt & M. Hersen (Eds.), *Handbook of social development.* New York: Plenum.

RUBIN, K. H., BREAM, L., & ROSE-KRASNOR, L. (1991). Social problem solving and aggression in childhood. In D. J. Pepler & K.

H. Rubin (Eds.), *The development and treatment of childhood aggression*. Hillsdale, NJ: Erlbaum.

RUBIN, K. H., BUKOWSKI, W., & PARKER, J. G. (1998). Peer interactions, relationships, and groups. In W. Damon (Series Ed.) & N. Eisenberg (Vol. Ed.), *Handbook of child psychology: Vol. 3. Social, emotional, and personality development* (5th ed.). New York: Wiley.

RUBIN, K. H., FEIN, G. G., & VANDEN-BERG, B. (1983). Play. In P. H. Mussen (Series Ed.) & E. M. Hetherington (Vol. Ed.), *Handbook of child psychology: Vol. 4. Socialization, personality, and social development*. New York: Wiley.

RUBIN, K. H., LYNCH, D., COPLAN, R., ROSE-KRASNOR, L., & BOOTH, C. L. (1994). "Birds of a feather . . .": Behavioral concordances and preferential personal attraction in children. *Child Development, 65,* 1778–1785.

RUBIN, K. H., LeMARE, L. J., & LOLLIS, S. (1990). Social withdrawal in childhood: Developmental pathways to peer rejection. In S. R. Asher & J. D. Coie (Eds.), *Peer rejection in childhood*. New York: Cambridge University Press.

RUBIN, K. H., STEWART, S. L., & CHEN, X. (1995). Parents of aggressive and withdrawn children. In M. H. Bornstein (Ed.), *Handbook of parenting. Vol. 1. Children and parenting*. Mahwah, NJ: Erlbaum.

RUBIN, K. H., WATSON, K. S., & JAMBOR, T. W. (1978). Free-play behaviors in preschool and kindergarten children. *Child Development, 49,* 534–536.

RUBIN, Z. (1980). *Children's friendships*. Cambridge: Harvard University Press.

RUBLE, D. N. (1994). A phase model of transitions: Cognitive and motivational consequences. In M. Zanna (Ed.), *Advances in experimental social psychology*. New York: Academic Press.

RUBLE, D. N., & DWECK, C. S. (1995). Self-conceptions, person conception, and their development. In N. Eisenberg (Ed.), *Review of personality and social psychology: Vol. 15. Development and social psychology: The interface*. Thousand Oaks, CA: Sage.

RUBLE, D. N., & FLETT, G. L. (1988). Conflicting goals in self-evaluative information seeking: Developmental and ability level analyses. *Child Development, 59,* 97–106.

RUBLE, D. N., & FREY, K. S. (1987). Social comparison and outcome evaluation in group contexts. In J. C. Masters & W. P. Smith (Eds.), *Social comparison, social justice, and relative deprivation*. Hillsdale, NJ: Erlbaum.

RUBLE, D. N., & FREY, K. S. (1991). Changing patterns of behavior as skills are acquired: A functional model of self-evaluation. In J. Suls & T. A. Wills (Eds.), *Social comparison: Contemporary theory and research*. Hillsdale, NJ: Erlbaum.

RUBLE, D. N., & MARTIN, C. A. (1998). Gender development. In W. Damon (Ed.), *Handbook of child psychology: Vol. 3. Social, emotional, and personality development*. New York: Wiley.

RUBLE, D. N., GROSOVSKY, E. H., FREY, K. S., & COHEN, R. (1990). Developmental changes and competence assessment. In A. K. Boggiano & T. S. Pittman (Eds.), *Achievement motivation*. New York: Cambridge University Press.

RUDDY, M. G. (1993). Attention shifting and temperament at 5 months. *Infant Behavior and Development, 16,* 255–259.

RUFF, H. A., & KOHLER, C. J. (1978). Tactual-visual transfer in six-month-old infants. *Infant Behavior and Development, 1,* 259–264.

RUFF, H. A., & ROTHBART, M. K. (1996). *Attention in early development*. New York: Oxford University Press.

RUFFMAN, T., PERNER, J., NAITO, M., PARKIN, L., & CLEMENTS, W. A. (1998). Older (but not younger) siblings facilitate false belief understanding. *Developmental Psychology, 34,*161–174.

RUFFMAN, T., PERNER, J., OLSON, D. R., & DOHERTY, M. (1993). Reflecting on scientific thinking: Children's understanding of the hypothesis-evidence relation. *Child Development, 64,* 1617–1636.

RUSHTON, J. P., FULKER, D. W., NEALE, M. C., NIAS, D. K. B., & EYSENCK, H. J. (1986). Altruism and aggression: The heritability of individual differences. *Journal of Personality and Social Psychology, 50,* 1192–1198.

RUSSELL, A., & SAEBEL, J. (1997). Mother-son, mother-daughter, father-son, father-daughter: Are they distinct relationships? *Developmental Review, 17,* 111–147.

RUSSELL, G., & RADOJEVIC, M. (1992). The changing role of fathers? Current directions and future directions for research and practice. *Infant Mental Health Journal, 13,* 296–311.

RUTTER, M. (1983). School effects on pupil progress: Research findings and policy implications. *Child Development, 54,* 1–29.

RUTTER, M. (1987). Continuities and discontinuities from infancy. In J. D. Osofsky (Ed.), *Handbook of infant development* (2nd ed.). New York: Wiley.

RUTTER, M., & CAESAR, P. (Eds.). (1991). *Biological risk factors for psychosocial disorders*. Cambridge: Cambridge University Press.

RUTTER, M., MacDONALD, H., LECOUTEUR, A., HARRINGTON, R., BOLTON, P., & BAILEY, A. (1990). Genetic factors in child psychiatric disorders: II. Empirical findings. *Journal of Child Psychology and Psychiatry, 31,* 39–84.

SAARNI, C. (1984). An observational study of children's attempts to monitor their expressive behavior. *Child Development, 55,* 1504–1513.

SAARNI, C. (1989). Children's understanding of strategic control of emotional expression in social transactions. In C. Saarni & P. L. Harris (Eds.), *Children's understanding of emotion*. Cambridge: Cambridge University Press.

SAARNI, C. (1990). Emotional competence: How emotions and relationships become integrated. In R. A. Thompson (Ed.), *Nebraska symposium on motivation: Vol. 36. Socioemotional development*. Lincoln: University of Nebraska Press.

SAARNI, C., MUMME, D., & CAMPOS, J. J. (1998). Emotional development: Action, communication, and understanding. In W. Damon (Ed.), *Handbook of child psychology: Vol. 3. Social, emotional, and personality development*. New York: Wiley.

SACHS, J., & DEVIN, J. (1976). Young children's use of age-appropriate speech styles in social interaction and role-playing. *Journal of Child Language, 3,* 81–98.

SACHS, O. (1993, May 10) A neurologist's notebook: To see and not see. *New Yorker*, pp. 59–73.

SADEH, A., & ANDERS, T. F. (1993). Sleep disorders. In C. H. Zeanah, Jr. (Ed.), *Handbook of infant mental development*. New York: Guilford.

SADKER, M., & SADKER, D. (1994). *Failing at fairness: How America's schools cheat girls*. New York: Scribner.

SAGI, A. (1990). Attachment theory and research from a cross-cultural perspective. *Human Development, 33,* 10–22.

SAGI, A., & LEWKOWICZ, K. S. (1987). A cross-cultural evaluation of attachment research. In L. W. C. Tavecchio & M. H. van IJzendoorn (Eds.), *Attachment in social networks. Contributions to the Bowlby–Ainsworth attachment theory*. Amsterdam: Elsevier.

SAGI, A., VAN IJZENDOORN, M. H., AVIEZER, O., DONNELL, F., KOREN-KARIE, N., JOELS, T., & HAREL, Y. (1995). Attachments in multiple-caregiver and multiple-infant environments: The case of the Israeli kibbutzim. In E. Waters, B. E. Vaughn, G. Posada, & K. Kondo-Ikemura (Eds.), *Caregiving, cultural, and cognitive perspectives on secure-base behavior and working models. Monographs of the Society for Research in Child Development, 60*(2–3, Serial No. 244).

St. PETERS, M., FITCH, M., HUSTON, A. C., WRIGHT, J. C., & EAKINS, D. J. (1991). Television and families: What do young children watch with their parents? *Child Development, 62,* 1409–1423.

SALTZ, E., CAMPBELL, S., & SKOTKO, D. (1983). Verbal control of behavior: The effects of shouting. *Developmental Psychology, 19,* 461–464.

SALTZSTEIN, H. D., SANVITALE, D., & SUPRANER, A. (1978). Social influence on children's standards for judging criminal culpability. *Developmental Psychology, 14,* 125–131.

SALTZSTEIN, H. D., WEINER, A. S., MUNK, J. J., SUPRANER, A., BLANK, R., & SCHWARZ, R. P. (1987). Comparison between children's own moral judgments and those they attribute to adults. *Merrill-Palmer Quarterly, 33,* 33–51.

SALZINGER, S., FELDMAN, R. S., HAMMER, M., & ROSARIO, M. (1993). The effects of physical abuse on children's social relationships. *Child Development, 64,* 169–187.

SAMARAPUNGAVAN, A., VOSNIADOU, S., & BREWER, W. F. (1996). Mental models of the earth, sun, and moon: Indian children's cosmologies. *Cognitive Development, 11,* 491–521.

SAMEROFF, A. J., SEIFER, R., BALDWIN, A., & BALDWIN, C. (1993). Stability of intelligence from pre-school to adolescence: The influence of social and family risk factors. *Child Development, 64,* 80–97.

SAMUELS, C. A. (1986). Bases for the infant's developing self-awareness. *Human Development, 29,* 36–48.

SANDER, L. W., SNYDER, P. A., ROSETT, H. L., LEE, A., GOULD, J. B., & OUELLETTE, E. (1977). Effects of alcohol intake during pregnancy on newborn state regulation: A progress report. *Alcoholism: Clinical and Experimental Research, 1,* 233–241.

SANSON, A., & ROTHBART, M. K. (1995). Child temperament and parenting. In M. H. Bornstein (Ed.), *Handbook of parenting: Vol. 4. Applied and practical parenting.* Mahwah, NJ: Erlbaum.

SANSON, A., PRIOR, M., & KYRIOS, M. (1990). Contamination of measures in temperament research. *Merrill-Palmer Quarterly, 36,* 179–192.

SANVITALE, D., SALTZSTEIN, H. D., & FISH, M. C. (1989). Moral judgments by normal and conduct-disordered preadolescent and adolescent boys. *Merrill-Palmer Quarterly, 35,* 463–481.

SARASWATHI, T. S., & SUNDARESAN, J. (1980). Perceived maternal disciplinary practices and their relations to development of moral judgment. *International Journal of Behavioral Development, 3,* 91–104.

SASANUMA, S. (1980). Do Japanese show sex differences in brain asymmetry? Supplementary findings. *Behavioral and Brain Sciences, 3,* 247–248.

SAUDINO, K. J., & PLOMIN, R. (1997). Cognitive and temperamental mediators of genetic contributions to the home environment during infancy. *Merrill-Palmer Quarterly, 43,* 1–23.

SAVIN-WILLIAMS, R. C. (1979). Dominance hierarchies in groups of early adolescents. *Child Development, 50,* 923–935.

SAVIN-WILLIAMS, R. C. (1987). *Adolescence: An ethological perspective.* New York: Springer-Verlag.

SAVIN-WILLIAMS, R. C., & BERNDT, T. J. (1990). Friendship and peer relations. In S. S. Feld-man & G. R. Elliott (Eds.), *At the threshold: The developing adolescent.* Cambridge: Harvard University Press.

SAWIN, D. G. (1990). Aggressive behavior among children in small playgroup settings with violent television. In K. D. Gadow (Ed.), *Advances in learning and behavioral disabilities* (Vol. 6). Greenwich, CT: JAI Press.

SAXE, G. B. (1988). The mathematics of child street vendors. *Child Development, 59,* 1415–1425.

SAXE, G. B. (1991). *Culture and cognitive development: Studies in mathematical understanding.* Hillsdale, NJ: Erlbaum.

SAYEGH, Y., & DENNIS, W. (1965). The effect of supplementary experiences upon the behavioral development of infants in institutions. *Child Development, 36,* 81–90.

SAYWITZ, K. J., GOODMAN, G. S., NICHOLAS, E., & MOAN, S. F. (1991). Children's memories of a physical examination involving genital touch: Implications for reports of child sexual abuse. *Journal of Consulting and Clinical Psyhology, 59,* 682–691.

SCARBOROUGH, H., & WYCKOFF, J. (1986). Mother, I'd still rather do it myself: Some further non-effects of "motherese." *Journal of Child Language, 13,* 431–437.

SCARR, S. (1981). *Race, social class, and individual differences in IQ: New studies of old problems.* Hillsdale, NJ: Erlbaum.

SCARR, S. (1983). An evolutionary perspective on infant intelligence: Species patterns and individual variations. In M. Lewis (Ed.), *Origins of intelligence: Infancy and early childhood* (2nd ed.). New York: Plenum.

SCARR, S. (1992). Developmental theories for the 1990s: Development and individual differences. *Child Development, 63,* 1–19.

SCARR, S. (1993). Biological and cultural diversity: The legacy of Darwin for development. *Child Development, 64,* 1333–1353.

SCARR, S. (1998). American child care today. *American Psychologist, 53,* 95–108.

SCARR, S., & KIDD, K. K. (1983). Developmental behavior genetics. In M. M. Haith & J. J. Campos (Eds.), *Handbook of child psychology: Vol. 2. Infancy and developmental psychobiology.* New York: Wiley.

SCARR, S., & KIDD, K. K. (1983). Developmental behavior genetics. In P. H. Mussen (Series Ed.) & M. M. Haith & J. J. Campos (Vol. Eds.), *Handbook of child psychology: Vol. 2. Infancy and developmental psychobiology.* New York: Wiley.

SCARR, S., & McCARTNEY, K. (1983). How people make their own environments: A theory of genotype–environment effects. *Child Development, 54,* 424–435.

SCARR, S., & WEINBERG, R. A. (1983). The Minnesota Adoption Studies: Genetic differences and malleability. *Child Development, 54,* 260–267.

SCARR, S., PAKSTIS, A. J., KATZ, S. H., & BARKER, W. B. (1977). Absence of a relationship between degree of white ancestry and intellectual skills within a black population. *Human Genetics, 39,* 69–86.

SCHACTER, F. F., SHORE, E., HODAPP, R., CHALFIN, S., & BUNDY, C. (1978). Do girls talk earlier? Mean length of utterance in toddlers. *Developmental Psychology, 14,* 388–392.

SCHAFFER, C. E., & BLATT, S. J. (1990). Interpersonal relationships and the experience of perceived efficacy. In R. J. Sternberg & J. Kolligian (Eds.), *Competence considered.* New Haven, CT: Yale University Press.

SCHAFFER, H. R. (1986). Some thoughts of an ordinologist. *Developmental Review, 6,* 115–121.

SCHAFFER, H. R., & EMERSON, P. E. (1964). The development of social attachments in infancy. *Monographs of the Society for Research in Child Development, 29*(3, Serial No. 94).

SCHIEFFELIN, B. (1985). The acquisition of Kaluli. In D. I. Slobin (Ed.), *The crosslinguistic study of language acquisition: Vol. 1. The data.* Hillsdale, NJ: Erlbaum.

SCHLEIDT, M. (1991). An ethological perspective on infant development. In M. E. Lamb & H. Keller (Eds.), *Infant development: Perspectives from German-speaking countries.* Hillsdale, NJ: Erlbaum.

SCHLESINGER, I. M. (1988). The origin of relational categories. In Y. Levy, I. M. Schlesinger, & M. D. S. Braine (Eds.), *Categories and processes in language acquisition.* Hillsdale, NJ: Erlbaum.

SCHMIDT, C. R., OLLENDICK, T. H., & STANOWICZ, L. B. (1988). Developmental changes in the influence of assigned goals on cooperation and competition. *Developmental Psychology, 24,* 574–579.

SCHMIDT, L. A., & FOX, N. A. (1998). The development and outcomes of childhood shyness: A multiple psychophysiologic measure approach. In R. Vasta (Ed.), *Annals of child development* (Vol. 13). London: Kingsley.

SCHMUCKLER, M. A. (1995). Self-knowledge of body position: Integration of perceptual and action system information. In P. Rochat (Ed.), *The self in infancy: Theory and research.* Amsterdam: Elsevier.

SCHNEIDER, B. A., & TREHUB, S. E. (1985a). Behavioral assessment of basic capabilities. In S. E. Trehub & B. A. Schneider (Eds.), *Auditory development in infancy.* New York: Plenum.

SCHNEIDER, B. A., & TREHUB, S. E. (1985b). Infant auditory psychophysics: An overview. In G. Gottlieb & N. A. Krasnegor (Eds.), *Measurement of audition and vision in the first year of postnatal life: A methodological overview.* Norwood, NJ: Ablex.

SCHNEIDER, B. H., & BYRNE, B. M. (1985). Children's social skills training: A meta-analysis. In B. H. Schneider, K. H. Rubin, & J. E. Ledingham (Eds.), *Children's peer relations: Issues in assessment and intervention.* New York: Springer-Verlag.

SCHNEIDER, B. H., RUBIN, K. H., & LEDINGHAM, J. E. (Eds.). (1985). *Children's peer relations: Issues in assessment and intervention.* New York: Springer-Verlag.

SCHNEIDER, W., & BJORKLUND, D. F. (1998). Memory. In W. Damon (Series Ed.) & D. Kuhn & R. S. Siegler (Vol. Eds.), *Handbook of child psychology: Vol. 2. Cognition, perception, and language* (5th ed.). New York: Wiley.

SCHNEIDER, W., & PRESSLEY, M. (1989). *Memory development between 2 and 20.* New York: Springer-Verlag.

SCHNEIDER, W., GRUBER, H., GOLD, A., & OPWIS, K. (1993). Chess expertise and memory for chess positions in children and adults. *Journal of Experimental Child Psychology, 56,* 328–349.

SCHNEIDER, W., KORKEL, J., & WEINERT, F. E. (1987). *The knowledge base and memory performance: A comparison of academically successful and unsuccessful learners.* Paper presented at the meeting of the American Educational Research Association, Washington, DC.

SCHNEIDER-ROSEN, K., & CICCHETTI, D. (1984). The relationship between affect and cognition in maltreated infants: Quality of attachment and the development of visual self-recognition. *Child Development, 55,* 648–658.

SCHNEIDER-ROSEN, K., & CICCHETTI, D. (1991). Early self-knowledge and emotional development: Visual self-recognition and affective reactions to mirror self-image in maltreated and nonmaltreated toddlers. *Developmental Psychology, 27,* 471–478.

SCHULMAN, A. H., & KAPLOWITZ, C. (1977). Mirror-image response during the first two years of life. *Developmental Psychobiology, 10,* 133–142.

SCHUNK, D. H. (1983). Reward contingencies and the development of children's skills and self-efficacy. *Journal of Educational Psychology, 75,* 511–518.

SCHUNK, D. H. (1984). Self-efficacy perspective on achievement behavior. *Educational Psychologist, 19,* 48–58.

SCHUNK, D. H. (1987). Peer models and children's behavioral change. *Review of Educational Research, 57,* 159–174.

SCHWARTZ, B. (1990). The creation and destruction of value. *American Psychologist, 45,* 7–15.

SCHWARTZ, D., DODGE, K. A., PETTIT, G. S., & BATES, J. E. (1997). The early socialization of aggressive victims of bullying. *Child Development, 68,* 665–675.

SCHWARTZ, R. G., & CAMARATA, S. (1985). Examining relationships between input and language development: Some statistical issues. *Journal of Child Language, 12,* 199–207.

SCHWARTZ, R. G., LEONARD, L. B., FROME-LOEB, D. M., & SWANSON, L. A. (1987). Attempted sounds are sometimes not: An expanded view of phonological selection and avoidance. *Journal of Child Language, 14,* 411–418.

SCHWEINHART, L. J., & WEIKART, D. P. (1991). Response to "Beyond IQ in Preschool Programs?" *Intelligence, 15,* 313–315.

SCOTT, J. P. (1987). Critical periods in the processes of social organization. In M. H. Bornstein (Ed.), *Sensitive periods in development: Interdisciplinary perspectives.* Hillsdale, NJ: Erlbaum.

SCOTT, M. M. (1997, April). *Children's problems and solution strategies in the natural habitat.* Paper presented at the meeting of the Society for Research in Child Development, Washington, DC.

SEARS, R. R. (1977). Sources of life satisfactions of the Terman gifted men. *American Psychologist, 32,* 119–128.

SEASHORE, M. J., LEIFER, A. D., BARNETT, C. R., & LEIDERMAN, P. H. (1973). The effects of denial of early mother–infant interaction on maternal self-confidence. *Journal of Personality and Social Psychology, 26,* 369–378.

SEBALD, H. (1989). Adolescent peer orientation: Changes in the support system during the last three decades. *Adolescence, 24,* 937–945.

SEGAL, L. B., OSTER, H., COHEN, M., CASPI, B., MYERS, M., & BROWN, D. (1995). Smiling and fussing in seven-month-old preterm and full-term black infants in the still-face situation. *Child Development, 66,* 1829–1843.

SEIDMAN, E., ALLEN, L., ABER, J. L., MITCHELL, C., & FEINMAN, J. (1994). The impact of school transition in early adolescence on the self-system and perceived social context of poor urban youth. *Child Development, 65,* 507–522.

SEIFER, R., & SCHILLER, M. (1995). The role of parenting sensitivity, infant temperament, and dyadic interaction in attachment theory and assessment. In E. Waters, B. E. Vaughn, G. Posada, & K. Kondo-Ikemura (Eds.), Caregiving, cultural, and cognitive perspectives on secure-base behavior and working models. *Monographs of the Society for Research in Child development, 60* (2–3, Serial No. 244).

SEIFER, R., SCHILLER, M., SAMEROFF, A. J., RESNICK, S., & RIORDAN, K. (1996). Attachment, maternal sensitivity, and infant temperament during the first year of life. *Developmental Psychology, 32,* 12–25.

SELMAN, R. L. (1980). *The growth of interpersonal understanding: Development and clinical analyses.* New York: Academic Press.

SELMAN, R. L., & JAQUETTE, D. (1977). *The development of interpersonal awareness.* Unpublished manuscript.

SERBIN, L. A., & SPRAFKIN, C. (1986). The salience of gender and the process of sex typing in three- to seven-year-old children. *Child Development, 57,* 1188–1199.

SERBIN, L. A., POWLISHTA, K. K., & GULKO, J. (1993). The development of sex typing in middle childhood. *Monographs of the Society for Research in Child Development, 58*(Serial No. 232).

SERBIN, L. A., SPRAFKIN, C., ELMAN, M., & DOYLE, A. (1994). The early development of sex differentiated patterns of social influence. *Canadian Journal of Social Science, 14,* 350–363.

SERBIN, L. A., TONICK, I. J., & STERNGLANZ, S. H. (1977). Shaping cooperative cross-sex play. *Child Development, 48,* 924–929.

SHAKIN, M., SHAKIN, D., & STERNGLANZ, S. H. (1985). Infant clothing: Sex labeling for strangers. *Sex Roles, 12,* 955–963.

SHANTZ, C. U. (1983). Social cognition. In P. H. Mussen (Series Ed.) & J. H. Flavell & E. M. Markman (Vol. Eds.), *Handbook of child psychology: Vol. 3. Cognitive development.* New York: Wiley.

SHANTZ, C. U. (1987). Conflicts between children. *Child Development, 58,* 283–305.

SHANTZ, C. U., & HARTUP, W. W. (Eds.). (1995). *Conflict in child and adolescent development.* New York: Cambridge University Press.

SHARPE, R. M., & SKAKKEBAEK, N. E. (1993). Are oestrogens involved in falling sperm counts and disorders of the male reproductive tract? *Lancet, 341,* 1392–1395.

SHATZ, M. (1983). On transition, continuity, and coupling: An alternative approach to communicative development. In R. M. Golinkoff (Ed.), *The transition from prelinguistic to linguistic communication.* Hillsdale, NJ: Erlbaum.

SHATZ, M. (1991). Using cross-cultural research to inform us about the role of language development: Comparisons of Japanese, Korean, and English, and of German, American English, and British English. In M. H. Bornstein (Ed.), *Cultural approaches to parenting.* Hillsdale, NJ: Erlbaum.

SHATZ, M., & GELMAN, R. (1973). The development of communication skills: Modifications in the speech of young children as a function of the listener. *Monographs of the Society for Research in Child Development, 38* (5, Serial No. 152).

SHATZ, M., & McCLOSKEY, L. (1984). Answering appropriately: A developmental perspective on conversational knowledge. In S. A. Kuczaj (Ed.), *Discourse development: Progress in cognitive developmental research.* New York: Springer-Verlag.

SHAYER, M., & WYLAM, H. (1978). The distribution of Piagetian stages of thinking in British middle and secondary school children: II. 14 to 16 year old and sex differentials. *British Journal of Educational Psychology, 48,* 62–70.

SHAYER, M., KUCHEMAN, D. E., & WYLAM, H. (1976). The distribution of Piagetian stages of thinking in British middle and secondary school children. *British Journal of Educational Psychology, 46,* 164–173.

SHELDON, A. (1990). Pickle fights: Gendered talk in preschool disputes. *Discourse Processes, 13,* 5–31.

SHELDON, A. (1992). Conflict talk: Sociolinguist challenges to self-assertion and how young girls meet them. *Merrill-Palmer Quarterly, 38,* 95–117.

SHEPARD, T. H. (1986). Human teratogenicity. *Advances in Pediatrics, 33,* 225–268.

SHERIF, M., HARVEY, O. J., WHITE, B. J., HOOD, W. R., & SHERIF, C. W. (1961). *Intergroup conflict and cooperation: The Robbers Cave experiment.* Norman: University of Oklahoma Press.

SHIGETOMI, C. C., HARTMANN, D. P., & GELFAND, D. M. (1981). Sex differences in children's altruistic behavior and reputations for helpfulness. *Developmental Psychology, 17,* 434–437.

SHORE, C. M. (1995). *Individual differences in language development.* Thousand Oaks, CA: Sage.

SHUCARD, J. L., & SHUCARD, D. W. (1990). Auditory evoked potentials and hand preference in 6-month-old infants: Possible gender-related differences in cerebral organization. *Developmental Psychology, 26,* 923–930.

SHUCARD, J. L., SHUCARD, D. W., CUMMINS, K. R., & CAMPOS, J. J. (1981). Auditory evoked potentials and sex-related differences in brain development. *Brain and Language, 13,* 91–102.

SHULMAN, S., & COLLINS, W. A. (Eds.). (1997). *New directions for child development: No. 78. Romantic relationships in adolescence: Developmental perspectives.* San Francisco: Jossey-Bass.

SHULTZ, T. R., & DARLEY, J. M. (1991). An information-processing model of retributive moral judgments based on "legal reasoning." In W. M. Kurtines & J. L. Gewirtz (Eds.), *Handbook of moral behavior and development: Vol. 2. Research.* Hillsdale, NJ: Erlbaum.

SHULTZ, T. R., & WRIGHT, K. (1985). Concepts of negligence and intention in the assignment of moral responsibility. *Canadian Journal of Behavioural Science, 17,* 97–108.

SHULTZ, T. R., WRIGHT, K., & SCHLEIFER, M. (1986). Assignment of moral responsibility and punishment. *Child Development, 57,* 177–184.

SHURE, M. B. (1989). Interpersonal competence training. In W. Damon (Ed.), *Child development today and tomorrow.* San Francisco: Jossey-Bass.

SHURKIN, J. N. (1992). *Terman's kids: The groundbreaking study of how the gifted grow up.* Boston: Little, Brown.

SHWE, H. I., & MARKMAN, E. M. (1997). Young children's appreciation of the mental impact of their communicative signals. *Developmental Psychology, 33,* 630–636.

SHWEDER, R. A., & MUCH, M. C. (1987). Determinations of meaning: Discourse and moral socialization. In W. M. Kurtines & J. L. Gewirtz (Eds.), *Moral development through social interaction.* New York: Wiley.

SHWEDER, R. A., GOODNOW, J., HATANO, G., LEVINE, H. M., & MILLER, P. (1998). The cultural psychology of development: One mind, many mentalities. In W. Damon (Ed.), *Handbook of child psychology: Vol. 1. Theoretical models of human development.* New York: Wiley.

SHWEDER, R. A., MAHAPATRA, M., & MILLER, J. (1987). Culture and moral development. In J. Kagan & S. Lamb (Eds.), *The emergence of morality in young children.* Chicago: University of Chicago Press.

SIEBER, J. E. (1992). *Planning ethically responsible research: A guide for students and internal review boards.* Newbury Park, CA: Sage.

SIEGAL, M. (1987). Are sons and daughters treated more differently by fathers than by mothers? *Developmental Review, 7,* 183–209.

SIEGAL, M. (1991). *Knowing children: Experiments in conversation and cognition.* Hillsdale, NJ: Erlbaum.

SIEGEL, L. S. (1984). Home environment influences on cognitive development in preterm and full-term children during the first 5 years. In A. W. Gottfried (Ed.), *Home environment and early cognitive development.* New York: Academic Press.

SIEGEL, L. S. (1989). A reconceptualization of prediction from infant test scores. In M. H. Bornstein & N. Krasnegor (Eds.), *Stability and continuity in mental development.* Hillsdale, NJ: Erlbaum.

SIEGEL, L. S. (1992). Infant, motor, and language behaviors as predictors of achievement at school age. In C. Rovee-Collier & L. P. Lipsitt (Eds.), *Advances in infancy research* (Vol. 7). Norwood, NJ: Ablex.

SIEGEL, L. S. (1993a). The development of reading. In H. W. Reese (Ed.), *Advances in child development and behavior* (Vol. 24). San Diego: Academic Press.

SIEGEL, L. S. (1993b). Phonological processing deficits as the basis of a reading disability. *Developmental Review, 13,* 246–257.

SIEGLER, R. S. (1976). Three aspects of cognitive development. *Cognitive Psychology, 8,* 481–520.

SIEGLER, R. S. (1978). The origins of scientific reasoning. In R. S. Siegler (Ed.), *Children's thinking: What develops?* Hillsdale, NJ: Erlbaum.

SIEGLER, R. S. (1981). Developmental sequences within and between concepts. *Monographs of the Society for Research in Child Development, 46* (2, Serial No. 189).

SIEGLER, R. S. (1988). Individual differences in strategy choices: Good students, not-so-good students, and perfectionists. *Child Development, 59,* 833–851.

SIEGLER, R. S. (1995). How does change occur?: A microgenetic study of number conservation. *Cognitive Psychology, 28,* 225–273.

SIEGLER, R. S. (1996a). *Emerging minds: The process of change in children's thinking.* New York: Oxford University Press.

SIEGLER, R. S. (1996b). A grand theory of development. *Monographs of the Society for Research in Child Development, 61* (1–2, Serial No. 246).

SIEGLER, R. S. (1998). *Children's thinking* (3rd ed.). Englewood Cliffs, NJ: Prentice Hall.

SIEGLER, R. S., & JENKINS, E. (1989). *How children discover new strategies.* Hillsdale, NJ: Erlbaum.

SIEGLER, R. S., & SHIPLEY, C. (1995). Variation, selection, and cognitive change. In T. J. Simon & G. S. Halford (Eds.), *Developing cognitive competence: New approaches to process modeling.* Hillsdale, NJ: Erlbaum.

SIEGLER, R. S., & SHRAGER, J. (1984). Strategy choices in addition and subtraction: How do children know what to do? In C. Sophian (Ed.), *Origins of cognitive skills.* Hillsdale, NJ: Erlbaum.

SIGELMAN, C. K., & WAITZMAN, K. A. (1991). The development of distributive justice orientations: Contextual influences of children's

resource allocations. *Child Development, 62,* 1367–1378.

SIGMAN, M. (1995). Nutrition and child development: More food for thought. *Current Directions in Psychological Science, 4,* 52–55.

SIGNORELLA, M. L. (1987). Gender schemata: Individual differences and context effects. In L. S. Liben & M. L. Signorella (Eds.), *New directions for child development: No. 38. Children's gender schemata.* San Francisco: Jossey-Bass.

SIGNORELLA, M. L., & LIBEN, L. S. (1984). Recall and reconstruction of gender-related pictures: Effects of attitude, task difficulty, and age. *Child Development, 55,* 393–405.

SIGNORELLA, M. L., BIGLER, R. S., & LIBEN, L. S. (1993). Developmental differences in children's gender schemata about others: A meta-analytic review. *Developmental Review, 13,* 147–183.

SIGNORIELLI, N. (1993). Television, the portrayal of women, and children's attitudes. In G. Berry & J. K. Asamen (Eds.), *Children and television: Images in a changing sociocultural world.* Newbury Park, CA: Sage.

SILVER, L. B. (1992). *Attention-deficit hyperactivity disorder.* Washington, DC: American Psychiatric Association.

SILVERMAN, I., & EALS, M. (1992). Sex differences in spatial abilities: Evolutionary theory and data. In J. H. Barkow, L. Cosmides, & J. Tooby (Eds.), *The adapted mind: Evolutionary psychology and the generation of culture.* New York: Oxford University Press.

SIMMONS, R. G., & BLYTH, D. A. (1987). *Moving into adolescence: The impact of pubertal change and social context.* Hawthorne, NY: Aldine de Gruyter.

SIMMONS, R. G., CARLTON-FORD, S. L., & BLYTH, D. A. (1987). Predicting how a child will age with the transition to junior high school. In R. M. Lerner & T. M. Foch (Eds.), *Biological-psychosocial interactions in early adolescence.* Hillsdale, NJ: Erlbaum.

SIMON, T. J. (1997). Reconceptualizing the origins of number knowledge: A "non-numerical" account. *Cognitive Development, 12,* 349–372.

SIMON, T. J., & HALFORD, G. S. (Eds.). (1995). *Developing cognitive competence: New approaches to process modeling.* Hillsdale, NJ: Erlbaum.

SIMON, T. J., HESPOS, S. J., & ROCHAT, P. (1995). Do infants understand simple arithmetic? A replication of Wynn. *Cognitive Development, 10,* 253–269.

SKINNER, B. F. (1953). *Science and human behavior.* New York: Macmillan.

SKINNER, B. F. (1957). *Verbal behavior.* New York: Appleton-Century-Crofts.

SKOWRONSKI, J. J., BETZ, A. L., THOMPSON, C. P., & LARSEN, S. F. (1995). Long-term performance in autobiographical event dating: Patterns of accuracy and error across a two-and-a-half year time span. In A. L. Healy & L. B. Bourne (Eds.), *Acquisition and long-term re-*

tention of knowledge and skills: The durability and specificity of cognitive procedures. Newbury Park, CA: Sage.

SLABY, R. G., & FREY, K. S. (1975). Development of gender constancy and selective attention to same-sex models. *Child Development, 46,* 849–856.

SLADE, A. (1987). Quality of attachment and early symbolic play. *Developmental Psychology, 23,* 78–85.

SLATER, A. (1995). Individual differences in infancy and later IQ. *Journal of Child Psychology and Psychiatry and Allied Disciplines, 36,* 69–112.

SLATER, A. (1995). Visual perception and memory at birth. In C. Rovee-Collier & L. P. Lipsitt (Eds.), *Advances in infancy research* (Vol. 9). Norwood, NJ: Ablex.

SLATER, A., & MORISON, V. (1985). Shape constancy and slant perception at birth. *Perception, 14,* 337–344.

SLATER, A., COOPER, R., ROSE, D., & MORISON, V. (1989). Prediction of cognitive performance from infancy to early childhood. *Human Development, 32,* 137–147.

SLATER, A., JOHNSON, S. P., BROWN, E., & BADENOCH, M. (1996). Newborn infants' perception of partly occluded objects. *Infant Behavior and Development, 19,* 145–148.

SLATER, A., JOHNSON, S. P., KELLMAN, P. J., & SPELKE, E. S. (1994). The role of three-dimensional depth cues in infants' perception of partly occluded objects. *Early Development and Parenting, 3,* 187–191.

SLATER, A., MATTOCK, A., & BROWN, E. (1990). Size constancy at birth: Newborn infant's responses to retinal and real size. *Journal of Experimental Child Psychology, 49,* 314–322.

SLATER, A., MATTOCK, A., BROWN, E., & BREMNER, J. G. (1991). Form perception at birth: Cohen and Younger (1984) revisited. *Journal of Experimental Child Psychology, 51,* 395–406.

SLAUGHTER-DeFOE, D. T., NAKAGAWA, K., TAKANISHI, R., & JOHNSON, D. J. (1990). Toward cultural/ecological perspectives on schooling and achievement in African- and Asian-American children. *Child Development, 61,* 363–383.

SLOBIN, D. I. (1982). Universal and particular in the acquisition of language. In E. Wanner & L. R. Gleitman (Eds.), *Language acquisition: The state of the art.* Cambridge: Cambridge University Press.

SLOBIN, D. I. (Ed.). (1985). *The cross-linguistic study of language* (Vols. 1 and 2). Hillsdale, NJ: Erlbaum.

SLOMKOWSKI, C., & DUNN, J. (1993, March). *Conflict in close relationships.* Paper presented at the meeting of the Society for Research in Child Development, New Orleans.

SLOMKOWSKI, C. L., & KILLEN, M. (1992). Young children's conceptions of transgressions with friends and nonfriends. *International Journal of Behavioral Development, 15,* 247–258.

SLUCKIN, A. (1980). Dominance relationships in preschool children. In D. R. Omark, F. F. Strayer, & D. G. Freedman (Eds.), *Dominance relations: An ethological view of human conflict and social interaction.* New York: Garland.

SMETANA, J. G. (1986). Preschool children's conceptions of sex-role transgressions. *Child Development, 57,* 862–871.

SMETANA, J. G. (1989). Toddlers' social interactions in the context of moral and conventional transgressions in the home. *Developmental Psychology, 25,* 499–508.

SMETANA, J. G. (1994). Morality in context: Abstractions, ambiguities, and applications. In R. Vasta (Ed.), *Annals of child development.* (Vol. 10). London: Kingsley.

SMETANA, J. G., & BRAEGES, J. L. (1990). The development of toddlers' moral and conventional judgments. *Merrill-Palmer Quarterly, 36,* 329–346.

SMETANA, J. G., KILLEN, M., & TURIEL, E. (1991). Children's reasoning about interpersonal and moral conflicts. *Child Development, 62,* 629–644.

SMETANA, J. G., SCHLAGMAN, N., & ADAMS, P. (1993). Preschoolers' judgments about hypothetical and actual transgressions. *Child Development, 64,* 202–214.

SMILEY, P., & HUTTENLOCHER, J. (1989). Young children's acquisition of emotion concepts. In C. Saarni & P. L. Harris (Eds.), *Children's understanding of emotion.* Cambridge: Cambridge University Press.

SMILEY, P. A., & DWECK, C. S. (1994). Individual differences in achievement goals among young children. *Child Development, 65,* 1723–1743.

SMITH, B. A., & BLASS, E. M. (1996). Taste-mediated calming in premature, preterm, and full-term human infants. *Developmental Psychology, 32,* 1084–1089.

SMITH, B. A., STEVENS, K., TORGERSON, W. S., & KIM, J. H. (1992). Diminished reactivity of postmature human infants to sucrose compared with term infants. *Developmental Psychology, 28,* 811–820.

SMITH, C. L. (1979). Children's understanding of natural language hierarchies. *Journal of Experimental Child Psychology, 27,* 437–458.

SMITH, E. A. (1989). A biosocial model of adolescent sexual behavior. In G. R. Adams, R. Montemayor, & T. P. Gullota (Eds.), *Biology of adolescent behavior and development.* Newbury Park, CA: Sage.

SMITH, P. K. (1978). A longitudinal study of social participation in preschool children: Solitary and parallel play reexamined. *Developmental Psychology, 14,* 517–523.

SMITH, P. K. (1995). Grandparenthood. In M. H. Bornstein (Ed.), *Handbook of parenting: Vol. 3. Status and social conditions of parenting.* Mahwah, NJ: Erlbaum.

SMITH, P. K., & CONNOLLY, K. J. (1981). *The ecology of preschool behavior.* Cambridge: Cambridge University Press.

SNAREY, J. R., & KELJO, K. (1991). In a *Gemeinschaft* voice: The cross-cultural expansion of moral development theory. In W. M. Kurtines & J. L. Gewirtz (Eds.), *Handbook of moral behavior and development: Vol. 1. Theory.* Hillsdale, NJ: Erlbaum.

SNAREY, J. R., REIMER, J., & KOHLBERG, L. (1985). Development of social-moral reasoning among kibbutz adolescents: A longitudinal cross-cultural study. *Developmental Psychology, 21,* 3–17.

SNAREY, J. R. (1985). Cross-cultural universality of social-moral development: A critical review of Kohlbergian research. *Psychological Bulletin, 97,* 202–232.

SNOW, C. E. (1981). The uses of imitation. *Journal of Child Language, 8,* 205–212.

SNOW, C. E. (1983). Saying it again: The role of expanded and deferred imitations in language acquisition. In K. E. Nelson (Ed.), *Children's language* (Vol. 4). Hillsdale, NJ: Erlbaum.

SNOW, C. E., & FERGUSON, C. (1977). *Talking to children: Language input and acquisition.* Cambridge: Cambridge University Press.

SNOW, C. E., & GOLDFIELD, B. A. (1983). Turn the page please: Situation-specific language acquisition. *Journal of Child Language, 10,* 551–569.

SNOW, C. E., PAN, B. E., IMBENS-BAILEY, A., & HERMAN, J. (1996). Learning how to say what one means: A longitudinal study of children's speech act use. *Social Development, 5,* 56–84.

SNOW, C. E., PERLMAN, R., & NATHAN, D. (1987). Why routines are different: Toward a multiple-factors model of the relation between input and language acquisition. In K. E. Nelson & A. VanKleeck (Eds.), *Children's language* (Vol. 6). Hillsdale, NJ: Erlbaum.

SNOW, R. E., & YALOW, E. (1982). Education and intelligence. In R. J. Sternberg (Ed.), *Handbook of human intelligence.* Cambridge: Cambridge University Press.

SNYDER, J. J., & PATTERSON, G. R. (1995). Individual differences in social aggression: A test of a reinforcement model of socialization in the natural environment. *Behavior Therapy, 26,* 371–391.

SNYDER, J., WEST, L., STOCKEMER, V., & GIBBONS, S. (1996). A social learning model of peer choice in the natural environment. *Journal of Applied Developmental Psychology, 17,* 215–237.

SOKOLOV, E. N. (1960). *Perception and the conditioned reflex.* New York: Macmillan.

SOLOMON, G. E. A., JOHNSON, S. C., ZAITCHIK, D., & CAREY, S. (1996). Like father, like son: Young children's understanding of how and why offspring resemble their parents. *Child Development, 67,* 151–171.

SOMMERVILLE, J. (1978). English Puritans and children: A social-cultural explanation. *Journal of Psychohistory, 6,* 113–137.

SOMMERVILLE, J. (1982). *The rise and fall of childhood.* Beverly Hills, CA: Sage.

SONNENSCHEIN, S. (1988). The development of referential communication: Speaking to different listeners. *Child Development, 59,* 694–702.

SONTAG, L. W. (1944). War and fetal maternal relationship. *Marriage and Family Living, 6,* 1–5.

SONTAG, L. W. (1966). Implications of fetal behavior and environment for adult personalities. *Annals of the New York Academy of Sciences, 134,* 782–786.

SOPHIAN, C. (1995). *Children's numbers.* Madison, WI: Brown & Benchmark.

SORCE, J. F., EMDE, R. N., CAMPOS, J. J., & KLINNERT, M. D. (1985). Maternal emotional signaling: Its effect on the visual cliff behavior of 1-year-olds. *Developmental Psychology, 21,* 195–200.

SOSTEK, A. M., SMITH, Y. F., KATZ, K. S., & GRANT, E. G. (1987). Developmental outcome of preterm infants with intraventricular hemorrhage at one and two years of age. *Child Development, 58,* 779–786.

SPEARMAN, C. (1927). *The abilities of man.* New York: Macmillan.

SPEER, J. R., & FLAVELL, J. H. (1979). Young children's knowledge of the relative difficulty of recognition and recall memory tasks. *Developmental Psychology, 15,* 214–217.

SPELKE, E. S. (1976). Infants' intermodal perception of events. *Cognitive Psychology, 8,* 533–560.

SPELKE, E. S. (1985). Perception of unity, persistence, and identity: Thoughts on infants' conceptions of objects. In J. Mehler & R. Fox (Eds.), *Neonate cognition: Beyond the blooming buzzing confusion.* Hillsdale, NJ: Erlbaum.

SPELKE, E. S. (1988). Where perceiving ends and thinking begins: The apprehension of objects in infancy. In A. Yonas (Ed.), *Minnesota symposia on child psychology: Vol. 20. Perceptual development in infancy.* Hillsdale, NJ: Erlbaum.

SPELKE, E. S. (1991). Physical knowledge in infancy: Reflections on Piaget's theory. In S. Carey & R. Gelman (Eds.), *The epigenesis of mind.* Hillsdale, NJ: Erlbaum.

SPELKE, E. S., & HERMER, L. (1996). Early cognitive development: Objects and space. In R. Gelman & T. Au (Eds.), *Perceptual and cognitive development.* San Diego: Academic Press.

SPELKE, E. S., & OWSLEY, C. J. (1979). Intermodal exploration and knowledge in infancy. *Infant Behavior and Development, 2,* 13–28.

SPELKE, E. S., BREINLINGER, K., MACOMBER, J., & JACOBSON, K. (1992). Origins of knowledge. *Psychological Review, 99,* 605–632.

SPENCE, J. T. (1985). Gender identity and its implications for concepts of masculinity and feminity. In T. B. Sonderegger (Ed.), *Nebraska symposium on motivation: Psychology and gender* (Vol. 32). Lincoln: University of Nebraska Press.

SPENCE, J. T., & HELMREICH, R. L. (1978). *Masculinity and femininity: Their psychological dimensions, correlates, and antecedents.* Austin: University of Texas Press.

SPENCE, J. T., HELMREICH, R. L., & HOLAHAN, C. K. (1979). Negative and positive components of psychological masculinity and femininity and their relationships to self-reports of neurotic and acting out behaviors. *Journal of Personality and Social Psychology, 37,* 1673–1682.

SPERGEL, I. A., & CURRY, G. D. (1993). The National Youth Gang Survey: A research and development process. In A. P. Goldstein & C. R. Huff (Eds.), *The gang intervention handbook.* Champaign, IL: Research Press.

SPERGEL, I. A., CHANCE, R. I., & CURRY, G. (1990, June). *National Youth Gang Suppression and Intervention Program* (National Institute of Justice Reports, No. 222, pp. 1–4).

SPERRY, L. L., & SPERRY, D. E. (1995). Young children's presentations of self in conversational narration. In L. L. Sperry & P. A. Smiley (Eds.), *Exploring young children's concepts of self and other through conversation.* San Francisco: Jossey-Bass.

SPIEKER, S. J., & BENSLEY, L. (1994). Roles of living arrangements and grandmother social support in adolescent mothering and infant attachment. *Developmental Psychology, 30,* 102–111.

SPITZ, R. (1945). Hospitalism: An inquiry into the genesis of psychiatric conditions in early childhood. *Psychoanalytic Study of the Child, 1,* 53–74.

SPRINGER, K. (1996). Young children's understanding of a biological basis for parent-offspring relations. *Child Development, 67,* 2841–2856.

SPRINGER, K., & KEIL, F. C. (1991). Early differentiation of causal mechanisms appropriate to biological and nonbiological kinds. *Child Development, 62,* 767–781.

SPRINGER, S. P., & DEUTSCH, G. (1989). *Left brain, right brain* (3rd ed.). New York: W. H. Freeman.

SROUFE, L. A., BENNETT, C., ENGLUND, M., URBAN, J., & SHULMAN, S. (1993). The significance of gender boundaries in preadolescence: Contemporary correlates and antecedents of boundary violation and maintenance. *Child Development, 64,* 455–466.

SROUFE, L. A. (1986). Bowlby's contribution to psychoanalytic theory and developmental psychology: Attachment: Separation: Loss. *Journal of Child Psychology and Psychiatry, 27,* 841–849.

SROUFE, L. A. (1990). An organizational perspective on the self. In D. Cicchetti & M. Beeghly (Eds.), *The self in transition: Infancy to childhood.* Chicago: University of Chicago Press.

SROUFE, L. A. (1996). *Emotional development.* New York: Cambridge University Press.

STACK, D. M., & MUIR, D. W. (1992). Adult tactile stimulation during face-to-face interactions modulates five-month-olds' affect and attention. *Child Development, 63,* 1509–1525.

STAKE, J. E. (1997). Integrating expressiveness and instrumentality in real-life settings: A new perspective on the benefits of androgyny. *Sex Roles, 37,* 541–564.

STAMBAK, M., & SINCLAIR, H. (1993). *Pretend play among 3-year-olds.* Hillsdale, NJ: Erlbaum.

STANGOR, C., & RUBLE, D. N. (1987). Development of gender role knowledge and gender constancy. In L. S. Liben & M. L. Signorella (Eds.), *New directions for child development: No. 38. Children's gender schemata.* San Francisco: Jossey-Bass.

STANHOPE, R. (1989). The endocrine control of puberty. In J. M. Tanner & M. A. Preece (Eds.), *The physiology of human growth.* London: Cambridge University Press.

STANOVICH, K. E. (Ed.). (1993). The development of rationality and critical thinking [Special issue]. *Merrill-Palmer Quarterly, 39* (1).

STANOVICH, K. E. (1993). Does reading make you smarter? Literacy and the development of verbal intelligence. In H. W. Reese (Ed.), *Advances in child development and behavior* (Vol. 24). San Diego: Academic Press.

STARK, R. E. (1986). Prespeech segmental feature development. In P. Fletcher & M. Garman (Eds.), *Language acquisition: Studies in first language development* (2nd ed.). New York: Cambridge University Press.

STARKEY, P., & COOPER, R. (1980). Perception of numbers by human infants. *Science, 210,* 1033–1034.

STAUB, E. (1996). Cultural-societal roots of violence: Examples of genocidal violence and of contemporary youth violence in the United States. *American Psychologist, 51,* 117–132.

STEELE, H., STEELE, M., & FONAGY, P. (1996). Associations among attachment classifications of mothers, fathers, and their infants. *Child Development, 67,* 541–555.

STEIN, A. H., & FRIEDRICH, L. K. (1975). The impact of television on children and youth. In E. M. Hetherington (Ed.), *Review of child development research* (Vol. 5). Chicago: University of Chicago Press.

STEINBERG, L. D. (1988). Pubertal maturation and family relations: Evidence for the distancing hypothesis. In G. Adams, R. Montemayor, & T. Gullotta (Eds.), *Advances in adolescent development.* Beverly Hills, CA: Sage.

STEINBERG, L., DARLING, N. E., FLETCHER, A. C., BROWN, B. B., & DORNBUSCH, S. M. (1995). Authoritative parenting and adolescent adjustment: An ecological journey. In P. Moen, G. H. Elder, Jr., & K. Luscher (Eds.), *Examining lives in context: Perspectives on the ecology of human development.* Washington, DC: American Psychological Association.

STEINBERG, L., LAMBORN, S. D., DARLING, N., MOUNTS, N. S., & DORNBUSCH, S. M. (1994). Over-time changes in adjustment and competence among adolescents from authoritative, authoritarian, indulgent, and neglectful families. *Child Development, 65,* 754–770.

STEINER, J. E. (1979). Human facial expressions in response to taste and smell stimulation. In H. W. Reese & L. P. Lipsitt (Eds.), *Advances in child development and behavior* (Vol. 13). New York: Academic Press.

STENBERG, C. R., CAMPOS, J. J., & EMDE, R. N. (1983). The facial expression of anger in seven-month-old infants. *Child Development, 54,* 178–184.

STEPHENS, T. (1990). Blocking fetal AIDS: Immune intervention paces science. *Journal of NIH Research, 3,* 53–54.

STERN, M., & KARRAKER, K. (1989). Sex stereotyping of infants: A review of gender labeling studies. *Sex Roles, 20,* 501–522.

STERN, M., & KARRAKER, K. (1992). Modifying the prematurity stereotype in matters of premature and ill full-term infants. *Journal of Clinical Child Psychology, 21,* 76–82.

STERNBERG, R. J., & POWELL, J. S. (1983). The development of intelligence. In P. H. Mussen (Series Ed.) & J. H. Flavell & E. M. Markman (Vol. Eds.), *Handbook of child psychology: Vol. 3. Cognitive development.* New York: Wiley.

STERNBERG, R. J. (1985). *Beyond IQ: A triarchic theory of human intelligence.* New York: Cambridge University Press.

STERNBERG, R. J. (1991). Death, taxes, and bad intelligence tests. *Intelligence, 15,* 257–269.

STEVENSON, H. W., & STIGLER, J. W. (1992). *The learning gap: Why our schools are failing and what we can learn from Japanese and Chinese education.* New York: Summit Books.

STEVENSON, H. W., CHEN, C., & LEE, S. Y. (1993). Mathematics achievement of Chinese, Japanese, and American children: Ten years later. *Science, 259,* 53–58.

STEVENSON, H. W., LEE, S., CHEN, C., STIGLER, J. W., HSU, C., & KITAMURA, S. (1990). Contexts of achievement: A study of American, Chinese, and Japanese children. *Monographs of the Society for Research in Child Development, 55* (1–2, Serial No. 221).

STEVENSON, H. W., LEE S. Y., & STIGLER, J. W. (1986). Mathematics achievement of Chinese, Japanese, and American children. *Science, 231,* 693–699.

STEVENSON, M. R., & BLACK, K. N. (1988). Paternal absence and sex-role development: A meta-analysis. *Child Development, 59,* 793–814.

STEWART, S. L., & RUBIN, K. H. (1995). The social problem solving skills of anxious-withdrawn children. *Development and Psychopathology, 7,* 323–336.

STIFTER, C. A., & BRAUNGART, J. M. (1995). The regulation of negative reactivity in infancy: Function and development. *Developmental Psychology, 31,* 448–455.

STIFTER, C. A., & FOX, N. A. (1990). Infant reactivity: Physiological correlates of newborn and 5-month temperament. *Developmental Psychology, 26,* 582–588.

STIFTER, C. A., COULEHAN, C. M., & FISH, M.

(1993). Linking employment to attachment: The mediating effects of maternal separation anxiety and interactive behavior. *Child Development, 64,* 1451–1460.

STIGLER, J. W., & FERNANDEZ, C. (1995). Learning mathematics from classroom instruction: Cross-cultural and experimental perspectives. In C. A. Nelson (Ed.), *Minnesota symposia on child psychology: Vol. 28. Basic and applied perspectives on learning, cognition, and development.* Mahwah, NJ: Erlbaum.

STIPEK, D. (1992). The child at school. In M. E. Lamb & M. H. Bornstein (Eds.), *Developmental psychology: An advanced textbook* (3rd ed.). Hillsdale, NJ: Erlbaum.

STIPEK, D., & MacIVER, D. (1989). Developmental change in children's assessment of intellectual competence. *Child Development, 60,* 521–538.

STIPEK, D., & TANNATT, L. (1984). Children's judgments of their own and their peers' academic competence. *Journal of Educational Psychology, 76,* 75–84.

STIPEK, D., GRALINSKI, J. H., & KOPP, C. B. (1990). Self-concept development in the toddler years. *Developmental Psychology, 26,* 972–977.

STIPEK, D., RECCHIA, S., & McCLINTIC, S. (1992). Self-evaluation in young children. *Monographs of the Society for Research in Child Development, 57*(1, Serial No. 226).

STJERNFELDT, M., BERGLUND, K., LINDSTEN, J., & LUDVIGSSON, J. (1986). Maternal smoking during pregnancy and risk of childhood cancer. *Lancet, 1,* 1350–1352.

STOCKER, C., & DUNN, J. (1990). Sibling relationships in childhood: Links with friendships and peer relationships. *British Journal of Developmental Psychology, 8,* 227–244.

STOCKER, C. M., & MANTZ-SIMMONS, L. M. (1993). *Children's friendship and peer status: Links with family relationships, temperament, and social skills.* Unpublished manuscript.

STODDART, T., & TURIEL, E. (1985). Children's concepts of cross-gender activities. *Child Development, 56,* 1241–1252.

STOLL, C., DOTT, B., ALEMBIK, Y., & ROTH, M. (1993). Evaluation of routine prenatal ultrasound examination in detecting fetal chromosomal abnormalities in a low risk population. *Human Genetics, 91,* 37–41.

STONE, C. A., & DAY, M. C. (1978). Levels of availability of a formal operational strategy. *Child Development, 49,* 1054–1065.

STOTT, D. H. (1969). The child's hazards *in utero.* In J. G. Howells (Ed.), *Modern perspectives in international child psychiatry.* Edinburgh: Oliver & Boyd.

STRAKER, G. (1992). *Faces in the revolution.* Cape Town, South Africa: David Philip.

STRAUGHAN, R. (1986). Why act on Kohlberg's moral judgments? (Or how to reach Stage 6 and remain a bastard). In S. Modgil & C. Modgil (Eds.), *Lawrence Kohlberg: Consensus and controversy.* Philadelphia: Falmer.

STRAYER, F. F. (1980). Social ecology of the preschool peer group. In W. A. Collins (Ed.), *Minnesota symposia on child psychology: Vol. 13. Development of cognition, affect, and social relations.* Hillsdale, NJ: Erlbaum.

STRAYER, F. F., & NOEL, J. M. (1986). The prosocial and antisocial functions of preschool aggression: An ethological study of triadic conflict among young children. In C. Zahn-Waxler, E. M. Cummings, & R. Iannotti (Eds.), *Altruism and aggression: Biological and social origins.* Cambridge: Cambridge University Press.

STRAYER, F. F., & STRAYER, J. (1976). An ethological analysis of social agonism and dominance relations among preschool children. *Child Development, 47,* 980–989.

STREISSGUTH, A. P., BARR, H. M., JOHNSON, J. C., MARTIN, D. C., & KIRCHNER, G. L. (1985). Attention and distraction at age 7 years related to maternal drinking during pregnancy. *Alcoholism: Clinical and Experimental Research, 9,* 195.

STREISSGUTH, A. P., SAMPSON, P. D., & BARR, H. M. (1989). Neurobehavioral dose-response effects of prenatal alcohol exposure in humans from infancy to adulthood. *Annals of the New York Academy of Sciences, 562,* 145–158.

STUDDERT-KENNEDY, M. (1986). Sources of variability in early speech in infancy. In G. Yeni-Konshian, C. Kavanaugh, & C. Ferguson (Eds.), *Child phonology: Perception and production.* New York: Academic Press.

SUE, S., & OZAKI, S. (1990). Asian-American educational achievements: A phenomenon in search of an explanation. *American Psychologist, 45,* 913–920.

SULLIVAN, M. W. (1982). Reactivation: Priming forgotten memories in human infants. *Child Development, 53,* 516–523.

SULLIVAN, M. W., LEWIS, M., & ALESSANDRI, S. M. (1992). Cross-age stability in emotional expressions: During learning and extinction. *Developmental Psychology, 28,* 58–63.

SULS, J., & WILLS, T. A. (Eds.). (1991). *Social comparison: Contemporary theory and research.* Hillsdale, NJ: Erlbaum.

SUN, M. (1988). Anti-acne drug poses dilemma for FDA. *Science, 240,* 714–715.

SUOMI, S. J., & HARLOW, H. F. (1975). The role and reason of peer relationships in rhesus monkeys. In M. Lewis & L. A. Rosenblum (Eds.), *Friendship and peer relations.* New York: Wiley.

SUPER, C. M. (1981). Cross-cultural research on infancy. In H. C. Triandis & A. Heron (Eds.), *Handbook of cross-cultural psychology: Vol. 4. Developmental psychology.* Boston: Allyn & Bacon.

SUPER, C. M., HERRERA, M. G., & MORA, J. O. (1990). Long-term effects of food supplementation and psychosocial intervention on the physical growth of Colombian infants at risk of malnutrition. *Child Development, 61,* 29–49.

SURBER, C. F. (1982). Separable effects of motives, consequences, and presentation order on children's moral judgments. *Developmental Psychology, 18*, 257–266.

SUSMAN, E. J., INOFF-GERMAIN, G., NOTTELMANN, E. D., LORIAUX, L., CUTLER, G. B., & CHROUSOS, G. P. (1987). Hormones, emotional dispositions, and aggressive attributes in young adolescents. *Child Development, 58*, 1114–1134.

SUZUKI, L. A., & VALENCIA, R. (1997). Race-ethnicity and measured intelligence. *American Psychologist, 52*, 1103–1114.

SVARE, B. (1983). Psychobiological determinants of maternal aggressive behavior. In E. C. Simmel, M. E. Hahn, & J. K. Walters (Eds.), *Aggressive behavior: Genetic and neural approaches.* Hillsdale, NJ: Erlbaum.

SVEJDA, M. J., PANNABECKER, B. J., & EMDE, R. N. (1982). Parent-to-infant attachment: A critique of the early "bonding" model. In R. N. Emde & R. J. Harmon (Eds.), *The development of attachment and affiliative systems.* New York: Plenum.

SWAAB, D. F., GOOREN, L. J. G., & HOFMAN, M. A. (1992). The human hypothalamus in relation to gender and sexual orientation. *Progress in Brain Research, 93*, 205–219.

SWAIN, I. U., ZELAZO, P. R., & CLIFTON, R. K. (1993). Newborn infants' memory for speech sounds retained over 24 hours. *Developmental Psychology, 29*, 313–323.

SWAIN, M. (1977). Bilingualism, monolingualism, and code acquisition. In W. Mackey & T. Andersson (Eds.), *Bilingualism in early childhood.* Rowley, MA: Newbury House.

SWANSON, H. L. (1996). *Swanson Cognitive Processing Test.* Austin, TX: PRO-ED.

St. PETERS, M., FITCH, M., HUSTON, A. C., WRIGHT, J. C., & EAKINS, D. J. (1991). Television and families: What do young children watch with their parents? *Child Development, 62*, 1409–1423.

TAGER-FLUSBERG, H., & CALKINS, S. (1990). Does imitation facilitate the acquisition of grammar? Evidence from a study of autistic, Down's syndrome and normal children. *Journal of Child Language, 17*, 591–606.

TAKAHASHI, K. (1986). Examining the Strange Situation procedure with Japanese mothers and 12-month-old infants. *Developmental Psychology, 22*, 265–270.

TAKAHASHI, K. (1990). Are the key assumptions of the "Strange Situation" procedure universal? A view from Japanese research. *Human Development, 33*, 23–30.

TAMIS-LEMONDA, C. S., & BORNSTEIN, M. H. (1994). Specificity in mother–toddler language-play relations across the second year. *Developmental Psychology, 30*, 283–292.

TANGNEY, J., & FISCHER, K. (Eds.). (1995). *Self-conscious emotions: The psychology of shame, guilt, embarrassment, and pride.* New York: Guilford.

TANNER, J. M. (1963). The regulation of human growth. *Child Development, 34*, 817–847.

TANNER, J. M. (1974). Variability of growth and maturity in newborn infants. In M. Lewis & L. A. Rosenblum (Eds.), *The effect of the infant on its caregiver.* New York: Wiley.

TANNER, J. M. (1987). Issues and advances in adolescent growth and development. *Journal of Adolescent Health Care, 8*, 470–478.

TANNER, J. M. (1990). *Fetus into man: Physical growth from conception to maturity* (2nd ed.). Cambridge: Harvard University Press.

TAPPAN, M. B. (1997) Language, culture, and moral development: A Vygotskian perspective. *Developmental Review, 17*, 78–100.

TATE, D. C., REPPUCCI, N. D., & MULVEY, E. P. (1995). Violent juvenile delinquents: Treatment effectiveness and implications for future action. *American Psychologist, 50*, 777–781.

TAYLOR, H. J. (1980). *The IQ game: A methodological inquiry into the heredity-environment controversy.* New Brunswick, NJ: Rutgers University Press.

TAYLOR, M. (1996). A theory of mind perspective on social cognitive development. In R. Gelman & T. Au (Eds.), *Perceptual and cognitive development.* San Diego: Academic Press.

TAYLOR, M., CARTWRIGHT, B. S., & BOWDEN, T. (1991). Perspective taking and theory of mind: Do children predict interpretive diversity as a function of differences in observers' knowledge? *Child Development, 62*, 1334–1351.

TAYLOR, M., ESBENSEN, B. M., & BENNETT, R. T. (1994). Children's understanding of knowledge acquisition: The tendency for children to report that they have always known what they have just learned. *Child Development, 65*, 1581–1604.

TAYLOR, M. G. (1996). The development of children's beliefs about social and biological aspects of gender differences. *Child Development, 67*, 1555–1571.

TELLER, D. Y., & BORNSTEIN, M. H. (1987). Infant color vision and color perception. In P. Salapatek & L. Cohen (Eds.), *Handbook of infant perception: Vol. 1. From sensation to perception.* New York: Academic Press.

TELZROW, R., CAMPOS, J., ATWATER, S., BERTENTHAL, B., BENSON, J., & CAMPOS,. (1988). Delays and spurts in spatial cognitive development in locomotor-handicapped infants. *Infant Behavior and Development, 11*, 312.

TEO, T., BECKER, G., & EDELSTEIN, W. (1995). Variability in structured wholeness: Context factors in L. Kohlberg's data on the development of moral judgment. *Merrill-Palmer Quarterly, 41*, 381–393.

TERMAN, L. M. (1925). *Genetic studies of genius: Vol. 1. Mental and physical traits of a thousand gifted children.* Stanford, CA: Stanford University Press.

TERRY, R., & COIE, J. D. (1991). A comparison of methods for defining sociometric status among children. *Developmental Psychology, 27*, 867–880.

TESSER, A. (1984). Self-evaluation maintenance processes: Implications for relationships and for development. In J. C. Masters & K. Yarkin-Levin (Eds.), *Boundary areas in social and developmental psychology.* New York: Academic Press.

TETI, D. M. (1992). Sibling interaction. In V. B. Van Hasselt & M. Hersen (Eds.), *Handbook of social development.* New York: Plenum.

THARP, R. G. (1989). Psychocultural variables and constants: Effects on teaching and learning in schools. *American Psychologist, 44*, 349–359.

THELEN, E. (1994). Three-month-old infants can learn task-specific patterns of interlimb coordination. *Psychological Science, 5*, 280–285.

THELEN, E. (1995). Motor development: A new synthesis: *American Psychologist, 50*, 79–95.

THELEN, E., & ADOLPH, K. E. (1992). Arnold L. Gesell: The paradox of nature and nurture. *Developmental Psychology, 28*, 368–380.

THELEN, E., & FISHER, D. M. (1982). Newborn stepping: An explanation for a "disappearing reflex." *Developmental Psychology, 18*, 760–775.

THELEN, E., & FISHER, D. M. (1983). The organization of spontaneous leg movements in newborn infants. *Journal of Motor Behavior, 15*, 353–377.

THELEN, E., & SMITH, L. B. (1998). Dynamic systems theories. In W. Damon (Ed.), *Handbook of child psychology: Vol. 1. Theoretical models of human development.* New York: Wiley.

THELEN, E., CORBETTA, D., & SPENCER, J. (1996). The development of reaching during the first year: The role of movement speed. *Journal of Experimental Psychology: Human Perception and Performance, 22*, 1059–1076.

THOMA, S. J. (1986). Estimating gender differences in the comprehension and preference of moral issues. *Developmental Review, 6*, 165–180.

THOMAN, E. B. (1990). Sleeping and waking states in infants: A functional perspective. *Neuroscience and Behavioral Reviews, 14*, 93–107.

THOMAN, E. B. (1993). Obligation and option in the premature nursery. *Developmental Review, 13*, 1–30.

THOMAN, E. B., INGERSOLL, E. W., & ACEBO, C. (1991). Premature infants seek rhythmic stimulation, and the experience facilitates neurobehavioral development. *Journal of Developmental and Behavioral Pediatrics, 12*, 11–18.

THOMAS, A., & CHESS, S. (1977). *Temperament and development.* New York: Bruner/Mazel.

THOMAS, A., & CHESS, S. (1984). Genesis and evaluation of behavioral disorder: From infancy to early adult life. *American Journal of Psychiatry, 141*, 1–9.

THOMAS, A., & CHESS, S. (1986). The New York Longitudinal Study: From infancy to early adult life. In R. Plomin & J. Dunn (Eds.), *The study of temperament: Changes, continuities and challenges.* Hillsdale, NJ: Erlbaum.

THOMAS, A., CHESS, S., & BIRCH, H. G. (1968). *Temperament and behavior disorders in children.* New York: New York University Press.

THOMAS, H. (1983). Familial correlational analyses, sex differences, and the X-linked gene hypothesis. *Psychological Bulletin, 93,* 427–440.

THOMAS, H. (1993). A theory explaining sex differences in high mathematical ability has been around for some time. *Behavioral and Brain Sciences, 16,* 187–215.

THOMAS, R. M. (1979). *Comparing theories of child development.* Belmont, CA: Wadsworth.

THOMPSON, C. P., SKOWRONSKI, J. J., LARSEN, S. F., & BETZ, A. L. (1996). *Autobiographical memory: Remembering what and remembering when.* Mahwah, NJ: Erlbaum.

THOMPSON, R. A. (1998). Early sociopersonality development. In W. Damon (Ed.), *Handbook of child psychology: Vol. 3. Social, emotional, and personality development.* New York: Wiley.

THOMPSON, R. A., & LIMBER, S. (1990). "Social anxiety" in infancy: Stranger wariness and separation distress. In H. Leitenberg (Ed.), *Handbook of social and evaluation anxiety.* New York: Plenum.

THOMPSON, R. A., CONNELL, J. P., & BRIDGES, L. J. (1988). Temperament, emotion, and social interactive behavior in the Strange Situation: A component process analysis of attachment system functioning. *Child Development, 59,* 1102–1110.

THOMPSON, R. A., FLOOD, M. F., & LUNDQUIST, L. (1995). Emotion regulation: Its relations to attachment and developmental psychopathology. In D. Cicchetti & S. L. Toth (Eds.), *Emotion, cognition, and representation. Rochester Symposium on Developmental Psychopathology* (Vol. 6). Rochester, NY: University of Rochester Press.

THOMPSON, T. L., & ZERBINOS, E. (1995). Gender roles in animated cartoons: Has the picture changed in 20 years? *Sex Roles, 32,* 651–674.

THOMPSON, T. L., & ZERBINOS, E. (1997). Television cartoons: Do children notice it's a boy's world? *Sex Roles, 37,* 415–432.

THOMPSON, W. R., & GRUSEC, J. E. (1970). Studies of early experience. In P. H. Mussen (Ed.), *Carmichael's manual of child psychology* (3rd ed., Vol. 1). New York: Wiley.

THOMSON, J. R., & CHAPMAN, R. S. (1977). Who is "Daddy" revisited: The status of two-year-olds' over-extended words in use and comprehension. *Journal of Child Language, 4,* 359–375.

THORNDIKE, R. L., HAGEN, E. P., & SATTLER, J. M. (1986). *Stanford–Binet Intelligence Scale* (4th ed.). Chicago: Riverside Publishing Company.

THORNE, B. (1986). Girls and boys together . . . but mostly apart: Gender arrange-

ments in elementary schools. In W. W. Hartup & Z. Rubin (Eds.), *Relationships and development.* Hillsdale, NJ: Erlbaum.

THURSTONE, L. L. (1938). *Primary mental abilities.* Chicago: University of Chicago Press.

THURSTONE, L. L., & THURSTONE, T. G. (1962). *SRA Primary Mental Abilities.* Chicago: Science Research Associates.

TIESZEN, H. R. (1979). Children's social behavior in a Korean preschool. *Journal of Korean Home Economics Association, 17,* 71–84.

TIETJEN, A. M., & WALKER, L. J. (1985). Moral reasoning and leadership among men in Papua New Guinea society. *Developmental Psychology, 21,* 982–992.

TINBERGEN, N. (1973). *The animal in its world: Explorations of an ethologist, 1932–1972* (Vols. 1 and 2). Cambridge: Harvard University Press.

TINSLEY, B. J., & PARKE, R. D. (1988). The role of grandfathers in the context of the family. In P. Bronstein & C. P. Cowan (Eds.), *Fatherhood today: Men's changing roles in the family.* New York: Wiley.

TISAK, M. S. (1995). Domains of social reasoning and beyond. In R. Vasta (Ed.), *Annals of child development* (Vol. 11). London: Kingsley.

TISAK, M. S., & TURIEL, E. (1988). Variation in seriousness of transgressions and children's immoral and conventional concepts. *Developmental Psychology, 24,* 352–357.

TITTLE, C. K. (1986). Gender research in education. *American Psychologist, 41,* 1161–1168.

TOBEY, A. E., & GOODMAN, G. S. (1992). Children's eyewitness memory: Effects of participation and forensic context. *Child Abuse and Neglect, 16,* 779–796.

TODA, S., & FOGEL, A. (1993). Infant response to the still-face situation at 3 and 6 months. *Developmental Psychology, 29,* 532–538.

TOMADA, G., & SCHNEIDER, B. H. (1997). Relational aggression, gender, and peer acceptance: Invariance across culture, stability over time, and concordance among informants. *Developmental Psychology, 33,* 601–609.

TOMASELLO, M. (1996). Piagetian and Vygotskian approaches to language acquisition. *Human Development, 39,* 269–276.

TOMASELLO, M., & FARRAR, M. J. (1986). Joint attention and early language. *Child Development, 57,* 1454–1463.

TOMASELLO, M., & MERRIMAN, W. E. (Eds.). (1995). *Beyond names for things: Young children's acquisition of verbs.* Hillsdale, NJ: Erlbaum.

TOMASELLO, M., CONTI-RAMSDEN, G., & EWERT, B. (1990). Young children's conversations with their mothers and fathers: Differences in breakdown and repair. *Journal of Child Language, 17,* 115–130.

TORRANCE, E. P. (1970). Influence of dyadic interaction on creative functioning. *Psychological Reports, 26,* 391–394.

TOUCHETTE, N. (1990). Evolutions: Fertilization. *Journal of NIH Research, 2,* 94–97.

TRACY, D. M. (1987). Toys, spatial ability, and science and mathematics achievement: Are they related? *Sex Roles, 17,* 115–138.

TRACY, R. L., & AINSWORTH, M. D. S. (1981). Maternal affectionate behavior and infant–mother attachment patterns. *Child Development, 52,* 1341–1343.

TRAUTNER, H. M. (1992). The development of sex-typing in children: A longitudinal analysis. *German Journal of Psychology, 16,* 183–199.

TRAVERS, J. R., & LIGHT, R. J. (Eds.). (1982). *Learning from experience: Evaluating early childhood demonstration programs.* Washington, DC: National Academy Press.

TREHUB, S. E. (1976). The discrimination of foreign speech contrasts by infants and adults. *Child Development, 47,* 466–472.

TREHUB, S. E., & HENDERSON, J. (1994, July). Caregivers' songs and their effect on infant listeners. *Proceedings of the Meeting of the International Conference for Music Perception and Cognition.* Liege, Belgium.

TREHUB, S. E., & SCHELLENBERG, E. G. (1995). Music: Its relevance to infants. In R. Vasta (Ed.), *Annals of child development* (Vol. 11). London: Kingsley.

TREHUB, S. E., & SCHNEIDER, B. A. (1983). Recent advances in the behavioral study of infant audition. In S. E. Gerber & G. T. Mencher (Eds.), *Development of auditory behavior.* New York: Grune & Stratton.

TREHUB, S. E., SCHNEIDER, B. A., MORRONGIELLO, B. A., & THORPE, L. A. (1988). Auditory sensitivity in school-age children. *Journal of Experimental Child Psychology, 46,* 273–285.

TREHUB, S. E., THORPE, L. A., & COHEN, A. J. (1991, April). *Infants' auditory processing of numerical information.* Paper presented at the meeting of the Society for Research in Child Development, Seattle.

TREXLER, R. C. (1973). The foundlings of Florence, 1395–1455. *History of Childhood Quarterly, 1,* 259–284.

TRICKETT, P. K., & McBRIDE-CHANG, C. (1995). The developmental impact of different forms of child abuse and neglect. *Developmental Review, 15,* 311–337.

TRIVERS, R. L. (1971). The evolution of reciprocal altruism. *Quarterly Review of Biology, 46,* 35–57.

TRIVERS, R. L. (1983). The evolution of cooperation. In D. L. Bridgeman (Ed.), *The nature of prosocial development.* New York: Academic Press.

TRONICK, E. Z. (1989). Emotions and emotional communication in infants. *American Psychologist, 44,* 112–119.

TSUSHIMA, T., TAKIZAWA, O., SASAKI, M., SIRAKI, S., NUSHI, K., KOHNO, M., MENYUK, P., & BEST, C. (1994). *Discrimination of English /r-l/ and /w-y/ by Japanese infants at 6–12 months: Language specific developmental changes in speech perception abilities.* Paper presented at the International Conference on Spoken Language Processing, 4, Yokohama, Japan.

TUBMAN, J. G., LERNER, R. M., LERNER, J. V., & VON EYE, A. (1992). Temperament and adjustment in young adulthood: A 15-year longitudinal analysis. *American Journal of Orthopsychiatry, 62,* 564–574.

TUDGE, J., & ROGOFF, B. (1989). Peer influences on cognitive development: Piagetian and Vygotskian perspectives. In M. H. Bornstein & J. S. Bruner (Eds.), *Interaction in human development.* Hillsdale, NJ: Erlbaum.

TURIEL, E. (1966). An experimental test of the sequentiality of developmental stages in the child's moral judgments. *Journal of Personality and Social Psychology, 3,* 611–618.

TURIEL, E. (1987). Potential relations between the development of social reasoning and childhood aggression. In D. H. Crowell, I. M. Evans, & C. R. O'Donnell (Eds.), *Childhood aggression and violence: Sources of influence, prevention, and control.* New York: Plenum.

TURIEL, E. (1998). The development of morality. In W. Damon (Ed.), *Handbook of child psychology: Vol. 3. Social, emotional, and personality development.* New York: Wiley.

TURIEL, E., & WAINRYB, C. (1994). Social reasoning and the varieties of social experiences in cultural contexts. In H. W. Reese (Ed.), *Advances in child development and behavior* (Vol. 25). San Diego: Academic Press.

TURIEL, E., HILDEBRANDT, C., & WAINRYB, C. (1991). Judging social issues. *Monograph of the Society for Research in Child Development, 56*(Serial No. 224).

TURIEL, E., KILLEN, M., & HELWIG, C. C. (1987). Morality: Its structure, functions, and vagaries. In J. Kagan & S. Lamb (Eds.), *The emergence of moral concepts in young children.* Chicago: University of Chicago Press.

TURKHEIMER, E. (1991). Individual and group differences in adoption studies of IQ. *Psychological Bulletin, 110,* 392–405.

TURNER, P. J., & GERVAI, J. (1995). A multidimensional study of gender typing in preschool children and their parents: Personality, attitudes, preferences, behavior, and cultural differences. *Developmental Psychology, 31,* 759–772.

TURNER-BOWKER, D. M. (1996). Gender stereotyped descriptors in children's picture books: Does "Curious Jane" exist in the literature? *Sex Roles, 35,* 461–488.

U. S. BUREAU OF THE CENSUS. (1990). *Current population reports.* Washington, DC: U.S. Government Printing Office.

UMBEL, V. M., PEARSON, B. Z., FERNANDEZ, M. C., & OLLER, D. K. (1992). Measuring bilingual children's receptive vocabularies. *Child Development, 63,* 1012–1020.

UNDERWOOD, B., & MOORE, B. (1982). Perspective-taking and altruism. *Psychological Bulletin, 91,* 143–173.

UNDERWOOD, M. K., COIE, J. D., & HERBSMAN, C. R. (1992). Display rules for anger and aggression in school-age children. *Child Development, 63,* 366–380.

UNGER, D., & COOLEY, M. (1992). Partner and grandmother contact in black and white teen parent families. *Journal of Adolescent Health, 13,* 546–552.

UNGERER, J. A., DOLBY, R., WATERS, B., BARNETT, B., KEIK, N., & LEWIN, V. (1990). The early development of empathy: Self-regulation and individual differences in the first year. *Motivation and Emotion, 14,* 93–106.

URBAIN, E. S., & KENDELL, P. C. (1980). Review of social-cognitive problem-solving interventions with children. *Psychological Bulletin, 88,* 109–143.

URBERG, K. A., DEGIRMENCIOUGLU, S. M., & PILGRIM, C. (1997). Close friend and group influence on adolescent cigarette smoking and alcohol use. *Developmental Psychology, 33,* 834–844.

UZGIRIS, I. C., & HUNT, J. McV. (1975). *Assessment in infancy: Ordinal scales of psychological development.* Urbana: University of Illinois Press.

VALDEZ-MENCHACA, M. C., & WHITEHURST, G. J. (1992). Accelerating language development through picture book reading: A systematic extension to Mexican day-care. *Developmental Psychology, 28,* 1106–1114.

VALIAN, V. (1996). *Parental replies: Linguistic status and didactic role.* Cambridge: MIT Press.

VALSINER, J. (1998). The development of the concept of development: Historical and epistemological perspectives. In W. Damon (Ed.), *Handbook of child psychology: Vol. 1. Theoretical models of human development.* New York: Wiley.

VAN DEN BOOM, D. C. (1994). The influence of temperament and mothering on attachment and exploration: An experimental manipulation of sensitive responsiveness among lower-class mothers with irritable infants. *Child Development, 65,* 1457–1477.

VAN DEN BOOM, D. C. (1995). Do first-year intervention effects endure? Follow-up during toddlerhood of a sample of Dutch irritable infants. *Child Development, 66,* 1798–1816.

Van der VEER, R., & VALSINER, J. (1988). Lev Vygotsky and Pierre Janet: On the origin of the concept of sociogenesis. *Developmental Review, 8,* 52–65.

VAN GIFFEN, K., & HAITH, M. M. (1984). Infant visual response to gestalt geometric forms. *Infant Behavior and Development, 7,* 335–346.

VAN IJZENDOORN, M. H. (1992). Intergenerational transmission of parenting: A review of studies in nonclinical populations. *Developmental Review, 12,* 76–99.

VAN IJZENDOORN, M. H. (1995). Associations between adult attachment representations and parent-child attachment, parent responsiveness, and clinical status: A meta-analysis on the predictive validity of the Adult Attachment Interview. *Psychological Bulletin, 117,* 387–403.

VAN IJZENDOORN, M. H., & De WOLFF, M. S. (1997). In search of the absent father—Meta-analyses of infant-father attachment: A rejoinder to our discussants. *Child Development, 68,* 604–609.

VAN IJZENDOORN, M. H., & KROONENBERG, P. M. (1988). Cross-cultural patterns of attachment: A meta-analysis of the Strange Situation. *Child Development, 59,* 147–156.

VAN IJZENDOORN, M. H., GOLDBERG, S., KROONENBERG, P. M., & FRENKEL, O. J. (1992). The relative effects of maternal and child problems on the quality of attachment: A meta-analysis of attachment in clinical samples. *Child Development, 63,* 840–858.

VAN IJZENDOORN, M. H., JUFFER, F., & DUYVESTEYN, M. G. C. (1995). Breaking the intergenerational cycle of insecure attachment: A review of the effects of attachment-based interventions on maternal sensitivity and infant security. *Journal of Child Psychology and Psychiatry, 36,* 225–248.

VAN LOOSBROEK, E., & SMITSMAN, A. W. (1990). Visual perception of numerosity in infancy. *Developmental Psychology, 26,* 916–922.

VAN TUINEN, I., & WOLFE, S. M. (1993). *Unnecessary cesarean sections: Halting a national epidemic.* Washington, DC: Public Citizens' Health Research Group.

VANDELL, D. L., MINNET, A. M., JOHNSON, B. S., & SANTROCK, J. W. (1990). *Siblings and friends: Experiences of school-aged children.* Unpublished manuscript, University of Texas at Dallas.

VANDELL, D. L., WILSON, K. S., & BUCHANAN, N. R. (1980). Peer interaction in the first year of life: An examination of its structure, content, and sensitivity to toys. *Child Development, 51,* 481–488.

VARGAS, E. A. (1986). Intraverbal behavior. In P. N. Chase & L. J. Parrott (Eds.), *Psychological aspects of language: The West Virginia Lectures.* Springfield, IL: Thomas.

VASTA, R. (1982a). Child study: Looking toward the eighties. In R. Vasta (Ed.), *Strategies and techniques of child study.* New York: Academic Press.

VASTA, R. (Ed.). (1982b). *Strategies and techniques of child study.* New York: Academic Press.

VASTA, R., & GREEN, P. J. (1982). Differential cue utilization by males and females in pattern copying. *Child Development, 53,* 1102–1105.

VASTA, R., & LIBEN, L. S. (1996). The water-level task: An intriguing puzzle. *Current Directions in Psychological Science, 5,* 171–177.

VAUGHN, B. E., & WATERS, E. (1990). Attachment behavior at home and in the laboratory: Q-sort observations and Strange Situation classifications of one-year-olds. *Child Development, 61,* 1965–1990.

VAUGHN, B. E., BRADLEY, C. F., JOFFE, L. S., SEIFER, R., & BARGLOW, P. (1987). Maternal characteristics measured prenatally are predictive of ratings of temperamental "difficulty" on the Carey Infant Temperament Questionnaire. *Developmental Psychology, 23,* 152–161.

VAUGHN, B. E., KOPP, C. B., & KRAKOW, J. B. (1984). The emergence and consolidation of self-control from eighteen to thirty months of age: Normative trends and individual differences. *Child Development, 55,* 990–1004.

VAUGHN, V. C., McKAY, J. R., & BEHRMAN, R. E. (1984). *Nelson textbook of pediatrics* (12th ed.). Philadelphia: Saunders.

VEDAM, S., & KOLODJII, Y. (1995). Guidelines for client selection in the home birth midwifery practice. *Journal of Nurse-Midwifery, 40,* 508–521.

VENTURA, S. J. (1989). Trends and variations in first births to older women, United States, 1970–1986 (Vital and Health Statistics Series 21, No. 47). Bethesda, MD: National Center for Health Statistics.

VERNON, P. A. (1993). *Biological approaches to the study of human intelligence.* Norwood, NJ: Ablex.

VERSCHUEREN, K., MARCOEN, A., & SCHOEFS, V. (1996). The internal working model of the self, attachment, and competence in five-year-olds. *Child Development, 67,* 2493–2511.

VESPO, J. E., & CAPLAN, M. (1993). Preschoolers' differential conflict behavior with friends and acquaintances. *Early Education and Development, 4,* 45–58.

VIETZE, P. M., & VAUGHAN, H. G. (1988). *Early identification of infants with developmental disabilities.* Philadelphia: Grune & Stratton.

VIHMAN, M. M. (1985). Language differentiation by the bilingual infant. *Journal of Child Language, 12,* 297–324.

VIHMAN, M. M., & MILLER, R. (1988). Words and babble at the threshold of language acquisition. In M. D. Smith & J. L. Locke (Eds.), *The emergent lexicon.* Orlando, FL: Academic Press.

VIHMAN, M. M., FERGUSON, C. A., & ELBERT, M. (1986). Phonological development from babbling to speech: Common tendencies and individual differences. *Applied Psycholinguistics, 7,* 3–40.

VINCENT, K. R. (1991). Black/White IQ differences: Does age make the difference? *Journal of Clinical Psychology, 47,* 266–270.

VINDEN, P. G. (1996). Junin Quechua children's understanding of mind. *Child Development, 67,* 1707–1716.

VOCATE, D. R. (1987). *The theory of A. R. Luria.* Hillsdale, NJ: Erlbaum.

VOLLING, B. L., & BELSKY, J. (1991). Multiple determinants of father involvement during infancy in dual-earner and single-earner families. *Journal of Marriage and the Family, 53,* 461–474.

VOLLING, B. L., YOUNGBLADE, L. M., & BELSKY, J. (1997). Young children's social relationships with siblings and friends. *American Journal of Orthopsychiatry, 67,* 102–111.

VOLTERRA, V., & TAESCHNER, T. (1978). The acquisition and development of language by bilingual children. *Journal of Child Language, 5,* 311–326.

VON HOFSTEN, C. (1982). Eye-hand coordination in the newborn. *Developmental Psychology, 18,* 450–461.

VON SENDEN, M. (1960). *Space and sight.* New York: Free Press.

VOORHEES, C. V., & MOLLNOW, E. (1987). Behavioral teratogenesis: Long-term influences on behavior from early exposure to environmental agents. In J. D. Osofsky (Ed.), *Handbook of infant development* (2nd ed.). New York: Wiley.

VOSNIADOU, S., & BREWER, W. F. (1992). Mental models of the earth: A study of conceptual change in childhood. *Cognitive Psychology, 24,* 535–585.

VOSNIADOU, S., & BREWER, W. F. (1994). Mental models of the day/night cycle. *Cognitive Science, 18,* 123–183.

VOYER, D., VOYER, S., & BRYDEN, M. P. (1995). Magnitude of sex differences in spatial abilities: A meta-analysis and consideration of critical variables. *Psychological Bulletin, 117,* 250–270.

VUCHINICH, S., BANK, L., & PATTERSON, G. R. (1992). Parenting, peers, and the stability of antisocial behavior in preadolescent boys. *Developmental Psychology, 28,* 510–521.

VURPILLOT, E. (1968). The development of scanning strategies and their relation to visual differentiation. *Journal of Experimental Child Psychology, 6,* 632–650.

VURPILLOT, E., & BALL, W. A. (1979). The concept of identity and children's selective attention. In G. A. Hale & M. Lewis (Eds.), *Attention and cognitive development.* New York: Plenum.

VYGOTSKY, L. S. (1962). *Thought and language.* Cambridge: MIT Press. (Original work published 1934).

VYGOTSKY, L. S. (1978). *Mind in society: The development of higher psychological processes.* Cambridge: Harvard University Press.

VYGOTSKY, L. S. (1987). *The collected works of L. S. Vygotsky: Vol. 1. Problems of general psychology.* New York: Plenum.

WAAS, G. A. (1988). Social attributional biases of peer-rejected and aggressive children. *Child Development, 59,* 969–975.

WACHS, T. D. (1988). Relevance of physical environment influences for toddler temperament. *Infant Behavior and Development, 11,* 431–445.

WACHS, T. D. (1992). *The nature of nurture.* Newbury Park, CA: Sage.

WACHS, T. D. (1994). Fit, context, and the transition between temperament and personality. In C. F. Halverson, Jr., G. A. Kohnstamm, & R. P. Martin (Eds.), *The developing structure of*

temperament and personality from infancy to adulthood. Hillsdale, NJ: Erlbaum.

WAGHORN, L., & SULLIVAN, E. V. (1970). The exploration of transition rules in conservation of quantity (substance) using film mediated modeling. *Acta Psychologica, 32,* 65–80.

WAGNER, B. M., & PHILLIPS, D. A. (1992). Beyond beliefs: Parent and child behaviors and children's perceived academic competence. *Child Development, 63,* 1380–1391.

WAGNER, R. K., & McBRIDE-CHANG, C. (1996). The development of reading-related phonological processing abilities. In R. Vasta (Ed.), *Annals of child development* (Vol. 12). London: Kingsley.

WAINRYB, C. (1993). The application of moral judgments to other cultures: Relativism and universality. *Child Development, 64,* 924–933.

WALDMAN, I. D. (1996). Aggressive boys' hostile perceptual and response biases: The role of attention and impulsivity. *Child Development, 67,* 1015–1033.

WALDMAN, I. D., WEINBERG, R. A., & SCARR, S. (1994). Racial-group differences in IQ in the Minnesota Transracial Adoption Study: A reply to Levin and Lynn. *Intelligence, 19,* 29–44.

WALDROP, M. F., & HALVERSON, C. F., JR. (1975). Intensive and extensive peer behavior: Longitudinal and cross-sectional analyses. *Child Development, 46,* 19–26.

WALKER, A. S. (1982). Intermodal perception of expressive behaviors by human infants. *Journal of Experimental Child Psychology, 33,* 514–535.

WALKER, L. J. (1980). Cognitive and perspective-taking prerequisites for moral development. *Child Development, 51,* 131–139.

WALKER, L. J. (1983). Sources of cognitive conflict for stage transition in moral development. *Developmental Psychology, 19,* 103–110.

WALKER, L. J. (1986). Cognitive processes in moral development. In G. L. Sapp (Ed.), *Handbook of moral development: Models, processes, techniques, and research.* Birmingham, AL: Religious Education Press.

WALKER, L. J. (1988). The development of moral reasoning. In R. Vasta (Ed.), *Annals of child development* (Vol. 5). Greenwich, CT: JAI Press.

WALKER, L. J. (1989). A longitudinal study of moral reasoning. *Child Development, 60,* 157–166.

WALKER, L. J. (1991). Sex differences in moral reasoning. In W. M. Kurtines & J. L. Gewirtz (Eds.), *Handbook of moral behavior and development: Vol. 2. Research.* Hillsdale, NJ: Erlbaum.

WALKER, L. J. (1995). Sexism in Kohlberg's moral psychology? In W. M. Kurtines & J. L. Gewirtz (Eds.), *Moral development: An introduction.* Needham Heights, MA: Allyn & Bacon.

WALKER, L. J., & RICHARDS, B. S. (1979). Stimulating transitions in moral reasoning as a function of stage of cognitive development. *Developmental Psychology, 15,* 95–103.

WALKER, L. J., & TAYLOR, J. H. (1991a). Family interactions and the development of moral reasoning. *Child Development, 62,* 264–283.

WALKER, L. J., & TAYLOR, J. H. (1991b). Stage transitions in moral reasoning: A longitudinal study of developmental processes. *Developmental Psychology, 27,* 330–337.

WALKER, L. J., DeVRIES, B., & BICHARD, S. L. (1984). The hierarchical nature of stages of moral development. *Developmental Psychology, 20,* 960–966.

WALKER, L. J., DeVRIES, B., & TREVARTHEN, S. D. (1987). Moral stages and moral orientations in real-life and hypothetical dilemmas. *Child Development, 58,* 842–858.

WALKER-ANDREWS, A. S. (1997). Infants' perception of expressive behaviors: Differentiation of multimodal information. *Psychological Bulletin, 121,* 437–456.

WALKER-ANDREWS, A. S., BAHRICK, L. E., RAGLIONI, S. S., & DIAZ, I. (1991). Infants' bimodal perception of gender. *Ecological Psychology, 3,* 55–75.

WALLACH, L., WALL, A. J., & ANDERSON, L. (1967). Number conservation: The role of reversibility, addition-subtraction, and misleading perceptual cues. *Child Development, 38,* 425–442.

WALLER, N. G., KOJETIN, B. A., BOUCHARD, T. J., JR., LYKKEN, D. T., & TELLEGEN, A. (1990). Genetic and environmental influences on religious interests, attitudes, and values: A study of twins reared apart and together. *Psychological Science, 1,* 138–142.

WALLERSTEIN, J. S., CORBIN, S. B., & LEWIS, J. M. (1988). Children of divorce: A 10-year study. In E. M. Hetherington & J. D. Arasteh (Eds.), *Impact of divorce, single parenting, and stepparenting on children.* Hillsdale, NJ: Erlbaum.

WALTON, G. E., BOWER, N. J., & BOWER, T. G. (1992). Recognition of familiar faces by newborns. *Infant Behavior and Development, 15,* 265–269.

WARD, M. J., & CARLSON, E. A. (1995). Associations among adult attachment representations, maternal sensitivity, and infant-mother attachment in a sample of adolescent mothers. *Child Development, 66,* 69–79.

WARK, G. R., & KREBS, D. L. (1996). Gender and dilemma differences in real-life moral judgment. *Developmental Psychology, 32,* 220–230.

WARKANY, J. (1977). History of teratology. In J. G. Wilson & F. C. Fraser (Eds.), *Handbook of teratology: Vol. 1. General principles and etiology.* New York: Plenum.

WARKANY, J. (1981). Prevention of congenital malformations. *Teratology, 23,* 175–189.

WARREN, K. R., & BAST, R. J. (1988). Alcohol-related birth defects: An update. *Public Health Reports, 103,* 638–642.

WARREN-LEUBECKER, A., & BOHANNON, J. N. (1989). Pragmatics: Language in social con-texts. In J. B. Gleason (Ed.), *The development of language* (2nd ed.). Columbus, OH: Chas E. Merrill.

WARTNER, U. G., GROSSMANN, K., FREMMER-BOMBIK, E., & SUESS, G. (1994). Attachment patterns at age six in south Germany: Predictability from infancy and implications for preschool behavior. *Child Development, 65,* 1014–1027.

WASHINGTON, J., MINDE, K., & GOLDBERG, S. (1986). Temperament in premature infants: Style and stability. *Journal of the American Academy of Child Psychiatry, 25,* 493–502.

WASSERMAN, G. A., & LEWIS, M. (1985). Infant sex differences: Ecological effects. *Sex Roles, 12,* 665–675.

WASSERMAN, P. M. (1988). Fertilization in mammals. *Scientific American, 259,* 78–84.

WASZ-HOCKERT, O., MICHELSSON, K., & LIND, J. (1985). Twenty-five years of Scandinavian cry research. In B. M. Lester & C. Z. Boukydis (Eds.), *Infant crying: Theoretical and research perspectives.* New York. Plenum.

WATERS, E. (1995). The Attachment Q-Set (Version 3.0) (Appendix A). In E. Waters, B. E. Vaughn, G. Posada, & K. Kondo-Ikemura (Eds.), Caregiving, cultural, and cognitive perspectives on secure-base behavior and working models. *Monographs of the Society for Research in Child Development, 60*(2–3, Serial No. 244).

WATERS, E., & DEANE, K. E. (1985). Defining and assessing individual differences in attachment relationships: Q-methodology and the organization of behavior in infancy and early childhood. In I. Bretherton & E. Waters (Eds.), Growing points of attachment theory and research. *Monographs of the Society for Research in Child Development, 50*(1–2, Serial No. 209).

WATERS, E., VAUGHN, B. E., POSADA, G., & KONDO-IKEMURA, K. (Eds.). (1995). Caregiving, cultural, and cognitive perspectives on secure-base behavior and working models. *Monographs of the Society for Research in Child Development, 60*(2–3, Serial No. 244).

WATERS, H. S., & SCHREIBER, L. L. (1991). Sex differences in elaborative strategies: A developmental analysis. *Journal of Experimental Child Psychology, 52,* 319–335.

WATERS, H. S., & TINSLEY, V. S. (1982). The development of verbal self-regulation: Relationships between language, cognition, and behavior. In S. Kuczaj (Ed.), *Language development: Language, cognition, and culture.* Hillsdale, NJ: Erlbaum.

WATERS, H. S. (1981). Organization strategies in memory for prose: A developmental analysis. *Journal of Experimental Child Psychology, 32,* 223–246.

WATSON, J. B., & RAYNER, R. (1920). Conditioned emotional reactions. *Journal of Experimental Psychology, 3,* 1–14.

WATSON, J. D. (1968). *The double helix: A personal account of the discovery of the structure of DNA.* New York: Atheneum.

WATSON, J. D. (1990). The Human Genome Project: Past, present, and future. *Science, 248,* 44–49.

WATSON, J. D., & CRICK, F. H. C. (1953). Molecular structure of nucleic acid: A structure for deoxyribose nucleic acid. *Nature, 171,* 737–738.

WAXMAN, S. R. (1990). Linguistic biases and the establishment of conceptual hierarchies. *Cognitive Development, 5,* 123–150.

WECHSLER, D. (1989). *Wechsler Preschool and Primary Scale of Intelligence—Revised.* New York: The Psychological Corporation.

WECHSLER, D. (1991). *Wechsler Intelligence Scale for Children—Third Edition.* New York: The Psychological Corporation.

WEGMAN, M. E. (1994). Annual summary of vital statistics—1993. *Pediatrics, 94,* 792–803.

WEINRAUB, M., & BROWN, L. M. (1983). The development of sex-role stereotypes in children: Crushing realities. In V. Franks & E. D. Rothblum (Eds.), *The stereotyping of women: Its effects on mental health.* New York: Springer.

WEINRAUB, M., & JAEGER, E. (1990). The timing of mothers' return to the workplace: Effects on the developing mother–infant relationship. In J. S. Hyde & M. J. Essex (Eds.), *Parental leave and child care: Setting a research and policy agenda.* Philadelphia: Temple University Press.

WEINRAUB, M., CLEMENS, L. P., SOCKLOFF, A., ETHRIDGE, T., GRACELY, E., & MYERS, B. (1984). The development of sex role stereotypes in the third year: Relationships to gender labeling, gender identity, sex-typed toy preference, and family characteristics. *Child Development, 55,* 1493–1503.

WEISNER, T. S., & EIDUSON, B. T. (1986). Children of the '60's as parents. *Psychology Today, 20,* 60–66.

WEISNER, T. S., & WILSON-MITCHELL, J. E. (1990). Nonconventional family life styles and sex typing in six-year-olds. *Child Development, 61,* 1915–1933.

WEISS, B., DODGE, K. A., BATES, J. E., & PETTIT, G. S. (1992). Some consequences of early harsh discipline: Child aggression and a maladaptive social information processing style. *Child Development, 63,* 1321–1335.

WEISS, M. G., & MILLER, P. H. (1983). Young children's understanding of displaced aggression. *Journal of Experimental Child Psychology, 35,* 529–539.

WEISSBERG, R. P. (1985). Designing effective social problem-solving programs for the classroom. In B. H. Schneider, K. H. Rubin, & J. E. Ledingham (Eds.), *Children's peer relations: Issues in assessment and intervention.* New York: Springer-Verlag.

WEISZ, J. R., CHAIYASIT, W., WEISS, B., EASTMAN, K. L., & JACKSON, E. W. (1995). A multimethod study of problem behavior among Thai and American children in school: Teacher reports versus direct observations. *Child Development, 66,* 402–415.

WEISZ, J. R., SIGMAN, M., WEISS, B., & MOSK, J. (1993). Parent reports of behavioral and emotional problems among children in Kenya, Thailand, and the United States. *Child Development, 64,* 98–109.

WEITZMAN, N., BIRNS, B., & FRIEND, R. (1985). Traditional and nontraditional mothers' communication with their sons and daughters. *Child Development, 56,* 894–898.

WEKSELMAN, K., SPIERING, K., HETTEBERG, C., KENNER, C., & FLANDERMEYER, A. (1995). Fetal alcohol syndrome from infancy to childhood: A review of the literature. *Journal of Pediatric Nursing, 10,* 296–303.

WELCH-ROSS, M. K. (1995). An integrative model of the development of autobiographical memory. *Developmental Review, 15,* 338–365.

WELCH-ROSS, M. K. (1997). Mother-child participation in conversation about the past: Relationships to preschoolers' theory of mind. *Developmental Psychology, 33,* 618–629.

WELCH-ROSS, M. K., & SCHMIDT, E. R. (1996). Gender schema development and children's constructive story memory: Evidence for a developmental model. *Child Development, 67,* 820–835.

WELD, N. (1968). Some possible genetic implications of Carthaginian child sacrifice. *Perspectives in Biology and Medicine, 12,* 69–78.

WELLMAN, H. M. (1977). Preschoolers' understanding of memory-relevant variables. *Child Development, 48,* 1720–1723.

WELLMAN, H. M. (1988). The early development of memory strategies. In F. E. Weinert & M. Perlmutter (Eds.), *Memory development: Universal changes and individual differences.* Hillsdale, NJ: Erlbaum.

WELLMAN, H. M., & GELMAN, S. A. (1998). Knowledge acquisition in foundational domains. In W. Damon (Series Ed.) & D. Kuhn & R. S. Siegler (Vol. Eds.) *Handbook of child psychology: Vol. 2. Cognition, perception, and language* (5th ed.). New York: Wiley.

WELLMAN, H. M., RITTER, K., & FLAVELL, J. H. (1975). Deliberate memory behavior in the delayed reactions of very young children. *Developmental Psychology, 11,* 780–787.

WENTZEL, K. R. (1988). Gender differences in math and English achievement: A longitudinal study. *Sex Roles, 18,* 691–699.

WENTZEL, K. R., & ERDLEY, C. A. (1993). Strategies for making friends: Relations to social behavior and peer acceptance in early adolescence. *Developmental Psychology, 29,* 819–826.

WERKER, J. F., & DESJARDINS, R. N. (1995). Listening to speech in the 1st year of life: Experiential influences on phoneme perception. *Current Directions in Psychological Science, 4,* 76–81.

WERNER, L. A., & BARGONES, J. Y. (1992). Psychoacoustic development of human infants. In C. Rovee-Collier & L. P. Lipsitt (Eds.), *Advances in infancy research* (Vol. 7). Norwood, NJ: Ablex.

WERTHEIMER, M. (1985). The evolution of the concept of development in the history of psychology. In G. Eckardt, W. G. Bringmann, & L. Sprung (Eds.), *Contributions to a history of developmental psychology.* Berlin: Mouton.

WERTSCH, J. V., & TULVISTE, P. (1992). L. S. Vygotsky and contemporary developmental psychology. *Developmental Psychology, 28,* 548–557.

WESTINGHOUSE LEARNING CENTER. (1969). *The impact of Head Start: An evaluation of the effects of Head Start on children's cognitive and affective development.* Washington, DC: Clearinghouse for Federal Scientific and Technical Information.

WHITAM, F. L., DIAMOND, M., & MARTIN, J. (1993). Homosexual orientation in twins: A report on 61 pairs and three triplet sets. *Archives of Sexual Behavior, 22,* 187–206.

WHITE, B. L., CASTLE, P., & HELD, R. (1964). Observations on the development of visually directed reaching. *Child Development, 35,* 349–364.

WHITE, B. L., KABAN, B. T., ATTANUCCI, J., & SHAPIRO, B. B. (1978). *Experience and environment: Major influences on the development of the young child* (Vol. 2). Englewood Cliffs, NJ: Prentice Hall.

WHITE, P. C., NEW, M. I., & DUPONT, B. (1987). Congenital adrenal hyperplasia. *New England Journal of Medicine, 316,* 1519–1524.

WHITE, S., & THARP, R. G. (1988, April). *Questioning and wait-time: A cross-cultural analysis.* Paper presented at the meeting of the American Educational Research Association, New Orleans.

WHITE, S. H. (1992). G. Stanley Hall: From philosophy to developmental psychology. *Developmental Psychology, 28,* 25–34.

WHITE, T. G. (1982). Naming practices, typicality, and underextension in child language. *Journal of Experimental Child Psychology, 33,* 324–346.

WHITEHURST, G. J. (1997). Language processes in context: Language learning in children reared in poverty. In L. B. Adamson & M. A. Romski (Eds.), *Research on communication and language disorders: Contributions to theories of language development.* Baltimore: Brookes.

WHITEHURST, G. J., & DeBARYSHE, B. D. (1989). Observational learning and language acquisition: Principles of learning, systems, and tasks. In G. E. Speidel & K. E. Nelson (Eds.), *The many faces of imitation in language learning.* New York: Springer-Verlag.

WHITEHURST, G. J., & LONIGAN, C. J. (in press). Child development and emergent literacy. *Child Development.*

WHITEHURST, G. J., & NOVAK, G. (1973). Modeling, imitation training, and the acquisition of sentence phrases. *Journal of Experimental Child Psychology, 16,* 332–345.

WHITEHURST, G. J., & SONNENSCHEIN, S. (1985). The development of communication: A functional analysis. In G. J. Whitehurst (Ed.), *Annals of child development* (Vol. 2). Greenwich, CT: JAI Press.

WHITEHURST, G. J., & VALDEZ-MENCHACA, M. C. (1988). What is the role of reinforcement in language acquisition? *Child Development, 59,* 430–440.

WHITEHURST, G. J., ARNOLD, D. H., EPSTEIN, J. N., ANGELL, A. L., SMITH, M., & FISCHEL, J. E. (1994). A picture book reading intervention in daycare and home for children from low-income families. *Developmental Psychology, 30,* 679–689.

WHITEHURST, G. J., EPSTEIN, J. N., ANGELL, A. L., PAYNE, A. C., CRONE, D., & FISCHEL, J. E. (1994). Outcomes of an emergent literacy intervention in Head Start. *Journal of Educational Psychology, 84,* 541–556.

WHITEHURST, G. J., FISCHEL, J. E., CAULFIELD, M., DeBARYSHE, B., & VALDEZ-MENCHACA, M. C. (1989). Assessment and treatment of early expressive language delay. In P. Zelazo & R. Barr (Eds.), *Challenges to developmental paradigms: Implications for theory, assessment, and treatment.* Hillsdale, NJ: Erlbaum.

WHITELY, B. E. (1985). Sex-role orientation and psychological well-being: Two meta-analyses. *Sex Roles, 12,* 207–225.

WHITING, B. B. (1983). The genesis of prosocial behavior. In D. Bridgeman (Ed.), *The nature of prosocial development: Interdisciplinary theories and strategies.* London: Academic Press.

WHITING, B. B., & EDWARDS, C. P. (1988). *Children of different worlds: The formation of social behavior.* Cambridge: Harvard University Press.

WHITLEY, R., & GOLDENBERG, R. (1990). Infectious disease in the prenatal period and the recommendations for screening. In I. R. Merkatz & J. E. Thompson (Eds.), *New perspectives on prenatal care.* New York: Elsevier.

WHYTE, M., & PARISH, W. (1984). *Urban life in contemporary China.* Chicago: University of Chicago Press.

WIDAMAN, K. F., LITTLE, T. D., GEARY, D. C., & CORMIER, P. (1992). Individual differences in the development of skill in mental addition: Internal and external validation of chronometric models. *Learning and Individual Differences, 4,* 167–213.

WIGFIELD, A., ECCLES, J. S., MacIVER, D., REUMAN, D. A., & MIDGLEY, C. (1991). Transitions during early adolescence: Changes in children's domain-specific self-perceptions and general self-esteem across the transition to junior high school. *Developmental Psychology, 27,* 552–565.

WILCOX, A. J., & SKJOERVEN, R. (1992). Birthweight and perinatal mortality: The effect of gestational age. *American Journal of Public Health, 82,* 378–382.

WILDER, G., MACKIE, D., & COOPER, J. (1985). Gender and computers: Two surveys of computer-related attitudes. *Sex Roles, 13,* 215–228.

WILLIAMS, J. (1987). *Psychology of women: Behavior in a biosocial context.* New York: Norton.

WILLIAMS, J. E., & BEST, D. L. (1990). Measuring sex stereotypes: *A multinational study.* Newbury Park, CA: Sage.

WILLIAMS, T. M. (1986). *The impact of television.* New York: Academic Press.

WILLINGER, M., JAMES, L., & CATZ, C. (1991). Defining sudden infant death syndrome (SIDS). *Developmental Pediatric Pathology, 11,* 677–684.

WILLINGER, M. (1995). SIDS prevention. *Pediatric Annals, 24,* 358–364.

WILSON, E. O. (1975). *Sociobiology: The new synthesis.* Cambridge: Harvard University Press.

WILSON, R. S. (1983). The Louis-ville Twin Study: Developmental synchronies in behavior. *Child De-velopment, 54,* 298–316.

WILSON, R. S. (1986). Growth and development of human twins. In F. Falkner & J. M. Tanner (Eds.), *Human growth: A comprehensive treatise.* New York: Plenum.

WINDLE, M., & LERNER, R. M. (1986). The "goodness-of-fit" model of temperament-context relations: Interaction or correlation? In J. V. Lerner & R. M. Lerner (Eds.), *New directions for child development: No. 31. Temperament and social interaction in infants and children.* San Francisco: Jossey-Bass.

WINDSOR, J. (1993). The functions of novel word compounds. *Journal of Child Language, 20,* 119–138.

WINEBERG, S. S. (1987). The fulfillment of the self-fulfilling prophecy. *Educational Researcher, 16,* 28–36.

WINSTON, R. M. L., & HANDYSIDE, A. H. (1993). New challenges in human in vitro fertilization. *Science, 260,* 932–936.

WITELSON, S. F., & KIGAR, S. (1989). Anatomical development of the corpus callosum in humans: A review with reference to sex and cognition. In D. L. Molfese & S. J. Segalowitz (Eds.), *Brain lateralization in children: Developmental implications.* New York: Guilford.

WITELSON, S. F. (1976). Sex and the single hemisphere: Specialization of the right hemisphere for spatial processing. *Science, 193,* 425–427.

WOLFF, P. H. (1959). Observations on newborn infants. *Psychosomatic Medicine, 21,* 110–118.

WOLFF, P. H. (1966). The causes, controls and organization of behavior in the neonate. *Psychological Issues, 5* (17).

WOLFF, P. H. (1969). The natural history of crying and other vocalizations in early infancy. In B. Foss (Ed.), *Determinants of infant behavior* (Vol. 4). London: Methuen.

WOLFNER, G. D., & GELLES, R. J. (1993). A profile of violence toward children: A national study. *Child Abuse and Neglect, 17,* 197–212.

WOODWARD, A. L., & MARKMAN, E. M. (1998). Early word learning. In W. Damon (Series Ed.) & D. Kuhn & R. S. Siegler (Vol. Eds.), *Handbook of child psychology: Vol. 2. Cognition, perception, and language* (5th ed.). New York: Wiley.

WOOLLETT, A., WHITE, D., & LYON, L. (1982). Observations of fathers at birth. In N. Beail & J. McGuire (Eds.), *Fathers: Psychological perspectives.* London: Junction Books.

WOROBEY J., & BLAJDA, V. M. (1989). Temperament ratings at 2 weeks, 2 months, and 1 year: Differential stability of activity and emotionality. *Developmental Psychology, 25,* 257–263.

WYNN, K. (1992). Addition and subtraction by human infants. *Nature, 358,* 749–750.

WYNN, K. (1995). Origins of numerical knowledge. *Mathematical Cognition, 1,* 36–60.

YANG, B., OLLENDICK, T. H., DONG, Q., XIA, Y., & LIN, L. (1995). Only children and children with siblings in the People's Republic of China: Levels of fear, anxiety, and depression. *Child Development, 66,* 1301–1311.

YATES, G. C. R., YATES, S. M., & BEASLEY, C. J. (1987). Young children's knowledge of strategies in delay of gratification. *Merrill-Palmer Quarterly, 33,* 159–169.

YEATES, K. O., SCHULTZ, L. H., & SELMAN, R. L. (1991). The development of interpersonal negotiation strategies in thought and action: A social-cognitive link to behavioral adjustment and social status. *Merrill-Palmer Quarterly, 37,* 369–406.

YONAS, A. (1981). Infants' responses to optical information for collision. In R. N. Aslin, J. R. Alberts, & M. R. Peterson (Eds.), *Development of perception: Psychobiological perspectives: Vol. 2. The visual system.* New York: Academic Press.

YONAS, A., & OWSLEY, C. (1987). Development of visual space perception. In P. Salapatek & L. Cohen (Eds.), *Handbook of infant perception: Vol. 2. From perception to cognition.* New York: Academic Press.

YOUNGBLADE, L. M., & BELSKY, J. (1992). Parent–child antecedents of 5-year-olds' close friendships: A longitudinal analysis. *Developmental Psychology, 28,* 700–713.

YOUNGER, A. J., & PICCININ, A. M. (1989). Children's recall of aggressive and withdrawn behaviors: Recognition memory and likability judgments. *Child Development, 60,* 580–590.

YOUNGER, A. J., SCHWARTZMAN, A. E., & LEDINGHAM, J. E. (1985). Age-related changes in children's perceptions of aggression and withdrawal in their peers. *Developmental Psychology, 21,* 70–75.

YOUNISS, J., & VOLPE, J. (1978). A relational analysis of children's friendship. In W. Damon (Ed.), *New directions for child development: No. 1. Social cognition.* San Francisco: Jossey-Bass.

YUILL, N., & PERNER, J. (1988). Intentionality and knowledge in children's judgments of actor's responsibility and recipient's emotional reaction. *Developmental Psychology, 24,* 358–365.

YUSSEN, S. R., & LEVY, V. M. (1975). Developmental changes in predicting one's own span of short-term memory. *Journal of Experimental Child Psychology, 19,* 502–508.

ZABRISKI, A. L., & COIE, J. D. (1996). A comparison of aggressive-rejected and nonaggressive-rejected children's interpretations of self-directed and other-directed rejection. *Child Development, 67,* 1048–1070.

ZAHN-WAXLER, C., CUMMINGS, E. M., & IANNOTTI, R. (Eds.). (1986). *Altruism and aggression: Biological and social origins.* Cambridge: Cambridge University Press.

ZAHN-WAXLER, C., RADKE-YARROW, M., WAGNER, E., & CHAPMAN, M. (1992). Development of concern for others. *Developmental Psychology, 28,* 126–136.

ZAHN-WAXLER, C., ROBINSON J. L., & EMDE, R. N. (1992). The development of empathy in twins. *Developmental Psychology, 28,* 1038–1047.

ZAMETKIN, A. J., NORDAHL, T. E., GROSS, M., KING, A. C., SEMPLE, W. E., RUMSEY, J., HAMBURGER, S., & COHEN, R. M. (1990). Cerebral glucose metabolism in adults with hyperactivity of childhood onset. *The New England Journal of Medicine, 20,* 1361–1366.

ZARBATANY, L., HARTMANN, D. P., & GELFAND, D. M. (1985). Why does children's generosity increase with age: Susceptibility to experimenter influence or altruism? *Child Development, 56,* 746–756.

ZARBATANY, L., HARTMANN, D. P., ELFAND, D. M., & VINCIGUERRA, P. (1985). Gender differences in altruistic reputation: Are they artifactual? *Developmental Psychology, 21,* 97–101.

ZELAZO, N. A., ZELAZO, P. R., COHEN, K. M., & ZELAZO, P. D. (1993). Specificity of practice effects on elementary neuromotor patterns. *Developmental Psychology, 29,* 686–691.

ZELAZO, P. D., HELWIG, C. C., & LAU, A. (1996). Intention, act, and outcome in behavioral prediction and moral judgment. *Child Development, 67,* 2478–2492.

ZELAZO, P. R. (1971). Smiling to social stimuli: Eliciting and conditioning effects. *Developmental Psychology, 4,* 32–42.

ZELAZO, P. R., WEISS, M. J. S., & TARQUINO, N. (1991). Habituation and recovery of neonatal orienting to auditory stimuli. In M. J. S. Weiss & P. R. Zelazo (Eds.), *Newborn attention: Biological constraints and the influence of experience.* Norwood, NJ: Ablex.

ZELAZO, P. R., ZELAZO, N., & KOLB, S. (1972). "Walking" in the newborn. *Science, 177,* 314–315.

ZESKIND, P. S. (1983). Production and spectral analysis of neonatal crying and its relation to other biobehavioral systems in the infant at risk. In T. Field & A. Sostek (Eds.), *Infants born at risk: Psychological and perceptual processes.* New York: Grune & Stratton.

ZESKIND, P. S., & MARSHALL, T. R. (1988). The relation between variations in pitch and maternal perceptions of infant crying. *Child Development, 59,* 193–196.

ZESKIND, P. S., & RAMEY, C. T. (1981). Preventing intellectual and interactional sequelae of fetal malnutrition: A longitudinal, transactional and synergistic approach to development. *Child Development, 52,* 213–218.

ZESKIND, P. S., KLEIN, L., & MARSHALL, T. R. (1992). Adult's perceptions of experimental modifications of durations of pauses and expiratory sounds in infant crying. *Developmental Psychology, 28,* 1153–1162.

ZIGLER, E. F., & FINN-STEVENSON, M. (1992). Applied developmental psychology. In M. H. Bornstein & M. E. Lamb (Eds.), *Developmental psychology: An advanced textbook* (3rd ed.). Hillsdale, NJ: Erlbaum.

ZIGLER, E. F., & MUENCHOW, S. (1992). *Head Start: The inside story of America's most successful educational experiment.* New York: Basic Books.

ZIGLER, E. F., & STYFCO, S. J. (Eds.). (1993). *Head Start and beyond: A national plan for extended childhood intervention.* New Haven, CT: Yale University Press.

ZIGLER, E. F., HOPPER, P., & HALL, N. W. (1993). Infant mental health and social policy. In C. H. Zeanah, Jr. (Ed.), *Handbook of infant mental health.* New York: Guilford.

ZILL, N., MORRISON, D. R., & COIRO, M. J. (1993). Long-term effects of parental divorce on parent-child relationships, adjustment, and achievement in young adulthood. *Journal of Family Psychology, 7,* 1–13.

ZIMMERMAN, B. J. (1983). Social learning theory: A contextualist account of cognitive functioning. In C. J. Brainerd (Ed.), *Recent advances in cognitive-developmental theory: Progress in cognitive development research.* New York: Springer-Verlag.

ZIMMERMAN, B. J., & BLOM, D. E. (1983). Toward an empirical test of the role of cognitive conflict in learning. *Developmental Review, 3,* 18–38.

ZINOBER, B., & MARTLEW, M. (1985). The development of communicative gestures. In M. D. Barrett (Ed.), *Children's single-word speech.* New York: Wiley.

ZIVIN, G. (1979). Removing common confusions about egocentric speech, private speech, and self-regulation. In G. Zivin (Ed.), *The development of self-regulation through private speech.* New York: Wiley.

ZUCKER, K. J. (1992). Gender identity disorder. In S. R. Hooper, G. W. Hynd, & R. E. Mattison (Eds.), *Child psychopathology: Diagnostic criteria and clinical assessment.* Hillsdale, NJ: Erlbaum.

ZUCKER, K. J., & BRADLEY, S. J. (Eds.). (1995). *Gender identity disorder and psychosexual problems in children and adolescents.* New York: Guilford.

ZUCKER, K. J., BRADLEY, S. J., & IPP, M. (1993). Delayed naming of a newborn boy: Relationship to the mother's wish for a girl and subsequent cross-gender identity in the child by the age of two. *Journal of Psychology and Human Sexuality, 6,* 57–68.

ZUCKER, K. J., WILD, J., BRADLEY, S. J., & LOWRY, C. B. (1993). Physical attractiveness of boys with gender identity disorder. *Archives of Sexual Behavior, 22,* 23–34.

ZUKOW, P. G. (Ed.). (1989). *Sibling interaction across cultures.* New York: Springer-Verlag.

ZUPAN, B. A., HAMMEN, C., & JAENICKE, C. (1987). The effects of current mood and prior depressive history on self-schematic processing in children. *Journal of Experimental Child Psychology, 43,* 149–158.

Photo Credits

Sources for Chapter-Opening Vignettes

Chapter 5 David Holmstrom, "U.S. Hospitals Are Flooded with Babies Abandoned by Alcohol and Drug Abusers," *Christian Science Monitor*, September 17, 1992; Donna O'Neal and Debbie Salamone, "Cocaine Mom's Case Thrown Out," *Orlando Sentinel*, July 24, 1992, p. B1; Mimi Hall, "Cocaine-Babies Case Appealed," *USA Today*, March 6, 1992, p. 3A; Andrew Stone, "Prosecutors Focus on Drug Use, Pregnancy," *USA Today*, February 26, 1990, p. 3A; Catherine Foster, "Fetal Endangerment Cases Increase," *Christian Science Monitor*, Ocober 10, 1989; Andrea Stone, "It's 'Tip of Iceberg' in Protecting Infants," *USA Today*, August 25, 1989, p. 3A.

Chapter 6 Brendan I. Koerner, "Outlook: Baby Talk," *U.S. News & World Report*, December 8, 1997; Linda Kulman, "Outlook: Cigars All Around," *U.S. News & World Report*, December 1, 1997; Jordan Lite, "Breaking News: Iowa Septuplets Are Doing Well," *U.S. News & World Report*, November 20, 1997; Pam Belluck, "Iowa Woman Gives Birth to 7 Children," *New York Times*, November 20, 1997.

Chapter 8 Debra Rosenberg and Larry Reibstein, "Pots, Blocks and Socks," *Newsweek Special Edition: Your Child*, Spring/Summer 1997, pp. 34–35; Doris Iarovici, "More!" *Parents*, November 1996, pp. 102–104; Karen S. Peterson, "Quest for Superkids," *USA Today*, August 22, 1988, p. 1D.

Chapter 9 Pam Belluck, "Woman Wins Suit Claiming Therapists Invoked Traumatic Memories," *New York Times*, November 6, 1997; Amy Argetsinger, "Maryland Court Rejects 'Repressed Memory' Argument," *Washington Post*, July 30, 1996, p. A7; Dan Morain, "Retrial in California Case Would Test Recovered Memory," *Washington Post*, December 27, 1995, p. A12; James H. Andrews, "Dredging the Past: Recovered Memory or False Memory?" *Christian Science Monitor*, July 25, 1994.

Chapter 12 Charmagne Helton, "Mom Loses Custody over Day Care," *USA Today*, July 27, 1994, p. 1A; Elizabeth Kastor, "The Maranda Decision," *Washington Post*, July 30, 1994, p. D1; Associated Press, "Court Gives Daughter Back to Mom: Ruling Overturned in Day Care Case," November 9, 1995; Jeanne May, "Parents to Share Maranda Equally: Long Custody Battle Ends with Settlement," *Detroit Free Press*, October 17, 1996, p. 1A.

Chapter 14 Blaine Harden, "Prom Night Mother Charged with Murder," *Washington Post*, June 25, 1997, p. A3; Faye Bowers, "Behind the Tragedy of Discarded Babies," *Christian Science Monitor*, June 18, 1997, p. 3; Laurie Goodstein and Blaine Harden, "Of Birth, Death and the Prom," *Washington Post*, June 10, 1997, p. A3; Marc Peyser, "Death in a Dumpster," *Newsweek*, December 2, 1996, pp. 92–94; Kari Vick, "Young Love and a Dead Baby Tear at the Heart of Delware," *Washington Post*, November 22, 1996, p. A1.

Chapter 16 Lucia Mouat, "Teens Take the Lead in Keeping Intoxicated Friends Off the Road," *Christian Science Monitor*, January 19, 1984, p. 7; Victoria Benning, "Bringing Peer Pressure to Bear on School Problems," *Washington Post*, September 20, 1997, p. A14; "News in Brief," *Christian Science Monitor*, October 9, 1997, p. 2.

Subject Index

Chapter 11: Language Development

This chapter discusses the role of parents in language learning in several sections:
- (p. 400)   Introduces the speech style known as "motherese."
- (pp. 410–411)   Considers parents' contribution to early individual differences in language.
- (pp. 415–416)   Discusses the role of parents' labeling practices in semantic development.
- (pp. 424–426)   Evaluates the role of modeling and feedback in grammatical development.
- (pp. 434–437)   ■ *Development in School Context:* Bilingualism: Teaching (and Learning) One Language or Two?
- (pp. 426–427)   ■ *Development in Cultural Context:* Cultural Variations in Language Learning Experiences

Chapter 12: Early Social and Emotional Development

- (pp. 451–454)   Examines parents' contribution to early emotional development.
- (pp. 467–470)   Discusses the child-rearing antecedents of different forms of attachment.
- (pp. 473–481)   "Family Influences"—Considers research on different styles of child rearing, issues of maternal employment and infant day care, the role of fathers, and the consequences of child abuse.
- (pp. 461–462)   ■ *Development in Cultural Context:* Ethnic Differences in Temperament: Biology or Culture?
- (pp. 471–472)   ■ *Development in Cultural Context:* Attachment Across Cultures
- (pp. 478–479)   ■ *Development in Cultural Context:* The Changing Roles of Fathers in China

Chapter 13: Development of the Self

- (pp. 491–492)   Provides an application of the Vygotskian approach in a section on parental directives as a source of children's self-regulation.
- (pp. 495–496)   Discusses the contribution of parents' caregiving to working models of the self.
- (p. 510)   Examines the relation between parenting styles and children's self-concept.
- (pp. 510–511)   Considers schools as one contributor to self-concept.
- (pp. 506–507)   Discusses academic self-concept and academic motivation.
- (pp. 506–507)   ■ *Development in Family Context:* Children's Self-Evaluation in Single-Parent Families
- (pp. 511–512)   ■ *Development in School Context:* Do Schools Depress Adolescents' Academic Self-Concept?
- (pp. 500–501)   ■ *Development in Cultural Context:* Self-Understanding Among Exceptional Inner-City Adolescents

Chapter 14: Moral Development

This chapter considers the contribution of the family to each of the major outcomes reviewed:
- (pp. 545–546)   Moral reasoning
- (p. 552)   Prosocial behavior
- (pp. 557–558)   Variations in levels of aggression